The Carlos S. Alvarado Archives

Volume 1

Essays in the History of Parapsychology and Psychology (1800–1899)

The Carlos S. Alvarado Archives

Volume 1

Essays in the History of Parapsychology and Psychology (1800–1899)

Edited by
NANCY L. ZINGRONE AND SONALI BHATT MARWAHA

BLOOMSBURY ACADEMIC
NEW YORK • LONDON • OXFORD • NEW DELHI • SYDNEY

BLOOMSBURY ACADEMIC

Bloomsbury Publishing Inc, 1359 Broadway, New York, NY 10018, USA
Bloomsbury Publishing Plc, 50 Bedford Square, London, WC1B 3DP, UK
Bloomsbury Publishing Ireland, 29 Earlsfort Terrace, Dublin 2, D02 AY28, Ireland

BLOOMSBURY, BLOOMSBURY ACADEMIC and the Diana logo are trademarks of Bloomsbury Publishing Plc

First published in the United States of America 2026

Cover design: Dustin Watson

Library of Congress Cataloging-in-Publication Data Available

ISBN: HB: 978-1-5381-9852-0
ePDF: 979-8-7651-5508-0
eBook: 978-1-5381-9853-7

Typeset by Lumina Datamatics Ltd
Printed and bound in the United States of America

For product safety related questions contact productsafety@bloomsbury.com.

To find out more about our authors and books visit www.bloomsbury.com and sign up for our newsletters.

To Carlos S. Alvarado, the unforgettable friend and brilliant scholar, who with wisdom and good humor built bridges between cultures and knowledge, leaving a legacy of academic rigor, friendship, and generosity that will forever live on with us.

Fatima R. Machado and Wellington Zangari

Contents

List of Tables

Foreword

Andreas Sommer

When the tragic news of Carlos Alvarado's death in July 2021 reached those of us who cherished him as a colleague, a teacher, and a friend, it came as a blow not only because of his towering standing as a historian of the modern empirical occult.[1] Those who were privileged to meet Carlos in the flesh were instantly impressed and humbled by his characteristic kindness, generosity, and cheeky-yet-always-warm sense of humor. One thing that always struck me in particular was that Carlos's aversion to unconstructive debate and confrontation seemed near absolute. It might therefore appear paradoxical that his lifelong intellectual attraction was to those perpetually controversial, and often aggressively contested, scientific questions and problems studied by parapsychological researchers.

No matter if you were sitting in one of his lectures or chatting over a meal, listening to Carlos made it evident that his curiosity in the figures and problems he studied was beyond deep and profound. Carlos's contagious enthusiasm and fascination are strikingly visible in the vast range of topics he studied: vitalist effluences like animal magnetism, the odylic force and related concepts; the persistence of mesmerism in medical hypnosis; interpretations of mediumistic phenomena and controversies around mediums (notably Eusapia Palladino, on whom Carlos was probably the world-leading authority); the pathologization of belief in psychic phenomena by medical and psychological communities, to name just a few of his areas of research.

As I noted in my obituary of Carlos (Sommer, 2021), our principal area of mutual interest was the significant role of 19th-century psychical researchers in the formation of modern concepts of mental dissociation and the subconscious mind. Carlos's work in this regard was thus very much in the intellectual history tradition of scholars such as Henri Ellenberger (1970), Adam Crabtree (1993), and Alan Gauld (1992).

This strong focus on ideas, written from an insider perspective that is interested mainly in empirical and conceptual questions, has been frowned on by some historians who are primarily concerned with wider social, cultural, and political contexts, and who are typically quite uninterested in questions of scientific validity. But in my view, such dogmatism is essentially misguided, as pluralism of methods and perspectives in history is just as vital as it is in the sciences. There is no one true way of looking at and understanding the past—saying that you should always get the actual concepts and ideas of your historical actors right.

In this regard, Carlos's work was more than just painstakingly rigorous. It was absolutely exemplary. Unfortunately, the latter can't be claimed to apply to all mainstream historical work on the occult. Carlos's writings therefore remain an indispensable guide to the past as it actually happened, serving as an important corrective to the work of writers (including some professional historians) who have forced past figures and events into line with their own worldviews and beliefs.

Adding to the mind-boggling range of topics studied by Carlos, what set his works apart from those of many other historians of 19th-century psychical research to 20th-century parapsychology was his mastery of various geographical contexts beyond the Anglophone literature, including but not limited to France, Italy, Spain, Switzerland, and Germany. Along with Carlos's uncompromising faithfulness to his source materials, the sheer vastness of topics and settings explored by him make the present volumes a veritable treasure trove for those refusing to subscribe to the widespread assumption that all that is worth investigating has already been filtered out and verified by current science, orthodox or otherwise.

It is for all these reasons that Carlos's wife and long-time collaborator, Nancy Zingrone, deserves our sincerest gratitude for saving these important texts from potential oblivion by collating them into the present volumes. May Carlos's legacy persist and inspire future generations of scholars to study past controversial science as faithfully and thoroughly as he did. After all, and as Carlos himself firmly believed, understanding the past is necessary in order to obtain a qualified comprehension of the present.

Note

1 I am grateful to acknowledge support of my current work by the Perrott-Warrick Fund, Trinity College, University of Cambridge.

References

Crabtree, A. (1993). *From Mesmer to Freud: Magnetic sleep and the roots of psychological healing*. Yale University Press.

Ellenberger, H. F. (1970). *The discovery of the unconscious: The history and evolution of dynamic psychiatry*. Basic Books.

Gauld, A. (1992). *A history of hypnotism*. Cambridge University Press.

Sommer, A. (2021). A remedy for historical split personalities: In memory of Carlos S. Alvarado. *Journal of Anomalous Experience and Cognition*, *1*, 159–162.

Acknowledgments

Heart-felt thanks to my colleague, Dr. Sonali Bhatt Marwaha, who brought the idea to me. I learned a great deal from her work on the *Archives*. She generously lent her extensive experience with every aspect of the process of this complex multivolume project. She was essential to the *Archives* in every way.

Nancy L. Zingrone

Preface

Nancy L. Zingrone

My late husband, Carlos S. Alvarado, passed away in the summer of 2021. I lost not only the love of my life but also my best friend. From the day we met, he was the source of my personal and professional inspiration, and my most cherished intellectual mentor and colleague. Our lives came together through our mutual fascination with the phenomena and histories of psychical research, psychology, parapsychology, and psychiatry.

For 38 years, we worked together, continually discussing psychic experiences, their contexts, and the men and women who presented or investigated them. I knew early on that he was extraordinary, fluent in English and Spanish, self-taught in French, Italian, and Portuguese. His linguistic ability allowed him to bring into his work so many others from around the world—friends who became colleagues, and colleagues who became life-long friends.

The process of the *Archives* and their three volumes started with an email exchange in January 2022. A complete list of Carlos's work was gathered. Most were peer-reviewed journal articles; some were chapters from anthologies, articles for websites, or essays printed in professional newsletters and magazines. Some were book reviews that included a group of books on the same topics but from different perspectives and languages. Others were more informal blog posts that brought an important corner of the field to students, researchers, and the public.

As Carlos's published works were organized, the decision was made to not arrange the volumes in the order of their publications but to focus on the timeline of phenomena, researchers, experiencers, and theorists. While reading and editing, the thread of Carlos's intellectual life came alive.

Constructing the tables of content, pouring over the figures, and editing the text sparked precious memories as well as a new understanding of his legacy. While I knew that the three volumes were going to be a lasting record of his contributions to the field, it became clear to me that they carried his understanding of history, the scholarly values he upheld, the multicultural questions he explored, and his nuanced view of the four intermingled disciplines that built his life's work.

Before I describe the volumes in the *Archives*, I wanted to honor our closest colleagues and friends in this work, Dr. Wellington Zangari and Dr. Fátima Machado of the University of São Paulo in Brazil, whose heartfelt dedication to Carlos begins each of these volumes.

In this volume 1, *Essays in the History of Parapsychology and Psychology (1800–1899),* the chapters cover the intellectual and institutional foundations of psychical research and related disciplines during the 19th century. There are 57 chapters, in which Carlos and his coauthors explore apparitions, the concepts of the subconscious and altered waking states of consciousness, mediumship, and Mesmerism through his investigations of the phenomena, and intellectuals and researchers from Richard Baxter (1615–1691) to Cesaré Lombroso (1835–1909).

Two more volumes have been published. In volume 2, *Essays in the History of Parapsychology and Psychology (1900–2022)*, the chapters cover the four fields and other related disciplines, even as psychology and psychiatry increasingly distanced themselves from the subject matter of psychical research and parapsychology. Carlos and his coauthors explored research, theory, and history developments, especially in psychical research and parapsychology. There are 59 chapters providing the historiography of the four fields, including the impact of the language barrier, the proliferation of journals, individuals whose impact on methods and theories was invaluable—among them, Ambroise August Liébault, William James, Frederic W. H. Myers, Eleanor M. Sidgwick, James H. Hyslop, Théodore Flournoy, Ernesto Bozzano, Eugène Osty, Charles Richet, Eileen J. Garrett, J. B. Rhine, and Robert van de Castle—and institutions such as the Society for Psychical Research, the Institut Métapsychique International, the American Society for Psychical Research, and the Parapsychology Foundation.

The third volume, *Essays and Investigations in Out-of-Body Experiences, Near-Death Experiences, and Associated Phenomena,* includes Carlos's overviews of the history of psi research, out-of-body experiences (OBEs), and near-death phenomena (NDEs), including critiques of theoretical work, the psychological correlates of experiencers, and other topics like deathbed experiences and auras. Carlos's original research, along with collaborative work with colleagues such as Massimo Biondi and myself, is featured there. The third volume highlights Carlos's ability to expand his perspectives on phenomenological and empirical work with a deep understanding of the evolution of theory, methods, and knowledge, their impact on psychical research, parapsychology, psychology, and psychiatry and on our understanding of what it means to be human.

Carlos was committed to illuminating areas of inquiry marginalized by prevailing academic consensus of accepted knowledge, to show that much of what was rejected in the process of disciplinary professionalization was, in fact, a legitimate part of that evolution—forgotten but not unimportant. He saw in this historical knowledge a source of clarity, inspiration, and continuity with the present.

I hope that these volumes will honor Carlos's memory while serving as a resource for those who, like Carlos, are ready to explore human experience with an open mind and an ability to apply enough rigor to see beyond the boundaries of the present to the past and the future.

Nancy L. Zingrone, PhD

1

Parapsychology and the Study of the Mind: Changing the Historical Record*

Carlos S. Alvarado

In a recent article in *Mindfield,* Chris Roe (2016) stated: "A powerful means of imposing scientific dogma is through textbooks, which do not passively and transparently describe a discipline, but instead actively circumscribe it. By the presence or absence of topics and by the way they are represented, the authors determine for the reader the boundaries of legitimate concern and appropriate practice. In this way the boundaries are policed and transmitted from generation to generation" (p. 86). I believe this has affected negatively views of the historical role of parapsychology in relation to psychology and psychiatry, as seen in the traditional historiography of these fields. In the rest of this paper I will discuss this issue, focusing, to a great extent, on some of the articles I have published during the last 15 years or so (with apologies for presenting various quotes).

Unfortunately, many historians have contributed to perpetuate the view that psychical research was not important to psychology or to psychiatry. An early example was Edwin G. Boring's (1886–1968) highly influential *A History of Experimental Psychology*, a book that influenced most of our older teachers of psychology and that was a standard textbook for many years (Boring, 1957). In this book psychical research was considered to be at the periphery of psychology, and it was only mentioned in the book in notes at the end of a chapter (p. 502). The lack of importance of psychical research is also assumed by many other writers who do not even mention psychical research in their writings (e.g., Robinson, 1995), or who mention it in passing as someone's interest with no details (e.g., Hergenhahn & Henley, 2013, p. 332), underscoring Roe's comment.

Fortunately, there are indications in the last decades that the situation is changing. Perhaps this is related to the attention historians of science and medicine have paid to "marginal" disciplines and movements, some of whom argued that these movements, and the ideas that came from them, contributed to science and to culture at large (see entries about alchemy, astrology, Hermeticism, mesmerism, occult sciences, Spiritualism, and phrenology in Hessenbruch, 2000). Although not all historians agree, many oppose the view that occult and mystical views were a factor that always hindered the development of science. In fact, the opposite has been argued, considering such topics as contributing factors to the development of science (see Applebaum 2005 for an overview).

An important early work bringing such a perspective to psychic phenomena was *The Discovery of the Unconscious* (1970) by Henri F. Ellenberger (1905–1993). Although the emphasis of the book was on the more conventional work of individuals such as Sigmund Freud (1856 1939), Pierre Janet (1859–1947), and Carl G. Jung (1875–1961), which led to the development of ideas about the unconscious mind and psychotherapy, Ellenberger gave a place to ideas coming from mesmerism, psychical research, and Spiritism affecting the study of the mind. Not only did he acknowledge the work of Frederic W. H. Myers (1843–1901), but he wrote: "Automatic writing, ... was taken over by

*Republished with permission from *Mindfield, 8*(1), 20–24, 2016.

scientists as a method of exploring the unconscious … A new subject, the medium, became available for experimental psychological investigations, out of which evolved a new model of the human mind' (Ellenberger, 1970, p. 85).

Later writers have argued for the importance of the study of psychic phenomena for the development of ideas about non-conscious activities of the mind, thus placing psychical research as a positive influence, not as a mere obstacle in the development of psychology as a science, or as an absurd field. Examples include Adam Crabtree's *From Mesmer to Freud* (1993), Régine Plas's *Naissance d'une Science Humaine* (2000), and Eugene Taylor's *William James on Consciousness Beyond the Margin* (1996), among others (see also Andreas Sommer's forthcoming book).

In her book, Plas (2000) resists the image of psychic studies as an "infantile malady" or as an "amusing bizarreness" of some psychologists (p. 13). Interest in the "marvelous" (including psychic phenomena) shown by psychologists is presented by Plas as an influential force in French psychological studies, particularly in terms of the development of ideas about the unconscious mind. Of course, we have to acknowledge that not everyone accepts this view. But it is encouraging to see the above-mentioned publications, and the fact that some mainstream historians argue that it would be a mistake to exclude psychic phenomena and other "marginal" topics from the canon, and that they "contributed mightily to the constitution of modern psychological medicine" (Micale, 2004, p. 11).

In my own work, consisting of various articles, I have tried to provide information about some of these issues, hoping to influence psychologists and psychiatrists. I *do not* write to defend the existence of psychic phenomena, nor the validity of their research findings, my intention is rather to present psychical research as an agent of influence, of change, just as so many have written about the role of fields such as neurology or concepts such as materialism, on ideas about the mind. The way I see it, the more practitioners and researchers in psychology and psychiatry see papers about psychical research in their journals about issues of historical relevance, the more they will get used to the new way of seeing these topics as part of the histories of psychology and psychiatry. In any case, at least they will be exposed to the topic, and to arguments defending the idea that psychical research is not an example of a peripheral or a useless pseudo-science.

With this purpose in mind in recent years I have published several papers in the Sage journal *History of Psychiatry*. These are contributions to a section of the journal called "Classic Text" devoted to presenting excerpts or whole articles or chapters relevant, in a broad way, to the history of psychiatry (Alvarado, 2010, 2014a, 2016; Alvarado & Zingrone, 2012). The reprinted text is presented with an introduction that provides contextual, biographical, and other information that justifies the inclusion of such material in the journal. This is not limited to mental illness, but includes much more, such as general psychological topics, and topics of general cultural and social concern believed to be relevant to the study of the mind and behavior. The journal, edited by historian of psychiatry German Berrios, is also open to psychic phenomena. I have never noticed any prejudice against the topic, as judged by my submissions, which to this day have all been accepted. I have presented much information about psychical research in these contributions.

The point of some of my papers has been to identify the psychical research writings of well-known psychologists (e.g., Alvarado, 2009; Alvarado, Maraldi, Machado, & Zangari, 2014). In one of the articles three colleagues and I discussed the work of Swiss psychologist Théodore Flournoy (1854–1920), which included his study of the medium Hélène Smith, as reported in his famous book *Des Indes à la Planète Mars* (Flournoy, 1900). My colleagues and I wrote:

> His main contribution, both to psychology and to psychical research, was conceptual, and referred to the development of the concept of the capabilities of the unseen mind. This he did

> mainly through his study of Smith's mediumship ..., but also with a few other case studies ... His contribution of the construction of this idea, while purely psychological, was developed and nurtured in the context of psychic investigations, as were the psychological ideas of Myers, and to some extent, those of others such as Janet and Richet ... From the early days after the publication of *Des Indes* to more recent developments, Flournoy's investigation of the Smith case has been cited by many to illustrate the capabilities of the subconscious mind for producing fictitious manifestations. It is an example of the vast influence that exemplary cases can have on the development of ideas and research, as seen both in psychology and in psychical research. (Alvarado, Maraldi, Machado, & Zangari, 2014, pp. 162–163)

Another example is William James (1842–1910; Alvarado, 2016; Alvarado & Krippner, 2010), who of course has been widely discussed by others. A colleague and I discussed William James as another example of how psychical research contributed to the study of dissociation (Alvarado & Krippner, 2010), with some studies accepting the existence of the supernormal. "Unlike Janet and others, James did not use dissociation to explain mediumship and other phenomena in the sense of reducing everything to suggestion and the workings of a secondary consciousness. Instead, he adapted ideas, such as Myers's, that assumed the existence of a secondary consciousness and that were not only relevant to pathology, but to the supernormal and the transcendental. James's acceptance of the supernormal in the case of Mrs. Piper represents a break with Janet and other conventional explorers of dissociation. It was in fact a plea to study and accept the possibility that dissociation and consciousness in general could transcend bodily limitations" (p. 37).

In my first paper exploring the contributions of psychical research to psychology I focused on the work that early members of the Society for Psychical Research conducted regarding dissociation (Alvarado, 2002). Because I wanted to inform contemporary dissociation researchers, I sent the paper to the *Journal of Trauma and Dissociation.* In the paper I focused on work about mediumship and hypnosis, and summarized aspects of Myers's contributions. I concluded that "it is far too simplistic in historical terms to dismiss psychical research as pseudoscientific or as an example of irrational or plainly wrong ideas that have been superseded as psychiatry and psychology have advanced and have become more scientific. Apart from the fact that psychical research deserves serious consideration, we need to realize that in the context of nineteenth-century developments this field made important contributions to the study of dissociation and to the development of the idea of a secondary self ... Such considerations remind us that much of our current understanding of the history of dissociation has been itself 'dissociated' in the sense of becoming separated from aspects of its origins" (p. 28).

I continued to explore dissociation in other articles. In one I focused on French psychologist Alfred Binet (1857–1911) and his discussion of mediumship to illustrate that, similarly to hypnosis and various cases apparently showing the existence of a secondary consciousness, this phenomenon was used in the psychological discourse of the nineteenth-century to argue for the existence of dissociation as a psychological process (Alvarado, 2010). Mediumship, I wrote with other colleagues in an essay published in the Brazilian psychiatry journal *Revista de Psiquiatria Clínica,* provided the context for the development of various ideas about the subconscious mind (Alvarado, Machado, Zangari, & Zingrone, 2007). Mediums, and others such as the hypnotized, "became part of a small group of special individuals who led students of the mind to see invisible regions of the psyche. This ... had implications for dissociation and for diagnostic matters" (p. 50). An example was the work of Pierre Janet, who did not accept the parapsychological aspects of mediumship, but used the phenomena (and the writings of Myers) to support the concept of dissociation and secondary personalities.

In later papers published in *History of Psychiatry*, I and other colleagues discussed pathological diagnoses informed by mediumship (Alvarado & Zingrone, 2012; Le Maléfan, Evrard, & Alvarado, 2013). Interestingly, and complicating the issue, there were also several formulations of the relation between dissociation, the subconscious mind, and mediumship, as discussed in another paper in the *Journal of Parapsychology* (Alvarado, 2014b). I wrote in the conclusion of this paper:

> Although most medical men held a closed model of the mind (and of dissociation) in which the phenomena were explained mostly by internal resources and a few external influences such as suggestion, few accepted a more open model of mind, such as the one some psychical researchers upheld based on powers that extend sensory and motor capacities beyond the confines of the body. Nonetheless, and as seen in the writings of some such as James ... these psychic or supernormal concepts were part of the same general interest in understanding the mind and its myriad of layers as the more accepted ideas of individuals such as Janet ... Interestingly, these ideas about the powers or capabilities of the subconscious mind were also connected in some cases to pathology. This was not only the case with those, like Janet ... [who] reduced everything to intrapsychic concepts, but also with those like Lombroso ... and Morselli ... who admitted the existence of the supernormal as a process related to pathologies such as hysteria. But most of the persons discussed here did not write about pathology. (p. 108)

Together with the authors mentioned above, I have been arguing for a more complete history of psychology and psychiatry. That is, one that represents better the past by recovering from the historical record research and ideas that have been neglected by many representatives of the traditional historiography of these fields. This includes other phenomena and issues not emphasized here, such as the study of hallucinations, hypnosis, eyewitness testimony, institutional developments, and other things. Although we should not forget that the past of these disciplines was influenced by multiple aspects and not only by psychical research, interest in the psychic or supernormal was a factor affecting positively some past inquiries about the mind.

References

Alvarado, C. S. (2002). Dissociation in Britain during the late nineteenth century: The Society for Psychical Research, 1882-1900. *Journal of Trauma and Dissociation, 3,* 9–33.

Alvarado, C. S. (2009). Ambroise August Liébeault and psychic phenomena. *American Journal of Clinical Hypnosis, 52,* 111–121.

Alvarado, C. S. (2010). Classic text no. 84: "Divisions of personality and spiritism" by Alfred Binet (1896). *History of Psychiatry, 21,* 487–500.

Alvarado, C. S. (2014a). Classic text no. 98: "Visions of the dying," by James H. Hyslop (1907). *History of Psychiatry, 25,* 237–252.

Alvarado, C. S. (2014b). Mediumship, psychical research, dissociation, and the powers of the subconscious mind. *Journal of Parapsychology, 78,* 98–114.

Alvarado, C. S. (2016). Classic Text No. 107: "Report of the Committee on Mediumistic Phenomena," by William James (1886). *History of Psychiatry, 27,* 85–100.

Alvarado, C. S., & Krippner, S. (2010). Nineteenth century pioneers in the study of dissociation: William James and psychical research. *Journal of Consciousness Studies, 17,* 19–43.

Alvarado, C. S., Machado, F. R., Zangari, W., & Zingrone, N. L. (2007). Perspectivas históricas da influência da mediunidade na construção de idéias psicológicos e psiquiátricas. *Revista de Psiquiatria Clínica, 34* (supp.1), 42–53.

Alvarado, C. S., Maraldi, E. de O., Machado, F. R., & Zangari, W. (2014). Théodore Flournoy's contributions to psychical research. *Journal of the Society for Psychical Research, 78*, 149–168.

Alvarado, C. S., & Zingrone, N. L. (2012). Classic text no. 90: "The pathology and treatment of mediomania," by Frederic Rowland Marvin (1874). *History of Psychiatry, 23*, 229–244.

Applebaum, W. (2005). *The scientific revolution and the foundations of modern science*. Greenwood Press.

Boring, E. G. (1957). *A history of experimental psychology* (2nd ed.). Appleton-Century-Crofts.

Crabtree, A. (1993). *From Mesmer to Freud: Magnetic sleep and the roots of psychological healing*. Yale University Press.

Ellenberger, H. F. (1970). *The discovery of the unconscious: The history and evolution of dynamic psychiatry*. Basic Books.

Flournoy, T. (1900). *From India to the planet Mars: A study of a case of somnambulism*. Harper & Brothers.

Hergenhahn, B., & Henley, T. (2014). *An introduction to the history of psychology* (7th ed.). Wadsworth Cengage Learning.

Hessenbruch, A. (Ed.). (2000). *Reader's guide to the history of science*. Fitzroy Dearborn.

Le Maléfan, P. Evrard, R., & Alvarado, C. S. (2013). Spiritist delusions and spiritism in the nosography of French psychiatry (1850–1950). *History of Psychiatry, 24*, 477–491.

Micale, M. S. (2004). The modernist mind: A map. In M. S. Micale (Ed.), *The mind of modernism: Medicine, psychology, and the cultural arts in Europe and America, 1880–1940* (pp. 1–19). Stanford University Press.

Plas, R. (2000). *Naissance d'une science humaine: La psychologie: Les psychologues et le "merveilleux psychique."* Presses Universitaires de Rennes.

Robinson, D. N. (1995). *An intellectual history of psychology* (3rd ed.). University of Wisconsin Press.

Roe, C. (2016). What are psychology students told about the current state of parapsychology? *Mindfield, 7*, 86-91.

Sommer, A. (n. d). *Psychical research and the formation of modern psychology in Europe and the US.*

Taylor, E. (1996). *William James on consciousness beyond the margin*. Princeton University Press.

2

The Role of Fraud in the Development of Parapsychology*

Carlos S. Alvarado

Chris A. Roe (2016) recently reminded us in *Mindfield* about the issue of fraud in parapsychology. His comments inspired me to briefly discuss the issue from another perspective. Discussions of fraud by parapsychologists generally consist of defenses or accusations about specific issues. Such emphasis is understandable because workers in the field are concerned mainly with the existence of the phenomena and their implications, so fraud is a threat to the field's database, and to the significance the phenomena entail to those involved in the research enterprise. However, there is another way to see fraud, or more precisely, its role in the development of parapsychology.

Like various practices and beliefs, the issue of fraud has been an agent of influence in the development of parapsychology in various ways. One of them has been the production of skepticism about the reality of the phenomena. Physical phenomena are a case in point, and materializations a specific one. Over the years many mediums have been found to fake materializations, as seen with one of the Bangs sisters, who was discovered using a mask to look like a materialized figure in the séance room (Anonymous, 1888). Many others were exposed in one way or another, as was medium Charles Eldred, who was hiding paraphernalia in a secret compartment of a chair to simulate materializations (Wallace, 1906).

As was to be expected exposures like these affected psychical research. Although some communities were more open than others, exposures not only created suspicions about materializations, but branded the more general area as false or too difficult to investigate. Although the topic was by no means abandoned in psychical research, as seen in the later work of individuals such as Albert von Schrenck-Notzing (1920), in some circles it never had the same status as mental phenomena.

Lessons have been learned via other cases. Several reports give us much information about the length some individuals will go to deceive others. This includes acting skills to defraud in the laboratory (Delanoy, 1987). Sidgwick has also pointed out that there are cases in which fraud is committed with no specific purpose, except perhaps "the pleasure of exciting the wonder of his deceived friends, and the pleasure of laughing in his sleeve at their credulity" (Sidgwick, 1894, p. 278).

In addition, and as pointed out by Beloff (1994), the issue of fraud affected modern parapsychologists interest in gifted individuals. Perhaps it was felt that professional psychics and mediums were more motivated than unselected study participants to commit fraud. Consequently, most modern published studies have been tests of college students and other volunteers not particularly psychic. If this impression is correct, and certainly there are other factors involved, the preoccupation with fraud, has been an important influence shaping research practice.

Fraud was an important factor in the development of the Society for Psychical Research. As shown by Gauld (1968) the discussions about fraud regarding mediums Eusapia Palladino

*Republished with permission from *Mindfield, 6,* 49-51, 2017.

and William Eglinton affected the course of the Society and produced many polarized views. This led to much more interest in mental phenomena than on physical and it affected the inner dynamics of the SPR due, to a great extent, to controversies about the very existence of the phenomena.

An important SPR user of the concept of fraud to define the field was Frank Podmore, as seen in his views about physical mediumship and poltergeists (Podmore, 1897). In Podmore's view fraud was a device to separate the wheat from the chaff, and thus define psychical research in terms of mental phenomena. "Whilst there is little room," he wrote, "to doubt that the great majority—at any rate—of the so-called physical manifestations were due to deliberate and preconcerted fraud, such phenomena as trance-speaking, automatic writing, and the visions seen at séances, were probably in many cases the genuine outcome of states more or less abnormal" (Podmore, 1897, p. 31).

It is also interesting to notice that the issue of fraud has affected the way histories are organized and conceived. Comparing *Modern Spiritualism* (Podmore, 1902) to *The History of Spiritualism* (Doyle, 1926), it is evident that Podmore put great emphasis on fraudulent accusations and exposures, particularly of mediums, while Doyle underemphasized the topic and defended specific cases from accusations. To some extent one is an example of a history of blunders and suspicion, while the other is a different, more positive, and perhaps rosy history. Such contrasts have come to more recent times, as seen in the views of Inglis (1992) and Brandon (1983).

The presence, or threat, of fraud, has also influenced parapsychology in other ways. One of them is the various ways devised to control for the problem, which has contributed to methodology. In terms of physical mediumship this includes new ways to control mediums, such as Cromwell Varley's electrical control with Florence Cook (Varley, 1874), and the detailed reporting of phenomena and various events with Eusapia Palladino (Feilding, Baggally & Carrington, 1909).

There has also been much concern for fraud in modern experimental work (e.g., Morris, 1986). Over the years many have conducted work with extra precautions in the detailed recording of laboratory work, as seen in Pratt et al.'s (1940) magnum opus *Extrasensory Perception After Sixty Years*, and in more recent discussions (e.g., Schmidt, Morris, & Rudolph, 1986). The shadow of fraud was one of the factors leading to the development of automated security measures for ESP testing in the ganzfeld (Dalton, Morris, Delanoy, Radin, Taylor, & Wiseman, 1996).

Finally, the existence of fraud led to the development of an influential explanation, that of unconscious fraud. Perhaps the most influential medium in this regard was Eusapia Palladino. In an article about her fraudulent performances, Julian Ochorowicz (1896) argued that the medium's seemingly suspicious movements may be accounted for as "*motor representations that rule in a given moment the medium's imagination*" (p. 100, italics in the original). In his view dissociative processes took place in the medium involving automatic centers of her nervous system, as well as somnambulistic states or suggestions, and the "dynamism" of her limbs. The last stage of this process involved fraud. This was when she was not conscious of the sensibility and position of her arms and legs, and was unable to distinguish real telekinesis from the action of her limbs. Furthermore, suggestions from the mediumistic circle, such as about ideas of fraud, were believed to influence the process. Such ideas were influential for years, especially in Europe.

Like other general and specific concepts—among them, nonphysicality—the idea of fraud has had an important impact on the development of parapsychology. This impact has gone far beyond an embarrassing problem limiting our ability to do scientific research.

References

Anonymous. (1888, April 3). Bogus spiritualists exposed: The lights turned up and the spook seized and arrested. *The Washington Post,* p. 4.

Beloff, J. (1994). Lessons of history. *Journal of the American Society for Psychical Research, 88,* 7–22.

Brandon, R. (1983). *The spiritualists: The passion for the occult in the nineteenth and twentieth centuries.* Knopf.

Dalton, K. S., Morris, R. L., Delanoy, D. L., Radin, D. I., Taylor, R., & Wiseman, R. (1996). Security measures in an automated ganzfeld system. *Journal of Parapsychology, 60,* 129–147.

Delanoy, D. L. (1987). Work with a fraudulent PK metal-bending subject. *Journal of the Society for Psychical Research, 54,* 247–256.

Doyle, A. C. (1926). *The history of spiritualism* (2 vols.). Cassell.

Feilding, E., Baggally, W. W., & Carrington, H. (1909). Report on a series of sittings with Eusapia Palladino. *Proceedings of the Society for Psychical Research, 23,* 309–569.

Gauld, A. (1968). *The founders of psychical research.* Routledge and Kegan Paul.

Inglis, B. (1992). *Natural and supernatural: A history of the paranormal from earliest times to 1914* (Rev. ed.). Prism.

Morris, R. L. (1986). Minimizing subject fraud in the parapsychological laboratory. *European Journal of Parapsychology, 6,* 137–149.

Ochorowicz, J. (1896). La question de la fraude dans les expériences avec Eusapia Paladino. *Annales des Sciences Psychiques, 6,* 79–123.

Podmore, F. (1897). *Studies in psychical research.* G. P. Putnam's Sons.

Podmore, F. (1902). *Modern Spiritualism: A history and a criticism* (2 vols.). Methuen.

Pratt, J. G., Rhine, J. B., Smith, B. F., Stuart, C. E., & Greenwood, J. (1940). *Extra-sensory perception after sixty years.* Henry Holt.

Roe, C. A. (2016). The problem of fraud in parapsychology. *Mindfield, 8*(1), 8–17

Schmidt, H., Morris, R. L., & Rudolph, L. R. (1986). Channeling evidence for a PK effect to independent observers. *Journal of Parapsychology, 50,* 1–15.

Schrenck-Notzing, Baron [A. von]. (1920). *Phenomena of materialisation* (Rev. ed.) Paul Trench, Trübner.

Sidgwick, H. (1894). Disinterested deception. *Journal of the Society for Psychical Research, 6,* 274–278.

Varley, C. F. (1874, March 20). Electrical experiments with Miss Cook when entranced. *Spiritualist Newspaper,* 134–135.

Wallace, A. (1906). Spiritualists unmask a pretender: Exposure of Mr. Eldred. *Light, 26,* 111.

Historical Aspects of Parapsychological Terminology*

Nancy L. Zingrone & Carlos S. Alvarado†

The authors review the past and recent concerns about the precision and applicability of parapsychological terminology and discuss the following points: (1) the proliferation of terminology across several eras; (2) the problems caused by this proliferation, including the increasing difficulties one has in determining the proper use of specific terms; (3) the attitudes towards specific terms, mainly technical ones; and (4) the standardization attempts expressed at congresses and conferences. It is pointed out that it has not been possible to standardize parapsychological nomenclature because of lack of agreement. The authors suggest that the formulation of a terminology may be a dynamic social process that, at least in the case of an underdeveloped discipline such as parapsychology, cannot be ordered in a methodical way.

A number of recent publications suggest a growing interest in parapsychological terminology. Several journals have published articles that criticize specific terms and examine the general theoretical assumptions underlying parapsychological terminology (Beloff, 1979; Lucadou, 1984; Neppe, 1984; Thalbourne, 1985). Braude (1979) has published a book that probes the philosophical and conceptual foundations of some currently used terms. In addition, recent conferences have featured presentations and discussions on some of the problems inherent in parapsychological terminology. Some authors have suggested that standardization and redefinition are long overdue.

Because we believe that no serious effort to refine the disciplinary language of parapsychology should proceed without the benefit of the lessons of the past, we have surveyed the parapsychological literature on this topic. What follows is a brief review of our findings. Among the points we discuss are: the proliferation of parapsychological terminology; the influence of laboratory work on terms; the past efforts to promote precise and useful coining; parapsychologists' attitudes, past and present, toward specific types of terms and toward terminological standardization; official efforts to impose a consensus; and finally, recent efforts to reopen the debate.

The Proliferation of Terminology

Before 1882, the year the Society for Psychical Research was founded, there was an abundance of lay terms for supernatural phenomena.[1] Among them were: *divination, miracles, necromancy, oracles, scrying,* and *wraiths*. The development of mesmerism and spiritualism added many new expressions,

*Republished with permission from *Journal of Parapsychology, 51,* 4–74, 1987.

†This is a modified version of a paper presented at the 28th Annual Parapsychological Association Convention, August 12–16, 1985, Tufts University, Medford, Massachusetts.

We want to thank Loyd M. Auerbach, Wayne Norman, J. Ricardo Musso, and Rhea White for helping us obtain some references quoted in this paper; Eric J. Dingwall and Emilio Servadio for information about past attempts to standardize terminology in which they were involved; and John Beloff, Gerd H. Hövelmann, and Michael A. Thalbourne for their encouragement and useful suggestions on improving this paper.

such as *animal magnetism, lucidity, medium, séance,* and *somnambulism.*[2] In the early period of formal parapsychology (the 1880s to the 1920s), a number of writers contributed terms. Among these writers were: Aksakof (1890/1895); Boirac (1893, 1908/1917); Myers (1896, 1903); Richet (1922); and finally, Sudre (1926). Table 3.1 lists some of the terms they proposed.[3]

During this early period, a creative and prolific neologist, P. T. Bret, devised one of the most complex and extensive classifications of psychic phenomena ever suggested.[4] In his *Précis de Métapsychique: Subconscient et Métapsychisme* (1927), he included an equally extensive terminology. The book contained a glossary of 185 terms, a fourth of which were of his own invention. In a later paper, Bret (1939a) outlined three basic principles for creating terminology: (1) to "have a single name for each modality" from which other parts of speech may be derived; (2) to use the prefix *meta* for all basic phenomena, the prefix *tele* for all varieties of phenomena produced from the basic ones, and the suffix *gnosie* to imply direct paranormal knowledge without sensory contact; and (3) to "never employ technical terms used in another science" (p. 244, our translation).[5] At the time when Bret emphasized the suffix *gnosie,* Richet (1922) and others (e.g., Fisher, 1926) preferred *esthesie* (e.g., *cryptaesthesie*).

It is likely that the majority of the new terms proposed between 1930 and 1959 originated in J. B. Rhine's parapsychology laboratory. Modern writers often wrongly assume that Rhine coined the terms *extrasensory perception* (J. B. Rhine, 1934) and *psychokinesis* (L. E. Rhine & J. B. Rhine, 1943). Both these terms, however, were in use before Rhine began his work in parapsychology.[6] Nonetheless, Rhine's laboratory was "a fertile source of nomenclature designed to meet the new demands which its pioneering work created" (Beloff, 1982, p. x). As can be seen in Table 3.2 rather

Table 3.1. Examples of Terms Coined by Psychical Researchers (1880s-1920s)

Psychical Researcher	Term	Definition
Aksakof (1890/1895)	Telekinetic	Movement of objects without *contact*
Boirac (1908/1917)	Metagnomy	ESP
Fisher (1926)	Metakinesis	Movement of objects without contact
Holt (1914)	Telepsychosis	A telepathic experience
Hyslop (1907c)	Telemnesia	Telepathy of subconscious memory
Myers (1895)	Retrocognition	ESP of past events
Prubusch (1929)	Parascopy	ESP
Richet (1922)	Cryptaesthesia	ESP
Sudre (1926)	Thorybism	Poltergeist disturbances

Table 3.2. Terms Used by J.B. Rhine and Associates at Duke University's Parapsychology Laboratory (1930s-1950s)

Card Testing Procedures	Dice Testing Procedures
Before touching	High dice test
Blind matching	Low dice test
Down through	Placement test
Open matching	Sevens test
Psychic shuffle	Single test
Screen touch matching	

Note: These terms are taken from Rhine (1934) and from the glossary of the *Journal of Parapsychology* for the period in question.

than using largely phenomenological terms as earlier authors did, Rhine's staff coined terms that literally described specific testing procedures.[7] Rhine introduced a number of important changes that precipitated the shift in emphasis from phenomenological to operational descriptions. For example, he and his workers reduced broad areas of study in psychical research to specific hypotheses amenable to laboratory testing (J. B. Rhine, 1934). They standardized test procedures and methods of analysis.[8] Rhine's laboratory disseminated the new methodology through the publication of their journal, the production of testing handbooks (Humphrey, 1948; Stuart & Pratt, 1937), and the publication of basic texts (Pratt, Rhine, Smith, Stuart, & Greenwood, 1940; Rhine & Pratt, 1957). The research production of Rhine's laboratory dominated American parapsychology during the 1940s and 1950s. Consequently, most terms in use in those years, although by no means all, were phenomenologically limited. Terms were coined to describe procedures rather than phenomena, and otherwise expressed methodological concerns. This was also true of English terms during the period.[9]

In languages other than English, however, terminology continued to encompass a wider range of phenomena and problems (e.g., spontaneous phenomena, physical mediumship). Non-English terms reflected a wider variety of underlying assumptions as well as widely differing degrees of acceptance of the objective reality of the phenomena (e.g., some terms implied energetic explanations for some phenomena instead of more spiritualistic descriptions). Sudre's (1956) terms *thorybism* (denoting noisy poltergeist activity) and *hylocasty* (apport) were in use in French. Cazzamalli (1954) coined *radio-cerebral-psychograph* and *psychobiophysics*. Non-English terminology is still quite different in emphasis from that used by English-speaking parapsychologists. Quevedo's (1969/1971) term *ecto-colo-plasm* and Andrade's (1970/1976) use of *psi-matter* are cases in point.[10]

New terms have also entered the literature during the modern period (1960s to 1980s). We have listed only a small sample of recently coined terms in Table 3.3. Many modern neologisms represent refinements in methodology, new phenomena under study, or proposed explanatory models and concepts.

Although, on the face of it, the introduction of new terms and the refinement of old terms signal progress in parapsychology, new terms also bring serious new problems. Not the least of these are, specifically, the increasing terminological isolation of some segments of the English-speaking parapsychological community from other segments, and, generally, the isolation of English-speaking parapsychologists from their non-English-speaking colleagues.[11]

Table 3.3. Terms of Recent Coinage (1960s-1980s)

Terms	Source
Allobiofeedback	Braud (1978)
Delta-afferentation	Neppe (1984)
Focusing effect	Ryzl and Pratt (1963)
Omega	Palmer (1986)
Preferential effect	Rao (1962)
Psi-in-process	Giesler (1984)
Psi trailing	Rhine and Feather (1962)
Psi-mediated instrumental response	Stanford (1974b)
Psychopraxia	Thalbourne (I 982b)
Remote viewing	Targ and Puthoff (1974)
Transtemporal inhibition	Tart (1978)

Problems of Proliferation

In 1921, Walter Franklin Prince reviewed a discussion of terminology that had taken place at a then recent congress. He said: "In general, the physical sciences have technical terms with fixed senses understood the world over ... But it is not so with psychical research" (p. 554). Prince identified a number of problems inherent in parapsychological terminology, most of which still persist:[12]

1. *Different meanings for the same terms.* The old term *telergy,* introduced by Myers (1896, p. 174; 1903, vol. 1, p. xxii) was meant to explain telepathy through a supposed physical action on the brain of the percipient. Constable (1918), however, used *telergy* in a more general way, implying "the power in us all which *must be* for telepathy to exist" (p. 41). Sudre (1926), and later Quevedo (1969/ 1971), used *telergy* to denote a specific psychic energy or supposed fluidic force that both writers believed to be fundamental to paranormal physical phenomena.
2. *Different terms for the same phenomena.* In the old literature writers used a variety of terms to denote *extrasensory perception,* among them *supernormal cognition* (Osty, 1922/1923), *cryptaesthesia* (Richet, 1922), *metagnomy* (Boirac, 1917/1918), and *metaesthesia* (Fisher, 1926). Later, Thouless and Wiesner (1947) suggested *psi-gamma.*
3. *New and confusing definitions of words already in use in common or in scientific language. Psychometry* and, to a lesser extent, *psychokinesis* are in use in other disciplines as well as in parapsychology. According to Thalbourne (1982b), the term *psychometry* was coined by J. R. Buchanan "to refer to the practice in which *sensitives* hold an object in their hands and obtain *paranormal* information about the object or its owner" (p. 62). However, the term is more widely in use in psychology and psychiatry to mean "the measurement of the duration and force of mental processes" (Hinsie & Campbell, 1960, p. 598). Its derivative, *psychometrics,* is widely used and refers to specific aspects of psychological and personality testing. *Psychokinesis* was also in use in psychiatry in the 1960s as "T. S. Clouston's term for defective inhibition; [and to refer] to the clinical syndrome known as *impulse insanity*" (Hinsie & Campbell, 1960, p. 596).

Some Attitudes about Terminology

Readers of parapsychological journals frequently complain about the unnecessary complexity of specific terms and about the unnecessary use of "jargon" in technical reports. Mrs. Salter was among the first to address the problem of jargon. In her review of Bret's *Précis de Métapsychique*, she said: "It is probably a drawback to any science to be too heavily encumbered with jargon'; it must certainly be a drawback in psychical research, which derives much of its material from ordinary men and women, and should strive therefore ... to be intelligible to them" (Salter, 1932, p. 225).

Complexity frequently obscures or inhibits the intelligibility of terms. New terms coined to correct the inadequacies of old terms are, unfortunately, often more complex than the old ones. This problem may have led Besterman to consider the coining of new terms "as a rule to be deprecated" (1929, p. 183). Criticisms of the writings of Bret (Amadou, 1954; Salter, 1932), Holt (Friend, 1915), and Richet (Anonymous, 1923b; Holt, 1922) contained admonitions against the creation and use of cumbersome terms. An anonymous writer (1923b), probably Ralph Shirley, editor of the *Occult Review,* wrote: "Surely the plentiful use of Greek composite words transmogrifed into modern language aids us not one whit in our knowledge of the essential meaning of psychical phenomena" (p. 136).

Some writers supported the creation of new terms if they were part of a carefully prepared terminology. Bret (1927), in particular, complained of "indifference," "negligence," and "disorder" (p. 6) in parapsychological terminology. In his opinion, "metapsychics" could not attain the status of a science until a well-crafted vocabulary had been completed. Bret's terms, however, like those coined by many contemporary parapsychologists with similar complaints, tended to exacerbate existing terminological problems instead of solving them.

Boirac's concern predated Bret's by a decade: "Unfortunately, the students of these sciences have not always been aware of the importance of having a really appropriate language. ... Many of the difficulties which have impeded the progress of the psychical sciences have been due to the insufficiency of their verbal equipment" (Boirac, 1917/1918, p. 7). Others, such as Anastasy (1902), Fisher (1926), Hayes (1893), Osty (1928), Prince, (1921), Prubusch (1929), and Sudre (1925), also supported the creation of a technical and widely used terminology.

It is probable that antipathy toward complex or unclear terms was fueled, at least in part, by the perceived importance of balancing the researcher's need for succinct and usable technical terms against the public's need for descriptive and easily understandable terms. Certainly Salter, quoted above, and indeed many modern parapsychologists have argued that parapsychology *must* effectively serve two masters—the public and the professional community. Although our opinion is that this perennial balancing act has been debilitating to both scientific progress and professionalization in parapsychology, a discussion of the point is beyond the scope of this paper. It is likely, however, that J. B. Rhine's view was closer to Salter's than to ours. Rhine published a number of popular books (1937c, 1947d). He was interested in marketing ESP test materials, and he relied on the public for data and funds.[13] The terms his staff coined were particularly successful in both laboratory and general usage. As can be seen in Table 3.2, Rhinean terms were easily abbreviated for daily use in the laboratory and in research reports (*before touching* became *BT, open matching* became *OM, screened touch matching* became *STM*), as well as for use in publications intended for the general reader, such as the earliest practical manual issued by the Parapsychology Laboratory, Stuart and Pratt's *Handbook for Testing Extra-Sensory Perception* (1937). The glossary of the *Journal of Parapsychology* continued the work of translation for the lay reader by "avoid[ing] constant redefining ... of commonly recurring terms in papers" (Anonymous, 1937, p. 156). Similarly, the revised manual, Humphrey's *Handbook of Tests in Parapsychology* (1948), while it did not include a glossary, paid particular attention to clear definitions of terms and abbreviations in the text. Humphrey's explicitly stated purpose was to make things easier for the lay reader who wished to test himself or herself, and for the student or new researcher beginning a series of experiments.

As is common in other sciences, different researchers devised different terms and abbreviations for their own use. What was clear to one laboratory was not necessarily clear to another. When Soal (1949) reviewed Humphrey's *Handbook* in the *Journal of the Society for Psychical Research,* he said: "The present reviewer has always found it difficult to remember the connotation of American terms like *BT, OM, STM* without referring to a glossary" (p. 20). Had Soal gone on to maintain that different terminology was a prerogative of different laboratories (instead he listed some of his own operational abbreviations), it is likely that Rhine would have agreed. Rhine did reserve the coining of new terms for the individual researchers, who, in the course of writing up specific experiments might coin terms for new effects or methods. A short exchange of letters between Rhine (1947a, 1947b, 1947c) and D. H. Rawcliffe (1947a, 1947b) in 1947 illustrates Rhine's tendency to connect terminological development with experimental work.

Before publication of *The Psychology of the Occult* (1952), Rawcliffe wrote Rhine to propose a variety of new terms, among them *psygnosis,* meant to indicate "the operative factor" behind all forms of ESP (Rawcliffe, 1947a). Rhine (1947a) replied that the term failed to cover the whole range of psychic phenomena because it did not include psychokinesis. Rhine noted that the term *psi* was already in use. It combined both phenomena and thus made Rawcliffe's term less useful.

Rawcliffe, in a reply (1947b) that included a more detailed description of his terms, invited Rhine and his research staff to discuss them. In the first of two replies to this letter Rhine (1947b) defended the terms already in use and added:

> It was decided that just as he who pays the piper calls the tune, those who are experimentally working with these phenomena will naturally determine by their usage in their published reports what terms are the most usable in their communications to one another.
>
> This is not to say that good suggestions may not come from some other and that they will not be welcome. What I do mean is that if you wish to introduce a term it is best to do it in connection with a report of experimental work.

Although a draft of Rhine's reply was given to his colleagues for comment, a copy was prematurely sent to Rawcliffe. The written reactions of B. M. Humphrey and J. G. Pratt were similar to those that we had upon first reading. Humphrey (1947), presumably unaware that Rhine's letter had already been sent, prepared an alternate version with comments in which she pointed out that Rhine's response could antagonize Rawcliffe and that Rhine had contradicted himself regarding previously published comments (Rhine, 1945) in which he had maintained that researchers should avoid accepting terms on any other grounds than their usefulness. The qualifications or prominence of the term's coiner, she said, should not be taken into consideration. Presumably this statement could be logically extended to the occupation of the neologist as well. Pratt (1947), in a note appended to Humphrey's draft, underscored this last point when he asserted that "signal contribution[s]" to parapsychology could also be made by those who had never done experiments.

Rhine forwarded a few of Humphrey's paragraphs in a second letter to Rawcliffe (Rhine, 1947c). These paragraphs are particularly instructive concerning the attitude of the laboratory staff as a whole, illustrating, as they do, a commitment to the public as consumers of parapsychological literature.

> We feel that a term should be as descriptive as possible and also that long usage of a term is a point in its favor. For these reasons, the group decided that it would be very difficult to adopt your terms. We are somewhat restricted in the choice of terms because of the fact that in this country at least, we are dependent upon the acceptance of our work by the general public and upon their understanding of our findings; that is, we have practically no select group of readers who are primarily parapsychologists ... Thus, at the present time at least, we would be greatly handicapped in our communications with our readers in general and with other scientists if we were to adopt the terms suggested since they are not descriptive and a definition would have to be included each time they were used. (Rhine, 1947c)

Nothing exists in the manuscript collection to suggest that Rawcliffe ever replied directly to either of the last two letters in the exchange.[14] The guidelines that Humphrey referred to in her note to Rhine were published in an editorial in the *Journal of Parapsychology* and predated the exchange with Rawcliffe by a few years. In the editorial, Rhine (1945) outlined his opposition to efforts to standardize parapsychological terminology. He felt the time was not "ripe for a discussion of existing terminology" (p. 149; see also Rhine, 1937a, p. 83). Until parapsychology reached a consensus on the nature of the phenomena and on the principles governing it, Rhine felt that parapsychology had little hope "of handling so delicate a problem as that of bringing about agreement in any actual instance" (p. 149).

Rhine's (1945) seven guidelines, although similar in some respects to previous ideas, are probably the clearest and most systematic expression of the principles involved:

> First, a term should be as descriptive as reasonable brevity will allow.
> Second, the adaptability of the term to general usage …
> Third, there should be no unwarranted assumptions or unsubstantiated hypotheses implied in the choice of the term.
> Fourth, it is advisable to consider the international character of the field of study and to try to use terms that offer little difficulty in translation …
> Fifth, long usage of a given term or acceptance by a considerable body of people … may be given weight in its favor, but not against serious defects it may have in respect to the points listed above.
> Sixth, no respect for authority should be shown in assigning a name.
> Seventh, consistency with already established scientific patterns of usage should be respected, along with any other factors that will aid the student to grasp and retain the meaning of the term more easily. (pp. 148–149)

When Humphrey pointed out the potential conflict between Rhine's sixth guideline and his second reply to Rawcliffe (Rhine, 1947b), she was uncovering relatively common behavior. Rhine certainly was not the first terminologist to break his own rules, nor probably would he be the last.[15]

Recent Attitudes

Much of the negative comment vented at the proliferation of terminology has been aimed specifically at jargon. Recently, Beloff (1982, pp. vii–viii) mentioned the necessity of maintaining a clear distinction between the two.

An exchange of letters published in the *Journal of the Society for Psychical Research* over the years between 1979 and 1983 touched on similar issues. Two readers complained about the increasing use of jargon in SPR articles (Grosse, 1979; Nisbet, 1979). Four others drew distinctions, albeit unclear ones, between jargon and technical language (Hövelmann, 1983a; Sargent, 1979; Thalbourne, 1982a; West, 1982). Although, in general, all the correspondents deplored the use of jargon "which obfuscates meaning" (Sargent, 1979, p. 195), the latter writers made a case for the usefulness of technical expressions and "appeal[ed] for tolerance of technical detail and language" (West, 1982, p. 398). It was felt that the use of technical language when done with a "virile sense of moderation in our recourse to technical expressions" (Thalbourne, 1982a, p. 397), as well as the use of "complex diagrams, or details of statistical calculations [are] often unavoidable" (Hövelmann, 1983a, p. 90) if writers hope to meet the requirements of a high standard of scientific reporting.

In a recent editorial statement in the same journal, Beloff (1985) wrote: "We wish to apologize to readers who may still be having problems with the terminology used in some of our more technical articles. However, psychical researchers need their technical vocabulary no less than other scientists" (p. 137).

The persistence of a commitment to popularization in parapsychology can be seen in the above exchanges, in Beloff's editorial, in the history of the SPR,[16] and most clearly in Rhine's (1947c) last letter to Rawcliffe. However, working parapsychologists, even those with *no* interest in popularization, have repeatedly made similar points about jargon.

Honegger and Hövelmann recently published criticisms along these lines.[17] Honegger (1982) objected strenuously to terminology that was "unnecessarily theory-laden" or "unintentionally demeaning and confusing" (p. 22). Hövelmann (1983b), in the *Zetetic Scholar,* put such criticism on stronger and more substantive ground in his "Seven Recommendations for the Future Practice of Parapsychology." The fourth recommendation read as follows: "Parapsychologists should cease to pretend that they are able to *explain* anything by means of their present terminology which is merely *descriptive* and build up a *standardized, methodically constructed* terminology as soon as possible" (p. 131). The *Zetetic Scholar* published a variety of responses to Hövelmann's recommendations. According to Palmer (1983a), the problem is that "we use the same set of terms to label what we seek to explain ... as we use to label the principle or process which ... might serve to explain it. ... What we need is one standardized set of descriptive, theoretically neutral terms and a separate set (or sets) of theoretical terms." Palmer continued in his reply: "Current usage of terms like 'psi' often create the illusion that we are explaining an anomaly when in fact we are only identifying one. ... Our present terminology ... serves to retard the development of genuine theory building in parapsychology by giving us this subtle illusion of understanding" (p. 164).[18,19,20] In a later paper, Hövelmann (1984) extended the argument. He laid the blame for the lack of replicability in parapsychological research partly at the doorstep of its inadequate terminology: "The obscure, inconsistent, and ambiguous terminological means, which presently are at our disposal, cannot be used for a clear, unmistakable, and unambiguous formulation of instructions, experimental purposes, etc." (p. 296).

An additional respondent to the *Zetetic Scholar* article (Stokes, 1983) took issue with Hövelmann's intent and suggested that a new terminology has to be developed hand in hand with testable theories in order for the first to have a firm empirical basis. The current lack of reliable findings suggests that such development may have to wait until a more consistent data base is obtained.

At first glance it appeared to us and to Stokes that a basic disagreement existed between the two authors; that is, Stokes seemed to argue for theory-bound terminology and Hövelmann seemed to argue for theory-free terminology. In fact, Hövelmann, in response to an earlier draft of this paper in which we used points made in his 1984 contribution to the *European Journal of Parapsychology,* argued that both inadequate terminology and replication problems were symptoms of a lack of understanding of the purpose of experimentation. He wrote: "Strictly speaking, the latter means that inadequate terminology is an inevitable consequence of inadequate philosophy/theory" (Hövelmann, 1986).

In general, controversies over the intellectual framework in which standardization should be couched have taken on a frustratingly circular bent. Some argue that terminology must be formed in advance of experimentation. Others argue that it must be formed in advance of theoretical development. And still others argue that terminology is a consequence of experimentation or theoretical development. Still others maintain that terminology, theory, and experimentation are all bound together and cannot be constructed separately or understood except in their interaction with one another. These arguments seem to us to be based on fundamental differences of opinion about what constitutes a proper theory, about how theories must develop, and about how methodology is categorized as adequate or reasonable for theoretical tasks at hand. Such fundamental disagreements were very much in evidence at the Dallas workshop on terminology.[21] Viewpoints similar to Palmer's, Hövelmann's, and Stokes's complicated the discussion. Participants voiced what seemed to us to be a justifiable defensiveness about the criteria by which they judged terms to be theory-laden or imprecise. These criteria, when articulated, were very often unshared by some or all of the other participants. There were *real* differences in degrees of confidence in parapsychological findings, and in the appropriateness of certain proposed theories that could not be minimized. There were *real* differences in methodological philosophies that could not be written off as consequences of incompetence or failures of training.

As can be seen in the attitudes reflected in print, and at other meetings, coming to grips with these types of fundamental differences, particularly when they constitute the hidden text of a debate rather than the acknowledged text, often severely inhibits the production of adoptable solutions to perceived terminological problems.

Efforts at Standardization

Congresses and Conferences

Although Forthuny (1923) speculated on the idea of an academy to regulate "metapsychic vocabulary," the only official attempts at regulating usage in parapsychology occurred at several of the international congresses held in the 1920s.

A motion proposed by Walter Franklin Prince at the 1921 congress at Copenhagen was unanimously approved. The resolution, published in the conference proceedings, read as follows:

> Resolved: that the proposition that a special committee be appointed to consider and if possible prepare a standard glossary of technical terms suited to the needs of psychical research, and to be employed internationally, is referred to the General Committee, with recommendation that they put it into effect and that a report be rendered at the second Congress. (Prince, 1922, p. 540)

At the second congress, held in Warsaw in 1923, delegates set up a committee comprised of one member from each nation represented at the meeting. The committee was to work on the problem and present guidelines at the third congress (Anonymous, 1924; Sudre, 1923). The committee developed several suggestions, among which were: (1) that new terms should be derived from Greek or Latin, and (2) that terms considered ambiguous or discredited from a scientific point of view should be eliminated (Sudre, 1923).

Suggestions for terminology were presented at the third congress, held in Paris in 1927. Although the proceedings of the conference do not present the text of the papers on terminology (Anonymous, 1928),[22] a report of the conference (Anonymous, 1927, p. 236) lists four papers on the topic. W. H. Salter (Anonymous, 1927, p. 315) opened the session by stating that the SPR had decided not to change any of the terms they had been using. Even if problems were inherent in the terms, the fact that they were convenient made it desirable to retain them (Anonymous, 1927, p. 315).[23] The conference report went on to say that "every name proposed by a delegate was consistently rejected by all the others for a variety of reasons" (Anonymous, 1927, p. 314, our translation).

Bret (1939b) reported that he unsuccessfully tried to interest Hans Driesch in using his influence to form a commission at the 1930 congress in Athens for the development of a terminology based on the prefix *meta.* To judge from the proceedings of the conference (Besterman, 1930) as well as those of the conference held in Oslo in 1935 (Anonymous, n. d. [ca. 1935]) there were no further discussions on the standardization of terminology in this particular series of congresses.

Other organizers, at other times and in other countries, however, have brought the topic of terminology before their meetings' attendees. At the First Italian Congress of Metapsychics, held in Sienna in 1949, one of the points agreed on was that the congress "accepts the proposition made by some delegates on the necessity and urgency for revision and unification of the vocabulary of metapsychics" (Anonymous, 1949, p. 250, our translation). However, like the resolutions that preceded it, this one produced no revised vocabulary, so far as we know.

In the early 1950s, the Parapsychology Foundation began their series of international meetings. The First International Conference of Parapsychological Studies, hosted by Tenhaeff at the University of Utrecht in 1953, recommended that the terms *psi-gamma* and *psi-kappa,* proposed as substitutes for *ESP* and *PK* by Thouless and Wiesner (1947), be adopted for general use (Anonymous, 1954). Although these terms are currently in use in some quarters, they have not found their way into general usage. (However, the shorter expression *psi* has been almost universally adopted.)

As a result of the Parapsychology Foundation's interest in international collaboration, another attempt was made. In the March-April 1957 edition, the *Newsletter of the Parapsychology Foundation* published a listing of parapsychological terms (Anonymous, 1957a). These terms were preparatory to a committee report to be given at the International Research Coordination Meeting of the Parapsychology Foundation, held in France the following August. At that meeting George Zorab presented a paper called "Clarification and Unification of Parapsychological Terms" (Anonymous, 1957b, pp. 1–2). He reported on the work already done by the committee devoted to terminology (of which the previously mentioned list of terms and an accompanying international table of translations were presumably a part). According to the conference report (Anonymous, 1957b), Zorab stressed "the importance of establishing definitions that will accurately represent the meaning of parapsychological terms while being readily translatable into several languages" (p. 2). One of the four resolutions passed at that conference established an official preparatory committee under Zorab's chairmanship with Eric J. Dingwall, Rosalind Heywood, and Emilio Servadio as committee members. Recent communication with the surviving members of the committee suggests that this attempt to standardize parapsychological terminology was as fruitless as preceding ones had been. Servadio (1985) wrote that "practically nothing" was done by the committee, while Dingwall (1985) said that the committee engaged only in "informal discussion at which it was decided that, in view of the various difficulties and complications, the matter should be dropped."

After a period of inactivity, interest in standardization has recently been revitalized. Hövelmann broached the subject in a presentation at the 1982 Parapsychological Association convention at Cambridge (Hövelmann, 1983b; see the above discussion of his paper). At the 1985 Parapsychological Association convention, in the context of a further discussion on the lack of "a sharp terminological distinction between the events in nature that need to be explained and the theoretical constructs proposed to explain them," Palmer (1986, p. 138) called for the Parapsychological Association's Council to "set up a committee to formulate recommendations for modifications in parapsychological terminology" (p. 141). An earlier version of the present paper (Alvarado & Zingrone, 1986), given in the same symposium, concurred with Palmer on this point (although we have since come to doubt the usefulness of such a committee). Of the other two "terminological" presentations (Ballard, 1986; Thalbourne, 1986), the first voted against an official committee, and the second focused on specific terms.

The Glossaries

In 1896, addressing the growing confusion over the meaning of specific terms, F. W. H. Myers wrote: "We have been repeatedly asked to furnish a glossary of the unfamiliar words which those inquiries [psychical research] oblige us to use" (p. 166). He eventually published a glossary, which was revised some years later (Myers, 1896, 1903). Myer's glossary was not the first, however.

Allan Kardec, in his book *Le Livre des Médiums* (1861), published one of the first glossaries dealing with paranormal phenomena. Mainly a collection of terms presumably coined by Kardec, the glossary reflected Kardec's spiritistic concepts. F. W. Hayes published another early glossary in 1893. This volume was mainly a list of spiritualistic terms.

Other later glossaries included Bret's "Vocabulaire Métapsychique" (1927, pp. 29–58), the dictionaries of Depascale and Rinaldini (1927), López Gómez (1929), and Fodor's (1933) well-known *Encyclopaedia of Psychic Science.* More recent works include the glossaries of Amadou (1954, pp. 358–364), Dale and White (1977), Jordán Peña (1975), Morel and Dalí Moral (1977), Teixera de Paula (1976), and Thalbourne (1982b). The glossary by Dietz, de Jong, and Zorab (1956) was particularly interesting because terms were translated into Dutch, English, and French.

However, many of these glossaries suffered from severe problems. Some were incomplete and focused on the terms of specific persons or countries. Aage Slomann urged the compilation, therefore, of an international glossary. Having unsuccessfully presented the idea to the Parapsychology Foundation in 1961, Slomann (1962) approached the SPR. His paper lists a number of alternate plans for a glossary, including one in which lists of equivalent terms in different languages would be published in either dictionary or encyclopedic form. Slomann presented the idea again at the Seventh Annual Parapsychological Association Convention in 1964. At that point Slomann was reporting encouragement from the SPR and some promise of funds from Rhine's Parapsychology Laboratory (Slomann, 1964, p. 297). However, to our knowledge, no dictionary resulted.

Some consensus on the usefulness of Thalbourne's (1982b) glossary is being reached. In addition to a recent SPR editorial urging its use (Beloff, 1985), a number of positive reviews have been published (Alvarado, 1983; Palmer, 1983b; White, 1983), and a committee at the Institute for Parapsychology has recently used Thalbourne's glossary in their major revision of the glossary of the *Journal of Parapsychology.* In addition to Thalbourne's recent effort, the best of the previously published glossaries (among them are Dietz, de Jong, & Zorab, 1956; Fodor, 1933; and Dale & White, 1977) may help to decrease terminological confusion in parapsychology, particularly that caused by the diversity of languages and national preferences extant in the discipline.

Although it has been proposed at least once that other parapsychological journals include a glossary (Thalbourne, 1982a, p. 398), the *Journal of Parapsychology* is currently the only journal that regularly prints one. Staff-written, the *Journal's* glossaries have been included in nearly all issues of the *Journal* from 1937 to 1938, and from 1942 to the present.[24] The impact of this glossary on the common usage of technical expressions in the English language literature has been considerable. Later glossaries have repeatedly relied on the *Journal's* definitions (see, for example, Dale & White, 1977; Rhine & Pratt, 1957; and Thalbourne, 1982b). For the most part, however, phenomenological, philosophical, and theoretical terms have been beyond its scope.

Concluding Remarks

In the course of this paper, we have mentioned the proliferation of terminology in different periods and by different means. We have catalogued some attitudes toward the coining and correct usage of terms and looked briefly at various working committees and other formal attempts to standardize parapsychological terminology. Two primary attitudes emerge. They are that: (1) it is (eternally) necessary to improve our nomenclature; and (2) it is difficult to resist solving terminological problems by coining entirely new and often more problematic terms. In addition, one distressing fact clouds the developments reviewed here. That is that terminological discussions evoke highly subjective and often emotionally laden discussion. It is possible that the tendency to personalize terminological debate is indicative only of the diversity of training and world views among parapsychologists. It is more likely, however, that some deeper entanglement of speaker and language is at the root of the problem.

We undertook our historical investigation to briefly and superficially review the chronology of terminological concerns in the hope that we might provide some perspective and guidance to those who are currently engaged in standardization attempts. While we have attempted to provide some historical context, we have not been able to provide any reassurance that terminological consensus can in fact be achieved. On the contrary, we have discovered that direct and formal attempts to impose consensus usually fail. Further, from what we have reviewed, it seems entirely possible that the formulation of any disciplinary language is a dynamic social process that *cannot* be ordered in a methodical way, at least in underdeveloped disciplines like parapsychology. (Studies of terminology in other fields are necessary before generalizing our points to science at large.)

In parapsychology, successful, albeit impermanent, terminological refinement has proceeded from an on-going, mainly indirect, negotiation between the individuals who produce our research literature, those who examine the philosophical and conceptual underpinnings of parapsychological theory, methodology, and terminology, and those who draw the synthesis on which the glossaries are based. Perhaps this is as it should be. Perhaps we are mistaken in seeking to enforce consensus, to obtain some *resolution* to our terminological crises. Perhaps it is the process itself that is of paramount importance to the progress of the field.

With that in mind, we will venture beyond our domain as historians and issue our best advice. Parapsychology must provide the environment in which continued terminological negotiation can take place. This can be accomplished by: (1) maintaining a willingness to commit meeting time and journal pages to terminological topics; (2) encouraging deeper and more substantive criticisms of theories, models, and terms from both parapsychologists and outside critics; (3) instilling an abiding sense that the coining and defining of terms is a difficult but often necessary business that calls for a reduction of emotional investment in, and the application of, reasonable and deliberate criteria to one's *own* terms (as opposed to only the terms of others); and (4) requiring that parapsychologists exercise more than a little restraint in the face of the often overwhelming urge to create yet another neologism.

Notes

1 For general reviews of these periods that are not, however, specifically concerned with terminology, see Ennemoser (1854) and Inglis (1977).

2 For more information on this period, see: Howitt (1863) and Inglis (1977).

3 See also Bret (1927), Fisher (1926), Hayes (1893), Holt (1914), Morselli (1908), and Prubusch (1929).

4 Bret (1878, ca. 1951) was a relatively unknown French physician who lived in Lisbon and published a number of books and papers on psychical research between 1920 and 1941. He discussed many classic mediumistic and spontaneous cases (e.g., Bret, 1927, 1939a, 1939b, 1940). According to Sibille (1951), Bret had a wide knowledge of metapsychics and other disciplines. However, Bret's contemporaries considered him to be dogmatic about the efficacy of certain controversial explanations and about the reality of certain contested phenomena.

5 Among the terms ending in *gnosie* that Bret proposed were *metagnosy* (originally suggested as the basic term from which all others were to be differentiated), *psychognosy* (a kind of mind-reading), *pragmanosy* (roughly equivalent to the current, popular definition of clairvoyance), *pathosy* (paranormal diagnosis of illness), and *hylosy* (defined as paranormal knowledge of "matter inaccessible to the senses, unknown, lost, or hidden") (1927, p. 36; our translation).

6 Pagenstecher used the term *extra-sensory perception* in 1924, Fisher in 1926, and Sainville in 1927. Each of these authors understood the term in essentially the same way Rhine did. Holt used *psychokinesis* in 1914 to denote the "power" necessary for mediumistic communication. Boirac's term (1908/1917, p. 129), *vital psychokynesia,* first used in 1908, was similar in meaning to Rhine's *psychokinesis.*

7 Operationalisms and terms that described or named various apparata designed to study physical phenomena did exist before Rhine (see Carrington, 1939, for examples). However, phenomenological terms were more widely used.

8 See also Mauskopf and McVaugh (1980) and L. E. Rhine (1971) for discussions of this period.

9 For good examples of English operationalisms see Soal's experimental reports (Soal, 1940; and Soal and Goldney, 1943), and West's (1945, 1954) reviews of British research. Soal (1949) also presents British reactions to American terms in his review of Humphrey's *Handbook.* In addition, a complete glossary of Soal's terms appears in Soal and Bateman (1954, pp. 362–367).

10 For other examples of earlier terms see Bret, 1940; Kherumian, 1948; Musso, 1954; and Van Rijnberk, 1952. Examples of more recent terms can be found in De Boni, 1960/1975; Dubrov and Pushkin, 1982; and Jordán Peña, 1975.

11 Part of the latter problem arises from the inability of English-speaking parapsychologists to read other languages or, even if they are fluent in other languages, from their general disinterest in non-English work. International collaboration is not much closer to being a reality in parapsychology today than it was when Murphy (1954) made a strong plea for it.

12 The headings of these paragraphs are taken from Prince's discussion. The examples are ours.

13 For evidence of this attitude see J. B. Rhine (1937b, p. 162) and also Mauskopf and McVaugh (1980, chapter 6).

14 Rawcliffe (1952) later published a harsh critique of parapsychology. J. B. Rhine (1953) reviewed the book and suggested that Rawcliffe may have turned against the field as a result of the indifferent reception his terminology encountered. In a brief reply to the review, Rawcliffe (1953) called Rhine's argument "the sheerest poppycock."

15 See, for example, Myers's (1885, p. 24) endorsement of descriptive terms and disagreement with terms first used as metaphors and later "incessantly sliding into an assertion of fact." See also his later complex and theory-laden neologisms (Myers, 1896) and our discussion of Bret in this paper.

16 For examples of this in the old literature, see statements by some prominent SPR members (e.g., Gurney, Myers, & Podmore, 1886, vol. 2, p. 273; and Myers, 1896, p. 166).

17 For similar discussions see Morris (1975) and Stanford (1974a).

18 For examples of this in the old literature, see statements by some prominent SPR members (e.g., Gurney, Myers, & Podmore, 1886, vol. 2, p. 273; and Myers, 1896, p. 166).

19 For similar discussions see Morris (1975) and Stanford (1974a).

20 This particular pitfall of imprecise use of terms was recognized relatively early on in parapsychology. See Barrett (1924), Bozzano (1922), and Hyslop (1907b). Hyslop (1907a) stated in the first issue of the *Journal of the American Society for Psychical Research* that the journal, as a policy, would use the terms *telepathy, clairvoyance,* and *premonition* in a purely descriptive way. Whether this policy was consistently applied, even in Hyslop's own work, is debatable.

21 This took place at the 1984 Parapsychological Convention in Dallas. The meeting, convened by M. A. Thalbourne, was informal and not a part of the convention's program. Our comments reflect our own opinions and are based on both our contemporary notes and on memory.

22 Quartier (1928), writing in the proceedings of the congress, implies that the presentations on terminology were not published because they were "fruitless sessions" (p. vi, our translation).

23 In an anonymous (n. d. [ca. 1927]), untitled report drafted by an SPR committee that we think may have been the text of Salter's presentation, the author suggested that "the terminology used by Myers in *Human Personality ... notwithstanding* certain defects in form be substantially preserved." It is not surprising, therefore, that the work of this section was described years later by Vesme (1934, p. 66) as being impeded by the "opposition of the Anglo-Saxons." See also Bird's (1927, p. 687) amusing account of this session.

24 From 1939 to 1941, the *Journal of Parapsychology* was edited in New York by an editorial team headed by Gardner Murphy. Murphy's group did not include a glossary in their issues.

References

Aksakof, A. (1895). *Animisme et spiritisme.* P. G. Leymarie. (Original work published in German, 1890)

Alvarado, C. S. (1983). Review of *A glossary of terms used in parapsychology*, by M. A. Thalbourne. *Journal of the American Society for Psychical Research, 77*, 347–349.

Alvarado C. S., & Zingrone, N. L. (1986). Historical aspects of parapsychological terminology. In D. H. Weiner & D. I. Radin (Eds.), *Research in parapsychology 1985* (pp. 136–137). Scarecrow Press. (Abstract)

Amadou, R. (1954). *La parapsychologie.* Denoël.

Anastasy, E. (1902). Avec une nomenclature rationalle des phénomènes de la science psychique. *Compte rendu du congrès spirite et spiritualiste international* (pp. 524–527). Société Française d'Étude des Phénomènes Psychiques.

Andrade, H. G. (1976). *The psi-matter.* (Monograph No. 2.) Instituto Brasileiro de Pesquisas Psicobiofísicas. (Original work published in Portuguese, 1970.)

Anonymous. (1923b). Notes of the month. *Occult Review, 38*, 129–140.

Anonymous. (1924). Sixième Journée. *L'état actuel des recherches psychiques.* (pp. 346–349). Presses Universitaires de France.

Anonymous. (1927). Le IIIe Congrès international de recherches psychiques. *Revue Métapsychique, 4*, 233–237; *5*, 313–317.

Anonymous. (Ed.). (1928). *Compte rendu du IIIème Congrès International de Recherches Psychiques à Paris.* Institut Métapsychique International.

Anonymous. (1937). Glossary. *Journal of Parapsychology, 1*, 156–157.

Anonymous. (1949). La vie métapsychique: Le premier congrès Italien de métapsychique. *Revue Métapsychique, 8*, 249–250.

Anonymous. (1954). Avant-propos. *Revue Métapsychique*, 29–30.

Anonymous. (1957a). Parapsychological terms. *Newsletter of the Parapsychology Foundation, Inc., 4*(2), 5–6.

Anonymous. (1957b). International Research Coordination Meeting. *Newsletter of the Parapsychology Foundation, Inc., 4*(5), 1–2.

Anonymous. (n. d. [ca. 1927]). *Report on psychical research terminology, drafted by a committee of the SPR, for submission to the 1927 International Congress of Psychical Research.* Archives of the American Society for Psychical Research.

Anonymous. (Ed.). (n. d. [ca. 1935]). Das Internasjonale Kongress für Psyckisk Forskning. n. p.

Ballard, J. A. (1986). Adequacy of some parapsychological terms. In D. H. Weiner & D. I. Radin (Eds.), *Research in Parapsychology 1985* (pp. 144–148). Scarecrow Press. (Abstract)

Barrett, W. (1924). Some reminiscences of fifty years' psychical research. *Proceedings of the Society for Psychical Research, 34*, 275–297.

Beloff, J. (1979). The categories of psi: The case for retention. *European Journal of Parapsychology, 3*, 69–77.

Beloff, J. (1982). Foreword. In M. A. Thalbourne (Comp.), *A glossary of terms used in parapsychology* (pp. vii–x). Heinemann.

Beloff, J. (1985). Letter to our readers. *Journal of the Society for Psychical Research, 53*, 137.

Besterman, T. (1929). Notes on periodicals. *Journal of the Society for Psychical Research, 25*, 183–186.

Besterman, T. (Ed.). (1930). *Transactions of the Fourth International Congress for Psychical Research.* Society for Psychical Research.

Bird, J. M., (1927). The Paris Congress-II. *Journal of the American Society for Psychical Research, 21*, 679–687.

Boirac, E. (1893). Un essai de classification des phénomènes parapsychiques. *Annales des sciences Psychiques, 3*, 341–354.

Boirac, E. (1917). *Our hidden forces.* Frederick A. Stokes. (Original work published in French, 1908)

Boirac, E. (1918). *The psychology of the future.* Frederick A. Stokes. (Original work published in French, 1917)

Bozzano, E. (1922). L'hypothese spirite et la "cryptesthesie." *Revue Métapsychique, 4*, 236–246.

Braud, W. (1978). Allobiofeedback: Immediate feedback for a psychokinetic influence upon another person's physiology. In W. G. Roll (Ed.), *Research in parapsychology 1977* (pp. 123–134). Scarecrow Press. (Abstract)

Braude, S. E. (1979). *ESP and psychokinesis: A philosophical examination.* Temple University Press.
Bret, P. T. (1927). *Précis de métapsychique: Subconscient et métapsychisme.* J. B. Baillière et Fils.
Bret, [P.] T. (1939a). La terminologie métapsychique. *Revue Métapsychique,* 4–6, 241–257.
Bret, P. T. (1939b). *Les métapsychoses: La métapsychorragie; la télépathie; la hantise* (Vol. 1). J. B. Baillière et Fils.
Bret, [P.] T. (1940). Vocabulaire de la métapsychique. *Revue Métapsychique, 21,* 35–52, 110–133.
Carrington, H. [1939]. *Laboratory investigations into psychic phenomena.* David McKay.
Cazzamalli, F. (1954). La metapsichica nuova disciplina scientifica. *Metapsichica, 9,* 5–27.
Constable, F. C. (1918). *Telergy. (The Communion of Souls).* Kegan, Paul, Trench, Trübner.
Dale, L. A., & White, R. A. (Comps.) (1977). Glossary of terms found in the literature of psychical research and parapsychology. In B. B. Wolman *(Ed.), Handbook of parapsychology* (pp. 921–936). Van Nostrand Reinhold.
de Boni, G. (1975). *L'uomo alla conquista dell'anima.* Armenia. (Original work published 1960)
Despascale, A., & Rinaldini, M. (1927). *Diccionario de metapsiquica, espiritismo y filosofía espiritualista.* Privately printed.
Dietz, P. A., de Jong, K. H. E., & Zorab, G. (1956). *Parapsychologische woordentalk.* H. P. Leopolds.
Dingwall, E. J. (1985). Personal communication, December 18.
Dubrov, A. P., & Pushkin, V. N. (1982). *Parapsychology and contemporary science.* Consultants Bureau.
Ennemoser, J. (1854). *The history of magic* (2 vols.). Henry G. Bohn.
Fisher, O. (1926). Zur Nomenklatur und Systematik des Okkultismus. *Zeitschrift für Parapsychologie, 1,* 304–310.
Fodor, N. (1933). *Encyclopaedia of psychic science.* Arthurs Press.
Forthuny, P. (1923). Chronique étrangère: Terminologie. *Revue Métapsychique, 5,* 333–335.
Friend, E. W. (1915). Mr. Henry Holt on the cosmic relations. *Journal of the American Society for Psychical Research, 9,* 132–147.
Giesler, P. (1984). Parapsychological anthropology: I. Multi-method approaches to the study of psi in the field setting. *Journal of the American Society for Psychical Research, 78,* 289–330.
Grosse, M. (1979). Correspondence. *Journal of the Society for Psychical Research, 50,* 39–40.
Gurney, E., Myers, F. W. H., & Podmore, F. (1886). *Phantasms of the living* (2 vols.). Trübner.
Hayes, F. W. (1893). A glossary of psychical phenomena. *Borderland, 1,* 71–72.
Hinsie, L. E., & Campbell, R. J. (1960). *Psychiatric dictionary.* Oxford University Press.
Holt, H. (1914). *On the cosmic relations* (2 vols.). Houghton-Mifflin.
Holt, H. (1922). A review of Richet. *Journal of the American Society for Psychical Research, 16,* 655–670.
Honegger, B. (1982). The necessity for theory-free terminology in parapsychology. In W. G. Roll, R. L. Morris, & R. A. White (Eds.), *Research in parapsychology 1981* (pp. 21–22). Scarecrow Press. (Abstract)
Hövelmann, G. H. (1983a). Correspondence. *Journal of the Society for Psychical Research, 52,* 90–91.
Hövelmann, G. H. (1983b). Seven recommendations for the future practice of parapsychology. *Zetetic Scholar, 11,* 128–138.
Hövelmann, G. H. (1984). Are psi experiments repeatable? A conceptual framework for the discussion of repeatability. *European Journal of Parapsychology, 5,* 285–306.
Hövelmann, G. H. (1986). Personal communication, May 21.
Howitt, W. (1863). *The history of the supernatural.* J. B. Lippincott.
Humphrey, B. (1947). *Note to J. B. Rhine's proposed draft of letter to answer Rawcliffe, undated.* J. B. Rhine Papers, Manuscript Department, Duke University Library, Durham, NC.
Humphrey, B. (1948). *Handbook of tests in parapsychology.* Parapsychology Laboratory.
[Hyslop, J. H.]. (1907a). Editorial: Explanation of terms. *Journal of the American Society for Psychical Research, 1,* 36.
Hyslop, J. H. (1907b). Telepathy. *Journal of the American Society for Psychical Research, 1,* 308–327.
[Hyslop, J. H.]. (1907c). Editorial. *Journal of the American Society for Psychical Research,* 1, 522–527.
Inglis, B. (1977). *Natural and supernatural.* Hodder and Stoughton.
Jordán Peña, J. L. (1975). Primeras aportaciones a un léxico parapsicológico. *Psi Comunicación, 1,* 129–152.
Kardec, A. (1861). *Le livre des médiums.* Didier.
Kherumian, R. (1948). Introduction à l'étude de la connaissance parapsychologique. *Revue Métapsychique, 1,* 23–35; *2,* 70–81; *3,* 142–157.
López Gómez, Q. (1929). *Diccionario de metapsíquica y espiritismo.* Maucci.

Lucadou, W. von. (1984). What is wrong with the definition of psi? *European Journal of Parapsychology, 5*, 261–283.
Mauskopf, S. H., & McVaugh, M. R. (1980). *The elusive science: Origins of experimental psychical research.* Johns Hopkins University Press.
Morel, H. V., & Dalí Moral, J. (1977). *Diccionario de parapsicología.* Kier.
Morris, R. L. (1975). Tacit communication and experimental theology. In J. D. Morris, W. G. Roll, & R. L. Morris (Eds.), *Research in parapsychology 1974* (pp. 179–198). Scarecrow Press.
Morselli, E. (1908). *Psicologia e "spiritismo"* (2 vols.). Fratelli Bocca.
Murphy, G. (1954). International collaboration in psychical research: Some reflections on the Utrecht Conference. *Journal of the American Society for Psychical Research, 48*, 81–95.
Musso, J. R. (1954). *En los limites de la psicología.* Periplo.
Myers, F. W. H. (1885). Automatic writing—II. *Proceedings of the Society for Psychical Research, 3*, 1–63.
Myers, F. W. H. (1895). The subliminal self. (Part 8). *Proceedings of the Society for Psychical Research, 11*, 334–407.
Myers, F. W. H. (1896). Glossary of terms used in psychical research. *Proceedings of the Society for Psychical Research, 12*, 166–174.
Myers, F. W. H. (1903). *Human personality and its survival of bodily death* (2 vols.). Longmans, Green.
Neppe, V. M. (1984). Extrasensory perception: An anachronism and anathema. *Journal of the Society for Psychical Research, 52*, 365–370.
Nisbet, B. C. (1979). Correspondence. *Journal of the Society for Psychical Research, 50*, 125.
Osty, E. (1923). *Supernormal faculties in man.* Methuen. (Original work published in French, 1922)
Osty, E. (1928). Rapport sur la préparation du Congrès. In *Compte rendu du IIléme Congrès International de Recherches Psychiques à Paris.* (pp. 27–32.). Institut Métapsychique International.
Pagenstecher, G. (1924). *Aussersinnliche Warhrnehmung.* C. Marhold.
Palmer, J. (1983a). Response to "Seven recommendations for the future practice of parapsychology." *Zetetic Scholar, 11*, 164–165.
Palmer, J. (1983b). Review of *A glossary of terms used in parapsychology,* by M. A. Thalbourne. *Journal of the Society for Psychical Research, 52*, 205–206.
Palmer, J. (1986). Terminological poverty in parapsychology: Two examples. In D. H. Weiner & D. I. Radin (Eds.), *Research in Parapsychology 1985* (pp. 138–141). Scarecrow Press. (Abstract)
Pratt, J. G. (1947). *Note appended to Humphrey's draft of Rhine's September 10th letter to Rawcliffe, undated.* J. B. Rhine Papers, Manuscript Department, Duke University Library, Durham, NC.
Pratt, J. G., Rhine, J. B., Smith, B. F., Stuart, C. E., & Greenwood, J. A. (1940). *Extra-sensory perception after sixty years.* Henry Holt.
Prince, W. F. (1921). The first international congress on psychical research. *Journal of the American Society for Psychical Research, 15*, 547–558.
Prince, W. F. (1922). Resolution. In C. Vett (Ed.), *Le compte rendu officiel du Premier Congrès International des Recherches Psychiques à Copenhagen* (p. 540). Copenhagen: n. p.
Prubusch, F. (1929). Zur Systematik und Nomenklatur in der Parapsychologie. *Zeitschrift für Parapsychologie, 4*, 697–713.
Quartier, C. (1928). Preface. *Compte rendu du IIème Congrès International de Recherches Psychiques à Paris* (pp. vi–viii). Institut Métapsychique International.
Quevedo, O. G. (1971). *Que es la parapsicología.* Buenos Aires: Columba. (Original work published,1969).
Rao, K. R. (1962). The preferential effect in ESP. *Journal of Parapsychology, 26*, 252–259.
Rawcliffe, D. H. (1947a). *Letter to J. B. Rhine, April 18.* J. B. Rhine Papers, Manuscript Department, Duke University Library, Durham, NC.
Rawcliffe, D. H. (1947b). *Letter to J. B. Rhine, August 24.* J. B. Rhine Papers, Manuscript Department, Duke University Library, Durham, NC.
Rawcliffe, D. H. (1952). *The psychology of the occult.* Derricke Ridgeway.
Rawcliffe, D. H. (1953). *Letter to J. B. Rhine, November 11.* J. B. Rhine Papers, Manuscript Department, Duke University Library, Durham, NC.
Rhine, J. B. (1934). *Extra-sensory perception.* Boston Society for Psychic Research.
Rhine, J. B. (1937a). Editorial comment. *Journal of Parapsychology, l*, 81–83.
Rhine, J. B. (1937b). Editorial comment. *Journal of Parapsychology, 1*, 159–162.
Rhine, J. B. (1937c). *New frontiers of the mind.* Farrar and Rinehart.

Rhine, J. B. (1945). Editorial: A proposed basis for choosing terms in parapsychology. *Journal of Parapsychology, 9*, 147–149.
Rhine, J. B. [1947a]. *Letter to D. H. Rawcliffe, undated.* J. B. Rhine Papers, Manuscript Department, Duke University Library, Durham, NC.
Rhine, J. B. (1947b). *Letter to D. H. Rawcliffe, September 10.* J. B. Rhine Papers, Manuscript Department, Duke University Library, Durham, NC.
Rhine, J. B. (1947c). *Letter to D. H. Rawcliffe, September 29.* J. B. Rhine Papers, Manuscript Department, Duke University Library, Durham, NC.
Rhine, J. B. (1947d). *The reach of the mind.* William Sloane.
Rhine, J. B. (1953). Review of *The psychology of the occult,* by D. H. Rawcliffe. *Journal of the American Society for Psychical Research, 47*, 125–127.
Rhine, J. B., & Feather, S. R. (1962). The study of cases of "psi-trailing" in animals. *Journal of Parapsychology,* 26, 1–22.
Rhine, J. B. & Pratt, J. G. (1957). *Parapsychology: Frontier science of the mind.* Charles C Thomas.
Rhine, L. E. (1971). The establishment of basic concepts and terminology in parapsychology. *Journal of Parapsychology, 35*, 34–56.
Rhine, L. E., & Rhine, J. B. (1943). The psychokinetic effect: I. The first experiment. *Journal of Parapsychology, 7*, 20–43.
Richet, C. (1922). *Traité de métapsychique.* Félix Alcan.
Ryzl, M., & Pratt, J. G. (1963). The focusing of ESP upon particular targets. *Journal of Parapsychology, 27*, 227–241.
Sainville, L. L. De. (1927). Perceptions extra-sensorielles (mes expériences). *Revue Métapsychique, 6*, 429–451.
Salter, H. de G. (1932). Review of *Precis de métapsychique* (Vols. 1–2), by P. T. Bret. *Journal of the Society for Psychical Research, 27*, 225–226.
Sargent, C. L. (1979). Correspondence. *Journal of the Society for Psychical Research, 50*, 195–196.
Servadio, E. (1985). Personal communication, December 2.
Sibille, Abbe. (1951). Nécrologie. *Revue Métapsychique,* 16, 222.
Slomann, A. (1962). A projected dictionary of parapsychology. *Journal of the Society for Psychical Research, 41*, 295–299.
Slomann, A. (1964). An international dictionary of parapsychology. *Journal of Parapsychology, 28*, 297–298. (Abstract)
Soal, S. G. (1940). Fresh light on card-guessing. Some new effects. *Proceedings of the Society for Psychical Research, 46*, 152–198.
Soal, S. G. (1949). Review of *Handbook of tests in parapsychology,* by B. M. Humphrey. *Journal of the Society for Psychical Research, 35*, 20–22.
Soal, S. G., & Bateman, F. (1954). *Modern experiments in telepathy.* Yale University Press.
Soal, S. G., & Goldney, K. M. (1943). Experiments in precognitive telepathy. *Proceedings of the Society for Psychical Research, 47*, 21–150.
Stanford, R. G. (1974a). Concept and psi. In W. G. Roll, R. L. Morris, & J. D. Morris (Eds.), *Research in parapsychology 1973* (pp. 137–162). Scarecrow Press.
Stanford, R. G. (1974b). An experimentally testable model for spontaneous psi events: I. Extrasensory events. *Journal of the American Society for Psychical Research, 68*, 34–57.
Stokes, D. (1983). Response to "Seven recommendations for the future practice of parapsychology." *Zetetic Scholar, 11*, 173–175.
Stuart, C. E., & Pratt, J. G. (1937). *A handbook for testing extra-sensory perception.* Farrar & Rinehart.
Sudre, R. (1923). Compte rendu du 2e congrès international des recherches psychiques. *Revue Métapsychique, 5*, 273–291.
Sudre, R. (1925). La classification et le vocabulaire métapsychique. *Revue Métapsychique, 6*, 391–398.
Sudre, R. (1926). *Introduction à la métapsychique humaine.* Payot.
Sudre, R. (1956). *Traité de parapsychologie.* Payot.
Targ, R., & Puthoff, H. (1974). Information transmission under conditions of sensory shielding. *Nature, 251*, 602–607.
Tart, C. T. (1978). Space, time and mind. In W. G. Roll (Ed.), *Research in parapsychology 1977* (pp. 197–249). Scarecrow Press.

Teixeira De Paula, J. (1976). *Diccionario enciclopédico ilustrado: Espiritismo; metapsíquica; parapsicología.* (Revised and enlarged, 3rd ed.). Bels.
Thalbourne, M. A. (1982a). Correspondence. *Journal of the Society for Psychical Research, 51*, 397–398.
Thalbourne, M. A. (Comp.) (1982b). *A glossary of terms used in parapsychology.* Heinemann.
Thalbourne, M. A. (1985). The conceptual framework of parapsychology: Time for a reformation. In R. A. White & J. Solfvin (Eds.), *Research in parapsychology 1984* (pp. 55–59). Scarecrow Press. (Abstract)
Thalbourne, M. A. (1986). Some further thoughts on living without "ESP" and "PK." In D. H. Weiner & D. I. Radin (Eds.), *Research in parapsychology 1985* (pp. 141–144). Scarecrow Press. (Abstract)
Thouless, R. H., & Wiesner, B. P. (1947). The psi processes in normal and "paranormal" psychology. *Proceedings of the Society for Psychical Research, 48*, 177–196.
van Rijnberk, G. (1952). *Les métasciences biologiques.* Adyar.
Vesme, C. De. (1934). Chronique: La terminologie métapsychique. *Revue Métapsychique, 1*, 65–66.
West, D. J. (1945). Experimental parapsychology in wartime Britain: A review. *Journal of Parapsychology, 9*, 230–248.
West, D. J. (1954). Experimental parapsychology in Britain: A survey of recent published work, 1948–1953. *Journal of the Society for Psychical Research, 37*, 323–347.
West, D. J. (1982). Correspondence. *Journal of the Society for Psychical Research, 51*, 398–399.
White, R. A. (1983). Review of *A glossary of terms used in parapsychology*, by M. A. Thalbourne. *Journal of Parapsychology, 47*, 75–76.

4

"The Dying Mother": Historical Citations of Mary Goffe's Seventeenth-Century Near-Death Apparition*

Carlos S. Alvarado

Traditionally, certain cases have been of particular importance to students of near-death phenomena. Such cases are more than mere examples or research data; they are resources that are generally used to defend particular theoretical ideas, such as the projection of the spirit or of some subtle body from the physical body around the time of death. One such case was that of Mary Goffe, a seventeenth-century apparition of a dying woman that Richard Baxter reported in his book *The Certainty of the Worlds of Spirits* (1691). This paper includes a reprint of the original case report and a discussion of how later writers used the case to defend the idea that something may leave the body during near-death states.

Over the years there have been many efforts to study psychic phenomena through attention to individual cases. Examples of this practice come from the seventeenth (Glanvil, 1682), nineteenth (Gurney, Myers, & Podmore, 1886), and twentieth centuries (Stevenson, 1974). In fact, one may say that many cases of apparitions, hauntings, and other phenomena have been essential to the development and construction of psychical research and its theories, as have been the performances of well-known mediums (Alvarado, 1993). Some cases are continuously cited as examples of the phenomena they represent.

These include several nineteenth-century apparition cases such as the one concerning an apparition of a dead person with a scratched cheek (Myers, 1889), the recurrent haunting apparition at Cheltenham (Morton, 1892), the Wilmot case of an apparition of a living person (Sidgwick, 1891), and poltergeist cases such as that of Angelique Cottin (Tanchou, 1846). Cases like these not only have become classic but have become resources by which to defend particular theoretical explanations.

Such reports, including the case discussed in this paper, have been used over the years in relation to near-death phenomena. As Carol Zaleski (1987) discussed, many accounts of near-death experiences (NDEs) were frequently cited in the Middle Ages to illustrate particular religious views. In later times the NDE cases of Wiltse (1889) and Bertrand (Myers, 1892), as well as more recent cases (Ring & Lawrence, 1993) including the famous Pam Reynolds case (Sabom, 1998), have been used by many authors to defend particular theoretical views.

The apparition case discussed in this paper provides an example to illustrate how some reports, and their continued citations, have been used in the past by students of the subject, a situation that continues to some extent to recent days.

The Mary Goffe Case

Writing in *The Book of Dreams and Ghosts*, Scottish author and folklorist Andrew Lang (1897) referred to the case discussed in this paper as "The Dying Mother" (p. 100). In this seventeen-century case, a dying woman named Mary Goffe was seen at a distance while she seemed to have been

*Republished with permission from *Journal of Near-Death Studies, 29*(1), 241–253, 2010.

conscious of the fact before she died. In this paper I will reprint the original account of the case and will make some comments about its citation in the literature. Rather than focus on the actual occurrence of the apparitions, or on its evidentiality, my interest is to briefly discuss how the case has been used in the literature to support a particular theoretical view.

The case was first published by English Puritan preacher and writer Richard Baxter (1615–1691) in chapter 7 (pp. 147–151) of his book *The Certainty of the Worlds of the Spirits. Fully Evinced by the Unqueftionable Hiftories of Apparations, Operations, Witchcrafts, Voices &c. Proving the Immortality of Souls, the Malice and Miferies of the Devils, and the Damned, and the Bleffednefs of the Juftified. Written for the Conviction of Sadduces and Infidels* (1691). The book, consisting of 12 chapters plus a preface, a conclusion, and a postscript, presented a variety of cases of apparitions and other phenomena, as well as witchcraft (on the book, and its historical context, see Handley, 2005; and Searle, 2007).

Like other seventeen-century writings (e.g., Glanvil, 1682; More, 1653), Baxter's work had as its purpose to convince people of the reality of a spiritual world and to combat skepticism. Alison Searle (2007) described it as a manifestation of Baxter's "prophetic voice," by which she meant religious preaching that offered "extra-scriptural proofs that will convince the unbeliever or sceptic about the supernatural truth of Christianity" (p. 66). As another author stated, Baxter's work was part of "an appeal to the wondrous activity found in nature … which required the constant, creative involvement of a hierarchy of spiritual agents" (Mandelbrote, 2007, p. 452; see also Handley, 2005).

Baxter (1691) saw apparitions and other phenomena as "a means that might do much with such as are prone to judge by Sense" (p. 5, preface, unnumbered). Such literary ministry was common in the seventeenth century (Finucane, 1984; Mandelbrote, 2007; Searle, 2007), representing an "invaluable weapon in the hands of both churchmen and conventionally Christian scholars" (Maxwell-Stuart, 2006, p. 164). This point does not mean that authors such as Baxter were not dealing with actual experiences, or that the cases were fictitious, a topic beyond the scope of this paper.

The case consists of a letter Thomas Tilson, a minister in Aylesford, Kent, sent to Baxter on July 6, 1681 about an apparition that reportedly had taken place in Rochester in the same year. Reflecting the ministerial use of these cases, Tilson wrote to Baxter that he wished "that God would bless your pious endeavours for the conviction of atheists and sadduces, and the promoting of true religion and godliness" (Baxter, 1691, p. 151). In reprinting the original account, I have kept the original spelling, capitalization, and the frequent use of italics in the text. It may be argued that Goffe should be spelled Gosse, but I have kept the former because it is the spelling that appears consistently in the literature.[1]

> *Mr.* Thomas Tilfon, *Minijter of* Aylefworth *in* Kent, *his Letter concerning an Apparition in* Rochefter, *this present year, 1691 Reverend Sir,*
>
> Being informed that you are writing about Witchcraft and Apparitions, I take the freedom, though a Stranger, to fend you this following Relation.
>
> *Mary,* the Wife of *John Goffe* of *Rochefter,* being afflicted with a long *Illnefs*, removed to her Father's Houle at *Weft-Mulling,* which is about nine Miles diftant from her own: There she died, *June* the 4th this prefent Year, *1691.*
>
> The Day before her departure, She grew impatiently defirous to fee her two Children, whom fhe had left at home, to the Care of a Nurfe. She prayed her Husband to hire a Horfe, for fhe muft go home, and die with the Children. When they perfuaded her to the contrary, telling her fhe was not fit to be taken out of her Bed, nor able to fit on Horfe back, fhe intreated them however to try: *If I cannot fit,* faid fhe, *I will lie all along upon the Horfe, for I muft go to fee my poor Babes.*"
>
> A minifter who lives in the Town was with her at Ten-a-clock that Night, to whom fhe exprefs'd good Hopes in the Mercies of God, and a willingnefs to die: *But*, said fhe, *it is my Mifery that I cannot fee my Children.*

Between One and Two-a-Clock in the Morning, fhe fell into a Trance. One Widow *Turner*, who watched with her that Night, fays, that her Eyes were open, and fixed, and her Jaw fallen: She put her Hand upon her Mouth and Noftrils, but could perceive no Breath; fhe thought her to be in a Fit, and doubted whether fhe were alive or dead.

The next Day this dying Woman told her Mother, that fhe had been at home with her Children. *That is impoffible*, faid the Mother, *for you have been here in bed all the while. Yes*, replied the other, *but I was with them laft Night, when I was afleep.*

The Nurfe at *Rochefter*, widow *Alexander* by Name, affirms, and fays, fhe will take her Oath on't before a Magiftrate, and receive the Sacrament upon it, that a little before Two a Clock that Morning fhe faw the Likeness of the faid *Mary Goffe* come out of the next Chamber (where the elder Child lay in a bed by it felf, the Door being left open, and ftood by her Bed-fide for about a quarter of an Hour; the younger Child was there lying by her; her Eyes moved, and her Mouth went, but fhe said nothing. The Nurfe, moreover fays, that fhe was perfectly awake; it was then Day-light, being one of the longeft days in the Year. She fate up in her Bed, and looked fteadfaftly upon the Apparition: In that time fhe heard the Bridge-Clock strike Two, and a while after faid, *In the Name of the Father, Son and Holy Ghoft, what art thou?* Thereupon the Appearance removed, and went away; fhe flipp'd on her Cloaths and followed, but what became on't fhe cannot tell. Then, and not before, fhe began to be grievoufly affrighted, and went out of doors, and walked upon the Wharf (the houfe is juft by the River fide) for some Hours, only going in now and then to look at the Children. At Five a-Clock fhe went to a Neighbour's Houfe, and knocked at the Door, but they would not rife: At Six fhe went again, then they arofe and let her in. She related to them all that had pafs'd: They would perfuade her fhe was miftaken, or dreamt: But fhe confidently affirmed, *If ever I faw her in all my Life, I faw her this Night.*

One of thofe to whom fhe made the Relation (*Mary,* the wife of *John Sweet*) had a Meffenger [who] came from *Mulling* that Forenoon, to let her know her Neighbour *Goffe* was dying, and defired to fpeak with her; fhe went over the fame day, and found her juft departing. The mother, amongft other Difcourfe, Related to her how much her Daughter had long'd to fee the Children, and faid fhe had feen them. This brought to Mrs. *Sweet*'s mind, what the Nurfe had told her that Morning, for till then, fhe had not thought to mention it, but difguifed it, rather as the Woman's difturbed Imagination.

The Subftance of this, I had Related to me by *John Carpenter*, the Father of the Deceafed, next day after the Burial: *July* the Second: I fully *Difcourfed* the Matter with the Nurfe and two Neighbours, to whofe Houfe fhe went that Morning.

Two days after, I had it from the Mother, the Minifter that was with her in the Evening, and the Woman who fat up with her that laft Night: They all agree in the same Story, and every one helps to ftrengthen the others Teftimony:

They all appear to be Sober Intelligent Perfons, far enough from Defigning to impofe a Cheat upon the World, or to manage a lye, and what Temptation they fhould lye under for fo doing, I cannot conceive (pp. 147–151).

Citations of the Case

As was the case with many other seventeen-century writings on unusual phenomena, later authors dismissed Baxter's (1691) writings. For example, in a biography of Baxter, Orme (1831, Vol. 2) stated that Baxter's cases were the result of the experiencers' "diseased imagination," coming from "imposition," and the "operation of natural causes" (p. 31). However, many other writers interested in psychic phenomena cited the Goffe case to support their belief in apparitions and, more specifically, in the projection of the spirit or some other principle from the confines of the physical body. In the discussion I will mention some examples published during the nineteenth century and, to a less extent, during the twentieth.

Edmund Gurney, Frederic W. H. Myers, and Frank Podmore cited the case in *Phantasms of the Living* (1886, Vol. 2, pp. 558–559). They presented it together with two other cases to show the existence of old cases of apparitions of the living while the person was dying. Presumably the authors were seeking validation of the type of experience they studied in their book by showing historical precedents. But this was by no means the first citation of the case in the nineteenth century (in addition to the citations mentioned below, see Brown, 1889, pp. 45–47; Ennemoser, 1854, Vol. 2, pp. 433–435; Ingram, 1886, pp. 212–215; and Lang, 1897, pp. 99–102).

Many of the individuals using the case presented it to support the idea that the spirit, or some subtle body, could leave the body at some moments, such as when the person was close to death. Whereas there is a long history of belief in such an "excursion" from antiquity to the late Middle Ages (Poortman, 1954/1978; Zaleski, 1987), there were also many similar ideas during the nineteenth century (e.g. Crowe, 1848; Jung-Stilling, 1808/1851), which is the period on which I am focusing (see also Alvarado, 1989, 2005, 2009a, 2009c; and Deveney, 1997).

In 1848, novelist Catherine Crowe included an account of the Goffe case in her famous book *The Night-Side of Nature* (1848, Vol. 1, pp. 230–231). It appeared in the book's seventh chapter entitled "Wraiths," which opened with the idea "that the spirit is freed from the body, when the latter becomes no longer a fit habitation for it" (p. 223). In some conditions of the body, Crowe continued,

> the spirit, in a manner unknown to us, resumes a portion of its freedom, and is enabled to exercise more or less of its inherent properties. It is somewhat released from those inexorable conditions of time and space, which bound and limit its powers. … (pp. 227–228)

The case was seen as an example of the emancipation of the spirit when close to death, a topic that was repeated in further citations over the years.

German student of mystical and religious phenomena Johan Joseph von Görres (1854, pp. 268–269) also cited the case. He referred to two bodies other than the physical, the "spectre of the soul, and … its plastic envelope" (p. 270). Görres believed that these two bodies may separate from the physical body at death and that there were states other than death that allowed for such a separation.

Social reformer and politician Robert Dale Owen included the case in a chapter on dreams in his book *Footfalls on the Boundary of Another World* (1860, pp. 187–190). Far from considering the case a simple dream, he referred to evidence about "the appearance of a living person at a greater or less distance from where that person actually is, and perhaps usually where the thoughts or affections of that person may be supposed, at the moment, to be concentrated. …" (p. 194). This passage referred to a discussion of apparitions of the living in a later chapter in the book. The Goffe case was a distinct type of cases in which "during a dream or a trance, partial or complete, the counterpart of a living person may show itself, at a greater or less distance from where that person actually is," and generally, "this counterpart appears where the thoughts or the affections, strongly excited, may be supposed to be" (p. 358).

An author writing in *Catholic World* presented the case as one of "presumably natural projection" (Anonymous, 1874, p. 163). A similar view regarding the separation of the spirit from the body came from English publisher and spiritualist William H. Harrison who, writing about apparitions of the dying, mentioned the case in his book *Spirits Before Our Eyes* (1879, pp. 34–36). According to Harrison:

> When the spirit of a man is partially loosened from his body at the approach of death, and when that spirit can make itself visible to a distant friend, the bodily powers are sometimes not so far destroyed but that the lips of the sufferer can tell those around the bed, that the far-off person has been seen by him. Thus direct evidence of the reality of the phenomenon is presented at both ends of the line. Similarly valuable evidence is, of course, not obtainable in connection with postmortem apparitions. (pp. 33–34)

Linguist Adolphe D'Assier used the case in his *Posthumous Humanity* (1883/1887, pp. 58–62) to support his contention that every human being had a fluidic phantom in the physical body that could project out of the body under certain circumstances and in some special individuals. In his view, the fact that Goffe's phantom's mouth moved and said nothing suggested that the "phantom had exerted all the vital force which still animated the dying woman. … It is presumable that the phonetic powerlessness of the image reflected the exhaustion of the dying woman" (pp. 61–62).

Theosophist Charles W. Leadbeater presented the Goffe case in his book *Clairvoyance* (1899, pp. 66–68) in the context of a discussion of intentional astral traveling. As he wrote: "This paying of intentional astral visits seems very often to become possible when the principles are loosened at the approach of death for people who were unable to perform such a feat at any other time" (p. 66).

Twentieth century authors also have discussed Goffe's case. Leaving aside G. G. Greenwood's (1903, pp. 277–280) skeptical examination, several other writers mentioned the case in contexts supporting the idea of a distant action or projection (e.g., Barrett, 1926, pp. 84–87; Davies, 1998, pp. 43–45; Evans, 2002, pp. 36–37; Hart and collaborators, 1956, pp. 162–163).

An interesting discussion was that of French magnetizer Hector Durville who summarized the Goffe case in a section of his book *Le Fantome des Vivants* (1909, pp. 108–110) about the manifestation of the phantom or double of the dying. According to Durville: "The soul, covered in the exterior with its astral body, and by its etheric body, goes with the swiftness of light" (p. 107, my translation) towards the persons that concern the person represented by the apparition. Those individuals with some psychic sensitivity could perceive the phantom. But the apparition, Durville believed, could also make its presence known through telepathy and physical effects.

Goffe's phantom, Durville noted, was one of those cases on which the "doubled" individual "remembered perfectly everything that they saw" (p. 137). In other cases, in which percipients had seen "doubled" individuals, the individuals themselves had only vague or no recollections of being in another location.

In a popular course of psychic phenomena, Swami Panchadasi (1916), pp. 217–219) cited the case. Just before presenting the case, the author stated:

> In many well authenticated cases, we may see that the soul of a dying person, one whose physical end is approaching, visits friends and relatives in the astral body, and in many cases materializes and even speaks to them. In such cases the dying person accomplishes the feat of astral manifestation without any special occult knowledge; the weakened links between the physical and the higher phases of the soul render the temporary passing-out comparatively easy, and the strong desire of the dying person furnishes the motive power necessary. Such visits, however, are often found to be merely the strongly charged thought of the dying person, along the lines of telepathy, as I have previously explained to you. But in many cases there can be no doubt that the phenomenon is a clear case of astral visitation and materialization. (pp. 216–217)

Similarly, the Goffe case was cited by a recent author whose purpose was not to demonstrate the reality of the apparition (Maxwell-Stuart, 2006, p. 127). Nonetheless, the author commented: "It may be significant that Mary was in a trance-like state and about to die, for this peculiar condition could have loosened the bond between her body and 'something other'—her soul, her spirit, her doppelganger—which would then have freed this 'something other' to move temporarily beyond its usual limitations" (pp. 127–128).

Concluding Remarks

Although Baxter presented the Goffe case as part of his ministry, many writers have used it over the years to support the idea that something is capable of leaving the physical body when the human organism is close to death. In fact, it is precisely the way past writers cited the Goffe case, and others like it, that has kept such a concept alive over the years.

The case certainly is not unique; many apparitions of the dying have been reported in the psychical research literature (e.g., Gurney, Myers, & Podmore, 1886). However, Goffe's account is particularly interesting for its emotional content. As Lang (1897) put it, the case involves a dying mother, and more than that, with her concern for her children. As such, the case also represents, and evokes, universal values regarding motherhood and family love. Such aspects may have been an important factor leading past writers to select the case for citation.

Interest in veridical phenomena associated with the dying continues to recent times. Some of it depends in part on the continuing citation of old cases, such as those of visual and other sensory impressions about a distant dying person recorded in Gurney, Myers, and Podmore's *Phantasms of the Living* (1886; e.g., Alvarado, 2006; Evans, 2002). Others have focused on more recent cases (e.g., Ring & Lawrence, 1993). In fact, the recent controversy surrounding the Pam Reynolds case shows the continuing importance veridical cases have for those seeking to understand the meaning of the near-death experience. This importance is exemplified by Keith Augustine's (2007a) critique of the case, of several counter-criticisms (Greyson, 2007; Sabom, 2007; Sharp, 2007; Tart, 2007), and of Augustine's (2007b) reply.

Like clinical cases in the histories of psychology and psychiatry (Alvarado, 2009b; Ellenberger, 1970), cases such as Goffe's have been instrumental in the development of conceptual aspects of near-death phenomena studies. In addition to evidential considerations (which are not strong in Goffe's case), such accounts have supported and maintained belief in the idea that there are aspects of these phenomena that cannot be easily reduced to conventional explanations. My discussion of the Goffe case has illustrated a historical example of this process.

Note

1 The use of f when writing the first s or the only s in a word was called the "long s." It was commonly used in writing and in printed books from the early medieval era through the end of the 1700s.

References

Alvarado, C. S. (1989). Trends in the study of out-of-body experiences: An overview of developments since the nineteenth century. *Journal of Scientific Exploration, 3,* 27–42.
Alvarado, C. S. (1993). Gifted subjects' contributions to parapsychology: The case of Eusapia Palladino. *Journal of the Society for Psychical Research, 59,* 269–292.
Alvarado, C. S. (2005). Ernesto Bozzano on the phenomena of bilocation. *Journal of Near-Death Studies, 24,* 207–238.
Alvarado, C. S. (2006). Neglected near-death phenomena. *Journal of Near-Death Studies, 24,* 131–151.
Alvarado, C. S. (2009a). Historical notes on doubles and travelling spirits: I—Introduction. *Paranormal Review, 50,* 6–15.
Alvarado, C. S. (2009b). Nineteenth-century hysteria and hypnosis: A historical note on Blanche Wittmann. *Australian Journal of Clinical and Experimental Hypnosis, 37,* 21–36.
Alvarado, C. S. (2009c). The spirit in out-of-body experiences: Historical and conceptual notes. In B. Batey (Ed.), *Spirituality, science and the paranormal* (pp. 3–19). Academy of Spirituality and Paranormal Studies.
Anonymous. (1874). Spiritualism. *Catholic World, 18,* 145–165.
Augustine, K. (2007a). Does paranormal perception occur in near-death experiences? *Journal of Near-Death Studies, 25,* 203–236.
Augustine, K. (2007b). "Does paranormal perception occur in near-death experiences?" defended. *Journal of Near-Death Studies, 25,* 261–283.
Barrett, W. F. (1926). *Death-bed visions.* Methuen.
Baxter, R. (1691). *The certainty of the worlds of the spirits fully evinced by the unqueftionable hiftories of apparitions and witchcrafts, operations, voices, &c. proving the immortality of souls, the malice and miferies of the devils and the damned, and the bleffednefs of the juftified: Written for the conviction of sadduces & infidels.* Printed for T. Parkhurft at the Bible and Three Crowns in Cheapfide, and J. Salusbury at the Rifing Sun over againft the Royal Exchange.
Brown, R. (1889). *Demonology and witchcraft: With especial reference to modern "spiritualism," so called.* John F. Shaw.
Crowe, C. (1848). *The night-side of nature; or, ghosts and ghost seers* (2 vols.). T. C. Newby.
D'Assier, A. (1887). *Posthumous humanity: A study of phantoms* (H. S. Olcott, Trans.) George Redway. (Original work published, 1883)
Davies, R. (1998). *Doubles: The enigma of the second self.* Robert Hale.
Deveney, J. P. (1997). *Astral projection or liberation of the double and the work of the early Theosophical Society (Theosophical history occasional paper,* Vol. 6). Theosophical History.
Durville, H. (1909*). Le fantôme des vivants: Anatomie et physiologie del'ame: Recherches experimentales sur le dedoublement des corps de l'homme.* Librairie du Magnétisme.
Ellenberger, H. F. (1970). *The discovery of the unconscious: The history and evolution of dynamic psychiatry.* Basic Books.
Ennemoser, J. (1854). *The history of magic* (2 vols.). Henry G. Bohn.
Evans, H. (2002). *Seeing ghosts: Experiences of the paranormal.* John Murray.
Finucane, R. C. (1984). *Appearances of the dead: A cultural history of ghosts.* Prometheus Books.
Glanvil, J. (1682). *Sadducismus triumphatus: Or full and plain evidence concerning witches and apparitions* (2nd ed.). Printed by Tho. Newcomb, for S. Lownds.
Görres, J. J. von. (1854). *La mystique divine, naturelle et diabolique: La mystique naturelle* (vol. 3, C. Saintse-Foi, Trans.). Mme Vve Pussielgue-Rusand.
Greenwood, G. G. (1903). Ghosts and telepathy. *Westminster Review, 160,* 271–291.
Greyson, B. (2007). Comment on "Does paranormal perception occur in near-death experiences?" *Journal of Near-Death Studies, 25,* 237–244.
Gurney, E., Myers, F. W. H., & Podmore, F. (1886). *Phantasms of the living* (2 vols.). Trübner.
Handley, S. (2005). Reclaiming ghosts in 1690s England. In K. Cooper & J. Gregory (Eds.), *Signs, wonders, miracles: Representations of divine power in the life of the Church* (pp. 345–355). Boydell Press.
Harrison, W. (1879). *Spirits before our eyes.* W. H. Harrison.

Hart, H., & collaborators. (1956). Six theories of apparitions. *Proceedings of the Society for Psychical Research, 50*, 153–239.

Ingram, J. H. (1886). *The haunted homes and family traditions of Great Britain.* W. H. Allen.

Jung-Stilling, J. H. (1851). *Theory of pneumatology; in reply to the question, what ought to be believed or disbelieved concerning presentiments, visions, and apparitions, according to nature, reason and scripture* (1st American ed.) (Jackson, S., Trans.; Bush, G., Ed.). J. S. Redfield. (Original work published 1808)

Lang, A. (1897). *The book of dreams and ghosts* (Rev. ed.). Longmans, Green.

Leadbeater, C. W. (1899). *Clairvoyance.* Theosophical Publishing Society.

Mandelbrote, S. (2007). The uses of natural theology in seventeenth-century England. *Science in Context, 20*, 451–480.

Maxwell-Stuart, P. G. (2006). *Ghosts: A history of phantoms, ghouls, and other spirits of the dead.* Tempus.

More, H. (1653). *An antidote against atheisme.* Roger Daniel.

Morton, R. (1892). Record of a haunted house. *Proceedings of the Society for Psychical Research, 8*, 311–332.

Myers, F. W. H. (1889). On recognised apparitions occurring more than a year after death. *Proceedings of the Society for Psychical Research, 6*, 13–65.

Myers, F. W. H. (1892). On indications of continued terrene knowledge on the part of phantasms of the dead. *Proceedings of the Society for Psychical Research, 8*, 170–252.

Orme, W. (1831). *The life and times of the Rev. Richard Baxter: With a critical examination of his writings* (2 vols.). Crocker & Brewster.

Owen, R. D. (1860). *Footfalls on the boundary of another world.* J. B. Lippincott.

Panchadasi, Swami. (1916). *A course of advanced lessons in clairvoyance and occult powers.* Advanced Thought.

Poortman, J. J. (1978). *Vehicles of consciousness: The concept of hylic pluralism (Ochema).* (N. D. Smith, Trans.). Theosophical Society in the Netherlands. (Original work published 1954)

Ring, K., & Lawrence, M. (1993). Further evidence for veridical perception during near-death experiences. *Journal of Near-Death Studies, 11*, 223–229.

Sabom, M. B. (1998). *Light & death: One doctor's fascinating account of near-death experiences.* Zondervan.

Sabom, M. B. (2007). Commentary on "Does paranormal perception occur in near-death experiences?" *Journal of Near-Death Studies, 25*, 257–260.

Searle, A. (2007). *The certainty of the worlds of spirits:* Richard Baxter's prophetic voice. *The Glass, 19*, 62–71.

Sharp, K. C. (2007). The other shoe drops: Commentary on "Does paranormal perception occur in near-death experiences?" *Journal of Near-Death Studies, 25*, 245–250.

Sidgwick, Mrs. H. [E. M.]. (1891). On the evidence for clairvoyance. *Proceedings of the Society for Psychical Research, 7*, 30–99.

Stevenson, I. (1974). *Twenty cases suggestive of reincarnation* (Rev. ed.). University Press of Virginia.

Tanchou, S. (1846). *Enquête sur l'authenticité des phénomènes électriques d'Angélique Cottin.* Germer Baillière.

Tart, C. T. (2007). Commentary on "Does paranormal perception occur in near-death experiences?" *Journal of Near-Death Studies, 25*, 251–256.

Wiltse, A. S. (1889). A case of typhoid fever with subnormal temperature and pulse. *St. Louis Medical and Surgical Journal, 57*, 355–364.

Zaleski, C. (1987). *Otherworld journeys: Accounts of near-death experience in medieval and modern times.* Oxford University Press.

The Ether and Psychic Phenomena: Some Old Speculations*

Carlos S. Alvarado

DeMeo's (2014) article about the idea of the ether in the *Journal of Scientific Exploration* brings to mind the historical relationship of this concept to psychic phenomena.

Much more than a simple physical theory of force, the ether was one of those powerful and overreaching concepts that captured the imagination of both scientists and the general public during parts of the nineteenth and the twentieth centuries (on the concept see Cantor & Hodge, 1981). As argued by Asprem (2014, p. 222):

> Ether metaphysics provided a worldview that emphasized the immanence of the divine, through the all-encompassing, interpenetrating, but invisible ether. This medium functioned as a kind of "world-soul"; it was the seat of animation in general, the source of life, and also the plane on which much mental functioning was thought to take place.

The metaphysical dimensions of the ether connected the topic to philosophical and religious views, as well as to ideas of the unity of nature, the transcendence of the spirit, and of human faculties. Such issues were discussed by Balfour Stewart and Peter G. Tait (1875) and Oliver Lodge (1925) (on the various dimensions of the ether see Asprem, 2014, Noakes, 2005, and Wynne, 1979), among others.

Several interesting speculations about the ether and psychic phenomena appeared during the Nineteenth Century. For example, magazine editor James T. Knowles wrote in *The Spectator* that assuming the existence of brain waves, these could spread via the ether in such a way that each "brain then would become a centre of undulations transmitted from it in all directions through space … with the varying nature and force of brain actions …" (Knowles, 1869, p. 136). Another writer in the *Melbourne Review* speculated along the same line about the possibility of propagation of thought from one person to another via brain waves. This, it was proposed, made sense supposing "the existence of a medium, analogous to that of the luminiferous ether" (Andrew, 1876, p. 109).

Several others had similar ideas. French physician Prosper Despine wrote about the possibility of a distant influence from a neuropathic person to another through the "intermediary of an ether fluid which fills all space, which penetrates all our organs, and which puts us in communication with all the beings of the universe" (Despine, 1880, p. 132).

American electrical engineer Edwin J. Houston speculated that:

> Cerebral energy … is dissipated by imparting wave motions to the surrounding ether, and such waves are sent out in all directions from the brain, possibly in greater amount, or of greater amplitude from some of the brain openings, as, for example, those of the eyes. (Houston, 1892, p. 490)

*Republished with permission from *Journal of Scientific Exploration, 29*(2), 295–297, 2015.

Similarly, the idea of vibrations propagating thought throughout the ether was speculated on by William Crookes (1897).

There are also examples of the use of the concept of the ether in nineteenth century Spiritualist publications. Some examples are as seen in Robert Hare's *Experimental Investigation of the Spirit Manifestations* (1855, p. 160, 163) and Hudson Tuttle's *Arcana of Spiritualism* (1871, p. 163). Tuttle expressed in a later book that there was a psychic ether "related to thought, as the luminiferous ether is to light." This ether, he thought, "may be regarded as the thought atmosphere of the universe. A thinking being in this atmosphere is a pulsating center of thought-waves, as a luminous body is of light." Furthermore: "All the so-called occult phenomena of mesmerism, trance, clairvoyance, mind reading, dreams, visions, thought transference, etc., are correlated to and explained by means of this psychic ether" (Tuttle, 1889, p. 5).

Another writer stated:

> We have seen that the ethereal medium interpenetrates all transparent bodies, and probably opaque bodies too. The Spiritual body is said to consist of a subtle form of ethereal matter interpenetrating the material body and bearing a definite correspondence to it. (Bryce, 1871, p. 126)

Referring to "ethereal" beings, presumably spirits, Alfred Russel Wallace (1875) speculated on the possibility that they could produce physical and visible effects "drawn perhaps from the boundless ether, perhaps from the vital energies of human beings" (p. 45).

The topic of the ether has also appeared in mediumistic communications. One example is discussions of the cosmic ether (as discussed in physics), and another is spiritual discussions about the attributes of God. The cosmic ether always stayed physical, while the spiritual one could continue to evolve, becoming more refined with time. The interplay between both ethers, as directed by spirits and by God, "have produced the universe, visible and invisible" (Anonymous, 1887).

Ideas of this sort come into the twentieth century, as seen in the writings of individuals such as Oliver Lodge (1919), and were also associated with various branches of occultism, such as Theosophy. My purpose here is not completeness, but a brief reminder of the fact that the ether was more than just a physical concept providing the media for the propagation in space of principles such as magnetism and light. For many thinkers it was a construct with wider implications about the nature of reality and of human beings, a meeting ground for matter and mind, a topic ably discussed recently by Asprem (2014).

References

Andrew, H. M. (1876). Brain waves. *Melbourne Review, 1,* 105-110.

Anonymous (1st M. B. [Lond.]) (1887). Cosmic and spiritual aethers. *Light, 7*, 460.

Asprem, E. (2014). *The problem of disenchantment: Scientific naturalism and esoteric discourse, 1900–1939.* Brill.

Bryce, J. P. (1871). *An essay on spiritual evolution considered in its bearing upon modern spiritualism, science and religion.* Trübner.

Cantor, G. N., & Hodge, M. J. S. (Eds.) (1981). *Conceptions of ether: Studies in the history of ether theories, 1740–1900.* Cambridge University Press.

Crookes, W. (1897). Address by the President. *Proceedings of the Society for Psychical Research, 12*, 338–355.

DeMeo, J. (2014). Does a cosmic ether exist? Evidence from Dayton Miller and others. *Journal of Scientific Exploration, 28*, 647–682.

Despine, P. (1880). *Etude scientifique sur le somnambulisme.* F. Savy.

Hare, R. (1855). *Experimental investigation of the spirit manifestations.* Partridge & Brittan.

Houston, J. (1892). Cerebral radiations. *Journal of the Franklin Institute, 133*, 488–497.
Knowles, J. T. (1869). Brain-waves: A theory. *The Spectator, 42*, 135–137.
Lodge, O. (1919). Ether, matter and the soul. *Hibbert Journal, 17*, 252–260.
Lodge, O. (1925). *Ether & reality: A series of discourses on the many functions of the ether of space*. Hodder & Stoughton.
Noakes, R. (2005). Ethers, religion, and politics in late-Victorian physics: Beyond the Wynne thesis. *History of Science, 43*, 415–455.
Stewart, B., & Tait, P. G. (1875). *The unseen universe: Or physical speculations on a future state* (3rd ed.). Macmillan.
Tuttle, H. (1871). *Arcana of spiritualism*. Adams.
Tuttle, H. (1889). *Studies in the out-lying fields of psychic science*. M. L. Holbrook.
Wallace, A. R. (1875). *On miracles and modern spiritualism: Three essays*. James Burns.
Wynne, B. (1979). Physics and psychics: Science, symbolic action and social control in late Victorian England. In B. Barnes & S. Shapin (Eds.). *Natural order: Historical studies of scientific culture* (pp. 167–187). Sage.

6

Some Forgotten Mesmeric Phenomena*

Carlos S. Alvarado

As is well known, animal magnetism was believed to be a universal force associated with the human body, and the principle behind mesmerism and its phenomena.[1] In his *Mémoire sur la Découverte du Magnétisme Animal,* Mesmer (1779) presented 27 propositions about animal magnetism, stating that it was a universal principle that could act on and through the human body. In the body it showed polarity and could cure various conditions. Furthermore, Mesmer stated that animal magnetism could act at a distance and could be propagated by sound and reflected by mirrors. Many of Mesmer's followers wrote at length about magnetism in various countries, as seen in the writings of Guidi (1863), Haddock (1851), and Petetin (1808), and discussed the power of this principle to produce a variety we impart: it moves like light rays sent out by bodies ablaze" (p. 89).[2]

Recent discussions of mesmerism by parapsychologists tend to focus on ESP phenomena. For example, Irwin and Watt (2007) refer to the "use of the magnetic trance as means of evoking telepathy, clairvoyance, travelling clairvoyance … and other parapsychological experiences" (p. 12). Although this is true, the repertoire of mesmeric phenomena was much wider. In this brief article I would like to present some examples of phenomena that I believe are generally not associated with mesmerism by current parapsychologists.

Seeing Animal Magnetism

There were reports of mesmerized individuals, referred to as somnambules or somnambulists, who could "see" this "magnetism," sometimes called a fluid. A. A. Tardy de Montravel (1785) referred to a somnambulist who showed this phenomenon:

> I put the thumb of my right hand in opposition to the thumb of the left hand of my patient, and separated our two hands horizontally; she saw the fluid out of her thumb & mine; she distinguished very well the two fluids. (pp. 27–28)

British physician John Elliotson (1848) also made relevant observations of a patient. As he wrote in the mesmeric journal *Zoist*:

> While I am drawing up her rigid arm in the waking state with her eyes free, she sees as soon as the limb begins to ascend, but not before, a colourless stream pass from it to my hand, of the same breadth as the number of the points of the fingers which I employ at the moment. Though I cover the part with a shawl, single or folded, the appearance is equal … If I stiffen her body and then make tractive passes from it, as soon as it advances the stream from it is seen. If I draw with both hands, there are two streams side by side from the part. The farther I stand from her, the fainter the stream appears; and, if at a great distance, there is no visible stream, nor traction. She compares it to moonlight, and it is stronger in the dark. She sees the same from my hand if I dart it at a stiffened part,

*Republished with permission from *Mindfield,* 7(1), 28–32, 2015.

> but not till this begins to relax. On darting my hand at a part not rigid, there is no such appearance. In tractive passes, the stream seems to wave back towards her when my hand moves towards her again before the next tractive pass. If I breathe upon a stiffened part she sees no stream of light. (p. 225)

Another observation came from Thomas Buckland (1850):

> I have myself a dear relative, in the enjoyment of good health, who can, in broad daylight, see this phenomenon in her normal state. When a glass of water is mesmerised in a dark room, she perceives 'bright little globules' pass from the fingers and sink about half way down the water before they disappear. If the same passes are made over an empty glass, she perceives at the bottom of it a bluish vapour, which remains there for some time afterwards. (p. 43)

Interestingly, one mesmerist discussed different perceptions as a function of the degree of clairvoyance manifested by the somnambulist, which he classified as threefold. Those of the first degree saw the fluid as "pale and wispy rays"; those of the second and third degree saw it, respectively, as flames or sparks, and as jets or strips of fire (Olivier, 1849, p. 36). He also wrote: "One of my somnambules saw it as bright stars" (p. 36), which he believed to be a rare occurrence.

Effects on the Growth of Plants

J. J. Ricard (1841) remarked in his *Traité Théorique et Pratique du Magnétisme Animal ou Méthode Facile Pour Apprendre à Magnétiser* that plants could be positively or negatively affected by willful magnetic action. He said he was able to affect shrubs through magnetization. In one case a sick and depleted shrub recovered after having being magnetized repeatedly every morning and afternoon for less than a month. However, a shrub of the same type that received the same care, was magnetized at the same time with negative intentions, and lost its leaves and looked depleted. He repeated such tests often and became convinced of the positive and negative influence of magnetism on plants.

The mesmeric literature offers many other examples of such effects, such as the one authored by Picard, a physician from Saint-Quentin. Out of six roses planted on April 5, Picard magnetized only one in the morning and in the evening for around five minutes. On the tenth, the one that was magnetized already had two shoots about one inch in length, and on the 20th the other five had barely started to grow. On May 10, the magnetized one had two shoots "40 centimeters high, with ten buttons on top, while the others had 5 to 10 centimeters, and the buttons were far from appearing. Finally, the first one bloomed on May 20, and gave successively ten beautiful roses! … Its leaves were about double in size than those of other roses" (Picard, 1845, p. 478).

Mediumistic-Like Manifestations

There were fascinating mediumistic-like phenomena recorded with magnetic somnambules. An example was recorded as part of the work of the Exegetic and Philantropic Society of Stockholm. The event took place on May 10, 1787, with a 40-year-old woman who was magnetized. According to the report the dialogue was:

> Is the patient asleep? *Yes.* Who are you, who speaks through the organ of the patient during her sleep? *My name is Marie.* Where are you? *I am in the Other world, in a happy state.* How long

> have you being in this world? *For 14 years.* Who were you when you lived here? *I died as a three year old infant.* Who was your father? *He was a carpenter in this town.* His name? *Lindstrom.* Where did he live? *In the Marais district.* Is he still alive? *No: he has been dead for seven years.* Is this woman, by whose body you are presently talking, the first person through whom you have come across since you have been in the other world? *Certainly not, there have been over 200 persons through whom I have presented myself successively.* (Lausanne, 1816, pp. 12–13)

Other examples include the reports of Cahagnet (1851) and Haddock (1851). The latter magnetized an English woman called Emma. According to Haddock:

> Frequently during the spring and summer of 1848, Emma would, in the mesmeric state, speak of the scenery and nature of the spirit-world, in such a way as to impress the beholder with a conviction, that the descriptions she gave could not be the result of any previously acquired knowledge, or of an active imagination. She also, occasionally, spoke of things which had actually occurred, but which it was impossible for her to know by any ordinary means. (p. 181)

Furthermore, as Haddock noted:

> I soon perceived, that one being, under whose influence she seemed to be, and of whom she frequently spoke, had been most nearly related to me, while in this world, but she had departed this life for about ten years when the first of these trances occurred. Emma always says that this 'lady,' as I will call her, following Emma's phraseology, 'helps her' in all serious cases of illness, and the like, but not in mere secular, or trifling cases. (p. 187)

Haddock also reported:

> In one case, where, as an experiment, an enquiry was being made relative to a missing will, she told me, not only what I asked her, but spoke of other things which neither myself nor she knew anything … about, nor had I been asked about what she said; but I was afterwards informed that what she said was correct. This was a description of some old furniture, and some bags with money in, in an Irish town, the existence of which things was perfectly unknown to me; but they were connected with the missing document, and Emma professed to derive her knowledge of the existence of these things, from the spirit of the departed. She asked me about the removal of this money, as if I knew of it. My correspondent afterwards informed me of the correctness of Emma's statements; but refused to continue the inquiry, from a superstitious dread of holding communication with the dead. (p. 201)

Concluding Remarks

Several other phenomena could have been mentioned here, phenomena that many contemporaries probably do not associate with mesmerism. Among them are reports of physical phenomena such as the appearance of objects, "travels" to other planets, transposition of the senses, the storage of magnetism on objects, and exteriorization of sensibility. These, and many other manifestations, were once very influential in maintaining belief in animal magnetism. In the case of mediumistic-like phenomena, the phenomena supported a spiritual outlook of mesmerism, another perspective forgotten by some students of psychic phenomena who seem to believe that mesmerism involved only the physical action of a mysterious agent.

Notes

1 For overviews of mesmerism and its phenomena see Crabtree (1993), Gauld (1992), and Méheust (1999). See also my bibliography (Alvarado, 2008).

2 Similar ideas continued in the neo-mesmeric movements of the 19th and part of the 20th centuries (Alvarado, 2009a, 2009b), and can be found today in various forms.

References

Alvarado, C. S. (2008). Mesmerism on-line: A bibliographic review. *Australian Journal of Clinical and Experimental Hypnosis, 36*, 115–120.

Alvarado, C. S. (2009a). Nineteenth and early twentieth century discussions of animal magnetism. *International Journal of Clinical and Experimental Hypnosis, 57*, 366–381.

Alvarado, C. S. (2009b). Modern animal magnetism: The work of Alexandre Baréty, Émile Boirac, and Julian Ochorowicz. *Australian Journal of Clinical and Experimental Hypnosis, 37,* 1–15.

Buckland, T. (1850). *The hand-book of mesmerism.* Hippolyte Baillière.

Cahagnet, L. A. (1851). The celestial telegraph, or, secrets of the life to come, revealed through magnetism. (1st American ed.). J. S. Redfield.

Crabtree, A. (1993). *From Mesmer to Freud: Magnetic sleep and the roots of psychological healing.* Yale University Press.

Deleuze, J. P. F. (1813). *Histoire critique du magnétisme animal.* (Vol. 1). Mame.

Elliotson, J. (1848). Cure of a true cancer of the female breast with mesmerism. *Zoist, 6*, 213–237.

Gauld, A. (1992). *A history of hypnotism.* Cambridge University Press.

Guidi, F. (1863). *Il magnetismo animale considerato secondo le leggi della natura e principalmente diretto.* Francesco Savito.

Haddock, J. W. (1851). Somnolism & psycheism; or, the science of the soul and the phenomena of nervation (2nd ed.). James S. Hodson.

Irwin, H. J., & Watt, C. A. (2007). *An introduction to parapsychology.* (5th ed.). McFarland.

Lausanne [pseudonym of Sarrazine de Montferrier, A. A. V.] (1816). Histoire du magnétisme animal. *Annales du Magnétisme Animale, 2*, 3–26.

Méheust, B. (1999). *Somnambulisme et médiumnité (1784–1930): Vol. 1: Le défi du magnétisme animal.* Institut Synthélabo pour le Progrès de la Connaissance.

Mesmer, F. A. (1779). *Mémoire sur la découverte du magnétisme animal.* Didot.

Olivier, J. (1849). *Traité de magnétisme suivi des paroles d'un somnambule et d'un recueil de traitements magnétiques.* L. Jougla.

Petetin, J. H. D. (1808). *Électricité animale: Prouvée par la découverte des phénomènes physiques et moraux de la catalepsie hystérique, et ses variétés.* Brunot-Labbe.

Picard, Dr. (1845). Application du magnétisme aux végétaux. *Journal du Magnétisme, 1*, 477–480.

Ricard, J. J. A. (1841). *Traité théorique et pratique du magnétisme animal ou méthode facile pour apprendre à magnétizer.* Germer Baillière.

Tardy de Montravel, A. A. (1785). Essai sur la théorie du somnambulisme magnétique. No publisher given.

Human Radiations: Concepts of Force in Mesmerism, Spiritualism and Psychical Research*

Carlos S. Alvarado†

The literature of mesmerism, Spiritualism and psychical research presents ideas of forces projected from the human body to acquire information and affect the environment. Franz Anton Mesmer and other workers developed the concept of animal magnetism to explain phenomena such as the induction of trances and healing. Nineteenth- and twentieth-century authors such as Edward Cox, Eduard Von Hartmann and Joseph Maxwell developed ideas of force as an attempt to explain the physical phenomena of mediumship. The studies of physical mediums conducted by Julian Ochorowicz, W. J. Crawford and others did much to support the belief that telekinesis and materialization were produced by forces coming from the body of the medium. With the rise of the Rhinean paradigm many parapsychologists set these ideas aside and adopted a mentalistic model. A study of these concepts helps us to understand how prevalent these ideas have been in the past, how they have been related to the body's vital processes and to physical radiations, and how they have been used to explain psychic phenomena.

Recent New Age, occult and frontier science literature is full of discussions about the role of little understood forces, radiations or fields in a variety of such phenomena as ESP, auras and healings (e.g., Benor, 2004). Furthermore, there are several organizations active today which are devoted to ideas of this sort.[1]

It is common to hear talk about ideas of "energies," "radiations" or "vibrations" that assume that human beings are virtual generators of vital force and that we live in a world of invisible forces intimately related to the phenomena studied by parapsychologists. Some, such as Guéret and Oudinot (1968), assume a continuum between the physical and biological forces accepted by modern science and ideas from occult traditions.

This hypothetical principle has been called a myriad of names: animal magnetism, magnetism, nervous force, neuric force, Od, psychic fluid, psychic force, vital energy and vital force, among other names. Since antiquity there have been discussions about subtle forces such as *prāṇa*, *chi*, the *mana*, as well as the ideas of such individuals as Maxwell, Van Helmont, Paracelsus and others (Amadou, 1953). In this paper I will discuss selected historical attempts to explain psychic or parapsychological phenomena through recourse to the idea of forces or radiations. My purpose is to make contemporary readers aware of aspects of a forgotten and difficult-to-obtain literature so as to provide some perspective for modern interests in similar topics. For pragmatic reasons I am focusing only on Western developments from the nineteenth century, with an emphasis on the literature published before the 1930s. I will not get into areas discussed outside of the mesmerism, Spiritualism and psychical research literatures, such as N-rays, mitogenic and other radiations from organic matter, Reich's orgone, radionics, or concepts from biology or from occult movements and philosophies (for overviews see Ungaro, 1992; Van Wijk, 2001). Furthermore, space considerations do not allow me to discuss force or field explanations of

*Republished with permission from *Journal of the Society for Psychical Research, 70*, 138–162, 2006.

†I wish to thank Debra H. Weiner and Nancy L. Zingrone for useful editorial suggestions for the improvement of this paper.

apparitions, auras, dowsing, luminous phenomena or psychometry, nor similar literature on "Od" force or ESP. Instead, my focus will be aspects of the literature of mesmerism, physical mediumship and the instrumental detection of those hypothetical radiations.

Humans as Magnets: Mesmerism and the Magnetic Force

In his *Mémoire sur la Découverte du Magnétisme Animal,* published in 1779, Mesmer presented 27 propositions about a universal fluid that could produce all kinds of effects (Mesmer, 1779/1970, pp. 54–56). Mesmer called this principle animal magnetism and related it to physical and organic matter. The human body was affected by it through the nerves; it was not localized only in the body. Mesmer saw it as emanating from the heavenly bodies and present in nature in general. Animal magnetism produced healing effects and could be reflected by mirrors, transmitted by sound and stored on different bodies. In a further attempt to relate this force to other aspects of nature, Mesmer compared it to magnetism, arguing that it was polarized. It is clear that Mesmer had great expectations for this fluid; he did not think animal magnetism would simply produce cures, but that it would revolutionize the medical profession (on Mesmer and his magnetic system see Pattie, 1994).

Both Mesmer and later writers believed that animal magnetism emanated from the magnetizer's body and could be conveyed to others through passes, or hand movements. A follower of Mesmer (Deleuze, 1852, pp. 1–2) wrote about this force:

> As we cannot comprehend how a body can act upon another at a distance, without there being something to establish a communication between them, we suppose that a substance emanates from him who magnetizes, and is conveyed to the person magnetized, in the direction given it by the will. This substance, which sustains life in us, we call the magnetic fluid. The nature of this fluid is unknown; even its existence has not been demonstrated; but everything occurs as if it did exist, and that warrants us in admitting it.

An influential early mesmerist, A. M. J. de Chastenet de Puységur (1807), argued in *Du Magnétisme Animal, Considéré dans ses Rapports avec Diverses Branches de la Physique Générale* for the importance of the will and the belief of the magnetizer to produce mesmeric phenomena. In addition, he thought that human beings were affected by surrounding forces such as gravity and magnetic currents. "The reciprocal influence between all bodies is called universal magnetism," (p. 133; this and other translations are mine) while "the particular influence of animated bodies on one another is animal magnetism" (p. 134). Humans are always surrounded and penetrated by the universal fluid. Their bodies behave like magnets in that the extremities are like poles, and this magnetic force may be reinforced by air, friction and by other bodies. Chastenet de Puységur referred to the magnetic fluid as a hypothesis, not necessarily a reality.

In his *Physiologie, Médecine et Métaphysique du Magnétisme,* L. J. J. Charpignon (1851, p. 15) proposed that electricity, light and heat were related to animal magnetism. This human magnetism, also described as a nervous fluid, was considered to be a modified form of the other physical forces, a process that operated through "additions and molecular combinations" (p. 41). The implication was that this was a universal principle animating matter that could be organized in different ways.

Phenomena such as the induction of trance, mental contact with the mesmerizer to the point of obeying his non-verbal commands, clairvoyance and transposition of the senses (for example, feeling that one was seeing from the pit of the stomach), were attributed by many to animal magnetism.

One writer argued that such transpositions of the senses were explained by the action of "animal electricity," an agent that could transfer sensory impressions to the nervous system in the absence of receptor organs such as eyes (Petetin, 1808).

But perhaps the best known and the most practical phenomena were the so- called magnetic cures of all kinds of conditions. Mesmer (1779/1970) himself became famous in part through some of his reported cures. Fatigue was felt occasionally by the magnetizer after the healing session. Some writers argued that the magnetizer "imparted of his own vital power to sustain that of the invalid" (Newnham, 1845, p. 148).

As late as the 1870s French mesmerist Baron J. D. Du Potet (1879) argued in the fourth edition of his *Traité Complet de Magnétisme Animal*: *Cours en douze leçons* (p. 43) that magnetism was involved in bodily processes such as digestion and circulation. To some extent, such ideas were a normal outgrowth of neurophysiological ideas prevalent in the eighteenth century that held that fluids and vital forces flowed through the nerves, allowing for movement and for the processing of sensory impressions (Clarke & Jacyna, 1987).[2]

Following this tradition, British physician James Esdaile argued that a fluid of the nervous system carried the orders of the brain within the body and that this fluid was also involved in perception. This fluid could produce mesmeric phenomena. For example, Esdaile said that the fluid "is transmitted to the mesmerised person's brain through the medium of his nerves: and the consequence is that the *thought-modified* nervous fluid of the active brain is both reflected and understood by the passive brain of the patient, exactly as the passive end of an electric telegraph records the impulses received from the active extremity of the battery" (Esdaile, 1852, p. 238). For Esdaile such ideas could account for the transmission of thought at a distance or the influence of the mesmerizer over the mesmerized without apparent conventional sensory commands.

For some, the fluid was not a mere physiological principle, but the instrument of the soul. Berruyer (1852) argued that the fluid emanated from Divinity, and hence to the human soul. "The human fluid ... is the link by which the body and the soul are united; it is the intermediary between spirit and matter." (Berruyer, 1852, p. 170). Ordinaire (1852) thought that the soul ruled and directed the fluid. Chastenet de Puységur (1807, p. 166) argued that in a mesmeric healing session the healer's compassion for the diseased person developed an intention or a will from the soul to help the patient. He intimated that the guiding principle of animal magnetism was a spiritual one (pp. 165–167).

Esdaile (1852) and other mesmerists (e.g., Du Potet, 1845–1846, pp. 392–393) believed that the mesmeric fluid could travel to distant places. The fluid was thought to be able to obtain information or to cause actions in these locations. One of these theorists, the American C. F. Durant, suggested that transference of thought could take place because the magnetic fluid travelled through physical barriers and great distances from the magnetizer to the magnetized person: "the magnetic fluid is composed of globular molecules which touch each other, and form strings or magnetic cords from one brain to the other brain" (Durant, 1837, p. 79).

Following on Tardy de Montravel's (1785) early observations, Charpignon (1851) noticed that some entranced individuals "say they see coming out of our hands, our eyes, our mouths, trails of light" (p. 32). He conducted tests to study this visual perception of the fluid. In one such test he used four bottles of clear glass, "charging" one of them with magnetic fluid. Charpignon mixed the bottles and presented all of them to the mesmerized person, who correctly identified the magnetized bottle, saying that there was a luminous vapor inside it. On another occasion, according to Charpignon (1851): "A flask was charged by three magnetizers immediately one after the other, and the somnambulist said she saw three fluids superimposed in layers, and she indicated their exact order." (p. 60).

While belief in magnetism became less fashionable as the century progressed, it is also true that it continued in some circles well into the late nineteenth century and beyond. Prominent examples include the work of Baréty (1887) and Boirac (1908/1917).

Physical Mediumship

Influential books such as Rogers's *Philosophy of Mysterious Agents* (1853) and Dods's *Spirit Manifestations Examined and Explained* (1854) postulated an externalized force to account for the mental and physical phenomena of Spiritualism. For Rogers the basic principle was nerve force, and the movement of objects in poltergeist cases or in séances could take place through unconscious direction of this force by the living agent or in an automatic way with no direction at all. Dods argued that the body's "electro-magnetic" forces were related to the "*involuntary powers* in the back of the brain" (Dods, 1854, p. 33), the section of the brain thought to control involuntary body functions.

The phenomenon of table-turning was particularly important because it provided a focus of attention for the development of theoretical concepts such as those discussed in this paper. In France, Count Agénor de Gasparin studied the problem, as reported in his book *Des Tables Tournantes* (1854). The movements and liftings of tables experienced by De Gasparin convinced him that some physical agent was involved. As he had more sittings, he postulated the existence of a fluid that acted through the hands of the chain of sitters around the table. De Gasparin wrote that "a physical agent ... similar to terrestrial magnetism, light, heat, electricity ... under the ... provisional name of hematonervous fluid" could explain table-turning, as well as other spiritualistic and mesmeric phenomena (Vol. 2, p. 407). This fluid was considered to be both physical and psychological; physical because of the effects it produced, and psychological because it depended on the (not always conscious) will of the sitters. As he wrote, the fluid "communicates to physical objects the movements determined by our will" (Vol. 1, p. 90).[3]

British Sergeant-at-Law Edward W. Cox named this principle "psychic force." Cox described his idea mainly in two books: *Spiritualism Answered by Science* (1872) and *What Am I?* (1874). Like previous writers, Cox argued that a force emanated from the nervous systems of psychics (his term). This force, directed by the psychic's intelligence, produced the physical phenomena of Spiritualism. He wrote:

> The Psychic is a person in whom there is an abnormal capacity for dislocation in the normal relationship of Soul and body. In such a condition, the Soul (or Psychic) Force ceases to flow through its usual channels and therefore manifests itself without them, as does the magnetic force, in disturbing effects upon molecular structure. Psychic Force ... penetrates and permeates molecular matter; and ... neutralises in matter the force of gravity. (Cox, 1874, pp. 417–418)

According to Cox this force is normally related to such body processes as movements. But the mediumistic trance is a catalyst in breaking the normal balance of the force and allowing it to leave the body. In another book, he wrote: "As the organism is itself moved and directed within its structure by a Force … it is an equally reasonable conclusion that the Force which causes the motions beyond the limits of the body is the same force that produces motion within the limits of the body" (Cox, 1872, p.101; on this issue see Alvarado, 1981).

Cox influenced English physicist William Crookes, who performed experimental studies of the psychic force with D. D. Home (Crookes, 1874). Crookes explored the ways in which this force interacted with the physical world. Telekinetic movements of an accordion were reported to occur inside a wire basket. To see if the hypothetical force was affected in some way, Crookes sent an electrical current around the wires. In other tests Home was able to use his psychic force through water. These tests reveal Crookes's training as a physicist, as he explored the characteristics of the force and its relationship to the physical world as opposed to seeking solely to prove the existence of this force.

Gracis Gerry Fairfield in his book, *Ten Years with Spiritual Mediums* (1875), also attempted to relate psychic forces to the human body, in this case the nervous system. Fairfield defended the existence of a "nerve-aura," a force he defined as "an emanating atmosphere having the molecular properties, motor and sensory, of nervous tissue itself, though of lessened intensity" (Fairfield, 1875, p. 122). Such a substance, Fairfield thought, could account for both the mental and the physical phenomena of Spiritualism. The author believed that the release of this force was associated with molecular disturbances of nerve-centers. Fairfield discussed epilepsy as an example of the pathological excitation of the nerve-centers, and as a disease involving the same molecular disturbance as that involved in the release of nerve force from the body.

Like Fairfield, the Reverend Asa Mahan explained spiritualistic phenomena as resulting from a force generated by the human body, rather than by a discarnate agency (Mahan, 1855, 1875). The force could be intelligent or not according to its locus in the nervous centers.

> When such centre is not immediately connected with the brain, then the action of this force, like that of magnetism, is simply that of a repulsive and attractive power, without the characteristics of intelligence. When that centre is the brain, then the direction of the action of this power bears, in many important particulars, the characteristics of intelligence, the action of the force, in such cases, being not only in accordance with, but evidently directed by, mental states. (Mahan, 1875, pp. 96–97)

Similar to previous writers, philosopher Eduard von Hartmann also attempted to explain mediumistic phenomena as a nervous force from the medium's body, and sometimes from the body of other persons around the medium (von Hartmann, 1885). This agent was said to produce 'lines' of force that could pull and push so as to cause movement of objects, direct writing and other phenomena. This process was related to the medium's state of consciousness:

> This liberation of directive radiation of nerve force is under all circumstances … not a function of those parts of the brain which serve as support to the conscious will, but of deeper-lying layers of the brain which either coincide with those supporting the somnambulic consciousness, or are more approximate to them than to the first. It is, therefore, no wonder that the development of a magnetic-mediumistic nerve force is stronger in the somnambulistic than in the waking state. (p. 442).

Of course, most of this literature was criticized by spiritualists. They generally argued that ideas of force without spiritual interpretations did not explain anything and were not supported by the evidence (Aksakof, 1890/n. d.; Force v. Spiritualism, 1867). But spiritualists also believed in these forces. What they objected to was the assumption that these forces were always directed by the conscious or unconscious mind of the medium. In their view, the spirits of deceased individuals directed the medium's energies.

One case in point was the ideas of Allan Kardec (the pseudonym of Léon Hyppolyte Denizard Rivail), considered by many as the codifier of spiritist doctrine. Kardec popularized the concept of the perispirit, "a fluidic envelope, which is semi-material, and constitutes the link between the soul and the body" (Kardec, 1876, p. 53). He followed the teachings of the spirits as "dictated" through mediums. Similar to previous ideas of subtle bodies and fluids (Poortman, 1954/1978), these teachings asserted that human beings consisted of the soul or spirit, the physical body and the perispirit. The perispirit was the "means by which the spirit acts upon its fleshy organs and transmits its will to all that is exterior to itself" (Kardec, 1876, p. 54). This fluid was described as universal (Kardec, 1875, pp. 9-10). As Kardec wrote, this principle "is drawn from the surrounding atmosphere, from the universal fluid; it participates at once in the nature of electricity, of the magnetic fluid and of inert matter" (Kardec, 1875, pp. 113–114). According to Kardec, it is through the perispirit that discarnate spirits can appear as apparitions, or materializations, and can move objects. In a physical medium, the fluid of the perispirit is strong and emanates from the body.

The idea that materialization phenomena were caused by an invisible force was common among many writers. Such ideas were consistent with the speculations that "invisible exudations from the human organisations" were used by spirits to create visible and tangible forms (Owen, 1871, p. 404). The spirits, according to another writer, "through the exercise of their united willpower attract and gather certain magnetic and material elements from the medium, the persons present and the atmosphere" (Crowell, 1879, pp. 181–182). Similarly, Brackett (1886, pp. 126–127) referred to luminous vapor as the matter from a medium's body used to create materializations.

There were many nineteenth-century speculations about materialization phenomena as the transformation of matter from the body of the medium and the sitters. In the words of an anonymous writer in *The Spiritualist Newspaper*, probably the editor:

> The power by which these duplications are effected seems to have something of the nature of a single force, and not of a complicated mixture of vital actions, because not merely are portions of the human body duplicated, but in some instances, the clothes also ... The law of conservation of energy points out that power cannot be gained in one direction without being lost in another, consequently the power which moves a visible or invisible spirit hand must come from somewhere, and on the hypothesis laid down in this sketch the power comes from the medium. On the withdrawal of much vital force from the whole or a particular part of the body of the medium, it would seem that of necessity that there must be a loss of heat to that part; such is actually the case in practice, for at all, or nearly all, materialisation *séances* for full forms, the medium becomes cold shortly before the manifestations begin. (Speculations, 1875, p. 135)[4]

While most of the materializations reported during the nineteenth century did not show a visible connection to the medium's body, there were exceptions which supported the speculation of projection of forces from the mediums. These consisted of actual observations of emanations or projections such as limbs from the body of the mediums (e.g., Spirit Faces, 1873) and forms such as clouds, drapery and other non-human shapes. The latter was reported on occasion with two extremely controversial British materialization mediums: William Eglinton (Farmer, 1886) and the so-called Dr. Monck (Francis Ward Monck: Oxley, 1876). An example with Monck was reported in a séance that took place on May 3, 1876. Observers had seen a spirit materialized named Lillie with no obvious connection to the medium:

> He [the medium] next stood close to the table ... and from his right side there issued a thin white vapour, which gradually assumed a form, at first as of gossamer outline like a garment or a robe, which became more dense or opaque; then appeared the head with a crown adorned by a luminous lily; and finally the full materialised form of Lillie ... and while thus standing Dr. Monck ... handled the drapery. ... This was repeated three times, the materialised form gradually dissolving each time before our eyes. (Oxley, 1876, p. 222)

The Russian Imperial Counsellor to the Czar and psychical researcher Alexander Aksakof argued that the matter used in materializations was taken in an act of dematerialization from the body of the medium (Aksakow, 1894–1895/1896).[5] Aksakof believed there were three stages of materializations. The first consisted of movement of objects and touches caused by an invisible force. The second consisted of the creation of visible and tangible but incomplete forms such as hands, heads and busts. Finally, the third stage was complete materialization, with the production of whole bodies (on stages of materialization, see De Rochas, 1897; and Richet, 1922/1923, p. 478). These stages, in Aksakof's view, were related to forces coming from the medium's body, a point he illustrated in his book with the case of the partial dematerialization of the body of medium Elizabeth D'Esperance (see also D'Esperance, 1897, and the criticism of Carrington, 1907).

Spiritualists' interests in forces also extended to a variety of physical processes such as magnetism and electricity. Many of these were limited to reports of current scientific developments (e.g., Electricity in the Body, 1875; Weaving by Electricity, 1854). These discussions did not mention Spiritualism or its phenomena. However, their inclusion in spiritualist publications indicated spiritualists' interests in dynamic ideas about the physical world. It was as if they felt that their phenomena—particularly mediumship—were a special case of mind- (or spirit)-matter interaction. In a world full of not completely understood forces, as seen in the nineteenth-century physics literature (D'Agostino, 2000; Harman, 1982), could there not be room for "new" imponderables?

Many twentieth-century researchers thought so. Astronomer Camille Flammarion (1907) referred to "an invisible prolongation of the organism of the medium" (p. 423) to account for physical phenomena. He compared this process to other natural emanations such as magnetism, electricity and heat. In Germany, physician and psychical researcher Albert F. von Schrenck-Notzing (1920/1925) referred to "energetic psychophysical emanations" (p. 63) coming from the medium's body. Charles Richet wrote that: "Materialization is a mechanical projection: we already know that projection of light, of heat and of electricity; it is not a very long step to think that a projection of mechanical energy may be possible. The remarkable demonstrations of Einstein show how close mechanical and luminous energy are to one another" (Richet, 1922/1923, p. 468).

In Italy, William Mackenzie (1923) argued in his *Metapsichica Moderna* for the "disaggregation (probably atomic) of the medium's organic substance" (p. 252). This process, considered by Mackenzie to be the central problem of metapsychics, was seen to be analogous to radioactive emanations from inorganic matter (pp. 270–271).

In another overview of psychical research, French psychical researcher René Sudre's *Introduction à la Métapsychique Humaine* (1926), the concept of the "psychic fluid" was related to all kinds of effects on physical and organic matter and to materialization. Sudre redefined the term telergy previously used by F. W. H. Myers, to mean "the phenomena by which the psychic fluid accomplishes more or less visibly an exterior work on ordinary matter" (p. 226).

The above-mentioned writers developed their ideas in part through the phenomena of physical mediumship. Similarly, French Attorney General and physician Joseph Maxwell believed that the force emitted by physical mediums was "kindred to the energy which circulates in our nerves and which provokes the contraction of our muscles" (Maxwell, 1903/1905, p. 51). To generate this force, Maxwell thought muscular contractions were useful. He wrote, "a movement without contact can be procured by tightly squeezing one another's hands, or by resting the feet very firmly on the floor" (p. 110). This was related to the possibility that this nerve energy may act "in proportion as it is able to acquire a sufficient tension for its emission" (p. 56). Tension was achieved by lack of motion of the medium. If the energy could not find a normal outlet, it increased the possibility of being exteriorized to produce telekinesis and other phenomena. But there could be exceptions. If there was enough tension, body movements could produce phenomena. That is, the movement could "liberate a quantity of energy superior to that which was utilised by the working of the muscle" (p. 57).[6]

One of the mediums Maxwell studied was Eusapia Palladino, who was very important for the development of concepts of paranormal forces, not only because of the phenomena reported to take place around her, but because she presented all kinds of behaviors (e.g., movements of the hands corresponding to movements of objects, statements about the force, exhaustion after séances) that supported the idea of the emission of a bodily force. While she was not unique in this, her performances were particularly influential in the development of these concepts of force (Alvarado, 1993).

For example, Italian psychiatrist Enrico Morselli derived his ideas from sittings with Palladino. Morselli's (1908) two-volume work *Psicologia e "Spiritismo"* was largely devoted to the physiology and psychology of Palladino's phenomena. In his view the medium could create phantasms and forms "through the radiant exteriorization of its force, the bio-psychic ondulatory emanation projected" from her (Morselli, 1908, Vol. 1, p. 449). This was further described as an "exopsychism, a vital dynamism" (Vol. l, p. 322). Like many previous writers, Morselli believed in collective agency to explain this force. He reported that dynamometric readings taken before and after séances showed that the force in the hand grip of medium and sitters decreased from the first to the second measurement, suggesting energy expenditure during the séance by all involved (Vol. 1, pp. 351–352).

Ideas of a force coming from the medium's body were also supported by observations of ectoplasm. Richet (1922/1923) referred to this as a "faculty of external projection, of "ectoplasmization." The emission of a material substance that can become organic" (p. 619). This substance—observed also during the nineteenth century (e.g., Oxley, 1876)—took mainly the form of clouds or nebulous formations, as well as a plaster-like and, more rarely, seemingly liquid forms. Ectoplasm was generally believed to be part of the vital force of the medium's body and the invisible principle behind most of the physical phenomena of mediumship.

French physician Gustave Geley described ectoplasm as consisting of an "anatomo-biologic decentralisation in the medium's body and an externalization of the decentralised factors in an amorphous state, solid, liquid, or vaporous" (Geley, 1924/1927, p. 358). In his view, this decentralization process could produce different effects, namely movement of objects, luminous effects and materializations. The latter were considered by Geley as the "final and superior phase" of the projection of the body's forces (Geley, 1922, p. 202).

Both Geley's (1919/1920,1924/1927) and others' observations of controversial medium Marthe Béraud, alias "Eva C.," (Schrenck-Notzing, 1920) did much to publicize the existence of strange forms, faces, cords and spaghetti-like structures that seemed to come from the medium's body or were seen close to it. As Geley described a particular observation:

> From the mouth of Eva there descends to her knees a cord of white substance of the thickness of two fingers; this ribbon takes under our eyes varying forms, that of a large perforated membrane,

> with swellings and vacant spaces; it gathers itself together, retracts, swells and narrows again. Here and there from the mass appear temporary protrusions, and these for a few seconds assume the form of fingers, the outline of hands, and then re-enter the mass. Finally the cord retracts on itself, lengthens to the knees, its end rises, detaches itself from the medium, and moves towards me. I then see the extremity thicken like a swelling, and this terminal swelling expands into a perfectly modelled hand. I touch it; it gives a normal sensation; I feel the bones, and the fingers with their nails. Then the hand contracts, diminishes and disappears in the end of the cord. The cord makes a few movements, retracts and returns into the medium's mouth. (Geley, 1919/1920, pp. 57–58)

Geley believed that the process of materialization, and the formation of ectoplasm in particular, was the same as the process behind the formation of a butterfly inside a chrysalis or of a fetus inside a woman's womb.[7] In his view "there is simply one substance, unique and basic, as the substratum of organic life" (Geley, 1919/1920, p. 64). Both organic and ectoplasmic forms were considered representations of this basic primal principle. In addition, Geley believed that the same superior dynamism or psychism shaped both organic life during fetal development and materialization phenomena in the séance room. It molded both organic and ectoplasmic formation through the process of ideoplasty, where an idea could direct both normal and "supernormal" materialization. The superior psychism, a principle independent of physiology, was seen to be the "very foundation of the living being; it centralises and directs the psychic whole; it binds together all present states of consciousness ... it possesses the so-called supernormal faculties" (Geley, 1919/1920, pp. 215–216).

Other researchers centered their speculations of subtle energies on more empirical work. Polish psychical researcher Julian Ochorowicz conducted particularly influential studies with physical medium Stanislawa Tomczyk. Ochorowicz studied the properties of fluidic projections from the medium that could move small objects. In his first paper he said he observed threads coming from the medium's fingers (Ochorowicz, 1909). According to him he could cut these threads and they would form back again. Tomczyk stated that there were different forces at work. She referred to: (1) the personal current of the medium, capable of acting a short distance from the body; (2) the etheric or fluidic hands of the medium's double, which could act at a distance without help from the medium's own force; and (3) the current from the hands of the medium's double, which could act at a short distance from the body (Ochorowicz, 1909, p. 98).

Ochorowicz kept defining the different emanations in different papers. In a later paper he said that the "current" was a combination of forces also related to what he conceived as rays (Ochorowicz, 1910). The latter were an external prolongation of the current, and were guided by the influence of the medium's subconscious mind. The rays could be further divided into two types: 'rigid' rays were concerned with mechanical phenomena but could not affect photographic plates or go through objects; on the other hand, 'X^{x}'-rays could affect photographic plates and could penetrate matter further than X-rays.

Ochorowicz (1911) conducted experiments to study the properties of the emanations. The 'fluidic thread' could carry objects and could be detected when passing through smoked paper and liquids. The 'current' or rays could carry water or humid particles that were able to cause chemical reactions when combined, thus showing the transfer of one substance to another. They were also found to be resistant to fire, unaffected by a magnetic field and capable of conducting electricity. Eventually, Ochorowicz (1911–1912, 1912) published pictures of hands. These were supposed to be the hands of the medium's double. The emanations that caused the pictures of the hands, Ochorowicz thought, came from Tomczyk's etheric body and were different from the other emanations that were related to the medium's nervous system.

Another important group of studies were those conducted by Irish mechanical engineer W. J. Crawford (1916/1918, 1919, 1921), who worked with a mediumistic circle—the Goligher circle — that produced such phenomena as table levitations. He conducted experiments that led him to postulate a 'psychic rod' theory of table levitations (Crawford, 1916/1918). On this theory, an invisible structure emanating from the body of the medium (but nurtured as well by the psychic forces of the sitters) could levitate tables. The observation that the weight of Kathleen Goligher, the main medium of the circle, increased when the table was levitated suggested that the table's weight was being transferred to her through an invisible structure projected by her body in cantilever shape (this change of weight had been reported before with Palladino by Courtier, 1908). On other occasions, Crawford believed that the cantilever had a point of contact on the floor and the weight was not transferred to the medium. He also postulated other modes of action of the rods. In addition, both the medium and the sitters lost weight after the séances.[8] This suggested that the phenomena depended on the forces of both medium and sitters. In his book, *The Reality of Psychic Phenomena,* Crawford stated that he believed that invisible "operators" or spirits manipulated the forces in question.

Attempts at Physical Detection

Other researchers worked with non-mediumistic individuals. French physician Hyppolyte Baraduc (1893) used an instrument he called a biometer consisting of a glass jar inside which was a needle suspended by a thread. The needle rotated on top of a circular surface with numbers that allowed Baraduc to obtain readings corresponding to the deviations of the movements of the needle. When people put their hands near the instrument the right hand effected an attraction of the needle whereas the left hand repelled it. These movements, described by Baraduc as "tangible and recordable expressions of a superior Force" (pp. 12–13), were considered to be evidence for the existence of a vital body in human beings. The movements of the needle showed that each person had a particular biometric formula consisting of "the expression of the vital state" (p. 22) at the moment of measurement. This formula, consisting of combinations of attraction and repulsion in the right and left hands, could change according to different states, dispositions and medical conditions. Baraduc believed that the conditions were caused by "primordial fluidic perturbations of the vital body" (p. 162). He was aware that the proximity of the hand to the biometer could induce some movements due to bodily heat. He conducted tests that showed that while candles and light produced movements of the biometer's needle, they did not produce the attraction and repulsion patterns observed with hands. In addition, Baraduc noticed that the movements could be produced at will by some individuals.

Similar to Kardec and others, Baraduc believed that the vital force or vital body was a semi-physical body that bridged the physical body and the spirit. The vital body influenced the physical body. It "rules, conserves, animates the material body" (p. 212). In turn, the spirit could influence the physical body through the vital body. The vital body obtained its nourishment through absorption of a universal life force surrounding everything, a concept similar to the universal animal magnetism of Mesmer and Reichenbach's (1849/1851) Od. In this vitalistic view, life was seen as much more than an energy emanating from the human body; the body was only a place where the spirit and vital body dwelled.

In addition to Baraduc, several French researchers argued that different types of instruments or devices showed the existence of a fluid or a nervous force by the movement of a needle or some other part of the instrument. One of the most influential workers in this area was physician Paul Joire, who published several papers about the influence of the nervous force on an instrument he called the sthenometer. The externalized nervous force, Joire maintained, could cause movements of a needle under glass. The right hand usually produced larger deflections of the needle than the left hand, but some medical conditions such as neurasthenia could reverse this pattern. Hysterics showed very low left-hand readings (Joire, 1905).

Typical of this literature, there were criticisms related to the possibility of alternate explanations to account for the movements of the sthenometer's needle. Stratton and Philips (1906) argued that the results could be explained through body heat, a conclusion disputed by Joire (1907). Such controversies continued in later years with similar devices, as seen in Carrington's (n. d.) discussion of these types of studies. During the nineteenth century (and later) there were many attempts to record human radiations using photographic plates. Because photography had been actively used to record materialization and other phenomena as well as to capture "invisible spirits" around the sitters (see Krauss, 1992/1995), it was logical to expect that photography could also be used to capture invisible human radiations as well. A pioneer in this area was the French Commandant Louis Darget (Darget, 1909; Tégrad, 1902). Darget reported he obtained "effluviographs," or pictures of the "fluid," around hands, fingers and plants without exposure to light. These pictures, he believed, reflected the moral state of the person, as well as emotional states and the state of health. Regarding the latter, Darget wrote that most diseases "are nothing but the accumulation of fluid in the diseased region or the absence of fluid" (Tégrad, 1902, p. 595). In addition, he obtained "thought photographs" by placing photographic plates a short distance from a person's body. In one such test Darget put a photographic plate for five minutes one centimeter from the head of his wife while she was sleeping. The plate showed what Darget interpreted to be the image of an eagle. Mme. Darget did not remember dreaming about an eagle but he speculated that the image represented the fluidic exteriorization of a dream. Darget obtained other pictures by placing fingers or hands on the plates. The images showed apparent radiations from the respective parts of the body.

Baraduc also conducted this type of work. In his *L'Âme Humaine: Ses Mouvements, ses Lumiéres, et l'Iconographie de I'lnvisible Fluidique,* he presented many pictures of vital radiations taken using a variety of methods, such as prolonged contact of hands with photographic plates (Baraduc, 1896). Like Darget, Baraduc claimed that pictures taken with regular photographic plates (with and without contact) reflected emotional and health states. The pictures present what look like fields and discrete energy particles, suggesting, as Baraduc argued, that there were different types of forces. This work led Baraduc to argue that: "Around us ... we attract, we aspire waves in the form of ellipsoidal curved surfaces drawn from the cosmos, which in form and delicacy are related to what we call a state of mind or soul. ... We throw back into this same cosmos, emanations more or less gross or subtle according to analogous states of the vibrating soul" (Dr. Baraduc's Discovery, 1897, p. 31).[9]

Concepts of Force and Modern Parapsychology

While popular interest in forces is as prevalent today as it was in the old days, the rise of modern experimental parapsychology in the Anglo-American milieu has decreased interest in the concept of human radiations among professionals in the field. The work of Joseph Banks Rhine and associates redefined modern parapsychological research. In his initial monograph, *Extrasensory Perception,* Rhine (1934) had written: "The Wave theory seems to be inapplicable to these results, in view of the distance experiments and the absence of any decline of results with distance. ... Likewise it is shown that E.S.P. is not a sensory phenomenon. The absence of any need of orientation, of any sensory localization, of any recognized stimulating energy such as the senses receive and of any awareness of reception all lead to the rejection of the sixth sense hypothesis as well" (p. 163).[10]

The new experimental parapsychology headed by Rhine (or at least some of its representatives) claimed that time, space and the physical characteristics of the target were irrelevant to ESP and PK test performance. This, as discussed by Warcollier (1953), led many parapsychologists to deny the existence of the 'fluid'. In *Parapsychology: Frontier Science of the Mind* (1957)—a textbook that articulated well the conclusions of the Rhinean paradigm derived from experimental work conducted since the 1930s—Rhine and Pratt stated that: "It is ... the manifestly nonphysical character of parapsychical phenomena that for the present constitutes their only general identifying feature and marks them off from the rest of general psychology. ... The distinction ... from physics is *not,* however, an absolute one. Rather they usually involve physical events or objects, either as stimuli or as effects. *But there is always some distinct point at which a completely physical interpretation is manifestly inadequate"* (Rhine & Pratt, 1957, p. 6, emphasis in original).

Rhine used the findings of his card and dice tests to defend a dualistic view of human beings, a perspective clearly seen in his books, *The Reach of the Mind* and *New World of the Mind* (Rhine, 1947, 1953). In his view, parapsychology was the science of the nonphysical. The mind was clearly the causative agent underlying psychic phenomena and no consideration of fluids or electromagnetic forces of any kind was deemed necessary. This was clear in Rhine's discussion of psychokinesis (e.g., Rhine, 1947), where he did not follow the ideas of projections of biophysical force from the body postulated by previous workers. While Rhine shared with previous writers the idea that the mind or will of the subject could to some extent direct the psychokinetic influence, he argued that the process was inherently non-physical.

In the face of experimental failures to find physical correlates of ESP and PK, many thought that the concept of psychic or fluidic forces seemed to lack explanatory power and could be forgotten. Nonetheless, others protested against Rhine and the like, arguing that the 'energetic' hypothesis had been rejected prematurely (e.g., Cazzamalli, 1954; Dufour, 1951).

Some figures from the period reviewed here—Carrington (1952-1953), Cazzamalli (1954), Mackenzie (n. d.) and Sudre (1956/1960)—have presented ideas of human radiations to a new generation of researchers. In addition, the interest in Soviet parapsychology, which is based largely on the concept of bioplasma, has kept alive the idea of vital, biological energies underlying psychic phenomena. The Soviet influence soon spread to the United States and elsewhere, where many claimed that the electrophotographic technique known as Kirlian photography could detect and document these auric or bioplasmic emanations (e.g., Krippner & Rubin, 1974). However, this claim was questioned by some (e.g., Burton, Joines, & Stevens, 1975; Ellison, 1982). Such criticisms have created distrust among many parapsychologists both concerning the validity of Kirlian photography and about most of the work claiming to detect subtle energies in general. Nonetheless concepts of force to explain psychic phenomena have been prevalent within the field of psychotronics (Second, 1975).

In recent times there have been many publications dealing with concepts of force. These include writings about auras and their instrumental detection (Korotkov, 2004; Lindgren, 2000), and about biofields in the context of alternative medicine (Rubik, 2002). Concepts of subtle energy have been discussed in recent decades within the parapsychological literature, as seen in Roll's work on poltergeists (e.g., Roll, Burdick & Joines, 1973) and Benor's (2004) and Grad's (1989) discussions about healing. Tiller's writings (e.g., Tiller, 1997) have also contributed to the modern articulation of the different meanings of the concept of subtle energies. Andrade (1983), Joines (1975), Wasserman (1956), and others, have promoted theoretical models for psychic phenomena that involve fields and emanating radiations. The concept is central to the parapsychology of such Asian countries as China (Leping & McConnell, 1991) and Japan (Kokubo & Kasahara, 2000). More recently, there has been some speculation about psychic phenomena and ambient energy in empty space, or zero-point energy (Puthoff, 2001; Roll, 2003).

The rejection of forces by many parapsychologists may also be related to the rise of concepts of non-locality that do not postulate a transmission mechanism (e.g., Oteri, 1975; Varvoglis, 1986). For example, the models developed by Schmidt (1975) and Walker (1975) do not involve projection of forces or radiations. The same may be said of more recent non-force-PK explanations (e.g., May, Utts & Spottiswood, 1995; Pallikari-Viras, 1997) and of other contemporary theoretical views (e.g., Jahn & Dunne, 2001; Rausher & Targ, 2001).[11]

Regardless of the causes of the neglect of force concepts, the fact is that many modern parapsychologists do not believe in these forces nor in physical models of psi in general and keep commenting on the apparent independence of distance and barriers of psi test performance (e.g., Braud & Schlitz, 1991, p. 36). As stated in a widely used textbook, "there is no generally acknowledged demonstration that an energy with the required characteristics actually exists" (Irwin, 2004, p. 134).

Concluding Remarks

Overview

The idea of a human radiation has been one of the main explanatory models of phenomena in the history of mesmerism, Spiritualism and psychical research. This hypothetical subtle energy was considered as the agent behind thought-transference, movement of objects, materializations, healings and many other phenomena.

It is clear that there are many differences between the concepts discussed in this paper. The concept of the magnetic fluid of Charpignon was more physiological than that of Ordinaire, who argued for the importance of the soul as the main driving principle behind the fluid. Similarly, Kardec's perispirit was a different principle than that proposed by Rogers or by Maxwell. While Kardec (as well as Mesmer) argued for a universal fluid connected to both the physical body and the spirit, Rogers and Maxwell referred to a nervous force of more limited dimensions.

It is interesting to see that many of these ideas associated these forces to functions of the body such as movement and to life itself (as seen in the ideas of Baraduc, Deleuze, Cox, and Geley). Even such concepts as animal magnetism, considered by Mesmer and others to be universal forces, have been described as being housed in the human body and related to its workings. In addition, many of the early writings (e.g., Esdaile, Fairfield, Mahan, Maxwell) argued that this force was intimately related to the nervous system or that it was the nerve force itself. But these ideas also played a different role: they naturalized psychic phenomena. For many, postulating an alternative view of the functioning of the nervous system to explain a variety of mysterious-looking phenomena was important in that the phenomena in question could then be related to the functions of the body, a kind of an extended chapter of human physiology. This seems to have been the thrust behind the writings of Cox, De Gasparin, Dods, Fairfield, Geley, Maxwell, Morselli, Rogers, Von Hartmann and others.

The emphasis on physiological explanations was in part an attempt to combat the notion of discarnate agency. Like the current idea that ESP and PK from the living can explain what seem to be survival phenomena, these ideas of force served as an explanatory concept that could be actively used to combat the basic tenet of Spiritualism. De Gasparin, Fairfield, Mahan, Morselli, Rogers and Von Hartmann, among others, were clearly interested in this goal. Nonetheless, others such as Kardec and Crawford presented views that postulated or at least admitted the possibility of the action of spirits of the dead.

Criticism

Regarding mesmerism, overt suggestion as well as the more subtle demands of the situation can perhaps account for such mesmeric phenomena as healing and reports of seeing and feeling the magnetic "current." This is especially true with the common practice of using the same subjects over and over again. As Carroy (1991) has argued, the history of hypnosis (and mesmerism) is full of the repeated use of the same person (or subject) to produce effects. This, in turn, may produce "professional" subjects who have been trained to produce particular effects that have nothing to do with animal magnetism as a force (a similar point may be made about mediums). Of course, suggestion may account for many of the reported effects even without training.[12] Many magnetizers did not control for the effects of suggestion, even though some of them were aware of and believed in its power. It is true that some effects were obtained at a distance. But such effects are at odds with the concept of a body-based "magnetic" action. A force based on nervous currents or other biological principles should not be able to function far away from the body. If long-distance action does take place, it is unlikely that it is based on biological principles. Some other principle must be invoked to explain the phenomena, as others have speculated (Rein, 2004).

The work of Baraduc, Darget and Joire needs to be replicated. These authors have described effects that do not necessarily represent the detection of a specific biophysical force. In addition to this ambiguity, researchers must confront the criticism that artifacts such as the influence of body heat have not been completely controlled for. Although such criticisms are controversial in and of themselves, the fact remains that artifacts may account for *some* results. Furthermore, we must be aware that researchers such as Baraduc were aware of these issues and controlled for them in some (but not all) tests. One hopes that researchers with the proper training will explore the use of these devices and put the artifact hypothesis to the test.

As for physical mediumship, we need to recognize that many of the claims that emanations from the bodies of mediums account for phenomena are based on such final effects as the perceived movement of an object or a materialization. In many cases, the supposition is not supported by any specific observation or measurement pointing to the idea that a force was projected. Of course, there are exceptions to this, among them the claim that mist or threads have been seen to come from the medium's body. Such observations were reported by Ochorowicz with the medium Stanislawa Tomczyk, by Crawford with Kathleen Goligher, and by Schrenck-Notzing and Geley with Eva C. Furthermore, the physiological phenomena shown by mediums were suggestive of some connection between bodily processes and physical manifestations. While none of these observations is conclusive, they help us to keep in mind the possibility of the existence of an emanation from the body.

While I agree with Braude (1997) that, in some cases, the evidence for physical mediumship is fairly good, one has to recognize the problem of fraud in such phenomena as materializations. Randall (2003), in a paper about a nineteenth-century medium, noted that it is very difficult to evaluate some of these phenomena evidentially. He suggested a provisional acceptance of the data in order to look for patterns and correlations. I agree that this is a good strategy for the development of theoretical ideas and procedures for future research. Such research has the potential of supporting the radiation hypothesis, particularly if it is conducted using modern technology. But in practice the prospect of finding a physical medium, and then persuading that person to submit to research is not encouraging, due to the apparent rarity of such individuals.

In any case, one must be very careful not to derive conclusions about the nature of this hypothetical force from the literature reviewed in this paper. This has been done in the past by many writers, including some who put too much faith in the validity of information obtained through spirit communications (Kardec, 1876), on their theoretical speculations (Von Hartmann, 1885), or on a very particular reading of the literature (Quevedo, 1971).

I am open to the idea that some type of measurable force may be identified at some point, and that it may account for some—though not necessarily all—phenomena. Perhaps the current literature on the subject, which was not the focus of this paper, will help us on this issue. We certainly cannot close our minds completely to the idea. However unfortunate, at present speculating on the basis of the old literature that vital forces are related to non-physical or spiritual processes (as Baraduc postulated), or to the body's nerve force (as Maxwell and Morselli believed), does not rest on adequate evidence as was believed in the past and is still believed today (e.g., Loureiro, 1998).

The Past and the Present

It is interesting to notice similarities between modern concepts and findings and some of the old material discussed in this paper. The Soviet parapsychological theory of bioplasma and its claimed detection using Kirlian photography, not to mention the recent work with Gas Discharge Visualization (Korotkov, 2004), is similar to previous ideas of psychic forces. Recent studies of the lowering of temperature during supposed qi emission (Nakamura et al., 2000) parallel observations about mediumistic energies (Speculations, 1875). Similarly, pictures of such unspecified radiations as those discussed by Korotkov (2004) and Rhead (2001), are reminiscent of those presented by Baraduc (1896). Benor's (2004) discussion of healing is reminiscent of aspects of the mesmeric literature. Certainly, these ideas have come to us from our past even if such an origin is not acknowledged.

From the point of view of those of us who are interested in the history of ideas, much more needs to be done to trace the development of these concepts, their relationship with ideas about physical forces prevalent at the time in which they were developed (for example, neurophysiological concepts, electricity, radioactivity, X-rays, radio waves), their relationship to other variables (e.g., distance), and to other such conceptual traditions as vitalism. In addition, there is much to explore regarding the factors that have contributed to the survival of such ideas. This has been described to some extent in another paper (Alvarado, 1993), in which I argued that ideas of human radiation are not wholly derived from research results but are also connected to other non-scientific aspects such as the behaviors of mediums during the séances.

Finally, it is important to state again that although most of the concepts discussed here were of biophysical forces, there are differences between these ideas. The same is true today, because the term "subtle force" or "subtle energy" is often used to refer to different hypothetical processes ranging from electromagnetic waves to unknown forces. In addition, the terms are also used as metaphorical (comparing the hypothetical forces to known forms of radiation), descriptive (to refer to ESP and PK phenomena), and as explanatory labels (to account for what we refer to as ESP and PK). There is indeed much to clarify both from our past and present literature.

Notes

1 Some examples are the International Society for the Study of Subtle Energy and Energy Medicine (http://www.issseem.org/) the BioEnergy Fields Foundation (http://www.bioenergyfields.org/), the International Center for Reiki Training (http://www.reiki.org/), Association for Comprehensive Energy Psychology (http://www.energypsych.org/), and the Center for Frontier Medicine in Biofield Science (http://biofield.arizona. edu/).

2 On the interactions between electricity and animal magnetism see Sutton (1981). Charpignon (1854) discusses vitalism and mesmerism.

3 I have not discussed here many other writings about table-turning (such as Marc Thury's), conveniently summarized by Crabtree (1993) and Wantuil (n. d.). These and similar ideas were challenged by those who argued that table-turning could be explained by postulating unconscious muscular movements produced by the persons sitting around the table (e.g., Faraday, 1853/2000).

4 There were also observations of cold winds in the séance room (e.g., Crookes, 1874, p. 86). For later observations—generally assumed to be related to the functioning of a force or with the transformation of power from ambient temperature—see Maxwell (1903/1905, pp. 114–115) and Price (1925, pp. 33–38). For a theoretical discussion see Dudley (1926).

5 I am grateful to Eberhard Bauer for informing me about the original publication date of this work. The published works of this author use different spellings of his surname. In the text I have used the spelling presented in the cited work. I am grateful to W. Peter Mulacz for pointing this out to me. For another example of dematerialization see Gissurarson and Haraldsson (1989, pp. 78–80).

6 There are many observations relating body processes and movements to physical phenomena. Palladino moved her feet against the floor before phenomena were produced (De Rochas, 1897, p. 17), and showed movements while telekinesis took place (e.g., De Rochas, 1897, p. 19; Lodge, 1894, p. 333). Hamilton (1934) reported movements of the mediums (stamping on the floor, rubbing their hands and the hands of others) presumably related to the release of forces to form materializations. Willy Schneider experienced clonic spasms, general body tension, penile erection and orgasm while physical phenomena were produced (Schrenck-Notzing, 1920/1925). Other mediums did 'passes' around sitters apparently to 'extract' energy (Farmer, 1886, p. 169; Price, 1926, p. 648). Pawlowski (1925) reported that with medium Franek Kluski rhythmic breathing of the sitters helped the 'growth' of a materialization from a small formation to one of a larger size. With Rudi Schneider, occlusion of infrared beams was apparently synchronized with the medium's breathing cycle (Osty & Osty, 1931–1932).

7 Years before, another writer described materializations as "another expression of uterine growth" (Donnelly, 1876). On vitalistic ideas see Carrington (1909) and Mulacz (2001).

8 See, for example, Crawford (1916/1918, pp. 24–25, 40–56). Regarding alterations of the weight of mediums as a physical phenomenon, see Courtier (1908), Grunewald (1920) and Olcott (1875).

9 During the following years there were many examples of the use of photographic plates, or actual photography, to detect the fluid or human thought (e.g., Warrick, 1939; for a review see Krauss, 1992/1995).

10 Radiation explanations of telepathy were criticized by many before Rhine (e.g., Driesch, 1932/1933; Gurney, Myers & Podmore, 1886). However, there were some supporters of these ideas as well (e.g., Cazzamalli, 1925/1926).

11 See Rogo's (1980) discussion of the old biological force paradigm and the more recent mentalistic and quantum mechanical approaches.

12 I say "of course" while recognizing that we still do not understand why suggestion has different effects on different individuals. My point is that there are certain effects that cannot be separated from suggestion considering the mesmerists' testing procedures.

References

Aksakof, A. (n. d., ca. 1906). *Animismo y Espiritismo: Ensayo de un examen crítico de los fenómenos medianímicos* (2 vols.). Carbonell y Esteva. (Original work published in German, 1890)

Aksakow, A. (1896). *Un cas de dématérialisation partielle du corps d'un medium: Enquête et commentaires.* Librairie de l'Art Indépendant. (Original work published in German, 1894–1895)

Alvarado, C. S. (1981). Correspondence. PK and body movements: A historical and semantic note. *Journal of the Society for Psychical Research, 51,* 116-118.

Alvarado, C. S. (1993). Gifted subjects' contributions to psychical research: The case of Eusapia Palladino. *Journal of the Society for Psychical Research, 59,* 269-292.

Amadou, R. (1953). Esquisse d'une histoire philosophique du fluide. *Revue Métapsychique, 21,* 5-33.

Andrade, H. G. (1983). *Morte, renascimiento, evolução: Uma biologia transcendental.* Pensamento.

Baraduc, H. (1893). *La force vitale: Notre corps vital fluidique, sa formule biométrique.* G. Carré.

Baraduc, H. (1896). *L'âme humaine: Ses mouvements, ses lumières et l'iconographie de l'invisible fluidique.* Georges Carré.

Barety, A. (1887). *Le magnétisme animal étudié sous le nom de force neurique rayonnante et circulante dans les propriétés physiques, physiologiques et thérapeutiques.* Octave Doin.

Benor, D. J. (2004). *Consciousness, bioenergy and healing: Self-healing and energy medicine for the 21st century.* Wholistic Healing Publications.

Berruyer, A. (1852). Études et théories: de l'union de l'âme et du corps. *Journal du Magnétisme, 11,* 169–191.

Boirac, E. (1917). *Our hidden forces: An experimental study of the psychic sciences.* Frederick A. Stokes. (Original work published in French, 1908)

Brackett, E. A. (1886). *Materialized apparitions: If not beings from another life, what are they?* Colby & Rich.

Braud, W. G. & Schlitz, M. (1991) Consciousness interactions with remote biological systems: anomalous intentionality effects. *Subtle Energies 2*(1), 1–44.

Braude, S. E. (1997). *The limits of influence: Psychokinesis and the philosophy of science.* (Rev. ed.). University Press of America.

Burton, L., Joines, W. & Stevens, B. (1975) Kirlian photography and its relevance to parapsychological research. *Research in Parapsychology, 1974,* 107–112.

Carrington, H. (1907). An examination and analysis of the evidence for 'dematerialization' as demonstrated in Mons. Aksakof's book. *Proceedings of the American Society for Psychical Research, 1,* 131–168.

Carrington, H. (1909). *Eusapia Palladino and her phenomena.* B. W. Dodge.

Carrington, H. (n. d., ca. 1939). *Laboratory investigations into psychic phenomena.* Rider.

Carrington, H. (1952-53). Psychic energy and physical phenomena. *Tomorrow, 1,* 104–111.

Carroy, J. (1991). *Hypnose, suggestion et psychologie: L'invention de sujets.* Presses Universitaires de France.

Cazzamalli, F. (1926). Telepsychic phenomena and cerebral radiations. *Journal of the American Society for Psychical Research, 20,* 1–17. (Original work published in French, 1925)

Cazzamalli, F. (1954). La metapsichica, nuova disciplina scientifica. *Metapsichica, 9,* 5–27.

Charpignon, [L. J.] J. (1851). *Physiologie, médicine et métaphysique du magnétisme.* Société Typographique Belgue.

Charpignon, Dr [L. J. J.] (1854). Études et théories: le vitalisme et le magnétisme. *Journal du Magnétisme, 13,* 197–203.

Chastenet de Puységur, A. M. J. (1807). *Du magnétisme animal, considéré dans les rapports avec diverses branches de la physique générale.* Imprimierie de Cellot.

Clarke, E. & Jacyna, L. S. (1987). *Nineteenth-century origins of neuroscientific concepts.* University of California Press.
Courtier, J. (1908). Rapport sur les séances d'Eusapia Paladino à 1'Institut Général Psychologique. *Bulletin de l'Institut General Psychologique, 8,* 415–546.
Cox, E. W. (1872). *Spiritualism answered by science: With the proofs of a psychic force* (Rev. ed.). Longman.
Cox, E. W. (1874). *What am I? A popular introduction to mental physiology and psychology. Vol. II. The mechanism in action.* Longmans.
Crabtree, A. (1993). *From Mesmer to Freud: Magnetic sleep and the roots of psychological healing.* Yale University Press.
Crawford, W. J. (1918). *The reality of psychic phenomena: Raps, levitations, etc.* (2nd ed.). John M. Watkins. (Original work published, 1916)
Crawford, W. J. (1919). *Experiments in psychical science: Levitation, 'contact' and the 'direct voice.'* John M. Watkins.
Crawford, W. J. (1921). *The psychic structures at the Goligher Circle.* E. P. Dutton.
Crookes, W. (1874). *Researches in the phenomena of spiritualism.* J. Burns.
Crowell, E. (1879). *The spirit world: Its inhabitants, nature, and philosophy.* Colby & Rich.
D'Agostino, S. (2000). *A history of the ideas of theoretical physics: Essays on the nineteenth and twentieth century physics.* Kluver.
Darget, Commandant [L.] (1909). Exposé des différentes méthodes pour l'obtention de photographies fluido-magnétiques et spirites: rayons V *(vitaux). L'lnitiation, 84(10),* 121.
De Gasparin, Comte A. (1854). *Des tables tournantes: du surnaturel en général et des esprits.* (2 vols.*).* E. Dentu.
Deleuze, J. P. F. (1852). *Practical instruction in animal magnetism.* (4th ed.). Hippolyte Baillière.
De Rochas, A. (1897). Les expériences de Choisy-Yvrec (prés Bordeaux) du 2 au 14 Octobre 1896. *Annales des Sciences Psychiques, 7,* 6–28.
D'Esperance, E. (1897). *Shadowland, or light from the other side.* George Redway.
Dods, J. B. (1854). *Spirit manifestations examined and explained: Judge Edmons refuted; Or, An exposition of the involuntary powers and instincts of the human mind.* De Witt & Davenport.
Donnelly, A. G. (1876, March 31). Correspondence. An American view of the spiritual phenomena. *Spiritualist Newspaper,* pp. 153–154.
Dr. Baraduc's discovery: Letter from the Doctor to Col. Olcott. *Borderland 4,* 30–32.
Driesch, H. (1933). *Psychical research: The science of the super-normal.* G. Bell. (Original work published in German, 1932).
Dudley, E. E. (1926). Energy transformation at séances. *Journal of the American Society for Psychical Research, 20,* 429–431.
Dufour, R. (1951). L'espace joue-t-il un rôle dans les phénomènes de télépathie? *Revue Métapsychique, 14 (ns),* 49–52.
Du Potet, [J. D.] (1845–1846). Manuel du magnétiseur. *Journal du Magnétisme 1,* 22–42, 77–94, 166–175, 192–207, 242–255, 299–304, 348–363, 392–400, 433–445, 489–491, 528–540; *2,* 8–11, 34–42, 75–76, 107–111.
Du Potet, Baron [J. D.] (1879). *Traité complet de magnétisme animal: Cours en douze leçons.* (4th Rev. ed.). Germer Baillière.
Durant, C. F. (1837). *Exposition, or a new theory of animal magnetism with a key to the mysteries: Demonstrated by experiments with the most celebrated somnambulists in America.* Wiley & Putnam.
Electricity in the body. (1875, February 5). *Spiritualist Newspaper,* pp. 68–69.
Ellison, A. J. (1982). Kirlian photography. In Grattan-Guinness, I. (Ed.) *Psychical Research* (pp. 188–192). Aquarian Books.
Esdaile, J. (1852). *Natural and mesmeric clairvoyance, with the practical application of mesmerism in surgery and medicine.* Hippolyte Baillière.
Fairfield, G. G. (1875). *Ten years with spiritual mediums: An inquiry concerning the etiology of certain phenomena called spiritual.* D. Appleton.
Faraday, M. (2000). Professor Faraday on table-moving. *International Journal of Parapsychology, 11,* 157–163. (Original work published, 1853)

Farmer, J. S. (1886). *'Twixt two worlds: A narrative of the life and work of William Eglinton.* Psychological Press.
Flammarion, C. (1907). *Mysterious psychic forces: An account of the author's investigations in psychical research, together with those of other European savants.* Small, Maynard.
Force v. spiritualism. (1867). *Spiritual Magazine, 2,* 223–237.
Geley, G. (1920). *From the unconscious to the conscious.* William Collins. (Original work published in French, 1919)
Geley, G. (1922). La lumière vivante métapsychique. *Revue Métapsychique, 3,* 187–203.
Geley, G. (1927). *Clairvoyance and materialisation: A record of experiments.* T. Fisher Unwin. (Original work published in French, 1924)
Gissurarson, L. R. & Haraldsson, E. (1989). The Icelandic physical medium Indridi Indridason. *Proceedings of the Society for Psychical Research, 57,* 53–148.
Grad, B. (1989). The healer phenomenon: Implications for parapsychology. *Research in Parapsychology, 1988,* 107–120.
Grunewald, F. (1920). *Physikalisch-mediumistische Untersuchungen.* Johannes Baum.
Guéret, A. & Oudinot, P. (1968) *L'homme et les impondérables: Science moderne et science occulte.* (2nd ed.). Dangle.
Gurney, E., Myers. F. W. H., & Podmore, F. (1886), *Phantasms of the living* (2 vols.). Trübner.
Hamilton, T. G. (1934). A study of the Winnipeg group-mediumship in its relations to the Dawn teleplasms. *Journal of the American Society for Psychical Research, 28,* 117–130.
Harman, P. M. (1982). *Energy, force and matter: The conceptual development of 19th century physics.* Cambridge University Press.
Irwin, H. J. (2004). *An introduction to parapsychology.* (4th ed,). McFarland.
Jahn, R. G. & Dunne, B. J. (2001). A modular model of mind/matter manifestations (M^5). *Journal of Scientific Exploration, 15,* 299–329.
Joines, W. (1975). A wave theory of psi energy. *Research in Parapsychology 1974,* 147–149.
Joire, P. (1905). Modifications in the nervous force externalised, according to the state of health of the subjects. *Annals of Psychical Science, 2,* 219–234.
Joire, P. (1907). On experiments with the sthenometer. *Journal of the Society for Psychical Research, 13,* 44–46.
Kardec, A. (1875). *Spiritualist philosophy: The spirits' book, containing the principles of spiritist doctrine.* Trübner.
Kardec, A. (1876). *Experimental Spiritism: The mediums' book; or, guide for mediums and for evocations.* Trübner.
Kokubo, H. & Kasahara, T. (2000). Japanese studies on anomalous phenomena in the 1990s. *International Journal of Parapsychology, 11,* 35–61.
Korotkov, K. (ed.) (2004). *Measuring energy fields: State-of-the-science.* Backbone.
Krauss, R. H. (1995). *Beyond light and shadow: The role of photography in certain paranormal phenomena: An historical survey.* Nazraeil Press. (Original work published in German, 1992).
Krippner, S., & Rubin, D. (Eds.). (1974). *The Kirlian aura: Photographing the galaxies of life.* Anchor.
Leping Zha, & McConnell, T. (1991). Parapsychology in the People's Republic of China. *Journal of the American Society for Psychical Research, 85,* 119–143.
Lindgren, C. F. (Ed.). (2000). *Capturing the aura: Integrating science, technology and metaphysics.* Blue Dolphin.
Lodge, O. J. (1894). Experience of unusual physical phenomena occurring in the presence of an entranced person (Eusapia Paladino). *Journal of the Society for Psychical Research, 6,* 306–336.
Loureiro, C. B. (1998). *Perispírito: Natureza, funções e propiedades.* Mnêmio Tulio.
Mackenzie, W. (1923). *Metapsichica moderna: Fenomeni medianici e problemi del subcosciente.* Librerie di Scienze e Lettere.
Mackenzie, W. (n. d.). Les limites de la métapsychique. In *La Métapsychique 1940–1946* (pp. 3–14). Presses Universitaires de France.
Mahan, A. (1855). *Modern mysteries explained and exposed, in four parts.* J. P. Jewett.
Mahan, A. (1875). *The phenomena of spiritualism scientifically explained and exposed.* Hodder.

Maxwell, J. (1905). *Metapsychical phenomena: Methods and observations.* Duckworth. (Original work published in French, 1903)

May, E. C., Utts, J. M., & Spottiswoode, S. J. P. (1995) Decision augmentation theory: Toward a model for anomalous mental phenomena. *Journal of Parapsychology, 59,* 195–220.

Mesmer, F. A. (1970). Dissertation on the discovery of animal magnetism. In M. M. Tinterow (Ed.)., *Foundations of hypnosis: From Mesmer to Freud* (pp. 32–57). Charles C Thomas. (Original work published in French, 1779)

Morselli, E. (1908). *Psicologia e 'Spiritismo': Note e impressioni critiche sui fenomeni medianici di Eusapia Paladino* (2 vols.). Fratelli Bocca.

Mulacz, P. (2001). Biology, vitalism and the 'golden era' of continental European parapsychology. *Proceedings of Presented Papers: The Parapsychological Association 44th Annual Convention,* pp. 191–204.

Nakamura, H., Kokubo, H., Parkhomtchouk, D. V., Chen, W., Tanaka, M., Zhang, T., Kokado, T., Yamamoto, M., & Fukuda, N. (2000) Biophoton and temperature changes of human hand during Quigong. *Journal of International Society of Life Information Science, 18,* 418–420.

Newnham, W. (1845). *Human magnetism; its claims to dispassionate inquiry: Being an attempt to show the utility of its application for the relief of human suffering.* John Churchill.

Ochorowicz, J. (1909). Un nouveau phénomène médiumique. *Annales des Sciences Psychiques 19,* 1–10, 45–51, 65–77, 97–106, 129–133.

Ochorowicz, J. (1910). Les rayons rigides et les rayons X^x: Études expérimentales. *Annales des Sciences Psychiques, 20,* 97–105, 129–136, 172–178, 204–209, 225–231, 257–263, 295–302, 336–344, 357–370.

Ochorowicz, J. (1911). Nouvelle étude expérimentale sur la nature des rayons rigides et du courant médiumnique. *Annales des Sciences Psychiques 21,* 161–166, 199–203, 230–236, 276–280.

Ochorowicz, J. (1911–1912). Radiographies des mains (monographie expérimentale). *Annales des Sciences Psychiques 21,* 296–303, 334–341; *22,* 1–8.

Ochorowicz, J. (1912). Les mains fluidiques et la photographie de la pensée. *Annales des Sciences Psychiques, 22,* 97–104, 147–153, 164–170, 204–210, 232–240.

Olcott, H. (1875) *People from the other world.* American Publishing.

Ordinaire, P. C. (1852). Des facultés de l'homme et de ses destínées: physiologie—philosophie—magnétisme. *Journal du Magnétisme, 11,* 598–608.

Osty, E. & Osty, M. (1931-1932). Les pouvoirs inconnus de l'esprit sur la matière. *Revue Métapsychique, 6,* 393–427, *No. 1,* 1–59, *No. 2,* 81–122.

Oteri, L. (ed.). (1975). *Quantum physics and parapsychology: Proceedings of an International Conference Held in Geneva, Switzerland, August 26–27, 1974.* Parapsychology Foundation.

Owen, R. D. (1871). *The debatable land between this world and the next.* Trübner.

Oxley, W. (1876, May 12). A spirit materialising under the eyes of the observers in Manchester. *Spiritualist Newspaper,* 222–223.

Pallikari-Viras, F. (1997). Further evidence for a statistical balancing in probabilistic systems influenced by the anomalous effect of conscious intention. *Journal of the Society for Psychical Research, 62,* 114–137.

Pattie, F. A. (1994), *Mesmer and animal magnetism: A chapter in the history of medicine.* Edmonston.

Pawlowski, F. W. (1925). The mediumship of Franek Kluski of Warsaw. *Journal of the American Society for Psychical Research, 19,* 481–504.

Petetin, J. H. D. (1808). *Électricité animale.* (2nd ed.). Brunot-Labbé.

Poortman, J. J. (1978). *Vehicles of consciousness: The concept of hylic pluralism (ochema)* Theosophical Society in the Netherlands. (Original work published in Dutch, 1954)

Price, H. (1925). *Stella C: An account of some original experiments in psychical research.* Hurst & Blackett.

Price, H. (1926). The phenomena of Rudi Schneider. *Journal of the American Society for Psychical Research, 20,* 641–665.

Puthoff, H. (2001). *On the relationship of quantum vacuum energy research to the role of 'metaphysical' processes in the physical world.* Retrieved from http://www.metanexus.net/

Quevedo, O. G. (1971). *As fôrças físicas da mente.* (2 vols.). Loyola.

Randall, J. L. (2003). Francis Ward Monck and the problems of physical mediumship. *Journal of the Society for Psychical Research, 67,* 243–259.

Rausher, E. A. & Targ, R. (2001). The speed of thought: Investigation of a complex spacetime metric to describe psychic phenomena. *Journal of Scientific Exploration, 15,* 331–354.

Reichenbach, C. von. (1851). *Physico-physiological researches on the dynamics of magnetism, electricity, heat, light, crystallization, and chemism, in their relation to vital force.* (2nd ed.). J. S. Redfield (Original work published in German, 1849)
Rein, G. (2004). Bioinformation within the biofield: Beyond bioelectromagnetics. *Journal of Alternative and Complementary Medicine, 10,* 59–68.
Rhead, G. (2001). Evidence for millimetre-wave radiation associated with paranormal activity. *Journal of the Society for Psychical Research, 65,* 138–145.
Rhine, J. B. (1934). *Extra-sensory perception.* Boston Society for Psychic Research.
Rhine, J. B. (1947). *The reach of the mind.* William Sloane.
Rhine, J. B. (1953). *New world of the mind.* William Sloane.
Rhine, J. B. & Pratt, J. G. (1957). *Parapsychology: Frontier science of the mind.* Charles C Thomas.
Richet, C. (1923). *Thirty years of psychical research: Being a treatise on metapsychics.* (2nd. ed.). Macmillan. (Original work published in French, 1922)
Rogers, E. C. (1853). *Philosophy of mysterious agents, human and mundane; Or, the dynamic laws and relations of man.* J. P. Jewett.
Rogo, D. S. (1980). Theories about PK: A critical evaluation. *Journal of the Society for Psychical Research, 50,* 359–378.
Roll, W. G., Burdick, D. S., & Joines, W. T. (1973). Radial and tangential forces in the Miami poltergeist. *Journal of the American Society for Psychical Research, 67,* 267–281.
Roll, W. G. (2003). Poltergeists, electromagnetism, and consciousness. *Journal of Scientific Exploration, 17,* 75–86.
Rubik, B. (2002). The biofield hypothesis: Its biophysical basis and role in medicine. *Journal of Alternative and Complementary Medicine, 8,* 703–717.
Schmidt, H. (1975). Toward a mathematical theory of psi. *Journal of the American Society for Psychical Research, 69,* 301–319.
Schrenck-Notzing, Baron [A. F.] von (1920). *Phenomena of materialisation: A contribution to the investigation of mediumistic teleplastics.* (Rev. ed.). Paul Trench, Trübner.
Schrenck-Notzing, A. [F.] de (1925). *Les phénomènes physiques de la médiumnité.* Payot. [Original work published in German, 1920]
Second International Congress on Psychotronic Research. (1975). International Association for Psychotronic Research.
Speculations relating to new facts in Spiritualism. (1875, March 19). *Spiritualist Newspaper,* pp. 133–135.
Spirit faces. (1873, February 1). *The Spiritualist,* 83.
Stratton, J. M. & Phillips, P. (1906). Some experiments with the sthenometer. *Journal of the Society for Psychical Research, 12,* 335–339.
Sudre, R. (1926). *Introduction à la métapsychique humaine.* Payot.
Sudre, R. (1960). *Parapsychology.* Citadel. (Original work published in French, 1956)
Sutton, G. (1981). Electric medicine and mesmerism. *Isis, 72,* 375–392.
[Tardy de Montravel, A. A.]. (1785). *Essai sur la théorie du somnambulisme magnétique.* No publisher given.
Tégrad, Comandant [Darget, L.]. (1902). Photographie des radiations magnético-psychiques. In *Compte rendu du Congrès Spirite et Spiritualiste International tenu à Paris du 16 au 27 septembre 1900* (pp. 592–595). Société d'Étude des Phénomènes Psychiques.
Tiller, W. A. (1997). *Science and human transformation: Subtle energies, intentionality and consciousness.* Pavior.
Ungaro, J. (1992). *Las radiaciones humanas: Historia de la radiónica.* Club de Estudio.
Van Wijk, R. (2001). Bio-photons and bio-communication. *Journal of Scientific Exploration, 15,* 183–197.
Varvoglis, M. P. (1986). Goal-directed-and observer-dependent PK: An evaluation of the conformance-behavior model and the observational theories. *Journal of the American Society for Psychical Research, 80,* 138–162.
Von Hartmann, E. (1885). Spiritism. *Light, 5,* 405–409, 417–421, 429–432, 441–443, 453–456, 466–470, 479–482, 491–494.
Walker, E. H. (1975). Foundations of paraphysical and parapsychological phenomena. In L. Oteri (Ed.). *Quantum Physics and Parapsychology: Proceedings of an International Conference Held in Geneva, Switzerland, August 26-27, 1974* (pp. 1–44). Parapsychology Foundation.

Wantuil, Z. (n. d.). As *Mesas girantes e o espiritismo.* Federação Espirita Brasileira.
Warcollier, R. (1953). Le fluide. *Revue Métapsychique, 1,* 1–4.
Warrick, F. W. (1939). *Experiments in psychics.* E. P. Dutton.
Wassermann, G. D. (1956). An outline of a field theory of organismic form and behavior. In G. E. W. Woltenholme, & E. C. P. Millar, (Eds.). *Ciba Foundation Symposium on Extrasensory Perception* (pp. 53–72). Little Brown.
Weaving by electricity. (1854). *Spiritual Telegraph, 3,* 133–134.

Further Notes on Historical Ideas of Human Radiations: On Electricity and Other Forces, Od and Psychometry, The Perispirit and Mediumistic Forces, and Mental Phenomena*

Carlos S. Alvarado†

I. On Electricity and Other Forces

The topic of human radiations—also called animal magnetism, fluids, and nervous, psychic or vital force—has a vast literature, as I have discussed in a recently published paper.[1] In that article I reviewed several ideas and observations from mesmeric, spiritualistic, and psychical research writings. The current notes, divided into four parts, are intended to be an addendum to the previous paper and are based to a great extent on material that had to be excluded due to space limitations. It is my hope that, together with the initial paper, these notes will guide interested readers to sources of information about past concepts of force and their relation to psychic phenomena.

Electrical Speculations and Other Forces

Darnton (1968) has reminded us that ideas of animal magnetism were developed by Mesmer and others in France in the context of a great interest in all kind of physical forces. For example, at the time the wonders of electricity were as mysterious to the intellectual and scientist as was animal magnetism. Electricity was considered by many to be a vital force, something related or identical to the process of life itself (Brazier, 1984; Clarke & Jacyna, 1987; for a later period see Morus, 1998). In fact, the concepts of electricity and animal magnetism were not completely independent of each other (Sutton, 1981). Certainly, some mesmerists drew their ideas from the studies of electricity of their times. In one mesmerist's view: "Mesmerism is probably only a modification of inorganic electricity" (Esdaile, 1852, p. 230). Esdaile further wrote: "If the electric fish can secrete electricity, and project it in the direction desired by the will, why should not man possess a modification of the same power?" (p. 233).

Another writer stated:

> Some consider Electricity to be the principle of life. We hear of Galvanism and Magnetic-electricity, or Electro-magnetism, and its efficacy through machines, upon the human body, in relieving paralysis and rheumatism, and different neuralgic disorders. Why might not Mesmerism, or Animal-magnetism … be Electricity under a different character? In our present imperfect knowledge of Mesmerism … it may be premature to adopt a theory: still I cannot help

*Republished with permission from *Psypioneer, 4*, 38–43, 63–69, 85–92, 119–126, 2008.

†I am grateful to Nancy L. Zingrone for useful editorial suggestions for the improvement of the four parts of this paper.

expressing an opinion that electricity, under some modification or other, is the immediate agent to which the Mesmeric action must be referred (Sandby, 1848, p. 71).

In this context, animal magnetism was only one among many unexplained forces of nature. Mesmer himself felt that animal magnetism could increase our understanding of such things as fire, light, gravity, and electricity, as seen in his *Mémoire sur la découverte du magnétisme* (1779, p. 80). Some years later Deleuze (1813, p. 81) wondered about the possibility that animal magnetism was a variant of such forces as light, magnetism, electricity, and heat. While this context did not ensure universal acceptance of the idea of animal magnetism in all quarters, it may have prepared the ground for receptive hearing.

Another example of attempts to associate animal magnetism to other forces of nature was John Ashburner's (1867) discussion of animal magnetism in his book, *Notes and Studies in the Philosophy of Animal Magnetism and Spiritualism*. In his view, we should consider the "evolutions of forces to be traced from the lowest grades of mineral crystal force by successive gradations up to that magnetic vital force culminating finally in the magnet, or grand crystal, Man; who remains subject even in the operations of his mind, to an inexorable magnetic law, acting through his phrenological organs, either from the force of his own soul, or from the force of the will of another" (p. vii). Such continuity of forces was assumed by many in the mesmeric literature.

Spiritualists also speculated that the phenomena produced by mediums were new and little-understood forces of nature, such as magnetism and electricity. This seemed to have been the perspective taken by Thomas Brevior (1864). After discussing such phenomena as evaporation, combustion, heat, electricity, and magnetism, Brevior stated: "If spirit is to us a mystery, matter of which we talk so gliby is no less so; for who can tell what matter is. ... What is the substance which underlies these properties? Who can tell me that? If we know spirit by its manifestations, we know matter only by its properties of the real—the inmost nature of both we are equally ignorant" (pp. 279–280). Similar arguments and comparisons appeared in other nineteenth century publications (e.g., Barkas, 1862, pp. 75–82), and it was not uncommon for spiritualists to write about the forces of nature, principles such as electricity, light, and magnetism (e.g., Dille, 1852). Many writers on spiritualism discussed the range of physical forces and its relation to spirit. One such example was the following:

> It is well known that, in its higher gradations, matter is so sublimated as to escape the observation of the senses. If we admit that, in this refined state, it may be organized, we have furnished our answer to the great question of the soul's independent existence. It is equally certain that the sphere of organic being comprehends millions of creatures, too minute to be perceived by the eye. Why may not other millions exist, invisible, not on account of their minuteness, but the refinement of their composition? ... But if disorganized matter may be so refined as to escape the sphere of sensuous observation, can a single reason be given for the hypothesis which denies the existence of invisible beings, possessing an organic structure of more refined elements, and adapted to sustain the relations, and perform the functions of a more exalted and spiritual life? To think of limiting the organic law to the contracted vision of mortals, indicates less of the immortal than appropriately belongs to man. If I am not in error concerning the general law which I have presumed to graduate the organization of matter by the specific degrees of its refinement, the argument would seem to be conclusive in proof of the existence of invisible spiritual beings. (Brittan, 1852, pp. 59–60)

Eugene Crowell asserted in his book *The Identity of Primitive Christianity and Modern Spiritualism* (1874): "Whatever may be the force employed, it soon becomes evident to all investigators of the spiritual phenomena, that electricity is not the cause of them, as some unscientific persons assert"

(Vol. 1, p. 493). Nonetheless, there were many speculations about the role of electricity in spiritualistic phenomena. This included a statement from a spirit communicator saying: "It is by that power all tangible bodies are moved—all the so-called miracles are performed" (Bradley, 1870, p. 186). Furthermore, such an influential writer as Andrew Jackson Davis believed that electricity was the "universal medium of spiritual vision" (Davis, 1853, p. 264).

In his book *Experimental Investigations of the Spirit Manifestations*, chemist Robert Hare (1855) saw raps as related to some sort of electricity. As discussed in mediumistic communications presented by Hare: "The raps are produced by voluntary discharges of the vitalized spiritual electricity, above mentioned, from the spirit, coming in contact with the animal electricity emanating from the medium" (p. 94). Certainly, many writers speculated on electricity, or its variants, to explain such phenomena as the movement of objects (e.g., Dods, 1854; Hitchman, 1875), an idea disputed by others (e.g., Rogers, 1853). One writer presented an elaborate and imaginative account of the process:

> The vertebrae are, as it were, the successive plates of a galvanic battery, of which the skull is the apex, while the spine, culminating in the brain, constitutes, like the acid in the artificial battery, a continuous and cumulative creator and channel of the electromagnetic force. Of this force the nerves of sensation and of voluntary motion are the conductors. ... The living battery, as ordinarily charged, may suffice to keep but one hemisphere of the brain in action, while an excessive charge may keep both hemispheres in simultaneous action.
>
> This theory may account for the rappings, phosphoric lights, table tippings, and other physical phenomena, reported in connection with the pretended spiritual intercourse. (Modern Necromancy, 1855, p. 521)

There were reports of electrical-like sensations that supported this belief. When Judge John Worth Edmonds was developing as a medium, he experienced "like a stream of electricity" touching him in different parts of the body (Edmonds and Dexter, 1853, p. 19). Another example appeared in Capron and Barron's *Explanation and History of the Mysterious Communion with Spirits* (1850). They stated in relation to rapping mediums: "Persons sometimes feel a sensation of electricity passing over their limbs when they stand in the vicinity of those who get the sounds most freely, although the particular persons who seem to be the medium feel no sensation at all. In one or two instances we have seen a perceptible shock as if caused by a galvanic battery especially when the persons were under the influence of Magnetism" (p. 29). Similarly, Sophia De Morgan (1863) referred to sensations of "tingling like that produced by the wires of a galvanic battery, and, during the raps, slight shocks like electricity passing through the arm of the medium" (p. 95).

The idea was also related late into the nineteenth-century to telepathy. One example was Mark Twain's (1891) belief that "the something which conveys on thoughts through the air from brain to brain is a finer and subtler form of electricity" (p. 101). Other cases helping to keep alive the belief in the electrical agency of physical phenomena were reports of poltergeist occurrences. The controversial "electrical girl" Angélique Cottin (Owen, 1864) was one of the better known and most widely cited cases (e.g., Rogers, 1853, pp. 52–59). She presented phenomena such as the apparent "repulsion" of chairs and other objects when in contact with her body. Another case was published in the *Atlantic Monthly* by H.A. Willis (1868, p. 133), who reported observations made to determine whether electricity accounted for both raps and movements of tables. The raps usually followed the presumed agent around but when she got into a bed that had the posts on glass with the purpose of preventing electrical discharges, the raps did not take place. Lack of raps in bed continued for six weeks and when they were heard once it was found that one of the posts was not on the glass. Other observations did not seem to support an electrical explanation.

In his book, *Essai sur les phénomènes électriques des etres vivants comprensant l'explication scientifique des phénomènes dits spirites*, Louis-Sophrone Fugairon (1894) claimed that "mediumistic phenomena are nothing but electrical phenomena" (p. 181). Under abnormal conditions this electricity could be projected from the body and could be enhanced by emission from the sitters in a mediumistic circle. The phantoms seen in these circles, according to Fugairon, were electrical vapors coming from the medium. These could be "an expansion of the vaporous body similar to the pseudopods or prolongations of the gelatinous body of amoebas" (p. 153). The electrical vapor could be formed also of organic substances from the medium's body. This vaporous body, called an aereosome, formed materializations.

Whiting (1871) recommended the use of a "magneto-electric" machine of his to improve table phenomena caused by the animal electricity used by the spirits. Along these lines, De Rochas (1897, p. 16) noticed that Palladino's phenomena seemed to be intensified by electricity from a Wimshurst machine. Years later Azam (1926) believed that the vital force was a current of electrons (p. 356) and that this current from mediums and sitters produced materializations (p. 410).

There is no question that electricity, and other forces and related technology, became part of the modern nineteenth-century world. Electricity was so integrated into culture that an author referred to an "age of electricity, just as former ones have been called, respectively, the ages of stone, bronze, and iron" (Brackett, 1889, p. 643). Such a principle, perceived by many as having limitless potential, was surely destined to be applied to all sorts of mysterious and little understood phenomena, such as the ones discussed in this paper.

II. Od and Psychometry

The Od Force

Like the mesmerists, Baron Karl von Reichenbach (1849/1851) believed in the existence of a universal force. He called this principle Od, and argued that it was not only generated by the human body, but also by magnetism, crystals, light (including sunlight and moonlight), heat, friction, chemical processes and electricity, among other causes. Describing the effects of this force, as channeled by magnets, Reichenbach wrote:

> The kind of impression … is rather disagreeable than pleasant, and combined with a slight sensation either of cold or warmth, resembling a cool or gently warm breath of air, which the patients imagine to blow softly upon them. Sometimes they feel sensations of drawing, pricking, or creeping; some complain of sudden attacks of headache. Not only women, but men in the very prime of life, are found distinctly susceptible of this influence; in children it is sometimes very active. (Reichenbach, 1849/1851, pp. 1–3)

In the human body such processes as digestion and respiration were believed to produce Od. Sensitive persons, Reichenbach thought, were able to perceive this force in different ways, such as visually (e.g., lights and auras around magnets, crystals and individuals) and as sensations of temperature and discomfort. According to Reichenbach:

> When I tried substances of another character—coal, selenium, iodine, Sulphur—they too were found to be luminous. The appearance of their bodies resembled the glow of phosphorescence. … Together with the glow, high-sensitives observed surrounding these substances … flame-like

> emanation[s] of light losing itself in smoke ... In colour the emanations were found to be by no means alike ... Everything made of copper, for instance, was seen in a red glow, surrounded by a green flame ... (Reichenbach, 1852/1968, p. 59)

In his discussion of the properties of Od Reichenbach stated that it could be stored on and transmitted to some bodies. Od, he stated, "is capable of mechanically attracting the hands of cataleptic patients ..." (Reichenbach, 1849/1851, p. 116).

Like magnetism, Reichenbach stated:

> The odic force possesses polarity. It appears at the two poles of the magnet with constantly different properties: at the northward ... it produces a sensation of coolness in the feeling, as a rule, in the pass downward, and in darkness a blue and bluish-grey light; the southward pole, on the other hand, a sensation of tepid warmth, ... and a red, reddish-yellow, and reddish-grey light. The former is connected with a decided pleasure, the latter with discomfort and uneasy pains. Next to magnets, crystals ... and living organic beings ... exhibit the odic polarity most distinctly. In crystals, the odic poles occur at the poles of the axes ...; in crystals with several axes, there are several odic axes, of unequal strength. (Reichenbach, 1849/1851, p. 283)

Reichenbach's claims were met with skepticism. For example, Scottish physician James Braid (1846/1970) argued that suggestion and expectation could account for the perceptions of Reichenbach's sensitives. Similarly, American physician William A. Hammond wrote in his booklet *The Physics and Physiology of Spiritualism* (1871) that "many of the experiments of the Baron von Reichenbach have no other foundation than that property of the human mind which causes it to be subjectively affected by suggestion" (p. 17).

Reichenbach's work was very influential on later developments. For example, he was widely cited by writers in the United States that discussed concepts of force to account for the phenomena of spiritualism (e.g., Beecher, 1853, p. 10; Rogers, 1853, pp. 21, 64). A physician combined the concept of Od with homeopathy, referring to "Od-preparations" relevant for health (Rohland, 1871). In this author's view: "The cause of every disease-phenomenon lies in the distemper of the *od-activity* in the organism" (p. 8).

Reichenbach also had an influence on the Society for Psychical Research, at least to the extent that one of the original purposes of the Society, as stated in the first issue of its *Proceedings*, was: "A critical revision of Reichenbach's researches with certain organisations called 'sensitive,' and an inquiry whether such organisations possess any power of perception beyond a highly exalted sensibility of the recognised sensory organs" (Objects of the Society, 1882, p. 3). This led to the establishment of a committee that conducted some research (e.g., Barrett et al., 1883; see also independent work by Barrett, 1884). This work explored the ability of individuals to perceive emanations from magnets. After tests with an electro-magnet, it was concluded:

> Firstly, that three observers, separately, on distinct occasions were in some way immediately aware when an electro-magnet was secretly "made" and "unmade," under such precautions as were devised to suppress ordinary means of knowing, and to exclude chance and deception; and identified such magnetization with luminous appearances which as described agreed generally with the evidence recorded by Reichenbach:
>
> Secondly, that there were, though less decisively, indications of other sensory effects of magnetism.
>
> In view of these apparent confirmations of previous testimony, the Committee incline to the opinion that, among other unknown phenomena associated with magnetism, there is a *primâ*

> *facie* case for the existence, under conditions not yet determined, of a peculiar and unexplained luminosity resembling phosphorescence, in the region immediately around the magnetic poles, and visible only to certain individuals. (Barrett et al., 1883, p. 236)

Further work conducted in the United States did not support Reichenbach's ideas. This included the work of Jastrow and Nuttell (1886), and Pickering (1886). But there were earlier observations conducted independently of Reichenbach that were similar to some of his claims. One example was English physician Joseph Haddock's studies of a woman called Emma, as reported in his book *Somnolism & Psycheism* (1851):

> Emma could see an aura, or fluid, passing into, along, and out of the magnet. Nothing was said to her respecting the poles of magnets, or their relation to terrestrial magnetism, lest any idea should be suggested to her, which might give a bias to her perceptions; but she invariably represented the fluid as passing *in* at the south pole of the magnet, and *out* at the north pole. This she did, whether the bar or horseshoe magnet was used. She describes the colours as "rainbow-like;" duller, with greenish and bluish colours predominating at the south end; and more brilliant colours, with *red* predominating, at the north end. In comparing the current with that in her hands, she said, That the current out of the *north* pole of the magnet, and out of her *right* hand, was warmest, and that was the reason she called her right hand, "the *warm* hand;" and the right side of the body, generally, "the *warm* side." (Haddock, 1851, pp. 168–169)[2]

Work with magnets, mentioned in the early mesmeric literature (e.g., Mesmer, 1779), was continued in later years by many individuals, but with the purpose of healing. Some examples include Hector Durville's *Traité expérimental de magnétisme* (1895), and Colonel Albert de Rochas's *Les forces non définies* (1887). In fact, the latter discussed and popularized Reichenbach his books *Le fluide des magnétiseurs* (1891) and in *Les frontières de la science* (1902). The latter work is organized in three parts: Reichenbach's predecessors, Reichenbach's work, and Reichenbach's successors.

De Rochas (1895) reported observations of effluvia from magnets and other substances while the observer was hypnotized. He considered Od a vital principle, a force intimately connected with the human body and its functions, and one centered in the brain and its ganglions of the human body. As he wrote in his 1891 book:

> The odic movement, called a *current*, comes mainly from the brain, descends down through the nerves of the face and goes to its corresponding ramifications. Finally, it is exhaled in the air, rendered sensible by impressions of heat and cold that it causes on the sensitives, is made visible in the form of effluvia in plain day, and as lights in darkness. The whole body seems bright; the head seems to have an aureole; the hands, the fingers and the toes throw long streams of odic light. (De Rochas, p. 104)

Psychometry

Another Od theoretician, physician Herbert Mayo, presented ideas to account for clairvoyant impressions obtained through touching objects such as hair or a letter in his book *Popular Superstitions, and the Theories Contained Therein* (1852). He wrote:

> I conceive that the lock of hair, or the letter … is charged with the Od-fluid emanating from the distant person; and that the clairvoyante measures exactly the force and quality of this dose of

> Od, and, as it were, individualizes it. Then … *distance being annihilated to the entranced mind*, it seeks for, or is drawn towards, whatever there is more of this same individual Od quality any where in space. When that is found, the party sought is identified, and brought into relation with the clairvoyante, who proceeds forthwith to tell all about him. (pp. 185–186)

During the 1840s Joseph Rodes Buchanan, Dean and Professor at the Eclectic Medical Institute (Covington, Kentucky), developed interesting ideas similar in some respects to those of some of the mesmerists. In his view human beings had an aura coming out of the nervous system. "This nerveaura, which is the agent by which one individual makes a physiological impression upon another when in contact, is radiated and conducted freely from the human hand" (Neurology in New York, 1849, p. 18).

Buchanan created the term psychometry to refer to the ability of some "sensitive" individuals to obtain impressions, sensations, and information from objects they touched. Early tests involved metals, and the sensitives could recognize the metal and perceived sensations of taste. In Buchanan's view: "It may be supposed that an impression made upon the nerves of the hand, is propagated by continuous sympathy to the head, or that some imponderable agent, proceeding from [materials and substances] conveyed their influence into the body" (Buchanan, 1849, pp. 52–53). Apparently, Buchanan thought that the person's "nerveaura" went into the substances and materials in question thus creating a link that brought information back to the individual. The fact that sensitives could obtain information also from writing and photographs suggested to Buchanan the emission of something from a person to an object, something indicating the possibility that "the mental and the physical were capable of entering into a psycho-material combination" (Buchanan, 1849, p. 60).

Years later, Buchanan (1885) still maintained these views in his *Manual of Psychometry*, but extended them to argue that "Psychometry is the earthly *irradiation of omniscience* and it will be known hereafter that it can penetrate all things" (p. 156). Like some of the mesmerists before him, Buchanan had extended the concept of psychic functioning and emanations to include the idea of divinity and transcendence. Buchanan clearly stated that after his first studies "in which emanations and influences were recognized" (p. 159), he was ready to take a deeper view of the subject. Psychometry was an indication of the divine element in man, an element that provided the key to access universal knowledge.

Writing in *Buchanan's Journal of Man*, physician B.W. Richardson (1855) believed that "while writing a letter, the paper imbibes the nervaura of our bodies from the hand, and that aura or vapor is subject to decomposition like all matter" (p. 34). In the same volume of the journal Dr. A. M. Potter (1855), a psychometrist, asserted that everything in nature had emanations. As he wrote:

> By this magnetism we impart to all we touch or are in relation with, we leave ourself stereotyped; and a psychometrist has but to reach our emanation to unfold our entire character as well morally, as intellectually and physically; and from the present follow down the linkwork of events to our earliest moment of existence or going forward, may by the aid of prevoyance unfold the future. (p. 246)

Many other ideas of force were related to psychometry. In *The Soul of Things* psychometrist Elizabeth Denton speculated on an ethereal fluid that "radiated to the surrounding atmosphere … which stamps upon it … images" (Denton & Denton, 1863, p. xv). James Coates (1906) considered psychometry to be a "sense by which we are placed in conscious relation to certain subtle forces—emanations, vibrations—in nature …" (p. 7), while another writer referred to a "network of vibrations, waves, influences, of nameless, numberless and uninterrupted fluids" (Maeterlinck, 1914,

p. 92). Somewhat later Ernesto Bozzano argued in his book *Les enigmes de la psychométrie et les phénomènes de télésthesie* (1927) that the vibrations corresponding to events are registered on a "transcendental and immanent medium on the object's matter, this medium is space ether" (p. 115).

Other force ideas related to psychometry included those discussed by Duchatel (1910), and Pagenstecher (1922). Some variants of these ideas were H. H. Price's (1939) and Warcollier's (1938, pp. 261–269) discussions of the "psychic ether" and "psychic charges," respectively.

III. The Perispirit and Mediumistic Forces

The Perispirit

In the past there have been many ideas about intermediary subtle bodies or fluids between the physical body and the spirit. Allan Kardec's ideas about the perispirit, basically a reformulation of previous concepts (e.g., Chardel, 1818; for older ideas see Poortman, 1954/1978), postulated that this agent was capable of conducting the effects of thought and will on the body, and was involved in the creation of visible apparitions, and physical phenomena. Using mediumistic communications as his source of information Kardec described the process by which he believed the fluid or the perispirit could move objects. He wrote:

> When an object is set in motion, carried away, or raised into the air, the spirit does not seize it, push it, or lift it, as we do with our hands; the spirit, so to say, *saturates* it with *his own* fluid combined with that of the medium, and the object, being thus vivified for the moment, acts as a living being would act ... [and] it follows the impulsion communicated to it by the will of the spirit (Kardec, 1876, pp. 76–77).

Followers of Kardec continued the speculations. Writing in the Italian journal *Annali dello Spiritismo in Italia*, Niceforo Filalete (1864, p. 292) argued that the perispirit was modeled after the physical body, but that when liberated from the body it was transformed by the spirit's will. The French engineer Gabriel Delanne discussed further the role of the perispirit in human affairs and in the production of psychic phenomena. In *L'évolution animique*, Delanne (1897) described the perispirit as a vital and directing principle that served as a model for the physical body's development. Delanne wrote:

> The perispirit is the directing idea, the imponderable plan for the structure of beings. It is it which stores, registers, and conserves all perceptions, all the volitions, all the ideas of the soul: not only does it embed in its substance all the states of the soul determined by the exterior world, but it is ... the unfailing receiver of the most fugitive thoughts ... In its incorruptible substance are fixed the laws of our development; it is the keeper par excellence of our personality, recollections reside on it. (p. 72)

The perispirit, Delanne believed, was the principle behind what some referred to as the subconscious, as seen in amnesia and changes of personality. He further assured us that the state of the perispirit could be modified through external means such as anaesthetics, hypnotic procedures and other agents capable of affecting the nervous system. This could produce secondary states of consciousness, "sort of an exaltation of the vital movement" (p. 227). Furthermore, it handled the automatic and reflex actions.

In later years Delanne continued to speculate along similar lines, while assuring us these were facts, as seen in his book *Le spiritisme devant la science* (Delanne, 1923; see also Geley, n. d., pp. 49–50). In his view the perispirit was formed of fluids of different degrees of condensation. The more material fluids were associated to the brain, while the more spiritual ones were closer to the soul. In addition, Delanne argued that the perispirit was capable of separating from the body with the soul, but keeping its connection to the body through a "fluidic cord."

Other writers also discussed the perispirit and its functions (Fedi, 1937; Geley, n. d.; Kudriavteff, 1909). Some argued that previous life memories were imprinted on this perispirit (Geley, n. d., pp. 49, 54). Others related the perispirit to health. In one view published in the English spiritualist periodical *Light*:

> The perispirit ... radiates a complex of rays and if it is in perfect harmony with the physical body, they find a free outlet beyond its limits; but if the physical body is unable to transmit the rays, they accumulate round the perispirit, producing a series of disturbances in both the psychical [the perispirit] and physical bodies, which may end in serious illnesses, such as neurasthenia, nervous swellings, &c. (Kudriavtzeff, 1909, p. 175)

While De Rochas did not use the term perispirit, he discussed similar concepts. In several other publications he argued that the nervous force of the body was spread through the nerves responsible for sensations and motor functions and that it took the form of the physical body, becoming a fluidic double (De Rochas, 1895a, 1895b, 1895c, 1896). In De Rochas' words:

1. There is in man a spiritual and fluidic body destined to serve as intermediary between the soul and the material body ...
2. This fluidic body, which, during life is the mold of the material body, can under some circumstances momentarily abandon the material body, and be perceived, even at a distance, by some of the human senses.
3. Some persons enjoy the property of secreting the substance that forms the fluidic body in fairly great quantity and with enough density for this substance to be perceived in the form of a luminous cloud ... (1895c, p. 125).

Following these thoughts, and echoing De Rochas and others, Flammarion mentioned the concept of a double in relation to mediums.

> "A fluidic and condensable double has ... the power of gliding momentarily out from the body of the medium ... How can this double, this fluidic body have the consistency of flesh and of muscles? We do not understand it" (Flammarion, 1907, pp. 424–425).

From the above, it is clear that some of the ideas discussed here intersect with several concepts of subtle bodies or doubles. While I will not discuss this literature here, I refer readers to the studies of Mead (1919) and Poortman (1954/1978).

Physical Mediumship

Many theoreticians explained physical mediumship through nervous forces coming from the body of the mediums. One of the best-known and more influential of these in the early days of spiritualism was Edward C. Rogers, as seen in his book *Philosophy of Mysterious Agents* (1853). Rogers summarized as follows some of his conclusions:

> It is evident … that the force which, emanating from such persons, produces these phenomena, is in some way intimately related to the nervous force, and the nerve-centres … In some instances, the regular periodical recurrence of these phenomena is precisely of the character of certain forms of intermittent fever, and nervous derangement … In all instances, when the normal tone of the nervous system is perfectly restored, the nervous symptoms have ceased, together with the phenomena in question … It follows, therefore, that the latter depend in all cases upon an abnormal condition of the nervous system … The Will and the Reason have no control of this force in its action from the nerve-centres in their abnormal condition, and it acts from the person without cognizance of the consciousness. (The reverse is the case in normal conditions.) … The physical agent belongs to the nerve-centres and the outer world, relating the one to the other (pp. 60–61).

Samuel Guppy discussed in his book *Mary Jane, or Spiritualism Chemically Explained* (1863) the action of "vapors" emanating from the human body. The emanations "under certain conditions … possess a living, acting, and thinking vitality; a vitality, in some cases, superior to the being they emanate from" (p. 332). The intellectual content of manifestations, such as table phenomena, was believed to reflect the mental content of the sitters.

He further speculated:

> "That this material vapour may have also the power of taking the shape of hands, &c., is credible, though I have not seen it; and that it may take the shape given it by the imagination of the medium, or of some person the medium is in communication with, is not absolutely deniable with the facts before us; and it is also conceivable that a phosphoric vapour, though invisible by day to the human eye, may affect a photographic plate, and so produce a spirit picture" (p. 336).

The beginning of the previous quote was a reference to the phenomena of materialization. "Unseen intelligences, versed in spirit chemistry," was stated in a column in the March 1876 issue of the *American Spiritual Magazine*, "have the power to collect and use the aura of mediums, the emanations of individuals and the elements of the atmosphere, manipulating and molding the same into shapes, forms, and garments of immortals, in which spirits appear" (Southern Notes, 1876, pp. 81–82). One observer of phenomena produced during the nineteenth-century referred to a "rapidly-moving luminous vapor, which quickly consolidates into a separate individualized form, complete in its organization, and capable, for the time, of physical and mental action" (Brackett, 1908, p. 126).

In France, Alphonse Chevillard discussed a variant of the nervous force idea in a pamphlet entitled *Études expérimentales sur le fluide nerveux et solution definitive du problème spirite* (1869). Table phenomena in séances were seen as the action of the medium's fluid, which could be aided by nervous force of the sitters. In cases in which the tables expressed messages, the medium's "interior diction is instantaneously translated" (p. 19) into outside action, producing the illusion of discarnate agency. But the idea that spirits of the dead influenced these forces was also discussed by many (e.g., Ballou, 1853; Hare, 1855; Kardec, 1876).

Another writer explaining mediumship in terms of vital forces was physician Robert H. Collyer. As he wrote: "If there is sufficient nervo-vital fluid at the command of the medium, he is enabled to produce an embodiment, which will for the time being, under the direction of the will power, manifest all the conditions of an independent existence …" (Collyer, 1871, p. 106). This included a variety of physical phenomena.

An early British psychical researcher, lawyer Edward William Cox, developed ideas about "psychic force" that influenced William Crookes (1874). While I mentioned some of his ideas in my previous paper (Alvarado, 2006, p. 142), much more could be said about Cox. In his book *The Mechanism of Man* (1879), Cox summarized what he believed was known about this force capable of performing physical effects. In addition to the fact that the force seemed to be guided by intelligence, it depended on the presence of a "Psychic," a term Cox defined as "a person possessing some peculiarity of constitution by reason of which the Psychic Force, that is in all of us, in him is either in excess or subject to abnormal development" (p. 377).

Cox also argued that the force: (1) Could be generated using surrounding people as a source; (2) was conducted better by wood than by metal; (3) could be impeded in its action by the presence of some individuals; (4) acted independently of beliefs and skepticism; (5) was diminished by the presence of many individuals, "instead of increasing the force" (p. 378); (6) depended on the state of being and health of the psychic, such as depression and sickness; (7) could be restored by drinking wine or coffee; (8) was enhanced by music; (9) developed slowly, as opposed of starting strong; (10) moved objects towards the psychic; and (11) was limited in action to twelve feet from the psychic, its effects being rarely seen beyond six or seven feet.

Another interesting theoretician, and one virtually unknown in the English-speaking world, was Spanish astronomer José Comas Solá. In his book, *El Espiritismo Ante la Ciencia*, Comas Solá (1908) expressed skepticism about mediumship due to negative personal experiences. Nonetheless, he conceded that in principle some phenomena could be real. He was skeptical of dematerialization phenomena, claiming that this process would produce an excess of force never seen with mediums. But later in his book he was willing to speculate in relation to ideas from modern physics.

Following ideas about atomic structure and the existence of a variety of states of energy, Comas Solá speculated on the existence of a process in the human body analogous to the decomposition of light, as studied spectrographically. Assuming the possibility of conducting spectographic analyses of the human body, this author wrote that:

> maybe we could decompose it in various *matters* or *elemental forces* of different types; that is, we may discover in the known complex of the individual the existence of different elemental individuals. Its whole in equilibrium constitutes the normal living body, such as the compositions of elementary rays form the color of light. Consequently, we can assume that in an anomalous bodily state these different energies that form the living being lack cohesion, and in specific cases it is completely or partially disaggregated in elementary bodies. (p. 86)

In this view, mediums were unstable individuals in a physical way. Their bodies showed different signs of lack of cohesion, such as trance during the phenomena and fatigue afterwards. The exteriorization of an element from the medium's body would consist of a diminished version of the medium's strength and mentality. This, Comas Solá argued, could in principle explain luminous phenomena and fluidic phantoms because the exteriorized element "could vibrate its *molecules* and transmit itself towards our retina through the ether" (p. 87).

As argued before (Alvarado, 1993), medium Eusapia Palladino provided a focus for discussion of concepts of force. In addition to the ideas of Morselli (1908), briefly discussed in my previous paper (Alvarado, 2006), she inspired many others. Lombroso speculated on the emission of motor forces related to "interruption of functions of … cerebral centers, while the activity of other centers is augmented, notably the motor centers" (1892, p. 150). Later, Lombroso (1909) was open to discarnate agency:

> Most potent, then, is the power of the medium in spiritistic matters, so much so that it explains the greater part of the phenomena, but not all; and the complete explanation can be found only by integrating the mediumistic force with another force, which, although it is more fragmentary and transitory, yet acquires, by identifying itself with the medium, a greater potency. And this force, authenticated by the tradition of all ages and all peoples and by experimental observation, is pointed out to us as found in the residual action of the dead. (p. 184)
>
> Polish researcher Julian Ochorowicz (1896) conceptualized some of Palladino's phenomena as a "collective psycho-physical creation" (p. 109). This involved a combination of nervous force and the ideas of the circle. The "medium is nothing but a mirror that reflects and directs the ideas and nervous forces of the sitters" (p. 111). The process was ideoplastic because the character of the phenomena was shaped by the expectations and beliefs of the sitters.

Another researcher with wide experience with Palladino was Hereward Carrington (1909). He believed that the medium's vital force, a force that constituted life and regulated processes in the body, could be exteriorized from her body and cause physical phenomena. In minor phenomena like movement of objects this force could be directed consciously or unconsciously by the medium. But Carrington believed that in complex materialization phenomena suggestive of personal identity spirits made use of this force.

French Astronomer Camille Flammarion also speculated on mediumistic forces, as seen in his *Mysterious Psychic Forces* (1907). He wrote:

> "We must admit … this prolongation of the muscular and nervous force of the subject … This prolongation is real, and only extends to a certain distance from the medium … We are forced to admit that this prolongation, usually invisible, and impalpable, may become visible and palpable; take, especially, the form of an articulated hand, with flesh and muscles; and reveal the exact form of a head or a body …" (p. 424)

Another Frenchman, science writer and psychical researcher René Sudre, discussed what he referred to as the "psychic fluid" in his book *Introduction a la métapsychique humaine* (1926). This was an "unknown substance-energy capable of imitating all forms of life and raw matter, and of accomplishing mechanical, physical, or chemical tasks of the greatest variety" (p. 209).

Many others speculated as well on such ideas as: radioactivity and transmutation of the medium's energy (Aggazzotti et al., 1907); projection of vital force "which can go as far as extra-organic manifestations, that is, out of the body" (Ochorowicz, 1909, p. 757); "magnetic aura and vital forces of the medium" (Sprague, 1912, p. 67); and transformation of unknown nature of the "biopsychic forces of the medium's organism" (Schrenck-Notzing, 1920/1925, p. 312). Several other ideas are summarized in a previous paper (Alvarado, 2006).

IV. Mental Phenomena

While I have emphasized physical phenomena in the previous sections of this paper, ideas of forces emanating from the human body were also associated to mental phenomena. This included mental mediumship, and telepathy and clairvoyance.

Mental Mediumship

Adin Ballou (1853) believed that mediums were characterized by having a good amount of "spiriticity," an ethereal principle employed by discarnate spirits when communicating through mediums. Spirit communicators quoted by Robert Hare in his book *Experimental Investigation of the Spirit Manifestations* (1855), affirmed they used "vitalized spiritual electricity" to influence the writing of mediums (p. 94). Hare also mentioned an aura that spirits used to communicate, an aura that "only a few are so endowed with" (p. 160).

Allan Kardec (1863, p. 279) cited spirit communications stating that the discarnate spirit's perispirit acted on the perispirit of the medium to produce such phenomena as writing. The communicators stated the importance of the "affinity that exists between our perispirit and the one of the medium that serves us as interpreter" (p. 280).

In later years others recorded observations about forces involved with mediumistic communications. Richard Hodgson (1898) summarized some relevant communications received through Leonora Piper:

> We all have bodies composed of "luminiferous ether" enclosed in our flesh and blood bodies. The relation of Mrs. Piper's etherial body to the etherial world, in which the "communicators" claim to dwell, is such that a special store of peculiar energy is accumulated in connection with her organism, and this appears to them as "a light." Mrs. Piper's etherial body is removed by them, and her ordinary body appears as a shell filled with this "light." Several "communicators" may be in contact with this light at the same time. There are two chief "masses" of it in her case, one in connection with the head, the other in connection with the right arm and hand. Latterly, that in connection with the hand has been "brighter" than that in connection with the head. If the "communicator" gets into contact with the "light" and thinks his thoughts, they tend to be reproduced by movements in Mrs. Piper's organism. Very few can produce vocal effects, even, when in contact with the "light" of the head, but practically all can-produce writing movements when in contact with the "light" of the hand. Upon the amount and brightness of this "light," coeteris paribus, the communications depend. When Mrs. Piper is in ill-health, the "light" is feebler, and the communications tend to be less coherent. It also gets used up during a sitting, and when it gets dim there is a tendency to incoherence even in otherwise clear communicators. In all cases, coming into contact with this "light" tends to produce bewilderment, and if the contact is continued too long, or the "light" becomes very dim, the consciousness of the communicator tends to lapse completely (p. 400).

Others also recorded communications about an emanation around the medium that was sensitive to the thoughts of spirits. An example was Charles Drayton's Thomas' (1928) discussion of medium Gladys Osborne Leonard. As he wrote summarizing the idea and referring to the medium's control:

> Medium and sitter are surrounded by a cloud of this power. Anything within this area is visible to Feda; but should a communicator remain outside it he would be invisible to her, and she could only with some difficulty obtain information from him by "sensing." Upon his entering the zone or sphere of influence, Feda would be able to see and hear him.
>
> This quasi-physical cloud emanates from the medium, and the sitter may contribute some small amount. Although usually visible to both control and communicator, the latter can, by passing out of it and then re-entering, feel its influence as a slight tingling. (p. 73)

Telepathy and Clairvoyance

Many writers, such as the mesmerists, discussed ideas of force to account for what we call today ESP. Physician Herbert Mayo discussed Od: "It cannot be doubted that … an Od-current … enables the mind of the clairvoyante to penetrate the interior being of the visiter [sic]—just as, in the humblest effects of common mesmerism, a relation is sensibly established between the party entranced and her mesmeriser, through the Od-current which he had previously directed upon her, in order to produce the trance" (1852, p. 185).

Chemist and physicist William Crookes (1897) discussed a variety of physical vibrations and x-rays in the hope of relating telepathy to physical processes. As he wrote:

> Let it be assumed that these rays, or rays even of higher frequency, can pass into the brain and act on some nervous centre there. Let it be conceived that the brain contains a centre which uses these rays as the vocal cords use sound vibrations (both being under the command of intelligence), and sends them out, with the velocity of light, to impinge on the receiving ganglion of another brain. In this way some, at least, of the phenomena of telepathy, and the transmission of intelligence from one sensitive to another through long distances, seem to come into the domain of law, and can be grasped. (p. 352)

Others saw telepathy as "sort of a natural telegraph and telephone … a magnetic communication without a conducting wire" (A. Denis, 1895, pp. 17-18). Mark Twain (1891) wrote about "mental telegraphy" based on electricity. In his view such cases as letters crossing in the mail, simultaneous development of ideas and discoveries, and other coincidences, were the result of a mind telegraphing another at a distance.

Héricourt's (1891) suggested that all bodies are connected to each other through unknown energies. Some evolve and develop receptive organs for "errant vibrations." Others acquire the sensibility by some form of unbalance. This sensitivity, another writer speculated, came from emotional bonds between people such as those that exist in familial relationships (Baudoin, 1900).

Houston (1892) stated in an article entitled "Cerebral Radiations" that: "An active brain may … be regarded as moulding the ether around it into thought waves that are spreading outward from it in all directions" (p. 152). A second brain may resonate with sympathetic vibrations coming from the thoughts of the first brain. These vibrations must travel at the speed of light. Similarly, Léon Denis (1900) argued that: "Thought vibrations may propagate through space like light and sounds and may affect other organisms that are in affinity with the one manifesting. The psychic waves, like hertzian waves in wireless telegraphy, propagate at a distance …" (p. 291). The response to the waves varies according to the person, manifesting as visions, voices, or movements.

In his book *Psychic Phenomena, Science and Immortality*, Henry Frank (1911) stated his belief in a physical transmission in telepathy, and the reasons it was not a common phenomenon:

> The reason that thought transference is at present so uncommon, at least to my mind, is because the forms of thought, or modes of vibration, which pass from individual brains, have been dissipated in the ether on account of not having found synchronous brains on which to impinge, and being without such paths their habits of action have not become fixed. (p. 341)

Some influential twentieth century research that has been forgotten by many was that conducted by Italian Ferdinando Cazzamalli. Cazzamalli (e.g., Cazzamalli, 1925/1926, 1928, 1947, 1960) used a variety of instruments to detect radiations from the brain. In his view the brain was a generator of electromagnetic energy responsible for telepathy, particularly during altered states of consciousness.

In an early paper entitled "Telepsychic Phenomena and Cerebral Radiations," Cazzamalli (1925/1926) presented results of studies with instruments that supposedly detected electromagnetic radiations and indicated their presence audibly through a frequency amplifyer. Using psychics and individuals suffering from psychiatric conditions, Cazzamalli argued that electromagnetic activity was detected at the time the participants—inside a shielded chamber—were experiencing hallucinations, trances and telepathic phenomena. These findings led him to state that: "The human subject, under particular psychic conditions … gives off electromagnetic oscillations of the type of radio waves" (Cazzamalli, 1925/1926, p. 16).

In later tests, conveniently summarized in his book *Il Cervello Radiante, Cazzamalli* (1960) presented tracings directly made on film of the oscillations of the radiations. These tracings, or "radiocerebropsychographs," recorded the intensity of these cerebral radiations, which varied according to a variety of factors such as the type of person and their state of consciousness.

In the case of dowsing, Cazzamalli (1947) argued, the dowser's brain emitted electromagnetic waves. These waves could hit water, metal and other materials and, as radar, would provide information to the brain by the variations in the waves' feedback. This allowed them to detect the desired target. Another possibility was for the brain to perceive radiations from the surrounding, that is, radiations emanations from water and other materials.

For Cazzamalli parapsychological phenomena were basically neuropsychological. As he wrote, "it is the brain which, having psycho-sensory centers in orgasm, [and having] electrical and electromagnetic currents with radiant effects, acquires the possibility of contacting directly the surrounding physical reality" (Cazzamalli, 1947, p. 87).

Cazzamalli was not the only one to argue for cerebral radiations during the twentieth century. Others such as Wilson (1925), Azam (1926), and Sinel (1927) speculated along similar, although less specific and less sophisticated lines. Sinel postulated that the pineal gland was the locus of the "sixth sense."

Charles Andry-Bourgeois (1935) compared ESP to television. He argued that on one hand scientists worked hard to transmit a "simple animated image at a distance," while the brain of a clairvoyant in trance, "this marvelous emitting and receptive post of 'psychic waves,' … does this automatically, unconsciously, instinctively, so to speak" (p. 487).

Although not specifically connected to the brain, one of the best-known physical ideas of ESP in psychical research literature was Charles Richet's concept of unknown vibrations to account for the "sixth sense." As Richet wrote: "The sixth sense is that one which gives us knowledge of a vibration of reality, a vibration which our normal senses are unable to perceive" (Richet, n. d., p. 224).

Another writer that wrote about physical transmission analogies of telepathy was engineer René Warcollier (1938). In his book of collected essays, *Experimental Telepathy*, Warcollier discussed the nature of the telepathic transmission. He cautioned the reader that he was using physical processes as analogies and that he was only speculating. Nonetheless, some of his writings suggest a more solid belief than Warcollier admitted. In an essay first written in 1921 Warcollier said that the process was one in which "the vibration of one of A's cerebral neurones producing by resonance, the corresponding vibration in one of P's cerebral neurons …" (Warcollier, 1938, p. 199).

As Warcollier wrote about the actual process:

> It seems to me that we can find in the disintegration of the atom the origin of radiations to account for distant and swift transmission. Psychic radioactivity, the breaking down of atoms of cerebral cells, is certainly pure hypothesis, but I feel it is necessary to explain the telepathic phenomenon … Modern physics has demonstrated that our organs, like other material bodies,

are made up of whirlwinds of forces, reacting on one another. The spirit is more at ease with the conceptions of these minute solar systems of ions and electrons than with the blood-filled particles that constitute the brain ... When we face the question from this angle ... we can conceive perfectly how the vibrations of the nervous system can be produced, how they can lead the vibrations of external bodies, through the nerve centers, to the centers of consciousness. We can conceive how motor nerves can transmit orders to muscles, how ideas can be associated with or without fibers of association, can pass beyond the cranium and influence, by induction, other nerve centers in other brains. (pp. 199, 202–203)

Not everyone interested in the phenomena took a physical approach involving vibrations or forces. Frederic W. H. Myers (1886) affirmed: "We may say that telepathy is a psychical agency, and that there is an impassable gulf between all agencies which can be classed as physical on the one hand, and on the other hand, all agencies, whether apparently operating in proximity or at a distance, which we can as yet cognise on the psychical side alone" (p. 178). Other individuals—such as Rudolf Tischner (1925), Hans Driesch (1932/1933), and J. B. Rhine (1934)—opposed radiation explanations of ESP and argued for non-physical models. For example, Driesch referred to the necessity of postulating a "mental field," described as "something superpersonal in addition to something non-spatial in general" (Driesch, 1932/1933, p. 133). This ambiguous statement referred to some sort of mental plane not bound by space that could connect different minds.

Concluding Remarks

This concludes this series of short notes on historical concepts of force related to psychic phenomena. The notes, readers should keep in mind, were not intended as complete reviews, but as offering supplementary material to a previous paper on the topic (Alvarado, 2006). Furthermore, I have not covered speculations on all possible phenomena, leaving aside, for example, psychic photography, hauntings, healing, and auras.

As argued before, the ideas discussed in these notes were related to a great extent to the scientific interests of the times. This included ideas about nerve fluids and animal electricity in past neurophysiology (Brazier, 1984; Morus, 1988). Furthermore, there were also multiple nineteenth-century developments about force and energy, including electricity and magnetism (Harman, 1982). The latter, as well as the rise of technology, was referred to by French popularizer of science Louis Figuier (1884) as the "new conquests of science." All of this—focusing on the transmission of electricity, nerve conduction, and on technologies such as telegraphy—encouraged the idea of transmission via a physical medium by assuming the extension of science into the unknown.

Such knowledge also brought us perspectives such as Flammarion's (1900), who argued that while x-rays, the telephone, and several physical processes showed what scientists had learned, they also served to remind us about how much was still to learn about the universe. Consequently, he said, we should open our minds to the domain of the unknown, which included telepathy and other phenomena.

The concepts discussed here were speculations developed from observations. In using the word speculation, I want to emphasize the supposed or hypothetical character of these concepts. The ideas I have mentioned were suppositions that were rarely generated through or supported by attempts to test the concept in scientific ways. Rather they were assumptions in which imagined extensions of physical concepts were used to make sense of the phenomena observed. These concepts of force are perhaps part of what Holton (1988) has referred to as thematic concepts in science, or general ideas that guide the course of science in different ways, while being resistant to proof or disproof, according to one's perspective.

Holton discussed concepts that ranged from the more general such as reductionism, atomism and evolution, to the more specific such as particular physical processes (e.g., inertia). Among these were ideas still considered valid, as well as those concepts that have been discarded over time, including such principles as humors, animal spirits, phlogiston, and the ether. While in some cases these ideas are now thought to have affected science negatively, they may also be seen as concepts that performed useful functions of creation and organization to those individuals who proposed them as true depictions of nature. This was the case of animal magnetism and the perispirit, which were central in mesmerism and spiritism. These concepts, interestingly enough, could be and were used to support different models, differentiating between ideas of human and discarnate agency.

In any case, the ideas presented here show the richness of the literatures in question. I offer my comments in the hopes that by presenting selected bibliography, I will awaken historical interest in these topics.

Notes

1 Readers should keep in mind that these notes are meant as supplementary material for a previous paper (Alvarado, 2006). See "Human Radiations: Concepts of Force in Mesmerism, Spiritualism and Psychical Research," this volume.

2 Other work following-up Reichenbach's observations is summarized by Sudre (1926, pp. 206–207).

References

Aggazzotti, A., Foa, C., Foa, P., & Herlitzka, A. (1907). The experiments of Prof. P. Foà, of the University of Turin, and three doctors, assistants of Professor Mosso, with Eusapia Palladino. *Annals of Psychical Science, 5*, 361–392.

Alvarado, C. S. (1993). Gifted subjects' contributions to psychical research: The case of Eusapia Palladino. *Journal of the Society for Psychical Research, 59*, 269–292.

Alvarado, C. S. (2006). Human radiations: Concepts of force in mesmerism, spiritualism and psychical research. *Journal of the Society for Psychical Research, 70*, 138–162.

Andry-Bourgeois, [C]. (1935). La télévision et la voyance. *Revue Spirite, 78*, 481–487.

Ashburner, J. (1867). *Notes and studies in the philosophy of animal magnetism and spiritualism.* H. Baillière.

Azam, H. (1926). Télégraphie sans fil et médiumnité: De la pratique de la médiumnité à l'evolution de l'âme dans l'universe. *Revue Spirite, 69*, 122–128.

Ballou, A. (1853). *An exposition of views respecting the modern spiritual manifestations* (2nd American ed.). Edward Howell.

Barkas, T. P. (1862). *Outlines of ten years' investigation into the phenomena of modern spiritualism, embracing letters, lectures, &c.* Frederick Pitman.

Barrett, W. F. (1884). Note on the existence of a "magnetic sense." *Proceedings of the Society for Psychical Research, 2*, 59–60.

Barrett, W. F., Close, M. H., Lane-Fox, G., Gurney, E., Myers, F. W. H., Myers, A. T., Pease, E. R., Ridley, H. N., Stone, W. H., & Coffin, W. H. (1883). First report of the "Reichenbach" committee. *Proceedings of the Society for Psychical Research, 1*, 230–237.

Baudoin, M. (1900). Un cas de télépathie: Manifestations d'une mourante sur sa soeur a l'état de veille constatée par un médicin en visite et charactérisé par un phénomène physique. *Annales des Sciences Psychique, 10*, 129–142.
Beecher, C. (1853). *A review of the "Spiritual manifestations."* G. P. Putnam.
Bozzano, E. (1927). *Les enigmes de la psychometrie et les phénomènes de télésthesie*. Jean Meyer.
Brackett, C. F. (1889). Electricity in the service of man: An introductory paper. *Scribner's Magazine, 5*, 643–659.
Brackett, E. A. (1908). *Materialized apparitions: If not beings from another life what are they?* Richard G. Badger.
Bradley, J. H. (1870). *Some examination of the theory of spiritualism*. Indiana State Sentinel Print.
Braid, J. (1970). The power of the mind over the body. In M. M. Tinterow (Ed.), *Foundations of hypnosis: From Mesmer to Freud* (pp. 331–364). Charles C Thomas. (Original work published 1846).
Brazier, M. A. B. (1984). *A history of neurophysiology in the 17th and 18th centuries*. Raven Press.
Brevior, T. (1864). Mysteries of nature and of spirit. *Spiritual Magazine, 5*, 271–280.
Brittan, S. B. (1852). Elements of spiritual science. *The Shekinah, 1*, 54–72.
Buchanan, J. R. (1849). Psychometry. *Buchanan's Journal of Man*, 1, 49–62, 97–113, 145–156, 208–227, 269–277.
Buchanan, J. R. (1885). *Manual of psychometry: The dawn of a new civilization* (2nd ed.). B. W. Dodge.
Capron, E. W., & Barron, H. D. (1850). *Explanation and history of the mysterious communion with spirit, comprehending the rise and progress of the mysterious noises in western New York* (2nd ed.). Capron and Barron.
Carrington, H. (1909). *Eusapia Palladino and her phenomena*. B. W. Dodge.
Cazzamalli, F. (1926/1925). Telepsychic phenomena and cerebral radiations. *Journal of the American Society for Psychical Research, 20*, 1–17.
Cazzamalli, F. (1928). Les ondes électro-magnétiques en correlation avec certains phénomènes psycho-sensoriales du cerveau humain. *Compte rendu du IIIème Congrès International de Recherché Psychiques* (pp. 45–55). Institut Métapsychique International.
Cazzamalli, F. (1947). De las posibles condiciones físicas de los fenómenos telepsíquicos. *Revista Médica de Metapsíquica, 1*(1), 80–90.
Cazzamalli, F. (1960). *Il cervello radianti: Fenomeni elettromagnetici radianti dal cervello umano durante l'intensa attivita psicosensoriale degli stati onirici, allucinatori e telepsichici*. Ceschina.
Chardel, C. (1818). *Mémoire sur le magnétisme animal, presenté a l'Academie de Berlin, en 1818*. Badouin.
Chevillard, A. (1869). *Études expérimentales sur le fluide nerveux et solution definitive du problème spirite*. Victor Masson.
Clarke, E., & Jacyna, L. S. (1987). *Nineteenth-century origins of neuroscientific concepts*. University of California Press.
Coates, J. (1907). *Seeing the invisible: Practical studies in psychometry, thought transference, telepathy, and allied phenomena*. L. N. Fowler.
Collyer, R. H. (1871). *Mysteries of the vital in connexion with dreams, somnambulism, trance, vital photography, faith and will, anaesthesia, nervous congestion and creative function* (2nd ed.). Henry Renshaw.
Comas Solá. J. [1908]. *El espiritismo ante la ciencia: Estudio critico sobre la mediumnidad*. Atlante.
Cox, E. W. (1879). *The mechanism of man: An answer to the question what am I? A Popular introduction to mental physiology and psychology: Vol. 2: The mechanism in action*. Longman.
Crookes, W. (1874). *Researches in the phenomena of spiritualism*. J. Burns.
Crookes, W. (1897) Address by the President. *Proceedings of the Society for Psychical Research, 12*, 338–355.
Crowell, E. (1874). *The identity of primitive Christianity and modern spiritualism* (2 vols.). G. W. Carleton.
Darnton, R. (1968). *Mesmerism and the end of the enlightenment in France*. Harvard University Press.
Davis, A. J. (1853). *The great harmonia, concerning the seven mental states* (Vol. 3). Benjamin B. Mussey.
De Morgan, S. J. (1863). *From matter to spirit: The results of ten years' experience in spirit manifestations*. Longman, Green, Longman, Roberts, & Green.
De Rochas, [A.] (1891). *Le fluide des magnetiseurs: Precis des experiences du Baron de Reinchenbach sur ses proprieties physiques et physiologiques*. Georges Carre.
De Rochas, A. (1887). *Les forces non définies: Recherches historiques et experimentales*. G. Masson.

De Rochas, A. (1895a). *L'extériorisation de la sensibilite: Étude expérimentale*. Chamuel.
De Rochas, A. (1895b). *Les fantômes des vivants. Annales des Sciences Psychiques, 5*, 257–275.
De Rochas, A. (1895c). Review of *Essai de spiritisme scientifique*, by D. Metzger, and *Le psychisme expérimentale*, by A. Erny. *Annales des Sciences Psychiques*, 5, 119–126.
De Rochas, A. (1896). *L'extériorisation de la motricité: Recueil d'expériences et d'observations*. Chamuel.
De Rochas, A. (1897). Les experiences de Choisy-Yvrec (prés Bordeaux) du 2 au 14 octobre 1896. *Annales des Sciences Psychiques, 7*, 6–28.
De Rochas, A. (1902). *Les frontières de la science (Series 1)*. Librairie des Sciences Psychologiques.
Delanne, G. (1897). *L'évolution animique: Essais de psychologie physiologique suivant le spiritisme*. Chamuel.
Delanne, G. (1923). *Le spiritisme devant la science*. Editions de la B. P. S.
Deleuze, J. P. F. (1813). *Histoire critique du magnetisme animal*. Mame.
Denis, A. (1895). Essai d'une théorie de la télépathie. *Annales des Sciences Psychiques, 5*, 14–32.
Denis, L. (1900). Psychologie expérimentale: Phénomènes d'extériorisation et de dédoublement. *Annales des Sciences Psychiques, 10*, 291–294.
Denton, W., & Denton, E. M. F. (1863). *The soul of things: Or, psychometric researches and discoveries*. Walker, Wise.
Dille, I. (1852). Matter, ether and spirit. *Brittan's Journal of Spiritual Science, Literature, Art, and Inspiration, 2*, 36–57.
Dods, J. B. (1854). *Spirit manifestations examined and explained: Judge Edmonds refuted; or, an exposition of the involuntary powers and instincts of the human mind*. De Witt & Davenport.
Driesch, H. (1933). *Psychical research: The science of the super-normal*. G. Bell. (Original work published in German, 1932)
Duchatel, E. (1910). *Enquete sur des cas de psychometrie: Janvier-Decembre 1909*. Leymarie.
Durville, H. (1895). *Traité experimental de magnétisme: Vol. 1: Physique magnétique*. Librairie du Magnétisme.
Edmonds, J. W., & Dexter, G. T. (1853). *Spiritualism* (4th ed., Vol. 1). Partridge & Brittan.
Esdaile, J. (1852). *Natural and mesmeric clairvoyance, with the practical application of mesmerism in surgery and medicine*. Hippolyte Baillière.
Fedi, R. (1937). Il perispirito. *La Ricerca Psichica, 37*, 221–225.
Figuier, L. [1884]. *Les nouvelles conquêtes de la science* (4 vols.). Librairie Illustrée.
Filalete, N. (1864). Azione degli spiriti sulla materia. *Annali dello Spiritismo in Italia, 1*, 289–309.
Flammarion, C. (1900). *L'inconnu: The unknown*. Harper.
Flammarion, C. (1907). *Mysterious psychic forces: An account of the author's investigations in psychical research, together with those of other European savants*. Small, Maynard.
Frank, H. (1911). *Psychic phenomena, science and immortality*. Sherman, French.
Fugairon, L. S. (1894). *Essai sur les phénomènes électriques des etres vivants comprensant l'explication scientifique des phénomènes dits spirites*. Chamuel.
Geley, G. (n. d.). *Ensayo de revista general y de interpretación sintética del espiritismo* (3rd French ed.). Maucci.
[Guppy, S.] (1863). *Mary Jane; or, spiritualism chemically explained*. John King.
Haddock, J. W. (1851). *Somnolism & psycheism; or, the science of the soul and the phenomena of nervation, as revealed by vital magnetism or mesmerism* (2nd ed.). James S. Hodson.
Hammond, W. A. (1871). *The physics and physiology of spiritualism*. D. Appleton.
Hare, R. (1855). *Experimental investigation of the spirit manifestations demonstrating the existence of spirits and their communion with mortals*. Partridge & Brittan.
Harman, P. M. (1982). *Energy, force and matter: The conceptual development of 19th century physics*. Cambridge University Press.
Hericourt, J. (1891). Review of *Les hallucinations télépatiques*, by E. Gurney, F. W. H. Myers, and F. Podmore. *Annales des Sciences Psychiques, 1*, 313–319.
Hitchman, W. (1875). Correspondence: Alleged evolution of electricity from the hands and feet. *Spiritualist Newspaper*, pp. 167–168.
Hodgson, R. (1898). A further record of observations of certain phenomena of trance. *Proceedings of the Society for Psychical Research, 13*, 284–582.

Holton, G. (1988). *Thematic origins of scientific thought: Kepler to Einstein* (Rev. ed.). Harvard University Press.
Houston, J. (1892). Cerebral radiations. *Psychical Review, 1*, 150–157.
Jastrow, J., & Nuttall, G. F. H. (1886). On the existence of a magnetic sense. *Proceedings of the American Society for Psychical Research, 1*, 116–126.
Kardec, A. (1863). *Spiritisme expérimental: Le livre des médiums ou guide des médiums et des évocateurs* (6th ed.). Didier.
Kardec, A. (1876). *Experimental spiritism: The mediums' book or guide for mediums and for evocations.* Trübner.
Kudriavtzeff, K. (1909). Human radiations and their applications to healing. *Light, 29*, 175–178.
Lombroso, C. (1892). Le spiritisme et la psychiatrie: Explication psychiatrique de certain faits spirites. *Annales des Sciences Psychiques, 2*, 143–151.
Lombroso, C. (1909). *After death—what? Spiritistic phenomena and their interpretation.* Small, Maynard.
Maeterlinck, M. (1914). *The unknown guest.* Dodd, Mead.
Mayo, H. (1852). *Popular superstitions, and the theories contained therein, with an account of mesmerism* (3rd London ed.). Lindsay and Blakiston.
Mead, G. R. S. (1919). *The doctrine of the subtle body in western tradition.* John Watkins.
Mesmer, F. A. (1779). *Mémoire sur la decouverte du magnétisme animal.* P. Fr. Didot.
Modern necromancy. (1855). *North American Review, 80*, 512–527.
Morselli, E. (1908). *Psicologia e "spiritismo:" Note e impressioni critiche sui fenomeni medianici di Eusapia Paladino* (2 vols.). Fratelli Bocca.
Morus, I. R. (1998). Galvanic cultures: Electricity and life in the early nineteenth century. *Endeavour, 22*, 7–11.
Myers, F. W. H. (1886). On telepathic hypnotism, and its relation to other forms of hypnotic suggestion. *Proceedings of the Society for Psychical Research, 4*, 127–188.
Neurology in New York (1849). *Buchanan's Journal of Man, 1*, 12–34.
Objects of the Society. (1882). *Proceedings of the Society for Psychical Research, 1*, 3–6.
Ochorowicz, J. (1896). La question de la fraude dans les expériences avec Eusapia Paladino. *Annales des Sciences Psychiques, 6*, 79–123.
Ochorowicz, J. (1909). Hypnotisme et mesmérisme. In C. Richet (Ed.), *Dictionnaire de physiologie* (Vol. 8, pp. 709–778). Félix Alcan.
Owen, R. D. (1864). The electric girl of La Perriere. *Atlantic Monthly, 14*, 284–292.
Pagenstecher, G. (1922). Past events seership: A study in psychometry. *Proceedings of the American Society for Psychical Research, 16*, 1–136.
Poortman, J. J. (1978). *Vehicles of consciousness: The concept of hylic pluralism (ochema).* Theosophical Society in the Netherlands. (Original work published in Dutch, 1954)
Potter, A. M. (1855). Psychometry. *Buchanan's Journal of Man, 5*, 244–249.
Price, H. H. (1939). Haunting and the "psychic ether" hypothesis; with some preliminary reflections on the present condition and possible future of psychical research. *Proceedings of the Society for Psychical Research, 45*, 307–343.
Reichenbach, C. von. (1851). *Physico-physiological researches on the dynamics of magnetism, electricity, heat, light, crystallization, and chemism, in their relation to vital force* (from German 2nd ed). J. S. Redfield (Original work published in German, 1849).
Reichenbach, K. von (1968). *The Odic force: Letters on Od and magnetism.* University Books. (Original work published in German, 1852)
Rhine, J. B. (1934). *Extra-sensory perception.* Boston Society for Psychic Research.
Richet, C. (n. d., ca 1928). *Our sixth sense.* Rider.
Richmond, B. W. (1855). Mental duality-psychometric dreaming, etc. *Buchanan's Journal of Man, 5*, 22–42.
Rogers, E. C. (1853). *Philosophy of mysterious agents, human and mundane; or, the dynamic laws and relations of man.* J. P. Jewett.
Rohland, R. (1871). *Od, or odo—magnetic force: And explanations of its influence on homeopathic medicines, from the odic stand-point.* Author.
Sandby. G. (1848). *Mesmerism and its opponents* (2nd ed.). Longman, Brown, Green, and Longmans.

Schrenck-Notzing, A. [F.] de. (1925). *Les phénomènes physiques de la médiumnité*. Payot. (Original work published in German, 1920)

Sinel, J. (1927). T*he sixth sense: A physical explanation of clairvoyance, telepathy, hypnotism, dreams, and other phenomena usually considered occult.* T. W. Laurie.

Southern notes. (1876). *American Spiritual Magazine, 2,* 81–83.

Sprague, E. W. (1912). *Spirit mediumship*. Author.

Sudre, R. (1926). *Introduction à la métapsychique humaine*. Payot.

Sutton, G. (1981). Electric medicine and mesmerism. *Isis, 72*, 375–392.

Thomas, C. D. (1928). The *modus operandi* of trance communication according to descriptions received through Mrs. Osborne Leonard. *Proceedings of the Society for Psychical Research, 38*, 49–100.

Tischner, R. E. (1925). *Telepathy and clairvoyance.* Harcourt, Brace.

Twain, M. (1891). Mental telegraphy: A manuscript with a history. *Harper's New Monthly Magazine, 84*, 95–104.

Warcollier, R. (1938). *Experimental telepathy*. Boston Society for Psychic Research.

Whiting, H. G. (1871). Correspondence. *Christian Spiritualist, 1,* 156–157.

Willis, H. A. (1868). A remarkable case of "physical phenomena." *Atlantic Monthly, 22,* 129–135.

Wilson, T. S. (1925). *Thought transference: Speculations upon psychology and religion.* George Allen and Unwin.

9

Altered Consciousness from the Age of Enlightenment Through Mid-20th Century*

Etzel Cardeña & Carlos S. Alvarado†

The alterations of consciousness, discernment strategies, and explanatory models were described throughout the 18th century, although the Age of Enlightenment would bring its own ideology to bear on these matters. Even earlier, the physician Duncan in 1634 had attributed the phenomena of the possessed nuns of Loudun to "folly and error of the imagination" and suggestion by the confessors rather than to supernatural causes (in de Certeau, 2000, pp. 135–136). The 17th century had a cadre of outstanding thinkers such as Leibniz and Descartes, but their rational models of the universe were still undergirded by God and religion; thus, the 18th century stands out thanks to a plethora of important works that pushed rational analyses above and beyond religious concerns. The groundbreaking works of Kant, Voltaire, and the French Encyclopedists set the stage for a search for knowledge perhaps unparalleled since the Al-Andaluz period during the Arabic reign of the Iberic peninsula in which rational and empirical concerns were harmoniously integrated with a mystical vision (Bakan, Merkur, & Weiss, 2009).

Similarly to classical Greece (see Dodds, 1951/1973), however, the age of enlightenment and rationality in Europe and the Americas had a corresponding and perhaps partly reactive set of religious and quasi-religious movements in which alterations of consciousness and behavior were a major concern for a large segment of the population, even though many of these manifestations had, earlier on, been condemned by the Christian church. Rosen (1969) provides a nonexhaustive list of movements that announced that their devotees could prophesize and be in contact with a divine realm, including the Camisard prophets and the Jansenist convulsionaries in France; the Shakers, the early Methodists, and the Great Awakening, especially in Great Britain and the USA; the Chlysti in Russia; and the Hassidic movement of the Baal-Shem Tov.

Similarly to contemporary Brazilian followers of Afro-Caribbean religions (see Frigerio, 1989), the prophetic state of consciousness among devotees of French sects included various degrees—the warning (*l'avertissement*), the whisper of inspiration (*le soufflé*), the prophecy (*la prophétie*), and the gift (*le don*)—besides physical manifestations including shivering, twitching convulsively, leaping, foaming in the mouth, speaking in tongues (i.e., glossolalia), and falling into stupor (Rosen, 1969, p. 211). The way to achieve such alterations in consciousness and behavior included, depending on the group, praying, singing, frenetic movements or dancing, fasting, sexual abstinence or license, and in more extreme cases whipping and even sexual automutilation (as among the Skopze, see Zacharias, 1980). Many of these religious movements are analyzed in detail by Garrett (1987) and the experiences and behaviors they manifested can be found across cultures and times, including ecstatic religions and Christian, Moslem, and Judaic traditions that continue to seek a direct religious experience of being possessed by spirits, saints, or the Divinity. Although there may be a temptation to assume that all or

*Republished with permission from E. Cardeña and M. Winkelman (Eds.), *Altering Consciousness: Multidisciplinary Perspectives: Vol. 1: History, Culture and the Humanities* (pp. 89–112). Santa Barbara, CA: Praeger, 2015.
†We are grateful for the editorial assistance of Alan Gauld.

most of the followers of these groups may have suffered from psychopathology, contemporary studies in different cultures suggests that practitioners in these sects are as a group at least as healthy as their cultural referent groups (Cardeña, van Duijl, Weiner, & Terhune, 2009; Moreira-Almeida, Lotufo Neto, & Cardeña, 2008). We will now discuss the most influential set of ideas and practices in the Western World concerning altered consciousness during the end of the 18th through beginning of the 20th centuries, namely animal magnetism/hypnosis and mediumship.

Mesmer and Animal Magnetism

The Age of Enlightenment was characterized by secular, rational explanations for many phenomena, including altered consciousness, previously understood only within a religious context. Perhaps the most influential was the development by the physician Franz Anton Mesmer (1734–1815) of *animal magnetism*. Although it may be the case that the priest Johann Joseph Gassner (1727–1779) used what would now be called psychotherapeutic strategies in his exorcisms (Peter, 2005), his explanation invoked the metaphysical battle between good and evil. In contrast, Mesmer developed in his medical dissertation a theory that purported to explain possession and exorcism phenomena in terms of his conception of an all-pervading magnetism in the universe (Mesmer, 1779; see also Pattie, 1994). Some of his tenets may bespeak of esoterism to some today, but they were compatible with the interpretation by Mesmer of what Benjamin Franklin and others researched about the electromagnetic forces of the universe. Furthermore, the astronomical underpinnings of Mesmer's theory, although suspect nowadays, were in agreement with a nonreligious explanation of the universe, as sought by Enlightenment authors (see Darnton, 1968). Mesmer (1779) declared that there is "an universally distributed fluid … which by its nature, is susceptible of receiving, propagating and communicating all the impressions of movement" (p. 74). This substance, which he postulated interacted with the rest of the forces in the universe, he called animal magnetism. Sickness was explained as a disturbance in the flow of this substance that could be exaggerated by the use of magnets or hands to the point that the system would go into a crisis and rebalance itself into its natural, healthy condition. Thus, the exorcism healings produced by the charismatic Father Gassner, the ironically named Father Hell (1720–1792), and others were explained by Mesmer through the skillful manipulation of animal magnetism rather than by the struggle between divine and demonic forces (Gauld, 1992).

At the beginning, Mesmer performed individual treatments touching or passing above the body magnets and, later on, his hands. After he traveled to Paris and became very well-known and sought after, he had group healing sessions in which he used music and appeared in a showy purple robe while the afflicted Parisian nobility sat around a *baquet* (tub) filled with *magnetized* water from which protruded metal tubes that could be moved to the afflicted bodily parts. Reports from the time mention the crises experienced by Mesmer's clients, particularly women. One writer stated that the crises started "by a small cough that becomes convulsive, which is soon followed by hiccups, a shriek, [and] by extraordinary singing," and by the imitation of dogs, cats, and chickens (Paulet, 1784, p. 22). In addition, some individuals cried, laughed, had gastric disturbances, experienced a sense of warmth or heat, went into convulsions, and even lost consciousness supposedly as a manifestation of the magnetic crisis (Gauld, 1992), phenomena previously observed in connection with spirit possession. Some of the behaviors seen at Mesmer's sessions seemed to spread once a person had manifested them, reminiscent of group manifestations occurring earlier as part of the Tarantella or St. Vitus's dances in which individuals affected with apparently uncontrollable dancing would end up affecting other onlookers. This phenomenon, when referring to a pathological manifestation, is currently called *medically unexplained epidemic illness* or *mass psychogenic illness* (Van Ommeren et al., 2001), probably mediated in part by an automatic emotional response, especially among some suggestible individuals (Cardeña, Terhune, Lööf, & Buratti, 2009).

As Gauld (1992) observes, Mesmer would explicitly state what physical manifestations the person could expect, which besides less direct suggestions probably had a strong effect on many individuals. Although it is not possible to ascertain with accuracy the effectiveness of Mesmer's treatments, he seemed to have had success in relief of pain and general unease and perhaps even in healing refractory medical cases. The two Royal Commissions ordered by Louis XVI to investigate the scandalous practices of Mesmer would not dispute their effectiveness, but would criticize his theory to explain his cures and point to the potential danger of the use of imagination and the implicit sexual tension fraught in the practices (Gauld, 1992).

Hypnotic Somnambulism

Although Mesmerism as a theory came into disrepute following the reports by the commissions, the idea of animal magnetism as a physical agent persisted longer than it is generally realized (Alvarado, 2009). A student of Mesmer, A. M. J. Chastenet, Marquis de Puységur (1751–1825), would introduce changes in practice that are the true predecessors of contemporary hypnotic practice. When he treated the peasant Victor Race for a lung condition, Puységur noticed that he did not go into a mesmeric crisis (perhaps because he did not have any models as to how he should behave and/or perhaps because he might have been delirious) but instead seemed to be experiencing and acting as if he were in a dream, which he could not recall once he seemed to come out of that state as if waking up. This and similar manifestations were called *somnambulism*, which means carrying out complex acts in a sleeplike state. This presumed association between mesmeric phenomena and sleep would be retained in the later term *hypnos*, which refers to the Greek god of sleep.

Puységur and other contemporary practitioners also noted a number of potential parapsychological phenomena, for instance, that patients in the state of magnetic somnambulism reputedly knew the cause of their own and others' diseases and were able to indicate the means of healing them (Chastenet de Puységur, 1820, p. 1). Crabtree (1993) has listed for us various described alterations in consciousness: a sleepwalking kind of consciousness, a different reservoir of knowledge and memory during that state, loss of the sense of identity, suggestibility to the mesmerist's communications, heightened memory, alterations in the senses, apparent insensibility to pain, and a special rapport with the magnetizer. Crabtree (1988) has also documented copious sources that describe potential psi phenomena during the magnetic state, including the apparent communication of the sensations or behaviors of the magnetizer to the magnetized without any known sensory or logical links (community of sensation and of muscular action), telepathy, becoming mesmerized at a distance without sensory or logical intermediation, clairvoyance of remote (in time and place) events and of medical conditions, and awareness of spiritual things and beings (see also Dingwall, 1967–1968).

Many, but not all, of these observations might be explained by unconscious sensory leakage, inferences, and similar ordinary mechanisms, but carefully described cases such as Pierre Janet's (1859–1947) patient Mme. B (the pseudonym of Leonie Leboulanger; Janet, 1885/1968a, 1886/1968b) or the extraordinary displays while mesmerized of the brothers Didier cannot be so easily explained away (see Gauld, 1992). Thus, the conclusion by Dingwall (1967-1968) regarding a possible connection between psi phenomena and hypnosis that "[A]n attitude of suspended judgment both as regards the past and the present is perhaps the most judicial (V. 1, p. 297)" is not farfetched, especially when controlled psi experiments generally suggest that hypnosis may be a context that facilitates psi phenomena (Cardeña, 2010).

In the early 19th century, Carl Alexander Ferdinand Kluge (1782–1844) categorized six levels or degrees of the phenomenology of magnetic somnambulism: waking state with increased warmth, half-sleep, "inner darkness" (sleep proper and insensitivity), "inner clarity" (perception through the body), "self-contemplation" (the ability to accurately see one's body and those of others), and "universal clarity" (perception unconstrained by time or space). He maintained that only a few people, such as the famous *seeress of Prevorst*, could attain the last three degrees (Kluge, 1811; see also Ellenberger, 1970, pp. 78–80). Current research on hypnotic phenomena has partly validated this categorization in the sense that only a minority of individuals (i.e., highly hypnotizables) spontaneously report transcendent experiences, and only when they feel that they are in self-evaluated "very deep hypnosis," whereas they experience mostly body sensation and image changes during "light hypnosis" and disembodied and imaginal experiences during "middle hypnosis" (Cardeña, 2005; Cardeña, Lehmann, Jönsson, Terhune, & Faber, 2007).

Other authors recorded interesting somnambulistic manifestations in their mesmeric participants. In France, the mesmerist Joseph Philippe François Deleuze (1753–1835) wrote in his book *Histoire Critique du Magnétisme Animal* that somnambulists could recover the "recollection of things that were forgotten during wakefulness" (Deleuze, 1813, p. 176). Also, events taking place during somnambulism were forgotten when the person was in his or her normal state, which Deleuze believed was an indication that "the two states are unfamiliar to one another," and that there were "two separate beings" (p. 176). He mentioned a case in which a woman in the somnambulistic state was opposed to the desire of her normal self to work in the theatre. Answering a question during her somnambulistic state about why she wanted to be in the theatre, she said, "It is not me, it is her ... she is mad" (p. 177).

There was also a discussion of what we would refer today as examples of state-specific memory. In France, Alexandre Bertrand (1795–1831) referred to the phenomenon as "one of the most constant properties" of the somnambulistic state (Bertrand, 1826, p. 409). In England, William Gregory (1803–1858) wrote as follows in his *Letters to a Candid Inquirer, on Animal Magnetism*:

> As a general rule ... the sleeper does not remember, after waking, what he may have seen, felt, tasted, smelled, heard, spoken, or done, during his sleep; but when next put to sleep, he recollects perfectly all that has occurred, not only in the last sleep, but in all former sleeps, and, as in the ordinary state, with greater or less accuracy, although usually very accurately indeed. He lives, in fact, a distinct life in the sleep, and has, what is called, a double or divided consciousness ... (Gregory, 1851, p. 82).

In later years, the leading English researcher of hypnosis and psychical phenomena Edmund Gurney (1847–1888) conducted more systematic studies of hypnotic state-specific memory. He described one test when his subject was hypnotized:

> In this condition he was able to read ... After reading a paragraph ... he was then woke [sic] completely as usual. But only one word of what he had read could be recalled, and he was very uncertain about that; he recollected distinctly, however, a paragraph that he had recently read in the normal state, and felt satisfied that that was the last one read. Again hypnotized, he had full recollection of the paragraph read in the hypnotic state with open eyes. (Gurney, 1888, p. 10)

Nowadays, hypnosis research has generally found that when controlling for implicit and explicit suggestions, amnesia is not a typical outcome of a hypnotic induction (e.g., Laurence & Perry, 1988).

Gurney (1884) also mentioned two hypnotic states, an alert and a deep hypnotic one. He believed that the identification of these states was difficult because

> (E)ach state admits of many degrees and the characteristics of either of them may be only slightly or only very transiently presented; and in the second place, unless special means are adopted, it is very easy to mistake the alert state for normal waking, and the deep state for sleep. (Gurney, 1884, p. 62)

According to Gurney (1884), individuals in the alert state may look vacant, the state resembling that of the usual consciousness, the eyes could be open and the person would be sensitive to pain but particularly open to suggestion. Gurney said that the deep stage could escape detection because it

> … is liable to be confounded with a contiguous condition, namely, the genuine hypnotic sleep into which it tends to merge. It resembles that condition in the fact that the eyelids are closed; that, if one of them be forcibly raised, the eyeball is found to be rolled upwards; in the general insensibility to pain and to ordinary modes of stimulation … If the … "subject" be left to himself, he will have no opportunity to manifest its characteristics, but … will soon lose consciousness and individuality in profound slumber. With some "subjects," moreover, the invasion of mental torpor is so rapid that it might be hard to fix and retain them in the genuine deep stage. … But many others, if taken in time, after their eyes are closed and they have become insensible to pain, but before sleep has intervened, will prove quite capable of rational conversation; they are mentally awake, even when their bodies are almost past movement. … The state is, however, harder to sustain at an even level than the alert one, owing to a stronger and more continuous tendency to lapse into a deeper condition. (p. 64)

Other observations documented changes of personality of different sorts. This was the case of a patient named Isabella:

> When in the state of what has been termed sleepwalking, or somnambulism, the patient always talks of herself as of another person. In the Mesmeric state she calls herself Martha, and she talks of Isabella (her real name) as of a totally different individual. When asked about the complaints with which Isabella was troubled, she described them with what seemed to be the greatest accuracy, and indicated the most suitable remedies. (Lang, 1843, p. 108)

Other changes were documented in a case reported by Gregory (1851):

> When the sleeper has become fully asleep, so as to answer questions readily without waking, there is almost always observed a remarkable change in the countenance, the manner, and the voice. On falling asleep at first, he looks, perhaps, drowsy and heavy … But when spoken to, he usually brightens up, and, although the eyes be closed, yet the expression becomes highly intelligent … a person of a much more elevated character than the same sleeper seems to be when awake … In the highest stages of the magnetic sleep, the countenance often acquires the most lovely expression … As to the voice, I have never seen one person in the true magnetic sleep, who did not speak in a tone quite distinct from the ordinary voice of the sleeper … softer and more gentle, well corresponding to the elevated and mild expression of the face … For the sleeper, in the magnetic state, has a consciousness quite separate and distinct from his ordinary consciousness. He is, in fact, if not a different individual, yet the same individual in a different and distinct phase of his being; and that phase, a higher one. (pp. 80–82)

These interpretations of mesmeric and hypnotic phenomena would be the basis for some later theories of double and multiple personalities, as well as for the notion of a superior self-described in the writings of Myers, James, and others.[1]

There were also examples of suppression of physical sensations through mesmeric procedures. This was clear in James Esdaile's (1808–1859) discussions of pain control, as seen in his book *Mesmerism in India* (1846). In his view, "in the mesmeric trance the most severe and protracted surgical operations can be performed, without the patients being sensible of pain" (p. 271), although some of his descriptions have been recently qualified (Chaves, 1997).

Mediumship

Besides putative exceptional powers, some of the anomalous experiences reported by gifted participants during magnetic/hypnotic sessions mentioned contact with angels and departed spirits, and there were some who interpreted these literally (Billot, 1839; Cahagnet, 1851; see Gauld, 1992, p. 3). One such mesmeric subject was an English woman called Emma. According to the report:

> Emma … began to speak frequently of spiritual objects and beings. I soon perceived, that one being, under whose influence she seemed to be, and of whom she frequently spoke, had been most nearly related to me, while in this world, but she had departed this life for about ten years when the first of these trances occurred. Emma always says that this "lady" … "helps her" in all serious cases of illness, and the like, but not in mere secular, or trifling cases. (Haddock, 1851, p. 187)

Mediumship, the experience and belief that an individual may be able to receive or be the medium for communications from spiritual entities, is an ancient and nearly universal phenomenon (Oesterreich, 1974/1921), and has been discussed in terms of dissociation and disruptions of an integrated identity. As argued by Podmore (1902), there seemed to be a connection between some of the manifestations of somnambulism and the performances of mediums from the movement referred to as "modern spiritualism." There was a short step from the *experimental metaphysics* of some magnetizers to the beginning of the spiritualist movement by the mid-19th century, which proposed that discarnate entities, especially the deceased, could communicate with the living in various ways. Although physical manifestations such as levitating tables were an innovation of this movement, "trance" mediumship, in which a gifted individual is supposed to communicate with the dead after entering some kind of altered state of consciousness (ASC), can partly trace its roots to mesmeric/hypnotic theories and practices; accordingly, historian Nicole Edelman (1995) has stated that mediums were both "the daughters and the sisters of somnambulists" (p. 9).

From the beginnings of modern spiritualism in the United States, mediums presented various unusual behaviors. Many of them, presumably under the influence of discarnate spirits, talked at length about the other world and about a variety of moral, philosophical, social, and scientific topics (e.g., Hatch, 1858). Others saw spirits, had impressions, personified the dead, and produced writing. Furthermore, there were mediums that painted, performed music, and sang. In their book *Spiritualism* (1853) Judge John W. Edmonds (1799–1874) and physician George T. Dexter discussed many of these manifestations. Commenting on the automatic writing produced by Dexter, Edmonds stated in the introduction of the book that some of the messages received came from the scientists Swedenborg and Bacon (presumably Sir Francis). He wrote:

> I call attention to the marked difference in thought and expression between ... papers purporting to be written by Bacon or Sweedenborg [sic], and to the remarkable resemblance between the style of each in those papers, and that which characterized the writings of each when on earth. There is something peculiar about the handwriting. All that purports to come from Bacon is always in the same handwriting; so it is with Sweedenborg [sic] ... when he is under the influence, he writes several different kinds of handwriting, and some of them more rapidly than he can write his own. This he can not do when he is not under the influence; and I have never seen any person that could, in his normal condition, write with such rapidity, at one sitting, four or five different kinds of handwriting, each distinctly marked, and having and always retaining its peculiar characteristic. (Edmonds and Dexter, 1853, Vol. 1, p. 50)

It was common for mediums to present communications from a variety of persons, some of which were famous individuals. In addition to the above-mentioned communications from Swedenborg and Bacon, there were many other examples. In Henry Spicer's *Sights and Sounds* (1853) there was mention of communications from such individuals as Washington (pp. 145–146) and Calvin (pp. 147–148). But there were also many mediumistic performances representing the action of common individuals, as well as ancient characters, as seen in the case of a purported Egyptian spirit (Berry, 1876, pp. 193–217). Even more exotic were the communications of spirits claiming to live on other planets, such as those the playwright Victorien Sardou (1831–1908) claimed to receive from planet Jupiter (Sardou, 1858). Impersonation in verbal or written communications was sometimes accompanied by apparent changes of mannerisms and personality. In one such example recorded by Sophia de Morgan (1809–1892), it was stated that the medium's "voice and manner differed much when under different influences" (De Morgan, 1863, p. 90).

Alterations of consciousness in mediums were commented upon by many. In one case the writer stated that "nervous hebetude is distinctly present, the operator is more or less taciturn and irritable, and the intellectual faculties are torpid" (Fairfield, 1875, p. 24). Carl G. Jung (1875-1961) wrote as follows about his cousin, a 15½-year-old medium he studied: "S. W. grew very pale, became cataleptic, drew several deep breaths, and began to speak" (Jung, 1902/1983, p. 19; see also Ellenberger, 1991). It is common to find mention of "trance" throughout the spiritualistic and psychical research literatures to refer to a variety of apparent ASC while mediums produced their phenomena, but from the beginnings it was noticed that not all mediums showed this feature. For example, commenting on their own mediumship, Edmonds and Dexter (1855, p. xviii) pointed out that the first was never "unconscious" while the second frequently was.

Some of the communications appeared to present information that could be verified as related to the ostensible discarnate communicator. An early example referred to communications from the writer's wife:

> The communications were perfectly characteristic of herself and when made in writing exactly corresponded with her original chirography. Besides on one occasion, she addressed me by a name she was in the habit of calling me, which name I had not thought of for years, and I did not at first recognise it. (Cooper, 1867, p. 75)

For our purposes, the paranormality or not of some of these communications is not relevant, although skeptical accounts have not explained away successfully the most spectacular and well-researched cases of some mediums, among them Leonora E. Piper (1857–1950) and Gladys Osborne Leonard (1881–1968; for overviews see Sage, 1904; Smith, 1964). Consequently, we focus on other aspects of their mediumship.

Mrs. Piper showed a variety of alterations of consciousness and corresponding phenomena (Sidgwick, 1915). Psychical researcher Richard Hodgson (1855–1905) observed what he described as an initial stage in which Mrs. Piper was "dreamily conscious of the sitter, and dreamily conscious of 'spirits'" (Hodgson, 1898, p. 397). This was followed by a "fuller and clearer consciousness—we may call it her subliminal consciousness—which is in direct relation ... not so much with our ordinary physical world as with 'another world'" (p. 397). Then came a state in which he thought the "subliminal consciousness (i.e., the subconscious mind) withdraws completely from the control of her body and takes her supraliminal consciousness (i.e., the conscious mind) with it" (p. 398). At the end it seemed to Hodgson that Mrs. Piper returned to her normal consciousness in a reverse order of the previous states. Hodgson wrote:

> But in passing out of trance, the stages are usually of longer duration than when she enters it. She frequently repeats statements apparently made to her by the "communicators" while she is in the purely "subliminal" stage, as though she was a "spirit" controlling her body but not in full possession of it, and, after her supraliminal consciousness has begun to surge up into view, she frequently has visions apparently of the distant or departing "communicators." (pp. 400–401).

In a very thorough account of Mrs. Leonard's mediumship, Una Lady Troubridge (1887–1963) described four different states of consciousness of Mrs. Leonard: (a) "normal," (b) slight drowsiness associated with automatic writing, (c) a "trance," including analgesia and amnesia and in which she manifested a different personality, and (d) a state in which she impersonated deceased individuals. The amnesia in the latter two states was not always present or sustained (Troubridge, 1922, p. 357), resembling spirit possession (Frigerio, 1989). Also, sometimes Mrs. Leonard's body seemed to lose all muscle tone, as has been observed in various ritual contexts, including Balinese dancers possessed by a spirit (Belo, 1960) and among a subgroup of highly hypnotizable and dissociative individuals (Barrett, 1990; Cardeña, 1989). Troubridge also described how the medium Stanislawa Tomczyk initially interpreted her control Moyenne as being an inner part of her personality before concluding that she was a spirit and mentions that it was common to find that the mediums' controls were disinhibited and undersocialized as compared with the mediums' regular personalities, as exemplified by the "alter" Margaret of Doris Fischer and the Feda control of Mrs. Leonard (Troubridge, 1922).

Trance mediumship was one of the phenomena studied during the latter part of the 19th century that contributed to the development of ideas of the subconscious mind and of dissociation (Alvarado, Machado, Zangari, & Zingrone, 2007; Crabtree, 1993). Two important examples of this were the ideas of Pierre Janet and of classical scholar and psychical researcher Frederic W.H. Myers (1843–1901). Janet discussed mediumship in his classic work *L'Automatisme Psychologique* (1889) to support the concept of dissociation. He believed that the phenomena of hypnotized individuals and of mediums were similar, showing the "disaggregation of personal perception and ... the formation of several personalities that developed both successively as well as simultaneously" (Janet, 1889, p. 413). Furthermore, probably following J. M. Charcot's (1825–1893) ideas of the link between hypnosis and psychopathology, Janet thought that mediumship was related to pathology because mediums showed phenomena similar to those shown by hysterics (e.g., partial anesthesias, unconscious acts), and "nervous accidents" (e.g., tremors and nervous crises).

In contrast, Myers did not equate mediumship and pathology and defined it in part as a manifestation of the subliminal (or subconscious) mind. He believed that the utterances of trance mediums "constitute one of many classes of phenomena which occur in sane subjects without entering the normal waking consciousness or forming part of the habitual chain of memory"

(Myers, 1890, p. 437). Myers saw mediumship as one of several psychological processes that illustrated the idea that the subliminal mind communicated with the supraliminal (or conscious) mind through a variety of automatism using sensory and motor means (e.g., hallucinations, speaking; Myers, 1884, 1885, 1889). Regardless of the differences between Janet and Myers, their work on mediumship shows that the phenomenon was part of the development of the constructs of the subconscious mind and of dissociation, a position that mediumship shared with hysteria and hypnosis, among other phenomena.

Into the 20th Century

A systematic study of "debatable phenomena designated by such terms as mesmeric, psychical, and Spiritualistic ... without prejudice or prepossession of any kind, and in the same spirit of exact and unimpassioned inquiry" would be initiated by the Society for Psychical Research (SPR) at the end of the 19th century (Society for Psychical Research, 1882). The foremost members of this society continued doing research on mediumship and hypnosis, both with regard to the nature of these phenomena as well as their possible relationship with potential parapsychological phenomena such as telepathy and precognition (Gauld, 1968; see Luke, 2011). One of their major works was *Phantasms of the Living* (Gurney, Myers, and Podmore, 1886), which presented a meticulous account of the phenomenology of hallucinations in the population at large and of how they provide consistent evidence for some type of anomalous transfer of information. Contemporary research has supported their findings at least with regard to the phenomenal experience of hallucinations among nonclinical samples (Aleman & Larøi, 2008, pp. 61–71). Although Edmund Gurney died fairly young, F. W. H. Myers continued working prolifically on all of these areas and his thoughts culminated in his posthumously published *Human Personality and Its Survival of Bodily Death* (1903; see also Alvarado, 2004).

Before the book was published, Myers had argued:

> I suggest ... that the stream of consciousness in which we habitually live is not the only consciousness which exists in connection with our organism. Our habitual or empirical consciousness may consist of a mere selection from a multitude of thoughts and sensations, of which some at least are equally conscious with those that we empirically know. (Myers, 1892, p. 301)

In articles and in *Human Personality* Myers presented a broad theory to explain apparent disparate phenomena such as dissociation, hypnosis, creativity, parapsychological phenomena, genius, and altered states of consciousness. He advanced the idea of a subliminal mind (which he defined as anything outside of the margins of ordinary consciousness) that also gave evidence of a link from our self to a larger Self, a concept that William James (1842–1910) would discuss as "consciousness at large." Myers wrote:

> I conceive also that no Self of which we can here have cognisance is in reality more than a fragment of a larger Self,—revealed in a fashion at once shifting and limited through an organism not so framed as to afford it full manifestation. (1903, Vol. 1, p. 15)

Although Myers's work was largely overshadowed by that of James, it has been recently championed by a discussion and update of his work in the light of contemporary psychology (Kelly et al., 2007).

It is to the towering figure of William James that we now turn. He is widely acknowledged as one of the most important psychologists of all time. His *Principles of Psychology* (James, 1890) provided a comprehensive summary of most of what was known in psychology at the time, with a philosophical depth and literary elegance that remain unmatched. James's attention to dissociation was evident in his early writings about Mrs. Piper and automatic writing in which he suggested the action of a secondary consciousness directing the phenomena (James, 1886, 1889). In the case of a 21-year-old student that produced writing with his hand and with a planchette, James wrote:

> Here ... we have the consciousness of a subject split into two parts, one of which expresses itself through the mouth, and the other through the hand, whilst both are in communication with the ear. The mouth-consciousness is ignorant of all that the hand suffers or does; the hand-consciousness is ignorant of pin-pricks indicted upon other parts of the body. (James, 1889, p. 551)

Regarding multiplicity, he wrote: "It must be admitted ... that *in certain persons, at least, the total possible consciousness may be split into parts which coexist but mutually ignore each other*, and share the objects of knowledge between them" (1890, Vol. 1, p. 206).

In the *Principles*, besides automatism he also discussed hypnotism, imagination, the mind-body problem (his discussion against jumping from neurological *correlation to causation* should be obligatory reading in neuroscience courses), and an extraordinary chapter on the *stream of thought* (later referred to as the *stream of consciousness*) that influenced not only psychological thought but literary practice through the "stream of consciousness" literary style of one of James's students, Gertrude Stein, and of James Joyce and others (see Cousins, 2011).

It is, however, another of James's masterpieces that has proven to be the cornerstone of the scientific studies of ASC. His *The Varieties of Religious Experience* provided the most cited justification for the study of alterations in consciousness:

> Our normal waking consciousness, rational consciousness as we call it, is but one special type of consciousness, whilst all about it, parted from it by the filmiest of screens, there lie potential forms of consciousness entirely different ... at a touch they are there in all completeness, definite types of mentality which probably somewhere have their field of application and adaptation. No account of the universe in its totality can be final which leaves these other forms of consciousness quite disregarded. (James, 1902/1961, p. 298)

But even before his treatise on religious experience, in his 1896 Lowell lectures he had discussed dreams, hypnosis, automatism, "hysteria," multiple personality (nowadays dissociative identity disorder), and a number of other alterations of consciousness (Taylor, 1983).

Besides Myers and James, many if not most of the pioneers in clinical psychology/psychiatry at the end of the 19th century and beginning of the 20th were very much involved in the study of altered consciousness. To give just some examples, besides his foundational work on dissociation, Pierre Janet (1926) provided a thorough account of various ASC of some of his patients including Madeleine, whom he treated for 22 years and who experienced mystical transports and other intense emotional events. The Swiss professor of psychology Théodore Flournoy (1854–1920) gave a detailed case analysis of the medium Hélène Smith (1861–1929, pseudonym of Catherine Elise Muller) who, among other things, experienced visiting the planet Mars (Flournoy, 1900). He described the creative abilities of the subconscious, particularly as it was expressed via mediumship. His work is also an exemplar of the influence of the psychosocial environment on subconscious creations, including the effects of suggestion and surrounding beliefs, topics of much concern in the study of "hysteria" and hypnosis during the late 19th century (Alvarado, 1991).

In addition to Flournoy, other students of mediumship contributed to develop the idea of the dramatizing powers of the medium's subconscious mind (Alvarado et al., 2007). This was the case of studies with Mrs. Piper (e.g., Sidgwick, 1915; Tanner, 1910). Eleanor Sidgwick (1845–1936) wrote about her:

> I think it is probably a state of self-induced hypnosis in which her hypnotic self personates different characters either consciously and deliberately, or unconsciously and believing herself to be the person she represents, and sometimes probably in a state of consciousness intermediate between the two. In the trance state her normal powers transcend in some directions those of her ordinary waking self. And further—what makes her case of great importance—she can obtain, imperfectly and for the most part fragmentarily, telepathic impressions. (Sidgwick, 1915, p. 330).

In Italy, psychiatrist Enrico Morselli (1852–1929) argued that mediums were persons showing an

> "anomalous psychic constitution, or, at least, on the extreme gradation of the scale of normal variability regarding the coalescence of the psychic elements. In mediums this coalescence is ... labile to the extreme ... with a facility for personal disaggregation." (Morselli, 1908, Vol. 1, p. 93)

Later, French psychical researcher René Sudre (1880–1968) discussed what he referred to as *prosopopesis* or the nonconscious tendency to impersonate, as seen in mediumship, as well as in hypnosis, possession and cases of double and multiple personality (Sudre, 1926). Relatedly, a dramatic aspect of spirit possession in other cultures was discussed by Metraux (1955).

Besides them, many other eminent psychological clinicians and researchers of the time from various countries took a keen interest in dissociation, hypnosis, depersonalization, and similar areas, but the ascent of psychoanalysis within clinical practice and behaviorism within academic psychology condemned the study of ASC to oblivion until a few decades ago (Spiegel & Cardeña, 1991). There were, however, a few exceptions here and there to this exile. Thus, despite Sigmund Freud's (1856–1939) dominant interest in the unconscious causes of symptomatology, his and Joseph Breuer's (1842–1925) *Studies on Hysteria* (1895/1955) contains extraordinary descriptions of altered, "hypnoid states," and Freud would also discuss other alterations of consciousness such as his own dissociative episodes (Freud, 1936), and a case of demonic possession (Freud, 1923).

There were also exceptions within academia such as the short-lived but extraordinarily fruitful research by Clark L. Hull (1884–1952; 1933) of hypnosis, although it was clear that even he was primarily interested in behavior rather than consciousness. After the impressive efforts of both the Society for Psychical Research and the American Society for Psychical Research, Joseph Banks Rhine (1895–1980) led an impressive program of investigation of parapsychological phenomena at Duke University, although, perhaps bccausc of his original training in botany, he did not seem to be as interested in the alterations of consciousness that have long been associated with them (see Alvarado, 1998).

With regard to the neurosciences, some of the most eminent minds during the first half of the 20th century devoted considerable time to researching altered consciousness. Santiago Ramón y Cajal (1852–1934), 1906 Nobel prizewinner and a towering figure for his work on the neuron, did research on hypnosis, mediumship, and parapsychological phenomena, although unfortunately a book he had written on the subject got lost during the Spanish Civil War (Sala et al., 2008). Hans Berger (1873–1941) created the EEG to try to obtain an "objective" measurement of possible telepathic communications, which his sister seemed to experience when he had an unexpected and serious accident (Millet, 2001). Charles Richet (1850–1935), another Nobel laureate for his work on physiology, devoted a substantial part of his life to research hypnosis, mediumship, and psi phenomena (Alvarado, 2008).

We will also mention briefly a tendency outside of both the academic and clinical spheres (some therapists such as C. G. Jung were clearly influenced by a non-academic visionary tradition). For lack of an accepted name, we can refer to it as the goal to radically change or expand one's ordinary state of consciousness. Although some religious and esoteric practices such as alchemy have had this goal (Cavendish, 1967), the period covered by this paper also includes other attempts, some of them still influential, to "expand" or "awaken" or, to paraphrase William Blake's (1757–1827) line, cleanse the doors of perception. This "cleansing" typically includes questioning the absolute value of rationality and the "given-ness" of reality as presented by the senses, an idea present in Plato and recurrent throughout history and in various places such as American transcendentalism. To achieve this goal, various esoteric traditions have advanced practices to alter one's state of consciousness and, at times, to "derange the senses" to use the phrase of the French poet, Arthur Rimbaud (1854–1891; see Cavendish, 1967).

Besides the use of psychoactive drugs, it is worth mentioning other proposals to achieve this altered consciousness. For instance, the anthroposophy of Rudolf Steiner (1861–1925) is not only a set of beliefs about spiritual matters but also includes a number of specific physical exercises (eurythmy) and pedagogical practices, some of which are currently practiced in the Waldorf educational system (see, Ahern, 2009). Also influential in some circles is the very controversial George Gurdjieff (1866–1949) whose "The Work" also proposed a set of movements and psychological practices to uncover one's automatic cognitions and become more mindful. More recently, Charles Tart (1986), while discarding much of the metaphysical baggage of Gudjieff, has discussed his valuable ideas on the automaticity of the mind in the context of meditation and contemporary psychology. Nonetheless, any history of psychology will show that consideration of ASC as a fundamental aspect of the human experience was to a large degree relegated to the academic dustbin during a great part of the 20th century. Although the study of ASC has re-emerged during recent decades (see Beischel, Rock, & Krippner, 2011), it may be still some time before the more comprehensive view of reality of such thinkers as Myers, James, and yes, even Steiner gets a full hearing.

Note

1 Even before mesmerism, there have been discussions of such phenomena as alternate consciousnesses and psychogenic amnesia (Gauld, 1992), and from early mesmerism onward it was proposed that mesmeric and—later—hypnotic techniques provided access to one or more selves that manifest different characteristics from the normal, waking self or identity (Crabtree, 1993; Ellenberger, 1970). Thus, the clinical phenomena that were first discussed under the umbrella of such terms as hysteria, double or multiple personality and, more recently, dissociative identity disorder became associated with hypnotic phenomena and techniques. This is evident, for instance, in the works of Pierre Janet (1889), Breuer and Freud (1895/1955), and many other pioneers of clinical psychology and psychiatry (Ellenberger, 1970; see also Spiegel and Cardeña, 1991). The relationship between hypnosis, suggestion, and identity multiplicity has been contentious. Suffice it to say here that although some authors have criticized the reality of identity multiplicity or fragmentation as mere cultural creation or, worse, iatrogenic suggestion, research has overwhelmingly shown a relationship between dissociation (including identity fragmentation), exposure to trauma, and hypnotic capacity (for a review, see Cardeña & Gleaves, 2007), although this relationship seems to occur only in a subgroup of highly hypnotizable individuals (Terhune, Cardeña, & Lindgren, 2011).

References

Ahern, G. (2009). *Sun at midnight.* James Clarke.

Aleman, A., & Larøi, F. (2008). *Hallucinations: The science of idiosyncratic perception.* American Psychological Association.

Alvarado, C. S. (1991). Iatrogenesis and dissociation: A historical note. *Dissociation, 4*, 36–38.

Alvarado, C. S. (1998). ESP and altered states of consciousness: An overview of conceptual and research trends. *Journal of Parapsychology, 62*, 27–63.

Alvarado, C. S. (2004). On the centenary of Frederic W. H. Myers's *Human personality and its survival of bodily death. Journal of Parapsychology, 68*, 3–43.

Alvarado, C. S. (2008). Aspects of the history of parapsychology: II. Charles Richet's (1850–1935) work in psychical research. *Parapsychology Foundation Lyceum.* http://www.pflyceum.org/447.html.

Alvarado, C. S. (2009). Late nineteenth and early twentieth century discussions of animal magnetism. *International Journal of Clinical and Experimental Hypnosis, 57*, 366–381.

Alvarado, C. S., Machado, F. R., Zangari, W., & Zingrone, N. L. (2007). Perspectivas históricas da influência da mediunidade na construção de idéias psicológicas e psiquiátricas. *Revista de Psiquiatria Clinica, 34*(supp. 1), 42–53.

Bakan, D., Merkur, D., & Weiss, D. S. (2009). *Maimonides' cure of souls: Medieval precursor of psychoanalysis.* State University of New York Press.

Barrett, D. (1990). Deep trance subjects: A schema of two distinct subgroups. In R. G. Kunzendorf (Ed.), *Mental imagery* (pp. 101–112). Plenum.

Beischel, J., Rock, A. J., & Krippner, S. (2011). Reconceptualizing the field of altered consciousness: A 50-year retrospective. In E. Cardeña, & M. Winkelman (Eds.), *Altered consciousness: Multidisciplinary perspectives. Volume 1: History, culture, and the humanities* (pp. 113–135). Praeger.

Belo, J. (1960). *Trance in Bali.* Columbia University Press.

Berry, C. (1876). *Experiences in spiritualism* (2nd ed.). James Burns.

Bertrand, A. (1826). *Du magnétisme animal en France.* J. B. Baillière.

Billot, J. P. (1839). *Recherchés psychologiques sur la cause des phénomènes extraordinaires observes chez les modernes voyans: Improprement dits somnambules magnetiques, ou correspondance sur le magnétisme vital, entre un solitaire et M. Deleuze.* Albanel et Martin.

Breuer, J., & Freud, S. (1955). *Studies on hysteria. The standard edition of the complete psychological works of Sigmund Freud* (Vol. 2). Hogarth Press. (Original work published 1895).

Cahagnet, L. A. (1851). *The celestial telegraph, or, secrets of the life to come, revealed through magnetism* (1st American ed.). J. S. Redfield.

Cardeña, E. (1989). The varieties of possession experience. Association for the *Anthropological Study of Consciousness Quarterly, 5*(2–3), 1–17.

Cardeña, E. (2005). The phenomenology of deep hypnosis: Quiescent and physically active. *International Journal of Clinical & Experimental Hypnosis, 53*, 37–59.

Cardeña, E. (2010). Anomalous experiences during deep hypnosis. In M. Smith (Ed.), *Anomalous experiences: Essays from parapsychological and psychological perspectives* (pp. 93–107). McFarland.

Cardeña, E., & Gleaves, D. (2007). Dissociative disorders. In M. Hersen, S. M. Turner, & D. Beidel (Eds.), *Adult psychopathology & diagnosis* (5th ed., pp. 473–503). Wiley.

Cardeña, E., Lehmann, D., Jonsson, P., Terhune, D., & Faber, P. (2007). The neurophenomenology of hypnosis. *Proceedings of the 50th Annual Convention of the Parapsychological Association*, pp. 17–30.

Cardeña, E., Terhune, D., Lööf, A., & Buratti, S. (2009). Hypnotic experience is related to emotional contagion. *International Journal of Clinical and Experimental Hypnosis, 57*, 33–46.

Cardeña, E., Van Duijl, M. Weiner, L., & Terhune, D. (2009). Possession/trance phenomena. In P. F. Dell & J. A. O'Neil (Eds.), *Dissociation and the dissociative disorders: DSM-V and beyond* (pp. 171–181). Routledge.

Cavendish, R. (1967). *The black arts.* Putnam.

Chastenet de Puysegur, A. M. J. (1820). *Du magnétisme animal consideré dans ses rapports avec diverses branches* (2nd ed.). J. G. Dentu.

Chaves, J. F. (1997). Hypnosis in dentistry: Historical overview and critical appraisal. *Hypnosis International Monographs, 3*, 5–23.

Cooper, R. (1867). *Spiritual experiences, including seven months with the brothers Davenport*. L. Heywood.

Cousins, W. E. (2011). Colored inklings: Altered states of consciousness and literature. In E. Cardeña, & M. Winkelman (Eds.), *Altered consciousness: Multidisciplinary perspectives. Volume 1: History, culture, and the humanities* (pp. 277–300). Praeger.

Crabtree, A. (1988). *Animal magnetism, early hypnotism, and psychical research 1766–1925: An annotated bibliography*. Kraus International.

Crabtree, A. (1993). *From Mesmer to Freud: Magnetic sleep and the roots of psychological healing*. Yale University Press.

Darnton, R. (1968). *Mesmerism and the end of enlightenment in France*. Harvard University Press.

De Certeau, M. (2000). *The possession at Loudun* (Michael B. Smith, Trans.) University of Chicago Press.

Deleuze, J. P. F. (1813). *Histoire critique du magnétisme animal*. Mame.

De Morgan, S. (1863). *From matter to spirit*. Longman, Green, Longman, Roberts & Green.

Dingwall, E. J. (Ed.). (1967–1968). *Abnormal hypnotic phenomena: A survey of nineteenth-century case*, (4 Vols.). J. & A. Churchill.

Dodds, E. R. (1973). *The Greeks and the irrational*. University of California Press. (Original work published 1951).

Edelman, N. (1995). *Voyantes, guérisseusses et visionnaires en France 1785–1914*. Albin Michel.

Edmonds, J. W., & Dexter, G. T. (1853). *Spiritualism* (Vol. 1). Partridge & Brittan.

Edmonds, J. W., & Dexter, G. T. (1855). *Spiritualism* (Vol. 2). Partridge & Brittan.

Ellenberger, H. F. (1970). *The discovery of the unconscious*. Basic Books.

Ellenberger, H. F. (1991). The story of Helene Preiswek: A critical study with new documents. *History of Psychiatry, 2*, 41–52.

Esdaile, J. (1846). *Mesmerism in India, and its practical application in surgery and medicine*. Longman, Brown, Green, and Longmans.

Fairfield, F. G. (1875). *Ten years with spiritual mediums*. D. Appleton.

Flournoy, T. (1900). *From India to the planet Mars: A study of a case of somnambulism*. Harper & Brothers.

Freud, S. (1923). *A seventeenth-century demonological neurosis. The standard edition of the complete psychological works of Sigmund Freud* (Vol. 19). Hogarth Press.

Freud, S. (1936). *A disturbance of memory on the Acropolis. The standard edition of the complete psychological works of Sigmund Freud* (Vol. 22). Hogarth Press.

Frigerio, A. (1989). Levels of possession awareness in Afro-Brazilian religions. *Association for the Anthropological Study of Consciousness Quarterly, 5*(2–3), 5–11.

Garrett, C. (1987). *Spirit possession and popular religion*. Johns Hopkins University Press.

Gauld, A. (1968). *The founders of psychical research*. Schocken.

Gauld, A. (1992). *A history of hypnotism*. Cambridge University Press.

Gregory, W. (1851). *Letters to a candid inquirer, on animal magnetism*. Blanchard and Lea.

Gurney, E. (1884). The stages of hypnotism. *Proceedings of the Society for Psychical Research, 2*, 61–72.

Gurney, E. (1888). Recent experiments in hypnotism. *Proceedings of the Society for Psychical Research, 5*, 3–17.

Gurney, E., Myers, F. W. H., & Podmore, F. (1886). *Phantasms of the living* (2 vols.). Trübner.

Haddock, J. W. (1851). *Somnolism and psycheism; Or, the science of the soul and the phenomena of nervation* (2nd Rev. ed.). James S. Hodson.

Hatch, C. L. V. (1858). *Discourses on religion, morals, philosophy and metaphysics* (Vol. 1). B. F. Hatch.

Hodgson, R. (1898). A further record of observations of certain phenomena of trance. *Proceedings of the Society for Psychical Research, 13*, 284–582.

Hull, C. L. (1933). *Hypnosis and suggestibility: An experimental approach*. D. Appleton-Century.

James, W. (1886). Report of the Committee on Mediumistic Phenomena. *Proceedings of the American Society for Psychical Research, 1*, 102–106.

James, W. (1889). Notes on automatic writing. *Proceedings of the American Society for Psychical Research, 1*, 548–564.

James, W. (1890). *The principles of psychology* (2 vols.). Henry Holt.

James, W. (1961). *The varieties of religious experience: A study in human nature*. Collier. (Original work published 1902).

Janet, P. (1889). *L'automatisme psychologique: Essai de psychologie experimentale sur les formes inférieures de l'activité humaine*. Félix Alcan.

Janet, P. (1926). *De l'angoisse a l'extase. Études sur les croyances et les sentiments*. Félix Alcan.

Janet, P. (1968a). Report on some phenomena of somnambulism. *Journal of the History of the Behavioral Sciences, 4*, 124–131. (Original work published 1885).

Janet, P. (1968b). Second observation of sleep provoked from a distance and the mental suggestion during the somnambulistic state. *Journal of the History of the Behavioral Sciences, 4*, 258–267. (Original work published 1886).

Jung, C. G. (1983). On the psychology and pathology of so-called occult phenomena. In C. G. Jung, *Psychiatric studies* (pp. 3–88). Princeton University Press. (Original work published 1902).

Kelly, E. F., Kelly, E. W., Crabtree, A., Gauld, A., Grosso, M., & Greyson, B. (2007). *Irreducible mind: Toward a psychology for the 21st century*. Rowman & Littlefield.

Kluge, C. A. F. (1811). *Versuch eine Darstellung des animalischen Magnetismus, als Heilmittel*. C. Salfeld.

Lang, W. (1843). *Mesmerism; its history, phenomena and practice*. Fraser.

Laurence, J. R., & Perry, C. (1988). *Hypnosis, will & memory: A psycho-legal history*. Guilford.

Luke, D. (2011). Anomalous phenomena, psi and altered consciousness. In E. Cardeña, & M. Winkelman (Eds.), *Altered consciousness: Multidisciplinary perspectives. Volume 2: Biological and psychological perspectives* (pp. 355–374). Praeger.

Mesmer, F. A. (1779). *Mémoire sur la découverte du magnétisme animal*. P. Fr. Didot le jeune, Librairie Imprimeur de monsieur.

Métraux, A. (1955). Dramatic elements in ritual possession. *Diogenes, 11*, 18–36.

Millett, D. (2001). Hans Berger: From psychic energy to the EEG. *Perspectives in Biology and Medicine, 44*, 522–542.

Moreira-Almeida, A., Lotufo Neto, F., & Cardeña, E. (2008). Comparison between Brazilian spiritist mediumship and dissociative identity disorder. *Journal of Nervous and Mental Disease, 196*, 420–424.

Morselli, E. (1908). *Psicologia e "spiritismo:" Impressioni e note critiche sui fenomeni medianici di Eusapia Paladino* (2 vols.). Fratelli Bocca.

Myers, F. W. H. (1884). On a telepathic explanation of some so-called spiritualistic phenomena: Part I. *Proceedings of the Society for Psychical Research, 2*, 217–237.

Myers, F. W. H. (1885). Automatic writing.—II. *Proceedings of the Society for Psychical Research, 3*, 1–63.

Myers, F. W. H. (1889). Automatic writing.—IV.—The daemon of Socrates. *Proceedings of the Society for Psychical Research, 5*, 522–547.

Myers, F. W. H. (1890). A record of observations of certain phenomena of trance (1). Introduction. *Proceedings of the Society for Psychical Research, 6*, 436–442.

Myers, F. W. H. (1892). The subliminal consciousness: Chapter I. General characteristics of subliminal messages. *Proceedings of the Society for Psychical Research, 7*, 298–327.

Myers, F. W. H. (1903). *Human personality and its survival of bodily death* (2 vols.). Longmans, Green.

Oesterreich, T. K. (1974). *Possession and exorcism among primitive races, in antiquity, the Middle Ages, and modern times*. Causeway. (Original work published 1921).

Pattie, F. A. (1994). *Mesmer and animal magnetism: A chapter in the history of medicine*. Edmonston.

Paulet, J. J. (1784). *Mesmer justifié* (Rev. ed.). No publisher given.

Peter, B. (2005). Gassner's exorcism—not Mesmer's magnetism—is the real predecessor of modern hypnosis. *International Journal of Clinical and Experimental Hypnosis, 53*, 1–12.

Podmore, F. (1902). *Modern spiritualism: A history and a criticism* (2 vols.). Methuen.

Rosen, G. (1969). *Madness in society: Chapters in the historical sociology of mental illness*. Harper.

Sage, M. (1904). *Mrs. Piper and the Society for Psychical Research*. Scott-Thaw.

Sala, J., Cardeña, E., Holgado, M. C., Añez, C., Perez, P., Periñán, R., & Capafons, A. (2008). The contributions of Ramón y Cajal and other Spanish authors to hypnosis. *International Journal of Clinical and Experimental Hypnosis, 56*, 361–372.

Sardou, V. (1858). Des habitations de la Planète Jupiter. *Revue Spirite, 1*, 223–232.

Sidgwick, E. (1915). A contribution to the study of the psychology of Mrs. Piper's trance phenomena. *Proceedings of the Society for Psychical Research, 28*, 1–657.
Smith, S. (1964). *The mediumship of Mrs. Leonard.* University Books.
Society for Psychical Research. (1882). Objects of the society. *Proceedings of the Society for Psychical Research, 1*, 1–4.
Spicer, H. (1853). *Sights and sounds: The mystery of the day.* Thomas Bosworth.
Spiegel, D., & Cardeña, E. (1991). Disintegrated experience: The dissociative disorders revisited. *Journal of Abnormal Psychology, 100*, 366–378.
Sudre, R. (1926). *Introduction* a *la métapsychique humaine.* Payot.
Tanner, A. (1910). *Studies in spiritism.* D. Appleton.
Tart, C. T. (1986). *Waking up: Overcoming the obstacles to human potential.* New Science Library.
Taylor, E. (1983). *William James on exceptional mental states. The 1896 Lowell lectures.* Scribner.
Terhune, D. B., Cardeña, E., & Lindgren, M. (2011). Dissociative tendencies and individual differences in high hypnotic suggestibility. *Cognitive Neuropsychiatry, 16,* 113–135.
Troubridge, U. L. (1922). The *modus operandi* in so-called mediumistic trance. *Proceedings of the Society for Psychical Research, 32*, 344–378.
Van Ommeren, M. V., Sharma, B., Komproe, I., Sharma, G. K., Cardeña, E., de Jong, J. T., Poudyal, B., & Makaju, R. (2001). Trauma and loss as determinants of medically unexplained epidemic illness in a Bhutanese refugee camp. *Psychological Medicine, 31*, 1259–1267.
Zacharias, G. (1980). *The satanic cult.* Allen & Unwin.

10

Mediumship and Psychical Research*

Carlos S. Alvarado

During the nineteenth century, many phenomena were important for the development of psychical research, or the systematic study of psychic phenomena. One of the most influential was mediumship. Similar to the role nineteenth-century hysterics and hypnotic subjects played in the development of ideas about pathology and the mind during the nineteenth century (Alvarado, 2009), mediums were instrumental in focusing the attention of researchers in ways that produced important methodological and conceptual developments in psychical research. My discussion of the topic will be confined to early nineteenth- and twentieth-century developments, periods that combined both the heyday of mediumship as well as the development of psychical research as a scientific discipline.

The Medium in Spiritualism

The appearance of the professional medium in the United States in the mid-nineteenth century was preceded by a tradition of communication from the dead that stretches back into antiquity (Ogden, 2001). Furthermore, the arrival of modem mediums was heralded by a variety of somnambulistic, trance, and visionary phenomena coming from both religious and lay settings (Crabtree, 1993).

Following the raps taking place in the presence of the Fox sisters in Hydesville, New York, in 1848, mediumship developed as a profession. The raps moved from the Hydesville home to other places where special meetings, later called séances, were held for the purpose of contacting the dead. This led the sisters to develop a reputation as intermediaries between the earthly and the spiritual worlds (Capron, 1885). Their well-known performances and the controversies they inspired led to what early historian of American Spiritualism and medium Emma Hardinge (later Britten, 1823–1899) described in her book, *Modern American Spiritualism*, as the formation of circles in every other house in town, and the rapid development of media in every other family" (Britten, 1870).

Spiritualism, and its tenet that the deceased could communicate with the living, spread thanks to the mental and physical manifestations of mediums, who became the ambassadors and the prophets of the new movements. Among them were Florence Cook (1856–1904), Ira E. (1839–1911) and William H. Davenport (1841–1877), George T. Dexter, Ermance Dufaux de la Jonchere (b. 1841), John W. Edmonds (1799–1874), William Eglinton (1858–1933), Emma Hardinge, Cora L.V. Hatch (1840–1923), D. D. Home (1833–1886), and Asa W. Sprague (1827–1862), among many others. These and countless other mediums were instrumental in spreading the movement of Spiritualism. But mediumship also affected psychical research.

*Republished with permission from C. Moreman (Ed.), *The spiritualist movement: Speaking with the dead in America and around the world* (Vol. 2, pp. 127–144). Praeger, 2013.

The Medium and Psychical Research

French physiologist Charles Richet (1850–1935) once wrote that "there is no metapsychics [psychical research] without a medium" (Richet, 1922). While this is an obvious exaggeration, there is no question that mediumship has been essential to the development of psychical research. Because mediums presented the possibility of observing phenomena repeatedly under conditions of some control, they were an important catalyst for the development of psychical research. That is, instead of depending solely on such difficult-to-observe spontaneous phenomena as poltergeists, hauntings, and apparitions of the dead, in mediumship, psychical researchers had a recurrent source of observable phenomena that allowed them to impose semi-experimental conditions under which more systematic observations were possible.

A good part of the psychical research of later years took place largely because of the performances of a great number of mediums who produced phenomena repeatedly. Mediumship had an important place in the work of the London-based Society for Psychical Research (SPR), which was founded in 1882. The SPR's original research program did not include mediumship as such except for a committee organized to look into "the various physical phenomena commonly called Spiritualistic; with an attempt to discover their causes and general law" (Society for Psychical Research, 1882). Nonetheless, both mental and physical mediumship were frequently discussed in the SPR's *Proceedings*. For the period from 1882 to 1900, out of 204 papers published in this journal, 23 percent were devoted to séance reports. I am not counting here conceptual and methodological discussions of mediumship that were also published in the *Proceedings*. In later years of this publication, as well as in other journals, mediumship continued to be an important topic (see Table 10.1).

Perhaps no other nineteenth-century mediums were as influential in the scientific study of mediumship than American mental medium Leonora E. Piper (1857–1950) and the Italian physical medium Eusapia Palladino (1854–1918). Mrs. Piper was brought to psychical research by the famous American philosopher and psychologist William James (1842–1910) (James, 1890). Representing the SPR, Richard Hodgson (1855–1905) started studying Mrs. Piper in 1887 and ended by publishing a report years later in the SPR Proceedings in which he accepted the veridical nature of some of her communications (Hodgson, 1892).

Mrs. Piper's willingness to take part in investigations provided psychical research for the first time in history with a great deal of systematic and controlled long-term studies of mental mediumship. Following Hodgson's initial studies, which appeared in print after later SPR work cited later in this chapter, Mrs. Piper traveled to England in 1889 to be investigated by the SPR. The researchers that investigated her insisted that some of her communications could not be explained by such

Table 10.1. Mediumship Papers in Psychical Research Journals, 1921-1930*

Journal	Place of Publication	Number of Papers	% Mediumship Papers
Proceedings of the Society for Psychical Research	England	67	57
Revue Métapsychique	France	284	25
Proceedings of the Society for Psychical Research American	United States	12	58

* The year 1921 was chosen because this was the first year of publication of the *Revue Métapsychique*, although under a different title. The *Proceedings of the American Society for Psychical Research* used here go up to 1927 and then start publication again in 1933. On the count of papers I have not included obituaries, short notes about the organizations that published the journals, and book notices or reviews.

conventional explanations as chance or fraud. (Leaf, 1890; Lodge, 1890). Later studies recorded Mrs. Piper's mentation with great care, contributing evidence for the existence of the supernormal or veridical elements in trance mediumship (Hodgson, 1898; Hyslop, 1901).

Palladino, on the other hand, as mainly a medium of telekinetic and materialization events, was an important catalyst for the investigation of mediumistic phenomena even though she was caught in fraud more than once (Alvarado, 2011). Several scientists and scholars were impressed by her, including German philosopher Carl du Prel (1839–1899), Polish psychologist Julian Ochorowicz (1850–1917), Russian diplomat and scholar Alexandre Aksakof (1832–1903), British physicist Oliver Lodge (1851–1940), Italian psychiatrist and criminologist Cesare Lombroso (1835–1909), and the previously mentioned French physiologist Charles Richet.

An early investigation conducted in Milan in 1892 marked the beginning of general scientific interest in and great controversy about her mediumship (Aksakof et al., 1893). After these sittings, Palladino attracted the attention of many researchers throughout Europe, as can be seen in the published literature (Lodge, 1894; Morselli, 1908).

Although the performances of Piper and Palladino encouraged the development of psychical research with mediums, the performances of other mediums indirectly encouraged a different sort of research. Those of controversial American medium Margery (Mina Stinson Crandon, 1889–1941) (Tietze, 1973), and the studies of mental mediums conducted by John F. Thomas (1874–1940) (Thomas, 1937), were influential in shaping the course of the famous laboratory ESP experiments conducted by Joseph Banks Rhine (1895–1980). Rhine and his wife and colleague Louisa E. Rhine (1891–1983) had had a séance with Margery that convinced them she used fraud. (J. B. Rhine & L. E. Rhine, 1927). Although in their mental mediumship work with Thomas, the Rhines obtained veridical communications, eventually they reached a state of doubt that they felt mediumistic séances could not resolve. The question in their minds was the following: Could the veridical impressions mediums conveyed be explained only as spirit influence, or was ESP between the medium and the sitters a better explanation? By the time J. B. Rhine published his now classic book *Extra-Sensory Perception* in 1934, he had decided to focus his research program on studying the psychic abilities of the living, implying that these abilities needed to be understood on their own terms and in relation to other phenomena before the problem of discarnate agency could be scientifically addressed (Rhine, 1934a). In an article published the same year, Rhine wrote that "as long as the natural powers of the sensitive are unknown and unmeasured, there can be only conjecture or uncertain belief as to the survival hypothesis" (Rhine, 1934b). Eventually, the Rhines turned to the experimental studies of ESP (and later psychokinesis) that affected the course of psychical research. What had been to a great extent the study of mediums in the séance room became a laboratory-based science studying such volunteer participants as college students (Mauskopf & McVaugh, 1980).

In time, the study of mediumship started to decline. However, this is not to say there were no studies of mediums published during the 1930s and later. Examples include work with mental mediums Gladys Osborne Leonard (1882–1968) (Irving, 1943) and Eileen J. Garrett (1893–1970) (Goldney & Soal, 1938) not to mention some work with physical mediums (Osty & Osty, 1932).

Methodological Aspects of the Study of Mediumship

Like other phenomena, among them telepathy, mediumship presented an opportunity for the development of methodology to study the claims of specific mediums. This was the case both with mental and physical mediumship.

Controlling the Mediums and Recording the Phenomena

Early critiques of physical mediumship in SPR circles (see, for example, Sidgwick, 1886) heightened the sensibilities of many to the problems of fraud and, more importantly, of malobservation, as seen in S. J. Davey's attempt to show the weakness of some testimony in favor of physical mediumship under specific conditions (Davey, 1887; also see Hodgson, 1887, 1892). Davey showed that witnesses of a mock séance were not able to recall the actual proceedings accurately. I am not saying that the results of these studies can be generalized to all séance contexts, but there is no doubt that these issues contributed not only to the raising of standards of evidence for physical mediumship, but simultaneously to the increase of skepticism about such phenomena.

Over time, a variety of mediums provided the opportunity for the development of better scientific controls. For example, Palladino's attempts at fraud involved liberating her hands. This habit of hers led to the development of techniques to control for such actions in later research (Courtier, 1908; Feilding, Baggally, & Carrington, 1909).

Palladino also provided the context for the development of research using instrumental recording and testing of physical phenomena, a trend that had started with some early nineteenth-century efforts (Crookes, 1874). For example, Italian physiologist Filippo Bottazzi (1867–1941) (Bottazzi, 1907) obtained recordings in séances of presumed telekinetic action on a variety of instruments, as did researchers at the séances conducted at the Institut General Psychologique in Paris (Courtier, 1905–1908). In the latter study, a table was outfitted so that whenever any of its legs was raised, a circuit closed and activated a recording needle, providing instrumental evidence of each elevation.

Work conducted with Mrs. Piper also raised methodological standards. She performed under controlled conditions designed to prevent fraud such as the selection of strangers as sitters. According to Oliver Lodge, "By introducing anonymous strangers, and by catechising her myself in various ways, I have satisfied myself that much of the information she possesses in the trance state is not acquired by ordinary commonplace methods, but that she has some unusual means of acquiring information" (Lodge, 1890, p. 443). Furthermore, Lodge stated that Mrs. Piper's correspondence was examined to control for normal sources of information.

Before work with Mrs. Piper, most sittings had been reported from memory and not recorded verbatim at the time (For an exception in the mid-nineteenth century, see Simon, 1923). Records compiled from memory were open to the criticisms of omission or embellishment. Early in Mrs. Piper's career, William James commented on the importance of having a stenographer take verbatim notes, which could then become permanent records of the sittings (James, 1886). James used this method to record some of his sittings with the medium. In his initial studies, Hodgson (1892) also used stenographic recordings, amplifying the records with notes made after the séances. There are also examples of note-taking during the séances (Hyslop, 1901; Lodge, 1890), and verbatim recording became standard in later research (Tanner, 1910, 1937), considerably improving the reliability of the records.

Quantitative and Qualitative Analyses of Mediumship

The study of statements provided by mental mediums has benefited psychical research methodologically because it provided impetus for the development of measurement tools to analyze verbal material. Characteristics of readings given by mediums led researchers to realize early on how difficult it was to evaluate chance as a possible explanation for the medium's veridical mentation. Several early researchers made concerted attempts to deal with the chance argument (see Hyslop, 1919; Prince, 1923; Sidgwick, 1921; Saltmarsh, 1929; Saltmarsh & Soal, 1930; Pratt, 1936; Thomas, 1937). For example, English researcher Herbert Francis Saltmarsh (1881–1943) devised a scoring system to evaluate the mentation of mental medium Mrs. Warren Elliott (Elliot, 1929). Saltmarsh assigned a score of one to general statements that might have applied to many individuals, a score of five to more specific statements that were less relevant to large numbers of people, and a score of 20 to statements that were particularly specific for the sitter. Following Hyslop (1919) before him, Saltmarsh attempted to exclude the possibility of coincidence by comparing the scores of the communications for the sitters against scores obtained from other individuals who had not sat with the medium and were not connected to the study.

Regardless of the validity of these early techniques, they must be regarded as an important part of the history of quantitative analysis in parapsychology. Later workers built on these efforts to develop statistical techniques that allowed for the study of free-response ESP in persons other than mediums. Pratt and Birge (1948) took this view when they presented a short literature review in their influential paper on the evaluation of verbal material in parapsychology.

These attempts at quantitative assessment notwithstanding, most of the studies with mediums were qualitative. Many of these early studies remain unrivaled in detail, depth, and incisiveness. An example was Swiss psychologist Theodore Flournoy's (1854–1920) study of medium Hélène Smith (pseudonym of Catherine Elise Muller, 1861–1929). Flournoy (1900) reported observations about the medium's life history, examples of dissociative and hallucinatory experiences in her daily life, examinations of her sensory and motor functioning and the different automatisms that characterized her mediumship, as well as a detailed description and analysis of her mediumistic utterances. He presented psychological analyses of the genesis, manifestation, and development of Smith's phenomena, which to this day is one of the most influential early examples on record of a psychological analysis of a single mediumistic case.

Other important studies in which trances, mediumistic mentation, and veridical statements were analyzed are summarized in Table 10.2.

Table 10.2. Further Examples of Qualitative Analyses of Mental Mediumship

Reference	Medium	Content
Hyslop (1912)	Mrs. Chenoweth (Minnie Soule, 1867-1936) and Mrs. Smead	Analysis of the process of communication seen as visual imagery from communicator to spirit control and to medium. Consideration of possible sources of mistakes.
Prince (1927)	Pearl Curran (1883-1937)	Description and analysis of literary productions. Exploration of possible normal sources of information such as the medium's education and exposure to literature.
Osty (1928)	Augustine Lesage (1874-1954)	Biography of medium. Discussion of paintings, techniques used in their production, changes in themes, and claims of authorship.
Deonna (1932)	Hélène Smith (Catherine Elise Muller 1861-1929)	Description of mediumistic paintings and how they were produced, and discussion of medium's visions, motivations, and opinions.
Balfour (1935)	Mrs. Willett (Mrs. Charles Coombe Tenant, 1874-1956)	Discussion of degrees of trance, visual imagery, feelings of presence, emotions, impulses, and verbal expressions.

Several reports of physical mediumship were very rich not only in the description of the phenomena, but in the use of instrumentation of different sorts, a topic briefly mentioned earlier in this chapter in relation to Palladino. Well-known early examples of such studies were those conducted by William Crookes (1874) with D. D. Home. Crookes was able to use a variety of devices to explore the properties of the "psychic force" he believed Home projected from his body during these events. His account included descriptions of tests designed to determine how much force Home could produce and whether this force could work through water.

Another example of instrumented studies was the use of balances to weigh both tables and the medium in the table levitation studies conducted by William J. Crawford (1881–1920) with Kathleen Goligher and her family circle (Crawford, 1918). A variety of ingenious devices were used by others to study physical phenomena (Grunwald, 1920; Osty & Osty, 1932). Others emphasized the use of photography for various purposes, such as the recording of phenomena, among them materializations (von Schrenck-Notzing, 1920).

Other studies consisted of analyses of published materials. In a remarkable study, Mrs. Sidgwick reviewed a great number of published observations with Mrs. Piper (Sidgwick, 1915). She focused on describing and analyzing specific spirit controls and communicators, the medium's different states of consciousness, the effects of sitters on the phenomena, fictitious communicators, the relationship of spirit controls to Mrs. Piper, and whether the medium remembered events from one state of consciousness to another.

Italian psychical researcher Ernesto Bozzano (1862–1943) also wrote overviews of the literature presenting many cases of mediumistic phenomena. This work included such topics as mediumistic xenoglossy (Bozzano, 1932), or speaking in languages unknown to the medium, and transfiguration (Bozzano, 1934), or those cases in which the medium's facial features were reported to change.

Conceptual Aspects of Mediumship

Mediumship presented to psychical research the opportunity to develop a variety of theoretical concepts. This included the idea of survival of death, concepts of force, and the concept of a nonconscious level of the mind.

Survival of Death

Early Spiritualism was full of nonevidential mediumistic communications about moral, religious, and philosophical topics (Edmonds & Dexter, 1853). Although these writings were popular among Spiritualists and the general public, they generally were unimpressive to the psychical researcher because they were too general in content and impossible to verify. What most psychical researchers were, and still are, looking for are evidential phenomena. Unlike philosophical, religious, and eschatological communications of uncertain origin, it was what could be checked, what could at the very least be identified as having a source different from the medium's own mind, that drew most researchers' interest. This included information about names, relationships, behaviors, and other incidents referring to a deceased individual communicated through a medium that could be investigated to see if it was truthful information about such individual. Such interest in the evidential was directly connected with its perceived potential to support the idea of survival of death.

The early SPR studies with Mrs. Piper, for example, were a case in point of evidential studies. Another example was the study of the famous cross-correspondences: communications received through different mediums that used allusions to classical literature and were understandable only when put together. Many SPR researchers believed these communications indicated the action of a discarnate organizing consciousness (Saltmarsh, 1938).

Opinions were divided on whether discarnate agency or ESP was the best explanation for the evidence. For example, regarding Mrs. Piper, British classical scholar and banker Walter Leaf (1852–1927) voted for telepathy, whereas American philosopher and psychical researcher James H. Hyslop (1854–1920) defended the theory of discarnate spirits (Leaf, 1890; Hyslop, 1901). Such discussions continue to the present day. But regardless of explanations, the phenomena of mental mediumship did much to maintain the issue of survival of death in the conceptual agenda of psychical researchers.

Concepts of Force

In addition to the survival issue, mediums fueled researchers' imaginations as they sought to develop many other ideas about the nature of mediumship. Among these was a concept that, while forgotten by many modern parapsychologists, formed part of old ideas related to mediumship. This was the idea that some sort of force or field was related to the workings of mediumship, a loosely postulated model that began to be used starting in the middle of the nineteenth century (Alvarado, 2006).

One early example from the Spiritualist literature was American social reformer Adin Ballou's (1803–1890) claim that mediums had an abundance of "spiricity" (Ballou, 1853) an ethereal substance used by spirits in their communications. These ideas were also promoted by the spirit communicators themselves. Mediumistic communications led Allan Kardec (pseudonym of Hippolyte Leon Denizard Rivail, 1804–1869) to affirm the existence of a "fluidic" semiphysical body called the "perispirit" that connected the physical body to the spirit (Kardec, 1863). Psychic phenomena were said to take place through the combination of the perispirits of both dead and living persons. In mental phenomena, the affinity between the perispirits could serve as a conduit for the transfer of information. That is, the discarnate spirit was able to communicate its thoughts to the medium through interperispiritual interaction.

Later in the nineteenth century, Hodgson recorded spirit communications about a "light," which was believed to facilitate communications in connection to Mrs. Piper's body (Hodgson, 1898). Such a concept and the idea that a "power" or an emanation existed around the medium that was particularly sensitive to thoughts from spirits were also mentioned through medium Gladys Osborne Leonard (Thomas, 1928).

There are more examples of concepts of mysterious substances or forces to account for mental phenomena, but such ideas were particularly popular as explanations for physical mediumship (Alvarado, 2006). From the beginning of interest in mediumship, nineteenth-century writers skeptical about the discarnate agency explanation argued that the medium's vital force was unconsciously guided by the medium or the sitters to produce physical effects (Rogers, 1853). Similar ideas based on the phenomena of physical mediums came into the twentieth century under different names. In Italy, psychiatrist Enrico Morselli (1852–1929) referred to a "bio-psychic ondulatory emanation" projected from Palladino (Morselli, 1908). In Germany, physician Albert F. von Schrenck-Notzing (1862–1929) wrote about an "energetic psychophysical emanation," (Schrenck-Notzing, 1925) while in France, physician Gustave Geley (1865–1924) said that materializations were "the medium herself, partially exteriorized" (Geley, 1920).

These ideas may not have general acceptance today among the scientific students of psychic phenomena, but they were influential at the time and contributed to the development of conceptual agendas in psychical research.

The Mediumistic Subconscious

Just as hypnosis produced much material interpreted as supporting the concept of a subconscious mind during the nineteenth century, mediumship, particularly mental mediumship, provided manifestations supporting the idea at a time when hypnosis was much less accepted than it is today. While there were several discussions of mediumship in relation to the subconscious and to dissociation, some of which came from outside psychical research (Janet, 1889), I will emphasize here a few examples developed by psychical researchers, whose enterprise was intimately associated with the workings of hidden levels of the mind (Alvarado, 2002; Crabtree, 1993).

While many used phenomena associated with mediumship, such as table turning, and other motor automatisms, to discuss unconscious muscular movements (Chevreul, 1854), the most sophisticated of the early models was that one produced by English classical scholar and psychical researcher Frederic W. H. Myers (1843–1901). He assumed the existence of an intelligent subconscious that, in addition to regulating the phenomena of hysteria, hypnosis, creativity, and dreams, also included manifestations such as telepathy. In an 1884 paper on automatic writing, Myers (1884) proposed that "*some* of the effects which Spiritualists ascribe to spirits are referable to the unconscious action of the writer's own mind" (p. 237). In a later paper discussing a case of intelligent communications, Myers (1885, p. 24) argued that the details of the communications went beyond simple unconscious cerebration. It was a case, he argued, "where the unconscious cerebral action was not subordinated to the conscious,—did not depend for its manifestation on the direction of the conscious attention elsewhere, but presented itself as co-ordinated with the conscious action, and as able to force itself upon the attention of the waking mind." Furthermore, the content of the case suggested telepathy, an element that expanded the scope of the psychological subconscious to "supernormal" processes. Myers (1885, p. 27) came to believe that an understanding of these phenomena required postulating the existence of a secondary self "which is apparently neither fugitive nor incidental merely—a delirium or a dream—but may possess, for a time at least, a kind of continuous individuality, a purposive activity of its own." The secondary self, Myers wrote in this second paper, concerned itself with handling telepathic information. Extending his psychological analysis further, Myers discussed other topics. He argued that automatisms could be the bearers of messages from the automatist's own mind. In his opinion: "They present themselves to us as messages communicated from one stratum to another stratum of the same personality. Originating in some deeper zone of a man's being, they float up into superficial consciousness as deeds, visions, words, ready-made and full-blown, without any accompanying perception of the elaborative process which has made them what they are" (Myers, 1889, p. 524).

Myers (1889, p. 525) considered the recognition of this message-bearing quality of automatisms an important conceptual development. But he was even more interested in pointing out that some of these messages were veridical. The automatic productions discussed in his 1885 paper seemed to show thought-transference from the automatist's husband. While Myers became convinced of spirit communication, he related this process to the subliminal mind. Writing in his well-known book *Human Personality and Its Survival of Bodily Death*, he referred to Mrs. Piper as a case in which the medium's subliminal mind was used by discarnate spirits to communicate, though he acknowledged the possibility of direct possession of the medium by a discarnate spirit (Myers, 1903, p. 250). Such ideas influenced many other workers in psychical research for generations to come, promoting a conceptual framework that presented the subconscious mind as a major theoretical idea with which to study psychic phenomena.

The existence of the subconscious was also accepted by other psychical researchers, such as Aksakof (1906), who defended the Spiritualistic point of view. Mediumship, he wrote, led to the belief that "In man there exists an interior consciousness, apparently independent from the exterior one, gifted with its own will and intelligence ... this interior consciousness is not under the dominion of the exterior one ... it is not a single manifestation of the latter, because the two consciousnesses do not always act simultaneously" (p. 194).

Similar in some ways to both Myers and Aksakof, Hyslop discussed spirit communications under the assumption that the subconscious of the medium could be involved in the process. This could take place by "intrusions of the subliminal of its own habits into the message" (Hyslop, 1910, p. 219). In his view, many communications consisted of telepathic images by a spirit to the medium's spirit control, who then relayed the message to the medium. These images could be "transferred to the subconsciousness of the medium and thus modify its stratum" (p. 88).

The normal psychological subconscious was also invoked to account for all sorts of personalities manifested through mediums. Theodore Flournoy's (1900) work with Hélène Smith's mediumistic communications, situated between psychology and psychical research, was particularly important in this regard. In Flournoy's view, such phenomena were subconscious creations showing no evidence of spirit influence. Writing about the medium's spirit control, Leopold, Flournoy stated that he was a secondary personality who acted like a "spirit-guide, giving good advice relative to the manner of acting towards the medium; of stage manager ...; of benevolently disposed interpreter willing to furnish explanations of all that is obscure; of censor of morals ...; of sympathetic physician" (p. 12).

Other researchers argued that changes of personality in mediums could be combined with veridical statements in particular mediumistic performances (Leaf, 1926). Later authors defended the existence of a mediumistic subconscious, including psychic phenomena such as telepathy and materializations in its functions (Morselli, 1908).

All of the previously mentioned ideas—from Myers's to those of today—have nurtured the generally made assumption that psychic phenomena are a function of the subconscious mind.

Concluding Remarks

Mediums have been important for the development of psychical research. To begin, mental and physical mediumship contributed to the agenda of psychical research, providing phenomena in need of study. The numerous reports of research with mediums gave much direction to the field.

Furthermore, the performances of mediums and their interaction with researchers have provided the context for a variety of methodological developments, such as control techniques and instrumented measurements. Conceptual contributions such as the idea of survival of bodily death and concepts of force and the nature of the subconscious mind are a result of this interaction. The latter has been particularly important for psychical research as a scientific discipline, providing the field both with a general conceptual framework, as well as with a link to psychology. All of these developments, nurtured in part by mediumship, contributed to the growth of psychical research as a scientific discipline.

References

Aksakof, A. (n. d., ca 1906). *Animismo y espiritismo: Ensayo de un exémen critico de los fenómenos medianímicos* (Vol. 2). Carbonell y Esteva

Aksakof, A., Schiaparelli, G., Du Prel, C., Brofferio, A., Gerosa, G., Ermacora, G. B., ... & Lombroso, C. (1893). Rapport de la commission réunie à Milan pour l'étude des phénomènes psychiques. *Annales des Sciences Psychiques, 3*, 39–64.

Alvarado, C. S. (2002). Dissociation in Britain during the late nineteenth century: The Society for Psychical Research, 1882–1900. *Journal of Trauma and Dissociation, 3*, 9–33.

Alvarado, C. S. (2006). Human radiations: Concepts of force in mesmerism, spiritualism and psychical research. *Journal of the Society for Psychical Research, 70*, 138–162.

Alvarado, C. S. (2009). Nineteenth-century hysteria and hypnosis: A historical note on Blanche Wittmann. *Australian Journal of Clinical and Experimental Hypnosis, 37*, 21–36.

Alvarado, C. S. (2011). Eusapia Palladino: An autobiographical essay. *Journal of Scientific Exploration, 25*, 77–101.

Ballou, A. (1853). *An exposition of views respecting the modern spiritual manifestations.* Edward Howell.

Bottazzi, F. (1907). The unexplored regions of human biology: Observations and experiments with Eusapia Paladino. *Annals of Psychical Science, 6*, 149–156, 260–290, 377–422.

Bozzano, E. (1932). *Polyglot mediumship (Xenoglossy).* Rider.

Bozzano, E. (1934). Dei fenomeni di "transfigurazione". *La Ricerca Psichica, 34*, 65–76, 140–150, 264–276, 330–342.

Britten, E. H. (1870). *Modern American spiritualism: A twenty year's record of the communion between earth and the world of spirits* (3rd ed.). Author.

Capron, E. W. (1855). *Modern spiritualism: Its facts and fanaticisms, its consistencies and contradictions.* Bela Marsh.

Chevreul, M. E. (1854). *De la baguette divinatoire, du pendule dit explorateur et des tables tournantes.* Mallet-Bachelier.

Courtier, J. (1908). Rapport sur les séances d'Eusapia Paladino à l'Institut General Psychologique. *Bulletin de l'Institut General Psychologique, 8*, 415–546.

Crabtree, A. (1993). *From Mesmer to Freud: Magnetic sleep and the roots of psychological healing.* Yale University Press.

Crawford, W. J. (1918). *The reality of psychic phenomena: Raps, levitations, etc.* (2nd ed.). John M. Watkins.

Crookes, W. (1874). *Researches in the phenomena of spiritualism.* J. Bums.

Davey, S. J. (1887). The possibilities of malobservation and lapse of memory from a practical point of view: Experimental investigation. *Proceedings of the Society for Psychical Research, 4*, 405–495.

Deonna, W. (1932). *De la planète Mars en terre sainte: Art et subconscient.* E. de Boccard.

Edmonds, J. W., & Dexter, G. T. (1853). *Spiritualism* (Vol. 1). Partridge and Brittan.

Feilding, E., Baggally, W. W., & Carrington, H. (1909). Report on a series of sittings with Eusapia Palladino. *Proceedings of the Society for Psychical Research, 23*, 309–569.

Flournoy, T. (1900). *From India to the planet Mars: A study of a case of somnambulism.* Harper and Brothers.

Geley, G. (1920). *From the unconscious to the conscious.* William Collins.

Gerald, W. Earl of Balfour (1935). A study of the psychological aspects of Mrs. Willett's mediumship, and of the statements of the communicators concerning process. *Proceedings of the Society for Psychical Research, 43*, 41–318.

Goldney, K. M., & Soal, S. G. (1938). Report on a series of experiments with Mrs Eileen Garrett. *Proceedings of the Society for Psychical Research, 45*, 43–87.

Grunwald, F. (1920). *Physikalisch-mediumistische Untersuchungen.* Johannes Baum.

Hodgson, R., & Davey, S. J. (1887). The possibilities of mal-observation and lapse of memory from a practical point of view. *Proceedings of the Society for Psychical Research, 4*, 381–495.

Hodgson, R. (1892). A record of observations of certain phenomena of trance. *Proceedings of the Society for Psychical Research, 8*, 1–167.

Hodgson, R. (1892). Mr. Davey's imitations by conjuring of phenomena sometimes attributed to spirit agency. *Proceedings of the Society for Psychical Research, 8*, 253–310.

Hodgson, R. (1898). A further record of observations of certain phenomena of trance. *Proceedings of the Society for Psychical Research, 13*, 284–582.
Hyslop, J. H. (1901). A further record of observations of certain phenomena of trance. *Proceedings of the Society for Psychical Research, 16*, 1–649.
Hyslop, J. H. (1910). Record and discussion of mediumistic experiments. *Proceedings of the American Society for Psychical Research, 4*(1), 1–812.
Hyslop, J. H. (1912). A record of experiments. *Proceedings of the American Society for Psychical Research, 6*, 1–976.
Hyslop, J. H. (1919). Chance coincidence and guessing in a mediumistic experiment. *Proceedings of the American Society for Psychical Research, 13*, 5–88.
Irving, W. S. (1943). Further tests with Mrs. Leonard. *Journal of the American Society for Psychical Research, 37*, 192–209.
James, W. (1886). Report of the Committee on Mediumistic Phenomena. *Proceedings of the American Society for Psychical Research, 1*, 102–106.
James, W. (1890). A record of observations of certain phenomena of trance: Part III. *Proceedings of the Society for Psychical Research, 6*, 651–659.
Janet, P. (1889). *L'automatisme psychologique: Essai de psychologic expérimentale sur les formes inferieures de l'activite humaine*. Félix Alcan.
Kardec, A. (1863). *Spiritisme experimental: Le livre des mediums, ou guide des mediums et des evocateurs* (6th ed.). Didier.
Leaf, W. (1890). A record of observations of certain phenomena of trance (3): Part II. *Proceedings of the Society for Psychical Research, 6*, 558–546.
Lodge, O. (1890). A record of observations of certain phenomena of trance (2): Part I. *Proceedings of the Society for Psychical Research, 6*, 443–457.
Lodge, O. J. (1894). Experience of unusual physical phenomena occurring in the presence of an entranced person (Eusapia Paladino). *Journal of the Society for Psychical Research, 6*, 306–336, 346–360.
Mauskopf, S. H., & McVaugh, M. R. (1980). *The elusive science: Origins of experimental psychical research.* Johns Hopkins University Press.
Morselli, E. (1908). *Psicologia e spiritismo: Impressioni e note critiche sui fenomeni medianici di Eusapia Paladino.* (2 Vols.). Fratelli Bocca.
Myers, F. W. H. (1884). On a telepathic explanation of some so-called spiritualistic phenomena: Part I. *Proceedings of the Society for Psychical Research, 2*, 217–237.
Myers, F. W. H. (1885). Automatic writing.—II. *Proceedings of the Society for Psychical Research 3*, 1–63.
Myers, F. W. H. (1889). Automatic Writing. IV. The Daemon of Socrates. *Proceedings of the Society for Psychical Research, 5*, 522–547.
Myers, F. W. H. (1903). *Human personality and its survival of bodily death.* (Vol. 2.). Longmans, Green.
Ogden, D. (2001). *Greek and Roman necromancy*. Princeton University Press.
Osty, E. & Osty, M. (1932). *Les pouvoirs inconnus de l'esprit sur la matiere*. Félix Alcan.
Osty, E. (1928). Aux confins de la psychologie classique et de la psychologie métapsychique: II. M. Augustin Lesage, peintre sans avois appris. *Revue Métapsychique, 1*, 1–35.
Pratt, J. G. (1936). Towards a method of evaluating mediumistic material. *Bulletin, Boston Society for Psychic Research, 23*, 5–53.
Pratt, J. G., & Birge, W. R. (1948). Appraising verbal test material in parapsychology. *Journal of Parapsychology, 12*, 236–256.
Prince, W. F. (1923). The Mother of Doris. *Proceedings of the American Society for Psychical Research, 17*, 1–216.
Prince, W. F. (1927). *The case of Patience Worth: A critical study of certain unusual phenomena.* Boston Society for Psychic Research.
Rhine, J. B. (1934a). *Extra-sensory perception*. Boston Society for Psychic Research.
Rhine, J. B. (1934b). Telepathy and clairvoyance in the normal and trance states of a "medium." *Character and Personality, 3*(2), 91–111.
Rhine, J. B., & Rhine, L. E. (1927). One evening's observation on the Margery mediumship, *Journal of Abnormal and Social Psychology, 21*(4), 401–421.
Richet, C. (1922). *Traité de métapsychique*. Félix Alcan.

Rogers, E. C. (1853). *Philosophy of mysterious agents, human and mundane; Or, the dynamic laws and relations of man*. J. P. Jewett.
Saltmarsh, H. F. (1929). Report on the investigation of some sittings with Mrs. Warren Elliott, *Proceedings of the Society for Psychical Research, 39*, 47–184.
Saltmarsh, H. F. (1938). *Evidence of personal survival from cross correspondences*. G. Bell.
Saltmarsh, H. H. & Soal, S. G. (1930). A method of estimating the supernormal content of mediumistic communications: I. The method. *Proceedings of the Society for Psychical Research, 39*, 266–271.
Schrenck-Notzing, A. de (1925). *Les phénomènes physiques de la mediumnite*. Payot.
Sidgwick, E. M. (1886). Mr. Eglinton. *Journal of the Society for Psychical Research, 2*, 282–334.
Sidgwick, E. M. (1915). A contribution to the study of the psychology of Mrs. Piper's trance phenomena. *Proceedings of the Society for Psychical Research, 28*, 1–657.
Sidgwick, E. M. (1921). An examination of book-tests obtained in sittings with Mrs. Leonard. *Proceedings of the Society for Psychical Research, 31*, 214–400.
Simon, G. (1923). *Chez Victor Hugo: Les tables tournantes de Jersey: Proçès-verbaux des séances*. Louis Conard.
Society for Psychical Research (1882). Objects of the Society. *Proceedings of the Society for Psychical Research, 1*, 4–6.
Sudre, R. (1926). *Introduction à la métapsychique humaine*. Payot.
Tanner, A. (1910). *Studies in spiritism*. D. Appleton.
Thomas, C. D. (1928) The modus operandi of trance communication according to descriptions received through Mrs. Osborne Leonard. *Proceedings of the Society for Psychical Research, 38*, 49–100.
Thomas, J. F. (1937). *Beyond normal cognition: An evaluative and methodological study of the mental content of certain trance phenomena*. Bruce Humphries.
Tietze, T. R. (1973). *Margery*. Harper and Row.
von Schrenck-Notzing, A. (1920). *Phenomena of materialisation: A contribution to the investigation of mediumistic teleplastics* (Rev. ed.). Paul Trench, Trübner.

Psychic Phenomena and the Brain Hemispheres: Some Nineteenth-Century Publications*

Carlos S. Alvarado†

This paper is an Essay Review of *The Night-Side of Nature: Or, Ghosts and Ghost Seers* (1843), *Modern Necromancy* (1855), *Automatic Writing*—II (1885), *Duality of the Brain: A Theory of Mind-Reading and Slate-Writing* (1888), *The Double Personality, and the Relation of the Submerged Personality to the Phenomena of Modern Spiritualism* (1893), and *Psychology and Spiritism* (1908).

Writing in 1839, physician Henry Holland stated: "I am not sure that this subject of the relation of the two hemispheres of the brain, has yet been followed into all the consequences which more or less directly result from it" (Holland 1839, p. 151). One of these "consequences" is the work about ESP and brain hemispheric functioning which started mainly in the 1970s (e.g., Braud & Braud, 1975; Broughton, 1976; Maher & Schmeidler, 1977; on these and other studies see Williams, 2012). The authors of reviews on the subject (Broughton, 1975; Williams, 2012) mentioned the speculations of Frederic W. H. Myers (1885a) about automatic writing, telepathy, and the hemispheres, but they presented few details, and did little with other early contributions, which is the point of this essay review (see also Harrington, 1987). I will summarize here ideas about the relationship between psychic phenomena and the brain's hemispheres published between the mid-nineteenth century and the first decade of the 1900s. These early ideas present examples of how neurological concepts filtered into beliefs and theoretical work about various psychic phenomena.

The Background for Ideas about Psychic Phenomena and the Brain's Hemispheres

Physiological ideas regarding the mind, and various psychological experiences, flourished during the nineteenth century as a consequence of the growth of the biological and medical sciences.[1] The field of neurology was particularly important, as it passed through a revolutionary stage during this period, in which various methodological, clinical, and theoretical developments changed the field (Brazier, 1961; Spillane, 1981; Young, 1970). These developments, including electrophysiology and localization of brain functions, led to the discussion of the immediate historical and theoretical context of the ideas about psychic phenomena and the hemispheres comprising them.

The rapid development of neurology in the nineteenth century led to an interest in physiological explanations for psychic phenomena and related psychological anomalies such as mediumistic and

*Republished with permission from *Journal of Scientific Exploration, 30*, 559–585, 2016.

†I wish to thank Rodger I. Anderson for informing me about Crowe's writings on the brain hemispheres. William G. Braud, Richard S. Broughton, and Jan Ehrenwald corresponded with me about the factors that led them to be interested in the topic in question. I am also grateful to Susan M. Adams, Arthur L. Benton, Gerd H. Hövelmann, and Nancy L. Zingrone for useful suggestions for the improvement of this paper. The author thanks the Society for Psychical Research for financial support.

hypnotic trance, and hysterical dissociation (e.g., Beard, 1877; Haddock, 1851; Prince, 1898). For example, Azam (1887) argued that the well-known double personality case of Félida X. could be explained through peculiarities of the circulation of blood in her brain. Among the hypotheses presented to explain reports of alleged psychic phenomena, particularly those reported to occur in the presence of mediums, one group of physicians offered a variety of neurologically- and psychophysiologically-based notions. Some of them were hallucinations, suggestion, unconscious reflexes or movements, and perceptual and memory errors (e.g., Beard, 1879; Carpenter, 1874; Hammond, 1870).

Another group, who felt that the reports provided evidence for the occurrence of genuine psychic phenomena, proposed that such phenomena manifested themselves by the action of some "force" acting through the brain, and through other parts of the nervous system, to produce external effects.[2] Although such concepts of force come from antiquity (Amadou, 1953), they were particularly influential in the Western world through the movement of mesmerism and its concept of animal magnetism. This force was considered by many during the eighteenth and nineteenth centuries to be intimately related to the vitality of the body and to be the agent behind the mesmeric trance, healings, and many other phenomena reported by the mesmerists (Gauld, 1992). One such explanation of physical phenomena was the speculation of John B. Dods (1795–1872), lecturer on Spiritualism and defender of the system of "electrical psychology," that "electro-nervous" or "electro-magnetic" forces existed that were related to the "*involuntary powers* in the back of the brain …" (Dods, 1854, p. 33). Dods emphasized that the brain was double, having a "front brain"—the cerebrum—in charge of "voluntary" powers (e.g., volition, reason, understanding), and a "back brain"—the cerebellum—related to "involuntary" powers (e.g., control of body functions, instincts) (Dods, 1854, p. 56–57). The authors of other books published around the same time also argued that these biological forces coming out of the human body could explain phenomena such as movements of objects, raps, and many of the phenomena of Spiritualism (Rogers, 1853; Samson 1860). In addition, other writers speculated on the role of the brain in the emission and reception of energies responsible for thought-transference (e.g., Houston, 1892).

Interest in the brain and in the functions of the hemispheres also flourished during these times. Although some researchers defended a unitary or an equipotential view of the functions of the cerebral cortex (Flourens, 1824, p. 236–241), the emphasis on localization began to be more widely accepted with the development of clinical and experimental neurology (Young, 1970).

Particularly important for the support of the localization model were later clinical observations of cases of aphasia induced by brain lesion or disease (Broca, 1861/1960; Dax, 1865; Jackson, 1878–1879)[3] and experimental studies with animals (Fritsch and Hitzig, 1870/1960) regarding the importance of the cortex in motor activity and electrical excitability of the hemispheres. Paul Broca's (1824–1880) work with aphasic patients in the 1860s led him to suggest that speech was regulated by the left hemisphere (Broca, 1861/1960).[4]

In general, a variety of ideas and controversies flourished during the period and reflected both the difficulties clinicians experienced in making sense of some of their observations, as well as the paucity of research. Nonetheless, these and further developments during the nineteenth century and the first two decades of the twentieth century led to the acceptance of the concept of left hemispheric dominance and the right hemisphere as the minor one (Benton, 1972, 1976; Harrington, 1987, Chap. 3).[5]

However, and regardless of dominance, the concept of duality of the brain was a popular subject for discussion during the nineteenth century (e.g., Brown-Sequard, 1874; Holland, 1839, p. 151–167, Maudsley 1889, Wigan 1844). Some physicians argued against the trend that the right hemisphere had no important function and suggested that this hemisphere was involved in a "geographical" vision center (Dunn, 1895), mirror writing (Ireland, 1881; Mills, 1894), "automatic speech" (Jackson, 1868/1915), and control of writing movements (Lichtheim, 1885). Others speculated on the possibility of discordant action of both hemispheres to explain some psychopathological syndromes (Ireland, 1891; Luys, 1888), particularly so-called cases of double personality (Holland, 1839; p. 162–163; Wigan, 1844, p. 391–398). Arthur Ladbroke Wigan (d. 1847), an influential writer in this line of thought, also tried to explain déjà vu, autoscopy, somnambulism, and sleep and dreaming using the concept of discordant or alternate function of the two hemispheres (Wigan, 1844, p. 84–87, 126–127, 370, 372–375). In addition, there was a hemi-hypnosis movement that assumed that each brain hemisphere could be hypnotized separately and cause different phenomena in opposite sides of the body (for a review, see Harrington, 1987, p. 185–205).

A New View of Insanity

Regardless of all this interest in the double brain, the idea of different hemispheric functions does not seem to have been generally accepted at the time. This may be appreciated in criticisms of Wigan's book (Anonymous, 1845), and in the comments of supporters of the idea (Lyon, 1895, p. 107–108; Wilks, 1872, p. 162).

Regardless of the acceptance of such ideas, the application of many of them reflected more than the progress obtained in the discipline of neurology. They represented attempts to naturalize the unusual and the paranormal, a trend discussed in other contexts (e.g., Alvarado & Zingrone, 2012; Gonçalves & Ortega, 2013). Harrington has argued that some of the nineteenth Century interest in the double brain was a strategy to naturalize the occult:

> There was no denying that both the medium and the madman gave evidence of possessing "two minds." ... Nevertheless, said the medical men, these phenomena all had their source in the lawful workings of the nervous system and were fully explicable in naturalistic terms. (Harrington, 1987, p. 110).

However, and as Harrington (1987, p. 153) has also discussed, these attempts to naturalize the phenomena of dissociation and of spiritualism did not consist only of a single reduction to brain activity. In addition to these arguments, a variety of neurological speculations, and the double brain in particular, was implied in what was considered true paranormal functioning (e.g., Beard, 1877). In the rest of this review, I will discuss the latter through examples of speculations of the functioning of the brain's hemispheres.

Speculations on Psychic Phenomena and the Brain's Hemispheres

Catherine Crowe's Ideas in The Night Side of Nature

Catherine Crowe (1790–1876), a well-known British novelist in Victorian times (Stephen & Lee, 1950, p. 257), published a two-volume work called *The Night Side of Nature* in 1848 (Crowe, 1848). Described as "one of the best collections of supernatural stories in our language," the book was also criticized for "being exceedingly credulous and uncritical" (Stephen & Lee, 1950, p. 257). Its chapters dealt with spontaneous experiences such as psychic dreams, apparitions of the living and of the dead, hauntings, and poltergeists. The book was influenced by the publications of German writers on occult and psychic topics, although the opinions of persons from other countries, particularly England, were also included.

In her book, Crowe showed that she was aware of Wigan's ideas on the duality of the brain and mentioned them to explain "double or alternate consciousness" and déjà vu involving the cerebral hemispheres. Crowe was not convinced by Wigan's speculations about déjà vu and pointed out that presentiments of future things were particularly difficult to explain in this way (Crowe, 1848, Vol. 1, pp. 98–99).[6]

Although ideas on the polarity of animal magnetism can be found in the writings of Franz Anton Mesmer (1734–1815) (Mesmer, 1779, p. 76) and others in the middle 1800s (Dods, 1854, pp. 54–55, 62–63, 148–214; Reichenbach, 1849/1851, p. 179–219), Crowe seemed to have been influenced mainly by the ideas of German writers regarding changes in the polarity of the organism during altered states of consciousness and illnesses (Crowe, 1848, Vol. 1, pp. 45–49).[7] Sleep and sickness, for example, were conceptualized as a change from a positive to a negative polarity in the human organism. As Crowe (1848, Vol. 1, p. 97) wrote to relate these ideas to the hemispheres as explanations for clairvoyance,

> the senses, being placed in a negative and passive state, the universal change of the immortal spirit within ... becomes more or less free to work unclogged. That the soul is a mirror in which the spirit sees all things reflected, is a modification of this theory. Another view ..., as maintained by Dr. Wigan and some other physiologists that our brains are double, it is possible that a polarity may exist between the two sides, by means of which the negative side may, under certain circumstances, become a mirror to the positive. (Crowe, 1848, Vol. 1, p. 98).

Crowe pointed out that this idea involving the brain seemed difficult to reconcile with the observation that the psychic impressions "occur most frequently when the brain is asleep" (Crowe, 1848, Vol. 1, p. 98), though she was aware of the uncertainty of knowing "how far the sleep is perfect" (Crowe, 1848, Vol. 1, p. 98).

Crowe further wrote: "The theory of one-half of the brain in a negative state, serving as a mirror to the other half, if admitted at all, may answer as well, or better, for those waking presentiments, than for clear-seeing in dreams" (Crowe, 1848, Vol. 1, pp. 108–109). However, Crowe preferred a more spiritual theory in which, under certain conditions, "the spirit may perceive, by its own inherent quality, without the aid of its material vehicle ..." (Crowe, 1848, Vol. 1, p. 109).

Anonymous Writer in the *North American Review*

Writing in the *North American Review* in 1855, an anonymous author tried to relate mediumistic phenomena to the cerebral hemispheres (Anonymous, 1855).[8] From the beginning of the paper it is made clear that the author believes that "the least tenable hypothesis of all is that which attributes the phenomena under discussion to the agency of departed spirits" (Anonymous, 1855, p. 513). It is said later in the paper that there is evidence which favors the belief that [mediumistic communications] have their origin in some peculiar mode of the medium's own consciousness, enlarged and modified indeed, in some instances, by the consciousness of members of the surrounding circle. (Anonymous, 1855, p. 515).

Such an idea was consistent with other nineteenth century attempts to counter spiritualistic explanations of psychic phenomena using the concept of psychic abilities of the living, in this case the projection of a biological or nervous force from the body of the medium (Dods, 1854; Rogers, 1853; Samson, 1860).

The brain was mentioned when the author suggested ideas to explain mediumistic phenomena. The concept of "duplication" of the organs of the body was stressed. "The right and the left half of the body are in more respects counterparts than complements of each other.

The brain, too, is double throughout ..." (Anonymous, 1855, p. 517). Each hemisphere was seen as capable of acting independently of the other in situations of cerebral disease. The concept was used to explain cases of "double consciousness," particularly that of Mary Reynolds (1785–1854), a well-known early case of multiple personality (Plumer, 1860).

The author considered electro-magnetism as the vital element in the human organism. This led him to explain double consciousness as "the consequence of some peculiar condition of animal electricity or sensitiveness to electro-magnetic influences ..." (Anonymous, 1855, p. 521), a topic consistent with ideas about electricity in the mesmeric and spiritualistic literatures (Alvarado, 2008). It was further said that:

> The vertebrae are, as it were, the successive plates of a galvanic battery, of which the skull is the apex, while the spine, culminating in the brain, constitutes, like the acid in the artificial battery, a continuous and cumulative creator and channel of the electromagnetic force. Of this force the nerves of sensation and of voluntary motion are the conductors. ... The living battery, as ordinarily charged, may suffice to keep but one hemisphere of the brain in action, while an excessive charge may keep both hemispheres in simultaneous action.
>
> This theory may account for the rappings, phosphoric lights, table tippings, and other physical phenomena, reported in connection with the pretended spiritual intercourse. (Anonymous, 1855, p. 521)

While the author implies that the accumulation of an overcharge of the nervous system inducing simultaneous action of both hemispheres is an important aspect of the explanation, no clarifying details are offered. Another postulate considered the possibility that the medium used environmental energy to produce the effects, and that veridical mediumistic communications in the presence of persons present who knew the correct answer could be explained by "electro-magnetic communication ... between the intensely stimulated brain of the medium and the brains of those composing the circle" (Anonymous, 1855, p. 522).

Frederic W. H. Myers on *Automatic Writing, Thought-Transference, and Other Phenomena*

Frederic W. H. Myers (1843–1901), a pioneer in psychology and psychical research, and a founding member of the London-based Society for Psychical Research (SPR), published in the 1880s interesting discussions on the nature of automatic writing and its possible ESP components (Myers, 1884, 1885a, 1885b, 1887a, 1889).[9] The idea of unconscious muscular movements to explain phenomena such as table turning and automatic writing was developed before Myers presented his ideas on the topic (e.g., Carpenter, 1874, p. 279–315; Chevreul, 1833; Faraday, 1853), but Myers further developed these ideas and incorporated various other concepts such as ESP information as well as psychological and physiological factors. "Unconscious cerebration" and telepathy were proposed by Myers to account for most of the cases he discussed in his papers;[10] he also argued that a secondary consciousness handled the telepathically acquired information in automatisms, and that automatic writing was only one example of several motor and sensory automatisms (e.g., vocal, visual, or auditory). For purposes of this review, I am primarily interested in Myers's speculations on the cerebral hemispheres and the above-mentioned phenomena.

Myers was influenced in his speculations on the brain's hemispheres by two main factors. First, by nineteenth century publications on aphasia and related problems (e.g., Bernard, 1885; Charcot, 1884; Ogle, 1867; Pitres, 1884). Second, by speculations by the Reverend P. H. Newnham regarding the role of the right hemisphere in explaining mediumistic communications of low moral character obtained through Newnham's wife's mediumship in 1871. Newnham, Vicar of Maker (Davenport, England), and an early SPR member, recorded in a diary in 1871 his observations of planchette-writing with his wife as medium. Myers (1885a, pp. 8–23) published extracts of Newnham's diary (but he seems to have been unaware of the previous ideas discussed here and of E. W. Cox's (1809–1879) brief reference to "unconscious activity of one of the brains" in relation to planchette writing [The Psychological Society of Great Britain, 1876, pp. 196–197]). Newnham's reference to low moral aspects of the communications referred to lies in the automatic script. In his opinion, such communications perhaps could be explained by postulating the action of the right hemisphere. Because of lack of education, the right hemisphere was considered by Newnham to show the same tendency for lying that children show in an early stage of their education process (Myers, 1885a, p. 22). This idea that the right hemisphere was the untrained and uneducated one was common in the nineteenth century and by no means unique to Newnham nor to Myers (e.g., Brown-Sequard, 1874, p. 333; Oglem 1867, pp. 89, 121–122; Wilks, 1872, p. 157).

Myers created his own terminology to refer to the operation of the two hemispheres. His terms indicated the use of both hemispheres (ambi-cerebral), the right (dextro-cerebral) and left hemispheres (sinistro-cerebral), as well as one hemisphere (hemi-cerebral) (Myers, 1885a, p. 42).

He considered the similarities between "supernormal" automatic writing and the "writing performed by patients who have … only the partially untrained half of the brain to rely on,—those centres which habitually initiate the graphic energy having been destroyed or rendered temporarily useless by accident or disease" (Myers, 1885a, p. 34). This is what many clinicians called *agraphia*, but which Myers preferred to call *agraphy*. In making this comparison, Myers pointed out that in both conditions the subject was occasionally unable to write and that sometimes repetition of letters or senseless words appeared. Transposition of letters and mirror writing were also considered as pointers to right-hemispheric action in writing problems (Myers, 1885a, p. 33–34).[11] A comparison was made between left-handed children's writing mistakes and mistakes in automatic writing scripts, finding similar problems in both. An attempt was also made to relate swearing and low moral communications in automatic writing and planchette scripts to the "swearing of the aphasic patient" (Myers, 1885a, p. 45). All this led Myers to conclude that:

> The inco-ordination of agraphy and the inco-ordination of rudimentary graphic automatism … arise from the same cause; from the employment in the act of writing of untrained centres in the right hemisphere of the brain. … (Myers 1885a, pp. 38–39)

In later publications, Myers (1885c, 1886a, 1886b) returned to the topic and suggested that the right hemisphere had in its "inferior evolution, traces of that savage ancestry which forms the sombre background of the refinements and felicities of civilised man" (Myers, 1886a, p. 228). Myers (1885a, pp. 31–33) discussed evolutionary concepts as related to telepathy and automatic writing, and was clearly influenced by John Hughlings Jackson's (1835–1911) ideas on the evolution and dissolution of the nervous system (Myers, 1885a, p. 24, 45).[12] In some of his publications, Jackson (1878–1879, 1884) discussed swearing and interjectional expressions in aphasics as emotional and rudimentary processes related to Thomas Laycock's (1812–1876) concept of reflex action, and affirmed that the right hemisphere was related to the automatic and involuntary use of words.

Myers wrote further to clarify these ideas and to relate them to thought-transference:

> I hold that in graphic automatism the action of the right hemisphere is predominant, because the secondary self can appropriate its energies more readily than those of the left hemisphere, which is more immediately at the service of the waking mind. ... Nevertheless, I hold that it uses the *right* hand habitually, being unable to overcome the incompetence of the *left*. But in its right-handed writing I should expect traces of dextro-cerebral influence occasionally to occur; and this I maintain that I have shown to be the case, first in the *reversed words* and secondly in the *mirror-writing*, which graphic automatism so frequently shows ...
>
> And here I must remind the reader that *occasional* indications are all that we can expect to find in tracing the "seat of election" of supernormal cerebral automatism. The lines will not be as sharply drawn as they sometimes are in cases of traumatic injury, or of congenital defect. For beside the alternated action of specialised centres, which I am here suggesting, other and profounder departures from normality are likely to be involved, and *their* results may be such as to leave no more than a mere hint discernible of such comparatively minor change as the replacement of some sinistro-cerebral by some dextro-cerebral centre of sight or speech.
>
> Such a hint ... I believe that we have got in experimental thought-transference, as well as in graphic automatism. The reader may remember that in [previous publications] we detailed some experiments in which the image of an arrow and other figures, were telepathically seen by Mr. Smith sometimes in an *inverted*, but more often in a laterally-inverted or *perverted* position (Myers, 1885a, pp. 43–44).[13]

Myers also presented an example of reversal of thought-transference impressions observed in 1884. The subject saw "letters appear in her field of mental vision in *reverse order* ... I placed the word NET behind her, and looked fixedly at the letters. She said that she saw successively the letters T, E, N. I next chose SEA, and she saw A, E, S ..." (Myers, 1885a, p. 44).

Later in the paper, Myers (1885a, pp. 50–60) related automatic writing to the ideas of Jean-Martin Charcot (1825–1893) on "word seeing" and "word writing" centers in his scheme of speech and writing (discussed by Bateman, 1890, pp. 39–41, see also Charcot, 1884 and Gasser, 1995) proposing that the "seat of election" of the secondary self that controlled automatic writing was in the right hemisphere and used the sensory and motor centers of that hemisphere in expressing itself. Myers basically extended this idea to include telepathically acquired information.

In later writings, Myers (1886a, pp. 651–652; 1886b, p. 227; 1887b, pp. 499–500) related the right hemisphere to multiple personality, and to genius (Myers, 1892, pp. 355–356). Particularly interesting were Myers's later speculations on spirit communication and the right hemisphere:

> I think it is possible that our left hemisphere, having been more constantly used than our right hemispheres, may be more crowded and blocked (so to say) with our own already fixed ideas. An external intelligence wishing to use my brain, might find it convenient to leave alone those more educated but also more preoccupied tracts, and to use the less elaborated, but less engrossed, mechanisms of my right hemisphere. (Myers, 1899, p. 386)[14]

R. C. Word on *Mind-Reading and Slate-Writing*

R. C. Word (died 1890), professor of physiology at Southern Medical College (Atlanta, Georgia) and Managing Editor of the monthly journal *Southern Medical Record*, published in that journal his ideas on the relationship of the brain's hemispheres to mind-reading and slate-writing (Word,

1888). Word accepted both mind-reading and slate-writing as real phenomena. Although he stated that he was aware of the problem of fraud in slate-writing, he went on to defend the reality of the phenomena on the basis of his personal experiences with mediums (Word, 1888, p. 88). However, Word was ambiguous about what he meant by slate-writing. In some parts of the paper, it seems that he referred to automatic writing rather than to the concept of "direct writing" (Word, 1888, pp. 87–88), in which letters or traces are supposed to appear on a surface without the use of the medium's or any person's limbs.

Like previously mentioned writers, Word related the concept of the double brain to double personality cases. He also related what we now call panoramic memory to the "doubly-aroused and excited brain" (Word, 1888, p. 86).

Word wrote that although "the two brains ordinarily act as a unit, they may, and sometimes do, act separately, and this possibly in cases wherein no disease exists in either hemisphere as a cause for non-action" (Word, 1888, p. 85). He then suggested "that under certain peculiar circumstances one side of the brain may converse with the other side" (Word, 1888, p. 85). This was offered as a hypothesis to explain the above-mentioned phenomena, as will be seen in the discussion that follows.

Word stated that the mesmerized person "is in a passive or receptive condition, which I will term electro-negative" (Word, 1888, p. 86). In this condition the person is under the influence of the mesmerizer. "He is wholly passive, and his brain and entire nervous system receives its impressions from the mesmerizer" (Word, 1888, p. 86). Word considered the mind-reader a highly developed "electro-negative subject" who became so sensitive as to be able to obtain information from other person's minds. These, and other phenomena, were ultimately explained through the action of a nervous electrical force presumably generated by the medium's nervous system. The ideas were extended to the concept of different electrical charges on each half of the brain in special circumstances. A "reversal or shutting off of the usual or normal electric or nerve currents passing between the two hemispheres" (Word, 1888, p. 87) deprived the brain of its normal work. As Word further wrote:

> In this condition the electro-positive side may ask questions which may be automatically answered by the electro-negative side. Herein we find an explanation of what is called slate-writing. …
>
> Under these circumstances any incident or memory which is latent in the brain is liable to be revived and to be automatically and unconsciously reproduced by the medium, and when thus presented comes with all the force of conviction of a communication from a third or an outside party.
>
> Thus the slate-writer gets messages from his or her own brain, or if brought into rapport with another party may get mental impressions from him also. (Word, 1888, p. 87)

Word later said in the same paper that an electro-negative subject could get mental impressions by rapport with persons in a circle. As he wrote to relate this concept to the brain's hemispheres:

> For this, it would seem to be sufficient that only one side of the brain be in the passive or electro-negative state, in which case the thoughts of the, as well as the thoughts of any member of the circle, are liable to be automatically written.
>
> It is possible with some mediums that both sides of the brain may become electro-negative, in which case they pass into a hypnotic or trance condition, which is no other than the mesmeric state. (Word, 1888, p. 88)

A. N. Somers, *Mediumship, and the "Submerged Personality"*

Another discussion of the topic comes from an article written by A. N. Somers (1893) in the American journal *Psychical Review*. Somers recognized from the beginning that human beings' neural systems were binary, or double, regarding its structure and their functions. Under abnormal physiological or psychological causes, the doubling of personality could take place.

Both brain hemispheres, Somers maintained, are connected by crossing fibers that kept them functioning together. This pattern of joint function was influenced by … hereditary factors and by early training. But "if deranged the activity may be double or alternating in acts of double personality (or mediumship)" (Somers, 1893, p. 316). These factors capable of changing the system thus included "disease, fatigue, or psychical inactivity of the dominant cerebral hemisphere" (Somers, 1893, p. 317); that is, the left hemisphere.

The author saw trance as one of the conditions helping human beings gain access to their submerged personality. This, and other states, also helped a person to contact aspects of the opposite sex that were hidden in every person, thus explaining sexual perversions. This was because the cerebral centers involved in these processes could become more active than the usual dominant ones. In Somers' view:

> Previous to these changes the only outlet for the cerebral contents of the submerged personality was in dreams, visions, or illusions, and occasional instances of equal activity with its double under intense excitement. … The various processes used in the 'development of mediumship' are sure to transfer this privilege from the ascendant to the submerged personality. (Somers, 1893, p. 319)

Following the prevalent tradition during the nineteenth century (Harrington, 1987), Somers considered the left hemisphere to be the dominant one. This was because he believed this hemisphere was formed early on around the same time as sex differentiation was taking place. If it were not for some influences from the maternal system (from the mother's side), everyone would be male and the right hemisphere would be atrophied. In Somers opinion: "Femaleness is a conservative check on that tendency. … Left-handedness, double personality, and mediumship could never exist but for this check" (Somers, 1893, p. 321).

Somers also made some interesting observations about temperature changes and pulse rates:

> I have found the right cerebral hemisphere of a right-handed medium rise in temperature one and a half degrees while in trance, and *vice versa* with a left-handed medium. In both instances the temperature of the quiescent hemisphere fell a degree during the trance, due to increased circulation in the hemisphere that took on greater activity when its opposite became hypnotic. I have gained the same results by hypnotism repeatedly. (Somers, 1893, p. 322)[15]

Somers also observed a diminution of pulse and respiration rate presumably related to a switch from the ordinary active hemisphere to the opposite one. Under these circumstances the submerged personality comes forward and can be shaped through suggestion. The medium, then, can impart information that is not in his or her consciousness nor in recollections.

Cesare Lombroso on *Observations of Handedness with Mediums*

Cesare Lombroso (1836–1909), a well-known Italian psychiatrist and criminologist, was interested in the topic of handedness.[16] His ideas should be considered in the context of his concepts on criminology, in which criminals were seen as examples of physical degeneration and atavism (Lombroso, 1884b). According to Lombroso, "motor and sensory left handedness" was one of the aspects in which criminals were similar to creatures "beyond our own race" (Lombroso, 1911, p. 368). As he further wrote,

> ... criminals are more left-handed than honest men, and lunatics are more sensitively left-sided than either of the two. That fact indicates that in criminals and lunatics the right lobe predominates very much more than in normal persons. While the healthy man thinks and feels with the left lobe, the abnormal thinks, wills, and feels more with the right. (Lombroso, 1903, p. 443)[17]

In the same paper, Lombroso speculated on the discordant action of "the two lobes of the brain" to explain double personality, and discussed mirror writing along similar lines (Lombroso, 1903, pp. 442–443). In an earlier paper, Lombroso (1892) argued that writing mediums are in

> a state of half somnambulism where, thanks to the preponderant action of the right hemisphere due to the inactivity of the left hemisphere, [the medium] does not have consciousness of the fact and believes he writes under the dictation of someone else. (Lombroso, 1892, p. 148)

Lombroso was also interested in right-left hand differences regarding mediumistic phenomena. As he wrote,

> almost all of the spiritistic phenomena of the medium have their origin on the left side ... [18] or are perceived on the left side even when they come from the right, and that sinistrality is temporarily transmitted also to the controllers of the medium. ... Hence it follows that in the trance the work of the right hemisphere of the brain prevails, the one least adapted to psychical work and which participates least in the activity of consciousness. (Lombroso, 1909, p. 182.)

Of particular interest here is the mention of the transfer of left-handedness, which is a reference to observations by psychiatrist Enrico Morselli (1852–1929) published about medium Eusapia Palladino (1854–1918) using hand dynamometers (Morselli, 1908).[19] A discussion of this requires a brief digression.

In the past, hand dynamometers have been used for neuropsychiatric examinations (e.g., Charcot, 1883–1884, p. 285; Morselli, 1884) and as a test of hand preference (Parsons, 1924, p. 72). A number of studies using this instrument to measure the level of hand-grip strength were done with Palladino and her sitters on the assumption that the measurements reflected expenditure of "psychic forces" in the production of physical phenomena (Lodge, 1894, pp. 326–327; Morselli, 1908, Vol. 1, pp. 315–319, 351–352). "Dynamometer readings," wrote physicist and psychical researcher Oliver J. Lodge (1851–1940), "were taken before and after each seance, in order to ascertain, if possible, the source of the energy. ..." (Lodge, 1894, p. 331). Morselli reported losses in group grip strength measures after séances, measured in kilograms, but emphasized differences in energy losses between the right and the left hands. On one occasion (N = 11, including the medium), the right hand had a loss of 46 Kg, while the left hand had a loss of 66 Kg (Morselli 1908, Vol. 1, p. 317). In a later experiment, the right hand had a loss of 40.5 Kg and the left 99 Kg (N = 12, including the medium) (Morselli 1908, Vol. 1, p. 352).

A particularly interesting observation was recorded in a séance held in 1901. According to Morselli, Palladino, usually left-handed, became right-handed after the séance. However, this does not refer to the medium's use of her right hand, but to the fact that she gained 6 Kg in the right hand and lost 2.5 Kg in the left hand after the séance (Morselli, 1908, Vol. 1, pp. 351–352).[20] Morselli found especially interesting the fact that his own "dynamometric type" was changed from right (his normal) to left. His readings showed a loss of 16 Kg in the right hand, while the left hand had a gain of 7 Kg after the séance. He noticed that before a materialization was observed in the séance, he had his left hand on the medium's head. Morselli speculated that a force emanating from the medium during the production of the materialization "came into my nervous centers. ..., passed partially into my arm, and rendered me left-handed" (Morselli, 1908, Vol. 1, p. 352, my translation).

Morselli did not speculate on the hemispheres, but Lombroso (1908, p. 378) related the incident to the action of the right hemisphere. Lombroso considered Morselli's observations a confirmation of "Audenino's hypothesis of transitory left-handedness in the abnormal state" (Lombroso, 1908, p. 378). This was a reference to Audenino's (1908) concepts postulating that temporary left-handedness could occur in abnormal states (e.g., epilepsy, intoxication, madness, somnambulism, trance) because they provided access to primitive and atavistic tendencies normally diminished by education.

Lombroso also had something to say regarding automatic writing mediums. In his opinion, the idea

> ... that only one hemisphere of the brain acts, preferably the right, while the left remains inert, thus explaining the unconsciousness of the right lobe,—an explication based on the extemporized left-handedness of many of the mediums ... (Lombroso 1909, p. 158)[21]

although considered of help to explain automatisms, may have some difficulties in explaining cases in which more than one spirit communicator manifested at the same time.

Discussion

The ideas discussed here may be considered an interesting but forgotten chapter of the history of hemispheric functions and attempts to explain or find physiological correlates of psychic phenomena. They were certainly influenced by the nineteenth century interest in finding specific cerebral localizations of diverse functions, and particularly by concepts and discussions on the duality of the brain (Harrington, 1987). In fact, the concepts of duality were discussed in the medical literature before and during the period covered in the present paper. While these ideas may be interpreted as part of the trend of nineteenth century science to conceptualize the phenomena of consciousness in natural terms, it was also an example of how spiritualists and psychical researchers appropriated neurological concepts as part of the workings of the supernormal.

There are some interesting differences in the concepts presented and the approaches taken by the writers discussed above. The concepts of unorthodox forces were emphasized or implied by Crowe, the writer in the *North American Review*, and by Word, but not by Myers, Somers, and Lombroso. The latter writer discussed concepts of psychic forces in relation to the Palladino mediumship, but not in terms of the brain and its hemispheres (Lombroso, 1892, 1909). Also, only three writers emphasized the importance or function of the right hemisphere (Myers, Somers, and Lombroso), although they considered it to be the primitive one. Likewise, only three presented their ideas with some attention to neurological aspects (Myers, the writer in the *North American Review*, and Somers), and two with ideas about polarity of energy in the nervous system (Crowe & Word).

Of the examples discussed here, Myers is of special interest in that he attempted to put his speculations into the context of knowledge of aphasia and agraphia in the 1880s.[22] As far as I know, he was the first person to point out that some of the mistakes in ESP reception may be indicative of right hemispheric function, a view considered by some modern writers (e.g., Ehrenwald, 1975, pp. 394–396).[23]

While some of Myers contemporaries were aware of his ideas regarding automatic writing and the brain hemispheres (e.g., James, 1889, p. 555; 1890, Vol. 1, p. 400; Janet, 1889, pp. 415–419), later commentators have not mentioned such ideas, as seen in texts about automatic writing (e.g., Honegger, 1980; Muhl, 1930; Stevenson, 1978). This suggests that his articles discussing the subject had little impact or influence after publication.

In fact, the five authors discussed in this Essay Review seem to have had little or no impact on psychical research at the time they proposed their ideas. (In addition, the authors themselves do not quote the publications of their predecessors.) We may speculate on some reasons for this: (1) the publications were scattered over a long period of time with occasional long intervals between them; (2) there was a general emphasis on the importance of the left hemisphere over the right during the period in question; and (3) the reports usually had a low circulation or were published in obscure sources (this may particularly apply to the *Annals of Psychical Science*, the *Southern Medical Record*, and the *Psychical Review*).

The first modern writers on the relationship between psychic phenomena and the hemispheres—William G. Braud, Richard S. Broughton, and Jan Ehrenwald—were not aware of the old speculations when they started to think about the topic, and claim they were influenced mainly by other factors,[24] particularly by developments in modern hemispheric research (for reviews of hemispheric research in those crucial years see Bryden, 1982 and Dimond, 1972). Ideas from Eastern traditions, research on altered states of consciousness, and studies of "split brain" patients, as seen in Robert Ornstein's (1972) influential book *The Psychology of Consciousness*, also may be considered an important factor that influenced modern parapsychologists to pay attention to right and left hemispheric differences. Other developments in parapsychology during the 1970s, such as EEG and other physiological correlate studies (Morris, 1977, pp. 705–710), also may have provided some theoretical background for the interest in the relationship between parapsychological phenomena and the hemispheres.

Regardless of these considerations, the material discussed herein is interesting in its own right. It illustrates an attempt to relate psychic phenomena to neurological processes, and thus normalize such controversial manifestations by association with the biological. In addition, these writings also show the wide range and impact of ideas about the brain on society since even psychic phenomena were seen through the neurological glass. Consequently, these ideas should be of importance to the history of views concerning the brain, as well as to the history of conceptual developments in parapsychology.

Notes

1 The progress of neurological thought during the nineteenth century has been discussed by Clarke and Jacyna (1987) and Finger (1994). On general ideas about physiology and the mind during the period, see Jacyna (1982), Smith (1973), and Young (1970). The idea of localizations of sensory and motor functions in the brain was an important aspect of neurological thought (Finger, 2010; Kaitaro, 2001; Young, 1970), as was the related study of aphasia (Benton, 1981, Tesak & Tod, 2008). A discussion of physiological ideas related to the mind in the context of developments in mesmerism, phrenology, Spiritualism, and psychical research in England is presented by Oppenheim (1985, pp. 205–266).

2 Ideas of psychic forces, fluids, and human radiations were developed during the nineteenth and twentieth centuries to explain psychic phenomena of all sorts, among them mediumship (Alvarado, 2006; Ungaro, 1992).

3 For reviews of nineteenth-century thoughts on the effects of hemisphere lesions and disease on aphasia and related disorders, see Bateman (1890), Benton (1981), and Harrington (1987). Among the many studies of nineteenth century aphasia, see the work of Henderson (2008), Jacyna (2000), Lorch (2016), and Roth (2002).

4 LaPointe (2012) discusses Broca's influential work (see also Harrington, 1987, Chap. 2). It has long been argued that Marc Dax (1770–1837) had precedence over Broca in his discovery of the role of the left hemisphere in relation to aphasia (e.g., Roe & Finger, 1996).

5 For an example of the lack of importance given to the right hemisphere in the non-medical literature, see Flammarion (1886, p. 786).

6 Discussing the "sentiment of pre-existence" in relation to reincarnation, spiritualist Hudson Tuttle wrote:

> To Plato ... such might be satisfactory evidence; but to us, with the knowledge we possess of physiology and of the brain, they are of no value. The double structure and double action of the brain, by which impressions are simultaneously produced on the mind, fully explain the sentiment of preexistence. For if these impressions ... are not simultaneously produced, the mind becomes confused, and the weakest impressions are referred to the past. (Tuttle, 1871, pp. 204–205)

7 A later discussant of the topic was Hector Durville (1900, pp. 40–45, 49). He questioned the idea that the "magnetic force" and the "nervous fluid" were the same agent in light of observations of contralateral hemispheric functions. Durville argued that "if the magnetic force were the nervous force it would follow, as does the nervous force, the length of the nerves and the hemispheres of the brain would be of opposite polarity to their corresponding sides" (Durville, 1900, p. 49). It is asserted that this is the case because the right side of the body is positive and the left side is negative. The concept of polarity was also present in the eighteenth and nineteenth century electrophysiological literature (Brazier, 1961, 1984).

8 According to Reeves (1979, p. 188, 199), the author was A. P. Peabody (1811–1893), editor of the *Review*.

9 On Myers, see Hamilton (2009). Myers is particularly known for his ideas about the subliminal mind and its relationship to psychological and parapsychological phenomena (for an overview, see Myers, 1903; see also Gauld, 1968, and Kelly, 2007).

10 "Unconscious cerebration" was Carpenter's term for unconscious creative automatic action (see Carpenter, 1874, pp. 515–543, and Cobbe, 1870).

11 In this instance, Myers follows the ideas of Ireland (1881, p. 367), who related mirror-writing to the right hemisphere. A paper by Lichtheim (1885, p. 450), also seen by Myers, mentions the right hemisphere in relation to writing (not mirror-writing).

12 Jackson, an important figure in nineteenth century neurology, has been discussed by Engelhardt (1975) and by Greenblatt (1977). Harrington (1987, Chap. 7) has reviewed Jackson's ideas on duality.

13 These experiments are a reference to the thought-transference studies of the early SPR researchers using Blackburn and Smith as agent and percipient (Gurney, Myers, & Barrett, 1882, p. 80; Gurney, Myers, Podmore, & Barrett, 1883, p. 166). Controversy was generated when Blackburn confessed (though Smith denied) that they were using trickery (Anonymous, 1911; Gauld, 1965; Hall, 1964, pp. 104–109).

14 For later speculations on the role of the hemispheres in the production of automatic writing, see Honegger (1980) and Muhl (1930, p. 36).

15 In a second-hand remark, it was stated that different temperatures were recorded on the two sides of the head of writing and trance mediums in France by Chavee (The National Association of Spiritists, 1876, p. 202).

16 On various aspects of Lombroso, see Knepper and Ystehede (2013). Bulferetti (1975, pp. 352, 439–458) discusses his psychical research. Harris (1980, pp. 53–54) presents a brief overview of Lombroso's ideas on left-handedness.

17 See also Lombroso (1884a). Other Italian physicians who shared Lombroso's ideas on handedness were Audenino (1907) and Lattes (1907). For a review of alleged connections between left-handedness and different forms of pathology or socially rejected or unacceptable behaviors, see Harris (1980, pp. 51–65).

18 In mentioning spirit communications on the left side of Mrs. Piper, a well-known medium, Lombroso (1909) referred to the "usual spiritualistic left-handedness ..." (p. 117). A more recent study on the relationship of the spatial position of perceptions of spirit guides and hemispheric pathology has been published by Fenwick, Galliano, Coate, Rippere, and Brown (1985).

19 On Morselli's interest in psychical research, see Brancaccio (2014). Eusapia Palladino was one of the most influential mediums in the history of psychical research (Alvarado, 1993). In an earlier publication,

Lombroso (1892) discussed Palladino, as well as hysterical and hypnotizable individuals, as pathological examples of the functioning of cerebral centers. With Palladino he proposed that the paralysis of some of those centers augmented the activity of the motor centers to the point of transmitting a force outside of the body that caused the physical phenomena of mediumship. This position was criticized in the Spiritualist press (Anonymous, 1893).

20 The significance of these findings may be questioned, among other things, by noticing that at least on one occasion the medium's right hand obtained a higher reading than her left before the séance (Lodge, 1894, p. 327, with readings of 47 vs. 38, respectively). This may be an indication of the unreliability of the use of dynamometers to determine hand preference, as discussed by Audenino (1907, p. 27). Other problems may be pointed out with this approach (e.g., lack of double-blind conditions), but my purpose in this review is not to discuss issues of validity nor to evaluate the material discussed here from the point of view of modern developments.

21 Théodore Flournoy's (1900, p. 64) observations of allochiria with medium Hélène Smith are of interest in this context.

22 This trend was followed years later by Jan Ehrenwald (1937, 1948) in a series of publications attempting to relate ESP with neuropsychiatric problems. However, and even though Ehrenwald (1931, p. 684) had discussed anosognosia in relation to the right hemisphere in a previous paper, his speculations on the role of the right hemisphere in ESP phenomena developed much later (Jan Ehrenwald, personal communication, August 10, 1985, and September 6, 1985; Ehrenwald, 1975, 1976).

23 Reversals and other distortions of ESP messages have been discussed by other writers from the point of view of psychological processes (e.g., Irwin, 1978, p. 118; Warcollier, 1931, pp. 334–335).

24 William G. Braud, personal communication, September 18, 1985; Richard S. Broughton, personal communication, September 9, 1985; and Jan Ehrenwald, personal communication, September 6, 1985. See also some discussions on the hemispheres in the parapsychological literature in relation to ESP and states of physical and mental relaxation and out-of-body experiences, as well as "transpersonal consciousness" (Braud & Braud, 1974, p. 242; Roll, 1974/1975, p. 159).

References

Alvarado, C. S. (1993). Gifted subjects' contributions to psychical research: The case of Eusapia Palladino. *Journal of the Society for Psychical Research, 59*, 269–292.

Alvarado, C. S. (2006). Human radiations: Concepts of force in mesmerism, spiritualism and psychical research. *Journal of the Society for Psychical Research, 70,* 138–162.

Alvarado, C. S. (2008). Further notes on historical ideas of human radiations: I. On electricity and other forces. *Psypioneer, 4*, 38–43.

Alvarado, C. S., & Zingrone, N. L. (2012). Classic text no. 90: 'The pathology and treatment of mediomania,' by Frederic Rowland Marvin (1874). *History of Psychiatry, 23*, 229–244.

Amadou, R. (1953). Esquisse d'une histoire philosophique du fluide. *Revue Métapsychique, 21*, 5–33.

Anonymous (1845). Review of *A new view of insanity: The duality of the mind* by A. L. Wigan. *British Foreign and Medical Review, 20*, 1–17.

Anonymous (1855). Modern necromancy. *North American Review, 80*, 512–527.

Anonymous (1893). Professor Lombroso's theories. *Light, 13*, 352–353.

Anonymous (1911). Confessions of a "telepathist." *Journal of the Society for Psychical Research, 15*, 115–132.

Audenino, E. (1907). L'homme droit, l'homme gauche et l'homme ambidextre. *Archivio di Psichiatria, Neuropatologia, Antropologia Criminale e Medicina Legale, 4*(3), 23–31.

Audenino, E. (1908). Mancinismo e destrismo. *Archivio di Psichiatria, Neuropatologia, Antropologia Criminale e Medicina Legale*, *5*(3), 292–301.

Azam, [E. E.] (1887). *Hypnotisme, double conscience et altération de la personnalité*. J. B. Baillière.

Bateman, F. [1890]. *On aphasia, or loss of speech, and the localization of the faculty of articulate language* (2nd ed.). J. & A. Churchill.

Beard, G. B. (1877). A new theory of trance, and its bearings on human testimony. *Journal of Nervous and Mental Disease, 4*, 1–47.

Beard, G. M. (1879). The psychology of spiritualism. *North American Review, 129*, 65–80.
Benton, A. L. (1972). The "minor" hemisphere. *Journal of the History of Medicine and Allied Sciences, 27*, 5–14.
Benton, A. L. (1976). Historical development of the concept of hemispheric cerebral dominance. In S. F. Spicker, & H. T. Engelhardt (Eds.), *Philosophical dimensions of the neuro-medical sciences* (pp. 35–57). D. Reidel.
Benton, A. [L.]. (1981). Aphasia: Historical perspectives. In M. T. Sarno (Ed.), *Acquired aphasia* (pp. 1–25). Academic Press.
Bernard, D. (1885). *De l'aphasie et de ses diverses formes*. Progrès Médical.
Brancaccio, M. T. (2014). Enrico Morselli's psychology and "spiritism": Psychiatry, psychology and psychical research in Italy in the decades around 1900. *Studies in History and Philosophy of Biological and Biomedical Sciences, 48*, 75–84.
Braud, L. W., & Braud, W. G. (1974). Further studies of relaxation as a psi-conducive state. *Journal of the American Society for Psychical Research*, *68*, 229–245.
Braud, W. G., & Braud, L. W. (1975). The Psi-conducive syndrome: Free response GESP performance following evocation of "left-hemispheric" vs. "right-hemispheric" functioning. In J. D. Morris, W. G. Roll, & R. L. Morris (Eds.). *Research in parapsychology 1974* (pp. 17–20). Scarecrow Press. (Abstract)
Brazier, M. A. B. (1961). *A history of the electrical activity of the brain: The first half-century*. Pitman Medical Publishing.
Brazier, M. A. B. (1984). *A history of neurophysiology in the 17th and 18th centuries*. Raven Press.
Broca, P. (1861/1960). Remarks on the seat of the faculty of articulate language, followed by an observation of aphemia. In G. von Bonin (Ed.)., *Some papers on the cerebral cortex* (pp. 49–72). Charles C Thomas. (Original work published in French, 1861)
Broughton, R. S. (1975). Psi and the two halves of the brain. *Journal of the Society for Psychical Research, 48*, 133–147.
Broughton, R. S. (1976). Possible brain hemisphere laterality effects in ESP performance. *Journal of the Society for Psychical Research, 48*, 384–399.
Brown-Sequard, [C. E.] (1874). The brain power of man: Has he two brains, or has he only one? *Cincinnati Lancet and Observer, 17*(n. s.), 330–333.
Bryden, M. P. (1982). *Laterality: Functional asymmetry in the intact brain*. Academic Press.
Bulferetti, L. (1975). *Cesare Lombroso*. Unione Tipografico-Editrice Torinese.
Carpenter, W. B. (1874). *Principles of mental physiology*. D. Appleton.
Charcot, J. M. (1883-1884). Lectures on the different forms of aphasia. *Medical Press Circular, 36*(2), 263–264, 285–287, 303–305, 325–326, 347–349, *37*, 21–23.
Charcot, J. (1884). *Differenti forme d'afasia*. Francesco Vallardi.
Chevreul, M. E. (1833). Lettre à M. Ampère sur une classe particulière de mouvements musculaires. *Revue des Deux Mondes*, *2*(2), 258–266.
Clarke, E., & Jacyna, L. S. (1987). *Nineteenth-century origins of neuroscientific concepts*. University of California Press.
Cobbe, F. P. (1870). Unconscious cerebration: A psychological study. *Macmillan's Magazine, 23*, 24–37.
Crowe, C. (1848). *The night-side of nature: Or, ghosts and ghost seers* (2 Vols.). T. Newby.
Dax, M. (1865). Lésions de la moitié gauche de l'encéphale coincïdant avec l'oubli des signes de la pensée. *Gazette Hebdomadaire de Médecine et Chirugie*, *2*(2), 259–260.
Dimond, S. (1972). *The double brain*. Churchill Livingstone.
Dods, J. B. (1854). *Spirit manifestations examined and explained*. De Witt & Davenport.
Dunn, T. D. (1895). Double hemiplegia with double hemianopsia and loss of geographical centre. *Transactions of the College of Physicians of Philadelphia, 17*(3), 45–55.
Durville, H. (1900). *The theory and practice of human magnetism*. Psychic Research.
Ehrenwald, J. (1931). Anosognosie und Depersonalisation: Ein Beitrag zur Psychologie der linksseitig Hemiplegischen. *Der Nervenarzt, 4*, 681–688.
Ehrenwald, H. (1937). Hirnpathologische Bemerkungen zu einem Falle von «paranormalen» Erscheinungen bei einem Kinde (F. von Neureiter). *Zeitschrift für die gesamten Neurologie und Psychiatrie, 157*, 734–742.

Ehrenwald, H. (1948). Neurobiological aspects of telepathy. *Journal of the American Society for Psychical Research, 4*, 132–141.
Ehrenwald, J. (1975). Cerebral localization and the psi syndrome. *Journal of Nervous and Mental Disease, 61*, 393–398.
Ehrenwald, J. (1976). Parapsychology and the seven dragons: A neuropsychiatric model of psi phenomena. In G. R. Schmeidler (Ed.), *Parapsychology: Its relation to physics, biology, psychology, and psychiatry* (pp. 246–263). Scarecrow Press.
Engelhardt, H. T., Jr. (1975). John Hughlings Jackson and the mind-body relation. *Bulletin of the History of Medicine, 49*, 137–151.
Faraday, M. (1853). Professor Faraday on table-moving. *The Athenaeum, 1340*, 801–803.
Fenwick, P., Galliano, S., Coate, M.A.N., Rippere, V., & Brown, D. (1985). 'Psychic sensitivity,' mystical experience, head injury and brain pathology. *British Journal of Medical Psychology, 58*, 35–44.
Finger, S. (1994). *Origins of neuroscience: A history of explorations into brain function.* Oxford University Press.
Finger, S. (2010). The birth of localization theory. In S. Finger, F. Boller, & K. Tyler (Eds.), *History of clinical neurology* (Vol. 95, pp. 117–128). Elsevier.
Flammarion, C. (1886). *Le monde avant la création de l'homme.* C. Marpon and E. Flammarion.
Flourens, P. (1824). *Recherches expérimentales sur les propriétés et les fonctions du système nerveux dans les animaux vertébrés.* Crevot.
Flournoy, T. (1900). *From India to the planet Mars.* Harper & Brothers.
Fritsch, G., & Hitzig, E. (1870/1960). On the electrical excitability of the cerebrum. In G. von Bonin (Ed.). *Some papers on the cerebral cortex* (pp. 73–96). Charles C Thomas. (Original work published in German, 1870)
Gasser, J. (1995). *Aux origines du cerveau moderne: Localisations, langage et mémoire dans l'œuvre de Charcot.* Fayard.
Gauld, A. (1965). Mr. Hall and the S. P. R. *Journal of the Society for Psychical Research, 43*, 53–62.
Gauld, A. (1968). *The founders of psychical research.* Routledge & Kegan Paul.
Gauld, A. (1992). *A history of hypnotism.* Cambridge University Press.
Gonçalves, V. P., & Ortega, F. (2013). Uma nosologia para os fenômenos sobrenaturais e a construção do cérebro "possuído" no seculo XIX. *História, Ciências, Saúde-Manguinhos, 20*, 373–390.
Greenblatt, S. H. (1977). The development of Hughlings Jackson's approach to diseases of the nervous system 1863–1866: Unilateral seizures, hemiplegia and aphasia. *Bulletin of the History of Medicine, 51*, 412–430.
Gurney, E., Myers, F. W. H., & Barrett, W. F. (1882). Second report on thought-transference. *Proceedings of the Society for Psychical Research, 1*, 70–97.
Gurney, E., Myers, F. W. H., Podmore, F., & Barrett, W. F. (1883). Third report on thought transference. *Proceedings of the Society for Psychical Research, 1*, 161–215.
Haddock, J. W. (1851). *Somnolism & psycheism* (2nd ed.). James S. Hodson.
Hall, T. H. (1964). *The strange case of Edmund Gurney.* Gerald Duckworth.
Hamilton T. (2009). *Immortal longings: F. W. H. Myers and the Victorian search for life after death.* Imprint Academic.
Hammond, W. A. (1870). The physics and physiology of spiritualism. *North American Review, 110*, 233–260.
Harrington, A. (1987). *Medicine, mind, and the double brain: A study in nineteenth-century thought.* Princeton University Press.
Harris, L. J. (1980). Left-handedness: Early theories, facts, and fancies. In J. Herron (Ed.), *Neuropsychology of left handedness* (pp. 3–78). Academic Press.
Henderson, V. W. (2008). Alexia and agraphia: Contrasting perspectives of J.-M. Charcot and J. Hughlings Jackson. *Neurology, 70*, 391–400.
Holland, H. (1839). *Medical notes and reflections.* Longman, Brown, Green, Longman.
Honegger, B. (1980). A neuropsychological theory of automatic verbal behavior. *Parapsychology Review, 11*(4), 1–8.
Houston, E. J. (1892). Cerebral radiations. *Journal of the Franklin Institute, 133*, 488–497.
Ireland, W. W. (1881). On mirror-writing and its relation to left-handedness and cerebral disease. *Brain, 4*, 361–367.
Ireland, W. W. (1891). On the discordant action of the double brain. *British Medical Journal, 1*, 1167–1169.

Irwin, H. J. (1978). ESP and the human information processing system. *Journal of the American Society for Psychical Research, 72*, 111–126.
Jackson, J. H. (1878–1879). On affections of speech from disease of the brain. *Brain, 1*, 304–330, *2*, 203–222, 323–356.
Jackson, J. H. (1884). The Croonian lectures on evolution and dissolution of the nervous system. *British Medical Journal, 1*, 591–593, 660–663, 703–707.
Jackson, J. H. (1868/1915). Notes on the physiology and pathology of the nervous system. *Brain, 38*, 65–71. (Original work published 1868)
Jacyna, L. S. (1982). Somatic theories of mind and the interests of medicine in Britain, 1850–1879. *Medical History, 26*, 233–258.
Jacyna, L. S. (2000). *Lost words: Narratives of language and the brain, 1825–1926*. Princeton University Press.
James, W. (1889). Notes on automatic writing. *Proceedings of the American Society Psychical Research, 1*, 548–564.
James, W. (1890). *The principles of psychology* (2 vols.). Henry Holt.
Janet, P. (1889). *L'automatisme psychologique: Essai de psychologie expérimentale sur les formes inféieures de l'activitè humaine*. Félix Alcan.
Kaitaro, T. (2001). Biological and epistemological models of localization in the nineteenth century: From Gall to Charcot. *Journal of the History of the Neurosciences, 10*, 262–276.
Kelly, E. W. (2007). F. W. H. Myers and the empirical study of the mind-body problem. In E. Kelly, E. W. Kelly, A. Crabtree, A. Gauld, M. Grosso, & B. Greyson, *Irreducible Mind: Toward a psychology for the 21st century* (pp. 47–115). Rowman & Littlefield.
Knepper, P., & Ystehede, P. J. (Eds.). (2013). *The Cesare Lombroso handbook*. Routledge.
LaPointe, L. L. (2012). *Paul Broca and the origins of language in the brain*. Plural.
Lattes, L. (1907). Destrismo e mancinismo in relazione con le asimmetrie funzionali del cervello. *Archivio di Psichiatria, Neuropatologia, Antropologia Criminale e Medicina Legale, 4*(3), 281–303.
Lichtheim, L. (1885). On aphasia. *Brain, 7*, 433–484.
Lodge, O. J. (1894). Experience of unusual physical phenomena occurring in the presence of an entranced person (Eusapia Palladino). *Journal of the Society for Psychical Research, 6*, 306–336.
Lombroso, C. (1884a). Sul mancinismo e destrismo tattile nei sani, nei pazzi, nei ciechi e nei sordomuti. *Archivio de Psichiatria, Scienze Penali, e Antropologia Criminale, 5*, 187–197.
Lombroso, C. (1884b). *L'uomo delinquente in rapporto all'antropologia, alla giurisprudenza ed alle discipline carcerarie: Delinquente nato e pazzo morale* (3rd ed.) Bocca.
Lombroso, C. (1892). Le spiritisme et la psychiatrie: Explication psychiatrique de certains faits spirites. *Annales des Sciences Psychiques, 2*, 143–151.
Lombroso, C. (1903). Left-handedness and left-sidedness. *North American Review, 177*, 440–444.
Lombroso, C. (1908). Psychology and spiritism. *Annals of Psychical Science, 7*, 376–380.
Lombroso, C. (1909). *After death—what? Spiritistic phenomena and their interpretation.* Small, Maynard.
Lombroso, C. (1911). *Crime: Its causes and remedies.* Little, Brown.
Lorch, M. P. (2016). The third man: Robert Dunn's (1799–1877) contribution to aphasia research in mid-nineteenth-century England. *Journal of the History of Neuroscience, 25*, 188–203.
Luys, J. (1888). Étude sur le dédoublement des operations cerebrales et sur le role isole de chaque hemisphere dans les phénomènes de la pathologie mentale. *L'Encéphale, 8*, 404–424, 516–537.
Lyon, S. B. (1895). Dual action of the brain. *New York Medical Journal, 62*, 107–110.
Maher, M., & Schmeidler, G. R. (1977). Cerebral lateralization effects in ESP processing. *Journal of the American Society for Psychical Research, 71*, 261–271.
Maudsley, H. (1889). The double brain. *Mind, 14*, 161–187.
Mesmer, F. A. (1779). *Memoire sur la découverte du magnétisme animal.* Didot.
Mills, C. K. (1894). Mirror-writing. *Journal of Nervous and Mental Disease, 19*(n. s.), 85–91.
Morris, R. L. (1977). Parapsychology, biology, and ANPSI. In B. B. Wolman (Ed.). *Handbook of parapsychology* (pp. 687–715.) Van Nostrand Reinhold.
Morselli, E. (1884). Sulla dinamografia e sue applicazioni al diagnostico dei disordini motori nelle malattie nervose. *Rivista Sperimentale di Freniatria, 10*, 265–290.

Morselli, E. (1908). *Psicologia e "spiritismo": Impressioni e note critiche sui fenomeni medianici di Eusapia Palladino* (2 vols.). Fratelli Bocca.

Muhl, A. (1930). *Automatic writing*. T. Steinkopff.

Myers, F. W. H. (1884). On a telepathic explanation of some so-called spiritualistic phenomena. *Proceedings of the Society for Psychical Research, 2*, 217–237.

Myers, F. W. H. (1885a). Automatic writing—II. *Proceedings of the Society for Psychical Research, 3*, 1–63.

Myers, F. W. H. (1885b). Automatic writing, or the rationale of planchette. *Contemporary Review, 47*, 233–249.

Myers, F. W. H. (1885c). Human personality in the light of hypnotic suggestion. *Proceedings of the Society for Psychical Research, 4*, 1–24.

Myers, F. W. H. (1886a). Multiplex personality. *Nineteenth Century, 20*, 648–666.

Myers, F. W. H. (1886b). Report to the general meeting. *Journal of the Society for Psychical Research, 2*, 224–229.

Myers, F. W. H. (1887a). Automatic writing—III. *Proceedings of the Society for Psychical Research, 4*, 209–261.

Myers, F. W. H. (1887b). Multiplex personality. *Proceedings of the Society for Psychical Research, 4*, 496–514.

Myers, F. W. H. (1889). Automatic writing—IV. The daemon of Socrates. *Proceedings of the Society for Psychical Research, 5*, 522–547.

Myers, F. W. H. (1892). The subliminal consciousness: Chapter 3: The mechanism of genius. *Proceedings of the Society for Psychical Research, 8*, 333–361.

Myers, F. W. H. (1899). Review of "Some peculiarities of the secondary personality" by G. T. W. Patrick. *Proceedings of the Society for Psychical Research, 34*, 382–386.

Myers, F. W. H. (1903). *Human personality and its survival of bodily death* (2 vols.). Longmans, Green.

The National Association of Spiritualists (1876, November 24). *Spiritualist Newspaper*, pp. 202–208.

Ogle, W. (1867). Aphasia and agraphia. *St. George's Hospital Reports, 2*, 83–122.

Oppenheim, J. (1985). *The other world: Spiritualism and psychical research in England, 1850–1914.* Cambridge University Press.

Ornstein, R. E. (1972). *The psychology of consciousness*. W. H. Freeman.

Parsons, B. S. (1924). *Left-handedness*. Macmillan.

Pitres, A. (1884). Considérations sur l'agraphie: À propos d'une observation nouvelle d'agraphie motrice pure. *Revue de Médicine, 4*, 855–873.

Plumer, W. S. (1860). Mary Reynolds: A case of double consciousness. *Harper's New Monthly Magazine, 20*, 807–812.

Prince, M. (1898). A contribution to the study of hysteria. *Proceedings of the Society for Psychical Research, 14*(34). (Original work published 1891)

The Psychological Society of Great Britain (1876, November 24). *Spiritualist Newspaper*, pp. 196–198.

Reeves, J. A. (1979). *Psychical phenomena in the United States in the nineteenth century.* (Doctoral dissertation.) Miami University, Oxford, Ohio.

Reichenbach, C. von (1849/1851). *Physico-physiological researches on the dynamics of magnetism, electricity, heat, light, crystallization, and chemism, in their relations to vital force.* J. S. Redfield. (Original work published in German, 1849)

Roe, D., & Finger, S. (1996). Gustave Dax and his fight for recognition: An overlooked chapter in the early history of cerebral dominance. *Journal of the History of the Neurosciences, 5*, 228–240.

Rogers, E. C. (1853). *Philosophy of mysterious agents*. John P. Jewett.

Roll, W. G. (1974/1975). A new look at the survival problem. In J. Beloff (Ed.). *New directions in parapsychology* (pp. 144–164). Scarecrow Press. (Original work published 1974)

Roth, H. L. (2002). Finding language in the matter of the brain: Origins of the clinical aphasia examination. *Seminars in Neurology, 22*, 335–348.

Samson, G. W. (1860). *Spiritualism tested.* Gould and Lincoln.

Smith, R. (1973). The background of physiological psychology in natural philosophy. *History of Science, 11*, 75–123.

Somers, A. N. (1893). The double personality, and the relation of the submerged personality to the phenomena of modern Spiritualism. *Psychical Review, 1*, 314–332.

Spillane, J. D. (1981). *The doctrine of the nerves: Chapters in the history of neurology.* Oxford University Press.

Stephen, L., & Lee, S. (Eds.) (1950). *The dictionary of national biography* (Vol. 5). Oxford University Press.

Stevenson, I. (1978). Some comments on automatic writing. *Journal of the American Society for Psychical Research, 72*, 315–332.

Tesak, J., & Code, C. (2008). *Milestones in the history of aphasia: Theories and protagonists.* Psychology Press.

Tuttle, H. (1871). *Arcana of spiritualism.* Adams.

Ungaro, J. (1992). *Las radiaciones humanas: Historia de la radiónica.* Club de Estudio.

Warcollier, R. (1931). Le dessin télépathique. *Revue Métapsychique, 5*, 321–335.

Wigan, A. L. (1844). *A new view of insanity: The duality of the mind.* Longman, Brown, Green, and Longmans.

Wilks, S. (1872). Cases of disease of the nervous system, with remarks: A case of aphasia, with remarks on the faculty of language and the duality of the brain. *Guy's Hospital Reports, 17*(2), 145–171.

Williams, B. J. (2012). Extrasensory perception and the brain hemispheres: Where does the issue stand now? *NeuroQuantology, 10*, 350–373.

Word, R. C. (1888). Duality of the brain: A theory of mind-reading and slate-writing. *Southern Medical Record, 18*, 81–89.

Young, R. M. (1970). *Mind, brain and adaptation in the nineteenth century: Cerebral localization and its biological context from Gall to Ferrier.* Clarendon Press.

Notes on Early Interpretations of Mediumship*

Carlos S. Alvarado, Michael Nahm, & Andreas Sommer

The purpose of this note is to dispel the notion that ideas of human agency to account for the veridical mental phenomena of mediums began with persons associated with the Society for Psychical Research (SPR) in England, or with certain later individuals. In fact, the appearance of these ideas preceded the founding of the Society in 1882. Examples of earlier writers who discussed these ideas include Carl Gustav Carus, Edward W. Cox, Justinus Kerner, Asa Mahan, André-Saturnin Morin, Maximilian Perty, B. W. Richmond, and Edward C. Rogers. In contrast to the speculation by later SPR authors and others, the concepts that appeared in the old literature often involved belief in physical forces.

The study of the possibility of survival of death is a traditional area of parapsychology, and one that has influenced the field in many ways (Alvarado, 2003). Within survival research much attention has been paid to the veridical statements of mental mediums delivered through such means as automatic writing or trance speaking. Among the information that could be corroborated in reports on the mediums of the past were specific names and information about relationships and events relevant to the life of the purported spirit communicator (e.g., Hodgson 1892; Radclyffe-Hall; and Troubridge; 1919).

Provided conventional explanations such as sensory cues and fraud have been ruled out or considered unlikely, much of this material has been interpreted by some as evidence of discarnate agency. However, as has been discussed in modern writings about mediumship, the psychic abilities of the mediums have been proposed as a frequent counter-explanation for discarnate agency (e.g., Braude, 2003; Gauld, 1982; Hart, 1959; Sudduth, 2009). Gauld (1982) stated that the assumption here is that mediums "obtain all their information by telepathically tapping the memory-stores of living persons, clairvoyantly scanning archives, etc." (Gauld, 1982, p. 127). The purpose of the present note is to provide the reader with examples of early ideas of this sort, generally neglected in the modern literature.

Recently one author argued that "the idea of explaining mediumistic communications in terms of extraordinary living agent psi originated in the late 19th century among members of the British and American societies of psychical research" (Sudduth, 2009, p. 190). Another recent author singled out Frank Podmore (1856–1910), an active member of the Society for Psychical Research (SPR) and a well-known writer, as someone who had developed this concept (Fontana 2005, p. 104). Similarly, authors of overviews of survival of death in psychical research have not mentioned early ideas of this sort (e.g., Almeder, 1992, Braude, 2003, Fontana, 2005, Gauld, 1982). Although work conducted by SPR researchers and others was important in the dissemination of the concept of living agency in mediumship (e.g., Leaf, 1890), and although their speculations may have been more detailed, the idea is older than that. In fact, it cropped up almost immediately after the rise of Spiritualism. Our review will present examples from the early mesmeric and spiritualistic literature (see also Crabtree, 1993, Podmore, 1902).

*Republished with permission from *Journal of Scientific Exploration, 26*, 855–865, 2012. The authors wish to thank Nancy L. Zingrone for useful editorial comments.

Some Authors Writing on Living Agency and Mediumship Previously to the Foundation of the SPR

The notion that the psychic powers of the living played a role in mediumistic communications attributed to the dead was present in the mesmeric movement. Writing in the journal Zoist, English clergyman the Reverend George Sandby (1799–1881) reduced the revelations some mesmeric subjects claimed to come from discarnate spirits to the "old mesmeric principles of thought-reading and clairvoyance" (Sandby, 1850, p. 423).[1] In France, lawyer André-Saturnin Morin (1807–1888) disagreed with the belief that mediumistic communications could be explained only by the action of spirits of the dead. In an account of a specific phenomenon, he wrote: "To imitate writings he has never seen ... the medium reads the thought of the consultant and sees the name of the evoked deceased [person] and the writing at the same time" (Morin, 1858, p. 96). In a later publication Morin (1860, p. 464) felt that the information conveyed by mediums was related to sources such as writings or books located in other places accessed through their lucidity (clairvoyance). Similarly, magnetizer Charles Lafontaine (1803–1892) argued that mediums could perceive the "unconscious thoughts of the persons present" (Lafontaine, 1866, p. 116).

Discussions of living agency have also been put forward in the early literature of spiritualism. Often, these authors referred to concepts based or derived from mesmerism and entailing the concept of vital, nervous, or psychic forces that were intimately related to the body of the medium. The projection of such a force was assumed by opponents of discarnate agency to be either an automatic process or one guided unconsciously by the medium. Most of these speculations referred to such physical phenomena as raps, table movements, and movement of other objects.[2] An early review of some of these publications in the English and French literature was presented by Alexander Aksakow (1832–1903) (Aksakow, 1886).[3] Many such examples existed (e.g., Oldfield, 1852; De Gasparin, 1854; Dods, 1854; Mahan, 1855; Samson, 1860;, Chevillard, 1869; Cox, 1879). Some of these discussions included the concept of Od, which became popular in the spiritualistic literature at the time.[4] An example was English spiritualist Thomas P. Barkas's (1862) summary of a popular explanation for the phenomena of spiritualism. The explanation rested on the assumption that the phenomena were produced by human agency, among which were

> the automatic action of the cerebral, spinal, and sympathetic nerve centers of mediums, acting through the agency of and using an imponderable and all-pervading fluid designated by Reichenbach, ODYLE. (Barkas, 1862, p. 15).

Traverse Oldfield (1852)—a pseudonym used by American minister George W. Samson (1819-1896)—argued that the

> communications of the clairvoyant and of the spiritual medium, as to facts that can be tested, have been only the knowledge, remembered or forgotten, and the surmise, right or wrong, of the person consulting. (Oldfield, 1852, p. 44)

He suggested that the explanation was "a united current of two persons' nervous influence" (Oldfield, 1852, p. 44) in which the thought of one person passed to the other, and then was expressed through rappings or automatic writing. Such process, Oldfield wrote,

> [I]s no more mysterious than that, by a connection of electric conductors, and by an excitement of the electric principle, I can control the electric influence of a series of electric conductors, reaching from New Orleans to Boston, and have my thought rapped or written out a thousand miles from the point where I exert the energy. (Oldfield, 1852, p. 44)

Physician B. W. Richmond believed that mental phenomena were caused by "mind acting on mind" (Brittan & Richmond, 1853, p. 149). The medium, in a magnetic state, was in rapport with another living mind. Phenomena such as automatic writing "follow the law of *mental reflection*—and the *reflected image* often corresponds to other minds than the medium ..." (Brittan & Richmond, 1853, p. 186). He believed that the mind of the medium could not realize that "she is being impressed by a book, a letter, or some human mind" (Brittan & Richmond, 1853, p. 204). Furthermore, Richmond asserted that in cases in which a medium produced a facsimile of a deceased person's signature that was unknown to her, the medium, being in rapport with a person familiar with the signature, "copied" it from that person's memory (Brittan & Richmond, 1853, p. 204). Another author, and one cited by many at the time, was the American writer Edward C. Rogers (1853). He believed that mediumistic physical phenomena were caused by human nervous forces related to the medium's brain centers. In mental mediums, there was the assumption of a fictitious "influence of external agencies," and of a "promptness of the brain to give a reflex action of these impressions back upon the outward world through the medium of the automatic apparatus in the bodily frame, or through the odylic agent" (Rogers, 1853, p. 176). The medium's brain, Rogers believed, "may, under certain circumstances in its action, assume any personality, from that of a divinity to that of a toad ..." (Rogers, 1853, p. 171).

The well-known American clairvoyant Andrew Jackson Davis (1826–1910) believed in different agencies. In his book *The Present Age and Inner Life* (1853) Davis wrote that "owing to the extraordinary attributes of man's mind, many experiences are by some individuals regarded as spiritually originated; which in truth, are only caused by the natural laws of our being" (Davis 1853, p. 160). Davis believed that 40% of the phenomena were due to discarnate spirits. The remaining possibilities included a variety of medical explanations, with 18% being accounted for by what would later be referred to as the psychic powers of the living. This living agency, Davis wrote, was due to "vital electricity" projected by the medium's body, and by clairvoyance. Like Davis, other writers accepted both spirit and human agency as explanations—for the phenomena of mediumship. One of them, Unitarian minister Adin Ballou (1803–1890), believed the phenomena "sometimes proceed from spirits in the flesh," and sometimes from discarnate spirits (Ballou 1853, p. 78). For Ballou the mind of the medium was open to "mesmeric and psychological influences, from controlling minds near them" (Ballou, 1853, p. 61). However, he believed it was possible to distinguish human from discarnate agency. Another author who accepted the notion of mixed agency was the writer Epes Sargent (1812–1880). In his book *Planchette; or, the Despair of Science* he wrote:

> It is not unlikely that many of the minor phenomena, attributed with sincerity by many partially developed mediums to spirits, may be produced by the unconscious exercise of spiritual powers latent in the individual; while other phenomena are of so extraordinary a character that the more rational explanation may be found in the theory of the application of an external spiritual intelligence or force. (Sargent, 1869, p. 233).

In Germany, Justinus Kerner (1786–1862), famous for his work with the "Seeress of Prevorst," argued that the spiritistic interpretation of table turning and mediumistic communication was misleading. In 1853, Kerner published *Die Somnambulen Tische*, a booklet in which he described experiences and experiments that had been performed on table turning and related phenomena. Some of the examples presented by Kerner concerned allegedly successful transmissions of mental suggestions by sitters, including cases of xenoglossy. Kerner argued that the peculiar movements of tables and other objects were caused by the "human nerve spirit" of the sitters (Kerner 1853, p. 52), a fluidic force expressed by their organisms. In addition, he attributed the received communications to a subconscious psychic aspect of this nerve spirit that would enable thought transference and clairvoyance.

Similar thoughts were expressed by noted physician Carl Gustav Carus (1789–1869). Along with Gotthilf Heinrich von Schubert (1780–1860), Carus is often regarded as one of the first writers who had laid foundations for exploring and understanding the subconscious layers of the human psyche. In his book *Über Lebensmagnetismus* (1857), Carus stated that table turning, rappings, and mediumistic communications "can be reduced to the rise of the subconscious into the region of the conscious" (Carus, 1857, p. 222). Like Kerner, he attributed table movements to influences of animal magnetism. The mediums would be especially prone to utilize this "stream of innervation" (Carus, 1857, p. 225) subconsciously. If veridical elements were contained in the received communications, Carus attributed them to the divining faculties of the human subconscious, sometimes also displayed in dreaming. He regarded the spreading of mediumship and sitter groups as an indication of an epidemic of regressive human madness.

The German zoologist Maximilian Perty (1804–1884) was another critic of belief in spirit communication in mediumship. Like Bruno Schindler (1797–1859) (Schindler, 1857) before him, in *Die Mystischen Erscheinungen der Menschlichen Natur* (1861/1872), Perty provided an alternative account of certain supernormal phenomena to that of such previous authors as Joseph Görres (1776–1848) (Görres 1836–1842), who held that they were usually caused by the supernatural agency of angels and demons, while Schindler and Perty proposed they were usually due to the vital or psychic forces of living persons.

Anticipating Carl du Prel's (1839–1899) philosophy of dissociation in somnambulism (du Prel, 1885), Perty argued that the "guides" of somnambulistic mediums, often assuming the appearance of deceased loved ones, were usually dramatized personifications from the somnambulist's own psyche (Perty, 1861/1872, Vol. 1, p. 244). Rather than suggesting evidence of spirit identity, Perty held that supernormal knowledge emerging in "spirit guides" was due to the somnambulist's own unconscious clairvoyance or "magic excitation." In a discussion of the literary products of Andréw Davis, the famous "Poughkeepsie Seer" and precursor of modern spiritualism we have mentioned above, Perty found them to be a mixture of inspiration and obvious errors, and he concluded that they were a "remarkable product of somnambulist ecstasy" (Perty, 1861/1872, Vol. 1, p. 339), combining certain cultural influences that Perty presumed Jackson must have been exposed to, but with glimpses of genius and supernormal knowledge. Similarly, in a contribution to the problem of demonic possession, Perty held that, in most cases, the possessing entities were "products of the own divided [entzweiten] psyche of those concerned" (Perty, 1861/1872, Vol. 1, p. 341), even if apparent possession episodes were accompanied by supernormal physical or mental phenomena. The second volume of *Die Mystischen Erscheinungen* opens with a chapter dedicated to the phenomena of spiritualism, i.e. table rapping, and automatic writing and speaking (Perty, 1861/1872, Vol. 2., pp. 1–77). Perty criticized spiritualists claiming that a "spirit's" opposition to views held by a medium counted as evidence for the alleged spirit's autonomy, for our normal dream life was replete with instances of opposing viewpoints of the dream self and the waking self (Perty, 1861/1872, Vol. 2, pp. 10–11). Perty therefore concluded: "In a considerable number of cases, the so-called spirits turn out to be products of the magically excited psyche of the mediums, appearing to be autonomous extraneous beings" (Perty, 1861/1872, Vol. 2, p. 60).[5]

Concluding Remarks

The material discussed in this note could be extended. It shows that explanations of veridical elements arising from the living medium rather than from discarnate influence preceded the founding of the SPR. Moreover, such ideas had been put forward during the early days of the SPR without being influenced by the SPR (e.g., von Hartmann, 1885a, 1885b). Nonetheless, the early ideas were often not exactly equivalent to those held by SPR workers and later writers engaged in controversies (e.g., Gasperini, 2011) and discussions of the so-called hypothetical construct referred to as super ESP (e.g., Gauld, 1982; Hart, 1959; Sudduth, 2009). Instead, early ideas were frequently associated with unorthodox concepts of force not discussed by the SPR workers who wrote about mental mediumship.[6] In addition, although earlier writers knew about such processes as those akin to unconscious cerebration, the SPR (and later) workers laid more emphasis on less physiological conceptions of subconscious processes that had a wider scope. The later interest took place in the context of observations of and research on dissociation and the subconscious mind during the late 19th century (Alvarado, 2002; Crabtree, 1993; Ellenberger, 1970). Similar to secondary personalities and the states observed in hypnosis, in hysterical patients, and in other circumstances, mediumship was discussed by some as an example of dissociation and of the existence of the subconscious mind.

Although other authors have discussed some of these ideas of the living medium as the source of veridical information before the foundation of the SPR (see the reviews of Aksakow, 1894; Crabtree, 1993; Podmore, 1902), or early after its foundation and independently from it (von Hartmann 1885a, 1885b), the literature we present is largely unknown among current writers. We hope that this note serves as a reminder that the concept of living agency in the interpretation of the phenomena of mediumship has a history that extends back to the middle of the 19th century.

Notes

1 On spiritualistic mesmerism, see Crabtree (1993, p. 196–212). See also Alvarado (2009).

2 Discussions of concepts of force in relation to mediumship include the works of Alvarado (2006, 2008b), Crabtree (1993), and Podmore (1902). Later authors who discuss such forces in the 19th century include Collyer (1871), Cox (1879), De Rochas (1897), and von Hartmann (1885a, 1885b). For example, referring to the medium's "nervo-vital fluid" affecting tables and other objects it was stated: "When this fact is admitted, there is no necessity of ascribing the phenomena to spiritual causes" (Collyer, 1871, p. 110). It should be kept in mind that believers in discarnate agency also accepted the existence of forces to explain the phenomena of mediums (e.g., Ballou, 1853; Kardec, 1863). But they postulated that spirits made use of such forces to produce both mental and physical phenomena.

3 This review was later included in his influential work Animismus und Spiritismus (Aksakow, 1894).

4 According to Baron Karl von Reichenbach (1849/1851), Od was a universal force similar to animal magnetism, that could be found in minerals, crystals, and living organisms including the human body, but that was also generated by several other means such as heat, light, friction, electricity, chemical reactions, and magnetism. The concept was used by many in the mid-19th century to explain mediumship and other psychic phenomena (e.g., Brittan & Richmond, 1853; Guppy, 1863; Mayo, 1852; Rogers, 1853; see also Alvarado, 2008a). Although in general spiritualists did not like phenomena explained in terms of Od—the writings of Samuel B. Brittan (c. 1815–1883) are one example (Brittan & Richmond, 1853)—there was widespread interest in the topic, as is evident in articles published in 19th-century spiritualist periodicals (e.g., Gregory, 1872; Howitt, 1860). However, von Reichenbach himself didn't relate the concept of Od

to mediumistic communications. When he wrote about mediumistic processes, he was more interested in physical phenomena (see, e.g., his presentation of the experiments he had performed on table turning in von Reichenbach, 1867, pp. 108–148). On Reichenbach and Od, see Nahm (2012).

5 Perty (1861/1872, Vol. 2, p. 65) also provided a brief discussion of the role of cryptomnesia in mediumship. That is, mediums seem to generate new information whereas they only reproduce forgotten memories without being aware of doing so.

6 The pre-SPR British literature on mediumistic forces in general (e.g., Cox, 1879; Crookes, 1874; Guppy, 1863), and of ideas of forces involved in mental mediumship in particular (Alvarado, 2008c) notwithstanding, the discussions of mental mediumship published by SPR leaders followed a mentalistic approach. Where force was discussed, it was in the context of physical phenomena, Lodge's (1894, pp. 334–335) and Myers's (1903, Vol. 2, pp. 544–546) works being examples.

References

Aksakow, A. (1886). Kritische Bemerkungen über Dr. Eduard von Hartmann's Werk: «Der Spiritismus."» Historische Überschau der anti-spiritistischen Theorien. *Psychische Studien, 13*, 62–76, 109–126.

Aksakow, A. (1894). *Animismus und spiritismus* (2nd Ed.). Mutze.

Almeder, R. F. (1992). *Death and personal survival: The evidence for life after death.* Littlefield Adams.

Alvarado, C. S. (2002). Dissociation in Britain during the late nineteenth century: The Society for Psychical Research, 1882–1900. *Journal of Trauma and Dissociation, 3*, 9–33.

Alvarado, C. S. (2003). The concept of survival of bodily death and the development of parapsychology. *Journal of the Society for Psychical Research, 67*, 65–95.

Alvarado, C. S. (2006). Human radiations: Concepts of force in mesmerism, spiritualism, and psychical research. *Journal of the Society for Psychical Research, 70*, 138–162.

Alvarado, C. S. (2008a). Further notes on historical ideas of human radiations: II. Od and psychometry. *Psypioneer, 4*, 63–69.

Alvarado, C. S. (2008b). Further notes on historical ideas of human radiations: III. The perispirit and mediumistic forces. *Psypioneer, 4*, 85–92.

Alvarado, C. S. (2008c). Further notes on historical ideas of human radiations: IV. Mental phenomena. *Psypioneer, 4*, 119–126.

Alvarado, C. S. (2009). Mesmeric mediumship: The case of Emma. *Psypioneer, 5*, 43–51.

Ballou, A. (1853). *An exposition of views respecting the principal facts, causes, and peculiarities involved in spirit manifestations* (2nd ed.). Bela Marsh.

Barkas, T. (1862). *Outlines of ten years' investigations into the phenomena of modern spiritualism, embracing letters, lectures, & etc.* Frederick Pittman.

Braude, S. E. (2003). *Immortal remains.* Rowman & Littlefield.

Brittan, S. B., & Richmond, B. W. (1853). *A discussion of the facts and philosophy of ancient and modern spiritualism.* Partridge & Brittan.

Carus, C. G. (1857). *Uber Lebensmagnetismus.* Brockhaus.

Chevillard, A. (1869). *Études expérimentales sur le fluide nerveux et solution définitive du problème spirite.* Victor Masson.

Collyer, R. H. (1871). *Mysteries of the vital in connexion with dreams, somnambulism, trance, vital photography, faith and will, anaesthesia, nervous congestion and creative function* (2nd ed.). Henry Renshaw.

Cox, E. W. (1879). *The mechanism of man: An answer to the question what am I: A popular introduction to mental physiology and psychology: Volume 2: The mechanism in action.* Longman.

Crabtree, A. (1993). *From Mesmer to Freud: Magnetic sleep and the roots of psychological healing.* Yale University Press.

Crookes, W. (1874). *Researches in the phenomena of spiritualism.* J. Burns.

Davis, A. J. (1853). *The present age and inner life: A sequel to spiritual intercourse: Modern mysteries classified and explained.* Partridge and Brittan.

De Gasparin, A., Count (1854). *Des tables tournantes: Du surnaturel en général et des esprits* (2 vols.). E. Dentu.

De Rochas, A. (1897). Les expériences de Choisy-Yvrec (près Bordeaux) du 2 au 14 octobre 1896. *Annales des Sciences Psychiques*, *7*, 6–28.

Dods, J. B. (1854). *Spirit manifestations examined and explained: Judge Edmonds refuted; or, an exposition of the involuntary powers and instincts of the human mind.* De Witt & Davenport.

du Prel, C. (1885). *Die philosophie der mystik.* Ernst Gunther.

Ellenberger, H. F. (1970). *The discovery of the unconscious: The History and evolution of dynamic psychiatry.* Basic Books.

Fontana, D. (2005). *Is there an afterlife?* O Books.

Gasperini, L. (2011). Criptestesia o ipotesi spiritica? Charles Richet ed E. Bozzano a confronto. *Luce e Ombra, 111*, 113–126.

Gauld, A. (1982). *Mediumship and survival.* Heinemann.

Gorres, J. von (1836-1842). *Die christliche Mystik* (4 vols.). G. Joseph Manz.

Gregory, W. (1872, November 15). Reichenbach's magnetic flames. *The Spiritualist*, 5–6.

[Guppy, S.] (1863). *Mary Jane; or, Spiritualism chemically explained.* John King. [Samuel Guppy wrote with the pseudonum "A Child at School".]

Hart, H. (1959). *The enigma of survival: The case for and against an after life.* Charles C Thomas.

Hartmann, E. von (1885a). *Der spiritismus.* Friedrich.

Hartmann, E. von (1885b). Spiritism. *Light*, *5*, 405–409, 417–421, 429–432, 441–443, 453–456, 466–470, 479–482, 491–494.

Hodgson, R. (1892). A record of observations of certain phenomena of trance. *Proceedings of the Society for Psychical Research*, *8*, 1–167.

Howitt, W. (1860). Correspondence: Reichenbach on Od. *Spiritual Magazine*, *1*, 566–567.

Kardec, A. (1863). *Spiritisme expérimental: Le livre des médiums ou guide des mediums et de évocateurs* (6th ed.). Didier.

Kerner, J. (1853). *Die somnambulen tische.* Johannes Baum.

Lafontaine, C. (1866). Avis aux spirites, la cause des effets dits spirites est dans le système nerveux. *Magnétiseur: Journal de Magnétisme Animal*, *7*, 113–116.

Leaf, W. (1890). A record of observations of certain phenomena of trance (3). Part II. *Proceedings of the Society for Psychical Research*, *6*, 558–646.

Lodge, O. J. (1894). Experience of unusual physical phenomena occurring in the presence of an entranced person (Eusapia Paladino). *Journal of the Society for Psychical Research*, *6*, 306–336.

Mahan, A. (1855). *Modern mysteries explained and exposed in four parts.* J. P. Jewett.

Mayo, H. (1852). *Popular superstitions, and the theories contained therein, with an account of mesmerism* (3rd London ed.). Lindsay and Blakiston.

Morin, A. S. (1858). Review of *Le monde spirituel ou science chrétienne de communiquer intimement avec les puissances célestres et les âmes heureuses* by G. de Candemberg. *Journal du Magnétisme*, *17*(2), 90–103.

Morin, A. S. (1860). *Du magnétisme et des sciences occultes.* Germer Baillière.

Myers, F. W. H. (1903). *Human personality and its survival of bodily death* (2 vols.). Longmans, Green.

Nahm, M. (2012). The sorcerer of Cobenzl and his legacy: The life of Karl Ludwig Baron von Reichenbach, his work and its aftermath. *Journal of Scientific Exploration*, *26*(2), 381–407.

Oldfield, T. (1852). *"To daimonion," or, The spiritual medium.* Gould and Lincoln.

Perty, M. (1872). *Die Mystischen Erscheinungen der Menschlichen Natur* (2 vols., 2nd enlarged ed.). Winter. (Original work published 1861)

Podmore, F. (1902). *Modern spiritualism: A history and a criticism* (2 vols.). Methuen.

Radclyffe-Hall, M., & Troubridge, U. (1919). On a series of sittings with Mrs. Osborne Leonard. *Proceedings of the Society for Psychical Research*, *30*, 339–554.

Reichenbach, K. von (1851). *Physico-physiological researches on the dynamics of magnetism, electricity, heat, light, crystallization, and chemism, in their relation to vital force.* J. S. Redfield. (Original work published in German, 1849)

Reichenbach, K. von (1867). *Die Od'sche lohe und einige Bewegungserscheinungen als neuent- deckte formen des Od'schen Prinzips in der Natur.* Braumuller.

Rogers, E. C. (1853). *Philosophy of mysterious agents.* J. P. Jewett.

Samson, G. W. (1860). *Spiritualism tested; Or, the facts of its history classified.* Gould and Lincoln.

Sandby, G. (1850). Review of M. Alphonse Cahagnet's *Arcanes de la Vie Future Dévoilés, &c. Zoist, 7,* 414–431.

Sargent, E. (1869). *Planchette; or, the despair of science.* Roberts Brothers.

Schindler, H. B. (1857). *Das magische Geistesleben. Ein Beitrag zur Psychologie.* Korn.

Sudduth, M. (2009). Super-psi and the survivalist interpretation of mediumship. *Journal of Scientific Exploration, 23*(2), 167–193.

13

Spiritist Delusions and Spiritism in the Nosography of French Psychiatry (1850–1950)*

Pascal Le Maléfan, Renaud Evrard, & Carlos S. Alvarado

At the turn of the twentieth century there was a wave of delusions which had a direct link to spiritism in their form and content. These so-called spiritist or mediumistic delusions were the object of detailed study, and clinicians assigned them a place in nosography, especially in France. This work of classification was carried out as a function of the convictions and paradoxes that these delusions aroused; it also made it possible to question the relationship between pathology and belief. It is therefore important to emphasize certain ideological views of psychiatry on para-normality. We observed both a reductionist discourse concerning these domains, and at the same time their utilization in the construction of psychiatric knowledge.

During the nineteenth century, spiritualism in the USA and spiritism in France developed as movements based on the claim that spirits of the dead residing in the spirit world had the ability to communicate with the living, especially through gifted humans called "mediums," generally during ritualized "séances" with a circle of open-minded participants (Cox, 2003; Sharp, 2006). The relation between these ideas and practices and psychiatry has received little attention by historians of the behavioral sciences. Yet many classic clinical psychopathologists have discussed the topic during subtle debates with nosographic purposes. In this paper we will review some interactions between spiritism and psychiatry around a specific case: the recalcitrant nosographic entity "spiritist delusions," born in French psychiatry at the turn of the twentieth century to account for a multiplicity of various clinical observations. While it is interesting to follow the different stages in the elaboration of this category, it is worth emphasizing that the relation between psychiatry and spiritism cannot be reduced merely to this classification. Psychiatric and psychopathological knowledge was genuinely gained from these confrontations with spiritism, as shown by Gilbert Ballet's (1914) use of mediumistic trances in the elaboration of "chronic hallucinatory psychosis" (CHP). In this study, we therefore propose first of all to trace the relations between spiritism and psychiatric thought, and then to examine the history of spiritist delusion in France.

Despite this lack of attention from historians, the few relevant studies reveal numerous and fruitful interactions between psychiatry and popular spiritism, for example Clervoy (2002), and Le Maléfan (1999) who made systematic review of the changing psychiatric discourse on the psychopathology of spiritism from 1850 to 1950. As often noted by these historians, since spiritist phenomena raised the question of automatism and subconscious activities, they would figure centrally in the work of Pierre Janet (2007), Max Dessoir (1889), Théodore Flournoy (1900) and especially Frederic W. H. Myers (1903), but not always in a psychopathological perspective. The study of mediums would play a foundational role in the development of dynamic psychiatry (Crabtree, 2003; Ellenberger, 1970). In the words of Ellenberger (1970, p. 85):

> The advent of spiritism was an event of major importance in the history of dynamic psychiatry, because it indirectly provided psychologists and psychopathologists with new approaches to

*Reprinted with permission from *History of Psychiatry*, *24*, 477–491, 2013.

> the mind. Automatic writing, one of the procedures introduced by spiritists, was taken over by scientists as a method of exploring the unconscious … A new subject, the medium, became available for experimental psychological investigations, out of which evolved a new model of the human mind.

Such a perspective has inspired later work (e.g. Alvarado, 2010; Crabtree, 1993; Shamdasani, 1994).

According to Plas (2000, 2012), before being rejected—partly because of a desire for respectability and professionalization—researches on "mental suggestion" and "telepathy" were the first sources of the psychological approach of a psychic unconscious in France. In England some members of the Society for Psychical Research, such as Myers, contributed to the study of dissociation and the workings of the subconscious mind (Alvarado, 2002). Indeed, conceptions originating in the early scientific study of spiritist phenomena would continue to influence scientific and medical approaches to the human psyche throughout the twentieth century (Alvarado, Machado, Zangari, & Zingrone, 2007; Kelly et al., 2007). One example of the way in which the early literature on spiritism continues to find relevance is Flournoy's (1900) famous account of the medium Hélène Smith; this continues to serve as an important case study in the field of psycholinguistics (for a review, see Engels, 2008), psychopathology (Maleval, 1996), and the history of the subliminal psychology (Shamdasani, 1994). Flournoy's "medium" Catherine-Elise Müller (alias Hélène Smith) had somnambulic trances during spiritist séances from which she developed four "cycles" of different personalities, with false memories and glossolalia, in the pure vein of multiple personalities. In such works, the history of spiritism and the history of clinical psychology find intersection points.

Among the many products of the historical intersection of science and popular religion was psychical research, more widely known in France during the twentieth century by the term "*métapsychique*" (Lachapelle, 2011; Richet, 1905). Metapsychics was an attempt to collect and critically assess "psychic marvels" as claimed by spiritists, using objective measures and rigorous methods, for example trying to repeat them in the controlled conditions of the laboratory. The development of metapsychics at the turn of the twentieth century owed much to the interest that the phenomena of mediumship held for the scientific elite. An important pioneering effort was the creation of the Society for Psychical Research in 1882. In France, Charles Richet, Professor of Medicine, 1913 Nobel laureate, and leading metapsychical researcher, for example with the Institut Métapsychique International (Brower, 2010; Lachapelle, 2005), served as a frequent point of reference among those in the medical community who debated the authenticity of mediumistic phenomena (Méheust, 1999). Baron Albert von Schrenk-Notzing, a pioneer in sexology, experimental hypnosis and parapsychology, played a similar role in German debates surrounding mediums (Wolffram, 2009). He was opposed by academic physicians and psychologists who proposed a psychology of occult belief as a means to discredit parapsychology and its practitioners. Such gestures led to increasing degrees of professionalization within the emerging discipline of psychology as it found ways of disassociating itself from "occult" practices and popular religious movements (Wolffram, 2006).

Historically, some of the rejection of psychical research / parapsychology / metapsychics relied on the presumption that spiritism represented a particular form of psychopathology; in other words, the extraordinary claims of the proponents of spiritism were simply fraud and madness (on the latter, see Alvarado & Zingrone, 2012; Le Maléfan, 1999; Owen, 1989). Throughout the first half of the twentieth century, psychiatric discourse consistently labelled mediumship as pathological and claimed that spiritism presented a form of mental contagion (for a review, see Moreira-Almeida, Silva de Almeida & Neto, 2005). Psychiatric disorders such as "Episodic Spiritist Delusion" (Roxo,

1938)—a diagnosis proposed in Brazil where spiritism has been important (Hess, 1991)—described spiritist experiences as "typical states of degeneration."

In the second half of the century, however, the prevailing position in psychiatry was moderated by developments in transcultural and ethnographic approaches which emphasized the culturally-relative value of knowledge, including psychiatric theory (Lewis-Fernandez & Kleinman, 1995). This revised approach is most likely attributable to the influence of French anthropologist Roger Bastide (1898–1974) who studied the Afro-Brazilian cults (many of which drew upon the basic forms of spiritism). Bastide (1958/2001, 1960, 1973/2002) catalogued the cultural biases that had influenced previous studies of these religions and argued that, although mental pathology was operative in some cases, in general, possession trance was sociological rather than pathological. Influenced by ethnopsychiatry, the field of psychiatry considers such religious experiences to be culturally-inflected and recognizes that that they can take non-pathological forms and even contribute to psychological well-being (Cardeña, Lynn, & Krippner, 2000; Reinsel, 2003).

The standpoint assumed by most of the international psychiatric community at the turn of the twentieth century was, however, quite different. In this earlier period, mediumistic practices were viewed above all as a threat to public health. When it was necessary to justify the treatment of people involved with spiritism, psychiatrists offered a variety of new nosological categories. In the rest of this article, we will describe the various categories that were applied to adepts of spiritism over the period 1850–1950 by focusing on one country, France, where the psychiatric discourse on that topic was particularly active and rich in its implications.

Dangers of Spiritism for Mental Health: The View of Kardec and the Spiritist Movement

Before focusing on the question of spiritist delusions, it is important to note that both in France and abroad certain individuals—philosophers and psychopathologists and also the clergy—tried to alert public opinion to the dangers that the practice of spiritism, and its ideology, represented for the human mind. Clerical and lay commentators proved increasingly willing to ascribe the new phenomena to demonic intervention (Cuchet, 2012; Monroe, 2008), but psychopathological notions were also used. The question of hallucinations, both individual and collective, and indeed of madness in general, could therefore not be fundamentally divorced from the question of the health status of spiritism, and the debates which animated Western bourgeois society when it began to spread towards the middle of the nineteenth century.[1]

Drawing on religious and social unrest, among other factors, the movement known as Modern Spiritualism started to develop in the USA during the mid-nineteenth century with the activities of mediums such as the Fox sisters (Weisberg, 2004). Capron (1855), an early historian of the movement, has discussed many of the early phenomena and controversies surrounding American mediums, and these soon spread to Europe. In France, *Tables tournantes* (turning tables) were an important manifestation in which tables moved spontaneously, with negligible physical effort, when touched by a group of people. These, according to Louis Figuier, a popularizer of science, writing in the *Dictionnaire universel des connaissances humaines*, were: "Strange phenomena that occupy much of the public, as well as the savants" (Figuier, 1859, p. 289). The range of these dramatic new phenomena was not limited to simple movement. Some sitters discovered that animated tables also had the ability to communicate, either by tapping the floor with their legs or by making mysterious cracking noises during recitations of the alphabet. These new manifestations, in which the phenomena appeared to convey messages, were named *tables parlantes* (speaking tables). During these séances, many attendees would hear, see and feel deceased people or apparently intelligent entities. "Some dismissed experimentation with the *tables* as a mere party game, while others saw it as a potential source of moral edification" (Monroe, 2008, p. 23, original italics).

The teacher and educator Hippolyte Léon Denizard Rivail (1804–1869), under the pseudonym of Allan Kardec, became the promoter and codifier of spiritism in France (Edelman, 1995; Sharp, 2006). In his *Livre des médiums*, Kardec (1861) gave rules for practicing mediums and defined this practice. He also devoted a chapter, "Drawbacks and dangers of practising as a medium," to the mental risks incurred by spiritists. He said that, even though practicing as a medium is not in itself pathological, it is nevertheless a state which is liable to cause great physical and moral fatigue, in particular for mediums susceptible to convulsions. For these persons, practicing the activity too often could have adverse effects on their nervous system. In this case mediumship may overtax one's strength and produce harmful disturbances. For this reason, Kardec warned, one must prevent the feeble-minded from becoming mediums, and direct them towards other activities in order to rest their sick organs.

It should be noted that Kardec was well acquainted with the doctrines of mental health of his time (Moreira-Almeida & Neto, 2005) and developed a definition of madness compatible with his doctrine. Moreover, some spiritist mediums also practiced as faith-healers or moral supports, and provided therapeutic help both to the insane spiritist (see Charuty, 1985), and those who were negatively affected by the death of close relatives.

Despite his knowledge of psychopathology, in chapter 6 of the *Livre des médiums*, Kardec gave an explanation of hallucinations that contradicted the view of his contemporaries (Kardec, 1861). This phenomenon, he wrote, has not yet received a satisfactory answer from physiologists and those he called "hallucinologists." He thought that the doctrine of Spirits—and in particular the doctrine of the eternal soul—could be of help here. Kardec argued that the issue was that of a physiological anomaly affecting imprints in the brain, and he thought fixed ideas had the same origin. Certain images are not erased; they remain fixed because certain parts of the brain, identified by phrenology, are paralyzed by a weakness. What the soul usually "sees" are fleeting "photographic" images in the brain, ephemeral traces of what has been seen, read and experienced. In the case of hallucinations, the soul only "sees" the same images over and over again. Thus, concludes Kardec, hallucinations are the vision by the soul of permanent images; they do not have the pathological character that medicine confers on them. Furthermore, Kardec discussed apparitions as the influence of spirits.

The Intervention of the Alienists

Since the arrival of spiritism in France in 1853, the opinion of the schools of medicine and philosophy on the phenomena of spiritism, especially on the widespread communication by "turning the tables" and "speaking tables" (Edelman, 1985), had been evident. However, it was only with the presentation by Jules Baillarger[2] to the Société Médico-Psychologique in 1861 that a full-blown confrontation emerged between alienism and spiritism, a confrontation that was to last for a century. Although he was alarmed, Baillarger was curious about the mediumistic experience because it supported his own nosographic entity of "psychical hallucinations" (xenopathic representation without externalization by sensory perception), as distinct from "psycho-sensorial hallucinations" (with externalization by sensory perception). According to Baillarger (1861), such mediumistic experiences may be ordinary psychological experiences, similar to the "doubling of personality" in dreams, until they become involuntary, automatic and under an emotional burden like that of spirit practices (Le Maléfan, 1999, 28–33).

Thus, the dangers of the spiritist practices were quickly denounced, in more or less measured terms. Philibert Burlet (1863), intern in the hospitals of Lyon, where Kardec lived, held spiritism to be one of the principal causes of insanity; on the other hand, the alienist Caliste Cavalier (1868) thought that it was less dangerous than witchcraft. However, in spite of these polemics, at this point the alienists were not really interested in spiritist practices. This began to change from 1870 onwards, when those who were seeking a basis for an experimental psychology different from the academic spiritualist[3] psychology found the material for a new theory of the mind in the study of that central person, the medium, and in particular in the phenomenon of automatic writing. The first initiative was taken by Hyppolite Taine (1870), who opened the way for Pierre Janet (1859–1947) to follow (see below). Janet did his doctoral dissertation in philosophy on psychological automatism (Janet, 1889), with careful studies of somnambulism, hypnotism, mancies, automatic writing with spirit mediums, etc., all practices that seem to allowed uprisings of a subconscious mind. Janet urged his colleagues to look at how these practices—beyond their insanity—might contribute to psychological knowledge. Some years later, Janet became a doctor of medicine with a thesis on hysterics (Janet, 1893), and then Professor of Psychology at the Collège de France, and he described all these subconscious activities in psychopathological terms.

Neurologists and Alienists Confronted with the Dangers of Spiritism

In the period which followed, the relations between spiritism and psychopathology intensified even more sharply along the two axes that we have just described. Were the peculiar perceptions during spiritist séances pathological in themselves, or was this an unwarranted generalization from isolated cases? Psychopathological discourse had to be refined because other arguments were also being aired. "Prodigious mediums" such as D. D. Home (1833–1886) and Eusapia Palladino (1854–1918) became famous at that time, because they agreed to be tested by scientists, though rarely in excellent scientific conditions (Brower, 2010; Monroe, 2008). The scientists convinced by these mediums participated in the questioning of the psychopathological discourse which reduced these phenomena to purely subjective hallucinations. On the one hand, more than with popular sitter groups, the era of prodigious mediums who claimed to play the scientific game provided a remarkably fruitful field for experimental investigation, in particular because of their trance-like states. On the other hand, the arguments concerning the morbid causality of spiritism were accentuated, notably by a new type of argument concerning the relation between spiritism and insanity in terms of "coloration," i.e., how the structure remains pathological when the superficial aspects vary.

One style of discourse concerning the morbidity of spiritism is best illustrated by the Salpêtrière School. Neurologist Jean-Martin Charcot (1825–1893) took it as the object of his sixteenth clinical lesson, and was widely followed by his colleagues and students. The objective was quite clear: spiritism is an agent which provokes hysteria and neurosis in individuals with a predisposition to those ailments (Charcot, 1890).

The alienists shared fairly similar views that were well summarized during the 10th Congress at Marseille in 1899 (Marie & Vigouroux, 1899): spiritism provokes psychosis in predisposed individuals. However, the conceptions of these clinicians showed that they had taken into account the studies of Janet concerning the trances of mediums; because they used these studies to argue that there was an analogy between the medium and the insane, and because both suffer from disintegration (a loss of their high mental function of conscious synthesis), the notion of a subconscious level and mental processes functioning outside consciousness was nevertheless taken into consideration. Secondly, they remarked that "spiritist psychosis" can occur even if the subject is not a spiritist, and even without ever having practiced spiritism. In this case, spiritism merely adds a "coloration" to a pre-existing delirium.

For Valentin Magnan (1835–1916), the question of the relation between spiritism and insanity can be summed up by this latter aspect of coloration (Magnan, 1890). According to this analysis, spiritism constitutes a form of excessive religiosity and corresponds to a symptom of degeneracy, that is, spiritist believers are maladjusted people who have a hereditary predisposition to mental disorders. The fact that they avoid reality with Kardec's doctrine or other forms of mysticism does not matter, as this is only a secondary aspect that operates within their imbalance.

This sort of psychopathological judgement fed into the moralistic discourse concerning these beliefs and practices, akin to those concerning occult practices in general. Many contemporary scholars denounced in this vein the mysticism and the decadence of the end of the nineteenth century. The psychopathologization of spiritism was part of a strong cultural background, visible in the administrative separation of the Church and the Government, the rise of positivism to the detriment of other epistemologies and, in return, a "crisis of factuality" that encouraged people to look beyond the Christian miracles for evidence of afterlife and the divine on earth (Monroe, 2008). So, spiritism was the great battlefield for a psychiatry that was urged to produce a new norm for religious beliefs.

Spiritist delusions, Mediumistic Delusions and Spiritist Madness (1901–1921)

At the beginning of the twentieth century there was a wave of delusions (or an inflation of diagnostics which was interpreted as an epidemic of delusions?), which arose quite suddenly and which lasted for quite a short time, in which spiritism took a prominent position as a recurrent topic related to phantasies and paranoias. This wave led to the creation of the category "spiritist delusions" in the nosography of French psychiatry. This new category was deeply affected by the transformation of psychiatric knowledge which was occurring at that time (Danion, Keppi, & Singer, 1985; Dowbiggin, 1991). Thus, it was initially linked to the dogma of degeneration; then, after 1910, it was linked to the new tendencies which were sweeping across the psychiatry of that period, and refashioning it: the doctrine of constitutions, the three great clinical entities (delusion of interpretation, delusion of imagination, and chronic hallucinatory psychosis), and also clinical and pathological psychology, including in particular the new study of neuroses.

In this work of construction, one author stands out: Jules Lévy-Valensi.[4] He gathered together practically everything that could be said in psychiatric circles and elsewhere concerning the relations between spiritism and insanity (Lévy-Valensi, 1910). Analysis of the psychiatric literature of the beginning of the twentieth century, and the article by Lévy-Valensi in particular, allows us to identify two dimensions which were present in the interpretation of this phenomenon: (1) a dimension of certainty: there were indeed a number of points on which a majority of clinicians were agreed; (2) a dimension of doubt, or at the very least of questioning: each certainty was coupled with a possible alternative interpretation.

The certainties. The first certainty of the psychiatrists in 1910 concerned the morbidity of spiritist practices. This was associated with a second certainty, which held that persons subject to spiritist delusion were predisposed thereto. The third certainty was more specific: the delusion in question was essentially hallucinatory. Three sorts of hallucinations were particularly well represented, which gave the syndrome its hallmark, to the extent that they were linked to spiritism: auditory and verbal hallucinations (the raps or knocks and the voice of the spirits that are heard, and the spirit that speaks through the mouth of a person); graphic hallucinations (automatic writing); sensations of levitation of the body, and the impression of the levitation of objects. On this last point, one can add the stories of astral voyages or reincarnation, which were most often considered as signs of dreamlike delirium.

Two further certainties were also widespread in the writing of alienists and psychiatrists. Firstly, it was well established that the subject involved in a spiritist delirium functioned in an automatic fashion. For such a subject, the automatism functioned quite unknown to the subject and against his or her will, to such an extent that there was the appearance of a truly split personality, which is not perceived by the subject, because there is a genuine dissociation, i.e., a shorting by the lower mental functions. This finding was of course based on clinical reality, but it drew its vocabulary and its references from psychopathological studies of mediums. This current was represented principally by Janet and by Joseph Grasset (1849–1918). The latter explicitly proposed the consideration of the phenomena involving mediums from a neurophysiological point of view (Grasset, 1904). In this way, it was generally admitted that there was a continuity between the medium and the delirious patient, since both of them exhibited a disintegration of the nervous system, one temporarily and the other permanently. Thus, Ballet and Dheur (1903) were able to state that the medium in a state of delirium was only an exaggeration of the normal state of the medium, which amounted to being on the same plane but at different angles.

For this reason, it was logical to warn the public against spiritism as an agent of disintegration and dissociation, and to proclaim that it was toxic for the mind, because it could well trigger a genuine mental contagion. This was the final established certainty, which summed up all the others, by making it quite clear that spiritism was a social and psychological danger.

Nevertheless, a half-certainty lingered on, allowing doubts and questions. This concerned the status of the facts that were alleged by the spiritists. In fact, the majority of clinicians gave attention to the phenomena of automatic writing, turning tables and raps, and also to alleged memories of other lives, in short, to everything that in a certain sense was supernatural, but which could be well explained by the psychology of the period with its notions of the unconscious and the subconscious, and indeed the subliminal as reinterpreted by Flournoy (1900). However, there was a sort of hesitation with respect to another category of unusual phenomena (telepathy, telekinesis, ectoplasms)—hesitation but not outright rejection, because although their character placed them at the borderline of official science, they were the object of a study carried out by a number of scientists in various countries. These "psychical researchers," including some renowned scientists, developed an objective study of paranormal events, for example with the promising use of photography. Not all researchers endorsed spiritist and occultist beliefs; in fact, they generally assumed the existence of latent powers in human intelligence, i.e., a kind of naturalistic point of view. Because psychical research argued for an alternative view, spiritist phenomena posed a dilemma: were they all due to hallucinations or to errors of interpretation by the scientists who studied them? If so, what was one to think of these scientists? But if not, might it not be that reality was more complex than it appeared?

The doubts and the questionings. All the certainties listed above have been revisited and challenged at one point or another during the elaboration of the entity "spiritist delusion" in the early twentieth century. First, it pointed out, following the analysis by Marie and Vigouroux (1899) mentioned above, that the appearance of a spiritist delusion was not purely due to the pathological action of the spiritist practices. It could also be encountered in subjects who were not spiritist adepts. For this reason, it was agreed to call the condition a mediumistic delusion, because all it took from spiritism was its particular coloration. In the same vein, Janet (1909) pointed out that a spiritist or mediumistic delusion induced by the spiritist practices did not occur only in the mediums themselves. In fact, many cases showed that the signs of true mediumship were not present in certain spiritists (these signs being amnesia with respect to the dissociation, and anesthesia). There was also insistence on the fact that it was not necessarily essential to be predisposed in order to become delirious. The trigger of delirium could also be depression, particularly in the case of grief and mourning. Here again it was Janet (1909) who contributed elements supporting this view, and who consequently gave a psychological explanation of spiritist delirium, even if this explanation was to remain fairly isolated.

In all this, one thing became obvious: there was no single, unified spiritist delusion but a multiplicity of diversified forms of spiritist delusion. Their classification depended on the course of their evolution, and on the mechanisms at work. Very often they were regrouped in the class of chronic systematic religious delusions, but making a distinction between those which could be considered as demonic manias and those closer to theo-manias. They were also classed as delusions of the imagination with emphasis being put on the florid richness of imagination which was very generally found in these cases; or as delusions of interpretation. They were also associated with psychasthenia and hysteria.

However, a number of questions remained in abeyance. In a large majority of cases the spiritist delusion was curable and only lasted for a short time. This was obviously reminiscent of delirious fits and acute hallucinatory psychoses, but there were certain elements which prevented them being classed in these frameworks. The problem was that they were too rich, too coherent in their structure, and above all that they maintained a certain continuity with the common belief in spiritism which marked that period. The philosopher, psychologist and alienist Charles Blondel (1876–1939) was thus led to remark, concerning the delirium of a patient, that it offered "the particular feature that it drew on the resources of the collective convictions adopted by the spiritist groups to which she belongs; many members of these groups could not be classified as insane. This feature thus raises a highly delicate question" (quoted in Lévy-Valensi & Génil-Perrin, 1912, p. 90). In other words, this amounts to questioning the value of a belief, and where the limits of psychiatric investigation should be placed.

From spiritist delusions to spiritist psychoses (1920–1959). After World War I, the world of psychiatry underwent a major evolution, especially with respect to the notions of "mental illness" and hence to the relations between the normal and the pathological. In the context of these changes in psychiatric knowledge, the designation of "spiritist delusion" was maintained. Rodiet and Heuyer (1931), in their review of the question of insanity in the twentieth century, note that cases of spiritist delusion were the contemporary form of cases of delusions of possession, themselves considered as a medieval form of being deluded under outside influence, and understood as belonging to the class of chronic hallucinatory psychoses. Nevertheless, this clinical entity was given different definitions according to the school which mentioned it, and especially whether it was the prestigious clinical school of Gaëtan de Clérambault (1872–1934) or that of Henri Claude (1869–1945).

The psychiatrist Clérambault, working at the special infirmary for the insane at the Préfecture de Police in Paris, discussed a case of spiritist delusion on three occasions. Although he claimed that he was the last person to question hallucinations with a psychological origin, his approach remained the same and consisted of considering that delirious symptoms could be taken as stemming from automatic mental processes. This amounts to saying that neither special practices nor particular emotions could be the cause of this type of delirium, but that its genesis was to be sought in a primordial organic dysfunction. Nevertheless, he did concede that only a thorough experimental study of the condition of mediums would be able to illuminate the true nature of the trance, and distinguish it from delirium (Clérambault & Brousseau, 1920).[5]

Other authors followed Clérambault, and the resulting current of thought became quite strong, to the point of seeing automatic mental processes at work in all the manifestations exhibited by the mediums. Nevertheless, certain authors hinted that, in spite of the similarities between the disorders presented by spiritists and automatic mental processes, the etiology of the spiritist disorders could possibly be related to neurosis, especially in the cases which were curable and where the hallucinatory polymorphism was dominant.

Among the clinicians, Claude (1869–1945), Lévy-Valensi and André Ceillier (1887–1954) used the cases of spiritist delusion to illustrate the relevance of the conceptual framework of "delusion of influence." A case of spiritist delusion was, according to them, an individual under the influence of a foreign force which directed and oriented his thoughts and commanded his acts and his behavior in a way which could be permanent or passing. Consequently, it was not surprising to find cases of this sort in syndromes of external action (Claude & Dublineau, 1933), of dispossession (Lévy-Valensi, 1927) or of influence (Ceillier, 1925). For Lévy-Valensi and Ceillier, it was above all the automatic constitution which predisposed an individual to delirium, as a result of practices (such as spiritism) or organic ailments. It is then the importance of the disintegration in these patients which makes them tip over into the automatisms. Among these patients there are many priests, religious persons, dreamers and so on, including the mediums themselves, and all those who "practice" disintegration deliberately and who are easily influenced, such as women (Ceillier, 1925).

However, the psychological origin of spiritist delusion could also have other and less tendentious explanations. Dr. Claude Vurpas (1875–1951), in an unpublished talk at the hospital St. Anne in Paris, considered that the cause was the result of the shock produced by the emotion involved in the practice of communication with the dead, especially for those who had recently suffered a bereavement. He classified them together with delirious dreams (Encausse, 1935/1943, 171–175).

These conceptions opened the way to a deeper understanding of the relation between spiritism and insanity. Thus, it became possible to envisage the relation between spiritist delusion and personality. This was the theme of the thesis of Kern (1936), under the direction of Claude and the impetus of Daniel Lagache (1903–1972); this thesis was also inspired by the thesis of Jacques Lacan (1901–1981) on paranoia taking psychoanalysis as a reference (Lacan, 1932). But if Kern does relate the single case that he analyses as paranoia as defined by Claude, he cannot refrain from evoking the possibility of another hypothesis, that of hysteria. Several points in the case he analyses allow him to consider this, notably the fact that the affection could be cured. However, this hypothesis was not fashionable at the time, as hysteria was disappearing from psychiatric nosography.

The End of an Entity

Conceived in a very specific context, the nosographic entity of "spiritist delusions" had disappeared coincidentally with spiritism's loss of popularity. But a few examples remain. In 1942 psychiatrist Jean Delay presented what was to be one of the last analyses of a case of spiritist delusion. His account is doubly interesting because he not only gives some indications for a dynamic understanding of the process of delirium, but also lays the ground for an ethno-psychiatric approach to this sort of delirium, based on a kind of cultural relativism and a non-judgmental approach of belief systems. The case he studied was that of a young West Indian woman who had grown up in a background of spiritist beliefs and who continued to cultivate an interest in the occult, which rendered this sort of approach more appropriate (Delay, 1942).

Finally, we find one of the last surviving traces of this entity in the *Traité de psychiatrie* of Henri Baruk (1959). Here, an ethno-psychiatric approach is overlaid in terms of social psychiatry where spiritism is quoted as an example of an epidemic agent.

Spiritism and Psychiatric Knowledge

Beyond descriptions of the harmful nature of spiritist practices, and judgements concerning the belief in communications with defunct spirits, at one time significant heuristic use was made of one of the most central aspects of spiritism: the capacity to function as a medium, that is, to access trance-like states and subconscious abilities. These influences are not very well known today, but they were frequent for almost a century.

As early as 1861, Baillarger sensed that the particular nature of the disturbances in spiritist practitioners could be of interest. Thus, in a communication delivered to the Société Médico-Psychologique, he took the example of a spiritist delusion that he presented in order to demonstrate the role of automatisms in the genesis of the disorder, and to illustrate his conception of psychic hallucination (Baillarger, 1861). According to him, it was indeed the "terrible nature of the emotions" induced by the practice of spiritism which caused a disturbance in the functioning of the brain and which allowed the inferior faculties to free themselves and to escape from voluntary control by realizing an actual "splitting of the personality."

This expression came to have considerable importance in the debates between spiritism and psychiatry, as well as the term "automatism," as we have seen. However, these phenomena were described and above all interpreted in diverse ways. We can see an opposition between a theory in terms of mental illness and a theory in terms of psychology. Thus, the "splitting" was open to two different interpretations: either it was the expression of inferior activities of the mind (sensations, imagination, memory), and in this case it was the sign of a pathological state; or else it was the manifestation of another part of the personality, the spirit in the case of the spiritists, or the unconscious for the psychologists, in which case it was envisaged as harboring a possibility for the individual to progress, an overflow or an uncovering of faculties.

Two clinicians made use of spiritism in order to illustrate these viewpoints, and to make them evolve: Janet and Jules Séglas.[6] Janet often referred to spiritism in the course of his theoretical production—this is why his opinion has been relevant throughout this discussion—and he held that the case of mediums provided a perfect example of a split personality. It was mainly at the beginning of his career that Janet addressed this phenomenon; his writings in the 1930s contain few references to it. His entry into the field of mental illness and his attachment to the medical profession gave him the opportunity to air his previous studies published in his doctoral thesis on psychological automatism (Janet, 1889). Among other things, these studies provided some clinical reference points for specialists in mental illness confronted with forms of hallucination where involuntary activity came to the forefront. Thus, in *Névroses et idées fixes* (Janet, 1898/2007), he took the example of a patient, LER, "a distinguished professor," who indulged in spiritism in the course of which he was invaded by the spirit with whom he was in communication. This spirit commanded his acts and led the professor to make painful and embarrassing utterances. Janet (1898/2007) cited this case to show that the phenomenon of split personality is not always attached to hysteria, but can actually be a symptom of a persecution mania. Conversely, in the course of many clinical discussions and particularly in the case of spiritist delusion, Janet had occasion to note that in spite of the presence of a theme of persecution, one could discern hysteria or psychasthenia.

These distinctions are obviously based on Janet's deep reflections on and interest in all these "lower" forms of mental activity as a whole. Among these forms, the case of mediums was prominent, largely because of its importance in the social landscape of the period. It taught Janet that the mind can disintegrate and split into two. This may be only a short-lived phenomenon, and often reflects "psychological wretchedness," but at times it reveals capacities which are astonishingly intelligent, to say the least.

Séglas did not ignore the teaching of Janet. This was particularly the case in the elaboration of psycho-motor hallucinations. More surprising, perhaps, is the use that Séglas (1888) made of mediumship in his efforts to clarify several aspects of such hallucinations; by comparing them and by elucidating their analogies, he advanced towards an understanding of their common underlying moving forces. But Séglas certainly knew that comparing was not the same thing as assimilating or identifying. Thus, at other points in his work, he insisted clearly on what differentiated a mental patient from a medium. Although there was a split personality in the two cases, in the case of mental illness the split was forced and reflected an influence and/or a persecution, and moreover went beyond a mere belief. In contrast, in the case of a medium the split was only temporary, unconscious, and triggered by the group that the medium belonged to. Nevertheless, Séglas (1888) also noted that spiritism favored "neo-mystical tendencies" and prepared the ground for the advent of psycho-motor hallucinations.

The alienist Gilbert Ballet (1853–1916), at that time Professor of History of Medicine in Paris, was another author who made use of spiritism in the construction of the diagnosis of "chronic hallucinatory psychosis" (CHP) in a series of publications appearing between 1911 and 1914. It was well known that, according to Ballet, a characteristic state of CHP resulted from disaggregation. This referred to dissociation or splitting of the personality. In 1914, in an article recapitulating the main features of CHP, he said that it was the nature of this psychosis (and of dissociation) which defined the affection. There were two aspects to this psychosis. One was the fact of being chronic, and the other was that it "exalts subconscious automatisms," the very same feature that is found in the trance of the medium. In other words, there is no difference in the *nature* of the two conditions (Ballet, 1914). This is why, in spite of the precautions taken to distinguish certain psychopathological and clinical fields, it appeared that the concept of "chronic hallucinatory psychosis" linked together two areas that were quite different. In our opinion this is the source of the confusion that this concept has generated (Le Maléfan, 2003).

These two areas are chronic hallucinatory delusions of persecution on the one hand and, on the other, the non-ordinary psychological state of the medium. It seems obvious to us that making disaggregation the basis of CHP caused mediumship, and with it the spirits, to be linked together and to share the same fate as hallucinatory psychosis. Furthermore, this made it difficult for psychiatric knowledge to detect anything other than "psychosis" in the most characteristic feature of disaggregation, automatism. This was all the more so when automatism occurred in patients who were involved with spiritism. Moreover, this connection favored an amalgam between hallucinosis and psychosis which has lasted in clinical practice to the present day.

There were other borrowings or references to spiritism during the first quarter of the twentieth century, and these continued up to the 1970s with Henri Ey (1900–1977) (see Ey, 1973/2004, Vol. 1, p. 306–307). During the 1920s most of these references had to do with the nebula of delusions of influence, and because of this they largely overlap with the history of spiritist delusions in the strict sense of the term. We may nevertheless note that, in parallel, the domain of psychical or metapsychical sciences was also drawn upon. In particular, again in the framework of delusions of influence, we mention a telepathic delusion (Lévy-Darras & Maillard, 1910) and a metapsychical delusion (Aubin, 1927). As for Ey, he made it clear that the experience of being a medium corresponded with a remarkable, but non-pathological, type of influence.

Conclusion

We have seen that the elaboration of spiritist delusions occurred during the same period as the construction of classic psychiatric knowledge in France, and that their presence had a number of repercussions and was at the origin of thorny questions and substantial challenges for psychopathologists. The nosographic and etiological problems related to spiritist delusions have never been entirely resolved, not indeed because of a lack of arguments or theoretical frameworks, but because they have always carried with them a sort of excessiveness which has made them impossible to reduce entirely. In this way they have been objects of resistance for psychiatric knowledge in its encounter with the field of beliefs.

An examination of the historical debates surrounding late-nineteenth and early-twentieth century spiritism may thus have important implications for psychiatric conceptions today. The differential diagnosis of mediumistic and psychotic experience, for example, still hinges on the question of belief and cultural relativism (Moreira-Almeida, Neto & Greyson, 2007). Although interest has waned in Kardecian *spiritisme* in France, the question of belief remains open in phenomena such as channeling (Trimble, 1995) or dissociative identity disorder (Moreira-Almeida, Neto & Cardeña, 2008), which, worldwide, continue to present the familiar forms of spiritist belief and practice. Spiritism is still practiced by many around the world and particularly in Brazil (Bragdon, 2011). It seems that clinical practice must still contend, to a greater or lesser extent, with forms of knowledge and belief that occupy the margins of the psychiatric field. In this respect, contemporary nosographic categories and concepts can only benefit from the lessons of the past.

Notes

1 In order to put the spread of spiritism in France in context, see Cuchet, 2007, 2012.
2 Baillarger (1809–1890) was a French neurologist and psychiatrist, a student of Esquirol and founder of the *Annalés Médico-Psychologiques*. He did research on automatism and the involuntary nature of hallucinations. He also described bipolar disorder which he referred to as *folie à double forme*; Baillarger, 1854.
3 Although the term "spiritualism" is the English word for "spiritisme," it refers in French to a philosophical school without any survivalist hypothesis, led by Victor Cousin during the nineteenth century.
4 Lévy-Valensi (1879–1943) was a neurologist and a psychiatrist. His name is associated with his syndrome of "*dépossession*" (Lévy-Valensi, 1927), described after studies of mental automatism and spiritism. As a teacher he had a considerable influence with his textbooks on delusions, for example, Lévy-Valensi, 1948.
5 The patient presented by Clérambault was Henriette Couédon, a famous clairvoyant of the end of the nineteenth century; see Le Maléfan, 2001.
6 Séglas (1856–1939) was a psychiatrist who made influential contributions to the nosology of delusions, hallucinations and pseudo-hallucinations. He did extensive research on the relationship between language and mental illness, describing, for instance, the symptoms of logorrhea, embolalia, near-mutism, automatic speech, alexia and agraphia.

References

Alvarado, C. S. (2002). Dissociation in Britain during the late nineteenth century: The Society for Psychical Research, 1882–1900. *Journal of Trauma and Dissociation, 3*, 9–33.

Alvarado, C. S. (2010). Classic text no. 84: 'Divisions of personality and spiritism' by Alfred Binet (1896). *History of Psychiatry, 21*(4), 487–500.

Alvarado, C. S. & Zingrone, N. L. (2012). Classic text no. 90: 'The pathology and treatment of mediomania,' by Frederic Rowland Marvin (1874). *History of Psychiatry, 23*(2), 222–244.

Alvarado, C. S., Machado, F. R., Zangari, W., & Zingrone, N. L. (2007). Perspectivas históricas da influência da mediunidade na construção de ideias psicológicas e psiquiátricas. *Archives of Clinical Psychiatry (São Paulo), 34*, 42–53.

Aubin, H. (1927). *Les délires de métapsychique*. (Medical thesis). University of Bordeaux.

Baillarger, J. (1854). De la folie à double forme. *Annales Médico-Psychologiques, 2*(6), 369–391.

Baillarger, J. (1861). Communication à la Société Médico-Psychologique. *Annales Médico-Psychologiques, 7*, 92–93.

Ballet, G. (1914). La psychose hallucinatoire chronique. *Revue Neurologique, 27*, 41–46.

Ballet, G. & Dheur, P. (1903). Sur un cas de délire de médiumnité. *Annales Médico-Psychologiques, 5*, 264–271.

Baruk, H. (1959). *Traité de psychiatrie*. Masson.

Bastide, R. (2001). *Le Candomblé de Bahia*. Pocket. (Original work published 1958).

Bastide, R. (1960). *Les religions africaines au Brésil: Vers une sociologie des interprétations de civilisations*. Presses Universitaires de France.

Bastide, R. (2002). *Poètes et dieux. Études afro-brésiliennes*. L'Harmattan. (Original work published 1978).

Bragdon, E. (ed.) (2011). *Spiritism and mental health. Practices from spiritist centers and spiritist psychiatric hospitals in Brazil*. Singing Dragon.

Brower, M. B. (2010). *Unruly spirits: The science of psychic phenomena in modern France*. Chicago University Press.

Burlet, P. (1863). *Du Spiritisme considéré comme cause d'aliénation mentale*. Richard.

Capron, E. W. (1855). *Modern spiritualism: Its facts and fanatisms, its consistencies and contradictions*. Bela Marsh.

Cardeña, E., Lynn, S. J., & Krippner, S. (eds.) (2000). *Varieties of anomalous experiences: examining the scientific evidence*. American Psychological Association.

Cavalier, C. (1868). *Étude médico-psychologique sur la croyance aux sortilèges à l'époque actuelle*. Editeurs du Montpellier médical.

Ceillier, A. (1925). Du rôle des hallucinations psychiques dans l'exploration de l'inconscient. *L'Évolution Psychiatrique, 1*, 142–154.

Charcot, J. M. (1890). *Œuvres complètes. Leçons sur les maladies du système nerveux*. Progrès Médical.

Charuty, G. (1985). *Le Couvent des fous*. Flammarion.

Claude, H., & Dublineau, J. (1933). Intuitions délirantes, obsessions et syndrome d'action extérieure. *L'Encéphale, 28*, 350–371.

Clérambault, G. G. de, & Brousseau, A. (1920). La fin d'une voyante. Présentation de malade. *Bulletin de la Société Clinique de Médecine Mentale, 12*, 223–230.

Clervoy, P. (2002). Esprit: Es-tu là? La psychiatrie face à l'engouement spirite. *Perspectives psychiatriques, 41*(3), 237–240.

Cox, R. S. (2003). *Body and soul: A sympathetic history of American spiritualism*. University of Virginia Press.

Crabtree, A. (2003). "Automatism" and the emergence of dynamic psychiatry. *Journal of the History of the Behavioral Sciences, 39*(1), 51–70.

Cuchet, G. (2007). Le retour des esprits, ou la naissance du spiritisme sous le Second Empire. *Revue d'Histoire Moderne et Contemporaine, 54*(2), 74–90.

Cuchet, G. (2012). *Les voix d'outre-tombe: Tables tournantes, spiritisme et société au XIXe siècle*. Seuil.

Danion, J. M., Keppi, J., & Singer, L. (1985). Une approche historique de la doctrine des dégénérescences et des constitutions psychopathiques. *Annales Médico-Psychologiques, 143*(3), 271–280.

Delay, J. (1942). Délire spirite avec écritures automatiques polymorphes. *Annales Médico-Psychologiques, 11*, 362–366.

Dessoir, M. (1889). *Das Doppel-Ich*. Siegismund.
Dowbiggin, I. (1991). *Inheriting madness. Professionalization and psychiatric knowledge in nineteenth-century France*. University of California Press.
Edelman, N. (1985). La vogue des tables tournantes. *L'Histoire, 75*(2), 16–23.
Edelman, N. (1995). *Voyantes, guérisseuses et visionnaires en France, 1785–1914*. Albin Michel.
Ellenberger, H. (1970). *The discovery of the unconscious: The history and evolution of dynamic psychiatry*. Basic Books.
Encausse, P. (1943). *Sciences occultes et déséquilibre mental* (Thèse à la Faculté de Médecine de Paris, 1935). Payot.
Engels, H. (2008). Understanding the glossolalia of Hélène Smith, the famous spiritist medium. In J. Arveiller (Ed.). *Psychiatries dans l'histoire* (pp. 141–148). Presses Universitaires de Caen.
Ey, H. (2004). *Traite des hallucinations* (2 vols.) Paris: Tchou (Original work published 1978).
Figuier, L. (1859). Tables tournantes. In B. Luna (Ed.). *Dictionnaire universel des connaissances humaines* (pp. 289–298). Magiaty.
Flournoy, T. (1900). *Des Indes à la planète Mars: Étude sur un cas de somnambulisme avec glossolalie*. Félix Alcan.
Grasset, J. (1904). *Le Spiritisme devant la science*. Masson.
Hess, D. (1991) *Spirits and scientists: Ideology, spiritism and Brazilian culture*. Pennsylvania State University Press.
Janet, P. (1889). *L'automatisme psychologique. Essai de psychologie expérimentale sur les formes inferieures de l'activité humaine*. Félix Alcan.
Janet, P. (1893). *L'état mental des hystériques*. Félix Alcan.
Janet, P. (2007). *Névroses et idées fixes*. L'Harmattan. (Original work published 1889).
Janet, P. (1909). *Les Névroses*. Flammarion.
Kardec, A. (1861). *Le livre des mediums*. Didier.
Kelly, E. F., Kelly, E. W., Crabtree, A., Gauld, A., Grosso, M., & Greyson, B. (2007) *Irreducible mind: Toward a psychology for the 21st Century*. Rowman & Littlefield.
Kern, S. (1936). *Contribution clinique et pathogénique à l'étude des délires spirites* (Thèse à la Faculté de Médecine de Paris). Jouve.
Lacan, J. (1932). *De la psychose paranoïaque dans ses rapports avec la personnalité*. Le François.
Lachapelle, S. (2005) Attempting science: the creation and early development of the Institut Métapsychique International in Paris, 1919–1931. *Journal of the History of the Behavioral Sciences, 41*(1), 1–24.
Lachapelle, S. (2011). *Investigating the supernatural: From spiritism and occultism to psychical research and metapsychics in France, 1853–1931*. The Johns Hopkins University Press.
Le Maléfan, P. (1999). *Folie et spiritisme: Histoire du discours psychopathologique sur la pratique du spiritisme, ses abords et ses avatars, 1850–1950*. L'Harmattan.
Le Maléfan, P. (2001). De Clerambault et la voyante H. C., *L'Évolution Psychiatrique, 66*(3), 506–511.
Le Maléfan, P. (2003). Gilbert Ballet et la médiumnité. Contribution à l'histoire de la PHC et des divisions subjectives. *L'Évolution Psychiatrique, 68*(1), 63–72.
Levy-Darras, A., & Maillard, N. (1910). Un cas de délire d'interprétation: Délire d'influence télépathique. *L'Encéphale, 5*, 401–412.
Levy-Valensi, J. (1910). Spiritisme et folie. *L'Encéphale, 5*(6), 696–716.
Levy-Valensi, J. (1927). *L'Automatisme mental dans les délires systématisés chroniques d'influence et hallucinatoires. Le syndrome de dépossession*. Masson.
Levy-Valensi, J. (1948). *Précis de psychiatrie (*3rd ed.) Baillière.
Levy-Valensi, J., & Genil-Perrin, G. (1912). Délire spirite. *L'Encéphale, 7*, 89–90.
Lewis-Fernandez, R., & Kleinman, A. (1995). Cultural psychiatry: theoretical, clinical and research issues. *Psychiatric Clinics of North America, 18*(3), 433–448.
Magnan, V. (1890). *Legons cliniques sur les maladies mentales. Le délire chronique*. Lecrosnier et Babe.
Maleval, J. C. (1996). *Logique du délire*. Masson.
Marie, P., & Vigouroux, A. (1899). *Spiritisme et folie. Xe Congrès des aliénistes et neurologistes de France et de l'étranger*. Masson.
Méheust, B. (1999). *Somnambulisme et médiumnité* (2 vols). Les Empêcheurs de Penser en Rond.
Monroe, J. W. (2008). *Laboratoires of faith. Mesmerism, spiritism, and occultism in modern France*. Cornell University Press.

Moreira-Almeida, A., & Neto, F. L. (2005). Spiritist views of mental disorders in Brazil. *Transcultural Psychiatry, 42*(4), 570–595.

Moreira-Almeida, A., Neto, F. L., & Cardeña, E. (2008). Comparison of Brazilian spiritist mediumship and dissociative identity disorder. *Journal of Nervous and Mental Disease, 196*(5), 420–424.

Moreira-Almeida A, Neto, F. L., & Greyson, B. (2007). Dissociative and psychotic experiences in Brazilian spiritist mediums. *Psychotherapy and Psychosomatics, 76*(1), 57–58.

Moreira-Almeida, A., Silva de Almeida, A. A., & Neto, F. L. (2005). History of "Spiritist madness" in Brazil. *History of Psychiatry, 16*(1), 5–25.

Myers, F. W. H. (1903). *Human personality and its survival of bodily death* (2 vols.). Longmans, Green.

Owen, A. (1989). *The darkened room: Women, power and spiritualism in late Victorian England.* Virago.

Plas, R. (2000). *Naissance d'une science humaine, la psychologie: les psychologues et le «merveilleux psychique»* Presses Universitaires de Rennes.

Plas, R. (2012). Psychology and psychical research in France around the end of the 19th century. *History of Human Sciences, 25*(2), 91–107.

Reinsel, R. (2003). Dissociation and mental health in mediums and sensitives: A pilot survey. *Proceedings of Presented Papers of PA 2003 Annual Convention,* pp. 200–221.

Richet, C. (1905). La métapsychique. *Proceedings of the Society for Psychical Research, 19*, 2–49.

Rodiet, A., & Heuyer, G. (1931). *La Folie au XXe siècle. Etude médico-sociale*. Masson.

Roxo, H. (1938). Delirio Espírita episódico nas classes populares do Rio de Janeiro. *Archivos Brasileiros de Medicina, 28*(2), 59–72.

Seglas, J. (1888). L'hallucination dans ses rapports avec la fonction du langage. Les hallucinations psychomotrices verbales. *Progrès Médical, 8*(33–34), 124–126.

Shamdasani, S. (1994). Encountering Hélène: Théodore Flournoy and the genesis of subliminal psychology. In T. Flournoy, *From India to the planet Mars: A case of multiple personality with imaginary languages by Théodore Flournoy* (pp. xi–li). University Press.

Sharp, L. L. (2006). *Secular spirituality: Reincarnation and spiritism in nineteenth-century France*. Rowman & Littlefield.

Taine, H. (1870). *De l'intelligence*. Hachette.

Trimble, S. M. (1995). Spiritualism and channeling. In T. Miller (Ed.). *America's alternative religions* (pp. 331–337). State of New York Press.

Weisberg, B. (2004). *Talking to the dead: Kate and Maggie Fox and the rise of spiritualism*. Harper.

Wolffram, H. (2006) Parapsychology on the couch: the psychology of occult belief in Germany, 1870–1939. *Journal of the History of the Behavioral Sciences, 42*(3), 237–260.

Wolffram, H. (2009). In the laboratory of the Geisterbaron: Experimental parapsychology in Germany. *Clio Medica, 88*, 131–189.

14

Historians of Science Explore Psychical Research*

A Review of *Los Límites de la Ciencia: Espiritismo, Hipnotismo y el Estudio de los Fenómenos Paranormales* (1850–1930), edited by Annette Mülberger

Carlos S. Alvarado

In recent years there has been a resurgence of interest in the history of psychical research. Some of this work has not only documented the interaction of psychical research with other fields, but has done much to argue that attention to psychic phenomena assisted the development of the concept of the unconscious mind. Examples include Adam Crabtree's *From Mesmer to Freud* (1993) and Regine Plas's *Naissance d'une Science Humaine* (2000). The recent historiography on the topic, some of which touches on aspects other than the unconscious, includes papers published in 2012 in an issue of *History of the Human Sciences* entitled "Relations Between Psychical Research and Academic Psychology in Europe, the USA and Japan" (Young, 2012), in a special section of papers published in *Studies in History and Philosophy of the Biological and Biomedical Sciences* in 2014 entitled "Psychical Research in the History of Science and Medicine" (Sommers, 2014), and in various contributions to the "Classic Text" section of *History of Psychiatry* (e.g., Alvarado & Biondi, 2017). Furthermore, others have explored aspects of the rejection of psychical research by psychologists (e.g., Sommers, 2012), work that reminds us of the negative views of scientists about psychical research, as well as of the strategies that assist some groups in shaping both the content and identity of scientific fields via various forms of rejection, something generally known as boundary work.

In addition, some of this new work has expanded our scope beyond the usual Anglo-American contexts. We are seeing more historical research about developments in such varied countries as Italy (Alvarado & Biondi, 2017), France (Plas, 2000), Japan (Takasuna, 2012) and Germany (Wolfram, 2009).

The collection of articles reviewed here, published in Madrid, follows the above-mentioned trends to some extent. That the topic of this specialized work was considered important in Spain is suggested by the fact that its publisher is a prominent institution in Spain, the Consejo Superior de Investigaciones Científicas (Superior Council of Scientific Research; referred to in English as the National Research Council). This is the largest Spanish government institution dedicated to the development and promotion of scientific and technological developments.

Los Límites de la Ciencia: Espiritismo, Hipnotismo y el Estudio de los Fenómenos Paranormales (1850–1930) is edited by Annette Mülberger, a historian of psychology at the Universitat Autònoma de Barcelona, who, in addition to psychical research, has conducted work on the history

*Republished with permission from *Journal of Parapsychology*, *83*(1), 101–106, 2019.

of mental testing in Spain. She states that the purpose of this work, published in Spanish, and with much information about developments in Spain, is to obtain a "greater knowledge and a better understanding of the intentions and beliefs defended in a different time period as 'scientific' and 'rational' by some groups of people" (p. 17). The point here is not to approve nor condemn psychic studies and beliefs, but to attempt to understand their historical context, and the motivations of the individuals involved.

Summarizing her approach, and that of those mentioned in the first paragraph of this review, Mülberger states that new perspectives in the history of science have allowed for more flexible views about what is scientific, and what is valid knowledge. The work discussed, she states, shows various conceptual frameworks and relationship to social and political issues.

After an introduction by the editor, the book is divided in three sections. The first one, "From Spiritism to Parapsychology," has three chapters written by Mülberger about the beginnings of Spiritism, its arrival to Spain, and research into psychic phenomena. The chapters present a good introduction to the topic, including the obligatory references to the Fox Sisters, and other mediums such as D. D. Home, not to mention the contributions of individuals such as Allan Kardec. Interestingly, much attention is given to Kardec, who was very influential in Spain. Like other writers in different contexts, Mülberger sees Spiritism as providing empirical facts that take the place of faith about spiritual truths, what she refers to as the "democratization of the epistemological power conferred to each communication with the beyond" (p. 53). In addition, she writes that Kardec "liberated Christians from the yoke of hell, enlarging at the same time the vital experience of people beyond the limits of organic life on planet Earth (pp. 52–53).

In the chapter about Spain, we are introduced to several figures that are little known in the English-speaking world. This includes philosopher Manuel Sanz y Benito, Viscount Antonio de Torres Solanot y Casas, and writer Amalia Domingo Soler, who did much to popularize, defend and organize Spiritism in Spain. An interesting example was Domingo Soler's *El Espiritismo Refutando los Errores del Catolicismo Romano* (1880), mainly a defense from religious attacks. This writer stated that the phenomena produced by spirits followed natural laws, and that many critiques showed ignorance about the topic. She emphasized that the acceptance of the manifestations of spirits did not imply that the movement considered everything described as marvelous, or tried to confirm it, nor "that it is the defender of all dreamers, of all utopias, of all systematic eccentricities, of all the romances and miraculous legends. It is necessary to know it little to consider it so" (Domingo Soler, 1880, p. 12).

The third chapter about research includes table turning, William Crookes, some of the early work of members of the Society for Psychical Research, the ideas of Frederic W. H. Myers and Pierre Janet about mediumship, studies of medium Eusapia Palladino, work conducted in France by Charles Richet and others, and Albert von Schrenck-Notzing's materialization research. The chapter is a good summary of a great amount of research and theory. I assume that the reason that some things are not mentioned is to keep the chapter short. For example, in the section about Myers and Janet, how Janet was influenced by Myers was not mentioned. In his book *L'Automatisme Psychologique*, Janet (1889) discussed dissociation and argued that this mental process was important in mediumship. He cited Myers repeatedly to support his points with cases and specific manifestation drawn from Myers' articles (Janet, 1889, pp. 78, 122, 393, 394, 402, 405). Janet actually wrote that Myers was "the author who has contributed the most to develop the scientific study of spiritistic phenomena" (Janet, 1889, p. 403).

This episode is important because it not only illustrates the influence of psychical research on psychology, but also presents an example of selective influence. In this case Janet, as was the case as well with Alfred Binet (1892), admitted the value of some of Myers's observations (summarized here, Myers, 1903), but not his beliefs in telepathy or the supernormal in general. So, while some of Myers's observations regarding the subliminal self were accepted to support the existence of unconscious processes, they were stripped of the full context of Myers's ideas in which supernormal meant "a faculty or phenomenon which goes beyond the level of ordinary experience, in the direction of evolution, or as pertaining to a transcendental world" (Myers, 1903, Vol. 1, p. xxii).

The second section of the book is "The Practice of Mediumship, Hypnosis, and Clairvoyance in Spain." Its first chapter, "'To Chase Away Spirits:' The Scientific Study of Mediumship," is by Andrea Graus. She argues that during the late nineteenth-century various scientists appropriated mediumship by separating it from spirit agency. Mediums were considered the "producing agent" of phenomena, something that led to a new view of the medium as an experimental subject (although it should be kept in mind that living agency was discussed as well before the period emphasized by Graus; see Alvarado, Nahm, & Sommer, 2012). This interest involved the "hope of finding extraordinary latent faculties in man" (p. 138), and the hope that mediumship would serve as a lesson for science in general, and for psychology in particular. Graus briefly mentions the interest in this perspective in Spain among such physicians as Víctor Melcior i Farre, Manuel Otero Acevedo (who eventually accepted the possibility of discarnate agency), and astronomer Josep Comas i Sola.

As I have argued before (Alvarado, 2014), discussions of the powers of the living medium were frequent in international psychical research circles. The writings of Theodore Flournoy, Charles Richet, Enrico Morselli, Frank Podmore, and Traugott Konstantin Oesterreich, among many others, are evidence of this. But there were others who defended discarnate agency (e.g., Oliver J. Lodge), and who changed their position from living to discarnate agency (e.g., Richard Hodgson). All of this work, as Graus said about Spain, indicated to most of the international community of psychical researchers that mediumship had to be accounted for by more than fraud, dissociation and other conventional explanations.

In the next chapter the focus changes in a paper by Ángel González de Pablo about hypnosis in Spain, "Consolidate, Colonize, Exclude: Strategies of Legitimation of Medical Hypnosis." The point of the article is to discuss the boundary work to obtain "epistemic identity for a branch of science (here, hypnosis) and epistemic authority over her by the specialists (here, physicians, hypnotists), that become in this way capable of impeding anyone else to intrude in their field" (p. 164). The devices of social control discussed by the author are consolidation (integration into medical practice in terms of expertise in theory, techniques, and therapeutic applications), colonization (non-medical applications of hypnosis, such as those in judicial and educational contexts), and exclusion (or the expulsion of some topics).

The strategy of expulsion, or rejection, was mainly used against what some perceived to be illegitimate applications of hypnosis, including those related to Spiritism and metapsychics. "Its purpose," writes González de Pablo, "consisted in 'cleaning up' hypnosis, that is, to purge it of any type of 'impurity' that casted a shadow over its scientific validity" (p. 183) so as to keep out what was perceived to be undesirable from medicine and from other areas of knowledge.

In fact, psychic phenomena were frequently discussed in the nineteenth-century literature of hypnosis, the period emphasized by the author of this chapter. Some individuals involved during this period in the use of hypnosis to produce psychic phenomena were Émile Boirac, Albert de Rochas, Paul Joire, Ambroise August Liébeault, Jules Bernard Luys, Julian Ochorowicz, and Charles Richet, not to mention the work of Pierre Janet and others regarding the telepathic induction of trance (for an overview, see Crabtree, 1993). Psychic phenomena were included in various hypnosis textbooks, including some authored by skeptical authors. An example of the latter was George Gilles de la Tourette (1889), who in *L'Hypnotisme et les États Analogues au Point de Vue Médico-Legal*, stated he did not believe in the transmission of thought because, to date, there had been no controlled demonstrations of the phenomenon. González de Pablo discusses Spanish physicians, some of who denied, while others defended, the reality of thought-transference in hypnosis. One case in point illustrating the latter was Abdón Sánchez Herrero.

The last chapter in this section, "The Practice of Metapsychics: A Marquis Investigating Clairvoyance," is authored by Mónica Balltondre. This is a study of clairvoyance experiments conducted by the Marquis of Santa Cara (Joaquín José Javier Argamasilla de La Cerda y Bayona). In his book *Un Tanteo en el Misterio*, Santa Cara (n. d.) reported clairvoyance experiments that he thought enlarged psychology by proving that knowledge could be acquired by human beings beyond their senses. He wrote that metapsychics had shown the existence of levels of thought which indicated the "antecedence of a dynamic spiritual principle as a permanent root of the Individual and an unchanging axis of the evolutionary process of the being" (Santa Cara, n. d., p. 270). Balltondre's chapter is a case study of psychic investigations drawing on the concepts of the unconscious mind, physical radiation, and spirituality. As stated by Balltondre:

> Santa Cara thought that the final nature both of beings and physical reality was a spiritual one ... [In his view] the physics studies of his time showed that the world was spiritual. He construed that the conception of matter was becoming spiritualized thanks to the new scientific theories, which explained it by means of energy and radioactivity (pp. 223–224).

The third part of the book, "Foresight and Spiritism in Europe and Russia," expands on the previous emphasis on the Spanish context. It includes two chapters translated from French and English. The first, authored by Nicole Edelman, is "Foresight in Occidental Europe (1900–1939)," and explores psychic sensitivity in relation to various topics such as psychoanalysis, astrology, and the media. The second one, "Russian Spiritism: Science and Public Knowledge," is by Michel D. Gordin. He discusses controversy, and the participation of scientific and non-scientific voices in a commission formed in Russia to study mediumship, which involved the chemist Dmitri Ivanovich Mendeléyev.

The book ends with general reflections by Mülberger. In addition, it has two appendices, one with poetry by Amalia Domingo Soler, and another with a glossary of, mainly, psychic terms.

On occasion I felt the book needed more information about specific topics. For example, it is stated that physician Otero Acevedo was not a spiritist, but that he believed that the phenomena presented proof of survival of death (p. 140). This, I think, deserved more discussion. Similarly, a brief reference to psychic concepts of force (pp. 142, 207–208) could have received more discussion, maybe in the chapters of the first section of the book, to establish the rich conceptual tradition and long history of attempts to explain telepathy, as well as mediumship, in terms of human radiations of different sorts. Similarly, Myers's ideas of the subliminal self are mentioned throughout the book (pp. 108, 151, 205), but I feel that, considering their influence, they could have been discussed in more detail.

Overall, the essays presented here are a welcome addition to the modern historiography of the topics in question. It is particularly interesting to see how these studies have developed in Spain, and how there are so many similarities with developments from other countries in such varied things as the debates to banish the topic from science, the various theoretical emphases of psychical researchers in terms of the issue of discarnate agency, and the use of ideas from psychology (the unconscious) and physics (the ether, radiations of various sorts). One hopes that this volume, and other recent work (e.g., Wolffram, 2009), will help to bring an expansion of studies focusing on other countries and cultures, such as those in Asia and in Latin America.

It is also of interest to see the attitude of the historians writing in this anthology, who treat students of psychic phenomena without dismissal, as serious and dedicated explorers. This is evident in one of Mülberger's final comments. In her view the work of psychical researchers cannot be understood without considering

> ... the intense enthusiasm they felt for the scientific, psychological and moral implications implied in the fact of discovering unknown intellectual capacities, occult physical forces or subliminal mental activity. If the physical sciences and technology could accomplish great achievements ... why was it not possible to discover a new psychic dimension or unknown mental capacities? (p. 292).

References

Alvarado, C. S. (2014). Mediumship, psychical research, dissociation, and the powers of the subconscious mind. *Journal of Parapsychology, 78*, 98–114.

Alvarado, C. S., & Biondi, M. (2017). Classic text no. 110: Cesare Lombroso on mediumship and pathology. *History of Psychiatry, 28*, 225–241.

Alvarado, C. S., Nahm, M., & Sommer, A. (2012). Notes on early interpretations of mediumship. *Journal of Scientific Exploration, 26*, 855–865.

Binet, A. (1892). *Les altérations de la personnalité*. Félix Alcan.

Crabtree, A. (1993). *From Mesmer to Freud: Magnetic sleep and the roots of psychological healing*. Yale University Press.

Domingo Soler, A. (1880). *El Espiritismo refutando los errores del Catolicismo Romano*. Juan Torrens.

Gilles de la Tourette, [G.] (1889). *L'hypnotisme et les états analogues au point de vue médico-legal.* (2nd ed.). E. Plon, Nourrit.

Janet, P. (1889). *L'automatisme psychologique: Essai de psychologie expérimentale sur les formes inférieures de l'activité humaine.* Félix Alcan.

Myers, F. W. H. (1903). *Human personality and its survival of bodily death* (2 vols.). Longmans, Green.

Plas, R. (2000). *Naissance d'une science humaine*: *La psychologie: Les psychologues et le "merveilleux psychique."* Presses Universitaires de Rennes.

Santa Cara, Marqués de. (n. d.). *Un tanteo en el misterio (Ensayo experimental sobre la lucidez sonambúlica).* M. Aguilar.

Sommer, A. (2012). Psychical research and the origins of American psychology: Hugo Münsterberg, William James and Eusapia Palladino. *History of the Human Sciences, 25*, 23–44.

Sommer, A. (2014, October 24). Free access to *Studies in History and Philosophy of Science C Special Section*, "Psychical Research in the History of Science and Medicine." https://forbidden-histories.wordpress.com/2014/10/24/free-access-to-studies-in-history-and-philosophy-of-science-c-special-section-psychical-research-in-the-history-of-science-and-medicine/

Takasuna, M. (2012). The Fukurai affair: Parapsychology and the history of psychology in Japan. *History of the Human Sciences, 25*, 149–164.

Wolffram, H. (2009). *The stepchildren of science: Psychical research and parapsychology in Germany, c. 1870–1939.* Rodopi.

Young, J. (2012, May 4). New! Special issue: *History of the Human Sciences*. https://ahp.apps01.yorku.ca/?p=2134

15

Mesmeric Mediumship: The Case of Emma*

Carlos S. Alvarado†

While a good part of the modern historical discussions of mediumship focuses on the nineteenth-century (e.g., Owen, 1990), it is well known that individuals claiming to receive recurrent, and sometimes controlled, communications from the dead existed in previous times, coming from antiquity (Ogden, 2001; Paton, 1921). Podmore (1902), among others, has reminded us of the activities of Swedenborg and several other individuals and movements that presented examples of mediumship before the appearance of the Fox sisters and of the development of modern spiritualism.[1] He also noticed that mesmerism also presented interesting cases of phenomena said to have been produced by spirits of the dead acting through mesmerized individuals (Podmore, 1902, Chap. 6, Vol. 1).[2] An example was Cahagnet (1851), who reported that his somnambules saw and interacted with presumed spirits of the dead. Another example, and the topic of this paper, was an English woman called Emma. The purpose of this article is to present excerpts of the "mediumistic" performances of Emma.

Emma's Mesmeric Performances

The performances of Emma are reported in the book of British physician Joseph W. Haddock *Somnolism & Psycheism* (1851).[3] Emma, whose initials were E. L., was described by Haddock to be a young woman, 24 years of age by December of 1850, from Worcestershire. Of "rather sallow complexion, and of a nervous-bilious temperament" (p. 84), she was said not to be able of much exertion. Emma started working in Haddock's house as a servant in 1846. Her phenomena, similar to those of many other somnambules, were quite varied. Haddock presented summaries of her clairvoyance at a distance, in some cases of which she was able to find lost money or property. In addition, Emma showed trances, amnesia of the trance state, and catalepsy. She also presented behaviours suggesting she was sensitive to Haddock's mental suggestions, to his mesmerizing other people at a distance, and to magnets located close by.

Emma and the "Other" World

In a section of his book Haddock described mediumistic phenomena involving apparent contact with spirits. This was chapter nine, entitled "Extasis, or Trance." Haddock referred to extasis as a "sort of swoon" under which "the mind became, as it were, loosened from its bodily connection, and could, by this means, obtain a perception of objects, and a knowledge of things not cognizable to the ordinary senses" (p. 180). The ancients, he wrote, used the word extasis to describe this "because the mind

*Republished with permission from *Psypioneer*, 5, 44–51, 2009.
†This paper was written while I enjoyed a grant from the Society for Psychical Research.

thus stood, comparatively, out of the body" (p. 180). Haddock stated that this condition appeared to be "a merely partial uncovering of the veil which conceals 'the things unseen;' and Extatics may be considered as travellers in an unknown country, enabled to see something of its nature, and to report, according to the degree of their perception, or powers of observation" (p. 180).

Haddock's account of the phenomena lacks many important details such as information about the identity of the "Lady" that Emma was in contact with. Furthermore, with the exception of some quotes coming from Emma's experiences, which most probably are reconstructions by the author, the book presents mainly Haddock's account of the events. The material reprinted here presents themes of spirit communications similar to those found in the early spiritualistic literature. Some of these includes discussions of death as the exit of the spirit from the body (Hare, 1855), the existence of spiritual spheres and places where spirits reside (Davis, 1867), and visions of people and places, including mentions of gardens (Edmonds & Dexter, 1854).

The following are long excerpts from Haddock's book, which I transcribe as a reminder of the existence of these mesmeric phenomenon:

> Frequently during the spring and summer of 1848, Emma would, in the mesmeric state, speak of the scenery and nature of the spirit-world, in such a way as to impress the beholder with a conviction, that the descriptions she gave could not be the result of any previously acquired knowledge, or of an active imagination. She also, occasionally, spoke of things which had actually occurred, but which it was impossible for her to know by any ordinary means ... (p. 181)
>
> In these states of spontaneous extasis she preserved a recollection, at times, of the place she was actually in, and of the persons by whom she was surrounded: and, at the same time, she had a distinct *sensational* perception of a higher and spiritual state of existence, and of a class of beings living in such a state. She would speak of these things while in the trance; and on her return to the normal state, she could recollect, and, with a feeling of awe and diffidence, again describe what she had seen and heard. During the first trance of four hours' duration, which occurred on the 28th of September, 1848, and was witnessed by several highly respectable gentlemen from Manchester, she was so far elevated in her perceptions, that she spoke of *this* world as the *other* world, just as if she had passed from this life by death. She said, also, that the persons in the room with her, appeared only *like shadows*, and *a long way from her*. Upon examination, she was found, in this and other trances, insensible to pain, and her eyes upturned, as in the ordinary mesmeric state, and her limbs continued flexible. At times, she would seem wholly indrawn; and then she would, as it were, return and speak of what was passing before her mental vision. But, in a subsequent trance, of six hours' duration, she became, for a part of it, quite insensible to all outward things, and perfectly cataleptic from head to foot. A gentleman, who was with me on this occasion, assisted me to raise her body, and we found it as stiff and inflexible as a log of wood. (p. 184)
>
> The subject of these trances would afford matter for many pages; but some were of a private character, and, although highly interesting to the parties concerned, would not be interesting to others, except as illustrating the nature of the spirit's home, and some of the general laws by which spiritual associations are regulated. (p. 184–185).
>
> A *general* statement of Emma's revealments while in the state of extasis, will enable the reader more fully to comprehend the *particular* details of individual trances. Man is represented as a spiritual being, rising from what she calls "the shell" of the dead material body, immediately after death; or as soon as the connection between the soul and its material covering is completely severed, which she says, does not sometimes occur, until a day or

two after what appears as death. The risen and emancipated spirit, is a perfectly organised existence, preserving the human form, and having a complete *sensational perception* of his fellow spiritual beings, and of the beautiful scenery of the spiritual spheres; that is, provided he possessed during his natural life, a moral state in harmony with those spheres. The male and female sex retaining all the characteristics necessary to a spiritual state of existence, and living together in a state of angelic union, being united as to their minds. Those who have been interiorly united here, coming into a state of union hereafter; those who have not been *mentally* united here, seek their true *mental* counterpart hereafter. She represents male and female spiritual beings thus united, appearing at a distance *as one*, and says they are not called two, nor the married, but THE ONE. Infants and young children who have passed from this world by death, are stated to grow to a state of adolescence, but more speedily than in the natural world. During infancy, and early childhood, they are confided to the care of good female spirits, or angels, whose delight it is, to instruct them by various methods, especially by *representations of things*, which form a sort of pictorial teaching. These spiritual spheres are not located in the distant regions of space, or in the sun, or heavenly bodies; but are connected apparently with our own planet, and the spiritual inhabitants are in close association with us, and exercise an influence over us, although we are unconscious of it. … In the highest state of extasis, *she appeared* to herself to be among spiritual beings *as one of themselves*, at home, and surrounded by objects which to her were real, and which appeared more real, than the shadowy beings, with whom she was naturally associated. At other times, she said, that she appeared to the spiritual beings as shadowy, and her own perceptions were proportionably obscure. The first receptacle, or common plane of departed spirits, she describes as a sort of middle state or place, from which the good, as they become prepared, ascend gradually, to higher and more delightful places; those that are the best having higher abodes than the others. All, she says, are welcomed by angelic spirits on their arrival in the spirit-world; but *the evil will not associate with the good,* and *recede of their own accord,* more or less rapidly, to darker places below this middle state, and which appeared also to be to the *left*: but of these darker places she had not seen so much, as of the abodes of the good … (pp. 185–187)

I have said, that before Emma became the subject of the extatic state, she had, in the ordinary mesmeric state, began to speak frequently of spiritual objects and beings. I soon perceived, that one being, under whose influence she seemed to be, and of whom she frequently spoke, had been most nearly related to me, while in this world, but she had departed this life for about ten years when the first of these trances occurred. Emma always says that this "lady," as I will call her, following Emma's phraseology, "helps her" in all serious cases of illness, and the like, but not in mere secular, or trifling cases. … She also spoke of a *fountain* of crystal water, in which, she said, the "lady" bathed her, before she could follow her to behold the scenery she afterwards described … The following narrative will shew that, at least, *some* of the matters connected with these trances, cannot be accounted for by resolving them into mere imaginative action; but that there is a *reality* in her extatic perceptions and that she then possesses a super-sensual gift. (pp. 187–188)

In the month of July, 1848, she told me, on a Saturday evening, while in the mesmeric state, that the "lady was coming to her, in the night between Sunday and Monday, and that she would show her a book *with some writing in*, which she was to take and shew to me;" and further, that the "lady would come to her again, at a quarter past nine on Monday morning when she would know more about it." I found her, as usual, on awaking, ignorant of what had transpired, and carefully concealed it from her. … From the general drift of her remarks, and her connecting the books and the writing with the "lady," I concluded, that, if there was any truth in her statements, one of three books was intended; two of these were in the house, the other, a small pocket-bible, *was not in the house*; but experience having convinced me of the correctness of her predictions, I got this little bible, *unknown to her*, and put it, with the other two books, on the shelves with many more, taking care not to put them together. In the night she got up in a state very similar, if not quite like *somnambulism*, and descending two flights of stairs, unheard by me, she went to the book-shelves, and selected *this very pocket-bible*, and ascending the stairs with it, came to my room, the opening of the door of which aroused me. She walked up to me, and addressing me in the peculiar way she then used to do, when mesmerised, she said,—"I have brought you a book which the 'lady' wishes you to read to me." She was holding the book open over the top of her head, with the inside of the book next her. This I could see by the twilight; but, as I could not see whereabouts the book was opened, I went to get a candle for that purpose, but, in doing so, owing to the darkness, I inadvertently knocked the book out of her hand. She picked it up, and speedily found the place again, by turning over the pages, right and left, *over her head*, in her usual mesmeric manner, until she said she had found the same place again. The passage selected was Joshua, ch. i. vv. 8, 9. … I read the passage to her; she said, "Yes! that is it,—'Be of good courage,' that is what the lady reads." When I began to read beyond the tenth verse, she stopped me, saying, "the lady did not read that." She appeared quite pleased and relieved by my reading to her, and soon spontaneously awoke. … She also told me circumstances connected with the history of that book [the Bible], which, she said, the lady told her, and in which the "lady was concerned; which *I am positive she could not know by any ordinary means*; for some were only known to myself! She was asked to tell by what means she found the passage, as she could not read, and was also in the dark? She replied, that the "'lady' had a similar book, but a larger one, open upon the left arm, where it lay without any weight, and that the 'lady' pointed, with the right hand, to the same pages and text: That her own hands seemed guided in their movements by the 'lady's' hand; and that when she had got to the right place, she could no longer turn the pages, either to the right or left!" How far this was fancy, or some real quasi magnetic drawing, it is impossible rightly to determine; but it is certain, that on trying her with the same bible a few months afterwards, when she had lost the connecting influence, she could not, after repeated trials, find the passage as she previously had done. (p. 188–190)

On Thursday, September 28th, 1848, Emma went into a trance she had foretold nearly two months before: this was the most remarkable she had, and lasted nearly four hours. … I … found her seated in a chair, partially *cataleptic*, with her eyes *fixed*, wide open, and staring, as it were, into vacuity. I spoke to her; but, at first, she did not hear me; I then saw her eyes roll *upwards* and *inwards*, as in the mesmeric state, and then the eyelids closed. She requested me "not to take her away," that is, not to interfere with the trance, which I promised, and led her to a more convenient place, where she might recline. I found it was with difficulty she could stand, and I had to support her to the seat prepared for her. She soon sunk into a complete sort of lethargy; occasionally moving her jaws, as if eating; at other times, speaking, as if to invisible personages: the principal remarks were questions, or such observations as seemed to repeat the *answers* she had received. After speaking, she appeared conscious of our presence, and rationally replied to what was said to her, and described what was visible to her perceptions. Then she relapsed into a state of unconsciousness to outward things, and, after a time, returned to the consciousness of our presence. These alternations continued to the close; but some minutes before arousing, her manner indicated that a change was passing over her. When she returned to the normal state, she was quite low and prostrated, and it was some hours before she could take any food. …

The following paragraphs contain, in nearly her own words, the substance of what she saw and heard during this, and another similar trance, as elicited by questions put during, and after, the trance, and from her own recollections of what had transpired. (pp. 191–193)

"When sitting in the chair, I felt as if something run up me, and I went mazy, and the room seemed as if it opened, and I was in another place, although I had some knowledge that I was still in the room; my eyes were open, and I could not shut them. Afterwards, when they were shut, it seemed as if they were open. At first, many beings came to me, and presently I seemed to be with them as one of themselves; this was after I was removed to the other seat; for taking me up stairs, seemed to draw me away from them. I did not feel strange, or any alarm, nor did they appear to think me strange or different to themselves. I felt with them just as I do now with you. There were many: some that I did not know, and some that I did know; some had been my companions when a child, and had been dead for years, but they knew me, and were glad to see me, and took me about gardens, like paradise gardens. The 'lady' came first, and many others with her; she was with me the whole time. When I took hold of your hand, she looked and smiled, and seemed pleased. It appeared to me nearly the same each time I have been. I saw each time that, from the place where I entered this spirit-world, there was a way leading to the *right, upwards,* to the good middle place; and away to the *left, downwards*, to the bad middle place, and there was a worse place lower down, but I did not see to it. All along the way leading to the good middle place, there were trees and flowers of various kinds growing, and *writings up* (inscriptions) in many places. The letters were of different kinds and colours, but I could not tell what they meant. It was told me, that they were directions and instructions, and that I must learn to read, that I may know what they mean. The good middle place seemed very large, and very many were there. Most that were there, *staying there*, were clothed in plain white loose dresses. I saw higher up, to the top of a hill, where, it was told me, angels lived. I did not go straight up, *but slanting to the side*; the angels who came to meet me, came a *nearer way* than I went. After going to the right, upwards, for some time, I came to a beautiful fountain, or lake (*pond*, she sometimes called it,) silvery looking. A beautiful brook, or river, flowed from the top of the hill, down into the fountain. I never saw such beautiful crystal and shining water anywhere else. Round this fountain, or lake, and on each side of the river, there grew the most beautiful flowers and trees I ever saw. The leaves which fell off these trees sparkled like gold and silver, as they lay along upon the ground. If a leaf fell off a tree, another leaf sprang forth directly, and the trees did not become bare, as here. The same, if a flower was plucked, another immediately sprang forth. No one can go up the hill until they have been bathed in that fountain; I had to bathe in it, and drink the water, before I could ascend; then you could go up on either side of the river. It was in this fountain I saw the beautiful fish I before spoke of, which was given me to eat; and it was in the walks about this river that I saw the fruit grow of which I ate. This fruit they eat as bread, but it is not bread, but most delicious fruit. It is something like an orange with seeds in it: "—afterwards, she compared it to a pear, sweet, and with seeds in it,—possibly something that seemed like a fig, or pomegranate." After bathing in the fountain, and going up the hill, I came down, and we sat down, round and near the fountain, and eat of the fruit, and many things were shown and told me." (pp. 193–195)

I … found that matters on which I had enquired in the mesmeric state, were sometimes referred to, and she has told me when those states of extasis would arise, in which she could learn things that she could not know by ordinary mesmerism. These, generally, were cases in which some person involved in the enquiry, had departed this life. (p. 201)

In one case, where, as an experiment, an enquiry was being made relative to a missing will, she told me, not only what I asked her, but spoke of other things which neither myself nor she knew anything … about, nor had I been asked about what she said; but I was afterwards informed that what she said was correct. This was a description of some old furniture, and some bags with money in, in an Irish town, the existence of which things was perfectly unknown to me; but they were connected with the missing document, and Emma professed to derive her knowledge of the existence of these things, from the spirit of the departed. She asked me about the removal of this money, as if I knew of it. My correspondent afterwards informed me of the correctness of Emma's statements; but refused to continue the inquiry, from a superstitious dread of holding communication with the dead. This case, as far as it went, was an excellent one, to prove the continued existence of man after death. I was desired by a gentleman to investigate a mysterious murder which occurred nearly twenty years ago. No particulars whatever were communicated to me, beyond that some bones which were sent me, were found in a very peculiar manner, and that there were reasons for supposing them to be the bones of a person long missing. I am precluded from going into the particulars of this case, further than that I found, from subsequent letters, that the skull was fractured in the part *she said it was*; that the bones were in the condition and found in such a place and manner as *she described*, and that her description of the supposed murderer, corresponded exactly with an *individual suspected*! I expended a good deal of time on this case, on account of its interest, and as another test of clairvoyance, and for the satisfaction of the gentleman, who had himself taken much trouble to procure the bones, and a portion of the clothing of the missing man, as a medium of enquiry. Emma several times spoke of this affair in the trance state, and, from the general correctness of her statements as far as the circumstances are known, it would seem that the whole transaction was *gradually* made known to her, and that she saw in the trances, *a representation of the occurrence. …* Another curious feature in enquiries where departed persons were involved, was observed. She would sometimes speak of these persons, and say she could see them, but that she could not communicate with them, because they had *not gone away long enough*, or had not passed *into the proper state*; and she has fixed the time, when, she said, such communication could be had, in conformity with what she represented as the law of the spirit-world. (pp. 201–202)

Notes

1 For a discussion of the Fox sisters as well as other early American mediums see Capron (1855).

2 For a more recent discussion of magnetic phenomena attributed to discarnate agency see Crabtree (1993, pp. 196–212).

3 Beloff (1997, pp. 25–28) discusses selected aspects of Emma's clairvoyant phenomena.

References

Beloff, J. (1997). *Parapsychology: A concise history*. St. Martin's Press.

Cahagnet, L. A. (1851). *The celestial telegraph, or, secrets of the life to come, revealed through magnetism* (1st American ed.) J. S. Redfield.

Capron, E. W. (1855). *Modern Spiritualism: Its facts and fanatisms, its consistencies and contradictions*. Bela Marsh.

Crabtree, A. (1993). *From Mesmer to Freud: Magnetic sleep and the roots of psychological healing*. Yale University Press.

Davis, A. J. (1867). *A stellar key to the summer land*. William White.

Edmonds, J. W., & Dexter, G.T. (1854). *Spiritualism* (Vol. 1, 9th ed.). Partridge & Brittan.

Haddock, J. W. (1851). *Somnolism & psycheism; or, the science of the soul and the phenomena of nervation* (2nd ed.). James S. Hodson.

Hare, R. (1855). *Experimental investigation of the spirit manifestations demonstrating the existence of spirits and their communion with mortals*. Partridge & Brittan.

Ogden, D. (2001). *Greek and Roman necromancy*. Princeton University Press.

Owen, A. (1990). *The darkened room: Women, power and spiritualism in late Victorian England*. University of Pennsylvania Press.

Paton, L. B. (1921). *Spiritism and the cult of the dead in antiquity*. Macmillan.

Podmore, F. (1902). *Modern spiritualism: A history and a criticism* (2 vols.). Methuen.

Early Spiritualist Discussions About the Distortions of Mediumistic Communications*

Carlos S. Alvarado

> ... The generality of communications ... are given in such a mode that they are liable to be affected by the mind of the medium, because they are given through their use, in some measure, of the medium's mental powers.
>
> John W. Edmonds (1858, p. 7)

In a previous article, I argued that the contributions of spiritualists to ideas about mediumship include more than defenses of discarnate agency (Alvarado, 2003; see "Human Radiations: Concepts of Force in Mesmerism, Spiritualism and Psychical Research," this volume). Among other things, they have contributed to the recognition of the existence of distortions and difficulties in spirit communications, a topic mentioned in a recent *Journal of Scientific Exploration* Editorial by Stephen Braude (2020) in which he cited statements about the subject by C. D. Broad (1962) and William James (1909). Although this was not the main topic of Braude's comments, I would like to refer to some nineteenth-century examples of the literature in question if only to recognize the pioneering role of various spiritualists in discussing the subject, what one writer referred to as "imperfect messages by the telegraph from heaven" (Spirit communications, 1858, p. 4).

One example includes the ideas of American Universalist minister Samuel B. Brittan. In an article entitled "Cerebral Influence on Revelation," Brittan (1852) wrote:

> In all ages, revelations from the Spiritual World have been essentially modified by the physical and mental characteristics of the persons through whom they have been given to mankind. In the process of influx, the elements of two minds are blended, and the revelation is the result of their mingled action. Sometimes this infusion is labored and difficult, and the spiritual influence is only perceptible in a slight abnormal quickening of the human faculties. Again the thought is directly inspired, but is left to be invested by the mind of the medium, from which it takes not only its coloring and clothing, but its specific form. (Brittan, 1852, pp. 39–40)

In his view the influence from the spiritual dimension, including biblical prophetic revelations, "usually conjoins itself to, and becomes cooperative with, the predominant elements of the mind" (p. 40). These elements were the usual patterns of thought and expression of the mind of the receiving person.

Similarly, another minister, social reformer Adin Ballou (1852), wrote that in mediums of inferior intellect: "Their own prejudices, will, imagination, low ideas, perverse sentiments, and peculiar absurdities of interior conception, must bias and characterize the communications, which any spirit should attempt to make through them" (p. 67). Thus, the meaning of communicating spirits would be conveyed incorrectly. "It would be like the message of a Frenchman to an Englishman, rendered

*Republished with permission from *Journal of Scientific Exploration, 34*(4), 710–716, 2020.

through an ignorant Dutchman, who had only a smattering of French and English. The Englishman might be puzzled to make anything decent of it" (p. 67).

The famous clairvoyant and visionary Andrew Jackson Davis also had something to say on the topic. He believed that:

> The mind which has been, through the formative influence of prevailing education and custom, moulded into a receptacle for the entertainment of any particular notion, theory, or creed extant, is almost certain to unconsciously alter, modify, and arrange all impressions, from whatever source received, invariably in accordance with the state and style of its own growth and individual culture. And furthermore, it may be accepted as a principle, fully demonstrated in the world's history, that the Divine cannot flow into Human structures—the celestial cannot blend, intimately, with the terrestrial, without the former (the Divine) participating to a degree more or less obvious, in the imperfections which are infinitely and eternally consequent upon, and inseparably connected with, a physical or material state of existence. Discord and contradiction, therefore, growing out of the intimate association or conjunction of the spiritual with the material, must invariably and everywhere be more or less apparent. This fact will certainly appear, notwithstanding the honesty or good intentions of the media,[1] or that entire passivity of mind which Truth requires. (Davis, 1853, p. 203)

Another example comes from the writings of a prominent spiritualist and student of mediumistic phenomena, American Judge John W. Edmonds. He wrote as follows in the second volume of *Spiritualism*, an early classic on the subject authored by Edmonds and physician George T. Dexter (1855), who wrote on the subject as students of the topic, but also in terms of their experiences as mediums. The following is from the volume's Introduction by Edmonds:

> The visions which I have are … impressed on my mind as vividly and distinctly as any material object possibly can be, yet in giving them to others, I must rely upon and use my own powers of observation, my own memory, my own command of language, and I not unfrequently labor under the difficulty of feeling that there is no word known to me that is adequate to conveying the novel idea communicated. I am often conscious that I fail, from poverty of language, in conveying the sentiment I receive with the same vigor and clearness with which it comes to me. So it is also with what I may call the didactic teachings through me. Sometimes the influence is so strong, that I am given, not merely the ideas, but the very words in which they are clothed, and I am unconscious of what I am going to say until I actually say it. At other times the thought is given me sentence by sentence, and I know not what idea or sentence is to follow, but the language used is my own and is selected by myself from my own memory's storehouse. And at other times the whole current of thought or process of reasoning is given me in advance, and I choose for myself the language and the illustrations used to convey it, and sometimes the order of giving it. But in all these modes there is more or less of myself in them, more or less of my individuality underlying it all … I have noticed the same thing in the Doctor [Dexter], and more than all that, I have observed in both of us that our communications not only at times contain what may be called Americanisms, but expressions peculiar to our respective professions.
>
> It is, therefore, rarely that either of us can say that the communications through us are precisely what the spirits designed they should be, and as they designed them; and consequently it will never do to receive them as absolute authority, however agreeable they may be or however consonant to other teachings …

> Sometimes it is more apparent than at others, owing to many causes ever at work around us; sometimes it is owing to the physical condition of the medium, and sometimes to his mental state; sometimes to the atmosphere; sometimes to locality—some localities, such as high and hilly places being more favorable than such as are low and swampy; sometimes to the condition of those who are present, whether in a state of harmony or discord, and very frequently to the state and condition of the spirits who are professing to commune, and their aptitude to the task …
>
> There is another cause, and that is, the passiveness or otherwise of the mediums to the influence at work with them. Sometimes they resist with a very determined will, and it is impossible for others, and often even for ourselves, to know when the operation of that will is entirely overcome, or how much of its influence may hang around and stain the communication with its taint of mortal life. Sometimes timidity and diffidence will color and sometimes vanity and fanaticism distort the teaching of the spirits. Often the want of confidence will warp them; for, strange as it may appear! there are mediums who are not Spiritualists, and who, unaccustomed to the examination of their own minds, can not discriminate between their operation and the spirit-influence; and as often an overweening credulity will put awry that which was designed to be plain and straightforward. (Edmonds & Dexter, 1855, pp. 39–41)

Another example was American attorney and inventor Joel Tiffany. He wrote in his book *Spiritualism Explained* that the significance of communications depended on the medium's translation of messages:

> Suppose the Spirits make a communication, they make it in words. These words only address your consciousness through your understanding, and you make them mean according to your understanding of them. If the Spirit makes a communication by Pantomime, it still appeals to your understanding, and depends upon your translation to give it significance. There may be error in the communication and in yourself, so that the error will be double. (Tiffany, 1856, p. 110)

My final example is from France, from the pen of Allan Kardec (pseudonym of educator Hippolyte-Leon Denizard Rivail). He wrote that when a spirit communicates in a language known to the medium, he uses the words he finds there to convey his thoughts. If the communicator uses a language different from the medium's the latter's mind would not have the necessary words, and letter-by-letter dictation would be required. "If the medium can neither read nor write, she does not even possess the letters; you must therefore lead her hand like a schoolgirl; and this is an even greater material difficulty to overcome" (Kardec, 1862, p. 281, my translation).

Many other examples could be cited (e.g., Crowell, 1879, Chap. 10; Inaccuracies in communications from the spirit life, 1857; Spicer, 1853, p. 150; Wolfe, 1874, p. 96), including many published later in the Twentieth Century (e.g., Carrington, 1937, Part 1, Chap. 7; Firebrace, Vigurs, & Leaf, 1954; Leaf, 1911).[2] Most of these writings focused on confusions between presumably veridical messages and the content of the medium's mind, including such things as imagery and recollections. But this literature did not include suggestions for research, nor actual studies of the problem. I have presented some ideas about possibilities for research on the subject in a discussion of mediumistic mentation published in this journal (Alvarado, 2010).

In the meantime, my main point is a strictly historical one. That is, we need to recognize the conceptual contribution of spiritualists to psychical research, which extends beyond generating interest in mediumship and providing a context for its development and practice. This contribution includes the development of various other theoretical ideas that, regardless of their validity, were influential in the study of mediumship and its conceptualizations.[3]

Notes

1 Mediums were sometimes called "media" in the early spiritualistic literature (e.g., Ballou, 1852, p. 61; Capron, 1855, p. 392; Hare, 1855, p. 159).

2 The psychical research literature also has interesting discussions, as seen in studies about medium Leonora E. Piper (Hodgson, 1898; Sidgwick, 1915). Also important were James H. Hyslop's numerous writings about the "pictographic" process (e.g., Hyslop, 1914, 1919, Chapter 10; see also Alvarado, 2009). This was a process in which "the communicator manages to elicit in the living subject a sensory phantasm of his thoughts, representing, but not necessarily directly corresponding to, the reality" (Hyslop, 1919, p. 111). The sensory impression could be in various modalities, depending on the medium. Hyslop argued that messages could be distorted when the content of the medium's subconscious mind interfered with the interpretation of the imagery involved or when stray or peripheral imagery came from the communicator.

3 This includes communications from the living and ESP from the living explanations of mediumship (Alvarado, 2003), as well as ideas of psychic forces, particularly in relation to physical mediumship (Alvarado, 2006).

References

Alvarado, C. S. (2003). The concept of survival of bodily death and the development of parapsychology. *Journal of the Society for Psychical Research, 67*(2), 65–95.

Alvarado, C. S. (2006). Human radiations: Concepts of force in mesmerism, Spiritualism and psychical research. *Journal of the Society for Psychical Research, 70*(3), 138–162.

Alvarado, C. S. (2009). James H. Hyslop and the pictographic process in mediumistic communications. *Paranormal Review, 49*, 3–7.

Alvarado, C. S. (2010). Investigating mental mediumship: Research suggestions from the historical literature. *Journal of Scientific Exploration, 24*(2), 197–224.

Ballou, A. (1852). *An exposition of views respecting the principal facts, causes, and peculiarities involved in spirit manifestations*. Bela Marsh.

Braude, S. E. (2020). Cosmic aesthetics [Editorial]. *Journal of Scientific Exploration, 34*(1), 5–12.

Brittan, S. B. (1852). Cerebral influence on revelation. *The Shekinah, 2*, 39–43.

Broad, C. D. (1962). *Lectures on psychical research*. Routledge & Kegan Paul.

Capron, E. W. (1855). *Modern spiritualism, its facts and fanaticisms, its consistencies and contradictions*. Bela Marsh.

Carrington, H. (1937). *The psychic world*. G. P. Putnam's Sons.

Crowell, E. (1879). *The spirit world: Its inhabitants, nature, and philosophy*. Colby & Rich.

Davis, A. J. (1853). *The present age and inner life: A sequel to spiritual intercourse: Modern mysteries classified and explained*. Partridge and Brittan.

Edmonds, Judge [J. W.] (1858). *Uncertainty of spiritual intercourse* (*Spiritual Tracts*, No. 4). No publisher given.

Edmonds, J. W., & Dexter, G. T. (1855). *Spiritualism* (Vol. 2). Partridge & Brittan.

Firebrace, R. C., Vigurs, H. L., & Leaf, H. (1954). *Spirit communication and the mind of the medium, the sitter, the communicator.* Almorris Press.

Hare, R. (1855). *Experimental investigation of the spirit manifestations*. Partridge & Brittan.

Hodgson, R. (1898). A further record of observations of certain phenomena of trance. *Proceedings of the Society for Psychical Research, 13*(33), 284–582.
Hyslop, J. H. (1914). A hypothetical process of communication. *Journal of the American Society for Psychical Research, 8*(8), 377–389.
Hyslop, J. H. (1919). *Contact with the other world.* Century.
Inaccuracies in communications from the spirit life. (1857, September 10). *Banner of Light*, 5–6.
James, W. (1909). Report on Mrs. Piper's Hodgson-control. *Proceedings of the Society for Psychical Research, 23*(58), 2–121.
Kardec, A. (1862). *Spiritualisme expérimentale: Le livre des mediums* (2nd ed.). Didier.
Leaf, H. (1911). Difficulties of spirit communication. *Light, 31*(1606), 496–497.
Sidgwick, Mrs. H. [E. M.]. (1915). A contribution to the study of the psychology of Mrs. Piper's trance phenomena. *Proceedings of the Society for Psychical Research, 28*(71), 1657.
Spicer, H. (1853). *Sights and sounds: The mystery of the day: Comprising an entire history of the American "spirit" manifestations.* Thomas Bosworth.
Spirit communications. (1858, January 9). *Banner of Light*, 4.
Tiffany, J. (1856). *Spiritualism explained.* Graham and Ellinwood.
Wolfe, N. B. (1874). *Startling facts in modern Spiritualism.* (n. p.)

Introduction to Michael Faraday's Essay on Table-Moving*

Carlos S. Alvarado†

The editors of the *International Journal of Parapsychology* are glad to inaugurate this section of classic papers from the literature of parapsychology with an important paper that represents early attempts to find conventional explanations for some of the early phenomena of spiritualism. I am referring to the essay that Michael Faraday (1791–1867) wrote in 1853 on table-turning (which he called "table moving," a phenomenon prevalent in early spiritualism, in which tables moved and through their movements answered questions when a group of people placed their hands or fingers on the tabletop (Crabtree, 1993, Chap. 12; Nisbet, 1973).

According to an early biographer, Faraday, an eminent nineteenth-century physicist well-known for his work with magnetism and electricity, "waged [an] implacable war with the Spiritualists" (Gladstone, 1872, p. 113). Some years after the 1853 essay, Faraday wrote an essay on education in which he argued that no contribution to knowledge had been obtained from the phenomena of spiritualism. He said: "How is it that not one new power has been added to the means of investigation employed by the philosophers, or one valuable utilitarian application presented to society?" (Faraday, 1855/1961, p. 14). More than a decade after the essay (1864), Faraday wrote to a believer in spiritualistic phenomena: "I've no evidence that any natural or unnatural power is concerned in the phenomena that requires investigation or deserves it" (Gladstone, 1872, p. 114).

Faraday's views on table-turning were first published in the *London Times* (June 30, 1853). Modified versions appeared in the same year in the intellectual review *The Athenaeum* and in the medical journal *The Lancet* (Faraday, 1853a, 1853b). We reprint here the essay as it was printed in *The Athenaeum*. In this article, Faraday proposed a normal explanation for table-turning. As Podmore (1902) summarized this work: "By the use of some ingenious apparatus Faraday showed conclusively that the movements were due to muscular action, and to that alone, exercised in most cases without the consciousness or volition of the sitters" (Vol. 2, p. 9).

During the nineteenth century, many attempted to explain mesmeric and spiritualistic phenomena by using all kinds of medical, psychological, and physiological explanations such as suggestion and hallucinations (for overviews, see Alvarado, 1989; Brown, 1983; and Shortt, 1984). Other explanatory notions proposed for mesmeric and spiritualistic phenomena included ideas of automatic and reflex actions of the nervous system. Examples of these ideas were those proposed by Carpenter (1853) and by Laycock (1851). The idea that unconscious muscular movements could explain such phenomena as dowsing and the use of pendulums existed before Faraday (e.g., Chevreul, 1833), and it was further developed in terms of its psychology by contemporaries of Faraday's during the 1850s and 1860s (see Crabtree, 1993, Chap. 12). Faraday himself, in this essay, acknowledges an 1852 address delivered by W. B. Carpenter at the Royal Institution in which the concept of ideo-motor phenomena had been discussed.

*Republished with permission from *International Journal of Parapsychology, 1*(1), 153–163, 2000.
†Thanks are due to Lorraine J. Haricombe, Associate Professor of Library Sciences and Associate Dean for Public Services, of the University Libraries at Northern Illinois University, USA, for helping us locate a copy of Faraday's paper.

However, the "mental physiology" of those days was barely beginning. More elaborate discussions of the psychology of motor automatisms had to wait for the later writings of Myers (1885), Janet (1889), Grasset (1907), and Flournoy (1911). The work of these writers represents what Ellenberger (1970) has described as the scientists' appropriation of spiritualistic phenomena for the purpose of exploring the subconscious mind: "A new subject, the medium, became available for experimental psychological investigations, out of which evolved a new model of the human mind" (Ellenberger, 1970, p. 85).

There were even ideas that extended the simple automatism proposed by Faraday into a collective psychism, as can be seen in the writings of Grasset (1907) and Warcollier (n. d.). According to René Sudre (1956/1960), table-turning "Is a question of collective psychism, for it is not a somnambulistic personality of the medium alone which makes the table turn and communicate; the contribution made by the other sitters is sometimes more important" (p. 116). Although Faraday postulated the influence of more than one person around the table, his ideas may seem very simple and underdeveloped to the modern reader. But it must be remembered that Faraday represents the beginning stages of theorization about motor automatisms and that the concept of a subconscious mind was fully developed only after his time. Consequently, his concept of automatism did not include discussion of the ideas that subconscious or secondary selves might be coordinating the production of the phenomena, but emphasized mainly involuntary movements.

It is not surprising that Faraday chose table-turning to perform his studies of unconscious movements. As Nisbet (1973) and Podmore (1902) have discussed, among others, the practice of table-turning was particularly popular in Britain and in other countries during the 1850s. An early description of this phenomena from France read as follows:

> In about ten minutes the table turned, in fifteen it answered questions by striking the floor with its feet. The replies were nearly all correct … (Gray, 1854, p. 520)

Several pamphlets described various facets of this phenomena, among which were Godfrey's *Table-Moving Tested and Proved to be the Result of Satanic Agency* (1853), and Nicholls' *Table Moving* (n. d.). While the first condemned the practice as one of satanic origin, the second encouraged its practice and presented instructions for inducing the phenomena. In addition, some systematic research was carried out by Count Agénor de Gasparin and Professor Marc Thury that suggested that table-turning phenomena could take place without contact, thus suggesting that Faraday's explanation was only part of the picture. This research has been conveniently summarized in English by Flammarion (1907).

Certainly, not everyone accepted Faraday's conclusions. Oliver Lodge stated that some of Faraday's ideas were unsound in the light of further work on the subject (General Meeting, 1906). Lodge was referring to many instances of table levitations and other phenomena reported under conditions in which there was no physical contact with the table (e.g., Barrett, 1917, p. 44; London Dialectical Society, 1871/1874, pp. 10–11). For this reason, it seems that Flammarion's (1907, p. 266) description of Faraday's explanations as "insufficient" is warranted as long as we do not discount it in circumstances in which it seems plausible.

Faraday's work was of key importance in pointing out a possible explanation for some types of table-turning phenomena, and it was certainly an important step in the history of automatic movement phenomena. It also alerts us to the importance of considering conventional explanations in psychical research before we accept other models. Unfortunately, as Lodge pointed out, Faraday's letter and essay had negative implications for research:

> The hostile influence of Faraday's great name has undoubtedly rendered more difficult the scientific examination of ultranormal physical phenomena. …, and has retarded the prosecution of our researches in that direction. … (General Meeting, 1906, p. 181)

But regardless of these negative effects, Faraday is a reminder of the conventional human processes one has to consider before one can embrace other explanations, such as the influence of spirits or the influence of psychic forces. His work is still cited today as an exemplar of research on conventional explanations (Irwin, 1999, p. 35). As such, the comments we reproduce here are still relevant to us as long as it is remembered that they are apt only when there is direct contact with the table, or with such other objects as a Ouija board.

Professor Faraday on Table-Moving[1]

The following account of the methods pursued and the results obtained by Prof. Faraday in the investigation of a subject which has taken such strange occupation of the public mind, both here and abroad, has-been communicated to our columns by that high scientific authority. The subject was generally opened by Mr. Faraday in the *Times* of Thursday: it being therein intimated that the details were to be reserved for our this day's publication. The communication is of great importance in the present morbid condition of public thought,—when, as Professor Faraday says, "the effect produced by table-turners has, without due inquiry, been referred to electricity, to magnetism, to attraction, to some unknown or hitherto unrecognized physical power able to affect inanimate bodies, to the revolution of the earth, and even to diabolical or supernatural agency":—and we are tempted to extract a passage from Mr. Faraday's letter to the *Times* which we think well worth adding to the experimental particulars and the commentaries with which he has favoured ourselves. "I have been," says the Professor, "greatly startled by the revelation which this purely physical subject has made on the condition of the public mind. No doubt, there are many persons who have formed a right judgment or used a cautious reserve,—for I know several such, and public communications have shown it to be so; but their number is almost as nothing to the great body who have believed and borne testimony, as I think, in the cause of error. I do not here refer to the distinction of those who agree with me and those who differ. By the great body, I mean such as reject all consideration of the equality of cause and effect,—who refer the results to electricity and magnetism, yet know nothing of the laws of these forces,—or to the attraction, yet show no phenomena of pure attractive power,—or to the rotation of the earth, as if the earth revolved round the leg of a table,—or to some unrecognized physical force, without inquiring whether the known forces are not sufficient,—or who even refer them to diabolical or supernatural agency, rather than suspend their judgment, or acknowledge to themselves that they are not learned enough in these matters to decide on the nature of the action. I think the system of education that could leave the mental condition of the public body in the state in which this subject has found it must have been greatly deficient in some very important principle."

Experimental Investigation of Table-Moving

The object which I had in view in this inquiry was not to satisfy myself, for my conclusion had been formed already on the evidence of those who had turned tables,—but that I might be enabled to give a strong opinion, founded on facts, to the many who applied to me for it. Yet the proof which I sought for, and the method followed in the inquiry, were precisely of the same nature as those which I should adopt in any other physical investigation. The parties with whom I have worked were very honourable, very clear in their intentions, successful table-movers, very desirous of succeeding in establishing the existence of a peculiar power, thoroughly candid, and very effectual. It is with me a clear point that the table moves when the parties, though they strongly wish it, do not intend, and do not believe that they move it by ordinary mechanical power. They say, the table draws their hands; that it moves first, and they have to follow it,—that sometimes it even moves from under their hands. With some the table will move to the right or left according as they wish or will it,—with others the direction of the first motion is uncertain:—but all agree that the table moves the hands and not the hands the table. Though I believe the parties do not intend to move the table, but obtain the result by a *quasi*-involuntary action,—still I had no doubt of the influence of expectation upon their minds, and through that upon the success or failure of their efforts. The first point, therefore, was, to remove all objections due to expectation, having relation to the substances which I might desire to use:—so, plates of the most different bodies, electrically speaking,—namely, sand-paper millboard, glue, glass, moist clay, tinfoil, cardboard, gutta percha, vulcanized rubber, wood, &c.,—were made into a bundle and placed on a table under the hands of a turner. The table turned. Other bundles of other plates were submitted to different persons at other times,—and the tables turned. Henceforth, therefore, these substances may be used in the construction of apparatus. Neither during their use nor at other times could the slightest trace of electrical or magnetic effects be obtained. At the same trials it was readily ascertained that one person could produce the effect; and that the motion was not necessarily circular, but might be in a straight line. No form of experiment or mode of observation that I could devise gave me the slightest indication of any peculiar natural force. No attractions, or repulsions, or signs of tangential power, appeared,—nor anything which could be referred to other than the mere mechanical pressure exerted, inadvertently by the turner. I therefore proceeded to analyze this pressure, or that part of it exerted in a horizontal direction:—doing so, in the first instance, unawares to the party. A soft cement, consisting of wax and turpentine, or wax and pomatum, was prepared. Four or five pieces of smooth slippery cardboard were attached one over the other by little pellets of the cement, and the lower of these to a piece of sand-paper resting on the table; the edges of these sheets overlapped slightly, and on the under surface a pencil line was drawn over the laps so as to indicate position. The upper cardboard was larger than the rest, so as to cover the whole from sight. Then, the table-turner placed the hands upon the upper card,—and we waited for the result. Now, the cement was strong enough to offer considerable resistance to mechanical motion, and also to retain the cards in any new position which they might acquire,—and yet weak enough to give way slowly to a continued force. When at last the tables, cards, and hands all moved to the left together, and so a true result was obtained, I took up the pack. On examination, it was easy to see by the displacement of the parts of the line, that the hand had moved further than the table, and that the latter had lagged behind;—that the hand, in fact, had pushed the upper card to the left, and that the under cards and the table had followed and been dragged by it. In other similar cases when the table had not moved, still the upper card was found to have moved, showing that the hand had carried it in the expected direction. It was evident, therefore, that the table had not drawn the hand and person round, nor had it moved simultaneously with the hand. The hand had left all things under it behind, and the table evidently tended continually to keep the hand back.

The next step was, to arrange an index, which should show whether the hand moved first, or the hand moved before the table, or both moved or remained at rest together. At first this was done by placing an upright pin fixed on a leaden foot upon the table, and using that as the fulcrum of a light lever. The latter was made of a slip of foolscap paper, and the short arm, about 1/4 of an inch in length, was attached to a pin proceeding from the edge of a slipping card placed on the table, and prepared to receive the hands of the table-turner. The other arm, of 11½ inches long, served for the index of motion. A coin laid on the table marked the normal position of the card and index. At first the slipping card was attached to the table by the soft cement, and the index was either screened from the turner, or the latter looked away; then, before the table moved, the index showed that the hand was giving a resultant pressure in the expected direction. The effect was never carried far enough to move the table, for the motion of the index corrected the judgment of the experimenter, who became aware that, inadvertently, a side force had been exerted. The card was now set free from the table, i.e., the cement was removed. This, of course, could not interfer with any of the results expected by the table-turner,—for both the bundle of plates spoken of and single cards had freely moved on the tables before; but now that the index was there, witnessing to the eye, and through it to the mind, of the table-turner, not the slightest tendency to motion either of the card or of the table occurred. Indeed, whether the card was left free or attached to the table all motion or tendency to motion was gone. In one particular case there was relative motion between the table and the hands: I believe that the hands moved in one direction; the table-turner was persuaded that the table moved from under the hand in the other direction:—a gauge, standing upon the floor, and pointing to the table, was therefore set up on that and some future occasions,—and then, neither motion of the hand nor of the table occurred.

A more perfect lever apparatus was then constructed in the following manner:—Two thin boards, 9½ inches by 7 inches, were provided; a board, 9 by 5 inches, was glued to the middle of the underside of one of these, (to be called the table-board), so as to raise the edges free from the table; being placed on the table, near and parallel to its side, an upright pin was fixed close to the further edge of the board, at the middle, to serve as the fulcrum for the indicating lever. Then, four glass rods, 7 inches long and ¼ [inch] in diameter, were placed as rollers on different parts of this table-board, and the upper board placed on them; the rods permitted any required amount of pressure on the boards, with a free motion of the upper on the lower to the right and left. At the part corresponding to the pin in the lower board, a piece was cut out of the upper board, and a pin attached there which, being bent downwards, entered the hole in the end of the short arm of the index lever: this part of the lever was of cardboard; the indicating prolongation was a straight hay-stalk 15 inches long. In order to restrain the motion of the upper board on the lower, two vulcanized rubber rings were passed round both, at the parts not renting on the table; these, whilst they tied the boards together, acted also as springs,—and whilst they allowed the first feeblest tendency to motion to be seen by the index, exerted before the upper board had moved a quarter of an inch sufficient power in pulling the upper board back from either side, to resist a strong lateral action of the hand. All being thus arranged, except that the lever was away,—the two boards were tied together with string, running parallel to the vulcanized rubber springs, so as to be immovable in relation to each other. They were then placed on the table, and a table-turner sat down to them:—the table very shortly moved in due order, showing the apparatus offered no impediment to the action. A like apparatus, with metal rollers, produced the same result under the hands of another person. The index was now put into its place and the string loosened, so that the springs should come into play. It was soon seen, with the party that could will the motion in either direction, (from whom the index was purposely hidden,) that the hands were gradually creeping up in the direction before agreed upon, though the party certainly thought that they were pressing downwards only. When shown it was so, they were truly surprised; but when they lifted up their hands and immediately saw the index return to its normal position, they were convinced. When they looked at the index and could see for themselves whether they were pressing truly downwards, or obliquely so as to produce a resultant in the right or left handed direction, then such an effect never took place. Several tried, for a long while together, and with the best will in the world; but no motion, right or left, of the table, or hand, or anything else, occurred.—[A passage from the letter in the *Times* is worth reproducing here, as illustrating in other words the value of this method of self-conviction.—"The result," says Prof. Faraday, "was, that when the parties saw the index it remained very steady; when it was hidden from them, or they looked away from it, it wavered about, though they believed that they always pressed directly downward; and when the table did not move, there was still a resultant of hand force in the direction in which it was wished the table should move, which, however, was exercised quite unwittingly by the party operating. This resultant it is which in the course of the waiting time while the fingers and hands become stiff, numb, and insensible by continued pressure, grows up to an amount sufficient to move the table or the substances pressed upon. But the most valuable effect of this test-apparatus (which was afterwards made more perfect and independent of the table) is the corrective power it possesses over the mind of the table-turner. As soon as the index is placed before the most earnest, and they perceive—as in my presence they have always done—that it tells truly whether they are pressing downwards only or obliquely, then all effects of table-turning cease, even though the parties persevere, earnestly desiring motion, till they become weary and worn out. No prompting or checking of the hands is needed—*the power is gone;* and this only because the parties are made conscious of what they are really doing, mechanically and so are unable unwittingly to deceive themselves. I know that some may say that it is the cardboard next [to] the fingers which moves first, and that *it* both drags the table and also the table-turner with it. All I have to reply is, that the cardboard may in practice be reduced to a thin sheet of paper weighing only a few grains, or to a piece of goldbeaters' skin, or even the end of the lever, and (in principle) to the very cuticle of the fingers itself. Then the results that follow are too absurd to be admitted: the table an incumbrance, and a person holding out the fingers in the air, either naked or tipped with goldbeaters' skin or cardboard, ought to be drawn about the room, &c.; but I refrain from considering imaginary yet consequent results which have nothing philosophical or real in them."]

Another form of index was applied thus:—a circular hole was cut in the middle of the upper board, and a piece of cartridge paper pasted under it on the lower surface of the board; a thin slice of cork was fixed on the upper surface of the lower board corresponding to the cartridge paper; the interval between them might be a quarter of an inch or less. A needle was fixed into the end of one of the index hay-stalks, and when all was in place the needle point was passed through the cartridge paper and pressed slightly into the cork beneath, so as to stand upright: then any motion of the hand, or hand-board, was instantly rendered evident by the deflection of the perpendicular hay-stalk to the right or left.

I think the apparatus I have described may be useful to many who really wish to know the truth of nature, and would prefer that truth to a mistaken conclusion; desired, perhaps, only because it seems to be new or strange. Persons do not know how difficult it is to press directly downward, or in any given direction against a fixed obstacle: or even to *know only* whether they are doing so or not; unless they have some indicator, which, by visible motion or otherwise, shall instruct them: and this is more especially the case when the muscles of the fingers and hand have been cramped and rendered either tingling, or insensible, or cold by long continued pressure. If a finger be pressed constantly into the corner of a window frame for ten minutes or more, and then, continuing the pressure, the mind be directed to judge whether the force at a given moment is all horizontal, or all downward, or how much is in one direction and how much in the other, it will find great difficulty in deciding; and will at last become altogether uncertain: at least such is my case. I know that a similar result occurs with others; for I have had two boards arranged, separated, not by rollers but by plugs of vulcanized rubber, and with the vertical index: when a person with his hands on the upper board is requested to press only downwards, and the index is hidden from his sight, it moves to the right, to the left, to him and from him, and in all horizontal directions; so utterly unable is he strictly to fulfil his intention without a visible and correcting indicator. Now, such is the use of the instrument with the horizontal index and rollers: the mind is instructed, and the involuntary or *quasi*-involuntary motion is checked in the commencement, and therefore never rises up to the degree needful to move the table, or even permanently the index itself. No one can suppose that looking at the index can in any way interfere with the transfer of electricity or any other power from the hand to the board under it or to the table. If the board tends to move, it may do so, the index does not confine it: and if the table tends to move, there is no reason why it should not. If both were influenced by any power to move together they may do so,—as they did indeed when the apparatus was tied, and the mind and muscles left unwatched and unchecked.

I must bring this long description to a close. I am little ashamed of it, for I think, in the present age, and in this part of the world, it ought not to have been required. Nevertheless, I hope it may the useful. There are many whom I do not expect to convince; but I may be allowed to say that I cannot undertake to answer such objections as may be made. I state my own convictions as an experimental philosopher, and find it no more necessary to enter into controversy on this point than on any other in science, as the nature of matter, or inertia, or the magnetization of light, on which I may differ from others. The world will decide sooner or later in all such cases, and I have no doubt very soon and correctly in the present instance. Those who may wish to see the particular construction of the test-apparatus which I have employed, may have the opportunity at Mr. Newman's, 122 Regent Street. Further, I may say, I have sought earnestly for cases of lifting by attraction, and indications of attraction in any form, but have gained no traces of such effects.

Finally, I beg to direct attention to the discourse delivered by Dr. Carpenter at the Royal Institution on the 12th of March 1852, entitled, "On the influence of Suggestion in modifying and directing Muscular Movement, independently of Volition":—which, especially in the latter part, should be considered in reference to table-moving by all who are interested in the subject.

M. Faraday, Royal Institution, June 27th, 1853.

Note

1 This paper is reprinted from *The Athenaeum*, No. 1340, pp. 801–803, published in 1853.

References

Alvarado, C. S. (1989). Nineteenth-century medical explanations of psychic phenomena. *Parapsychology Review*, *20*(3), 4–7.

Barrett, W. F. (1917). *On the threshold of the unseen*. Kegan Paul, Trench, Trübner.
Brown, E. M. (1983). Neurology and spiritualism in the 1870s. *Bulletin of the History of Medicine, 37*, 563–577.
Carpenter, W. B. (1853). Electro-biology and mesmerism. *Quarterly Review, 93*, 501–557.
Crabtree, A. (1993). *From Mesmer to Freud: Magnetic sleep and the roots of psychological healing*. Yale University Press.
Chevreul, E. (1833). Lettre à M. Ampère sur une classe particulière de mouvements musculaires. *Revue des Deux Mondes, 2* (s. 2), 258–266.
Ellenberger, H. F. (1970). *The discovery of the unconscious: The history and evolution of dynamic psychiatry*. Basic Books.
Faraday, M. (1853a). Professor Faraday on table-moving. *The Athenaeum*, No. 1340, 801–803.
Faraday, M. (1853b). The table turning delusion. *Lancet, 2*, 466–467.
Faraday, M. (1961). Observations on mental education. In F. Gudas (Ed.), *Extrasensory perception* (pp. 13–15). Charles Scribner's Sons. (Original work published 1855.)
Flammarion, C. (1907). *Mysterious psychic forces: An account of the author's investigations in psychical research, together with those of other European savants*. Small, Maynard.
Flournoy, T. (1911). *Spiritism and psychology*. New York: Harper & Brothers. General Meeting (1906). *Journal of the Society for Psychical Research, 12*, 179–184.
Gladstone, J. H. (1872). *Michael Faraday*. Macmillan.
Godfrey, N. S. (1853). *Table-moving tested and proved to be the result of satanic agency* (4th ed.). Seeley.
Grasset, J. (1907). *L'occultisme hier et aujourd'hui: Le merveilleux préscientifique*. Coulet et Fils.
Gray, C. (1854). Table turning in Paris. *Spiritual Telegraph, 3* (n. s.), 520–523.
Irwin, H. J. (1999). *An introduction to parapsychology* (3rd ed.). McFarland.
Janet, P. (1889). *L'automatisme psychologique: Essai de psychologie expérimentale sur les formes inferieures de l'activité humaine*. Félix Alcan.
Laycock, T. (1851). Odyle, mesmerism, electrobiology, &c. *British and Foreign Medico-Chirurgical Review, 8*, 378–431.
London Dialectical Society. (1874). *Report on spiritualism, of the Committee of the London Dialectical Society, together with the evidence, oral and written, and a selection from the correspondence*. J. Burns. (Original work published 1871.)
Myers, F.W. H. (1885). Automatic writing.—II. *Proceedings of the Society for Psychical Research, 3*, 1–63.
Nicholls, [no initial]. (n. d.). *Table moving, its causes and phenomena: With directions how to experiment*. John Wesley.
Nisbet, B. (1973). Table turning: A brief historical note mainly for the period 1848–1853. *Journal of the Society for Psychical Research, 47*, 96–106.
Podmore, F. (1902). *Modern spiritualism: A history and a criticism* (2 vols.). Methuen.
Shortt, S. E. D. (1984). Physicians and psychics: The Anglo-American medical response to spiritualism. *Journal of the History of Medicine and Allied Sciences, 39*, 339–355.
Sudre, R. (1960). *Parapsychology*. Citadel Press. (Original work published in French, 1956.)
Warcollier, R. (n. d.). Polyzoisme et polypsychisme. In *La Métapsychique, 1940–1946* (pp. 2–72). Presses Universitaires de France.

18

Frederic W. H. Myers, Psychical Research and Psychology: An Essay Review of Trevor Hamilton's Immortal Longings: F. W. H. Myers and the Victorian Search for Life After Death*

Carlos S. Alvarado†

The history of psychical research is full of fascinating figures who devoted their lives, or significant parts of it, to the study of telepathy, apparitions, mediumship, and other phenomena. A particularly important one, and the topic of the book reviewed here, was classical scholar and inspector of schools Frederic William Henry Myers (1843–1901). Myers, who was also an early pioneer in psychical research and psychology and the leading theoretician of the Society for Psychical Research (SPR), was criticized and appreciated by many during his lifetime. The latter was typically the case among those open to psychical research. Examples include physicist Oliver Lodge (1903, p. 6), who compared Myers to Francis Bacon, and psychologist and philosopher William James (1903), who believed Myers showed a "genius not unlike that of Charles Darwin" (p. 30). In his Presidential Address to the SPR, French physiologist Charles Richet (1905, p. 4) described Myers as the soul of the Society, while American physician Rufus Osgood Mason (1893) referred to him in the pages of the *New York Times* as a man of "acute intellect and scholarly attainments" (p. 20).

There has been a small resurgence of interest in Myers in the last decade or so, as I will discuss further in the next section. His ideas are the Centre of an important defense of the existence of the mind as separate from the body (E. F. Kelly et al., 2007), and he has been included in recent reference works (Gregory, 1998, p. 507; J. B. Taylor, 2007, pp. 25–29) and in the section of brief historical articles of the prestigious *American Journal of Psychiatry* (Kelly & Alvarado, 2005). Some celebratory events accompanied the centenary of Myers's *Human Personality and Its Survival of Bodily Death* (1903) in parapsychology forums. These consisted of a panel discussion of the book at the 2003 Convention of the Parapsychological Association[1] and an article examining the content, context, reception, and other aspects of the book (Alvarado, 2004). While no one denies the great importance of Myers in the history of psychical research—he was involved in the founding of the SPR, in the empirical study of psychic phenomena and survival of death, and in the development of the concept of the subliminal mind—until now he has not been the subject of a full-length biography.

In this essay, I will review Trevor Hamilton's biography of Myers, *Immortal Longings: F. W. H. Myers and the Victorian Search for Life After Death.* The book is organized into eight chapters. The first two, "Keswick to Cambridge" and "Life, Love and Letters," include information about Myers's early life, education, and social milieu. His career as an inspector of schools, as well as his first explorations in spiritualism, are discussed in the third chapter, "A Career in the Seen and Unseen World." Myers's actual psychical research appears in the rest of the book, mainly in Chapters 4 through 7: "Myers and

*Republished with permission from *Journal of the Society for Psychical Research, 73*(896), 150–170, 2009.
†I am grateful to Nancy L. Zingrone for editorial suggestions that have improved this essay.

the SPR in the 1880s," "Myers as a Psychologist," "Myers and the Great Mediums of the 1890s," and "Myers, Haunted Houses and Miss Goodrich-Freer." Finally, Hamilton assesses Myers and his work in "Myers, Science and the SPR," and in "The Legacy of Myers."

I will present my comments about the book in the context of what I refer to as "Myers Studies," or the scholarly attempts to understand the life and work of Myers from a variety of perspectives.[2] My focus will be on Myers's psychical and psychological work, as opposed to his literary publications (on this aspect, see J. W. Beer, 1998). In addition to comments on Hamilton's work, I will present some general information about Myers not included in the book.

Myers Studies

Hamilton's *Immortal Longings* was preceded by several publications. This work reflects two general orientations briefly outlined below.

Like other research fields, parapsychology has a literature in which its practitioners write about their history and its pioneers. The writers of such literature tend to focus on the current use and validity of phenomena and theories, and the anticipation of current ideas. Myers has been discussed in his role as an SPR pioneer (e.g., Salter, 1957), in terms of his ideas supporting the existence of the mind separate from the body, which is a topic of current concern (Kelly et al., 2007), and on the anniversary of his best-known publication (Alvarado, 2004). Recent authors of historical publications about dissociation (Dorahy & Van der Hart, 2007) and hypnosis (Pintar & Lynn, 2008) have also discussed Myers, if only briefly.

We may also mention the work of Emily Cook, now Emily Kelly (Cook, 1992, 1994; Kelly, 2001, 2007), which falls between the practitioner and the historical approach. She has argued that psychology needs to return to fundamental questions and that Myers offered possibilities for the empirical study of such issues (Kelly, 2007). Furthermore, she stated: "In the century since Myers's death, many of the observations he made have been powerfully reinforced by subsequent research" (p. 115). Kelly's main contribution, her as yet unpublished doctoral thesis, is a pioneering study entitled *The Intellectual Background and Potential Significance of F. W. H. Myers' Work in Psychology and Parapsychology* (Cook, 1992).

Other works have as a goal the understanding of Myers in his own context, regardless of the validity of the concepts and phenomena involved and of their relevance for present-day concerns. The first important study of Myers's personal life and intellectual context, as well as of aspects of his work, appeared in Alan Gauld's *The Founders of Psychical Research* (1968). Gauld presented Myers in the context of English nineteenth-century crises of faith and the development of spiritualism. Furthermore, here we find for the first time a detailed description and analysis of Myers's work in psychical research, including his early and later experiences with mediums, his role in *Phantasms of the Living* (Gurney, Myers, & Podmore, 1886), and his ideas about the subliminal mind. This book remains today a basic source of information about Myers, and a classic in the modern historiography of psychical research. Frank M. Turner (1974) also explored the intellectual context of Myers, presenting him as one of several Victorian figures located between the realms of science and religion. That is, Myers and others were disenchanted with Christianity, but were not able to accept fully the tenets of scientific naturalism.

In addition, there are historical works that touch on various aspects of psychic phenomena which, while not devoted completely to Myers, have informed readers about his work and his role in the development of psychical research in England (e.g., Cerullo, 1982; Luckhurst, 2002; Meheust, 1999; Oppenheim, 1985).

Furthermore, Myers, who used to be almost completely ignored in the traditional historiography of psychology and psychiatry,[3] has started to be recognized in books and papers about these specialties. Henri F. Ellenberger mentioned Myers in his celebrated *The Discovery of the Unconscious* (1970) and even referred to him as "one of the great systematisers of the notion of the unconscious mind" (p. 314). But regardless of this praise, Ellenberger did not devote a chapter to him as he did for Janet, Freud, Adler, and Jung, a situation that we may regret today but one that reflected the state of the historiography of psychical research at the time.[4] The only study to date with a chapter about Myers from the perspective of the history of the subconscious mind is Adam Crabtree's *From Mesmer to Freud* (1993). Following Ellenberger but improving on him in terms of details and general perspective, Crabtree located mesmerism, spiritualism, and psychical research as important factors influencing the development of the concepts of the subconscious mind and dissociation.

Some assessments have been negative. In his concise history of British psychology, Hearnshaw (1964) presented Myers as lacking a truly scientific spirit, being guided in his quest by personal yearnings. Similarly, Starobinski (1970) argued that Myers was naive because he was motivated by an "obstinate desire to obtain experimental proof of the existence of a 'spiritual world'" (p. 337). But such perspectives are far from being universal. Goldstein (1963) wrote that "Myers's theory of the subliminal self, along with the incipient psychoanalytic movement, helped to overturn the view of nonconscious states as static or pathological" (pp. 588–589). In a more general evaluation, Kelly (2001) argued that more than his model of the subliminal mind, Myers's contribution to psychology included ideas about the mind-matter relationship, as well as the need to develop unique psychological methods of study and to consider comprehensive theoretical models that accounted for a wide range of human phenomena.

In addition, there are sections about Myers and psychology and psychiatry in publications with different emphases, such as those on dissociation (Alvarado, 2002), hypnosis (Gauld, 1992), and psychology at the end of the nineteenth century (J. B. Taylor, 2007; see also Crabtree, 2003; Shamdasani, 1993; Taves, 1999; Williams, 1985). The growing industry of studies about William James has included considerations of Myers's ideas and their influence on James (e.g., Leary, 1990; Taves, 2004; E. Taylor, 1996).

The end result of these publications has been the still-in-progress creation of a new image of Myers as an important nineteenth-century figure in the study of dissociation and the subconscious mind. Hamilton's *Immortal Longings* covers many of the above-mentioned issues. But it is different from these publications in that it espouses a more general view than anyone else who has written about Myers.

Early Years

Hamilton presents us with a fascinating and detailed discussion of Myers's early development, education, and social environment. Before the Introduction, Hamilton presents three family trees (pp. xi–xiii), Myers's and the trees representing his mother, Susan Marshall, and his wife, Eveleen Tennant. The main individuals in these family trees are discussed in these chapters.

The author cites the opinions of different people about Myers's character and personality. Some of them are not flattering to Myers. In fact, one of the things I like about this book is that while Hamilton defends Myers from some attacks, he is also critical of him on occasion. In his view, "Myers was a snob" (p. 265) and "had a strong histrionic side to his character" (p. 266). But there is no question that most psychical researchers who knew Myers liked and admired him. An example not mentioned by Hamilton was Charles Richet, who presented his impressions in his book *Le savant* (1923). "What I admired in Myers," Richet stated, "was his scrupulous scientific integrity" (p. 78). Richet also praised Myers for his detailed memory and wrote: "His courtesy, his good graces, his erudition, were enhanced by a very delicate sense of humour that made his conversation charming" (p. 78).

Hamilton writes that Myers had a tendency to "push on towards his goal" and that this "could involve a certain economy with the truth" (p. 93). This observation is presented in the context of an incident involving Lord Rayleigh. But unfortunately, the existence of such "tendency" is not substantiated with other incidents. In fact, it is puzzling that Hamilton does not develop this point, because it has obvious implications for the reader's assessment of Myers.

Myers started his life with some social advantages. Hamilton writes: "Myers was born ... into an environment of powerful cultural, social and political connections ... The milieu was positive, supportive, stimulating and hierarchical, and, in conjunction with his outstanding natural gifts, fostered in the young Myers a considerable, even overweening, sense of his own worth and status" (p. 16). Such a sense was not only an issue of self-perception. His early work was recognized by others as well. By the time he was 22 years old, Myers had obtained "two first classes at Cambridge, a clutch of other awards, and a burgeoning reputation as a scholar and a poet" (p. 33). Other information presented focuses on Myers's education, family life, his alleged homosexuality, the influence of Josephine Butler, and his work as an inspector of schools. Myers was also interested in women's education and suffrage. In fact, an 1870 report of a meeting of the National Association for Women's Suffrage printed in *The Times* stated: "A resolution declaring that by the deprivation of the Parliamentary franchise not only do women suffer much grievous social injustice, but the State loses an influence which would tend to soften and purify laws and morals, was adopted unanimously on the motion of Mr. F. W. H. Myers ..." (Women as Suffrage, 1870, p. 12). In an article published in *Macmillan's Magazine* about lectures for women, Myers (1868) wrote: "That a man should be pleased with ignorance in a woman is a folly; that a woman should therefore acquiesce in ignorance is a crime: for the first duty of women ... is to please, not men, but God, who has set us here to help each other and to glorify Him, tasks which need all the wisdom that life or death can teach" (p. 163).

In a discussion of Myers's "Career in the Seen and Unseen World" the first is a reference to his work as an inspector of schools, and the second to his work on psychic phenomena. From early on, Myers was interested in unusual phenomena: "Myers had shown an interest in mesmerism and abnormal behavior in the 1860s. Indeed, as early as 26th June 1863 he had visited a lunatic asylum ... In February 1867 he visited the London Mesmeric Hospital, and in his diary for the same month there is a reference to Henry Sidgwick's being involved in mesmeric experiments. There were also a number of diary references to his mesmerising or being mesmerised" (p. 83). One wishes there were more details about these events. As seen in the pages of the journal Zoist and in such works as Joseph W. Haddock's *Somnolism and Psycheism* (1851), there was much mesmeric activity in England. Mesmerism and hypnotism were topics that Myers would write about at length in later years. For example, in a paper on the subject co-authored with Edmund Gurney, they wrote:

> It is the key which seems likeliest to unlock the mysteries of attention and memory; of sleep, dreams, and hallucination; of 'double consciousness' and of religious ecstasy. It is by thus throwing the mental machinery slightly out of gear that we discern the secrets of its adjustment, or (to use a more fanciful metaphor) "the soul that rises in us, our life's star," acquires from

> this displacement a sensible parallax, and reveals laws of its motion which direct introspection could never discover. (Gurney & Myers, 1885, p. 422)

Myers had séances with many mediums during the 1870s as a member of what Hamilton calls—referring to the Cambridge moral philosopher and former teacher of Myers, Henry Sidgwick—the Sidgwick group. This group included Eleanor Balfour, Edmund Gurney, Walter Leaf, and others. The author describes the group as follows: "Very few people ... had ... the time, leisure, status and finance to work with mediums in the very intensive way that the Sidgwick group did in the 1870s" (pp. 95–96). These séances were held with Fay, and with other mediums (Wood, Fairlamb, the Petty family) including Henry Slade, who was at the center of many controversies in England when he was taken to court (e.g., The Slade Prosecution, 1876). Some of these early séances in which physical phenomena were reported were discussed by Mrs. Sidgwick (1886), who concluded that the evidence for physical mediumship was deficient.

Myers and Psychical Research

Discussions of the SPR—sometimes neutral, critical, or appreciative—were common in many popular and scientific publications. For example, the August 1882 issue of the *Eclectic Magazine of Foreign Literature, Science and Art* included the following news item:

> A "Society for Psychical Research" has been started under the presidency of Mr. Henry Sidgwick. Several men of note who have leanings in the direction of Spiritualism, but who have hitherto avoided declaring themselves so openly, are connected with it: Mr. A. J. Balfour, M. P., Prof. Balfour Stewart, Mr. R. H. Button, Hon. Roden Noel, Mr. F. Myers, Dr. Lockhart Robertson, and others. It makes one rub one's eyes to find a society founded in 1882 gravely announcing a "Committee on Apparitions, Haunted Houses", etc., presided over by Mr. Hensleigh Wedgwood. It is a pity that the Cock Lane ghost is extinct. There is a committee on "Thought Reading", headed by Prof. Barrett. [Science and Art, 1882, p. 282]

Myers was to become an important contributor to the SPR, a topic discussed by Hamilton. In fact, he was described at one point as "one of the leading spirits of the Psychical Research Society ..." (*Our London Letter*, 1893, p. 5). This is supported by my analysis of the single-author papers appearing in the *SPR Proceedings* between 1882 and 1900, which shows that Myers published more papers than other authors did (see Table 18.1). In addition, reports published in the *SPR Journal* indicate that he was a frequent presenter and discussant at the Society's meetings.

We also find Myers early on writing articles for the general public in intellectual reviews, some of which were written with other authors. These articles, which publicized the work of the SPR in England, and elsewhere, were about topics such as automatic writing (Myers, 1885b), thought transference (Barrett, Gurney & Myers, 1882), and a future life (Myers, 1891b). I wonder how Myers's articles (particularly those written solely by him) compare in style and structure with other articles appearing in similar publications designed to present scientific topics to the public in Victorian times, a period that had a considerable popular scientific literature (Lightman, 2007).

Many ideas guided Myers's work. In addition to the issue of survival of death, Hamilton mentions that Myers had a "strong strain of Platonic mysticism in his intellectual repertoire ... and had been encouraged to apply the concept of Darwinian evolution to the spiritual sphere through contact with Alfred Russel Wallace" (p. 137).

Table 18.1. Papers in the Proceedings of the Society for Psychical Research by Single Authors, 1882-1900 (N = 152)

Author	%
Frederic W. H. Myers	21
Henry Sidgwick	7
Edmund Gurney	6
Richard Hodgson	5
William F. Barrett	4
Eleanor Sidgwick	3
Balfour Stewart	3
J. Milne Bramwell	3
Oliver J. Lodge	3
Andrew Lang	2
Frank Podmore	2
Other	41*

* This includes several authors with one per cent each, such as Thomas Barkworth, William Crookes, Alice Johnson, C. C. Massey, W. R. Newbold and Charles Richet.

Note: This analysis does not include anonymous papers, articles by more than one author, correspondence, book/article reviews, conference reports or news. Papers with more than one part were counted individually.

The book contains good summaries of Myers's involvement with such topics as automatic writing, telepathy, and the veridical hallucinations that led to the production of *Phantasms of the Living* (Gurney, Myers & Podmore, 1886), the first major study of the SPR. It was in the context of crisis apparitions that Myers "began to display his considerable gifts of organisation, pattern identifying and classification" (p. 139).

Hamilton also discusses Myers's introduction to *Phantasms of the Living,* in which the whole enterprise was justified. Myers defended the scientific character of psychical research, and pointed out what he believed were the connections of the field to anthropology and religion. The introduction could be further analyzed from the point of view of the rhetoric of science to identify the specific arguments that Myers used to convince his readers to take seriously the topic of the book. For example, Myers assured readers that the authors of the book did not want to upset the order of things:

> It is necessary … to state at once that we have no wish either to mystify or to startle mankind … we wish distinctly to say that so far from aiming at any paradoxical reversion of established scientific conclusions, we conceive ourselves to be working (however imperfectly) in the main track of discovery, and assailing a problem which, though strange and hard, does yet stand next in order among the new adventures on which Science must needs set forth, if her methods and her temper are to guide and control the widening curiosity, the expanding capacities of men. (Gurney, Myers & Podmore, 1886, p. xxxvi)

Myers's studies of automatic writing were of key importance for the development of his ideas. His early writings on the topic mention the concept of a subliminal self (e.g., Myers, 1885a). But Hamilton covers a wide range of topics in which Myers was involved, such as hauntings, apparitions of the dead, and mediums. The latter include mental mediums Leonora E. Piper and Rosalie Thompson, and physical medium Eusapia Palladino. In addition, there is a section discussing *Human Personality.*

Myers and Psychology

From the historical record it is clear that Myers did not represent orthodox psychology. In fact, in a letter Myers (1891a) wrote to Charles Richet, he referred to his "psychological heterodoxy." Hamilton discusses many reasons why Myers was at odds with nineteenth-century psychology. Differing from the views of many that the subconscious was mainly concerned with pathology, Myers believed, Hamilton writes, that: "From the subliminal emerged the insights, the skills, the inspirations, that one associates with genius and the highest creative achievement" (p. 191; see also Williams, 1985). Relevant to this, Méheust (1999, pp. 52–53) has argued that Myers did not reduce the subliminal as an impoverished region of the mind, as Janet did, nor to primary processes, as Freud did with his theory of the unconscious. In Méheust's view, Myers's originality consisted of including "levels of existence that are superior and inferior at the same time from the waking ordinary consciousness" (p. 53). If we add to subliminal manifestations such phenomena as telepathy and also add discussions of survival of death, a topic generally neglected by psychologists, one can see why they did not like Myers's system of thought at all.

Another problem for psychologists was what Hamilton refers to, in the title of a chapter section, as "The Cosmic Myers" (p. 195). This included "pre-existence in a Platonic sense" and the idea that "the soul, after death, progressed through a number of spheres where eventually ... the soul united with the ultimate principle while still retaining its individuality" (p. 195).

Myers's more metaphysical ideas led Swiss psychologist Theodore Flournoy (1903) to caution his readers about the need to distinguish Myers's subliminal psychology from his "philosophical-religious system" (p. 295). Another European commentator, Italian alienist Enrico Morselli, commented in his book *Psicologia e 'Spiritismo'* (1908) that Myers's writings showed traces of "primitive mysticism, of deistic sensibility, of ethical candor, which combine spiritism-science with spiritism-religion, 'cold and serene research of the facts,' with 'the aspirations of the soul, the basis of every moral and religious life, sublime, strengthening, and comforting truth'" (Vol. l, p. 42). Nonetheless, both Flournoy and Morselli praised Myers's empirical approach.

There is no doubt that Myers was an important nineteenth-century theorist of the subconscious, as well as of phenomena related to this construct, such as automatisms, creativity, dissociation, and dreams. However, there are aspects of this perspective that, probably for reason of space, are not fully articulated by Hamilton. Therefore, I will discuss some additional issues below.

First, Myers's reviews of psychological literature, such as those covering the influential French studies with hysterical and/or hypnotic subjects (Carroy, 1991), were valuable beyond the expression of his own views. They probably assisted in the transmission of knowledge about those studies into the English-speaking worlds. This included the work of Pierre Janet (Myers, 1889b) and Alfred Binet (Myers, 1892a). We may also include here Myers's discussion of Breuer and Freud mentioned by Hamilton (p. 190). According to Hearnshaw (1964), Myers's (1893, pp. 7, 12-13, 15) presentation of Breuer and Freud's early ideas about hysteria earned him the "distinction of being the first Englishman to give an account of the work of Freud" (p. 159) in England.

Second, there is no question that Myers was cited by many in a variety of psychological works. Examples of these include such books as William James's *The Principles of Psychology* (1890),

Pierre Janet's *L'automatisme psychologique* (1889), Joseph Jastrow's *The Subconscious* (1906), and Charles L. Tuckey's *Treatment by Hypnotism and Suggestion or Psycho-Therapeutics* (1907). He was also mentioned in articles, such as those discussing hypnosis (De Sarlo, 1893), one of which was devoted to Myers's ideas (Mangin, 1902).

The attitudes of several students of the subconscious mind towards Myers's concept of the subliminal can be seen in *Subconscious Phenomena,* a book containing several articles about concepts of the subconscious mind by influential workers in the field originally published in the *Journal of Abnormal Psychology* (Münsterberg et al., 1910). The book opened with an acknowledgment that the concept of the subconscious was controversial and that there were no generally accepted definitions or agreements about the phenomena that illustrated its functioning. Three of the participants in the discussions mentioned Myers's concept of the subliminal and criticized it. Théodule Ribot stated that Myers's concept "bears the stamp of a peculiar biologic mysticism" (p. 35). In Morton Prince's opinion, it is "a wasteful expenditure of intellectual energy to indulge in metaphysical speculations regarding the existence and functions of a mystical subliminal self (Myers), transcending as it does all experience and everything that even a 'subconscious self' can experience" (p. 74). Finally, Bernard Hart said: "Myers ascribes to the subconscious various supernatural properties which take his conception altogether beyond the limits of science" (p. 127).

Those open to psychical research, such as Mason (1897), were more positive towards Myers than those who opposed the movement. But even those who reduced psychic phenomena to such conventional explanations as dissociation made use of Myers. However, theirs was a *selective use.*

A prominent example of this can be found in the writings of Pierre Janet. In Janet's classic study, *L'automatisme psychologique* (1889), he mentioned many phenomena, including mediumship, to support the concept of dissociation. In this context, Janet cited Myers to provide examples of cases or phenomena (pp. 78, 122, 393, 394, 402, 405). Furthermore, Janet wrote: "To my knowledge, the author that has contributed the most to develop the scientific study of spiritistic phenomena certainly is M. Fr. Myers. This author … has presented a very ingenious theory, at once psychological and physiological of mental disaggregation … [Myers's theories] are more developed than previous ones" (p. 403).

Interestingly, and for reasons similar to those of Janet, Alfred Binet (1892) also cited and praised Myers in the context of his discussion of secondary personalities and referred to him as one of the authors "who has better understood the true nature of spiritist phenomena," having summarized in a precise way the "theory of multiple personalities at a time in which the studies of M. Janet … had not started yet" (p. 299). Both French authors focused on the fact of the subconscious and on dissociation, neglecting the supernormal discussed by Myers as an integral part of his system of thought. Such neglect, commented on by Myers (1892a, p. 420), shows a common pattern in the way Myers was cited in some psychological works. In addition to Binet and Janet, other students of the subconscious used Myers as a source for what they found acceptable—namely, the existence of the subconscious—but stripped Myers's discourse of such aspects as the occurrence of telepathy and the issue of survival of bodily death (e.g., Jastrow, 1906; Sidis, 1898).[5]

Hamilton also discusses Myers's participation in the international congresses of psychology held between 1889 and 1900. But the author could have presented more details, such as summaries of Myers' participation in the discussions in the congresses. An example of a particularly interesting moment was the following that took place during the 1889 congress held in Paris (Statistique des Hallucinations, 1890). In addition to Myers, others such as Joseph Delboeuf, Pierre Janet, Charles Richet, Henry Sidgwick, and Julian Ochorowicz were present. Richet reminded the group that some members of the congress wanted to discuss the phenomena of "transmission of ideas" (p. 152), while Janet asked the representatives of the SPR present at the discussion to summarize their work. Myers followed Janet and talked about aspects of the SPR's thought-transference work. Examples of dialogues such as this are important because they show Myers interacting with other figures in the congress, illustrating his transcendence of SPR circles.

I agree with Hamilton's comments about the congresses, but I wish he had used as sources the proceedings of the conferences (e.g., *Congrès International de Psychologic Physiologique,* 1890; Janet, 1901) as opposed to relying only on published accounts of some of the congresses in the *SPR Proceedings.* While an analysis of the first two congresses, held in 1889 and 1892, suggests that psychical research was "accepted," this does not mean there were not some dissenters from this view. Wilhelm Wundt (1892/2000) was not happy with Henry Sidgwick as president of the 1892 congress for fear that telepathy would be overrepresented, a charge that Sidgwick (1892) rebutted in his Presidential Address. Hamilton mentions that there were protests at the 1900 congress, and that is certainly visible in the conference proceedings (Discussion, 1901). He states that the "1900 congress was the last at which there was any significant consideration" of psychic phenomena and, among other factors, "this reflected the growing professionalism of psychology" (p. 185). As discussed by many in the past, the rejection of psychical research from the congress in 1900 represented the "expulsion of intruders" (Paicheler, 1992, p. 248) and what Le Maléfan 1995) has referred to as the separation of "the acceptable from the unacceptable in psychology" (p. 624). I would frame the issue as one of boundary work, in which members of particular fields or groups engage in active separation from individuals, ideas, or methodology "for the purpose of drawing a rhetorical boundary between science and some less authoritative residual non-science" (Gieryn, 1999, pp. 4–5). Such demarcations were partly an attempt to acquire prestige and control over the domain of human experience and behavior through the elimination of competition. The history of psychology presents several such episodes in relation to psychic phenomena (e.g., Alvarado, 2009b; Coon, 1992).

While discussions of psychic phenomena in the congresses declined considerably after 1900, to the point of disappearing, they were still present at a low level at the 1905 congress, held in Rome under the presidency of Giuseppe Sergi. For example, Richet (1906) defended psychical research, arguing that the field—which he called metapsychics—would eventually develop more and obtain general acceptance. Favre (1906) reported work testing the effects of the human hand on the growth of grains and microbes.

The Reception of Myers's Work

Studies of how Myers influenced others are needed. An interesting one is Powell's (1979) discussion of the role of the concept of Myers's subliminal in the acceptance of psychoanalysis in the United States. Eugene Taylor (1996), among others, has discussed Myers's influence on William James. According to Fuller (1986), both Boris Sidis and Morton Prince incorporated some of Myers's ideas in their thinking. Sidis was cited by Bruce (1910) as saying to him that "Myers … first opened my eyes to the close relationship between psychology and medicine" (p. 452). However, as mentioned above, in many cases, this influence was stripped of its supernormal content.

In reality, we have not done justice to the study of the reception of Myers's work, such as *Human Personality.* Most contemporary writers have limited their discussions to English-language material and then to individuals such as James, Mallock, and Stout, as Hamilton has done (pp. 279–280), neglecting lesser-known authors and the popular press (e.g., Chadwick, 1903; De Wyzewa, 1903; Jankelevitch, 1904; Riley, 1905; Review of Human Personality, 1903). *Human Personality* also received a two-part review in the *New York Times* written by physician Rufus Osgood Mason (1903). In his view, even if it would take a generation for the value of Myers's work to be recognized, "he has called the attention of the thinking world to a new line of human development, and sooner or later it will be recognized" (p. BR1). The book was also mentioned in American newspapers. Among these was the announcement that Longmans, Green "will publish next month the long expected book" (Book Gossip in London, 1903), as well as advertisements listing the chapters of the book (Advert, 1903). There is a need to widen the range of study to other authors who reviewed *Human Personality.* The current boundaries have limited our understanding of both the positive and the negative reception of Myers's work.[6]

Much of the material ignored to date was published in languages other than English. Hamilton briefly mentions that Myers was rejected by some in countries such as France and Germany (p. 187), but his work does not cover these aspects of Myers's reception. There is actually much to be learned about the international reception of scientific work, as can be seen in studies of Darwin's reception in many countries (Glick, 1988).

The abridged French translation of Myers's *Human Personality, La personnalité humaine, sa survivance, ses manifestations supranormales* (Myers, 1905), was reviewed in many generally ignored forums. These include *L'annee psychologique* (Maxwell, 1906). Maxwell believed that Myers was original only in the way in which he presented and supported his ideas, but in Maxwell's view, Myers's ideas were not very different from spiritistic doctrine.

Going beyond *Human Personality,* many French publications included mention of Myers's work. An example was Erny's (1895) book *Le psychisme expérimental.* An anonymous writer in the newspaper *Les temps* stated, "Myers ... is one of the more universally recognized authorities on matters of subconscious psychology. The scientific research work he founded and inspired with systematic and exact observations of second sight, of correspondences of thought, is one of the most solid that there are." (Nouvelles de l'Étrangere, 1904). Myers was mentioned, and criticized, in an article about novelties in psychology published in the *Journal des débats politiques et littéraires* (Bordeau, 1906). This author credited Myers with rejuvenating animism and providing a scientific framework for its support. This entailed bringing together mysticism and an empirical approach, something that made Myers a "positivist Swedenborg." Another critic, philosopher Émile Boutroux (1908), wrote a paper about the subliminal self in which he stated that Myers showed the existence of subconscious processes but said that some of the facts Myers used were "very difficult to prove" (p. 114).

An author writing in *La Ciudad de Dios,* a Spanish journal published by members of the Augustine order, discussed Myers as an example of a new theorist about personality (Gutiérrez Marcelino, 1890). In Italy, De Sarlo (1893, p. 173) mentioned Myers, together with Janet and Max Dessoir, as examples of individuals interested in dissociation and automatisms.

Another area of note is the reaction of English spiritualists to the SPR and Myers's work. Their reaction to *Human Personality* deserves more attention than it has received so far. Some interesting comments about the book appeared in *Light,* both positive (The Myers Book, 1903) and negative (Robertson, 1903). Hamilton covers some of the critiques that spiritualists, such as Roden Noel (p. 158), made of Myers's ideas. He further points out that Myers, and particularly the early Myers (1884, 1885a), was perceived as "undermining the spiritualist position by attributing most of their phenomena to a psychological source" (p. 159).[7] Spiritualists's reactions were not surprising: they were defending their beliefs against a newcomer to the neighborhood, the young psychical research movement as represented by the SPR since 1882. Their reactions, as Hamilton is aware, were part of an overall response to the perception that much of the SPR's work was critical of some of the claims of spiritualists. I would add to this that spiritualists' reactions can also be seen against the background of previous developments. Spiritualists were used to, and perhaps tired of, those who reduced their beliefs to the conventional workings of the nervous system (Carpenter, 1853) and to the action of thought transmission and psychic forces unrelated to spirits (Mahan, 1855).

But Hamilton also argues that the SPR-spiritualism relationship had other facets. To some extent, the empirical work of psychical researchers brought support to spiritualists in the sense that evidence was provided for some of the psychic phenomena in which spiritualists believed.

Myers and Scientific Research

As Hamilton says, regardless of Myers's "emotional longing" for survival of death, his work was empirical: "Phenomena had to be probed, examined and discarded, no matter how comforting, if they failed to meet the standards of evidence required" (p. 256). Myers (1900) himself wrote: "No attachment to Christian tradition, no recognition of the need and value of high intuitions, should blind us to the fact that only on truths scientifically demonstrated can a world-philosophy or world-religion be based" (p. 110). But Hamilton points out that, regardless of his recognition of the importance of science, Myers's "own writing sometimes soared too far from that disciplined base" (p. 187).

Defending the SPR from Robert Thouless's criticism to the effect that its members did not understand the concept of experimentation, Hamilton remarks: "An experiment is not just a designed intervention into the natural order. It can also be deliberate and careful observation intended to reveal particular information" (p. 256). It is important to state here that many of the uses of the terms 'experimental' and 'experimental psychology' during the nineteenth century were different from the current use in psychology, or from its use when Thouless was writing. Furthermore, many, such as Ribot (1870), used the terms to mean an empirical approach to psychological problems. Myers (1886) wrote about "experimental psychology" as "the attempt to attack the great problems of our being not by metaphysical argument, nor by merely introspective analysis, but by a study, as detailed and exact as in any other natural science, of all such phenomena of life as have both a psychical and a physical aspect" (p. 1). But as Henry Sidgwick (1892) noted in his Presidential Address at the Second Congress of Experimental Psychology, the term 'experimental' was used in different ways by different psychologists. The situation was one in which many groups had their own definitions that were used, more importantly, in the quest for scientific legitimacy.[8]

As chronicled by Hamilton, Myers made many empirical observations during his career, such as attending séances for physical phenomena and studying cases of automatic writing and apparitions, among other phenomena. "Myers travelled ceaselessly at home and abroad to investigate promising cases" (p. 247). His analyses of published observations of hypnotic, hysterical, apparitional, mediumistic, and telepathic phenomena (e.g., Myers, 1886, 1889a, 1893, 1903) show he had a particular ability not only to summarize countless observations of phenomena made by others, but to organize such observations in a coherent way so as to support the existence and capabilities of the subliminal mind. The way Myers analyzed cases is what Gillian Beer (2000) refers to as a mid-nineteenth-century "literary, non-mathematical discourse" (p. 4) used by some scientists in their writings. This style allowed for a wide range of material to be classified and compared, and in addition, it was accessible to non-scientists. Hamilton states that Myers "was trying to use Darwinian classification methods to show that the normal, abnormal and paranormal phenomena were related manifestations of the same core process" (p. 4). In fact, Myers had been compared to Darwin before, both by James (1903, p. 30) and by American journalist B. O. Flower (1903, p. 193). But regardless of brief remarks about classification and comparison of phenomena (Gauld, 1968, pp. 277–278; James, 1901, p. 16; Meheust, 1999, pp. 47–48; Podmore, 1901, pp. 30–31), the fact is that no one has analyzed Myers in detail to assess how he organized his ideas, or to reconstruct the sequence of his thinking and reasoning, as has been done for other figures in the history-of-science literature (e.g., G. Beer, 2000).[9]

Myers emphasized bibliographic research in a good part of his work, frequently reorganizing and reinterpreting the work published by others, as in the case of hypnosis (e.g., Myers, 1886, 1903, Vol. 1, Chap. 5). He was less of a 'hands on' hypnosis researcher (for exceptions see Myers, 1886, pp. 6, 14–15) than others who actually used hypnosis frequently to produce specific manifestations (e.g., Beaunis, 1887; Janet, 1889). But Myers was not unique in his approach. Théodule Ribot, for example, made fundamental contributions to the orientation of the new French psychology during the last quarter of the nineteenth century in a similar fashion. Brooks (1998) has stated that while Ribot inspired scientific psychology in France, "his psychological works consisted of observations culled from the works of others—primarily physiologists and psychiatrists—and interpreted systematically from a biological and evolutionary point of view" (pp. 67–68). Brooks further wrote about Ribot—and this also applies to Myers—that "it was his general, philosophical, conception of the field of psychology that allowed him to rise above compartmentalized scientific disciplines and to unite elements from various sources" (p. 96). While I believe Myers was more original than Ribot in his combinations of data as well as deeper in his analyses, it would be interesting to compare their analytic styles systematically, keeping in mind their conceptual differences.

The Legacy and Future of Myers's Ideas and of Myers Studies

Hamilton asks at the end of his book: "Was Myers' quest successful?" (p. 302). He argues that the fact that Myers became convinced of survival of death was a personal form of success. Another form of success was that, through *Human Personality,* Myers "kept alive … the key issues of the mind-body relationship. He has been a force for good in terms of opposition to over-simple mechanistic and reductionistic approaches to the human psyche" (p. 302).

However, the story is different when it comes to the acceptance of Myers's work. In a letter William James wrote in 1901, he mentioned Myers and stated: "Fifty or a hundred years hence, people will know better than now whether his instinct for truth was a sound one" (H. James, 1920, p. 157). More than a hundred years have gone by and Myers still is not part of the mainstream. He may have been strongly defended by Kelly et al. (2007), and featured in other forums (e.g., Kelly & Alvarado, 2005; J. B. Taylor, 2007), but this does not mean that Myers has gained general acceptance in the modern context. In fact, it is unusual to find modern papers citing Myers either to justify or to provide theoretical context for research (an exception is Alvarado & Zingrone, 2007–2008). Of course, it is always possible that the situation may change. As has been pointed out before (Alvarado, 2004; Kelly et al., 2007), there are many areas in psychology and parapsychology today that are consistent with, and that may be explored by following Myers's side. Kelly et al.'s *Irreducible Mind* (2007), in which areas of modern psychology are reviewed and critiqued using

Myers, is an important and necessary beginning that brings attention to Myers's relevance. But such an effort, if it is going to change psychology *à la* Myers, needs to be followed by actual research designed to test Myers's ideas where possible. What is needed now is the development of a research program that will provide new empirical evidence for Myers's tenets with the potential of expanding his system of thought.

Many ideas from Myers's writings could guide a modern research program. These include the speculation of a "transition from hyperaesthesia to telaesthesia, so that when peripheral sensation is no longer possible, central perception may be still operating across obstacles otherwise insurmountable" (Myers, 1903, Vol. 1, p. 276). An important hypothesis, and one that has the potential to help us to integrate the supernormal, the normal, and the pathological, is the following statement:

> It may be expected that supernormal vital phenomena will manifest themselves as far as possible through the same channels as abnormal or morbid vital phenomena, when the same centres or the same synergies are involved … [Assuming] there be within us a secondary self-aiming at manifestation by physiological means, it seems probable that its readiest path of externalisation—its readiest outlet of visible action,—may often lie along some track which has already been shown to be a line of low resistance by the disintegrating processes of disease. Or, varying the metaphor, we may anticipate that the partition of the primary and the secondary self will lie along some plane of cleavage which the morbid dissociations of our psychical synergies have already shown themselves disposed to follow. If epilepsy, madness, &c., tend to split up our faculties in certain ways, automatism is likely to split them up in ways somewhat resembling these. (Myers, 1903, Vol. 2, p. 84)

But regardless of the validity of Myers's ideas, and of the possibility of developing a psychology following his lead, we need to remember that Myers is also important for history, as I have pointed out throughout this essay. Even considering previous historical studies concerning Myers, there is much more work to be done. Further study will bring a better understanding of the man, his work, his influence, and his place in psychology and psychical research.

The variety of topics studied in relation to such figures as Charles Darwin (Kohn, 1985), Sigmund Freud (Rozen, 2001), and Wilhelm Wundt (Reiber & Robinson, 2001) can provide many suggestions about research directions that may develop our historical understanding of Myers. Some possibilities are detailed studies of: (1) early personal and intellectual factors affecting Myers (e.g., Josephine Butler, classical training); (2) later influence of particular individuals on Myers's thought (Carl du Prel, Pierre Janet); (3) guiding concepts in Myers's work (e.g., previous ideas about the subconscious mind, ideas of evolution); (4) development of Myers's ideas (from early 1880s writings to later years); (5) Myers's analytical methods (e.g., study of gradations of the phenomena, classifications); (6) comparisons of Myers's subliminal to the concepts of the subconscious of others (e.g., Janet, Prince); (7) specific topics discussed by Myers (e.g., apparitions of the dead, physical phenomena); (8) Myers's writing style (e.g., rhetoric, use of metaphors); (9) Myers's use of knowledge from other areas (e.g., psychology, neurology); (10) relationship between Myers and other figures (e.g., Henri Bergson, Charles Richet); (11) reception of Myers's work (e.g., in different countries, in areas such as religion); (12) the influence of Myers on other individuals (e.g., Oliver Lodge, Theodore Flournoy); (13) the influence of Myers on movements or fields (e.g., spiritualism, psychical research); and (14) the dissemination and popularization of Myers's ideas (by authors such as Frank Podmore and Rufus Osgood Mason).

Concluding Remarks

While Hamilton could have included more details in his discussions of some topics, his work is successful in presenting an overview of Myers's life and work. In fact, no author before Hamilton has presented such a global and integrative perspective of Myers. Hamilton combines well the personal and intellectual aspects of Myers with his psychical and psychological work. Furthermore, he covers areas of Myers that have previously been neglected, or only briefly discussed. In fact, I would recommend that Hamilton's work must be the first step in obtaining a good panoramic view of Myers for anyone who wishes to embark on more detailed studies.

One can only hope that the general tapestry woven by Hamilton in *Immortal Longings,* together with previous work by authors such as Gauld and Kelly, will help others to move forward both in the empirical explorations of the phenomena and concepts that mattered to Myers, and in the historical studies of his accomplishments and related areas.

Notes

1 The session included the following brief presentations: "Human Personality and Its Survival of Bodily Death: An Overview" by Jeffrey Mishlove; "The Reception of Human Personality and Its Survival of Bodily Death" by Nancy L. Zingrone and Carlos S. Alvarado; "Myers and Modem Parapsychology" by John Palmer; and "F. W. H. Myers and the Future of Psychology" by Robert L. Morris.

2 It may not be proper to refer to the few published studies of Myers as comprising an area I am referring to as "Myers Studies." Such an area barely exists and is poorly developed.

3 In a section of notes at the end of a chapter of his influential book, *A History of Experimental Psychology*, E. G. Boring (1957, p. 502) briefly mentioned Myers, saying that he was very influential. However, he did not discuss Myers in the text and referred to psychical research as work at the periphery of the new psychology. The latter view has started to change in recent years, as seen in the works of Crabtree (1993), Plas (2000), and others (e.g., Alvarado, 2002; Shamdasani, 1993). For a short review, see Alvarado (2005).

4 One must not be too hard on Ellenberger. His pioneering work did much to show the importance of mesmerism and spiritualism in the development of ideas about the subconscious mind. The same lack of detailed discussions about Myers's concept of the subliminal mind is evident in Tallis's (2002) book and in overview histories of psychical research (e.g., Beloff, 1993; Gutierez & Maillard, 2004).

5 Another author who used Myers's writings selectively was Joseph Grasset (1906), who had a different (reductionist) model of the subconscious from Myers. He referred to Myers as a leading author on the topic and one who had provided him with valuable source material (pp. 8–9).

6 See also my bibliography of online psychical research and psychology materials about Myers (Alvarado, 2009a), which includes many generally ignored reviews of *Human Personality*.

7 This also applies to critiques presented by French spiritists (e.g., Vincent, 1886).

8 Carroy and Schmidgen (2006) wrote about the differences between the German and French approaches to psychological experimentation. The situation was further complicated by the fact that spiritists also used the term "experimental" in works partly based on non-veridical mediumistic communications (e.g., Kardec, 1863). In a paper he delivered at the 1900 International Psychology Congress, spiritist Gabriel Delanne (1901) referred to "experimental psychology" in a discussion of observations of telepathy and apparitions. A similar situation existed regarding the terms, "psychology" and "psychological."

9 Similarly, it may be possible to study Myers using Holmes' (2004) concept of the "investigative pathway," which shows the "expression of the distinctiveness and continuity of the individual scientific personality" (p. xx) slowly developing over time as the individual progresses in his or her work.

References

[Advert] (1903, May 7) *New York Times*, BR1.

Alvarado, C. S. (2002). Dissociation in Britain during the late nineteenth century: the Society for Psychical Research, 1882–1900. *Journal of Trauma and Dissociation, 3,* 9–33.

Alvarado, C. S. (2004). On the centenary of Frederic W. H. Myers's *Human Personality and Its Survival of Bodily Death. Journal of Parapsychology, 68,* 3–43.

Alvarado, C. S. (2005). Historical writings on parapsychology and its contributions to psychology. *Psypioneer, 1,* 270–274.

Alvarado, C. S. (2009a). Frederic W. H. Myers online: I. General materials and reviews of *Human Personality and Its Survival of Bodily Death. Psypioneer, 5,* 162–169.

Alvarado, C. S. (2009b). Psychical research in the *Psychological Review,* 1894–1900: A bibliographical note. *Journal of Scientific Exploration, 23,* 211–220.

Alvarado, C. S. & Zingrone, N. L. (2007–2008). Interrelationships of psychic experiences, dream recall, and lucid dreams in a survey with Spanish participants. *Imagination, Cognition and Personality, 27,* 63–69.

Barrett, W. F., Gurney, E. & Myers, F. W. H. (1882). Thought-reading. *Nineteenth Century, 11,* 890–900.

Beaunis, H. (1887). *Le somnambulism provoqué* (2nd ed.). J. B. Baillière.

Beloff, J. (1993). *Parapsychology: A concise history.* St. Martin's Press.

Beer, G. (2000). *Darwin's plots: Evolutionary narrative in Darwin, George Eliot and nineteenth-century fiction* (2nd ed.). Cambridge University Press.

Beer, J. W. (1998). *Providence and love: Studies in Wordsworth, Channing, Myers, George Eliot and Ruskin.* Oxford University Press.

Binet, A. (1892). *Les altérations de la personnalité.* Félix Alcan.

Book gossip in London. (1903, January 10). *Chicago Daily Tribune*, p. 13.

Bordeau, J. (1906, August 28). Nouveautés en psychologie. *Journal des débats politiques et littéraires,* 1.

Boring, E. G. (1957). *A history of experimental psychology* (2nd ed.). Appleton-Century-Crofts.

Boutroux, E. (1908). Le moi subliminal. *Bulletin de l'Institut Général Psychologique, 8,* 107–122.

Brooks, J. I. (1998). *The eclectic legacy: Academic philosophy and the human sciences in nineteenth-century France.* University of Delaware Press.

Bruce, H. A. (1910). The ghost society and what came of it. *Outlook, 94,* 451–462.

Carpenter, W. B. J. (1853). Electro-biology and mesmerism. *Quarterly Review, 93,* 501–557.

Carroy, J. (1991). *Hypnose, suggestion et psychologie: l'invention de sujets.* Presses Universitaires de France.

Carroy J. & Schmidgen, H. (2006). Psychologies expérimentales: Leipzig-Paris-Würzburg (1890–1910). *Mil neuf cent, 24,* 171–204.

Cerullo, J. J. (1982). *The secularization of the soul: Psychical research in modern Britain.* Institute for the Study of Human Issues.

Chadwick, J. W. (1903). The opus magnum of Frederic W. H. Myers. *The Critic, 42,* 461–463.

Congrès International de Psychologie Physiologique (1890). Bureau de Revues.

Cook, E. W. (1992). *The intellectual background and potential significance of F. W. H. Myers' work in psychology and parapsychology.* (Doctoral thesis). University of Edinburgh.

Cook, E. W. (1994). The subliminal consciousness: F. W. H. Myers' approach to the problem of survival. *Journal of Parapsychology, 58,* 39–58.

Coon, D. J. (1992). Testing the limits of sense and science: American experimental psychologists combat spiritualism, 1880–1920. *American Psychologist, 47,* 143–151.

Crabtree, A. (1993). *From Mesmer to Freud: Magnetic sleep and the roots of psychological healing.* Yale University Press.

Crabtree, A. (2003). 'Automatism' and the emergence of dynamic psychiatry. *Journal of the History of the Behavioral Sciences, 39,* 51–70.

Delanne, G. (1901). La psychologie expérimentale. In P. Janet (Ed.), *IVe Congrès International de Psychologie* (pp. 610–612). Félix Alcan.

De Sarlo, F. (1893). La teorie moderne sulla psicologia della suggestione. *Rivista Italiana di Filosofia, 8,* 172–205.

De Wyzewa, T. (1903). Une théorie scientifique de la vie future. *Revue des deux mondes, 17,* 935–946.
Discussion (1901). In P. Janet (Ed.), *IVe Congrès International de Psychologie* (pp. 662–663). Félix Alcan.
Dorahy, M. J., & Van der Hart, O. (2007). Relationship between trauma and dissociation: A historical analysis. In E. Vermetten, M. J. Dorathy, & D. Spiegel (Eds.), *Traumatic dissociation: Neurobiology and treatment* (pp. 3–30). American Psychiatric Association.
Ellenberger, H. F. (1970). *The discovery of the unconscious: The history and evolution of dynamic psychiatry.* Basic Books.
Erny, A. (1895). *Le psychisme expérimental: étude des phénomènes psychiques.* Ernest Flammarion.
Favre, L. (1906). Hypnotisme et magnétisme animal. In S. De Sanctis (Ed.), *Atti del V Congresso Internazionale di Psicologia* (pp. 552–553). Forzani.
Flournoy, T. (1903). F. W. H. Myers en son œuvre posthume. *Archives de psychologie, 2,* 269–296.
Flower, B. O. (1903). Science and a future life. *Arena, 30,* 190–199.
Fuller, R. G. (1986). *Americans and the unconscious.* Oxford University Press.
Gauld, A. (1968). *The founders of psychical research.* Routledge & Kegan Paul.
Gauld, A. (1992). *A history of hypnotism.* Cambridge University Press.
Gieryn, T. F. (1999). *Cultural boundaries of science: Credibility on the line.* University of Chicago Press.
Glick, T. F. (Ed.). (1988). *The comparative reception of Darwinism.* University of Chicago Press.
Goldstein, R. (1963). Inclined toward the marvelous: Romantic uses of clinical phenomena in the work of Frederic W. H. Myers. *Psychoanalytic Review, 79,* 577–589.
Grasset, J. (1906). *Le psychisme inférieur: Étude de physiopathologie clinique des centres psychiques.* Chevalier & Rivière.
Gregory, R. L. (Ed.). (1998). *The Oxford companion to the mind.* Oxford University Press.
Gurney, E., & Myers, F. W. H. (1885). Some higher aspects of mesmerism. *Proceedings of the Society for Psychical Research, 3,* 401–423.
Gurney, E., Myers, F. W. H., & Podmore, F. (1886). *Phantasms of the living* (2 vols.). Trübner.
Gutierez, G., & Maillard, N. (2004). *Les adventuriers de l'esprit: Une histoire de la parapsychologie.* Presses du Châtelet.
Gutiérrez Marcelino, Fr. (1890). Nueva teoría de la personalidad. *La Ciudad de Dios, 21,* 17–34, 95–113, 204–224.
Haddock, J. W. (1851). *Somnolism and psycheism.* (2nd ed.). James S. Hodson.
Hearnshaw, L. S. (1964). *A short history of British Psychology: 1840–1940.* Barnes & Noble.
Holmes, F. L. (2004). *Investigative pathways: Patterns and stages in the career of experimental scientists.* Yale University Press.
James, H. (Ed.). (1920). *The letters of William James* (Vol. 2). Atlantic Monthly Press.
James, W. (1890). *The principles of psychology* (2 vols.). Henry Holt.
James, W. (1901). Frederic Myers' service to psychology. *Proceedings of the Society for Psychical Research, 17,* 13–23.
James, W. (1903). Review of *Human personality and its survival of bodily death. Proceedings of the Society for Psychical Research, 18,* 22–33.
Janet, P. (1889). *L'automatisme psychologique: Essai de psychologie expérimentale sur les formes inférieures de l'activé humaine.* Félix Alcan.
Janet, P. (Ed.) (1901). *IVe congrès international de psychologie.* Félix Alcan.
Jankelevitch, S. (1904). Review of *Human personality. Revue philosophique de la France et de l'étranger, 57,* 201–208.
Jastrow, J. (1906). *The subconscious.* Houghton Mifflin.
Kardec. A. (1863). *Spiritisme expérimental: Le livre des médiums ou guide des mediums et des évocateurs* (6th ed.). Didier.
Kelly, E. F. (2001). The contributions of F. W. H. Myers to psychology. *Journal of the Society for Psychical Research, 65,* 65–90.
Kelly, E. F. (2007). F. W. H. Myers and the empirical study of the mind-body problem. In E. Kelly et al., *Irreducible Mind* (pp. 47–115). Rowman & Littlefield.
Kelly, E. F., & Alvarado, C. S. (2005). Frederic William Henry Myers, 1843–1901. *American Journal of Psychiatry, 162,* 34.

Kelly, E. F., Kelly, E. W., Crabtree, A., Gauld, A., Grosso, M. & Greyson, B. (2007). *Irreducible mind: Toward a psychology for the 21st century.* Rowman & Littlefield.
Kohn, D. (ed.) (1985). *The Darwinian heritage.* Princeton University Press in Association with Novoa Pacifica.
Leary, D. E. (1990). William James on the self and personality: clearing the ground for subsequent theorists, researchers, and practitioners. In M. G. Johnson & T. B. Henley (Eds.), *Reflections on the principles of psychology: William James after a century,* (pp. 101–137). Lawrence Erlbaum.
Le Maléfan, P. (1995). Sciences psychiques, métapsychique et psychologie: Côtoiement et divorce: Histoire d'un partage. *Bulletin de Psychologie, 48,* 624–630.
Lightman, B. (2007). *Victorian popularizers of science: Designing nature for new audiences.* University of Chicago Press.
Lodge, O. (1903). Presidential address. *Proceedings of the Society for Psychical Research 18,* 1–21.
Luckhurst, R. (2002). *The invention of telepathy, 1870–1901.* Oxford University Press.
Mahan, A. (1855). *Modern mysteries explained and exposed in four parts.* J. P. Jewett.
Mangin, M. (1902). Le mécanisme de la suggestion d'après les travaux de M. F. Myers (de Cambridge). *Revue de l'hypnoisme et de la psychologie physiologique, 16,* 259–266, 295–300.
[Mason, R. O.]. (1893, November 26). In the field of psychology. *New York Times,* p. 20.
Mason, R. O. (1897). *Telepathy and the subliminal self.* Henry Holt.
Mason, R. O. (1903, March 21, March 28). Life after death: the late F. W. H. Myers' posthumous work on the survival of human personality. *New York Times,* BR2, BRI.
Maxwell, J. (1906). Revue de métapsychique (Spiritisme, télépathie, sciences occultes). *L'Année psychologique, 12,* 525–549.
Méheust, B. (1999). *Somnambulisme et médiumnité (1784–1930) ; Vol. 2 ; Le choc des sciences psychiques.* Le Plessis-Robinson: Institut Synthélabo pour de Progrès de la Connaissance.
Morselli, E. (1908). *Psicologia e 'spiritismo': Impressioni e note critiche sui fenomeni medianici di Eusapia Paladino* (2 vols.). Fratelli Bocca.
Münsterberg, H., Ribot, T., Janet, P., Jastrow, J., Hart, B. & Prince, M. (1910). *Subconscious phenomena.* Richard G. Badger.
The Myers book (1903). *Light, 23,* 90–91.
Myers, F. W. H. (1868). Local lectures for women. *Macmillan's Magazine, 19,* 159–163.
Myers, F. W. H. (1884). On a telepathic explanation of some so-called spiritualistic phenomena: Part I. *Proceedings of the Society for Psychical Research, 2,* 217–237.
Myers, F. W. H. (1885a). Automatic writing.—II. *Proceedings of the Society for Psychical Research, 3,* 1–63.
Myers, F. W. H. (1885b). Automatic writing, or the rationale of planchette. *Contemporary Review, 47,* 233–249.
Myers, F. W. H. (1886). Human personality in the light of hypnotic suggestion. *Proceedings of the Society for Psychical Research, 4,* 1–24.
Myers, F. W. H. (1889a). On recognised apparitions occurring more than a year after death. *Proceedings of the Society for Psychical Research, 6,* 13–65.
Myers, F. W. H. (1889b). Professor Pierre Janet's "Automatisme Psychologique." *Proceedings of the Society for Psychical Research, 6,* 186–199.
Myers, F. W. H. (1891a). *Letter to Charles Richet (26 April).* Frederic W. H. Myers Papers. Cambridge University.
Myers, F. W. H. (1891b). Science and a future life. *Nineteenth Century, 29,* 628–647.
Myers, F. W. H. (1892). Review of *Les altérations de la personnalité* by A. Binet. *Mind, 1,* 417–421.
Myers, F. W. H. (1893). The subliminal consciousness: Chapter VI: The mechanism of hysteria. *Proceedings of the Society for Psychical Research, 9,* 2–25.
Myers, F. W. H. (1900). Presidential Address. *Proceedings of the Society for Psychical Research, 15,* 110–127.
Myers, F. W. H. (1903). *Human personality and its survival of bodily death* (2 vols.). Longmans, Green.
Myers, F. W. H. (1905). *La personnalité humaine, sa survivance, ses manifestations supranormales.* Félix Alcan. (Original work published in English, 1903).
Nouvelles de l'étangere (1904, January 4). *Les Temps,* 2.
O'Donnell, J. M. (1985). *The origins of behaviorism: American psychology, 1879–1920.* New York University Press.

Oppenheim, J. (1985). *The other world: Spiritualism and psychical research in England, 1850–1914.* Cambridge University Press.
Our London letter (1893, May 18). *Liverpool Mercury,* p. 5.
Paicheler, G. (1992). Du métaphysicien au bricoleur: Les débuts de la psychologie dans les universités américaines. *Communications, 54,* 241–261.
Pintar, J., & Lynn, S. J. (2008). *Hypnosis: A brief history.* Wiley-Blackwell.
Plas, R. (2000). *Naissance d'une science humaine: La psychologie: Les psychologues et le 'merveilleux psychique'.* Presses Universitaires de Rennes.
Podmore, F. (1901). F. W. H. Myers and the Society for Psychical Research. *Proceedings of the Society for Psychical Research, 17,* 29–32.
Powell, R. C. (1979). The 'subliminal' versus the 'subconscious' in the American acceptance of psychoanalysis, 1906–1910. *Journal of the History of the Behavioral Science, 15,* 155–165.
Reiber, R. W., & Robinson, D. K. (Eds.) (2001). *Wilhelm Wundt in history: The making of a scientific psychology.* Kluwer Academic/Plenum.
Review of *Human personality and its survival of bodily death* (1903). *American Journal of Psychology, 14,* 116.
Ribot, T. (1870). *La psychologie anglaise contemporaine (école expérimentale).* Librairie Philosophique de Ladrange.
Richet, C. (1905). La métapsychique. *Proceedings of the Society for Psychical Research, 19,* 2–49.
Richet, C. (1906). L'avenir de la psychologie. In S. De Sanctis (Ed.), *Atti del V Congresso Internazionale di Psicologia* (pp. 166–173). Forzani.
Richet, C. (1923). *Le savant.* Hachette.
Riley, I. W. (1905). The new thought and its literature. *The Bookman, 21,* 635–637.
Robertson, J. (1903). Mr. Myers'limitations and hesitations. *Light, 22,* 247–249, 259–261.
Rozen, P. (2001). *The historiography of psychoanalysis.* Transaction Publishers.
Salter, W. H. (1957). Our pioneers II: Frederic W. H. Myers. *Journal of the Society for Psychical Research, 39,* 261–266.
Science and art (1882). *Eclectic Magazine of Foreign Literature, Science, and Art, 36* (n. s.), 282–285.
Shamdasani, S. (1993). Automatic writing and the discovery of the unconscious. *Spring, 54,* 100–131.
Sidgwick, H. (1892). [Presidential address]. *International Congress of Experimental Psychology,* (pp. 1–8). Williams & Norgate.
Sidgwick, Mrs. H. (1886). Results of a personal investigation into the physical phenomena of spiritualism, with some critical remarks on the evidence for the genuineness of such phenomena. *Proceedings of the Society for Psychical Research, 4,* 45–74.
Sidis, B. (1898). *The psychology of suggestion: A research into the subconscious nature of man and society.* D. Appleton.
The Slade prosecution (1876, October 23). *The Times,* p. 11.
Starobinski, J. (1970). *L'Œil vivant II: La relation critique.* Gallimard.
Statistique des hallucinations (1890). *Congrès international de psychologie physiologique,* 151–157. Bureau de Revues.
Tallis, F. (2002). *Hidden minds: A history of the unconscious.* Arcade.
Taves, A. (1999). *Fits, trances, and visions: Experiencing religion and explaining experience from Wesley to James.* Princeton University Press.
Taves, A. (2004). The fragmentation of consciousness and *The Varieties of Religious Experience:* William James' contribution to a theory of religion. In W. Proudfoot (Ed.), *William James and a science of the religious: Reexperiencing The varieties of religious experience* (pp. 48–72). Columbia University Press.
Taylor, E. (1996). *William James on consciousness beyond the margin.* Princeton University Press.
Taylor, J. B. (2007). Psychology at the fin de siècle. In G. Marshall (Ed.), *The Cambridge companion to the Fin de Siècle* (pp. 13–30). Cambridge University Press.
Tuckey, C. L. (1907). *Treatment by hypnotism and suggestion or psycho-therapeutics* (5th ed.). G. P. Putnam's Sons.
Turner, F. M. (1974). *Between science and religion: The reaction to scientific naturalism in late Victorian England.* Yale University Press.

Vincent, A. (1886). L'écriture automatique et la science. *Revue spirite, 29,* 716–720, 779–781.
Williams, J. P. (1985). Psychical research and psychiatry in late Victorian Britain: Trance as ecstasy or trance as insanity. In W. F. Bynum, R. Porter, & M. Shepherd (Eds.), *The anatomy of madness* (Vol. 1, pp. 233–254). Tavistock.
Women as suffrage (1870, February 7). *The Times,* p. 12.
Wundt, W. (2000). *Hipnotismo y sugestión.* Del Lunar. (Original work published 1892)

19

Table Turning in the Early 1850s: The Séance Reports of Agénor de Gasparin*

Carlos S. Alvarado

The phenomena of table-turning flourished during the 1850s, providing many people a context for belief in spirit action and for the development of explanations such as unconscious muscular movements and the exteriorization of nervous forces from the sitters. This paper consists of the presentation of excerpts from the classic study of these phenomena by Agénor de Gasparin, who reported his work on the subject in his book *Des Tables Tournantes* (1854, 2 vols., translated into English in 1857). De Gasparin believed that unconscious muscular action could not explain the movements of tables and postulated the emission of a force from the sitters around the table to account for the movements. I present a long excerpt from de Gasparin's book in which he described the phenomena he obtained, preceded by a short review of interest in table phenomena in the 1850s, and followed by critiques showing the general skepticism about these phenomena during and after de Gasparin's lifetime.

Most people shrug their shoulders when we speak to them of Turning Tables, but they find it very simple to believe in the infallibility of the electric telegraph, and in the fact that physical and moral resemblances are transmitted from them to their children! The tables could not escape the common fate. Absurd to-day and evident to-morrow, they will have their theory, a theory, scientific and official, before which I respectfully bow in advance.

(Agénor de Gasparin 1857, Vol. 1, p. 99)

Writing in June 1853 in the *Illustrated London News*, an anonymous author mentioned a delusion threatening to become epidemic: "Thousands of people in Europe and America are turning tables, and obstinately refusing to believe that physical and mechanical means are in any way concerned in the process ..." (Anonymous, 1853a, p. 481). Another commentator, physician and mesmerist John Elliotson (1791–1868), wrote: "Every body now sees the tables turn in his own dwelling, be it Buckingham Palace or a room which serves for kitchen and parlour and all ..." (Elliotson, 1853, p. 191).

These were references to the appeal table turning held for many in some societies. The practice was, in fact, one of the most influential ones in the development of middle-nineteenth-century belief in Spiritualism, leading a writer to state that the phenomenon "is as well-established as any fact in history or science" (Dibdin, 1853, p. 2).

The purpose of this paper is to reprint descriptions of table-turning séances, those published by Agénor de Gasparin (1854; English translation and later abridged edition de Gasparin, 1857, 1889). My purpose is not to discuss their evidential value today but to remind current students of this phenomenon and of this important pioneering work and its importance in psychic history. While these séances have been discussed in various historical overview works (e.g., Evrard, 2016, Chap. 2, Gutierez & Maillard, 2004, pp. 20–23, Inglis, 1992, pp. 218–219, Podmore, 1902, Volume 2,

*Republished with permission from *Journal of Scientific Exploration*, *32*, 702–741, 2018.

pp. 187–188), de Gasparin's work does not seem to be well-known today and has not been cited by more recent writers covering the topic of physical phenomena (e.g., Nicol, 1977; Robinson, 1981; for an exception see Gimeno, 2015). Furthermore, these studies deserve to be better known because they were very influential at the time they appeared. Although there are many reports and discussions of table phenomena throughout the late Nineteenth Century and later (Willin, 2015), I focus my comments in most of this paper on material published in the 1850s. I extend the later discussion at the end of this paper to the reception of the work in later periods.

Table turning, also known as table moving, table talking, table tipping, dancing tables, and by various other names, was widely discussed during the Nineteenth Century to the point that in some places, it became a fashionable social practice.[1] In addition to being entertaining, in some places, the tables had fit into the prevailing political and religious contexts (Monroe, 2008). The practice spread fast in the United States and in Europe for many reasons. Furthermore, it may be argued that the terrain for such acceptance had been prepared by highly publicized accounts of unusual physical phenomena. These included physical effects from the early literature of American Spiritualism (Capron, 1855; Capron & Barron, 1850) and reports of poltergeist-type cases.[2]

Here is a fairly typical account of table-turning:

> I witnessed at the house of an American gentleman in Paris, a series of experiments … It may be proper to say that some fifty persons were present …, In the first place, a light mahogany tea-table, with six legs, was placed on the waxed floor of the saloon, and the palms of the hands of four persons (two ladies and two gentlemen) were placed upon it … In three minutes, the table cracked, undulated, and then moved on being directed by the will of one of the party; it moved along the floor slowly or rapidly to the right or left, forward or backward, when thus directed it also rose on two legs, and resisted strong pressure before it would come down. While standing on two legs, it also turned round to the right and the left, as directed by the will. (Anonymous, n. d., p. 4)

But not all the effects were purely physical. Some presented veridical information, as in the following account:

> The writer has seen a gentleman enter a room who was a perfect stranger to the medium, and ask if the table would spell his name. The alphabet was called over, the table tipping to the different letters which spelt his proper name. It then spelt, in the same manner the name of his deceased sister, the name of the disease with which she died, told many events in her life, &c. (Wharton, 1853)

According to a commentator, lawyer André Saturnin Morin (1807–1888), the behavior and tone of the communications produced by the tables varied greatly. Some were graceful and novel, others presented platitudes. They showed gaiety, mocking, and solemnity and could be bad-tempered and pedantic. Similarly, they presented various political and religious views (Morin, 1860, pp. 354–355). This, and other issues such as knowledge of literature, was, in Morin's view, a function of the composition of the circle. In his view, communications were "in harmony with the ideas of the operators and it [the table] does not express knowledge other than that belonging to the latter" (p. 359; this, and other translations, are mine).

In some communications, such as those the famous writer Victor Hugo (1802–1885) and his family and friends had in Jersey in the early 1850s, the tables produced messages from communicators identifying themselves as Galileo, Moliere, Mozart, and Shakespeare, among others. There were also more abstract communicators who called themselves The Drama, The Idea, and the Shadow of the Sepulcher (Simon, 1923).

Many writers believed that spirit agency accounted for table phenomena, be it Satan (Godfrey, 1853) or deceased spirits. In a defense of the latter, it was argued that spirits of the dead could charge the table with their perispirit, a vital principle allowing the spirit to cause intelligent movements of a table (and other objects) (Kardec, 1862).

The previous idea is a variant of the concept of a force coming out of the body of mediums and sitters, a kind of nervous force that some believed was unrelated to spirits. This idea was proposed by many and was, in a way, an extension of the concept of animal magnetism (e.g., Charpignon, 1848; Deleuze, 1813).[3] In fact, several writers discussing mesmerism included table-turning in their writings (e.g., Baragnon, 1853; Bersot, 1864; Gathy, 1853). One of them wrote that, in his opinion, table-turning was "an undeniable magnetic phenomenon" (Baragnon, 1853, p. 358), while another stated that the magnetic agent affecting tables was the same principle that was used to magnetize people (Du Potet, 1853, p. 581).

Within the context of American Spiritualism, this force was discussed:

> Tables are *moved* by a mysterious power, when a circle of interested spectators, with a medium, are seated around it ... Stretch forth your arm, and grasp a heavy weight and raise it. How mighty that power put forth! Trace it back to its origin, and how wonderful! You *willed* to perform that act. Instantly in your brain, as in a Leyden jar, a nervous influence was generated, which, coursing along your nerves as on metallic wires, entered your muscles and there the mere shrinking of the fibres of a little muscle, the shortening of a small cord, drew up the large weight in your hand. How immeasurable, how unaccountable, such a power! And now think of that circle around the table. When they first sit calmly down, no movement is seen; none can be produced. But when for a few moments in intense mental action, a nervous energy has been generated in the frame of each, until, like a circle of Leyden jars, a whole battery is surcharged, and there are negatives as well as positives in the circle, who can wonder if currents of nervous influence should leap over from one to the other, and if tables, chairs, or anything else intervening, should be moved? We should not wonder at any phenomena which might show themselves under such circumstances. We should only fear that, like inexperienced experimenters in electricity, we should thoughtlessly inflict upon ourselves an incurable injury ... If I overcharge myself with it, if I strain the vital organs which generate it, I may weaken my own energies for life. (Oldfield, 1852, p. 37–38)

As we shall see, de Gasparin wrote along similar lines. In addition to Oldfield (the pseudonym of George W. Samson [1819–1896]), many others discussed similar concepts of force during the period in question. This was the case of Marc Thury (1822–1905) (Thury, 1855) and others (Rogers, 1853; Mahan, 1855).[4]

A somewhat later example from France was Alphonse Chevillard, a professor at the Ecole des Beaux-Arts. He argued that when the medium's magnetic fluid charged the table, this acted like a limb of the body, obeying the medium's will (Chevillard, 1869, p. 15). This idea was also discussed by de Gasparin.

In addition to articles in journals dedicated to psychic phenomena (e.g., Kardec, 1859; Gathy, 1853), there were discussions in the general press (e.g., de Gasparin, 1853b), some of which were humorous. This was the case with cartoons and other humorous writings published in France

(Doré & Paulin, 1853; see also Monroe, 2008, p. 22–26). In France, a commentator wrote that the tables are not only trained to talk, but they beat people who do not accept their statements (Kendall, 1853).

Furthermore, some discussions of table-turning were published in medical and science journals (e.g., Anonymous, 1853b; Seguin, 1853). In Spain, a physician justified the inclusion of the topic in the *Bolétin de Medicina, C'irugía y Farmacia*, saying that turning tables may have important theoretical implications for physiology, pathology, and therapeutics (D, 1853).

Perhaps the most famous publication by a scientist was that of English physicist Michael Faraday (1791–1867), who conducted tests that suggested that the movement of tables observed was caused by small unconscious movements (Faraday, 1853a),[5] an idea defended as well by several others (e.g., Babinet, 1854; Carpenter, 1853; Chevreul, 1854; Orioli, 1853).

One version of this idea, with some psychological concepts, was that of Scottish physician James Braid (1795–1860). He postulated that various phenomena could be produced provided there was a state of concentration opening the person to the influence of suggestion and dominant ideas. He wrote:

> Thus, let the mind of the person be engrossed with the notion, that he is to be irresistibly drawn, repelled, or paralysed, or catalepsed, and the ideo-dynamic or ideational condition of the muscles corresponding to this idea will take place, without any conscious volition of the subject to that effect. It is this very ideational or unconscious muscular action which is the cause of "Table-moving," ... The experimenters perceive the fact that the table moves; but not being conscious of putting out any voluntary effort, they imagine that the table is drawing them, whilst all the while their own muscles are imparting the requisite impulse to the table, although they are unconscious that they are doing so. (Braid, 1853, p. 38)

Such ideas of unconscious movements were developed in opposition to explanations involving spirits and psychic forces of various kinds. But they were, in turn, criticized as well by others. For example, one writer considered ideas of unconscious movements to be "ingeniously ridiculous explanations" (Morin, 1854, p. 676). This was probably because proponents of unconscious movements ignored the various reports of movements of tables without physical contact (for some examples of phenomena, see Capron & Barron, 1850, p. 6; Capron, 1855, p. 349; Edmonds & Dexter, 1853, p. 426; Hare, 1855, p. 46).[6]

Interestingly, and one of the reasons to reprint de Gasparin's work in this article, is that most of the literature on table turning consists of discussions of the topic or informal accounts of séances. Not many individuals conducted what may be described as tests with some controls. In addition to the studies of Faraday and de Gasparin, there were other tests. These include the accounts of Thury (1855) and a few others (e.g., Delgras, 1853; Orioli, 1853; Terzaghi 1853).

Agénor de Gasparin and Table Turning

The son of Count Adrien de Gasparin (1783–1862), Minister of the Interior in France, statesman and author Count Agénor Etienne de Gasparin (1810–1871), was born in Orange, France, and later lived in Switzerland.[7] His mother was Adèle de Daunant (1784–1834), and he married Valérie Boissier (1813–1894), a well-known writer on social and religious topics (Gilman, Peck, & Colby, 1907, p. 471).

An obituarist referred to him as a noble and chivalrous man who showed "grace that charmed his adversaries as well as his friends" (N, 1871). He held various political appointments, such as a member of the Chamber of Deputies from Bastia (Corsica) in 1842. Furthermore, de Gasparin was interested and active in issues related to economics, history, politics, and religion.

A biographer presented de Gasparin as a man always willing to fight for causes, such as the abolition of slavery (Borel, 1879). This was evident in his various books, among them *De l'Affranchissement des Esclaves et des Rapports avec la Politique Actuelle* (1839), *Intérêts Généraux du Protestantisme Français* (1843), *Les États-Unis en 1861* (1861), *L'Amérique devant l'Europe* (1862), *La Liberté Morale* (1868), and *L'Égalité* (1869).

Although de Gasparin's book about table turning appeared in 1854, he had discussed the topic in print before that in some letters published in various reviews (de Gasparin 1853a, 1853b). In one of these, he expressed his approach. He wrote:

> I denounce ... scientific intolerance that concludes without examination that seeks to stifle under anathema and sarcasms a physical phenomenon that troubles it. (de Gasparin, 1853b).

Entitled *Des Tables Tournantes: Du Surnaturel en Général et des Esprits*, de Gasparin's (1854) book consisted of two volumes, which were translated into English a few years later (de Gasparin, 1857; there was also a later abridged French edition in 1889). The first volume has two parts. The first one, and the one relevant to this article, is about table-turning. Here, he presented accounts of séances, which I reproduce here, and discussed various methodological and evidential considerations.

The second part is about "The Supernatural in General." The third part, entitled "Spirits," is about the "supernatural apocrypha." Chapters about miracles, sorcery, animal magnetism, and spirits appeared in the second volume. The discussion consists of attempts to explain the supernatural, including the action of spirits, in natural terms. This includes things such as fraud, testimony problems, nervous excitement producing physiological and psychological changes, and hallucinations. In some cases, the author considers fluid action. This was not confined to physical effects but also included mental ones, such as obtaining information from the thoughts of others.

De Gasparin was critical of all spiritual agency arguments to account for phenomena. Among others, he was critical of the French writer about miracles and psychic phenomena, Jules Eudes de Mirville (1802–1873), a well-known defender of satanic agency (e.g., de Mirville, 1854).[8]

"My deductions," wrote de Gasparin, "have been of a nature to destroy all superstitious fables, modern as well as ancient, and, at the same time, to strengthen historical, scientific, and religious certainty" (de Gasparin, 1857, Volume 2, p. 469). In this sense, de Gasparin's work was similar to that of previous critics who attempted to reduce all unusual phenomena to deception, physiological and psychological explanations (e.g., Dendy, 1841; Newnham, 1830).[9] But his emphasis on the action of a nervous fluid outside the physical body separated him from this line of thought and placed him in line with mesmeric ideas and the ideas of other nervous force critics of Spiritualism (e.g., Rogers, 1853).

The analyses of previous traditions led French physician Auguste Debay (1802–1890) to remark that the book, unlike other works, was not an "indigestible compilation" of information (Debay, 1854, p. 370). He believed de Gasparin's analyses were "a monument of reason, against the disorders of the imagination" (p. 370), a kind of antidote against superstition.

Writing about this nervous force, de Gasparin referred to it as a hypothetical one consistent with the facts. He stated that although he did not accept all the mesmeric ideas of a universal fluid, he thought that an "hemato-nervous fluid" could explain much in mesmerism and Spiritualism (de Gasparin, 1857, p. 331). He wrote further:

> If my brain, acting like a Leyden jar, emits and directs a fluid current along my nerves, if this fluid is also emitted by the other members of the chain, it is evident that our combined action will soon form a sort of electric battery, the influence of which will be felt conformably to our thought; we shall communicate a rotation, we shall produce, even at a distance, energetic elevations. (de Gasparin, 1857, Vol. 1, p. 430–431)

The fluid was seen as an agent connected to the will of the sitters.[10] As mentioned above, this principle was seen by him as related to body movements. He wrote that

> the table identifies itself in some sort with us, becomes one of our members, and executes the motions conceived in our minds, in the same way that our arm does. (de Gasparin, 1857, Volume 1, p. 98).

De Gasparin also discussed in the first part of his book the objections to new phenomena. He noticed how new facts were rejected by many without examination. According to a reviewer of his work, he examined in detail many objections, and refuted them "with a clarity, a reason, a dialectic superiority which makes this part of his work a masterpiece of an essay; he victoriously crushes his opponents" (Morin, 1854, p. 676).

The section about séances reprinted here includes reports on 12 meetings held by de Gasparin and his collaborators at Valleyres, Switzerland, from September 20 to December 2, 1853. These do not represent all the séances conducted, since there were many held before and after the ones that appear below. But those extra séances were not reported. Not much is said about the sitters, but de Gasparin (1857, Vol. 1, p. 178) stated:

> The persons engaged in these experiments were two scientific botanists, MM. Muret and Reuter, M. Tachet, the clergyman, M. Boissier, several domestics, three children from eleven to fifteen years of age, my wife, and myself.

The number of sitters varied between 8 and 12 sitters but was generally 10. Thury (1855) also attended some séances.

The Count's wife, Valerie Boissier, wrote in a letter to her father dated March 31, 1853: "The day before yesterday, we placed Agénor on the table, and under this weight of nearly a quintal, she rose on two legs and turned" (Barbey-Boissier, 1902, p. 243). In a later letter she stated that the table danced the waltz, as well as the gavotte and the minuet.

Excerpt about Table Turning

Presented here are the séance accounts from the English-language translation of de Gasparin's 1857 work.

Sitting of September 20th

> I leave out … everything that has not been sufficiently studied, everything that ulterior experiments have rendered in the slightest degree doubtful, everything that is merely a repetition of the facts already stated. This deduction performed, there still remain some results to notice.

And first, to speak of the table that has served us most frequently. The top is of ash, about 32 inches in diameter, and rests upon a heavy pillar from which project three feet, 22 inches distant from each other. Another table, the top of which is a little larger, the pillar less heavy, has also been employed. In fact, we have sometimes put in motion tables with four feet, both round and square, all of respectable dimensions. The number of experimenters forming the chain at a time is ordinarily ten; it has varied between the two extremes of eight and a dozen. The rotation usually manifests itself after five or ten minutes. In certain cases—very rare—we have waited nearly half an hour.

On the 20th of September, then, we desired to put to the proof the pretended faculty of divination ascribed to the tables. For this purpose, we submitted to the one around which we were sitting, and which operated to admiration, the most elementary question assuredly, that can be proposed to a spirit. We placed three nuts in the pocket of one of the experimenters; the table, interrogated as to their number, promptly struck nine blows! The same person, after having succeeded in obtaining several numbers indicated by his will—among which was a cypher—entered upon a contest with his vis-à-vis [facing person]. This constituted a particularly interesting experiment, which we termed *the balance of forces*. It cannot be said in this case that the motion was communicated by the vis-à-vis acting as a lever, for the interests were opposed. The vis-à-vis struggle against each other, the one wills a large number, the other a small number. Were the impulsion of a mechanical nature, the champion of the small number would determine to cease furnishing the balance from the moment his number had been struck, he would even lean in such a manner as to obtain judgment! But, no! The most powerful operator carries it; if he is charged with the high number, the high number is attained. One thing must be remarked, however, that from the moment his adversary's limit is passed, and the wills have ceased to coincide, the blows become less strong; the foot which previously obeyed both thoughts is no longer sustained by more than one.

We then changed the conditions of the struggle. A coalition was formed to the advantage of the small numbers; they were confined to two, afterwards to three members of the chain, and it was only then that the knight of the large numbers was vanquished, and the foot in front of him (a foot over which he was deprived of all mechanical action), ceased to follow the impulsion of his will, in spite of the experimenters opposite, who alone would have been sufficient to put and maintain it in motion, had that motion been produced by muscular force.

It is to be taken for granted that different combinations were tried and produced results not less decisive. We made a variation in the feet, sending the blows from one foot to another. We inverted the *roles*—the most powerful experimenter was in his turn charged with the small numbers; and he regularly succeeded in stopping his adversaries, no matter which foot was designated.

It was at last proposed to try the counterproof of one of our most conclusive experiments; that which consists in making the table turn and knock while supporting the weight of a man weighing 174 pounds. The man was placed upon it; the twelve experimenters, taking care not to form the chain, applied their fingers to the table and exerted themselves to obtain by the tension of their muscles what they had obtained some days previous without tension or effort. The energy with which they worked was astonishing! and yet—nothing! The rotation took place in a feeble degree, scarcely turning half round; the poor table all the time trembling and creaking as though it were about to split into pieces. To raise it from the ground was out of the question. Not one of the feet would give the least sign of docility. It is useless to add, that, for the strongest possible reason, we gave up all hopes of obtaining the complete revolution, which our simplest commands had effected but a short time before.

September 22nd Sitting

We have not established any new fact worthy of mention here; but among the old facts reproduced, I think it useful to describe the motions of the table while bearing the same person who was placed on it three days before. The inutility of muscular action had then been seen; we were this time about to see the power of the fluid, or whatever physical agent it may be, of which the operators dispose when they form the chain and when command with a firm will. We were indeed very glad of the opportunity to make this comparison.

In the habit of criticizing our experiments, and not willing to accept as a certainty what we had observed only once or twice, we were anxious to begin by placing ourselves in the identical positions. The success has this time been complete. The table has turned; it has struck several blows; it has stood entirely upright, so as to throw off the man.

I desire, in passing, to be permitted to record a general remark. We had already held numerous meetings; our experimenters, among whom were several young, delicate women, had acted with uncommon perseverance and energy; their physical fatigue, at the termination of each sitting, was naturally very great; it might consequently have been expected that nervous accidents, more or less grave, would have occurred. If the explanations based upon the involuntary acts accomplished in a state of extraordinary excitement, had rested upon any real foundation, we should have had ecstasies, almost possessions, and in all cases nervous attacks.[11] Now, it did not happen, during the five months we thus met, animated and noisy as our experiments frequently were, that one of us, for a single moment, experienced the slightest discomfort.

Still further, when one is in a state of nervous tension, he becomes absolutely incapable of acting on the table. It must be taken cheerfully, briskly, with confidence and authority, but without passion. This is so true, that the moment my interest in it becomes too great, I cease to make it obey me; and in all our sittings, I invariably found that whenever, by reason of the public discussion in which I was engaged, I allowed myself to desire success too ardently, and became impatient at our numerous delays, I lost my influence over the table.

September 26th Sitting

Our début was discouraging enough, and led us to think that the entire results of the day would be limited to the two following observations, which are in fact well worth their price, and which our practice has not ceased to confirm: First, there are some days when we can do nothing, however numerous, strong, or animated we may be. This proves that the motions of the table are not obtained by fraud, nor by involuntary pressure of the muscles. Second, there are persons (among others, those who are unhealthy or fatigued) whose presence in the chain, is not merely useless, but injurious; themselves deprived of fluid, they seem also to hinder its transmission and circulation; their good will, their faith in the table, go for nothing; so long as they are there, the rotations are feeble, the elevations are languid; the commands are not executed, the foot placed in front of them is particularly affected by paralysis; induce them to retire, and immediately, life reappears and everything succeeds as by enchantment.

It was not, indeed, until after we had taken this course that the movements became as free and energetic as usual. We had already met with several checks, and especially when the purpose was to dislodge a man placed on the table. In vain did we issue our commands impressively and with spirit; no rotation, no perpendicular motion! We were forced to substitute a child for the man, and then alone could we succeed in producing action.

We were thus almost disheartened, when the purification of which I just now spoke was tried, and immediately, what a metamorphosis! Nothing seemed difficult to us; those even, who, like me, ordinarily succeeded only tolerably well, now caused the numbers indicated by our thoughts to be correctly rapped out, with the occasional exception of one rap too many, resulting from the tardy issue of the mental order which should have arrested the blows.

Finding that everything progressed according to our wishes, and determined to attempt the impossible, we undertook an experiment which marks our entrance into quite a new phase, and puts our previous experience under the guarantee of an irrefutable demonstration. We were about to forsake probabilities for evidence. We were about to make the table move *without touching it*.

Our first success was brought about as follows:

Choosing a moment when the table was impelled by an energetic and truly spirited rotation, we all raised our hands at a given signal; then, maintaining them united by means of the little finger, and continuing to form the chain at about an inch above the table, we pursued our course, and, to our great surprise, the table also pursued its course, making thus three or four turns!

We could scarcely believe in such a success; the witnesses of the experiment could not refrain from clapping their hands. And not less remarkable than the rotation without contact, was the manner in which it was effected. Once or twice, the table had ceased to follow us, because the accidents resulting from our change of place had separated our fingers from their regular position above the margin; once or twice the table came to life again, if I may dare thus to express myself, as soon as the revolving chain returned to its proper relative position. We all had a perception that each hand had carried, by a sort of attraction, the portion of the table underneath it.

September 29th Sitting

We were naturally impatient to submit the rotation without contact to a new proof. In the confusion incidental to a first success, we had not thought either to vary or renew this decisive experiment. Since then, we had reflected on it; we had felt that it was important to do the thing over again more carefully, and in the presence of new witnesses; that it was especially important to produce the motion in place of continuing it, and to produce it under the form of elevations, rather than confine ourselves to the rotations.

Such was the programme for the meeting of the 29th of September. Never was a programme more implicitly followed.

First of all, we resumed our experiments of the 26th. The table being in full rotation, the hands were separated and continued to turn above it, in forming the chain. The table followed, making sometimes one or two revolutions, sometimes half, or nearly a quarter of a revolution. The success, more or less prolonged, was certain. We verified it several times.

But it might be said that the table being already started, preserved a certain impetus which it mechanically obeyed, while we imagined it to obey our fluid power. The objection is absurd, and we would have challenged anyone to obtain merely a quarter of a revolution without forming the chain, no matter how great the velocity of the rotation; we would especially have challenged them to succeed in renewing the race, after it had been momentarily suspended. Nevertheless, it is well in such matters to anticipate objections, however absurd, as long as they are plausible: and this might appear so to the eyes of the careless observer. It was necessary, therefore, to produce rotation from a condition of complete repose.

We did so. The table being motionless as well as ourselves, the chain of hands separated from it and began to turn slowly a short distance above its margin. After a moment, the table made a slight motion, and each person endeavoring by his will to incite the portion underneath his fingers, we drew the body of the table after us. The same circumstances then occurred as in the preceding case; it is a difficult matter to maintain the chain in the air without breaking it, without removing it from the edge of the table, without moving too quickly and thus interrupting the established relation, that the rotation is often arrested after one, or even less than one, revolution. Nevertheless, it is sometimes prolonged during three or four.

We expected to encounter still more obstacles, when it came to the point of raising it without contact. But we were agreeably disappointed—the fact was entirely otherwise, and we accounted for it in the following manner: There being in this instance no circular movement demanded from us, we found it much easier to retain the normal position of the hands above the table. The chain then being formed a short distance above the top of the table, we ordered one of the feet to rise, and it instantly obeyed.

We were in raptures. This beautiful experiment was renewed many times. We ordered the table, likewise without touching it, to stand erect, and to resist the witnesses who should attempt to bring it to the ground. We ordered it to turn over, and it fell with the feet in the air, although our fingers at no time touched it, but always remained at the same distance from it.

These were the essential results of this meeting. They are such that I hesitate to mention by their side other incidents of secondary importance.

I will merely add in passing that the sitting had commenced very discouragingly; that not only had it been necessary to send away some new operators, but several of the old ones were deprived of their usual enthusiasm. The table obeyed badly; blows were struck feebly, and as if with regret the numbers demanded were not expressed. Therefore, we took a new approach, from which good results flowed without number: We persevered and persevered cheerfully; we sung, we made the table dance, we banished from our minds all new experiments, insisting upon easy and amusing operations. After a certain time, the order of things was changed, the table overflowed with activity and willingness, its obedience almost anticipating our commands; we were prepared to approach matters of grave import.

October 6th Sitting

Notwithstanding the distraction created by too many spectators, and the lassitude caused by the stifling heat, we obtained in this long sitting the most essential confirmation of previous results.

Numbers indicated by the thought, the balance of forces, the elevation and resistance of the table, all were renewed. With regard to resistance in particular, we measured it. A weight of 80 lbs. did not suffice to lower the table over which we made the chain, when it formed with the floor an angle of 35 degrees. The same table forming the same angle, fell heavily under the force of a weight of about 60 lbs. when not sustained by the influence of the chain. Note, moreover, that the hands placed opposite the weight of 80 lbs. had been raised, and did not again touch the table while it continued to resist. But I do not offer this as a conclusive experiment, because I know that there is a certain point of equilibrium, where a table the most destitute of fluids, would, of itself, resist a considerable pressure; notwithstanding, therefore, the difference above established, I discard the fact (very real to my eyes) that I have just related, for I am determined to adduce only such proofs as cannot be controverted.

We tried also to set in motion the table bearing the weight of a heavy man. The rotation was at that time impossible, but the feet struck several heavy blows.

Passing then to the counterproof, we remarked that when we act mechanically, precisely the contrary result takes place. By energetic muscular efforts, a slight rotatory movement is obtained, but it is impossible to raise the feet.

Finally, we resumed the great experiment, that of motion without contact.

It seemed at first that we were not in a condition to obtain good results. But soon, however, we succeeded in continuing the rotation and in producing it from a state of repose. Its most remarkable feature was, that our commands effected a small rotation, about one-quarter of a revolution, although we ourselves remained entirely motionless. The table thus gently glided from under our fingers.

The perpendicular motions without contact were produced many times and with energy. The table, influenced by our hands, which were extended a short distance above it, stood erect, resisted efforts to lower it, and turned itself over completely several times.

October 7th Sitting

Another long and fatiguing *réunion.* It was principally devoted to the trial of divers pieces of mechanism, which had no success: metal rings, frames of canvas or paper placed above the table, platforms turning on pivots, and the keyboard of a piano. Whether a view of the machines in question suppressed the emission of the fluid in the operators, whether the machines themselves suppressed its circulation in the table, whether, in fact, the natural conditions of the phenomenon were disturbed in another manner, it is certain that the results were either nothing or questionable.

Only one new experiment succeeded. A platform turning on a pivot supported a bucket. After filling the bucket with water, I and two others plunged our hands into it. There we formed the chain, and began to turn round, avoiding touching the bucket; it was not long before the bucket also put itself in motion. The same thing was done several times in succession.[12]

As the objection might be offered that the impulsion given to the water was sufficient to impel a thing so easily moved as a bucket, we immediately proceeded to the counterproof. The water was agitated circularly, and with much more rapidity than when we formed a chain in it, but the bucket did not stir. It remains to know, doubtless, if one of us three did not touch the interior of the bucket in order to influence its motion. To this I reply, first, that the manner in which our hands were plunged into the bucket was evident proof that none of our fingers could, corporally, touch the bottom; second, that being careful to form the chain in the center, we might as easily have brought our fingers in contact with the walls of the room.

The doubt, however, not being absolutely inadmissible, I continue to rank this experiment among those of which I do not pretend to make any use. I desire to show myself difficult on the point of proofs.

That which is furnished by the expression of numbers indicated by the thought, is still one of the most substantial in my estimation.

What rendered it particularly convincing, in the sitting of which I speak, was that each of the ten operators, in turn, received the communication of a sum in writing, from some member of the audience, the others having their eyes closed. Now, of the ten, all, with one exception, obtained perfect obedience from the foot designated by the most suspicious witnesses. Whoever reflects on the above-mentioned experiment, will see for himself that it is entirely beyond the circle of things admissible, that fraud could not have any agency in producing the combination of motions here communicated. The objection needs to invent a prodigy far more surprising than ours.

Let us return to the demonstration *par excellence*—the elevation without contact. We began by accomplishing it three times. Then, as it was suggested that the presence of witnesses exercised a more certain influence over a small table than a large one, over five operators than ten, we caused a round table, made of spruce, to be brought in, and which the chain reduced by one-half, sufficed to put in rotation. Whereupon, the hands being raised, and all contact having ceased, the table elevated itself perpendicularly seven times at our command.

October 8th Sitting

This sitting was accomplished under such circumstances that I ought, perhaps, to pass over it in silence. The death of a valued friend had plunged us all into profound grief, and the moral depression resulting from it took away the fluid power even of those in whom it was usually most abundant.

Had it not been for the presence of a visitor, who had come a long distance to assist at our experiments, and who could not prolong his stay, we should certainly not have attempted to act at such a moment.

Among the new trials, I will mention one, the object of which was to raise entirely from the ground a table suspended from a pulley and balanced by a counterweight. Only one of its feet touched the ground, and the weight to overcome it was reduced to a trifle. The chain having been formed, the foot that touched the ground rose clear from it, and the table thus accomplished some vibrations without encountering the floor.

Had it been raised? I am far from affirming this to be the fact. It might have been simply impelled by the fluid, so as to change the mode of suspension, and put a space between the earth and its foot. It might also have been that the action of the hands on it was purely mechanical, that the cord which sustained it had been removed from the vertical, and that the friction had ceased because the table was forcibly drawn to the right or left, at the precise instant when its foot would have been impelled to strike the ground.

Consequently, this fact possesses no value either in favor of or against my theory. I will say as much of various analogous experiments, and also of the keyboard of the piano, over which we formed the chain anew without obtaining any rotation. The fluid is probably lost in this labyrinth of springs and platforms; moreover, the confidence and will are weakened.

To conclude with something less negative, I will state two more facts confirmatory of the preceding results.

Among the numbers called for, the malice of a witness had placed a cypher, and the foot designated for its expression at the left of the operator, beyond the sphere of his muscular action. Now, the command having been issued without producing any response, we were all extremely annoyed, convinced as we were that our powerlessness for the time being was so great as to prevent our obtaining even the simple elevation. I confidently assert that if the experimenters placed in front of the foot ever were tempted fraudulently to apply mechanical action, they were at that moment. Our nerves were intensely excited, and our impatience was at its height; nevertheless, no motion was observed, and to our great relief the figure was announced to be a cypher.

We at length twice effected the motion without contact. At such times, it was great movement, and we considered ourselves happy in having accomplished it.

October 27th Sitting

I relate things as they occurred, and have no wish to describe ourselves as more triumphant than we actually were. The reader must judge for himself. I confess that here again is a sitting by no means brilliant.

Moreover, this lack of uniformity is of interest. We were, for example, deprived of a great portion of our power, by the single fact of the indisposition of the person who has the most influence over the table. Now, let the enemies of the tables try to explain that! If it were the result of mechanical action, it and we would have succeeded as in the past, for our muscular force was not diminished.

If it were the result of fraud, we should also have succeeded equally well, for our *personnel* was the same, and nothing prevented the dishonest hands from performing their office. If it were the consequence of unconscious and involuntary motion, the success ought likewise to have been complete, for never had we been more ardent and energetic. But there we sat, real objects of pity, sometimes passing an entire quarter of an hour without obtaining a rap or a simple rotation.

Nevertheless, we finally arrived at some results, which were as follows:

Seeing that we did not succeed in effecting the perpendicular motion without contact, starting from a state of immobility, we contented ourselves with effecting it under the more modest form of a continuation of the motion; thus, we commanded the table to strike eight blows; at the third, the hands were raised, and the table, no longer touched by any one, pursued its task, at one time striking four, at another five, and at another eight.

Such was our principal exploit. I will cite another, the exact value of which I do not pretend to determine.

It had been objected to in our experiment in which the table was made to strike while it bore the weight of a man, that this man could lend himself to the motion, and in a measure provoke it. As earnest seekers after truth, we felt that there was plausibility in this objection, and consequently decided to give it our particular attention. The living being, endowed with intelligence, and consequently subject to suspicion, was replaced by inert matter; retorts, filled with sand, were put on the exact center of the table, which was then summoned to display its skill.

But the day was badly chosen. After having thus deposited, one upon the other, two retorts, weighing 130 lbs., we found that we were incapable of producing the elevations; we were obliged to content ourselves with continuing them; the retorts were therefore removed, the table set in motion, and the retorts replaced while the rotation was going on did not check it; they were jostled about with considerable force, and the sand was spilled out on all sides. The remainder of the sitting was devoted to new experiments on the pretended power of divination. Let me here recapitulate the results of those we had attempted in this and in other sittings.

When the table is requested to divine anything that is known to one of the members of the chain, it happens frequently enough, and very naturally, that it divines. The operation is the same as that of numbers indicated by the thought, neither more nor less.

When the table is asked to divine something which is known to one of the audience who takes no part in the chain, it sometimes happens that it divines. This occurs when the person in question is endowed with great fluid power, and can exercise it at a distance. We obtained no such demonstration; but others have succeeded, and their testimony appears too well-established to be called into question.

Up to the present time, we perceive not the slightest trace of divination; fluid action, either near or distant, accounts for those results which at first glance would appear to resemble it.

If tables divine, if they think, if they are under the control of spirits, we ought to obtain conclusive responses under circumstances where the facts are not known, either in or out of the chain. With the problem thus stated, its solution is not difficult.

Take a book; do not open it, but invite the table to read the first line of any page you may choose to designate—page 162 or page 354.[13] The table will not recoil; it will strike blows and you will compose words. It is thus, at least, that we have always been treated. Be that as it may, one thing is certain: no spirit, either here or elsewhere, now or at a future time, however cunning or clever he may be, has read, or will read this simple line. I recommend this experiment to the partisans of the thinking tables and of mysterious evocations.

As for the examples of nuts, pieces of money contained in a purse, the hours, playing cards, the tables conform themselves exactly to the calculation of probabilities, they divine just as much as you and I do. As regards the question of small numbers of which we get a proximate idea, the circle of possible combinations is very little extended; the mind fixes upon a figure, which has tolerable chances of being correct; the proportion between the failure of the table and its success, is about the same as it would be, independent of all miraculous divination. We are here very far from those uniform results obtained by fluid action: numbers indicated by the thoughts, for example, which succeed ten or twenty times in succession, during moments of excitement. This cannot certainly explain itself by any casual conjunction of circumstances.

November 9th Sitting

We were in haste to take our revenge; and it far anticipated our hopes.

Before commencing my relation of this sitting, the most remarkable of all, I wish to observe that neither the thermometer nor the compass have furnished the slightest, interesting indication. I have thought it my duty to note this in passing, in order to show the reader that we have not neglected to employ instruments which, it would seem, might have put us on the road to a scientific explanation. In general, I pass over in silence the various trials that have remained under the conditions of the trials and have led to nothing positive.

Our first care was to renew the experiment of raising an inert weight. This time it was agreed that we should begin with a condition of absolute immobility. The question was to produce, not to continue the motion.

The center of the table having been determined with precision, a bucket, filled with sand and weighing 42 lbs., was placed upon it. The feet raised themselves easily as soon as the order was given.

A second bucket weighing 38 lbs. was then placed in the center of the first. They were both raised, less easily, but very distinctly.

A third and smaller bucket, weighing 26 lbs., was likewise added, and placed upon the other two. The elevation took place.

We had prepared, in addition to these, some enormous stones, weighing about 44 lbs. We put them on the third bucket. After considerable hesitation, the table raised each of its three feet successively and several times, with a force, a decision, and a spirit which surprised us. But its strength, already subjected to so many trials, was unequal to this. Staggering under the energetic impulse communicated to the entire mass of 150 lbs., it suddenly gave way, and its pillar was rent from top to bottom, to the great peril of the operators on the side toward which the load fell.

I do not pause to comment on such an experiment; it covers the whole ground. Our muscular force would not have sufficed to determine the motion that took place. An inert and noncomplying weight had replaced the person whose complicity was to be feared. In fine, the three feet having been raised, each in its turn, there could be no excuse for insinuating that we had put the weight more on one side than on the other.

Our poor table was wounded on the field of honor. Not being able to cure it immediately, we took a new one strongly resembling it, but which was in reality a little larger and a little lighter.

It remained to be seen if we should be obliged to wait until it had become charged with fluid. The occasion was favorable to the resolution of an important problem: Where does the fluid reside? In the operators or in the table? The solution was as prompt as decisive. Hardly had our hands, forming the chain, been placed on the table, than it turned with the most unexpected and comical rapidity. Evidently the fluid was in us, and we were free to apply it to any other table.

Our time had not been lost. In the condition in which we found ourselves, the motions without contact ought to have succeeded better than ever. We were not deceived in supposing it.

The rotations without contact were first obtained up to the number of five or six. The motion under our fingers, and under the will that attached itself to this or that particular point of the table, was slow at the beginning, gradually accelerating toward the end; several rotations lasted during three or four revolutions.

As to the elevations without contact, we discovered a new process that rendered success easy. The chain, formed a short distance above the bed of the table, is so arranged as to pursue its course in the direction of the point where the motion is expected to take place. The hands nearest the foot called upon to rise are outside the bed of the table, which they gradually approach and pass over; while the hands opposite, and which at first had advanced toward the same foot, move off to one side, drawing it with them. It is during this progression of the chain, while all the wills are fixed on one particular spot in the wood, and the orders to rise are uttered with force, that the foot quits the earth and follows the hands to the point of overturning the table if not prevented from doing so.

This is not an isolated result. We reproduced it about thirty times. We caused it to be executed by each of the three feet successively, in order to deprive the critic of all pretext for cavil. We, moreover, watched the hands with scrupulous attention; and when it is observed that this watchfulness was continued during thirty operations, without surprising us with the slightest contact, it will be concluded, I think, that the reality of the phenomenon is henceforth established beyond all reasonable contestation; especially, if it be added that during the last elevations one of the spectators, kneeling down, applied his eye to the plane of the table in such a manner as to assure himself that it was the whole time free from touch or other improper influence.

One word more. It seemed to us that the table once made a movement forward instead of perpendicularly, and that it had thus followed on the floor the progress of the chain. This was a fact to verify.

Confirmed, as will be seen by our subsequent experiments, it manifests under a new form, the impulse to which the table yields. It is curious to see it submit to our action from a distance, and glide over the ground, when it has not force enough to rise. In fact, the same thing occurred when the hands rested on it. If the fluid power does not suffice for the elevation demanded, the table takes flight and makes its escape, sometimes in a straight line, sometimes by commencing an unlooked-for rotation—now in one direction, now in another. The impulse communicated, whether great or small, produces a proportionate effect.

November 24th Sitting

The peculiar characteristic of this sitting was the absence of the person who exercised the greatest authority over the table. By operating without him we were enabled to establish two things: the first, an experimenter cannot with impunity be dispensed with; the second, that he can be dispensed with in case of extremity, and that success, although less brilliant at first, is not impossible. I underline this last point, along with the frequent modifications caused by our personnel, for the benefit of the suspicious portion of the community, who, not knowing the moral value of the persons in question, would be disposed to impute to their dexterity, results to which they, themselves, essentially contribute.

First of all, and when there was in none of us any fluid developed, we desired to ascertain if it could not be produced by the simple process of mechanical rotation. Applying, then, our hands to the table without forming the chain, we turned it rapidly for nearly a quarter of an hour. We then commanded the table to resume this motion of itself; we commanded it to raise one foot, and although our fingers rested on it the whole time, it was impossible for us to obtain the feeblest movement.

Still more significant was the fact that having formed the chain, but having determined its rotation by the mechanical action of our hands, we were thus able to continue it for a quarter of an hour, without inducing any fluid manifestation; in vain did we address various orders to the table—not one of them was obeyed. We exercised no power over it.

It is consequently clear that the phenomenon is of a mixed nature; that a given position and a circular course are not of themselves sufficient to call it into existence. There must still be another force—the will.

Our wills being finally brought into cooperation with the other powers, and the muscular pressure having ceded its place to the pressure of commands, we produced the fluid rotation after five or six minutes concentration of our thoughts. We clearly felt that we lacked some person of importance, and that we did not possess all our usual power; nevertheless we were determined to overcome the obstacle, even at the price of greater moral fatigue.

The great difficulty, motion without contact, was thus attacked frontally.

The rotations without contact were obtained three times. I should add that they were very incomplete, a quarter or a half revolution at most.

The success of the elevations without contact was more decisive; but it was bought by the expenditure of a very considerable amount of strength. After each elevation we were obliged to take a rest, and when we had reached the figure nine, yielding to lassitude, we were compelled to stop entirely. It is necessary to go through with such experiments in order to know how much attention and energy they exact, to what degree it is indispensable to will, to will absolutely that such a knot in the wood of the table follow the extended fingers that attract it from a distance.

Be that as it may, our attempt was crowned with success, and we felt at liberty to terminate the sitting by exercises less exhausting.

The idea then occurred to us to make the trial on a large table with four feet. It had often been claimed that the round tables with three feet alone lent themselves to our operations; it was time to furnish demonstrative proof to the contrary. We therefore selected a table whose diameter was 3/2 feet, and the half of which, independent of the foot that supported it when drawn out, folded up at will.

Hardly had our fingers touched it, than it surrendered itself with a loud noise to a rotation, the vivacity of which surprised us, thus showing that tables with four feet diameter were not more rebellious than others. It furnished, besides, a new argument in favor of one of our preceding observations; the fluid is in the individuals, not in the tables. Indeed, the motion was produced almost immediately, and before the large table could be considered as charged.

It was afterwards requested to strike blows with its different feet. We began with those that supported the top and one of the leaves; they were three in number. They raised themselves, two by two, with such force as to break one of the casters in splinters ... Now it would be difficult to accept the idea that the intensity of this motion could result from the fraudulent action of the fingers as a lever upon so heavy a piece of inert matter, or that they could impel it to such a height.

It remained to try the foot that was independent of the bed of the table. We thought it would obey as readily as the others; but no! In vain we lavished the most pressing invitations; it did not once consent to rise, whether in company with its neighbor on the right, or whether associated with its neighbor on the left. Supposing that this reluctance might be owing to the persons placed near it, we changed the position of the members of the chain. Useless efforts! All the combinations were doomed to be successively foiled.

We already anticipated an important consequence from this fact. But as it was afterwards proved incorrect, the rebel foot yielding us its perfect obedience on another occasion, I shall not confide our process of reasoning to the public; I will only beg them to remark two things: first, the care which we constantly took to confirm the accuracy of our proofs by repeated experiments; second, the impossibility of having recourse to explanations based on muscular action. This action could have been exercised as easily to raise the foot that was independent of the table, as to raise the feet confined to it; and yet, by the operation of some unknown cause, evidently foreign to all mechanical laws, the latter alone consented to move.

November 28th Sitting

We were all assembled; but two or three of the operators were slightly indisposed. In fact, from some cause or other, the meeting was only remarkable because of the almost total absence of fluid power. For a single moment we had a little half an hour of action, and then two hours and a half of inertia.

I always state the fact as it is; first, out of respect for truth, and also because it seems to me that nothing better refutes the vulgar objections than to show that the same individuals are incapable of constantly obtaining the same results. Their muscles have not changed; their susceptibility is as great; their dexterity in fraud (we need not fear to speak thus) has not vanished, and yet, behold them unable to do that which but a short time previous they had done with extreme facility.

Our wounded victims had been cured; the old table reappeared with its pillar repaired; the large table with four feet was supplied with a new caster. It was with this that we commenced. Inauspicious beginning! That which the other day had whirled and leaped about with so much vigor, now scarcely stirred. And as for inducing either of the feet to strike a single blow, we were compelled to renounce the idea.

Then, passing to the table with three feet, we entered upon our phase of animation, which did not, however, long continue.

Nevertheless, we profited by it to the extent of effecting five elevations without contact. After which, our slender provision of fluid being exhausted, it was no longer possible to effect anything. The rotations without contact, as we had foreseen, were utterly out of the question.

Nothing could be more lamentable and curious at the same time, than to see us sitting round the various tables, passing from one to the other, resorting to all sorts of expedients, and yet unable to obtain more than a languid rotation, which soon ceased entirely.

December 2nd Sitting

I should have been sorry to close the relation of my experience with a report so little brilliant. Happily, the result of our last meeting gives me the right to leave quite a different impression on the mind of the reader.

We were all in excellent spirits; to which the fine weather perhaps contributed, and this is not the first time I have remarked the coincidence. One thing is certain, that the same persons who, on the 27th of November, had obtained but a half-hour of success, passing the rest of the sitting in vainly soliciting for something better than poor, imperfect rotations, or languid blows, ruled the table today with an authority, a promptness, and if I may be allowed the expression, with an elasticity that left nothing to be desired.

The large table, with four feet, had been put in motion, and this time the facility with which the foot at liberty raised its portion of the top, proved that we were right in not drawing from its preceding refusal a too positive conclusion.

We did not succeed in raising this table without contact, or in folding up its movable leaf. None of us were surprised at this, for the weight was very considerable; our attempts, however, were not entirely without fruit, for they brought about a result of which we had not dreamed.

Each time that we endeavored to elevate without contact the portion of the table farthest from me, I felt the foot, whose neighbor I was, gradually approach, and lean itself against my leg. Struck with this fact, which was repeated several times, I inferred from it that the table was sliding forward, in consequence of not having enough force to raise itself. We thus exercised a sensible action upon this large table without touching it in any way.

In order better to assure myself of the fact, I left the chain, and observed the progress of the feet of the table on the floor. It varied from less than an inch to several inches. Having afterwards tried to fold up without contact, the movable leaf of a card table, covered with cloth, we obtained the same result. The top did not yield to our influence, but the whole table was carried forward in the direction of the ordered motion. I should add that it was far from easy for it to slide along thus, for the floor of the hall in which we carried on our experiments is rough and uneven.

It is not less interesting to note here, the moment when the movement usually occurs. It is precisely the same as that in which the elevation without contact takes place whenever it is effected. When the portion of the chain which presses forward is about to pass beyond the edge of the table where it is brought back, and the portion of the chain that draws, is about to pass over it in making a retreat, then is manifested, either the ascensional, or in default of that, the sliding motion. Our fluid power is at its maximum, just at the point where our mechanical power is at its minimum, where the hands that push have ceased to be able to act (supposing fraud is intended), and where the hands that draw cannot yet act.

Returning to the table we generally employed, we tried to produce the rotations and elevations without contact. Our success was complete.

The rotations numbered three. We obtained the elevations, one after another, with the most satisfactory regularity. Setting aside as uncertain four movements which, although real, did not terminate in a complete elevation of the top (even leaving out of consideration two energetic overtures that were separately produced), we effected an uninterrupted series of fourteen elevations, and so emphatic, in general, that we were several times obliged to catch the table thus subdued, in order to prevent its becoming wrecked.

The reader is now as well-acquainted with the results of our sittings as though he had personally assisted at them. I have concealed nothing; I have related the best and the worst, the experiments that were failures, and the experiments crowned with success.

(de Gasparin, 1854/1857, Vol. 1, p. 43–66)

[Added Observations in the Preface]

Some distinguished men of science to whom I communicated the results obtained, were unanimously of the opinion that the elevations without contact would possess the character of absolutely certain proof, provided we could succeed in verifying them by any material process. They said:

Strew some flour over the table the instant the hands are separated from it; in these conditions, cause it to effect one or several elevations; then, if the layer of flour does not bear the impress of fingers, or give any other evidence of having been touched, there can no longer be a word offered in objection to your theory.

Well! we have recently and on several occasion, performed this very experiment. I briefly present a few of the details.

Our first attempts were most unsuccessful. Making use of a coarse sieve, which it was necessary to move about over the entire surface of the table, we met with a double inconvenience; first, of suspending for too long a time, and consequently, annulling the action of the operators; second, our layer of flour was much too thick. The enthusiasm of will was weakened, the fluid action impeded, the ardor of the table diminished; in short, nothing progressed. The effect was even so injurious that the table not only refused elevations and rotations without contact, it almost refused ordinary elevations and rotations.

After a while, a brilliant idea suggested itself to one of the operators. We possessed a pair of bellows, such as are used in sprinkling sulphur over vines infested with *oidium*. Substituting flour for sulphur, we renewed the operation.

> We were in the most favorable conditions; the weather was dry and warm, the table bounded beneath our fingers, and, indeed, before the order to raise the hands was given, the majority of them had spontaneously ceased to touch the table. The command being issued, the entire chain separated from the table, which was, at the same instant, covered by the bellows with a light cloud of flour. Not a second had been lost, the elevation without contact had already taken place, and, in order to leave no doubt in our minds, it was repeated three or four times in succession.
>
> That done, the table was scrupulously examined: It bore not the faintest token of having been touched or even grazed.
>
> The fear of inadvertently touching it was indeed so great among the operators as to cause them to raise their hands much higher from the table than in the previous sittings, without, however, producing any diminution of the fluid action. I should also mention that we resorted to none of the maneuvers, none of the passes of which we had made use at other times. Remaining in its place above the table to be raised, the chain had preserved its form; it had scarcely effected a slight motion in the direction of that which it provoked at a distance.
>
> I add, in conclusion, that we did not rest contented with one experiment. We produced several elevations in succession, at the close of which, a minute examination of the flour that covered every portion of the surface of the table, convinced us that it had been absolutely untouched.[14]
>
> (de Gasparin, 1854/1857, Vol. 1, pp. xix–xxi)

Perspective: Critiques and Influence

De Gasparin wrote about the table movements: "Thus the fact is established. Multiple experiments, various irrefutable proofs, mutually supporting each other, give to fluid action an entire certainty" (de Gasparin, 1857, Volume 1, p. 81). But he also discussed various other things about the séances, such as the use of instruments, psychological conditions, occasional unproductive séances, and the implausibility of the issue of fraud and unconscious movements.

But how did others react to this work? Here, I limit myself to table-turning and not to examinations of other phenomena in different time periods nor to views of de Gasparin's use of the concept of the fluid.[15]

There is no question that de Gasparin's tests can be considered "classic" studies. Castellan (1960, pp. 53–55) opened her chapter about "The Classic Period in Europe" in her brief history of psychical research with this work,[16] which has traditionally been included in older and more recent overviews of these topics (e.g., Podmore, 1902, Vol. 2, pp. 187–188; Inglis, 1992, pp. 218–219).

In addition, de Gasparin's work frequently has been mentioned in encyclopedia entries (e.g., Felton, 1898, p. 673; Sidgwick, 1890, p. 407) and has been summarized in various textbook overviews (e.g., Holms, 1927, pp. 276–277; Richet, 1922, p. 521), as well as in other psychical research books (e.g., de Rochas, 1896, pp. 317–320; Flammarion, 1907, Chap. 6).

Thury (1855) was certainly positive about the work in question. In his view, the experiments at Valleyres established that the will "can act at a distance on inert bodies by means different than muscular action" (p. 11). Students of Spiritism and magnetism were also positive about the séances. One stated that the main aspect of the work was "the evidential constatation, indelible, REAL FACTS ..." (Auguez, 1857, p. 101). Another was also positive, stating he found the work imposing. But he regretted it had little impact on scientists. In summary, "no attention was paid to him [de Gasparin]" (Morin, 1860, p. 378).

In fact, various writers in later years discussed explanations of table-turning and unconscious movements without mention of de Gasparin's work (e.g., Hahn & Thomas, 1883, pp. 286–287; Maira & Benavente, 1887, pp. 204–209; Maury, 1861, pp. 419–424). Two further important examples were French physicist Jacques Babinet (1794–1872) and English physiologist William B. Carpenter (1813–1885), whose writings (or reprints) on the topic published after the appearance of *Des Tables Tournantes* in 1854 did not mention de Gasparin (Babinet, 1856, pp. 9–56, 237–254; Carpenter, 1877, pp. 97–100, 1882, pp. 292–311).

G. Mabru (1858) stated that:

> [if de Gasparin had used] the Faraday apparatus to control his experiments, he would have avoided the trouble of writing two volumes on things which do not exist. He would have seen that the movement of the tables was not due to any supernatural cause, that it comes simply from the impulse of the fingers of the operators. (Mabru, 1858, p. 386)

No mention was made of effects inconsistent with the unconscious movement explanation.

A further example was Joseph Grasset (1849–1918) discussing his model of polygons, consisting of subconscious centers of superior and inferior mental functioning capable of managing cognitive, motor, and other functions, including unconscious movements related to table-turning (Grasset, 1908, pp. 105–111). While Grasset mentioned de Gasparin in relation to the importance of having confidence in the phenomena (p. 110), he did not mention de Gasparin's evidence regarding actual movement of tables, as opposed to coordinated polygonal activity of the sitters pushing the table around.

Skepticism was the tone of the reviewer in *Harper's New Monthly Magazine*. The writer suggested that testimony of sitters would not be convincing to establish facts that science now considers to be in the realm of the supernatural. "The monks who imprisioned Galileo," he wrote, "only evinced the bigotry of common sense. With their light they were entitled to consider him an impostor; and with ours, we laugh at turning tables" (Anonymous, 1857b, p. 772).

Such also was the case of French physician and popularizer of science Louis Figuier (1819–1894), who discussed de Gasparin's studies in the fourth volume of his classic examination of psychic-related topics *Histoire du Merveilleux dans des Temps Modernes* (Figuier, 1860). He started out assuming that the movement of tables without physical contact was not possible and that the phenomena was never produced beyond his small group of sitters. Then he speculated that a too-zealous sitter in the circle produced such phenomena fraudulently. While not doubting the honesty of de Gasparin, he wrote:

> All that can be said is that he saw the movement without contact occur, without being able to recognize the secret engine. But in order to admit the scientific reality of this fact, it should have been reproduced several times, and at will, in later experiments, at the hands of other experimenters. Now this is what has never happened … (Figuier, 1860, p. 306)[17]

The issue of fraud, something discussed by de Gasparin, was also mentioned by others. Although A. Petit d'Ormoy (1856) wrote that de Gasparin's descriptions of the test seemed to exclude some sources of error, it was not impossible to conceive that some sitters played pranks on the others. Another skeptical response came from Adrien Delondre (1857). He started by raising suspicions about the sitters, saying that in situations like those described by de Gasparin there could a strong desire to cheat. Then he argued that the sitters could deceive themselves via unconscious muscular movements, to which he added suggestion and dissociation as complicating factors. While Delondre did not deal with movements without contact, he decided that de Gasparin's rejection of unconscious movements obtained when no one was touching the table led "the astonished to reasonably ask whether such a statement is serious" (p. 21).

Finally, Delondre suggested that sitters may have hallucinated the movements of the table without contact. He preferred "the marvels of hallucination" to "the prodigies of the volitive fluid" (Delondre, 1857, p. 277).

The possibility of fraud was also raised by Frank Podmore (1856–1910), a well-known critic of mediumship and other psychic phenomena. In his book *Studies in Psychical Research*, Podmore stated that de Gasparin did not control well for potential fraud, as some sitters could have used their knees to move the table (Podmore, 1897, p. 47). In a later work, Podmore wrote:

> It will be seen that the results depend for their acceptance on the sufficiency of the precautions taken to exclude action of the hands, feet, knees, and other parts of the person below the table. These precautions appear to me, so far as can be gathered from the scanty records, to have been wholly insufficient. The records of the experiments are extremely brief, and hardly any detailed accounts of individual experiments are given; the names of the assistants nowhere appear; but we learn that the persons present numbered on some occasions as many as twelve, that this number included several servants and children, and that, generally speaking, the children were found to be more successful operators than their elders.[18] Neither de Gasparin nor Thury appear to have sufficiently appreciated the possibilities of unconscious muscular action or of fraud; nor the extreme difficulty of detecting the kind of half-conscious fraud which later experience has shown that children and young persons are prone on such occasions to practise.[19] (Podmore, 1902, Vol. 2, p. 188)

Positive comments came from William Crookes (1832–1919), well-known for his studies of mediums, who mentioned de Gasparin's work as the "only good series of test experiments" of physical phenomena he had found (Crookes, 1874, p. 5). Some later discussions suggest that the work was influential and held in high regard (e.g., de Rochas, 1896, pp. 317–320; Flammarion, 1907, Chap. 6). One writer considered the work to have been conducted under rigorous control and that "the movement of heavy bodies without mechanical contact was recognized, proved, and demonstrated" (Aksakof, 1895, p. 10).

Morin (1854) reviewed *Des Tables Tournantes* in the *Journal du Magnétisme*, praising de Gasparin's scientific spirit. He concluded by saying: "Honor to the courageous athlete who defends with equal energy and talent the rights of reason and truth!" (p. 684).

Two writers confessed that their skepticism was diminished after reading about de Gasparin's séances (Debay, 1854, p. 347; J., 1855). In addition, an author who was critical of de Gasparin's use of the concept of the fluid to explain things such as miracles and spiritualistic phenomena characterized his research with the tables as "scrupulous" and as providing an "incontestable service" for truth (Gougenot de Mousseaux, 1860, p. 253).

Comments also came from American magician and student of the history of magic Henry Ridgely Evans (1861–1949). While he believed that most mediumship was accomplished via tricks, he included in his debunking book *Hours with the Ghosts* the work of de Gasparin (together with the work of Crookes and others) as "a class of cases not ascribable to trickery" (Evans, 1897, p. 207).

Concluding Remarks

De Gasparin's work was ignored by many, particularly by strong defenders of the unconscious movement explanation. While the reports could have been more detailed, something not common at the time, the critics ignored aspects of de Gasparin's results inconsistent with unconscious movements and simple fraud explanations. This is a pattern that has been common in the evaluation of past work, such as that conducted by Crookes and others. While it may be argued that there are issues of interpretation in terms of the evidential strength of séance reports such as the ones discussed here, I would also argue that it is the duty of the critic to criticize keeping the argument close to the evidence, and at least taking into account aspects of the phenomena inconsistent with the critiques.

The assumption here, and again a common one in psychical research, is that there is nothing to consider, no testimony worth credence to support the existence of unconventional psychic action. Carpenter (1853) argued that the testimony of believers was worthless because they were possessed by their own ideas, a form of insanity. Similarly, later versions of this also declared positive testimony in favor of mediumistic phenomena as delusional and the effects of a weak mentality, as discussed by Brown (1983) and Le Maléfan (1999).

To account for the rejection of de Gasparin's work, it has been stated that he "made the mistake of reopening the old controversy of animal magnetism, which had been closed by a final verdict from the Academies" (Sudre, 1962, p. 33). Such association with the magnetic fluid must have certainly been an important factor in the perception of the work as tainted. But other contributing factors to this rejection must be considered. The tables Monroe (2008, Chap. 1) has shown were associated with entertainment and ridicule, not with scientific analysis. Similarly, they were also connected to the development of mediumship in Western societies, and to the spread of American Spiritualism, topics that were not appealing to many people.

Several commentators on de Gasparin's work—Delondre, Figuier, and Podmore—raised the issue of fraud. While this has to be considered, it is important to recognize that there was no actual evidence for such an explanation. But as a consequence of this situation, the work was not generally accepted, something quite common in the history of physical mediumship and other areas of psychical research.

Although by modern standards, de Gasparin's accounts could have been more detailed, his work was an improvement in reporting in terms of providing support for non-conventional explanations. His contribution would have been more valuable, however, if he had reported more séances and had he worked with others in addition to Thury (1855). But I have the impression that de Gasparin, who was not a scientist, did not seem particularly interested in further careful work. In fact, his interests seemed to lay elsewhere. The séances in question take only a short section of his book. His concerns seemed mainly exegetic, as seen in his explanations of miracles and various other phenomena recorded through history in the greater part of the book. Furthermore, he was not only interested in séances. As seen in his biography (Borel, 1879), most of his time after the publication of the tables book seems to have been taken by work and writings about social, religious, and political issues (e.g., de Gasparin, 1861, 1868).

Regardless of evidential considerations, de Gasparin's work was certainly important in many ways. He contributed to rescuing table turning from the casual discussions in the press and popular books, and from the "learned" attempts to reduce all phenomena related to tables to delusion and unconscious muscular movements. It is less clear, however, how influential he was on later studies of table movements (e.g., Crawford, 1916).

Regardless of his lack of further work, de Gasparin, it has been stated recently, upheld "reproducible experimentation" and showed in his work "an empiricist will denouncing prejudices and refusals of examination" (Evrard, 2016, p. 86). Because of this, he raised the bar in various ways in the study of table-turning. This work presented important instances of tests attempting to counter objections empirically, and emphasizing phenomena inconsistent with the unconscious movement explanations of others. While a few conducted tests to see if they could support this hypothesis (e.g., Faraday, 1853a), *many* others just accepted the argument without empirical examination (e.g., Chevreul, 1854).

Even if de Gasparin's work was not successful in countering skepticism at the time, his effort inspired some, like Thury (1855) and Crookes (1874) to conduct later work.[20] In addition, it is probable that it provided an impetus both for the development of then-current ideas of nervous forces and, more important, the empirical approach typical of later developments in psychical research.[21]

Notes

1 For discussions of the topic, see Crabtree (1993, Chap. 12), Figuier (1860, Volume 4, Chaps. 14–17), Gonzalez de Pablo (2006), Monroe (2008, Chap. 1), Nisbet (1973), Podmore (1902, Volume 2, Chap. 1), and Wantuil (circa 1957).

2 Some examples were accounts of knockings and movement of objects in the Friederike Hauffe (1801–1829) case (the famous Seeress of Prevorst, Germany, Kerner 1845), the Angelique Cottin case (France, Tanchou 1846), the Phelps and family case (Stratford, Connecticut; Capron 1855, Chapter 7), and the Cideville case (France; Owen, 1860, pp. 272–283). See also the summaries of cases presented by Owen (1860, Book 3) and Podmore (1902, Volume 1, Chapter 2). Furthermore, the idea of physical phenomena connected to human beings was supported by claims of the influence of animal magnetism on plants and instruments (e.g., Picard, 1845; Rutter, 1851).

3 I have discussed this rich tradition of unorthodox concepts of force—fluids, human radiations, magnetism, and nervous forces—in various papers (e.g., Alvarado, 2006, 2009, 2016; Alvarado & Nahm, 2011). For ideas about animal magnetism, see Gauld (1992).

4 Another writer argued that the tables were affected by a nervous fluid directed by the will. This was the same will and fluid "which puts your fingers in movement when you write, and your legs in action when you walk" (Debay, 1854, p. 355; see also Alvarado, 1981). For some later examples of nervous and vital force speculations, see my papers listed in Note 3 (Alvarado).

5 Faraday's work received much publicity and was reprinted in publications in many countries, such as Australia (Faraday, 1853b), France (Faraday, 1853c), and the United States (Faraday, 1853d). See also Alvarado (2000).

6 In addition to veridical table communications mentioned above, there were other phenomena hardly explained by unconscious movements, among them difficulties in raising a table (Capron & Barron, 1850, p. 69). One author mentioned that a young girl could raise a table, but men and women could not (Tiffany, 1851, p. 200).

7 For biographical information, see Anonymous (1871, pp. 332–333), Borel (1879), N (1871), and Ripley and Dana (1868, p. 104).

8 De Mirville (1855) answered many of the critiques throughout his book *Question des Esprits*. There were other critiques about de Gasparin's remarks about clairvoyant and other phenomena (Almignana, 1889), spirit agency (Hare 1857), and sanctuaries in Palestine (Mislin, 1858, pp. 485–513). An anonymous reviewer of the English translation felt that de Gasparin's comments were testy and lacking in calmness (Anonymous, 1857a). Samson (1860, pp. 175–183) summarizes de Gasparin's arguments to naturalize the supernatural (see also Anonymous, 1857c).

9 It may be argued that de Gasparin's work is also part of nineteenth-century attempts to present overarching interpretations of many phenomena, as seen in the works of Crowe (1848), de Mirville (1854), and Gougenot de Mousseaux (1860).

10 De Gasparin may have been influenced by similar previous discussions of the will in relation to animal magnetism (e.g., Chastenet de Puységur, 1809, p. 247, Deleuze, 1813, Volume 1, p. 90). Others writing about table turning also referred to the directing role of the will (e.g., Roubaud, 1853, p. 39). Rogers (1853, p. 179) argued that the force responsible for phenomena

> is not, as a general rule, controllable by the will; not at all directly, as it is the agent of the unconscious organs, and plays its part automatically, as the organs of the brain are affected. That it is not acted upon, therefore, directly by the will, but indirectly.

11 Silas (1853, pp. 20, 22, 23, 25) presents some possible cases of nervous reactions related to table-turning, but the cause of these reactions is ambiguous at best. Another writer stated that somnambules were the best table turners, followed by persons of nervous and sanguine temperaments (Ogier, 1855, p. 114). Physician Félix Roubaud (1820–1878) (Roubaud, 1853) stated that women in morbid states made tables move more than other sitters (p. 42), and that in rare cases headaches were associated with table turning. But he observed no relationship with nervous or epileptic attacks (p. 92).

12 Crookes (1874, pp. 30, 36) and Hare (1855, Plate 3, pp. 48–49, 51) also used water in some tests.

13 Book tests became an important part of the study of mental mediumship years later (e.g., Thomas, 1922).

14 Ogier (1855, p. 120) wrote that he covered a table with cork sawdust and that it moved without disturbing the dust. For another mention of talc, see Hebert (de Garnay) (1854, p. 84). In a letter sent to Abbot Francois Moigno (1804–1884), chief editor of the popular science magazine *Cosmos*, a professor Stroumbo from the University of Athens (perhaps D. S. Stroumbo) communicated some tests he conducted in which sitters placed their hands on a plate over a table. In a summary of the tests, Moigno (1853, p. 94) wrote that when dust was placed on the plate the table did not move. It was assumed that the dust prevented the adherence of fingers Stroumbo believed was necessary to produce table movements.

15 See Dingwall's (1921) discussion of de Gasparin's fluid in terms of W. G. Crawford's (1921) later work.

16 After mentioning de Gasparin, Castellan summarized aspects of the work of French researchers, among them Camille Flammarion (1842–1925), Albert de Rochas (1837–1914), and Joseph Maxwell (1858–1938).

17 Years later Figuier (n. d., p. 579) repeated his accusation, once again, without presenting supporting evidence. Both the Countess de Gasparin (1889) and Marc Thury (1889) criticized Figuier, arguing he had omitted important information from the séance reports that did not support his assertions.

18 Sidgwick (1890, p. 407) pointed out that de Gasparin did not present the testimony of his sitters.

19 Podmore (1896) wrote earlier on about naughty children and poltergeists.

20 For later work with tables, including physical effects without contact, see Willin (2015).

21 Guy Lyon Playfair, who refereed this paper, pointed out that Kenneth Batcheldor's "work was strongly influenced by de Gasparin's book, of which he had a copy and knew well." It is a matter of speculation how much he was also influenced by other early table-turning literature, as well as by later students of table phenomena such as Crawford (1916).

References

Aksakof, A. (1895). *Animisme et spiritisme.* P. G. Leymarie. (Original work published in German, 1890)

Almignana, Abbé (1889). Du somnambulisme, des tables tournantes et des médiums considérés dans leurs rapports avec la théologie et la physique. *Revue Spirite: Journal d'Études Psychologiques, 32*, 129–137.

Alvarado, C. S. (1981). PK and body movements: A historical—and semantic—note. *Journal of the Society for Psychical Research, 51*,116–118.

Alvarado, C. S. (2000). Introduction to Michael Faraday's essay on table-moving. *International Journal of Parapsychology, 11* (1), 153–163.

Alvarado, C. S. (2006). Human radiations: Concepts of force in mesmerism, spiritualism, and psychical research. *Journal of the Society for Psychical Research, 70,* 138–162.

Alvarado, C. S. (2009). Modern animal magnetism: The work of Alexandre Baréty, Émile Boirac, and Julian Ochorowicz. *Australian Journal of Clinical and Experimental Hypnosis, 37*, 1–15.

Alvarado, C. S. (2016). On psychic forces and doubles: The case of Albert de Rochas. *Journal of Scientific Exploration, 30*, 63–84.

Alvarado, C. S., & Nahm, M. (2011). Psychic phenomena and the vital force: Hereward Carrington on "Vital Energy and Psychical Phenomena." *Journal of the Society for Psychical Research, 75*, 91–103.

Anonymous (1853a, June 18). The mystery of the tables. *Illustrated London News*, pp. 481–482.

Anonymous (1853b). –*Medical Times and Gazette, 6*, 603–604.

Anonymous (1857a, January 20). Review of *Science vs. modern spiritualism. New-York Daily Tribune*, p. 6.

Anonymous (1857b). Table-turning in France. *Harper's New Monthly Magazine, 14*, 767–772.

Anonymous (1857c). Table turning-spiritualism. *United States Magazine, 4*, 296–303.

Anonymous (1871). *The American annual cyclopaedia and register of important events for the year 1871* (Vol. 11). D. Appleton.
Anonymous (no date). *Table moving, its causes and phenomena: With directions how to experiment.* John Wesley.
Auguez, P. (1857). *Les manifestations des esprits.* E. Dentu.
Babinet, [J.] (1854). Des tables tournantes au point de vue de la mécanique et de la physiologie. *Revue des Deux Mondes, 5* (seconde série), 408–419.
Babinet, M. [J.] (1856). *Études et lectures sur les sciences d'observation et leurs applications pratiques* (Vol. 2). Mallet-Bachelier.
Baragnon, P. P. (1853). *Étude du magnétisme animal sous le point de vue d'une exacte pratique, suivie d'un mot sur la rotation des tables* (2nd ed.). Germer-Bailliere.
Barbey-Boissier, C. (1902). *La Comtesse Agénor de Gasparin et sa Famille* (Vol. 2). Plon- Nourrit.
Bersot, E. (1864). *Mesmer et le magnétisme animal: Les Tables tournantes* (3rd ed.). L. Hachette.
Borel, T. (1879). *Le Comte Agénor de Gasparin* (6th ed.). J. Bonhoure.
Braid, J. (1853). *Hypnotic therapeutics, illustrated by cases: With an appendix on table-moving and spirit-rapping.* (Reprint from the 1853 July issue of *The Monthly Journal of Medical Science*).
Brown, E. M. (1983). Neurology and spiritualism in the 1870s. *Bulletin of the History of Medicine, 57*, 563–577.
Capron, E. W. (1855). *ModernSpiritualism: Its facts and fanaticisms, its consistencies and contradictions.* Bela Marsh.
Capron, E. W., & Barron, H. D. (1850). *Singular revelations. Explanation and history of the mysterious communion with spirits, comprehending the rise and progress of the mysterious noises in western New York* (2nd ed.). Capron and Barron.
Carpenter, W. B. (1853). Electro-biology and mesmerism. *Quarterly Review, 93*, 501–557.
Carpenter, W. B. (1877). *Mesmerism, spiritualism, &c.: Historically & scientifically considered, 2 lectures.* Longmans, Green.
Carpenter, W. B. (1882). *Principles of mental physiology* (4th ed.). D. Appleton.
Castellan, Y. (1960). *La Metapsíquica.* Paidos. (Original work published in French, 1955).
Charpignon, J. (1848). *Physiologie, médecine et métaphysiques du magnétisme.* Germer Baillière.
Chastenet de Puységur, A.- M.- J. (1809). *Du magnétisme animal, considéré dans ses rapports avec diverses branches de la physique générale* (2nd ed.). Cellot.
Chevillard, A. (1869). *Études expérimentales sur le fluide nerveux et solution définitive du problème spirite.* Victor Masson.
Chevreul, M. E. (1854). *De la baguette divinatoire, du pendule dit explorateur et des tables tournantes au point de vue de l'histoire de la critique et de la méthode expérimentale.* Mallet-Bachelier.
Crabtree, A. (1993). *From Mesmer to Freud: Magnetic sleep and the roots of psychological healing.* Yale University Press.
Crawford, W. J. (1916). *The reality of psychic phenomena: Raps, levitations, etc.* John M. Watkins.
Crawford, W. J. (1921). *The psychic structures at the Goligher Circle.* E. P. Dutton.
Crookes, W. (1874). *Researches in the phenomena of spiritualism.* J. Burns.
Crowe, C. (1848). *The night-side of nature, or ghosts and ghost seers* (2 vols.). T. C. Newby.
D. M. (1853). Mesas giratorias. *Boletín de Medicina, Cirugía y Farmacia, 3*, 190.
Debay, A. (1854). *Les mystères du sommeil et du magnétisme; ou, Physiologie anecdotique du somnambulisme naturel et magnétique* (5th ed.). E. Dentu.
de Gasparin, A. (1839). *De l'affranchissement des esclaves et de ses rapports avec la politique actuelle.* Joubert.
de Gasparin, Compte A. (1843). *Intérêts généraux du Protestantisme Français.* L. R. Delay.
de Gasparin, A. (1853a, August 30). Au rédacteur. *Journal des Débats*, pp. 1–2.
de Gasparin, A. (1853b, November 26). Correspondance. *L'Illustration: Journal Universel*, p. 351.
de Gasparin, Cte A. (1854). *Des tables tournantes: Du surnaturel en général et des esprits* (2 vols.). E. Dentu.
de Gasparin, A. (1857). *Science vs. modern spiritualism: A treatise on turning tables, the supernatural in general, and spirits* (2 vols.). Kiggins & Kellogg.
de Gasparin, A. (1861). *Les États-Unis en 1861: Un grand peuple qui se relève.* Michel Lévy.
de Gasparin, Cte A. (1862). *L'Amérique devant l'Europe: Principes et intérêts.* Michel Lévy.

de Gasparin, Cte A. (1868). *La liberté morale* (2 vols.). Michel Lévy.

de Gasparin, Cte A. (1869). *L'égalité* (2nd ed.). Michel Lévy.

de Gasparin, Cte A. (1889a). *Les tables tournantes* (4th vol.). Calmann Lévy.

de Gasparin, Ctesse A. (1889). Au lecteur. In A. de Gasparin, *Les tables tournantes* (4th ed., pp. i–ix). Calmann Lévy

Deleuze, J. P. F. (1813). *Histoire critique du magnétisme animal* (Vol. 1). Mame.

Delgras, M. (1853). Nuevo descubrimiento magnético. *Boletín de Medicina, Cirugía y Farmacia, 3,* 157–158.

Delondre, A. (1857). La magie et les magiciens au XIXme siècle. *Revue Contemporaine et Athenaeum Française, 32,* 5–32, 251–284.

de Mirville, J. E. (1854). *Pneumatologie: Des esprits et de leurs manifestations fluidiques* (3rd ed.). H. Vrayet de Surcy.

de Mirville, J. E. (1855). *Question des esprits: Ses progrès dans la science.* Delaroque.

Dendy, W. C. (1841). *The philosophy of mystery.* Longmans, Orme, Brown, Green & Longmans.

de Rochas, A. (1896). *L'exteriorisation de la motricite: Recueil d'experiences et d'observations.* Chamuel.

Dibdin, B. W. (1853, November 8). *A lecture by the Rev. B. W. Dibdin. M. A. Delivered in the Music-Hall, Store Street, on Tuesday evening.* J. W. Alexander Esq., Chairman

Dingwall, E. J. (1921). De Gasparin's experiments in the light of recent research. *Journal of the American Society for Psychical Research, 15,* 370–377.

Doré, G., & Paulin (1853, May 21). Les tables et les têtes tournantes. *Le Journal pour Rire,* p. 1.

Du Potet, Baron (1853). [Editorial comments]. *Journal du Magnétisme, 12,* 580–582.

Edmonds, J. W., & Dexter, G. T. (1853). *Spiritualism.* Partridge & Brittan.

Elliotson, J. (1853). The departed spirits. *Zoist: A Journal of Cerebral Physiology & Mesmerism, 11,* 191–201.

Evans, H. R. (1897). *Hours with the ghosts: Or nineteenth century witchcraft.* Laird & Lee.

Evrard, R. (2016). *Enquête sur 150 ans de parapsychologie: La légende de l'esprit.* Escalquens, Trajectoire.

Faraday, M. (1853a). Professor Faraday on table-moving. *The Athenaeum: Journal of Literature, Science, and the Fine Arts, 1340,* 801–803.

Faraday, M. (1853b, October 10). Professor Faraday on table turning. *Courier* (Tasmania), p. 3.

Faraday, M. (1853c, July 9). Recherches expérimentales sur les tables tournantes, *L'Illustration: Journal Universel,* 27.

Faraday, M. (1853d, August 20). Table turning. *Opelousas Courier* (Louisiana), p. 2.

Felton, T. C. (1898). Spiritualism. In C. K. Adams (Ed.), *Johnson's universal cyclopedia* (Vol. 7, pp. 672–673) D. Appleton.

Figuier, L. (1860). *Histoire du merveilleux dans les temps modernes* (Vol. 4). L. Hachette.

Figuier, L. (n. d.). *Les mystères de la science: Aujour d'hui.* Librairie Illustrée.

Flammarion, C. (1907). *Mysterious psychic forces.* Small, Maynard.

Gathy, A. (1853). Faits et expériences: 2. Électro-magnétisme. *Journal du Magnétisme, 12,* 183–186.

Gauld, A. (1992). *A history of hypnotism.* Cambridge University Press.

Gilman, D. C., Peck, H. T., & Colby, F. M. (1907). *The international encyclopaedia* (Vol. 8). Dodd, Mead.

Gimeno, J. (2015). Shortage of rabbits or insufficient traps? Table-turning and the discovery of a presumably PK-gifted person in Argentina. *Journal of Scientific Exploration, 29,* 585–600.

Godfrey, N. S. (1853). *Table-moving tested, and proved to be the result of satanic agency.* Sealeys.

González de Pablo, A. (2006). Sobre los inicios del espiritismo en España: La epidemia psíquica de las mesas giratorias de 1853 en la prensa médica. *Asclepio: Revista de Historia de la Medicina y de la Ciencia, 58,* 63–96.

Gougenot de Mousseaux, R. (1860). *La magie au dix-neuvième siècle: Ses agents, ses vérités, ses mensonges.* E. Dentu.

Grasset, J. (1908). *L'occultisme hier et aujourd'hui: Le merveilleux pré-scientifique* (2nd ed.). Coulet et Fils.

Gutierez, G., & Maillard, N. (2004). *Les aventuriers de l'esprit: Une histoire de la parapsychologie.* Presses du Châtelet.

Hahn, L., & Thomas, L. (1883). Spiritisme. In A. Dechambre (Ed.), *Dictionnaire encyclopédique des sciences médicales* (Vol. 11, pp. 277–294). P. Asselin.

Hare, R. (1855). *Experimental investigation of the spirit manifestations.* Partridge & Brittan.

Hare, Dr. [R.] (1857, April 18). The principles of nature: Strictures on the work of Count de Gasparin, entitled "Science versus spiritualism; or a treatise on turning tables." *Banner of Light,* 401–403.

Hébert (de Garnay) (1854). Controverses: 2. Tables tournantes. *Journal du Magnétisme, 13*, 83–84.
Holms, A. C. (1927). *The facts of psychic science and philosophy*. Occult Press. (Original work published 1925)
Inglis, B. (1992). *Natural and supernatural: A history of the paranormal from earliest times to 1914* (Rev. ed.). Prism Press.
J., R. (1855). Review of *Des tables tournantes*. *Revue Franco-Italienne, 2*(1), 4.
Kardec, A. (1859). Les tables volantes. *Revue Spirite: Journal d'Études Psychologiques, 2*, 229–230.
Kardec, A. (1862). *Spiritisme expérimental: Le livre des médiums* (2nd ed.). Didier.
Kendall, Mr. (1853, September 15). The rappers in trouble. *Planter's Banner* (Louisiana), p. 1.
Kerner, J. (1845). *The seeress of Prevorst: Being revelations concerning the inner-life of man*. J. C. Moore. (Abridged translation of Kerner's *Die Seherin von Prevorst,* 1829)
Le Maléfan, P. (1999). *Folie et spiritisme: Histoire du discourse psychopathologique sur la P-pratique du spiritisme, ses abords et ses avatars (1850–1950)*. L'Harmattan.
Mabru, G., (1858). *Les magnétiseurs jugés par eux mêmes: Nouvelle enquête sur le magnétisme animal.* Mallet-Bachelier.
Mahan, A. (1855). *Modern mysteries explained and exposed in four parts*. J. P. Jewett.
Maira, O., & Benavente, D. (1887). *Hipnotismo y sugestión.* Imprenta Nacional.
Maury, L. F. A. (1861). *Le aommeil et les rêves*. Didier.
Mislin, Mgr. (1858). *Les saints lieux: Pèlerinage à Jérusalem* (Vol. 3). Jacques Lecoffre.
Moigno, F. (1853). Tables tournantes. *Cosmos: Revue Encyclopédique Hebdomadaire des Progrès des Sciences, 3*, 92–101.
Monroe, J. W. (2008). *Laboratories of faith: Mesmerism, spiritism, and occultism in modern France*. Cornell University Press.
Morin, A. S. (1854). Review of *Des tables tournantes*. *Journal du Magnétisme, 13*, 674–684
Morin, A. S. (1860). *Du magnétisme et des sciences occultes.* Germer Baillière.
N, A. (1871, May 16). Le Compte Agénor de Gasparin. *Journal de Genève*, p. 1.
Newnham, W. (1830). *Essay n superstition; Being an inquiry into the effects of physical influence on the mind, in the production of dreams, visions, ghosts, and other supernatural appearances*. J. Hatchard and Son.
Nicol, J. F. (1977). Historical background. In B. B. Wolman, L. A. Dale, G. R. Schmeidler, & M. Ullman (Eds.), *Handbook of parapsychology* (pp. 305–323). Van Nostrand Reinhold.
Nisbet, B. (1973). Table turning: A brief historical note mainly for the period 1848–1853. *Journal of the Society for Psychical Research, 47*, 96–106.
Ogier (1855). Des tables tournantes et des divers phénomènes qui s'y rattachent. *Journal du Magnétisme, 14*, 113–124.
Oldfield, T. [pseudonym of G. W. Samson] (1852). *"To Daimonion," or, the spiritual medium*. Gould and Lincoln.
Orioli, F. (1853. *Delle Tavole e degli altri corpi giranti per l'applicazione delle mani a cert speciali modi.* Rome: Tipografi e Legale.
Owen, R. D. (1860). *Footfalls on the boundary of another world: With narrative illustrations*. J. B. Lippincott.
Petit d'Ormoy, A. (1856). De la nouvelle direction au journal. *Journal du Magnétisme, 15*, 85–105.
Picard, Dr. (1845). Application du magnétisme aux végétaux. *Journal du Magnétisme, 1*, 477–480.
Podmore, F. (1896). Poltergeists. *Proceedings of the Society for Psychical Research, 12*, 45–115.
Podmore, F. (1897). *Studies in psychical research.* G. P. Putman's Sons.
Podmore, F. (1902). *Modern spiritualism: A history and a criticism* (2 vols.). Methuen.
Richet, C. (1922). *Traité de métapsychique*. Félix Alcan.
Ripley, G., & Dana, C. A. (Eds.). (1868). *The new American cyclopaedia: A popular dictionary of general knowledge* (Vol. 8). D. Appleton.
Robinson, D. (1981). *To stretch a plank: A survey of psychokinesis*. Nelson-Hall.
Rogers, E. C. (1853). *Philosophy of mysterious agents, human and mundane; or, the dynamic laws and relations of man*. J. P. Jewett.
Roubaud, F. (1853). *La danse des tables: Phénomènes physiologiques démonstrés.* Librairie Nouvelle.
Rutter, J. O. N. (1851). *Magnetoid currents, their forces and directions; with a description of the magnetoscope: A series of experiments.* J. W. Parker & Son.

Samson, G. W. (1860). *Spiritualism tested, or, the facts of its history classified, and their cause in nature verified from ancient and modern testimonies.* Gould and Lincoln.

Seguin, M. (1853). Expériences relatives à la faculté attribuée aux êtres animés de développer, dans des corps inertes, une électricité particulière. *Compte Rendu Hebdomadaires des Séances de l'Académie des Sciences, 36*, 890–893.

Sidgwick, E. M. (1890). Spiritualism. In *Encyclopaedia Britannica: A dictionary of arts, sciences and general literature* (9th ed., Vol. 22; pp. 404–407). Henry G. Allen.

Silas, F. (1853). *Instruction explicative et pratique des tables tournantes: D'après les publications Allemandes, Américaines, et les extraits des journaux Allemands, Français et Américains* (3rd ed.). A. Houssiaux.

Simon, G. (1923). *Chez Victor Hugo: Les tables tournantes de Jersey: Procès-verbaux des séances.* Louis Conard.

Sudre, R. (1962). *Parapsychology*. Grove Press. (Original work published in French, 1956).

Tanchou, Dr. [S.] (1846). *Enquête sur l'authenticité des phénomènes électriques d'Angelique Cottin.* Germer Baillière.

Terzaghi, G. (1853). *Sulla potenza motrice transfuse dall'uomo nella materia bruta: Fenomeno comunemente noto sotto il titulo di tavola girante.* Gugleilmini.

Thomas, C. D. (1922). *Some new evidence for human survival.* W. Collins & Son.

Thury, M. (1855). *Les tables tournantes considérées au point de vue de la question de physique générale qui s'y rattache, le livre de M. le Comte A. de Gasparin et les expériences de Valleyres.* J. Kessman.

Thury, M. (1889). Trente ans après. In A. de Gasparin (Ed.), *Les tables ournantes* (4th ed., pp. 291–303). Calmann Lévy.

Tiffany, J. (1851). *Lectures on spiritualism.* J. Tiffany.

Wantuil, Z. (circa 1957). *As mesas girantes e o espiritismo.* Federação Espirita Brasileira.

Wharton, W. D. (1853, July 30). Professor Faraday and table moving. *Sunbury American*, p. 1.

Willin, M. (2015). Table turning. In R. McLuhan (Ed.), *Psi encyclopedia*, Society for Psychical Research.

20

The Influence of Reichenbach's Concept of Od*

Carlos S. Alvarado

Michael Nahm's (2012) recent article about Reichenbach and his concept of Od reminds us of important work done in the past that has been forgotten by many current students of psychic phenomena and related topics. I find particularly interesting how the concept of Od influenced a variety of conceptual developments, something I would like to briefly discuss in this Commentary. While Nahm is aware of this, and addresses the issue briefly, he appropriately in my view did not make this the focus of this paper because his purpose was a general overview of Reichenbach for the modern reader.

One of the main influences of Reichenbach was how his work was used by others to develop and support the development of unorthodox concepts of force in relation to psychic phenomena, a model that existed before in the mesmeric movement and in other contexts. A prominent example of this was how Reichenbach's Od was one of the inspiring factors behind the development of ideas of forces to explain physical manifestations such as those associated with mediums during the beginnings of spiritualism. This is clearly seen in American books published during the 1850s in which various authors speculated on the powers of the living medium to explain various mediumistic manifestations. A prominent one was Edward C. Rogers's (1853) *Philosophy of Mysterious Agents, Human and Mundane*. Reichenbach's work was used by Rogers repeatedly throughout the book to justify his acceptance of the existence of a new force associated with the nervous system. This was basically a biophysical force coming from the bodies of mediums and others, an idea that allowed him to apply the concept of a non-spirit-based agency to explain spiritualistic manifestations such as movement of objects, raps, and luminous effects. He wrote in his Introduction:

> In our researches with regard to the phenomena treated in the following pages, we have found so many of the characteristics of an agent differing so essentially from those of Electricity and Magnetism proper, and bearing so many of the characteristics of identity with the Odyle of Reichenbach, that *we* feel forced to admit this identity. (Rogers, 1853, pp. 20–21)

Rogers also used Reichenbach as a guide to analyze several cases, such as the so-called electrical girl Angelique Cottin, a once-well-known poltergeist case, in whose presence objects were reported to move (Owen, 1864; Tanchou, 1846). In his view, the attraction and repulsion phenomena of Cottin followed Reichenbach's ideas of polarity. He also related Od to the phenomena of the divining rod (p. 272).

The concept of Od was also important to support the notion of forces responsible for mediumistic phenomena in other writings (e.g., Guppy, 1863, Mahan, 1855). An interesting example of the centrality of Od in speculations of this sort were the ideas of physician B. W. Richmond (1853) presented in his book with Samuel B. Brittan *A Discussion of the Facts and Philosophy of Ancient and Modern Spiritualism*.

*Republished with permission from *Journal of Scientific Exploration, 27*, 111–115, 2013.

> The Od-force of Reichenbach [wrote Richmond] comes to our aid in the "modern mysteries." It is an imponderable fluid. The human body having it in abundance transmits it to inanimate matter—the human will having control over it—as easily grasps and impels it, when chairs and tables have been charged with it, as when a muscle or a nerve has been charged with it. (Brittan & Richmond, 1853, p. 70)

Such influences were not limited to the United States. Od made its way to the writings of individuals in other countries. Examples in England and in Germany were Herbert Mayo (1851) and Carl du Prel (1899/1907), respectively. The latter, who was discussing the subject in the later part of the nineteenth century, believed that: "The key of magic is in animal magnetism, what Reichenbach has designated with the name of *od.* It is the *physics of magic* ..." (p. 13). In his view Od accounted for psychic phenomena and other manifestations.

The influence of Reichenbach was also evident in France in the work of Albert de Rochas. In fact, de Rochas greatly popularized Reichenbach's work in France in several books (de Rochas 1887, pp. 45–50, 1891, 1895, pp. 2–5, 189–190). A presentation of Reichenbach's lectures was preceded by various essays authored by de Rochas introducing the Baron and presenting a discussion of those who conducted work relevant to his.

Like Reichenbach, de Rochas believed Od was a vital principle related to the human body. He wrote in *Le Fluide des Magnetiseurs*:

> The odic movement, called a *current*, comes mainly from the brain, descends down through the nerves of the face and goes to its corresponding branches. Finally, it is exhaled in the air, rendered sensible by impressions of heat and cold that it causes on the sensitives, is made visible in the form of effluvia in plain day, and as lights in darkness. The whole body seems bright; the head seems to have an aureole; the hands, the fingers, and the toes throw long streams of odic light. (de Rochas 1891, p. 104)

Reichenbach's Od was an important part of the context in which de Rochas (1895) conducted his well-known studies of the exteriorization of sensibility. In a later work entitled *Les Frontieres de la Science,* de Rochas (1902) discussed the concept of a psychic force and Reichenbach's work and referred to him as "the man who is, without any possible comparison, the one who has studied the issue with the most care and talent" (de Rochas, 1902, p. 29). He organized the discussion of psychic forces in sections about the precursors of Reichenbach, Reichenbach's work, and Reichenbach's successors. Interestingly, de Rochas also related Od to the astral double (de Rochas, 1906).

Spiritualists received the gospel of Od in different ways. Some were not convinced that it had the explanatory power to account for spiritualistic manifestations in the way Rogers, Mahan, and others suggested, as was the case of Samuel B. Brittan (Brittan & Richmond, 1853). Others had different views. One of them stated:

> Mediumship seems to depend upon the presence in, and evolution from, the persons of its subjects, of a very subtle fluid—that which the German Von Reichenbach calls "human-od." When this "od" is electrical or negative, the party becomes a rapper or "physical medium." When it is positive or magnetic, the subject is a trance or mental medium of some sort ... (Randolph, 1860, p. 27)

John W. Edmonds wrote about the existence of an electric body, a principle bridging the soul and the physical body. According to Edmonds: "In the earth-life its presence is manifested by that odic light of which Reichenbach speaks ..." (Edmonds, 1874, p. 119).

In later years, French spiritist Gabriel Delanne (1900) discussed Reichenbach's Od. He implied that such a principle was consistent with spiritist teachings. In particular he referred to the idea that spirits of the dead cannot act on matter without taking the "necessary force from a living being" (Delanne, 1900, p. 641). This force, Delanne said, was visible to "the *sensitives* discovered by Baron Reichenbach, and by some magnetic or hypnotic subjects" (Delanne, 1900, p. 641).

Reichenbach's work served yet another function. A small group of people utilized Reichenbach's work to argue for the power of the mind to create illusory phenomena, a topic discussed before in relation to mesmerism and other phenomena. The individuals in question saw the performances of Reichenbach's sensitives as the product of suggestion and expectation. This was the case of James Braid in *The Power of the Mind Over the Body* (1846). As he wrote:

> But it is an undoubted fact that with many individuals, and especially of the highly nervous, and imaginative, and abstractive classes, a strong direction of inward consciousness to any part of the body, especially if attended with the expectation or belief of something being about to happen, is quite sufficient to *change the physical action of the part, and to produce such impressions from this cause alone, as Baron Reichenbach attributes to his new force*. Thus every variety of feeling may be excited from an *internal* or *mental* cause. (Braid, 1846, p. 6)

Later writers—Thomas Laycock (1851, p. 389), William A. Hammond (1870, p. 240), and Willliam B. Carpenter (1877, p. 31), among others—presented variations of Braid's ideas assuming the influence of suggestion and expectation. Henri Beaunis (1884) stated that Reichenbach's tests showed the "influence of imagination, or, better, of a dominant idea in the production of sensations" (p. 197). However, the discussions presented by those men were less detailed than Braid's.

In summary, like the theoretical construct of animal magnetism, Reichenbach's concept of Od had many influences and uses. It provided the basis for speculation about a physical force to account for spiritualistic phenomena, and it inspired many to develop the idea of imagination to account for the unexplained perceptions of luminosities. The discussions and reactions to the concept of Od affected the conceptual development of spiritualism and psychical research.

References

Beaunis, H. (1884). *Recherches expérimentales sur les conditions de l'activité cérébrale et sur la physiologie des nerfs* (Vol. 1). J. B. Bailliere.

Braid, J. (1846). *The power of the mind over the body: An experimental inquiry into the nature and cause of the phenomena attributed by Baron Reichenbach and others to a "new imponderable."* John Churchill.

Brittan, S. B., & Richmond, B. W. (1853). *A discussion of the facts and philosophy of ancient and modern spiritualism*. Partridge & Brittan.

Carpenter W. B. (1877). *Mesmerism, spiritualism, &c.: Historically & scientifically considered.* Longmans, Green.

Delanne, G. (1900). Les recherches de Reichenbach et la science moderne. *Revue Scientifique & Morale du Spiritisme*, *5*, 641-648.

de Rochas, A. (1887). *Les forces non définies: Recherches historiques et expérimentales.* G. Masson.

de Rochas, A. (1891). *Le fluide des magnétiseurs*. Georges Carré.

de Rochas, A. (1895). *L'extériorisation de la sensibilité: Étude expérimentale et historique*. Chamuel.

de Rochas, A. (1902). *Les frontières de la science*. Librairie des Sciences Psychologiques.

de Rochas, A. (1906). New experiments relative to the astral body and magnetic "rapport." *Annals of Psychical Science*, *4*, 120–125.

du Prel, C. (1907). *La magie: Science naturelle*. H. Vaillant-Carmanne. (Original work published in German, 1899)

Edmonds, J. W. (1874). *Letters and tracts on spiritualism* (J. Burns, Ed.). J. Burns.

[Guppy, S.] (1863). *Mary Jane; or, spiritualism chemically explained.* John King.

Hammond, W. A. (1870). The physics and physiology of spiritualism. *North American Review, 110*, 233–260.

Laycock, T. (1851). Odyle, mesmerism, electro-biology, & etc. *British and Foreign Medico-Chirurgical Review, 8*, 378–431.

Mahan, A. (1855). *Modern mysteries explained and exposed in four parts*. J. P. Jewett.

Mayo, H. (1851). *On the truths contained in popular superstitions* (3rd ed.). William Blackwood.

Nahm, M. (2012). The sorcerer of Cobenzl and his legacy: The life of Baron Karl Ludwig von Reichenbach, his work and its aftermath. *Journal of Scientific Exploration, 26*, 381–407.

Owen, R. D. (1864). The electric girl of La Perrière. *Atlantic Monthly, 14*, 284–292.

Randolph, P. B. (1860). *The unveiling: Or what I think of spiritualism*. William H. Husc.

Rogers, E. C. (1853). *Philosophy of mysterious agents, human and mundane*. J. P. Jewett.

Tanchou, S. (1846). *Enquête sur l'authenticité des phénomènes électriques d'Angélique Cottin.* Germer Baillère.

On First Volumes and Beginnings in the Study of Psychic Phenomena: Varieties of Investigative Approaches

Revue Spirite: Journal d'Études Psychologiques (1858), *Proceedings of the Society for Psychical Research*, (1882–1883), and *Journal of Parapsychology* (1937)*

Carlos S. Alvarado†

Much has been written about the various existing research styles and approaches in science. An example is Alistair Crombie's *Styles of Scientific Thinking in the European Tradition* (1994), in which the author presented a widely cited classification that included axiomatic, experimental, and taxonomic approaches to the study of nature, among others (*see also* Kwa, 2005/2011). Similarly, many approaches coexisted during the nineteenth century in the study of the human experience, as seen in the field of psychology. This brought debates and conflicts between case and experimental studies, as seen in the German and French traditions, respectively (Carroy & Schmidgen 2006), and between the use of introspection and studies based on the study of observable phenomena (Brooks 1998). As Danzinger (1990) has argued, the situation was not simply one of differing approaches, but also one of different assumptions and different social research styles and practices.

A similar situation and the topic of this essay review is the different approaches in the study of psychic phenomena over time. The purpose of this essay review is to introduce to modern readers some of these approaches in the forms of summaries of the contents of three different journals from the past. These are comments about the first volumes of influential publications concerned with the study of psychic phenomena that are probably not familiar to current students of psychic phenomena. Consequently, I hope this essay review will inform the readers [of the *Journal of Scientific Exploration*] about aspects of the beginnings of these publications and about the beginnings of specific research styles, thus providing a more complete historical perspective of the history of research of psychic phenomena that is generally lacking in non-specialists.

To accomplish this, I could have selected a variety of journals representing different methodological approaches to psychic phenomena, some of which have been discussed elsewhere (Alvarado, Biondi, & Kramer, 2006). I have focused only on three for two main reasons. First, and for practical considerations, this review would be too long if other journals—publications such as *Annales des Sciences Psychiques*, *Journal of the American Society for Psychical Research*, *Light*, *Luce e Ombra*, *Psychische Studien*, or the *Revue Métapsychique*—had been included. Second, I feel that the publications I review below—the *Revue Spirite*, the *Proceedings of the Society for Psychical Research*, and *The Journal of Parapsychology*—represent well the various approaches to the study of psychic

*Republished with permission from *Journal of Scientific Exploration*, *29*, 131–153, 2015.
†I am grateful to the Society for Psychical Research for financial support.

phenomena. These were foundational journals that clearly articulated the approaches discussed below, and which influence comes to our own time, although the latter topic is not discussed in any detail.

As mentioned before, my comments are limited to the beginnings of the journals and not to their development, nor to their content and philosophy in later years. Rather than a general study of the journals in question, I am merely presenting some comments about what they represented when they started.

Revue Spirite: Journal d'Études Psychologiques

"It is a 'sign of the times' …," wrote an anonymous author in *The Spectator*, published in London, "that a 'Revue Spirite', containing reports of table turning, spirit-rapping, and other like manifestations, has been recently established at Paris" (Anonymous 1859). The *Revue Spirite: Journal d'Études Psychologiques* was founded by the French educator Hippolyte Leon Denizard Rivail (1804–1869), better known by his pseudonym Allan Kardec, to help spread the movement of spiritism, which has received some scholarly attention in recent decades.[1] Together with several books that were reprinted many times (e.g., Kardec 1857, 1861), the *Revue* allowed Kardec to organize spiritism in France and to develop its basic tenets. This took place through the publication of multiple topics such as mediumistic communications and through discussions of phenomena, their cause, and the progress and development of the movement.

Kardec explained in his "Introduction" (pp. 1–6) to the volume why the expression psychological studies was part of the title of the *Revue*:

> Our scope … includes everything connected to knowledge about the metaphysical part of man; we will study it in its present state and in its future state, because studying the nature of Spirits, is to study man, since one day he will form part of the world of Spirits: This is why we have added to our main title the one of journal of psychological studies so as to include the whole range. (p. 6, this and other translations are mine).

This grandiose view of spiritism, an overall philosophy of life and death, was elaborated on by others, including an author who wrote years later:

> What is Spiritism? It is the revelation of the history of man, with its relations to various elements of creation; it is the justification of the place that the Creator has impressed on the chain of beings; it is psychology illuminated by revelation. Philosophy directs us to Spiritism, and Spiritism brings us back to philosophy. (Bonnamy, 1868, p.1)

The title of the journal also illustrated how spiritists during the nineteenth century and later used the terms *psychology* and *psychological* to refer to spiritism (e.g., Kardec 1857, p.79; see also the use of *physiological psychology* and *experimental psychology* by Delanne 1897, 1901). This usage represented many things, among them attempts to expand the scope of psychology, to bring spiritism into the academic disciplines that studied human beings, and to legitimize the topic.

Kardec stated in his Introduction that spiritism was not an empirical science in the same way that other disciplines used the term, but that it was a science more in the philosophical sense. The movement, he wrote, had the beginnings of a science in its attempts to deduce explanatory principles. After all, Kardec stated, facts alone do not form a science, "science is born from the coordination and the logical deduction of facts" (p. 3). The main deduction and the most important implications of the phenomena were for Kardec "the communication that men can establish with beings of an incorporeal world" (p. 4). But he also appreciated the philosophical and moral consequences of the movement.

In his view spiritist doctrine presented humankind with the "only possible and rational solution of a multitude of moral and anthropological phenomena which we witness daily …" (p. 5).

One way in which spiritism was not like the sciences was the sources of information used. While nineteenth century science, like all science, was not based solely on facts, it had a strong component of work based on observations of the natural world, as seen in astronomy and geology, and on experiment, as seen in physics. But spiritism, as presented in the first volume of the *Revue*, and elsewhere, was based on revelatory "truth" coming from the spirits. That is, most of Kardec's efforts were in organizing knowledge given by mediums, as opposed to the more direct observations of nature used by others. A good part of his work was the compilation of the teachings of the spirits, many of which consisted of answers to questions presented to and answered by mediums.

The way this was done was briefly described in Kardec's *Le Livre des Esprits* (1857), which first edition appeared before the *Revue* was published. Kardec stated in the book that the principles discussed came from the spirits in answer to questions, or from spontaneously given communications. Furthermore, Kardec wrote: "Everything was coordinated so as to present a regular and methodical ensemble and has been made public after having been carefully reviewed many times and corrected by the spirits themselves" (Kardec, 1857, p. 31). The topic was briefly discussed in the *Revue* in an article entitled "Différents Ordres d'Esprits" (Different Orders of Spirits, pp. 37–44), which, like most articles in the journal, did not have a particular author. Here it was stated that the work reported in the *Revue* was done following the classification approaches of Linnaeus and others. We are told that spirits were not invented, but that their messages were classified by their similarities (p. 38).

The definition of empirical in the *Revue* comes from the fact that information was taken from the above-mentioned sources, but it did not carry any systematic verification. The volume of the *Revue* is full of non-evidential communications that will not impress most serious students of psychical research. Examples of this throughout the volume were communications from St. Louis (pp. 55–56), potter and ceramicist Bernard Palissy (pp. 108–114), Pasha Mehmet-Ali (pp. 114–117), Mozart (pp. 137–142), Louis XI (pp. 144–145), St. Vincent of Paul (pp. 215–218), as well as from an executed murderer (pp. 79–81), an insane person (pp. 164–166), and a suicide (pp. 166–168).

Almost all of these communications referred to spiritual, philosophical, and moral issues. Two examples were those received through Ermance Dufaux (b. 1841), a young medium who specialized in evoking famous historical figures (Dufaux 1855). The *Revue* contains transcriptions of her written communications about topics such as avarice (pp. 55–56) and pride (pp. 132–133). There were also summaries of Dufaux's writings conveying messages from Jeanne d'Arc (ca 1412–1431, p. 32) and King Louis XI (1423–1483, pp. 73–75).

An example of a communication appeared in "Entretiens d'Outre-Tombe" (Interviews from Beyond the Grave, pp. 57–58). The communicating spirit, frequently evoked by her family, was Miss Clary D., who died in 1850 when she was 13 years old. In a séance dated January 12, 1857, they communicated with her through her medium brother. The following is part of the transcribed proceedings (p. 57). Q. and R. stand for question and reply:

Q. Do you have a precise recollection of your corporeal existence?
R. The spirit sees the present, the past, and a little of the future depending on its perfection and its closeness to God.
Q. This condition of perfection is only about the future, or does this also relate to the present and to the past?
R. The spirit sees the future more clearly as it gets closer to God. After death the soul's sight is embraced by a glance at all its past emigrations, but she cannot see what God has prepared …

Q. Do you know when you will reincarnate?
R. In 10 years or in 100 years.
Q. Will it be on this earth?
R. In another world.

As mentioned before, some communications were valued for their content with no external verification other than similarities in content between communications. In a two-page paper entitled "Utilité de Certaines Évocations Particulières" (Utility of Some Particular Evocations, pp. 77-78), it was stated that these messages were valuable because the spirits in question "have acquired a high degree of perfection" (p. 77) that allowed them to "penetrate the mysteries that exceed the vulgar reach of humanity. ..." (p. 78).

There are also some interesting discussions of spirit life on other planets that illuminate the degree of critical spirit prevalent in this publication.[2] In one article entitled "Des Habitations de la Planète Jupiter" (Dwellings on Planet Jupiter, pp. 223–232), playwright Victorien Sardou (1831–1908) mentioned communications and drawings he received from Bernard Palissy (1510–1590) and Wolfgang Amadeus Mozart (1756–1791), who were supposed to live on Jupiter. In addition, he had several other things to say as communicated by spirits. This included the fact that Jupiter had many highly evolved spirits, that the bodies of the habitants had a light density, and that they also had animals there.[3]

This was preceded by an article entitled "Jupiter et Quelques Autres Mondes" (Jupiter and Some Other Worlds, pp. 67–73) in which readers were told in all seriousness, and based on spirit communications, that spirits of different spiritual advancement lived on different planets and that Jupiter was the one with the most advanced inhabitants. The author of the article also stated that the residents of Jupiter had a longer lifespan and grew faster than earthlings. In addition, two other things were published in the first volume of the *Revue* about Jupiter. One was a communication from Palissy about Jupiter (pp. 108–114) that had an introductory editorial note saying that the content of the message was similar to those received before. Those similarities were said to be a "remarkable fact that at the very least is a presumption of exactitude" (p. 108). Probably anticipating incredulity, a note was inserted entitled "Observation à Propos de Dessins de Jupiter" (Observations Regarding the Jupiter Drawings, p. 222), which reminded the reader that the purpose of the *Revue* was the study of all phenomena and that nothing should be neglected. Readers were told that even assuming that the drawings were the product of a spirit's fantasy they were worth studying, but the possibility that the communications were produced by the medium's imagination was not discussed, which was consistent with the belief system presented in the *Revue*.[4]

Spirit communications were also used to develop explanations for the phenomena, as seen in a two-part article entitled "Théorie des Manifestations Physiques" (Theory of Physical Manifestations, pp. 121–125, 149–153), presumably authored by Kardec. According to the spirits, physical phenomena were produced by the perispirit, a semi-physical principle separate from the spirit and the physical body that acted following the will of the spirit. Some apparitions and materializations consisted of the spirit surrounded by its semi-physical envelope, which could assume material properties: "The condensation may reach the point of producing resistance and tangibility; ... but the condensation ... or better, a solidification of ethereal matter, is not in its normal state, it is but temporary" (pp. 123–124). It was argued that explanations of physical phenomena were based on "the observation and on a logical deduction of facts: We have concluded from what we saw" (p. 149). But it is evident from the article that instead of observing, Kardec and his followers listened and read the words of the presumed spirits.

Many articles are accounts of cases, mainly taken from the press or from other sources. Examples include "Visions" (pp. 24–26), "Le Revenant de Mademoiselle Clairon" (The Ghost of Miss Clairon, pp. 44–48), "L'Esprit Frappeur de Dibbelsdorf—Basse-Saxe" (The Rapping Spirit of Dibbelsdorf—Lower Saxony), pp. 219–222), and "Phénomène d'Apparition" (Apparition Phenomena, pp. 291–292). These were not original case investigations, but reprints of accounts from other publications that were accompanied by commentary. In addition, there are many other articles about such varied topics as "Different Ordres d'Esprits" (Different Types of Spirits, pp. 37–44), "Le Magnétisme et le Spiritisme" (Magnetism and Spiritism, pp. 91–92), "Propagation du Spiritisme" (The Spread of Spiritism, pp. 237–243), and "De la Pluralité des Existences Corporelles" (On the Plurality of Corporal Existences, pp. 295–302). The *Revue* also carried articles about medium D. D. Home (1833–1886, pp. 59–63, 88–91, 117–119), spirit photography (pp. 180–183), spirit obsession (pp. 265–276), clairvoyance in somnambules (pp. 313–315), apparitions (pp. 321–324), and "bicorporeity" (on the separation of the soul and apparitions of the living, pp. 328–331).

Although I am focusing my comments on only the first issue of the *Revue*, there is no question that historically this was an important journal and one that articulated the philosophy of spiritism. In later years the journal continued to feature Kardec's initial teachings and inspired many other generations.[5] The *Revue* was important in spreading the movement, and has continued to our day after many changes and after having suspended publication for a period.

The *Revue*, according to an anonymous critic, "seems to provide us with good buffoonery" (Anonymous, 1858, 235). I would not put it in these terms, but more in terms of another contemporary of Kardec, André Saturnin Morin (1807–1888), who argued that Kardec was not critical enough in his evaluation of the truthfulness and identity of his communicators (Morin, 1858). Leaving aside the historical perspective, many of us interested in the systematic and scientific study of psychic phenomena cannot see the *Revue* as a good start for what later became psychical research, other than publicizing the existence of psychic phenomena and inspiring a positive attitude toward the topic.

Furthermore, there was no serious consideration in the first volume of the *Revue* of the possibility that the communications were imaginary, or the possibility that they were influenced in various ways, such as through knowledge of other communications obtained by the mediums who were active in spiritist meetings and presumably read the literature. Admittedly, this is speculation, but not farfetched considering what we have learned over the years about the indirect influence of suggestion and the expectations of groups, not to mention the theoretical possibility of personation.[6] This possibility renders the use of mediumistic communications, at best, a problematic way of obtaining knowledge.

In addition, to consider the content of the *Revue*, and Kardec's work, as a scientific research program (Moreira-Almeida, 2008) begs the question of what science is. It is one thing to observe nature and develop hypotheses based on observed patterns, or to be tested by further observations or actual experimentation, and another thing to use communications through séances, which source is uncertain, as shown in this volume of the *Revue*, to get teachings and answers to questions about the nature of topics such as the workings of psychic phenomena and a variety of moral and philosophical issues. Similarly, it is one thing to report on non-evidential spirit communications and on cases of apparitions and other phenomena discussed in the press and other sources, and it is another to study these phenomena with attention to evidence.

In some ways psychical research was developed to do better than this. It was not only a response to crises of faith and the search for alternate worldviews, but also an attempt to be empirical without depending on difficult-to-interpret revelations from "spiritual" sources. As Frederic W. H. Myers (1843–1901) stated about the approach of British psychical researchers: "We endeavour to approach the problems of that [spiritual] world by careful collection, scrutiny, testing, of particular facts" (Myers,

1900a, 117). Neither the first volume of the *Revue*, nor later ones, achieved this agenda. It is true that there was an empirical spirit in the journal in terms of breaking with metaphysics and religion, and in collecting information (Chibeni, 2014). But the collection of cases was anything but "careful," there was little "scrutiny" (if any) and no "testing" to speak of unless one considers that asking questions of mediums and selecting and arranging communications was akin to scrutiny and testing in the conventional way. Such an approach was developed in the next publication reviewed here.

Proceedings of the Society for Psychical Research

> The four reports of the Society for psychical research which have been issued at intervals during 1882 and 1883 have now appeared in the form of a handsome volume, and it cannot be denied that they constitute a formidable body of evidence in favor of certain beliefs that have hitherto been looked upon with peculiar suspicion and distrust. (Anonymous, 1884, 40)

These were comments appearing in the journal *Science*, which, with some exceptions, became less positive toward the contents of the *Proceedings of the Society for Psychical Research* (PSPR) in later years.

The *PSPR* was the main organ of the Society for Psychical Research (SPR), which was of basic importance for the development of parapsychology. Its work, conducted by figures such as the above-mentioned Myers, by the Society's President Henry Sidgwick (1838–1900), and by others such as Eleanor Sidgwick (1845–1936), Edmund Gurney (1847–1888), and William F. Barrett (1844–1925), systematized research into psychic phenomena in England, but it was also influential in other countries.[7] The first volume of the PSPR bears witness to this.

The volume opens with the "Objects of the Society" (pp. 3–6), in which the purpose of the SPR was stated to be to make "an organised and systematic attempt to investigate that large group of debatable phenomena designated by such terms as mesmeric, psychical, and Spiritualistic" (p. 3), topics referred to as "residual phenomena" (p. 3).[8] These phenomena and associated matters were entrusted to committees responsible for:

> 1. An examination of the nature and extent of any influence which may be exerted by one mind upon another, apart from any generally recognised mode of perception.
> 2. The study of hypnotism, and the forms of so-called mesmeric trance, with its alleged insensibility to pain; clairvoyance, and other allied phenomena.
> 3. A critical revision of Reichenbach's researches with certain organisations called "sensitive," and an inquiry whether such organisations possess any power of perception beyond a highly exalted sensibility of the recognised sensory organs.[9]
> 4. A careful investigation of any reports, resting on strong testimony, regarding apparitions at the moment of death, or otherwise, or regarding disturbances in houses reputed to be haunted.
> 5. An inquiry into the various physical phenomena commonly called Spiritualistic; with an attempt to discover their causes and general laws.
> 6. The collection and collation of existing materials bearing on the history of these subjects. (pp. 3–4)

The tone was set with Henry Sidgwick's Presidential Address (pp. 7–12) delivered at the first general meeting of the Society held on July 17, 1882. He reminded members that their work "should be carried on with a single-minded desire to ascertain the facts, and without any foregone conclusion as to their nature" (p. 8), acknowledging that different positions were allowed within the Society, including skepticism. In addition to recognizing previous efforts, Sidgwick clearly stated that more evidence was needed to convince the scientific world. Their main task, he said, was to "carefully sift the evidence, and guard against the danger of illusion or deception … and then, when the evidence has been sifted by accumulation of personal experiments, make it more available for the purpose of producing general conviction" (p. 11). But he was aware of the incredulity they would have to fight. As he put it: "We have done all that we can when the critic has nothing left to allege except that the investigator is in the trick. But when he has nothing else left to allege he will allege that" (p. 12).

The first volume, containing four issues appearing in 1882 and 1883, was formed of papers reporting on the collection and analysis of evidence for psychic phenomena coming from accounts and from experiments. Some of these were reports of the above-mentioned committees, among them Barrett, Gurney, and Myers's "First Report of the Committee on Thought-Reading" (1882, pp. 13–34) and Gurney, Myers, and Barrett's "Second Report of the Committee on Thought-Transference" (1882, pp. 70–97), which dealt mainly with experimental studies of the Creery sisters. Reverend Creery informed the SPR of cases of thought-transference observed in his family. According to the first report:

> He has a family of five girls, ranging now between the ages of ten and seventeen … The father stated that any one of these children (except the youngest), as well as a young servant-girl who had lived with the family for two years, was frequently able to designate correctly, without contact or sign, a card or other object fixed on in the child's absence. (p. 20)

Several tests were done, many with positive results. Unfortunately, in later tests with cards, two of the girls, "acting as 'agent' and 'percipient,' were detected in the use of a code of signals; and a third has confessed to a certain amount of signaling in the earlier series to which reference has been made" (Gurney,1888, p. 269). However, even though it was decided not to continue to use work with the Creery sisters in support of telepathy, we must notice the precautions taken by the investigators and mentioned in the original report, some of which included means to prevent the sisters, or other members of her family, from having knowledge of the target material.

Other reports included Barrett, Keep, Massey, Wedgwood, Podmore, and Pease's "First Report of the Committee on 'Haunted Houses'" (1882, pp. 101–115), and Barrett, Massey, Moses, Podmore, Gurney, and Myers' "Report of the Literary Committee" (1882, pp. 116–155). These, and other reports such as Barrett's "On Some Phenomena Associated with Abnormal Conditions of Mind" (1883, pp. 238–244) and Malcolm Guthrie and James Birchall's "Record of Experiments in Thought-Transference, at Liverpool" (1883, pp. 263–283), point to the empirical approach prevalent in the SPR even if such attempts seem methodologically crude by modern standards.

Such standards are illustrated in the above-mentioned "First Report of the Committee on 'Haunted Houses'" (1882, pp. 101–115). Different from brief and secondhand accounts characterizing most older reports of ghosts, the SPR researchers acted as follows:

> In the first place, we, of course, begin by tracing every story to the fountain-head. But we do not consider that every first-hand narration of the appearance of a ghost, even from a thoroughly trustworthy narrator, gives us adequate reason for attempting further investigation. On the contrary, our general principle is that the unsupported evidence of a single witness does not constitute sufficient ground for accepting an apparition as having a prima facie claim

> to objective reality. To distinguish any apparition from an ordinary hallucination … it must receive some independent evidence to corroborate it. And this corroboration may be of two kinds; we may have the consentient testimony of several witnesses; or there may be some point of external agreement and coincidence—unknown, as such, to the seer at the time—(e.g., the periodic appearance on a particular anniversary, or the recognition of a peculiar dress), or give to the vision an objective foundation. (pp. 101–102)

Interestingly, the SPR encouraged the participation of its members in conducting research. In doing so, they both exemplified the less professional nature of the enterprise in those early days and its emphasis on data collection. An example was a circular printed in the *PSPR*: "To Members and Associates of the Society for Psychical Research: Circular No. 1. (Second Edition). On the General Work of the Society" (1883, pp. 295–302). But in addition to encouraging research into thought-transference, the circular contained statements about our limited knowledge regarding the phenomena and about some precautions needed in its study:

> We must specially urge, however, that those who are willing thus to cooperate with us will accurately record the results of every experiment made; we do not desire selected results. If the experiment is made with cards the whole pack should be used, and not a selected portion of it. If with numbers, names, &c., the principle on which the selection is made should be indicated (e.g., that the number consists of two figures, or that the name is a Christian name), in order that some estimate may be formed of the chances against success … Absolute silence should be secured during the progress of the experiments. If the first trial is a failure, the percipient should learn that fact from the silence of the experimenter, or "agent," as we prefer to call him. It should further be stated what precautions, if any, have been taken to preclude the possibility of learning the object selected by ordinary means. (pp. 297–298)

This, and other cautionary advice regarding other topics such as physical mediumship, shows how the early SPR did not simply care for "facts." Its members, or at least most of those who conducted the work, were mindful of the way they were collected, of possible artifacts and conventional explanations.

In Henry Sidgwick's first untitled Presidential Address to the SPR (1882, pp. 7–12) he stated that he believed it was a scandal "that the educated world, as a body, should still be simply in the attitude of incredulity" (p. 8) regarding psychic phenomena, and that the main aim of the SPR was to end this situation. He admitted that previous efforts had been valuable but affirmed that more work was necessary, work that would carry conviction in the scientific world. Part of this work, he stated, should be carried out using mediums who do not get money for their performances, a way to control for motives for fraud. Regarding this research, Sidgwick believed that

> In a matter so strange to ordinary experience I think we may say that it is only gradually that a man learns the complicated precautions that have to be taken in order to exclude all conceivable possibility of illusion or deception. (p. 11)

In the above-mentioned report of the Literary Committee, we find the SPR's early attempts to classify apparitional and other experiences collected by the Society via public appeals. This was an initial attempt to classify the cases, seeing them in terms of thought-transference, an idea they would continue to develop later in the PSPR and in the first major publication of the Society (Gurney, Myers, & Podmore 1886). It was stated in the report: "In a chaos such as this subject presents, classification, however rude and provisional, is itself light-bringing; it is at any rate an indispensable pre-requisite of any true analysis" (p. 118). The tentative classification, an attempt to bring order into many confusing cases, included: agent and percipient in a normal condition; percipient in an abnormal condition (exalted perception during sleep; exalted perception during trance; exalted perception at or during death); agent in an abnormal condition (impression from a person in sleep; impression from a person in a state of trance; impression from a dying person; impression from a person who is excited or in danger); agent and percipient both in an abnormal condition (two persons dying or in peril at the same moment; simultaneous dreams; percipient asleep and agent excited; and percipient asleep and agent dying). The state of the situation regarding the classification, it was stated in the report, was "very much in the position which zoology and botany occupied in the time of Aristotle, or nosology in the time of Hippocrates" (p. 149).

In addition, the authors of the report of the Literary Committee mentioned the problem of chance in relation to dreams. This was consistent with interest in conventional explanations, and with discussions of coincidences regarding psychic dreams found during the nineteenth century (Alvarado, 2012).

Interestingly, there was little in the first volume of the *PSPR* regarding theory. An exception was Barrett's ideas in his paper "On Some Phenomena Associated with Abnormal Conditions of Mind." He wrote regarding thought-transference:

> The energy of electricity exerts itself in two ways, by transmission along a material conductor and by influence, or induction as it is termed, across space. May not nerve energy, whatever be its nature, also act by influence as well as conduction? (p. 244)

There was more attention to theory in later volumes regarding such topics as telepathic explanations of apparitions, and the ideas of Myers about the subliminal mind.[10] But the publication of the PSPR's initial volume marks an important contribution, an attempt to systematize the study of psychic phenomena that had much impact on the development of psychical research.

As expected, the reception of the *PSPR* varied according to the reviewer. Two contrasting opinions came from American psychologists G. Stanley Hall (1844–1924) and William James (1842–1910). Hall (1887), a skeptic in all things regarding psychic phenomena, was not convinced by the quality of the material. James was more positive and stated that there was a big difference between most of the literature about the "supernormal" and the *PSPR*. In his words, the *PSPR* emphasized quality of evidential material over quantity. "Outside of these 'Proceedings,'" he wrote, "I know of no systematic attempt to weigh the evidence for the supernatural" (James 1892, p. 728–729).

Journal of Parapsychology

While the *PSPR* included some reports of experiments (and this became more frequent in later volumes), this approach was not the main one taken by SPR researchers. But it was the research style predominant in the *Journal of Parapsychology*.

Joseph Banks Rhine (1895–1980) promoted in the United States during the 1930s a parapsychological experimental research program. These efforts consisted at first of the now-classic ESP card-guessing studies initially reported in *Extra-Sensory Perception* (Rhine, 1934), a tradition that was continued in the *Journal of Parapsychology* (*JP*).[11]

The *JP* was first published in 1937 and was printed by Duke University Press. It was first edited by William McDougall (1871–1938) and Joseph Banks Rhine, with Assistant Editor Charles E. Stuart

(1907–1947). It has been argued that: "With the 1937 publication of the first volume of the *Journal of Parapsychology*, a new era of psychical research began" (Tietze, 1973, p. 176). Furthermore, the journal has been considered "one of the vehicles through which J. B. Rhine and his associates at Duke University articulated their experimental research program" (Alvarado, Biondi, & Kramer, 2006, pp. 74–75).

This emphasis was stated in the initial unsigned "Editorial Introduction" (pp. 1–9), which has been attributed to William McDougall (Mauskopf & McVaugh, 1980, p. 147). In the Editorial it was stated:

> Parapsychology is a word that comes to us from Germany,[12] where for some dozen years past it has been used to denote the stricter inquiries into obscure and questionable forms of mental activity. We think it may well be adopted into the English language to designate the more strictly experimental part of the whole field implied by psychical research as now pretty generally understood. It is these strictly laboratory studies which most need the atmosphere and conditions to be found only in the universities; and it is these which the universities can most properly promote, leaving the extra-academic groups the still-important task of collecting and recording all such reports of phenomena apparently expressive of unusual mental powers as occur spontaneously ... We do not claim that any sharp line can be drawn marking off the field of parapsychology within the larger vaguer province of psychical research. Rather, we anticipate that the stricter experimental methods will gradually invade other parts of the province annexing them to their own more special field, until possibly the two shall coincide. But we regard the differentiation of the two terms as useful at the present time; and it is our intention to admit to this journal only contributions that properly fall within the narrower sphere implied by its title; that is to say, reports of experimental studies in the stricter sense and discussions of methods and interpretations of such work. (p. 7)

The experimental emphasis was well-represented in the four issues of the *JP* which appeared in its first volume in 1937. According to my count of types of paper in the first volume, excluding correspondence and notes, there were 16 experimental reports, 4 editorials, 3 reviews of specific topics, 3 summaries and reviews of specific experiments, and 3 discussions of statistical issues.

Examples of experiments include ESP studies such as J. G. Pratt's (1910–1979) "Clairvoyant Blind Matching" (pp. 10–17), J. L. Woodruff and R. W. George's "Experiments in Extra-Sensory Perception" (pp. 18–30), Lucien Warner's "The Role of Luck in ESP Data" (pp. 84–92), and Vernon Sharp and C. C. Clark's "Group Tests for Extra-Sensory Perception" (pp. 123–142).

The experimental approach was not limited to proving the existence of ESP. The *JP* carried interesting experiments to study ESP in relation to other variables, such as J. B. Rhine's "The Effect of Distance in ESP Tests" (pp. 172–184), Margaret H. Pegram's "Some Psychological Relations of Extra-Sensory Perception" (pp. 191–205), and Edmond P. Gibson's "A Study of Comparative Performance in Several ESP Procedures" (pp. 264–275). In addition, several studies were reported about ESP tests with special participants. These were: Louisa E. Rhine's (1891–1983) "Some Stimulus Variations in Extra-Sensory Perception with Child Subjects" (pp. 102–113), Esther May Bond's "General Extra-Sensory Perception with a Group of Fourth and Fifth Grade Retarded Children" (pp. 114–122), Margaret M. Price and Margaret H. Pegram's "Extra-Sensory Perception Among the Blind" (pp. 143–155), and Joseph F. Kubis and Fabian L. Rouke's "An Experimental Investigation of Telepathic Phenomena in Twins" (pp. 163–171).

As is common today with much parapsychological research, the early *JP* reports were full of procedural details and statistical analyses. An example was the following excerpt from the above-mentioned Price and Pegram study with blind participants:

> For a total of 2,024 runs there were 11,518 correct calls, or a positive deviation of 1,398. This gives an average of 5.69 hits per 25 calls from a mean expectation of 5. This deviation is 16.99 times the standard deviation. The odds against so large a deviation occurring by chance in this number of trials are 1,054 to one. 28 of the entire 66 subjects had individually significant total scores; that is had positive deviations which were at least 2.5 times the standard deviation. (p. 148)

Because Rhine's work was involved in many criticisms from the beginning (Mauskopf & McVaugh, 1980), the *JP* included much about methodology and critiques to show the validity of the ESP work. One of these was J. B. Rhine's "The Question of Sensory Cues and the Evidence" (pp. 276–291). Other defenses were about the statistical analyses used. C. E. Stuart and J. A. Greenwood commented in "A Review of Criticisms of the Mathematical Evaluation of ESP Data" (pp. 295–304) that

> [critiques] have been irrelevant in regard to the mean chance expectation, mathematically valid but experimentally trivial in regard to the standard deviations, and mathematically and experimentally valid in regard to the probability statements. (p. 304)

Whatever mistakes or problems were pointed out "in no way affect any of the conclusions heretofore established in ESP research" (p. 304).

Also related to statistics was the reprint of a press release by Dr. Burton H. Camp, President of the Institute of Mathematical Statistics, presented in a section about "Notes" in which Camp stated:

> Dr. Rhine's investigations have two aspects; experimental and statistical. On the experimental side mathematicians of course have nothing to say. On the statistical side, however, recent mathematical work has established the fact that assuming that the experiments have been properly performed, the statistical analysis is essentially valid. If the Rhine investigation is to be fairly attacked it must be on other than mathematical grounds. (p. 305)

Interestingly, the publication of the *JP* received publicity in prominent publications such as *Science* and *The New York Times* (Anonymous, 1937a, 1937b). The writer of the latter comment summarized the research style of the Duke group, and of the *JP*, in the following words: "We seem to breathe the bracing air of the laboratory rather than the sticky incense of darkened rooms in which frauds hold forth."

Concluding Remarks

The journals discussed here, surrounded by different social and national contexts, started publication in different eras (1858, 1882, and 1937), and they are still published today. All of them had to carve out their own territory, so to speak, when they started. The *Revue* appeared in a context in which mesmerism was better known, a movement that was not always open to spiritism (e.g., Morin, 1858). Similarly, to some extent the *PSPR* and the *JP* represented "new" beginnings in terms of spiritualism and psychical research, respectively. However, it would be wrong to reduce everything to breaks and discontinuities. In fairness, the issue was more one of general trends, and it is important to recognize that there were clear conceptual and methodological connections between the movements.

Mediumship was not the sole province of spiritism during the nineteenth century, as seen in phenomena that may be termed mediumistic in magnetic somnambules (e.g., Haddock 1851, Chapter 9; Lausanne, 1816, pp. 12–26).[13] Similarly, the concern of early psychical research with hauntings and apparitions (not to mention the examinations of mediumship included in later *PSPR* volumes) shows a connection with the interests of spiritualists (e.g., Ambler, 1850; Harrison, 1879), and Rhine's parapsychology inherited a previous interest in experiments and statistical evaluation (e.g., Coover, 1917; Richet 1884).

While different, the three journals presented in their pages material showing empirical attempts to study psychic phenomena, even though they represent different research styles. Of the three approaches—the teaching of the spirits, the analyses of testimony, and the conducting of experiments—only the last two are still pursued in parapsychology. In fact, I doubt that today many parapsychologists and readers of the *JSE* [*Journal of Scientific Exploration*] will consider the use of mediumistically obtained teachings as a reliable approach to study psychic phenomena, although one may argue that it may be useful to generate hypotheses that may be put to test by other means. But leaving aside modern standards and practices, we must admit that Kardec saw his work as empirical, different from faith, an attempt to collect information from the natural world, albeit from an unusual source.

The emphasis of the *Revue* on the teachings of the spirits as a source of knowledge about psychic phenomena was obviously associated with the conviction that the communications came from spirits. Lacking this belief, most psychical researchers, including those convinced of survival, did not pay attention to such sources and placed their efforts on verifiable mediumistic communications and observable phenomena (e.g., Myers, 1903, Vol. 2, 117–118). This, and the fact that psychical researchers traditionally have taken the capabilities of the non-conscious level of the mind more seriously than spiritists and spiritualists,[14] led to the rejection, or at least the classification of this material as uncertain. This was not limited to early French spiritism, but applied as well to many other claims associated with unverifiable psychic sources of information, such as descriptions of the afterlife and philosophical and moral communications (e.g., Davis, 1867, Moses, 1883). In some ways it may be argued that one of the reasons psychical research developed was to be able to study phenomena without depending on such ambiguous sources of information.

Different from the above, the *PSPR* and the *JP*, not to mention other journals (Alvarado, Biondi, & Kramer, 2006), emphasized cases and experiments as the means to generate knowledge for psychical research. Later developments within the SPR and the Duke group, as articulated in the *PSPR* and the *JP*, significantly affected the study of psychic phenomena, transforming it into a more systematic endeavor.[15]

While I have written only about the first volume of each of these journals, it is important to remember that they have expanded their coverage over the years. I invite readers to explore these changes to appreciate how the content of the journals and the assumptions behind the content have changed, while, I believe, staying the same in terms of initial purposes.

Notes

1 Some examples of this scholarship, which include information about Kardec, are the works of Edelman (1995), Monroe (2008), and Sharp (2006). The most detailed biographical study of Kardec, although disorganized, is that presented by Wantuil and Thiesen (1984). Moreira-Almeida (2008) has argued that Kardec's work represents a research program into psychic phenomena.

2 Kardec (1857, 37, 159) had discussed before the *Revue* was published the idea that other planets were inhabited, that earthlings could reincarnate on Jupiter, and that spirits from that planet could visit Earth. Previous discussions of planetary topics include the experiences of Emmanuel Swedenborg (1688–1772) with spirits from Mars, Mercury, Jupiter, Saturn, and Venus (Swedenborg, 1758/1828), and the "trips" of a young somnambulist to places such as Ceres, Mercury, Jupiter, and the Moon (Anonymous, 1837).

3 Sardou later expressed doubts about the identity of Palissy (Claretie, 1897, de P. 1897).

4 Referring to Sardou's productions, Camille Flammarion (1842–1925) wrote:

> At that time we all thought Jupiter was inhabited by a superior race of beings. The spiritistic communications were the reflex of the general ideas in the air. To-day, with our present knowledge of the planets, we should not imagine anything of the kind about that globe. (Flammarion, 1907, p. 26)

5 The movement was very influential in France (e.g., Edelman, 1995; Sharp, 2006). It spread to countries such as Italy and Brazil (e.g., Biondi, 1988; Machado, 1983), but much less so to the Anglo-American world. Historically, reticence to accept some of the claims of spiritism can be seen in the writings of some believers in discarnate agency who assumed, without clear evidence, that the communications coming from Kardec's mediums were affected by his beliefs (e.g., Aksakof 1875; Home, 1877, Part 3, Chapter 3; Myers, 1903, Vol. 2, 135). In addition, several were skeptical about reincarnation, a main tenet of spiritism (e.g., Coleman, 1878; Howitt 1876).

6 See, for example, the later writings of Flournoy (1900), Janet (1889), Myers (1900b), and Sudre (1946) (*see also* Alvarado, 2011a). While such concepts were developed in detail after Kardec's times, the idea of psychological influences on phenomena traditionally believed to be produced by spirits was around before Kardec started being involved with mediums. Examples include seeing demonopathy as a contagious condition (Calmeil, 1845, Vol. 1, p. 86) and hallucinations as manifestations open to be influenced by the "force of example, by a true moral contagion" (Brierre de Boismont, 1845, p. 308).

7 The best source about early SPR developments is still Gauld (1968). Other perspectives appear in Alvarado (2002) and Cerullo (1982). The SPR also published the *Journal of the Society for Psychical Research*, which circulated only among members. The *PSPR* was the public voice of the Society and it soon became well-known and was received by many libraries in various countries. In addition to the individuals mentioned, there were many who helped the development of the SPR, among them Vice Presidents Arthur Balfour (1848–1930), William Stainton Moses (1839–1892), and Hensleigh Wedgwood (1803–1891), and Council Members Charles Massey (1828–1907), Frank Podmore (1856–1910), and George Wyld (1821–1906), among others.

8 In the United States William James (1842–1910) wrote years later about psychic phenomena as an "unclassified residuum" (James, 1890, p. 362).

9 Karl Ludwig von Reichenbach (1788–1869) postulated the existence of Od, a universal force that was seen and perceived in other ways by sensitive people (*see* Nahm, 2012).

10 There were many ideas of forces and waves of different sorts to account for telepathy during the nineteenth century (Alvarado, 2008). Two examples before and after Barrett's paper are those of Houston (1892) and Knowles (1869). Examples of later *PSPR* theoretical discussions include Barrett, Massey Moses, Podmore, Gurney, and Myers (1884), and Myers (1884).

11 On Rhine, see Berger (1988, p. 194–231), Brian (1982), Mauskopf and McVaugh (1980), and Rao (1982). There are also discussions about different aspects of the *JP* (Alvarado, 2011b; Alvarado, Biondi, & Kramer, 2006, pp. 73–75; Broughton, 1987; and Mauskopf, 1987).

12 The term parapsychology was used in the title of a journal, *Zeitschrift für Parapsychologie* (1926–1934), and in many works, among them those of Oesterreich (1921) and Driesch (1932). For context information, see Sommer (2013).

13 For discussions of this interesting issue, see Crabtree (1993, pp. 196–212) and Crockford (2013).

14 The skeptical attitude of spiritists and spiritualists about the capabilities of the subconscious mind and of dissociation as an explanatory principle of mediumship was evident in several publications (e.g., Delanne, 1902), and it continues to our day. The use of the subconscious mind to explain mediumship in the French context has received some scholarly attention (Alvarado, 2010; Lachapelle, 2011; Le Maléfan, 1999; Monroe, 2008).

15 While some may see the *PSPR* and the *JP* as examples of methodological progress in the scientific study of psychic phenomena, others may see them as too reductionistic, as having limited too much both the possible methodologies of study as well as the phenomena.

References

Aksakof, A. (1875, August 13). Researches on the historical origin of the reincarnation speculations of French spiritualists. *Spiritualist Newspaper,* 74–75.

Alvarado, C. S. (2002). Dissociation in Britain during the late nineteenth century: The Society for Psychical Research, 1882–1900. *Journal of Trauma and Dissociation*, 3, 9–33.

Alvarado, C. S. (2008). Further notes on historical ideas of human radiations: IV. Mental phenomena. *Psypioneer, 4,* 119–126.

Alvarado, C. S. (2010). Classic text No. 84: 'Divisions of personality and spiritism' by Alfred Binet (1896). *History of Psychiatry*, *21*, 487–500.

Alvarado, C. S. (2011a). On mediumistic personation phenomena [Letter to the Editor]. *Journal of the Society for Psychical Research, 75,* 59–61.

Alvarado, C. S. (2011b). Prescribing for parapsychology: Note on J. B. Rhine's writings in the *Journal of Parapsychology. Australian Journal of Parapsychology, 11*, 89–99.

Alvarado, C. S. (2012). Dream ESP studies before Maimonides: An overview, 1880s –1950s. In *Aquém e Além do Cerebro: Behind and Beyond the Brain* (pp. 77–101). Fundação Bial.

Alvarado, C. S., Biondi, M., & Kramer, W. (2006). Historical notes on psychic phenomena in specialised journals. *European Journal of Parapsychology, 21*, 58–87.

Ambler, R. P. (1850). Haunted houses. *Spirit Messenger, 1*, 155.

Anonymous. (1837). *Journeys into the moon, several planets and the sun: History of a female somnambulist.* Vollmer and Haggenmacher.

Anonymous. (1858). Du 29 au 30 Avril 1858. *Revue Anecdotique des Excentricites Contemporaines, 6,* 225–244.

Anonymous. (1859). Literary news. *The Spectator, 32*, 959.

Anonymous. (1884). The Society for Psychical Research. *Science, 4*, 40–43.

Anonymous. (1937a). A journal of "parapsychology." *Science, 85,* 171–172.

Anonymous. (1937b, April 12). Parapsychology. *The New York Times*, 16, April 12.

Barrett, W. E., Massey, C. C., Moses, W. S., Podmore, F., Gurney, E., & Myers, F. W. H. (1884). Third report of the Literary Committee: A theory of apparitions, Part I. *Proceedings of the Society for Psychical Research, 2*, 109–136.

Berger, A. S. (1988). *Lives and letters in American parapsychology: A biographical history, 1850–1987.* McFarland.

Biondi, M. (1988). *Tavoli e medium: Storia dello spiritismo in Italia*. Gremese.

Bonnamy, M. (1868). *La Raison du Spiritisme*. Librairie Internationale.

Brian, D. (1982). *The enchanted voyager: The life of J. B. Rhine.* Prentice-Hall.

Brierre de Boismont, A. (1845). *Des hallucinations ou histoire raisonnée des apparitions, des visions, des sognes, de l'extase, du magnétisme et du somnambulisme*. Germer Baillière.

Brooks, J. I., III (1998). *The eclectic legacy: Academic philosophy and the human sciences in nineteenth-century France*. University of Delaware Press.

Broughton, R. S. (1987). Publication policy and the *Journal of Parapsychology. Journal of Parapsychology, 51*, 21–32.

Calmeil, L. -F. (1845). *De la Folie Considérée Sous le Point de Vue Pathologique, Philosophique, Historique et Judiciaire* (2 vols.). J. -B. Baillière.

Carroy J., & Schmidgen, H. (2006). Psychologies expérimentales: Leipzig-Paris-Würzburg (1890–1910). *Mil Neuf Cent, 24*, 171–204.

Cerullo, J. J. (1982). *The secularization of the soul: Psychical research in modern Britain*. Institute for the Study of Human Issues.

Chibeni, S. (2013). Spiritism: An experimental approach to the issue of personal post-mortem survival. *Spiritist Knowledge Letters, 4*.

Claretie, J. (1897, February 11). La vie a Paris. *Le Temps*, 2.

Coleman, W. E. (1878, November 1). Re-incarnation. Its fancies and follies: II—Inconsistencies and contradictions. *Religio Philosophical Journal*, 1.

Coover, J. E. (1917). *Experiments in psychical research at Leland Stanford Junior University*. Stanford University.

Crabtree, A. (1993). *From Mesmer to Freud: Magnetic sleep and the roots of psychological healing*. Yale University Press.

Crockford, S. (2013). From spiritualist magnetism to spiritism: The development of spiritualism in France, 1840–1870. In C. Moreman (Ed.), *The Spiritualist movement: Speaking with the dead in America and around the world: Volume 1: American origins and global proliferation* (pp. 129–143). Praeger.

Crombie, A. C. (1994). *Styles of scientific thinking in the European tradition: The history of argument and explanation especially in the mathematical and biomedical sciences and arts.* Duckworth.

Danzinger, K. (1990). *Constructing the subject: Historical origins of psychological research.* Cambridge University Press.

Davis, A. J. (1867). *A stellar key to the summer land* (5th ed.). Colby & Rich.

Delanne, G. (1897). *L'évolution animique: Essais de psychologie physiologique suivant le spiritisme.* Chamuel.

Delanne, G. (1901). La psychologie expérimentale. In P. Janet (Ed.), *IVe Congrés International de Psychologie* (pp. 610–612). Félix Alcan.

Delanne, G. (1902). *Recherches sur la médiumnité.* Librairie des Science Psychiques.

de P., C. (1897). Interview with M. Sardou. *Borderland, 4*, 150–151.

Driesch, H. (1932). *Parapsychologie: Die Wissenschaft von Den "Okkulten" Erscheinungen.* F. Bruckmann.

Dufaux, E. (1855). *Vies Dictées d'outre-tombe á ermance Dufaux, agée de 14 ans, et publiées par elle.* Desrues.

Edelman, N. (1995). *Voyantes, guérisseuses et visionnaires en France 1785–1914.* Albin Michel.

Flammarion, C. (1907). *Mysterious psychic forces: An account of the author's investigations in psychical research, together with those of other European savants.* Small, Maynard.

Flournoy, T. (1900). *From India to the planet Mars: A study of a case of somnabulism.* Harper & Brothers.

Gauld, A. (1968). *The founders of psychical research.* Routledge and Kegan Paul.

Gurney, E. (1888). Note relating to some of the published experiments in thought-transference. *Proceedings of the Society for Psychical Research, 5*, 269–270.

Gurney, E., Myers, F. W. H., & Podmore, F. (1886). *Phantasms of the living* (2 vols.). Trübner.

Haddock, J. W. (1851). *Somnolism & psycheism; or, the science of the soul and the phenomena of nervation* (2nd ed.). James S. Hodson.

[Hall, G. S.] (1887). Review of *Proceedings of the Society for Psychical Research*, and *Phantasms of the living*, by E. Gurney, F. W. H. Myers, and F. Podmore. *American Journal of Psychology, 1*, 128–146.

Harrison, W. H. (1879). *Spirits before our eyes.* W. H. Harrison.

Home, D. D. (1877). *Lights and Shadows of spiritualism.* Virtue.

Houston, J. (1892). Cerebral radiations. *Psychical Review, 1*, 150–157.

Howitt, W. (1876). Re-incarnation, its champions and delusions. *Spiritual Magazine, 2*(s. 3), 49–60.

James, W. (1890). The hidden self. *Scribner's Magazine*, 7, 361–173.

James, W. (1892). What psychical research has accomplished. *Forum, 13*, 727–742.

Janet, P. (1889). *L'Automatisme psychologique: Essai de psychologie expérimentale sur les formes inférieures de l'activité humaine.* Félix Alcan.

Kardec, A. (1857). *Le livre des esprits.* E. Dentu.

Kardec, A. (1861). *Le livre des médiums.* Didier.

Knowles, J. T. (1869). Brain-waves—A theory. *The Spectator, 42*, 135–137.

Kwa, C. (2011). *Styles of knowing: A new history of science from ancient times to the present.* University of Pittsburgh Press. (Original work published in Dutch, 2005)

Lachapelle, S. (2011). *Investigating the supernatural: From spiritism and occultism to psychical research and metapsychics in France, 1853–1931.* Johns Hopkins University Press.

Lausanne [pseudonym of A. A. V. Sarrazin de Montferrier] (1816). Histoire du magnétisme animal. *Annales du Magnérisme Animal, 2*(25), 3–26.

Le Maléfan, P. (1999). *Folie et spiritisme: Histoire du discourse psychopathologique sur la pratique du spiritisme, ses abords et ses avatars (1850–1950).* L'Hartmattan.

Machado, U. (1983). *Os intelectuais e o espiritismo.* Antares.

Mauskopf, S. H. (1987). The origin of the *Journal of Parapsychology. Journal of Parapsychology, 51*, 9–19.

Mauskopf, S. H., & McVaugh, M. A. (1980). *The elusive science: Origins of experimental psychical research.* John Hopkins University Press.

Monroe, J. W. (2008). *Laboratories of faith: Mesmerism, spiritism, and occultism in modern France.* Cornell University Press.

Moreira-Almeida, A. (2008, August). Allan Kardec and the development of a research program in psychic experiences. Paper presented at the Joint *Annual Convention of the Parapsychological Association and the Society for Psychical Research.*

Morin, A. S. (1858). [Review of *Revue Spirite*]. *Journal du Magnétisme, 17*(s. 2), 162–168.

Moses, W. S. [published under the pseudonym M. A. Oxon] (1883). *Spirit teachings*. Psychological Press Association.

Myers, F. W. H. (1884). On a telepathic explanation of some so-called spiritualistic phenomena: Part I. *Proceedings of the Society for Psychical Research, 2*, 217–237.

Myers, F. W. H. (1900a). Presidential address. *Proceedings of the Society for Psychical Research, 15*, 110–127.

Myers, F. W. H. (1900b). Pseudo-possession. *Proceedings of the Society for Psychical Research, 15*, 384–415.

Myers, F. W. H. (1903). *Human personality and its survival of bodily death* (2 vols.). Longmans, Green.

Nahm, M. (2012). The sorcerer of Cobenzl and his legacy: The life of Baron Karl Ludwig von Reichenbach, his work and its aftermath. *Journal of Scientific Exploration, 26*, 381–407.

Oesterreich, T. K. (1921). *Grundbegriffe der Parapsychologie: Eine Philosophische Studie*. Johannes Baum.

Rao, K. R. (Ed.). (1982). *J. B. Rhine: On the frontiers of science*: McFarland.

Rhine, J. B. (1934). *Extra-sensory perception*. Boston Society for Psychic Research.

Richet, C. (1884). La suggestion mentale et le calcul des probabilités. *Revue Philosophique de la France et de l'Étranger, 18*, 609–674.

Sharp, L. L. (2006). *Secular spirituality: Reincarnation and spiritism in nineteenth-century France*. Lexington Books.

Sommer, A. (2013). Normalizing the supernormal: The formation of the "Gesellschaft für Psychologische Forschung" ("Society for Psychological Research"), c. 1886–1890. *Journal of the History of the Behavioral Sciences, 49*, 18–44.

Sudre, R. (1946) *Personnages d'au-dela*. Société des Éditions de Noel.

Swedenborg, E. (1828). *Concerning the earths in our Solar System, which are called planets and concerning the earths in the starry heaven*. Adonis Howard. (Original work published 1758).

Tietze, T. R. (1973). *Margery*. Harper & Row.

Wantuil, Z., & Thiesen, F. (1984). *Allan Kardec* (3 vols., 2nd ed.). Federação Espirita Brasileira.

22

Dissociation and the Unconscious Mind: Nineteenth-Century Perspectives on Mediumship*

Carlos S. Alvarado†

There is a long history of discussions of mediumship as related to dissociation and the unconscious mind during the nineteenth century. After an overview of relevant ideas and observations from the mesmeric, hypnosis, and spiritualistic literatures, I focus on the writings of Jules Baillarger, Alfred Binet, Paul Blocq, Théodore Flournoy, Jules Héricourt, William James, Pierre Janet, Ambroise Auguste Liébeault, Frederic W. H. Myers, Julian Ochorowicz, Charles Richet, Hippolyte Taine, Paul Tascher, and Edouard von Hartmann. While some of their ideas reduced mediumship solely to intra-psychic processes, others considered veridical phenomena as well. The speculations of these individuals, involving personation, and different memory states, were part of a general interest in the unconscious mind, and in automatisms, hysteria, and hypnosis during the period in question. Similar ideas continued into the twentieth century.

Dissociation, a process involving the disconnection of a sense of identity, physical sensations, and memory from conscious experience, has been related to mediumship due to the latter's sensory and motor automatism and changes of identity. In recent years there have been some conceptual discussions of dissociation and mediumship (e.g., Maraldi et al., 2019) as well as empirical studies exploring their relationship (e.g., Vencio, et al., 2018). This is not a new interest, as seen in my discussion below of speculations and observations about dissociative aspects of mediumship during the nineteenth century. Considering some of this material has generally been forgotten by current mediumship and dissociation researchers, and that some of it has not been translated into English, my purpose in this article is to make the content of these writings more available, and to provide some historical context to current ideas on the subject with additional references, several of which appear in Notes.[1]

Readers should be aware that most of the discussions about the topic during the nineteenth century were attempts to reduce mediumship to psychological, physiological, and medical ideas. In addition, much of what I discuss as examples of dissociation was not seen as such by believers in the spiritual interpretation of mediumship.

Dissociation During the Nineteenth Century

Trances and Secondary Personalities

The concept of dissociation and of hidden levels of the mind was widely discussed throughout the nineteenth century in relation to manifestations such as amnesia, somnambulism, and secondary personalities appearing spontaneously or via hypnosis, and specific features such as state-specific

*Republished with permission from *Journal of Scientific Exploration, 34*(3), 537–596, 2020.
†I am grateful to the Research Grants Committee of the Society for Psychical Research for funding the research that supported this paper.

memories (Crabtree, 1993; Gauld, 1992). For example, natural somnambulism, or sleepwalking, was discussed by many (e.g., Abercrombie, 1838; Bertrand, 1823; Macario, 1857; Prichard, 1835), and several cases were presented during the period (e.g., A., 1869; Abercrombie, 1838, pp. 296–298; Chambord, 1879; Moore, 1870). One of them was of a medical student who, in addition to having seen a patient, played the piano, played cards, and did anatomical drawings while he was in his somnambulistic state (A., 1869).

Many cases of somnambulistic behavior became well-known, such as that of American Rachel Baker (born 1794), who preached to audiences about moral and religious topics with no recollection of her actions. "This modest damsel," wrote a commentator about her case, "falls into a devotional exercise as soon as she loses her consciousness" (Mais, 1814, p. 6). Interestingly, other cases of somnambulistic speakers were also reported during the nineteenth century (e.g., Belden, 1834; Mitchell, 1876).[2]

This was part of a long history of examples of "inspired," "entranced," or "somnambulistic" revelations about all kinds of topics, but particularly moral, philosophical, religious, and spiritual ones. Such cases came from antiquity and are to be found in the literatures of mesmerism, possession, religious movements, Spiritualism, trance, and other topics (e.g., Baxter, 1833; Casaubon, 1655; Gauthier, 1842; Oesterreich, 1930), which have also been discussed in more recent times (e.g., Crabtree, 1993; Garrett, 1987; Gauld, 1992; Taves, 1999). Examples of these "revelations" were the discourses of visionary and magnetic patient Friederike Hauffe (1801–1829) (Kerner, 1845), the mesmeric subject Emma (Haddock, 1851), and the well-known clairvoyant Andrew Jackson Davis (1826–1910) (Davis, 1847).

The mesmeric literature, embedded in the theoretical concept of animal magnetism, presented many examples of the induction of magnetic somnambulism. This was generally described as similar to sleep in some aspects:

> If his magnetizer speaks to him he responds without waking up; he can even perform various movements, and when he returns to the natural state he retains no memory of what has happened. His eyes are closed, he usually hears only those who have been put in rapport with him. The external organs of his senses are all, or almost all, dormant, and yet he feels sensations, but by some other means. (Deleuze, 1825, p. 98) [This, and other translations, are mine.]

The state was interpreted by a writer to be one in between sleep and wakefulness (Gauthier, 1845, p. 566), while another mesmerist stated that it sometimes seemed to be a nervous disturbance, but in other occasions it appeared as a tranquil sleep (Charpignon, 1848, p. 67). English chemist and physician William Gregory (1803–1858) wrote in his *Letters to a Candid Inquirer, on Animal Magnetism* that: "The state of somnambulism is not a true sleep, but a state in which ordinary vision is cut off, while the mind is, in other respects, not only awake, but, intellectually and morally, more active than usual ..." (W. Gregory, 1851, p. 57).

Magnetic somnambulism, as seen in historical treatises (Crabtree 1993; Gauld 1992), was associated with phenomena such as thought-transference, clairvoyance, healing, pre-vision of future events, and other occurrences. This is what German philosopher Carl du Prel (1839 1899) referred to as "new faculties, new connections with nature, in apparent contradiction with all the laws of physiology" (du Prel, 1907, p. 62).

Dissociative phenomena were discussed and observed as well by the mesmerists. Some of these reports can be found before the nineteenth century, such as Armand Marie Jacques de Chastenet Puységur's (1751–1825) *Mémoires pour Servir à l'Histoire et a l'Établissement du Magnétisme Animal*. Here he presented his now classic observations of Victor Race, a peasant he magnetized to treat his ailments. Described as quiet and shy, Race changed when magnetized. He became outspoken, and very friendly, "his heart poured out; … as if it was filled with friendship and gratitude … " (Puységur, 1784, p. 36).

French mesmerist Joseph Philippe François Deleuze (1753–1835) noticed that during the mesmeric state a person could recover the "recollection of things that were forgotten during wakefulness" (Deleuze, 1813, p. 176), leading him to postulate the existence of separate beings. Another interesting case was the patient Estelle L'Hardy, who showed various changes in the magnetic state (Despine, 1840). In addition to an apparent secondary personality and visions of someone called Angeline (among others), who "served as a guide to the patient" (p. 35), it was recorded that some of these changes were: "The remarkable development of intelligence, memory, imagination, and of all physical and moral faculties …" (Despine, 1840, p. 40).

Another mesmerist reported the case of a "magnetized" woman who referred to herself using a different name than usual, saying she was a different individual (Lang, 1843, pp. 95–96, 108). In addition, there were occasional reports of communications from the deceased (e.g., Lausanne, 1816, pp. 12–14). Louis Alphonse Cahagnet (1809–1885) presented many accounts of the spiritual world and of encounters with spiritual entities narrated by his mesmerized subjects in his *Magnétisme: Arcanes de la Vie Future Dévoilés* (Cahagnet 1848–1854; see also Haddock, 1851). Such accounts were believed by some to be the result of the influence of the magnetizer's interests and the somnambule's imagination (Sandby, 1850).[3]

Reminiscent of dissociative effects, mesmeric procedures could make people insensitive to pain, as seen in cases of amputations and removal of teeth (Elliotson, 1843; Esdaile, 1847). An interesting testimonial came from English writer of literature and social topics Harriet Martineau (1802–1876), who had a disease that caused her much pain that was alleviated by the use of opiates. She wrote in her book *Letters on Mesmerism* (Martineau, 1845) that once, when magnetized, she felt "a delicious sensation of ease spread through me,—a cool comfort, before which all pain and distress gave way, oozing out, as it were, at the soles of my feet" (p. 9).

Persons in the magnetic state have been described as forgetting events during their trance, but remembering them later during another magnetic induction. In this situation, according to Gregory, the person "lives … a distinct life in the sleep, and has … a double or divided consciousness" (W. Gregory, 1851, p. 82).

In addition to mesmeric procedures, later explorers of hypnosis were able to document the existence of state-specific memories during their observations (e.g., Gurney, 1884). Some changes took place under hypnosis, as in the case of a woman named Lucie. When she was hypnotized, it was noticed that the idea that appeared in her consciousness after a sudden awakening is not the recollection of somnambulism, it is the next part of the act started and interrupted during wakefulness. It is as if somnambulism never existed and the two waking moments seem to join. In the middle of a conversation L. was asleep before she could finish her phrase. After a quarter of an hour of sleep she woke up and calmly finished the conversation started without doubting that she had slept (Janet, 1886, p. 579).

So-called personalities were also induced through suggestion (Richet, 1883), leading to the speculation that suggestion could produce in the hypnotized a "dissociation of their psychic elements" (p. 233). This was sort of the illusion of being a different person, while maintaining their sense of self, which could disappear with a deeper hypnotic state. The process not only involved affecting recollections, but also an overstimulation of the person's imagination. Similarly, it was argued that suggestion could induce ideas of spiritual agency during automatic writing (e.g., Barkworth, 1891, p. 24).

This was part of an interest by the end of the nineteenth century on conducting psychology from an empirical perspective, as compared to philosophical speculations. Much of this took place, particularly in France, in studies of pathology of memory and other phenomena using the single case study approach (Carroy & Plas, 1996; Foschi, 2003; Lombardo & Foschi, 2003). It was assumed that much could be learned about the normal aspects of human beings by the study of their abnormalities (e.g., Ribot, 1885). The emphasis on pathology was the province of the work of individuals such as Jean-Martin Charcot (1825–1893) and Pierre Janet (1859–1947) (Bourneville, 1886; Janet, 1889). Others had a less pathologically oriented outlook, but still maintained that the induction of unusual mental states by hypnosis could illuminate the workings of the mind (e.g., Beaunis, 1885; Myers, 1886). As stated at the time, "throwing the mental machinery slightly out of gear" allows us to "discern the secrets of its adjustment" (Gurney & Myers, 1885, p. 422).

Furthermore, much was learned about dissociation from those who studied motor automatisms (e.g., Binet, 1890; Binet & Féré, 1887; James, 1889; Janet, 1889), and from cases of spontaneous secondary personalities. The latter included the cases of Mary Reynolds (1793–1854; Mitchill, 1817), Félida X. (born 1843) (Azam, 1887), Ansel Bourne (born 1826) (Hodgson, 1891), and Mollie Fancher (1848–1916) (Dailey, 1894), among many others (e.g., Bourru & Burot, 1888; Dewar, 1823; Mason, 1893; Mayo, 1847, Chap.18).[4]

Some interesting observations of these personalities were those conducted under hypnosis with Léonie Leboulanger (born 1837) in France.

When first hypnotized Léonie adopted the name L Léontine, who claimed she was not Léonie:

> This new character, Léonie2, claims to have all the sensations and all the actions, in a word, all the psychological phenomena she has been conscious of during somnambulism ...; she attributes the opposite to Léonie1, that is, to the normal awake person, all phenomena that have been conscious during wakefulness. (Janet, 1889, p. 132)

Cases of this sort, as well as many of the phenomena of hysteria and hypnosis, led some to speculation about the "doubling" of conscious thoughts. This, in the words of a student of the subject, suggested the existence of other aspects of the self "each of which may have its perceptions, its memories, and even its moral character" (Binet, 1891, p. 839). Furthermore, "there may exist successions of ... intelligent, self-conscious operations that are accomplished without our help and even without our knowledge" (Binet, 1891, p. 855).

Eventually all of these phenomena, and others such as dreams, imagination, and memory, contributed to support the notion of the existence of non-conscious regions of the mind, and of dissociation. This was frequently discussed during the late nineteenth century in works such as *On Double Consciousness* (Binet, 1890), *Das Doppellch* (Dessoir, 1890), *L'Automatisme Psychologique* (Janet, 1889), *The Psychology of Suggestion* (Sidis, 1898), as well as in influential articles (e.g., James, 1890a; Prince, 1890).

These investigations coincided with the development of psychical research in the nineteenth century, as seen in countries such as Italy (Biondi, 1988), England (Gauld, 1968), the United States (Moore, 1977), France (Plas, 2000), and Germany (Wolffram, 2009). There is scholarly work showing that some of the studies of the unconscious mind, and the process of dissociation, not only took place within psychical research work, but that psychical research contributed to the development of these ideas (Alvarado, 2002; Crabtree, 1993; Plas, 2000). This was particularly the case in the study of mediumship, a phenomenon that played a central role in the development of Spiritualism in the nineteenth century (e.g., Cox, 2003; Edelman, 1995; Podmore, 1902), and that was pathologized by many students of the topic (Janet, 1889; Marvin, 1874).[5]

Mediumship

References to mediums include the assertion that they were "simply incomplete somnambules" (Perrier, 1854, p. 79), that they were "possessed with certain dominant ideas" (Carpenter, 1853, p. 547), that they showed a "mixed state" they were not aware of (Lafontaine, 1860, p. 31), and that trance made them automatons, liable to produce unconscious reflex actions (Beard, 1879).

Lawyer André-Saturnin Morin (1807–1888) wrote in *Du Magnétisme et des Sciences Occultes* that mediums had, like mesmeric somnambulists,

> a mental state different from the waking state, and at times his opinions, his feelings, are seriously modified, so it is no wonder that the language he addresses the table with, bears a particular character that does not seem to belong to the person of the medium. (Morin, 1860, p. 368)

In this state, Morin assured us, it is not possible to distinguish if thoughts came from within or from outside the medium.

Another writer referred to suggestion bringing out the medium's "submerged personality" (Somers, 1893, p. 322). Others shared the belief that suggestion could condition the medium's subconscious mind to assume the shape of communications from the dead (e.g., Ermacora, 1893, pp. 42–43; Hudson, 1893, p. 213). This was the case even if the phenomena were veridical, a topic further discussed below.

American Judge John W. Edmonds (1799–1874), a medium himself, noticed that mediums sometimes were unaware that they were writing and knew nothing of the content of the written message (Edmonds, 1860). This was the case of Edmond's friend and writing medium, American physician George T. Dexter (Edmonds & Dexter, 1853, p. 93), and of later mediums (e.g., Flournoy, 1900, p. 5; Myers, 1902, p. 70). Other variants of the experience of mediums witnessed by Edmonds were being conscious but with no control, and cases "when the medium was in the full possession of consciousness and volition, and yet was uttering the thoughts of an intelligence not his own" (Edmonds, 1860, p. 62). In fact, not every medium was entranced. As American reverend and spiritualist Samuel B. Brittan (1815–1883) noticed, while performing many mediums are in their usual mental states, some "write letters and converse on subjects altogether foreign to the manifestations" (Brittan & Richmond, 1853, p. 72).

The famous medium D. D. Home (1833–1886) described his experience of trance as follows:

> I feel for two or three minutes in a dreamy state, then I become quite dizzy, and then I lose all consciousness. When I awake I find my feet and limbs cold, and it is difficult to restore the circulation … I have no knowledge on my own part of what occurs during the trance. (London Dialectical Society, 1871, p. 188)

There are also accounts of Home behaving as if he were possessed by a spirit (e.g., L. M. Gregory, 1866). In one of them it was stated:

> All who have seen Mr. Home in this state of trance, are aware how clearly he sees and communicates with spirits … The gestures, the most trivial actions of bodily life, the mode of walking and speaking, the voice, the infirmities of persons who have passed away long before he was born, and concerning whose peculiarities in all these particulars Mr. Home had not the least possible means of obtaining any knowledge, are all repeated by him when in this state with an accuracy of detail which leaves no doubt, either that he is at the moment possessed by the spirit whose earthly characteristics he is delineating, or that he is receiving from them or from other spirits impressive communications which enable him to reproduce them. (D., 1867, p. 112)

Such experiences could vary, showing various degrees of trance (an ill-defined concept), and the production of phenomena without apparent alteration of consciousness (Edmonds, no date). There were even a few accounts showing awareness during trance (e.g., Hill-Tout, 1895).

An interesting introspective account about trance lectures comes from English medium and author Emma Hardinge (1823–1899), who stated in *Six Lectures on Theology and Nature* that when she talked to audiences inspired by spirits:

> There is an absolute compulsion to perform a certain part, whilst I retain sufficient consciousness to appreciate and hopelessly to struggle against the control exercised. In these spiritual lectures I can equally clearly recognize the presence of psychological control. The unprompted flow of words is not my own. Every gesture and movement appears to me, at times, compelled, and yet the compulsion is accompanied by a dreamy indifference on my part, a perfect absence of care, and sense of safety and protection from my precious invisible masters, that renders my servitude an exceedingly happy one … The details of my addresses I can only realize very imperfectly at the time, my own state being too dreamy for acute perception. (Hardinge, 1860, pp. 11–12)

Another account, this one about automatic writing, showed no awareness of the process. For example, the above-mentioned writing medium George T. Dexter wrote: "Let it also be understood that the spirit-manifestation by my arm is absolutely involuntary. I have no direction in the act. My muscles are the medium of spirit-communication, not my thought … " (Edmonds & Dexter, 1853, p. 89).

One writer referred to common characteristics of the secondary mediumistic personalities. In addition to claims to be a spirit, the list included suggestibility, eloquence, enhanced memory and imagination, and a propensity for vulgarity and profanity (by no means universal), and there was "a certain faculty of lucky or supernormal perception" (Patrick, 1898, p. 559), something the writer was skeptical of.

Much was written about veridical information obtained through mediums, which did much to sustain the belief in the reality of spirit communication (e.g., Cridge, 1854, Chap. 8; Moses, 1879). Physician William Gregory, said that although mediums believed that their communications came from spirits of the dead, he thought that "being more or less somnambulists and lucid, these answers come from their own intelligences, but without any consciousness of this fact" (W. Gregory, 1856, p. 320). Another defender of living agency was physician Carl Gustav Carus (1789–1869), who said in *Über Lebensmagnetismus* (1857) that mediumistic communications were phenomena that source the medium's unconscious divining powers (Carus, 1857).

The veridical trances and behavior changes of American medium Leonora E. Piper (1857–1950) were particularly influential (e.g., Hodgson, 1892, 1898; James, 1886; Lodge, 1890).[6] One of her investigators wrote:

> The personality active and speaking in the trance is apparently so distinct from the personality of Mrs. Piper that it is permissible and convenient to call it by another name … It strikes one as a different personality altogether, and the name by which it introduces itself when asked, viz., "Dr. Phinuit," is as convenient as any other … and can be used wholly irrespective of hypothesis … At the same time the name is useful as expressing compactly what is naturally prominent to the feeling of any sitter, that he is not talking to Mrs. Piper at all. The manner, mode of thought, tone, trains of idea, are all different. You are speaking no longer to a lady but to a man, an old man … (Lodge, 1890, p. 448)

Changes of behavior consistent with the identity of spirit communicators were observed with many mediums. In the opinion of an early author, automatic actions in the brain could allow a medium to "assume any personality, from that of a divinity to that of a toad" (Rogers, 1853, p. 171). In one case a medium "was first controlled by an influence which purported to be the spirit of Pocahontas, during which she combed her hair down upon her shoulders, and assumed the actions and even the physiognomy of an Indian woman, and sang what appeared to be an Indian song" (Anonymous, 1854, p. 202). Another example with the medium Emma Jay, recorded in the well-known book *From Matter to Spirit*, was the observation that "her voice and manner differed much when under different influences" (De Morgan, 1863, p. 90).[7]

Those types of observations led Russian Alexander Aksakof (1832–1903) to discuss the "doubling of consciousness" as a fundamental phenomenon of mediumship (Aksakof, 1895/1890, p. xxiv). This included the phenomenon of personation, which shows the "duality of the psychic being" (p. xxiv) presenting an unconscious life. In mediumship and other phenomena, this author stated, the self "can have a multiple character—normal, abnormal, or fictional—according to the conditions of the organism (natural sleep, somnambulism, mediumship)" (p. xxiv).

This has led to many discussions about the topic. Among them, those concerning the similarities between secondary personalities in non-mediumistic cases and the communicators and controls manifested by mediums (e.g., Leaf, 1890, p. 567).

Also relevant to the concept of dissociation in mediumship were various ideas of unconscious action in mental and physical mediumship, including the reality of the manifestations, and which were akin to the concept of unconscious cerebration (e.g., Lum, 1873; Rogers, 1853). In addition, there were ideas of unconscious muscular action to account for table turning (e.g., Braid, 1853; Faraday, 1853).[8]

Further Examples of Discussions of Mediumship and Dissociation

Paul Tascher

The topic was discussed in Paul Tascher's (1855) *Seconde Lettre de Grosjean à son Évèque au Sujet de Tables Parlantes, des Possessions, des Sibylles, du Magnétisme et Autres Diableries*, published anonymously under the pseudonym Gros Jean. Tascher's ideas have been popularized by later authors (e.g., Crabtree, 1993, pp. 264–265; Janet, 1889, Part 2, Chap. 3, Section 4). He believed that in adolescence, and in the case of young girls, there may be a separation of the action of the will on the body, affecting sensibility and recollections, which could be manifested in mediumistic ways. He wrote about table turning and mediumship and listed five stages of the process.

In the first stage, Tascher wrote, the will and the sense of self were not separated. This separation commenced in the second stage in which the young person's will started to separate from the mind and the body, and could act without willful action (automatism). Writing, speech, and movements of the table (with contact) started to take place in the third stage: "The girl knows the answer that forms in her intellect, but she knows it as if it did not come from her: Attention is engaged, but without establishing the link between the mind and the self" (p. 11).

Finally, Tascher wrote about the fourth stage:

> The girl has no internal knowledge of the response that is made in her mind, apart from the self; she does not know that as the movements of the table take place: the mental division is complete.
>
> At the same time dissenting thoughts increase their domain. It is no longer a question addressed to the table, to the contrary she spontaneously interrogates one or other of the persons present … distant recollections are revealed without the girl's awareness, romantic inventions, sentimental fantasies, ramblings [are produced] … (Tascher, 1855, pp. 10–11)

Jules Baillarger

Other interesting comments were authored by French physician Jules Baillarger (1809–1890) well-known for his studies of mental illness and one of the founding members of the Société Médico-Psychologique (Ritti, 1891). His short comments were published in the *Annales Médico-Psychologiques* in the context of a presentation made at the aforementioned society on February 27, 1860, in which it was assumed that mediumistic practices could lead to mental illness, an idea shared by many French psychiatrists (Le Maléfan, 1999).

Baillarger wrote about a woman who believed she was in contact with her deceased daughter, to whom she spoke continuously. The lady claimed the daughter guided her. According to Baillarger: "There is a doubling of personality similar to that which occurs during a dream; a fraction belonging to the individual, it seems there is another outside her" (Baillarger, 1861, p. 93).

Hippolyte Taine

French historian and critic Hippolyte Taine (1828–1893) is by all accounts an important figure in the development of positivistic approaches to knowledge in nineteenth century France (Nias, 1999). In his book *De l'Intelligence* (1878), he referred to a person's internal dialogue and abolition of the senses and of functions. Furthermore, Taine stated:

> In this respect, the *spiritist* manifestations themselves put us on the path of discovery, showing us the coexistence at the same time, in the same individual, of two thoughts, two wills, two different actions, one of which is conscious, the other of which he is unaware of and which he attributes to invisible beings. The human brain is then a theatre in which different plays are performed at the same time ... Nothing is more worthy of study than this basic plurality of the self; it goes much further than we imagine. I have seen a person who, [while] talking, singing, wrote, without looking at the paper, phrases and even entire pages, without been aware of what she wrote. In my eyes, her sincerity is perfect: She says that after the last page she has no idea of what she has written on the paper; when she reads it, she is surprised, sometimes alarmed. The writing is different from her ordinary writing. The movement of the fingers and the pencil is stiff and seems automatic. The writing always ends with a signature, that of a dead person, and bears the imprint of intimate thoughts, of a mental back-ground that the author does not want to disclose.—Certainly we observed a *doubling* of the self, the simultaneous presence of two series of parallel and independent ideas, two centers of action ... juxtaposed in the same brain, each with its own work and each with different work, one on stage and the other behind the scenes, the second as complete as the first, since, alone and out of sight of each other, they build ideas followed and linked with phrases and related sentences which the other has no part of. (Taine, 1878, pp. 16–17)

Frederic W. H. Myers

An example of an influential theorist, mainly in psychical research, but also in psychology, was classical scholar Frederic W. H. Myers (1843–1901). [9] In his view, there were a variety of states and conditions affecting the threshold between the conscious and unconscious (or subliminal) regions of the mind. These included dreams, hypnosis, hysteria, mediumistic trance, natural somnambulism, and some medical conditions, which could "afford examples of the development of what I have called secondary mnemonic chains,—fresh personalities, more or less complete, alongside the normal state" (Myers, 1888, p. 387).

Myers wrote about automatic writing stating, that there were many cases in which the person produced writing without being aware of its content. On occasion, "the involuntary movement of the pen is altogether puzzling to the writer,—is something which he has to make out with difficulty as if it were the product of another brain …" (Myers, 1884, p. 226; see also Myers, 1885).

In Myers' view the trance utterances of medium Mrs. Piper were automatisms "which occur in sane subjects without entering the normal waking consciousness or forming part of the habitual chain of memory" (Myers, 1890, p. 437). It was for him, as he wrote in his well- known work *Human Personality and Its Survival of Bodily Death* (1903), an extreme case of automatism affecting "the whole psychical area;—where a secondary consciousness not only crops up here and there through the primary, but for a time displaces it;—where, in short, the whole personality appears to suffer intermittent change" (Myers, 1903, Vol. 2, p. 237).

Possession in mediumship, Myers (1903) believed, was akin to apparent possession by one's own subliminal self, as seen in some cases of creativity and hypnotic secondary personalities. In this way Myers saw a continuity of the action of the subliminal mind and dissociation that was not limited to mediumship.

While Myers accepted spirit communication via mediumship (e.g., Myers, 1902), he believed that, even with the best mediums, not all trances came from spirits, and that the medium's mind could interact with spiritual influence. He wrote: "I think that the depth of the trance has varied greatly on different occasions, and that sometimes the subliminal self of the sensitive is vaguely simulating, probably in an unconscious dream-like way, an external intelligence" (Myers, 1903, Vol. 1, p. 205). Such dynamics of the subliminal accounted for the mixed source of messages, which could be further complicated, Myers thought, by the content of the medium's supraliminal (conscious) mind. Furthermore, Myers (1903, Vol. 2, p. 250) conceived of "a kind of mixed telepathy between the sitter, the sensitive's spirit, and the extraneous spirit," which could appear during the same seance.[10]

In addition, Myers also observed varieties in the trance and behaviors of Mrs. Piper during séances. The spirit control "Phinuit" sometimes was fairly quiet. At times no veridical information was given, while at other times it seemed to flow freely. Also:

> The trances could not always be induced at pleasure. A state of quiet expectancy would usually bring one on; but sometimes the attempt altogether failed. The trance when induced usually lasted about an hour, and there was often a marked difference between the first few minutes of a trance and the remaining time. On such occasions almost all that was of value would be told in the first few minutes; and the remaining talk would consist of vague generalities or mere repetitions of what had already been given. (Myers, 1903, Vol. 2, p. 239).

Eduard von Hartmann

In Germany philosopher Eduard von Hartmann (1842–1906) (see Treitel, 2004, pp. 13–15, 21–22) believed that mediums had a "a certain disorganization of the nervous system; that is, the lower and the middle nerve centres are too independent of the highest, reflex-prohibiting centre of consciousness self control; they are, in other words, … hysterical ..." (von Hartmann, 1885, p. 406). Mediums, according to him, showed two forms of somnambulism, an automatic one, with no intelligence, and an intelligent one.

The somnambulistic consciousness, he believed, had a tendency to form personalities. "A medium in the somnambulistic state can play the part of a spirit and do things of which afterwards, when awake, he knows nothing, and which from the reports of the witnesses he must take for immediate spirit actions" (von Hartmann, 1885, p. 5).

This could involve veridical information. But according to von Hartmann these unconscious processes could also guide physical mediumship via the exteriorization of the medium's nervous forces.[11] In his view:

> This liberation of directive radiation of nerve force is under all circumstances ... not a function of those parts of the brain which serve as support to the conscious will, but of deeper-lying layers of the brain which either coincide with those supporting the somnambulic consciousness, or are more approximate to them than to the first. (von Hartmann, 1885, p. 442)

Charles Richet

The famous physiologist Charles Richet (1850–1935) was also well-known during the nineteenth century for his work in psychical research, particularly his studies of what we would refer to today as ESP (e.g., Richet, 1884, 1889) (on Richet, see Alvarado, 2019a, and S. Wolf, 1993). In the 1884 article, the classic "La Suggestion Mentale et le Calcul des Probabilités," he wrote about mediumship and dissociation, expressing his belief that

> ... all the intelligent manifestations attributed to the spirits are due to an individual that is unconscious and active at the same time. In addition, he is surprised by everything produced; because he is ignorant of the intellectual operations he performs, which are translated into action, and are not less removed from his awareness. (Richet, 1884, p. 650)

Richet stated that some individuals could perform actions without conscious awareness. The medium, he thought, was a person "who has the ability of *hemisomnambulism* or *partial unconsciousness*, an ability by which a part of his intelligence, his memory, his will, operates outside of awareness, however, consciousness remains quite awake" (Richet, 1884, pp. 650–651).

In a later paper, entitled "Les Mouvements Inconscients," Richet said that in mediums two states succeed each other and are mixed, that is, regular normal consciousness persists at the same time as another consciousness appears, coinciding with it without mixing, performing acts exempted from the first normal consciousness, and continuing, without the aid of the normal consciousness, a series of logical developments. It is therefore *hemi-uncon-sciousness*, or *hemi-somnambulism.* (Richet, 1886, p. 93)

Richet eventually defended the reality of veridical mediumship, as I point out at the end of this paper.

William James

American psychologist and philosopher William James (1842–1910), well-known for his interest in psychic phenomena, also contributed to the study of mediumship (Alvarado, 2016; Knapp, 2017). Writing in *Scribner's Magazine*, James (1890a) summarized the work of French researchers on dissociative states. In his view trances were not necessarily pathological and were far from understood.

He wrote: "A comparative study of trances and sub-conscious states is meanwhile of the most urgent importance for the comprehension of our nature" (W. James, 1890a, p. 373).

When James discussed automatic writing in his *Principles of Psychology,* he stated:

> The lowest phase of mediumship is automatic writing ... Inspirational speaking, playing on musical instruments, etc., also belong to the relatively lower phases of possession, in which the normal self is not excluded from conscious participation in the performance, though their initiative seems to come from elsewhere. In the highest phase the trance is complete, the voice, language, and everything are changed, and there is no after-memory whatever until the next trance comes. (W. James, 1890b, pp. 393–394; see also W. James, 1889)

Also in *Principles*, James considered the similarities between many spirit communications and wondered if "sub-conscious selves are peculiarly susceptible to a certain stratum of the Zeitgeist, and get their inspiration from it," something which "is obviously the case with the secondary selves which become 'developed' in spiritualist circles" (W. James, 1890b, p. 394). Nonetheless, he was not willing to explain all the content of communications using that explication.[12]

In various papers, James (1886, 1890c, 1909) reported his observations of medium Leonora E. Piper, who eventually convinced him her mentation could be veridical. He wrote that he was "as absolutely certain as I am of any personal fact in the world that she knows things in her trances which she cannot possibly have heard in her waking state, and that the definitive philosophy of her trances is yet to be found" (W. James, 1890c, pp. 658659). But James also wrote that, regardless of showing good memory of previous communications, "Phinuit," the medium's spirit control, appeared to him to be fictitious. On occasion, James complained, he produced "tiresome twaddle" (W. James, 1890c, p. 656).

The importance of James' (1886) earlier Piper report has been pointed out elsewhere (Alvarado, 2016). In addition to being the first scientific study of a mental medium (and of Piper) published, this was a call for the study of special individuals,[13] and an example of the innovative use of stenographic records for that purpose. More relevant for the topic of dissociation, James paid attention to the features of Piper's trances (which unfortunately he did not describe in the report), and used hypnosis to study them.

Regarding hypnosis, James (1886) wrote about his modest results:

> My first two attempts to hypnotize her were unsuccessful. Between the second time and the third, I suggested to her "Control" in the medium-trance that he should make her a mesmeric subject for me. He agreed. (A suggestion of this sort made by the operator in one hypnotic trance would probably have some effect on the next.) She became partially hypnotized on the third trial; but the effect was so slight that I ascribe it rather to the effect of repetition than to the suggestion made. By the fifth trial she had become a pretty good hypnotic subject, as far as muscular phenomena and automatic imitations of speech and gesture go: But I could not affect her consciousness, or otherwise get her beyond this point. Her condition in this semi-hypnosis is very different from her medium-trance. The latter is characterized by great muscular unrest, even her ears moving vigorously in a way impossible to her in her waking state. But in hypnosis her muscular relaxation and weakness are extreme. She often makes several efforts to speak ere her voice becomes audible; and to get a strong contraction of the hand, for example, express manipulation and suggestion must be practised. The automaticimitations I spoke of are in the first instance very weak, and only become strong after repetition. Her pupils contract in the medium-trance. Suggestions to the "Control" that he should make her recollect after the

> trance what she had been saying were accepted, but had no result. In the hypnotic-trance such a suggestion will often make the patient remember all that has happened. (W. James, 1886, pp. 105–106)[14]

While Piper showed some evidence of veridical communications that impressed James, she was not consistently successful in thought-transference tests conducted in her normal state, during hypnosis, or during her mediumistic trance.

In a later publication by James (1909), "Report on Mrs. Piper's Hodgson-Control," he presented more examples of trances and communications via Piper by the presumed personality of Richard Hodgson (1855–1905), one of the medium's main investigators while he was alive. Referring to Rector, a later spirit control, he wrote:

> He appears like an aged and, when he speaks instead of writing, like a somewhat hollow-voiced clergyman, a little weary of his experience of the world, endlessly patient and sympathetic, and desiring to put all his tenderness and wisdom at your service while you are there. (W. James, 1909, p. 3)

James also commented about how life-like the conversations with Rector and Hodgson could be, a feeling not possible to obtain by reading the transcripts. He discussed how difficult it was for him to decide if the drama presented by Piper was from a spirit source, or the result of psychological personation, perhaps with flashes of telepathy. This fascinating discussion presents a good example of how dissociative processes and spirit agency permeated the theoretical thoughts of some psychical researchers.

At the end of the Hodgson report, James wrote that he felt there was a will to communicate that went beyond telepathy. "But if asked whether the will to communicate be Hodgson's, or be some mere spirit-counterfeit of Hodgson, I remain uncertain and await more facts, facts which may not point clearly to a conclusion for fifty or a hundred years" (W. James, 1909, p. 121).

Pierre Janet

When it comes to dissociation, the above-mentioned psychopathologist Pierre Janet (1859–1947), who was also interested in psychic phenomena, was one of the central figures of the nineteenth century (Evrard et al., 2018; Nicolas, 2002, Chap. 7; Van der Hart & Horst, 1989). In a reference to automatic writing, Janet (1887) stated that this phenomenon represented the separation of some psychological aspects of the mind that are "grouped in a new synthesis that has the appearance of a personality" (p. 452). This practice common in mediums, he believed, was a "way … to penetrate further into the thoughts of somnambules" (Janet, 1886, p. 452).

In *L'Automatisme Psychologique*, published in 1889, Janet discussed various phenomena such as automatisms, hypnotic memory, and mediumship (on Janet and mediumship, see Le Maléfan, 1999, pp. 66–84).[15] He argued that when someone was psychologically healthy their synthesis of mental functions such as memory was cohesive, but that the opposite was the case when unhealthy conditions predominated. This produced a state of "disaggregation" (or dissociation) that could be part of hysteria and other conditions, presenting changes of personality, and the above-mentioned memory and sensory-motor disturbances. The person would be more sensitive to suggestion, and to other manifestations, among them catalepsy and automatic writing. "This is the state in which spiritists are so happy to see their mediums in order to evoke the spirits through the disaggregated phenomena" (Janet, 1889, p. 338). Because he believed that automatic activity and dissociation in general were inferior mental manifestations (see also Beard, 1879, and Hammond, 1876), mediumship was consequently pathologized (see Note 5).

Janet wrote that most mediums "are neuropaths, when they are not frankly hysterics" (Janet, 1889, p. 404). Furthermore, he said that "we see from time to time that the medium has some choreic movements …, or that the experience of automatic writing causes them great exhaustion which forces them to stop because of delicate health …" (p. 405).[16]

Janet believed that changes in the writing of the hypnotized and of mediums were of the same nature, and that both showed "the disintegration of personal perception" as well as "the formation of several personalities which sometimes succeed and sometimes develop simultaneously" (Janet, 1889, p. 413). He stated that "perfect" or fully dissociated mediums showed "the most complete type of division in which the two personalities are completely unaware and develop independently of each other" (p. 419).

In later writings Janet continued discussing the topic (Janet, 1892, 1904; Raymond and Janet 1908). "The medium," he wrote in *Névroses et Idées Fixes*, "is an individual who dreams while awake, but who has completely lost the personal consciousness of his reverie" (Janet, 1904, pp. 394–395). Such a person is unaware of the things he has said or written, which are attributed to a deceased spirit, and sometimes to a famous one. He also maintained that in some mediums automatic writing was accompanied by a "temporarily anesthesia of the hand and even an anesthesia of hearing" (Raymond & Janet, 1908, p. 404).[17]

Jules Héricourt

"The state of the problem of the unconscious," wrote Henri F. Ellenberger in his well-known work *The Discovery of the Unconscious* (1970), "as it was in the late 1880s, was sketched by Héricourt in a survey published in 1889, stating that the unconscious activity of the mind is a scientific truth established beyond any doubt …" (p. 314). This was a reference to French physician Jules Héricourt (1850–1938), who distinguished himself in military medicine, serotherapy, hygiene, tuberculosis, and other areas (on Héricourt, see Anonymous, 1914). Interestingly, but similar to some of his colleagues at the time, Héricourt was also interested in psychic phenomena (e.g., Héricourt, 1886).

The paper in question, entitled "L'Activité Inconsciente de l'Esprit," was published in the French journal *Revue Scientifique*, a publication edited by Charles Richet that was devoted to discussions of developments in all areas of science (Héricourt, 1889). The article was a review of some of the phenomena considered to provide evidence for the workings of the unconscious mind, considering such topics as hysteria, hypnosis, and cases of spontaneous secondary personalities. In addition, Héricourt considered mediumship.

Mediumship, our author wrote, presents a state of trance in which "the conscious and the unconscious appears to have an independent existence, not successive, but simultaneous" (p. 265). In automatic writing the medium may write without showing awareness of what he or she is doing. In his view

> … some mediums, in the state of *trance*, completely have the appearance of somnambules or of hypnotized subjects; and, in fact, one can observe in them all the degrees between a kind of hemisomnambulism, as Mr. Richet well named the state of mediums who were awake, and the state of complete somnambulism. (Héricourt, 1889, p. 265)

Conscious mediums feel, wrote Héricourt, that the medium's writing is produced by a deceased spirit. It is a real foreign personality to the conscious medium, but one in which the unconscious mind communicates to the conscious mind without the latter's awareness. "This second personality is most frequently a simpleton and extremely childish, but sometimes, …on the contrary, it shows a true originality and a memory and a subtleness of which the conscious person seems completely deprived …" (Héricourt, 1889, p. 265).

Héricourt concluded:

> The conditions of mediumship are still rather badly known. However, it seems that the aptitude for somnambulism and for suggestions is a very favorable condition. The preparation of the medium with its exercises can also explain the nature of the results obtained. Such preparation consists, indeed, in a kind of auto-hypnotization which takes the subject midway between the waking state and the state of complete hypnotism. The unconscious person appears without the conscious person, whose disintegration undoubtedly relates only to a few elements, which have disappeared or are greatly reduced. It is the hemisomnambulism of Mr. Richet. (Héricourt, 1889, pp. 265–266).

Ambroise Auguste Liébeault

Another French physician who contributed to ideas about mediumship and dissociation was Ambroise Auguste Liébeault (1823–1904) well-known for his influence on the Nancy school of hypnosis through his psychotherapeutic use of suggestion (on Liébeault, see Carrer, 2002, and Gauld, 1992, pp. 319–324). In addition, he was interested in psychical research topics (Alvarado, 2009).

Liébeault (1889) stated in his book *Le Sommeil Provoqué et les États Analogues* that people could answer their own questions without awareness when in hypnotic states. This was an explanation for table turning, generally explained by the action of spirits. Those acting as mediums around tables, he wrote, were in a mental state analogous to that of the dreamer who believes in unreal characters as long as he is not awake.

In Liébeault's view mediums and the hypnotized were similar. He wrote that both of these individuals do not show any difference in their passive state: Concentration of thought to enter their dreams in action, isolation, automatism, insensibility, loss of memory upon awakening, all these signs are common to them; but the medium, entering his dream with the idea that he will remember the revelation of spirits and their appearance, keeps more often than the somnambule the memory of the acts of his passive state (Liébeault, 1889, p. 250).

Paul Blocq

Physician Paul Blocq (1860–1896), once at the Salpêtrière, and a researcher of various aspects of internal medicine and neurology (Walusinski, 2014), believed that automatic writing produced by mediums and non-mediums, such as hysterics, were similar. Both, he stated in his article "L'Écriture Médianimique.—Le Spiritisme au Point de Vue Scientifique," involved lack of awareness of producing writing (Blocq, 1889).

Spiritists beliefs in discarnate agency, Blocq stated, could be questioned on the basis of the content of spirit communications. "Massillon lost his eloquence, Mozart his genius, and a good number of other no less illustrious people expressed themselves in a coarse, sometimes incomprehensible way, committing inadmissible anachronisms" (Blocq, 1889, p. 1436). He believed that such communications were produced unconsciously by the medium.

The process involved suggestions given by the sitters, and recollections from the medium's memories. "On the occasion of special influences, memory takes, as we know, an extraordinary acuteness: Its abnormal development means that in the medium, the facts, usually completely forgotten, come back as a precise memory that will animate their pen" (Blocq, 1889, p. 1436). Blocq believed that "some hysterical states, and hypnotic somnambulism in particular, come close to becoming confused with the psychic disposition which characterizes the state of the medium" (p. 1437).

Alfred Binet

French psychologist Alfred Binet (1857–1911) is well-known for his studies of hypnosis, intelligence, and other topics (on Binet, see Alvarado, 2010; Nicolas and Ferrand, 2002; T. H. Wolf, 1973). He discussed dissociation in some of his writings (e.g., Binet, 1889, 1890). In one article he commented that mediums "manage to express in a variety of ways, and often without being aware of it, a thought which is not theirs" (Binet, 1891, p. 852). In automatic writing, Binet continued, the medium presents thoughts outside of conscious awareness. There are "two coexisting personalities; because the thought that directs the automatic writing is not a disjointed thought, it has a character of its own, and even has a name, the name given to the spirit that has been evoked" (Binet, 1891, p. 854).

In a book about alterations of personality, Binet (1896/1892) wrote about mediumship. The book had three sections about various phenomena of dissociation such as spontaneous secondary personalities, hysteria, automatic writing, and alterations of personality using suggestion. As before, Binet affirmed that in automatic writing via mediumship there were two coexistent personalities.

Furthermore, in his view:

> As with experiments in suggestion, those in spiritism succeed best on a certain class of subjects, among whom hysterical patients hold an important place. Hysterical patients, and somnambulists generally, furnish the greater part of the good mediums. One may see that by glancing over the works on spiritism. Every now and then the most discreet author finds himself obliged to say that such and such an excellent medium had a nervous crisis or was soon fatigued, in consequence of delicate health. It is, moreover, generally admitted that spiritist performances predispose to nervous complications. (Binet, 1896/1892, pp. 229–230)

Binet also stated that mediumship also presented a tendency toward personation, believed by many to be spirits of the deceased (see Note 8). "In any case this person does not consider himself as a part of the medium, and does not apply his special memories to the medium" (Binet, 1896/1892, p. 339). Personation, Binet stated, is affected by expectations from the medium, or communicated to her from sitters at a séance. Discussing this in more detail, Binet wrote that it was the secondary self who performed the suggestion, "and who, sustaining this illusion or obligingly complying with it—for we do not know exactly how it occurs—goes on to write messages in the style of the person conjured up, whose name he signs" (Binet, 1896/1892, p. 340).

It is this suggestion, Binet postulated, that led to a dissociated state. Eventually, this caused the emergence of a subconscious personality.

Julian Ochorowicz

Polish philosopher Julian Ochorowicz (1850–1917) was a philosopher and psychologist of many interests, including hypnotism and psychical research (Hess, 2018; Weaver, 2019). Among other things, he was an inventor, published on mental suggestion and physical mediumship (e.g., Ochorowicz, 1887, 1910), and was also interested in unusual mental states, such as dissociation.

This interest is clear in "La Question de la Fraude dans les Expériences avec Eusapia Paladino," a paper authored by Ochorowicz (1896) about fraud in séances with the famous Italian medium Eusapia Palladino (1854–1918), well known for her séances for physical phenomena such as movement of objects, touches, lights, and materializations.[18] The paper is basically a critique of the attitude taken by researchers from the Society for Psychical Research in their investigation of Palladino (H. Sidgwick, 1895; see also Gauld 1968), but it contains much about mediumship and dissociation.

In that investigation, Ochorowicz wrote, the researchers "did not admit in their report but two alternatives: *real phenomena*, and *conscious fraud*" (Ochorowicz, 1896, p. 96). He criticized them on the basis that they did not consider unconscious fraud. This form of fraud, Ochorowicz believed, was commonly practiced by Palladino in her séances, and it was a manifestation of what he considered to be inferior mediumship, as compared to superior mediumship, consisting of true physical phenomena.[19]

The English researchers, he wrote further, did not make sure that she was in trance, a state which facilitated unconscious fraud. This was a problem when they accused Palladino of premeditated fraud, a fraud she would not remember consciously. Part of this consisted of bodily movements which may have been "*motor representations that rule in a given moment the medium's imagination*" (Ochorowicz, 1896, p. 100, italics in the original).

To support his belief in Palladino's dissociative actions, Ochorowicz recounted an experience he had with the medium while she was visiting Warsaw for a series of séances. Everyone had turned in to sleep, when he saw in darkness that the medium, who was in a nearby room to that where he was with his wife, entered their room and opened and closed a drawer of his wife's dressing table. Then she left silently. They went to her room and found her in bed, apparently sleeping. She woke up and denied having been in the other room, a denial that continued the next day when asked about the incident again.

Ochorowicz, who believed that Palladino was in a somnambulistic state, decided to use table tilting to question the medium's spirit control about the incident. The improvised séance, with the medium out of trance, revealed, to Palladino's surprise, that she had in fact been in Ochorowicz's room looking for matches, and that she was neither in her normal nor trance state, but sleepwalking. This is a woman, Ochorowicz wrote, "who is capable to be in an entirely different psychic state from one moment to another" (Ochorowicz, 1896, p. 102).

Ochorowicz argued that at the beginning of a séance the medium produced inferior phenomena (automatisms leading to fraud), so she needed some time before every séance to go deeper into "physiological doubling" (dissociation) to produce real phenomena. This involved separation between the medium's brain and her nervous centers and separation from the "dynamism" of her bodily limbs. Ochorowicz wrote:

> Before arriving at this last point, which constitutes the node of higher mediumship, the medium must necessarily cheat, because she is not aware of the position of her members, which sometimes become hyperesthetized and insensitive, or of the difference that there is between a movement performed remotely and a direct movement, since this is always *her* arm, sometimes palpable and sometimes impalpable, executing the ordered movement. Gradually the doubling increases, subjective differences are accentuated, and then we *can* be expected to watch her reflexes; her hand, which naturally seeks to free itself and to follow the direction of her thoughts, does not go too far in that direction, and does not execute the movement herself. (Ochorowicz, 1896, pp. 109–110)

Without any influence to contradict these factors, Ochorowicz affirmed, "*the medium will always cheat*" (Ochorowicz, 1896, p. 107).

Ochorowicz saw the phenomena of Palladino as produced by psychic forces related to the medium and the sitters (on this concept see Note 12). He believed that John King, the medium's spirit control, was a "special psychic state that allowed the vital dynamism of the medium … to act out at a distance in certain exceptional conditions" (p. 104). In his view the action of the spirit control could change according to the suggestive influences of the circle. As he wrote:

> After recognizing that the medium is only a mirror that reflects and directs the ideas and nerve forces of the sitters towards an ideoplastic goal,[20] we will not be surprised to see that suggestion plays an important role. It is not doubtful that the sitters can suggest to the medium the desired act, and there is no doubt that manifestations take on the character of the surrounding beliefs. I have seen "John" in the company of materialists dissolve into an impersonal force that the medium simply called: "*questa forza*;" [this force] while in intimate circles of spiritists, he took the form of dead people, more or less clumsily. Similarly, with controllers imbued with the idea of fraud … *the medium will remain under the influence of a suggestion of fraud.* (Ochorowicz, 1896, p. 111)

Théodore Flournoy

Swiss psychologist Théodore Flournoy (1854–1920) became well-known for his studies of mediumship and various psychological phenomena (see Alvarado et al., 2014; Claparède, 1921). In an early paper, "Genèse de Quelques Prétendus Messages Spirites," Flournoy (1899) explained cases of mediumship via the "medium's subconscious imagination, working on recollections or latent concerns" (Flournoy, 1899, p. 144). Flournoy concluded the paper stating that in healthy and normal persons the psychological state may be affected by mediumship, producing simulations of communications from spirits, being instead "the results of the subliminal operation of the ordinary faculties of the subject" (Flournoy, 1899, p. 158). The powers of this subconscious imagination, he wrote in a different paper, were able to "attain a degree of complexity and extension in no way different from the compositions and reflexions of the thinker and the novelist" (Flournoy, 1897, p. 419).

In the now classic study *From India to the Planet Mars: A Study of a Case of Somnambulism*, Flournoy (1900) focused on Héléne Smith (pseudonym for Catherine Elise Muller [1861–1929]), a medium who showed various automatisms and who became well-known about her communications involving planet Mars, including a Martian language, and previous lives in India and in France.[21] Various communicators manifested through Smith, among them Victor Hugo, Marie Antoinette, and Leopold, who claimed to be Giuseppe Balsamo, the famous Cagliostro.

We are told that Smith had visions since childhood, and that she later experienced spontaneous episodes of daydreaming and reverie in which she saw images in her field of vision and heard voices. She also had impressions of solitude and of not belonging to her family. Her years of puberty showed a "wildness of … dreams and automatisms, which were symptoms of a tendency to mental disintegration" (Flournoy, 1900, p. 33).

Smith showed trance, which could be partial (when she was in contact with a sitter, and with waking visons) or complete. During the latter she would awake "slowly through phases of deep sleep, alternating with relapses into somnambulistic gestures and attitudes, moments of catalepsy, etc. The final awakening is always preceded by several brief awakenings, followed by relapses into sleep" (p. 61).

Flournoy further wrote about her:

> In her daily life she has only passing hallucinations limited to one or two of the senses, superficial hemisomnambulisms, compatible with a certain amount of self-possession ... ephemeral perturbations of no importance from a practical point of view ... In the séances, on the contrary, she presents the most grave functional alterations that one can imagine, and passes through accesses of lethargy, catalepsy, somnambulism, total change of personality ... (Flournoy, 1900, pp. 47–48).

As a medium she showed automatic writing and what Flournoy referred to as a "tendency of the subliminal imagination to reconstruct the deceased and to feign their presence" (p. 425). She also painted images that she perceived, some of which were related to Mars, and was susceptible to suggestions during the séances that could affect her waking experiences.

The spirit personalities and "romances" by the medium were considered to be produced via

> the enormous suggestibility and auto-suggestibility of mediums, which render them so sensitive to all the influences of spiritistic reunions, and are so favorable to the play of those brilliant subliminal creations in which, occasionally, the doctrinal ideas of the surrounding environment are reflected together with the latent emotional tendencies of the medium herself. (Flournoy, 1900, p. 443)

One of the communicators, Leopold, was seen by the medium, but also wrote automatically, producing different calligraphy than the medium, a phenomenon recorded from the early days of Spiritualism (e.g., Edmonds & Dexter, 1853, Appendix A). Leopold's communications, considered by Flournoy to originate from "that deep and delicate sphere in which we so often encounter the roots of hypnoid phenomena" (Flournoy, 1900, p. 91), were seen as a function of the interaction between the spiritistic context of the séance and the medium's suggestibility. This communicator "spoke with a deep bass voice, and a strong, easily recognizable Italian accent" (p. 104). The medium, Flournoy said, sometimes looked different when Leopold came through. Her "eyelids drop; her expression changes; her throat swells into a sort of double chin, which gives her a likeness of some sort to the well-known figure of Cagliostro" (p. 104).[22]

Final Thoughts

Overview

It is my hope that the brief summaries presented here of the writings of Tascher, Baillarger, Taine, Richet, Myers, von Hartmann, James, Janet, Ochorowicz, Héricourt, Liébeault, Blocq, Binet, and Flournoy will inform modern readers about some important, and somewhat forgotten nineteenth century ideas on the subject. To a great extent discussions of nineteenth century mediumship in terms of dissociation, and the unconscious regions of the mind, were part of a common trend to reduce unusual phenomena to known concepts of medicine and psychology (Gongalves & Ortega, 2013), a strategy seen frequently with mediumship (Le Maléfan, 1999). But there were different degrees of reductionism. Some, more consistent with the scientific establishment, only included dissociation (with manifestations such as changes of personality and state-specific memory), while others combined both dissociation and the supernormal.[23]

While some of the authors of these writings emphasized the potential of the unconscious mind (Myers, Flournoy), others, as seen in the writings of Baillarger, von Hartmann, Janet, Blocq, and Binet, wrote in the context of pathology, something common in the writings of many French physicians and other nineteenth century students of mediumship (see Note 6).

Certainly, sampling biases may account for the association with pathology. If physicians looked for mediums among mental patients it is not surprising that many of them showed some degree of psychopathology. In addition, one wonders if physicians such as Janet actually saw enough mediums to make proper generalizations. But the idea did not escape criticism at the time.

The pathology of mediumship, an idea that seems to be less prevalent now, was combated by many (e.g., Crowell, 1877; Delanne, 1897b).[24] An example is Myers' critique of Pierre Janet, consisting of the point that Janet's observations were limited to hysterics and other medical patients, which biased his ideas (Myers, 1889, p. 188; see also Maxwell, 1905/1903, p. 261). Furthermore, Gabriel Delanne (1857–1926), an engineer and leading French spiritist, was also critical of Janet and ideas of pathology. In his *Le Phénomène Spirite* Delanne (1897b) stated he had never seen hysterical crises in mediums (p. 137), and that pathology did not explain veridical phenomena with mediums (p. 143).[25] The latter point was also made by Italian student of psychic phenomena Ernesto Bozzano (1862–1943), known for his strong defenses of discarnate agency. Bozzano (1899) also stated that "no theory of mental disaggregation or of subconscious automatism" could explain the evidence for supernormal knowledge found in the above-cited work of Richard Hodgson with Mrs. Piper (p. 364). In his view, ideas of subconscious activity and telepathy were too "elastic" and insufficient to explain mediumship without the inclusion of discarnate agency (see also the critiques published by other defenders of the spirit agency explanation such as Brofferio, 1892, pp. 323–324, and Noel, 1885).[26]

Myers was an example of a student of mediumship who not only discussed dissociative aspects of mediums' performances, but also believed there was evidence to accept that mediums produced veridical phenomena, such as information about sitters that could not be accounted for by conventional mechanisms. But he went beyond this. In his view the subliminal self-manifesting via dissociative means and other ways was the real self, and one that was not material, so it was the part that would survive bodily death (Myers, 1903, Vol. 1, p. 222; for similar views see du Prel, 1889/1884, and Geley, 1899). His ideas were controversial, not only for their emphasis on veridical cases, but because at the time many speculations about the unconscious emphasized pathological processes. Perhaps Myers would have furthered his position if instead of depending mainly on the work of others, he had conducted his own observations and experiments as did Gurney (1884) and Janet (1889).

There were others who accepted veridical mediumship (e.g., Hodgson, 1892; Lodge, 1890), as did James. His work represents an important early empirical attempt to study mediumship, and to relate it to dissociation and "supernormal" aspects of the medium's performance (Alvarado, 2016). But the majority of students of dissociation seemed to be skeptical about this possibility and ignored this aspect of the work of psychical researchers. In fact, this prejudice, a problem with which psychical researchers still have to contend with today, led to the rejection of work that had the potential of enlarging conceptions of dissociation. Most of the time the veridical aspects of mediumship were just ignored or glossed over, or explained via suppositions that were not empirical, that expressed skepticism without showing actual mistakes. Such glossing over the issue was the case with both Binet and Janet, discussed above. Von Hartmann and Flournoy were exceptions, as was Richet. But both Richet and Flournoy wrote about veridical mediumship later, which brings us to twentieth century writings.

Into the Twentieth Century

The perspective of the joint action of dissociation and veridical inform – ation was further discussed by several later students of the subject (e.g., Flournoy, 1911; Kotik, 1908; Richet, 1922; Sudre, 1926). Flournoy (1911) stated the need to consider the combination of "mental transmission [telepathy] with the products to which memory and subconscious imagination of the sitters can give birth" (p. 213). All the evidential cases with Mrs. Piper, wrote German philosopher Traugott Konstantin Oesterreich (1880–1949), might be accounted for by the medium's creative imagination and telepathy working together (Oesterreich, 1923, pp. 44–45).

An important member of the Society for Psychical Research, Eleanor Sidgwick (1845–1936), who later became convinced of the possibility of communication with the dead, stated in her study "A Contribution to the Study of the Psychology of Mrs. Piper's Trance Phenomena":

> I think it is probably a state of self-induced hypnosis in which her hypnotic self personates different characters either consciously and deliberately, or unconsciously and believing herself to be the person she represents, and sometimes probably in a state of consciousness intermediate between the two. In the trance state her normal powers transcend in some directions those of her ordinary waking self … And further … she can obtain, imperfectly and for the most part fragmentarily, telepathic impressions. (E. Sidgwick, 1915, p. 330)

While such ideas are plausible if one accepts both dissociation (with its dynamics and need-serving capabilities), they are also speculative to a great degree. The analyses to support them are not always clear, and on many occasions they seem to depend on the preferences of the analyst, as compared with some clear evidence in the case, a problem shared with many psychodynamic analyses.

Nonetheless, these, and other issues, continued to be discussed during the twentieth century. Both Geley (1920/1919) and Myers (1903) disagreed with those who played down the importance of the unconscious mind and dissociation, arguing that mediumship and other phenomena showed the transcendental nature of the unconscious self, one that was not material and survived death. In Geley's words, when the higher faculties of the unconscious are released by the "decentralization" of limiting factors, we need to realize that they "are more completely accessible to us after the final rupture of those limitations by death" (Geley, 1919/1920, p. 262).[27]

Other relevant twentieth century discussions included the writings about specific mediums such as Mrs. Smead (Hyslop, 1906a), Helene Preiswerk (1881–1911) (Jung, 1975/1902), Hélène Smith (Flournoy, 1901), Eusapia Palladino (Morselli, 1908), and Leonora E. Piper (Tanner, 1910). The personalities manifested by Preiswerk, wrote psychologist Carl G. Jung (1875–1961), "are nothing but dramatized split-offs from her dream-ego" (Jung, 1975/1902, p. 78). Similarly, Ochorowicz referred to one of Stanislawa Tomczyck's controls as an "unconscious creation" that communicated via the "complementary unconscious imagination of the medium" (Ochorowicz, 1910, p. 130).

The concept of dissociation was present in discussions of pathology (e.g., Ballet, 1911; Janet, 1909; Lévy-Valensi, 1910), including French physician Joseph Grasset's (1849–1918) complex model of automatisms involving multiple unconscious processing centers (Grasset, 1908).[28] Automatic writing, wrote a physician from a psychiatric hospital, was a form of psychological doubling in mediums developed due to emotional shocks, similar to those observed in the insane (Viollet, 1908, p. 25).

There were also later discussions of personation that assumed the workings of the unconscious imagination of mediums (Flournoy, 1911; Lebiedzinski, 1924; Maxwell, 1905/1903). This included French writer and psychical researcher's René Sudre's (1880–1968) essays about different aspects of the phenomenon, *Personnages d'Au-Dela* (Sudre, 1946), where he discussed pathological personation, such as that seen in hysteria, in mediumship, and in other contexts. In his view, the workings of the subliminal imagination produced personalities in both pathology and mediumship. But in mediumship, "thanks to the metapsychic faculties of the medium, they are satisfactory copies of an original that lived in the real scene of the world" (p. 59).[29]

Writing in his well-known *Traité de Métapsychique*, Richet (1922, pp. 55–62) devoted space in the book to argue for the existence of the unconscious capabilities of mediums to create characters and stories surrounding them (see also Alvarado, 2019a, Chap. 6). In his view: "The talents of the unconscious have more variety than the talents of the conscious" (Richet, 1922, p. 50). Echoing others such as Flournoy (1900, 1911), Richet argued that such talents were a combination of the workings of the unconscious mind of the medium and its memories, which were never forgotten, a phenomenon he called "pantomnesia" (Richet, 1922, p. 59).

There were also some discussions of the different gradations of mediumistic trance and of apparent different states of consciousness (Morselli, 1908, Vol. 1, pp. 258, 272–273; E. Sidgwick, 1915, Chaps. 6 and 7). It was argued by some that medium Eusapia Palladino showed phenomena of higher magnitude in deeper stages of trance (Lombroso, 1909, pp. 104–105; Visani Scozzi, 1901, pp. 392–393). However, Morselli (Vol. 1, p. 209) disagreed, arguing that the medium showed no "absolute correspondence with the depth or phase of her trance states."

The idea that unconscious memories could account for some of the productions of mental mediums was accepted by some (e.g., Hyslop, 1906a, p. 215). This was also the case of American neurologist Morton Prince (1854–1929), who postulated that when the mind is in states lacking balance it may exteriorize unconscious memories. "Such phenomena," including mediumship and automatisms, "may then be interpreted as the *flowering of functioning of the unconscious*" (Prince, 1914, p. 260)?[30]

But mention must also be made of those who argued for discarnate influence as compared with secondary personalities (e.g., Bozzano, 1923; Thomas, 1922). This included, among many, Myers' statement regarding Mrs. Thompson about his belief that most of her communications "are uttered through Mrs. Thompson's organism by spirits who for the time inform or 'possess' that organism" (Myers, 1902, p. 73).

To conclude, perhaps the last word should be left to American philosopher and psychical researcher James H. Hyslop (1854–1920), who, while a strong believer in the supernormal and in survival of death, also saw that some cases could be explained by dissociation and other workings of the unconscious mind. He wrote:

> The skeptic has apparently still to learn that the phenomena of secondary personality, while they indicate decided limitations to the supernormal, do not exclude the use of subliminal conditions for the transmission of it; and the ready believer in spirits has still to learn that these agencies are not so frequently active as he imagines. (Hyslop, 1906b, p. 297)

Concluding Remarks

We need to keep in mind that, in addition to dissociation, and the general workings of the unconscious mind, there are probably several other factors influencing mediumship, among them the health of mediums, the effects of practice, and the psycho-social environment in which séances are conducted. Writing about physical mediums, German physician and psychical researcher Albert F. von Schrenck-Notzing (1862–1929) mentioned the suggestive influences of sitters and experimenters, and, on the side of the mediums, their spiritualistic ideas and training, and unknown physical dispositions

(Schrenck-Notzing, 1920, pp. 182–183). Certainly these, and other ideas, need to be considered in the context of the discussion presented above.

In the meantime, we would do well to remember that the ideas presented in this article belong to the various attempts—be they from psychical research, psychiatry, psychology, or Spiritualism—to explore the human mind empirically. For psychological science, ideas about mediumship were one more strand supporting the development of concepts about secondary mental states, what William James (1890a) referred to as the "hidden self."

Notes

1 For some discussions about the historical interrelationships between mediumship and dissociation see my previous papers (e.g., Alvarado, 2010, 2014) and the work of Crabtree (1993) and Le Maléfan (1999).

2 On this, and other relevant phenomena, see Friedman (2014) and Taves (1999). Many of these cases were referred to as trance, a term that has had different meanings and that remains to this day a vague and unprecise expression. In addition to its use to refer to alterations of consciousness in the literatures of mesmerism, hypnosis, and Spiritualism, during the last century the term was applied to automatic actions of habitual alcohol drinkers, lethargy, catalepsy, and deathlike states with near-death experiences elements. Interestingly, and reflecting various theoretical emphases, the terms dream, sleep, and somnambulism were used during the nineteenth century to cover a variety of visionary and dissociative phenomena (T. James, 1995, pp. 7–8).

3 Magnetic somnambulists were also credited with producing discourses about such things as God, evil, and religion (e.g., Olivier, 1854), and about other planets and celestial bodies (e.g., Peabody, 1838, Chaps. 9, 11). Deleuze (1813, Vol. 1, pp. 181–182) refers to somnambulistic dissertations about metaphysical and medical topics, and about a case he saw of a six-year-old girl who talked about and answered questions about several diseases.

4 Azam (1892), Binet (1892/1896), Elliotson (1846), and Myers (1888) presented discussions of cases of secondary personalities during the nineteenth century, as did Guinon (1891–1892) in his discussion of published cases and cases studied at the Salpêtrière. See also the work of Crabtree (1993), Hacking (1995), Kenny (1986), and Taylor and Martin's (1944) review of cases.

5 One theorist stated: "It is undeniable that the tendency of mediumship is to unhinge the mind, to destroy the mental balance, and often to produce the worst forms of insanity" (Hudson, 1893, p. 329). For overviews of pathological ideas about mediumship, see Alvarado (2018a), Alvarado and Zingrone (2012), and Le Maléfan (1999).

6 For overviews of the Piper case, see Gauld (1982, Chap. 3) and Tymn (2013). She became one of those paradigmatic cases that, in addition to her role as a producer of evidence for survival of death, and for the workings of dissociation, provided a focus that assisted in the development of methodological and conceptual issues in psychical research, and views about the workings of mental mediumship. Regarding dissociation, her case presented much information about the complexity of various shades and stages of trance (e.g., Hodgson, 1898, pp. 397-399; see also the detailed overview by E. Sidgwick, 1915).

7 On personation see Maxwell (1903/1905, pp. 64–71), Myers (1903, Vol. 2, Chap. 9), and Sudre (1926, 1946).

8 Unconscious cerebration referred to non-conscious production of ideas and actions via automatic brain processes (Carpenter, 1874, Chap. 13). On early nineteenth-century discussions of table turning, and its explanation by the idea of unconscious muscular movements, see Alvarado (2018b).

9 On Myers' ideas see Kelly (2007). Myers was influential in terms of ideas about unconscious action, but his defense of the supernormal was not well-received by many outside psychical research circles. Writing about automatists, he stated that some authors who cited him ignored his evidence for veridical information (Myers, 1892, p. 420).

10 Several writers in the early spiritualist literature argued for the influence of the medium's mental content on mediumistic communications (e.g., Ballou, 1852, p. 67; Brittan, 1852; Davis, 1853, p. 203; Edmonds and Dexter, 1855, pp. 39–41). There are also discussions about problems from the side of the presumed spirit communicators (see the later writings of Hyslop, e.g., 1901b, 1914).

11 The spiritualistic and psychical research literatures have many examples of discussions of these forces, presumed to come from the human body, as the agent behind mediumistic phenomena, such as movement of objects and materializations (for reviews, see Alvarado, 2006, and Alvarado & Nahm, 2011).

12 James wrote about this: "But the odd thing is that persons unexposed to spiritualist traditions will so often act in the same way when they become entranced … I have no theory to publish of these cases, several of which I have personally seen" (W. James, 1890a, Vol. 1, p. 394).

13 This interest in case studies is evident in W. James' lectures about exceptional mental states (E. Taylor, 1983) and in several of his publications (W. James, 1886, 1889, 1909). The importance of research "subjects" and clinical patients in the development of psychology and psychical research has been discussed elsewhere (e.g., Alvarado, 1993; Carroy, 1991; Hustvedt, 2011).

14 Another investigator of Piper reported he was not successful in making Piper perform acts with post-hypnotic suggestion, nor to obtain "some manifestation of Phinuit by gesture, speech, or automatic writing, in reply to our inquiries and commands, and during the trance state some manifestation of Mrs. Piper" (Hodgson, 1892, p. 56).

15 Janet cited many of Myers' observations in his discussion of mediumship (Janet, 1889, pp. 78, 121–122, 135–136, 371, 392–394, 403, 405, 415–419). He disagreed in several ways with Myers, but he credited him with presenting a theory involving "mental disintegration" in his articles about automatic writing, which Janet thought was more developed than previously published ideas (p. 403). Crabtree (2003) has compared the approaches of both men.

16 Janet was citing Myers about a medium presenting choreic movements. What Myers (1885, p. 32) mentioned was "a stage of inco-ordinated movements, which might almost be taken for choreic," a comment referring to a case reported to him that involved writing in "an abruptly, jerking, and irregular way" (Myers, 1885, p. 27), not necessarily of choreic origin. Writing about Mrs. Piper, others have referred to jerking, twitching, and convulsive movements, sometimes taking place at the beginning of her trance (Hodgson, 1898, pp. 483, 587; Hyslop, 1901a, pp. 303, 304, 312; Leaf, 1890, pp. 618–619; Lodge, 1890, p. 444). According to Hodgson (1899, p. 55), these convulsions eventually stopped. A writer discussing mediumistic trance mentioned the "more or less tonic or clonic spasms" sometimes presented by mediums (Loveland, 1889, p. 49), while another stated that six cases of mediums showing convulsions, he knew about were probably influenced by suggestion because they had seen other mediums doing the same (Anonymous, 1888, p. 285). Medium Eusapia Palladino said in 1902 that she was suffering from convulsions, which descriptions suggested Jacksonian epilepsy (Morselli, 1908, Vol. 1, p. 126).

17 James (1889, p. 549) found tactile anesthesia in two out of three automatic writers, as did others with various mediums (Magnin, 1903, p. 233; Newbold, 1898, p. 12; Morselli, 1908, Vol. 2, p. 14; Ochorowicz, 1896, p. 100). But Flournoy (1900, p. 42) did not. In the United States, physician William A. Hammond (1828–1900) claimed that mediums frequently experienced sensations of formication, numbness, prickling, and water on the skin, which he believed were an indication of nervous problems (Hammond, 1876, p. 118). Troubles of sensibility, such as loss of sensation in parts of the body, and hyperesthesia, were frequently discussed during the nineteenth century as symptoms of hysteria (e.g., Gilles de la Tourette, 1891, Vol. 1, Chaps. 4 through 7).

18 For information about Palladino's life and phenomena see the classic overviews of Carrington (1909) and de Rochas (1896, pp. 1–315), and more recent writings (e.g., Alvarado, 1993, 2011; Inglis, 1992, Chaps. 35, 38).

19 There are many instances of (presumably unconscious) fraud throughout Palladino's career (e.g., Carrington, 1909, p. 182; Flammarion, 1907, pp. 520–521). For an early mention of possible unconscious fraud with the Fox sisters see Figuier (1860, pp. 334, 344).

20 In this context ideoplasty referred to the use of psychic forces to fulfill an idea involving physical phenomena, a topic I have briefly discussed elsewhere (Alvarado, 2019c, pp. 79–80, see also Bozzano, 1926–1927; Hess, 2018). Ochorowicz speculated about collective agency to explain physical phenomena. This was the creation of a "separate dynamic body, at the expense of the sitters, including the medium" (Ochorowicz, 1896, p. 107), an idea similar to previous speculations about collective agency to account for physical phenomena (e.g., Anonymous, 1875; de Gasparin, 1854). The exteriorization of nerve force referred to was more clearly conceptualized later as a form of physical dissociation "between the organs [of the body] and the dynamic principle animating them, which can go as far as extra-organic manifestations, that is, outside the body" (Ochorowicz, 1909, p. 757). Similar versions of this idea were presented by others (Mackenzie, 1923, p. 200; Purdon, 1889, p. 1).

21 Flournoy's (1900) account of the case became a classic of turn-of-the-century ideas about the creative capabilities of the subconscious mind, attracting much attention in various circles (on the reception of the book, see Alvarado & Zingrone, 2015). The book has been frequently discussed as an influential example of subliminal creative ability (e.g., Maraldi & Alvarado, 2018). In addition, Flournoy's study "became a key addition to the other paradigm cases of mediumship and multiple personality that defined the era" (E. Taylor, 2009, p. 41).

22 In a long paper Flournoy (1901) later continued discussing the case along the same lines. In addition, he discussed new communications about the Moon and Uranus, the dynamics of the Leopold communicator, and the influence of investigators on the unconscious productions of the medium. In later years the medium produced many paintings focusing on religious topics (Deonna, 1932; Lemaitre, 1908).

23 It has been argued that inhibition (or dissociation?) of interfering material such as the content of the medium's mind and irrelevant spirit communications, could facilitate spirit action. Hodgson (1898, p. 401) referred to the need to avoid or to lessen confusions coming from various spirit communicators and from the medium's mind (see also Hyslop, 1910, p. 379; Hyslop, 1918, pp. 226, 231). This last author also argued, rather unclearly, that dissociation may be essential to real spirit mediumship, even in non-veridical cases (Hyslop, 1919, p. 403).

24 There were also more complex views involving the coexistence of both pathology and supernormal phenomena (e.g., Lombroso, 1909; Lum, 1873; Morselli, 1908). See also Alvarado (2019b) and Alvarado & Biondi (2017).

25 Interestingly, Delanne (1897a), like other spiritists, defended the existence of the perispirit, a fluidic body surrounding the spirit that was believed to provide a bridge between the spirit and the physical body involved with sensations, memories, and other processes. It was said that this principle explained unconscious memories and dissociation due to changes in the vibratory rate of the perispirit (p. 226). Delanne's views were consistent with some ideas of mesmeric pathology (Alvarado, 2019b).

26 For reviews of such critiques in the context of Flournoy and the Society for Psychical Research, see Alvarado & Zingrone (2015) and Cerullo (1982). Independently of this, the validity and usefulness of the concept of the unconscious mind was put in doubt for other reasons during the early twentieth century by some psychologists (e.g., Angell, 1909, p. 456; Titchener, 1915, pp. 327-328). Lack of interest in mediumship and dissociation by psychologists and psychiatrists was probably related to the lack of regard many had about the psychical researchers' emphasis in veridical mediumistic communications and the fact that there were many different concepts about the unconscious, most of which were not open to veridical manifestations (Münsterberg et al., 1910).

27 Geley (1905) had already written about this in an earlier book in which he defended the existence of a subconscious mind with supernormal faculties. This self, he maintained, operated independently of the physical body, and preexisted and survived the physical body.

28 He proposed the existence of a superior psychism (our usual state of consciousness) and of an inferior psychism, made of a series of "polygons," or supposed centers in the nervous systems in charge of specific sensory and motor functions, generally automatic and unconscious. The polygons could coordinate the phenomena of mediumship (and other processes such as imagination, memory, and motor activity), during trance and during pathological states. Grasset also postulated that polygonal action did not involve veridical manifestations. In his view a medium was an individual with a facility to manifest polygonal action more than most persons. See also Grasset (1904, 1906).

29 Another discussion of personation, and other mediumistic productions, came from the Italian psychiatrist Enrico Morselli (1852–1929), who discussed the topic in his book *Psicologia e "Spiritismo"* (Morselli, 1908, Vol. 2, pp. 63–67, 115–119). He argued that ideas in the unconscious minds of mediums, characterized by an infantile mentality, emerged when the medium was in the proper state. These ideas were organized by "the subconscious Imagination [which] … arranges them in its own way, fertilizes and complicates them, and builds spirit romances" (Vol. 2, p. 468). Morselli was also keen to point out that phenomena took place when Palladino presumably was in her waking state, and that the medium "follows with her conscious attention all the developments of the phenomena …" (Morselli, 1908, Vol. 1, p. 385).

30 Many other topics were considered during the early twentieth century, among them the concept of unconscious fraud (Hamilton et al., 1911), the similarity of spirit communicators to the phenomena reported in double and multiple personality cases (Troubridge, 1922), and analyses of automatic writing in terms of the authorship of the messages (anonymous and signed messages), the content of the messages (length, meaningless phrases), and language issues (meaningless words, poetic expressions) (Verrall, 1906).

References

A., J. A. (1869). Remarkable case of somnambulism. *Chicago Medical Journal, 26*(20), 650–655.

Abercrombie, J. (1838). *Inquiries concerning the intellectual powers and the investigation of truth* (8th ed.). J. Murray.

Aksakof, A. (1895). *Animisme et spiritisme* (B. Sandow, Trans.). P.-G. Leymarie (Original work published in German, 1890)

Alvarado, C. S. (1993). Gifted subjects' contributions to psychical research: The case of Eusapia Palladino. *Journal of the Society for Psychical Research, 59*(833), 269–292.

Alvarado, C. S. (2002). Dissociation in Britain during the late nineteenth century: The Society for Psychical Research, 1882–1900. *Journal of Trauma and Dissociation, 3*(2), 9–33.

Alvarado, C. S. (2006). Human radiations: Concepts of force in mesmerism, spiritualism and psychical research. *Journal of the Society for Psychical Research, 70.3*(884), 138–162.

Alvarado, C. S. (2009). Ambroise August Liébeault and psychic phenomena. *American Journal of Clinical Hypnosis, 52*(2), 111–121.

Alvarado, C. S. (2010). Classic text no. 84: 'Divisions of personality and spiritism' by Alfred Binet (1896). *History of Psychiatry, 21*(4), 487–500.

Alvarado, C. S. (2011). Eusapia Palladino: An autobiographical essay. *Journal of Scientific Exploration, 25*(1), 77–101.

Alvarado, C. S. (2014). Mediumship, psychical research, dissociation, and the powers of the subconscious mind. *Journal of Parapsychology, 78*(1), 98–114.

Alvarado, C. S. (2016). Classic text no. 105: 'Report of the Committee on Mediumistic Phenomena,' by William James (1886). *History of Psychiatry, 27*(1), 85–100.

Alvarado, C. S. (2018a). Mediumship and pathology. In R. McLuhan (Ed.), *Psi encyclopedia.*

Alvarado, C. S. (2018b). Table turning in the early 1850s: The séance reports of Agénor de Gasparin. *Journal of Scientific Exploration, 32*(4), 723–762.

Alvarado, C. S. (2019a). *Charles Richet: A Nobel Prize winning scientist's explorations of psychic phenomena.* White Crow Books.

Alvarado, C. S. (2019b, September). Classic text no. 119: Jules Bernard Luys on magnetic pathology. *History of Psychiatry, 30*(3), 359–374.

Alvarado, C. S. (2019c). Musings on materializations: Eric J. Dingwall on "The Plasma Theory." *Journal of Scientific Exploration, 33*(1), 73–113.

Alvarado, C. S., & Biondi, M. (2017, June). Classic text no. 110: Cesare Lombroso on mediumship and pathology. *History of Psychiatry, 28*(2), 225–241.

Alvarado, C. S., Maraldi, E. O., Machado, F. R., & Zangari, W. (2014). Théodore Flournoy's contributions to psychical research. *Journal of the Society for Psychical Research, 78.3*(916), 149–168.

Alvarado, C. S., & Nahm, M. (2011). Psychic phenomena and the vital force: Hereward Carrington on "Vital energy and psychical phenomena." *Journal of the Society for Psychical Research, 75.2*(903), 91–103.

Alvarado, C. S., & Zingrone, N. L. (2012). Classic text no. 90: 'The Pathology and Treatment of Mediomania', by Frederic Rowland Marvin (1874). *History of Psychiatry, 23*(2), 229–244.

Alvarado, C. S., & Zingrone, N. L. (2015). Note on the reception of Théodore Flournoy's study of Des Indes à la Planète Mars. *Journal of the Society for Psychical Research, 79.3*(920), 156–164.

Angell, J. R. (1909). *Psychology: An introductory study of the structure and function of human consciousness* (4th rev. ed.). Henry Holt.

Anonymous. (1854, April 22). Spirit personations—Death scenes. In *The Spiritual Telegraph* (Vol. III: *Telegraph Papers*), 201–206. Partridge & Brittan.

Anonymous. (1875, March 19). Speculations relating to new facts in spiritualism. *Spiritualist Newspaper*.

Anonymous. (1888). The connection of hypnotism with the subjective phenomena of spiritualism. *Proceedings of the Society for Psychical Research, 5*(13), 279–287.

Anonymous. (1914). Le Docteur Jules Héricourt—Notice biographique. *Science et Vie, 4*(11), 277.

Azam, [E. E.]. (1887). *Hypnotisme, double conscience et altérations de la personnalité: Le cas Felida X.* J.-B. Baillière et fils.

Azam, E. (1892). Double consciousness. In D. H. Tuke (Ed.), *A dictionary of psychological medicine* (Vol. 1, pp. 401–406). J. & A. Churchill.

Baillarger, J. (1861). [Untitled communication to the Société Médico-Psychologique]. *Annales Médico-Psychologiques, 7*(3), 92–93.
Ballet, G. (1911). La psychose hallucinatoire chronique et la désagrégation de la personnalité. *L'encéphale, 8*(6), 501–508.
Ballou, A. (1852). *An exposition of views respecting the principal facts, causes, and peculiarities involved in spirit manifestations.* Bela Marsh.
Barkworth, T. (1891–1892). Some recent experiments in automatic writing. *Proceedings of the Society for Psychical Research, 7*(18), 23–29.
Baxter, R. (1833). *Narrative of facts, characterizing the supernatural manifestations in members of Mr. Irwin's congregation and other individuals, in England and Scotland, and formerly in the writer himself.* James Nisbet.
Beard, G. M. (1879). The psychology of spiritualism. *North American Review, 129,* 65–81,
Beaunis, H. (1885). L'expérimentation en psychologie par le somnambulisme provoqué. *Revue Philosophique de la France et de l'Étranger, 20,* 1–36, 113–134.
Belden, L. W. (1834). *An account of Jane C. Rider, the Springfield somnambulist: The substance of which was delivered as a lecture before the Springfield Lyceum, Jan. 22, 1834.* G. and C. Merriam.
Bertrand, A. (1823). *Traité du somnambulisme et des differentes modifications qu'il présente.* J. G. Dentu.
Binet, A. (1889). Recherches sur les altérations de la conscience chez les hystériques. *Revue Philosophique de la France et de l'Étranger, 27,* 135–170.
Binet, A. (1890). *On double consciousness: Experimental psychological studies.* Open Court.
Binet, A. (1891, February 15). Les altérations de la personnalité d'après les travaux récens. *Revue des deux Mondes, 103,* 839–855.
Binet, A. (1896). *Alterations of personality.* D. Appleton. (Original work published in French, 1892])
Binet, A., & Féré, C. (1887). Recherches expérimentales sur la physiologie des mouvements chez les hystériques. *Archives de Physiologie Normale et Pathologique, 9*(s. 3), 320–373.
Biondi, M. (1988). *Tavoli e medium: Storia dello Spiritismo in Italia.* Gremese.
Blocq, P. (1889). L'écriture médianimique. *Bulletin Médical, 3,* 1435–1437.
Bourneville, [D. M.] (Ed.). (1886). *Oeuvres complètes de J. M. Charcot* (Vol. 1). Bureaux du Progrès Médical.
Bourru, H., & Burot, P. (1888). *Variations de la personnalité.* J.-B. Baillière.
Bozzano, E. (1899). Spiritualismo e critica scientifica. *Rivista di Studi Psichici, 5*(11–12), 356–379.
Bozzano, E. (1923, May 31–June 30). La storia di "Stasia". *Luce e Ombra, 23*(5–6), 171–179.
Bozzano, E. (November 1926–July 1927). Pensiero e volontà: Forze plasticizzante e organizzanti. *Luce e Ombra, 26*(11), 481–488; *26*(12), 556–563; *27*(1), 34–44; *27*(2–3), 60–69, *27*(4), 164–175; *27*(5), 223–230; *27*(6)250–262.
Braid, J. (1853). *Hypnotic therapeutics, illustrated by cases: With an appendix on table- moving and spirit-rapping.* Murray and James.
Brittan, S. B. (1852). Cerebral influence on revelation. *The Shekinah, 2,* 39–43.
Brittan, S. B., & Richmond, B. W. (1853). *A discussion of the facts and philosophy of ancient and modern spiritualism.* Partridge & Brittan.
Brofferio, A. (1892). *Per lo Spiritismo.* Domenico Briola.
Cahagnet, L.A. (1848–1854). *Magnetisme* (3 vols.). Author (Vol. 1). Germer Baillière (Vols. 2 & 3).
[Carpenter, W. B.]. (1853). Electrobiology and mesmerism. *Quarterly Review, 93*(186), 501–557.
Carpenter, W. B. (1874). *Principles of mental physiology.* D. Appleton.
Carrer, L. (Comp. & Trans.) (2002). *Ambroise-August Liébeault: The hypnological legacy of a secular saint.* Virtualbookworm.com
Carrington, H. (1909). *Eusapia Palladino and her phenomena.* B. W. Dodge.
Carroy, J. (1991). *Hypnose, suggestion et psychologie: L'invention de sujets.* Presses Universitaires de France.
Carroy, J., & Plas, R. (1996). The origins of French experimental psychology: Experiment and experimentalism. *History of the Human Sciences, 9*(1), 73–84.
Carus, C. G. (1857). *Über Lebensmagnetismus und über die magischen Wirkungen überhaupt.* F. A. Brockhaus.
Casaubon, M. (1655). *A treatise concerning enthusiasme.* Printed by R. D.
Cerullo, J. J. (1982). *The secularization of the soul: Psychical research in modern Britain.* Institute for the Study of Human Issues.

Chambard, E. (1879, April). Sur un cas d'hystérie avec somnambulisme. *Revue Mensuelle de Médecine et de Chrirugie, 3*, 273–288.

Charpignon, J. (1848). *Physiologie, médecine et métaphysique du magnétisme*. Germer Baillière.

Claparède, E. (1921). Théodore Flournoy: Sa vie et son oeuvre. *Archives de Psychologie, 18*(69–70), 1–125.

Cox, R. S. (2003). *Body and soul: A sympathetic history of American Spiritualism.* University of Virginia Press.

Crabtree, A. (1993). *From Mesmer to Freud: Magnetic sleep and the roots of psychological healing.* Yale University Press.

Crabtree, A. (2003). "Automatism" and the emergence of dynamic psychiatry. *Journal of History of the Behavioral Sciences, 39*(1), 51–70.

Cridge, A. (1854). *Epitome of spirit-intercourse*. Bela Marsh.

Crowell, E. (1877). *Spiritualism and insanity.* Colby & Rich.

D., M. (1867, March). Guardians of strength. *Spiritual Magazine, 2*(n. s.), 112–118.

Dailey, A. H. (1894). *Mollie Fancher, the Brooklyn enigma*. Eagle Book Printing.

Davis, A. J. (1847). *The principles of nature, her divine revelations, and a voice to mankind* (3rd ed.). S. S. Lyon and Wm. Fishbough.

Davis, A. J. (1853). *The present age and inner life: A sequel to spiritual intercourse: Modern mysteries classified and explained.* Partridge and Brittan.

de Gasparin, Cte A. (1854). *Des tables tournantes* (2 vol.). E. Dentu.

Delanne, G. (1897a). *L'evolution animique: Essais de psychologie suivant le spiritisme*. Chamuel.

Delanne, G. (1897b). *Le phénomène spirite: Témoignages des savants* (5th ed.). Chamuel.

Deleuze, J. P. F. (1813). *Histoire critique du magnétisme animal* (Vol. 1). Mame.

Deleuze, J. P. F. (1825). *Instruction pratique sur le magnétisme animal*. J. -G. Dentu.

De Morgan, S. E. [originally published with the pseudonym CD] (1863). *From matter to spirit*. Longman, Green, Longman, Roberts, & Green.

Deonna, W. (1932). *De la planète Mars en Terre Sainte: Art et subconscient*. E. de Boccard.

de Rochas, A. (1896). *L'extériorisation de la motricité*. Chamuel.

Despine, A. (1840). *De l'emploi du magnétisme animal et des eaux minérales dans le traitement des maladies nerveuses*. Germer Baillière.

Dessoir, M. (1890). *Das Doppel-Ich*. Ernest Günther.

Dewar, H. (1823). Report on a communication from Dr. Dyce of Aberdeen, to the Royal Society of Edinburgh, "On uterine irritation and its effects on the female constitution." *Transactions of the Royal Society of Edinburgh, 9*(2), 365–379. [Republished by Cambridge University Press 2013].

Du Prel, C. (1889). *The philosophy of mysticism* (2 vols.). George Redway. (Original work published in German, 1884].

Du Prel, C. (1907). *La magie: Science naturelle* (Vol. 1). H. Vaillant-Carmanne. (Original work published in German, 1899).

Edelman, N. (1995). *Voyantes, guérisseuses et visionnaires en France 1785–1914*. Albin Michel.

Edmonds, Judge [J. W.]. (1860). Letters to the "New York Tribune," on Spiritualism [Spiritual Tracts, No. 10). No publisher.

Edmonds, Judge [J. W.]. (n. d., ca 1875). *Letters and tracts on Spiritualism* (J. Burns, Ed.). J. Burns.

Edmonds, J. W., & Dexter, G. T. (1853). *Spiritualism*. Partridge & Brittan. Edmonds, J. W., & Dexter, G. T. (1855). *Spiritualism*. Partridge & Brittan.

Ellenberger, H. F. (1970). *The discovery of the unconscious: The history and evolution of dynamic psychiatry.* Basic Books.

Elliotson, J. (1843). *Numerous cases of surgical operation without pain in the mesmeric state.* H. Baillière.

Elliotson, J. (1846). Instances of double states of consciousness independent of mesmerism. *Zoist, 4*(14), 157–187.

Ermacora, G. B. (1894). Attività subcosciente e spiritismo. *Lux: Bolletino dell'Accademia Internazionale per gli studi psicologici, 6*(2), 37–48.

Esdaile, J. (1847). *Mesmerism in India, and its practical application in surgery and medicine*. Silas Andrus and Son.

Evrard, R., Pratte, E. A., & Cardeña, E. (2018). Pierre Janet and the enchanted boundary of psychical research. *History of Psychology, 21*(2), 100–125.

Faraday, M. (1853, July 2). Professor Faraday on table-moving. *The Athenaeum: Journal of Literature, Science, and the Fine Arts*, no. 1340, 801–803.
Figuier, L. (1860). *Histoire du merveilleux dans les temps modernes.* (Vol. 4). Hachette.
Flammarion, C. (1907). *Mysterious psychic forces.* Small, Maynard.
Flournoy, T. (1897). Quelques faits d'imagination subliminale chez les médiums. In *Dritter Internationaler Congress für Psychologie in München vom 4. bis 7. August, 1896.* (pp. 419–420). J. F. Lehmann.
Flournoy, T. (1899, February). Genèse de quelques prétendus messages spirites. *Revue Philosophique de la France et de l'Étranger, 47*, 144–158.
Flournoy, T. (1900). *From India to the Planet Mars: A study of a case of somnambulism with glossolalia.* Harper & Brothers.
Flournoy,T. (1901). Nouvelles observations sur un cas de somnambulisme avec glossolalie, *Archives de Psychologie, 1*(2), 101–255.
Flournoy, T. (1911). *Spiritism and psychology*. Harper & Brothers.
Foschi, R. (2003). L'indagine sulla personalità alle origini della psicologia scientifica francese (1870-1885). *Physis, 40*(1–2), 63–105.
Friedman, K. A. K. (2014). *Soul sleepers: A history of somnambulism in the United States, 1740–1840.* (Doctoral dissertation). Harvard University.
Garrett, C. (1987). *Spirit possession and popular religion: From the Camisards to the Shakers.* John Hopkins University Press.
Gauld, A. (1968). *The founders of psychical research.* Routledge and Kegan Paul.
Gauld, A. (1982). *Mediumship and survival: A century of investigations*. Heinemann.
Gauld, A. (1992). *A history of hypnotism.* Cambridge University Press.
Gauthier, A. (1842). *Histoire du somnambulisme chez tous les peuples* (2 vols.). Félix Malteste.
Gauthier, A. (1845). *Traité pratique du magnétisme et du somnambulisme.* Germer Baillière.
Geley, G. [under the pseudonym E. Gyel]. (1899). *L'être subconscient.* Félix Alcan.
Geley, G. (1905). *L'être subconscient* (2nd ed.). Félix Alcan.
Geley, G. (1920). *From the unconscious to the conscious.* Williams Collins Sons. (Original work published in French, 1919).
Gilles de la Tourette, [G.]. (1891). *Traité clinique et thérapeutique de l'hystérie d'après l'enseignement de la Salpêtrière* (Vol. 1). E. Plon, Nourrit.
Gonçalves, V. P., & Ortega, F. (2013). Uma nosologia para os fenômenos sobrenaturais e a construção do cérebro "possuído" no século XIX. *Historia, Ciências, Saude-Manguinhos, 20*(2), 373–390.
Grasset, J. (1904). *Le Spiritisme devant la science*. Coulet et Fils.
Grasset, J. (1906). *Le psychisme inferieur*. Chevalier et Rivière.
Grasset, J. (1908). *L'occultisme hier et aujourd'hui* (2nd ed.). Coulet et Fils.
Gregory, L. M. (1866, May). A séance with Mr. Home. *Spiritual Magazine, 1*(n.s.), 226–227.
Gregory, W. (1851). *Letters to a candid inquirer, on animal magnetism*. Blanchard & Lea.
Gregory, W. (1856). Le spiritualisme en Angleterra. *Journal du Magnétisme, 15*(238), 309–334.
Guinon, G. (1891–1892). Documents pour server à l'histoire des somnambulismes. *Progrès Médical, 13*(s. 2), (20), 401–404, (21), 425–429, (23) 460–466, (26), 513–517; *14*(s. 2), (29), 41–49, (34) 137–141; *15*(s. 2), (11), 193–196, (13), 236–238, (19), 361–364, (21), 401–402; *16*(s. 2), (27), 1–4, (28), 17–21, (31), 73–76, (34), 131–134.
Gurney, E. (1884). The stages of hypnotism. *Proceedings of the Society for Psychical Research, 2*(5), 61–72.
Gurney, E., & Myers, F. W. H. (1885, May-June). Some higher aspects of mesmerism. *Proceedings of the Society for Psychical Research, 3*(9), 401–423.
Hacking, I. (1995). *Rewriting the soul: Multiple personality and the sciences of memory.* Princeton University Press.
Haddock, J. W. (1851). *Somnolism & psycheism* (2nd ed.). James S. Hodson.
Hamilton, W. H., Smyth, J. S., & Hyslop, J. H. (1911). A case of hysteria. *Proceedings of the American Society for Psychical Research, 5*(10), 1–656.
Hammond, W. A. (1876). *Spiritualism and allied causes and conditions of nervous derangement.* G. P. Putnam's Sons.
Hardinge, E. (1860). *Six lectures on theology and nature.* Hitt.

Héricourt, J. (1886). Un cas de somnambulisme à distance. *Revue Philosophique de la France et de l'Étranger, 21*, 200–203.
Héricourt, J. (1889). L'activité inconsciente de l'esprit [The unconscious activity of the mind]. *Revue Scientifique, 44*(9), 257–268.
Hess, K. M. (2018). The idea of ideoplasty and occult phenomena in the theoretical and empirical research of Julian Ochorowicz. *Preternature, 7*(2), 239–274.
Hill-Tout, C. H. (1895). Some psychical phenomena bearing upon the question of spirit control. *Proceedings of the Society for Psychical Research, 11(28)*, 309–316.
Hodgson, R. (1891). A case of double consciousness. *Proceedings of the Society for Psychical Research, 7*(19), 221–255.
Hodgson, R. (1892). A record of observations of certain phenomena of trance. *Proceedings of the Society for Psychical Research, 8*(21), 1–167.
Hodgson, R. (1898). A further record of observations of certain phenomena of trance. *Proceedings of the Society for Psychical Research, 13*(33), 284–582.
Hodgson, R. (1899, February 4). Miss Freer and Mrs. Piper. *Light, 19*(943), 55–56.
Hudson, T. J. (1893). *The law of psychic phenomena: A working hypothesis for the systematic study of hypnosis, spiritism, mental therapeutics, etc*. A. C. McClurg.
Hustvedt, A. (2011). *Medical muses: Hysteria in nineteenth-century Paris*. W. W. Norton.
Hyslop, J. H. (1901a). A further record of observations of certain trance phenomena. *Proceedings of the Society for Psychical Research, 16*(41), 1–649.
Hyslop, J. H. (1901b, March). Nature of life after death. *Harper's Monthly Magazine, 102*(610), 632–639.
Hyslop, J. H. (1906a). Apparent subconscious fabrication. *Journal of Abnormal Psychology, 1*(5), 201- –215.
Hyslop, J. H. (1906b). *Borderland of psychic research.* Herbert B. Turner.
Hyslop, J. H. (1910). A record and discussion of mediumistic experiments. *Proceedings of the American Society for Psychical Research, 4*(1), 1–812.
Hyslop, J. H. (1914). A hypothetical process of communication. *Journal of the American Society for Psychical Research, 8*(8), 377–389.
Hyslop, J. H. (1918). *Life after death: Problems of the future life and its nature. E. P.* Dutton.
Hyslop, J. H. (1919). *Contact with the other world: The latest evidence as to communication with the dead.* Century.
Inglis, B. (1992). *Natural and supernatural: A history of the paranormal from earliest times to 1914* (rev. ed.). Prism.
James, T. (1995). *Dream, creativity, and madness in nineteenth-century France.* Oxford University Press.
James, W. (1886). Report of the Committee on Mediumistic Phenomena. *Proceedings of the American Society for Psychical Research, 1*(2), 102–106.
James, W. (1889). Notes on automatic writing. *Proceedings of the American Society for Psychical Research, 1*(4), 548–564.
James, W. (1890a, March). The hidden self. *Scribner's Magazine, 7*(3), 361–373.
James, W. (1890b). *The principles of psychology* (Vol. 1). Henry Holt.
James, W. (1890c). A record of observations of certain phenomena of trance (5) Part III. *Proceedings of the Society for Psychical Research, 6*(17), 651–659.
James, W. (1909). Report on Mrs. Piper's Hodgson-control. *Proceedings of the Society for Psychical Research, 23*(58), 2–121.
Janet, P. (1886, December). Les actes inconscientes et la dédoublement de la personnalité pendant le somnambulisme provoqué. *Revue Philosophique de la France et de l'Étranger 22*, 577–592.
Janet, P. (1887). L'anesthésie systématisée et la dissociation des phénomènes psychiques. *Revue Philosophique de la France et de l'Étranger, 23*, 449–472.
Janet, P. (1889). *L'automatisme psychologique*. Félix Alcan.
Janet, P. (1892). Le spiritisme contemporain. *Revue Philosophique de la France et de l'Étranger, 33*, 413–442.
Janet, P. (1904). *Névroses et idées fixes* (2nd ed., Vol. 1). Félix Alcan.
Janet, P. (1909). Dèlire systématique à la suite de pratiques du spiritisme. *L'Éncephale, 4*(4), 363–367.
Jung, C. G. (1975). On the psychology and pathology of so-called occult phenomena. In C. G. Jung, *Psychiatric studies* (*The collected works of C. G. Jung*, Vol. 1, pp. 3–8). Princeton University Press (Original work published in German, 1902).

Kelly, E. W. (2007). F. W. H. Myers and the empirical study of the mind-body problem. In E. Kelly, E. W, Kelly, A. Crabtree, A. Gauld, M. Grosso, & B. Greyson, *Irreducible mind: Toward a psychology for the 21st century* (pp. 47–115). Rowman & Littlefield.

Kenny, M. G. (1986). *The passion of Ansel Bourne: Multiple personality in American culture*. Smithsonian Institution Press.

Kerner, J. A. C. (1845). *The seeress of Prevorst*. J. C. Moore. [Abridgement of Kerner's *Die Seherin von Prevorst*, 1829, C. Crowe (tr.)]

Knapp, K. D. (2017). *William James: Psychical research and the challenge of modernity*. University of North Carolina Press.

Kotik, N. G. (1908). *Die Emanation der psychophysischen Energie*. J. F. Bergmann.

Lafontaine, C. (1860). *L'art de magnétiser, ou le magnétisme animal considéré sous le point de vue théorique, pratique et thérapeutique* (3rd ed.). Germer Baillière.

[Lang, W.]. (1843). *Mesmerism*. Fraser.

Lausanne [pseudonym of Sarrazine de Montferrier, A. A. V.]. (1816, July 1). Histoire du magnétisme animal. *Annales du Magnétisme Animal, 2*, 3–26.

Leaf, W. (1890). A record of observations of certain phenomena of trance (3). Part II. *Proceedings of the Society for Psychical Research, 6*(17), 558–646.

Lebiedzinski, P. (1924). L'ideoplastie comme hypothèse directrice des études métapsychiques. In *L'Etat Actuel des Recherches Psychiques d'après les travaux du IIme Congrès International tenu à Varsovie en 1923 en l'honneur du Dr Julien Ochorowicz* (pp. 286–300). Presses Universitaires de France.

Lemaître, A. (1908). Un nouveau cycle somnambulique de Mlle Smith. *Archives de Psychologie, 7*, 63–83.

Le Maléfan, P. (1999). *Folie et Spiritisme (1850–1950)*. L'Harmattan.

Lévy-Valensi, J. (1910). Spiritisme et folie. *L'Encéphale, 5*(6), 696–716.

Liébeault, A.-A. (1889). *Le sommeil provoqué et les états analogues*. Octave Doin.

Lodge, O. (1890). A record of observations of certain phenomena of trance (2). Part I. *Proceedings of the Society for Psychical Research, 6*(17), 443–557.

Lombardo, G. P., & Foschi, R. (2003). The concept of personality in 19th-century French and 20th-century American psychology. *History of Psychology, 6*(2), 123–142.

Lombroso, C. (1909). *After death—What?: Spiritistic phenomena and their interpretation*. Small, Maynard.

London Dialectical Society. (1871). *Report on Spiritualism*. Longmans, Green, Reader & Dyer.

Loveland, J. S. (1889). *Mediumship: A course of seven lectures*. Moses Hull.

Lum, D. D. (1873). *The "Spiritual" delusion*. J. B. Lippincott.

Macario, M. M. A. (1857). *Du sommeil des rêves et du somnambulisme dans l'état de santé et de maladie*. Perisse Frèrs.

Mackenzie, W. (1923). *Metapsichica moderna*. Librerie di Scienze e Lettere.

Magnin, E. (1903, April 1). Un bon médium à l'horizon. *Revue Spirite: Journal d'Études Psychologiques, 46*(4), 232–235.

Mais, C. (1814). *The surprising case of Rachel Baker, who prays and preaches in her sleep* (2nd ed.). Whiting and Watson.

Maraldi, E. de O., & Alvarado, C. S. (2018). Classic text no. 113: Final chapter, *From India to the planet Mars: A study of a case of somnambulism with glossolalia* by Théodore Flournoy (1900). *History of Psychiatry, 29*(1), 110–125.

Maraldi, E. de O., Ribeiro, R. N., & Krippner, S. (2019). Cultural and group differences in mediumship and dissociation: Exploring the varieties of mediumistic experiences. *International Journal of Latin American Religions, 3*(1), 170–192.

Martineau, H. (1845). *Letters on mesmerism* (2nd ed.). Edward Moxon.

Marvin, F. R. (1874). *The philosophy of spiritualism and the pathology and treatment of mediomania: Two lectures*. A. K. Butts.

Mason, R. O. (1893, September). Duplex personality. *Journal of Nervous and Mental Disease, 18*(9), 593–598.

Maxwell, J. (1905). *Metapsychical phenomena: Methods and observations* (trans. Laura I. Finch). Duckworth. (Original work published in French, 1903).

Mayo, T. (1847). *Clinical facts and reflections: Also, remarks on the impunity of murder in some cases of presumed insanity*. Longman, Brown, Green, and Longmans.

Mitchell, G. W. (1876). *X + Y = Z: or the sleeping preacher of North Alabama: Containing an account of most wonderful mysterious mental phenomena, fully authenticated by living witnesses*. W. C. Smith.
Mitchill, S. L. (1817). A double consciousness, or a duality of person in the same individual. *Medical Repository of Original Essays and Intelligence Relative to Physic, Surgery, Chemistry, and Natural History, 3*(n. s., 2), 185–186.
Moore, J. S. (1870). A case of somnambulism. *Medical Archives, 4*(6), 331–332.
Moore, R. L. (1977). *In search of white crows: Spiritualism, parapsychology, and American culture*. Oxford University Press.
Morin, A. -S. (1860). *Du magnétisme et des sciences occultes*. Germer Baillière.
Morselli, E. (1908). *Psicologia e "spiritismo:" Impressioni e note critiche sui fenomeni medianici di Eusapia Paladino* (2 vols.). Fratelli Bocca.
Moses, W. S. [under the pseudonym M. A. Oxon] (1879). *Spirit identity*. W. H. Harrison.
Münsterberg, H., Ribot, T. A., Janet, P., Jastrow, J., Hart, B., & Prince, M. (1910). *Subconscious phenomena*. Richard G. Badger.
Myers, F. W. H. (1884). On a telepathic explanation of some so-called spiritualistic phenomena: Part I. *Proceedings of the Society for Psychical Research, 2*(7), 217–237.
Myers, F. W. H. (1885). Automatic writing.—II. *Proceedings of the Society for Psychical Research, 3*(8), 1–63.
Myers, F. W. H. (1886). Human personality in the light of hypnotic suggestion. *Proceedings of the Society for Psychical Research, 4*(10), 1–24.
Myers, F. W. H. (1888). French experiments on strata of personality. *Proceedings of the Society for Psychical Research, 5*(13), 374–397.
Myers, F. W. H. (1889). Professor Pierre Janet's 'Automatisme Psychologique.' *Proceedings of the Society for Psychical Research, 6*(15), 186–199.
Myers, F. W. H. (1890). A record of observations of certain phenomena of trance (1) Introduction. *Proceedings of the Society for Psychical Research, 6*(17), 436–442.
Myers, F. W. H. (1892). Review of *Les Altérations de la Personnalité*, by A Binet. *Mind, 1*(13), 417–421.
Myers, F. W. H. (1902). On the trance-phenomena of Mrs. Thompson. *Proceedings of the Society for Psychical Research, 17*(44), 67–74.
Myers, F. W. H. (1903). *Human personality and its survival of bodily death* (2 vols.). Longmans, Green.
Newbold, W. R. (1898). A further record of observations of certain phenomena of trance. *Proceedings of the Society for Psychical Research, 14*(34), 6–49.
Nias, H. (1999). *The artificial self: The psychology of Hippolyte Taine*. Legenda.
Nicolas, S. (2002). *Histoire de la psychologie française*. Editions.
Nicolas, S., & Ferrand, L. (2002). Alfred Binet and higher education. *History of Psychology, 5*(3), 264–283.
Noel, R. (1885, November 28 & December 5). Spiritism versus other theories (being an answer to Messrs. von Hartmann, Myers, and Gurney). *Light, 5*(256), 587–588; (257), 599–600.
Ochorowicz, J. (1887). *De la suggestion mentale*. Octave Doin.
Ochorowicz, J. (1896). La question de la fraude dans les expériences avec Eusapia Paladino. *Annales des Sciences Psychiques, 6*(2), 79–123.
Ochorowicz, J. (1909). Hypnotisme et mesmérisme. In C. Richet (Ed.), *Dictionnaire de Physiologie* (Vol. 8, pp. 709–778). Félix Alcan.
Ochorowicz, J. (1910). Les rayons rigides et les rayons Xx. *Annales des Sciences Psychiques, 20*(7–8), 97–105; (9–10), 129–136; (11–12), 172–178; (13–14), 204–209; (15–16), 225–231; (17–18), 257–263; (19-20), 295–302; (21-22), 336–344; (23–24), 357–370.
Oesterreich, T. K. (1923). *Occultism and modern science* (2nd German ed.). McBride.
Oesterreich, T. K. (1930). *Possession: Demoniacal and other*. Kegan Paul, Trench, Trübner. (Original work published in German, 1921).
Olivier, J. (1854). *Traité de magnétisme suivi des paroles d'un somnambule et d'un recueil de traitements magnétiques*. Germer Baillière.
Patrick, G. T. W. (1898). Some peculiarities of the second personality. *Psychological Review, 5*(6), 555–578.
Peabody, J. R. (1838). *A world of wonders, or, divers developments, showing the triumph of animal magnetism in New England* (3rd ed.). Robert S. Davis.
Perrier, A. (1854). Études et théories: Recherches médico-magnétiques. *Journal du Magnétisme, 13*(181), 65–80.

Plas, R. (2000). *Naissance d'une science humaine: La psychologie*. Presses Universitaires de Rennes.
Podmore, F. (1902). *Modern spiritualism: A history and a criticism* (2 vols.). Methuen.
Prichard, J. C. (1835). Somnambulism and animal magnetism. In J. Forbes, A. Tweedie, & J. Conolly (Eds.), *The cyclopaedia of practical medicine* (Vol. 4, pp. 21–39). Sherwood, Gilbert, and Piper, and Baldwin and Cradock.
Prince, M. (1890). Some of the revelations of hypnotism: Post hypnotic suggestion, automatic writing, and double personality. *Boston Medical and Surgical Journal, 122*(20), 463–467; (21), 493–495.
Prince, M. (1914). *The unconscious: The fundamentals of human personality, normal and abnormal.* Macmillan.
Purdon, J. E. (1889). Animal magnetism, and the supplementary working hypothesis of scientific spiritualism. *Religio-Philosophical Journal, 45*(23), 1, 8.
Puységur, A. M. J., de C. (1784). *Mémoires pour servir à l'histoire et à l'établissement du magnétisme animal.* No publisher.
Raymond, F., & Janet, P. (1908). *Névroses et idées fixes* (2nd ed., Vol. 2). Félix Alcan.
Ribot, T. (1885). *Les maladies de la personnalité*. Félix Alcan.
Richet, C. (1883). La personnalité et la mémoire dans le somnambulisme. *Revue Philosophique de la France et de l'Étranger, 15,* 225–242.
Richet, C. (1884). La suggestion mentale et le calcul des probabilités. *Revue Philosophique de la France et de l'Étranger, 18*, 609–674.
Richet, C. (1886). Les mouvements inconscients. In M. Berthelot (Ed.), *Hommage à Monsieur Chevreul a l'occasion de son centenaire 31 Aôut 1886* (pp. 79–94). Félix Alcan.
Richet, C. (1889). Further experiments in hypnotic lucidity or clairvoyance. *Proceedings of the Society for Psychical Research, 6*(15), 66–83.
Richet, C. (1922). *Traité de métapsychique*. Félix Alcan.
Ritti, A. (1891). Mort de M. le Dr. Baillarger. *Annales Médico-Psychologiques, 13*(s. 7), 161–168.
Rogers, E. C. (1853). *Philosophy of mysterious agents, human and mundane* J. P. Jewett.
Sandby, G. (1850). Review of M. Alphonse Cahagnet's *Arcanes de la Vie Future Dévoilés, &c. Zoist, 7*(28), 414–431.
Schrenck-Notzing, A. F. von. (1920). *Physikalische Phaenomene des Mediumismus*. Ernst Reinhardt.
Sidgwick, H. (1895). Eusapia Paladino. *Journal of the Society for Psychical Research, 7*(123), 148–159.
Sidgwick, Mrs. H. [E. M.]. (1915). A contribution to the study of the psychology of Mrs. Piper's trance phenomena. *Proceedings of the Society for Psychical Research, 28*(71), 1–657.
Sidis, B. (1898). *The psychology of suggestion: A research into the subconscious nature of man and society.* D. Appleton.
Smith, J. E. (1837). *Legends and miracles, and other curious and marvellous stories of human nature, collected from scarce works and ancient records.* (No. 8). B. D. Cousins.
Somers, A. N. (1893). The double personality, and the relation of the submerged personality to the phenomena of modern spiritualism. *Psychical Review, 1*(4), 314–323.
Sudre, R. (1926). *Introduction à la métapsychique humaine*. Payot.
Sudre, R. (1946). *Personnages d'au-dela*. Société des Éditions de Noël.
Taine, H.-A. (1878). *De l'intelligence* (Vol. 1, 3rd Tev. ed.). Hachette.
Tanner, A. E. (1910). *Studies in spiritism.* D. Appleton.
Tascher, P. (1855). *Seconde lettre de Gros Jean à son évêque au sujet de tables parlantes, des possessions, des sibylles, du magnétisme et autres diableries*. Ledoyen.
Taves, A. (1999). *Fits, trances, and visions: Experiencing religion and explaining experience from Wesley to James*. Princeton University Press.
Taylor, E. (1983). *William James on exceptional mental states: The 1896 Lowell Lectures.* Charles Scribner's Sons.
Taylor, E. (2009). *The mystery of personality: A history of psychodynamic theories.* Springer.
Taylor, W. S., & Martin, M. F. (1944). Multiple personality. *Journal of Abnormal Psychology, 39*(3), 281–300.
Thomas, C. D. (1922). *Some new evidence for human survival.* W. Collins Sons.
Titchener, E. B. (1915). *A beginner's psychology*. Macmillan.
Treitel, C. (2004). *A science for the soul: Occultism and the genesis of the German modern.* John Hopkins University Press.

Troubridge, U. (1922). The *modus operandi* in so-called mediumistic trance. *Proceedings of the Society for Psychical Research, 32*(84), 344–378.

Tymn, M. E. (2013). *Resurrecting Leonora Piper: How science discovered the afterlife*. White Crow Books.

Van der Hart, O., & Horst, R. (1989). The dissociation theory of Pierre Janet. *Journal of Traumatic Stress, 2*(4), 397–412.

Vencio, S., Caiado-Vencio, R., & Caixeta, L. (2018). Differential diagnosis between anomalous experiences and dissociation disorder using the Dissociative Disorders Interview Schedule (DDIS). *Journal of Trauma and Dissociation, 20*(2), 165–178.

Verrall, Mrs A. W. [M.]. (1906). On a series of automatic writings. *Proceedings of the Society for Psychical Research, 20*(53), 1–432.

Viollet, M. (1908). *Le Spiritisme dans ses rapports avec la folie: Essai de psychologie normale et pathologique*. Bloud.

Visani Scozzi, P. (1901). *La medianità*. R. Bemporad & Figlio.

von Hartmann, E. (1885). *Spiritism*. Psychological Press.

Walusinski, O. (2014). Biographies des internes de Jean-Martin Charcot à La Salpêtrière entre 1862 et 1893.

Weaver, Z. (2019). Julian Ochorowicz and his contribution to psychical research. *Journal of Parapsychology, 83*(1), 69–78.

Wolf, S. (1993). *Brain, mind, and medicine: Charles Richet and the origins of physiological psychology*. Transaction Publishers.

Wolf, T. H. (1973). *Alfred Binet*. University of Chicago Press.

Wolffram, H. (2009). *The stepchildren of science: Psychical research and parapsychology in Germany, c. 1870–1939*. Rodopi.

23

Psychical Physics: On the Borderland of Physics and Psychic Phenomena*

Carlos S. Alvarado

Review of *Physics and Psychics: The Occult and the Sciences in Modern Britain* (2019) by Richard Noakes.

In an address presented on August 20, 1891, at the Sixty-First Meeting of the British Association for the Advancement of Science, the President of the Association's Section of Mathematics and Physical Science discussed various scientific developments. The speaker started with brief mentions of Michael Faraday's centenary, and the death of Wilhelm Weber, and then went on to detailed discussions of a binary system of stars, the discovery of ways to achieve color photography, and the importance of professional systematic physics research leaving behind amateur efforts. Then he changed directions and said he was going to discuss a "topic which is as yet beyond the pale of scientific orthodoxy" (p. 551). The topic, the study of psychic phenomena, was called by the speaker the "borderland of physics and psychology," an area "bounded on the north by psychology, on the south by physics, on the east by physiology, and on the west by pathology and medicine" (p. 553).

> "I have spoken of the apparently direct action of mind on mind, and of a possible action of mind on matter. But the whole region is unexplored territory … I care not what the end may be. I do care that *inquiry shall be conducted by us*" (p. 555, my italics).

The speaker was English physicist Oliver J. Lodge (1892), who by that time was well-known for his interest and work in psychical research.[1] The "us" in the last quote above was a reference to the community of physicists. Such interest in the topic by some physicists, of which Lodge was a main player, is the subject of the book reviewed here.

Richard Noakes, author of *Physics and Psychics: The Occult and the Sciences in Modern Britain*, is an Associate Professor of the History of Science and Technology at the University of Exeter. For years he has been working on the topics covered in *Physics and Psychics*, writing about subjects such as the reasons behind the interest of physicists in psychic phenomena (Noakes, 2008), and how particular individuals combined physics and psychical research in their actual work (Noakes, 2004). The book reviewed here, an important contribution to the historiography of psychical research, includes this material and much more.

Although the interaction between physics and psychic phenomena has been discussed before by others (e.g., Oppenheim, 1985; Wynne, 1979), this is the first detailed study of what Noakes calls "physical- psychical scientists", or the community of physicists and other physical scientists interested in the phenomena of Spiritualism and psychical research. More than previous writers, Noakes, who focuses on British developments roughly around 1870–1930, argues that these individuals were more interested in the topic than has been previously realized, or emphasized.

*Republished with permission from *Journal of Scientific Exploration*, 35(3), 646-661, 2021.

In his introduction Noakes makes it clear that the historical discourse has changed, from labeling these topics pseudo-science, to viewing them as alternative ways of knowing that were a reflection of the needs of the times and of attempts to redefine science. Such ideas are conceptually related to work published in the history of science literature about the positive influence of magic, and generally occult beliefs and practices, on the development of science and thinking about human beings.[2] Examples of specific claims of influences presented over the years include the nurturing effects of Platonic, neo-Platonic, and Hermetic teachings on Renaissance science (Debus, 1978), and of mesmeric phenomena, nineteenth-century psychiatry, and psychology (Ellenberger, 1970). Also related to Noakes's approach is the work of many historians who have questioned the universal application of long- held ideas about modern science. This includes the secularization of the soul and the banishment of magic (Josephson-Storm, 2017), as well as what many still believe was the perennial conflict between science and religion (Lightman, 2019).

Noakes refers to historical work seeing "mesmerism, spiritualism and psychical research ... as new forms of psychology or sciences of the mind, ... [that] played significant roles in the nineteenth-century debates about the proper nature and scope of psychology" (p. 11). Some examples are the work of Adam Crabtree (1993), Andreas Sommer (2013), and Regina Plas (2000). In fact, the latter affirms in her study of French developments that various attempts to understand thought-transference supported the existence of the concept of the unconscious mind.

The author also reminds us that some individuals within Spiritualism and psychical research attempted to widen the scope of scientific naturalism to explain the world "by showing how scientific methods could ... challenge what they perceived to be scientific naturalism's 'materialistic' philosophy, which proclaimed that everything in the cosmos, including life, mind, and spirit, could be reduced to matter and force" (p. 11). However, we are also reminded that not all physicists were strictly materialists. In fact, James Clerk Maxwell and others were "devout Christians who maintained that professionalized physics could fulfill the religious purposes that the sciences had carried for centuries: to evidence a cosmos designed and ruled by divine agency" (p. 17). Some even argued that some ideas in physics supported religious ideas, as did Balfour Stewart and Peter Guthrie Tait in their controversial and widely read book *The Unseen Universe or Physical Speculations on a Future State* (1875), a work discussed later by Noakes. Stewart and Tait argued for the existence of a universe that could not be perceived by our senses but was connected with the known universe, and for the lack of incompatibility between religion and science. They wrote in the second edition of their book:

> If in the course of our discussion we are to some extent constructors, and find analogies in nature which seem to us to throw light upon the doctrines of Christianity, yet in the main our object is rather to break down unfounded objections than to construct apologetic arguments ... The Bishop of Manchester has very clearly described our position by stating that [*from a purely physical point of view* ...] we "contend for the possibility of immortality and of a personal God." (Stewart and Tait, 1875, p. vii)

Physics and Psychics has six chapters covering a variety of individuals and conceptual issues. It starts with one covering a variety of concepts of force from physics, but also from mesmerism and Spiritualism. Writing about animal magnetism, a universal force popularized by Franz Anton Mesmer and many others, the author states:

> By the late eighteenth century, physical sciences divided the material cosmos into ponderable matter and a host of forces and imponderable (weightless) and invisible fluids such as gravity, mineral magnetism, frictional electricity and heat ... The apparent discovery of

> another invisible force or imponderable fluid fitted well within programmes of enquiry in these sciences. The ideas of a universal force or fluid linking the microcosm of animate and inanimate bodies on earth to the macrocosm of celestial bodies and of the therapeutic benefits arising from the manipulation of such a fluid made sense within contemporary scientific and medical discourses. (p. 25)

Such discourses, as seen in a classic of mesmeric historiography, Robert Darnton's *Mesmerism and the End of the Enlightenment in France* (1968), included those developed at a time of interest in the wonders of electricity and in other physical forces. General interest in these ideas helped the popular reception of the mesmeric movement. In Darnton's words, consistent with Noakes's: "Frenchmen could read descriptions of fluids very like Mesmer's under the articles 'fire' and 'electricity' in the Encyclopédie ... In fact, there were enough fluids, sponsored by enough philosophers, to make any eighteenth-century reader's head swim." (p. 11)

Soon after, magnetic ideas, sometimes through their transformation into the Od force, affected Spiritualism by providing physical explanations for phenomena, particularly ideas of nervous-vital forces emanating from the medium during séances. Some early examples were applied to explain table turning, as seen in the views of French Count Agénor de Gasparin (1854). He argued for the existence of a fluidic force emanating from the sitters that set tables in movement, a force "similar to terrestrial magnetism, light, heat, electricity ... under the ... provisional name of hematonervous fluid" (Vol. 2, p. 407).

Those interested in these unorthodox concepts of force will find much of interest in this chapter and in the book in general. However, even if this is a recurring topic, the purpose of the book is not a history of these specific ideas, but instead of the general ideas and work of British "physical-psychical scientists,",which included much about these mysterious emanations from the bodies of mediums and others.

The British spiritualistic literature had many examples of speculations about forces. One was an article by electrician Desmond G. FitzGerald, who wrote about the basis of physical phenomena in séances:

> The moment we have satisfied ourselves that this energy, or 'power,' is derived or 'drawn' from the medium and sitters, it becomes from our point of view almost certain that something material—ponderable matter, or 'psychical matter'—in which potential energy has been previously stored up by the separation of molecules, and through which work may be done by the conversion of energy as those fall together, is actually taken from them by the manifesting agent. (Fitzgerald, 1878, p. 251)

A general history of this topic would include the work of many other individuals who did not have a particular physics background, some of whom are mentioned by Noakes. Some of those individuals and publications that come to mind are French physician Hippolyte Baraduc's *L'Âme Humaine* (1896), English attorney Edward W. Cox's *What Am I?* (1874), German philosopher Eduard von Hartmann's *Spiritism* (1885), and American abolitionist writer Edward C. Rogers' *Philosophy of Mysterious Agents* (1853). These forces, German philosopher Carl du Prel believed, "do not wait for their discovery and baptism to become active; they have been operating for a long time before and give rise to phenomena of unknown physics ..." (du Prel, 1896, p. 447).[3]

As chronicled by Noakes, such unknown physics developed in the context of more orthodox but still not fully understood topics of nineteenth century British physics. These were important times when influential physical concepts were developed from previous ideas, such as the all-pervasive ether and its implications for the transmission of signals in space, not to mention its metaphysical dimensions (Cantor & Hodge, 1981). Another important conceptual development were ideas of electromagnetism, and the principle of conservation of energy (Hunt, 1991) which, in addition to having an impact on conceptions of energy, matter, and signal transmission, brought together theory and practice, as seen in many practical applications involving electricity (including telegraphy), and the development of new engines, a process described by Morus (2005).

In the third chapter Noakes presents the community of "physical-psychical scientists," or those who were interested by training in physical aspects of psychic phenomena, without necessarily reducing them to materialistic processes. Because the professions were not strictly defined as they are today, this includes individuals who did not train exclusively in physics, but also those with a background in astronomy, engineering, chemistry, or telegraphy. A long table (pp. 86–92) presents the names and other details of many of these individuals affiliated with the Society for Psychical Research (SPR), including non-British persons (1882–ca 1940), while another table lists non-SPR "physical-psychical scientists" for the same period (pp. 95–103). Among the better-known British persons in the first table are William F. Barrett, William Crookes, Edmund E. Fournier d'Albe, Oliver J. Lodge, Eleanor M. Sidgwick, Balfour Stewart, John William Strutt, and George N. M. Tyrrell but there are also many others not particularly known for their psychic interests, at least in terms of research and publications (e.g., John Cox, John Herschel, William Ramsay, Joseph J. Thomson, Charles J. Young). Some non-SPR foreign individuals mentioned are Pierre Curie, Fritz Grunewald, Giovanni Battista Ermacora, Amos E. Dolbear, William Gregory, Robert Hare, Dimitri I. Mendeleev, and Francesco Porro.

Interestingly, and mentioned by Noakes (p. 77), it was physicist William F. Barrett, who sent a letter out to several individuals in December 1881 inviting them for a meeting to be held in January. This meeting, to "consider the advisability of having a select Central Society organised, under some such name as the London Psychical Society," led to the founding of the SPR (Barrett, 1924, p. 395).

Like others with no physics training, for these individuals, psychic phenomena seemed to express or fulfill needs of a philosophical, religious, and scientific nature. More specifically, and related to their interest in physical processes, was the "belief in the possibility that psychical phenomena represented a possible extension of the knowledge and practice of the physical sciences" (p. 135).

The actual work and ideas of the individuals studied in this book are the subject of Chapters 3–5. This includes actual physical theories, among them ideas of brain waves to account for telepathy, ideas of a psychic force in mediumship, and various other topics involving methodology and the concept of scientific expertise. Regarding the ideas of some of these individuals Noakes writes:

> Most of them were acutely aware, not least from critics near and far, of the risks of applying physical principles, analogies, theories and explanations to psychical puzzles. Despite their increasing caution about the psychical applications of physical theories, they never gave up the hope that some theories and ideas in physics might constitute the basis for more satisfactory interpretations of psychical phenomena and this partly depended on new understandings of the physics of the ether, energy and matter as they unfolded in the early 1900s. (pp. 183–184)

Finally, in Chapter 6 the author comments on the lack of success of physical approaches to psychic phenomena, and how the new generation continued speculating. Some of the discussion focuses on the writings of Hereward Carrington, who, without formal training in physics or engineering, fomented public interest in the physical detection of psychic forces and in radio models of telepathy (pp. 317–319). Like Lodge, Carrington was a proponent of laboratory investigations of psychic phenomena. In his book, *Laboratory Investigations into Psychic Phenomena* (n. d.) he gave much attention to concepts of force and to past attempts to instrumentally detect those hypothetical forces. In his view "a whole world of forces and curious phenomena is thrown open to the impartial inquirer calling for exact observation and scientific interpretation" (Carrington, 1917, p. 20).

This chapter also extends the discussion to later individuals and ideas published up to the 1930s. For example, Noakes comments on the wide interest in speculations about wireless communications both in Britain as well as in the United States. While he is clear that the "physical-psychical scientists" did not succeed in finding physical correlates of psychic phenomena, and thus develop a research program based on physics, he points out similarities between the old period he reviews, and more recent developments. But he also reminds us in the conclusion that some figures's orthodox physical interests were probably influenced by unorthodox ideas:

> William Thomson was probably not completely wrong in suggesting that mesmerism informed Crookes's path to the novel idea of matter in a radiant state; Varley's earlier contribution to the pre-history of the electron—his study of the mechanical effect of electrical discharge—was almost certainly fueled by a spiritualist preoccupation with the apparent materiality of immaterial agents; and the problem of the mechanisms of telepathy, telekinesis and survival undoubtedly spurred Lodge's major experimental and theoretical contributions to ether physics. (p. 338)

It is interesting to see that although many of the "physical-psychical scientists" in question tended to see, at least on occasion, psychic phenomena through the prism of physical processes, very few of them followed this influence in the actual investigation of phenomena. Such influence is seen in the work of William Crookes (1874), who clearly acted like a physicist when he tested D. D. Home's telekinesis in ways to explore physical parameters. For example, Crookes was interested to see if Home's psychic force could affect an accordion even when the instrument was enclosed in a basket surrounded by an electrical current, or when the force presumably had to go through water to exert an effect. A different approach, but still related to physical ideas, was that of Cromwell Varley who used an electrical current as a means of control to make sure that medium Florence Cook was in a particular location while the materialized form of Katie King appeared in the séance room. According to Varley, "Miss Cook took the place of a telegraph cable, under electrical test" (Varley, 1874, p. 134).

Although much has been published about the relationship between physics and other topics, among them religion (Gregory, 2003), less has been done with psychic phenomena. Noakes's book is the first major effort to study the history of physics and its relation to psychic phenomena. His work expands our knowledge of the interests and motivations of British "physicist-psychical scientists" considerably, which, in turn, helped the development of conceptions about matter, and the role of mind in the physical world. In doing so, Noakes not only has contributed to the historiography of physics (and science in general) but also to that of psychic phenomena and their role in both science and society.

Noakes gives us a generally neglected detailed view of a physically oriented community whose work and ideas complement the usual emphasis on psychology shown by figures such as Edmund Gurney and Frederic W. H. Myers (Gauld, 1968). Furthermore, while there is still plenty of emphasis on individuals such as Barrett, Crookes, and Lodge, whose contributions were essential, the author's discussion of the "physical-psychical scientists" enlarges the cast of characters of this orientation.

I was glad to see generally forgotten figures such as Edmund E. Fournier d'Albe, and Cromwell Varley, among others, brought to the attention of modern readers. But other figures are even less-known to students of psychic literature because they did not publish their ideas. A case in point was civil engineer Samuel Tolver Preston, who speculated privately about physical explanations of telepathy (pp. 172–174). For example, in an unpublished letter to physicist George F. FitzGerald, another interesting figure, Preston mentioned in relation to telepathy the theoretical possibility that the "electromagnetic aether may be found ultimately to be capable of giving a sufficient explanation without looking at anything additional" (Preston, 1890).

Noakes's analysis goes beyond the expression of ideas of members of this group, arguing, on the basis of unpublished correspondence, that some of these "silent" physical scientists provided a nurturing intellectual environment for the speculations and actual research of the more active "physical-psychical scientists." The identification of this invisible college reminds us of the importance of intellectual groups in the construction of knowledge, of the socio-collective aspects of idea development, a topic explored before in other specialties, an example being the role of Oxford physiologists in the work of William Harvey (Frank, 1980).

A major contribution by Noakes is the restoration of a physicalistic tradition that influenced many developments. But he also reminds us that the search for an expansion of physical horizons was not a materialistic quest for many of the individuals involved, as was clear in some of the writings of Barrett and Lodge.

The case of Barrett is interesting. He argued in a paper presented at the British Association for the Advancement of Science in 1876 that thought-transference may resemble "grosser cases of electric or magnetic induction" (Barrett, 1876, p. 87). However, and as discussed by Noakes, Barrett changed his mind later. Writing in the *Proceedings of the Society for Psychical Research*, he affirmed that now he thought that more knowledge about the phenomena in question "will shew the insufficiency of any physical analogy or materialistic explanation, and thus should tend to accelerate the passage of the existing wave of materialism ..." (Barrett, 1882, p. 62). By 1918 he was ready to say: "The paramount importance of psychical research lies in its demonstration of the fact that the physical plane is not the whole of Nature" (Barrett, 1918, p. 179). Such change may have been caused by various factors. Two possible ones are Barrett's increased experience with the features of thought-transference and other phenomena, and his interaction with individuals with different ideas, such as Myers.

I also enjoyed Noakes's discussions of the interactions of "physical-psychical scientists" with non-physicists. This includes Myers's influence on Lodge (pp. 294–295). Some conceptual opposition is also covered, as seen in critiques by prominent SPR members of signal transmission explanations of telepathy. Noakes refers (p. 164) to the classic first major work of the Society, *Phantasms of the Living*, which I cite below in greater length:

> Let us use every analogy which helps us, but let us recognize that nothing has been discovered which shows that thought-transference has anything to do with ether or with vibrations. Everything in the universe may be reducible to vibrations, for aught we know; but until some definite experiment, as of reflection, interference, or the like, can be brought forward to connect telepathy with ether-waves, it is surely safer to avoid using that analogy in a way which suggests that it has a prior right over many others which that be proposed. (Gurney, Myers, & Podmore, 1886, Vol. 2, p. 315)

My only critique of *Physics and Psychics* is that, on a few occasions, I wish the author had the opportunity to explore some issues in more detail. I say the opportunity, because, as Noakes informed me, he had to shorten his manuscript, a practical consideration many authors face.

An example in which more information would have been desirable is the discussion of the above-mentioned Hereward Carrington, which omits mention of his interest in vitalistic concepts (Alvarado & Nahm, 2011). That is, regardless of Carrington's belief in the exteriorization of a biophysical force from the human body, he maintained that this force was part of life itself, which was a principle that animated the body, while transcending physical aspects of it. Interestingly, similar ideas presenting physical properties of psychic forces were postulated by many, *while at the same time indicating the existence of a transcendental reality*, as seen in the ideas about ectoplasm of French physician Gustave Geley (1919/1920).

Although Noakes mentioned William J. Crawford in the book, I wish he had included more details about his physical mediumship investigations. Crawford, a lecturer of mechanical engineering, lived in Ireland, where he conducted physical measurements of table levitations (Crawford, 1916, 1919). In his view, most table levitations he studied were caused by an invisible cantilever structure emanating from his medium, Kathleen Goligher, but supported as well by forces emanating from the sitters. He noticed that the medium's weight increased indicating that the weight of the table was transferred to her. But he also reported cases in which there was no increase in weight suggesting other mechanisms, such as a fulcrum on the floor. His research program, based on mechanical principles, is another example of how physical concepts guided some investigators to try to map the hidden physical workings of some phenomena. Crawford in fact wrote: "I desire to help in the discovery of the psychic laws, which are as real as physical ones, so that in the years to come there may be no more mystery" (Crawford, 1919, p. 144).

Another area that could have been explored further are the reasons for the lack of careful empirical studies exploring physical aspects of psychic phenomena. Unlike Crookes and Crawford mentioned above, "physical-psychical scientists" such as Barrett, Fournier d'Albe, Lodge, and Stewart discussed in the book presented much speculation but no empirical work to test for physically-based hypotheses or to search for physical correlates of psychic phenomena. For example, regardless of Lodge's studies of telepathy, and mediumship, his published work has little actual research following physical assumptions, an exception being his recording of dynamometric readings of sitters in séances with medium Eusapia Palladino (Lodge, 1894, pp. 326–327).[4]

But these, and other thoughts, are minor points. They show to a great extent my interests and in no way detracts from Noakes's detailed and contextually sensitive study.

Outside the scope of *Physics and Psychics,* Noakes's excellent study makes me wish for similar examinations of physical-psychic theorization and research conducted in other countries, and sometimes by individuals with no training in physics. Examples of this are the séances held in France at the Institut Général Psychologique with Eusapia Palladino (Courtier, 1908, briefly mentioned by Noakes, p. 288). In these séances researchers documented increases in the medium's weight at the time of table levitations, and the discharge of an electroscope without contact. They also unsuccessfully conducted tests for ionization, temperature changes, and chemical changes in the atmosphere around the medium. Also relevant is German engineer Fritz Grunewald's ideas and measurements of a field in the human body that had "ferro-magnetic properties and can therefore be objectively detectable" (Grunewald, 1922, p. 82). One hopes that studies of such developments will follow Noakes's lead and thus place such research work in the context of each country's traditions of physics, psychical research, and other relevant concerns, studies that could also be guided by the ideas of other fields, among them the biological and medical sciences.

Notes

1 Perhaps the most important of Lodge's early contributions was his detailed report of séances with medium Leonora E. Piper, which presents several instances of veridical communications and information about the medium's mentation (Lodge, 1890). For a bibliography see Sommer (n.d.).

2 For a bibliography see Sommer (n. d.).

3 On this literature see Alvarado (2006) and Montandon (1927).
4 On the assumption that dynamometric measures of grip strength reflected the expenditure of energy in sitters, see Alvarado (2016, pp. 573–574).

References

Alvarado, C. S. (2006). Human radiations: Concepts of force in mesmerism, spiritualism and psychical research. *Journal of the Society for Psychical Research, 70*(884), 138–162.
Alvarado, C. S. (2016). Psychic phenomena and the brain hemispheres: Some nineteenth-century publications. *Journal of Scientific Exploration, 30*(4), 559–585.
Alvarado, C. S., & Nahm, M. (2011). Psychic phenomena and the vital force: Hereward Carrington on "Vital energy and psychical phenomena." *Journal of the Society for Psychical Research, 75*(903), 91–103.
Baraduc, H. (1896). *L'âme humaine: Ses mouvements, ses lumieres et I'iconographie de l'invisible fluidique*. Georges Carré.
Barrett, W. F. (1876, September 22). On some phenomena associated with abnormal conditions of mind. *Spiritualist Newspaper*, pp. 85–88.
Barrett, W. F. (1882). Appendix to the report on thought-reading. *Proceedings of the Society for Psychical Research, 1*(1), 47–64.
Barrett, W. F. (1918, February). The deeper issues of psychical research. *Contemporary Review*, *113*, 169–179.
Barrett, W. F. (1924, June 21). The early years of psychical research. *Light, 44*(2267), 395.
Cantor, G. N., & Hodge, M. J. S. (Eds.). (1981). *Conceptions of ether: Studies in the history of ether theories 1740–1900*. Cambridge University Press.
Carrington, H. (1917). The need of a psychical laboratory. *Psychical Research Review*, *3*(4), 17–23.
Carrington, H. (n. d., ca 1939). *Laboratory investigations into psychic phenomena.* Rider.
Courtier, J. (1908). Rapport sur les séances d'Eusapia Paladino à l'Institut Général Psychologique. *Bulletin de l'Institut Général Psychologique*, *8*(5–6), 415–546.
Cox, E. W. (1874). *What am I? A popular introduction to mental physiology and psychology: Vol. II.: The mechanism in action.* Longman.
Crabtree, A. (1993). *From Mesmer to Freud: Magnetic sleep and the roots of psychological healing*. Yale University Press.
Crawford, W. J. (1916). *The reality of psychic phenomena: Raps, levitations, etc.* John M. Watkins.
Crawford, W. J. (1919). *Experiments in psychical science: Levitation, "contact," and the "direct voice."* John M. Watkins.
Crookes, W. (1874). *Researches in the phenomena of spiritualism*. J. Burns.
Darnton, R. (1968). *Mesmerism and the end of the enlightenment in France*. Harvard University Press.
Debus, A. G. (1978). *Man and nature in the renaissance*. Cambridge University Press.
de Gasparin, Cte A. (1854). *Des tables tournantes: Du surnaturel en général et des esprits* (2 vols.). E. Dentu.
du Prel, C. (1896). Les rayons de Rontgen et l'occultisme. *Revue des Revues, 16*, 439–447.
Ellenberger, H. F. (1970). *The discovery of the unconscious: The history and evolution of dynamic psychiatry*. Basic Books.
Fitzgerald, D. G. (1878, May 24). The "conservation of energy" in relation to certain views of the theosophists. *Spiritualist Newspaper,* pp. 249–251.
Frank, R. G., Jr. (1980). *Harvey and the Oxford physiologists.* University of California Press.
Gauld, A. (1968). *The founders of psychical research.* Routledge & Kegan Paul.
Geley, G. (1920). *From the unconscious to the conscious.* William Collins. (Original work published in French, 1919).
Gregory, F. (2003). Intersection of physical science and Western religion in the nineteenth and twentieth centuries. In M. J. Nye (Ed.), *The Cambridge history of science: Vol. 5: The modern physical and mathematical sciences* (pp. 36–53). Cambridge University Press.
Grunewald, F. (1922). Ferromagnetische Erscheinungen am Menschen. *Psychische Studien, 49*(2), 65–83.
Gurney, E., Myers, F. W. H., & Podmore, F. (1886). *Phantasms of the living* (2 vols.). Trubner.

Hunt, B. J. (1991). *The Maxwellians*. Cornell University Press.

Josephson-Storm, J. A. (2017). *The myth of disenchantment: Magic, modernity, and the birth of the human sciences*. University of Chicago Press.

Lightman, B. (Ed.). (2019). *Rethinking history, science, and religion: An exploration of conflict and the complexity principle*. University of Pittsburgh Press.

Lodge, O. (1890). A record of observations of certain phenomena of trance (2). Part I. *Proceedings of the Society for Psychical Research, 6*(17), 443–557.

Lodge, O. (1892). [Address]. *Report of the sixty-first meeting of the British Association for the Advancement of Science held at Cardiff in August 1891* (pp. 547–557). John Murray.

Lodge, O. J. (1894, November). Experience of unusual physical phenomena occurring in the presence of an entranced person (Eusapia Paladino). *Journal of the Society for Psychical Research, 6*(114), 306–336.

Montandon, R. (1927). *Les radiations humaines: Introduction à la demonstration expérimentale de l'existence des corps subtils de l'homme*. Félix Alcan.

Morus, I. R. (2005). *When physics became king*. University of Chicago Press.

Noakes, R. (2004). The "bridge which is between physical and psychical research": William Fletcher Barrett, sensitive flames, and spiritualism. *History of Science, 42*(4), 419–464.

Noakes, R. (2008). The 'world of the infinitely little': Connecting physical and psychical realities circa 1900. *Studies in History and Philosophy of Science, 39*(3), 323–334.

Noakes, R. (2019). *Physics and psychics: The occult and the sciences in modern Britain*. Cambridge University Press.

Oppenheim, J. (1985). *The other world: Spiritualism and psychical research in England, 1850–1914*. Cambridge University Press.

Plas, R. (2000). *Naissance d'une science humaine: La psychologie: Les psychologues et le « merveilleux psychique »*. Presses Universitaires de Rennes.

Preston, S. T. (1890, September 3). Letter to George F. FitzGerald. *George F. FitzGerald Letters*, Royal Dublin Society.

Richet, C. (1922). *Traité de Métapsychique*. Félix Alcan.

Rogers, E. C. (1853). *Philosophy of mysterious agents, human and mundane; or, the dynamic laws and relations of man*. J. P. Jewett.

Sommer, A. (n.d.). From 'natural magic' to 'scientific naturalism': Key readings in the history of science & magic. *Forbidden histories*.

Sommer, A. (2013). *Crossing the boundaries of mind and body: Psychical research and the origins of modern psychology*. (Doctoral dissertation). University College London.

[Stewart, B., & Tait, P. G.]. (1875). *The unseen universe or physical speculations on a future state* (2nd ed.). Macmillan.

Varley, C. F. (1874, March 20). Electrical experiments with Miss Cook when entranced. *Spiritualist Newspaper*, pp. 134–135.

von Hartmann, E. (1885). *Spiritism*. Psychological Press.

Wynne, B. (1979). Physics and psychics: Science, symbolic action and social control in late Victorian England. In B. Barnes & S. Shapin (Eds.), *Natural order: Historical studies of scientific culture* (pp. 167–186). Sage.

Early Studies of Psychic Phenomena: The Contributions of Psychologist and Psychiatrists*

Carlos S. Alvarado†

The purpose of this article is to provide some historical perspective to current interest in psychic phenomena such as ESP and mediumship, and to argue that research and theorization about these phenomena affected both psychiatry and psychology. This included George M. Beard's and William B. Carpenter's ideas of automatic nervous action, Frederic W. H. Myers's and William James' concepts of subconscious selves, Edmund Gurney's and Charles Richet's telepathic and clairvoyance studies, and Pierre Janet's and Joseph Grasset's psychopathological views of mediumship. Some of these individuals explained these phenomena as normal processes such as dissociation, while others believed the phenomena required explanations other than those offered by science. Together with other factors, research and theorization about psychic phenomena contributed to the development of aspects of modern psychiatry and psychology, such as the elaboration of the concept of the subconscious mind.

Phenomena traditionally called in the past psychic, supernormal, parapsychological, or paranormal, have been a topic of interest for physicians, psychologists, and others over the years. This includes phenomena suggesting that consciousness can obtain information (ESP) and affect the environment without the usual sensorimotor mechanisms (psychokinesis), topics discussed in detail in the contemporary literature (Cardeña, Palmer, and Marcusson-Clavertz, 2015; May and Marwaha, 2015). Furthermore, there have also been discussions in many articles published in psychology journals (Alvarado & Martínez-Taboas, 2002; Storm, Tressoldi, and Di Risio, 2010).

The study of and theorization about these phenomena has a long history that, unfortunately, is sometimes neglected by current workers. Consequently, I will present a summary of some of these developments, referring readers to other works presenting more detailed historical perspectives (Crabtree, 1993; Gauld, 1968; Inglis, 1977; Plas, 2000).[1]

I will summarize aspects of the interest in phenomena such as telepathy and mediumship, with emphasis on the work of physicians and psychologists interested in the workings of the mind during the nineteenth and part of the twentieth centuries. Such phenomena were studied from early times even though then, as well as now, there was much skepticism and criticism of explanations requiring principles beyond known psychological and physiological processes. My discussion will focus on selected aspects of the work of the Society for Psychical Research, French studies of mental suggestion (or the apparent transmission of thoughts), and research and theories about mediumship.

In addition, I will argue in the paper that the study of these unexplained phenomena was one of several factors that influenced the development of selected psychological and psychiatric ideas. Historian of

*Republished with permission from *Ciencias de la Conducta, 32*, 71–98, 2017.

†Thanks are due to the Society for Psychical Research (London) for financial support. I am grateful to Ursula Bielski for useful editorial suggestions that improved this paper.

psychology Regine Plas (2000) has stated in reference to French psychology that what we call now parapsychological phenomena was a component of the beginnings of organized psychology, a topic that has also been explored by Sommer (2013). Other writings have shown that interest in psychic phenomena and their study made important contributions to ideas of the subconscious mind, a line of thought pioneered by Ellenberger (1970). According to this historian, both mesmerism and Spiritualism promoted phenomena such as trances, automatism and secondary personalities which, when brought to the attention of physicians and others, provided manifestations that were interpreted by assuming that the human mind had different levels of functioning. Later studies also expanded our perspectives of the role of the "extraordinary" in psychology and psychiatry (Alvarado, 2010; Crabtree, 1993; Plas, 2000; Shamdasani, 1993). What follows is a reminder of selected examples of some of that history.

From the beginning of recorded history there has been a myriad of accounts of prophetic dreams, clairvoyance, possessions, miraculous healings, and apparitions (Inglis, 1977). The first movement to bring systematic attention to psychic phenomena such as healing and clairvoyance, and to manifestations such as trances and double consciousness, was mesmerism, which developed during the late eighteenth and nineteenth centuries.[2] This was followed by (but also coexisted with) Spiritualism, which centered around the figure of the medium. The medium was said to be the means by which the dead could cause physical effects such as table levitations and materializations, or convey information from deceased persons through automatic writing and speaking, among other ways (for overviews in selected countries see Biondi, 1988, Braude, 2001; Oppenheim, 1985; Sharp, 2006).

All of this interest in unusual mental states and phenomena led to the founding of the Society for Psychical Research (SPR) in London in 1882.[3] The SPR's purpose was to learn about human nature through "an organised and systematic attempt to investigate that large group of debatable phenomena designated by such terms as mesmeric, psychical, and Spiritualistic" (Anonymous, 1882, p. 3). SPR members conducted many investigations that included spontaneous cases of what was later called ESP (Gurney, Myers, and Podmore, 1886), as well as studies of apparitions of deceased persons (Podmore, 1889), haunted houses (Barrett et al., 1883), communications of "spirits" through mediums (Lodge, 1890), and thought-transference experiments (Guthrie and Birchall, 1883). In addition to these parapsychological interests, some prominent SPR members wrote about and investigated dissociative phenomena and the subconscious mind, contributing significantly to psychiatry and psychology (Alvarado, 2002).

Edmund Gurney (1847–1888) was one of the most prominent early SPR researchers. He contributed to nineteenth century hypnosis research, producing important studies of hypnotic memory (Gurney, 1887), and the creative abilities of the hypnotic subconscious (Gurney, 1888), among other topics. But Gurney was also a researcher of spontaneously occurring telepathy. In one of the central classics of early SPR work, *Phantasms of the Living* (Gurney, Myers, and Podmore, 1886), Gurney developed a theoretical model to explain a variety of veridical experiences the SPR had collected. In his view, a telepathic message, which nature was unknown, was manifested through the psychological resources of the person receiving the message (e.g., imagery). This produced such experiences as visual and auditory impressions about people or events that corresponded to incidents that had taken place at a distance. The information in many cases referred to death or some crisis such as an accident or a medical problem occurring to someone important to the person having the experience. The following account from the collection illustrates the experiences in question:

> On one occasion (I am unable to fix the date, but I must have been about 10 years old) I was walking in a country lane … I was reading geometry as I walked along, a subject little likely to produce fancies or morbid phenomena of any kind, when, in a moment, I saw a bedroom known as the White Room in my home, and upon the floor lay my mother, to all appearance dead. The vision

> must have remained some minutes, during which time my real surroundings appeared to pale and die out; but as the vision faded, actual surroundings came back, at first dimly, and then clearly.
>
> I could not doubt that what I had seen was real, so, instead of going home, I went at once to the house of our medical man and found him at home. He at once set out with me for my home, on the way putting questions I could not answer, as my mother was to all appearance well when I left home.
>
> I led the doctor straight to the White Room, where we found my mother actually lying as in my vision. This was true even to minute details. She had been seized suddenly by an attack at the heart, and would soon have breathed her last but for the doctor's timely advent (Gurney, Myers, and Podmore, 1886, Vol. 1, p. 19)

Another well-known SPR member was classical scholar Frederic W. H. Myers (1843–1901), probably the most knowledgeable psychical researcher on the subconscious mind of the nineteenth century.[4] Myers discussed in his writings what he called the subliminal mind, or the subconscious. In a widely cited statement Myers wrote:

> I suggest … that the stream of consciousness in which we habitually live is not the only consciousness which exists in connection with our organism. Our habitual or empirical consciousness may consist of a mere selection from a multitude of thoughts and sensations, of which some at least are equally conscious with those that we empirically know. I accord no primacy to my ordinary waking self, except that among my potential selves this one has shown itself the fittest to meet the needs of common life (Myers, 1892a, p. 301).

According to Myers the subliminal self was the common principle behind normal, abnormal and supernormal phenomena. This included dreams, creativity, hallucinations, hysteria, telepathy, apparitions, and the phenomena of mediums discussed in a later section of this paper (Myers, 1903). Different from other theoreticians of the mind such as Janet, Myers did not believe that the subliminal was limited to the pathological. In fact, Myers (1887) argued that in some multiple personality cases the personality changes were positive and illustrated evolution instead of degeneration or mental weakness, as most of his contemporaries believed (Janet, 1889).

The workings of the subliminal, both normal and supernormal, Myers wrote, were "habitually received, not by aid of those sensory adits or operations which the supraliminal [conscious] self directly commands, but by aid of adits and operations peculiar to the subliminal self …" (Myers, 1892a, p. 306). These adits and operations were the sensory (hallucinations, impressions) and motor automatisms (automatic writing, trance speaking) that brought psychological and supernormal information to the conscious mind (Myers, 1892b, 1893).

Myers influenced an important American psychologist and philosopher, the well-known William James (1842–1910).[5] Similar to Myers, James considered the existence of what he referred to as the "hidden self," an intelligence behind many of the phenomena of dissociation and of psychical research. In an article written for the general public, James (1890a) summarized the work of French psychiatrists (mainly Janet) as well as aspects of the work of the SPR. In fact, Taylor (1996) has argued that James was an important mediator of the French work on the subconscious mind coming to the United States, and that James took some of this information from the SPR.

Throughout his life James showed much interest in psychical research, as seen in his numerous writings on the subject (Burkhardt, 1986). In his 1896 lectures on exceptional mental states he focused on dreams and hypnosis, automatism, multiple personality and possession, among other topics (Taylor, 1982). Some of this material appeared in his later study of religious experiences (James, 1902).

Furthermore, it has been argued that in his study of the famous American medium Leonora E. Piper (1857–1950)[6] James did not follow Janet and others in reducing mediumship to dissociation. He accepted that the medium presented veridical communications transcending conventional views of dissociation (James, 1886, 1890b; see also Alvarado, 2016; and Alvarado and Krippner, 2010). As he did in other publications, James argued for an expansion of human experience to include what Myers and others referred to as the supernormal.

The SPR work, as well as the general interest in hysteria and hypnosis, also led others to the observation of parapsychological phenomena. The patient Léonie Leboulanger (b. 1837) connected the fields of pathological dissociation and psychical research, as seen in the prominent careers of Pierre Janet (1859–1947) and Charles Richet (1850–1935) (Gauld, 1996).[7] Both men showed much interest in what we would call today ESP phenomena around the same time that they were conducting their better known studies of hypnosis and dissociation (Janet, 1889; Richet, 1883). Janet (1930) admitted in an autobiographical essay that his career in abnormal psychology started with his studies of mental suggestion at a distance with Leonie. His initial observations, presented at a meeting of the *Société de Psychologie Physiologique* in 1885 presided by Charcot, were about the induction of the hypnotic trance at a distance (Janet, 1885/1968a, see also Janet, 1886/1968b). These observations, which Janet made together with J. H. A. Gibert, a physician with more experience than Janet had at the time with hypnosis, were very influential in the study of mental action at a distance, especially in France.

One of the tests was summarized as follows:

> Without warning Mrs. B. of his intention, Dr. Gibert went into an adjoining room and placed himself six or seven meters from his subject. From this other room, he tried mentally to give her the order to sleep. I remained with the subject and noticed that after a few minutes her eyes closed and sleep began. But what seemed particularly strange to me was that in her lethargy she was not at all under my influence. I could not provoke in her either contracture or attraction, although I was in her presence when she went to sleep. On the other hand, she completely obeyed Dr. Gibert who was not present, and finally it was Dr. Gibert who had to awaken her. This proved that it was he who had to put her to sleep. (Janet 1885/1968a, p. 127)

Soon after Janet presented his observations others read similar reports of mental suggestion at the same society (Gley, 1886; Hericourt, 1886). A commission of both French and foreign observers witnessed Janet and Gibert's efforts to induce trance and actions at a distance and documented effects similar to those reported by Janet. According to this report, when Janet and Gibert's observations were combined with those done in the presence of the commission, it was found that of 25 tests, 19 were successful and six were not (Myers, 1886, p. 136).

Janet did not show interest in these investigations in posterior years, as seen in his autobiography (Janet, 1930). The studies were not emphasized in his *L'Automatisme Psychologique*, where Janet (1889) discussed Léonie's dissociations. But as seen in this book, and elsewhere (Janet, 1892), Janet continued throughout his life to be interested in the "extraordinary" in psychiatry, arguing the phenomena could be explained through either the concept of dissociation or other conventional explanations.

On the other hand, Richet devoted a good part of his life to the study of psychical research and to defend the reality of their phenomena beyond explanations such as fraud, dissociation and sensory information. In an influential article on mental suggestion, Richet (1884) introduced the use of probability theory to psychical research in card guessing tests. In the same article he wrote that "instead of acting on the conscious faculties," mental suggestion "makes its influence felt on the unconscious faculties of intelligence. It follows that the individual who receives the suggestion will not be able to realize it" (p. 639).

He also studied Léonie from the parapsychological point of view. In an article published in England by the SPR, Richet (1888) reported on further attempts to induce trance at a distance and to test for clairvoyance. In a later report, he used playing cards inside opaque envelopes. Richet hypnotized Léonie and her secondary personalities took the clairvoyance tests. According to Richet: "She spent two months and a half in my house. ... As I could keep her entranced for a long time without injury to her—generally during the night—I have repeatedly sat by her side from 8 p.m. till 6 a.m. For it was not in the earliest moments of her trance that she could tell the cards under the envelope, but after long and apparently very laborious endeavor" (Richet, 1889, p. 68). Léonie put the envelopes between her hands and talked for hours before guessing each card's identity. Richet became convinced of the existence of a faculty to obtain knowledge without the usual means but admitted that the phenomenon was not consistent and that he was ignorant about the conditions under which good results could be obtained in the tests. Another interesting observation was that Léonie tended to be successful in guessing cards with kings, queens and aces. In a footnote Richet stated that she could do trickery when she was left alone at night with the cards inside envelopes (something that was not Richet's usual testing procedure). There was no doubt that Léonie opened the envelopes, but Richet believed trickery was done by one of her secondary personalities (Richet, 1889, p. 77). In later years Richet (n. d.) continued to be interested in what he referred to as the "sixth sense."

But not everyone in France followed Richet. In his book *L'Hypnotisme et les États Analogues au Point de Vue Médico-Légal*, Gilles de la Tourette (1857–1904) tried unsuccessfully to follow up Richet's card guessing studies using healthy subjects and somnambules in and out of trance. "The number of cards guessed never went beyond what was indicated by the calculus of probability" (Gilles de la Tourette, 1887, p. 167). No success was found in tests in which the participants had to guess names and phrases. This led this author to conclude that "in the current state of science the phenomena of mental suggestion do not exist ... or are not proven" (pp. 167–168).

Several skeptical psychiatrists and psychologists in the nineteenth century were active arguing that Spiritualism in general was basically a problem of unreliable testimony. This was the position of such individuals as Americans George M. Beard (1839–1883) and William A. Hammond (1828–1900), Englishman William B. Carpenter (1813–1885), and German Wilhelm Wundt (1832–1920). The evidence for spiritualistic phenomena, including mediumship, they suggested, came from persons without proper training in observation and scientific thinking and from suggestible individuals (Beard, 1879; Carpenter, 1876; Hammond, 1870; Wundt, 1879). As Carpenter stated:

> Everything which tends to prove the reality of the occult influence, is exaggerated or distorted; everything which would help to explain it away, is quietly (no doubt quite unintentionally) dropped out. ... And the degree in which such constructions involve ascriptions of supernatural power, can be shown in many instances to depend upon the prevalent notions entertained as to what the individual might be expected to do (Carpenter, 1876, pp. 290–291).

Many individuals with medical training believed that mediumship could be explained by the workings of the nervous system. Carpenter's (1853, 1877) ideas about the reflex, automatic action of the nervous system to produce phenomena such as seemingly intelligent messages received through table turning or trance mediumship was a case in point. As he wrote, "the tilting—like the turning—of tables, may be unhesitatingly attributed to the unconscious muscular action of the operators; while the answers which are brought out by its instrumentality may be shown to be the expressions, either ... of ideas actually present to the mind of one or other of the performers; or ... of past ideas which have left their traces in the brain, although they have dropped out of the conscious memory" (Carpenter, 1877, p. 100; see also Chevreul, 1854; and Faraday 1853).

In Beard's (1879) view, trance consisted of a pathology of the nervous system in which "the cerebral activity is concentrated in some limited region of the brain, the activity of the rest of the brain being for the time suspended" (p. 67). The sense of the marvelous or of the supernatural was able to induce trance in those with psychological or pathological predispositions such as mediums. Beard believed that while one was in a trance they became an automaton prone to automatic behaviors, visions and ideas related to the context that induced the trance:

> It is this which causes the table to move beneath the hands of the expectant circles, performs the writing and varied motions of planchette ...; it is this that unfolds the marvels and all the genuine developments of trance orators and preachers ...; it is this, finally, that makes it easy, if not inevitable, that enraptured and entranced inquirers after tidings from departed loved ones should see their faces and hear their voices, in dreams, in the darkness of night, or in the dim light of organized *séances*" (Beard, 1879, p. 69).

The French were particularly interested in the pathology of mediumship, as seen in Le Maléfan's study (1999). Mediums, Janet (1889) wrote, are "neuropaths if not frankly hysterical" (p. 404). In his view mediumship "depends on a particular morbid state similar to that which can later become hysteria or madness: mediumship is a symptom and not a cause" (Janet, 1889, p. 406). In fact, Janet (1892, p. 424) clarified he did not believe that the medium was always a hysteric. He observed a case of somnambulism and of automatic writing that did not show hysteria, although it had fixed ideas and lack of contact with reality. Janet believed cases like this were examples of "mental disaggregation as a disease larger than hysteria that may manifest through hysterical symptoms or in other forms" (Janet, 1892, p. 424).

Alfred Binet (1892) also discussed the pathology of mediums in his book *Les Altérations de la Personnalité*. According to him, "on occasion the most discrete authors cannot avoid saying that some excellent medium has had a nervous crisis, or is quickly fatigued due to delicate health. ..." (p. 299). Gilles de la Tourette (1887) mentioned a case of a 13-year-old girl who had had a "violent attack of hysteria" (p. 309) after performing as a medium for two days.

Other French physicians commented along similar lines. One of them classified mediums in three groups: the frauds, the insane and those suffering from degeneration or mental weakness (Duhem, 1904, p. 131). Joseph Grasset (1849–1918) wrote that "mediums belong to the neuropathic family" (Grasset, 1904, p. 256). This author speculated on the existence of "polygons," a chain of several centers or mental structures that produced many psychological and psychophysiological manifestations. According to Grasset this system had superior centers that were connected with inferior centers related to the production of images, motor processes and many other functions. During disease or other pathological states such as mediumistic trance this polygonal system could produce complex phenomena such as the coordination of the movements needed to coordinate automatic writing, table turning, or the ideas involved in spirit communications. The polygonal system of the medium, according to Grasset, could act by itself with the medium's own polygons or in collaboration with the polygons of the persons forming the mediumistic circle. The final product of this polygonal activity was the simulation of the action of an external intelligence.

Such ideas of pathology continued into the twentieth century in the works of other French physicians (Ballet, 1913; Lévy-Valensi, 1910). Furthermore, these concepts were discussed as well in other countries, such as the United States and Brazil (Alvarado & Zingrone, 2012; Moreira-Almeida, Silva de Almeida, Lotufo Neto, 2005).

As argued by many writers, attention to mediumship contributed to the study of the capabilities of the subconscious mind (for a review see Alvarado, 2010). But for Janet, Grasset and others, there was no transcendence of the medium's sensory and motor activities, and the manifestations were produced through the internal resources of both mediums and sitters. In contrast, other individuals saw mediumship as a phenomenon open to supernormal influence. That is, the phenomena were real in the sense that mediums obtained information beyond their sensory powers, and some could produce physical manifestations beyond their motor abilities.

Some students of mediumship combined the belief in the supernormality of mediumship with the view that mediums were hysterics. This was the case of studies with the famous Italian physical medium Eusapia Palladino (1854–1918), who influenced psychical research in various ways (Alvarado, 1993). The Italian psychiatrist and criminologist Cesare Lombroso (1836–1909) accepted that Palladino produced movement of objects and materializations while maintaining his belief that she was a hysteric and an epileptic (see also Alvarado & Biondi, 2017). Lombroso (1892) believed that Palladino, like hysterics and hypnotized individuals, had the activity of some of her nervous centers arrested. This allowed her to project nervous energy outside her body to produce physical phenomena. He later extended this idea of projection of vital force to include the action of spirits of the dead (Lombroso, 1909).

Similar to Lombroso, Italian psychiatrist Enrico Morselli (1852–1929) accepted Palladino's physical phenomena as objective and viewed her as a hysteric, as seen in his book *Psicologia e "Spiritismo"* (Morselli, 1908). The exteriorization of force by the medium was stronger when her consciousness changed, from lighter to more profound stages of trance. In Morselli's view, trance inhibited the superior nervous centers allowing the lower ones to become more active in the exteriorization of "bio-psychic" force. Such automatic processes, Morselli believed, were forms of inferior mental activity associated with hysteria and related to the restriction of consciousness documented in hysterical patients by Janet and others.

Several other psychologists and psychiatrists were interested in mediumship but did not necessarily assumed pathology. This was the case of the above-mentioned Frederic W. H. Myers. In his view, the statements of trance mediums "constitute one of many classes of phenomena which occur in sane subjects without entering the normal waking consciousness or forming part of the habitual chain of memory" (Myers, 1890, p. 437). Mental mediumship was one of the phenomena that allowed Myers to argue that the subliminal mind had specific ways to communicate knowledge to the conscious (or supraliminal) mind. Myers argued that automatisms such as trance speaking and automatic writing were forms that the subliminal mind used to convey information to the supraliminal. This information consisted mainly of the content of the medium's mind but could on occasion be telepathically derived (Myers, 1884, 1885). In fact, in Myers's view: "It is the *secondary* self ... which receives or recognizes the telepathic impact ... and in some way or other furnishes an intelligent reply" (Myers, 1885, p. 28). Myers eventually accepted that spirits could communicate using the contents of the medium's mind to craft their messages (Myers, 1903, Vol. 2, p. 249).

William James also accepted that some mediumistic communications were veridical. As is well known, James (1886, 1890b) had many sittings with the above-mentioned medium Leonora E. Piper. This medium was actively studied by many SPR researchers, most of whom became convinced of the veridical nature of her communications (Sage, 1902/1904). One of these communications was summarized in the *Proceedings* of the Society:

> During the sitting Mrs. Piper was constantly moving, sometimes writhing, and frequently uttering inarticulate sounds. In her writhing she frequently clutched her throat with both hands; this reminded me of the curious affection of the throat—a very large external swelling—of which my friend E ...

> had died within a few weeks ... Thus he came into my head; within a half hour or so she had tolerably described and distinctly named him. A similar phenomenon preceded the naming of my uncle ... her inarticulate utterances took a form that reminded me strongly of the gasping which I had heard him utter during the interval of nearly a day which elapsed between a stroke of apoplexy and his death. Once in my head, she named him before long (Hodgson, 1892, p. 98).

It was James who introduced Piper to nineteenth century psychologists and psychical researchers. In his opinion, "taking everything that I know of Mrs. P. into account, the result is to make me feel as absolutely certain as I am of any personal fact in the world that she knows things in her trances which she cannot possibly have heard in her waking state, and that the definitive philosophy of her trances is yet to be found" (James, 1890b, pp. 658–659).

Another relevant figure was Swiss psychologist Théodore Flournoy (1854–1920), who was interested in the mental dynamics of mediums. In an early article Flournoy argued that some communications received through mediums were the "product of the medium's subconscious imagination, working from recollections and latent worries" (Flournoy, 1899, p. 144). Flournoy (1900) made psychological and psychical research history with his study of the fictitious communications received through medium Hélène Smith (pseudonym of Catherine Élise Müller, 1861–1929). This medium produced romances of previous lives in India and France as well as of life on planet Mars. Her subconscious, Flournoy believed, guided the medium to paint Martian houses and to invent a Martian language (see also Alvarado, Maraldi, Machado, & Zangari, 2014).

But Flournoy (1911) also believed that mental mediums could obtain information in supernormal ways, information that was presented as if coming from a discarnate source. He suggested that the personification of a dead person presented by the medium perhaps was accomplished by the subconscious dramatization of telepathically-obtained information. Ideas of this sort were also presented by others (reviewed in Alvarado, 2014a).

In this short and certainly incomplete overview I have presented several examples of the interest of physicians and psychologists in psychic or supernormal phenomena during the nineteenth century and part of the twentieth. Other than those few who have devoted themselves to the study of parapsychological phenomena, most scientists today are not concerned with this topic. As seen in this paper and elsewhere (e.g., Alvarado, 2002; Crabtree, 1993; Plas, 2000; Shamdasani, 1993), many students of the mind have been concerned with these phenomena in the past, including some eminent ones we have not discussed (such as Freud and Jung; see Fodor, 1971). In fact, these concerns have been part of their psychiatric and psychological work. Janet, for example, not only started his career in abnormal psychology through the study of mental suggestion at a distance, but he actively used the phenomena of mediumship to develop his ideas about dissociation. He cited cases of mediumship and some of the work of Myers to illustrate the occurrence of psychological "disaggregation" in persons who were not clinical patients. In some ways mediumship was used by Janet to validate the ideas he had developed with patients such as Léonie. One may speculate that this validation was, in part, based on the need of some medical and mental health professionals who had to contain the claims of Spiritualism while at the same time establish their profession as the only one competent to deal with these claims scientifically (Brown, 1983; Coon, 1992).

A similar view may be taken regarding Carpenter's ideas of ideo-motor and automatic action of the nervous system. Those ideas were not only used within the small technical field of "mental physiology," but were believed by some to be useful in explaining the practice of mediumship. Such applications furthered both Janet and Carpenter's systems of thought and contributed to theoretical ideas in psychology in general. Furthermore, and as Le Maléfan (1999) has argued, many French psychiatrists were both influenced by the phenomena of mental mediumship in their creation of psychiatric syndromes. The medium was used to illustrate principles of mental dynamics in the same way as hysterics and others were used by many psychiatrists to develop ideas about mental illness and the subconscious mind (on mediumship see also Alvarado & Zingrone, 2012).

The influential writings of Flournoy, Myers and James were intimately related to the phenomena of psychical research. These ideas, in turn, influenced many others in their conceptions of the subconscious mind. As Ellenberger (1970) and later writers have argued (Alvarado, 2002; Crabtree, 1993; Plas, 2000), the parapsychological was one of several factors influencing the development of ideas of dissociation and the subconscious mind. This was the case regardless of whether the theoretician believed in conventional explanations of psychic phenomena such as suggestion, dissociation or fraud (Beard, Binet, Grasset, Janet), or the idea that the mind could obtain information at a distance using presently unknown means (Flournoy, James, Richet, Myers).

Mental suggestion and mediumship influenced psychiatry and psychology regardless of the explanations these phenomena received. They were part of the context in which ideas of the subconscious developed. Janet (1892) himself stated: "I insist in believing that the spiritists were the first to bring attention to subconscious movements and to the indeed extraordinary manifestations of mental disaggregation" (p. 413). Of course, the acceptance of the idea that the mind could transcend the limitations of the body was important in that it led some, such as Myers, to have a wider conception of human potential and of the mind-body relationship. In other words, acceptance of the supernormal affected the actual ideas of some theoreticians.

Some of the early studies with mental suggestion were also influential in other ways. Richet (1884) helped to bring probability theory into psychology, as seen in Hacking's (1988) article. Many of the early studies of telepathy and the like also taught us much about normal explanations such as muscle reading and other sensory cues (Luckhurst, 2002).

It is clear, however, that the psychic, defined as phenomena requiring new explanatory models, was not accepted by the majority of students of the mind who were influenced by such ideas as Myers' concepts of the subliminal and its manifestations.[8] Nonetheless, Myers's work, as well as that of Flournoy and others with mediums, illustrated the possibilities of the subconscious mind in terms of its imaginative and plastic potential, something also learned from the history of hypnosis (Gauld, 1992). All of this suggests that interest in the psychic should be considered as a factor of some influence in specific areas of the histories of psychiatry and psychology, a trend we are starting to see in the work of the above-mentioned historians.

Notes

1 For a short overview of aspects of the history of parapsychology see Zingrone & Alvarado (2015). Other general accounts include Beloff (1993) and Gutierez & Maillard (2004).

2 For overviews of mesmerism see Crabtree (1993) and Gauld (1992). The movement centered around the belief of the existence of animal magnetism, a universal force that was postulated to induce trances, healing and various phenomena such as clairvoyance.

3 On the early SPR see Gauld (1968). Later discussions include Alvarado (2002) and Cerullo (1982).

4 In terms of connecting psychology and psychical research Myers was the most important of the early SPR members. In addition to Gauld's (1968) classic account of his life and work, see Hamilton (2009) and Kelly (2007). Ellenberger (1970) considered that Myers was "one of the great systematisers of the notion of the unconscious mind" (p. 314).

5 There has been much scholarship about James (e.g., Bordogna, 2008; Taylor, 1996). Discussions about his involvement with psychical research include Alvarado & Krippner (2010), Knapp (2017), and Junior, Araujo, & Moreira-Almeida (2013). See also his collected psychical research writings (Burkhardt, 1986).

6 Piper was studied by many others, as seen in reviews of her mediumship (e.g., Tymn, 2013; Sage, 1902/1904).
7 Janet and Richet were important figures in French psychology interested in psychic phenomena. Janet is better known today for his studies of dissociation (Van der Hart & Friedman, 1989), and Richet for his work in physiology (Wolf, 1993).
8 Many individuals were involved in the rejection of psychic phenomena from psychology. In addition to Carpenter, Janet and Wundt, this includes Hippolyte Bernheim (1840–1919), G. Stanley Hall (1844–1924), Joseph Jastrow (1863–1944), and Hugo Munsterberg (1863–1916). On aspects of this rejection of psychic phenomena see Alvarado (2014b, 2017), Coon (1992), Sommer (2012), and Taves (2014).

References

Alvarado, C. S. (1993). Gifted subjects' contributions to psychical research: The case of Eusapia Palladino. *Journal of the Society for Psychical Research, 59*, 269–292.
Alvarado, C. S. (2002). Dissociation in Britain during the late nineteenth century: The Society for Psychical Research, 1882–1900. *Journal of Trauma and Dissociation, 3*, 9–33.
Alvarado, C. S. (2010). Classic text No. 84: 'Divisions of personality and spiritism' by Alfred Binet (1896). *History of Psychiatry, 21*, 487–500.
Alvarado, C. S. (2014a). Mediumship, psychical research, dissociation, and the powers of the subconscious mind. *Journal of Parapsychology, 78*, 98–114.
Alvarado, C. S. (2014b). G. Stanley Hall on "Mystic or Borderline Phenomena." *Journal of Scientific Exploration, 28*, 75–93.
Alvarado, C. S. (2016). Classic text no. 105: 'Report of the Committee on Mediumistic Phenomena,' by William James (1886). *History of Psychiatry, 27*, 85–100.
Alvarado, C. S. (2017). Telepathy, mediumship and psychology: Psychical research at the international congresses of psychology, 1889–1905. *Journal of Scientific Exploration, 31*, 255–292.
Alvarado, C. S., & Biondi, M. (2017). Classic text no. 110: Cesare Lombroso on mediumship and pathology. *History of Psychiatry, 28*, 225–241.
Alvarado, C. S., & Krippner, S. (2010). Nineteenth century pioneers in the study of dissociation: William James and psychical research. *Journal of Consciousness Studies, 17*, 19–43.
Alvarado, C. S., Maraldi, E. de O., Machado, F. R., & Zangari, W. (2014). Théodore Flournoy's contributions to psychical research. *Journal of the Society for Psychical Research, 78*, 149–168.
Alvarado, C. S., & Martmez-Taboas, A (2002). Parapsicología: Mitos y falacias que todo psicólogo debe reconocer. *Revista Puertorriquena de Psicología, 13*, 99–125.
Alvarado, C. S., & Zingrone, N. L. (2012). Classic text no. 90: 'The pathology and treatment of mediomania,' by Frederic Rowland Marvin (1874). *History of Psychiatry, 23*, 229–244.
Anonymous. (1882). Objects of the Society. *Proceedings of the Society for Psychical Research, 1*, 3–6.
Ballet, G. (1913). La psychose hallucinatoire chronique et la désagrégation de la personnalité. *L'Encéphale, 8*, 501–519.
Barrett, W. F., Keep, A. P. P., Massey, C. C., Wedgwood, H., Podmore, F., & Pease, E. R. (1883). First report of the Committee on Haunted Houses. *Proceedings of the Society for Psychical Research, 1*, 101–115.
Beard, G. M. (1879). The psychology of spiritualism. *North American Review, 129*, 65–80.
Beloff, J. (1993). *Parapsychology: A concise history*. Athlone Press.
Binet, A. (1892). *Les altérations de la personnalité*. Félix Alcan.
Biondi, M. (1988). *Tavoli e medium: Storia dello spiritismo in Italia*. Gremese.
Bordogna, F. (2008). *William James at the boundaries: Philosophy, science, and the geography of knowledge*. University of Chicago Press.
Braude, A. (2001). *Radical spirits: Spiritualism and women's rights in nineteenth-century America*. Indiana University Press.
Brown, E. M. (1983). Neurology and spiritualism in the 1870s. *Bulletin of the History of Medicine, 37*, 563–577.

Burkhardt, F. H. (Ed.). (1986). *Essays in psychical research (The Works of William James, Vol. 16).* Harvard University Press.

Cardeña, E., Palmer, J., & Marcusson-Clavertz, D. (Eds.). (2015). *Parapsychology: A handbook for the 21st century*. McFarland

Carpenter, W. B. (1853). Electro-biology and mesmerism. *Quarterly Review, 93,* 501–557.

Carpenter, W. B. (1876). On the fallacies of testimony in relation to the supernatural. *Contemporary Review, 27,* 279–295.

Carpenter, W. B. (1877). *Mesmerism and spiritualism, &c. historically and scientifically considered.* Longmans and Green.

Cerullo, J. J. (1982). *The secularization of the soul: Psychical research in modern Britain.* Institute for the Study of Human Issues.

Chevreul, E. M. (1854). *De la baguette divinatoire, du pendule dit explorateur et des tables tournantes.* Mallet-Bachelier.

Coon, D. J. (1992). Testing the limits of sense and science: American experimental psychologists combat spiritualism, 1880–1920. *American Psychologist, 47,* 143–151.

Crabtree, A. (1993). *From Mesmer to Freud: Magnetic sleep and the roots of psychological healing.* Yale University Press.

Duhem, P. (1904). *Contribution a Vetude de la folie chez les spirites*. G. Steinheil.

Ellenberger, H. F. (1970). *The discovery of the unconscious: The history and evolution of dynamic psychiatry.* Basic Books.

Faraday, M. (1853). Professor Faraday on table-moving. *The Athenaeum, 1340,* 801–803.

Flournoy, T. (1899). Genèse de quelques prétendus messages spirites. *Revue Philosophique de la France et de L'Étranger, 47,* 144–158.

Flournoy, T. (1900). *From India to the planet Mars: A study of a case of somnambulism.* New York: Harper & Brothers.

Flournoy, T. (1911). *Spiritism and psychology*. Harper and Brothers.

Fodor, N. (1971). *Freud, Jung and occultism*. University Press.

Gauld, A. (1968). *The founders of psychical research*. Routledge and Kegan Paul.

Gauld, A. (1992). *A history of hypnotism.* Cambridge University Press.

Gauld, A. (1996). Notes on the career of the somnambule Leonie. *Journal of the Society for Psychical Research, 61,* 141–151.

Gley, G. (1886). A propos d'une observation de sommeil provoqué a distance. *Revue Philosophique de la France et de l'Étranger, 21*, 425–428.

Gilles de la Tourette, G. (1887). *L'hypnotisme et les états analogues au point de vue médico-legal.* E. Plon, Nourrit.

Grasset, J. (1904). *Le spiritisme devant la science* (Rev. ed.). Coulet.

Gurney, E. (1887). Stages of hypnotic memory. *Proceedings of the Society for Psychical Research, 4*, 515–531.

Gurney, E. (1888). Recent experiments in hypnotism. *Proceedings of the Society for Psychical Research, 5*, 317.

Gurney, E., Myers, F. W. H., & Podmore, F. (1886). *Phantasms of the living* (2 vols.). Trübner.

Guthrie, M., & Birchall, J. (1883). Record of experiments in thought-transference. *Proceedings of the Society for Psychical Research, 1*, 263–283.

Gutierez, G., & Maillard, N. (2004). *Les aventuriers de l'esprit.* Presses du Chatelet.

Hacking, I. (1988). Telepathy: Origins of randomisation in experimental design. *Isis, 79*, 427–451.

Hamilton, T. (2009). *Immortal longings: F. W. H. Myers and the Victorian search for life after death.* Imprint Academic.

Hammond, W.A. (1870). The physics and physiology of Spiritualism. *North American Review, 110*, 233–260.

Héricourt, J. (1886). Un cas de somnambulisme à distance. *Revue Philosophique de la France et de l'Étranger, 21*, 200–203.

Hodgson, R. (1892). A record of observations of certain phenomena of trance. *Proceedings of the Society for Psychical Research, 8*, 1–167.

Inglis, B. (1977). *Natural and supernatural: A history of the paranormal from earliest times to 1914.* Hodder and Stoughton.

James, W. (1886). Report of the Committee on Mediumistic Phenomena. *Proceedings of the American Society for Psychical Research, 1*, 102–106.

James, W. (1890a). The hidden self. *Scribner's Magazine, 7*, 361–173.

James, W. (1890b). A record of observations of certain phenomena of trance (5). Part III. *Proceedings of the Society for Psychical Research, 6*, 651–659.

James, W. (1902). *The varieties of religious experience: A study in human nature*. Longmans, Green.

Janet, P. (1889). *L'automatisme psychologique: Essai de psychologie experimentale sur les formes inferieures de Vactivite humaine*. Félix Alcan.

Janet, P. (1892). Le spiritisme contemporain. *Revue Philosophique de la France et de l'Étranger, 33*, 413–442.

Janet, P. (1930). Autobiography of Pierre Janet. In C. Murchison (Ed.), A history of psychology in autobiography (pp. 123–133). Clark University Press.

Janet, P. (1968a). Report on some phenomena of somnambulism. *Journal of the History of the Behavioral Sciences, 4*, 124–131. (Original work published 1885).

Janet, P. (1968b). Second observation of sleep provoked from a distance and the mental suggestion during the somnambulistic state. *Journal of the History of the Behavioral Sciences, 4*, 258–267. (Original work published, 1886).

Junior, A. S., Araujo, S. de., & Moreira-Almeida, A. (2013). William James and psychical research: Towards a radical science of mind. *History of Psychiatry, 24*, 62–78.

Kelly E. W. (2007). F. W. H. Myers and the empirical study of the mind-body problem. In E. Kelly, E.W. Kelly, A. Crabtree, A. Gauld, A. Grosso, & B. Greyson, (Eds.), *Irreducible mind: Toward a psychology for the 21st Century* (pp. 47–115). Rowman & Littlefield.

Knapp, K. D. (2017). *William James, psychical research, and the challenge of modernity.* University of North Carolina Press.

Le Maléfan, P. (1999). *Folie et spiritisme: Histoire du discourse psychopathologique sur la pratique du spiritisme, ses abords et ses avatars (1850–1950)*. L'Hartmattan.

Lévy-Valensi, J. (1910). Spiritisme et folie. *L'encéphale, 5*, 696–716.

Lodge, O. (1890). A record of observations of certain phenomena of trance (2). Part I. *Proceedings of the Society for Psychical Research, 6*, 443–557.

Lombroso, C. (1892). Le spiritisme et la psychiatrie: Explication psychiatrique de certains faits spirites. *Annales des Sciences Psychiques, 2*, 143–151.

Lombroso, C. (1909). *After death — what? Spiritistic phenomena and their interpretation.* Small, Maynard.

Luckhurst, R. (2002). *The invention of telepathy 1870–1901.* Oxford University Press.

May, E. C., & Marwaha, S. B. (Eds.). (2015). *Extrasensory perception: Support, skepticism, and science* (2 vols.). Praeger.

Moreira-Almeida, A., Almeida, A.A.S., & Lotufo Neto, F. (2005). History of "spiritist madness" in Brazil. *History of Psychiatry, 16*, 5–25.

Morselli, E. (1908). *Psicologia e "spiritismo:" Impressioni e note critiche sui fenomeni medianici di Eusapia Paladino* (2 vols.). Fratelli Bocca.

Myers, F. W. H. (1884). On a telepathic explanation of some socalled spiritualistic phenomena: Part I. *Proceedings of the Society for Psychical Research, 2*, 217–237.

Myers, F. W. H. (1885). Automatic writing. II. *Proceedings of the Society for Psychical Research, 3*, 163.

Myers, F. W. H. (1886). On telepathic hypnotism, and its relation to other forms of hypnotic suggestion. *Proceedings of the Society for Psychical Research, 4*, 127–188.

Myers, F. W. H. (1887). Multiplex personality. *Proceedings of the Society for Psychical Research, 4*, 496–514.

Myers, F. W. H. (1890). A record of observations of certain phenomena of trance (1). Introduction. *Proceedings of the Society for Psychical Research, 6*, 436–442.

Myers, F. W. H. (1892a). The subliminal consciousness: Chapter I. General characteristics of subliminal messages. *Proceedings of the Society for Psychical Research, 7*, 298–327.

Myers, F. W. H. (1892b). The subliminal consciousness: Chapter V: Sensory automatism and induced hallucinations. *Proceedings of the Society for Psychical Research, 8*, 436–535.

Myers, F.W. H. (1893). The subliminal consciousness: Chapter VII: Motor automatism. *Proceedings of the Society for Psychical Research, 9*, 26–128.

Myers, F.W. H. (1903). *Human personality and its survival of bodily death* (2 vols.). Longmans, Green.

Oppenheim, J. (1985). *The other world: Spiritualism and psychical research in England, 1850–1914.* Cambridge University Press.
Plas, R. (2000). *Naissance d'une science humaine: La psychologie: Les psychologues et le « merveilleux psychique. »* Presses Universitaires de Rennes.
Podmore, F. (1889). Phantasms of the dead from another point of view. *Proceedings of the Society for Psychical Research, 6,* 229–313.
Richet, C. (1883). La personnalité et la mémoire dans le somnambulisme. *Revue Philosophique de la France et de l'Étranger, 15,* 225–242.
Richet, C. (1884). La suggestion mentale et le calcul des probabilités. *Revue Philosophique de la France et de l'Etranger, 18,* 609–674.
Richet, C. (1888). Relation de diverses experiences sur la transmission mentale, la lucidité, et autres phénomènes non explicables par les données scientifiques actuelles. *Proceedings of the Society for Psychical Research, 5,* 18–168.
Richet, C. (1889). Further experiments in hypnotic lucidity or clairvoyance. P*roceedings of the Society for Psychical Research, 6,* 66–83.
Richet, C. (n. d.). *Our sixth sense*. Rider.
Sage, M. (1904). *Mrs. Piper and the Society for Psychical Research.* Scott-Thaw.
Shamdasani, S. (1993). Automatic writing and the discovery of the unconscious. *Spring, 54,* 100–131.
Sharp, L. L. (2006). *Secular spirituality: Reincarnation and Spiritism in nineteenth-century France.* Rowman & Littlefield.
Sommer, A. (2012). Psychical research and the origins of American psychology: Hugo Munsterberg, William James, and Eusapia Palladino. *History of the Human Sciences, 25,* 23–44.
Sommer, A. (2013). *Crossing the boundaries of mind and body: Psychical research and the origins of modern psychology.* (Doctoral dissertation). University College London, London.
Storm, L., Tressoldi, P. E., & Di Risio, L. (2010). Meta-analyses of free-response studies 1992-2008: Assessing the noise reduction model in parapsychology. *Psychological Bulletin, 136,* 471–485.
Taves, A. (2014). A tale of two congresses: The psychological study of psychical, occult, and religious phenomena, 1900–1909. *Journal of the History of the Behavioral Sciences, 50,* 376–399.
Taylor, E. (1982). *William James on exceptional mental states: The 1896 Lowell lectures.* Charles Scribner's Sons.
Taylor, E. (1996). *William James on consciousness beyond the margin.* Princeton University Press.
Tymn, M. (2013). *Resurrecting Leonora Piper: How science discovered the afterlife.* White Crow Books.
Van der Hart, O., & Friedman, B. (1989). A reader's guide to Pierre Janet on dissociation: A neglected intellectual heritage. *Dissociation: Progress in the Dissociative Disorders, 2,* 3–16.
Wolf, S. (1993). *Brain, mind and medicine: Charles Richet and the origins of physiological psychology.* Transaction Publishers.
Wundt, W. (1879). Spiritualism as a scientific question: An open letter to Professor Hermann Ulrich, of Halle. *Popular Science Monthly, 15,* 577–593.
Zingrone, N. L., & Alvarado, C. S. (2015). A brief history of psi research. In E. C. May & S. B. Marwaha (Eds.), *Extrasensory perception: Support, skepticism, and science: Vol. 1: History, controversy, and research* (pp. 35–79). Praeger.

Classic Text No. 90: 'The Pathology and Treatment of Mediomania', by Frederic Rowland Marvin (1874)*

Carlos S. Alvarado & Nancy L. Zingrone

During the nineteenth century there were several examples of attempts to pathologize mediumship. One of them was the work of US physician Frederic Rowland Marvin (1847–1918), who is the author of this Classic Text. The excerpt presented here comes from the second part of Marvin's book, *The Philosophy of Spiritualism and the Pathology and Treatment of Mediomania* (1874). Marvin argued for a diagnosis he called 'mediomania,' conceived by him as a neurosis of uterine etiology that could assume epidemic dimensions. His views are consistent with nineteenth-century somatic ideas of psychopathology as well as with ideas about the weaknesses and vulnerabilities of women.

Traditionally there have been many attempts to explain unusual phenomena through a variety of conventional psychological and medical processes, such as the action of the imagination, expectation, and the workings of the nervous system.[1] This trend can be found in writings about apparitions (Ferriar, 1813), possession (Calmeil, 1845) and mesmerism and hypnosis, examples of which are the rejection of animal magnetism by such writers as Bertrand (1826) and Braid (1843). This was also true for mediumship. The purpose of this Classic Text is to discuss the pathologizing of mediumship through the presentation of a segment of the writings of US physician Frederic Rowland Marvin (1874b).

Spiritualism and Mediumship

The development of spiritualism in the middle of the nineteenth century brought mediumship into a prominent position in society in the USA.[2] Mediums, referred to by some as the 'modern Pythia' (Luce, 1877), were individuals believed by many to be able to contact the dead. Acting in a trance or not, they conveyed communications said to come from deceased spirits via verbal statements, writing, visions and impressions. Many messages purported to come from historical personages such as Thomas Jefferson and John Calvin (Spicer, 1853, p. 146–148). But there were also reports of spirit communications conveying verifiable information (e.g. Cooper, 1867, p. 75), something that convinced many that their loved ones survived bodily death.

In addition, there were mediums in whose presence physical manifestations were reported to take place. The spirits were thought to communicate via rapping sounds, through the movement of objects and through materializations, or appearances of phantoms in the séance room that represented the deceased, among other phenomena reported at the time (e.g., Crookes, 1874; Owen, 1871).

Many prominent individuals—among them chemist and physicist William Crookes (1832–1919), Judge John W. Edmonds (1799–1874) and naturalist, evolutionist and anthropologist Alfred Russel

*Republished with permission from *History of Psychiatry, 23*, 229–244, 2012.

Wallace (1823–1913)—defended spiritualism and the phenomena of mediums, giving prominence to their performances (Crookes, 1874; Edmonds & Dexter, 1853; Wallace, 1875). Actual work claiming evidence for mediumship was very influential on public opinion, as seen in the studies of Crookes (1874) with medium D. D. Home (1833–1886), among other investigations and observations (e.g. London Dialectical Society, 1871).

As Galvan (2010, p. 2) says, the medium was "at once emblematic and pliable: she signifies diversely across individual narratives and spans multiple genres." For many, these individuals were considered to be the prophets of a new revelation, one that did not depend on the Bible or organized religion. Nevertheless, the spiritual origin of mediumship defended by spiritualists was questioned. There were many who considered mediums a disruptive force in society. Some argued that mediums in particular, and spiritualism in general, were the instruments of the devil (e.g., Gordon, 1856). Others assumed that the performances were all fraudulent (e.g., Jewett, 1873). In addition, there were others who saw mediumship as a disease, a condition related to a variety of mental and physical diseases. This is the topic of both the present introduction and the Classic Text.[3]

The idea that spiritualism could cause all kinds of mental problems, including 'insanity,' was discussed frequently (e.g., Burlet, 1863; Winslow, 1877). One author wrote in the US journal *Medical World*: "Clearly, Spiritualism is an extensive mental epidemic, which in extreme cases has repeatedly terminated in confirmed madness. Nearly every asylum for the insane, throughout the Union, bears melancholy evidence of the truth of this declaration." (Anonymous, 1856, p. 310).[4]

An anonymous writer in the *North American Review* said that the brain could lose its balance due to strong emotional experiences. It was stated that mediums were exposed to "much unnatural and unhealthy excitement, the brains of many are agitated beyond their power of healthy endurance, and of these some become insane" (Anonymous, 1859, p. 334). A contributor to *The Lancet* wrote: "The counterpart of the wretched medium we find in the half-deluded and half-designing hysterical patient ..." (Anonymous, 1860, p. 466). Another commentator said: "The abnormal conditions of mediumship are apt to be connected with bodily derangements more or less marked" (Anonymous, 1869, p. 602).

Others also mentioned hysteria. George M. Beard (1839–1883), a US physician who specialized in nervous disorders, referred to the "strange performances of hysterical mediums ..." (Beard, 1874, p. 2). Similarly, William A. Hammond (1828–1900), also a prominent physician of the time, wrote in his book, *Spiritualism and Allied Causes of Nervous Derangement*: "At most of the spiritualistic meetings which I have attended there have been hysterical phenomena manifested" (Hammond, 1876, p. 256).

Such concepts of pathology interacted with two other ideas. The first was the somatic understanding of mental illness prevalent through a great part of the nineteenth century (e.g., Bucknill & Tuke, 1862; Winslow, 1866). Physiological views were also prevalent among the phenomena discussed in conjunction with hypnotism, mesmerism, somnambulism and trance (Beard, 1877; Braid, 1843; Carpenter, 1877; Laycock, 1851).

Ideas about pathology were also related to nineteenth-century beliefs that female physiology was ruled by the system of reproduction, problems with which produced a weaker nervous system than that of men (Smith-Rosenberg & Rosenberg, 1973). It was assumed that women were not strong enough to inhabit the public sphere and were better confined to domestic tasks because inherent emotion or too much education could upset the balance of their nervous system. Many believed that exposing women to an education similar to that enjoyed by men would undermine their health and make it impossible for women to enjoy "a future secure from neuralgia, uterine disease, hysteria, and other derangements of the nervous system" (Clarke, 1873, p. 18).

Later in the nineteenth century, as well as in the twentieth century, others continued to associate mediumship with pathology (e.g. Charcot, 1888: 1–12; Duhem, 1904; Janet, 1889; Levy-Valensi, 1910). This short review is sufficient to show that Marvin's ideas were part of a general trend in discussions of mediumship by the medical profession of the day.

Marvin's Life

Frederic Rowland Marvin (1847–1918) was born in the town of Troy in upstate New York.[5] He attended Union College in Schenectady, New York, and Lafayette College in Easton, Pennsylvania, before graduating with his MD from the College of Physicians and Surgeons in New York in 1870. From 1872 to 1875, Marvin was a Professor of Psychological Medicine and Medical Jurisprudence at the New York Free Medical College for Women.[6] He married Persis Anne Rowell, seven years his senior, in 1874. His wife held the distinction of being the first woman elected to the Middletown, New York, School Board. The couple had no children (Reynold, 1911, p. 502).

In 1876 Marvin entered the Theological Seminary of the Reformed Church in Brunswick, New Jersey, graduated in 1877 and was ordained as a Dutch Reform minister in 1879. A possible explanation for his change in profession so early in his career lies in excerpts from his writing published in *An Ethical Problem or Sidelights Upon Scientific Experimentation on Man and Animals* by Alfred Leffingwell, a past President of the American Humane Association. An extract from a letter Marvin wrote to the Association says: "Though now a Minister of the Gospel, I was educated to the profession of medicine ... In the class-room I saw vivisections so unqualifiedly cruel that even now they remain in my memory as a nightmare" (Leffingwell, 1916, p. 429).

Marvin held pastorates in Congregational Churches in Middleton, New York (1879–1883), Portland, Oregon (1883–1886), and Great Barrington, Massachusetts (1887–1895). He was remembered as "a cultivated Christian gentleman ... an effective and interesting speaker ... [who] had a most interesting personality and maintained a warm interest in the common affairs of life" (Corwin, 1922, p. 415–416). From 1895 through 1900, Marvin traveled and studied in Europe, following which he returned to Albany, New York. Although he did not take up another pastorate after his return, he was in great demand as a supply preacher for Presbyterian and Congregational churches in the Albany area until the end of his life.

Marvin was also a prolific writer who published a wide variety of titles during his long life, ranging from poetry to collected sermons, and essays to medical and theological monographs. Among these were *Epidemic Delusions* (1874a), *Literature of the Insane* (1875), *Christ Among the Cattle* (1899), and *The Last Words (Real and Traditional) of Distinguished Men and Women* (1900), and other works (e.g., Marvin, 1870, 1874b, 1903, 1907, 1910, 1915).

The Philosophy of Spiritualism and the Pathology and Treatment of Mediomania (Marvin, 1874b)

Marvin's 68-page booklet consists of two lectures, delivered at the New York Liberal Club on March 20th and 27th, 1874, respectively.[7] The lectures are preceded by a preface in which the author expresses sadness that his lectures are necessary. He writes: "These lectures are not written for spiritual media.[8] Spiritual media are beyond the reach of lectures like these. They are in need of treatment which can be but faintly indicated in these pages. These lectures are written to save those who are about to be drawn into the meshes of Spiritualism …" (Marvin, 1874b, p. iii).

In the first part of the book, *The Philosophy of Spiritualism*, the author criticizes spiritualism on the unusual ground that it is a materialistic philosophy: "Its ghosts are material and appeal to the five senses—they have shape, color, and density; they walk and talk like men and women … Other forms of Materialism have left the soul out and ignored its existence, but Spiritualism is an organized effort to drag it into view and exhibit its earthiness" (p. 5).

According to Marvin the phenomena of spiritualism are of nervous origin:

> Certain physiological and natural laws which have been recently discovered are explaining many of the wonders of spiritual intercourse. Cerebro-physiology, with its marvelous doctrines of unconscious cerebration, automatic thought and action, the corelation [*sic*] of thought with other forces in the universe, and the physical basis of memory, is sending light into the dark things of modern witchcraft. (p. 24)

In the second part of the book, from which we have taken excerpts for the Classic Text below, Marvin presents his diagnosis of 'mediomania,' the pathological condition of mediumship that presented trance, convulsions and ideas of communication with spirits. This condition was more frequent in women than in men, was allied to hysteria and chorea, and was contagious to the point of being epidemic.

Marvin's book was noted or reviewed in several publications, but we will present only those that agreed with or criticized him. In the *Popular Science Monthly* the reviewer declared the book's conclusions were "in accordance with the existing tendencies of scientific thought" (Anonymous, 1874c), while another commented that "all minds that are now sane should imbue themselves with the ideas of this work to guard them from the taint of a spreading infection …" (Anonymous, 1874d, p. 550). Praise also came from a commentator who considered Marvin "a healthy mind, armed with scientific knowledge and common sense …" (Anonymous, 1874e). The reviewer in the *Chicago Medical Journal* agreed with Marvin's intention, but took issue with his discussion of the sexual aspects of the condition (H., 1874).

Others were more negative. In the *Atlantic Monthly* the reviewer doubted if Marvin's arguments would do any good: "Their own philosophy is vague; their rhetoric, though clever, is somewhat shrill …" (Anonymous, 1874b, p. 629). 'Mediomania,' wrote the commentator in the journal *Medical Record*, "is hardly more than a common form of melancholia dished up with a dash of hysteria" (Anonymous, 1874f, p. 633). The writer went on to say that the writing style of the book "is exceedingly bombastic," and shows "a reckless poetical license' (pp. 633–634). Another medical journal said that those who wasted the time to read the book "will be doubtful which most to deplore, the insanity of media … or that of the author" (Anonymous, 1874g).

Negative comments also came from believers in the phenomena of spiritualism. For example, the minister, spiritualist and physician Samuel B. Brittan (*c.* 1815–1883) said Marvin "runs a reckless tilt against something which he suspects is Spiritualism" (Brittan, 1874, p. 477). He pointed out that there were many male mediums who, by virtue of their sex, could not suffer from uterine pathology.

Furthermore, he stated that Marvin brought dishonour to his profession:

> We are surprised that the Free College for Women …, will even tolerate—in the chair of Psychological Medicine—a man who only trifles with the great problems of life and immortality!—questions that demand of him an honest statement and a logical explanation. It is time for all such pseudo-scientific expounders of Spiritual Phenomena to stop airing their egotism and to engage in prayer. (Brittan, 1874, p. 481–482)

Years later Marvin (1905) referred to his book on spiritualism and wrote: "I do not now defend the conclusions I arrived at in that work, but I do hold that mediums and phenomena are not now any more respectable or worthy of confidence than they were when the book was written. The mediums are a sorry lot at the very best." Another reference to spiritualism appears in his book *Poems and Translations,* in which he presents a poem entitled 'Modern Spiritualism' (Marvin, 1907, p. 44). The movement is described as one based on lies, and one that goes against reason.

In another book Marvin wrote an essay about 'human derelicts' and refers to visionaries and to the Fox sisters. In his view "our fathers had no definitive knowledge of hypnotic influence or control" (Marvin, 1915, p. 84). Although he classes mediums and other inspired writers as derelicts, gone were the references to pathology of his earlier work (Marvin, 1874b).

Marvin's book has become an exemplar for modern scholars interested in nineteenth-century ideas about women. This is especially the case for those who focus on some aspect of mediumship (e.g., Braude, 2001, p. 159; McGarry, 2008, p. 125; Owen, 1990, p. 149; Zingrone, 1994).

Notes for Introduction

1 Other examples of this skeptical tradition include: Carpenter, 1877; Grellety, 1876; Madden, 1857; Newnham, 1830; Tissot, 1868.

2 For historical discussions of American spiritualism see: Braude, 2001; Carroll, 1997; Cox, 2003. These, and other authors (e.g. Alvarado, Machado, Zangari & Zingrone, 2007; Tromp, 2006), have discussed mediumship.

3 Most medically-oriented writers on the subject did not believe there was anything in mediumship but pathological and psychological processes, e.g. Alvarado et al., 2007; Brown, 1983; Le Maléfan, 1999; Moreira-Almeida, Silva de Almeida & Lotufo Neto, 2005; Owen, 1990; Zingrone, 1994.

4 There were cases in which individuals, mainly women, were committed to asylums due to their spiritualistic belief and practices; Haber, 1986; Owen, 1990; Porter, Nicholson and Bennett, 2003. Spiritualists disagreed with affirmations of the wide prevalence of spiritualistic-related madness; Anonymous, 1857; Anonymous, 1863. One spiritualist physician conducted a survey by writing to various asylums and presented statistics to the contrary; Crowell, 1877.

5 Biographical material compiled from the following sources: Anonymous, 1904a: 471; Anonymous, 1904b: 401; Anonymous, 1910, p. 254; Anonymous, 1918; Coffin, 1879, pp. 230-231.

6 This college was free to women and was said to represent three schools of medicine: the old allopathic one (of which Marvin was a practitioner), and the homeopathic and the eclectic; Holbrook, 1873. The college was incorporated at the New York Legislature on 12 Apr. 1871; Anonymous, 1873a, p. 348. It was reported to have graduated students in 1873, 1874 and 1875, and to have closed in 1876; Anonymous, 1914, p. 14. There is much information about students and the faculty in a report of the trustees to the regents of the university for the academic years ending on 10 Apr. 1875; Anonymous, 1876, p. 342–344. The report mentions Marvin as faculty member and as President of the Faculty, and presents some topics of his course of psychological medicine, including: Outlines of Insanity, Affective Insanity, Obscure Neuroses and Insane Diatheses, and Epidemic Delusions. Newspaper reports for 1875 also mention Marvin as President of the College; Anonymous, 1875a; Robinson, 1875.

7 The Club, founded in 1869, was dedicated to the discussion and presentation of intellectual, social and political topics; Putnam, 1894, p. 569. The *New York Times* presented reports of two lectures Marvin gave at the Club about 'disordered mental action' and the 'aetiology of insanity'; Anonymous, 1873b; Anonymous, 1874a. Marvin also lectured at the Cooper Institute in New York City on Madame Roland and the French Revolution; Anonymous, 1875b.

8 The term 'media' was used in the early literature of spiritualism as the plural of mediums: e.g., Capron, 1855, p. 171; Gordon, 1856, p. 69.

Classic Text No. 90: 'The Pathology and Treatment of Mediomania' by Frederic Rowland Marvin (1874)*

Insanity is a word used to signify the whole family of intellectual derangements. This family is a large one and we have selected for this evening's study that member of it known as mediomania, or the insanity of mediums. Mediomania is a very ancient form of derangement—the name is modern, the phenomena ancient.[1] The earliest histories of civilization record both rare and typical cases of this interesting disorder, and mediaeval chronicles are filled with the fairy-tales, marvelous revelations, and cruel fate that marked the progress of the disorder. Uncivilized men in uncivilized ages observed the phenomena but mistook their import, and modern science is only just beginning to ravel the mystery and suggest methods of rational treatment. …

Mediomania, though usually sympathetic, is occasionally idiopathic. Its causes are predisposing and exciting. With regard to the predisposing causes of mediomania and its allied neuroses, conflicting opinions are held by eminent pathologists. There are those who mention among the prominent predisposing causes of mediomania—sex, age, natural heritage and civilization. Sex, age, and Civilization enter into the account; they frequently determine the nature and modify the phenomena of insanity, but the absurdity of mentioning them among the causes of any form of intellectual disorder must be evident to the most careless observer. No one is insane because she is a woman, nor because she is civilized, nor because she has reached a certain age; and yet if she be insane, the existing civilization will largely determine the nature of her derangement, and her sex and age will play their part in deciding the character of the disorder and the fate of her intellect.

Sex and age, though not in themselves predisposing causes of mediomania, modify the phenomena of that derangement and make possible many of those conditions which give rise to it. There are certain physical conditions, arising from functional and organic disturbances of the sexual organs, which occasion this and other forms of insanity. Sexual insanity is such insanity as arises from or results in sexual derangement. In women the sexual system is more complicated, both as to structure and function, than in men, hence those forms of insanity which are associated with derangements of that system are more frequent among women than among men. Mediomania, while it often attacks men, and from other than sexual causes, more frequently assails women, and is usually preceded by a genito or venerio-pathological history. Men are more likely to suffer from such cerebral disorders as apoplexy, hemiplegia, rainollissement, and general paralysis, while women are subject to such disorders as chorea, hysteria, and utromania. More women become insane than men, but more men die from insanity than women. The word mediomania, though not actually synonymous with the word utromania, is very closely allied to it in meaning. The word mediomania does not positively designate a pathological condition, for it has grown out of a vulgar belief with regard to certain phenomena, yet it fills a previously unoccupied space and must not be discarded until a better word shall have been coined.

Uterine disorders, whether functional or organic, seldom fail to result in some form of hysteria or of its allied neuroses, and no nervous disorder is oftener thus exhibited than mediomania.[2]

Mediomania has its own peculiar phenomena, and the best way of bringing them before you is by reciting a case, with the history of which I am familiar:

Mrs. W., aged 23, of nervous temperament, and delicate habit, was seized with a sharp pain over the axis of the lumbar vertebra. This pain was repeated at irregular intervals and followed by syncope. The

*The original spelling and punctuation are followed.

syncope alternated with a state of nervous exaltation known as ecstasis.[3] During the ecstasis she was, to use her own words, "entranced with joy." The ecstasis would last from a few minutes to many hours. When I first saw the patient she was recovering from a prolonged attack of ecstasis and was suffering profound exhaustion. Her pulse was rapid, feeble, and irregular; her limbs were cold; pupils dilated; cheeks flushed; lips dry; tongue heavily coated and bordered with a broad red line running from base to apex and sharply defined; and the respiration was rapid, shallow and sighing. To such questions as I asked her she returned evasive answers and seemed to be endeavoring to conceal her thoughts and emotions. I saw her the second time while she was entranced and remained with her until she recovered normal consciousness. About this time visions were presented to her of which she spoke with great reserve. Her husband told me she had spoken to him of a communication which she had received from their dead child. Desiring to discover the patient's intellectual condition, I held with her a long and somewhat enthusiastic conversation concerning the immortality of the soul. At first I received nothing but a general consent to the doctrine, but suddenly and without preparing her mind for the declaration, I confessed to her not only a belief in the doctrine of personal immortality, but possession of convincing proof of a life to come; I declared myself able to see a spirit child, and, having previously examined the husband on the subject and inspected the family photographs, I accurately described the little spirit of her child. This was more than she could endure. Turning her keen, luminous eyes toward the window, she said in a hoarse whisper, "It is my little Harry! where do you see him?" Following the direction of her eyes I took the hint and promptly replied, "In front of the window." Before the conversation ended the patient confessed that she was in daily communication with the spirit of her child and that her whole life was spent in the alternate excitement and depression which accompanied these spiritual communications. She was afflicted with obstinate amenorrhea, and physical examination revealed retroversion of the uterus. The case passed at my request into the hands of an obstetrician with whom I visited the patient. …

The trances which accompany and are part of the phenomena of mediomania may, like other forms of hysteria, be divided into convulsive and non-convulsive. The non-convulsive is the form usually met with.

The convulsions of mediomania resemble very closely those of epilepsy, but are usually less violent. The limbs and trunk are agitated, the head is thrown backward, the legs are violently retracted and extended, the body twists and writhes as if in great agony, the *pomum Adami* projects, the face is flushed, the eyelids are closed and tremulous, the nostrils distended, the jaws shut, the hands are flung wildly in every direction—they sometimes beat the breast with rapid and mechanical strokes or are thrown into the air as if endeavoring to grasp something; occasionally the patient plucks her hair or rends her clothing. The respiration is labored, deep, and irregular. The heart palpitates. Frequently in the intervals of the paroxysms the patient gives utterance to disconnected sentences or fragments of sentences more or less connected with the delusion occupying her mind.

Now with all this there is usually little or no distortion of the countenance, and the face wears a very calm and satisfied expression. Soon the convulsions cease and the patient becomes quiet. The quiet is sometimes complete, but usually broken and watchful. The patient is exceedingly tremulous, and a sudden draft or a slight noise will induce a repetition of the convulsion. A word or look of sympathy or tenderness will act like magic. The moment the patient finds herself the object of attention or conversation she will be seized with a most violent convulsion. These attacks may be repeated many times, with short intervals of quietness.

Another and more common form of mediomaniacal convulsion is that in which the patient becomes suddenly unconscious, and in which such phenomena as slow and interrupted breathing, turgid neck, and flushed cheeks are prominent, while the violence of convulsion is greatly abated. The patient recovers weary in body and melancholy in mind. After the paroxysm a large quantity of pale, limpid urine is passed. These phenomena, like those of kindred forms of hysteria, seem to be dependent on functional disturbance of abdominal or thoracic viscera, for the symptoms are such as naturally arise from disturbance of the ganglionic system.

In mediomania of a non-convulsive character the loss of consciousness is seldom complete, and it frequently happens that a mediomaniac is able to answer questions and converse fluently while deeply entranced. They who have attended spiritual meetings and lectures will call to mind many examples of this wonderful power. The partial loss of consciousness which occurs in this disorder does not attend the onset of the attack, but is gradual in its invasion. The larynx is never closed, hence that peculiar, heavy, sighing inspiration which is almost characteristic of the non-convulsive spiritual trance.

Mediomania occurs in both sexes, but more frequently in women, especially at puberty or the menopausis, or at some period between puberty and the menopausis. It seldom occurs early or late in life; children and old women are not often its victims.

Mediomaniacs are usually young women in whom the process of menstruation is interfered with. They are feeble and debilitated; they have pale faces and cold extremities; they have feeble and depraved appetites, and a dislike for animal food; they will eat strange and unwholesome things and will, frequently, refuse all kinds of food, pretending to their friends that they have eaten nothing for whole weeks. A very public and remarkable example of this morbid propensity for deception is found in a Mrs. J. O. Darling, of Canawaugus, N.Y.—a mediomaniac who pretends to have remained twenty days without eating. During this time she was busily engaged in watching a corpse which she believed would be reanimated in six months.

Another prominent predisposing cause of mediomania is found in Natural Heritage … Now, if it be true that like produces like, our organisms must be, within certain limitations, like the organisms of our parents, and not only must we inherit physiological or pathological lungs, livers, and stomachs, but normally or abnormally organized brains. And if it be true that organic disease leads to functional derangement, it follows that since thought is a function of the brain, abnormally organized brains are productive of disordered mental action, and such brains may be inherited. What is true, in this respect, of one portion of the nervous system is true of all portions—the ganglionic nervous system as well as the cerebro-spinal.

Mediomaniacs do not always reproduce their disorder in their progeny, nor does their neurosis always assume the same type when reproduced. Like other disorders, mediomania is a member of a family from which it is not easily alienated. Hysteria, chorea, utromania, and mediomania are all in one group, and though not always attended by the same causes they are very closely related. Hysteria or mediomania in the first generation may become chorea or melancholia in the second, open insanity in the third, and idiocy in the fourth: the merciful laws of nature usually forbid that there should be a fifth generation.

The exciting causes of mediomania are, so far as have been ascertained, in no way essentially different from causes which bring about other forms of insanity. They are usually divided into physical and moral or psychical, but in the last instance there is no such thing as a moral or psychical cause, since every phenomenon occurring in the system has a physical basis for its antecedent.

Mediomania occasionally manifests itself in sporadic cases, but is usually epidemic. Its present manifestation is in connection with modern Spiritualism, from the practices of which it has derived the prefix of its name. The epidemic does not appear to be decreasing, though fortunately its victims are now almost altogether from the vulgar and illiterate classes, and scientific men do not seem to be liable to the contagion. It numbers among its victims a few men and women of talent and genius, but they were attacked years ago. Had they remained free from the disorder up to the present day, they would not now be very susceptible to its influence. The fact is, Spiritualism has lost its hold on the higher classes, and is spreading with fearful rapidity among the rude and illiterate. Whole communities are given over to its influence. Its believers have their organizations, places of worship, mediums, books, and papers, and they are as sincere, earnest, and fearless as were the Flagelants, Lycanthropes, and Crusaders of the Middle Ages.[4]

Mediomania, hysteria, and allied neuroses are contagious—not by the reception of morbific particles into the system, but through that tendency to imitate which haunts the nervous system like a ghost, urging it to strange and frantic deeds. This tendency to imitate is seated in all minds, whether educated or ignorant, but its most prominent parts are played in the lives of the rude and illiterate ...

In the Middle Ages two thirds of the witches were women, and now more than two thirds of the spiritual media are women. This has always been so, and I suppose it is right it should be so. Women are naturally more sensitive, impulsive, and enthusiastic than men, and it is well for them that they are so; but they must exercise great care that these fine qualities do not become deranged, and it is necessary to such care that they cultivate many of those qualities of mind which are more completely developed in the male temperament. That woman has the most symmetrical, balanced, healthy, and perfect temperament who with the sweetness of womanhood unites the strength of manhood, and that man has the most complete and rounded temperament who to the strength of manhood joins the fineness, gentleness, and sweetness of womanhood.

A neurosis in no way essentially different from hysteria is what is known as utromania. Utromania frequently results in mediomania; indeed, at the present day the two are seldom entirely dissociated. Many women undergo perceptible mental disturbance at every menstrual epoch. The dangers of puberty are greater to girls than to boys, and more girls between the ages of twelve and eighteen become insane than boys. ... I dread to treat no form of insanity more than utromania, for of all derangements it is the most violent and persistent, and yet it is a very common disorder. The angle at which the womb is suspended in the pelvis frequently settles the whole question of sanity or insanity. Tilt the organ a little forward—introvert it, and immediately the patient forsakes her home, embraces some strange and ultra ism—Mormonism, Mesmerism, Fourierism, Socialism, oftener Spiritualism. She becomes possessed by the idea that she has some startling mission in the world. She forsakes her home, her children, and her duty, to mount the rostrum and proclaim the peculiar virtues of free-love,[5] elective affinity, or the reincarnation of souls. Allow the disorder to advance and it becomes a chronic malady, and, alas! the once intelligent, cultivated, and pure woman sinks through a series of strange isms and remarkable affinities until she reaches the despicable level of the *demi monde.*

Utromaniacs imbibe very strange notions, and, what is remarkable, they reflect the spirit of the age with great accuracy. In the classic ages of Greece and Rome they were sibyls, priestesses, and vestal virgins. ... in the darker days of the Middle Ages they were witches, saints, and worshipers at sacred shrines; and in these times they are what the age makes them. They drift with neither rudder nor compass on the tide of human affairs, the sport of every wind that blows. They usually conceive the idea that they are reformers, though themselves wofully [*sic*] in need of reformation. They adopt strange modes of dress, and conduct themselves in so eccentric a manner as to attract attention. They entertain bitter and unnatural dislike for everything which has helped to make their lives happy, useful and pure. They trample upon the sacredness of their marriage relations and despise their religious obligations. They regard their husbands as tyrants bent on their enslavement, and they are likely to forsake their homes for positions of public trust for which they are unfitted.

Every one is acquainted with utromaniacs, for this is the age of utromania. They assemble in strange and eccentric meetings, which they advertise with sad audacity in every daily print. …

The treatment of convulsive mediomania regards (1) the paroxysm interim between the paroxysms, and (2) the interim between the paroxysm. During the paroxysm it is the duty of the physician to do all in his power to prevent the patient from injuring herself. Her clothing should be loosened; and if she uses her hands and teeth so as to injure herself or others, she should be forcibly restrained. Open the windows or doors so as to give her plenty of fresh air, but be careful that you do not expose her to a draft. If the patient is willing to swallow, the attack may be shortened by the exhibition of such articles as asafoetida, valerian, and ammonia. Asafoetida and spiritus ammonise may be combined. …

If the patient will not or can not swallow, she may be induced to do so by the application of some stimulating volatile substance to the nostril. If this fails, resort may be had to enema. An excellent enema is made by mixing asafoetida and turpentine. Mediomaniacs are usually constipated, and it is the duty of the physician when first called to a case to discover the condition of the intestinal viscus.

In mediomaniacal insanity favorable results have followed the administration of cannabis indica or Indian hemp—not the tincture, which is unreliable, but the extract, and if you choose you may combine it with the bromide of potassium. Where the insanity is associated with dysmenorrhea, I can not do better than recommend camphor combined with opium and hyoscyamus or conium. If necessary you may exhibit your sedative by hypodermic injection; medicines so exhibited act with greater promptness than when given by the stomach, and are less likely to irritate that organ. The injection should be made upon the inner side of the upper arm or in some other place where the skin is thin.

Attention has been called to the fact that the erotic element is likely to enter very prominently into all forms of hysterio-mania. Hysteriomaniacs and mediomaniacs are proverbially erotic, egotistic, and religious.

The first symptoms of sexual derangement which a physician is likely to detect are love of solitude, irritability of temper, offensive and steadily increasing egotism, and, a little later, great irresolution and profound and unnatural religiosity. Soon the face betrays the derangement—its features droop, the eye gains a sudden and spasmodic brilliance, the lips and tongue become dry and hot; and, sometimes, the glands in the neck and axilla become enlarged and tender. The face is subject to sudden flushes, followed by great pallor, and, as the disease progresses, persistent thirst, loss of appetite, and insomnia supervene. Strange and interesting psychological phenomena now make their appearance. The patient shuns society, and is suspicious and revengeful. He divides his time between devotional and sexual rapture. Soon the intellect becomes involved, and some pronounced form of mental derangement appears.

Profound and protracted religious excitements are productive of aidoiomania. Religious revivals, spiritual seances, and Romish pilgrimages seldom fail to result in epidemics of sexual impropriety. The lives of saints, priests, ecstatics, devotees, and media, are so many records of sexual derangement. St. Theresa and St. Catherine de Siene, who, in nightly trances, believed themselves folded in the arms of Jesus, were nymphomaniacs; and the love festivals, holy loves, and seraphim- kisses, are believed by physiologists to have indicated points of union between religion and sexual erethism. … .[6]

It is frequently said that a man's religion stamps itself upon his temperament and comes to so affect his nervous system as to appreciably modify its phenomena. This is true, but the converse is as true. The religious faith not only determines but is determined by the nervous status. … Under one religion you will find a certain family of diseases prevalent, and under another, and physicians, especially cerebro-pathologists, will find, in studying cases, that they can not afford to leave the religious tenets of the patients out of consideration. Women of certain denominations are more prolific than women of other denominations, and this is owing to the fact that the organs of generation both in themselves and their husbands are under the control of the nervous system, and the nervous system in the face of a great religious conviction is, like the sensitive leaf, a plant in a rushing wind.

Now all this is especially true of Spiritualism. There is no religion on earth so exciting as Spiritualism. No religion burns up so much tissue or uses so much nervous energy as Spiritualism. Operating upon the human organism, it converts more oxygen into carbonic acid than any other religion with which I am acquainted; consequently it is more injurious to health than any other religious faith, and its occurrence in the sensitive nervous system of a young girl is dangerous in the extreme.

In order to discover the pathological conditions established in the system by Spiritualism, I instituted several experiments which, though not sufficiently exact to be conclusive, indicate some of the physical results of mediomania.

I selected ten patients under treatment for nervous disorders, of which seven were women and three men. Of these ten five professed to be media in one way or another. Four of the five were sufferers from disorders peculiar to their sex; the other subject was a man. I subjected three specimens of urine from each patient to careful and comparative analysis and discovered that in every case the urine of the media was loaded with phosphates. There was also a deficiency in the amount of urea, the average quantity being only about 240 grains per diem. The deficiency in urea I suppose to be due to the nonnitrogenous diet of the patients, for you remember that I directed your attention to the fact that hysteriomaniacs and mediomaniacs usually avoid animal food. The exhibition of a moderate quantity of animal food to one patient increased the number of grains of urea eliminated in a very few hours. …

Deposits of uric acid exhibited broken and fragmental crystals. Why the crystals were fractured I do not know.[7]

A healthy adult usually consumes about seven pounds of food *per diem,* and in the same time discharges from the system the same amount, of effete material. He takes into the system oxygen, water, albumen, starch, fat, and salts; and he discharges carbonic acid, aqueous vapor, perspiration, water of the urine, urea, salts, and feces. Food having been taken into the system combines with the tissues and becomes part of their substance, and the condition of these tissues determines the character of their several functions, and among them that of thought. …

It is difficult to prescribe a regular and uniform diet in any form of mental disorder, for circumstances so modify cases as to make exceptions to all rules. But in general it may be said that the spiritual medium should be placed on a partially meat diet. The diet which I employ in ordinary melancholia might be appropriately employed in the treatment of mediomania. Give plain, nutritious food, poultry, game, fish, mutton, and beef, and in many cases you will find alcoholic stimulants useful adjuncts.

The constipation which marks mediomania, and of which I have spoken, will frequently disappear under the influence of the stimulus of the increased amount of food.[8] If, however, the colon is distended by hardened masses of scybala they must be removed by enema. Active purgation should be avoided. A lady who was more of a medium than she cared to confess was frequently disturbed at night by what she took for a spirit-hand. This hand was very cold and when placed in contact with her sensitive skin caused great nervous disturbance. The spirit-hand was usually placed over the pit of the stomach. When once thoroughly awakened by the hand, she found it difficult to sleep again. I advised her to eat a sandwich and drink a glass of wine immediately after waking. This she did and obtained partial relief, and a few grains of chloral completed the cure.

Before closing this lecture, I again direct your attention to the relations which the sexual and religious instincts bear to each other. It is an interesting and singular fact that the special indulgence in religious exercises undermines the fabric of morality. Moderate use of the various instincts and faculties is right and healthful, and the religious instinct is as much entitled to exercise as other instincts; but I wish to make you believe that its over-exercise or exclusive exercise is productive of sexual immorality. Those men and women who in all ages of the world have been set apart for religious purposes have been notoriously impure. The same thing is true to-day. Priests, monks, nuns, saints, media, ecstatics, and devotees, are famous for their impurities. But scientific pursuits tend in another direction. By liberating the intellect, enlarging the affections, and cooling the temper, they encourage and foster calmness and purity. Geologists, botanists, doctors, and chemists, are, on the average, healthier and purer people. …

Notes to Marvin's text (added by Alvarado and Zingrone)

1 On mediumship in ancient times, see: Howitt, 1863; Ogden, 2004; Paton, 1921.
2 Here Marvin was following a conceptual tradition prevalent in the nineteenth century before he published his book, e.g. Landouzy, 1846; Lightfoot, 1857; Storer, 1871; Tilt, 1862. One physician stated "there is no doubt that insanity is often the result of uterine irritation in patients who are hereditarily predisposed to it"; Byford, 1864, p. 41.
3 It was affirmed that ecstasy was a "neurosis of the nervous centers, mainly the brain", which was affected by "exaggerated fasting and by the excitation of religious feelings" (Despine, 1868, p. 598). See also: Bertrand, 1826; Desages, 1866; Maury, 1861.
4 On epidemic delusion and mental epidemics, see: Anonymous, 1851; Calmeil, 1845; Gilmore, 1868; Marvin, 1874a. For later discussions, see Tuke, 1892; also Rosen, 1968.
5 While some spiritualists advocated various positions regarding the ill-defined term 'free love', such ideas were not exclusive to spiritualists and were in fact present in the USA before the advent of spiritualism; Spurlock, 1988. Braude (2001, p. 128) has argued that such association was used as an idelogical weapon: "Those wary of radicals classed Spiritualists, socialists, and woman's rights advocates together as sympathizers with the bogeyman of radicalism, free love." See also Hardinge's (1870, p. 233) complaints about the generalizations of the critics of spiritualism.
6 Writing about 'salacious delusions' English physician Henry Maudsley (1835–1918) stated: "In every large asylum are to be met women who believe themselves to be visited every night by their lovers, or violently ravished in their sleep; and in some of these, as in St. Catherine de Sienne and St. Theresa, a religious ecstasy is united with their salacious delusions. Indeed, a religious fanaticism carried to a morbid degree is not seldom accompanied by a corresponding morbid lewdness; while religious feeling of a less extreme kind in some women, especially certain unmarried and childless women, is very much a uterine affection"; Maudsley, 1867, p. 241. See also Mazzoni, 1996.
7 On urine analysis in relation to psychiatric conditions, see Bucknill & Tuke, 1862; Lindsay, 1856.
8 Some physicians have mentioned constipation as a frequent event in cases of mental illness, e.g., Winslow, 1866, p. 97, 421.

References (added by Alvarado and Zingrone)

Alvarado, C. S., Machado, F. R., Zangari, W., & Zingrone, N. L. (2007). Perspectivas históricas da influência da mediunidade na construção de idéias psicológicas e psiquiátricas. *Revista de Psiquiatria Clínica,* 34(suppl. 1), 42–53.

Anonymous. (1851). The mental aspects of epidemics. *Journal of Psychological Medicine and Mental Pathology, 4*, 171–186.
Anonymous. (1856). Spiritual manifestations. *Medical World 1*, 309–310.
Anonymous. (1857). Insanity. *Tiffany's Monthly, 3*, 316–320.
Anonymous. (1859). Causes of mental disease. *North American Review, 89*, 316–339.
Anonymous. (1860). The delusions of spiritualism. *Lancet* (2), 466–467.
Anonymous. (1863). Sur la folie spirite: reponse a M. Burlet, de Lyon. *Revue Spirite, 6*, 51–59.
Anonymous. (1869). Table-talk. *Appleton's Journal, 1*, 601–602.
Anonymous. (1873a). *Documents of the Assembly of the State of New York: Ninety-Sixth Session–1873* (Vol. 3, Nos 28–33). Argus Company.
Anonymous. (1873b, March 22). New York Liberal Club—lecture by Prof. Marvin. *New York Times*, p. 2.
Anonymous. (1874a, December 5). Aetiology of insanity: Lecture by Prof. F. R. Marvin before the Liberal Club. *New York Times*, p. 3.
Anonymous. (1874b). Recent literature. *Atlantic Monthly,* 34, 624–633.
Anonymous. (1874c). Review of *The philosophy of spiritualism and the pathology and treatment of medio-mania. Popular Science Monthly* 5, 751.
Anonymous. (1874d). Review of *The philosophy of spiritualism and the pathology and treatment of mediomania. Western Lancet, 3*, 550–557.
Anonymous. (1874e). Review of *The philosophy of spiritualism and the pathology and treatment of mediomania. The Inter Ocean* (Aug. 14), 12.
Anonymous. (1874f). Review of *The philosophy of spiritualism and the pathology and treatment of mediomania. Medical Record, 9*, 633–634.
Anonymous. (1874g). Review of *The philosophy of spiritualism and the pathology and treatment of mediomania. Medical and Surgical Reporter,* 31, 174.
Anonymous. (1875a, April 10). Commencement of the Free Medical College for Women. *New York Times*, p. 10.
Anonymous. (1875b, January 28). Mme. Roland and the French revolution. *New York Times*, p. 9.
Anonymous. (1876). *Documents of the Assembly of the State of New York: Ninety-Ninth Session - 1876* (Vol. 8, Nos. 133–136). Jerome B. Parmenter.
Anonymous. (1904a). *National cyclopaedia of American biography* (Vol. 12). James T. White & Company.
Anonymous. (1904b). *Who's who in New York City and state*. L. R. Hamersly Company.
Anonymous. (1910). *Progressive Americans of the Americas*. Progressive Publishing.
Anonymous. (1914). *Medical twentieth century containing biographical sketches of distinguished Colleges of the United States and of Foreign Countries*. American Medical Association.
Anonymous. (1918, July 26). Former pastor dead: Dr. F. R. Marvin dies at 70 in his home at Albany, N.Y. *Oregonian*, p. 15.
Beard, G. M. (1874). Spiritualism: the counterfeits of science and how to detect them. *New York Times* (Nov. 20), 2.
Beard, G. M. (1877). A new theory of trance, and its bearings on human testimony. *Journal of Nervous and Mental Disease,* 4, 1–47.
Bertrand, A. (1826). *Du Magnétisme animal en France, et des jugements qu'en ont portes les sociétés savantes*. J. B. Baillière.
Braid, J. (1843). *Neurypnology or the rationale of nervous sleep considered in relation with animal magnetism*. John Murray.
Braude, A. (2001). *Radical spirits: Spiritualism and women's rights in nineteenth-century America*. Indiana University Press.
Brittan, S. S. (1874). Dr. Marvin on mediomania. *Brittan's Journal of Spiritual Science, Literature, Art, and Inspiration,* 2, 475–482.
Brown, E. M. (1983). Neurology and spiritualism in the 1870s. *Bulletin of the History of Medicine, 37*, 563–577.
Bucknill, J. C., & Tuke, D. H. (1862). *A manual of psychological medicine* (2nd ed.). John Churchill.
Burlet, P. (1863). *Du Spiritisme considere comme cause d'alienation mentale.* Imprimerie de Richard.
Byford, W. H. (1864). *A treatise on the chronic inflammation and displacements of the unimpregnated uterus*. Lindsay & Blakiston.

Calmeil, L. -F. (1845). *De la folie considérée sous le point de vue pathologique, philosophique, historique et judiciaire* (2 vols.). J. -B. Bailliere.
Capron, E. W. (1855). *Modern spiritualism: Its facts and fanatisms, its consistencies and contradictions*. Bela Marsh.
Carpenter, W. B. (1877). *Mesmerism and spiritualism, &c. historically & scientifically considered*. Longmans and Green.
Carroll, B. E. (1997). *Spiritualism in antebellum America*. Indiana University Press.
Charcot, J. M. (1888). *Clinical lectures on certain diseases of the nervous system*. Geoge S. Davis.
Clarke, E. H. (1873). *Sex in education; or, a fair chance for the girls*. James R. Osgood.
Coffin, S. J. (1879). *Record of the men of Lafayette: Brief biographical sketches of the alumni of Lafayette College*. Skinner & Finch.
Cooper, R. (1867). *Spiritual experiences, including seven months with the brothers Davenport*. L. Heywood.
Corwin, C. E. (1922). *A manual of the Reformed Church in America (Former Reformed Protestant Dutch Church) 1628–1922* (5th ed.). Board of Publication and Bible-School Work of the Reformed Church in America.
Cox, R. S. (2003). *Body and soul: A sympathetic history of American spiritualism*. University of Virginia Press.
Crookes, W. (1874). *Researches in the phenomena of spiritualism*. J. Burns.
Crowell, E. (1877). Spiritualism opposed to insanity. *Spiritual Magazine of Phenomena Spiritual-Ethereal-Physical*, 3(s. 3), 160–162.
Desages, L. (1866). *De la extase ou des miraclescomme phénomènes naturels*. F. Henry.
Despine, P. (1868). *Psychologie naturelle: Étude sur les facultés intellectuelles et morales dans leur état normal et dans leurs manifestations anomales chez les aliénés et chez les criminels* (Vol. 1). F. Savy.
Duhem, P. (1904). *Contribution a l'tude de la folie chez les spirites*. G. Steinheil.
Edmonds, J. W., & Dexter, G. T. (1853). *Spiritualism*, Vol. 1. Partridge & Brittan.
Ferriar, D. (1813). *An essay towards a theory of apparitions*. Cadell and Davies.
Galvan, J. (2010). *The sympathetic medium: Feminine channeling, the occult, and communication technology, 1859–1919*. Cornell University Press.
Gilmore, J. S. (1868). *Mental epidemics: Two lectures*. Edward Ponsonby.
Gordon, W. R. (1856). *A three-fold test of modern spiritualism*. Charles Scribner.
Grellety, L. (1876). *Du Merveilleux, des miracles et des peèlerinages, au point de vue médical*. J. B. Baillière.
H. (1874). Review of *The philosophy of spiritualism and the pathology and treatment of mediomania*. *Chicago Medical Journal, 31*, 751–753.
Haber, C. (1986). Who's looney now? The insanity case of John Armstrong. *Bulletin of the History of Medicine*, 60, 177–193.
Hammond, W. A. (1876). *Spiritualism and allied causes and conditions of nervous derangement*. G. P. Putnam's.
Hardinge, E. (1870). *Modern American spiritualism: A twenty year's record of the communion between earth and the world of spirits* (3rd ed). Author.
Holbrook, M. L. (1873). Topics of the month: The New York Free Medical College for Women. *Herald of Health Devoted to the Culture of Body and Mind, 2*, 275.
Howitt, W. (1863). *The history of the supernatural in all ages and nations and in all churches christian and pagan demonstrating a universal faith* (2 vols.). J. B. Lippincott.
Janet, P. (1889). *L'Automatisme psychologique: Essai de psychologie experimentale sur les forms inferieures de l'activite humaine*. Félix Alcan.
Jewett, P. L. (1873). *Spiritualism and charlatanism; or, the tricks of the media*. S.W. Green.
Landouzy, H. (1846). *Traite complet de l'hysterie*. J. -B. et G. Baillière.
[Laycock, T.] (1851). Odyle, mesmerism, electro-biology, &c. *British Foreign Medico-Chirurgical Review, 8*, 378–431.
Leffingwell, A. (1916). *An ethical problem or sidelights upon scientific experimentation on man and animals*. G. Bell & Sons.
Le Maléfan, P. (1999). *Folie et spiritisme: Histoire du discourse psychopathologique sur la pratique du spirit- isme, ses abords et ses avatars (1850–1950)*. L'Hartmattan.

Levy-Valensi, J. (1910). Spiritisme et folie. *L'encephale, 5*, 696–716.
Lightfoot, T. (1857). On the mental, nervous and convulsive disorders traceable to physiological or pathological conditions of the sexual organs in woman, and more especially, to the ovaria. *Lancet, 1*, 86–88, 135–137; *2*, 79–80.
Lindsay, W. L. (1856). Contributions to the chemistry and histology of the urine in the insane. *Journal of Psychological Medicine and Mental Pathology, 9*, 488–496.
London Dialectical Society. (1871). *Report on spiritualism, of the Committee of the London Dialectical Society, together with the evidence, oral and written, and a selection from the correspondence*. Longmans, Green, Reader, and Dyer.
Luce, S. B. (1877). The modern pythia. *The Galaxy, 23*, 209–216.
Madden, R. R. (1857). *Phantasmata or Illusions and fanaticisms of protean forms productive of great evils* (2 vols.). T. C. Newby.
Marvin, F. R. (1870). *Dream music: A volume of poems*. Carleton Publisher.
Marvin, F. R. (1874a). *Epidemic delusions: A lecture read before the New York Liberal Club, May 9th, 1873*. Asa K. Butts.
Marvin, F. R. (1874b). *The philosophy of spiritualism and the pathology and treatment of mediomania: Two lectures read before the New York Liberal Club, March 20 and 27, 1874*. New York: Asa K. Butts.
Marvin, F. R. (1875). *Literature of the insane*. Truth Seeker.
Marvin, F. R(1899). *Christ among the cattle: A sermon preached in the first congregational church, Portland, Oregon*. J. O. Wright & Co.
Marvin, F. R. (1900). *The last words (real and traditional) of distinguished men and women*. C. A. Brewster.
Marvin, F. R. (1903). *Consecrated womanhood: A sermon preached in the first congregational church, Portland, Oregon*. J.O Wright & Co.
Marvin, F. R. (1905). Spiritism, hypnotism and telepathy. *Medico-Legal Journal, 23*, 29.
Marvin, F. R. (1907). *Poems and translations*. Prafaets Book Company.
Marvin, F. R. (1910). *The excursions of a book lover: Being papers on literary themes*. Sherman, French & Company.
Marvin, F. R. (1915). *Fireside papers*. Sherman, French & Company.
Maudsley, H. (1867). *The physiology and pathology of the mind*. D. Appleton.
Maury, L. F. A. (1861). *Le Somneil et les reves*. Didier.
Mazzoni, C. (1996). *Saint hysteria: Neurosis, mysticism, and gender in European culture*. Cornell University Press.
McGarry, M. (2008). *Ghosts of futures past: spiritualism and the politics of nineteenth-century America*. University of California Press.
Moreira-Almeida, A., Silva de Almeida, A. A., & Lotufo, Neto F. (2005). History of 'spiritist madness' in Brazil. *History of Psychiatry, 16*, 5–25.
Newnham, W. (1830). *Essay on superstition; being an inquiry into the effects of physical influence on the mind, in the production of dreams, visions, ghosts, and other supernatural appearances*. J. Hatchard and Son.
Ogden, D. (2004). *Greek and Roman necromancy*. Princeton University Press.
Owen, A. (1990). *The darkened room: Women, power and spiritualism in late Victorian England*. University of Pennsylvania Press.
Owen, R. D. (1871). *The debatable land between this world and the next*. Trübner.
Paton, L. B. (1921). *Spiritism and the cult of the dead in antiquity*. Macmillan.
Porter, R., Nicholson, H., & Bennett, B. (Eds). (2003). *Women, madness and spiritualism*. Routledge.
Putnam, S. P. (1894). *400 years of freethought*. Truth Seeker Company.
Reynold, C. (Ed.). (1911). *Hudson-Mohawk genealogical and family memoirs* (Vol. 2.). Lewis Historical Company.
Robinson, M. G. (1875). How New York is doctored. *New York Observer and Chronicle* (July, 29), 237.
Rosen, G. (1968). *Madness in society: Chapters in the historical sociology of mental illness*. Routledge & Kegan Paul.
Smith-Rosenberg, C., & Rosenberg, C. (1973). The female animal: medical and biological views of woman and her role in nineteenth-century America. *Journal of American History, 60*, 332–356.
Spicer, H. (1853). *Sights and sounds: The mystery of the day: comprising an entire history of the American "spirit" manifestations*. Thomas Bosworth.

Spurlock, J. C. (1988). *Free love: Marriage and middle-class radicalism in America, 1825–1860.* New York University Press.

Storer, H. R. (1871). *The causation, course, and treatment of reflex insanity in women.* Lee and Shepard.

Tilt, E. J. (1862). *On uterine and ovarian inflammation*, 3rd ed. John Churchill.

Tissot, J. (1868). *L'Imagination: ses bienfaits et ses égarements surtout dans le domaine du merveilleux.* Didier.

Tromp, M. (2006). *Altered states: Sex, nation, drugs, and self-transformation in Victorian spiritualism.* SUNY Press.

Tuke, D. H. (1892). Imitation; or mental contagion. In D. H. Tuke (Ed.), *A Dictionary of Psychological Medicine* (Vol. 2, pp. 676–678). J. & A. Churchill.

Wallace, A. R. (1875). *On miracles and modern spiritualism: Three essays.* J. Burns.

Winslow, F. (1866). *Obscure diseases of the brain and mind* (2nd American ed., based on 3rd rev. British ed). Henry C. Lea.

Winslow, L. F. S. (1877). *Spiritualistic madness.* Baillière, Tindall & Cox.

Zingrone, N. L. (1994). Images of women as mediums: Power, pathology and passivity in the writings of Frederic Marvin and Cesare Lombroso. In L. Coly & R. A. White (Eds)., *Women and parapsychology* (pp. 90–121). Parapsychology Foundation.

Note on the Intellectual Work of William Stainton Moses*

Carlos S. Alvarado

Most discussions about William Stainton Moses have focused on his mediumship. This note is a reminder that, in addition to mediumship, such as the spirit communication recorded in *Spirit Teachings* (1883), he contributed in other ways to the study of psychic phenomena, including studies of direct writing, materializations, and spirit photography. Furthermore, Moses wrote about apparitions of the living and out-of-body experiences, and veridical mediumistic communications, and criticized the writings of others, among them physiologist William B. Carpenter. A consideration of this and other neglected aspects of Moses's work, enlarges our view of his contributions to Nineteenth-Century British Spiritualism and psychical research.

In a previous paper published in the *Journal of Scientific Exploration*, I discussed the fact that some individuals connected to the history of psychical research are sometimes neglected in historical accounts (Alvarado, 2012). I also mentioned that some historical figures are only partially remembered for aspects of their work, to the detriment of others. One example I briefly discussed, and which I would like to present more information about here, is William Stainton Moses.

Reverend William Stainton Moses (1839–1892) has generally been discussed as a medium (e.g., Myers 1894–1895, Tymn 2015). One of his best–known publications was his book about spirit communications *Spirit Teachings* (Moses, 1883), which, like other writings, appeared under his pseudonym M. A. Oxon. My point in this note is to remind current readers of the somewhat forgotten fact that Moses's work on behalf of Spiritualism, and the study of psychic phenomena in general, consisted of more than his performances as a mental or physical medium.[1] He also contributed to the description and analysis of phenomena, and to the critique of theoretical ideas, some of which I will briefly summarize.

William Stainton Moses

Some Important Publications and Studies of William Stainton Moses

In addition to holding positions such as Vice-President of the Society for Psychical Research (SPR) and editor of the journal *Light*, Moses wrote about general issues related to Spiritualism. For example, in his *Higher Aspects of Spiritualism* (Moses, 1880) had sections about the current state and the future of the movement in England, and about its religious aspects. He wished for better séance conditions that would not look suspicious, and this included "the abolition of all means of secluding the medium, and—though I do not lay so much stress on this—of dark circles also" (pp. 36–37). Of mediums, he further wrote,

> … instead of producing a number of astounding phenomena in the dark, would devote their powers to evolving a very few simple experiments in the light, the whole aspect of the matter would be changed. (Moses, 1880, p.122)

*Republished with permission from *Journal of Scientific Exploration, 32*, 592–603, 2018.

A few years later, after he joined the SPR, Moses's name appeared in the proceedings of the Society as one of the workers on the Literary Committee (e.g., Barrett et al. 1884). But his main intellectual work was published in other forums.

One of these forums was the journal *Human Nature*. Here Moses (1874a, 1874b, 1875c) published a series of articles about physical mediumship.[2] In the first one he focused on general developments and his own conviction in the phenomena. He wrote,

> Most of the phenomena which have been evoked in this country have at different times come under my notice, and have been recorded by me, at the time, as carefully and accurately as has been possible. (Moses, 1874a, p. 99).

In other articles in the same series, he wrote about raps and movement of objects, the production of perfumes, and lights and music.

Most of the installments of this article were about spirit photography (Moses, 1874b, 1875c). Moses accepted the reality of this phenomenon and stated that he was surprised that he found there was so much evidence on its behalf. He was convinced of spirit agency, but believed that in many cases the spirits involved were of a low moral order. Moses recommended students of the topic not to consider some cases produced by this agency that were suspicious, but instead to focus on clear-cut cases, and on those in which communication (presumably mediumistic) had shown the "reliability" and "truthfulness" of the spirits. However, he cautioned,

> Experience, if it prove that some manifestations look tricky, proves also that "second thoughts are best," and that some which appears at first sight most suspicious, turn out in the end to be suspicious only in appearance, but real and true in fact. (Moses, 1875c, p. 195)

In another long paper, Moses (1876–1877) presented discussions and classifications of cases of what he referred to as the "Trans-Corporeal Action of Spirit." This included various cases of out-of-body experiences and of apparitions of the living. Moses wrote that the cases he presented here were scattered and in need of "classification and arrangement" (Moses, 1876–1877, p. 241). The cases, he stated, were arranged with a principle in mind.

> The principle is the Transcorporeal Action of Spirit. The fact is the possession by man of a spirit which manifests its action in diverse ways irrespective of and beyond the power of the body. (Moses, 1876–1877, p. 241)

This action of the spirit beyond the confines of the body led Moses to argue the survival of that spirit after death.[3]

In *Psychography, A Treatise on One of the Objective Forms of Psychic or Spiritual Phenomena*, Moses (1878) reviewed the evidence for the phenomenon of direct writing obtained via mediums. He presented examples of cases attested by the senses (vision, hearing), cases presenting writing in languages unknown by the medium, and cases obtained in conditions preventing the previous preparation of writing to fake the phenomenon. In Moses's view, psychography was only one of many phenomena "which testify to the existence of a soul in man, and to its independent action beyond his physical body; an earnest of its survival and independent life when released by death from its earthly prison-house" (Moses, 1878, p. 6).

Another book was *Spirit Identity*, in which Moses (1879) studied veridical mediumistic communications. This included personal experiences, and communications recorded by others. The author concluded, "Intelligence is perpetuated after the body is dead" (p. 69), and that the "human spirit after its separation from the body loses none of its individuality" (p. 70).

Moses was also very interested in the phenomenon of materialization. He published in *Light* one of the most detailed studies available of the varieties of features of this phenomenon and tests performed as they were recorded in the literature (Moses, 1884–1886). Rather than be concerned with evidential considerations, Moses wrote,

> My task is to sift by ordinary methods evidence already published, to classify and arrange it, to indicate its value as a contribution to the study of a very difficult problem, and, whenever I can, to illustrate from my own experience what I am quoting on the published authority of others. (Moses, 1884–1886, p. 9)

Some of the topics covered by Moses were appearances of inanimate objects (e.g., drapery, flowers), hands, faces, full forms (both shadowy and well-defined), as well as forms that were seen to dematerialize, and that were recognized. Furthermore, mention is made of the weighing of mediums and materialized forms.

Like the previous publications, this one about materializations presented a great number of references that are useful today to locate published discussions about this phenomenon. The cases referred to many mediums such as Florence Cook, William Eglinton, Kate Fox, Mary J. Hollis, Cecil Husk, Francis Ward Monck, Mary Showers, Henry Slade, Charles Williams, and C. E. Wood.

While Moses's articles were rich on descriptions of materializations, he also stated that little was known for certain about the process involved in their production, something he had stated a few years earlier (Moses, 1877c). Nonetheless, he believed, as many did in his era, that the phenomenon involved forces processed through the medium's body.

Other Writings

Various other topics in articles include reports of séances for physical phenomena such as spirit photography (Moses, 1875d), voices and materializations (Moses, 1877e), cases of spirit identity (Moses, 1885a), discussions about the defense of mediums (Moses, 1877f), mental healing (Moses, 1885b), and psychometry (Moses, 1885c). Regarding psychometry, Moses wrote that he sent three writing samples from very different individuals to a psychometrist. The writing samples were dissimilar to each other and were only identified by numbers from one to three. Leaving aside some general statements, Moses said that he

> … could have easily picked out half a dozen such specific statements in each, which were at once strikingly true of the writer, and quite inapplicable to the authors of the other writings sent by me. (Moses, 1885c, p. 217).

Although Moses was convinced of the reality of the human spirit, its survival of death, and of spirit agency as an explanation for phenomena, he reminded his fellow spiritualists about the resistance others had to these ideas. As he wrote,

> I do not expect much from any attempt to force upon the present generation what it is quite unfit for. A study of the pages of the *Zoist* will show how the objective, palpable facts of mesmerism, especially of healing of disease, advocated with infinite skill and courage, failed to make any permanent effect on a generation that did not want to believe them; that had no place for them in its mind, no use for them in the economy of its life. So it is with all these matters. There is a time and a place for them, and it is our business to have them ready when that conjunction occurs. (Moses, 1884a, p. 6).

Moses also admitted his inability to explain phenomena. Focusing on physical mediumship, he stated,

> I do not know … how a rap is produced, how luminous bodies are created in the seance room, how in vacant space is built up before my eyes a body organised as my own … (Moses, 1890, p. 156).

But he had no doubt about the existence of these phenomena.

In addition, he criticized many of the critics of Spiritualism. This included Frederick George Lee and Asa Mahan (Moses, 1875e), and Edwin Ray Lankaster (Moses, 1876b). Another was the well-known William B. Carpenter (Moses, 1877a, 1877b). Moses did not hold back his contempt for Carpenter's explanations of spiritualistic phenomena, "Dr. Carpenter seems either to write in reckless haste without understanding or grasping his subject, or to answer his opponents without ever reading their arguments" (Moses, 1877a, p. 532).

Moses was also critical of the SPR. For example, he wrote,

> The Society for Psychical Research seems to be drifting into the attitude of the Sadducee, believing neither in angel nor spirit, but only in a sub-conscious self. That is a pity, but can do no particular harm, for angels and spirits will still persist in spite of denial. (Moses, 1890, p. 157)

In the September 17, 1881, issue of *Light*, Moses took over the responsibility of writing a column that lasted for several years and that included summaries, commentaries, and critiques about publications, the phenomena, the issues, the critics, and the social aspects of Spiritualism. Regarding explanations of phenomena, in his first column he commented about narratives of stone-throwing, and theosophical ideas about them,

> I have repeatedly seen phenomena which might far more reasonably be attributed to the gambols of a monkey than to the calculated malice of a fiend. These aimless antics, and many perplexing phenomena of a kindred nature, suggest Puck rather than Satan, a sub-human intelligence devoid of moral consciousness, rather than the serious attempts of a departed human Spirit to demonstrate its continued existence. … It is extremely difficult to refer such pranks to departed human Spirits. Nor is it fair to say broadly that all Spiritualists assume this position. The present writer, speaking solely for himself, is free to confess that he has long felt it to be one of the most considerable stumbling-blocks in the way of intelligent acceptance of the creed of Spiritualism that such tricks should be put down to the action of our own departed friends. (Moses, 1881, p. 292).

Moses also compiled bibliographies (Moses, 1889), and published many book reviews. This included comments about the books of Henry S. Olcott (Moses, 1875a), Eugene Crowell (Moses, 1876a), Hudson Tuttle (Moses, 1877d), Alfred Percy Sinnett (Moses, 1881), and Epes Sargent (Moses, 1882). In an introduction to a book about mesmerism by William Gregory, Moses related the topic to Spiritualism,

> The Mesmeric Trance, again, accidental or induced; the Ecstatic state, in which the mesmerised subject seems to enjoy communion with the world of spirit, and to live in a state sometimes entirely detached from the world of sense; will readily be seen to have their bearing on such experiences as those of Andrew Jackson Davis, and on the familiar state of Trance into which almost all well-developed psychics are accustomed to pass while utterances purporting to come from an alien spirit are made through their lips; or while their vital forces are being utilised for the production of such phenomena as, for instance, those of Materialisation, or Form-manifestation. (Moses, 1884b, p. v).

Concluding Remarks

My discussion is certainly not complete, for I have omitted topics such as Moses's work in the organization of spiritualist organizations and his critiques of theosophical ideas. But I believe that the information I have presented shows that Moses had a wide range of interests and made many intellectual contributions to both Spiritualism and psychical research in addition to his work as a medium. Moses in fact reminds us of the multiple roles that some figures played in Nineteenth-Century Spiritualism and psychical research.

Regardless of evidential and theoretical considerations, much of this work, particularly the publications about the "transcorporeal action of the spirit," direct writing, mediumistic communications, and materializations (e.g., Moses, 1876–1877, 1878, 1879, 1884–1886), remain valuable reference works to locate Nineteenth-Century publications about those topics.

Notes

1 I do not want to play down the contributions of mediumship (and mediums) to the development of psychical research, a topic I have discussed elsewhere (Alvarado, 2013).

2 The first three articles were entitled "Researches in Spiritualism during the Years 1872–1873" (1874a), while the rest appeared under the shorter title "Researches in Spiritualism" (1874b, 1875c).

3 See Moses's (1875b) account of the photographs of his spirit while he was sleeping taken at a distance by controversial spirit photographer Edouard Isidore Buguet.

References

Alvarado, C. S. (2012). Distortions of the past. *Journal of Scientific Exploration, 26*, 611–633.

Alvarado, C. S. (2013). Mediumship and psychical research. In C. Moreman (Ed.), *The spiritualist movement, speaking with the dead in America and around the torld* (Vol. 2, pp. 127–144). Praeger.

Barrett, W. F., Massey, C. C., Moses, W. S., Podmore, F., Gurney, E., & Myers, F. W. H. (1884). Third report of the Literary Committee, A theory of apparitions, Part I. *Proceedings of the Society for Psychical Research, 2*, 109–136.

Moses, W. S. [under the pseudonym M. A. Oxon] (1874a). Researches in spiritualism during the years 1872–1873, together with a discussion of theories advanced in explanation of the phenomena. *Human Nature, 8*, 97–11, 161–176, 193–207.

Moses, W. S. [under the pseudonym M. A. Oxon] (1874b). Researches in spiritualism. *Human Nature, 8*, 313–326, 337–350, 387–397, 425–430, 473–488, 513–527.

Moses, W. S. [under the pseudonym M. A. Oxon] (1875a). People from the other world, by H. S. Olcott. *Human Nature, 9*, 269–286.

Moses, W. S. [under the pseudonym M. A. Oxon] (1875b). Photographing the spirit of a medium in Paris, while his body was asleep in London. *The Spiritualist*, March 5, 119.

Moses, W. S. [under the pseudonym M. A. Oxon] (1875c). Researches in spiritualism. *Human Nature, 9*, 12–21, 81–86, 97–104, 145–157, 193–213, 334–335.

Moses, W. S. [under the pseudonym M. A. Oxon] (1875d). Some recent experiments in spirit photography with Buguet and Firman. *Human Nature, 9*, 157–160.

Moses, W. S. [under the pseudonym M. A. Oxon] (1875e). Spiritualism and some of its recent critics, A reply to certain arguments and objections. *Human Nature, 9*, 337–350.

Moses, W. S. [under the pseudonym M. A. Oxon] (1876a). Dr. Crowell on primitive Christianity and modern spiritualism. *Human Nature, 10*, 76–91.
Moses, W. S. [under the pseudonym M. A. Oxon] (1876b). Notes on the present crisis. *Human Nature, 10,* 548–567.
Moses, W. S. [under the pseudonym M. A. Oxon] (1876–1877). On the trans–corporeal action of spirit. *Human Nature, 10*, 97–125, 145–157; *11*, 241–264, 289–312, 337–351, 385–400, 433–441.
Moses, W. S. [under the pseudonym M. A. Oxon] (1877a). Carpenterian criticism, A reply to Dr. W. B. Carpenter. *Human Nature, 11*, 529–549.
Moses, W. S. [under the pseudonym M. A. Oxon] (1877b). Dr. Carpenter's theories, and Dr. Carpenter's facts. *Medium and Daybreak*, January 12, 17–18.
Moses, W. S. [under the pseudonym M. A. Oxon] (1877c). Form manifestations. *Spiritualist Newspaper*, May 18, 232–233.
Moses, W. S. [under the pseudonym M. A. Oxon] (1877d). Hudson Tuttle's "Arcana of Spiritualism." *Human Nature, 11*, 145–164.
Moses, W. S. [under the pseudonym M. A. Oxon] (1877e). A séance with Mr. Williams, and some reflections thereon. *Medium and Daybreak*, March 2, 137–138.
Moses, W. S. [under the pseudonym M. A. Oxon] (1877f). What have been the results of the defence of mediums? *Medium and Daybreak*, May 4, 276.
Moses, W. S. [under the pseudonym M. A. Oxon] (1878). *Psychography, A treatise on one of the objective forms of psychic or spiritual phenomena.* W. H. Harrison.
Moses, W. S. [under the pseudonym M. A. Oxon] (1879). *Spirit identity.* W. H. Harrison.
Moses, W. S. [under the pseudonym M. A. Oxon] (1880). *Higher aspects of spiritualism.* E. W. Allen.
Moses, W. S. [under the pseudonym M. A. Oxon] (1881). The claims of occultism. *Light, 1,* 194.
Moses, W. S. [under the pseudonym M. A. Oxon] (1882). Planchette; or the despair of science. *Psychological Review, 4*, 124–131.
Moses, W. S. [under the pseudonym M. A. Oxon] (1883). *Spirit teachings.* Psychological Press.
Moses, W. S. [under the pseudonym M. A. Oxon] (1884a). Notes by the way. *Light, 4*, 6–7.
Moses, W. S. [under the pseudonym M. A. Oxon] (1884b). Preface to the third edition. In W. Gregory (Ed.), *'Animal magnetism' or mesmerism & its phenomena* (3rd Rev. ed, pp. iii–iv). Psychological Press.
Moses, W. S. [under the pseudonym M. A. Oxon] (1884–1886). Phases of materialization, A chapter of research in the objective phenomena of spiritualism. *Light*, *4*, 9–10, 19–20, 31–32, 41–42, 51–52, 61–62, 71–72, 81–82, 91–92, 101–102, 111, 121–122, 131–132, 141–142, 151–152, 161–162, 289–290, 299–300, 309–310, 319–320, 329–330; *5*, 485, 497, 508–509, 525–526, 536–537, 548–549, 560, 580–581, 592, 603–605, 615–616, 627–628; *6*, 8, 19–20, 32–33, 44, 58, 68, 80–82, 92–94, 105, 129–130, 135–136, 166, 188, 195, 211–212, 220, 233–234, 253, 263–264, 273–274, 281–282.
Moses, W. S. [under the pseudonym M. A. Oxon] (1885a). A case of spirit identity. *Light, 5*, 547–548.
Moses, W. S. [under the pseudonym M. A. Oxon] (1885b). Mental healing in Boston, U.S.A. *Light, 5*, 267–268.
Moses, W. S. [under the pseudonym M. A. Oxon] (1885c). Psychometry. *Light, 5*, 217–218.
Moses, W. S. [under the pseudonym M. A. Oxon] (1889). Bibliography of spiritualism. *Light, 9*, 84.
Moses, W. S. [under the pseudonym M. A. Oxon] (1890). Personal experiences of spiritualism, with some deductions therefrom. *Light, 10*, 155–158.
Myers, F. W. H. (1894–1895). The experiences of W. Stainton Moses. *Proceedings of the Society for Psychical Research, 9*, 245–353; *11*, 24–113.
Tymn, M. (2015). William Stainton Moses. *Psi Encyclopedia.* Retrieved from https://psi-encyclopedia.spr.ac.uk/ articles/william-stainton-moses. C. Moreman

Supernormal-Pathological Ideas About Mediumship: The Case of Francis Gerry Fairfield*

Carlos S. Alvarado†

During the nineteenth century, and later, there were discussions of mediumship and other psychic phenomena as examples of pathology. While many reduced mediumship to pathology, a few others upheld a different model, basically the idea that supernormal phenomena, or phenomena involving actual instances of acquisition of knowledge and physical effects on matter, coexisted with, or were facilitated by, pathological conditions. This article includes a long excerpt about the ideas of supernormal pathology defended by American journalist Francis Gerry Fairfield in his book *Ten Years with Spiritual Mediums* (1875d), who postulated the existence of a nervous aura, or emanation from mediums and other individuals who had a nervous predisposition and evident or slight signs of epilepsy. Fairfield's writings are part of a small nineteenth-century movement about such ideas.

One of the ways physicians and others dealt with mediumship during the nineteenth century was to label the phenomenon as pathological (e.g., Janet, 1889; Marvin, 1874). This implied that mediums suffered from psychological and physical ailments and that their performances did not include "real" supernormal manifestations, or the acquisition of information or physical effects claimed by spiritualists as evidence of discarnate action.[1] However, little has been written about the possibility that pathology and supernormal phenomena are not necessarily exclusive. That is, that mediumship providing evidence for the acquisition of information and for physical effects not explained by conventional means may appear together with, or may be facilitated by, actual pathological processes. Because this form of pathology is seldom discussed today, I would like to summarize here a few other similar ideas relevant to the pathology-genuine psychic phenomena overlap, with emphasis on the writings of American journalist Francis Gerry Fairfield. Rather than presenting an evaluation of pathological ideas, my intent is to contribute to the history of such speculations. I hope to remind those interested in the history of mediumship about the generally neglected ideas of supernormal pathology, and about Fairfield's ideas. Regarding the latter, I present a long excerpt from a book by Fairfield that I believe conveys well his ideas on the subject.

Supernormal-Pathological Mediumship

The nineteenth-century background for belief in the pathology of mediumship includes many social and scientific factors. In addition to the general rise of rationalism and naturalistic views of nature, there were prevailing somatic concepts of mental illness (e.g., Bucknill & Tuke, 1874), and the belief that unusual mental states were explained by various psychological, medical and physiological

*Republished with permission from *Journal of the Society for Psychical Research*, *84*(3), 220–236, 2020.
†I wish to thank Fatima R. Machado and Everton de Oliveira Maraldi for suggestions of relevant references.

explanations (e.g., Braid, 1843), such as disturbances of the nervous system. This included hysteria. According to French physician Paul Briquet (1796–1881) "most of the so-called magnetic somnambules, are hysterical women" (Briquet, 1859, p. 413; this, and other translations, are mine). In later years these ideas, and their concomitant physiological ones, were applied to hypnosis (e.g., Charcot, 1882; Richer, 1885, p. 535).

Some mesmerists believed that susceptibility to magnetic influence was better in those suffering from organic and chronic problems and in "weak individuals, with a lymphatic and nervous temperament" (Pigeaire, 1839, p. 282), something consistent with the beliefs of later neo-mesmerists (e.g., Bourru & Burot, 1887). Interestingly, magnetism was believed by some to be the cause of bodily disturbances (e.g., Petetin, 1808, p. 58). The neuric, or magnetic force, wrote French physician and neo-mesmerist Alexandre Barety (1844–1918), was related to hysteria due to "a change in the direction, strength and distribution of nervous or neural currents" (Barety, 1887, p. 627).[2] Also of interest here are Karl von Reichenbach's (1788–1869) studies of the Od force, a universal force the existence of which he defended based in part on tests with sensitive individuals capable of seeing luminous emanations from magnets and crystals. Many of the individuals' degrees of perception "depended on the varying conditions of disease of the observers" (von Reichenbach, 1849/1851, p. 245).

Many reduced mediumship to pathology. One thought that mediums were the counterpart of hysterics (Anonymous, 1860), while another writer stated that the "abnormal conditions of mediumship are apt to be connected with bodily derangements more or less marked" (Anonymous, 1869, p. 602). In influential writing several physicians contributed to maintain alive the idea that mediumship was pathological (e.g., Janet, 1889; Marvin, 1874). One of them stated that the majority of mediums "are neuropaths, when they are not frankly hysterics" (Janet, 1889, p. 404; for additional bibliography see footnote 2).

Supernormal mediumship was also considered to be associated to pathology. B. W. Richmond (Brittan & Richmond, 1853) believed séance, and other psychic phenomena, were real, but caused by the medium's Od force or vital force (von Reichenbach, 1849/1851), and not by spirits, an idea shared by others (Alvarado, 2013). He believed that mediums were "abnormal-magnetic-biologic-mesmeric-cataleptic-hysteric-impressive-sick-sensitive persons" (Brittan & Richmond, 1853, p. 106). The family of mediums, Richmond stated, consisted of individuals with nervous, hysterical, and epileptic antecedents.

American anarchist Dyer D. Lum (1839–1893), stated in his book *The "Spiritual" Delusion* (1873) that mediumship was detrimental to health because: "Anything which tends to sap or destroy the natural activity of the organs through which man holds converse with objective nature tends to lower the standard of health, for the abnormal use of any faculty being 'irregular' must so far weaken it for normal service" (Lum, 1873, p. 92). Another writer, educator and phrenologist John Hecker (1868), believed that mediumship perverted the normal faculties in mediums and led to a loss of the spiritual faculties and "the propensities, of physical command and control, even in the natural order of social life" (p. 125).

Related to the idea of the pathology of supernormal mediumship were various reports by physicians of ESP phenomena produced by individuals said to have nervous or hysterical problems (e.g., Dailey, 1894; Fontan, 1887; Mason, 1894; Tolosa-Latour, 1893). Another example was the belief that openness to thought-transference depended on a rare "state of impressionability" on the brain, an "extreme abnormal, pathological, and fortunately rare sensibility" (Despine, 1880, p. 226). Similarly, Italian criminologist and psychiatrist Cesare Lombroso (1835–1909) believed that telepathy was related to a sensitivity showed by individuals having a "nervous excitability to an extreme degree" (Lombroso, 1891, p. 68).

Francis Gerry Fairfield

Born in Stafford, Connecticut, Francis Gerry Fairfield (1844–1887) worked as a journalist in various newspapers during his career. He studied at the Pennsylvania College (Gettysburg), and finished his degree in a Lutheran seminary. At twenty years of age, he was in charge of a church in Waterloo, New York, but only pursued his religious duties for two years, and then left to be a journalist (Wilson & Fiske, 1888, p. 403). It is evident from some of his publications that Fairfield (1875d, 1880) showed knowledge of neurology and anatomy. According to some sources he practiced veterinary medicine for a short time (Wilson & Fiske, 1888, p. 403), and practiced medicine (Anonymous, 1887a), which presumably exposed him to medical literature.

Fairfield was a man of many interests, as seen in publications about short stories (Fairfield, 1872b), clubs in New York (Fairfield, 1873), Edgar Allan Poe (Fairfield,1875a), and various other topics (Fairfield, 1872a, 1874, 1876, 1880), including the phenomena of mediumship (Fairfield, 1875b, 1875c, 1875d). However, some of his literary production was criticized in terms of his writing style (Didier, 1883, pp. 34–42).

His career was cut short by drug addiction, which caused his death (Anonymous, 1887b). According to the writers of a biographical entry, Fairfield's addiction "gave way to mental vagaries and irregularities that eventually reduced him to poverty" (Wilson & Fiske, 1888, p. 403).

As mentioned above, Fairfield (1875b, 1875c, 1875d) wrote about mediumship. He had experiences with mediums starting in the late 1850s. This led him to propose explanations excluding spirit agency based on a nerve atmosphere, or aura, that manifested in exceptional individuals when stimulated by nervous disorders, and its exteriorization from the body allowed the person to obtain information or to produce physical phenomena. The idea owed much to the mesmeric movement, and to the concepts of force of authors cited by Fairfield (e.g., Crookes, 1874; Philips, 1855; von Reichenbach, 1849/1851).

The phenomena of Spiritualism, Fairfield wrote, "are the exponents of nervous lesions … [which] belongs to the epileptic type …" (Fairfield, 1875d, p. 101). Such pathology was believed by Fairfield to produce a nerve-aura, or an emanation from a person's body "having the molecular properties, motor and sensory, of nervous tissue, though in lessened intensity" (p. 122). This was consistent with several other explanations of supernormal phenomena using the idea of forces exteriorized from the human body proposed during the nineteenth century (Alvarado, 2006), which were used by some individuals without recourse to spirit agency (e.g., Cox, 1871; Mahan, 1855; Rogers, 1853; von Hartmann, 1885)[3].

In the next section, I present a long excerpt about ideas of this sort taken from Fairfield's *Ten Years with Spiritual Mediums* (1875d). By the time Fairfield published this book, Spiritualism had spread widely, not only in terms of its phenomena, but in terms of the development of its literature, as well as in institutional, philosophical, and conceptual ways (for overviews see Tuttle and Peebles, 1871). The movement, and the practice of mediumship, received much publicity from both critiques (e.g., Hammond, 1871) and defenses (e.g., Wallace, 1874) of the reality of the phenomena, as well as from the publication of important investigations (e.g., Crookes, 1874; London Dialectical Society, 1871).

> I was a boy of sixteen when, in the winter of 1856–1857, the first wave of spiritualism swept over the little town of Stafford, Connecticut, now one of its New-England centres of activity. Mediums had occasionally dropped in and run brief careers previous to that date. Among them was Mr. Home …[4], and at several of his *séances* I was present.
>
> When, in 1864, I became a resident of New York City, it devolved on me, as the representative of a daily newspaper, to study the phenomena … as well as to attend all private *séances* at

which admission was attainable. The first result of this practice, attended with every possible device to detect imposition, was naturally a somewhat critical familiarity, not only with the *personnel* of mediums themselves, but with the mental aura of trance, clairvoyance, and the kindred sensorial phenomena. Secondly, after duly testing the more remarkable feats of Mr. C. H. Foster,[5] and other celebrated mediums, in every available manner, I was reluctantly forced to dismiss one scientific explanation after another, as inadequate to the facts, and either to suspend opinion, or to cast about for an explanation, both adequate to the phenomena and rigidly scientific in its terms …

I was very particular in testing the question whether these phenomena were merely illusive—a phantasmagoria of the senses—having frequently witnessed the phenomenon at mesmeric *séances*, of that kind of psychic control that enables the operator to impress illusions at will upon the senses of his subject. I was accordingly careful to note that no drowsiness nor nervous shock on my part preceded the phantom appearances; also, not to permit my attention to be fixed upon any one article in the room, and to avoid personal contact with the medium previous to the exhibition. These precautions are more important than they at first appear; for many facts, both experimental and observed, have convinced me that the semi-mesmeric state is more easily induced than most scientific observers are aware …

Thus, taking every possible precaution to avoid those nervous states in which illusions spring up naturally, or are easily imposed upon the senses, I was soon able to state authoritatively that the phenomena are not phantasmagorial, or mere imaginings, incident to an unnatural nervous or cerebral state, but actual objective existences—real to the senses, real as matters of fact. The theory that the phenomena are due to conscious or unconscious cerebral action, unless cerebral action is competent to lift heavy bodies without hands, though it applies to a considerable series of the facts, breaks down in view of the more important series. Morbid cerebral action may cause its victim to see phantoms, but it cannot endow him with the power to make others see them. Nevertheless, there is a great deal of unconscious cerebration[6] interwoven with the phenomena of spiritualism …

The experimental and observational investigations into the nature and physiology of mesmeric phenomena were, however, though the psychological theory did break down, of value in one important particular: as they led to a careful study of the literature of the subject and a careful examination of the phenomena in common between mesmerism and spiritualism. One of these, namely, clairvoyance, in some of its aspects, is the pivot and centre of the psychical states associated with spiritualism as well as of those associated with mesmerism; and to the physiology of this state—for there is no psychical phenomenon without its physiological exponents—it seemed to me worth the while to direct my attention. It might or might not furnish the clew to the production of the phantom phenomena, of which Prof. Crookes[7] has since recorded very full memoranda; but, whether it did or did not, its results would contribute somewhat to the stock of physiological observation.

But the investigation gradually enlarged and opened new vistas, finally extending itself further and further into the domain of medical psychology, with observations from life of morbid psychical states and of their physiological causes, microscopic studies of nervous tissue and of cerebral structure, and experimental inquiries as to the functions of the various nerve-centres.

I was led in this direction, from finding that clairvoyance is often the psychological exponent of a certain morbid nervous condition, and with a view to ascertain whether it is ever dissociated from nervous perversion. This, of course, eventuated in my gathering as many memoranda from life as possible, of instances in which clairvoyance and its associate states were confessedly morbid, with a view to compare symptoms and note points of difference. I commenced these special studies in the summer of 1868, and have since pursued them in the interstices of work as a journalist and contributor to scientific literature—with what result scientific men must judge.

My own observations of spiritualism since that period, with an eye sharpened by long study of nervous disturbances, have convinced me of three things: First, that its phenomena are invariably associated with nervous and generally with mental perversion, and that the moral aberrations and morbid impulses associated with mediums are the exponents of that perversion; secondly, that mediums, as a rule, particularly those addicted to trance, are persons of defective physical organization; thirdly, that the *séances* rapidly exhaust the nervous energies of the operator.[8] I have notes of one instance in which the medium died of the exhaustion consequent upon his most celebrated feat, that of tearing an iron sink, incorporated into the solid masonry of a wall, from its moorings, by simply placing his hand upon the edge of it. Mr. Benjamin Hawkes,[9] of Liverpool, England, a medium of some celebrity, fell dead under circumstances somewhat similar in the autumn of 1873, and, notwithstanding his magnificent *physique*, Mr. Home is an invalid at forty. So with Miss Kate Fox ...[10]

Again, in *séances* given by trance-mediums, I have observed that those significant prodromata of the fit in its ordinary aspects, sudden cadaverous pallor, a kind of fading of the eye, accompanied with dilatation of the pupil, and a slight nervous shock, invariably precede and announce the supervention of the trance. In table-tipping this shock occasions the slight tremor of the table before the manifestations occur, and is frequently visible in slight convulsive jerkings of the medium's hands.[11] The same shock precedes the supervention of the mesmeric trance ...

... in its more ordinary aspects, the mental impressions in clairvoyance invariably consist of the two elements, nervous perception and cerebration, in the same manner as impressions received through the media of the senses; the only difference consisting in the fact that the former originate in a peripheral nervous aura. I shall not attempt to say that all the trances of spiritual mediums are so limited in their manner of receiving impressions—for I am satisfied, from personal observation and from physiological study, that there is a higher type of trance, that has its origin in the gray matter of the brain, and is more immediate in its processes. This, however, is but a cerebral stage of the same type of nervous perversion, and will be adverted to again by-and-by. What I wish to impress on the reader's mind at this juncture is, that the peripheral aura, that produces the sensory phenomena of clairvoyance, independent of the media of the senses, is a symptom of nervous degeneracy; that—to employ a medical term—it is an exponent of neurosis.

Comparing, then, the series of psychical phenomena upon which spiritualism rests with the more pronounced series familiar to medical psychologists, from Esquirol to Maudsley[12] and other living masters, the first observation of the student will be that a singular parallelism exists between the two series; that trance is the exponent of the latter equally with the former, and that the physical precursors of the trance incident to the latter series are invariably present in the former.[13] If he is of an inquiring turn of mind, he will, at this stage, furnish himself with a microscope, and make a thorough study of nervous tissue, then address himself to the careful investigation of function. He will put himself to the pains to investigate the various phases of morbid function, particularly as relates to the nerve-centres, remembering always that one fact is worth fifty clever but unverified hypotheses, and that it is not advisable to have an opinion at all, unless the facts not only warrant but command it. Having pursued this course for a few years, he is competent to investigate the nature and relations of morbid psychical phenomena, and will long mightily to dissect the cerebral and nervous organism of a spiritual medium, by way of determining its pathological condition.

The point I wish to impress is, that of the three kindred groups of phenomena—that pertaining to mesmerism, the more pronounced group incident to spiritualism, and the still more interesting series illustrated in morbid psychology—it is impossible thoroughly to investigate the middle series without examining the other two with equal thoroughness. It was his accurate and extensive acquaintance with morbid psychology, amassed by years of practical contact with nervous disorders, that enabled Dr. Maudsley, with unerring sagacity, to diagnose epilepsy as the cause of the trances of Swedenborg, and finally to collect and sift the facts of his visit to London in a manner to demonstrate the diagnosis.[14]

Prof. Crookes and Mr. A. R. Wallace[15]— the one not a physiologist, the other more attentive to structure than to function—have erred, therefore, it seems to me, in having pursued an incorrect method of investigation, and in neglecting to subject the physiological traits of mediums to the minutest scrutiny. The true method seems to me to be obvious. Here are so many persons—one in a thousand possibly—who are competent to produce certain phenomena. They are not persons of superior organization, physical or cerebral. Some of them, indeed, are of very low type physically and intellectually. The question for scientific inquiry, then, is not whether these phenomena involve the presumption of superhuman intervention, but by what perversion of nervous function the medium is enabled to produce them.

Now, to answer the conditions of the problem as a scientific one, any proposed explanation of the phenomena must put order of sequence and relation into the facts, protean as they are. It must demonstrate the agency by which they are produced, and indicate the special perversion of nervous function concerned in their production. Finally, it must lie within the circle of verifiable hypotheses, which, unfortunately, is *Supernormal-Pathological Ideas About Mediumship: The Case of Francis Gerry Fairfield* not the case with the psychic-force theory—a beautiful but romantic dream, having no relation to the demonstrated laws of physics and physiology.

In accordance with this method of investigation, the phenomena appear to me to present two very distinct series, seldom present in the same person, which I shall style respectively nervo-psychic and nervo-dynamic—meaning, under the former, to include clairvoyance in its ordinary aspects, trance, prevision, presentiment, and the like; under the latter, table-tipping, rappings, levitation of bodies, writing with phantom-hands, production of visible phantoms from luminous clouds, and other feats involving the presumption of an invisible dynamic agency. That both series have the same etiology my memoranda of cases will, I think, show beyond reasonable doubt.

I have thus briefly indicated my own course of studies, pursued somewhat fitfully for the last ten years, and the method of investigation to which they have led, by way of preface to a series of conclusions that I shall state first, and verify afterward:

1. That there is no pathological difference between the trances of mediums, the induced trances of mesmerism, and the trances incident to epileptic and cataleptic attacks; the three types equally involving reflex excitability of the gray matter of the brain, during partial suspension of the motor centres and, in catalepsy, of the medullary centres. The same sudden pallor and perceptible fading of the eye, with slight nervous shock, precede the supervention of the fit, and the same exponent of heat in the coronal region of the cranium is more or less developed in all cases.
2. That spirit-seeing, as illustrated in the cases of Judge Edmonds, A. J. Davis, Mrs. Woodhull,[16] and mediums of that class, is a well-marked symptom of a single type of nervous and cerebral lesion; which lesion is accompanied by a mental aura, distinguished by a vague, generalizing

tendency, and by morbid sensorial impressions, such as those of which the literature of spiritualism largely consists.

3. That this lesion develops as one of its exponents a peculiar sensory and motor aura (or atmosphere), which, entering into intimate molecular relations and contact with surrounding objects within a circle of greater or less periphery, eventuates in the phenomenon of clairvoyance in cephalic, and of table-tipping, rappings, and the like, in vital temperaments. This law is constant and invariable. The nervo-dynamic series occur only in connection with mediums of strong vital temperament; the nervo-psychic mainly in connection with mediums in whom the cerebral predominates, and both in cases where the cerebral and the vital are more or less evenly balanced, but whose manifestations are extraordinary in neither.
4. That this aura is of nervous origin, and consequent upon molecular disturbance of the nerve-centres developed by nervous disorder. That, as such, it is more or less subject to the volition of the medium.
5. That, in its motor aspect, this nervous atmosphere is correlated with light, and susceptible of transformation into luminous clouds, into spectral apparitions, and other objective phenomena; and that the production of these phenomena constitutes a problem in nervo-molecular physics, to be investigated carefully, but having no ascertained relation to the higher spiritual aspects of human life.
6. That in its sensory aspects it enters into intimate relations with nervous organisms surrounding it, is impressed with their thoughts at greater or less distance, transmits what they know or remember to the brain of the medium, and renders the organism whence it proceeds *en rapport* with the minds of persons within the circle of its operations.
7. That both groups of phenomena are, therefore, morbid nervous phenomena, having their cause in nervous lesion, and their physiological basis in reflex excitability of the nerve-centres.
8. That, therefore, there is no occasion to refer them to the operations of an hypothetical psychic force, nor to the intervention or agency of departed spirits …

As Prof. Crookes remarks, it is obvious that a medium possesses something that is not possessed by ordinary men. Neither is it disputed, by those who have observed the phenomena, that, under certain conditions and within a limited distance from certain persons of special nervous organization, a force operates by which, without muscular contact, action at a distance is caused, and visible motions and audible sounds are produced in solid substances. As this force acts intelligently, Prof. Crookes and Sergeant Cox[17] style it psychic force—or soul-force—and identify it with a psychic organism supposed to pervade and inhabit the material. Hence, in their terminology, a medium is designated as a *psychic*.[18]

Although this theory constitutes the scientific basis of spiritualism, a man may nevertheless accept it, without accepting the cardinal tenet of the spiritualists, that the psychic is *en rapport* with the spirits of the dead. It is, on the other hand, illogical and fragmentary to accept the latter and deny the former.

Scientific progress—so far from tending to overturn a real religious faith—is gradually gathering the materials, the generalizations, let me say, for profounder conceptions of life and destiny, of religion in the larger acceptation of the word, than the last century had. The great law of the correlation of forces—the same force always present in Nature, now actual, now potential, now heat, now light, now electricity, now nervous, force, now mental, but the same in all its transformations—opens new vistas for metaphysical dreamers.[19] Alone, disconnected from phenomena, of itself only, what is the substratum of this tremendous and universal energy? This is the problem upon which, in its different aspects, every scientist labors—to the solution of which

> every discovery tends. Analytically, it is a mere problem of molecular physics; synthetically, it dips deep into the question of life and destiny; and though, in the strictly empirical work of the experimentalist, the idea of teleology is excluded from science, yet in the hands of men like Herbert Spencer[20] its teleological aspects have already assumed some prominence, and will presently eventuate in a new era of profoundly speculative inquiry. So this law of correlation, to the true thinker, asks, "What is the real?" No dreaming metaphysician, with his dialect of terms for airy nothings, ever put the question more pertinently or more directly; and the psychic-force theory, it seems to me, while at war with the deeper aspects of this, according to Faraday,[21] the highest law in physical science, fails to answer the important question in a manner that commends itself to men of real scientific aptitude, and stultifies the tendency to deeper religious conceptions, now beginning to be felt as an active force in scientific thought.
>
> It is no doubt true, and can be established from careful comparison of ancient forms of civilization with modern, and of ancient types of the human race with modern, that there has been a general progress toward more psychical types of organization, involving a greater complexity of emotional and intellectual life. The question is, whether the average spiritual medium is an earnest of the advanced type potential in the existing; and this question can only be answered by rigid physiological investigation.

Fairfield's Ideas

In the third chapter of his book, "Cases of Nervous Psychic Phenomena," Fairfield (1875d) presented cases to support his ideas, with aspects such as supposed nervous and epileptic problems. He mentioned Andrew Jackson Davis as a person "subject to spontaneous attacks of trance" (p. 46), and John W. Edmonds as having "an almost monomaniac persistency in discussing the subject of death and future destiny" (p. 49) and symptoms of nervous disorder. Victoria Woodhull's trances and talking to spirits were considered as "larvated epilepsy" (p. 57), or masked epilepsy without observable convulsions.[22]

Interestingly, Fairfield did not exempt himself from diagnosis. Presenting a summary of his mental psychic experiences he pointed out he had a neurotic tendency and that his experiences took place "only at periods of exceeding nervous disturbance and of reduced physical condition" (p. 80).

Fairfield emphasized the connection of cases to nervous conditions and epilepsy (sometimes without observable epileptic symptoms), as well as to hereditary predisposition. The latter was part of a larger nineteenth-century interest in the inheritance of mental illness (Porter, 2018).

Like previous critiques of the diagnosis of insanity in mediums (e.g., Anonymous, 1863; Crowell, 1877), the ideas presented by Fairfield received some criticism. One author believed that, even if the nervous disorder approach seemed reasonable in some cases, Fairfield

> … does not make the connection between the effect and its cause very clear; and in other cases it is impossible to see any connection or relation whatever between the phenomena and the alleged nervous disorder and even the existence of the latter seems to be a matter of assumption (Anonymous, 1875e, p. 68).

Two other critics stated that Fairfield's ideas were nonsense (Anonymous, 1875a), and that in addition to lacking enough evidence for the theory, Fairfield had too many unproven assumptions (Hammond, 1875).

In one review the writer took issue with the statements made about John W. Edmonds, accusing Fairfield of slander. In this reviewer's view Fairfield had ignored facts that were not consistent with his theory (Anonymous, 1875d).

One critic argued that Fairfield's ideas did not explain everything. In fact, it was stated that some specific phenomena showed the theory to be inapplicable (Anonymous, 1875b). In another review, Fairfield's explanation was described as an example of using the obscure to account for the more obscure (Anonymous, 1875c).

It is not surprising that most of the critiques, coming from authors in spiritualist publications, were negative. This was consistent with other defenses of mediumship from accusations of pathology (e.g., Anonymous, 1863; Crowell, 1877).

Although Fairfield's views were commented in the spiritualist literature, and elsewhere, it is a matter of speculation if he was influential at the time. Fairfield's views were not as well-known as those of other individuals writing about the pathology of mediumship during the nineteenth century. Furthermore, Fairfield did not have the medical reputation nor clinical experience of physicians who attempted to pathologize mediumship, individuals such as William Hammond (1876), Pierre Janet (1889), and L. S. Forbes Winslow (1877). This may have curtailed his influence in general. Then, and this is also speculation, his defense of supernormal aspects of mediumship in the context of pathology may have also diminished acceptance of his views. Some were probably reluctant to accept the connection between pathology and the supernormal because it tainted the meaning of psychic phenomena (spiritualists and other believers in psychic phenomena), while others may have felt that pathology need not be associated with the supernormal (physicians and other students of mental pathology).

Nonetheless, Fairfield's ideas are important in their own context. They illustrate a hidden history of attempts to combine the supernormal with pathology which, in turn, inform us about the variety of ideas about mediumship, psychology and health.

Later Ideas by Other Investigators

Similar to Fairfield, there were later writers who accepted the reality of mediumistic phenomena and their association with pathology. German philosopher Eduard von Hartmann (1842–1906) affirmed that mediums "are without exception individuals with a certain disorganisation of the nervous system ... they are, in other words ... hysterical ..." (von Hartmann, 1885, p. 4). This force, von Hartmann believed, could produce some genuine phenomena.

Other examples of similar theoretical positions may be seen in relation to the Italian medium Eusapia Palladino (1854–1918). Italian criminologist and psychiatrist Cesare Lombroso (1835–1909), became convinced of the reality of Palladino's physical phenomena, but also of her hysterical pathology (Alvarado & Biondi, 2017). Initially, he wrote that the medium showed brain anomalies diminishing and increasing the functions of various cerebral centers. When the motor centers activity was enhanced, there was an overflow of nervous force that caused actual physical phenomena (Lombroso, 1892). Later he stated that the medium showed some symptoms consistent with epilepsy, and with hysteria. In terms of the latter, he wrote: "She has the hyperaesthesic zone, especially in the ovary. She has the bole in the oesophagus that women with hysteria have, and general weakness, or paresis, in the limbs of the left side" (Lombroso, 1909, p. 107).

Italian psychiatrist Enrico Morselli (1852–1929), wrote in his book about Palladino, *Psicologia e 'Spiritismo'*: "Mediumship is a metahysterical condition" (Morselli, 1908, Vol. 2, p. 310), which for him included other medical problems. Palladino had occasional convulsions that Morselli suspected were epileptic (Vol. 1, p. 126). He also considered her emotional behaviors and changing moods hysterical. Furthermore, Morselli listed various mediums that he thought presented symptoms of both organic and functional nervous disturbances (Vol. 1, pp. 103–104).

Also from Italy, other physicians had ideas similar to Morselli's regarding Palladino (Arullani, 1907; Visani-Scozzi, 1901). The latter referred to a "general mediumistic neurosis which at its highest degree associates often with real diseases of the cerebrospinal axis" (Visani-Scozzi, 1901, p. 193), which he said allowed for the extension of the functions of the motor zones of the medium outside her body.

Another forgotten theorist was Spanish physician Víctor Melcior i Farré (1860–1929), who was interested in mediumship and psychic phenomena in general. He wrote that "mediums are beings who produce currents of a sort of electricity that has not been defined yet" (Melcior, 1901, p. 415). Such currents are formed in the medullary bulb, something indicated by the fact that "in all physical mediums there is a predominance of the functions of vegetative life; the antecedent or the presence of a deep nervous affliction, such as neurasthenia, hysteria or hysteroepilepsy," conditions related to "drowsiness, suspension or hindrance in the functions of the higher cerebral centers (reflection and will)" (p. 415). This may lead to a diminution of intellectual functions, and then, to automatisms. While the physical phenomena of mediums were believed by Melcior to be genuine, "such phenomena can never be produced by a healthy person, but must be produced by a sick person with a psychological ailment" (p. 415).

Concluding Remarks

In this paper I have attempted to remind the reader about past ideas combining pathology and genuine mediumistic phenomena, something that is sometimes neglected in the study of the relationship between mediumship and pathology. As part of the discussion, I have presented an excerpt of a generally forgotten publication by Francis Gerry Fairfield. His ideas, and other ideas similar to his enlarge our conceptions of the history of explanations for mediumship, and more broadly, show the complexity of medical views about psychic phenomena.

Except for papers about the pre-1930s literature (e.g., Alvarado, 2014), ideas about mediumship similar to Fairfield's are rarely mentioned today. Modern authors discussing psychopathology in mediumship do not get into this topic, confining their discussion to generally failed attempts to find pathology in mediums regardless of parapsychological aspects involving acquisition of veridical information and physical effects (e.g., Bastos et al., 2015). Different from some of the old medical literature, this recent literature does not relate psychopathology to mediumship (see also Maraldi, Ribeiro, & Krippner, 2019).[23] However, and not necessarily related to psychopathology, see a recent study that found more medical problems in mediums than in a control group (Beischel, Tassone, & Boccuzzi, 2019).

But while supernormal-pathological ideas about mediumship may not prevail today, it is of interest to mention briefly more recent ideas involving genuine psychic functioning and pathology. Some have argued that those showing psychic phenomena are at risk for nervous, volition, and dissociative problems (Quevedo, 1960/1971; see also Machado, 1996). In addition to what I mentioned above, there have been ideas about ESP and maladjustment in the psychotherapeutic context (Devereux, 1953), and generally unsupported suggestions of ESP-functioning behind schizophrenic delusions (Ehrenwald, 1947). Another area of speculation centered on pathological ideas in the psychodynamics of poltergeist agency, as seen in early (Winterstein, 1926) and later writings (Roll, 1972). All of this is beyond the scope of the present article, but conceptually-related to the ideas of Fairfield and other individuals mentioned in the previous section.

Notes

1 On mediumship and pathology see Alvarado (2020), Alvarado & Biondi (2017), Alvarado & Zingrone (2012), Ferguson (2012, Chapter 2), Gutierrez (2003), Le Maléfan (1999), Moreira-Almeida, Silva de Almeida & Lotufo Neto (2005), Owen (1990), & Porter, Nicholson, & Bennett (2003).

2 Some students of the subject also believed that vital or nervous force emanations from the body presented features reflecting medical pathology (e.g., Baraduc, 1893; Luys, 1892). Further examples of this idea appeared in writings about auras (e.g., Leadbeater, 1895), and about the action of a "plastic mediator" or fluidic body (Rouget, 1870).

3 However, it is important to be aware that similar ideas of forces were also used by some believers in discarnate agency (e.g., Ballou, 1853).

4 This was the famous D. D. Home (1833–1886), who greatly popularized Spiritualism and mediumship via his séances, travels, and writings (Lamont, 2005).

5 This was American medium Charles H. Foster (d. 1885), who, among other phenomena, was reported to produce skin writing and pellet reading (Bartlett, 1891).

6 Unconscious cerebration was a term used to refer to the unconscious generation of actions and ideas through the reflex (automatic) action of the brain (Carpenter, 1874, Chapter 13).

7 Fairfield refers here to the well-known studies of English chemist and physicist William Crookes (1832–1919) of the physical phenomena of mediumship, particularly those reported to take place around mediums D. D. Home and Florence Cook (Crookes, 1874).

8 There were several references to the exhaustion of physical mediums after séances during the 1870s (e.g., Barkas, 1876, p. 43; Fitz-Gerald, 1877, p. 126). Crookes (1874) wrote about "the painful state of nervous and bodily prostration" of D. D. Home after experiments, where he was "lying in an almost fainting condition on the floor, pale and speechless" (p. 41).

9 Benjamin Hawkes (d. 1873) was a toy dealer in England and also a medium who fell dead during a séance. According to his wife he suffered from heart problems (Anonymous, 1873, p. 562).

10 This was Catherine Fox (1837?–1892), one of the famous Fox sisters, who was very influential in the development of early Spiritualism and mediumship (Weisberg, 2004).

11 Some years later it was commented that on occasion choreic movements were seen in mediums (Janet, 1889, p. 405). Some of those who studied medium Leonora E. Piper (1857–1950) mentioned that she showed convulsive and twitching movements when she was starting to fall in trance (Hodgson, 1898, pp. 483, 587). See also Fairfield's (1875d, p. 102) observations with mediums and clairvoyant physicians.

12 This refers to Jean-Etienne-Dominique Esquirol (1772–1840) and Henry Maudsley (1835–1918), physicians known for their work with mental disturbances who published influential treatises (e.g. Esquirol, 1838; Maudsley, 1868).

13 American physician George Beard (1839–1883) considered trance a pathological state characterized by the concentration of cerebral activity on "some limited region of the brain, the activity of the rest of the brain being for the time suspended" (Beard, 1879, p. 67).

14 Maudsley (1873, pp. 205–206) speculated about epileptic tendencies, and stated Swedenborg was insane (p. 263). He also said that there was nothing in his revelations showing superhuman insight and "nothing which is inconsistent or incompatible with the wild imaginations of a person the balance of whose faculties has been lost" (pp. 261–262).

15 This was the famous British naturalist Alfred Russel Wallace (1823–1913), well known for his strong defenses of Spiritualism (e.g., Wallace, 1874).

16 These are references to three Americans, Judge, medium, and writer about Spiritualism John Worth Edmonds (1799–1874), visionary and clairvoyant Andrew Jackson Davis (1826–1910), and activist for women rights Victoria Woodhull (1838–1927).

17 Edward W. Cox (1809–1879) was a prominent lawyer in London and a somewhat forgotten researcher and theorist of spiritualistic and psychological phenomena (Richards, 2001). He wrote to Crookes in 1871 to suggest the use of the term "psychic force" (Crookes, 1871, p. 349, Cox 1871, 1874) and discussed in detail his ideas about this force.

18 This term had been proposed earlier by Baradiuc to refer to a force of unknown properties behind the production of mediumistic phenomena (Flammarion, 1865, p. 135).

19 The correlation of forces, or the idea that forces such as heat and electricity were interrelated and could be converted into the other, was an important feature of nineteenth-century physics intimately related to the idea of the conservation of force (e.g., Grove, 1846). Many others wrote on the subject (Youmans, 1865), which suggested to some that nature had balance and harmony in its processes.

20 English philosopher and sociologist Herbert Spencer (1820–1903) was a very influential philosopher in many areas, among them evolution. He argued that the principle of correlation of forces was active in terms of social processes (Spencer, 1862, pp. 281–284).

21 English physicist Michael Faraday (1791–1867) was well known for his work on topics such as electromagnetism. In addition, he wrote about phenomena such as table turning, explaining it through unconscious movements (Faraday, 1853).

22 Fairfield (1875a) defined this term as "sudden attacks of maniacal type, without contemporaneous convulsions" (p. 691). He was influenced by Benedict A. Morel's (1809–1873) ideas about epilepsy (Morel, 1860, pp. 480–481).

23 Others have also denied the association with pathology in the past (e.g., Prince, 1923).

References

Alvarado, C. S. (2006). Human radiations: Concepts of force in mesmerism, spiritualism and psychical research. *Journal of the Society for Psychical Research, 70*, 138–162.

Alvarado, C. S. (2013). The influence of Reichenbach's concept of Od. *Journal of Scientific Exploration, 27,* 111–115.

Alvarado, C. S. (2014). Mediumship, psychical research, dissociation, and the powers of the subconscious mind. *Journal of Parapsychology, 78*, 98–114.

Alvarado, C. S. (2020). Dissociation and the unconscious mind: Nineteenth century perspectives on mediumship. *Journal of Scientific Exploration, 34*, 539–598.

Alvarado, C. S., & Biondi, M. (2017). Classic text no. 110: Cesare Lombroso on mediumship and pathology. *History of Psychiatry, 28*, 225–241.

Alvarado, C. S., & Zingrone, N. L. (2012). Classic text no. 90: 'The pathology and treatment of mediomania,' by Frederic Rowland Marvin (1874). *History of Psychiatry, 23*, 229–244.

Anonymous. (1860). The delusions of spiritualism. *Lancet, 2*, 466–467.

Anonymous. (1863). Sur la folie spirite: Reponse a M. Burlet, de Lyon. *Revue spirite, 6*, 51–59.

Anonymous. (1869). Table-talk. *Appleton's Journal, 1*, 601–602.

Anonymous. (1873). Notes and gleanings. *Spiritual Magazine, 8*(n. s.), 561–569.

Anonymous. (1875a, August 26). Explaining the obscure by the more obscure. *Spiritual Scientist,* 291.

Anonymous. (1875b, November 16). Exposures of "Spiritualism." *Spiritual Scientist*, 123.

Anonymous. (1875c, April 24). Fairfield's "Ten years with spiritual mediums." *Banner of Light*, 4.

Anonymous. (1875d, April 3). A queer book. *Religio-Philosophical Journal*, 19.

Anonymous. (1875e, April 15). Spiritualism and epilepsy. *Spiritual Scientist*, 68.

Anonymous. (1887a, April 5). Francis Gerry Fairfield dead also. *The Sun*, p. 2.

Anonymous. (1887b, April 10). The poison of the poppy: The sad story of the life and death of Francis G. Fairfield and his wife. *Indianapolis Journal*, p. 5.

Arullani, P. F. (1907). *Sulla medianit a della Eusapia Paladino.* Rosenberg and Sellier.

Ballou, A. (1853). *An exposition of views respecting the principal facts, causes, and peculiarities involved in spirit manifestations* (2nd ed.). Bela Marsh.

Baraduc, H. (1893). *La force vitale: Notre corps vital fluidique, sa formule biometrique*. G. Carre.

Barèty, A. (1887). *Le magnètisme animal: Etudie sous le nom de force neurique rayonnante et circulante dans ces proprietes physiques, physiologiques et thèrapeutique.* Octave Doin.

Barkas, T. P. (1876, August 25). An extraordinary materialization seance. *Spiritualist Newspaper*, pp. 42–43.

Bartlett, G. C. (1891). *The Salem seer: Reminiscences of Charles H. Foster*. United States Book Company.

Bastos, M. A. V., Bastos, P. R. H. de O., Goncalves, L. M., Osorio, I. H. S., & Luccheti, G. (2015). Mediumship: Review of quantitatives studies published in the 21st century. *Archives of Clinical Psychiatry, 42*, 129–138.

Beard, G. M. (1879). The psychology of spiritualism. *North American Review, 129*, 65–80.
Beischel, J., Tassone, S., & Boccuzzi, M. (2019). Hematological and psychophysiological correlates of anomalous information reception in mediums: A preliminary exploration. *Explore: Journal of Science and Healing, 15,* 126–133.
Bourru, H., & Burot, P. (1887). *La suggestion mentale et l'action à distance des substances toxiques et medicamenteuses*. J. -B. Baillière.
Braid, J. (1843). *Neurypnology or the rationale of nervous sleep considered in relation with animal magnetism.* John Murray.
Briquet, P. (1859). *Traite clinique et thérapeutique de l'hystérie.* J. -B. Baillière.
Brittan, S. B., & Richmond, B. W. (1853). A *discussion of the facts and philosophy of ancient and modern Spiritualism*. Partridge and Brittan.
Bucknill, J. C. & Tuke, D. H. (1874). *A manual of psychological medicine* (3rd. ed). John Churchill.
Carpenter, W. B. (1874). *Principles of mental physiology*. D. Appleton.
Charcot, J. M. (1882). Sur les divers états nerveux determines par hypnotisation chez les hystériques. *Comptes Rendus Hebdomadaires des Seances de l'Academie des Sciences, 94*, 403–405.
Cox, E. W. (1871). *Spiritualism answered by science.* Longman.
Cox, E. W. (1874). *What am I? A popular introduction to mental philosophy and psychology: Vol. 2: The mechanism in action.* Longman.
Crookes, W. (1871). Experimental investigation of a new force. *Quarterly Journal of Science, 1*(n. s.), 339–349.
Crookes, W. (1874). *Researches in the phenomena of spiritualism*. J. Burns.
Crowell, E. (1877). Spiritualism opposed to insanity. *Spiritual Magazine of Phenomena Spiritual-Ethereal-Physical, 3*(s. 3), 160–162.
Dailey, A. H. (1894). *Mollie Fancher, the Brooklyn enigma*. Press of Eagle Book Printing Department.
Despine, P. (1880). *Etude scientifique sur le somnambulisme.* F. Savy.
Devereux, G. (Ed.). (1953). *Psychoanalysis and the occult.* International University Press.
Didier, E. L. (1883). *A primer of criticism*. People's Publishing.
Ehrenwald, J. (1947). *Telepathy and medical psychology*. G. Allen and Unwin.
Esquirol, E. (1838). *Des maladies mentales consiérées sous les rapports médical, hygiénique et médico-légal* (2 vols., and atlas). J. -B. Baillière.
Fairfield, F. G. (1872a). Building progress in New York—statistically and artistically considered. *Manufacturer and Builder, 4*, 21-22.
Fairfield, F. G. (1872b). Timothy Tot: A prose story with poetic passages. *The Radical, 10*, 66–75.
Fairfield, F. G. (1873). *The clubs of New York.* Henry L. Hinton.
Fairfield, F. G. (1874). The confession of a reformed smoker: A record of observations and experiments concerning the physiological action of tobacco. *Popular Science Monthly, 6*, 76–87.
Fairfield, F. G. (1875a). A mad man of letters. *Scribner's Monthly, 10,* 690–699.
Fairfield, F. G. (1875b). An appendix to the "new solution." *Scribner's Monthly, 10*, 374–378.
Fairfield, F. G. (1875c). A new solution of an old puzzle. *Scribner's Monthly, 9*, 333–341, 483–488.
Fairfield, F. G. (1875d). *Ten years with spiritual mediums: An inquiry concerning the etiology of certain phenomena called spiritual.* D. Appleton.
Fairfield, F. G. (1876). The problem of crime. *Appleton's Journal, 15*, 15–19.
Fairfield, F. G. (1880). A study in apparent death. *Scribner's Monthly, 21*, 249–257.
Faraday, M. (1853). Professor Faraday on table-moving. *The Athenaeum: Journal of Literature, Science, and the Fine Arts, 1340,* 801–803.
Ferguson, C. (2012). *Determined spirits: Eugenics, heredity and racial regeneration in Anglo-American spiritualist writing, 1848–1930.* Edinburgh University Press.
Fitz-Gerald, D. (1877, March 16). Physical science and spiritual psychology. *Spiritualist Newspaper*, pp. 124–126.
Flammarion, C. [under the pseudonym Hermes]. (1865). *Des forces naturelles inconnues: À propos des phénomènes produits par les frères Davenport et par les médiums en général.* Didier.
Fontan, J. (1887). Hystéro-épilepsie masculine: Suggestion-inhibition-transposition de sens. *Revue philosophique de la France et de l'etranger, 24,* 213–221.
Grove, W. R. (1846). *On the correlation of physical forces.* Samuel Highley.

Gutierrez, C. (2003). From electricity to ectoplasm: Hysteria and American Spiritualism. *Aries, 3*, 55–81.
Hammond., W. A. (1875, March 5). Fairfield's spiritual mediums. *New York Daily*, p. 6.
Hammond, W. A. (1871). *The physics and physiology of Spiritualism*. D. Appleton.
Hammond, W. A. (1876). *Spiritualism and allied causes and conditions of nervous derangement.* G. P. Putnam's Sons.
Hecker, J. (1868). *The scientific basis of education* (2nd ed.). A. S. Barnes.
Hodgson, R. (1898). A further record of observations of certain phenomena of trance. *Proceedings of the Society for Psychical Research, 13*, 284–582.
Janet, P. (1889). *L'automatisme psychologique: Essai de psychologie expérimentale sur les formes inférieures de l'activité humaine*. Félix Alcan.
Lamont, P. (2005). *The first psychic: The peculiar mystery of a notorious Victorian wizard.* Little, Brown.
Leadbeater, C. W. (1895). The aura. *The Theosophist, 17,* 134–141.
Le Maléfan, P. (1999). *Folie et spiritisme: Histoire du discours psychopathologique sur la pratique du spiritisme, ses abords et ses avatars (1850–1950).* L'Hartmattan.
Lombroso, C. (1891). Inchiesta sulla trasmissione del pensiero. *Archivio di Psichiatria, Scienze Penali, ed Antropologia Criminale, 12,* 58–108.
Lombroso, C. (1892). Le spiritisme et la psychiatrie: Explication psychiatrique de certains faits spirites. *Annales des Sciences Psychiques, 2*, 143–151.
Lombroso, C. (1909). *After death—what? Spiritistic phenomena and their interpretation.* Small, Maynard.
London Dialectical Society. (1871). *Report on Spiritualism of the Committee of the London Dialectical Society, together with evidence oral and written, and a selection from the correspondence*. Longmans, Green, Reader, and Dyer.
Lum, D. D. (1873). *The "spiritual" delusion; its methods, teachings, and effects.* J. B. Lippincott.
Luys, J. (1892). De la visibilité des effluves magnetiques and électriques chez les sujets en état hypnotique. *Annales de Psychiatrie et Hypnologie dans Leurs Rapports avec la Psychologie et la Médicine Légale, 2,* 193–195.
Machado, F. R. (1996). *A causa dos espíritos: Um estudo sobre a utilização da parapsicologia para a defesa da fé católica e espírita no Brasil*. Masters' thesis, Pontifícia Universidade Católica de São Paulo.
Mahan, A. (1855). *Modern mysteries explained and exposed in four parts*. J. P. Jewett.
Maraldi, E. de O., Ribeiro, R. N., & Krippner, S. (2019). Cultural and group differences in mediumship and dissociation: Exploring the varieties of mediumistic experiences. *International Journal of Latin American Religions, 3*(1), 170–192.
Marvin, F. R. (1874). *The philosophy of spiritualism and the pathology and treatment of mediomania.* A. K. Butts.
Mason, R. O. (1894). Case of hysteria, catalepsy and unstable consciousness accompanied by supernormal perception. *Journal of the Society for Psychical Research, 6,* 361–365.
Maudsley, H. (1868). *The physiology and pathology of mind* (2nd ed.). Macmillan.
Maudsley, H. (1873). *Body and mind* (Rev. ed.). Macmillan.
Melcior, V. (1901). La dinamita anulada por una potencia invisible. *Luz y Union, 2*, 414–416.
Moreira-Almeida A, Silva de Almeida, A. A., & Lotufo Neto, F. (2005). History of 'spiritist madness' in Brazil. *History of Psychiatry, 16,* 5–25.
Morel, B. A. (1860). *Traité des maladies mentales*. Victor Masson.
Morselli, E. (1908). *Psicologia e 'Spiritismo': Impressioni e note critiche sui fenomeni medianici di Eusapia Paladino* (2 vols.). Fratelli Bocca.
Owen, A. (1990). *The darkened room: Women, power and spiritualism in late Victorian England.* University of Pennsylvania Press.
Petetin, J. H. D. (1808). *Électricite animalé* (2nd ed.). Brunot-Labbe.
Philips, A. J. P. (1855). *Électro-dynamisme vital ou, les relations physiologiques de l'esprit et de la matière, demontrées par des experiences entièrement nouvelles et par l'histoire raisonnée du système nerveux.* J. B. Baillière.
Pigeaire, J. (1839). *Puissance de l'électricité animale, ou, du magnétisme vital et de ses rapports avec la physique, la physiologie et la médecine*. Dentu.
Porter, R., Nicholson, H., & Bennett, B. (Eds). (2003). *Women, madness and spiritualism.* Routledge.

Porter, T. M. (2018). *Genetics in the madhouse: The unknown history of human heredity.* Princeton University Press.
Prince, W. F. (1923). Is the possession of "psychical' faculty pathological? *Journal of the American Society for Psychical Research, 17,* 430–436, 473–480.
Quevedo, O. G. (1971). *Que es la parapsicología.* Buenos Aires: Columba. (Original work published 1969)
Richards, G. (2001). Edward Cox, the Psychological Society of Great Britain (1875–1879) and the meanings of an institutional failure. In G. C. Bunn, A. D. Lovie, & G. D. Richards (Eds.), *Psychology in Britain: Historical essays and personal reflections* (pp. 33–53). BPS Books.
Richer, P. (1885). *Études cliniques sur la grande hystérie ou hystéro-épilepsie* (2nd ed.). Adrien Delahaye et Emile Lecrosnier.
Rogers, E. C. (1853). *Philosophy of mysterious agents.* J. P. Jewett.
Roll, W. G. (1972). *The poltergeist.* Doubleday.
Rouget, F. (1870). *La photographie mentale des esprits dévoilée.* Bompard.
Spencer, H. (1862). *First principles.* Williams and Norgate.
Tolosa-Latour, M. (1893). Expériences de suggestion mentale à distance. *Annales des Sciences Psychiques, 3,* 268–273.
Tuttle, H., & Peebles, J. M. (Eds.). (1871). *The year-book of Spiritualism for 1871.* William White.
Visani Scozzi, P. (1901). *La medianita.* R. Bemporad.
von Hartmann, E. (1885). *Spiritism.* Psychological Press.
von Reichenbach, C. (1851). *Physico-physiological researches on the dynamics of magnetism, electricity, heat, light, crystallization, and chemism, in their relation to vital force.* J. S. Redfield. (Original work published in German, 1849)
Wallace, A. R. (1874). A defence of modern Spiritualism. *Fortnightly Review, 15*(n. s.) 630¬657, 785–807.
Weisberg, B. (2004). *Talking to the dead: Kate and Maggie Fox and the rise of spiritualism.* Harper San Francisco.
Wilson, J. G., & Fiske, J. (Eds.). (1888). *Appleton's cyclopaedia of American biography* (Vol. 2). D. Appleton.
Winslow, L. S. F. (1877). *Spiritualistic madness.* Baillière, Tindall and Cox.
Winterstein, A. (1926). Psychoanalytische Bemerkungen zum Thema Spuk. *Zeitschrift für Parapsychologie, 1,* 548–553.
Youmans, E. L. (Ed.). (1865). *The correlation and conservation of forces.* D. Appleton.

28

Experimenter and Other Effects in the Historical Séance Literature*

Carlos S. Alvarado

Various reviews on the topic of experimenter effects have been published in parapsychology (Palmer & Miller, 2015; Roe, 2016; White, 1977). Many have argued that investigators and sitters can affect the phenomena produced by mediums, a topic extended by some to surrounding beliefs and the traditions of Spiritualism. Here I present some examples of such discussions published before the 1930s. While it is possible to talk about psi experimenter effects, I am also concerned with effects apparently mediated by attitudes and other socio-psychological processes, including suggestion and expectation.

An example of psychological influences on mediums appeared in the *Spiritualist Newspaper*—Russian student of psychic phenomena Alexander Aksakof (1875) wrote a critique of Allan Kardec, arguing that Kardec affected the content of the mediumistic communications of his mediums. He was particularly concerned with the support French communications gave to the idea of reincarnation. Aksakof emphasized that Kardec used writing mediums, "who it is well known pass so easily under the psychological influence of preconceived ideas" (p. 75).

An anonymous (1875) writer in the same publication suggested that if reincarnation was discussed in England,

> ... plenty of spirits will begin to teach it, the reason being that the minds of the various mediums will be set buzzing by the arguments on the subject mooted by persons around them, after which there will be plenty of spirit messages about reincarnation. (p. 170)

In Germany Eduard Von Hartmann (1885), commented as follows about the influence of spiritist tradition:

> As mediums learn to know the tradition of Spiritist circles before they get beyond physical manifestations and thought-reading, it is explicable that certain figures are of stereotyped reproduction with quite different mediums, as Harlequin, Pierrot, Columbine, &c., in the Harlequinade; they call themselves John King, Katie King, &c, ... (p. 82)

Similarly, William James (1890) discussed the issue in the first volume of *The Principles of Psychology* in terms of the influence of the zeitgeist. After commenting on similarities in the personalities manifested in mediums' controls, and some common topics mentioned by them, James wrote:

> Whether all sub-conscious selves are peculiarly susceptible to a certain stratum of the Zeitgeist, and get their inspiration from it, I know not; but this is obviously the case with the secondary

*Republished with permission from *Mindfield*, *10*(1), 36–39, 2018.

> selves which become 'developed' in spiritualist circles ... The subject assumes the role of a medium simply because opinion expects it of him under the conditions which are present; and carries it out with a feebleness or a vivacity proportionate to his histrionic gifts. But the odd thing is that persons unexposed to spiritualist traditions will so often act in the same way when they become entranced .... (p. 394)

The topic was also discussed in relation to the mediumship of Eusapia Palladino.

> Eusapia is ... eminently suggestible. This suggestibility, which may be increased in the state of trance, may have psychological consequences such that the will of the medium is largely influenced by that of the experimenters, by their desires, by their suspicions, by their prejudices." (de Rochas, 1896, p. 259)

This lead a group of researchers to state in the introduction of a séance report that they were aware that the medium was not an instrument and that negative attitudes and extreme suspicion could produce negative effects (Sabatier, de Rochas, de Gramont, Maxwell, Dariex, & de Watteville, 1896).

French physician Gustave Geley, writing under the pseudonym of E. Gyel (1899), wrote that one of many possible causes of mediumistic communications was "notions suggested voluntarily or not by the sitters" (p. 92).

In his classic *From India to the Planet Mars* Theodore Flournoy (1900) analyzed communications produced by Hélène Smith, whose real name was Élise Catherine Müller. The communications consisted in part of stories about previous lives and travels to planet Mars. In his conclusion, Flournoy wrote:

> We must also take into consideration the enormous suggestibility and auto–suggestibility of mediums, which render them so sensitive to all the influences of spiritistic reunions, and are so favorable to the play of those brilliant subliminal creations in which, occasionally, the doctrinal ideas of the surrounding environment are reflected together with the latent emotional tendencies of the medium herself. (p. 443)

Flournoy stated that he talked to the medium and explained to her his reasons to believe these were creations of her subliminal mind, failing to convince her. But he believed that his critiques about Mars and the Martian language had some impact on Smith, leading her to produce new phenomena.

In an article Flournoy (1901) published later about Hélène Smith in the *Archives de Psychologie*, he speculated about the effect his book had on the medium, that it basically gave her ideas for new subconscious flights of fancy, which he discusses in some detail (including more descriptions of Mars and romances about Uranus and the Moon). Interestingly, Flournoy wrote: "In my opinion, contrary to what is advocated often in this field, it is not good for a medium to be studied too long by the same investigator, because the latter, despite its precautions, inevitably ends by shaping the suggestible subconsciousness of its subject ..." (p. 116), which prevents new developments. This situation, he stated, is "sort of a psychological ankylosis" (p. 116) affecting the medium who reacts to being observed by having difficulties in showing phenomena other than those he or she believes are expected by the observer.

The well-known astronomer Camille Flammarion (1907) suggested that Victorien Sardou's (1858) drawings of houses on planet Jupiter were "the reflex of the general ideas in the air" (p. 26). Many others believed that the ideas of the circle could affect mediumistic communications (e.g., Lebiedzinski, 1924; Maxwell, 1903/1905; Sudre, 1926). Maxwell believed that spirit personalities, or personifications, were suggestible. He wrote "that the role played by the personification varies with the composition of the circle. It will always be the spirit of a dead or living person with spiritists. But the roles are more varied if the circle be composed of people who are not spiritists …" (p. 65).

Amy Tanner (1910) believed that Mrs. Piper's controls were educated by some of her researchers. In her view, "the various believers have framed a theory, which, being offered to the control, was accepted as everything is which is given it sympathetically. The controls themselves have thus been given a spiritistic education for over twenty years in all, so that whatever they were in the beginning, they are now thoroughly dyed-in-the-wool Spiritists" (p. 311). In later years René Sudre (1926) wrote about this, particularly in his book *Personnages d'au-delà* (Sudre, 1946).

Another interesting mention of the influence of sitters was that presented by Eleanor Sidgwick (1915) in her study of séances held with Mrs. Piper. In her view:

> That the sitters must influence the trance communications to some extent is … obvious. For one thing, they are themselves personages in the drama, and the part they play in it and the way they play it must affect the way the trance personalities play theirs … And in the trance drama the sitters not only largely determine the subjects of conversation, but the personages who shall take part in it. They explicitly or tacitly demand that their own friends shall manifest themselves and produce evidence of identity, or give information on particular points. (Sidgwick, 1915, p. 294)

Interestingly, there were also speculations about physical mediumship. I will refer here only to ideas related to two mediums. Referring to Eusapia Palladino, Julian Ochorowicz (1896) stated that the sitters could project ideas on the medium. This included suspicions of fraud that could produce actual fraudulent actions in the medium. Also, materialist sitters could influence the medium to produce phenomena looking as a force with no apparent consciousness or independence, but in spiritist-oriented circles the manifestations could be of a more spiritist character. This was actually the case with reports coming from the Circolo Scientifico Minerva, from Italy, which had many members convinced of discarnate agency (Venzano, 1907).

Enrico Morselli also wrote about Palladino. In his view, spiritism illustrates the "general law of imitation" (Morselli, 1908, p. 122). He was referring to the suggestions delivered by Giovanni Damiani, an early supporter of Palladino, who he believed "educated" the medium, a process continued by a later supporter, Ercole Chiaia. According to Morselli's suggestion always "shapes, or modifies, or enlivens the phenomena of which the highly susceptible nervous system of patients and mediums is capable of" (p. 122).

Other speculations were also presented about W. J. Crawford's studies of medium Kathleen Goligher and her mediumistic circle (e.g., Crawford, 1916). An aspect of this work consisted of Crawford's ideas of psychic levers responsible for table levitations, which were supported by weigh measurements. Various writers, among them Ernesto Bozzano (1929), René Sudre (1926), and Albert von Schrenck-Notzing (1920/1925), argued that Crawford's results were influenced by his ideas and expectations as a mechanical engineer. According to Barrett (1921): "In the case of Dr. Crawford's experiments the ideas of the medium, Miss Goligher, were derived from the mechanical conceptions of Dr. Crawford; which he freely expressed to all." That is, instead of having findings confirming mechanical principles behind table levitations, it was believed that Crawford influenced the medium with his conceptions of the process, conceptions which "shaped" the phenomena following mechanical ideas. The reality of the phenomena was not questioned, but the nature of the process was.

To conclude, I would like to remind my readers that the above-mentioned ideas consisted of theoretical speculations presented after the fact, and not necessarily descriptions of what actually took place in the séance room, or more precisely, in the mind of the medium and sitters. Second, we also need to remember that many similar ideas were also prevalent in the hypnosis literature.

These, and other ideas mentioned here, are somewhat different from our current conception of experimenter's effects generally limited to the modern experimental setting. But they are conceptually related, at least in terms of the influence of unexpected variables.

References

Aksakof, A. (1875, August 13). Researches on the historical origin of the reincarnation speculations of French spiritualists. *Spiritualist Newspaper*, pp. 74–75.

Anonymous. (1875, October 8). Allan Kardec's "Spirits book." *Spiritualist Newspaper*, pp. 169–170.

Ballou, A. (1852). *An exposition of views respecting the principal facts, causes and peculiarities involved in spirit manifestations.* Bela Marsh.

Barrett, W.F. (1921). Ectoplasms. *Light*, 41, 347.

Bozzano, E. (1929). *Pensée & volonté.* Jean Meyer.

Crawford, W. J. (1916). *The reality of psychic phenomena.* John M. Watkins.

de Rochas, A. (1896). *L'extériorisation de la motricité.* Chamuel.

Flammarion, C. (1907). *Mysterious psychic forces.* Small, Maynard.

Flournoy, T. (1900). *From India to the planet Mars: A study of a case of somnambulism with glossolalia.* Harper & Brothers.

Flournoy, T. (1901). Nouvelles observations sur un cas de somnambulisme avec glossolalie. *Archives de Psychologie, 1,* 101–255.

Gyel, E. [pseudonym of Gustave Geley]. (1899). *L'être subconscient.* Félix Alcan.

Harrison, W. (1873, December 5). Certain problems connected to mediumship. *The Spiritualist*, pp. 436–440.

James, W. (1890). *The principles of psychology* (Vol. 1). Henry Holt.

Lebiedzinski, P. (1924). *L'idéoplastie comme hypothèse directrice des études métapsychiques. Dans L'état actuel des recherches psychiques d'après les travaux du IIme Congrès International tenu à Varsovie en 1923 en l'honneur du Dr Julien Ochorowicz* (pp. 286–300). Presses Universitaires de France

Maxwell, J. (1905). *Metapsychical phenomena.* Duckworth. (Original work published 1903)

Morin, A. S. (1860). Du magnétisme et des sciences occultes. Germer Baillière.

Morselli, E. (1908). *Psicologia e 'Spiritismo'* (Vol. 1). Fratelli Bocca.

Ochorowicz, J. (1896). La question de la fraude dans les expériences avec Eusapia Paladino. *Annales des Sciences Psychiques, 6,* 79–123.

Palmer, J., & Miller, B. (2015). Experimenter effects in parapsychology research. In E. Cardeña, J. Palmer, & D. Marcusson-Clavertz (Eds.), *Parapsychology: A handbook for the 21st century* (pp. 293–300). McFarland.

Roe, C. (2016). Experimenter as participant: What can we learn from the experimenter effect? *Mindfield, 8,* 89–97.

Sabatier, A., de Rochas, A., de Gramont, A., Maxwell, J., Dariex, X., & de Watteville, C. (1896). Expériences de l'Agnelas sur Eusapia Paladino. *Annales des Sciences Psychiques, 6,* 1–55.

Sardou, V. (1858). Des habitations de la planète Jupiter. *Revue Spirite: Journal d'Études Psychologiques, 1,* 223–232.

Schrenck-Notzing, A. de. (1925). *Les phénomènes physiques de la médiumnité.* Payot. (Original work published in German, 1920).

Sidgwick, Mrs. H. [E. M.]. (1915). A contribution to the study of the psychology of Mrs. Piper's trance phenomena. *Proceedings of the Society for Psychical Research, 28,* 1–657.

Sudre, R. (1926). *Introduction a la métapsychique humaine*. Payot.
Sudre, R. (1946) *Personnages d'au-delà*. Société des Éditions de Noël.
Tanner, A. (1910). *Studies in spiritism*. D. Appleton.
Venzano, J. (1907). A contribution to the study of materialisations. *Annals of Psychical Science, 6*, 75–119, 157–195.
Von Hartmann, E. (1885). *Spiritism*. Psychological Press.
White, R. A. (1977). The influence of experimenter motivation, attitudes, and methods of handling subjects on psi test results. In B. B. Wolman (Ed.), *Handbook of parapsychology* (pp. 273–301). Van Nostrand Reinhold.

ESP Displacement Effects: A Review of Pre-1940 Concepts and Qualitative Observations*

Carlos S. Alvarado†

Displacement ESP effects, a situation in which a percipient's response corresponds to a target other than the intended one, have traditionally been of interest to experimental parapsychologists. This may be seen in the publications of Carington (1940), Pratt and Foster (1950), and Soal (1940),[1] and in more recent studies (e.g., Child and Levi, 1980; Crandall and Hite, 1983; Palmer, Bogart, Jones, and Tart, 1977; for reviews of the literature see Braud, 1987; and Milton, 1986, 1988a, 1988b).

The concept of and evidence for displacement have generally been considered a modern development.[2] Thouless (1942, p. 11) gave credit to Whately Carington for its discovery. Braud (1987, pp. 209–210, 216) traced the concept from Abbot's (1938) publication to recent discussions. Neglect of the history of the concept, however, precedes these authors. Neither Abbot (1938) nor Carington (1940) mentioned previous discussions of displacement. In his initial publication on the topic, Soal (1940, pp. 152–153) said that Carington suggested that Soal look for displacement in the records of his card experiments. Soal did not mention previous observations on displacement except for remarks regarding some problems gifted subjects seem to have with ESP impressions. As Soal wrote: "They will refer to some trifling event known to the sitter, which happened last week or yesterday or a year ago, and make no mention at all of what is occupying their client's mind at the moment" (p. 153). (Soal had experienced phenomena of this type before, as reported in his paper on sittings with Mrs. Blanche Cooper [Soal, 1925].)

This paper is not a history of displacement but a review of publications that show that the concept of displacement is older than previously thought. It is possible that many of the observations to be discussed may be explained by normal means (e.g., sensory cues, chance coincidence, response bias) or criticized on methodological grounds (e.g., post hoc arguments, artifacts resulting from a small number of trials, or selected examples). Accordingly, they are not presented as evidence of ESP functioning.

Observations and Concepts of Displacement

Mesmerist Joseph W. Haddock (1851) reported an early example of displacement with his subject Emma. In a traveling clairvoyance test, after the subject had been hypnotized, Haddock asked Emma to "find" a relative of his in London. As he wrote: "She speedily found her, and began to describe her residence, etc.; but suddenly her attention ceased to be directed to my relative, and she became engrossed with the description of a magnificent residence, with its elegant and costly furniture" (p. 105). Haddock suspected that this referred to Buckingham Palace, an opinion he thought was confirmed when his relative (the ESP target) told him that she wanted Emma to

*Republished with permission from *Journal of the American Society for Psychical Research, 83*(3), 227–239, 1989.
†I am grateful to the Parapsychology Foundation for financial support of my bibliographic research in parapsychology. I wish to thank Richard S. Broughton, James Crandall, John Palmer, and Nancy L. Zingrone for useful suggestions for the improvement of this paper.

describe the palace. In Haddock's opinion, the cause of the unexpected description was that his "relative had wished her to go there; when brought into mesmeric connection with her, the active sentiment of her mind was communicated to Emma's mind, and by this means, her attention was unconsciously directed to the royal residence" (p. 106).[3] Displacement was also reported in ESP studies published by the Society for Psychical Research during the 1880s. Guthrie (1883) mentioned some "failures" during some of his thought-transference studies. In one trial, Guthrie reported "that although a certain article was placed for observation, a picture hanging on the wall a little above it was described" (p. 28).

This was attributed to the "wandering attention" of the agent. In later tests, Guthrie (1885) referred to "reminiscence" effects with the transmission of taste sensations and of drawings. In his words:

> In some taste experiments … it happened three times running that the taste which the percipient described was not the one which the agent was at that moment tasting, but the one which he had been tasting in the preceding trial a minute before, none of the substances having been named during the course of the experiments. In looking back over the volumes of diagrams I possess, I find that a good many which I considered failures at the time are evidently due to reminiscence of the preceding diagram which had not, in the majority of instances, been shown to the percipient in the interval. (p. 426)

In one of the earliest reports of ESP tests using statistics to evaluate the results, French physiologist Charles Richet (1884, pp. 643–645) described a series of trials in which the subjects had to select objects or cards through the movements of a wand (sort of like a divining rod) held in their two hands. Some of the failures mentioned by Richet were interesting. The subjects chose the wrong target on several occasions when they had reduced their selection to two similar cards or objects (e.g., two cards with, pictures of a man on a horse, two medallions). Regarding a trial using cards as targets, Richet wrote that there had been a "confusion between the two cards representing the same object" (p. 644, my translation).[4] On another occasion it was noticed that in three consecutive trials the card selected by the percipient was "the card exactly adjacent to the card thought" (p. 645, my translation) by the agent. Richet considered that the mistake was due to a misinterpretation of the movement of the wand.

In later tests, Richet (1888, p. 133) described medical diagnosis through ESP in which, on occasion, subjects produced veridical impressions about patients other than the intended ones.[5]

In other thought-transference tests, Rawson (1887, pp. 147–148; 1895, p. 5) noted that some of the reported successes were obtained with targets that had been originally selected to be used in the study but were then replaced by other targets. Similar observations have been reported by other investigators (e.g., Hodgson, 1892, p. 14; Hyslop, 1914b, pp. 155, 169; Schrenck-Notzing, 1891, p. 20).[6]

Sidgwick, Sidgwick, and Smith's (1889)[7] report of thought-transference experiments with numbers contained the following passage about the performance of a subject called P:

> After two successive correct guesses by P., the number 19 was drawn. We waited for 5½ minutes, and then, as P. had no impression, gave it up, and drew another number, which turned out to be 43. Twenty-five seconds after the new number was drawn P. said 19. This was recorded and another number drawn, viz., 75, 13 seconds after which P. said 43. Thus two numbers in succession were rightly given, but one stage later. (p. 161)

In later experiments, Sidgwick and Johnson (1892) reported instances of veridical guesses of numbers the agent "had been looking at in the trial immediately preceding, without having had any opportunity of learning by normal means what that number was" (p. 548). These observations, and those of the previously mentioned report, were interpreted as deferred telepathic impressions. That is, the telepathic message was received by the percipient, but it took some time to come to consciousness.[8]

Northcote W. Thomas (1905), once secretary of the Society for Psychical Research, reported the results of thought-transference experiments with playing cards. Thomas himself was occasionally a subject. Thomas noticed what he called "postponed success" in the results, that is, a "tendency for the suits and numbers of the card drawn for one experiment to appear in the guess following" (p. 156). The results of three series of experiments were reported (series A, C, and another one with no particular identification). In series A, postponed success was observed. Thomas noted that "successes and failures in direct results corresponded to failures and successes in postponed results" (p. 161). This he called an "inverse relation" (p. 159). Thomas also wrote about the tendency to guess in "cycles" (response biases or preferences) and about the relation of this response pattern to postponed successes:

> If, for example, hearts has been guessed, one of the other three suits is more likely to be guessed ... in the next trial, and, to a less extent, one of the two remaining ones in the following trial, and so on. The effect of this is, where the series is on the whole unsuccessful, to render a postponed success more probable than if chance alone regulated the choice of a suit. On the other hand, it tends to eliminate any effect due to telepathy, inasmuch as the selection is not made at random, so far as the percipient's conscious action is concerned ... It seems clear that, so far as direct successes are concerned, the result is to diminish the chances of success if there is any tele pathic element; the case is less clear in the case of postponed successes, but probably the chances of success are, after a previous failure, increased; for quite apart from any telepathic element, the chance of guessing right is nearer 1 in 3 than in four, and the cyclic tendency would not conflict perceptibly with any telepathic impulse to choose the right suit. (pp. 161–162)

The results of a later series C were not considered to provide evidence for telepathy. In other trials with two simultaneous percipients it was noticed that one percipient showed postponed success of the preceding guesses of the other percipient (p. 173).

Miles and Ramsden (1907, 1914) conducted ESP experiments in which Ramsden had to describe places that Miles was visiting or observing at a distance at a prearranged time. Some of the successes were not of the intended targets, but of other things seen by Miles earlier in the day or around the moment of the test (for examples see Miles & Ramsden, 1907, p. 74; 1914, pp. 284–285).

Alexander (1910) conducted telepathic drawing experiments in which he was the agent and his wife was the percipient. He noticed that in some of the series of trials, the percipient's response seemed to correspond to other drawings already used in previous tests or to be used in the next trial. In Alexander's words: "Where the response does fail to synchronize exactly it usually occurs immediately after or before the trial figure" (p. 284). He decided to count as a success a response anywhere in the individual series, because when he tried to send thc picture he had "nearly the whole series in mind at once" (p. 284) and because he had already drawn the target or he had been thinking about the next one.

German physician Carl Bruck (1924)[9] reported telepathic drawing tests with four subjects in two conditions: with and without hypnosis. In some trials it was observed that the subjects responded to the previously used target (not known to the subject) and to targets to be used in later trials, which were kept all together in a portfolio by the experimenter. The following is an example:

> In this case the original was a bottle; and the subject drew something like a hat. ... He then left the hat *in statu quo,* and proceeded to make a new drawing below it, of the top of a street lantern; and this corresponded in every detail to the original, waiting in the portfolio, for the next test. (Bruck, 1924, p. 305)

Bruck also mentioned that a possible explanation for this phenomenon was that the subject may have "telepathic access to the whole experimental complex prepared by the investigator" (Bruck, 1924, p. 305).[10]

The literature discussing the performance of well-known mediums and psychics also presents examples of displacement. As Hyslop (1907) has said in a discussion of confusions and errors in the mentations of mental mediums, it is possible that the information given by a medium "may be true in relation to some other incident or person than the sitter" (p. 582).[11] Examples of this, and other types of displacements, may be found with Gladys Osborne Leonard. Several reports on sittings with Mrs. Leonard contain examples of displacement because instead of the expected communications, the medium's statements referred to veridical events corresponding to the activities of distant individuals (e.g., Crandon, 1929; Salter, 1926, pp. 202–203). Some researchers noticed in Mrs. Leonard's well-known book tests that there were confusions (spatial displacements) between nearby books and particular pages inside the books (Irving, 1927, pp. 565–566; Sidgwick, 1921, pp. 262, 338–347). As Mrs. Sidgwick wrote regarding one of the examples she quoted: "There is a method in the errors which certainly suggests mistakes or confusion rather than reck less statements aided by chance" (p. 269).

Saltmarsh (1929, pp. 107–108) noticed with Mrs. Warren Elliott in stances in which the information given by the medium applied to the note taker instead of to the sitter.[12]

The phenomenon was also noticed with Polish psychic Stephan Ossowiecki. Schrenck-Notzing (1924/1972, p. 73) briefly reported that Ossowiecki described his studio in the middle of a reading about other persons. Geley (1924/1927, pp. 42, 78–79) published other examples of possible displacement in which Ossowiecki's ESP impressions corresponded to the persons that had prepared the ESP target in addition to the target itself.

French researcher Eugene Osty was interested in displacement, because he made special studies of errors during ESP performance. As he wrote regarding his studies of Mme. Morel and other subjects:

> "It happens sometimes ... that a subject instead of receiving and revealing knowledge concerning the individual desired, reveals states of life of another person, usually belonging to the same surroundings, or whom enquiry enables us easily to identify" (Osty, 1922/1923, p. 190). In chair tests conducted with psychic Pascal Forthuny, Osty (1926, p. 192) noticed that on occasion Forthuny's impressions did not correspond to the person in the selected chair, but to someone sitting in the front, back, or to the side of the target chair. Osty also mentioned that some impressions seemed to be a mixture of ESP information from two or three persons sitting nearby the target person.[13] In an article about Forthuny, Sudre (1926) said that because proximity in space was the factor leading to these confusions, a hypothesis could be proposed: "There exists a spatial element, likely a material one, a kind of 'fluid' which favors metagnomy" (p. 70).

In drawing tests Upton Sinclair did with his wife Mary Craig as percipient, "anticipations," that is, responses to existing targets to be used later, were observed (Sinclair, 1930, pp. 113–120, 124–136).[14] In a particularly interesting example there were several "anticipations." As Sinclair reported:

> Drawing number one was a tooth; Craig wrote: "First see a rooster. Then elephant." Drawing number two was an elephant; and Craig wrote: "Elephant came again. I try to suppress it, and see lines, and a spike sticking some way into something." She drew it, and it seems clear that the "spike" is the elephant's tusk, and the head of the "spike" is the elephant's eye … Next, number three was the rooster. But Craig had set "rooster" down in her mind as a blunder. (Sinclair, 1930, p. 124)

Although the drawing the percipient made resembled the target (the rooster) in some ways, Mrs Sinclair did not identify it as such. As Sinclair wrote, his wife resisted correct images if they had been "anticipated," because they were attributed to memory (p. 136).

Concluding Remarks

I have already stated that it was not my intention to present evidence for displacement, but rather to document the existence of the concept before the studies of Abbot (1938) and Carington (1940). Nonetheless, it should be stated again that most of this material is open to criticisms such as reliance on post hoc analysis and chance coincidence.

As was seen in the previous section, instances of alleged displacement have been observed in different contexts (mediumistic and nonmediumistic settings, experimental and quasi-experimental conditions), with a variety of methodologies (forced choice and free response, with and without a designated agent) and using different target types (numbers, drawings, persons). It is interesting to note that several explanations for the phenomenon have been offered, such as: competing ESP signals (Osty, 1927), confusion due to target similarity (Richet, 1884), confusion due to target associations and memory images (Warcollier, 1938), wandering attention of agent (Guthrie, 1883), spatial proximity (Sudre, 1926), deferred ESP impressions (Sidgwick & Johnson, 1892), response biases (Thomas, 1905), ESP of the whole target pool (Bruck, 1924). These explanations have been proposed after the fact because, unlike more recent studies (e.g., Crandall & Hite, 1983), past researchers have considered the phenomenon as an incidental occurrence and did not pursue displacement as the primary objective of their studies.

Some concepts about displacement in the recent literature have precedents in some of the material discussed in the preceding section. For example, Thomas's (1905) "inverse relation" seems similar to more recent observations regarding psi-missing results on the intended targets when significant displacement was observed (e.g., Child and Levi, 1980; Crandall and Hite, 1983; Palmer et al., 1977). Also, Thomas's comments about the effects of response biases (pp. 161–162) are similar to later discussions of the "tendency to avoid repeating calls [that] will increase the probability of obtaining displaced scores in the direction *opposite* to the direct scores" (Burdick & Broughton, 1987, pp. 117–118; see also Bartlett, 1949).[15]

Braud (1987) observed that in some free-response ESP experiments he has conducted, the percipient's impressions "match very closely those of the immediately preceding percipient" (p. 214). Influence between percipients was also noted by Thomas (1905, p. 173) and by Warcollier (1938, pp. 22, 241, 243–244).

Crandall's (1987; Crandall & Covey, 1986) study of background stimuli in relation to displacement may be related to observations and conjectures of the effectiveness of peripheral, forgotten, or subconscious material as ESP targets (e.g., R[awson], 1887, pp. 147–148; Schrenck-Notzing, 1891, p. 20; Warcollier, 1938, pp. 166–185).

Regardless of possible evidential problems with the above-mentioned ideas and observations, they may provide hypotheses for further research on displacement. One line of investigation that may prove fruitful is an examination of the occurrence of deferment. Another idea deserving study is the notion of obtaining information about subconscious material, associations, and peripheral stimuli through ESP. Perhaps it may be possible to induce displacement by manipulating knowledge about the target in selected individuals (e.g., subliminally), or in the handling of objects by different persons, following psychometric ideas.

In summary, the concept of displacement has a long tradition in parapsychology. Perhaps an awareness of this material, even if methodologically weak, may prove of some use to those currently interested in the subject.

Notes

1 Soal's work has probably been the best known and most influential set of studies on displacement (see also Soal and Bateman, 1954, pp. 124–128, 148–167, 176–190, 208–211, 216–218; Soal and Goldney, 1943; Soal and Pratt, 1951). Unfortunately, there are good reasons to suspect that Soal altered some of his figures to simulate significant results (Markwick, 1978).

2 Two exceptions are Milton (1986, pp. 49–50) and Thalbourne (1981, p. 19), who mentioned two studies discussed in this paper (Guthrie, 1885; Sinclair, 1930).

3 The idea that ESP information from sources other than the subject may interfere with the subject's mentation by providing veridical information unrelated to the target is frequently found in the literature. Balfour (1888, pp. 353–354), Hettinger (1940, p. 184), and Osty (1927, pp. 262–264, 267–270) have speculated on the ESP influence of the experimenter and other observers. Warcollier (1938, pp. 22, 241–244) thought that in group telepathy experiments "mental contagion," or influence between percipients, could occur instead of responses to the target. Prince (1924) speculated on similar lines when he wrote that mediumistic communicators fail to get through a medium "because of the interference of the thoughts of others" (p. 168). For a more recent discussion of the concept of interference in relation to displacement, see Rogo (1979).

4 Regarding these observations, Edmund Gurney (1884) speculated on the possibility that a telepathic impression "is to reveal itself when—and only when—the other element, the image, finds its fellow in a conscious percept, the actual picture of the object" (p. 246). Presumably, Gurney meant that the association of similar images could facilitate confusions when there were two similar targets.

5 Osty (1930, pp. 99–104) discussed errors in paranormal diagnosis that he attributed to false beliefs acquired through ESP from observers about the illnesses.

6 The underlying assumption here is that ESP of the memory, subconscious impressions, or material in the back of the mind of (or peripherally perceived by) an individual can influence or be perceived even when an attempt to receive or transmit a different target is made. Quevedo (1968/1972, pp. 347–381) and Warcollier (1938, pp. 166–185) discuss this topic with examples.

7 For questions about Smith's honesty, see Gauld (1965, pp. 55–57) and Hall (1964, pp. 104–149).

8 Regarding deferment or latency of ESP impressions, see Gurney, Myers, and Podmore (1886, Vol. I, pp. 56, 70–71, 201, 519–520), Sidgwick et al. (1889, p. 161), and Salt marsh (1929, p. IOI). Despard and Campbell ("Experiments in Thought-Transference," 1893, p. 5) also reported "deferred successes" in some of their thought-transference experiments with playing cards.

9 The official report of these tests, which I have seen but have not used in this paper, was published in book form a year later (Bruck, 1925). For further examples of displacement in Bruck's research, see Murphy and Dale (1943, pp. 10–12).

10 Commenting about the explanation for the above-mentioned example with the street lantern, two reviewers of Brock's work have expressed different opinions. One said that because the experimenter knew the

content of the target pool, the percipient could have obtained the information telepathically from his mind (Schiller, 1925, p. 468), whereas the other said that the incident shows that "telepathy is nothing but a particular case of metagnomy [clairvoyance]" (Sudre, 1925, p. 184, my translation).

11 Regarding Hyslop, it is of interest to study his ideas on the process of mediumistic communication (Hyslop, 1914a, 1919, pp. 107–121). What we may consider to be examples of displacement were discussed by Hyslop (1919) as examples of crossed communications (pp. 119–120) and of the "diversion of the medium's subconscious attention from the persons wanted" (p. 120). Salter (1930) considered, in relation to Mrs. Leonard's mediumship, that confusions and irrelevance in the communications could be created when information obtained through the sitters' minds "may be wrongly associated with the communicator" (p. 320).

12 There are examples of this phenomenon with Mrs. Piper (Hodgson, 1892, p. 109) and with Mrs. Soule, known as Mrs. Chenoweth (Hyslop, 1919, p. 120).

13 Similar phenomena have been reported elsewhere. For example, Hettinger (1940, p. 38) noticed in his psychometry experiments that "readings" of objects not only corresponded to the object's owners but also to persons related to the owners in some way. See also Hyslop's (1919, p. 121) discussion of cases of "interfusion" of thought of more than one person in mediumistic communications.

14 See also Prince's (1932, pp. 57–60) description and comments about the "anticipations." In a review of Sinclair's book, Sidgwick (1930, p. 345) argued that because the agent was acquainted with the target pool, telepathy was a more likely explanation of "anticipations" than precognition.

15 For a previous discussion on the statistical implications of number habits not related to displacement, see R. A. Fisher's comments appended to Jephson's (1928, pp. 269–271) report.

References

[Abbot, C. G.]. (1938). A scientist tests his own ESP ability. *Journal of Parapsychology, 2,* 65–70.

Alexander, H. B. (1910). Experiments in telepathy. *Journal of the American Society for Psychical Research, 4,* 281–306.

Balfour, A. B. (1888). Some remarks on Professor Richet's experiments on the possibility of clairvoyant perceptions of drawings. *Journal of the Society for Psychical Research, 3,* 348–354.

Bartlett, M. S. (1949). The statistical significance of "dispersed hits" in card-guessing experiments. *Proceedings of the Society for Psychical Research, 48,* 336–338.

Braud, W. (1987). Dealing with displacement. *Journal of the American Society for Psychical Research, 81,* 209–231.

Bruck, C. (1924). Experimental telepathy: Tests by Dr. Carl Bruck, M.D., Berlin, on the transmission of drawings. Adapted by Dr. Alfred Gradenwitz from the investigator's report. *Scientific American, 130,* 304–305.

Bruck, C. (1925). *Experimentelle telepathie.* Julius Puttmann.

Burdick, D. S., & Broughton, R. S. (1987). Conditional displacement analysis. *Journal of Parapsychology, 51,* 117–123.

Carington, W. (1940). Experiments on the paranormal cognition of drawings: I. Experiments I to IVB. *Proceedings of the Society for Psychical Research, 46,* 34–151.

Child, I. L., & Levi, A. (1980). The use of judges' ratings to test hypotheses about psi processes. *Journal of the American Society for Psychical Research, 74,* 171–181.

Crandall, J. E. (1987). Further studies of the effects of background stimuli in psi-missers. *Journal of the American Society for Psychical Research, 81,* 11–21.

Crandall, J. E., & Covey, M. K. (1986). A model for receptivity to background stimuli in ESP research, with further data. *Journal of the American Society for Psychical Research, 80,* 393–408.

Crandall, J. E., & Hite, D. D. (1983). Psi-missing and displacement: Evidence for improperly focused psi? *Journal of the American Society for Psychical Research, 77,* 209–228.

Crandon, L. R. G. (1929). Feda and Walter: Cross correspondences between the mediumship of Mrs. Leonard and of Margery; brought out in a sitting with Mrs. Leonard. *Psychic Research: Journal of the American Society for Psychical Research, 23,* 295–313.

Experiments in Thought–Transference. (1893). *Journal of the Society for Psychical Research, 6,* 4–9.

Gauld, A. (1965). Mr[.] Hall and the S.P.R. *Journal of the Society for Psychical Research, 43,* 53–62.

Geley, G. (1927). *Clairvoyance and materialisation* (S. de Brath, Trans.). T. Fisher Unwin. (Original work published 1924)

Gurney, E. (1884). M. Richet's recent researches in thought-transference. *Proceedings of the Society for Psychical Research, 2,* 239–264.

Gurney, E., Myers, F. W. H., & Podmore, F. (1886). *Phantasms of the Living* (2 vols.). Trübner.

Guthrie, M. (1883). An account of some experiments in thought–transference. *Proceedings of the Society for Psychical Research, 2,* 24–42.

Guthrie, M. (1885). Further report on experiments in thought-transference at Liverpool. *Proceedings of the Society for Psychical Research, 3,* 424–452.

Haddock, J. W. (1851). *Somnolism & psycheism* (2nd ed.). James S. Hodson.

Hall, T. H. (1964). *The strange case of Edmund Gurney.* Gerald Duckworth.

Hettinger, J. [1940]. *The ultra-perceptive faculty.* Rider.

Hodgson, R. (1892). A record of observations of certain phenomena of trance. *Proceedings of the Society for Psychical Research, 8,* 1–167.

Hyslop, J. H. (1907). Preliminary report on the trance phenomena of Mrs. Smead. *Proceedings of the American Society for Psychical Research, 1,* 525–722.

Hyslop, J. H. (1914a). A hypothetical process of communication. *Journal of the American Society for Psychical Research, 8,* 377–389.

Hyslop, J. H. (1914b). Telepathic experiments. *Proceedings of the American Society for Psychical Research, 8,* 152–199.

Hyslop, J. H. (1919). *Contact with the other world.* Century.

Irving, W. S. (1927). More thoughts on trance phenomena. *Proceedings of the Society for Psychical Research, 36,* 555–572.

Jephson, I. (1928). Evidence for clairvoyance in card-guessing: A report on some recent experiments. *Proceedings of the Society for Psychical Research, 38,* 223–271.

Markwick, B. (1978). The Soal-Goldney experiments with Basil Shackleton: New evidence of data manipulation. *Proceedings of the Society for Psychical Research, 56,* 250–277.

Miles, C., & Ramsden, H. (1907). Experiments in thought-transference. *Proceedings of the Society for Psychical Research, 21,* 60–93.

Miles, C., & Ramsden, H. (1914). Experiments in thought-transference. *Proceedings of the Society for Psychical Research, 27,* 279–317.

Milton, J. (1986). *Displacement effects, role of the agent and mentation categories in relation to ESP performance.* Unpublished doctoral dissertation, University of Edinburgh, Scotland.

Milton, J. (1988a). Critical review of the displacement effect: I. The relationship between displacement and scoring on the intended target. *Journal of Parapsychology, 52,* 29–55.

Milton, J. (1988b). Critical review of the displacement effect: II. The relationship between displacement and psychological and situational variables. *Journal of Parapsychology, 52,* 127–156.

Murphy, G., & Dale, L. A. (1943). Concentration versus relaxation in relation to telepathy. *Journal of the American Society for Psychical Research, 37,* 2–15.

Osty, E. (1923). *Supernormal faculties in man: An experimental study* (S. de Brath, Trans.). Methuen. (Original work published 1922)

Osty, E. (1926). Un metagnome: M. Pascal Forthuny. *Revue Métapsychique, 3,* 171–214.

Osty, E. (1927). Une utilisation practique de la connaissance supranormale. *Revue Métapsychique, 4,* 238–274.

Osty, E. (1930). Le diagnostic des maladies par Jes sujets doues de connaissance paranormale. *Revue Métapsychique, 2,* 97–141.

Palmer, J., Bogart, D. N., Jones, S. M., & Tart, C. T. (1977). Scoring patterns in an ESP ganzfeld experiment. *Journal of the American Society for Psychical Research, 71,* 121–145.

Pratt, J. G., & Foster, E. B. (1950). Displacement in ESP card tests in relation to hits and misses. *Journal of Parapsychology, 14,* 37–52.
Prince, W. F. (ED.) (1924). Five sittings with Mrs. Sanders. *Proceedings of the American Society for Psychical Research, 18,* 1–177.
[Prince, W. F.]. (1932). The Sinclair experiments demonstrating telepathy. *Bulletin of the Boston Society for Psychic Research, 16,* 1–86.
Quevedo, O. G. (19 2). *El Rostro Oculto de la Mente* (A. M. Sancho, Trans.). Santander, Spain: "Sal Terrae." (Original work published 1968)
Rawson, H. G. (1887). Letter to the editor. *Journal of the Society for Psychical Research, 3,* 146–148.
Rawson, H. G. (1895). Experiments in thought-transference. *Proceedings of the Society for Psychical Research, 11,* 2–17.
Richet, C. (1884). La suggestion mentale et le calcul des probabilités. *Revue Philosophique de la France et de l'Étranger, 18,* 609–674.
Richet C. (1888). Relation de diverses experiences sur la transmission mentale, la lucidité, et autres phénomènes non explicables par les données scientifiques actuelles. *Proceedings of the Society for Psychical Research, 5,* 18–168.
Rogo, D. S. (1979). The concept of extrasensory "noise." *Research Letter, 9,* 40–54.
Salter, Mrs. W. H. [H. DEG.]. (1926). A report on some recent sittings with Mrs. Leonard. *Proceedings of the Society for Psychical Research, 36,* 187–332.
Salter, Mrs. W. H. [H DE G.]. (1930). Some incidents occurring at sittings with Mrs. Leonard which may throw light upon their *modus operandi. Proceedings of the Society for Psychical Research, 39,* 306–332.
Saltmarsh, H. F. (1929). Report on the investigation of some sittings with Mrs. Warren Elliott. *Proceedings of the Society for Psychical Research, 39,* 47–184.
Schiller, F. C. S. (1925). Review of *Experimentelle Telepathie* by C. Bruck. *Proceedings of the Society for Psychical Research, 35,* 466–469.
Schrenck-Notzing, Baron [A. F.] VON. (1891). Experimental studies in thought-transference. *Proceedings of the Society for Psychical Research, 7,* 3–22.
Schrenck–Notzing, A. F. Von. (1972). Un experimento de clarividencia con Stephan Ossowiecki. In A. F. von Schrenck-Notzing, *Problemas Básicos de la Parapsicologiá* (G. Walther, Ed.; S. Belaieff, Trans.) (pp. 71–79). Troquel. (Original work published 1924)
Sidgwick, Mrs[.] H. [E. M.]. (1921). An examination of book-tests obtained in sittings with Mrs. Leonard. *Proceedings of the Society for Psychical Research, 31,* 241–400.
Sidgwick, E. M. (1930). Review of *Mental Radio* by U. Sinclair. *Proceedings of the Society for Psychical Research, 39,* 343–346.
Sidgwick, Mrs. H. [E. M.], & Johnson, A. (1892). Experiments in thought-transference. *Proceedings of the Society for Psychical Research, 8,* 536–596.
Sidgwick, Professor [H. J.], Sidgwick, Mrs. H. [E. M.], & Smith, G. A. (1889). Experiments in thought-transference. *Proceedings of the Society for Psychical Research, 6,* 128–170.
Sinclair, U. (1930). *Mental Radio.* Author.
Soal, S. G. (1925). A report on some communications received through Mrs. Blanche Cooper. *Proceedings of the Society for Psychical Research, 35,* 471–594.
Soal, S. G. (1940). Fresh light on card-guessing—Some new effects. *Proceedings of the Society for Psychical Research, 46,* 152–198.
Soal, S. G., & Bateman, F. (1954). *Modern experiments in telepathy.* Yale University Press.
Soal, S. G., & Goldney, K. M. (1943). Experiments in precognitive telepathy. *Proceedings of the Society for Psychical Research, 47,* 21–150.
Soal, S. G., & Pratt, J. G. (1951). ESP performance and target sequence. *Journal of Parapsychology, 15,* 192–215.
Sudre, R. (1925). Transmission mentale de dessins. *Revue Métapsychique, 3,* 184–185.
Sudre, R. (1926). A new clairvoyant: The French writer, Pascal Forthuny. *Journal of the American Society for Psychical Research, 20,* 65–77.

Thalbourne, M. A. (1981). Some experiments on the paranormal cognition of drawings: With special reference to personality and attitudinal variables. Unpublished doctoral dissertation, University of Edinburgh, Scotland.

Thomas, N. W. (1905). *Thought transference: A critical and historical review of the evidence for telepathy, with a record of new experiments, 1902–1903.* Alexander Moring.

Thouless, R. H. (1942). The present position of experimental research into telepathy and related phenomena. *Proceedings of the Society for Psychical Research, 47,* 1–19.

Warcollier, R. (1938). *Experimental telepathy* (G. Murphy, Ed.; J. B. Gridley & M. K. Murphy, Trans.). Boston Society for Psychic Research.

Historical Notes on Doubles and Travelling Spirits*

Carlos S. Alvarado†

I. Introduction

In the past a variety of authors have discussed phenomena such as apparitions of the living, out-of-body (OBEs) and near-death experiences (NDEs), as examples of the existence of a double, or a subtle body (overviews include Battersby, 1942; Bozzano, 1934/1937; Davies, 1998; Shirley, n.d.). This hypothetical body (or bodies), said to interpenetrate the physical body, has a long history of discussion dating from antiquity, as has the idea that human consciousness can travel out of its body.

In a series of papers, of which this is the introductory part, I will discuss the topic using some of the literature published from the nineteenth century on. Rather than present systematic discussions of the history of these ideas in the papers that follow, my purpose is to present excerpts from the mesmeric, spiritualistic and psychical research literatures illustrating ideas about travels out of the body and subtle bodies. I will first present an overview of ideas and experiences, while in later instalments I will focus on specific issues.

Accounts of Phenomena

Accounts of experiences have created the belief in the possibility of leaving the body and in concepts of subtle bodies. In the seventh book of his *Natural History* Pliny the Elder (1890, p. 210) wrote that:

> … the soul of Hermotinus of Clazomenae was in the habit of leaving his body, and wandering into distant countries, whence it brought back numerous accounts of various things, which could not have been obtained by anyone but a person who was present. The body, in the meantime, was left apparently lifeless. … At last, however, his enemies, the Cantharidae … burned the body, so that the soul, on its return, was deprived of its sheath, as it were.

Plutarch, who died around 125 A.D., recorded such an experience in one of his essays (Schilleto, 1888):

> Thespesius of Soli … who lived in this city with us for some time, had been very profligate during the early part of his life, and had quickly run through his property, and for some time owing to his straits had given himself up to bad practices. … He fell headlong down from a great height, and though he had received no wound (p. 357) nor even a blow, the fall did for him, but three days after (just as he was about to be buried) he recovered. He soon picked up his strength again, and went home, and so changed his manner of life that people would hardly credit it … [Thespesius said]

*Republished with permission from the Society for Psychical Research. *Paranormal Review* (2009–2011), *50*, 6–15; 51, 3–7; 52, 13–16; 53, 3–6; 54, 6–9; 56, 3–8; 57, 3–7; 58, 12–18; 59, 18–21; 60, 3–6; 61, 3–11.

†I thank the Society for Psychical Research for a grant that allowed me to prepare this series of papers. Nancy L. Zingrone provided useful editorial suggestions for the improvement of this paper.

that, when his soul left the body, the change he first underwent was as if he were a pilot thrown violently into the sea out of a ship. Then raising himself up a little, he thought he recovered the power of breathing again altogether, and looked round him in every direction, as if one eye of the soul was open. But he saw none of the things he had ever seen before, but stars enormous in size and at immense distance from one another, sending forth a wonderful and intense brightness of colour, so that the soul was borne along and moved about everywhere quickly and easily, like a ship in fair weather. But omitting most of the sights he saw, he said that the souls of the dead mounted into the air, which yielded to them and formed fiery bubbles, and then, when each bubble quietly broke, they assumed human forms, light in weight but with different kinds of motion, for some leapt about with wonderful agility and darted straight upwards, while others like spindles flitted round all together in a circle, some in an upward direction, some in a downward, with mixed and confused motion, hardly stopping at all, or only after a very long time. As to most of these he was ignorant who they were, but he saw two or three that he knew, and tried to approach them and talk with them, but they would not listen to him, and did not seem to be in their right minds, but out of their senses and distraught, avoiding every sight and touch, and at first turned round and round alone, but afterwards meeting many other souls whirling round and in the same condition as themselves, they moved about promiscuously with no particular object in view, and uttered (p. 358) inarticulate sounds, like yells, mixed with wailing and terror. Other souls in the upper part of the air seemed joyful, and frequently approached one another in a friendly way, and avoided those troubled souls, and seemed to mark their displeasure by keeping themselves to themselves, and their joy and delight by extension and expansion. At last he said he saw the soul of a relation, that he thought he knew but was not quite sure, as he died when he was a boy, which came up to him and said to him, "Welcome, Thespesius". And he wondering, and saying that his name was not Thespesius but Aridseus, the soul replied, "That was your old name, but henceforth it will be Thespesius. For assuredly you are not dead, but by the will of the gods are come here with your intellect, for the rest of your soul you have left in the body like an anchor; and as a proof of what I say both now and hereafter notice that the souls of the dead have no shadow and do not move their eyelids'. Thespesius, on hearing these words, pulled himself somewhat more together again, and began to use his reason, and looking more closely he noticed that an indistinct and shadow-like line was suspended over him, while the others shone all round and were transparent, but were not all alike; for some were like the full-moon at its brightest, throwing out one smooth even and continuous colour, others had spots or light marks here and there, while others were quite variegated and strange to the sight, with black spots like snakes, while others again had dim scratches. … [p. 360]

After he had said this, Thespesius' kinsman [who had shown him many things] hurried him at great speed through immense space, as it seemed to him, though he travelled as easily and straight as if he were carried on the wings of the sun's rays. At last he got to an extensive and bottomless abyss, where his strength left him, as he found was the case with the other souls there: for keeping together and making swoops, like birds, they flitted all round the abyss, but did not venture to pass over it. To internal view it resembled the caverns of Bacchus, being beautiful throughout … with trees and green foliage and flowers of all kinds, and it breathed a soft and gentle air, laden with scents marvellously pleasant, and producing the effect that wine does on those who are topers; for the souls were elevated by its fragrance, and gay and blithe with one another: and the whole spot was full of mirth and laughter, and such songs as emanate from gaiety and enjoyment. And Thespesius' kinsman told him that this was the way Dionysus went up to heaven by, and by which he afterwards took up Semele, and it was called the place of Oblivion. But he would not let Thespesius stay there, much as he wished, but forcibly dragged him away. … [p. 361]

> Next Thespesius travelled as far in another direction, and seemed to see a great crater into which several rivers emptied themselves, one whiter than the foam of the sea or snow, another like the purple of the rainbow, and others of various hues whose brightness was apparent at some distance, but when he got nearer the air became thinner and the colours grew dim, and the crater lost all its gay colours but white. And he saw three genii sitting together in a triangular position, mixing the rivers together in certain proportions. ... [p. 362]
>
> After this Thespesius and his guide turned to see those that were undergoing punishment. And at first they saw only distressing and pitiable sights, but after that, Thespesius, little expecting it, found himself among his friends and acquaintances and kinsfolk who were being punished, and undergoing dreadful sufferings and hideous and bitter tortures, and who wept and wailed to him. And at last he descried his father coming up out of a certain gulf covered with marks and scars, stretching out his hands, and not allowed to keep silence, but compelled by those that presided over his torture to confess that he had been an accursed wretch and poisoned some strangers that had gold, and during his lifetime had escaped the detection of everybody; but had been found out here, and his guilt brought home to him, for which he had already suffered much, and was being dragged on to suffer more. So great was his consternation and fear that he did not dare to intercede or beg for his father's release, but wishing to turn and flee he could no longer see his gentle and kind guide, but he was thrust forward by some persons horrible to look at, as if some dire necessity compelled him to go through with the business, and saw that the shades of those that had been notorious criminals and punished in their lifetime were not so severely tortured here or like the others, but had an incomplete ... though toilsome punishment for their irrational passions. ... [p. 363]
>
> So much did Thespesius behold, but as he intended to return a horrible dread came upon him. For a woman, marvellous in appearance and size, took hold of him and said to him, "Come here that you may the better remember everything you have seen". And she was about to strike him with a red-hot iron pin, such as the encaustic painters use, ... when another woman prevented her; and he was suddenly sucked up, as through ... a pipe, by a strong and violent wind, and lit upon his own body, and woke up and found that he was close to his tomb [p. 365].

Several other experiences, which we will refer today as NDEs, were reported in later times, including the ones written up by Hill (1711) and by Wiltse (1889). But there were also many OBEs that did not take place while the person was near death. One example is those experiences reported to take place in magnetized individuals. One of these, Bruno Binet, stated: "In the state I am now ...I am out of my body, I perceive it seated on the chair; I walk about in my room without being seen or felt by you whom I touch" (Cahagnet, 1851, Vol. 1, p. 19).

Other experiences were reported in different circumstances. Italian spiritist Ernesto Volpi (1890) was under the influence of chloroform. He wrote, "my self, that is, my soul and my thinking reason, clothed in corporeal form, was two meters from my body ... I saw my body immobile on the bed" (p. 319).

In another report a Mrs Stone wrote about an experience when she was a girl in school: "I was in an upper room in the school, standing with some others, in a class opposite our teacher ...; suddenly I found myself by her side, and looking towards the class saw myself distinctly—a slim, pale girl, in a white frock and pinafore" (Gurney, Myers and Podmore, 1886, Vol. 2, p. 85, footnote).

Medium D. D. Home had an unusual and complex OBE while he was thinking about death. He wrote in his autobiography, *Incidents in My Life* (1864):

> One evening I had been pondering deeply on that change which the world calls death, and on the eternity that lies beyond, until wearied I found relief in prayer, and then in sleep. My last

waking consciousness had been that of perfect trust in God, and a sense of gratitude to Him for the enjoyment I received from contemplating the beauties of the material creation. … It appeared to me that, as I closed my eyes to earthly things, an inner perception was quickened within me, till at last reason was as active as when I was awake. I, with vivid distinctness, remember asking myself the question, whether I was asleep or no? when, to my amazement, I heard a voice which seemed no natural, that my heart bounded with joy as I recognised it as the voice of one who while on earth was far too pure for such a world as ours, and who, in passing to that brighter home, had promised to watch over and protect me. … She said, "Fear not, Daniel, I am near you; the vision you are about to have is that of death, yet you will not die. Your spirit must again return to the body in a few hours. Trust in God and his good angels: all will be well". Here the voice became lost [p. 43] … away. … This was but momentary, for almost instantaneously came rushing with a fearful rapidity memories of the past; my thoughts bore the semblance of realities, and every action appeared as an eternity of existence. During the whole time I was aware of a benumbing and chilling sensation which stole over my body, but the more inactive my nervous system became, the more active was my mind, till at length I felt as if I had fallen from the brink of some fearful precipice, and as I fell, all became obscure, and my whole body became one dizzy mass, only kept alive by a feeling of terror, until sensation and thought simultaneously ceased, and I knew no more. How long I had lain thus I know not, but soon I felt that I was about to awaken in a most dense obscurity; terror had now given place to a pleasurable feeling, accompanied by a certitude of some one dearly loved being near me, yet invisible … instinctively I realized that beyond the surrounding obscurity lay an ocean of silver-toned light. I was at this instant brought to a consciousness of light, by seeing the whole of my nervous system, as it were, composed of thousands of electrical scintillations, which here and there, as in the created nerve, took the form of currents, darting their rayons over the whole body in a manner most marvellous; still this was but a cold electrical light and besides, it was external. Gradually, however, I saw that the extremities were less luminous, and the finer membranes surrounding the brain became as it were glowing, and I felt that thought and action were no longer connected with the earthly tenement, but that they were in a spirit-body in every respect similar to the body which I knew to have been mine, and which I now saw lying motionless before me on the bed. The only link which held the two forms together [p. 44] seemed to be a silvery-like light, which proceeded from the brain; and, as if it were a response to my earlier waking thoughts, the same voice, only that it was now more musical than before, said, "Death is but a second birth, corresponding in every respect to the natural birth, and should the uniting link now be severed, you could never again enter the body. As I told you, however, this will not be". …

It now appeared to me that I was waking from a dream of darkness to a sense of light; but such a glorious light. Never did earthly sun shed such rays, strong in beauty, soft in love, warm in life-giving glow, and as my last idea of earthly light had been the reflex of my own body, so now this heavenly light came from those I saw standing about me. Yet the light was not of their creating, but was shed on them from a higher and purer source … and now I was bathed in light, and about me were those for whom I had sorrowed. … One that I had never known on earth then drew near and said, "You will come with me, Daniel" I could only reply, that it was impossible to move, inasmuch as I could not feel that my nature had a power over my new spirit body. To this he replied, "Desire and you will accomplish your desires which are not sinful, desires being as prayers to the Divinity, and He answereth the every prayer of His children", [p. 45]

> For the first time I now looked to see what sustained my body, and I found that it was but a purple tinted cloud, and that as I desired to go onward with my guide, the cloud appeared as if disturbed by a gentle breeze, and in its movements I found I was wafted upward until I saw the earth, as a vision, far, far below us. Soon, I found that we had drawn nearer, and were just hovering over a cottage that I had never seen; and I also saw the inmates, but had never met them in life. The walls of the cottage were not the least obstruction to my sight, they were only as if constructed of a dense body of air, yet perfectly transparent, and the same might be said of every article of furniture. I perceived that the inmates were asleep, and I saw the various spirits who were watching over the sleepers. ...
>
> I was most deeply interested in all this, when my guide said, "We must now return". When I found myself near my body, I turncd to thc onc who had remained near my bed, and said, "Why must I return so soon, for it can be but a few moments I have been with you, and I would fain see more, and remain near you longer?" She replied, "It is now many hours since you came to us; but here we take no cognizance of time, and as you are here in spirit, you too have lost this knowledge; we would have you with us, but this must not be at present. Return to earth, love your fellow-creatures, love truth, and in so doing, you will serve the God of infinite love, who careth for and loveth all. May the Father of mercies bless you, Daniel!"
>
> I heard no more, but seemed to sink as in a swoon, [p. 46] until consciousness was merged into a feeling that earth with its trials lay before me. ... And when I opened my eyes to material things, I found that the little star had given way to the sun, which had been above the horizon about four hours; making in all about eleven hours that this vision had lasted. My limbs were so dead, that at least half an hour elapsed before I could reach the bell rope, to bring any one to my assistance, and it was only by continued friction that, at the end of an hour, I had sufficient force to enable me to stand upright [p. 47].

The idea that consciousness or a subtle body (not the same concept) could leave the body was spread by the writings of individuals representing a variety of movements. According to Annie Besant (1892):

> "Man, according to the Theosophical teaching ... has a septenary constitution. Putting it in yet another way, man's nature has seven aspects ... is composed of Seven Principles. ... Man's consciousness is able to function through as many of these aspects, on as many of these planes, as have been already evolved in him into activity" (p. 6).
>
> William Q. Judge stated in *The Ocean of Theosophy* (1893):
>
> "In the ordinary man who has not been trained in practical occultism or who has not the faculty by birth, the astral body cannot go more than a few feet from the physical one. ... But there are those who, by reason of practices pursued in former lives on the earth, have a power born with them of unconsciously sending out the astral body. These are mediums, some seers, and many hysterical, catalcptic, and scrofulous people" (p. 41).

There were also ideas coming from other movements. An example was the French spiritistic tradition, whose representatives argued that, in addition to the physical body and the spirit, there was a perispirit that provided a link between both bodies and was involved in the various manifestations of the double. In his *Spiritisme Expérimentale: Le Livre des Médiums* (1863), Allan Kardec wrote about the phenomena of bicorporeity. In later papers I will present parts of the writings of Kardec and of his follower Gabriel Delanne (1904/1899).

The topic received some discussion in the nineteenth-century spiritualist literature. Examples include "The Travelling of the Spirit During the Life of the Body" (Hardinge, 1875), "Spirit Travelling During Bodily Sleep" (Kislingbury, 1875), and "Do Mediums Leave their Bodies?" (Peebles, 1872). Furthermore, a variety of occultists discussed the topic (e.g., Encausse, 1902; Hartmann, 1888). Ernest Bose (1896) described the astral body as a perfect double of the physical body, emanating from it in the form of rays. He wrote:

> Man can project … its astral body through a strong concentration of will, at least in part, because if it is projected completely, this will be death, [p. 137] … The astral body is … sort of a light, intangible, imponderable entity absolutely imperceptible to our material senses, yet it wraps, surrounds, and penetrates us. … The astral body is the very life of man [p. 138]. It is the astral which serves as balsam to our wounds, our scars, our injuries of all sorts. … The astral is the essential principle of life, so when the astral body leaves man, he dies. [p. 139]

The concept of projection or exteriorization was also supported by those cases in which veridical information was obtained by the experient. An example is those cases of mesmerized individuals who visited distant locations unknown to them and described correctly the surroundings or events taking place thereof (e.g., Haddock, 1851). A later paper in this series will focus on this topic. In addition, there were cases in which the person having an experience in contexts other than being mesmerized obtained veridical information.

Also related to the mesmeric tradition were the magnetic experiments of Albert De Rochas (1899) regarding the so-called exteriorization of sensibility. In those tests De Rochas claimed that the tactile sensations of magnetized individuals could be projected out of the physical body. De Rochas (1895, 1906) conducted further work to separate subtle bodies from the physical one. Similarly, in his book *Le Fantôme des Vivants*, Hector Durville (1909) reported tests he conducted with magnetized individuals to detect the double physically and to observe its perceptual capabilities.

Furthermore, OBEs were popularized by other types of publications, notably, the writings of individuals having recurrent OBEs that appeared during the twentieth century. These included authors such as Vincent Turvey (n.d.), Cora L.V. Richmond (1915), Sylvan Muldoon (Muldoon and Carrington, 1929) and Oliver Fox (n.d.)—a tradition that continues to more recent times. There were also collections and discussions of cases, such as Hill's *Man is a Spirit* (1918), Mattiesen's "Der Austritt des Ich als spiritistisches Argument" (1931), Bozzano's Les Phénomènes de Bilocation (1934/1937), and Muldoon's *The Case for Astral Projection* (1936).

In addition to OBEs and NDEs, apparitions of the living led many to believe in the projection of spirits and doubles. Examples of this include Catherine Crowe's *The Night-Side of Nature* (1848), William H. Harrison's *Spirits Before Our Eyes* (1879), Johann Heinrich Jung-Stilling's *Theory of Pneumatology* (1808/1851), and Robert Dale Owen's *Footfalls on the Boundary of Another World* (1860). An example of such an apparition from antiquity comes from the historian Tacitus:

> Vespasian conceived a … desire to visit the sanctuary of Serapis, in order to consult the god about affairs of the empire. He ordered all persons to be excluded from the temple; and lo, when he entered, and his thoughts were fixed on the deity, he perceived behind him a man of principal note among the Egyptians, named Basilides, whom, at that moment, he knew to be detained by illness at a distance of several days' journey from Alexandria. … Vespasian inquired of the priests whether Basilides that day had entered the temple. He asked of others whom he met whether he was seen in the city. At length, from messengers whom he dispatched on horseback,

> he received certain intelligence that Basilides was at that instant of time eighty miles distant from Alexandria. He then concluded that it was a divine vision, and deduced the import of the response from the name of Basilides (Tacitus, 1874, p. 260).

While some of these apparitions included the consciousness of the experient, most of them did not. Many of these reports were of apparitions of persons who were dying, or were passing through a crisis such as an accident or illness. Other accounts were about apparitions that were seen before someone died, or that arrived at a place before the person reached the location, as well as recurrent, and induced apparitions (Gurney, Myers & Podmore, 1886). I will present examples of such apparitions in a later paper.

There were also apparitions of the self, those cases referred to as autoscopy, which were redefined into a psychiatric condition by the work of many researchers (e.g., Sollier, 1903). Writers such as Bozzano (1934/1937) considered visions of the self to be a manifestation of the double (see also Alvarado, 2005).

The idea that these apparitions had some physical dimension, while not believed by some (e.g., Myers, 1886), was defended by others. As one of these theorists stated:

> We now know that human intelligence may act beyond its bodily limits; that a man may react to the psychic activity of another man and produce on him impressions that correspond to those that he feels himself, transmit his thoughts and sensations, evoke in him the view of his image. … And this extracorporeal activity may reach the [actual] doubling of the organism, presenting a simulacra of the person, which acts for a while independently of its prototype and presents incontestable attributes of corporeality (Aksakof, 1890/n.d., Vol. 2, pp. 269–270).

Another phenomenon supporting belief in the possibility of projection from the body—conscious or not—was the numerous mediumistic communications about the experience of dying, an example being the communications about "spiritual birth" that Robert Hare published in his book *Experimental Investigation of the Spirit Manifestations* (1855), in which death was 'described' as the projection of the spirit from the dead physical body. His deceased brother was said to have communicated that "when the vital cord which bound me to the physical body was parted, I experienced a full consciousness of my personality. I enjoyed perfect freedom from pain and sickness, and an unwonted degree of strength and buoyancy of spirit; sensations of the most exalted character took possession of me, and a holy calm pervaded the sanctuary of my soul. It was not, however, until I saw my body lying upon the bed that the true nature of my situation flashed across my mind" (p. 111).

The double, or spirit action, was also invoked to explain communications of the living through mediums. In Kardec's (1863, p. 379) view invocations of living spirits could take place better while the person was sleeping, a time where the spirit was free to respond to the invocation. Turvey (n.d.) claimed he could project and communicate through mediums.

Furthermore, there was the belief that the medium's double could explain materializations, as argued by Benjamin Coleman in relation to the Davenport brothers (Coleman, 1865) and Florence Cook (Coleman, 1873), an idea that was not accepted by everyone (e.g., Brevior, 1874). Samuel Watson (1876) argued that "there is deception often practised by [spirit] controls, in palming off the double of the medium for a relative or friend of someone present" (p 187). De Rochas (1897c) related the exteriorization of sensibility to mediumistic materializations. In his view there were four stages or degrees of fluidic body exteriorization. The first one was when the individual's sensibility was projected in layers close to the surroundings of their physical body. The second was a "coagulation of the effluvia in a double" (pp. 26–27) invisible to human eyes. This was followed by two more stages consisting of the visible and tangible materialization of body parts, and, finally, materializations of whole bodies.

In later years others speculated on this topic. One of them was Cesare Lombroso (1909):

> The double may furnish an explanation of many spiritistic phenomena without having recourse to the spirits of the dead, substituting for these the action of the medium,—the body of the double, or a part of it, acting at a certain distance from the medium's living body, just as this itself would act. Perhaps to the double belong also those more or less incomplete limbs which are seen to emerge from the body (the shoulders or the skirts) of the medium; so also, perchance, with some of those floating hands or arms which exactly resemble those of the medium, so much so that they have given rise to suspicion of deceit (p. 256).

In addition to phenomena related to mediums there have been a variety of observations of spirits leaving the body at death. An influential case was the clairvoyant observation of Andrew Jackson Davis (1850), in which he saw the spirit of a woman emerge from her physical body at death. Other descriptions of emanations from the dying body were recorded during the nineteenth century (e.g., De Morgan, 1863), as well as in later years (Monk, 1922; Tweedale, 1921). The spirit, or so it seemed to many, was clearly exiting the physical body at death. In a later paper I will present examples of these observations.

Dreams were also believed by some to involve projection phenomena (Bose, 1896; Leadbeater, 1903). In his book *Mind and its Relations* the Reverend Samuel B. Brittan (1864) argued that

> the soul is not necessarily confined by its corporeal restraints to any specific locality; but … it is free to traverse the world. … The facts of this class are very numerous. … In the hours of sleep we often visit distant places, and the scenes that pass before the inward vision have at once the semblance and the substance of reality. Indeed, in some essential sense, the soul leaves the body, and makes excursions into remote regions; and in many cases our dreams, no less than the mental impressions of our waking life, are found to be faithful representations of actual circumstances and events (p. 337).

Finally, but not exhausting the topic, the phantom limb sensations of amputees have been related to the idea of a double (Bozzano, 1934/1937; D'Assier, 1887/1883). Some clairvoyant visions have supported this idea, as in those of Friedericke Hauffe, the famous Seeress of Prevost studied by Justinus Kerner (1845). As Kerner wrote:

> When she saw people who had lost a limb, she still saw the limb attached to the body; that is, she saw the nerve-projected-form of the limb. … From this interesting phenomenon, we may, perhaps, explain the sensations of persons, who still have feeling in a limb that has been amputated: the invisible nerve-projected-form of the limb is still in connexion with the visible body; and this is a satisfactory proof, that after the destruction of the visible husk, the form is preserved by the nerve-spirit. (p. 77).

Concluding Remarks

While I have mentioned several phenomena cited in the past to support the idea of the human double, OBEs, and the like, I have not discussed all possible manifestations. These include photographs of doubles, reports of auras and of the exteriorization of nervous forces, and many OBE and NDE features such as sensations of repercussion or shocks to the physical body, and seeing oneself in a replica of the physical body during the experience.

Flammarion (1921/1922) represents the thinking of many when, considering some of the phenomena mentioned in this article, he argued: "It can no longer be doubted that human beings possess fluid phantasms which may, under certain conditions, become visible and tangible" (p. 66). As we have seen, many others—writers such as Bozzano (1934/1937), D'Assier (1883/1887), Durville (1909), Harrison (1879), Jung-Stilling (1808/1851)—believed the above mentioned phenomena supported both the existence of a subtle body and of the exteriorization of consciousness.

I am not trying to validate the concepts under discussion either in this or in the forthcoming articles. Instead, I will present excerpts from specific theorists and researchers to highlight a literature that has contributed to the construction of the idea of projection of consciousness and of the existence of subtle bodies.

II. J. H. Jung-Stilling on the Soul

The mesmeric literature has many speculations about the soul and its independence from the body. Colquhoun (1836) believed that acceptance of animal magnetism supported the existence of the soul because its phenomena were "capable of exercising its various functions ... without the assistance or co-operation of any of those material organs, by means of which it usually maintains a correspondence with the external world" (Vol. 2, p. 166). In his *Memoire sur le Magnétisme Animal,* Chardel (1818) discussed a vital principle bridging and putting in communication the physical body and the soul. He stated that the somnambulist could show clairvoyance because the soul was temporarily detached from the usual sensory pathways and received, directly from this 'life' principle, the impression that constituted the images of perceptions.

Another believer in the spiritual dimensions of mesmerism was J. H. Jung-Stilling (1740–1817), a physician as well as a practitioner in other disciplines. He developed ideas about the soul that gave prominence to mesmerism. This is discussed in his 1808 book, *Théorie der Geisterkunde,* translated as *Theory of Pneumatology; in Reply to the Question, What Ought to be Believed or Disbelieved Concerning Presentiments, Visions, and Apparitions, According to Nature, Reason and Scripture* (1834/1808). According to Podmore (1902), his "special distinction is that he placed the doctrine of the psychic body on a new and surer basis, first by associating it with the conception—then for the first time beginning to gain general acceptance in the scientific world—of the luminiferous ether; and secondly, by supporting and explaining it by means of illustrations drawn from the observed phenomena of somnambulism" (Vol. 1, p. 95).

In his book, Jung-Stilling (1808/1834) stated: "Animal magnetism undeniably proves that we have an inward man, a soul, which is constituted of the divine spark, the immortal spirit, possessing reason and will, and of a luminous body, which is inseparable from it" (p. 227). Among the chapters in his book were those entitled: "On Presentiments, Predictions, Enchantments, and Prophesying", and "On Visions and Apparitions". The following excerpt is taken from the second chapter of Jung-Stilling's work, which is entitled *"Remarks Upon the Nature of Man".*

Jung-Stilling on Subtle Bodies and Spirit Travelling

We must divide man into three different parts, mutually united to each other. First—The outward mechanical body, which has no material preference above the brutes; or, at least, is not essentially different from them: by this body, the man is united with the visible world as long as he lives. Secondly—The ethereal fluid, which is, properly speaking, the corporeal principle of life, which the man has in common with the brutes, and [p. 57] which may be called, abstractedly, soul, (anima—animans). Thirdly—The immortal spirit of man, which is peculiarly created after the image of God: and on this account stands in this singular connexion with the material world, in order that it may strive for the re-attainment of its lost inherent dignity.

The ethereal fluid and the spirit together, which, in eternity, make inseparably one, I will in future call the human soul, to distinguish it from the animal soul; in the sequel, all this will be clearer, and become convincingly certain.

The human soul is present in every part of its body; it is conscious of itself in every part, according as the organs of the body give occasion; it sees with the eyes, hears with the ears, smells with the nose, tastes with the tongue and palate, and feels with the whole skin, or the whole superficies of the body. All this it has in common with the animal soul; but there is something more superadded, which gives it a rank far different and more elevated than the brutes: it is an intelligent being that is capable of knowing and loving God, and of ripening to an angel, but also of becoming a devil. Considered, therefore, in this point of view, it is a citizen of the world of spirits, and can also be brought into connexion with them [p. 58].

The human soul is invisible to us in our natural state; but those that are in the magnetic sleep see it like an azure radiance, which surrounds the whole body to a certain extent, so that every man has around him a psychical atmosphere. ... What is called magnetizing is also performed solely in this atmosphere, by which operation the wonderful effects of magnetic sleep are produced.

The human soul is directed, in the natural state, by the nerves, wherever feeling, consciousness, and motion are necessary. It appears to have the principal seat in the brain; but by magnetizing, it is more or less detached from the brain and nerves, and consequently becomes, more or less, a free agent; for, as the clear-seeing somnambulist does not see with the eyes, but out of the region of the pit of the heart, and as this is always the case, without exception, it is clear from hence, that the human soul of itself can not only see without the aid of the body, but also so much clearer than in its fleshly prison, nor does it stand in need of our material light; for magnetic sleepers read what is laid on the pit of the heart, and the contents of closed letters. Nay, they can read at a distance, when the book or writing is separated from them by dense and opaque bodies, as soon as that which is to be read, is held by a person, with whom the [p. 59] somnambulist stands in psychical contact or connexion. ...

The human soul, in this state, not only sees but also feels every thing more acutely, than in its natural waking state, without requiring for this purpose any one of the bodily senses; but it is very remarkable, that it is not susceptible of the smallest thing belonging to the visible world, except when brought into a psychical contact, connexion, or rapport, which is effected when another person is magnetically brought into unison with the soul of the magnetic sleeper, by certain graspings of the hand, so that both touch each other; the somnambulist can then, particularly when he is in a very exalted and clear-sighted state, perceive every thing that the person thinks, suffers, feels, and enjoys, who stands in connexion with him [p. 60].

... It is indispensably necessary, that the rational spirit of man which is immortal, and proceeded forth from God, should have an organ by which it can act upon other beings, and they in return upon it; without this, it would have no knowledge of any thing out of itself, and would be itself a pure nonentity to every other being. Now this organ is ether, which is indestructible by any natural power, and is eternal and unchangeable. The spirit, during its sensible existence upon earth, forms to itself a spiritual luminous body, with which it continues eternally united.

The magnetic facts and experiments above stated prove, to a demonstration, the existence of this spiritual luminous body, or the human soul: they further prove that this human soul has need of its gross and animal body, solely with reference to its earthly life, in which man must necessarily stand in reciprocal operation with the sensible or material world, but that it is able without it to think and feel, and to act upon others, both near and at a distance, in a much more perfect manner, and is also more susceptible of suffering and enjoyment [p. 61], …

If the human soul during its existence in its material body, from which it is not entirely detached, be capable of such wonderful things; what will its capability be when totally separated from it by death! Let the reader reflect upon this. In dying, the person loses his consciousness, he falls into a perfect trance or profound sleep. As long as the mass of blood is still warm and not congealed, all the members of the body continue pliant; and as long as this is the case, the soul remains in it; but as soon as the brain and the nerves lose their warmth and become frigid, they can no longer attract the ethereal part of the soul, nor retain it any longer; it therefore disengages itself, divests itself of its earthly bonds, and awakes. It is now in the state of a clear-seeing magnetic sleeper, but being entirely separated from the body, its state is much more perfect: it has a complete recollection of its earthly existence from beginning to end; it remembers those it has left behind, and can form to itself a very clear idea of the visible world, of which it is now no longer susceptible, whilst on the contrary, it is conscious of the invisible world and its objects: namely, that part of it to which it belongs, or to which it has here adapted itself [p. 62], …

The somnambulist has no perception of any thing in the visible world, with the exception of the souls of those individuals that are brought into a corresponding connexion, or into rapport with him: through these he learns what passes in the visible world. The soul, after death, enters into connexion with those that bear the greatest affinity to its own nature: if it enters into this kind of contact with others, it feels a pain, the extent of which corresponds with the degree of difference [p. 63].

The highest species of apparitions, which have their foundation in human nature is, incontestibly, when a person still living can show himself in some distant place. However much this may have been ridiculed as the most absurd superstition, yet so certain and positive are the facts narrated, that the matter is placed beyond a doubt; and many of my readers will probably remember some incident or other of this kind. I do not speak here of such apparitions as have shewn themselves, immediately after death, to some particular friend, but of those that have made such a visit, whilst the individual still animated a living body. Instances are known [p. 73] to me, in which persons who were sick, were seized with an indescribable longing to see a certain friend; they soon after fell into a swoon, and, during the time, they appeared to the distant object of their longing. But the following narrative exceeds all I ever read or heard upon this subject; it comes from a credible source, and possesses all the characteristics of historic veracity.

About sixty or seventy years ago, a man of piety and integrity arrived in Germany, from Philadelphia, in North America, to visit his poor old parents, and with his well-earned wealth to place them beyond the reach of care. He went out to America whilst he was still young, and had succeeded so far as to become overlooker of various mills on the Delaware river, in which situation he had honourably laid up a considerable sum. This respectable individual related to one of my friends, upon whose veracity I can depend, the following wonderful tale.

In the neighbourhood of Philadelphia, not far from the mills above-mentioned, there dwelt a solitary man in a lonely house. He was very benevolent, but extremely retired and reserved, and strange things were related of him, amongst which were his being able to tell a person things that were unknown to every one else. Now it happened, that the captain of a vessel belonging to [p. 74] Philadelphia, was about to sail to Africa and Europe. He promised his wife that he would return again in a certain time, and also that he would write to her frequently. She waited long, but no letters arrived: the time appointed passed over, but her beloved husband did not return. She was now deeply distressed, and knew not where to look either for counsel or consolation. At length, a friend advised her for once to go to the pious solitary, and tell him her griefs. The woman followed his advice, and went to him. After she had told him all her troubles, he desired her to wait a while there, until he returned and brought her an answer. She sat down to wait, and the man opening a door, went into his closet. But the woman thinking he stayed a long time, rose up, went to the window in the door, lifted up the little curtain, and looking in, saw him lying on the couch or sofa like a corpse: she then immediately went back to her place. At length he came and told her that her husband was in London, in a coffee-house which he named, and that he would return very soon: he then told her also the reason why he had been unable to write. The woman went home pretty much at ease.

What the solitary had told her was minutely fulfilled, her husband returned, and the reasons of his delay and his not writing were just the same as the man had stated. The woman was now curious to know what would [p. 75] be the result, if she visited the friendly solitary in company with her husband. The visit was arranged, but when the captain saw the man, he was struck with amazement; he afterwards told his wife that he had seen this very man, on such a day; (it was the very day that the woman had been with him), in a coffee-house in London; and that he had told him that his wife was much distressed about him; that he had then stated the reason why his return was delayed, and of his not writing, and that he would shortly come back, on which he lost sight of the man among the company. …

This most singular narrative, which is totally inexplicable and incredible, according to the common system of materialism, can be explained only according to my theory of human nature, and its possibility demonstrated. For this purpose, I must refer to the indubitable facts, for which we are indebted to animal magnetism.

It is now an evident and established truth, that there is, in the human frame, a subtle luminous body, an ethereal covering of the immortal rational spirit, which has undeniably manifested itself in magnetism, galvanism, electricity, and in sympathy and antipathy, and shewn itself operative in a variety of ways: with this body the [p. 76] rational spirit is eternally and inseparably connected. In the foregoing pages, I have denominated this eternal luminous body, the human soul.

This human soul, by an artificial stroking, or magnetizing, can be detached from the nervous system in a numberless variety of degrees, and become a free agent, according to the extent of the degree of detachment; certain diseases, and like wise certain medicines, or rather, poisonous plants, are capable of producing the same effect.

In the inferior degrees of this detachment, consciousness remains, but the imagination is more lively, so that the man believes he really sees and hears what he merely imagines.

Natural sleep is also one species of detachment. When the organic machine of the body, or rather the nerves, become wearied to a certain extent, the human soul forsakes these organs, in so far as they belong to the senses; for, from the latter alone proceeds our consciousness of the visible world; the soul, however, continues to act of itself; and if this take place in so lively a manner, as to make an impression on the inward organs of sense, we then remember it on awaking, and call it a dream [p. 77].

This detachment is some degrees more complete in the common sleep-walkers, and has a similarity to magnetic somnambulism: in this case the human soul acts more freely, it dreams more connectedly and distinctly, and to such a degree, that the nervous system, and consequently the body also, is set in motion, although the senses are all at rest; and as the man in this state is not actuated by the sensible world, but by the connexion of ideas in the soul, actions ensue which do not belong to the natural order of things: but these very actions, as every one knows, are much more perfect in themselves, than when performed in a wakeful state; from whence it is again evident, that the human soul, when delivered from the bonds of the body, can act much more freely, perfectly, and actively; it then neither sleeps nor slumbers, nor is wearied any more for ever.

In the common fits of hypochondriacal and hysterical persons, as also of those who are afflicted with worms, the degrees of detachment are likewise very various, consequently the exhibitions and actions also which proceed from them; but at death it is complete. …

It is, therefore, an incontestable experimental truth, that the human soul can be detached in an infinite number and variety of degrees, even to entire separation from [p. 78] the body, and is able to act freely of itself, according to the degree of this detachment.

There may be those to whom this detachment is a very easy matter, and assisted by secret means, may even be carried so far, that the human soul leaves the body for a short time, performs something at a distance, and returns to the body again: but this, however, must take place in a very short time, before the blood loses its fluidity, We have several instances of the occurrence of this in diseased persons. I will now explain, according to my theory, this rare and most remarkable phenomenon, with reference to the American instance above related, which is the most perfect of its kind.

When the soul is in a state of detachment from its sensitive organs, whilst still in the body, consciousness of the visible world ceases, so long as the detachment lasts; the soul, however, lives and acts in the sphere of its knowledge, and enters, at length, by frequent repetition of this state, into connexion with the world of spirits; it is no longer sensible of any thing in the visible world; it sees and hears no one except those with whom it is placed in rapport, which is accomplished by bringing the psychical atmospheres of both into contact with each other, according to certain laws. With such persons the soul can have intercourse and converse, and from them [p. 79] it learns what is passing around it in the visible world at the time.

Now, supposing the American abovementioned, possessed the capability, either from nature, or by some secret means, or by both, to detach his soul at pleasure, entirely from the body, and unite it again with the body, he could therefore place himself in a state of the most perfect somnambulism; by the phenomena and experiments of which, every thing must now be explained. His soul, therefore, forsook its body, with the will to ask the captain the reason of his protracted stay and of his not writing. As soon as it left the body, it was no longer sensible of any thing in the material world, and was in the world of spirits, where no space can separate. The moment, therefore, the soul forsook the body, it was already in London with the captain of the vessel; and if he had been in China, or any where else, its magic mil would have carried it thither.

The human soul, abstractedly considered, is invisible, it is naturally not obvious to the senses, but it can make itself visible in two ways: first, by attracting atmospheric substances, and forming out of them a body like its own; and secondly, by placing itself in rapport with the person to whom it wishes to appear. In the former case, it may be seen by many persons; but then [p. 80] every one perceives that the apparition is no human being, but a spirit: in the latter case, it is only visible to him, with whom it stands in rapport, by acting in such a lively manner on his soul and organs of sense, that he sees the person before him as clearly, as if he were present in his own body. This remark I shall also subsequently elucidate, very clearly and completely, in the chapter on the apparition of spirits.

The American certainly appeared to the captain according to the second mode, for in the first, a great sensation would have been excited amongst those that were present: and who knows what might have been the consequence of it to the individual himself? …

The singular phenomenon when persons see themselves, or appear to themselves, is not rare, and may take place in two ways: first, when the person, who sees himself, is alone conscious of the apparition,[1] whilst others who are present see nothing. In this case, the appearance may be merely natural, and founded in human nature; but where it is seen by several, it then belongs to [p. 81] the invisible world….

Should any one ask, how it is possible for a man to appear to himself, or how this self-sight is founded in human nature: I answer that, in order to this, nothing more is requisite, than to see angels and spirits where there are none, or at least where they are not obvious to the senses…Now just as other forms may be so vividly impressed upon the imagination, as to resemble the external sensible impressions, so the same impression may also be made by one's own figure [p. 82], …

Animal Magnetism, and an extensive medical experience have taught and incontrovertibly convinced me that the immortal spirit, the divine spark in man, is inseparably united with an ethereal or luminous body; that this human soul, which is destined to be a citizen of the world of spirits, is, as it were, exiled into this earthly life and animal body, to which it is fettered by means of the nerves, and must be thus fettered to it, for the purposes of its ennoblement and perfection: that this inward and luminous being, during such incarceration, is destined to receive its instruction through the five organs of sense, and not through intercourse with the world of spirits; but that by means of magnetism, by certain diseases, and by other instrumentality, it may be more or less divested of the bonds of the body, and enter into connexion with the invisible world, which however is always something unnatural, and contrary to [p. 95] the principles of the Christian religion; and finally, that its actions are so much the more perfect and volatile, the more it is divested of the body, in order to think, imagine, or in a word, to make use of its understanding, reason, and will; on the contrary, all the faculties of the soul or spirit are much more perfect when the inward man is freed from the body, it possesses the latter only for the purpose of being conscious of the visible world, and of acting in it [p. 96].

III. William Gregory on Travelling Clairvoyance

The literature of mesmerism presents many examples of phenomena such as healing, medical diagnosis, mental suggestion and transposition of the senses (for reviews see Dingwall, 1967–1968; Gauld, 1992). The excerpt presented in this paper is about the phenomenon of travelling clairvoyance, in which a mesmerized individual was asked to go to a distant place to describe the place or events taking place there. Instances of this phenomenon were reported by several mesmerists (e.g., Haddock,

1851, pp. 105–108), and raised the issue of the actual displacement of the soul, and controversies on the topic.[2]

Some mesmeric subjects described their experiences. One example was the famous French somnambule Alexis Didier,[3] who wrote: "The whole Universe is in front of me; and I can transport from a pole to another with the speed of lightning; I can talk with the Caffres, walk in China, descend on the mines of Australia, enter the harem of a sultan in less than an hour, without fatigue" (Didier, 1856, p. 15).

The passage that follows, discussing travelling clairvoyance, was published by the physician William Gregory (1803–1858), who taught chemistry at the University of Edinburgh (Kaufman, 2008). Gregory discussed mesmerism in his book *Letters to a Candid Inquirer, on Animal Magnetism* (1851). The book had two parts. The first one was about general aspects of mesmeric phenomena, and the second about cases and personal observations.

William Gregory on Travelling Clairvoyance

The sleeper, at the request of the operator, and frequently of his own accord, visits distant places and countries, and describes them, as well as the persons in them. This may, as I have already said, be done, in some cases, by sympathy, but there are many cases in which ordinary sympathy will not explain it.

Thus, the clairvoyant will often see and describe accurately, as is subsequently ascertained, places, objects, and people, totally unknown to the operator, or to any one present; and he will likewise, in describing such as are known to the operator, notice details and changes which could not be known to him.

The clairvoyant appears, as it were, mentally to go to the place named. He often finds himself, first, in no place, but floating, as it were, on air, or in space, and in a very short time exclaims, "Now, I am there". The place named is the first, as a general rule, that presents itself to him. But whether it be so, or whether he see, first, some other place, a certain internal feeling tells him when he is right. If it be a distant town, and no house be specified to him, he will either see a general panoramic view of it, as from a neighbouring hill, or from a height in the air, and describe this as he would a map or bird's-eye view, or he will find himself in some street, place, square, or promenade, which, although not specified to him, is at once recognised from his account of it. He sees and describes the trees, roads, streets, houses, churches, fountains, and walks, and the people moving in them, and his expressions of delight and surprise are unceasing. If sent thither, to use his almost invariable phrase, a second or a third time, the sleeper will see the same objects, but remarks the change on the living part of the picture.

For example, Mr D., a clairvoyant, magnetised by myself, when in an early and imperfect stage of lucidity, was asked by me to go to Aix-la-Chapelle, he never having left Scotland. He agreed, and after a very short, apparently an aerial voyage, said he was there. He was in a beautiful walk, bordered with trees, saw green turf, and the walk stretched on both sides, till lost, at either end, by a turning, not sharp, but gradual. This was evidently the boulevard. Another time, I specified the Friedrich Wilhelmsplatz, where he saw houses on one side, and at both ends, [p. 124] some much higher than others, the place itself of irregular oblong form, wider at one end than the other, and partly shrouded in a mist, of which he long complained; on the other side a long building, not a house. In the middle, a road, with small trees, having no branches till the stem rose rather higher than a man, and then a number, but the top obscured by mist.

Another time, he saw the door of Nuellen's Hotel, large enough, he thought, to allow a carriage to enter, but not more, if that; people were going in and out; and a man stood at the door, with a white neckcloth and vest, and no hat; as he thought, a waiter. In the saloon, he saw tables, all brown, no one there. Another time, some tables were white, and people sat at them eating, while others moved about. According to the hours of experiment, he was most likely right both times, although their dinner hour differs so much from ours. One day, I sent him to Cologne. There he noticed, from a bird's-eye position, a large building, seen rather misty, but much higher than the houses. He got into a street near it, and described its long pointed windows, showing with his fingers their form, and its buttresses, which he described, but could not name. In the street, he saw people, indistinctly, moving; but he saw, pretty clearly, one "old boy", as he called him, fat and comfortable, standing in his shop-door, and idling. He had no hat, and wore an apron. Mr D. was much surprised, without any question being asked, at the fact that about half of the men he saw, both in Aix and Cologne, wore beards, and he described different fashions of beards and moustaches. One time, when I sent him to Bonn, he gave a beautiful account of the view from the hills to the west of it, of the town, arid the Rhine, stretching out and winding through the plain, with the rising grounds on the other side, such as the Ennertz. But it was remarkable that he stoutly maintained, that the hill on which he stood was to the east of the town, the town to the east of the Rhine, between the hill and the river, and the Rhine running towards the south; whereas I knew every one of these directions to be reversed.

The same subject has often spontaneously visited other places, unknown to me, but has given such minute and graphic accounts of the localities, the people, houses, dress, occupations, and topography of these places, that I should [p. 125] recognise them at once, were I to see them. …

It often happens, that a clairvoyant, who can see and describe very well all that is in the same room, or the next room, or even in the same house, cannot thus travel to a distance, without passing into a new stage. This generally occurs spontaneously, but may sometimes be effected by passes, or by the will of the operator.

The new or travelling stage, in such cases, is marked by peculiar characters. Thus, in one very fine case, which I had the opportunity of studying, the clairvoyant, in her first lucid state, could tell all that passed behind her, or in the next room, and could, by contact, perceive, and accurately describe, the state of body of other persons. She could hear, and she very readily answered, every question put to her by any one present, but could not go to a distant place. Yet, as I saw, she would often spontaneously pass from that state or stage into another, in which she was deaf to all sounds, even to the voice of her magnetiser, unless he spoke with his mouth touching the tips of the fingers of her right hand. Anyone else might also converse with her in this way, but when first addressed, she invariably started. And now, not only could she go to a distance, and see very plainly what passed, but she was already in some distant place, and much occupied with it. She called this going away, or, when it was done by her magnetiser, being taken away, and when tired, would ask him to bring her back, which he did by some trifling manipulations. She then remembered (in her first state, to which she came back) what she had seen on her travels [p. 126]. …

[Gregory described further observations with Mr D.] One day, while observing the town above mentioned, and describing it spontaneously, as I always encouraged him to do, he became suddenly silent, and after a short time told me, that he was travelling through air or space, to a great distance. I soon discovered that he had spontaneously passed into a higher stage. … As soon as he had come to the end of his journey, he began to describe a beautiful garden, with avenues of fine trees, of which he drew a plan. It was near a town, in which he could see no spires. At the end of one principal avenue was a round pond, or fountain, enclosed in stone and gravel, with two jets of water, and close to this fountain or pond stood an elderly man, in what, from the description, seemed to be the ancient Greek dress, the head bare, long beard, flowing white robes, and bare feet in sandals. He was surrounded by about a dozen younger men, most of whom had black beards, and wore the same dress as their master. He seemed to be occupied in teaching them, and after a time, the lecture or conversation being finished, they all left the fountain, by twos and threes, and slowly walked along the avenues. Looking down these avenues, Mr. D. saw glimpses of the neighbouring hills, and of the town, which lay nearer to the garden than the hills, although still at some distance. This singular vision also recurred spontaneously two or three times; that is, Mr. D. saw the gardens and the localities, but not again the group at the fountain, although other persons were seen enjoying the walks, and on one occasion two ladies were noticed, whose dress seemed also to be ancient Greek. But what particularly struck me was, that this vision only occurred in a peculiar state, of which the consciousness was quite distinct, not only from his ordinary consciousness. … This peculiar, third consciousness was interpolated, and he always slept out his full time, as previously fixed, in the more common magnetic state, while the time spent in this new state was added. On returning, which he always did of himself, to his first magnetic state, he had not the slightest recollection of the new vision, nor did he ever remember [p. 322] it, except when he came into the new state. It certainly seems probable that, in that new state, he was transported to distant times and past events.

Another time he spontaneously passed into a similar state, but which I think had a fourth consciousness of its own, divided from all the others. He told me one day that he was travelling through the air or through space, as before, but all at once began to appear uneasy and alarmed, and told me he had fallen into the water, and would be drowned, if I did not help him. I commanded him to get out of the water, and after much actual exertion and alarm, he said he had got to the bank. He then said he had fallen into a river in Caffraria, at the place where a friend of his was born. But what was very remarkable was, that he spoke of the river, the fields, farm-houses, people, animals, and woods, as if perfectly familiar to him, and told me he had spent many years as a boy in that country, whereas he has never been out of Scotland. Moreover, he insisted he was not asleep, but wide awake, and although his eyes were closed, said they were open, and complained that I was making a fool of him, when I said he was asleep. He was somewhat puzzled to explain how I, whom he knew to be in Edinburgh, could be conversing with him in Caffraria, as he declared he was; and he was still more puzzled when I asked him, how he had gone to that country, for he admitted he had never been on board a ship. But still he maintained that he was in Caffraria, and had long lived there, and that he knew every man and every animal at the farm he described. It was evident that he had heard of Caffraria from his friend; but as he described all that he saw, precisely as a man would do who was looking at the place and the people, and as he maintained that all were familiar to him, I could hardly avoid supposing, that, his mind having been interested in what he had heard, he had, in some of his previous sleeps visited Caffraria by clairvoyance, without telling me of it at the time; for it often happened, that he would sleep for an hour or half an hour without speaking; that when he had spontaneously passed into that state on this occasion, he not only saw, but recognised as well known, and as seen in previous portions of that peculiar consciousness, the localities, persons, &c. whom he described. Certainly his descriptions were such as to convey to me the [p. 323] impression that he actually saw these things as they exist. On two other occasions, he spontaneously got into the same state, and always then spoke as he had done the first time; but he retained not a trace of recollection of this South African vision in any other state but that one. Nay, when I asked him about Caffraria in his ordinary magnetic sleep, he seemed not to understand me, and thought I was making fun of him when I asked whether he had ever been in Africa.

In these three distinct kinds of vision, that of R., that of the Greek garden and philosopher, and that of Caffraria, it is hardly possible to verify the visions; but when I reflect, that Mr D. was able, in a certain state, to see and describe accurately towns, such as Aix and Cologne, countries, and persons, at a great distance, and quite unknown to him, I am disposed to think that in these visions also he saw the real places actually before him. It would have been most interesting to have studied more minutely the powers exhibited, or which might have been developed, in this very interesting case; but, as I have mentioned, Mr D., whose extreme susceptibility at that time may have depended on the very unsatisfactory state of his health, was taken ill, and confined to bed with an affection of the chest, for five or six weeks; and when he had recovered, I found that his general health was far better than when he was first magnetised, but his extreme susceptibility was gone. I can still magnetise him, although with far more difficulty; and since his recovery, I have only once been able to get him to see the town formerly described, and R. [p. 324].

IV. Allan Kardec on Bicorporeity

French educator Hippolyte-Leon Denizard Rivail (1804–1869), known as Allan Kardec, became known for his compilations of the teachings of "spirits". Some of these teachings were ideas about God, creation, the nature of spirits, spiritual life, and reincarnation (Kardec, 1860). Others were about specific phenomena such as apparitions, hauntings, mediumistic communications and physical phenomena, and about the variety of mediums (Kardec, 1863).[4] An important part of this discussion was the existence of the perispirit, a fluidic or semi-physical envelope providing a link between the body and the spirit. Such a vehicle, the principle behind the actions of the spirit on the body, physical phenomena and the visibility of apparitions, was believed to leave the physical body at death with the spirit.[5]

In Kardec's view phenomena such as somnambulism and clairvoyance were examples of the independence of the soul from the physical body. He believed that dreams were "the product of the emancipation of the soul rendered more independent by the suspension of the active and relational life" (Kardec, 1860, p. 179). In his discussion of phenomena Kardec (1863, Part 2, Chapter 8) considered "bicorporeity", those cases in which apparitions of living individuals were perceived. The excerpt that follows was taken from *Experimental Spiritism: Book on Mediums* (Kardec, 1891).

Kardec on Bicorporeity

We know that during sleep the spirit partly recovers its liberty; that is, it is isolated from the body; and it is in this state that we have, many times, had occasion to observe it. But the spirit, be the man dead or living, has always its semi-material envelope [the perispirit], which, for the same causes that we have described, can acquire visibility and tangibility. Very positive facts leave no doubt of this; we will cite some examples of our own personal knowledge, whose truth we can guarantee; every one can, no doubt, remember analogous ones, by searching his memory. ...

The wife of one of our friends several times saw a fruit merchant of the neighborhood, whom she [p. 151] knew by sight, but to whom she had never spoken, enter her room in the night, whether she had a light or not. This apparition caused her great terror, greater because at that time she had no knowledge of Spiritism, and the phenomenon happened very often. But the merchant was perfectly alive, and probably sleeping at that hour: while his material body was at home, his spirit and his fluidic body was with this lady; with what motive? No one knows. ... Each time the apparition vanished without her knowing how, and each time, also, after its disappearance, she went to the doors to assure herself that they were perfectly shut, and that nobody could have been introduced into her room. This precaution proved to her that she was perfectly awake, and not the sport of a dream. At other times she saw, in the same way, a man she did not know; but one day she saw her brother, who was then in California. He had so much the appearance of a real person, that, at the first moment, she thought he had returned, and was going to speak to him; but he disappeared without giving her time. A letter, afterwards received, proved that he was not dead. This lady was what was called a natural seeing medium, but at that time, as we have said, she had never heard of mediums. ...

Another lady, who lives in the country, being very seriously ill, saw, about ten o'clock one evening, an aged gentleman, living in the same town, whom she had sometimes met in society, but of no intimate acquaintance. This gentleman was seated in an armchair, at the foot of her bed, and from time to time took snuff; he seemed to be watching. Surprised at [p. 152] such a visit at such an hour, she wished to ask the cause of it; but he signed to her not to speak, but to go to sleep: several times she was about to address him, but each time with the same result. She ended by going to sleep. Some days after, being convalescent, she received a visit from this same gentleman, but at a more suitable hour; and this time it was himself: he was dressed the same, had the same snuffbox, the same manners. Persuaded that he had come during her illness, she thanked him for the trouble he had taken. The gentleman, much surprised, said he had not had the pleasure of seeing her for a very long time. The lady, who understood spirit phenomena, saw at once what it was, but not wishing to explain it to him, contented herself with telling him she had probably dreamed it. "Very probably", will say the skeptical, the strong-minded, for them the synonym of men of mind; but it is certain she slept not at all, no more than the preceding. Then she dreamed awake; in other words, she had a hallucination. That is the great word, the universal explanation of everything that is not understood. As we have already refuted this objection, we will continue, addressing ourselves to those who can understand us. ...

Here is another and more characteristic fact, and we should be curious to see how it can be explained by the play of the imagination. A gentleman, living in the country, had never wished to marry, in spite of the importunity of his family. They had constantly insisted in favor of a person living in a neighboring town, and whom he had never seen. One day, being in his room, he was astonished to find himself in the presence of a young girl, dressed in white, her head crowned with flowers. She told him she was his [p. 153] betrothed, held out her hand to him, which he took in his, and on which he saw a ring. In a few moments she disappeared. Surprised at this apparition, and being sure that he was fully awake, he asked if any one had come during the day, but was answered no person had been seen. A year after, yielding to the renewed solicitations of a relative, he decided to go and see the person proposed to him. He arrived the day of the Fête-Dieu (festival of Corpus Christi day). They returned from the procession, and one of the first persons he saw, on entering the house, was a young girl, whom he recognized as the one who had appeared to him, dressed in the same manner; for the day of the apparition was also that of the Fête-Dieu. He remained speechless, and the young girl uttered a cry of surprise, and fainted. Restored to her senses, she said she had already seen this gentleman, the same day in the preceding year. The marriage was concluded. This was about 1835; at that time there was no question about spirits, and besides, both were persons of extreme positivism, and imagination the least exalted possible.

It may be said, perhaps, that both had their minds occupied with the idea of the proposed union, and that this preoccupation brought about a hallucination; but it must not be forgotten, that the husband was so indifferent that he was a year without going to see his intended. Admitting even this hypothesis, the double apparition remains to be explained, the coincidence of the costume with the day of the *Fête-Dieu*, and then the physical recognition between persons who had never seen each other—circumstances that could not be the effect of imagination. …

Before going further, we should answer immediately [p. 154] a question that will not fail to be asked; this is, to know how the body can live while the soul is absent. We can say that the body can live with the organic life, which is independent of the presence of the spirit, and the proof of this is, that plants live, and have no spirit; but we would add that during life the spirit is never completely detached from the body. Spirits, as also some seeing mediums, recognize the spirit of a living person by a luminous train joined to its body, a phenomenon that never occurs when the body is dead,[6] for then the separation is complete. Thus, the body can never die during the absence of the spirit, and it can never happen that the spirit on its arrival finds the door shut, as some romancers have said, in their fairy histories.

To return to our subject. The spirit of a living person isolated from the body can appear the same as that of a dead person, and have all the appearance of reality; and further, for the same causes that we have explained, it can acquire a momentary tangibility. It is this phenomenon called bi-corporeity that has given foundation to the stories of double men, that is to say, individuals whose simultaneous presence has been verified in two different places. Here are two examples, drawn not from our popular legends, but from ecclesiastical history.[7]

St. Alphonse de Liguori was canonized before the usual time, for having been seen simultaneously in two different places, which passed for a miracle.

St. Antoine de Padua was in Spain, and at the time he was preaching, his father, who was in Padua, was going to the torture, accused of murder. At this moment St. Antoine appeared, showed the innocence [p. 155] of his father, and pointed out the true criminal, who was afterward punished. It was proved that St. Antoine had not left Spain.

St. Alphonse, having been invoked and interrogated by us on this fact, gave us the following answers: —

1. "Can you give us the explanation of this phenomenon?"

"Yes; man, when he is completely dematerialized by his virtue, when he has elevated his soul toward God, can appear in two places at once, and in this way. The incarnated spirit, feeling sleep come, can ask God to transport him to some especial place. His spirit, or his soul, as you would call it, then leaves his body, followed by a *part of his perisprit*, and leaves the unclean matter in a state *bordering* on death. I say, bordering on death, because there remains in the body a tie which attaches the *perisprit* and the soul to the matter, and this tie cannot be defined. The body appears then in the place desired. I believe this is all you wish to know."

2. "This does not give us the explanation of the visibility and tangibility of the *perisprit*."

"The spirit, finding himself freed from matter, can, according to his degree of elevation, become tangible."

3. "Is the sleep of the body indispensable to the spirit appearing in other places?"

"The soul can divide itself, when it feels itself taken to a different place from where the body is. It may happen that the body does not sleep, though that is very rare; but then the body is not in a perfectly normal condition; it is always in a state more or less ecstatic."

Remark. The soul does not divide itself in the [p. 156] literal sense of the word; it radiates on different sides, and thus can be manifested on several points without being divided; the same as a light, which can be reflected simultaneously in several glasses.

4. "A man being asleep while his spirit appears elsewhere, what would happen were he awakened suddenly?"

"That could not happen, because, if any one had such an intention, the spirit would reenter the body, and foresee the intention, for the spirit reads the thought."

This identical explanation has been given to us several times, by the spirit of persons dead or living. St. Alphonse explains the fact of this double presence, but does not give the theory of its visibility and tangibility. …

Tacitus relates an analogous fact.[8] During the months that Vespasian passed in Alexandria to await the periodical return of the spring winds, and the season when the sea should become safe, several prodigies took place, showing the favor of the heavens, and the interest which the gods seemed to take in this prince.

These prodigies redoubled in Vespasian the desire of visiting the sacred dwelling-place of the god, to consult him about the empire. He ordered that the temple should be closed to every one, entered himself, and just as the oracle was about to be pronounced, he perceived behind him one of the principal Egyptians, named Basilidus, who, he knew, had been left sick several days' journey from Alexandria. He inquired of the priests if Basilidus had come that day to the temple, and asked of the passers-by if he had been seen in the city; finally, he sent some men on horse [p. 157] back, and was assured that, at that moment, he was eighty miles distant. Then he no longer doubted that the vision was supernatural, and the name of Basilide was to him instead of an oracle. …

The individual who is seen in two different places simultaneously has, then, two bodies, but only one of them is real; the other is but an appearance; we might say the first has the organic life, the second the life of the soul; at the awakening, the two bodies reunite, and the life of the soul reenters the material body. It does not appear possible, at least we have no example of it, and reason seems to disprove it, that in the state of separation the two bodies can enjoy, simultaneously, and to the same degree, active and intelligent life. It results, moreover, from what we have said, that the real body could not die if the apparent body remained visible; the approach of death always recalling the spirit into the body, were it but for an instant. It equally results that the apparent body could not be killed, because it is not organic, and is not formed of flesh and bones; it would disappear the moment a person might desire to kill it (p. 158)

V. Adolphe D'assier's Ideas of Doubles

Another example of ideas about the double came from Adolphe D'Assier (1827–1889). D'Assier was a member of the Bordeaux Academy of Sciences who wrote about many topics, among them language and grammar. His thoughts on doubles and apparitions appeared in his book *Essai sur l'Humanité Posthume et le Spiritisme* (1883), translated as *Posthumous Humanity: A Study of Phantoms* (1887).

The translation was done by theosophist Henry Olcott, who annotated the book and disagreed with the author on occasion.

D'Assier discussed the existence of a phantom associated to the physical body, and able to manifest during life and after death. While his work is not cited frequently today by most contemporary writers considering apparitions, he was reviewed and discussed during the 1880s and 1890s in many places. This includes publications such as Science (Jordan, 1899), *Cornhill Magazine* (The Manners of Posthumous Man, 1883), and the theosophical magazine *Lucifer* (Posthumous Humanity, 1888).

D'Assier's Ideas

The existence of the posthumous personality being demonstrated by some thousands of facts, observed in all ages and among all peoples, it remains to seek out its nature and origin. Evidently it proceeds [p. 30] from the living personality, whose continuation it shows itself, with its form, habits, prejudices, &c. Let us, then, inquire if there is not found in man a principle which, detaching itself from the body while the vital forces abandon the latter, continues for some time the action of the human individuality. Numerous facts show that this principle exists, and that it sometimes manifests itself during life, exhibiting, at the same time, the characteristics of the living personality and those of the posthumous personality [p. 31]. …

I compared the post-sepulchral phantom with the living phantom, and I had not much trouble in convincing myself that it was the same personage. I could not, however, establish such a conclusion save upon the basis of a great number of proofs. I then consulted the works of those writers who, after a more or less direct method, had treated [p. 34] this question. I found in the reports of the theologians, magistrates, physicians, magnetizers, &c., a harvest of facts much more abundant than I had dared to hope for. The doubling of the human personality, and, as a consequence, the existence of the posthumous phantom, became for me a matter of certainty [p. 35]. …

The phenomena of "doubling" present … all the shades of difference, from the complete and living apparition of the human form to the simplest dreams. These different manifestations evidently depend upon the degree of moral energy in the individual, the tension of his mind toward a determined result, his physical constitution, his age, and probably other causes as well, of which we are ignorant …. The same applies to the memory of what passes during the "doubling." Certain persons recollect most accurately all that they have done, seen, or heard. Others only catch vague and broken reminiscences alternated with perfect blanks; others have no remembrance of the part which they have played during their lethargic sleep. Such is the case of some somnambules, about whom I shall soon have occasion to remark [p. 41]….

If it is surprising to see a vocal organ in the human phantom, it is still more so to learn that the latter also possesses a digestive apparatus. A glass of water, for example, can be swallowed by the fluidic image of a person and instantaneously pass into that person's body. … I will but add that this apparatus can only be the gaziform replica of that which exists in the body, and that it is united to the latter by a plexus of invisible capillaries [p. 49]. … It would not be impossible, however, to find analogies in the physical world. … Let us [p. 50] only bear in mind this principle of natural philosophy, so familiar to all who devote themselves to the study of science: there is no solution of continuity in nature. The child who comes out of the body of its mother is attached to her by a vascular system which brought it strength and life. It is the same in this doubling; the human phantom is constantly in immediate relation with the body whence it has wandered for some moments. Invisible bonds, and of a vascular nature, so intimately connect the two extremities of the chain, that any accident happening to one of the two poles reacts . . . instantaneously upon the other [p. 51]. …

The phantom possesses a circulatory apparatus as well as the body of which it is the double. Invisible capillaries unite the one to the other, and the whole forms a system so homogeneous, so closely connected, that the slightest prick received by the phantom at once reacts … on all the vascular apparatus up to the extremity of the chain, and blood flows immediately [p. 57]. …

In nearly all the narratives of phantasmal doubling that we have seen unfold themselves up to this point, the person who was the subject of it has been in bed, motionless, and plunged either in sleep or lethargy. The same rule holds with the greater part of analogous facts, which I either pass without remark or which I shall have occasion to cite in the following chapters. Hence follows this natural conclusion, that a lethargic sleep is the first necessary condition for producing the phenomenon of the Double [p. 65]. …

Innumerable facts, observed from antiquity to our own day, demonstrate in our being the existence of an internal [p. 68] reality—the internal man. Analysis of these different manifestations has permitted us to penetrate its nature. Externally it is the exact image of the person of whom it is the complement. Internally, it reproduces the mould of all the organs which constitute the framework of the human body. We see it, in short, move, speak, take nourishment; perform, in a word, all the great functions of animal life. The extreme tenuity of these constituent molecules, which represent the last term of organic matter, allow it to pass through the walls and partitions of apartments. Hence the name of phantom, by which it is generally designated. Nevertheless, as it is united with the body from which it emanates by an invisible vascular plexus, it can, at will, draw to itself by a sort of aspiration the greater part of the living forces which animate the latter. One sees, then, by a singular inversion, life withdraw from the body, which then exhibits a cadaverous rigidity, and transfer itself entirely to the phantom, which acquires consistency, sometimes even to the point of struggling with persons before whom it materializes. It is but exceptionally that it shows itself in connexion with a living person. But as soon as death has snapped the bonds which attach it to our organism, it definitely separates itself from the human body and constitutes the posthumous phantom [p. 69]. …

Let us return to the posthumous man. Being the continuation beyond the tomb of the inner personality that we have seen manifest itself in the phenomenon of duplication, it becomes easier to observe it. The living phantom and the post- sepulchral phantom have, in fact, as their common origin would indicate, numerous points of resemblance, so that the study of the one completes that of the other. I shall pass in review the principal traits which characterize them, so that we may inform ourselves as to the nature of the posthumous being. At the same time, we must not forget that we are entering the shadow-world, and that more than one point of interrogation will go unanswered.

Let us first study its physical constitution. What I have already said of the living spectre in the examples of duplication, cited in the second chapter, throws light upon the structure of the post-sepulchral spectre. It is the phantasmal replica of all the organs of the human body. It has been seen, in [p. 84] fact, to move, speak, take nourishment, accomplish, in a word, the different functions of animal life. This applies to the posthumous phantom as well as to its elder brother, as I shall have occasion to show, especially in the chapter on the post-mortem vampire. The molecules which constitute it are evidently borrowed from the organism which gave it birth. It may then be defined as a gaseous tissue offering a certain resistance. …

The fluidic constitution of the phantom offers the explanation of several peculiarities which it presents. In the first place, it clearly accounts for the ease with which it penetrates houses.

Some spectres open and close the doors of rooms, but others disdain these precautions, and know how to pass through when the entrances are all shut. They pass through partitions, or at least wooden ones. This phenomenon involves nothing contrary to the laws of nature. It is a direct consequence of the structure of the phantom. We know that all bodies, however great their density, are pierced with innumerable pores which give passage to fluid. Platinum, the densest of metals, is penetrated by hydrogen, and we have the record of the famous experiment of the Florentine academicians, who, submitting to a heavy pressure a hollow sphere of gold filled with water, saw tiny liquid drops ooze through the surface. One deduces from this, that the fissures of wood [p. 85] work of doors imperfectly joined may give access to the gaseous and elastic tissue of the spectre. …

By analogous considerations may be explained the rapidity with which the phantom, whether living or posthumous, may move [p. 86]. …

The living phantom is clothed, like the post- sepulchral phantom, with the costume that he habitually wore; he carries also with him the objects which are familiar to him. …

It seems indispensable to admit that garments and material objects in general have their fluidic duplicates as much as men and animals—duplicates that the phantom can detach and make use of [p. 92]. …

Besides its exterior and organic form, the human body possesses an interior and fluidic form moulded after the former. When a person's Double is projected, the person and his image are seen simultaneously [p. 103]. …

Every man possessing his Double should, it seems, enter after death the region of shadows; it is not at all certain, however, judging from the small number of posthumous apparitions and the exceeding rarity of projection of the Double with living persons. It is probable that the phantasmal image, inert of itself, has need to be stimulated, and in some sort completed, by another agent of the organism, which imparts to it the necessary energy to give it self-consciousness [p. 104], …

Let us now resume our inquiry upon a higher level. Why the exceeding rarity of the projection of the Double?

The answer to this question, which we have had to leave in suspense until now, has become possible, since the elements of the problem have been brought out in the successive analyses that we have made above. These elements are two in number—the fluidic being, which is virtually in each of us, and the mesmeric ether. The first is the gasiform [p. 249] duplicate of the human body. Its existence has been proven by the phenomena of duplication, and by this fact, that persons who have lost an arm or a leg often experience pains in the missing member—a member which the Seeress of Prevorst[9] perceived distinctly on all amputated persons. It plays a purely passive part, and only becomes animated under the action of the vital fluid. The latter, whose reservoir is the nervous apparatus, is developed in great quantity as the result of a very strong mental strain, a moral commotion, certain diseases, or other physiological causes. Under its vivifying influence, the inner being awakens, and, although remaining always in the latent state, reveals itself by unequivocal manifestations. One would say, then, that there was in man a second personality entirely different from the ordinary personality, and putting itself at times in antagonism with the latter. If the energies that it receives from the thaumaturgic fluid are so potent as to enable it to burst the bonds of its prison and assume momentarily an independent existence, it detaches itself from the body and shows itself under its visible form. This is duplication. This phenomenon is observed only in some organizations exceptionally gifted in the matter of sensitiveness; and this explains its extreme rarity [p. 250] …

Let us return to the posthumous phantom. Its visible manifestations are as rare as those of the living phantom. This comes evidently from the same causes. It is not enough that death frees the fluidic being from its bonds for the latter to become an independent and active personality, endowed with a life of its own ; it is further necessary that at this moment it shall be suitably saturated with mesmeric ether. Now this fluid decreasing with age and illness, and losing at the same time its essential qualities, it is excessively rare that it should have sufficient strength and energy to vivify the phantom at the instant when the latter is about to open the doors of its prison [p.255], ...

The living spectre and the spectre from beyond the tomb, having the same origin, can present in their manifestation the same common characteristics. Such are the noises that occur in certain habitations, where the chairs, furniture, crockery, &c., are seen to change place or to shake under the impulse of an invisible hand. When the hubbub is nocturnal, and the family has lost-one of its members, the phenomenon should be attributed to the actions of the posthumous being. If the noises occur during the day, and no death has happened, the cause of the prodigy must be sought in the effects of mesmerism. By scrutinizing closely, we shall probably find that there is in the house some electric person whose fluidic self is the cause of all these disorders; usually it is a young girl.[10] When it is a case of visions occurring in sleep, it is not so easy to discern the nature of the agent and to know if one has to do with a phenomenon of the objective or subjective order. We think, however, that the principle may be laid down that it must be ascribed in greater part to mesmerism [p. 256].

VI. Apparitions of the Living

In previous sections I have mentioned apparitions of the living as a phenomenon interpreted by many during the nineteenth century as the production or projection of a double from the physical body (e.g., Alvarado, 2009a). This idea was discussed by other authors in later years (e.g., Carrington, 1915; Flammarion, 1922/1921). Hornell Hart's work was a pioneering modern study of the features of apparitions of the living (Hart and Collaborators, 1956).

The purpose of this paper is to familiarize the reader with apparitions of the living through the presentation of nineteenth century examples of the phenomenon. Most of the cases are taken from Gurney, Myers and Podmore's *Phantasms of the Living* (1886), in which they were interpreted by Gurney as telepathic phenomena.[11]

Auditory Experience

Not all of the experiences reported were visual. The following case involved an auditory experience that corresponded to an action performed by the person who felt that he was out of the body. The reader should note that, while there are some cases of apparitions of the living involving out-of-body experiences, most of them do not include the recollection of being in a different location from the physical body.

> My mother and grandmother were together in the dining room of their house in the Isle of Wight, occupied in some domestic matter knock at the door caused my grandmother to hasten to it with a view to taking the [II, p. 598][12] stranger into the drawing-room. The knock was

heard by both mother and daughter. On opening the door with the least loss of time possible, my grandmother was surprised to find not only no one there but no one even in the long corridor which led to the dining-room. My mother distinctly remembered the look of astonishment in her mother's face as she returned from the door. Nothing more was said on the subject, but in a short time afterwards a letter was received from London from my grandmother's sister, or rather her family, saying that she (the sister) had been most seriously ill, at death's door indeed, but was now a little better, and wished my grandmother to come and see her. The latter went up to town and found her sister still very ill, but slowly recovering. After the mutual endearments natural to such an occasion, my grandmother said:

"Do you know, such a strange thing occurred, exactly at the time, it seems, when you were supposed to be dead or dying".

"I know what you are going to say", said the other. "When I was in the trance which was mistaken for death, I thought I went to your house in the Isle of Wight and knocked at your dining room door. You opened it instantly and looked much affrighted at not seeing me or any one, though I saw you".

The singular point in the story is the anticipation by the one sister of what the other sister was going to say.

No theory or inference was ever deduced by my relations from the circumstance, and it was only mentioned as an odd coincidence by them and their friends, who, as well as my mother, have often told me the story, [p. 599]

Apparition of a Sleeping Person

Some apparitions take place when the person seen is not in the waking state. The following took place when the man that appeared was sleeping and felt he was located in a place where he was heard and felt by someone in the distant location.

In March, 1854, I was up at Oxford, keeping my last term, in lodgings. I was subject to violent neuralgic headaches, which always culminated in sleep. One evening, about 8 p.m., I had an unusually violent one; when it became unendurable, about 9 p.m., I went into (I, p. 225) my bedroom, and flung myself, without undressing, on the bed, and soon fell asleep.

I then had a singularly clear and vivid dream, all the incidents of which are still as clear to my memory as ever. I dreamed that I was stopping with the family of the lady who subsequently became my wife. All the younger ones had gone to bed, and I stopped chatting to the father and mother, standing up by the fireplace. Presently I bade them goodnight, took my candle, and went off to bed. On arriving in the hall, I perceived that my fiancée had been detained downstairs, and was only then near the top of the staircase. I rushed upstairs, overtook her on the top step, and passed my two arms round her waist, under her arms, from behind. Although I was carrying my candle in my left hand, when I ran upstairs, this did not, in my dream, interfere with this gesture.

On this I woke, and a clock in the house struck 10 almost immediately afterwards.

So strong was the impression of the dream that I wrote a detailed account of it next morning to my fiancée.

Crossing my letter, not in answer to it, I received a letter from the lady in question: 'Were you thinking about me, very specially, last night, just about 10 o'clock? For, as I was going upstairs to bed, I distinctly heard your footsteps on the stairs, and felt you put your arms round my waist.'

> The letters in question are now destroyed, but we verified the statement made therein some years later, when we read over our old letters, previous to their destruction, and we found that our personal recollections had not varied in the least degree therefrom. The above narratives may, therefore, be accepted as absolutely accurate.
>
> *P. H. Newnham*
>
> The following is Mrs. Newnham's account.
>
> I remember distinctly the circumstance which my husband has described as corresponding with his dream. I was on my way up to bed, as usual, about 10 o'clock, and on reaching the first landing I heard distinctly the footsteps of the gentleman to whom I was engaged, quickly mounting the stairs after me, and then I as plainly felt him put his arms round my waist. So strong an impression did this make upon me that I wrote the very next morning to the gentleman, asking if he had been particularly thinking of me at 10 o'clock the night before, and to my astonishment I received (at the same time that my letter would reach him) a letter from him describing his dream, in almost the same words that I had used in describing my impression of his presence.
>
> *M. Newnham [p. 226]*

Apparition of a Dying Person

Many of the accounts presented in *Phantasms of the Living* referred to crisis apparitions in which the person perceived at a distance was passing through some sort of crisis such as an accident or was dying. The following is an example of the latter.

> In 1856 I was engaged on duty at a place called Roha, some 40 miles south of Bombay, and moving about in the districts (as it is termed in India). My only shelter was a tent, in which I lived for several months in the year. My parents, and only sister, about 22 years [II, p. 41] of age, were living at K., from which place letters used to take a week reaching me. My sister and I were regular correspondents, and the post generally arrived about 6 a.m., as I was starting to my work. It was on the 18th April of that year (a day never to be forgotten) that I received a letter from my mother, stating that my sister was not feeling well, but hoped to write to me the next day. There was nothing in the letter to make me feel particularly anxious. After my usual out-door work, I returned to my tent, and in due course set to my ordinary daily work. At 2 o'clock my clerk was with me, reading some native documents that required my attention, and I was in no way thinking of my sister, when all of a sudden I was startled by seeing my sister (as it appeared) walk in front of me from one door of the tent to the other, dressed in her nightdress. The apparition had such an effect upon me that I felt persuaded that my sister had died at that time. I wrote at once to my father, stating what I had seen, and in due time I also heard from him that my sister had died at that time. [p. 42]

Producing an apparition

Over the years there have been reports of individuals who can produce apparitions of themselves through willing it. The following is an example.

> On a certain Sunday evening in November, 1881, having been reading of the great power which the human will is capable of exercising, I determined with the whole force of my being that I

would be present in spirit in the front bedroom on the second floor of a house situated at 22, Hogarth Road, Kensington, in which room slept two ladies of my acquaintance, viz., Miss L. S. V. and Miss E. C. V., aged respectively 25 and 11 years. I was living at this time at 23, Kildare Gardens, a distance of about 3 miles from Hogarth Road, and I had not mentioned in any way my intention of trying this experiment to either of the above ladies, for the simple reason that it was only on retiring to rest upon this Sunday night that I made up my mind to do so. The time at which I determined I would be there was 1 o'clock in the morning, and I also had a strong intention of making my presence perceptible [I, p. 104].

On the following Thursday I went to see the ladies in question, and, in the course of conversation (without any allusion to the subject on my part), the elder one told me, that, on the previous Sunday night, she had been much terrified by perceiving me standing by her bedside, and that she screamed when the apparition advanced towards her, and awoke her little sister, who saw me also.

I asked her if she was awake at the time, and she replied most decidedly in the affirmative, and upon my inquiring the time of the occurrence, she replied, about 1 o'clock in the morning.

This lady, at my request, wrote down a statement of the event and signed it.

This was the first occasion upon which I tried an experiment of this kind, and its complete success startled me very much.

Besides exercising my power of volition very strongly, I put forth an effort which I cannot find words to describe. I was conscious of a mysterious influence of some sort permeating in my body, and had a distinct impression that I was exercising some force with which I had been hitherto unacquainted, but which I can now at certain times set in motion at will.

S. H. B.

[Of the original entry in the almanack diary, Mr B. Says: "I recollect having made it within a week or so of the occurrence of the experiment, and whilst it was perfectly fresh in my memory".]

Miss Verity's account is as follows:

On a certain Sunday evening, about twelve months since, at our house in Hogarth Road, Kensington, I distinctly saw Mr B. in my room, about 1 o'clock. I was perfectly awake and was much terrified. I awoke my sister by screaming, and she saw the apparition herself. Three days after, when I saw Mr B., I told him what had happened; but it was some time before I could recover from the shock I had received, and the remembrance is too vivid to be ever erased from my memory.

L. S. Verity

Miss E. C. Verity says:

I remember the occurrence of the event described by my sister in the annexed paragraph, and her description is quite correct. I saw the apparition which she saw, at the same time and under the same circumstances.

Miss A. S. Verity says:

I remember quite clearly the evening my eldest sister awoke me by calling to me from an adjoining room; and upon my going to her bedside, where she slept with my youngest sister, they both told me they had seen S. H. B. standing in the room. The time was about 1 o'clock. S. H. B. Was in evening dress, they told me. [p. 105]

Arrival Apparition

Some apparitions are seen arriving at a location before the person represented by them actually gets there. These experiences seem to be recurrent with these persons.

> In the autumn of 1877, while at Sholebrook Lodge, Towcester, Northamptonshire, one night, at a little after 10 o'clock, I remember I was about to move a lamp in my room to a position where I usually sat a little while before retiring to bed, when I suddenly saw a vision of my brother. It seemed to affect me like a mild shock of electricity. It surprised me so that I hesitated to carry out what I had intended, my eyes remaining fixed on the apparition of my brother. It gradually disappeared, leaving me wondering what it meant. I am positive no light or reflection deceived me. I had not been sleeping or rubbing my eyes. I was again in the act of moving my lamp when I heard taps along the window. I looked towards it—the window was on the ground-floor—and heard a voice, my brother's, say, 'It's I; don't be frightened.' I let him in; he remarked, 'How cool you are; I thought I should have frightened you.'
>
> The fact was that the distinct vision of my brother had quite prepared me for his call. He found the window by accident, as he had never been to the house before; to use his own words, 'I thought it was your window, and that I should find you.' He had unexpectedly left London to pay me a visit, and when near the house lost his way, and had found his way in the dark to the back of the place. [II, p. 96]

Apparition before Death

Apparitions of individuals before they die have created the belief that this is a presage of death. I have presented some examples of these apparitions from the old literature (Alvarado, 2008b). The following is a case in point.

> The house being a small one, I occupied a bedroom which communicated with a sitting room on the upper storey, and, being some way from the other sleeping rooms, it was my habit to keep a lamp burning during the entire night. On the 29th of September I retired as usual in the best possible health and spirits, quite unaware of the then critical state of my relative, and had just got into bed, with face turned towards the wall, when I became aware of another presence in the room.
>
> Turning towards the door of communication, I there saw, as I imagined, my relative who was ill, standing looking at me and smiling. He was dressed as I had been accustomed to see him; the light was bright, and I observed every detail. I lay for a few seconds and then spoke, but getting no answer, jumped out of bed with hands outstretched towards the figure, which, on my approach, retreated to the outer room still smiling with peculiar sweetness. I followed it, and watched it vanish through the outer door, which was closed. After a moment's pause I opened the door and looked out, but saw nothing but a bare passage and narrow staircase, dimly lit from the room in which I stood. I was not afraid, only wondering, for though we had been in the habit of telling 'ghost' stories, it did not strike me at the time to associate this with anything of the kind.
>
> On the following morning I told the other members of the family of my experience, and somebody suggested that it was just possible that the bright light at that hour might have alarmed the man who had care of the house, an old servant, and that he might have come upstairs to see that all was safe. Though personally quite sure of the identity of the apparition, I made inquiries, and found that there was no foundation for the suggestion.
>
> My relative died the following night (Sidgwick et al., 1894, pp. 286–287).

Recurrent Apparition

In addition to arrival apparitions there are some rare cases in which some persons are seen repeatedly by others for no apparent cause. The following is an example of such cases which the late George Zorab (1975) grouped with other phenomena as representing a "phantom–forming predisposition."

Lucy Hawkins was seen repeatedly by family and friends in her youth. She wrote:

> The event described in the enclosed accounts took place at Cherington, near Shipston-on-Stour, in Warwickshire, the residence of my uncle, Mr William Dickins who was for many years chairman of Quarter Sessions in [II, p. 78] the county. The ladies who saw the appearance are two of his daughters, one of them a little older than myself, the other 3 or 4 years younger. I was then just 17.
>
> The only mistake that I can discover in either of the accounts is that Mrs Malcolm says I had been hiding with her 'brother,' whereas I had really been all the time with her sister, Miss Lucy Dickins—a fact of no importance except that she (Miss D.) might (if necessary) bear witness that I had really been with her all the time in the washhouse, and so could not have been near where I was seen.
>
> I remember we were all somewhat awed by what had happened, and that it broke up our game. I myself quite thought it was a warning of speedy death; but as I was not a nervous or excitable girl, it did not make me anxious or unhappy, and in course of time the impression passed off.

Writing to Mrs Hawkins in September, 1884, Miss Dickins said:

> Georgie [Mrs Malcolm] is coming here on Friday, and I propose then to show her your letters, and Mr Gurney's, and that we should each write our impressions of what we saw independently, and see how far they agree, and we will send the result to you. It is all very fresh in my memory, and I can at this moment conjure you up in my mind's eye, as you appeared under that tree and disappeared in the yard. I even recollect distinctly the dress you wore, a sort of brown and white, rather large check, such as was in fashion then, and is now, but was in abeyance in the intermediate years.

Shortly afterwards Miss Dickins wrote:

> I send the two accounts which Georgie and I wrote about your apparition. We wrote them independently, and so I think they are wonderfully good evidence, as they tally to almost every particular, except the little fact that I thought she joined me in searching the yard for you, and she thinks not—but that has nothing to do with the main fact of the story, our entire belief that we saw you in the body.
>
> In the autumn of 1845, we were a large party of young ones staying in the house, and on one occasion were playing at a species of hide-and-seek, in which we were allowed to move from one hiding-place to another, until caught by the opposite side. At the back of the house there was a small fold-yard opening on one side into the orchard, on the other into the stable yard, and there were other buildings to the left. I came round the corner of these buildings, and saw my cousin standing under some trees about 20 yards from me, and I distinctly saw her face; my sister, who at the moment appeared on the other side, also saw her and shouted to me to give chase. My cousin ran between us in the direction of the fold-yard, and when she reached the door we were both close behind her and followed instantly, but she had entirely disappeared, though scarcely a second had elapsed. We looked at one another in amazement, and searched every corner of the yard in vain; and when found some little time afterwards, she assured us that she had never been on that side of the house at all, or anywhere near the spot, but had remained hidden in the same place until discovered by one of the enemy.
>
> *S. F. D.* [p. 79]

I well remember the incident of your 'fetch' appearing to us. I believe I wrote down the details at the time, but do not know what has become of that record, so must trust to my memory to recall the circumstances, and do not fear its [not] being faithful though nearly 40 years have passed.

We were playing our favourite game of Golowain, which consisted in dividing into sides at hide-and-seek, the party hiding having the privilege of moving on from place to place until they reached the 'Home,' unless meanwhile caught by the pursuing party.

As I stood towards the end of the game, as a seeker, in the orchard, I saw you, who belonged to the opposite party, stealing toward me. As your dress was the same as your sister's, and there was the possibility of my mistaking you for her, who was on my side, I shouted her name, and she answered me from the opposite side of the wood. I then gave chase, and you turned, and looked at me laughing, and I saw your face distinctly. But at the same instant, Nina, also my friend, but your enemy, appeared round some corner, and being still nearer to you than I was, I left the glory of your capture to her. She was close upon you as you fled into a cow yard. I was so sure your fate was sealed that I followed more slowly, and hearing the bell ring, that, according to the rules of our game, recalled us to the 'Home', I went on there, to find Nina upbraiding you for having so mysteriously escaped her in this cow-yard.

In astonishment you said you never had been near the place. Of course I supported my little sister in her assertion; whilst our brother supported you, saying he had been hiding with you, and that, being tired, you had both remained hidden in one place until the bell warned you that the game was over—that place being a washhouse in a distinct part of the premises from the cow or fold-yard, into which we believed we had chased you.

G. M. (nee Dickins).

Mrs Hawkins continues:

The second appearance of my 'double' was in the spring (February or March) of 1847, at Leigh Rectory, in Essex, my father, the Rev. Robert Eden (now Primus of Scotland), being rector of the parish.

The person who saw it was the nursery maid. I am not quite sure of her name; but if, as I think, she was a certain 'Caroline,' she has been dead many years, therefore I can only give you my own very vivid recollections of her story, told with tears of agitation.

But first I should mention that I had the mumps at that time, and was going about with my head tied up, and the only other person in the house who had it was my little brother, nearly 10 years younger than myself, who could not possibly be mistaken for me.

On the first floor of Leigh Rectory there is a passage which runs the length of the house, terminated at one end by the door of a room that was then the nursery. One morning, about 10.30, 'Caroline' came out of the nursery, and, walking along the passage, had to pass a doorway opening on to the stairs which led down into the front hall. As she passed, she glanced down, and saw me (conspicuous by the white handkerchief round my head, [p. 80] and facing her) come out of the drawing-room door and walk across the corner of the hall to the library. She proceeded along the passage, and, coming to the foot of the attic stairs, met our maid, who said to her, 'Do you know where Miss Eden is? I want to go to her room.' 'Oh yes,' answered Caroline, 'I just saw her go into the library. So they came together up to my room, which was one of the attics, and found me sitting there, where I had been for at least half an hour, writing a letter. After a moment's pause of astonishment, they fled, though I called to them to come in. When I went downstairs a few minutes afterwards, and reached the passage, I saw in the nursery a group of maids, all looking so perturbed that, instead of proceeding down the front stairs, I went on to the nursery and asked what was the matter. But as no one answered, and I saw the nurserymaid was crying, I thought they had been quarrelling, and went away, quite unconscious that it was on my account they were so disturbed.

Lucy Hawkins

The following account is from Mrs Hawkins' son:

In the autumn of 1877, I was living at my father's house, Beyton Rectory, Bury St. Edmunds. The household consisted of my father, mother, three sisters, and three maid servants. One moonlight night I was sleeping in my room, and had been asleep some hours, when I was awakened by hearing a noise close to my head, like the chinking of money. My waking idea, therefore, was that a man was trying to take my money out of my trousers pocket, which lay on a chair close to the head of my bed. On opening my eyes, I was astonished to see a woman, and I well remember thinking with sorrow that it must be one of our servants who was trying to take my money. I mention these two thoughts to show that I was not thinking in the slightest degree of my mother. When my eyes had become more accustomed to the light, I was more than ever surprised to see that it was my mother. … Dressed in a peculiar silver-grey dress, which she had originally got for a fancy ball. She was standing with both hands stretched out in front of her as if feeling her way; and in that manner moved slowly away from me, passing in front of the dressing-table, which stood in front of the curtained window, through which the moon threw a certain amount of light. Of course, my idea all this time was that she was walking in her sleep. On getting beyond the table she was lost to my sight in the darkness. I then sat up in bed, listening; but hearing nothing, and, on peering through the darkness, saw that the door, which was at the foot of my bed, and to get to which she would have had to pass in front of the light, was still shut. I then jumped out of bed, struck a light, and instead of finding my mother at the far end of the room, as I expected, found the room empty. I then for the first time supposed that it was an 'appearance,' and greatly dreaded that it signified her death.

I might add that I had, at that time, quite forgotten that my mother had ever appeared to any one before, her last appearance having been about the year 1847, three years before I was born.

Edward Hawkins [p. 81]

VII. Visions of Death

The old idea that death is the permanent separation of the spirit and the physical body is the first thing that comes to mind when we hear about those cases referred to by William Barrett as "Visions of the Spirit of a Dying Person Leaving the Body" (Barrett, 1926, Chapter 6). These are instances in which death-bed witnesses see something—lights, mist, or a spirit body—coming out of the body of a dying person.[13]

Cases of this sort were published during the nineteenth century (e.g., Moses, 1887/1904), as can be seen in the excerpts presented below. One such observation was recorded in Sarah Cartwright's *Magnetism Clairvoyantly Discerned* (1884), whose "spiritual sight" perceived the separation of the spirit of an eighteen year old young woman: "Death came to her through the delirium of fever … and as the separation gradually progressed from the extremities I saw the spirit body contract, withdrawing from the flesh leaving the feet cold, the hands, arms, limbs until life centered around the heart and base of the brain, and the spinal cord, which gradually loosened its hold … The spirit body of the young girl, when withdrawn from the larger development of the physical, was less than two-thirds in size" (p. 118–119).

Some cases of this type have been reported during the twentieth century. These include the luminous emanations described by Tweedale (1921) and Monk (1922), and the observations of spirit bodies presented by Snell (1918; see also Hallucinations, 1908). More recently there have been reports of vague emanations, as seen in McAdams's (1984) paper, and in the short descriptions presented by Wills–Brandon (2000).

The purpose of the current paper is to reprint some descriptions of this phenomenon published in the nineteenth century. I present accounts written by Sophia De Morgan and Andrew Jackson Davis.

Sophia de Morgan

Several examples of these death visions were recorded by Sophia de Morgan (1809–1892), who was involved with mesmerism, spiritualism and women's rights. Both Sophia, and her husband, mathematician Augustus De Morgan (1806–1871), explored spiritualism and accepted the reality of its phenomena.[14]

The observations presented here appeared in Sophia De Morgan's book *From Matter to Spirit* (1863), a book devoted to spiritualism. The book included several chapters about mediumistic phenomena (e.g., writing, visions), apparitions, and the topic of this article. The latter, the ninth chapter of the book, was entitled "Process of Death and Formation of the Spiritual Body".

The following excerpts include several accounts, starting with an experience by the author:

> I was myself once standing with a person who had sometimes the gift of spiritual vision, beside a bed on which lay one whose life was departing. The breathing was ceasing slowly when I noticed a thin white mist which seemed to rise two or three inches above the bed. My companion appeared also to be looking at something. Her eyes, which always had a strange glitter when they encountered any object unseen by others, were raised gradually from the recumbent form to the top of the bed; then, returning, seemed to rest half-way between, gazing, as far as I could see, on vacancy. This earnest gaze lasted more than a minute. I looked at her enquiringly, but she did not speak. She told me a few minutes after what she had seen, thus:
>
> "I was looking at a mist which seemed to be rising from the bed, and which I have noticed some time, when my attention was drawn upwards, and I saw a pillar of light, between sunshine and moonlight, rising three or four feet. Within this was a still brighter light, becoming more brilliant at the centre; and from the centre to the circumference, from within outwards, it was all working together with intense rapidity. I saw it once again, but slightly afterwards, just as the last breath was drawn. It seemed then to pass off by the top of the bed."
>
> The seer has been a trusted friend of my own for many years; her character for truthfulness is quite above suspicion [p. 128].
>
> On giving an account of this appearance to a friend, he told me that a similar statement had been made by a girl in whose character for truth he had entire confidence … The young woman had nursed her mother, who was confined to her bed by long and wasting illness. The poor invalid died gradually; the feet first, then the legs, becoming numb and powerless. At length life seemed to be confined to the head and upper part of the body. One night, or rather towards morning, the poor girl awoke suddenly and saw a strong light rising to some height above the sick woman, from whom it seemed to emanate. It passed away in an upward direction, and disappeared. The girl in great terror called out to her mother, but received no answer. She then ran to a friend (a confidential servant of my informant), and told her what she had seen. Her friend returned to the cottage, where they found the mother quite dead.

The late Miss W—, well known at one time in the mesmerising world, told me that she once nursed an uncle through his last illness. As he died, a very small bright cloud, appearing to come from the nostrils, passed away, and rising while she watched it, disappeared by the ceiling. This is another instance of a difference in the power of vision [p. 129].

My readers who are old enough to remember some of the early observations on magnetised girls, may recall the assertion made by one of the Okeys,[15] who, being taken by her mesmeriser into one of the hospital wards, declared that she always saw a cloudy figure, to which she gave some slang name, rising from the beds of certain patients. It was asserted by her mesmeriser, that in all those cases where she had represented the form as *tall*, the patient died; but there was a chance of recovery for those from whom it only seemed to emanate to a lesser height … The shorter figure was probably an efflux of the most external spiritual fluid of the sick person [p. 130].

Andrew Jackson Davis

Clairvoyant and visionary Andrew Jackson Davis (1826–1910) was well known for his numerous visions and descriptions of the other world.[16] Davis (1866) stated: "I have had the periscopic and clairvoyant ability to see through man's iron coating [the physical body] for the past fifteen years …" (p. 14), an ability he used at death-beds. The following excerpt is taken from Davis's *The Great Harmonia* (1850), and refers to his observations of a dying woman:

> Now the head of the body became suddenly enveloped in a fine—soft—mellow—luminous atmosphere; and, as instantly, I saw the cerebrum and the cerebellum expand their most interior portions; I saw them discontinue their appropriate galvanic functions; and then I saw that they became highly charged with the vital electricity and vital magnetism which permeate subordinate systems and structures … This phenomenon invariably precedes physical dissolution.
>
> Now the process of dying, or of the spirit's departure from the body, was fully commenced … The head became intensely brilliant; and I particularly remarked that just in the same proportion as the extremities of the organism grew dark, and cold, the brain appeared light and glowing.
>
> Now I saw, in the mellow, spiritual atmosphere, which [p. 165] emanated from, and encircled, her head, the indistinct outlines of the formation of another head! … This new head unfolded more and more distinctly; and so indescribably compact and intensely brilliant did it become, that I could neither see through it, nor gaze upon it as steadily as I desired. While this spiritual head was being eliminated and organized from out of, and above, the material head, I saw that the surrounding aromal atmosphere which had emanated from the material head was in great commotion; but, as the new head became more distinct and perfect, this brilliant atmosphere gradually disappeared. …
>
> With inexpressible wonder, and with a heavenly and utterable reverence, I gazed upon the holy and harmonious processes that were going on before me. In the identical manner in which the spiritual head was eliminated and unchangeably organized, I saw, unfolding in their natural, progressive order, the harmonious development of the neck, the shoulders, the breast, and the entire spiritual organization [p. 166] … The defects and deformities of her physical body, were, in the spiritual body which I saw thus developed, almost completely removed … her spiritual constitution, being elevated above those obstructions, was enabled to unfold and perfect itself.
>
> The spirit arose at right angles over the head or brain of the deserted body. But immediately previous to the final dissolution of the relationship which had for so many years subsisted between the two spiritual and material bodies, I saw—playing energetically between the feet of the

elevated spiritual body and the head of the prostrate physical body—a bright stream or current of vital electricity. This taught me, that what is customarily termed *Death* is but a *Birth* of the spirit from a lower into a higher state; that an inferior body and mode of existence are exchanged for a superior body and corresponding endowments and capabilities [p. 167] of happiness. I learned that the correspondence between the birth of a child into this world, and the birth of the spirit from the material body into a higher world, is absolute and complete—even to the *umbilical cord*, which was represented by the thread, of vital electricity, which, for a few minutes, subsisted between, and connected the two organisms together. And here I perceived, what I had never before obtained a knowledge of, that a small portion of this vital electrical element returned to the deserted body, immediately subsequent to the separation of the umbilical thread; and that that portion of this element which passed back into the earthly organism, instantly diffused itself through the entire structure, and thus prevented immediate decomposition [p. 168].

As soon as the spirit, whose departing hour I thus watched, was wholly disengaged from the tenacious physical body, I directed my attention to the movements and emotions of the former; and I saw her begin to breathe the most interior or spiritual portions of the surrounding terrestrial atmosphere ... At first it seemed with difficulty that she could breathe the new medium; but, in a few seconds, she inhaled and exhaled the spiritual elements of nature, with the greatest possible ease and delight. And now I saw that she was in the possession of exterior and physical proportions, which were identical, in every possible particular—improved and beautified—with those proportions which characterized her earthly organization. That is to say, she possessed a heart, a stomach, a liver, lungs, &c., &c., just as her natural body did previous to (not her, but) *its* death [p. 169], ...

The period required to accomplish the entire *change*, which I saw, was not far from two hours and a half ... Without changing my position, or spiritual perceptions, I continued to observe the movements of her new-born spirit. As soon as she became accustomed to the new elements which surrounded her, she descended from her elevated position, which was immediately over the body, by an effort of the will-power, and directly passed out of the door of the bedroom, in which she had lain [p. 171] (in the material form) prostrated with disease for several weeks. It being in a summer month, the doors were all open, and her egress from the house was attended with no obstructions. I saw her pass through the adjoining room, out of the door, and step from the house into the atmosphere! ... She walked in the atmosphere as easily, and in the same manner, as we tread the earth, and ascend an eminence. Immediately upon her emergement from the house, *she was joined by two friendly spirits from the spiritual country*; and, after tenderly recognising and communing with each other, the three, in the most graceful manner, began ascending obliquely through the ethereal envelopment of our globe. They walked so naturally and fraternally together, that I could scarcely realize the fact that they trod the air—they seemed to be walking upon the side of a glorious but familiar mountain! I continued to gaze upon them until the distance shut them from my view; whereupon I returned to my external and ordinary condition [p. 172].

VIII. Frederic W. H. Myers

Of all the early researchers of the Society for Psychical Research (SPR), Frederic W. H. Myers (1843–1901) was the one who addressed the topic of the current series of papers in greatest detail.[17] At the time the excerpts presented below appeared Myers was already known for his publications in the SPR *Proceedings*. Among these were his articles about the subliminal mind (Myers, 1892b) and about such topics as automatic writing (Myers, 1885) and apparitions of the dead (Myers, 1892a).

Myers (1886) started discussing the topic of the present excerpt as an alternate explanation to Edmund Gurney's telepathic model of apparitions of the living, particularly of collective apparitions (Gurney, Myers & Podmore, 1886). In what follows I will present Myers's ideas as he expressed them in his *Human Personality and Its Survival of Bodily Death* (1903). Here, and to some extent in the context of the phenomenon of apparitions of the living,[18] he referred to psychical excursion, an experience "involving some kind of perception as from a new standpoint, which perception may or may not include material objects in its purview" [1: p. 230].[19] Assuming this could take place, Myers suggested that "it is conceivable that this should involve not only the migrant spirit's perception from that point, but also perception of that point by persons materially present near it" [1: p. 232]. Such space would be a phantasmogenetic centre, which was different from a double. The centre was seen by Myers as a modification of "a certain portion of space, not materially nor optically, but in such a manner that specially susceptible persons may perceive it" [I, pp. xix–xx],

Myers on Psychical Invasions, Psychical Excursions, Phantasmogenetic Centres and the Psychorrhagic Diathesis

Now one advantage of the conception *of psychical invasion or excursion* ... is that it is at any rate sufficiently fundamental to allow of our arrangement of all our recorded cases—perhaps of all possible cases of apparition—in accordance with its own lines. And even though there be many cases for which the metaphor of invasion seems needlessly strong, and the older metaphor of "telepathic impact" quite sufficient, yet these cases also, although in some sense less complete, will arrange themselves naturally in the same divisions.

Let us take A for the "agent", or the spirit supposed in each case to be invasive or excursive: P for the "percipient", the spirit which plays the more passive role, receiving and sometimes observing the visit of A. Naturally the agent is often—perhaps in reality *always*—a percipient also. He goes forth to acquire information as well as to give it; but his subliminal self, which makes this excursion, cannot always report the results to his supraliminal self—from whom we outsiders are forced to make our inquiry. His power of giving us information, indeed, is ... particularly liable to be cut short by his death.

We want, then, a scheme which is to include, on the lines of this conception of *invasion* or *excursion*, all observable telepathic action, from the faint currents which we may imagine to be continually passing between man and man, up to the point ... where one of the parties to the telepathic intercourse has definitely quitted the flesh. The *first* term in our series must be conveniently vague: the last must lead us to the threshold of the spiritual world. ...

I must begin with cases where the action of the excursive fragment of the personality is of the weakest kind—the least capable of [I: p. 254] affecting other observers, or of being recalled into the agent's own waking memory.

Such cases, naturally enough, will be hard to bring up to evidential level. It must depend on mere chance whether these weak and aimless psychical excursions are observed at all; or are observed in such a way as to lead us to attribute them to anything more than the subjective fancy of the observers.

How can a casual vision—say, of a lady sitting in her drawing-room,—of a man returning home at six o'clock—be distinguished from memory-images on the one hand and from what I may term "expectation-images" on the other? The picture of the lady may be a slightly modified and externalised reminiscence; the picture of the man walking up to the door may be a mere projection of what the observer was hoping to see.

I have assumed that these phantoms coincided with no marked event. The lady may have been thinking of going to her drawing-room; the man may have been in the act of walking home;—but these are trivial circumstances which might be repeated any day.

Yet, however trivial, almost any set of human circumstances are sufficiently complex to leave room for coincidence. If the sitter in the drawing room is wearing a distinctive article of dress, never seen by the percipient until it is seen in the hallucination;—if the phantasmal homeward traveller is carrying a parcel of unusual shape, which the real man does afterwards unexpectedly bring home with him;—there may be reason to think that there is a causal connection between the apparent agent's condition at the moment, and the apparition [I: p. 255]. …

In these *arrival* cases,[20] there is, I say, a certain likelihood that the man's mind may be fixed on his return home, so that his phantasm is seen in what might seem both to himself and to others the most probable place. …

But there are other cases where a man's phantasm is seen in a place where there is no special reason for his appearing, although these places seem always to lie within the beat and circuit of his habitual thought.

In such cases there are still possible circumstances which may give reason to think that the apparition is causally connected with the apparent agent. The phantasm of a given person may be seen *repeatedly* by different percipients, or it may be seen *collectively* by several persons at a time; or it may combine both these evidential characteristics, and may be seen several times and by several persons together.

Now considering the rarity of phantasmal appearances, considering that not one person in (say) five thousand is ever phantasmally seen at all; the mere fact that a given person's phantasm is seen even *twice*, by different percipients (for we cannot count a second appearance to the same percipient as of equal value), is in itself a remarkable fact; while if this happens *three or four times* we can hardly ascribe such a sequence of rare occurrences to chance alone [I: p. 257]. …

Impressive as is the *repetition* of the apparition in these cases, it is yet less so to my mind than the *collective* character of some of the perceptions [I: p. 260], …

The question of the true import of collectivity of percipience renews in another form that problem of *invasion* to which our evidence so often brings us back. When two or three persons see what seems to be the same phantom in the same place and at the same time, does that mean that that special part of space is somehow modified? Or does it mean that a mental impression, conveyed by the distant agent—the phantom-begetter—to one of the percipients is reflected telepathically from that percipient's mind to the minds of the other—as it were secondary—percipients? The reader already knows that I prefer the former of these views. And I observe—as telling against that other view, of psychical contagion—that in certain collective cases we discern no probable link between any one of the percipient minds and the distant agent.

In some of that group of collective cases which we are at this moment considering, this absence of link is noticeable in a special way. The agent may indeed be acquainted with the percipients. … But there is nothing to show that any thought or emotion was passing from agent to percipients at the moment of the apparition. On the contrary, the indication is that there is no necessary connection whatever between the agent's condition of mind at the moment and the fact that such and such persons observed his phantasm. The projection of the phantasm, if I may so term it, seems a matter wholly automatic on the agent's part, as automatic and meaningless as a dream.

Assuming, then, that this is so—that these bilocations do occur without any appreciable stimulus from without, and in moments of apparent calm and indifference—in what way will this fact tend to modify previous conceptions?

It suggests that the continuous dream-life which we must suppose to run concurrently with our waking life is potent enough to effect from time to time enough of dissociation to enable some element of the personality to be perceived at a distance from the organism. How much of consciousness, if any, may be felt at the point where the excursive phantasm is seen, we cannot say. But the notion that a mere incoherent quasi-dream should thus become perceptible to others is fully in accordance with the theories suggested in this work. For I regard subliminal operation as *continuously* going on, and I hold that the degree of dissociation which can generate a perceptible phantasm is not necessarily a profound change, since that perceptibility depends so largely upon idiosyncrasies of agent and percipient as yet wholly unexplained. [I: p. 263]

One of Myers' most interesting ideas was that of a predisposition to produce apparitions of oneself while alive, which he speculated could be both physiological and psychological. "Psychorrhagy" was defined by him in his glossary as: "A special idiosyncrasy which tends to make the phantasm of a person easily perceptible; the breaking loose of a psychical element, definable mainly by its power of producing a phantasm, perceptible by one or more persons, in some portion of space" (I, p. xx). Some elements of this idea had been presented before by others. For example, Jung-Stilling, whom I discussed in a previous paper (Alvarado, 2009c), stated that there could be individuals "to whom this detachment is a very easy matter" (Jung-Stilling, 1808/1834, p. 79). He also speculated on a particular case in which the appearer may have had "the capability, either from nature, or by some secret means, or by both, to detach his soul at pleasure" (p. 80).

Another idea along these lines came from the English spiritualist and publisher, William H. Harrison. He suggested that some individuals "are so physiologically constituted that their spirits are not infrequently seen in the place to which their thoughts are directed" (Harrison, 1879, p. 161). Interestingly, German philosopher Carl du Prel (1888) referred to a "disposition of the nervous system" (p. 211) related to these phenomena.[21]

That special idiosyncracy on the part of the agent which tends to make his phantasm easily visible has never yet, so far as I know, received a name, although for convenience sake it certainly needs one. I propose to [I: p. 263] use the Greek word ψυχορραγῶ, which means strictly "to let the soul break loose", and from which I form the words *psychorrhagy* and *psychorrhagic*, on obvious analogies. When I say that Mrs. Beaumont or Mr Williams,[22] … was born with the *psychorrhagic diathesis*, I express what I believe to be an important fact, physiological as well as psychological. … That which "breaks loose" on my hypothesis is not (as in the Greek use of the word) the whole principle of life in the organism; rather it is some psychical element probably of very varying character, and definable mainly by its power of producing a phantasm, perceptible by one or more persons, in some portion or other of space. I hold that this phantasmogenetic effect may be produced either on the mind, and consequently on the brain of another person—in which case he may discern the phantasm somewhere in his vicinity, according to his own mental habit or prepossession—or else directly on a portion of space, "out in the open", in which case several persons may simultaneously discern the phantasm in that actual spot.

Here Myers analysed the case of Canon Bourne (I: 651–653). This involved a father and two daughters who went out hunting. The daughters went back to the house without the father. Then, at one point the daughters (and a coachman) saw the father at a distance riding his horse and waving his hat at them. The coachman believed Bourne had had an accident because the horse looked muddy. One of the sisters said that her father waved his hat at them and she saw the mark of the hat's make inside it, something that was not possible at a distance. On approaching Bourne they lost sight of him and only encountered him later when they went back to their house. The father assured them he had not been where he was seen and that he had not waved at them and had not had an accident of any sort. Myers stated:

> Let us apply the view to one of our most bizarre and puzzling cases—that of Canon Bourne. ... Here I conceive that Canon Bourne, while riding in the hunting-field, was also subliminally dreaming of himself (imagining himself with some part of his submerged consciousness) as having had a fall, and as beckoning to his daughters—an incoherent dream indeed, but of a quite ordinary type. I go on to suppose that, Canon Bourne being born with the psychorrhagic diathesis, a certain psychical element so far detached itself from his organism as to affect a certain portion of space—near the daughters of whom he was thinking—to affect it, I say, not materially nor even optically, but yet in such a manner that to a certain kind of immaterial and non- optical sensitivity a phantasm of himself and his horse became discernible. His horse was of course as purely a part of the phantasmal picture as his hat. The non-optical distinctness with which the words printed inside his hat were seen indicates that it was some inner non-retinal vision which received the impression from the phantasmogenetic centre. ...
>
> That explanation, indeed, suffers from the complexity and apparent absurdity inevitable in dealing with phenomena which greatly transcend known laws; but on the other hand it does in its way colligate Canon Bourne's case with a good many others of odd and varying types. Thus these appearances ... are in my view exactly parallel to the *hauntings* ascribed to departed spirits. There also we find a psychorrhagic diathesis—a habit or capacity on the part of certain spirits of detaching some psychical element in such [I: p. 264] a manner as to form a phantasmal picture, which represents the spirit as going through some dream-like action in a given place.
>
> The phantasmogenetic centre may thus, in my view, be equally well produced by an incarnate or by a discarnate spirit.
>
> These psychorrhagic cases are also, I think, important as showing us the earliest or feeblest stages of self-projection—where the dissociation belongs to the dream-stratum—implicating neither the supraliminal will nor the profounder subliminal strata. ...
>
> And now let us pass on from these psychorrhagic cases, which hardly concern anybody beyond the phantom-begetter himself—and do not even add anything to his own knowledge—to cases where there is some sort of communication from one mind to another, or some knowledge gained by the excursive spirit.
>
> It is impossible to arrange these groups in one continuous logical series. But, roughly speaking, the degree in which the psychical collision is *recollected* on either side may in some degree indicate its *intensity*, and may serve as a guide to our provisional arrangement.
>
> And following this scheme I shall begin with a group of cases which seem to promise but little information,—cases, namely, where A, the agent, in some way impresses or invades P, the percipient,—but nevertheless neither A nor P retains in supraliminal memory any knowledge of what has occurred.
>
> Now to begin with we shall have no difficulty in admitting that cases of this type are likely often to occur. The psychical *rapprochement* of telepathy takes place, *ex hypothesi*, in a region which is subliminal for both agent and percipient, and from whence but few and scattered impressions rise for either of them above the conscious threshold. Telepathy will thus probably operate far more continuously than our scattered glimpses would in themselves suggest.

> But how can we outside inquirers know anything of telepathic incidents which the principals themselves fail altogether to remember?
>
> In ordinary life we may sometimes learn from bystanders incidents which we cannot learn from the principals themselves. Can there be bystanders who look on at a psychical invasion?
>
> The question is of much theoretical import. On my view that there is a real transference of something from the agent, involving an alteration of some kind in a particular part of space, there might theoretically be some bystander who might discern that alteration in space more clearly than the person for whose benefit, so to say, the alteration was made. If, on the other hand, what has happened is merely a transference of some impulse "from mind to mind";—then one can hardly understand how any mind except the mind aimed at could perceive the telepathic impression. Yet, in collective cases, persons in whom the agent feels no interest, nay, of whose presence along with the intended percipient he is not aware, do in fact receive the impression in just the same way as that intended [I: p. 265] percipient himself [I: p. 266]. ...

Myers then went on to discuss cases in which the agent remembered having an experience.

> And here I note a gradual transition to the next large class of cases on which I am about to enter. I am about to deal with *telaesthesia;*—with cases where an agent-percipient—for he is both in one—makes a clairvoyant excursion (of a more serious type than the mere psychorrhagies already described), and brings back some memory of the scene which he has psychically visited. Now, of course, it may happen that he fails to bring back any such memory, or that if he does bring it back, he tells no one about it. In such cases, just as in the telepathic cases of which I have just spoken, the excursive phantom may possibly be observed by a bystander, and the circumstances may be such as to involve some coincidence which negatives the supposition of the bystander's mere subjective fancy [I: p. 270]. ...
>
> The cases which I have lately been recounting can be called telaesthetic only by courtesy. There has been a psychical excursion, with its possibilities of clairvoyance; but the excursive element has not brought home any assignable knowledge to the supraliminal personality [I: p. 275].

Myers discussed cases of this type.

> We now come ... to that class of cases where B invades A and A perceives the invasion; but B retains no memory of it in supraliminal life. From one point of view, as will be seen, this is just the reverse of the class last discussed—where the invader remembered an invasion which the invaded person (when there was one) did not perceive.
>
> We have already discussed some cases of this sort which seemed to be *psychorrhagic*—to have occurred without will or purpose on the part of the invader. What we must now do is to collect cases where there may probably have been some real projection of will or desire on the invader's part, leading to the projection of his phantasm in a manner recognisable by the distant friend whom he thus invades—yet without subsequent memory of his own. These cases will be intermediate between the *psychorrhagic* cases already described and the *experimental* cases on which we shall presently enter [I: p. 286]. ...
>
> Of still greater interest is the class which comes next in order in my ascending scale of apparent *intensity*; the cases, namely, where there is recollection on both sides, so that the experience is *reciprocal*. ... They deserve study, for it is by noting under what circumstances these spontaneously reciprocal cases occur that we have the best chance of learning how to produce them experimentally. ...

It is plain that just as we are not confined to noting small spontaneous telepathic transferences when they occur, but can also endeavour to reproduce them by experiment, so also we can endeavour to reproduce experimentally these [I: p. 291]. … more advanced telepathic phenomena of the invasion of the presence of the percipient by the agent. It is to be hoped, indeed, that such experiment may become one of the most important features of our inquiry. The type of the experiment is somewhat as follows. The intending agent endeavours by an effort at self-concentration, made either in waking hours or just before sleep, to render himself perceptible to a given person at a distance, who, of course, must have no reason to expect a phantasmal visit at that hour. Independent records must be made on each side, of all attempts made, and of all phantoms seen. The evidential point is, of course, the coincidence between the *attempt* and the *phantom*, whether or not the agent can afterwards remember his own success.[23] …

Now the *experimental* element here is obviously very incomplete. It consists in little more than in a concentrated desire to produce an effect which one can never explain, and seldom fully remember. I have seen no evidence to show that any one can claim to be an adept in such matters—has learned a method of thus appearing at will … We are acting in the dark. Yet nevertheless the mere fact that on some few occasions this strong desire has actually been followed by a result of this extremely interesting kind is one of the most encouraging phenomena in our whole research. The successes indeed have borne a higher proportion to the failures than I should have ventured to hope. But nowhere is there more need of persistent and careful experimentation [I: p. 292], …

It will be observed that in all these instances the conditions were the same—the agent concentrating his thoughts on the object in view before going to sleep. …

In these experimental apparitions … we naturally wish to know all that we can about each detail in the experience. Two important points are the *amount of effort* made by the experimenter, and the degree of his *consciousness of success*. The amount of effort in [two cases cited] … seems to have been great: and this is encouraging, since what we want is to be assured that the tension of will has really some power. It seems to act in much the same way as a therapeutic suggestion from the conscious self … It is therefore quite in accordance with analogy that a suggestion from without, given to a hypnotised person, should be the most promising way of inducing these self-projections. It should be strongly impressed on hypnotised subjects that they can and must temporarily "leave the body," as they call it, and manifest themselves to distant persons. …

That subsequent memory should be an eminently *educable* thing. The carrying over of recollections from one stratum of personality into another—as hypnotic experiment shows us—is largely a matter of patient suggestion. It would be very desirable to hypnotise the person who had succeeded in producing an experimental apparition … and to see if he could then recall the psychical excursion. Hypnotic states should be far more carefully utilised in connection with all these forms of self-projection.[24]

In the last section reprinted here Myers related self-projection to death.

In these self-projections we have before us, I do not say the most useful, but the most extraordinary achievement of the human will. What [I: p. 296] can lie further outside any known capacity than the power to cause a semblance of oneself to appear at a distance? What can be a more *central* action—more manifestly the outcome of whatsoever is deepest and most unitary in man's whole being? Here, indeed, begins the justification of the conception … that we should now see the subliminal self no longer as a mere chain of eddies or backwaters, in some way secluded from the main stream of man's being, but rather as itself the central and potent current, the most truly

> identifiable with the man himself. Other achievements have their manifest limit; where is the limit here? The spirit has shown itself in part dissociated from the organism; to what point may its dissociation go? It has shown some independence, some intelligence, some permanence. To what degree of intelligence, independence, permanence, may it conceivably attain? Of all vital phenomena, I say, this is the most significant; this self-projection is the one definite act which it seems as though a man might perform equally well before and after bodily death [I: p. 297].[25]

IX. Alma Haemmerle's "Experiments in Bilocation"

In a previous paper about apparitions of the living I presented a case of an "experimental apparition" (Alvarado, 2010a). These are cases in which a person has been able to produce an apparition of themselves intentionally at a distance. Some examples of these apparitions were published in *Phantasms of the Living* (Gurney, Myers & Podmore, 1886, Vol. 1, pp. 103–109, Vol. 2. pp. 675–676), and elsewhere (e.g., 'Experimental Thought-Transference', 1891; James, 1909). While these experiences are sometimes presented in the context of belief in a double and in the idea that something is leaving the body, not everyone who has been successful in projecting their image was aware of being in a different location or of feeling separated from their physical body. But the following excerpt presents some evidence concerning this.

I reprint here an account entitled "Experiments in Bilocation" authored by Alma Haemmerlé (1906). In the introduction to the paper by French psychical researcher Albert de Rochas we are told that the author was the eighteen-year-old daughter of Agathe Haemmerlé.[26] The account is remarkable in that it is rare to find a group of gifted people who are able to produce effects in distant locations, and to have the experience of visiting such locations.

In the first "experiment" two persons at a distance felt that they went to the place where the Haemmerlé family was, and were seen and felt tactilely by Alma, as well as seen by her sister and her brother. It is clear from the account of the first test that all the persons who perceived something were aware that the "visits" were going to take place at particular moments. But this was not the case in other instances mentioned below.

Mlle. Haemmerlé was particularly sensitive. In addition to being able to perceive "visits", she had out-of-body experiences (OBEs). In a note at the end of the paper de Rochas referred to an OBE she had when trying to visit his home from a distance. He presented her account:

> In the evening, when retiring to rest, I felt in the mood for producing the "double". I made a preliminary attempt, and I saw my own body lying on the bed, at a distance of six feet from me. When I had come back to myself I concluded that I was in a condition to make a more extended experiment. I felt myself transported into France; but as I had not re-read the directions contained in your letter, I asked myself where L'Agnelas might be. Then, at the same moment, the idea came to me that it was only necessary to think of you. An instant later I found myself at the foot of your bed. I saw you stretched on it, and I fixed my attention on you to make you look at me. You then sat up, looking round you, as if searching for something, blinking as a person does when awakened suddenly in the middle of the night. You were wearing a rather large night-shirt with a turned down collar; your neck was partially uncovered and your hair somewhat disordered. Around you I only perceived the white pillows and the white border of the sheet, which was turned back over your counterpane. I am sorry I did not think of looking at the whole room. I was at your right, at the corner of the foot of the bed" (in Haemmerlé, 1906, p. 118).

De Rochas stated that the details were correct but that the observations were too commonplace to be impressive. He did not remember having awakened. But Mlle. Haemmerlé's account supplies us with independent evidence about her OBE talents.

Mlle. Haemmerlé's paper has not been cited very often in recent times (for an exception see Blackmore, 1982, p. 202), but it was discussed in the old literature (e.g., Peter, 1907; Richet, 1922, p. 708). The account appears below.

Haemmerlé's "Experiments in Bilocation"

First experiment

The first experiment took place at Kherson (in Southern Russia), where my brother was completing his studies at the college. His classmates frequently visited our house; and as my mother was studying psychic matters, in which we were all interested, we determined one evening to try an experiment.

We therefore arranged that, on the following night, two of these young men, M Stankewitch and M Serboff, should endeavour to send their doubles to us; the former at 11 p.m., the latter at 11.30 p.m.

We timed our watches together and it was agreed that M Stankewitch should go to my brother in his bedroom, whilst M Serboff should manifest in the drawing-room.

On the following evening my sister Irma sat in the dining-room, from whence she could see the open door which led into the drawing-room. My brother, as had been agreed, remained in his bedroom and stretched himself on his bed, in order the better to concentrate his attention on the phenomenon he expected. The bedroom adjoined the dining-room.

After having been with my sister for a few minutes, I entered my brother's room, and leaning my elbow on the rail at the foot of his bed, I asked him what o'clock it was. He pulled out his watch and said it was just 11 o'clock. The hanging lamp in the dining-room gave light enough to make it possible to distinguish objects in the bedroom. At the same moment I felt something push against my shoulder and I saw at my side, very distinctly, the form of M Stankewitch; I could distinguish his dark uniform with the white metal buttons. At the same moment my brother said, "There he is, beside you," adding, almost immediately, "Did you see him?" for after the first remark the apparition had disappeared.

My sister, hearing us talking, came in, saying that she had just seen M Stankewitch enter by the drawing-room door, pass near the table in the dining-room, and then disappear from her sight. She also had seen him in uniform, and was able to distinguish the white metal buttons.

We then immediately, all three of us, entered the drawing-room, which was lighted by the lamp in the dining-room, and awaited the apparition of M Serboff. He did not appear until nearly midnight. This apparition seemed to us paler and less distinct than the preceding one. He entered the drawing-room by the ante-chamber, where he paused for a moment near the door, advancing now to the right towards one of the book-cases, then to the left towards the other one; then he suddenly disappeared. We kept silence for a while, thinking he might appear again, but he did not do so.

My brother then wrote out the results of our experiment, in detail, on two sheets of paper, enclosed them in envelopes and sealed them. The following day at the college my brother asked his two friends whether they had not forgotten their promise. They at once described, in the presence of their comrades, details which corresponded exactly with all that my brother had written. He then put into their hands the sealed envelopes, which were opened, the contents being read aloud before the whole class. After having read the account of his own appearance, M Serboff said that, at the moment when he entered the drawing room, he was undecided which cupboard he would approach, because he had intended to open the bookcase and take out a book; but he had lost his power of concentration and returned to his normal self. He felt too fatigued to try again. M Stankewitch added that he was surprised to feel a resistance on approaching the bed, for he had not expected me to be present. He thought the resistance was due to his having approached too near to the wall, since he only saw my brother. …

Second experiment

My sister Irma went to spend a few days in the country with one of our friends, whilst I remained with my parents. It was the first time that I had been separated from my twin sister; and, as her absence was a great trial to me, I determined to go and see what she was doing.

It was 11 p.m. and I was in bed. Soon I saw myself in the room which she was sharing with our friend, and I saw my sister in her bed, a book in her hand, and reading by the light of a lamp, which had a green shade. She felt my presence, raised her eyes and saw me standing by the stove. When I saw that she was looking at me I tried to hide myself behind the stove, being afraid that she would be frightened at the apparition, not being sure that she would recognise me.

On the following day I wrote her the details which I have just related, and I received a letter, dated the same day, telling me that she had seen me on the previous evening at 11 p.m., near the stove.

My sister and I have repeated this experiment several times, not always with success.

Third experiment

One evening, when I was with four of my friends, sisters belonging to the family Spechnieff, the eldest, Mlle Anna, said, with some anxiety, that her brother (who was an officer and who was to leave on the following day for Vladivostok) had suddenly been seized with a bad attack of fever. Seeing that my friends were so anxious, I resolved, on returning home, to try and cure him by mental suggestion.

I saw myself transported into the room of the sick man, and I fixed my attention upon him with all my will, mentally making the suggestion to him of a complete cure. When I went, on the following day, to see my friends and to ask after their brother, Mlle Anna told me that he had set off in good health, and that he had told her, on that very morning, that he had seen an apparition during the night: he had seen me at the further end of his room, and had felt my presence as a calming influence, and at the same moment the feverish condition had left him.

The other sisters also saw me on a day on which we had agreed that I should appear to them.

Fourth experiment

One of my cousins who was much interested in psychology has made numerous experiments in producing her own "double".

We were passing a few days in the country at the house of an aunt. One evening, wishing to know whether she would perceive my presence, I resolved to go and see her without previously informing her of my intention.

We were living in the right wing of the house, at the far end of the courtyard. Her room was on the ground floor and I wished to enter by the window that looked out on to the courtyard. I first tried to open the shutter, but did not succeed; I then determined to get in by a simple act of will. The noise I had made in attempting to open the shutter awakened my cousin, who jumped out of bed to see what the noise could be. She saw me in front of her, and guessing my object, she became calm. The following day she told me of her astonishment at having observed that the astral body had the power of moving objects.

X. Albert de Rochas and Doubles

An important figure in the history of ideas about the double was French scholar Lieutenant Colonel Eugène-Auguste-Albert de Rochas d'Aiglun (1837–1914), better known as Albert de Rochas.[27] He was well known for his studies in military history, fortifications, and ancient technology, as well as for his investigations of animal magnetism, hypnosis, and psychic phenomena. De Rochas's name is associated with ideas of forces projected from the body (e.g., de Rochas, 1887), as seen in his study of the exteriorization of sensitivity (de Rochas, 1899), a topic he related to the double. He also published about mediumistic physical phenomena, hypnosis, and reincarnation (see, respectively, de Rochas, 1896, 1897a, 1911), among other topics (e.g., de Rochas, 1902, 1905a, 1905b).

de Rochas (1895, 1906) reported how he released the double of some special subjects using magnetic passes. In a paper devoted to medium Eusapia Palladino, de Rochas related the concept of a fluidic double to the exteriorization of sensitivity and to mediumistic materialization phenomena, which he argued manifested in four degrees or stages (de Rochas, 1897b). The first consisted of "the exteriorization of sensibility in the form of concrete layers on the body of the subject" (p. 26). The second involved the "coagulation of its effluvia in a sensitive double, but still not visible to ordinary eyes" (pp. 26–27). While the third involved visible tangible materializations of parts of the body, the fourth consisted of whole materializations of bodies. He wrote that the last two stages presented a "galvanoplastic transport of the matter of the physical body of the medium, matter that leaves from the physical body to occupy a similar place on the fluidic double" (p. 27).

In a later book, *Les frontieres de la science*, de Rochas (1902) equated the "fluidic body of man" with the "nervous agent" running along nerves and through the physical body. This force, he argued, had the "same form as the body because it occupies the same portion of space" (p. 22).

The excerpts from the article appearing below, published in 1906 in the *Annals of Psychical Science*, illustrate some of the ideas and work of de Rochas about the double.

New Experiments Relative to the Astral Body and the Magnetic "Rapport"

The hypothesis of the astral body, among all those which have been put forward to explain psychical phenomena, is the most ancient, the most widespread, and the most rational.[28] … There is therefore great interest attaching to those experiments which make for proof of the reality of that intermediary. …

If we magnetise certain sensitives by passes, or send them to sleep by means of electric currents, we produce in them the exteriorisation of that agent which appears to be the vehicle of sensitivity, so that the sense of touch can be exerted at some distance from the skin, greater or less according to the energy of the action and the sensitiveness of the subjects.

In some cases, that agent which I shall call *Od*[29] … is projected towards the exterior normally from the surface of the body, and seems in some way connected with the rhythmical movement of the organism (the respiration and the pulsations of the heart and brain, which have three distinct measures), in such manner as to present *maxima*, and *minima*, forming a series of concentric envelopes whose sensitivity diminishes according to the distance. As the operation progresses, the Od seems to rarefy itself before and behind the subject, so as to condense itself at each side, forming there two poles analogous to those of a magnet. That condensation finally becomes intense enough to form at the right and left of the subject two luminous phantoms, reproducing in a more or less exact manner the corresponding halves of his body. Finally, the two half-phantoms, which are at about a yard distant from the physical body on either side, reunite themselves between the magnetiser and the subject, so as to form a complete phantom, which must be the *double* of the Egyptians and the *astral body* of the occultists.

I have recently had the opportunity of observing a lady in whom that process of formation was notably shortened. The *Od* exteriorised itself well; but as soon as it had gone from the physical body, it ascended and went to form the *double* over the head. That lady, who could see the *Od* herself, compared its progress to that of the hot air which ascends along the sides of a stove-pipe.[30]

In any case, the astral body, which the subject can displace by an effort of will, is united to the physical body by a fluidic bond which is sensitive and becomes more tenuous as the distance increases between the two bodies. It is the magnetiser who should furnish the *Od* permitting the extension of the fluidic bond, seeing that the subject always demands the continuation of the passes when his double must go to a distance, sometimes insisting that the rupture of that bond would result in his immediate death.

With certain subjects, the astral body behaves itself as if it was very dense and could not rise. It remains nearly level with the earth,[31] a thing which one can verify by testing the sensitivity of the air round the physical body. In the case of others, on the contrary, it tends always to rise. All of these last, without any exception, manifest a true beatitude when they have attained the higher regions which they are loath to leave to return to their "miserable rag"—the body.

The unanimity of the subjects, on this point, has certainly great value, especially when it has been possible to verify that their indications of the position of their astral body are consistently confirmed by the reactions which occur in the physical body, when one acts on the position in space where they say that their double is; but until now, I had made these verifications in some subjects only, and in such a way that they may have followed my movements and reacted consciously or unconsciously in order to support my theories.

Some time ago, however, some favourable circumstances permitted me to make a more rigorous experiment.

I had asked Mrs Lambert,[32] one of my best trained subjects, to come to my country house, L' Agnelas. ...[33] One evening some friends begged me to show them how the disengagement of the astral body was effected. After having placed Mrs Lambert in the ecstatic state, of which I have spoken above, I left her, according to her desire, in that state and continued the conversation without paying any attention to her. Then, the idea came to my mind to verify if the fluidic bond uniting her physical body to her astral body, which she said was then floating in the air at a great height, really had travelled over to those higher regions; so, under some pretext, I left the drawing-room on the ground floor where we were. I ascended cautiously to the first floor, went into the apartment just over the drawing-room, and put my hand forward with great caution until I reached a point which I judged to be vertically above the head of the subject.

When I came down again, I found the spectators in great agitation; during my absence, Mrs Lambert had suddenly leapt from her chair, uttering a violent cry of pain and joining her hands over her head. Her whole body was contracted, the movements of the heart and of the respiration had stopped.

It was only after some minutes that, by means of warm insufflations on the principal hypnogenetic points,[34] I enabled her to recover her senses. Then she complained about some dreadful pains in the head, which I tried vainly to relieve by means of energetic suggestions. I was obliged to have the poor woman put to bed, where she remained, without being able to eat or sleep, during all the night and a part of the following day. A kind of cerebral rupture had occurred, by which the *Od* was escaping in great abundance; any object approaching her head was insupportable to her, and the inferior extremities were very cold. I succeeded in diminishing her sufferings only by making prolonged descending passes several times a day, in order to relieve the head and to charge the legs. …

On thinking over what had occurred, I asked myself how it was that a similar accident had not happened during a period of experiments lasting over ten years, seeing that I had effected some hundreds of times the exteriorisation of the astral bodies of different subjects, either in my own house, or in houses where the higher floors were inhabited by strangers. …

Each time that I had had the occasion to verify the action of a stranger upon the astral body or the fluid bond, I had, for precaution, myself guided the hand of that stranger or followed with much attention his movements, I was led to suppose that *the astral substance of a living person was capable of being impressed only by agents "en rapport" with that person.* However, I verified the hypothesis by observing that the fluid escape from the vertex of Mrs Lambert, which was so painful when I touched it, was insensible to the touch of another, as long as that person was not "en rapport" with me, either by contact or by a look. It is probable that, if a stranger remained exposed for some time to one of these fluid escapes, he would finish by entering "en rapport" with the subject and producing in him the same feelings as the magnetiser. In view of the painful state into which I had thrown Mrs Lambert, I had no wish to attempt the experiment. The interests of science must not make us forget the rights of humanity.

XI. Hector Durville

Over the years there have been attempts to physically detect the existence of a double or of a projected spirit, as seen in claims of photographs of the spirits of the living (e.g., Moses, 1875). An important attempt in the history of the topic I am discussing in this series of articles were the tests for physical detection (and sensory aspects) of subtle bodies conducted by Hector Durville (1849–1923). A representative of the French neo-mesmeric movement, Durville was a well-known French student of the powers of magnetism.[35] He believed that magnetism was a real force capable of producing healing and other phenomena. His two-volume work *Traité Expérimentale de Magnétisme* (Durville, 1895–1896) was one of the most detailed discussions of magnetism of the late mesmeric movement (see also Durville, 1899, 1905).

Durville also explored the topic of the "doubling" of the human body. This took place mainly in his book *Le Fantôme des Vivants* (1909) and in other publications such as *Manifestations du Fantôme des Vivants* (n.d.), which consisted of a lecture presented in 1910 (see also Durville, 1908a, 1908b). He wrote in the second book:

The phantom of the doubled subject is composed of several bodies that double over again. When it is located near the subject… it is the etheric body, which is animated by the astral body. When it is away for some time, it abandons its etheric form and parts with the astral, which from then on is animated by the mental body. At this moment the etheric body, seat of vitality, reenters into the subject to animate it, because without it physical life cannot be prolonged for a long time.

The phantom is all the individual. On it live the sensations, thoughts, will, judgement; it has become the seat of consciousness … In talking about themselves all the doubled subjects … declare that the visible body is nothing … "The phantom is me … ," said one of my subjects (Durville, n.d., p. 15).

Durville's main publication on the subject, *Le Fantôme des Vivants*, was divided into two sections. The first one was devoted to the history of the topic and to conceptual issues. Durville was convinced that doubling involved the projection of consciousness from the physical body and that this double could obtain information and influence the environment. The second part of the book was devoted to reports of tests the author conducted to test the perceptual and motor manifestations of the doubles, which may have been inspired by the work of Albert de Rochas (1837–1914, Alvarado, 2011a; de Rochas, 1895). Durville experimented with several women who he magnetized to project their doubles or phantoms. One of them, Mme. Lambert, was also one of the persons studied by de Rochas.[36]

This work has received some citation over the years (e.g., Blackmore, 1982, pp. 185–187; Irwin, 1985, p. 62; Muldoon & Carrington, 1929, pp. xxix–xxx; Rogo, 1983, pp. 20–22). In addition, some of the material has appeared in English (Durville, 1908a, 1908b). But it does not seems to be well known today, at least in detail. In what follows I present Durville's descriptions of some of his tests as they appeared in the *Annals of Psychical Science* (Durville, 1908a).[37]

Durville's Tests

My first experiments were made in October last, in conjunction with M. Andre, a young artist and student of magnetism, upon two subjects introduced by him. I reproduce word for word the notes which I made at the end of each séance:

Séance, October 22nd, 5 p.m. Experimenters, M. Andre and Durville. Subjects, Mademoiselles Marthe and Nénette. The experiments took place in my study.

M. Andre put Nénette into the magnetic sleep, and I did the same for Marthe. The doubles were disengaged in accordance with the usual procedure for each subject. After some experiments as to the perception of sound-waves, we endeavoured to ascertain if the double of the one could influence the double of the other at a distance. In order to do this M. Andre took Nénette into the lecture room of the society, while I remained in the study with Marthe.

First Experiment.—Without my knowing what he was about to do, M. Andre commanded Nénette to send her double to that of Marthe and tread on her feet. Marthe quickly drew her feet back, complaining that someone was treading on them.

Second Experiment.—M. Andre desired Nénette to send her double and strike that of Marthe a hard blow with the fist on the head. Marthe raised both hands to her breast, and, seemingly in pain, said that someone had fallen on her chest. I remarked to her that from her position it was not possible for anyone to fall on her chest, but she still persisted that she had experienced a violent blow.

Third Experiment.—M. Andre told Nénette to send her double and vigorously pull the left leg of Marthe's double. This resulted in a powerful stretching of the limb, causing sharp pain.

It was evident that Marthe felt very distinctly the various actions of Nénette's double on her own, except that in the second experiment she felt the blow on the chest instead of on the head, as had been commanded.

We then desired to see whether Nénette would similarly feel the action of Marthe's double. M. Andre and Nénette remained in the lecture room and Marthe and I stayed in the study. Neither M. Andre nor Nénette knew the nature of the commands given to Marthe's double.

First Experiment.—I said to Marthe: "You felt pain a little while ago: that wretched Nénette hurt you; her double trod on your feet, struck you on the breast, and strained your leg. It is only right that you should make her suffer also. You are willing, are you not?" On her replying in the affirmative, I added: "Very well, then, send your double to Nénette and pull her hair hard".

She made with her hands a series of movements as of a person pulling the hair of another, but Nénette declared that she felt nothing.

Second Experiment.—I said to Marthe: "Your double will go and pull hard the leg of the double of Nénette". Nénette felt a twitching throughout her body.

Third Experiment.—I said to Marthe: "You are not putting forth sufficient energy; Nénette has not felt anything; you must put more strength into your actions. She has her arms bare; now let your double go and pinch her right arm". Nénette complained that someone had scratched her right arm.

Marthe now showed signs of fatigue, and we decided to awaken both subjects, when a surprise awaited us. Even before she had become fully conscious, Marthe complained of a pain in her left leg, "As though someone had pulled it very hard", she said; and Nénette said that her right arm had been scratched and was very painful and felt as if it was bleeding. While she was saying this she rubbed her arm with her left hand. When both subjects were fully awake, Marthe, who was still seated, continued to complain of pain in her left leg. I took hold of her hands to help her to rise; for a moment or so she stood up, but was unable to remain standing, and fell back on the chair. Nénette continued to rub her right arm, and, seemingly in pain, said: "My arm certainly is bleeding, someone has scratched it". I lifted up the sleeve of her garment: the arm certainly was red, probably because she had rubbed it, but there was no trace of any scratch…[38]

When the double is projected under magnetic influence all impressions are received by the double and transformed by it into sensation

On submitting a highly sensitive person to vigorous and prolonged magnetic action, it will soon be observed that when the sleep is sufficiently profound there is an externalisation of the self, in all directions, in the form of sensitive layers, which soon condense to the right and to the left and form the phantom, or the double of the subject.[39] This phantom, which forms to the left of the subject, remains there for a greater or less period, almost always in the same attitude at a distance of about two feet, but it can also move about and even go to a distance. The constituent parts of this double escape under the form of emanations from all parts of the body of the subject, but chiefly from the forehead, the top of the head, the throat, the epigastric region, and the spleen. In their formation, in the earlier stages of the experiments, they cause a more or less disagreeable sensation, amounting in some instances to pain. The subject sometimes complains of pain in the head, as happened in the instances of Edmée and Madame Francois; others experience an itching sensation in the throat, causing them to cough, though not suffering from chill, as was the case with Leontine and also with Edmée. These disagreeable sensations quickly pass away, and at the end of the séance the subject always feels entirely well.

After the double is properly condensed it assumes exactly the form of the subject, and appears to the latter as more or less luminous. Some sensitives, whom I regard as the best, see it as blue to the right; yellow, orange or red to the left; others only see a more or less distinct glimmer of white light. In perfect darkness highly sensitive persons, without being asleep, see it very distinctly with the colours I have mentioned. Ordinary sensitives only see a white light, more or less bright. Those partially sensitive perceive it in an undefined form, generally that of a bust, or rather of a dressmaker's dummy, which seems as though formed of mist or greyish vapour.

The double is connected with the physical body by a cord of the thickness of the little finger, which nearly always runs from the navel of the physical body to the corresponding point in the double.[40] There are exceptions: Mme. Francois is connected to her double by a cord issuing from the top of the head, almost at the cerebro-spinal centre and terminating at the corresponding point in the double. There are even a few subjects who say that this cord starts from the epigastric region, in front of the stomach, and even from the spleen—that is to say, on the same level but more to the left.

In most subjects this cord, which is not everywhere of the same thickness, forms in places swellings like ganglia, which apparently nourish the cord when the double is projected. In all subjects this cord is the seat of a very intense luminous circulation, and to sensitives it presents the aspect of a mixed nerve, the luminous fluid circulating from the subject to the double in the one part, and from the double to the subject in the other portion.

The physical senses are completely inhibited; the subject sees nothing with her eyes, hears nothing with her ears, nor perceives any smell with the olfactory sense, and has no feeling of contact. All these impressions appear to be perceived by distinct senses located in the double.

"When the double is touched", she said, "the impression of contact comes as a shock to the physical brain, and the sensation strikes upon it. When we talk, it seems as though my physical body hears, because it replies; but that is not the case. It hears nothing; that which hears is the double. The question and the reply are transmitted along the cord to the physical brain as by a movement, by something which vibrates. It is also the double which sees, and the sight is conveyed to the physical body by a movement, as though the physical brain were caused to vibrate by electricity, and then it sees what the double has seen. All the impressions received by the double are transmitted to the senses of the brain, but these centres perceive nothing of themselves".

It is, however, very easy to verify all these affirmatives by direct experiment. I will describe a series of experiments relating to the various senses:—

Touch

We know that nearly all subjects in the magnetic sleep are insensible; but we do not know whither the sensibility has transferred itself. When the subject is externalised, the sensibility always radiates around the body, at a little distance from it; and if we pinch, burn or prick the sensitive zones, the subject feels sharp pain, though she feels nothing when we prick the body. It is the same in the projection of the double. The subject feels neither pricks nor pinches on the physical body; but she experiences a disagreeable and even painful sensation as soon as we touch the double or the connecting cord. This phenomenon has been verified at all the stances and with all the subjects without exception. ...

Sight

M. Andre and I tried the following experiment with Marthe, which has been verified many times by M. Andre himself:—A paper with large letters printed on it was placed before the half-open eyes of the subject, who declared that she could see nothing. The paper was then placed before different parts of the body by which the somnambulistic subjects sometimes see: the top of the head, the nape of the neck, or the epigastrium; the subject again declared that she could see nothing. The paper was placed before the eyes of the double, but it could see nothing, nor yet at the top of the head; but at the nape of the neck it could read without hesitation.

The projected double can see, but rather confusedly, from one room into another. While I was at the end of my study with Edmée, whose double was projected, I asked three of the witnesses of the experiment—Mme. Stahl, Mme. Fournier, and M. Bonnet—to go into the lecture room of the society and perform some simple and easily-described movements, so that we could ascertain whether the double, which I would send there, could see anything. Dr. Pau de Saint Martin stood near the window, between my study and the hall where the witnesses were, in order to see almost at the same time both the subject and what these experimenters were doing.

First Experiment.—Mme. Fournier seated herself on the table. "I see", said the subject, "Mme. Fournier seated on the table".

Second Experiment.—The three persons walked into the room and gesticulated. "They walk and make gestures with their hands; I do not know what it means".

Third Experiment.—Mme. Stahl took a pamphlet from the table and handed it to Mme. Fournier. "The two ladies are reading", said the subject.

Fourth Experiment.—The three persons joined hands, formed a chain and walked round the table. "How funny!" said the subject; "they are dancing round the table like three lunatics". ...

Hearing

Marthe's double being projected, I placed my watch at the place corresponding to the left ear of the double. Marthe heard the ticking very distinctly. I placed the watch on the nape of the neck, on the epigastrium at the feet of the double; the subject still heard. I then placed the watch successively on the external orifices of the subject's ears, on the nape of her neck, on the epigastrium, and on her feet; she heard absolutely nothing. The experiment was repeated many times with the same subject, under different conditions, but always with the same results.

Edmée's double hears very distinctly the ticking of the watch, but she hears absolutely nothing when it is placed on the physical ears. I wished to ascertain whether she could hear, from one room to another, the words of a person uttered in a low voice. For this purpose I placed a chair in the middle of the lecture room, and asked Mme. Stahl to come close to this chair, to which, from the end of my study, I would send Edmée's double, to find out whether the double would hear her speak. Mme. Fournier was stationed by the window, between the two rooms, so that she could see Mme. Stahl and the subject almost at the same time. I sent Edmée's double to sit on the chair beside Mme. Stahl and told it to listen attentively to hear if she spoke to it. The double was on the chair. Mme. Stahl drew near to the chair, stooped and spoke in a low voice.

Edmée at first complained that Mme. Stahl had touched her, which was disagreeable to her; she heard her speak, but she changed her place, and this unnerved her and she could not understand what was said. I asked her to give her attention to what was said by Mme. Stahl. "She gives me advice", she said; "she tells me to be calm and less nervous".

Mme. Stahl told us that she had said to the double: "I am here; can you hear me? Do not be nervous, be calm". These words were uttered in so low a tone that Madame Fournier, seven feet away, had not heard a single word.

The double of Leontine heard distinctly the ticking of a watch, and the physical body, notwithstanding suggestions, heard nothing.

I passed my watch to Dr Pan de Saint-Martin and, unknown to the subject, I asked him to ascertain whether it was the double or the physical body that heard the ticking of the watch. The doctor cautiously approached the physical body and placed the watch close to the ears, but without touching them. The subject said nothing. The doctor drew her attention and said that he was holding a watch to her ear, and that she certainly ought to hear it. The subject declared that she could hear nothing. A few moments afterwards the doctor brought the watch close to the left ear of the double. The subject immediately declared that she could hear the ticking of a watch.

In order to more fully verify the fact that the physical body heard nothing, I asked the doctor to hand me back my watch, and opened the mouth of the subject. I inserted the ring of the watch, and asked the subject to close her teeth and to listen attentively. I then asked the subject to open her mouth, and withdrew the watch. She had seen the watch but had heard nothing. …

Smell

Without Edmée knowing it, Dr Pau de Saint-Martin put an uncorked bottle of ammonia under her nose, and kept it there for about a minute, but the subject perceived nothing. A few moments later he put the same bottle in front of the face of the double. "Oh!" she cried, turning round, "it is a bottle, and it smells bad". He withdrew the bottle noiselessly and put in its place a bottle containing essence of bergamot. "That smells better", said the subject at the same moment.

The same experiment was tried with Leontine, and gave even more decided results. Dr Pau de Saint-Martin put the bottle of ammonia under the nose of the double. In a moment the subject seized her nose with her right hand, and turned away making a grimace. "It is sedative water", she said; then added, "no, it is ammonia".

After five or six minutes, and without the subject suspecting it, the doctor placed the bottle of ammonia under the nose of the physical body. The subject said nothing and did not appear to perceive any unpleasant odour. On being questioned as to whether she smelt anything, either agreeable or otherwise, she declared that she smelt absolutely nothing. The doctor tried to find out whether suggestion might not, in spite of all appearances, play some part in these manifestations. "It was ammonia", he said "that I was holding under your nose a moment ago; you ought not only to smell it, but the odour should be very disagreeable". The subject, as though vexed that she was not believed, replied sharply, "I tell you that I smell nothing; I don't care whether you believe me or not".

The doctor withdrew, and a few moments later he gently advanced towards the double with the bottle of bergamot, which he held out towards the place occupied by the head of the double. "I see", said the subject, "that you are holding a bottle to my ear; you want to make me smell something"; and she added, with a malicious smile, "but I do not smell with my ear". The doctor then placed the bottle in front of the place occupied by the nose, and the subject immediately declared that she smelt an agreeable odour. "That is better than the ammonia," she added. …

Taste

Subject of the experiments, Mme. Leontine; witnesses, MM. Combe, Dubois and G. Durville. We were in a dim light.

I projected the double in the usual manner, and proposed to ascertain whether it was the subject or the double that perceived savours. In order to do this I had arranged two armchairs in my study, in front of a long table—one chair for the subject, the other for the double—in such a way that when the subject leaned forward she could place her forearms on the table without inconvenience. As the double naturally assumes the attitude of the subject, it would also rest its forearms on the table. A pile of books was placed on the table in front of the double, in the space between its arms. This pile was as high as the double's chin, so as to serve as a mark for the position of its mouth.

The double being on the left of the subject, in the place prepared for it, when the condensation appeared sufficient, I requested the subject to lean forward and place her forearms on the table, as I have just described, and I asked the double to assume the same position.

The subject was not informed of the nature of the substances to be used in the experiment. These substances had very little smell and were intended to affect only the sense of taste.

I. I placed a morsel of aloes in the subject's hand, and asked her to put it into her mouth, to chew it, and tell us whether it tasted good or bad. She chewed the morsel and declared that it had no taste. To avoid any purgative action I told her to spit it out.

II. I put a small piece of sugar into her hand, and asked her to chew it and tell us how it tasted. The reply was the same as before.

III. By means of forceps I took a chip of quassia and put it towards the lower part of the face of the double, at the place where I supposed the mouth to be. I asked the double to open its mouth and take into it what I presented to it, then to close it so as to perceive the taste. "It is not good", the subject immediately said; "it is bitter". I withdrew the forceps and chip cautiously, put the chip into the subject's hand and asked her to put it in her mouth and taste it. She did so, and declared that she tasted nothing: "It has no taste", she added.

IV. I took a morsel of aloes with the forceps and put it towards the mouth of the double, with the same request. "I know what that is", said the subject; "but it is not good, it is bitter". After withdrawing the morsel of aloes I put it into the subject's mouth and asked her to suck it. She did so, and said she tasted nothing.

V. I put a few drops of sulphate of quinine into a small spoon and placed it near the mouth of the double, with the same request. "It is not good", was the answer; "it is bitter".

VI. I put a pinch of nux vomica into a small spoon with a few drops of water, and proceeded as in the last experiment. "It is nasty", said the subject; "it is bitter, it is harsh to the tongue".

VII. With a forceps I took a piece of an orange and put it towards the mouth of the double, with request as before. "That is good", said the subject; "it is orange". I withdrew the piece of orange and placed it in the subject's mouth, asking her to tell us what it was. "I don't know at all", she answered; "just now you made me taste orange, but now I taste nothing".

VIII. I put a pinch of salt into a small spoon and brought it to the mouth of the double, with the usual request. "That's salt", said the subject.

XI. I took a lump of sugar with the forceps and put it to the mouth of the double, with the same request. "Oh, that's sugar", said the subject. I withdrew it and laid it on the table. After a few moments, wishing to see whether, in spite of all appearances, suggestion did not enter into the production of the phenomena, I took it up again, and put it into the subject's mouth for her to chew, telling her it was a piece of aloes. She chewed it, and I told her it was nasty, and she ought certainly to find it so. "I don't care if it is nasty", she answered; "I cannot taste it at all". …

How the presence and position of the phantom can be proved

I. When the phantom approaches the spectators, nine out of ten of them become aware of its presence by a feeling of coolness which comes over them and which disappears soon after it has gone away again.[41] Some perceive distinctly a sort of breath, which somewhat resembles that felt when standing near an electrostatic machine in operation. When the phantom has stood for six or eight minutes near persons placed at one end of my study, it seems to them that that part of the room has become sensibly colder. There are a few persons who do not perceive this sensation of coolness, but who receive other impressions. Thus, on the approach of the phantom, especially when it has stood before him for forty or fifty seconds, M. Dubois feels a moisture in his hands, and especially at the ends of his fingers. If the phantom remains longer, this moisture spreads to the upper part of his body. Others feel a slight trembling, a sort of shivering, which is curious without being disagreeable.

If a person approaches the phantom without touching it, and then plunges his hand into it, the hand is rapidly affected by this impression of coolness or moisture. When the hand which has remained for a few moments in the phantom is looked at in the dark it almost always appears slightly luminous, especially at the tips of the fingers.

II. The phantom gives off N-rays in great abundance, which illuminate phosphorescent screens in a very remarkable manner. .. ,[42]

I had two large screens and a number of small ones. For the experiments which I am about to relate, I took the two large screens and a small one, which I had exposed to sunlight. The following is the result of an experiment made in complete darkness. The subject was Mme. Francois; the witnesses were M. Francois and M. Sigogne, Professor at the University of Brussels.

The double of the subject having been projected, I took the three screens and showed them to the witnesses, who observed that they were completely dark. Laying the small screen aside for a moment, I placed one of the large ones on the abdomen of the subject and held the other in the phantom, which was seated on an arm-chair to the left of the subject.

The screen placed in the phantom became rapidly illuminated, and the one on the subject remained completely dark. After several minutes I took both screens and showed them to the witnesses, who were much astonished by the phenomenon. I then took the screen which had been on the subject, and remained dark, and placed it in the phantom. It immediately became illuminated like the first. I again showed them to the witnesses, who saw that they were sufficiently illuminated to allow them easily to count the spots of sulphide of calcium at a distance of a yard.

I then took the small screen which had not been used, and placed it on the abdomen of the subject for two or three minutes without obtaining the slightest trace of luminosity. I then placed it in the phantom, and it became very strongly illuminated. The witnesses found that it gave enough light to enable one of them to tell the time by a watch.

These experiments, repeated about ten times with seven or eight different subjects, always gave similar results, which were very intense when the screens had been well exposed to the sun, less so when the exposure had been insufficient.

It is as well to add here that I had previously observed the action of nearly all the subjects on the same screens when the double was not projected. When they approached their hands to the screen in the dark, especially when they closed their fists firmly, the screen was more or less illuminated, as, in fact, is the case with anyone. But it is worthy of notice that the luminosity is always considerably less than that which is observed when the screen is placed in the phantom.

This series of experiments with phosphorescent screens shows once more that the physical body, when the phantom is projected, is no longer the seat of any radio-activity; at all events, it does not emit X-rays, while the phantom becomes an extraordinarily powerful source of these rays.

Action of the phantom on matter

I first attempted to photograph the phantom, to obtain an impression of its hand on flour, and to get it to move a piece of paper suspended by a thread; but, except for traces of luminous action on one or two plates, traces which, however, disappeared in the course of development, I obtained absolutely nothing, although I had the patience to repeat each attempt four or five times at intervals of a week. …

Raps.—The subject of the experiment was Mme. Francois, who knows nothing of spirit phenomena. M. and Mlle. Rubenstein, MM. François and Dubois were present at the experiment. We were in darkness; it was 9 p.m.

I caused the projection of the phantom, and when it appeared to be sufficiently condensed I said to the subject: "Since we did not obtain the moving of the sheet of paper, I will leave to the phantom the choice of the action to be performed. It can do what it pleases, but I should be glad if it would strike two blows on the table". This was a black varnished drawing-room table without a cloth, placed about a yard in front of the arm-chair occupied by the phantom, in front of me to my right, in such a way that without ceasing to touch the subject, and simply by extending my arm in that direction, I could ascertain the presence of the phantom. The witnesses were seated near my desk, about two-and-a-half yards from the edge of the table.

After about twenty or thirty seconds we all heard, very distinctly, two sharp blows struck on the table. …

Somewhat astonished at this result, I said to the phantom: "If it is you who have struck on the table, please strike on it again". I had scarcely uttered these words when two raps, less strong than the former ones, were again heard on the table.

The next séance, with the same subject, at the same hour, and under the same conditions, was held in the presence of MM. Dubois and Francois. Profiting by what I had learnt at the two previous séances, I only tried to obtain raps. I caused the double to be projected, and when it seemed sufficiently condensed I asked it, when it could, to strike more blows on the table. After two or three minutes we heard some crackings in the table, which no one was touching, then two light blows were distinctly heard, as though struck with the tip of a finger. I asked the phantom to give two more raps. I had scarcely expressed this desire when two blows similar to the former ones were heard. I allowed the subject to rest for a few moments, then I asked the phantom to give three more raps. Crackings were heard in the table and immediately afterwards three blows similar to the former ones were distinctly heard….

The phantom had returned to the chair, but was disorganised, and the subject was enervated. I calmed her, and then tried to condense the phantom. When this appeared to be sufficiently accomplished I asked it to approach the table and give two raps. After two or three minutes, crackings were heard in the table, and then three raps were heard, as though struck with the fleshy part of the fingers of the open hand.

Notes

1 This is a reference to autoscopy.

2 See, for example, discussions on the subject published in the Journal du Magnétisme that started with Morin's (1857) review of Didier (1856) and continued with De Guilr (1857), Lamothe (1857) and Berruyer (1858).

3 On Didier, see Méheust (2003), and Gauld (1992, pp. 235–239).
4 Wantuil and Thiesen (1984) present a detailed examination of Kardec's life and work. More recent discussions in the context of French developments appear in Edelman (1995) and Sharp (2006).
5 I have summarized other views of the perispirit elsewhere (Alvarado, 2008a). Gabriel Delanne (1897) discussed its functions as regards the place where memory was stored, and as a metabolic and embryological organizing principle.
6 The so-called astral cord, which became better known later with the descriptions of Sylvan J. Muldoon (Muldoon & Carrington, 1929), was also mentioned during the nineteenth century (e.g., Blavatsky, 1892, p. 484; Davis, 1850, pp. 167–168). D'Assier (1883/1887, p. 51) referred to invisible bonds uniting the physical body and the double.
7 On bilocation in Catholic saints see Thurston (1952).
8 See Church and Brodribb (1876, Book 4, Chapter 82, p. 189).
9 This was a reference to Friederike Hauffe (1801–1829), studied by Justinus Kemer (1786–1862; see Kerner, 1845).
10 On this topic see Rogers (1853) as well as Tanchou's (1846) discussion of the famous case of Angelique Cottin.
11 But see also Myers' (1886) ideas in the book, to be discussed later.
12 The Roman numeral preceding the page number indicates the volume of the book.
13 The topic has been discussed by many authors, among them Becker (1993), Bozzano (1934/1937), Crookall (1967) and Rogo (1973). See also my papers (Alvarado, 1987, 2005, 2006a).
14 On Augustus and Sophia De Morgan and spiritualism see Smith (2002, Chapter 3).
15 This is a reference to Elizabeth and Jane Okey, studied by John Elliotson (see Gauld, 1992, pp. 201–203).
16 See, for example, his descriptions of spiritual spheres and spirit communities (Davis, 1868). Davis has been discussed by Delp (1967) and De Salvo (2005).
17 Myers has received some attention in recent years, as seen in Hamilton's (2009) biography, and in other writings (e.g., Alvarado, 2004; Kelly, 2007). I have summarized Myers's views about OBEs and apparitions of the living in a previous paper (Alvarado, 2009b).
18 See a previous paper in this series (Alvarado, 2010a), as well as Gurney, Myers and Podmore (1886).
19 This and later similar indications, refer to the volume number of Myers's Human Personality (1903).
20 For an arrival case see a previous paper in the current series (Alvarado, 2010a, p. 6). I have presented references for many other cases (Alvarado, 2003).
21 I owe du Prel's reference to Michael Nahm.
22 These are the presumed agents in cases cited by Myers (I, pp. 646–651).
23 I have presented an example of an experimental case in a previous paper (Alvarado, 2010a, p. 5).
24 Myers mentioned the studies of Backman (1891). In this context it is also relevant to remember the mesmeric travelling clairvoyance performances (Alvarado, 2009b).
25 In his comments about a "vital faculty" Myers included a section about "Death; as an Irrevocable Self-projection of the Spirit" (II, p. 524). On the issue of death see one of the papers in the current series (Alvarado, 2010b).
26 Agathe Haemmerlé was described as "that most gifted woman … of Russia, the friend and correspondent of Du Prel and many other men of intellectual and scientific repute in Europe" (Olcott, 1897, p. 66). She was a member of the Theosophical Society and translated Carl du Prel into French (Du Prel, 1905).
27 On de Rochas see Albert de Rochas Papers (2004), Alvarado (2009e), and Necrologie (1914).
28 On the antiquity of the concept see Mead (1919) and Poortman (1954/1978).
29 Od was a term used by Karl von Reichenbach (1849/1851) to refer to an universal force emanating from the human body as well as from magnets, crystals, minerals, light, heat, and other sources. See also Alvarado (2008c) and de Rochas (n. d.).
30 De Rochas added the following note in the paper: "I am inclined to believe that this mode of exteriorisation is peculiar to subjects whose mentality is highly developed; I had already encountered it, but without understanding the process, in another extremely intelligent lady".
31 de Rochas added this note: "According to the cases, the subject perceives his physical body alone, or his astral body alone, or the two at the same time. Another clairvoyant subject professed to see a kind of brilliant flame in the first case in the physical body, in the second in the astral body, in the third in the fluidic

bond which unites them. That flame should be the soul". He referred readers to one of his articles for more details (de Rochas, 1895).

32 Mrs. Lambert was also studied by others, such as Hector Durville (1909). She was described as a medium in whose presence physical phenomena took place both outside and inside the séance room (Lefranc, 1911a).

33 de Rochas (1896, chapter 9; Sabatier et al., 1896) also tested Palladino in his house in L'Agnelas.

34 These were points in the body that, when pressured, produced or stopped hypnosis or other manifestations.

35 For biographical details see Pleasants (1964, p. 89). On the late mesmeric movement see Alvarado (2009e, 2009f).

36 Lefranc (1911a) said Lambert was a medium who produced physical phenomena. De Rochas used her as a subject to study the exteriorization of sensitivity, and the projection of the double. Lefranc also investigated her doubling manifestations (Lefranc, 191 1 a, 191lb).

37 For reviews of the book see Alvarado (201lb, pp. 566–569), Brieu (1909), and Frollo (1909).

38 On this see the "repercussion" producing a wound on Lambert, illustrated with photographs (Lefranc, 1911c).

39 On the issue of layers, typical of the exteriorization of sensitivity, see Alvarado (2011a) and de Rochas (1895).

40 For earlier references to the cord, popularized by later writers (e.g., Muldoon & Carrington, 1929) see the account of medium D. D. Home's (1833–1886) out-of-body experience (1863, p. 73) and also Andrew Jackson Davis' (1826–1910) clairvoyant visions of the spirit leaving the body at death (Davis, 1850, p. 168). Mentions of the cord appeared during the nineteenth-century in many sources (e.g., Besant, 1893, pp. 17–18; Colville, 1886, p. 7).

41 On sensations of cold in relation to apparitions see Tyrrell (1953, pp. 73–74).

42 N rays, believed to be a new form of radiation from physical and biological bodies, were studied in France by Rene Blondlot (1849–1930; Blondlot, 1904/1905) and others. Although many papers were published supporting their existence there was also much skepticism and eventually N rays were discredited (Ashmore, 1993; Nye, 1980). Durville, who believed the double gave off N rays, followed Blondlot in using screens covered with calcium sulphide to detect the radiation. The latter wrote that after calcium sulphide was made phosphorescent by exposure to sunlight its "phosphorescent glow is observed to increase in a very marked fashion" (Blondlot, 1904/1905, p. 22). In addition to Durville, others related N rays to the concept of radiations and fluids prevalent in psychic literature (Regnault, 1905); however, occultist Gerard Encausse (1865–1916) pointed out many differences between the forces of psychic literature and N rays (Encausse, 1904).

References

Aksakof, A. (n.d., ca 1906). *Animismo y espiritismo: Ensayo de un examen critico de los fenómenos medianlmicos.* Carbonell y Esteva. (Original work published 1890).

Albert de Rochas Papers, American Philosophical Society. (2004). Online, retrieved September 10, 2011, http://www.amphilsoc.org/mole/view7docld=ead/Mss.Ms.Coll. 106-ead.xml

Alvarado, C. S. (1987). Observations of luminous phenomena around the human body: A review. *Journal of the Society for Psychical Research, 54,* 38–60.

Alvarado, C. S. (2003) Note on "arrival" cases (letter to the editor). *Journal of Scientific Exploration,* 17, 534–535.

Alvarado, C. S. (2004). On thc centenary of Frederic W. H. Myers's *Human Personality and Its Survival of Bodily Death. Journal of Parapsychology,* 68, 3–43.

Alvarado, C. S. (2005). Ernesto Bozzano and the phenomena of bilocation. *Journal of Near–Death Studies, 23,* 207–238.

Alvarado, C. S. (2008a). Further notes on historical ideas of human radiations: II. The perispirit and mediumistic forces. *Psypioneer, 4,* 83–92.

Alvarado, C. S. (2008b). Apparitions of the living seen shortly before their deaths [Letter to the editor]. *Journal of Near-Death Studies,* 27, *11*–80.

Alvarado, C. S. (2008c). Further notes on historical ideas of human radiations: II. Od and psychometry. *Psypioneer, 4,* 63–69.
Alvarado, C. S. (2009a). Historical notes on doubles and travelling spirits: V. Adolphe d'Assier's ideas of doubles. *Paranormal Review, 54,* 6–9.
Alvarado, C. S. (2009b). The spirit in out-of-body experiences: Historical and conceptual notes. In B. Batey (Ed.), *Spirituality, Science and the Paranormal* (pp. 3–19). Academy of Spirituality and Paranormal Studies.
Alvarado, C.S. (2009c). Historical notes on doubles and travelling spirits: II—J. H. Jung-Stilling on the soul. *Paranormal Review,* 51, 3–7.
Alvarado, C. S. (2009d). Historical notes on doubles and travelling spirits: III—William Gregory on travelling clairvoyance. *Paranormal Review,* 52, 13–16.
Alvarado, C. S. (2009e). Late nineteenth and early twentieth century discussions of animal magnetism. *International Journal of Clinical and Experimental Hypnosis, 57,* 366–381.
Alvarado, C. S. (2009f). Modern animal magnetism: The work of Alexandre Barety, Emile Boirac, and Julian Ochorowicz. *Australian Journal of Clinical and Experimental Hypnosis, 37,* 1–15.
Alvarado, C. S. (2010a). Historical notes on doubles and travelling spirits: VI: Apparitions of the living. *Paranormal Review, 56,* 3–8.
Alvarado, C. S. (2010b). Historical notes on doubles and travelling spirits: VII: Visions of death. *Paranormal Review, 57,* 3–7.
Alvarado, C. S. (2011a). Historical notes on doubles and travelling spirits: X. Albert de Rochas. *Paranormal Review, 60,* 3–6.
Alvarado, C. S. (2011b). On doubles and excursions from the physical body, 1876–1956. *Journal of Scientific Exploration, 25,* 563–580.
Ashmore, M. (1993). The theatre of the blind: Starring a promethean prankster, a phony phenomenon, a prism, a pocket, and a piece of wood. *Social Studies of Science, 23,* 67–106.
Backman, A. (1891). Experiments in clairvoyance. *Proceedings of the Society for Psychical Research, 7,* 199–220.
Barrett, W. (1926). *Death-bed visions.* Methuen.
Battersby, H. F. P. (n. d., 1942). *Man outside himself: The facts of etheric projection.* Rider.
Becker, C. B. (1993). *Paranormal experience and survival of death.* State University of New York Press.
Berruyer, [A.]. (1858). Controverse sur le somnambulisme: Faits curieux et divers. *Journal du Magnétisme,* 17(s. 2), 42–54.
Besant, A. (1892). *The seven principles of man* (*Theosophical Manuals No. 1*). Theosophical Publishing Society.
Besant, A. (1893). *Death and after?* (Theosophical Manuals No. 3). Theosophical Publishing Society.
Biondi, M. (1984). Pagine d'appunti di Ernesto Bozzano. *Luce e Ombra, 84,* 156–164.
Blackmore, S. J. (1982). *Beyond the body.* Heinemann.
Blavatsky, H. P. (1892). *Isis unveiled: A master-key to the mysteries of ancient and modern science and theology: Vol. 1: Science* (6th ed.). J. W. Bouton.
Blondlot, R. (1905). *"N" rays: A collection of papers communicated to the Academy of Sciences.* Longmans, Green. (Original work published in French, 1904.)
Bose, E. (1896). *Dictionnaire d'orientalisme, d'occultisme et de psychologic ou dictionnarie de la science occulte* (Vol. 1). Chamuel.
Bozzano, E. (1934/1937). *Les phénomènes de bilocation.* Jean Meyer. (Original work published 1934)
Brevior, T. (1874). Spiritual problems.—Materialisation of spirit forms.—The double. *Spiritual Magazine,* 9 (n. s.), 152–160.
Brieu, J. (1909). Esoterisme et sciences psychiques. *Mercure de France, 80,* 144–147.
Brittan, S. B. (1864). *Mind and his relations: Illustrating the influence of the mind on the body.* W.A. Townsend.
Cahagnet, L. A. (1851). *The celestial telegraph; or, secrets of the life to come, revealed through magnetism* (1st American ed., 2 vols.). J. S. Redfield.
Carrington, H. (1915). *True ghost stories.* J. S. Ogilvie.
Cartwright, S. (1884). *Magnetism clairvoyantly discerned.* Detroit, Gulley, Bornman.
Chardel, C. (1818). *Mémoire sur le magnétisme animal, présente a l'Académie de Berlin, en 1818.* Badouin.

Church, A. J., & Brodribb, W. J. (Eds. and trans.). (1876). *The history of Tacitus* (3rd ed.). Macmillan.
Coleman, B.]. (1865). Spiritualism at Brighton—The Davenport's double. *Spiritual Magazine, 6*, 125–128.
Coleman, B. (1873). A séance with Miss Cook, held at the residence of J. C. Luxmoore, Esq., 16, Gloucester Square, Hyde Park, November 18, 1873. *Spiritual Magazine, 8*, 555–559.
Colquhoun, J. C. (1836). *Isis revelata: An inquiry into the origin, progress and present state of animal magnetism* (2 vols.). Maclachlan & Stewart.
Colville, W. J. (1886). *Spiritual, ethical and historical discourses, delivered under inspiration.* Cochrane.
Crookall, R. (1967). *Events on the threshold of the after-life.* Darshana International.
Crowe, C. (1848). *The night-side of nature; or, ghosts and ghost seers* (2 Vols.). T. C. Newby.
D'Assier, A. (1883). *Essai sur l'humanité posthume et le spiritisme.* A. Ghio
Davies, R. (1998). *Doubles: The enigma of the second self.* Robert Hale.
Davis, A. J. (1850). *The great harmonia: Being a philosophical revelation of the natural, spiritual and celestial universe* (Vol. 1). Benjamin B. Mussey.
Davis, A.J. (1868). *A stellar key to the summer land.* William White.
de Guilr, C. (1857). Fait et expériences: Le somnambule voit-il a distance, ou son ame se déplace-t-elle? *Journal du Magnétisme, 16*(2), 433–439, 495–504.
de Morgan, S.]. (1863). *From matter to spirit.* Longman, Green, Longman, Roberts, & Green.
de Rochas, A. (1887). *Les forces non définies: Recherchés historiques et expérimentales.* G. Masson.
de Rochas, A. (1895). Les fantômes des vivants. *Annales des Sciences Psychiques, 5*, 257–275.
de Rochas, A. (1896). L'extériorisation de la motricité: Recueil d'experiences et d'observations. Chamuel.
de Rochas, A. (1897a). *Les etats superficiels de l'hypnose* (5th ed.). Chamuel.
de Rochas, A. (1897b). Les experiences de Choisy-Yvrec (pres Bordeaux) du 2 au 14 octobre 1896. *Annales des Sciences Psychiques, 7*, 6–28.
de Rochas, A. (1897c). Les expériences de Choisy-Yvrac (pres Bordeaux) du 2 au 14 octobre 1896. *Annales des Sciences Psychiques,* 7, 6–28.
de Rochas, A. (n.d., ca 1897). Les effluves odiques. Ernest Flammarion.
de Rochas, A. (1899). *L'extériorisation de la sensibilité: Etude expérimentale & historique* (5th ed.). Chamuel.
de Rochas, A. (1902). *Les frontières de la science* (Series 1). Librairie des Sciences Psychologiques.
de Rochas, A. (1905a). The regression of memory: Case of Mayo. *Annals of Psychical Science, 2*, 1–52.
de Rochas, A. (1905b). Concerning spirit photography. *Annals of Psychical Science, 2*, 216–218.
de Rochas, A. (1906). New experiments relative to the astral body and the magnetic "rapport". *Annals of Psychical Science, 4,* 120–125.
de Rochas, A. (1911). *Les vies successives: Documents pour l'étude de cette question.* Chacomac.
de Salvo, J. (2005). *Andrew Jackson Davis: The First American Prophet and Clairvoyant (18261910).* Np: Lulu.com.
Delanne, G. (1897). *L'evolution animique: Essais de psychologic physiologique suivant le spiritisme.* Chamuel.
Delanne, G. (1904). *Evidence for a future life.* Philip Wellby. (Original work published 1899)
Delp, R. W. (1967). Andrew Jackson Davis: Prophet of American Spiritualism. *Journal of American History, 54,* 43–56.
Didier, A. (1856). *Le sommeil magnétique explique par le somnambule Alexis en état de lucidité.* R. Dentu.
Dingwall, E. J. (Ed.). (1967–1968). *Abnormal hypnotic phenomena* (4 vols.). J. & A. Churchill.
du Prel, C. (1888). *Die monistische Seelenlehre.* Gunthers.
du Prel, C. (1905). *La mart, l'au dela, la vie dans l'au dela.* Chacornac.
Durville, H. (1895–1896). *Traité expérimentale de magnétisme* (2 vols.). Librairie du Magnétisme.
Durville, H. (1899). *Application de l'aimant au traitement des maladies* (th ed.). Librairie du Magnétisme.
Durville, H. (1905). *Magnétisme personnel ou psychique.* Librairie du Magnétisme.
Durville, H. (1908a). Experimental researches concerning phantoms of the living. *Annals of Psychical Science, 7*, 335–343.
Durville, H. (1908b). New experiments with phantoms of the living. *Annals of Psychical Science, 7*, 464–470.
Durville, H. (1909). *Le fantôme des vivants: Anatomie et physiologie de l'amé: Recherches expérimentales sur le dédoublement des corps de l'homme.* Librairie du Magnétisme.
Durville, H. (n.d., ca 1911). *Manifestations du fantôme des vivants: Pour dedoubler le corps humain* (3rd ed.). Henri Durville.

Edelman, N. (1995). *Voyantes, guerisseuses et visionnaires en France 1785–1914.* Albin Michel.
Encausse, G. (1902). *Occultisme et le spiritualisme.* Félix Alcan.
Encausse, G. [under the pseudonym of Papus]. (1904). Le radium, les rayons N et l'occultisme. *L'initiation, 62,* 99–144.
Experimental thought-transference from a distance with apparition of agent. (1891). *Journal of the Society for Psychical Research, 5,* 21–30.
Flammarion, C. (1922). *Death and its mystery: at the moment of death.* Century. (Original work published 1921).
Fox, O. [1939]. *Astral projection: A record of out-of-the-body experiences.* Rider.
Frollo, J. (1909, June 20). Les fantômes. *Le Petit Parisien,* p. 1.
Gauld, A. (1992). *A history of hypnotism.* Cambridge University Press.
Gregory, W. (1851). *Letters to a candid inquirer, on animal magnetism.* Blanchard and Lea.
Gurney, E., Myers, F. W. H., & Podmore, F. (1886). *Phantasms of the living* (2 vols.). Trübner.
Haddock, J. W. (1851) *Somnolism & Psycheism* (2nd ed.). James S. Hodson.
Haemmerlé, A. (1906). Experiments in bilocation. *Annals of Psychical Science, 4,* 113–119.
Hallucinations experienced in connection with dying persons. (1908). *Journal of the Society for Psychical Research, 13,* 308–312.
Hamilton, T. (2009). *Immortal longings: F. W. H. Myers and the Victorian search for life after death.* Imprint Academic.
Hardinge, E. (1875, December 24). The travelling of the spirit during the life of the body. *Spiritualist Newspaper,* pp. 303–304.
Hare, R. (1855). *Experimental investigation of the spirit manifestations, demonstrating the existence of spirits and their communion with mortals.* Partridge & Brittan.
Harrison, W. H. (1879). *Spirits before our eyes.* W. H. Harrison.
Hart, H., and collaborators. (1956). Six theories of apparitions. *Proceedings of the Society for Psychical Research, 50,* 153–239.
Hartmann, F. (1888). *Magic, white and black: Or, the science of finite and infinite life, containing practical hints for students of occultism* (3rd Rev. ed.). George Redway.
Hill, J. A. (1918). *Man is a spirit: A collection of spontaneous cases of dream, vision, and ecstasy.* Cassell.
Hill, W. (1711). *Full account of the life and visions of Nicholas Hart.* John Baker.
Home, D. D. (1863). Incidents in my *life*. Carleton.
Home, D. D. (1864). *Incidents in my life* (2nd ed.). F. Pitman.
Irwin, H. J. (1985). *Flight of mind: A psychological study of the out-of-body experience.* Scarecrow Press.
James, W. (1909). A possible case of projection of the double. *Journal of the Society for Psychical Research, 3,* 253–254.
Jordan, D. S. (1899). The posthom phantom: A study in the spontaneous activity of shadows. *Science, 9* (n. s.), 674–681.
Judge, W. Q. (1893). *The ocean of theosophy* (2nd ed.). The Path.
Jung-Stilling, J. H. (1834). *Theory of pneumatology, in reply to the question, what ought to be believed or disbelieved concerning presentiments, visions, and apparitions, according to nature, reason and scripture.* Longman, Rees, Orme, Brown, Green, and Longman. (Original work published 1808.)
Jung-Stilling, J. H. (1851). *Theory of pneumatology; in reply to the question, what ought to be believed or disbelieved concerning presentiments, visions, and apparitions, according to nature, reason and scripture* (1st American ed.). J. S. Redfield. (Original work published 1808)
Kardec, A. (1860). *Philosophie spiritualiste: Le livre des esprits* (2nd ed.). Didier.
Kardec, A. (1863). *Spiritisme expérimentale: Le livre des médiums* (6th ed.). Didier.
Kardec, A. (1891). *Experimental spiritism: Book on mediums* (5th ed.). Colby & Rich.
Kaufman, M.H. (2008). William Gregory (1803–1858): Professor of chemistry at the University of Edinburgh and enthusiast for phrenology and mesmerism. *Journal of Medical Biography, 16,* 128–133.
Kelly, E. W. (2007). F. W. H. Myers and the empirical study of the mind-body problem. In E. F. Kelly et al. *Irreducible Mind* (pp. 47–115). Rowman & Littlefield.
Kemer, J. (1845). *The Seeress of Prevorst: Being revelations concerning the inner-life of man.* J. C. Moore. (Abridged from German original; Original work published 1829)
Kislingbury, E. (1875, April 9). Correspondence: Spirit travelling during sleep. *Spiritualist Newspaper,* p. 178.

Lamothe, L. (1857). Controverse: Vue a distance; deplacement de Fame. *Journal du Magnétisme, 16*(s. 2), 505–508.
Lannuzzo, G. (1983). *Ernesto Bozzano: La Vita e l'Opera* (Le Monografie di Luce e Ombra, No. 2). Luce e Ombra.
Leadbeater, C. W. (1903). *Dreams: What they are and how they are caused* (3rd Rev. ed.). Theosophical Publishing Society.
Lefranc, L. (1911a). Comment il faut etudier le probleme spirite. *Le Monde Psychique, 1*(6), *161–172;* (7), 195–199
Lefranc, L. (1911b). Les etats du sommeil magnétique du fantôme du vivant ou corps éthérique. *Le monde psychique, 1*(2), 3–7.
Lefranc, L. (1911c). Cas fortuit de repercussion sur le corps physique d'une lesion produite sur le fantôme d'un sujet. *Le mondepsychique, 1*(3), 84–88.
Lombroso, C. (1909). *After death—What?* Small, Maynard.
Mattiesen, E. (1931). Der Austritt des Ich als spiritistisches Argument. *Zeitschrift für Parapsychologie, 6*, 413–437, 481–494.
McAdams, E. (1984). Reported near-death observations in a hospice in California. In M. C. Rose (Ed.). *The Synergy of Religion and Psychical Research* (pp. 57–64). Academy of Religion and Psychical Research.
Mead, G. R. S. (1919). *The doctrine of the subtle body in western tradition.* J. M. Watkins.
Méheust, B. (2003). *Un voyant prodigieux, Alexis Didier.* Les Empecheurs de penser en rond-Le Seuil.
Morin, A.S. (1857). Review of *Le sommeil magnetique explique par le somnambule Alexis en etat de lucidite,* by A. Didier. *Journal du Magnétisme,* 16(s. 2), 76–84.
Moses, W. S. [under the pseudonym M.A. Oxon]. (1875, March 5). Photographing the spirit of a medium in Paris, while his body was asleep in London. *Spiritualist Newspaper,* p. 119.
Moses, W.S. (1904/1887). A vision of death. *Light, 24,* 167–168.
Muldoon, S. J. (1936). *The case for astral projection.* Ariel Press.
Muldoon, S. J., & Carrington, H. (1929). *The projection of the astral body.* Rider.
Myers, F. W. H. (1886). Note on a suggested mode of psychical interaction. In E. Gurney, F. W. H. Myers, & F. Podmore, *Phantasms of the Living* (Vol. 2, pp. 277–316). Trübner.
Myers, F. W. H. (1892a). On indications of continued terrene knowledge on the part of phantasms of the dead. *Proceedings of the Society for Psychical Research, 8,* 170–252.
Myers, F. W. H. (1892b). The subliminal consciousness: Chapter I. General characteristics of subliminal messages. *Proceedings of the Society for Psychical Research, 7,* 298–327.
Myers, F. W. H. (1903). *Human personality and its survival of bodily death* (2 vols.). Longmans, Green.
Necrologie: Albert de Rochas. (1915). *Annales des sciences psychiques*, 25, 243–245.
Nye, M. J. (1980). N-rays: An episode in the history and psychology of science. *Historical Studies in the Physical Sciences, 11*, 125–156.
Olcott, H. S. (1897). Old diary leaves: Second oriental series, chapter VIL. *The Theosophist, 19*, 65–68.
Owen, R. D. (1860). *Footfalls on the boundary of another world: With narrative illustrations.* J. B. Lippincott.
Peebles, J. M. (1872). Do mediums leave their bodies? *Human Nature, 6,* 376–378.
Peter, J. (1907). Versuche uber Bilokation von A. de Rochas und Mlle Alma Haemmerlé. *Psychische Studien, 34,* 79–80.
Pleasants, H. (Comp.). (1964). Biographical *dictionary of parapsychology.* Garrett Publications.
Pliny the Edler. (1890). *The natural history of Pliny* (Vol. 2). George Bell & Sons.
Podmore, F. (1902). *Modern spiritualism: A history and a criticism* (2 vols.). Methuen.
Poortman, J. J. (1978/1954). *Vehicles of consciousness: The concept of hylic pluralism (Ochema)* (4 vols.). Utrecht: Theosophical Society in the Netherlands.
Posthumous Humanity. (1888). *Lucifer, 1*, 399–401.
Ravaldini, S. (1993). *Ernesto Bozzano e la Ricerca Psichica: Vita e Opere di un Pioniere della Parapsicologia.* Mediterranee.
Regnault, J. (1905). Odic phenomena and new radiations. *Annals of Psychical Science, 1*, 145–163.
Reichenbach, C. von. (1851/1849). *Physico-physiological researches on the dynamics of magnetism, electricity, heat, light, crystallization, and chemism, in their relation to vital force* (from German 2nd ed.). J. S. Redfield.
Richet, C. (1922). *Traité de métapsychique.* Félix Alcan.

Richmond, C. L. V. (1915). *My experiences while out of my body and my return after many days.* Christopher Press.
Rogers, E. C. (1853). *Philosophy of mysterious agents.* J. P. Jewett.
Rogo, D. S. (1973). *The welcoming silence.* University Books.
Rogo, D. S. (1983). *Leaving the body: A practical guide to astral projection.* Prentice-Hall.
Sabatier, A., de Rochas, A., de Gramont, A., Maxwell, J., Dariex, X., & de Watteville, C. (1896). Experiences de l'Agnelas sur Eusapia Paladino. *Annales des Sciences Psychiques, 6,* 1–55.
Schilleto, A. R. (Ed. & Trans.). (1888). *Plutarch's morals: Ethical essays.* George Bell and Sons.
Sharp, L. L. (2006). *Secular spirituality: Reincarnation and spiritism in nineteenth-century France.* Lexington Books.
Shirley, R. (n. d., 1938). *The mystery of the human double.* Rider.
Sidgwick, H., Johnson, A., Myers, F. W. H., Podmore, F., & Sidgwick, E. M. (1894). Report on the Census of Hallucinations. *Proceedings of the Society for Psychical Research, 10,* 25–422.
Smith, E. L. (2002). *Evelyn Pickering De Morgan and the allegorical body.* Farleigh Dickinson University Press.
Snell, J. (1918). *The ministry of angels: Here and hereafter.* G. Bell & Sons.
Sollier, P. (1903). *Les phenomenes d'autoscopie.* Félix Alcan.
Tacitus. (1874). *The works of Tacitus* (Vol. 2). Harper and Brothers.
Tanchou, Dr. [S.]. (1846). *Enquete sur l'authenticite des phenomenes electriques d'Angelique Cottin.* Germer Baillière.
The manners of posthumous man. (1883). *Cornhill Magazine, 1* (n. s.), 214–224.
Thurston, H. (1952). *The physical phenomena of mysticism* (J. H. Crehan, Ed.). Burns, Oates.
Turvey, V. (n. d., ca 1911) *The beginnings of seership; or, Super-normal mental activity.* Stead's Publishing House.
Tweedale, C. L. (1921). The passing of Mary Burnett: Wonderful purple light precedes transition. *Light, 41,* 551.
Tyrrell, G. N. M. (1953). *Apparitions.* Pantheon Books.
Volpi, E. (1890). Memoire de M. Ernesto Volpi. In *Compte rendu du Congres Spirite et Spiritualiste tenu a Paris du 9 au 16 septembre 1889* (pp. 317–325). Librairie Spirite.
Wantuil, Z., & Thiesen, F. (1984). *Allan Kardec* (3 vols.) (2nd ed.). Fédéraçao Espirita Brasileira.
Watson, [S.]. (1876). The double. *American Spiritual Magazine,* 2, 187–188.
Wills–Brandon, C. (2000). *One last hug before I go: The mystery and meaning of deathbed visions.* Health Communications.
Wiltse, A.S. (1889). A case of typhoid fever with subnormal temperature and pulse. *St. Louis Medical and Surgical Journal, 57,* 355–364.
Zorab, G. (1975). Have we to reckon with a special phantom-forming predisposition? *Journal of the Society for Psychical Research,* 48, 19–30.

On Doubles and Excursions from the Physical Body, 1876–1956*

Carlos S. Alvarado

This essay review is about the ideas of a group of authors who contributed to constructing and maintaining the concept that some principle inherent in human beings was capable of leaving the physical body, and thus accounted for phenomena such as apparitions of the living and what later came to be called out-of-body and near-death experiences (OBEs and NDEs). The authors in question believed the phenomena were explained by the projection of a spirit, or some sort of subtle body sometimes referred to as a "double," from the physical body. In fact, such ideas of subtle bodies come from ancient times (Mead, 1919; Poortman, 1954/1978) and were widely discussed in the past by many writers (e.g., Jung-Stilling, 1808/1851), including those representing theosophy (e.g., Besant, 1896). But there have been others, such as prominent members of the Society for Psychical Research (Gurney, Myers & Podmore, 1886; Myers, 1903), who have not conceptualized OBEs and apparitions of the living as produced by the projection of a subtle body.

Referring to the implications of excursions of consciousness for the issue of survival of bodily death, German philosopher Carl du Prel (1839–1899) argued that the astral body could "exist independently of the material body and be separated from it, in other words it is immortal" (du Prel, 1899/1907(1), 186). The authors reviewed in this essay believed that OBEs supported belief in survival of death, something accepted as well by many others (e.g., Mattiesen, 1931; Myers, 1903). These ideas have been included in popular books published in relatively modern times, such as *The Mystery of the Human Double* (Shirley, n. d.), and *The Enigma of Out-of-Body Travel* (Smith, 1965), among others (e.g., Battersby, n. d.; Pilloni, 1978). All of this is part of the conceptual history of OBEs, a topic that has received some attention as seen in my writings (Alvarado, 1989, 2005, 2009b, 2009c) and those of others (Crookall, 1961, Appendix 1; Deveney, 1997).

In this essay review I will comment on three articles and five books published between 1876 and 1956 whose authors have postulated that something leaves the body in an OBE, as opposed to the ideas of those who have theorized that the experience is hallucinatory, even if accompanied by veridical perceptions (Alvarado, 2009a). I am not including in this eview writings based on the repeated OBEs of single individuals (e.g., Muldoon & Carrington, 1929), nor on single accounts of NDEs (Wiltse, 1889), literatures that deserve to be separately reviewed.

William Stainton Moses

William Stainton Moses (1839–1892) was a clergyman, as well as an influential English spiritualist and medium. He wrote about many aspects of spiritualism and psychic phenomena, among them the identity of mediumistic communicators and direct writing (Moses, 1879, 1882). In one of his private

*Republished with permission from *Journal of Scientific Exploration, 25*(3), 563–580, 2011.

notebooks, he recorded an interesting OBE he had in January of 1874 while he was writing (Myers, 1895, p. 36–37).

His article "On the Trans-Corporeal Action of Spirit," published in the English *journal Human* Nature in 1876, is one of those nineteenth-century forgotten discussions on the topics of apparitions of the living and OBEs. Like other writers discussed here, Moses considered cases that did not involve recollection of being out of the body while the person in question was seen as an apparition. Moses wrote:

> The testimony of all sensitives, psychics, or mediums, i.e. persons in whom the spirit is not so closely bound to the body as in the majority of individuals, agrees in the consciousness they all have of standing in places, and observing people, and scenes from a spot removed from that which they know their bodies to be. Whilst employed in some occupation compatible with quietness and passivity, e.g., reading, meditating, or quiet conversation, they feel frequently a strange second consciousness, as though the *ego* had moved away through space and were busied with other scenes. (p. 102)

Moses classified the cases he discussed in two groups. The first were those cases happening spontaneously: (1) seeing oneself (later called autoscopy) and unconscious apparitions of the living; (2) apparitions apparently providing warnings of an oncoming death; (3) apparitions taking place when the physical body was not in movement or was in some other state (including mediumistic materializations), and (4) apparitions showing consciousness and those apparently without consciousness while the person seen was experiencing anxiety.

The second group discussed by Moses was what he considered to be phenomena connected to some form of volition. This group consisted of cases having a strong emotional content (such as apparitions of the dying), and those seemingly dependent on the will of the person represented by the apparition.

Adolphe D'Assier

The topic of a double with physical properties was the main concept discussed by Adolphe D'Assier (1827–1889), once member of the Académie des Sciences de Bordeaux, and known for his writings about matters such as grammar and language (e.g., D'Assier, 1861). His book *Posthumous Humanity: A Study of Phantoms* (1887) was translated from the original French edition *Essai sur l'Humanité Posthume et le Spiritisme* (1883).

In the book, D'Assier speculated on the posthumous personality as manifesting with phenomena such as apparitions, and argued that during life there was a principle that could leave the body and that could continue after physical death. Some cases of doubling during life, the author argued, were remembered by the experiencer, but others were forgotten.

D'Assier speculated about this principle, which he believed had physical properties. He wrote:

> The child who comes out of the body of its mother is attached to her by a vascular system which brought it strength and life. It is the same in this doubling; the human phantom is constantly in immediate relation with the body whence it has wandered for some moments. Invisible bonds, and of a vascular nature, so intimately connect the two extremities of the chain, that any accident happening to one of the two poles reacts (*se répercute*) instantaneously upon the other (p. 51) … The phantom possesses a circulatory apparatus as well as the body of which it is the double. Invisible capillaries unite the one to the other, and the whole forms a system so homogeneous, so closely connected, that the slightest prick received by the phantom at

> once reacts ... on all the vascular apparatus up to the extremity of the chain, and blood flows immediately. (p. 57)

Like Moses, D'Assier presented many cases of apparitions in his book. In his view, the phenomenon of duplication "is observed only in some organizations exceptionally gifted in the matter of sensitiveness; and this explains its extreme rarity" (p. 250). The posthumous apparition, he believed, was the same entity manifested in doublings and apparitions of the living:

> The living spectre and the spectre from beyond the tomb, having the same origin, can present in their manifestation the same common characteristics. Such are the noises that occur in certain habitations, where the chairs, furniture, crockery, &c., are seen to change place or to shake under the impulse of an invisible hand. (p. 256)

Hector Durville

Hector Durville (1849–1923) was a well-known French student of magnetism and psychic phenomena. He founded the Société de Magnétisme de France and defended the existence of a magnetic force that could cause healing and other phenomena, a topic he discussed in his two-volume work *Traité Expérimentale de Magnétisme* (1895–1896). In the book reviewed here, *Le Fantôme des Vivants* (1909), Durville focused on the projection of phantoms of the living, or what he termed doubling.

The first part of the book was about the history and conceptual aspects of the topic. This included the idea of subtle bodies and their manifestations. The latter part consisted of OBEs as well as apparitions of the living with and without the consciousness of the person represented by the apparition. Durville concluded the section stating:

> The physical body is seen at the place that it really occupies; and at the same moment its phantom is seen at a distance ... The sensations felt by the phantom are reflected on the physical [body] ... The physical [body] is never in its normal state during doubling. The mystics are always in ecstasy; the sorcerers and nearly all the common people are more or less profoundly asleep, the mediums are in trance, the somnambules in a state of magnetic somnambulism and the dying delirious or in syncope ... Some of the doubled recollect perfectly everything that was seen, said, or that took place ...; others remember vaguely ..., most others do not keep any recollection. (pp. 136–138; this and other translations are mine)

Durville believed that doubling showed that the thinking principle could leave the physical body while the person was alive and that this double could perceive and sometimes act on the environment, an idea consistent with the beliefs of other individuals mentioned in this essay review.

In the second part of the book, Durville reported tests he conducted to study intentionally projected phantoms of the living. In this work Durville followed on the previous investigations of Albert de Rochas (1837–1914), a pioneer in the laboratory study of phantoms of the living (de Rochas, 1895) and of the exteriorization of sensibility, a topic I have discussed before in the *Journal of Scientific Exploration* (Alvarado, 2011a). Durville worked with several ladies whom he magnetized repeatedly, asking them to project their phantom in order to explore its perceptual and motor capabilities. He said very little about his participants but they were obviously sensitive to magnetization (or suggestion). One of the ladies in question, Mme. Lambert, was also studied by de Rochas. She was later described as a medium who had physical phenomena at home as well as in the séance room (Lefranc, 1911a).

Durville wrote that he considered the exteriorization of sensibility and doubling to be similar. The first was a state in which the sensibility was believed to radiate around the person, while the second was a state in which the sensibility was contained in the phantom. Durville wrote:

> We have seen that the subjects submitted to the action of magnetism … exteriorize …, all of them keep their usual state of consciousness, their sensibility which had disappeared at the beginning of somnambulism … radiates now around them, up to a distance that may reach a distance 2 meters 50 and even 3 meters. At some moment … such *sensibility*, which all the subjects see in the form of vapour, a whitish fluid, gray or grayish, sometimes with light iridescent shades, is condensed and localized on each side of them, at a distance that may vary from 20 centimeters … to 80 centimeters. (p. 178)

Several chapters contain descriptions of such aspects as the appearance of the phantom, its perceptual capabilities, influences on other persons, and physical effects presumably produced by it. The point of the studies was to obtain evidence that perceptions and physical effects could take place from a location distant from the physical body of the projected persons, at the place where the phantom was supposed to be. Because some aspects of Durville's reports have been published in English in the *Annals of Psychical Science* (Durville, 1908a, 1908b), I will cite some descriptions from one of them to take advantage of the translations.

Some tests were performed to test for vision. In Durville's words:

> The projected double can see, but rather confusedly, from one room into another. While I was at the end of my study with Edmee, whose double was projected, I asked three of the witnesses of the experiment … to go into the lecture room of the society and perform some simple and easily described movements, so that we could ascertain whether the double, which I would send there, could see anything. Dr. Pau de Saint-Martin stood near the window, between my study and the hall where the witnesses were, in order to see almost at the same time both the subject and what these experimenters were doing.
>
> *First Experiment.*—Mme. Fournier seated herself on the table. 'I see,' said the subject, 'Mme. Fournier seated on the table.'
>
> *Second Experiment.*—The three persons walked into the room and gesticulated. 'They walk and make gestures with their hands; I do not know what it means.'
>
> *Third Experiment.*—Mme. Stahl took a pamphlet from the table and handed it to Mme. Fournier. 'The two ladies are reading,' said the subject.
>
> *Fourth Experiment.*—The three persons joined hands, formed a chain and walked round the table. 'How funny!' said the subject; 'they are dancing round the table like three lunatics.' (Durville, 1908a, p. 338)

Durville believed that the phantom emanated N-rays, a controversial form of radiation prominent during the first decade of the twentieth century that was eventually dismissed by the scientific community as being due to artifactual observations (Ashmore, 1993; Nye, 1980). To detect the projected phantom, he used screens covered with calcium sulphide, a substance believed to produce brightness in contact with the rays. Durville wrote as follows:

> The double of the subject having been projected, I took the three screens and showed them to the witnesses, who observed that they were completely dark. Laying the small screen aside for a moment, I placed one of the large ones on the abdomen of the subject and held the other in the phantom, which was seated on an armchair to the left of the subject.

> The screen placed in the phantom became rapidly illuminated, and the one on the subject remained completely dark. After several minutes I took both screens and showed them to the witnesses, who were much astonished by the phenomenon. I then took the screen which had been on the subject, and remained dark, and placed it in the phantom. It immediately became illuminated like the first. I again showed them to the witnesses, who saw that they were sufficiently illuminated to allow them easily to count the spots of sulphide of calcium at a distance of a yard.
>
> I then took the small screen which had not been used, and placed it on the abdomen of the subject for two or three minutes without obtaining the slightest trace of luminosity.
>
> I then placed it in the phantom, and it became very strongly illuminated. The witnesses found that it gave enough light to enable one of them to tell the time by a watch.
>
> These experiments, repeated about ten times with seven or eight different subjects, always gave similar results, which were very intense when the screens had been well exposed to the sun, less so when the exposure had been insufficient. (Durville, 1908a, p. 341)

The double was said to be able to produce raps and movement of objects, which was taken by Durville to indicate its objective nature. This body, Durville wrote in his book, carried the "very principle of life, as well as will, intelligence, memory, consciousness, the physical senses, while the physical body does not have any faculty" (p. 354). This suggests that the subject's awareness was out of the body, something that is not always clear throughout the experiments reported in the book.

The tests reported by Durville represent a historically important attempt to empirically study the topic through the induction of experiences. This is a break with the rest of the work discussed in this essay review, which depended on the collection and interpretation of cases. The book was repeatedly cited by later writers on the topic such as the following ones mentioned below. Some aspects of his work were replicated and extended, but the reports have fewer methodological details than Durville's (e.g., Lefranc, 1911b).

Ernesto Bozzano

Italian psychical researcher Ernesto Bozzano (1862–1943) was well-known for his publications presenting many cases of psychic phenomena from the international literature on the subject, for his classifications of phenomena, and for his ardent defenses of survival of bodily death. Such work was evident in his discussions of phenomena related to death, such as deathbed visions, the hearing of music, and the perception of physical phenomena related to a distant death (Bozzano, 1923). Bozzano discussed the topic under the name of "bilocation," a term he used to group a variety of phenomena he explained using the concept of a subtle body (Alvarado, 2005). He first wrote in detail about the topic in a paper (Bozzano, 1911), and expanded this article into a short book published in Italian (Bozzano, 1934). I am commenting here on the French translation of this book, *Les Phénomènes de Bilocation,* published in 1937.

This study consisted of the compilation and interpretation of published cases. Bozzano discussed: (1) the phantom limb sensation of amputees and the "doubling" sensations of the body of hemiplegics; (2) apparitions of the self, or autoscopy; (3) cases of apparitions perceived by another person (such as those manifestations seen apparently coming out of the body of dying persons); and (4) a variety of cases difficult to classify as those of doubling or of telepathy, including many apparitions of the living.

In some cases, Bozzano noticed, “the personal consciousness is transferred to the phantom” (p. 41). He believed consciousness was in the etheric body, which he referred to as “the supreme, immaterial envelope of the discarnate spirit” (p. 8). But many cases discussed by him did not involve the *experience* of being out of the body.

In the book Bozzano mentioned twenty published cases of individuals who found themselves out of their physical body in a variety of circumstances. These were taken from published discussions of psychic phenomena. Bozzano noticed that these cases rarely happened when the person was in their waking state. Many of the cases he presented happened “during absolute rest of the body” (p. 41). Five of them took place when the person was under the effects of anesthesia, while the rest were experiences that took place during illness (2 cases), hypnosis (2 cases), and one each in the following circumstances: exhaustion and stress, being shot, giving birth, under depression, during asphyxia, smoke inhalation, coma, a fall, sleep, during automatic writing, and falling asleep.

Bozzano considered veridical perceptions during the experience to be very important. These cases suggested to him that the phenomenon was not hallucinatory. Similarly, Bozzano placed great importance on those perceptions of deathbed observers in which mists or lights were seen emanating from the dying person, phenomena that are not frequently discussed today (for an exception, see Alvarado, 2006b). In his view, these cases indicated an initial stage of doubling representing the beginnings of death. This was conceptualized as the separation of a fluidic matter from the body that showed fluctuations due to changes in the vitality of the dying person, ending with the formation of an etheric body.

For Bozzano, when all the phenomena he mentioned in his book were considered together they showed the existence of an etheric body capable of leaving the body. Furthermore, he believed that such etheric body implicated the existence of an etheric brain through which a spirit manifested. In his view bilocation demonstrated survival of bodily death.

Sylvan J. Muldoon and Hereward Carrington

Sylvan Muldoon (1903–1969) became known for his classic book written with psychical researcher Hereward Carrington (1880–1958), *The Projection of the Astral Body* (Muldoon and Carrington, 1929). In this book Muldoon analyzed his multiple OBEs, some of which he could induce. His interest on the topic led him to publish books about psychic phenomena (e.g., Muldoon, 1942), as well as the two books reviewed here. By the time Carrington published his 1929 book with Muldoon, he had been involved in psychical research for more than 20 years and was well- known through publications such as *The Physical Phenomena of Spiritualism*, where he discussed mediumistic fraud (Carrington, 1920).

In his first case collection, *The Case for Astral Projection* (1936), Muldoon presented previously published cases, as well as new cases from people who wrote to him. The first part of the book was devoted to the concept of astral projection, while the second included many actual cases.

Some accounts included projections presented with headings such as “Floats Horizontally in Air,” “A Mother Projects, Finds Her Baby Well,” “Finds Her Dog in Astral World,” “Finds Her Astral Body Beautiful,” and “Spends Several Days in Spirit World.” There were also accounts such as Wiltse’s (1889) NDE, and other experiences taking place under anesthesia, during sleep, relaxing, and in other circumstances. Muldoon was convinced that people could leave their bodies, but he was also open to other explanations in some particular cases.

Muldoon's work was continued in a study published fifteen years later with Carrington as coauthor. This was *The Phenomena of Astral Projection* (1951), one of the most influential of the modern case collections of OBEs and NDEs. The authors presented more than 100 cases, most of which were organized in chapters including deliberately induced projections (such as those under hypnosis), and those taking place under the influence of drugs, suppressed desire and other emotional factors, during accidents or illness, and during the waking state. The latter included cases where the person was lying down (eight cases), sitting down playing an organ (six cases consisting of the same individual's repeated experiences), sitting down (three cases), and one each for the following: walking, standing and assisting a surgical operation, standing inactive, kneeling in prayer, and no information.

Like Bozzano, Muldoon and Carrington included in their book several cases in which observers at deathbeds saw emanations such as mists and lights from the body of dying persons. Those accounts present no evidence that the persons were conscious of leaving the body while they were dying.

The authors commented in their conclusion about the commonality of features in the narratives presented in the book:

> In a large percentage of the cases we find mention of floating and soaring, of being above the body and looking down upon it, of floating above the physical body, of being suspended in the air, of the astral cord uniting the two bodies, of cracking and snapping sensations and sounds in the head, of catalepsy, physical numbness and the inability to move, of the momentary blanking of consciousness when entering and leaving the body, of the feeling of depression just before projection, of the feeling of "repercussion" when again entering the body, of the belief that one is dead, etc. These characteristics are repeatedly found throughout the cases reported, and it is interesting to note that they are seemingly so universal and so identical. (p. 216)

Muldoon and Carrington also presented descriptions of rare features of astral projection. Among them were returning to the body through the head of the physical body (p. 77), seeing both the physical body and a replica of it from a different position (p. 133), being perceived by others while out of the body (p. 187), and shifts of visual perception location in terms of alternately seeing from the physical body and from another location (p. 190).

Like so many before them, Muldoon and Carrington argued that astral projection involved a spiritual body and that it supported the concept of survival of bodily death. They wrote about the latter idea: "Death is nothing more than the permanent separation of the two bodies …" (p. 31)

Hornell Hart

As the inheritor of the previous literature, sociologist Hornell Hart (1888–1967) focused on the study of spontaneous cases and the idea of survival of bodily death. One of his initial studies, "Visions and Apparitions Collectively and Reciprocally Perceived," appeared in the *Proceedings of the Society for Psychical Research* (Hart and Hart, 1933). In later years he expressed his ideas about survival in his book The Enigma of Survival (1959). He is to be credited for bringing the topic of OBEs to parapsychology journals at a time in which there was little discussion of the topic.

In his paper "ESP Projection: Spontaneous Cases and the Experimental Method," published in the *Journal of the American Society for Psychical Research* in 1954, Hart compiled published OBE cases to study what he referred to as "ESP projection." These were experiences that included the sensation that one was located out of the body, veridical perceptions during that state, and that had a "consistent orientation to the out-of-body location" (p. 121). His efforts led him to find 288 published cases, out of which he used 99 reports in which the experience had been reported before it was verified.

Hart analyzed cases in terms of various concerns. One was the way in which the experience took place. Some were induced via the use of hypnosis (20 cases), concentration (15), and methods other than concentration (12), while others took place spontaneously (22). He found that "neither the concentration method nor the hypnotic method usually produce full-fledged ESP projection" (p. 128).

The "full-fledged projections" had several features. In addition to veridical features, the cases also included reports of seeing the physical body, sensations of floating, being aware of having a different body, and being able to pass through matter.

Some of the features seemed related to the circumstances in which the OBE took place. For example, features such as going to other dimensions and seeing spirits took place more often in spontaneous OBEs than in induced ones. Those induced by hypnosis had veridical perceptions, but few other features. Perhaps the hypnotically-induced experiences tended to be veridical because the induction procedure included suggestions to visit and observe distant places. With some exceptions, such focusing of attention is not necessarily present in spontaneous OBEs.

Hart said he used a scale to rate cases for evidentiality, details of which appear in his 1956 paper "Six Theories about Apparitions." The article presented an early example of the use of quantification to analyze OBE features.

The overall purpose of the paper was to discuss explanations of apparitions and to assess empirically if the features of apparitions of the living and apparitions of the dead were similar. Hart collected 165 published apparition cases out of which 25 were OBE apparitions. Some of the features of the latter cases were full figures (100%), adjustment to physical surroundings (80%) and to persons (72%), normal body movements (28%), descriptions of features as vivid (24%), and of the apparitions as solid and life-like (12%).

Hart believed that OBEs were "internal views of the phenomena observed externally in connection with apparition of the living" (p. 177). For this reason, he argued that similarities between different types of apparitions—apparitions of the dead, of the dying (but not conscious), and OBE apparitions—suggested "something of the nature of the experiences undergone at and (to a limited extent) after death" (p. 177). Statistical analyses were reported by Hart showing that all apparitions had similar features.

He summarized the hypotheses and findings of the study as follows:

1. That full-fledged ESP projection consists in a conscious apparition of a living person, within which the projected personality carries full memories and purposes, and from which, on returning to his physical body, this personality carries back the full memory of the observations and operations performed while projected.
2. That these conscious projections of living persons are in most respects essentially indistinguishable from apparitions of the dying, of those who have been dead for periods up to a few hours, and those who have been dead for days, months, or years.
3. That since this is the case, some of the most frequent types of apparitions of the dead presumably carry with them the memories and purposes of the personalities which they represent, and thus constitute evidence of survival of personality beyond bodily death. (pp. 234–235)

As mentioned in my discussion of D'Assier, and as I have pointed out before in the *Journal of Scientific Exploration* (Alvarado, 2011b), the idea that apparitions of the living are similar to apparitions of the dead, and that this similarity supports a survivalist explanation, was discussed by others before Hart.

Critical Remarks

An interesting issue regarding work with cases is how much the authors in question imposed a theoretical framework onto the accounts they compiled. This seems to be the case when D'Assier assured us that the phantoms he studied had "invisible capillaries" and when Bozzano wrote about an "etheric brain." These were speculations derived from the author's interpretation of cases.

Related to this is the continuity the above-mentioned authors and others (e.g., Myers, 1903) assumed existed between apparitions of the living and OBEs. But this continuity, as assumed by authors such as Moses, D'Assier, and Bozzano, is not clear in many cases. The same may be said about the various phenomena Bozzano connected to each other: OBEs, autoscopy, emanations from the dying, and apparitions of the living. While the connections assumed to exist may be real and may reveal we are dealing with the same class of phenomena, they are not clearly observable and instead of being "uncovered" from the data they may be the result of conceptual impositions guided by projection assumptions. After all, many of the same phenomena these authors have interpreted on a projection OBE model have been interpreted in different ways by others (Braude, 2003, Bret, 1939, Gurney, Myers, & Podmore, 1886).

Most of the authors relied on their impression of the cases to argue for similarities and continuities, and this may have produced erroneous conclusions. To check for Muldoon and Carrington's statements about the commonality of OBE features, I analyzed their cases for a few of the features Muldoon and Carrington said were frequently reported: reports of cords, catalepsy, sounds (such as snapping, clicking, and roaring sounds), and "repercussion" (shocks or jolts felt on the physical body on return). Except for the chapter of cases in brief (Chap. 9), and those cases of emanations from the body at death which did not include cases in which individuals felt they were located outside of their physical bodies, I used the 87 cases reported in chapters 1–2 and 4–8 of their book. This showed the following: cords (6 cases, or 7%), catalepsy (5 cases, or 6%), sounds (7 cases, or 8%), and shocks (3 cases, or 3%). Such results do not support the claim that such features were found in a "large percentage of the cases" (p. 216), casting doubt on Muldoon and Carrington's generalizations, as well as on impressionistic analyses which fail to include the most elementary counts of features. This reminds us of the importance of reaching conclusions on the basis of estimates of the actual proportion of OBE features as opposed to general impressions based on what we remember from reading cases.

Hart brought more precision to OBE studies when he conducted quantitative analyses of the features of OBE apparitions, and apparitions of the dying and of the dead. With his work we have specific proportions of features while before him the issue was only addressed with general descriptions. But was such precision unambiguous? His conclusion regarding the survival implications of the above-mentioned apparitions did not depend solely on his statistical comparisons. The interpretations of his results depend on the validity of his assumption that OBEs represent consciousness located out of the physical body.

Furthermore, it may be argued that some of the cases used by Hart are problematic. Six of the 25 OBE apparition cases analyzed by Hart were taken from secondary sources that did not present the actual testimony of the experiencer. This, and the fact that most of the other cases with firsthand testimony included few details about the OBEs suggest that the profile of features coded by Hart may not be reliable. In any case, his effort was a valuable one deserving follow-up with a higher number of cases.

There are also questions about Durville's work. It is not always clear how isolated the magnetized subjects were from the information they were asked to perceive. The physical results reported by Durville are puzzling, but one wonders if they can be explained by ideas other than the exteriorization of a phantom. Similar effects have been interpreted in the past in the physical mediumship and psychokinesis literatures using concepts that do not necessarily involve the idea of a double. In addition, because perceptions of the phantom depended on the testimony of the subjects, one wonders about the role of suggestion, particularly with repeatedly used individuals who knew what Durville and his collaborators wanted to obtain. One wonders if different effects would have been obtained with special subjects who had different beliefs than the ones used by Durville or with subjects with less "training."

I do not mean to say that the work of the authors discussed here is not valid or that it has no value for us today. But the above-mentioned critiques are methodological issues that need to be considered both in the evaluation as well as in the replication of such research.

Concluding Remarks

Works such as the ones commented on here have kept alive the idea of subtle bodies and projection over time. However, some of them, such as Moses and D'Assier, have been almost forgotten in the modern scholarly and scientific OBE literature. Durville and Bozzano are cited mainly by European authors, partly because their work has not been translated into English. There was a period when most authors writing about OBEs cited Muldoon and Carrington's 1951 book as well as Hart's 1954 paper. This work has not been completely forgotten, but, as happens in most fields, citations from these years decline because more recent publications tend to be cited instead.

In addition to the usual forgetfulness that writers in modern fields show about the old literature over time, there have been other influences in the neglect of this past. Perhaps the main one is that the academic contemporary OBE literature has been heavily influenced by psychological ideas (Murray, 2009), and more recently by neurophysiological approaches (Blanke, 2004). In such climate—affecting both parapsychology and psychology—ideas of projection such as the ones discussed here are not seriously considered in academic circles. This has led to the neglect of empirical studies about veridical aspects of OBEs in recent times, a topic that has received more attention in NDE studies (Holden, 2009).

Another reason for the neglect of this old literature is that some of the concepts of subtle bodies discussed here (mainly those of D'Assier and Durville) may seem to be too physical for some current students of psychic phenomena. As I have argued elsewhere, many modern parapsychologists have argued that experimental evidence for psi is inconsistent with a belief in physical forces (Alvarado, 2006a). Furthermore, some have presented higher-space theoretical speculations that do not assume a projection into physical space (Poynton, 2001).

We also need to remember that during the 1980s and later, most OBE researchers focused on studies of the features, the psychology, and other correlates of OBEs, and ideas of projection and subtle bodies became less popular in parapsychology (for overviews, see Alvarado, 1989, 2000). Examples of this were the works of Gabbard and Twemlow (1984) and Irwin (1985).

Regardless of changes in approach, the tradition represented by the publications reviewed here has been important in modern times. These ideas have been influential in discussions of the topic of survival of death (e.g., Fontana, 2005), and have inspired the few modern laboratory studies of veridical perception and detection (Alvarado, 1982a, 1982b) that deserve follow-up. In fact, successful laboratory work along these lines and the compilation and study of new well-documented cases would be valuable to balance the view held by many today that the OBE is purely hallucinatory.

Some of this past work, such as Muldoon and Carrington's, has reminded us about the variety and complexity of OBE features. Much remains to be done with cases to examine the basic features of the

OBE, including the less frequent ones, as well as studying if specific features, or features profiles, are related to other features, to circumstances of occurrence, or to other variables (Alvarado, 1997). Hart provides us with ideas for research, such as the difference between spontaneous and induced OBEs.

Although the writings of Moses, D'Assier, Durville, Bozzano, Muldoon and Carrington, and Hart represent different time periods, they can still inspire new research on the subject. Furthermore, these old writings help us to understand the development of OBE studies. But we need to realize that such development did not depend solely on projection ideas. In addition to these, the field was influenced by other concepts, such as those coming from psychology. Like the OBE, the history of the topic is more complex than what it seems on the surface.

References

Alvarado, C. S. (1982a). ESP during out-of-body experiences: A review of experimental studies. *Journal of Parapsychology, 46,* 209–230.

Alvarado, C. S. (1982b). Recent OBE detection studies: A review. *Theta, 10*(2), 35–37.

Alvarado, C. S. (1989). Trends in the study of out-of-body experiences: An overview of developments since the nineteenth century. *Journal of Scientific Exploration, 3,* 27–42.

Alvarado, C. S. (1997). Mapping the characteristics of out-of-body experiences. *Journal of the American Society for Psychical Research, 91,* 13–30.

Alvarado, C. S. (2000). Out-of-body experiences. In E. Cardeña, S. J. Lynn, & S. Krippner (Eds.), *Varieties of anomalous experience* (pp. 183–218). American Psychological Association.

Alvarado, C. S. (2005). Ernesto Bozzano on the phenomena of bilocation. *Journal of Near-Death Studies, 23,* 207–238.

Alvarado, C. S. (2006a). Human radiations: Concepts of force in mesmerism, spiritualism and psychical research. *Journal of the Society for Psychical Research, 70,* 138–162.

Alvarado, C. S. (2006b). Neglected near–death phenomena. *Journal of Near-Death Studies, 24,* 131–151.

Alvarado, C. S. (2009a). Early and modern developments in the psychological approach to out-of-body experiences. In C. D. Murray (Ed.), *Psychological scientific perspectives on out-of-body and near-death experiences* (pp. 1–22). Nova Science.

Alvarado, C. S. (2009b). Historical notes on doubles and travelling spirits: I—Introduction. *Paranormal Review, 50,* 6–15.

Alvarado, C. S. (2009c). The spirit in out-of-body experiences: Historical and conceptual notes. In *Spirituality, science and the paranormal* (pp. 3–19). Academy of Spirituality and Paranormal Studies.

Alvarado, C. S. (2011a). Unorthodox concepts of force and psychic phenomena. *Journal of Scientific Exploration, 25*(1), 121–130.

Alvarado, C. S. (2011b). Essay review. Apparitions of the living: The views of William H. Harrison and Gabriel Delanne. *Journal of Scientific Exploration, 25*(2), 351–360.

Ashmore, M. (1993). The theatre of the blind: Starring a promethean prankster, a phony phenomenon, a prism, a pocket, and a piece of wood. *Social Studies of Science, 23,* 67–106.

Battersby, H. F. P. (n. d., 1942). *Man outside himself: The facts of etheric projection.* Rider.

Besant, A. (1896). *Man and his bodies* (Theosophical Manual 7). Theosophical Publishing.

Blanke, O. (2004). Out of body experiences and their neural basis. *British Medical Journal, 329,* 1414–1415.

Bozzano, E. (1911). Considérations et hypothèses sur les phénomènes de « bilocation. » *Annales des Sciences Psychiques, 21,* 65–72, 109–116, 143–152, 166–172.

Bozzano, E. (1923). *Phénomènes psychiques au moment de la mort.* Editions de la B. P. S.

Bozzano, E. (1934). *Dei fenomeni di « bilocazione. »* Tipografia Dante.

Bozzano, E. (1937/2006). *Les phénomènes de bilocation* by Ernesto Bozzano. JMG Editions.

Braude, S. E. (2003). *Immortal remains: The evidence for life after death.* Rowman & Littlefield.

Bret, P. T. (1939). *Les metapsychoses: La metapsychorragie, la télépathie, la hantise: Vol. 1: Introduction et la metapsychorragie fantasmale.* J. -B. Baillière.

Carrington, H. (1920). *The physical phenomena of spiritualism: Fraudulent and genuine* (Rev.ed). Dodd, Mead.

Crookall, R. (1961). *The study and practice of astral projection.* Aquarian Press.

D'Assier, A. (1861). *Essai de grammaire générale d'àpres la comparaison des principales langues Indo-Européennes*. Benjamin Duprat.

D'Assier, A. (1883). *Essai sur l'humanité posthume et le spiritisme.* Paris: Auguste Ghio.

de Rochas, A. (1895). Les fantômes des vivants. *Annales des Sciences Psychiques, 5*, 257–275.

D'Assier, A. (1887/1981). Posthumous humanity: A study of phantoms. George Redway.

Deveney, J. P. (1997). *Astral projection or liberation of the double and the work of the early Theosophical Society* (Theosophical History Occasional Paper, Vol. 6). Theosophical History.

du Prel, C. (1899/1907). *La magie: Science naturele: I: La physique magique*. H. Vaillant-Carmanne, 1907. (Original work published, 1899).

Durville, H. (1895–1896). *Traité expérimental de magnétisme* (2 vols.). Librairie du Magnetisme.

Durville, H. (1908a). Experimental researches concerning phantoms of the living. *Annals of Psychical Science 7*, 335–343.

Durville, H. (1908b). New experiments with phantoms of the living. *Annals of Psychical Science, 7*, 464–470.

Durville, H. (1909). Le fantôme des vivants: Anatomie et physiologie de l'âme: Recherche expérimentale sur le dédoublement des corps de l'homme. Librairie du Magnétisme.

Fontana, D. (2005). *Is there an afterlife?* O Books.

Gabbard, G. O., & Twemlow, S. W. (1984). *With the eyes of the mind: An empirical analysis of out-of-body states*. Praeger Scientific.

Gurney, E., Myers, F. W. H., & Podmore, F. (1886). *Phantasms of the living* (2 vols.). Trübner.

Hart, H. (1954). ESP projection: Spontaneous cases and the experimental method. *Journal of the American Society for Psychical Research, 48*, 121–146.

Hart, H. (1956, May). Six theories about apparitions. In *Proceedings of the Society for Psychical Research, 50*(185), 53–239).

Hart, H. (1959). *The enigma of survival: The case for and against an after-life.* Charles C Thomas.

Hart, H., & Hart, E. B. (1933). Visions and apparitions collectively and reciprocally perceived. *Proceedings of the Society for Psychical Research, 41*, 205–249.

Holden, J. M. (2009). Veridical perception in near-death experiences. In J. M. Holden, B. Greyson, & D. James (Eds.), *The handbook of near-death experiences: Thirty years of investigation* (pp. 185–211). Praeger.

Irwin, H. J. (1985). *Flight of mind: A psychological study of the out-of-body experience.* Scarecrow Press.

Jung-Stilling, J. H. (1808/1851). *Theory of pneumatology; in reply to the question, what ought to be believed or disbelieved concerning presentiments, visions, and apparitions, according to nature, reason and scripture* (1st American ed.). J. S. Redfield. (Original work published 1808).

Lefranc, L. (1911a). Comment il faut étudier le problème spirite. *Le Monde Psychique, 1*, 162–172, 195–199.

Lefranc, L. (1911b). Les états du sommeil magnétique du fantôme du vivant ou corps éthérique. *Le Monde Psychique, 1*(2), 3–7.

Mattiesen, E. (1931). Der Austritt des Ich als spiritistisches Argument. *Zeitschrift für Parapsychologie, 6*, 413–437, 481–494.

Mead, G. R. S. (1919). *The doctrine of the subtle body in western tradition.* J. M. Watkins.

Moses, W. S. (under pseudonym of M. A. Oxon). (1879). *Spirit identity.* W. H. Harrison.

Moses, W. S. (under pseudonym of M. A. Oxon). (1882). *Psychography: A treatise on one of the objective forms of psychic or spiritual phenomena* (2nd ed.). Psychological Press Association.

Moses, W. S. (under the pseudonym M. A. Oxon). (1876). On the trans-corporeal action of "spirit," *Human Nature, 10,* 1876, 97–125, 145–157.

Muldoon, S. J. & Carrington, H. (1951/1981). *The phenomena of astral projection.* Samuel Weiser. (Original work published by Rider, 1951).

Muldoon, S. J. (1936/2004). *The case for astral projection.* Kesinger.

Muldoon, S. J. (1942). *Famous psychic stories.* New Horizon.

Muldoon, S. J., & Carrington, H. (1929). *The projection of the astral body.* Rider.

Murray, C. D. (Ed.) (2009). *Psychological scientific perspectives on out-of-body and near-death experiences.* Nova Science.

Myers, F. W. H. (1895). The experiences of W. Stainton Moses—II. *Proceedings of the Society for Psychical Research, 11*, 24–113.
Myers, F. W. H. (1903). *Human personality and its survival of bodily death* (2 vols.). Longmans, Green.
Nye, M. J. (1980). N-rays: An episode in the history and psychology of science. *Historical Studies in the Physical Sciences, 11*, 125–156.
Pilloni, W. (1978). *La nilocazione: Esperience e testimonianze*. Mediterranée.
Poortman, J. J. (1954/1978). *Vehicles of consciousness: The concept of hylic pluralism (ochema)* (4 vols.). Theosophical Society in the Netherlands. (Original work published 1954).
Poynton, J. (2001). Challenges of out-of-body experience: Does psychical research fully meet them? *Journal of the Society for Psychical Research, 65*, 194–206.
Shirley, R. (n.d./1938). *The mystery of the human double*. Rider.
Smith, S. (1965). *The enigma of out-of-body travel*. Helix Press.
Wiltse, A. S. (1889). A case of typhoid fever with subnormal temperature and pulse. *St. Louis Medical and Surgical Journal, 57*, 355–364.

Nineteenth-Century Hysteria and Hypnosis: A Historical Note on Blanche Wittmann*

Carlos S. Alvarado†

There were many patients and hypnotic subjects in the nineteenth century who influenced the development of psychology. An example was Blanche Wittmann, one of the star hysterical patients and hypnotic subjects at the Salpêtrière. In addition to producing phenomena for Jean-Martin Charcot, Wittmann performed for others such as Gilbert Ballet, Alfred Binet, Charles Féré, Jules Janet, and Paul Richer Wittmann produced phenomena such as muscle contractions, transfer of symptoms from one side of the body to another, hysterogenic zones, hallucinations, and apparent secondary states or personalities. The performances of such individuals, together with the actual work of clinicians and researchers, contributed to the spread of clinical and theoretical views of psychological phenomena. In fact, they worked together complementing each other.

While we generally study the history of psychology through the contributions of clinicians and researchers—individuals such as Sigmund Freud (1856–1939), Pierre Janet (1859–1947), Edward B. Titchener (1867–1927), and Wilhelm Wundt (1832–1920)—it is also possible to focus on the performances of patients and research subjects as contributors to the field. Henri F. Ellenberger (1970) reminded us of this perspective. Since then, there have been several discussions of the topic. A prominent example are writings about Freud's patients (e.g., Decker, 1991; Guttmann, 2001), and about famous cases of dissociation (e.g., Faure, Kersten, Koopman, & Van der Hart, 1997; Kenny, 1986).[1] These individuals did more than allow themselves to be studied. They interacted with clinicians and researchers in a joint process that contributed to the cataloguing of clinical symptoms and the developing of theoretical ideas. In this short paper, I discuss Blanche Wittmann, whose hysteric and hypnotic performances contributed to the development of French psychology and psychiatry.

French Explorations of Hysteria and Hypnosis

The French specialised in the study of a variety of clinical conditions which showed that "the normal unity of consciousness is broken" (Binet, 1892, p. viii; this, and other translations, are mine).[2] Many explorations of dissociative phenomena were published during these years, including cases of amnesia, somnambulism, and double and multiple personality (e.g., Azam, 1887; Binet, 1892; Bourru & Burot, 1888; Burot, 1889). A particularly well-known case was that of Félida X. (Azam, 1887), whose double existence influenced ideas of dissociation during the last quarter of the nineteenth century.

*Republished with permission from *Australian Journal of Clinical and Experimental Hypnosis*, *37*, 21–36, 2009.
†I am grateful to Nancy L. Zingrone for editorial suggestions to improve this paper.

Another concern of late nineteenth-century French psychopathologists was hysteria, defined by a writer as an "ensemble of functional or dynamic problems of the nervous system, very numerous, very diverse," manifesting in "thousands of ways" (Dutil, 1894, p. 1322). Neurologist Jean-Martin Charcot (1825–1893) embarked into the best known and most influential research program of this condition at the Salpêtrière Hospital at Paris, which was a woman's hospital and insane asylum (Gauchet & Swain, 1997/2000). Some of his early lectures on the topic include hysterical ischuria, hemiplegia, and contractions, as well as ovarian hyperesthesia and hystero-epilepsy (Charcot, 1872–1873, Chapters 9–13). Many followers of Charcot have described the proteic phenomenology of hysteria, while claiming that there were particular patterns and stages (e.g., Bourneville & Regnard, 1879–1880; Gilles de la Tourette, 1887; Pitres, 1891; Richer, 1881). Paul Richer (1849–1933) discussed the stages of grand hysteria in his influential study *Études Cliniques sur l'Hystéro-épilepsie ou Grande Hystérie* (1881). In addition to a prodomic period consisting of mood changes and a variety of problems of digestion, circulation, and sensibility, there were four stages. These were an epileptoid period (trembling, convulsions), and periods of contortions (large movements of the body, may include hallucinations), passionate attitudes (vivid hallucination and "plastic" poses expressing religious fervour and emotions), and delirium (hallucinatory and movement problems).

Hypnosis was also a French concern (Barrucand, 1967), and one studied as well by Charcot, who saw the phenomenon as a hysterical one (Bourneville, 1890, Part 2, Chapters 1–17; Charcot, 1882). In a famous communication to the Academy of Sciences, entitled "Sur les Divers États Nerveux Determinés par l'Hypnotisation chez les Hystériques," Charcot (1882) described hypnosis as a phenomenon frequently observed in women with hystero-epilepsy that presented three "nervous states." These were the cataleptic, lethargic, and somnambulistic states. In addition to studies of hypnosis as a hysterical manifestation, something questioned by others (e.g., Bernheim, 1884, 1891), many used hypnotic techniques to learn about the making of the mind and its plasticity. As stated by physiologist Henri Beaunis (1830–1921), "hypnotism constitutes … a true method of experimental psychology; it is for the philosopher what vivisection is for the physiologist" (Beaunis, 1887, p. 115). Some examples of this were the use of magnets on the hypnotised to transfer motor and mental phenomena such as paralyses and hallucinations from one side of the body to another (Binet & Féré, 1885, 1887), the exploration (Janet, 1889) and induction (Richet, 1883) of secondary personalities, and the effects of hypnosis on somatic processes such as heart rate, cutaneous congestion, and auditive acuity (Beaunis, 1887).

Most of this research was done with hysterics and particularly suggestible individuals. These were the individuals that physiologist Charles Richet (1850–1935) referred to as the "demoniacs of today," by which he meant that the old descriptions of the possessed were "absolutely identical to today's hystero-epileptic access" (Richet, 1880, p. 356). One of the "demoniacs" during Richet's times was Blanche Wittmann.

Wittmann's Early History

Writing in 1889, English classical scholar and psychical researcher Frederic W. H. Myers (1843–1901) stated:

> Blanche Wittmann is one of the best known personalities—or groups of personalities—in Paris. A hystero-epileptic of the most pronounced type, she has never been able for long together to meet the stresses of ordinary life. She has long been an inmate of the Salpêtrière; and some of my readers may have seen her exhibited there, at Prof. Charcot's lectures, or by the kindness of Dr. Féré or other physicians, as the type—I may almost say the prototype—of the celebrated

"three stages" of lethargy, catalepsy, and somnambulism, of which she realised every characteristic detail with marvellous precision. (Myers, 1889, p. 216)

Blanche Wittmann was immortalised in the famous 1887 painting by Andre Broulliet (1857–1914) representing a lecture on hypnosis by Charcot at the Salpêtrière.[3] In addition to Charcot and Wittmann, the painting includes 29 additional persons, most of them physicians. Some of them are Joseph Babinski (1857–1932), Charles Féré (1852–1907), Georges Gilles de la Tourette (1857–1904), and Théodule Ribot (1838–1916). At the time Charcot was at the heyday of his clinical and research work on hysteria and hypnotism (Gauchet & Swain, 1997/2000; Owen, 1971).

Wittmann was one of the star subjects of Charcot and his followers who displayed phenomena supporting the ideas of hysteria and hypnosis developed by the so-called Salpêtrière School.[4] Signoret (1983) has reminded us that her actual name is uncertain, and that she was referred to in the literature as Marie, W… W, Wit, Witt and as Blanche Witt. Archival research shows the existence of a record of a Marie Wittman, born on 15 April 1859 in Paris, who entered the hospital as an epileptic on 6 May 1877 (Signoret, 1983, p. 692). This is similar to a publication about BW, and contemporary with her, that stated that a 19-year-old woman "W … Marie, seamstress … entered the service of M. Charcot on May 5, 1877" (Bourneville & Regnard, 1879–1880, p. 5).

She was said to have a barely average intelligence, and a good memory. However, the patient thought her memory had diminished after the administration of ether. She was described as a woman with a large and strong body, weighing 70 kilograms (154 pounds). Another description read: "She is blond and of a lymphatic complexion. The skin is white and also presents several ephelides …. The bosom is very large" (Bourneville & Regnard, 1879–1880, p. 7).

In a volume of the famous *Iconographie Photographique de la Salpêtrière*, serial publications that articulated Charcot's interest in objectifying hysteria as a medical phenomenon with specific symptoms and stages (Didi-Huberman, 1982/2003), Bourneville and Regnard (1879–1880, pp. 4–39) presented the early history of B W according to herself. Her father, a Swiss carpenter, had a violent character to the point that once he put Wittmann inside a coffin. Eventually he was institutionalised as insane. Her mother, a seamstress, who had died, suffered from nervous attacks. Wittmann had nine siblings, five of whom were deceased. One of them had convulsions and another suffered from possible epilepsy. She was the oldest of the surviving children, one of whom coughed blood and another who suffered from "weakness."

When Wittmann was 22 months of age, she suffered from convulsions. In addition, she became unable to walk, left-handed, and speechless. Her conditions improved by the time she was seven years old. At 12 Wittmann had "nervous accidents" in which she lost consciousness and urinated on herself, while at 13 her condition included body tremors. In her own words: "Everything I had in my hands fell down" (Bourneville & Regnard, 1879–1880, p. 6). In later years she had sexual relations with her employer, having some "attacks" during intercourse, and once after the act. After she left this man she had two other lovers.

Alphonse Baudouin (1876–1956), who was an intern at the Salpêtrière in 1905, met Wittmann when she was no longer having her hysterical crises and was working at the hospital's radiology laboratory. He described her as "authoritarian and capricious" (Baudouin, 1925, p. 519). Baudouin asked her about the possibility that her hysterical crises were purposely simulated, and she is reported to have said: "Do you believe that it was easy to deceive M. Charcot? Yes, there were fakes that tried it; he would throw a simple glance and say: 'Be still'" (p. 520). Unfortunately, Baudouin observed that she had suffered several amputations due to the "abominable cancer of radiologists" (p. 519).

Wittmann had a long career of performances of hysterical and hypnotic phenomena, some of which is summarised below.

Observations of and Phenomena Produced by Wittmann

Wittmann worked with different clinicians and researchers. Her performances, sometimes quite dramatic, presented a wide variety of phenomena related to different sensory, motor, and cognitive functions.

Tactile and Visual Functions

In an 1878 paper with other authors, Charcot stated: "Wittmann, 18 years old … has painful points in the ovarian regions; she is anaesthesic in all parts of the body" (Charcot, Luys, & Dumontpallier, 1878, p. x). Others observed changes in sensations: "1877. May 7.—*Hemianesthesia* of the right side; diminishment of the sensibility of the left arm.—*Right ovarian hyperesthesia*, magnified at the approach of the attacks" (Bourneville & Regnard, 1879–1880, p. 7).

Wittmann lost sensibility in the skin and those parts with membranes such as around the eyes and the vaginal area. She also had other problems: "The eyes closed, W … is incapable to indicate with exactitude the position of her members, to name the objects she holds on her hands, and to walk with confidence" (Bourneville & Regnard, 1879–1880, p. 25).

Sometimes the patient experienced the hysterical ball. In some circumstances the "ball oscillates from the pit of the stomach to the inferior part of the neck," and cardiac palpitations appeared (Bourneville & Regnard, 1879–1880, p. 38).

In both the waking and the hypnotic state Wittmann showed anaesthesia, loss of muscular sense (such as awareness of the position of body members), color blindness and poor vision in the left eye. Overall, the vision in the right eye was normal, but the report for the other eye read: "Left eye: complete achromatopsia for all colours, save for saturated red, normal luminous sense" (J. Janet, 1888, p. 617).

Body Movements

Wittmann showed many of the classic stages and motor manifestations of "grand hysteria," such as the following:

> *Epileptoid period.*—Rigidity augments; breathing becomes faster, it is suspended, congestion of the face is accentuated more …. Sometimes there are tetanic tremblings.
>
> *Clonic period.*—After a short rest, one observes the swinging movements of the head that, before long, is raised …
>
> *Delirium period.*—The breathing is very frequent; the pupils are dilated; small groans; movements of the lips; the patient talks in a low voice …. She complains of feeling bad in the head, that the vision is confused, and of being fatigued. (Bourneville & Regnard, 1879–1880, p. 8)

In addition, she showed an arched position in which "the body rests on the top of the head … and on the point of the feet," a position "W … keeps … nearly a minute; afterwards she falls heavily on her bed" (Bourneville & Regnard, 1879–1880, p. 30).

Physical Stimuli Affecting Hysterical and Hypnotic Phenomena

Charcot and others conducted research that supported the assertions that hysterics could be affected by metals applied externally as well as ingested internally (Charcot, Luys, & Dumontpallier, 1877,

1878). The later referred to solutions with different metals ingested for therapeutic purposes. As they wrote in a test with Wittmann: "With the internal administration of gold the patient recovered the peripheral sensibility and a good part of her muscular force. She did not have hysterical attacks during 9 months" (Charcot et al., 1878, p. xi).

One of the most interesting manifestations was the effect of touching or pressing the so-called hysterogenic zones of the body of the hysteric capable of causing or arresting manifestations. With Wittmann, and with other hysterics, the compression of the ovarian region was an effective zone. On one occasion, after compression of the right ovarian region it was noticed that "before long the eyelids move apart, the pupils are greatly dilated" (Bourneville & Regnard, 1879–1880, p. 10).

The patient was "wakened" from her hysterical attacks through the use of ovarian compressions (Bourneville & Regnard, 1879–1880, p. 17), and from hypnosis by blowing on her eyes (Ballet, 1891, p. 523). In 1890, as reported by Georges Guinon (1859–1932) and Sophie Woltke, Wittmann was asked to stare at a bright object until she fell into the hypnotic lethargic state (Guinon & Woltke, 1891, p. 78).

There were also examples in which attacks were arrested by the inhalation of ethylic iodine (Bourneville & Regnard, 1879–1880, p. 11). On another occasion, in January 1879 it was observed that: "Under the influence of static electricity ... the sensibility returns in all the right half of the body" (Bourneville & Regnard, 1879–1880, p. 13).

Gilbert Ballet (1853–1916) observed the patient in the hypnotic lethargic state and noticed that "it is enough to exert a slight rubbing of the vertex to throw Wit. ... into ... the somnambulistic state" (Ballet, 1891, p. 523).

In other tests reported by Guinon and Woltke (1891), Wittmann experienced different emotions when colored glass was put in front of her eyes. For example, a red glass seemed to induce joy and pleasure (p. 78). Other observations were reported as follows:

> *Blue glass.* – She frowned and her physiognomy showed sadness.
> *Yellow glass.* – She showed all the signs of great fear.
> *Dark green glass.* – Her physiognomy expressed astonishment followed by admiration .... The patient raised her arms and moved them apart [in admiration]. (p. 78)

Other stimuli included smells. Substances put under Wittmann's nose produced disgust (sulphur of carbon), contentment (cologne, and camphor of ether), and disgust and repulsion (chloroform) (pp. 78–79). Light drumming produced violent contractions (p. 79).

Neuromuscular Hyperexcitability

Charcot (1882) described neuromuscular excitability as the tendency of "muscles to have a contraction under the influence of a mechanical excitation endured on the tendon, on the muscle itself, or on the nerve of which it is a tributary" (p. 404). The stimuli in question could be actions such as pressure or massage. While this phenomenon appeared during the lethargic state, it did not do so either during the cataleptic or the somnambulistic states. Richer (1881, p. 366) noted that it was easy to induce in "Witt ... contractions of facial muscles." In a study published by Charcot and Richer (1881/1890) they observed that during the lethargic state of hypnosis, Wittmann presented "modifications of the reflex muscular contraction" (p. 320). They obtained instrumental graphic recordings of this muscular activity. It was normal during the waking state, but contracted during hypnosis.

Dermography

"During the attacks," Bourneville and Regnard (1879–1880, p. 19) wrote, "we traced on the chest, with the point of a pin, the name of the patient and the name Salpêtrière on the stomach. An erythemic band of several centimetres of elevation was produced and on this band the letters were drawn in relief, having about two centimetres in length; the erythema disappeared slowly, the letters lasted [longer]." While uncommon, similar phenomena have been reported with other persons (Mesnet, 1890).

Hallucinations

Richer (1881) reported several interesting hallucinations. In one of them "W … saw a red lion on her left" (p. 10). Sometimes the hallucinations represented things from the patient's life: "She talked about a certain Alphonse, called him an 'ingrate,' and directed very bitter reproaches at him" (p. 116). According to Bourneville and Regnard (1879–1880, p. 7) one of Wittmann's former lovers was called Alphonse.

At other times hallucinations were suggested. Ballet (1891, p. 523) did this with a bird, which the patient saw and caressed.

While Wittmann was in the arch position she was brought out of her stupor through ovarian compressions and she seemed to have had "nightmares." In one of these instances she recollected that she fell into a precipice, while in another she was persecuted by a villain (Richer, 1881, p. 92). Similarly, after the above-mentioned effect of drumming, Wittmann fell into a "bizarre state of semi-consciousness" (Guinon & Woltke, 1891, p. 79). She said that she saw extraordinary things during it. This included seeing herself in the arms of her lover, "full of contentment and pleasure" (p. 79). There were also images of the sea, a great fire, a ballroom, a place with dead bodies, and a garden with flowers. Finally, the scene changed and she perceived a smell like wet terrain and felt dead. She saw all of this but did not seem to take part in the visions.

Transfer

Transfer phenomena referred to the act of "transferring" sensory, motor, or cognitive phenomena from one side of the body of a hypnotised person to the other through the use of magnets, which was one of the early specialties of Alfred Binet (1857–1911) and the previously mentioned Charles Féré (Binet & Féré, 1885, 1887). In Wittmann's case they argued that it was "probable that the state of her nervous system favours the action of the magnet at a high degree" (Binet & Féré, 1885, p. 15).

An example of transfer of motor phenomena was the occasion when Binet and Féré had Wittmann under hypnosis and suggested to her to scratch the arm rest of an armchair with her left index finger. She started to do this and they placed a magnet some distance from her right hand. After about 30 seconds, not only the left index finger was doing the task, but the right one started to do so as well. The "movement was intensified in the right, while it declined at the left" (Binet & Féré, 1885, p. 8). Other observations focused on the transfer of acts, a "phenomenon not only formed from movement, but from thoughts, reasoning and will" (p. 9).

Myers (1886) wrote about transfer experiments he observed in Paris: "Witt—is in the somnambulic state. The hypnotiser suggests to her to make figures, 1, 2, 3, &c., with her right hand. She is awakened;

a magnet being hidden near her left hand. She writes the numerals up to twelve with her right hand, then hesitates, takes the pen in her other hand, and begins to write in mirror-writing with her left hand. I have witnessed this experiment, (Aug. 25th, 1885)" (p. 444).

Secondary States

Following on the work of Pierre Janet (1859–1947) with hypnotic secondary states published in the *Revue Philosophique* (Janet, 1886, 1887, 1888), and later in a book (Janet, 1889), Jules Janet (1861–1945), Pierre's brother, conducted explorations with Wittmann. Janet attempted to take his subject beyond the hypnotic lethargic stage. In that state, different from the somnambulistic one, she was cheerful, which was in contrast with her usual serious behaviour out of that state. While the "normal" state had problems such as anaesthesia and colour blindness, the secondary state was completely normal.

Janet described Wittmann's new hypnotic state as Blanche 2, and her usual state as Blanche 1. In his view: "Blanche 1 is incomplete. Blanche 2 is complete" (J. Janet, 1888, p. 619). This meant that the secondary state had access to the experiences and recollections of the other state, but not the other way around. Janet conducted tests in which he determined that when stimuli were presented to Blanche 1, she did not perceive them but Blanche 2 did. This included sensations of pricking and seeing colors. Communication with Blanche 2 while the stimuli were presented to Blanche 1 took place through ideomotor action, namely a prearranged response of raising a finger when something was felt or perceived.

In a review of Janet's paper, Myers (1889) wrote that: "M. Janet tells me that last year he kept Blanche Witt—for months together in her second state, with much comfort to her; and that now, though he has ceased to attend her, he understands that her condition in the first state is much better than of old" (p. 219).

Concluding Remarks

Like so many other patients and research subjects, Wittmann formed a partnership with clinicians and researchers that articulated the phenomenology of hysteria and hypnosis. While her case was not cited as often as that of Félida X., the classic French example of "doubling" of personality (Azam, 1887), it was studied by more researchers than Félida was. This allowed her to become a human laboratory in the French tradition of the study of single individuals as a method of exploration and knowledge-gathering. Brouillet's painting presents a visual representation of this process, one that had many examples in nineteenth-century French hypnosis work (for an overview see Carroy, 1991).

There is no question that Wittmann's performances, together with the performances of others, provided phenomena that sustained the existence and illustrated the phenomenology of hysteria and hypnosis. Furthermore, her phenomena were used to support the ideas of Binet, Charcot, Féré, Janet, and Richer, ideas that influenced their generation when it came to pathology, hypnotic stages, and the workings of dissociation. This included the "usual" phenomena such as lack of sensibility, contractions, hallucinations, and hysterogenic zones, as well as less common ones such as dermography and controversial issues including the therapeutic use of metals and the effectiveness of magnets to induce transfer phenomena.

Such developments, as has been argued before (Carroy, 1991; Didi-Huberman, 1982/2003), should not be interpreted simply as the results of objective observations. To start, we must be open to the possibility that some hysterics and hypnotic subjects were openly lying, as suggested in the past (e.g., Munthe, 1929, p. 302). It is conceivable that many of Wittmann's phenomena could have been intentionally produced by her to obtain attention, or to comply with the desire of her investigators to observe hysteria and hypnosis. Fraudulent performances could have been instrumental to maintain her identity as a star patient/research subject, or to fulfil other needs.

But her performance could also have been genuine while still affected by the demand characteristics of the clinical-research context, including specific theoretical ideas and the suggestive influence of previous performances by other patients. This is what some nineteenth-century critics of the Salpêtrière referred to when they wrote about the influence of education and imitation in the production of hypnotic phenomena (Delboeuf, 1886).

Following Bernheim (1884, p. 5), who stated that his researches did not confirm the existence of Charcot's hypnotic states and phases, the writer of a popular article about hypnosis described the Salpêtrière patients as "'drilled' hysterical subjects" (O'Connor, 1890, p. 579). Bernheim (1891) also proposed that the Salpêtrière hysterics were affected by suggestion, and by the example of other hysterics. The phenomena, he argued, showed a tendency for "imitation, acting through auto-suggestion" (p. 168). In Bernheim's view the specific stages of hysteria were created by the theoretical environment of the Salpêtrière, what he referred to as "an hysteria of culture" (p. 169). In one way or another Wittmann responded to the conceptual "culture" of her surroundings and researchers when she produced her phenomena.

Another important variable to consider was the presence of a special individual such as Wittmann. Assuming some of the phenomena were not fraudulently produced, we need to remember that not everyone can have hallucinations, sensory, tactile and muscular changes, produce writing on their bodies, or respond to the procedures to induce transfer. This suggests the presence of a high-level propensity for the production of imaginative-dissociative and psychophysiological phenomena such as that hypothesised to exist in high hypnotisable and fantasy-prone individuals (Wilson & Barber, 1983).

Finally, the above-mentioned variables probably interacted with Wittmann's personal makeup. Her motivations and needs, both as a person and as a Salpêtrière star performer, may have been involved in the production of either real or fraudulent phenomena.

In addition to these psychological considerations, there are other social aspects that probably affected Wittmann's interactions with her researchers. Charcot's physicians, Evans (1991) has argued, came from a higher social class than the patients did and this created authoritative attitudes in their treatment. This, in turn, "fed into the positivist mission of nineteenth-century French doctors and created an emphasis on scientific discovery that strangely elided the human existence of the patients" (p. 36).

In any case, Wittmann continues to serve as a reminder of the importance, and ambiguity, surrounding patients and research subjects in the development of psychology and psychiatry. Developments in nosography and theory would not have been possible without individuals like her. More than objects studied by past scholars and clinicians, persons such as Blanche Wittmann were active agents in the construction of the concepts of hysteria and hypnosis.

Notes

1 There is also a literature consisting of accounts of madness from the patient's point of view (e.g., Porter, 1987), feminist critiques of the study of cases (e.g., Bernheimer & Kahane, 1990), and discussions of hypnotic subjects (e.g., Carroy, 1991) and mediums (e.g., Alvarado, 1993).
2 For overviews see Crabtree (1993), Ellenberger (1970), Gauld (1992), Lopez Pinero and Morales Meseguer (1970), & Nicolas (2004). An overview of French psychology appears in Nicolas (2002).
3 The painting can be seen in the web ("Psychosomatic Medicine: 'The Puzzling Leap,' (n. d.) and has been discussed by Perez-Rincon (1998, chaps. 4–5) and by Signoret (1983).
4 Other patients at the Salpêtrière mentioned in the first chapter of Richer's (1881) book include Alphonsine Bar, Ang., Gen., Gl ., Ler., and Marc. Another famous patient, Augustine, has been discussed by Didi-Huberman (1982/2003).

References

Alvarado, C. S. (1993). The case of Eusapia Palladino: Gifted subjects' contributions to parapsychology. *Journal of the Society for Psychical Research, 59*, 269–292.

Azam, [E. E.]. (1887). *Hypnotisme, double conscience et altération de la personnalité.* J. B. Baillière.

Ballet, G. (1891). La suggestion hypnotique au point de vue médico-légal. *Gazette Hebdomadaire de Médecine et de Chirurgie, 28*, 522–525.

Barrucand, D. (1967). *Histoire de l'Hypnose en France.* Presses Universitaires de France.

Baudouin, A. (1925). Quelques souvenirs de la Salpêtrière. *Paris Médical, 56*, 517–520.

Beaunis, H. (1887). *Le somnambulisme provoqué* (2nd ed.). J. -B. Baillière.

Bernheim, Dr [H.]. (1884). *De la suggestion dans l'état hypnotique: Réponse à M. Paul Janet.* Octave Doin.

Bernheim, Dr. [H]. (1891). *Hypnotisme, suggestion, psychothérapie: Études nouvelles.* Octave Doin.

Bernheimer, C., & Kahane, C. (Eds). (1990). *In Dora's case: Freud-hysteria-feminism* (2nd ed.). Columbia University Press.

Binet, A. (1892). *Les altérations de la personnalité.* Félix Alcan.

Binet, A., & Féré, C. (1885). L'hypnotisme chez les hystériques: Le transfert. R*evue philosophique de la France et de l'étranger, 19*, 1–25.

Binet, A., & Féré, C. (1887). *Animal magnetism.* Kegan Paul, Trench.

Bourneville, D. M. (Ed.). (1890). *Œuvres complètes de J. M. Charcot* (Vol. 9). Bureaux de Progres Mèdical/ Lécrosnier et Babe.

Bourneville, [D. M.], & Regnard, P. (1879–1880). *Iconographie photographique de la Salpêtrière* (Vol. 3). Bureaux du Progrès Médical/Delahaye & Lécrosnier.

Bourru, H., & Burot, P. (1888). *Variations de la personnalité.* J. -B. Baillière.

Burot, P. (1889). Un cas de somnambulisme spontané. *Revue de l'hypnotisme expérimentale et thérapeutique, 3*, 132–136.

Carroy, J. (1991). *Hypnose, suggestion et psychologie: L'invention de sujets.* Presses Universitaires de France.

Charcot, J. -M. (1872–1873). *Leçons sur les maladies du système nerveux faites à la Salpêtrière* (D. M. Bourneville, Ed.). Adrien Delahaye.

Charcot, J. -M. (1882). Sur les divers états nerveux déterminés par l'hypnotisation chez les hystériques. *Comptes-rendus Hebdomadaires des Séances de l'Académie des Sciences, 94*, 403—405.

Charcot, [J. -M.], Luys, [J. B.], & Dumontpallier, [A.] (1877). Rapport fait à la Société de Biologie sur la métalloscopie du Docteur Burq. *Comptes Rendus des Séances de la Société de Biologie, 30*, 1–24.

Charcot, [J. -M.], Luys, [J. B.], & Dumontpallier, [A.] (1878). Second rapport fait à la Société de Biologie sur la métalloscopie et la métallothérapie du Docteur Burq. *Comptes Rendus des Séances de la Société de Biologie, 31*, I–XXXII.

Charcot, J.-M., & Richer, P. (1890). Contribution à l'étude de l'hypnotisme chez les hystériques; du phénomène de l'hyperexcitabilité neuro-musculaire. In *Œuvres completes de J. -M. Charcot* (Vol. 9, pp. 309–421). Bureaux du Progrés Médical. (Original work published 1881).

Crabtree, A. (1993). *From Mesmer to Freud: Magnetic sleep and the roots of psychological healing*. Yale University Press.
Decker, H. S. (1991). *Freud, Dora, and Vienna 1900*. Free Press.
Delboeuf, J. R. L. (1886). De l'influence de l'éducation et de l'imitation dans le somnambulisme provoqué. *Revue Philosophique de la France et de l'Étranger*, *22*, 146–171.
Didi-Huberman, G. (2003). *The invention of hysteria: Charcot and the photographic iconography of the Salpêtrière* (A. Hartz, trans.). MIT Press. (Original work published 1982).
Dutil, Dr (1894). Neurasthénie—épilepsie—hystérie. In J. -M. Charcot, C. J. Brochard, & E. Brissaud (Eds), *Traité de Médicine* (pp. 1281–1386). G. Masson.
Ellenberger, H. F. (1970). *The discovery of the unconscious: The history and evolution of dynamic psychiatry*. Basic Books.
Evans, M. N. (1991). *Fits and starts: A genealogy of hysteria in modern France*. Cornell University Press.
Faure, H., Kersten, J., Koopman, D., & Van der Hart, O. (1997). The 19th century DID case of Louis Vivet: New findings and re-evaluation. *Dissociation*, *10*, 104–113.
Gauchet, M., & Swain, G. (2000). *El verdadero Charcot: Los caminos imprevistos del inconsciente.* (M. I. Fontao, trans.). Nueva Visión. (Original work published 1997)
Gauld, A. (1992). *A history of hypnotism*. Cambridge University Press.
Gilles de la Tourette, [G.] (1887). *L'hypnotisme et les états analogues au point de vue médico-légal*. E. Plon, Nourrit.
Guinon, G., & Woltke, S. (1891). De l'influence des excitations sensitives et sensorielles dans les phases cataleptique et somnambulique du grand hypnotisme. Dans J. -M. Charcot, G. Gilles de la Tourette, A. Londe, G. Guinon, & P. Bloq (Eds), *Nouvelle iconographie de la Salpêtrière: Clinique des maladies du système nerveux* (Vol. 4, pp. 77–88). Veuve Babé.
Guttman, M. G. (2001). *The enigma of Anna O.: A biography of Bertha Pappenheim*. Moyer Bell.
Janet, J. (1888). L'hystérie et l'hypnotisme, d'après la theorie de la double personnalité. *Revue Scientifique*, *25*, 616–623.
Janet, P. (1886). Les actes inconscients et le dédoublement de la personnalité pendant le somnambulisme provoqué. *Revue Philosophique de la France et de l'Étranger*, *22*, 577–592.
Janet, P. (1887). L'anesthésie systématisée et la dissociation des phénomènes psychiques. *Revue Philosophique de la France et de l'Étranger*, *23*, 449–472.
Janet, P. (1888). Les actes inconscients et la mémoire pendant le somnambulisme. *Revue Philosophique de la France et de l'Étranger*, *25*, 238–279.
Janet, P. (1889). *L'automatisme psychologique: Essai de psychologie expérimentale sur les formes inférieures de l'activité humaine*. Félix Alcan.
Kenny, M. G. (1986). *The passion of Ansel Bourne: Multiple personality in American culture*. Smithsonian Institution Press.
López Pinero, J. M., & Morales Meseguer, J. M. (1970). *Neurosis y psicoterapia: Un estudio histórico*. Espasa-Calpa.
Mesnet, Docteur [U. A. E.]. (1890). Autographisme et stigmates. *Revue de l'Hypnotisme et de la Psychologie Physiologique*, *4*, 321–335.
Munthe, A. (1929). *The story of San Michel*. John Murray.
Myers, F. W. H. (1886). Report of the General Meeting. *Journal of the Society for Psychical Research*, *2*, 443–453.
Myers, F. W. H. (1889). Dr. Jules Janet on hysteria and double personality. *Proceedings of the Society for Psychical Research*, *6*, 216–221.
Nicolas, S. (2002). *Histoire de la psychologie française: Naissance d'une nouvelle science*. In Press.
Nicolas, S. (2004). *L'hypnose: Charcot face à Bernheim: L'école de la Salpêtrière face à l'école de Nancy*. L'Harmattan.
O'Connor, J. T. (1890). Hypnotism. *Catholic World*, *1*, 574–582.
Owen, A. R. G. (1971). *Hysteria, hypnosis and healing: The work of J. -M. Charcot*. Garrett Publications.
Perez-Rincon, H. (1998). *El teatro de las histéricas: De cómo Charcot descubrió, entre otras cosas, que también había histéricos*. México: Fondo de Cultura Económica.
Pitres, A. (1891). *Leçons cliniques sur l'hystérie et l'hypnotisme faites à l'Hôpital Saint-André de Bordeaux* (2 vols). Octave Doin.
Porter, R. (1987). *A social history of madness: Stories of the insane*. Weidenfeld & Nicolson.

Psychosomatic Medicine: "The puzzling leap." (n. d.). US National Library of Medicine.
Richer, P. (1881). *Études cliniques sur l'hystéro-épilepsie ou grande hystérie*. Adrien Delahaye et Emile Lécrosnier.
Richet, C. (1880). Les démoniaques d'aujourd'hui. *Revue des Deux Mondes*, *50*, 340–372.
Richet, C. (1883). La personnalité et la mémoire dans le somnambulisme. *Revue Philosophique de la France et de l'Étranger*, *15*, 225–242.
Signoret, J. L. (1983). Une leçon clinique à la Salpêtrière (1887) par André Brouillet. *Revue Neurologique*, *139*, 687–701.
Wilson, S. C., & Barber, T. X. (1983). The fantasy-prone personality: Implications for understanding imagery, hypnosis, and parapsychological phenomena. In A. A. Sheikh (Ed.), *Imagery: Current theory, research, and application* (pp. 340–387). John Wiley.

33

Dream ESP Studies Before Maimonides: An Overview, 1880s–1950s*

Carlos S. Alvarado†

Writing in her influential and widely-cited book *The Night-Side of Nature*, published in 1848, English writer Catherine Crowe referred to "dreams ... which partake of the nature of second sight, or prophecy ... some being plain and literal in their premonitions, others allegorical and obscure; whilst some also regard the most unimportant, and others the most grave events of our lives" (Crowe, 1848, Vol. 1, p. 57). These dreams, now referred to as ESP dreams, are the topic of this paper.

Crowe illustrated the features of these dreams with accounts such as the following one:

> Mrs. W. dreamed that she saw people ascending by a ladder to the chamber of her step-son John; wakes, and says she is afraid he is dead, and that there was something odd in her dream about a watch and a candle. In the morning a messenger is sent to inquire for the gentleman, and they find people ascending to his chamber-window by a ladder, the door of the room being locked. They discover him dead on the floor, with his watch in his hand, and the candle between his feet. (Vol. 1, p. 64)

As can be seen in Crowe's volume, ESP was not only associated with dreams but also with various other altered states of consciousness. Nonetheless dreams have always commanded a special interest in writings about psychic phenomena. In addition to Crowe, numerous nineteenth-century authors mentioned psychic dreams in their works, among them German philosopher Carl du Prel (1899/1907), German physician J. H. Jung-Stilling (1808/1851), British physician Herbert Mayo (1851), and Scottish social reformer Robert Dale Owen (1860). Not only have authors such as these mentioned many cases, but the relationship of dreams with ESP has received attention in modern times as well (e.g., Child, 1985; Krippner, 1991, 2007; Sherwood & Roe, 2003; Ullman, Krippner, with Vaughn, 2001; Van de Castle, 1977). However, except for some brief mentions, in this paper I will not enter into antiquity nor into the modern era. I will confine my discussion to an overview of trends in the study of ESP dreams conducted before the well-known experimental studies that took place at the Maimonides Medical Center in Brooklyn, New York, from the 1960s to the early 1970s (e.g., Krippner, 1970; Krippner, Ullman, and Honorton, 1971; Ullman and Krippner, 1969; Ullman, Krippner, and Feldstein, 1966; for overviews see Child, 1985; Ullman & Krippner, 1970; and Ullman, Krippner, with Vaughn, 2001).

*Reprinted with permission from Behind and *Beyond the Brain* (pp. 77–101). Porto, Portugal: Fundação Bial.

†I wish to thank the Bial Foundation for their past support of my research as well as for inviting me to present this paper as part of the panel discussion "Dreams and Anomalous Cognition." I am also grateful to Caroline Watt and Dick Bierman for organizing the panel, to Massimo Biondi and Lori Derr for help with references, and to Nancy L. Zingrone for useful editorial suggestions to improve this paper.

Rather than defend the existence of ESP in dreams, or focus on theoretical ideas, in this paper I will highlight trends, approaches, methodology, and both study findings and observations that took place between the late nineteenth-century and the 1950s. Because of the paucity of experimental work in the area for the period in question I concentrate on the study of cases, generally referred to in parapsychology as spontaneous cases.

Prolegomena

The topic of ESP dreams is part of the general topic of the relationship between altered states of consciousness and a variety of unusual phenomena which, in addition to ESP, include possession, mediumship, healings and the various phenomena that have been reported in religious contexts, somnambulism, and hypnosis throughout history (Cardeña & Alvarado, 2011; Inglis, 1989; Sluhovsky, 2011; Taves, 1999; Ustinova, 2011). Alterations of consciousness, including that which occurs in dreams, have been part of the research and theoretical agenda of parapsychology from the beginnings of the movement (Alvarado, 1998; Kelly & Locke, 2009; Luke, 2011; Parker, 1975; Shapin & Coly, 1978).

One of the oldest relationships between dreams and unusual phenomena come from discussions and experiences of divination. As argued by Auguste Bouché-Leclercq in his classic work *Histoire de la Divination Dans l'Antiquité*: "If there is a form of divination in support of which we can invoke testimony of universal approval, it is definitively the interpretation of dreams … There is no people during antiquity, and almost no individuals who have not believed in a divine revelation through dreams …" (Bouché-Leclercq, 1879, Vol. 1, p. 277; this, and other translations, are mine). In fact—and in addition to works such as those of Bouché-Leclercq and others (e.g., Halliday, 1913, pp. 128–134; Maury, 1860, 2nd Part, Ch. 1)—there is much information about the ancient history of the topic in recent studies of dreams covering antiquity to the nineteenth-century (e.g., Holowchak, 2002; James, 1995; Miller, 1994; Pick & Roper, 2004; Van de Kemp, 1981).

Many writers from antiquity—among them Aristotle (1902) and Cicero (1853)—discussed divination in dreams. Dream divination in particular, and ESP in altered states of conscious in general, have been related since antiquity to the idea that the soul has unexplained powers that are inhibited by the physical body. It is believed that these powers manifest when the workings of the body are weakened or diminished through the use of drugs or under the influence of a variety of natural states of consciousness, such as dreams. Cicero entertained this notion when he presented dialogues for and against divination. In a section of his treatise he argued that nature "teaches us how great is the energy of the mind when abstracted from the bodily senses, as it is most especially in ecstasy and sleep," going on to state that "when the soul of man is disengaged from corporeal impediments, and set at freedom, either from being relaxed in sleep, or in a state of mental excitement, it beholds those wonders which, when entangled beneath the veil of the flesh, it is unable to see" (Cicero, 1853, p. 198).[1]

In addition to such works as Aristotle's (1902) and Cicero's (1854) many discussions of the topic were made public in antiquity (Egidi, 1949), and many of these included what we would now call dream ESP cases. An interesting later example appears in John Aubrey's Miscellanies (1721), in which the fifth chapter included a variety of ESP dreams published in ancient to medieval sources. In addition, Aubrey included a case he himself had heard about: "A Gentlewoman of my acquaintance dreamed, that if she slept again, the House would be in danger to be Robb'd. She kept awake, and anon Thieves came to break open the House; but were prevented" (p. 64).

Accounts of this sort continued into the nineteenth-century, the period at which I will start my discussion. For example, ESP dreams are mentioned in works of mesmerism such as William Gregory's *Letters to a Candid Inquirer, on Animal Magnetism* (1851), in which he stated "I think it probable, a priori, that the state of spontaneous clairvoyance, like natural somnambulism, occurs much more frequently in the sleeping than in the waking state. We all know how heterogeneous dreams often are; but it is very far from being impossible, or even improbable, that, in certain persons, many of their dreams are the result of true clairvoyance" (p. 142). Similarly, some of the spiritualistic literature—works such as Robert Dale Owen's *Footfalls on the Boundary of Another World* (1860, Book 2, Ch. 2)—both contained cases and a defense of the reality of these dreams even though authors were aware of the possibility that many ESP dreams might possibly be explained through more conventional means.

A skeptical tradition did exist during the nineteenth-century through which period (following on ideas from the previous century, Tavera, 2000) many seemingly ESP dreams were understood as physiologically-based and shaped by the experiences of the preceding day. An example was the case of French physician Alfred Maury who, in his book *Le Sommeil et les Rêves* (1861), saw dreams as "open to instinctive and automatic impulses" (p. 7). For Maury sleep was described as a state in which there was a diminution of functions: "The circulation gets slower; breathing and digestion are less active; the muscular movements have ceased almost completely, and the senses are dulled, or three quarters abolished" (p. 7). Other writers of the era reminded us that dreams consisted of "past remembrances and associations following each other" (Briere de Boismont, 1855, p. 202).

Many authors accounted for psychic dreams as coincidences, malobservation, forgotten ideas, anxiety, or unconscious perception (e.g., Delage, 1891; Macnish, 1834; Maury, 1861; Simon, 1888). English physician John Addington Symmonds, in his book *Sleep and Dreams* (1851), presented some criteria for the acceptance of "prophetic" dreams. He wrote:

> 1stly. We must remember that the testimony is single, and, so far, less to be trusted than were it confirmed by the experience of others ...
>
> 2ndly. If the dream comes to us second-hand, we must remember that the love of the marvellous, so inherent in man, renders the hearer as prone to believe, as the narrator to dress up a wonderful story. The relaters of the most real events are but too prone to modify and add to their stories, or to suppress circumstances, in order to make them fit some particular view ...
>
> 3rdly. We must reject all cases in which the verification of the dream may be explained on other principles than that of a real prophetic power. Of these principles, the first that occurs to our notice is casual or fortuitous fulfilment. The sense I here attach to fortuitous is this. The event in the dream, and its subsequent corresponding event, happen near together, but are dependent on different trains of causes ... The principle of mere coincidence, then, will explain many fulfilments of dreams as they are called; and it must not be presumed that it is not mere coincidence, because the dreams are of an unusually interesting character. When one thinks of the vast number of dreams which happen to every one in proportion to the number that come true, I only wonder the fulfilments are so rare. (pp. 74–76)

Psychical research developed out of the movements of mesmerism and spiritualism.[2] For example the Society for Psychical Research (SPR) was founded in London in 1882 by scientists, scholars and others, including members of the spiritualist community, to test the evidentiality of claims raised in mesmerism and spiritualism. The Society's initial studies of ESP—both in terms of cases as in experiments—as well as studies of apparitions, mediumship, and dissociation in general, were very important for the development of parapsychology (for overviews see Alvarado, 2002; and Gauld, 1968). Although much of this work emphasized the reality of the phenomena the SPR's work also contributed to the study of features, methodology, as well as a critical outlook in that SPR members routinely presented a variety of conventional possible explanation, among them coincidence, fraud, hallucination and sensory and motor automatisms.

For example, in a book on telepathic experiences the authors argued:

> The first objection to dreams, as evidence for transferred impressions of distant conditions or events, is this—that dreams being often somewhat dim and shapeless things, subsequent knowledge of the conditions or events may easily have the effect of giving body and definiteness to the recollection of a dream. When the actual facts are learnt, a faint amount of resemblance may often suggest a past dream, and set the mind on the track of trying accurately to recall it. This very act involves a search for details, for something tangible and distinct; and the real features and definite incidents which are now present in the mind, in close association with some general scene or fact which actually figured in the dream, will be apt to be unconsciously read back into the dream …
>
> But there is a more general and sweeping objection. Millions of people are dreaming every night; and in dreams, if anywhere, the range of possibilities seems infinite; can any positive conclusion be drawn from such a chaos of meaningless and fragmentary impressions? Must not we admit the force of the obvious a priori argument, that among the countless multitude of dreams, one here and there is likely to correspond in time with an actual occurrence resembling the one dreamed of; and that when a dream thus "comes true," unscientific minds are sure to note and store up the fact as something extraordinary, without taking the trouble to reflect whether such incidents occur oftener than pure chance would allow? …
>
> In the first place, it is to be noted that there has, so far, been a complete lack of the statistics which alone could form the basis for an answer to these questions. It has never been known with any certainty what proportion of people habitually dream, what proportion of dreams are remembered at all, in what proportion of these remembered dreams the memory is evanescent, and in what proportion it is profound and durable … . (Gurney, Myers & Podmore, 1886, Vol. 1, pp. 298–300)

Another psychical researcher and SPR leader, Eleanor Sidgwick (1889, p. 289), wrote about aspects of the recollection of dreams. In her view "our memory for dreams being less vivid and less trustworthy than our memory for waking experiences, details are more apt to be unconsciously read back into dreams, so that the dreams assume a definiteness and precision and fullness of detail which do not really belong to them. This source of weakness is excluded, if the dream has been told to some one else before the fulfilment arrives …" (p. 312). Similarly, psychical researcher and classical scholar Frederic W. H. Myers (1892a, 1892b) also focused on conventional explanations of some psychic dreams. In his view the subliminal mind could inspire dreams from knowledge the person may have acquired through sense perception but that was not consciously recalled.

With this as a background I will discuss observations and research with such cases (single cases and groups of cases) that were conducted from the nineteenth-century up to the late 1950s. I will only discuss studies of cases because of the scarcity of experimental attempts to induce ESP in dreams (for a few exceptions see Daim, 1954; Ermacora, 1895, 1898; and Weserman, 1820) in that period of history.

The scene changed from the 1960s because of the experimental program established at the Maimonides Medical Center (Ullman, Krippner, with Vaughn, 2001) and elsewhere (Sherwood & Roe, 2003).

Single Case Studies

Similar to other areas of the study of human experiences and behavior, work on the topic of psychic dreams began with attention paid to specific accounts. Not only do we find those reports in many of the above-mentioned books (e.g., Crowe, 1848; Owen, 1860), but also in a variety of other sources. For example the mesmeric English journal *Zoist* (e.g., Cottrell, 1853; Davey, 1850; Roffe, 1848), as well as the periodicals of the spiritualist movement (e.g., A Child's Life, 1869; Wallace, 1878; Warning Dream, 1849) published such cases. However, these accounts, and many others like them, were reported by the experiencers or narrated second-hand by someone else with no attempt to corroborate the testimony of the original experiencers. In some ways these early case reports were testimonies to the marvelous, called to bear witness on the power of the mind and the spirit and did not represent a scientific approach to the topic. In later years many single case reports appeared that improved the situation somewhat, but in general very little was done with the cases in these early times, particularly in the documentation of the psychology of the persons having the experiences. Such criticism may also be raised about some late 19th and early 20th century case reports (e.g., Bozzano, 1905; De Witt, 1897; Dream, 1907; Newbold, 1901; Paulhan, 1892; Warcollier, 1908).

In one such case report Swiss psychologist Théodore Flournoy (1905) documented what seemed to be an ESP dream and leaned towards a telepathic interpretation of it after considering such aspects as fraud, subconscious inference, suggestion, and coincidence. Interestingly Flournoy noticed that the case showed two elements at the same time. This was "on one hand remarkable exactitude of the recollections about the essential content of the oniric prediction, and on the other hand a considerable alteration of related circumstances, in terms of a simplification of the topic of the dream, and a dramatization of the case as a whole to make it more impressive ..." (p. 62). Here Flournoy intimated that even in veridical dreams the content could be distorted by the mind of the experiencer, or by the normal process of recollection.

The idea that the mind could distort the telepathic content of a dream was one prevalent in the case studies of psychoanalysis. Sigmund Freud discussed the topic in several papers, "Dreams and Telepathy" (Freud, 1922) being one example.[3] Here he clearly said he was not going to address the issue of the existence of telepathy. In his view: "Telepathy has no relation to the essential nature of dreams; it cannot deepen in any way what we already understand of them by analysis. On the other hand, psycho-analysis may do something to advance the study of telepathy, in so far as, by the help of its interpretations, many of the puzzling characteristics of telepathic phenomena may be rendered more intelligible to us ..." (Freud, 1922, p. 304). Telepathy, he speculated, may be related to the Oedipus complex. In a later article Freud argued that one may arrive at a provisional opinion about the existence of telepathy. He wrote: "There would ... be nothing contradictory in the material that had been telepathically communicated being modified and transformed in the dream like any other material" (Freud, 1925/1953a, p. 90).

Freud (1933/1953b) later specified some of these dynamics. In one case a man wrote to him about a dream he had about his wife having twins. The man had a daughter who was expecting a baby in December and the dream took place in November. The dream referred to his second wife, the stepmother of his daughter, with whom he did not have sexual relations and whom he did not consider fit to raise a child. He wrote to Freud because his daughter had twin babies before December, presumably the night of the dream. Freud analyzed the dream as follows:

> Here is a man, dissatisfied with his second wife, who would prefer to have a wife like his daughter by his first marriage. In the unconscious this "like" is naturally omitted. Now during the night he receives the telepathic communication that his daughter has had twins. The dream work seizes on this information, allows his unconscious wish that his daughter should replace his second wife to act upon it, and thus emerges the singular manifest dream in which the wish itself is veiled and the message distorted. We must admit that only dream interpretation has shown us that this is a telepathic dream; psychoanalysis has discovered a telepathic event which we should not otherwise have recognized as such. (p. 97)

Later psychoanalysts continued along the same line in their analyses of cases. For example Nandor Fodor (1942) stated in relation to telepathy that "the clue to a complete understanding of a dream sometimes lies in an event which we cannot know about through the patient's associations alone and that, in some instances, we may find the missing clue by analysing our own dreams in relationship to our patients" (p. 85). Similar discussions, as well as analyses of dynamics such as transference and counter-transference, were present in the works of other psychoanalysts who treated the topic of telepathic dreams (e.g., Ehrenwald, 1950; Eisenbud, 1948; Servadio, 1956; see also Devereux, 1953).

Incidental work also was reported with single dream cases, but most of this consisted only of the recording of the events so as to determine whether such dreams could yield to conventional explanations or not (e.g., Bozzano, 1905; Case, 1947; Grensted, 1950; Incidents, 1911). The interest in establishing veridicality—a central point in parapsychology—has guided most case research on the subject.

Studies of Groups of Cases

The most important of studies of groups of cases began with members of the SPR. An initial examination of cases was published in the first report of the Society's Literary Committee (Barrett, Massey, Moses, Podmore, Gurney, & Myers, 1882). But the deepest and most thorough review appeared in the first major work of the SPR, Gurney, Myers and Podmore's *Phantasms of the Living* (1886). *Phantasms* almost immediately became one of the central works of nineteenth-century psychical research. The authors of *Phantasms* undertook a systematic study of cases of spontaneous telepathy. In the book they developed the idea that a telepathic message from a distant agent could be expressed by another person at a distance, usually a spouse or a family member of the agent, manifesting through various senses such as vision and hearing, as well as in dreams, and through intuitions, and somatosensory experiences. The authors of *Phantasms* were particularly interested, from their initial examination of published cases and their own preliminary collection (Barrett et al., 1882), in cases that coincided with the death of someone at a distance, or with some crisis such as illness and accident. Seven hundred and one cases were collected gleaned from a larger collection, many of which were obtained through public appeals. Each case was checked for evidentiality, with specific attention paid to the manner in which the veridical element was corroborated. The book is arguably the best nineteenth-century discussion of the evidential problems posed by telepathy cases on record. In addition to painstaking attempts to obtain corroboration—all of which was presented together with each case—the researchers discussed various forms of distortion of testimony, as well as the problem of chance.

One of the questions the authors had circulated in the press was: "Since January 1st 1874, have you ever had a dream of the death of some person known to you, which dream you marked as an exceptionally vivid one, and of which the distressing impression lasted for as long as an hour after you rose in the morning?" (Gurney, Myers & Podmore, 1886, Vol. 1, p. 304). The question was answered by 5360 individuals of which 173 gave a positive reply. However, after corrections for repeated dreams, it was concluded that 202 was a more representative number:

> With this substitution, 1/26 of the whole number of persons asked may be taken to have given an affirmative answer. Now, the persons asked were a quite promiscuous body, and a body large enough to be safely regarded as a fair average sample of the population; just as a similar number of persons, taken at random, would be accepted as a fair sample for purposes of statistics on short sight, or colour-blindness. We may conclude, then, that the number of persons who can recall having had—during the twelve years 1874–1885, and without special assignable cause—the experience named in the question, amount to about 1 in 26 of the population of this country. (Vol. 1 pp. 304–305)

While we cannot assume representativeness in a sample collected from the press and in other ways,[4] this was an important pioneering effort to address the issue of prevalence empirically. Before this work no one had tried to do anything about the problem. Previous writers only mentioned that chance could account for what was perceived as meaningful coincidences.

Other questions asked for experiences while the person was awake. The book included 701 telepathy cases, out of which 163 (23%) were dreams. There were 149 actual dream cases included in the book, 79 (53%) of which were about someone's death. The authors of *Phantasms* engaged in statistical speculations and arrived at the conclusion that reports of dreams about death were "larger than doctrine of chances would have allowed us to expect" (Vol. 1, p. 307). Once again, and regardless of the validity of such analyses, the authors of the study pioneered an empirical approach to the subject that had not been seen in this scale in the prior literature on the topic.

Such empirism is further seen in the fact that the authors pointed out they had 107 first-hand testimony dream cases included in their analysis:

> 72 are alleged to have been described, 11 more to have been recorded in writing (in one instance by a relative of the dreamer's), and 9 more to have been in some marked way acted on, before the corresponding event was known; and in 46 of the 72 cases where the dream was at once described, we have also the testimony of the person to whom it was described. In 18 other cases, we have the testimony of the person to whom the dream was described before the corresponding event was known, but not the dreamer's own account. (Vol. 1, p. 309)

The *Phantasms* authors speculated that the telepathic element (of which there was no actual explanation) combined with the percipient's dream imagery to form a veridical dream that manifested in the typical way of dreams. That is, sometimes using fantastic and symbolic imagery.

Some dream cases were also collected in the United States on behalf of the American Society for Psychical Research (Royce, 1889), but they were not analyzed in detail. Another SPR worker, Eleanor Sidgwick (1889), discussed dreams in a paper she wrote in which she evaluated the evidence for premonitions, and found it to be inconclusive. She stated that about two-thirds of the premonitions examined took place during dreams. Sidgwick discussed the content of these dreams, including those that referred to death, accidents, winning races, and trivial incidents. She noticed both the occurrence of symbolic dreams and their lesser evidential value. Sidgwick argued:

> Two kinds of dreams may be called symbolic: firstly, those where the dream is unlike the real fact but yet has in it an underlying idea which suggests the fact … Such dreams may vary to any extent in the degree of their correspondence with the supposed fulfilment, and in some cases might perhaps be more properly called grotesque or distorted dreams rather than symbolic ones. In the other kind of symbolic dreams the symbol has no resemblance to the fact supposed to be indicated. The interpretation is, so to speak, purely conventional … There is no difficulty in supposing that the mind might clothe a premonitory (or telepathic) idea in a symbolic form once the "convention" is started, and this might be done either by tradition, or by the first coincidence of the dream and event in the dreamer's experience, the same dream afterwards recurring in apparent connection with similar events. (p. 351)

Sancte de Sactis, an important Italian psychologist, wrote about the topic in his book *I Sogni* (1899). He referred to his "numerous inquiries on the dreams of ordinary and abnormal people" (p. 370) in which he looked for those dreams but found that "a large part of these tales are so vague and poorly documented that they do not deserve the attention of the psychologist" (p. 370). Later in the book he stated: "I have to confess that from a total of at least 55 dreams designated as extraordinary or marvellous by the dreamer I did not find a single one that … resists scientific critique" (p. 384). Like other commentators in the psychological literature, de Sanctis was skeptical of the phenomena and offered the usual conventional explanations.

Another nineteenth-century skeptic was American psychologist Mary Whiton Calkins, who discussed the topic briefly in her "Statistics of Dreams" (1893). She analyzed 375 dreams recorded by two persons finding five cases of dreams about the future. Following on Calkins, others found one participant who had reported several veridical dreams (Weed, Hallam, & Phinney, 1895). Most of the dreams referred to trivial topics but a few were about "more significant events, as when a dream-letter announcing illness is followed by an actual letter of the same sort, and as when a death which later really occurs is announced in a dream" (p. 411).

Many cases were presented and discussed in terms of both evidentiality and specific features (e.g., Rogers, 1916; Vesme, 1901). French astronomer and psychical researcher Camille Flammarion (1900) compiled numerous ESP cases—including dreams, intuitions and visions—after having appealed for such cases in the Annales *Politiques et Litteraires*. Many of the dreams he collected centered on dying persons. Although Flammarion did not consider dreams to be the best evidence for telepathy, he stated that "a large number of these dreams ought to be accepted as positive evidence of a relation of cause and effect between the mind of the dying person and that of the percipient. The exactitude of detail is clearly established" (p. 364).

Ernesto Bozzano (1907) analyzed the symbolic character of different types of psychic phenomena, noting that symbols took place during dreams. In his view if a symbol of a premonitory dream took place several times "it gradually gains in distinctness, so that sometimes it loses its symbolic character and takes a more directly representative form" (p. 351). In a later study of published precognitive experiences Bozzano (1913, pp. 7–8) remarked that precognitive dreams were more labile than other dreams. They were more vivid than ordinary dreams but, according to Bozzano, were also easier to forget even though the dream had been seen as more vivid than ordinary dreams more likely to have been discussed.

An interesting investigation was that of psychology Professor Ágúst Bjarnason's (1915) who studied seemingly psychic dreams produced by Icelandic dreamer Jóhannes Jónson, known locally as "Dreaming Joe." While asleep this person was reported to tell "people the whereabouts of lost things … besides informing them of various things that they are desirous of knowing" (pp. 54–55).

Jónson concentrated his thoughts before he went to sleep to get the information requested of him. Bjarnason collected testimonies that he felt supported the claims for veridical dreams. His attempts to elicit dreams to test Jónson were not successful (for comments on Bjarnason's research, see Verrall, 1915).

Over the years many others compiled veridical dream cases with little attempt to analyze them beyond illustrating what the authors believed were their veridical elements (Hill, 1918, Chapter 2; Prince, 1918, 1919, 1922). French psychical researcher Réne Warcollier discussed in his book *La Télépathie* (1921, Chapter 5, Part C) many cases of such dreams, some of which were his own (see Warcollier, 1908). He noted that some cases were symbolic and that many announced various things such as visits, letters and death. Other writers recorded their own dreams (e.g., Shipley, 1908). The best known example was J. W. Dunne's (1927) compilation of many of his own precognitive dreams, which inspired him to develop theoretical ideas about time. This line of research—the self-recording of dreams—was followed by Kooy (1934) in Holland, and by others in more recent times, the content of which lie beyond the scope of this paper (de Pablos, 1998; Sondow, 1988).

In a later analysis of questionnaire data originally collected by Royce (1889), Prince (1921) stated that there were 7969 replies to a question about dreams about someone's death which was exceptionally vivid and which produced distress at least for an hour after waking up. Four hundred forty-nine replies to the initial solicitation claimed such dreams.

In England Theodore Besterman (1933) analyzed the dreams of persons that agreed to participate in an investigation of precognitive dreams. He wrote:

> Forty-three subjects sent in 430 records of dreams, an average of ten each … These forty-three subjects, then, put forward forty-five events in their dreams as being possibly precognitive, or an average of just over one apiece. Of these forty-five cases I regard eighteen as having a prima facie case, of which two have a good case. I do not regard any of these eighteen cases as capable of being regarded as conclusive instances of precognition. (p. 204)

Some case collection studies were published by various authors in later years (Hart & Hart, 1933; Levi Bianchini, 1946, 1950; Marulli, 1953). In one of them, Hart and Hart (1933) presented 15 examples of reciprocal dreams, in which there was a "reciprocal perception of each other by two or more percipients, in a common dream environment" (p. 234). Saltmarsh (1934) studied different forms of precognition experiences. His collection had 94 dreams and the rest were experiences during mediumistic communications (41), hallucinations (23) impressions (17), crystal gazing (4) and borderland states (4). He saw dreams as a form of dissociation in which subliminal messages could come to conscious attention easily.

A particularly interesting study was a collection of 1300 dreams analyzed for details related to the kidnapping of the 20-month-old son of aviator Charles Lindbergh, an event that took place in 1932 in the United States and attracted an immense amount of publicity. Murray and Wheeler (1937) solicited dream accounts in the press and analyzed the cases they received for evidence of specific details that became known after the kidnapping. The authors reported that about 5% of the dreams mentioned the baby was dead "and only seven dreams … suggested the actual location of the body, its nakedness and the manner of its burial" (p. 310). The authors, who were aware that their methodology did not control for elaboration of information after the details of the kidnapping were known, were disappointed with the low number of dreams providing veridical details. They concluded: "The findings do not support the contention that distant events and dreams are causally related" (p. 313).

In the United States Louisa E. Rhine discussed dream cases as part of her analyses of ESP experiences, most of which had been sent to J. B. Rhine or to the Parapsychology Laboratory then in existence at Duke University. She noticed that experiencers showed less conviction in the experience if they took place in dreams, as compared to waking experiences (Rhine, 1951). She also classified cases as realistic and unrealistic (symbolic) dreams (Rhine, 1953) and noticed that dreams were more likely to convey precognitive information than such waking experiences as intuitions and hallucinations and that of the dreams submitted this was especially true of realistic dreams (Rhine, 1954). Another observation was that "in both types of dreams, realistic and unrealistic, one would look in vain for an internal distinction, between those of psi and those of non-psi nature. Thus it seems that psi converts itself into a conscious experience by utilizing methods already well known in psychology and in common experience" (Rhine, 1953, p. 109).

Two researchers introduced a methodological innovation, the recording of the precognitive dreams of two ladies before the dreams were fulfilled, finding some encouraging results (Dommeyer, 1955; Marabini, 1956). Both researchers also documented symbolic aspects in the dreams. Marabini studied an Italian 34-year-old midwife. In his work he deviated from previous case studies in that he paid more attention to the personal, medical and psychological history of this person. According to Marabini psychological tests did not reveal any intellectual or emotional abnormality. He was able to determine that this lady lived in a family environment open to the idea of psychic experiences: "As a child she loved sitting on the knees of the father when he told her of his past life. The most beautiful stories were always those in which there was talk of strange things that happened to the father; for example the dreams that he had and that 'came true', or the stories of 'spirits' in which the father believed firmly and comfortably" (p. iv).

Concluding Remarks

The material discussed here presents some clear trends about empirical interest in ESP in dreams prior to 1960. As we have seen there has been a long tradition of criticism surrounding the evidence for the existence of psychic dreams. The writings of Delage (1891), Macnish (1834), Maury (1861), Simon (1888), and Symmonds (1851) provide examples of this. The critical tradition has informed the evolution of the analysis of such cases. This was particularly the case in the discussions of evidentiality in Gurney Myers and Podmore's *Phantasms of the Living* (1886), in which the issue was examined by the presentation of an unprecedented detail along with the discussion of "best cases" in the evidential sense. All cases that were included were first hand, while most of the previous literature included many summaries of cases that were not narrated by the experiencers. All corroborating testimony was included. This style of case reporting both improved the evidence for dream ESP considerably as well as inspired later work, such as the studies conducted by psychiatrist Ian Stevenson (1961, 1992), among others (e.g., Beloff, 1973).

An important lesson of the history of the investigation of seemingly psychic dreams is that some of the best criticisms, and most of the attempts to deal with them in the empirical analysis of cases, came from psychical researchers and not from "outside" skeptics. Regardless of the common sense or validity of the points raised by "outside" critics, very few of them conducted research themselves.

Although there were a few attempts to induce ESP dreams in the period of history I have covered, it is clear that before the Maimonides studies there was no experimental research tradition on the subject as such. But there were many observations and analyses of cases, some of them focusing on single cases and others on case collections. Most of these works were simple reports of cases designed to present evidence for ESP. *Phantasms of the Living* differed from that tradition because while the study documented the existence of evidence for coincidental dreams it also included dream features. Unfortunately little work was conducted in which dream ESP was studied in terms of interactions with other variables, nor there many attempts to understand more about the experiencers, with the exception of the work of Flournoy (1905) and Marabini (1956). One other exception was the attempt to explore dream and non-dream ESP in relation to conviction about the experience (Rhine, 1951).

The period I have covered was clearly one of qualitative analyses. The only early attempt to use quantification appeared in *Phantasms of the Living*, in which analyses of the issue of chance were presented. In addition some presented the prevalence of certain characteristics as percentages (e.g., Rhine, 1953; Saltmarsh, 1934). This type of description was then in evidence in more general studies of seemingly ESP experiences.

Later researchers, whose work was published from the 1960s forward continued the type of work discussed here. Although beyond the scope of this paper, I will mention that this later work included reports of single dream cases (e.g., Beloff, 1973; Bender, 1966; Hearne,1982; Stevenson, 1961; Tart, 1964) as well as analyses of groups of cases (e.g., Barker, 1967; Rhine, 1962; Schredl, Gotz & Ehrhardt-Knudsen, 2010; Schreiver, 1987; Stevenson, 1992). Furthermore, a question about ESP dreams has been included in some recent surveys (e.g., Alvarado & Zingrone, 2007–2008; Kohr, 1980; Palmer, 1979; Prasad & Stevenson, 1968).

These, and later developments, have brought experimental approaches and systematic study of psychological variables to dream ESP research. The shift was to be expected as parapsychology evolved methodologically and followed psychology proper as it develop a new interest in the study of consciousness.

Notes

1 Other examples from antiquity include Apuleius (1853, p. 291), Iamblichos (1911, p. 111) and Xenophon (1847, p. 328). The idea continued into later periods (e.g., Macario, 1857, p. 234) and has been modified in more recent times, particularly in removing the concept of the soul from the discussion, as can be seen in ideas of noise reduction (e.g., Honorton, 1977).

2 For discussions of the development of psychical research in different countries see Biondi (1988), Monroe (2008), Moore (1977), Oppenheim (1985), and Wolffram (2009).

3 I will not discuss here all of Freud's writings about telepathy and dreams. A short overview of the topic is Smith's (2002). Freud's writings on the issue have been reprinted by Devereux (1953, Part 2). Wilhelm Stekel discussed the topic before Freud in his book *Der telepathische Traum* (1920), in which he proposed that such emotions as love and jealousy predisposed people (or his patients) to telepathy.

4 In the book it was not specified who was targeted with the question. In another publication members of the SPR were mentioned as possible participants in the survey and hopes were expressed that the question may be presented to others who "without any selection of those persons only who have unusual facts to relate" (Circular, 1883, p. 303).

References

Alvarado, C. S. (1998). ESP and altered states of consciousness: An overview of conceptual and research trends. *Journal of Parapsychology, 62*, 27–63.

Alvarado, C. S. (2002). Dissociation in Britain during the late nineteenth century: The Society for Psychical Research, 1882–1900. *Journal of Trauma and Dissociation, 3*, 9–33.
Alvarado, C. S., & Zingrone, N. L. (2007–2008). Interrelationships of psychic experiences, dream recall and lucid dreams in a survey with Spanish participants. *Imagination, Cognition and Personality, 27*, 63–69.
Apuleius. (1853). *The works of Apuleius*. H. G. Bohn.
Aristotle. (1902). *Aristotle's psychology* (W. A. Hammond, trans.). Swan Sonnenschein.
Aubrey, J. (1721). *Miscellanies, upon the following subjects* (2nd ed.). A. Bettesworth and J. Battley.
Barker, J. C. (1967). Premonitions of the Aberfan disaster. *Journal of the Society for Psychical Research, 44*, 169–181.
Barrett, W. F., Massey, C. C., Moses, W. S., Podmore, F., Gurney, E., & Myers, F. W. H. (1882). Report of the Literary Committee. *Proceedings of the Society for Psychical Research, 1*, 116–155.
Beloff, J. (1973). A note on an ostensibly precognitive dream. *Journal of the Society for Psychical Research, 47*, 217–221.
Bender, H. (1966). The Gotenhafen case of correspondence between dreams and future events: A study of motivation. *International Journal of Neuropsychiatry, 2*, 398–407.
Besterman, T. (1933). Report of inquiry into precognitive dreams. *Proceedings of the Society for Psychical Research, 41*, 186–204.
Biondi, M. (1988). *Tavoli e medium: Storia dello spiritismo in Italia.* Gremese.
Bjarnason, A. (1915). An Icelandic seer (edited by H. de G. Verrall). *Journal of the Society for Psychical Research, 17*, 53–76.
Bouché-Leclercq, A. (1879). *Histoire de la divination dans l'antiquite* (Vol. 1). Ernest Leroux.
Bozzano, R. (1905). A veridical dream: Telepathy or telaesthesia? *Annals of Psychical Science, 2*, 383–384.
Bozzano, E. (1907). Symbolism and metapsychical phenomena. *Annals of Psychical Science, 6*, 235–259, 335–366.
Bozzano, E. (1913). Des phénomènes prémonitoires. *Annales des Sciences Psychiques.*
Brierre de Boismont, A. (1855). *History of dreams, visions, apparitions, ecstasy, magnetism, and somnambulism* (1st American ed. from 2nd French ed.). Lindsay and Blakiston.
Calkins, M. W. (1893). Statistics of dreams. *American Journal of Psychology, 5*, 311–343.
Cardeña, E., & Alvarado, C. S. (2011). Altered consciousness from the age of Enlightenment through mid-20th century. In E. Cardeña & M. Winkelman (Eds.), *Altering consciousness: Multidisciplinary perspectives: Vol. 1: History, culture and the humanities* (pp. 89–112). Praeger.
Case: Precognitive dream. (1947). *Journal of the Society for Psychical Research, 34*, 21–22.
Child, I. L. (1985). Psychology and anomalous observations: The question of ESP in dreams. *American Psychologist, 40*, 1219–1230.
A child's life saved by a dream. (1869). *Spiritual Magazine*, 4(n. s.), 134.
Cicero, M. T. (1853). *The treatises of Cicero* (C. D. Yonge, trans.). Henry Murray.
Circular No. 2 (Third edition). On dreaming and allied states. (1883). *Proceedings of the Society for Psychical Research, 1*, 303–305.
Cottrell, C. H. (1853). A very recent and remarkable clairvoyant dream. *Zoist, 11*, 79–80.
Crowe, C. (1848). *The night-side of nature; or, ghosts and ghost seers* (2 Vols.). T. C. Newby.
Daim, W. (1953). Studies in dream telepathy. *Tomorrow, 2*, 35–48.
Davey, Dr. (1850). Instance of clairvoyance during sleep. *Zoist, 8*, 328–329.
Delage, Y. (1891). Essai sur la théorie du rêve. *Revue Scientifique, 48*, 40–48.
de Pablos, F. (1998). Spontaneous precognition during dreams: Analysis of a one-year naturalistic study. *Journal of the Society for Psychical Research, 62*, 423–433.
de Sanctis, S. (1899). *I sogni: Studi psicologici e clinici di un alienista.* Fratelli Bocca.
Devereux, G. (Ed.). (1953). *Psychoanalysis and the occult.* International University Press.
De Witt, A. (1897). Sogno premonitorio. *Archivio di Psichiatria, Scienze Penali ed Antropologie Criminale per Servire allo Studio dell'Uomo Alienato e Delinquente, 18*, 268–269.
Dommeyer, F. C. (1955). Some ostensibly precognitive dreams. *Journal of the American Society for Psychical Research, 40*, 109–117.
Dream.—Coincidental. (1907). *Journal of the American Society for Psychical Research,* 1, 361–363.
Dunne, J. W. (1927). *An experiment with time.* A. & C. Black.

du Prel, C. (1907). *La magie: Science naturelle: I: La physique magique*. H. Vaillant-Carmanne. (Original work published, 1899)
Egidi, F. (1949). Sogni nell'antichità classica. *Luce e Ombra, 49*, 3-25, 67-82.
Ehrenwald, J. (1950). Presumptively telepathic incidents during analysis. *Psychiatric Quarterly, 24*, 726–743.
Eisenbud, J. (1948). Analysis of presumptively telepathic dream. *Psychiatric Quarterly, 22*, 103–135.
Ermacora, G. B. (1895). Telepathic dreams experimentally induced. *Proceedings of the Society for Psychical Research, 11*, 235–308.
Ermacora, G. B. (1898). *La telepatia*. L. Crescini.
Flammarion, C. (1900). *L'inconnu: The unknown*. Harper & Brothers.
Flournoy, T. (1905). Note sur un sogne prophétique réalisé. *Archives de Psychologie, 4*, 58–72.
Fodor, N. (1942). Telepathic dreams. *American Imago, 3*, 61–85.
Freud, S. (1922). Dreams and telepathy. *International Journal of Psycho-Analysis, 3*, 283–305.
Freud, S. (1953a). The occult significance of dreams. In G. Devereux (Ed.), *Psychoanalysis and the occult* (pp. 87–90). International University Press. (Original work published 1925)
Freud, S. (1953b). Dreams and the occult. In G. Devereux (Ed.), P*sychoanalysis and the occult* (pp. 91–109). International University Press. (Original work published 1925)
Gauld, A. (1968). *The founders of psychical research*. Routledge & Kegan Paul.
Gregory, W. (1851). *Letters to a candid inquirer, on animal magnetism*. Blanchard and Lea.
Grensted, L. W. (1950). A paranormal dream? *Journal of the Society for Psychical Research, 35*, 339–341.
Gurney, E., Myers, F. W. H., & Podmore, F. (1886). *Phantasms of the living* (2 vols.). Trübner.
Halliday, W. R. (1913). *Greek divination: A study of its methods and principles*. Macmillan.
Hart, H., & Hart, E. B. (1933).Visions and apparitions collectively and reciprocally perceived. *Proceedings of the Society for Psychical Research, 41*, 205–249.
Hearne, K. M. T. (1982). An ostensible precognition of the accidental sinking of H. M. submarine Artemis in 1971. *Journal of the Society for Psychical Research, 51*, 283–287.
Hill, J. A. (1918). *Man is a spirit: A collection of spontaneous cases of dream, vision and ecstasy*. George H. Doran.
Holowchak, M. A. (2002). *Ancient science and dreams: Oneirology in Greco-Roman antiquity*. University Press of America.
Honorton, C. (1977). Psi and internal attention states. In B. B. Wolman (Ed.), Handbook *of Parapsychology* (pp. 435–472). Van Nostrand Reinhold.
Iamblichos (1911). *Theurgia or the Egyptian mysteries* (A. Wilder, trans.). Metaphysical Publishing.
Incidents: A symbolic and apparently premonitory dream. (1911). *Journal of the American Society for Psychical Research, 5*, 369–370.
Inglis, B. (1989). *Trance: A natural history of altered states of mind.* Grafton.
James, T. (1995). *Dream, creativity, and madness in nineteenth-century France*. Oxford University Press.
Jung-Stilling, J. H. (1851). *Theory of pneumatology; in reply to the question, What ought to be believed or disbelieved concerning presentiments, visions, and apparitions, according to nature, reason and scripture* (1st American ed). J. S. Redfield. (Original work published, 1808)
Kelly, E. F., & Locke, R. G. (2009). *Altered states of consciousness and psi: An historical survey and research prospectus* (Parapsychological Monographs No. 18) (2nd ed.). Parapsychology Foundation.
Kohr, R. L. (1980). A survey of PSI experiences among members of a special population. *Journal of the American Society for Psychical Research, 74*, 395–411.
Kooy, J. M. J. (1934). Introspectief onderzoek naar het Dunne-effect. *Tijdschrift voor Parapsychologie, 6*, 144–169.
Krippner, S. (1970). Electrophysiological studies of ESP in dreams: Sex differences in seventy-four telepathy sessions. *Journal of the American Society for Psychical Research, 64*, 277–285.
Krippner, S. (1991). An experimental approach to the anomalous dream. In J. Gackenbach & A. A. Sheikh (Eds.), *Dream images: A call to mental arms* (pp. 31–54). Baywood Publishing.
Krippner, S. (2007). Anomalous experiences and dreams. In D. Barrett & P. McNamara (Eds.), *The new science of dreaming* (Vol. 2, pp. 285–306). Praeger.
Krippner, S., Ullman, M., & Honorton, C. (1971). A precognitive dream study with a single subject. *Journal of the American Society for Psychical Research, 65*,192–203.
Levi Bianchini, M. (1946). Sogno metafisico: Psicobiofi sica e mesencefalo. *Metapsichica, 1*(1), 28–45.

Levi Bianchini, M. (1950). Ulteriori contributi al problema dei sogni metapsichici e della psicobiofisica. *Metapsichica, 5*(4), 23–35.

Luke, D. (2011). Anomalous phenomena, psi, and altered consciousness. In E. Cardeña & M. Winkelman (Eds.), *Altering consciousness: Multidisciplinary perspectives: Vol. 2: Biological and psychological perspectives* (pp. 355–374). Praeger.

Macario, M. (1857). *Du sommeil: Des rêves et du somnambulisme dans l'état de santé et de maladie.* Périsse Frérès.

Macnish, R. (1834). *The philosophy of sleep* (1st American ed.). D. Appleton.

Marabini, E. (1956). Sogno Paragnosico (Contributo casistico). *Minerva Medica, 47* (Supplement), II–XII.

Marulli, G. (1953). Il sogno telepatico di Giuseppina Perlasco: Contributo alla documentazione dei fenomeni metapsichici. *Rivista di Psicopatologia, Neuropsichiatria e Psicoanalisi, 21*, 419–422.

Maury, L. F. A. (1860). *La magie et l'astrologie dans l'antiquité et au Moyen Âge: ou étude sur les superstitions païnnes qui se sont pérpetuées jusqu'à nos jours.* Didier.

Maury, L. F. A. (1861). *Le sommeil et les rêves: Études psychologiques sur ces phénomènes et les divers états qui s'y rattachent.* Didier.

Mayo, H. (1851). *On the truths contained in popular superstitions with an account of mesmerism* (3rd ed.). William Blackwood and Sons.

Miller, P. C. (1994). *Dreams in late antiquity: Studies in the imagination of a culture.* Princeton University Press.

Monroe, J. W. (2008). *Laboratories of faith: Mesmerism, spiritism, and occultism in modern France.* Cornell University Press.

Moore, R. L. (1977). *In search of white crows: Spiritualism, parapsychology, and American culture.* Oxford University Press.

Murray, H. A., & Wheeler, D. R. (1937). A note on the possible clairvoyance of dreams. *Journal of Psychology, 3*, 309–313.

Myers, F. W. H. (1892a). The subliminal consciousness: Chapter IV: Hypermnesic dreams. *Proceedings of the Society for Psychical Research, 8*, 362–404.

Myers, F. W. H. (1892b). The subliminal consciousness: Chapter V: Sensory automatism and induced hallucinations. *Proceedings of the Society for Psychical Research, 8*, 436–535.

Newbold, W. R. (1901). Cases: P. 266. Dream. *Journal of the Society for Psychical Research, 10*, 22–24.

Oppenheim, J. (1985). *The other world: Spiritualism and psychical research in England, 1850–1914.* Cambridge University Press.

Owen, R. D. (1860). *Footfalls on the boundary of another world.* Lippincott.

Palmer, J. (1979). A community mail survey of psychic experiences. *Journal of the American Society for Psychical Research, 73*, 221–251.

Parker, A. (1975). *States of mind: ESP and states of consciousness.* Taplinger.

Paulhan, F. (1892). Un cas de télépathie ou de lucidité dans le rêve. *Annales des Sciences Psychiques, 2*, 2–4.

Pick, D., & Roper, L. (Eds.). (2004). *Dreams and history: The interpretation of dreams from ancient Greece to modern psychoanalysis.* Brunner-Routledge.

Prasad, J, & Stevenson, I. (1968). A survey of spontaneous psychical experiences in school children of Uttar Pradesh, India. *International Journal of Parapsychology, 10*, 241–261.

Prince, W. F. (1918). Four dreams. *Journal of the American Society for Psychical Research, 12*, 395–403.

Prince, W. F. (1919). Some coincidental dreams. *Journal of the American Society for Psychical Research, 13*, 61–93, 172–182.

Prince, W. F. (1921). Analysis of the results of an old questionnaire. *Journal of the American Society for Psychical Research, 15*, 169–184.

Prince, W. F. (1922). Dreams seeming, or interpreted, to indicate death. *Journal of the American Society for Psychical Research, 16*, 164–189.

Rhine, L. E. (1951). Conviction and associated conditions in spontaneous cases. *Journal of Parapsychology, 15*, 164–191.

Rhine, L. E. (1953). Subjective forms of spontaneous psi experiences. *Journal of Parapsychology, 17*, 77–114.

Rhine, L. E. (1954). Frequency and types of experience in spontaneous precognition. *Journal of Parapsychology, 18*, 93–123.

Rhine, L. E. (1962). Psychological processes in ESP experiences: Part II. Dreams. *Journal of Parapsychology, 26*, 172–199.
Roffe, A. (1848). Clairvoyance in a dream. *Zoist, 6*, 54–56.
Rogers, L. W. (1916). *Dreams and premonitions*. Theosophical Book Concern.
Royce, J. (1889). Report of the Committee on Phantasms and Presentiments. *Proceedings of the American Society for Psychical Research, 1,* 350–528.
Saltmarsh, H. F. (1934). Report on cases of apparent precognition. *Proceedings of the Society for Psychical Research, 42*, 49–103.
Schredl, M., Gotz, S., & Ehrhardt-Knudsen, S. (2010). Precognitive dreams: A pilot diary study. *Journal of the Society for Psychical Research, 74,* 168–175.
Schriever, F. (1987). A 30-year "experiment with time:" Evaluation of an individual case study of precognitive dreams. *European Journal of Parapsychology, 7*, 49–72.
Servadio, E. (1956). A presumptively telepathic-precognitive dream during analysis. *International Journal of Psycho-Analysis, 36*, 27–30.
Shapin, B., & Coly, L. (1978). (Eds.). *Psi and altered states of awareness*. Parapsychology Foundation.
Sherwood, S. J., & Roe, C. A. (2003). A review of dream ESP studies conducted since the Maimonides dream ESP programme. *Journal of Consciousness Studies, 10*, 85–109.
Shipley, M.F. (1908). A record of dreams and other coincidental experiences (comments by J. H. Hyslop). *Proceedings of the American Society for Psychical Research, 2,* 454–535.
Sidgwick, E. (1889). On the evidence for premonitions. *Proceedings of the Society for Psychical Research, 5*, 288–354.
Sluhovsky, M. (2011). Spirit possession and other alterations of consciousness in the Christian Western tradition. In E. Cardeña & M. Winkelman (Eds.), *Altering consciousness: Multidisciplinary perspectives: Vol. 1: History, culture and the humanities* (pp. 73–88). Praeger.
Simon, P. M. (1888). *Le monde des reves* (2nd ed.). J. -B. Baillière et Fils.
Smith, D. L. (2002). *Occult, and Freud.* In E. Erwin (Ed.), *The Freud encyclopedia: Theory, therapy, and culture* (pp. 395–397). Routledge.
Sondow, N. (1988). The decline of precognized events with the passage of time: Evidence from spontaneous dreams. *Journal of the American Society for Psychical Research, 82*, 33–51.
Stekel, W. (1920). *Der Telepathische Traum.* Johannes Baum.
Stevenson, I. (1961). An example illustrating the criteria and characteristics of precognitive dreams. *Journal of the American Society for Psychical Research, 55*, 98–103.
Stevenson, I. (1992). A series of possibly paranormal recurrent dreams. *Journal of Scientific Exploration, 6,* 281–289.
Symmonds, J. A. (1851). *Sleep and dreams*. John Murray.
Tart, C. T. (1964). A possible "psychic" dream. *Journal of the Society for Psychical Research, 42*, 283–99.
Tavera, M. (2000). Le rêve naturel: Physiologie de l'onirisme au XV^{IIIe} siecle. *Gesnerus, 57*, 5–26.
Taves, A. (1999). *Fits, trances, & visions: Experiencing religion and explaining experience from Wesley to James.* Princeton University Press
Ullman, M., & Krippner, S. (1969). A laboratory approach to the nocturnal dimension of paranormal experience: Report of a confirmatory study using the REM monitoring technique. *Biological Psychiatry, 2,* 259–270.
Ullman, M., & Krippner, S. (1970). *Dream studies and telepathy* (Parapsychological Monographs No. 12). Parapsychological Foundation.
Ullman, M., Krippner, S., & Feldstein, S. (1966). Experimentally induced telepathic dreams: Two studies using EEG-REM monitoring. *International Journal of Neuropsychiatry, 2*, 420–437.
Ullman, M., Krippner, S., & Vaughn, A. (2001). *Dream telepathy: Scientific experiments in nocturnal extrasensory perception* (3rd ed.). Hampton Roads.
Ustinova, Y. (2011). Consciousness alteration practices in the West from prehistory to late antiquity. In E. Cardeña & M. Winkelman (Eds.), *Altering consciousness: Multidisciplinary perspectives: Vol. 1: History, culture and the humanities* (pp. 45–72). Praeger.
Van de Castle, R.L. (1977). Sleep and dreams. In B. B. Wolman (Ed.), *Handbook of parapsychology* (pp. 473–489). Van Nostrand Reinhold.

Van de Kemp, H. (1981). The dream periodical literature: 1860–1910. *Journal of the History of the Behavioral Sciences, 17*, 88–113.

Verrall, H. de G. (1915). An Icelandic seer: Further comments on professor Bjarnason's report. *Journal of the Society for Psychical Research, 17*, 78–82.

Vesme, C. (1901). A propos de rêves prémonitoires et de paramnésie. *Revue des Etudes Psychiques, 1*, 225–242, 331–350, 361–371.

Wallace, W. (1878, September 13). A remarkable dream or vision. *Medium and Daybreak*, p. 583.

Warcollier, R. (1908). Rêve symbolique prémonitoire. *Annales des Sciences Psychiques, 18*, 81–83.

Warcollier, R. (1921). *La télépathie: Recherches expérimentales*. Félix Alcan.

Warning dream, and trance. (1849). *Univercoleum and Spiritual Philosopher, 4*, 23.

Weed, S. C., Hallam, F. M., with the assistance of Phinney, E. D. (1895). Minor studies from the psychological laboratory of Wellesley College: III. A study of the dream consciousness. *American Journal of Psychology, 7*, 405–411.

Wesermann, H. M. (1820). Versuche willkuhrlicher Traumbildung. *Archives für den Thierischen Magnetismus, 6*, 135–142.

Wolffram, H. (2009). *The stepchildren of science: Psychical research and parapsychology in Germany, c. 1870–1939*. Rodopi.

Xenophon. (1847). *The anabiosis* (vol. 2). Harper & Brothers.

Modern Animal Magnetism: The Work of Alexandre Barety, Émile Boirac, and Julian Ochorowicz*

Carlos S. Alvarado†

Historical discussions of animal magnetism as a concept of force generally emphasize publications appearing before the mid-nineteenth century. This article focuses on selected aspects of a later neo-magnetism that flourished between the late nineteenth and the first two decades of the twentieth century, namely the work of Alexandre Barety, Émile Boirac, and Julian Ochorowicz. They used the concept of magnetism to explain the induction of trance and anesthesia, as well as mental suggestion. Outside of the neo-magnetic movement, contemporary comments of the work of these men were generally negative. Regardless of this, and of current skepticism on the subject, this work should be recognized as part of the context in which the field of hypnosis developed.

General histories of the investigations and ideas of hypnotic phenomena always mention the concept of animal magnetism as a factor in the development of hypnosis (e.g., Gauld, 1992; Pintar and Lynn, 2008). Because the concept was important, we need to be aware that certain aspects of its history are sometimes neglected. In this article, I will focus on selected examples of late nineteenth- and early twentieth-century magnetism.

Animal Magnetism

Animal magnetism was considered by many to be a force that could be used to induce trance, and other phenomena such as healing, clairvoyance, and the transference of thoughts and sensations from one person to another (for overviews see Barrucand, 1967; Crabtree, 1993; Gauld, 1992; Méheust, 1999). Writing in 1779, Franz Anton Mesmer (1734–1815) listed 27 propositions concerning this force, which he defined as a universal fluid that emanated from the heavenly bodies and that was present in nature (Mesmer, 1779/1980).[1] Mesmer related animal magnetism to physical and organic matter, the human body being affected by it through the nerves. In an attempt to relate this force to other principles, Mesmer compared it to magnetism, arguing that it was polarized. He not only believed that this force could heal, but was convinced that it could be reflected and intensified by mirrors, propagated by sound, and stored in matter (Mesmer's system is thoroughly discussed by Pattie, 1994).

This concept was elaborated by later mesmerists who published their ideas and observations during the eighteenth (Tardy de Montravel, 1785), nineteenth (Du Potet, 1868), and twentieth (Durville, 1920) centuries. In the opinion of Baron Jean du Potet de Sennevoy (1796–1881), the phenomena of magnetism could be explained as follows: "The nervous, active atmosphere of the magnetiser, no doubt augmented by the impulse of his will ... enters in rapport with the passive nervous atmosphere of the magnetised person, and augments the latter to the point that, in some cases, it seems that there is a

*Republished with permission from *Australian Journal of Clinical and Experimental Hypnosis*, *37*, 1–15, 2009.

†Research for this paper was funded by a grant from the Society for Psychical Research (London). I am grateful to Nancy L. Zingrone for editorial suggestions to improve this paper.

real saturation of the nervous system" (Du Potet, 1868, p. 316; this and other translations are mine). By all accounts, the mesmeric literature was vast and varied (Alvarado, 2008; Gauld, 1992, pp. 631–668).

The development of a variety of theoretical views about hypnosis (e.g., Braid, 1843; Charcot, 1882) contributed to the decline of magnetic theory. As stated by a writer in the *Revue Scientifique de la France et de la Étranger*, hypnosis was seen either as a "particular case of induced hysteria," or as the absorption of "animal magnetism into hypnotism according to Braid's formula" (Héricourt, 1884, p. 813).

Skepticism about this hypothetical force was rampant. One author saw the "hypothesis of magnetic fluid" as one unsupported by "any good experimental demonstrations" (Richet, 1884a, p. 221). Hippolyte Bernheim (1840/1919), the leader of the Nancy school of hypnosis, affirmed that the phenomena of hypnosis "are not due to a magnetic fluid"; instead, he wrote "everything is due to suggestion" (Bernheim, 1884, p. 73).

But this is far from saying that the mesmeric tradition was over. As stated in a recent overview: "Hypnosis had not replaced mesmerism at the end of the nineteenth century, but still existed alongside it" (Pintar & Lynn, 2008, p. 91). In fact, magnetism, and its variants, continued to be defended by serious students during the late nineteenth and into the twentieth centuries. While it may be argued that ideas, similar to the concept of animal magnetism, are still with us in many guises (e.g., Movaffaghi & Farsi, 2009; Nelson & Schwartz, 2005), my interest in this article is to discuss some partly forgotten figures who were active at the end of the nineteenth and the first decades of the twentieth centuries. In a previous article, I discussed two such figures (Alvarado, 2009). In this article, I will focus on the work of other overlooked theorists, namely Alexandre Barèty, Émile Boirac, and Julian Ochorowicz.[2]

Some Modern Magnetic Ideas

Mesmer's view (1779/1980), that the efficacy of the magnet to heal was due to animal magnetism, was echoed by others who saw the magnet as one of the means by which human magnetism could be transmitted (Durville, 1895). In this context, it is of interest to mention that the influence of the magnet was explored at the Salpêtrière by many physicians such as Alfred Binet (1857–1911) and Charles Féré (1852–1907), who focused on transfer phenomena. This was the belief that a magnet applied on a hypnotized subject could be used to move a motor or a sensory phenomenon from one side of the body to another (and later from one person to another). However, instead of animal magnetism, these authors explained their successes with the idea that the magnet "acts like a faint electric current on the nervous system, and produces a continuous peripheral excitement" (Binet & Féré, 1887, p. 262). This, and studies on the physiological effects of metals applied internally (in liquid form), or externally on contact with the skin (Charcot, Luys, & Dumontpallier, 1877, 1878), while not using the concept of animal magnetism, had a conceptual relationship to the old mesmeric claims of the efficacy of magnets as healing agents (Harrington, 1988).

In England, Edmund Gurney (1847–1888) explored the possible effect of a physical influence from the fingers of a person to induce anesthesia and other effects (e.g., Gurney, 1884). The French were particularly interested in these ideas as seen in Ambroise-Auguste Liébeault's (1823–1904) exploration of the effects of "zoomagnetism" on the medical condition of small children (Liébeault, 1883), in Albert de Rochas' (1837–1914) studies of the projection of tactual sensations beyond the periphery of the body during hypnosis, a phenomenon referred to as the "exteriorisation of sensibility" (De Rochas, 1899), and in Jules Bernard Luys' (1828–1897) descriptions as the abilities of hypnotized individuals to perceive "effluvia" emanating from human beings (Luys, 1892). In addition, many others defended a variety of concepts of force that formed what may be termed the late neo-mesmeric movement. The individuals discussed below represent prominent exponents of this tradition.[3]

The Contributions of Julian Ochorowicz (1850–1917)

Polish psychologist and philosopher Julian Ochorowicz created a simple instrument to measure susceptibility to hypnosis and to magnetism. This consisted of a tubular magnet, called an hypnoscope, that was placed around the finger of a person (Ochorowicz, 1885). In some persons, the magnet produced physical sensations that indicated to Ochorowicz openness to hypnosis and to magnetism. Out of 100 tests, there were reports of sensations in 30 of them.

Ochorowicz believed that the effects could not be accounted for by suggestion, even though he accepted that both suggestion and magnetism could act together. In his view, the magnet "is merely the substratum of another action, which is so weak ... that it hides itself from our instruments, and exhibits itself only through the intermedium of exceptionally sensitive nervous systems" (p. 281).

In a test conducted in darkness, a woman was able to differentiate a magnetized from a non-magnetized hypnoscope (Ochorowicz, 1909, p. 750). The magnetized hypnoscope elicited sensations of cold and tingling, while the non-magnetized one felt hot and agreeable.[4]

Ochorowicz (1887/1891, p. 348) referred to "psycho-physical transmission" to account for such phenomena as differences in performance between hypnotizers. Furthermore, he discussed this transmission in terms of the ups and down of what the French called "mental suggestion," defined by one author as "the transmission of thought or sensations of an individual to another without perceptible exterior signs to our senses" (De Rochas, 1887, p. 372).[5] He believed that rapport between operator and subject did not take place in hypnosis. However, magnetic action could bring rapport in different stages. In this view, rapport showed "the action upon the subject of a centre of radiation from without ... and an adjustment in conformity with the dynamic nature of that centre ... effected little by little" (Ochorowicz, 1887/1891, pp. 273–274).

Ochorowicz discussed other phenomena that, in his opinion, provided evidence for the existence of a physical influence. One of these was the subject's recognition of the magnetizer's touch from that of other individuals. This also happened, he said, when the touch was applied through a rod or a pencil. On the latter, he wrote: "*It proves that molecular dynamic differences pass beyond the surface of the body*; that a certain vibratory tonic movement peculiar to a given organism is propagated beyond its periphery, and can influence the subject so definitively, so palpably, that there is a real action" (Ochorowicz, 1887/1891, p. 223).

The Polish researcher also said that it was possible to produce healing effects without actual physical contact and without the patient's knowledge. This effect was further evidence for "an inductive action that overpasses the superficies of the body" (Ochorowicz, 1887/1891, p. 328). In addition, he argued that "moral" or psychological means could not explain the differences in the effects of the magnetic action on different people: "One hand acts differently from the other hand. Hence, there is a physical action, and a personal physical action" (p. 329). Nevertheless, he stated later that he did not believe that the right and left hands had different polarities and that he had not found that they produced different effects (Ochorowicz, 1909, p. 759).

The Contributions of Alexandre Barety (1844–1918)

French physician Alexandre Barety became interested in magnetism during the 1880s. His preliminary studies were presented to the Société de Biologie de Paris on July of 1881 (Barety, 1881/1882) and later expanded into a long monograph entitled *Le magnétisme animal: Étudié sous le nom de force neurique rayonnante et circulante dans ces propriétés physiques, physiologiques et thérapeutiques* (Barety, 1887; see also Barety, 1888).

Barety's monograph, over 600 pages long, was described by another proponent of magnetism as "the greatest scientific effort which has been made hitherto to establish the reality of animal magnetism" (Boirac, 1912/1917, p. 92). This book was about the field of "neurodynamics," or "the study of actions of neuric currents of a neuraliser subject on the neuric currents of a neuralised subject" (Barety, 1887, p. xiv). Neuric force, a principle analogous to animal magnetism, was believed to be a bodily force "probably from the nervous system, which circulates along the nerves or *radiates* out of them ... and is susceptible to producing certain sensitive, motor and psychic modifications on other human bodies" (p. xii). The book was divided into two parts. The first consisted of physical and physiological phenomena observed with one person, a Mlle C., and the second included phenomena observed with other individuals.

The neuric force, Barety believed, circulated within the nerves of the body and could be projected out of it as well. The latter was accomplished by means of passes, by pointing the fingers to the desired target, as well as through eyesight, and breath. The rays were said to travel in a straight line when coming out of the body, and could be reflected by some surfaces such as mirrors, or dispersed when passing through a prism.

Its effects included anesthesia, hyperesthesia, loss of sight or hearing, contractions and trance. For example, when Barety affected the sensibility of Mlle C, he was able to "anaesthetise and hyperesthesise the integuments of different regions ... abolish or exalt one or another sense" (p. 326).

The neuric force was said to have both internal and external properties. The internal ones were physical properties similar to heat, light and electricity. The external ones were the effects on animate and inanimate matter out of the body. The effects of this force were similar to the effects of a magnet, and some metals could augment the neuric force. Furthermore, Barety noticed that those susceptible to "neuricity" were also susceptible to atmospheric electricity.

Direct neurisation involved radiation from the magnetiser to the patient. But it could also be achieved through reflection (when the neuric force bounced off another surface) or through refraction (through lenses or prisms). Barety also referred to mediated neurisation, or an effect produced by another body or substance that had been charged with neuric force. An example of such a substance was water, which could "acquire the inherent properties of the neuric force" (p. 56). But water did not retain the force for long. Barety presented a list of common objects that he was able to charge with neuric force to use in mediated neurisation (pp. 271–272). In addition to water, this included paper, a table, a wall, a mirror, a book, a flower, a ruler, dice, and a handkerchief. Barety believed that the hand could project this force through a sewing needle.

Neurisation also took place through induction. As Barety explained: "The sole presence of a person close to another may affect the specific nervous state of one of them ..." (p. 234).

The neuric force could produce therapeutic effects. Barety believed it could affect general sensations, the functioning of the senses, movement and mental functions. These effects could take place while the subject was awake, or in a trance induced by the force, or appear spontaneously while the force was acting.

The first passes with Mlle. C. were carried out on 30 October 1880. Barety passed his open hand up and down the patient's body, and she soon fell into trance and exhibited anesthesia throughout the body. "Some days later, on 2 November, I saw that I could produce anaesthesia without trance by passes on different regions of the body, and limited to the region covered by the passes. I could thus anaesthetise a finger, the nose, and ear, one of the eyelids, [and] half of the side of the body" (p. 211).

Barety attempted to control Mlle. C.'s stomach pain. "Her pain," he wrote, "disappeared in a few seconds when we directed our fingers" to the region of her body that was in pain (p. 98).

Digital rays could go through different obstacles, he thought, such as walls, wool, and a shawl folded in eight sections. But the effects of the force passing through obstacles were weaker than those obtained with the direct projection of "neuric radiation." In November of 1880, Baréty tested the possibility of neuralization through a brick wall; the wall was 50 cm thick. His patient was situated between 10 to 12 cm from the wall's surface. From another room, Baréty placed his hand 50 to 60 cm from the wall pointing his fingers at the subject. He was able to induce contractions in the patient's hand and wrist (p. 116).

Baréty believed the neuric force could explain some medical conditions. Hysteria was a case in point, representing a "modification in the direction, the force and the distribution of nervous or neuric currents" (1887, p. 627).[6]

The Contributions of Émile Boirac (1851–1917)

French philosopher Émile Boirac, a professor of philosophy at the Lycée Condorcet (Paris), and chancellor of the Academié de Grenoble and of the Université de Dijon, was well known for his strong defenses of magnetism. In an early essay written to classify what we refer to today as parapsychological phenomena, Boirac (1893) referred to "psychodynamy," or the phenomena in which an individual could affect persons or physical matter at a distance through a force housed in the human body that was "different from all known forces, but analogous to radiating or circulating forces such as heat, light, electricity and magnetism" (pp. 346–347). Later, in a similar way, he referred to magnetism as "a personal and psychophysical action of the operator, an action emanating from its brain, which is exerted by currents more or less analogous to electrical and magnetic currents ..." (Boirac, 1895b, p. 60). The effects of this force on individuals included sensations of attraction and healing, but also such effects as the exteriorization of sensibility (Boirac, 1895a) and the induction of trance at a distance (Boirac, 1896a).[7]

For all the merits of the Nancy School of Hypnosis, Boirac (1895b) argued, suggestion was not enough to explain all the phenomena produced. But he believed that mesmeric hypothesis had acquired a bad reputation and was ignored by most scientists: "Animal magnetism is [like] an America [in] that [it] has been lost and recovered during the [last] twenty or thirty years" (Boirac, 1907, pp. 1–2).

Boirac was aware of the influence of suggestion, but wondered "whether the ancient hypothesis of animal magnetism, in a more or less modified expression, was not the source" of some hypnotic phenomena (Boirac, 1912/1917, p. 80), as he wrote about a force he called "biactinism":

> [This] is the agent which transmits to the nerve centres the excitations coming from the periphery and gives birth to the sensations. It is this also which transmits to the muscles the orders of the will, and determines the movements of the exterior organs. It is this, too, which excites and regulates the different vital functions; respiration, circulation, assimilation, and catabolism. But we do not know what constitutes it. (Boirac, 1917/ n.d., p. 158)

Boirac classified the phenomena dependent on this nervous force as "magnetoid." He argued that, when acting on a person, their physical basis could be separated from suggestion by keeping information from the subject, by conducting observations in complete silence, and "by acting only at a distance, without contact, through the supposed radiation of some organ of the operator, principally the hand" (Boirac, 1917/n. d., p. 60).

In attempting to show the existence of this force, Boirac used passes and a steady gaze to influence a 16-year-old young man: "Seated in front of the subject ... I slid my right foot slowly over the carpet, the toe pointing toward the subject's left foot. I noticed immediately a slight movement, a sort of tremor, in his foot. Again I slid my right foot, very slowly and without noise; this time the subject's foot glided visibly toward mine" (Boirac, 1917/n. d., pp. 165–166). Similar effects were reported when Boirac moved his hand nearer to the subject's own hand. In these movements, the subject "behaved as if his nervous system were, so far as voluntary movements are concerned, in communication with my own" (pp. 166–167).

Contemporary Critiques

The work of Ochorowicz, Barêty, and Boirac was not accepted by most of their contemporaries involved with hypnosis. An indication of this was an editorial note published in the *Revue de l'Hypnotisme Expérimental & Thérapeutique* on the first page of an article about the neuric force authored by Barêty (1888). The note stated that Barêty's opinions were in "complete opposition with the ideas generally admitted today" (p. 80). Suggestion was the generally accepted explanation for the phenomena of hypnosis, and ideas of magnetism, fluids and the like were considered unscientific and unacceptable by many.

An example of incredulity about the dynamic ideas of Ochorowicz was the reviewer of his book on mental suggestion. The reviewer, who praised Ochorowicz for his empirical approach, simply stated that he was not convinced (Colas, 1888). Another reviewer, English psychical researcher, Frank Podmore (1856–1910), referred to the hypnoscope as a "dubious little toy," and considered that it was premature to discuss the merits of Ochorowicz's force concepts to explain mental suggestion (Podmore, 1887).

Barêty was said not to have taken (or reported) proper precautions against suggestion, especially because most of his results were obtained with a single subject and "everyone knows that hypnotisable subjects are susceptible, through training, to a special education of incredible perfection, that renders them suitable to seize the suggestions" (Anonymous, 1887, p. 566). Similarly, the reviewer of the *American Journal of Psychology* saw the book as a document suggestive of a "joint product of pseudo-scientific methods gradually evolving a set of systematised symptom-reaction in an interesting hysterical subject, half whimsical originations, half subtle divination of theories of the experimenter almost before they are known to himself" (Anonymous, 1888, p. 502).

Pierre Janet, well known for his studies of dissociation, suggested that Barêty's beliefs led him to accept ambiguous responses of his subjects that may have had explanations other than the projection of a neuric force (Janet, 1888, p. 94). Janet also felt that the psychological aspects of the subjects were not explored, something that could explain or interact with other factors. However, he admitted that ideas such as Barêty's could contain some truth.

Boirac's ideas were also debated by several individuals. One of them wrote that he used a "truly scientific spirit" (Jankelevitch, 1908, p. 552), while another saw his work as possibly being the effect of "unsuspected sources of error rather than the existence of a psychic force" (Pierce, 1908, p. 471).

It was noticed that Boirac's concept of a force was ambiguous, but seemed to be analogous to physical magnetism (Leaf, 1895, p. 600). As this critic wrote: "We know far too little to say that it is not so; but I am not aware of any experiments which tend to prove it, and M. Boirac's seem to me to go certainly against it" (p. 600).[8] Furthermore, another critic accused Boirac of showing a "loose and vague way of handling theories" (Sidgwick, 1908, p. 288).

Another reason for the rejection of the work discussed here was the psychical research work these men engaged in, particularly Boirac and Ochorowicz.[9] Both of them wrote about mental suggestion

(Boirac, 1896a; Ochorowicz, 1887/1891). Similarly, both men discussed telekinesis, assuming that it was explained by the projection of a biophysical force of a person's body (Boirac, 1912/1917; Ochorowicz, 1910). Such interests were demonstrated as well by other neo-mesmerists (e.g., Durville, 1909; De Rochas, 1887). Closely related to the late magnetic movement, there was a spiritualistic and psychical research literature on concepts of forces emanating from the human body to explain mental and physical phenomena that preceded, and later overlapped with, the neo-mesmeric movement (Alvarado, 2006).

Conclusion

Compared to earlier authors, Baréty, Boirac and Ochorowicz represent a late mesmeric tradition. Among other aspects, they used magnetic theory to explain action at a distance. In addition, both Baréty and Boirac discussed magnetic effects on the human body.

While their ideas were not widely accepted at the time, and may seem to many today to be methodologically weak, this does not mean that they were the work of cranks, or that they should be treated with disdain, as some have done in the past (Barrucand, 1967). Such ideas were part of the history of attempts to understand hypnosis, interacting in many ways with other developments that became part of the accepted canon.

Following the interest historians of science have in rejected practices such as alchemy and phrenology, and in constructs, such as the ether and phlogiston, a proper history of hypnosis should not be made only of past work and ideas that resemble the present. Studying the work of such men as Baréty, Boirac and Ochorowicz illuminates the context in which Charcot, Bernheim and others worked to develop their ideas. In a wider context, re-examining such ideas is helpful to understand the development of science itself (e.g., Hanen, Osler, & Weyant, 1980), a topic beyond the scope of this article.

Notes

1 Note: when searching for the details of this and similar double dates, go to name first and then the second date mentioned of the two; e.g., Mesmer 1980.

2 Regarding the late magnetic movement, see Alvarado (2009), De Rochas (1902), and Harrington (1989). Gauld (1992) and Pintar and Lynn (2008) paid little attention to this literature. Aspects of it were discussed by authors such as Barrucand (1967), Crabtree (1993), Dingwall (1967–1968), and Plas (2000).

3 There were many other representatives of this tradition (e.g., Alrutz, 1921; Bertholet, 1927; Chazarain and Declé, 1886; Magnin, n. d.). Both Delboeuf (1887) and Grasset (1887) reported instances in which subjects did not show reactions differently to magnetised and non-magnetised hypnoscopes.

4 Both Delboeuf (1887) and Grasset (1887) reported instances in which subjects did not show reactions differently to magnetised and non-magnetised hypnoscopes.

5 For an overview of examples of this phenomenon and methodological issues in its study see Ochorowicz (1887/1891). Plas (2000, pp. 87–109) also discussed French interest in mental suggestion, such as Richet's (1884b).

6 For other late magnetic views of hysteria see Baraduc (1893, p. 162), and Bonnaymé de la Flachere (1917, p. 137). Ochorowicz (1884, p. 558) believed that sensitivity to the effects of magnets indicated that a person could be cured of nervous maladies through the influence of "magnetism, of hypnotism, of imagination, of metallotherapy, of weak electrical influences and of other minimal stimulants."

7 Caratelli (1996, pp. 146–171) reviews accounts of induction of trance at a distance. See also Ochorowicz (1887/1891) and Myers (1886).
8 A later exchange between Boirac (1896b) and Leaf (1896) did not solve the controversy. One of the issues discussed was the hypothetical distinction between thought transference and the effects of a physical effluence to explain the effects reported by Boirac.
9 On nineteenth–century European psychical research, see Biondi (1988), Oppenheim (1985), Plas (2000), and Wolffram (2005).

References

Alrutz, S. (1921). Problems of hypnotism: An experimental investigation. *Proceedings of the Society for Psychical Research, 32*, 151–178.

Alvarado, C. S. (2006). Human radiations: Concepts of force in mesmerism, spiritualism and psychical research. *Journal of the Society for Psychical Research, 70,* 138–162.

Alvarado, C. S. (2008). Mesmerism online: A bibliographic review. *Australian Journal of Clinical and Experimental Hypnosis, 36,* 115–120.

Alvarado, C. S. (2009). Late 19th- and early 20th-century discussions of animal magnetism. *International Journal of Clinical and Experimental Hypnosis, 57*, 366–381.

Anonymous. (1887). [Review of the book *Le magnétisme animal*]. *Revue Scientifique, 13* (s. 3), 565–566.

Anonymous. (1888). [Review of the book *Le magnétisme animal*]. *American Journal of Psychology, 1*, 501–502.

Baraduc, H. (1893). *La force vitale: Notre corps vital fluidique, sa formule biométrique*. G. Carré.

Barèty, A. (1882). *Contribution à l'étude des propriétés du système nerveux : Des proprietes physiques d'une force particulière du corps humain (force neurique rayonnante), connue vulgairement sous le nom de magnétisme animal.* Octave Doin. (Original work published, 1881).

Barèty, A. (1887). *Le magnétisme animal : Étudié sous le nom de force neurique rayonnante et circulante dans ces propriétés physiques, physiologiques et thérapeutiques*. Octave Doin.

Barèty, A. (1888). La force neurique. *Revue de L'Hypnotisme Expérimental & Thérapeutique, 2*, 80–85.

Barrucand, D. (1967). *Histoire de l'hypnose en France*. Presses Universitaires de France.

Bernheim, Dr [H.]. (1884). *De la suggestion dans l'état hypnotique et dans l'état de veille*. Octave Doin.

Bertholet, E. (1927). *Le fluide des magnétiseurs : Réponse aux adversaires des effluves humains*. H. Held.

Binet, A., & Féré, C. (1887). *Animal magnetism.* Kegan Paul, Trench.

Biondi, M. (1988). *Tavoli e medium: Storia dello spiritismo in Italia.* Gremese.

Boirac, E. (1893). Un essai de classification des phénomènes parapsychiques. *Annales des Sciences Psychiques, 3,* 342–354.

Boirac, E. (1895a). Expériences sur l'extériorisation de la sensibilité. *Annales des Sciences Psychiques, 5,* 169–173.

Boirac, E. (1895b). [Review of the book Le magnétisme curatif]. *Annales des Sciences Psychiques, 4*, 58–64.

Boirac, E. (1896a). Un cas de somneil provoqué à distance. *Annales des Sciences Psychiques, 6*, 56–58.

Boirac, E. (1896b). Correspondence. *Journal of the Society for Psychical Research, 7,* 221–224.

Boirac, E. (1907). Préface. In E. Gasc-Desfossés, *Magnétisme vital: Contributions expérimentales à l'étude par le galvanomètre de l'électro-magnétisme vital* (pp. 1–13, 2nd ed.). F. R. de Rudeval.

Boirac, E. (1917). *Our hidden forces: An experimental study of the psychic sciences* (from 2nd French ed.) (W. de Kerlor, trans.). Frederick A. Stokes. (2nd ed., published in French, 1912).

Boirac, E. (1917). *The psychology of the future* (W. de Kerlor, trans.). Frederick A. Stokes.

Bonnaymé de la Flachere, Dr (1917). Hystérie, neurasthénie et force. *Journal du Magnétisme et du Psychisme Expérimental, 45*, 130–139, 146–150.

Braid, J. (1843). *Neurypnology or the rationale of nervous sleep considered in relation with animal magnetism.* John Murray.

Caratelli, G. (1996). *Psicologia psicoanalisis.* Sovera.

Charcot, J. M. (1882). Sur les divers états nerveux déterminés par l'hypnotisation chez les sujets. *Comptes-rendus Hebdomadaires des Séances de l'Academie des Sciences, 94*, 403–405.
Charcot, [J. M.], Luys, [J. B.], & Dumontpallier, [A.]. (1877). Rapport fait à la Société de Biologie sur la métalloscopie du Docteur Burq. *Comptes Rendus des Séances de la Société de Biologie, 30,* 1–24.
Charcot, [J. M.], Luys, [J. B.], & Dumontpallier, [A.]. (1878). Second rapport fait à la Société de Biologie sur la métalloscopie et la métallothérapie du Docteur Burq. *Comptes Rendus des Séances de la Société de Biologie, 31*, I–XXXII.
Chazarain, Dr [L. T.], & Decle, C. (1886). *Découverte de la polarité humaine ou démonstration expérimentale des lois suivant lesquelles l'application des aimants, de l'électricité et les actions manuelles ou analogues du corps*. O. Doin.
Colas, A. (1888). [Review of the book De la suggestion mentale]. *Revue de l'Hypnotisme Expérimental & Thérapeutique, 2*, 60–62.
Crabtree, A. (1993). *From Mesmer to Freud: Magnetic sleep and the roots of psychological healing*. Yale University Press.
Delboeuf, J. (1887). Note sur l'hypnoscope et sur les phénomènes de transfert par les aimants. *Revue de l'Hypnotisme Expérimental & Thérapeutique, 1,* 370–372.
Dingwall, E. J. (Ed.). (1967–1968). *Abnormal hypnotic phenomena: A survey of nineteenth-century cases.* Barnes and Noble.
Durville, H. (1895). *Application de l'aimant au traitement des maladies* (5th ed.). Librairie du Magnétisme.
Durville, H. (1909). *Le fântome des vivants*. Librairie du Magnetisme.
Durville, H. (1920). *Cours de magnétisme personnel : Magnétisme expérimental & curatif, hypnotisme, suggestion* (5th ed.). Henri Durville.
Gauld, A. (1992). *A history of hypnotism*. Cambridge University Press.
Grasset, Docteur [J.]. (1887). Note sur l'hypnoscope d'Ochorowicz. *Revue de l'Hypnotisme Expérimental & Thérapeutique, 1*, 316–317.
Gurney, E. (1884). An account of some experiments in mesmerism. *Proceedings of the Society for Psychical Research, 2,* 189–206.
Hanen, M. P., Osler, M. J., & Weyant, R. G. (1980). (Eds.). *Science, pseudo-science and society*. Wilfrid Laurier University Press.
Harrington, A. (1988). Metals and magnets in medicine: Hysteria, hypnosis, and medical culture in fin-de-siècle Paris. *Psychological Medicine, 18*, 21–38.
Harrington, A. (1989). Hysteria, hypnosis, and the lure of the invisible: The rise of neo-mesmerism in fin-de-siècle French psychiatry. In W. F. Bynum, R. Porter & M. Shepherd (Eds.), *The anatomy of madness: Essays in the history of psychiatry* (Vol. 3, pp. 226–246). Tavistock.
Héricourt, J. (1884). Le magnétisme animal en dehors de l'hystérie. *Revue Scientifique de la France et de L'Étranger, 7* (s. 3), 812–813.
Janet, P. (1888). [Review of the book Le magnétisme animal]. *Revue Philosophique de la France et de L'Étranger, 25*, 91–95.
Jankelevitch, S. (1908). [Review of the book La psychologie inconnue]. *Revue Philosophique de la France et de l'Étranger, 66*, 550–552.
Leaf, W (1895). [Review of the article "L'Hypothèse du magnétisme animal"]. *Proceedings of the Society for Psychical Research, 11*, 599–600.
Leaf, W (1896). Correspondence. *Journal of the Society for Psychical Research, 7,* 224–228.
Liébeault, A. A. (1883). *Étude sur le zoomagnétisme*. Georges Masson.
Luys, J. B. (1892). De la visibilité, par les sujets en état hypnotique, des effluves dégagés par les êtres vivants. *Compte rendu hebdomadaires des séances el memoires de la Société de Biologie, 4* (s. 9), 657–659.
Magnin, E. (n.d. ca. 1905). *L'art et l'hypnose: Interprétation plastique d'œuvres littéraires et musicales.* "Atar."
Méheust, B. (1999). *Somnambulisme et mediumnité (1784–1930) : Vol. 1. Le defi du magnétisme animal.* Le Plessis-Robinson: Institut Synthelabo pour de Progres de la Connaissance.
Mesmer, F. A. (1980). Dissertation on the discovery of animal magnetism. In G. Bloch (Ed.), *Mesmerism: A translation of the original scientific and medical writings of F. A. Mesmer* (pp. 43-78). William Kaufmann. (Original work published 1779).

Movaffaghi, Z., & Farsi, M. (2009). Biofield therapies: Biophysical basis and biological regulations? *Complementary Therapies in Clinical Practice, 15*, 35–37.
Myers, F. W. H. (1886). On telepathic hypnotism, and its relation to other forms of hypnotic suggestion. *Proceedings of the Society for Psychical Research, 4,* 127–188.
Nelson, L. A., & Schwartz, G. E. (2005). Human biofield and intention detection: Individual differences. *Journal of Alternative and Complementary Medicine, 11*, 93–101.
Ochorowicz, J. (1884). Le sens du toucher et les sens du magnétisme. *Revue Scientifique de la France et de l'Étranger, 7* (s. 3), 553–538.
Ochorowicz, J. (1885). A new hypnoscope. *Journal of the Society for Psychical Research, 1*, 277–282.
Ochorowicz, J. (1891). *Mental suggestion* (J. Fitzgerald, trans.). Humbolt. (Original work published 1887).
Ochorowicz, J. (1909). Hypnotisme et mesmérisme. In C. Richet (Ed.), *Dictionnaire de physiologie* (Vol. 8, pp. 709–778). Félix Alcan.
Ochorowicz, J. (1910). Les rayons rigides et les rayons Xx: Études expérimentales. *Annales des Sciences Psychiques, 20*, 97–105, 129–136, 172–178, 204–209, 225–231, 257–263, 295–302, 336–344, 357–370.
Oppenheim, J. (1985). *The other world: Spiritualism and psychical research in England, 1850–1914.* Cambridge University Press.
Pattie, F. A. (1994). *Mesmer and animal magnetism: A chapter in the history of medicine*. Edmonston.
Pierce, A. H. (1908). [Review of the book *La psychologie inconnue*]. *Journal of Philosophy, Psychology and Scientific Methods, 5*, 470–471.
Pintar, J., & Lynn, S. J. (2008). *Hypnosis: A brief history*. Wiley–Blackwell.
Plas, R. (2000). *Naissance d'une science humaine: La psychologie: Les psychologues et le «merveilleux psychique.»* Presses Universitaires de Rennes.
Podmore, F. (1887). [Review of the book De la suggestion mentale]. *Proceedings of the Society for Psychical Research, 4*, 562–566.
Du Potet, Baron. (1868). *Manuel de l'étudiant magnétiseur* (4th ed.). Germer Baillière.
Richet, C. (1884a). *L'homme et l'intelligence: Fragments de physiologie et de psychologie*. Félix Alcan.
Richet, C. (1884b). La suggestion mentale et le calcul des probabilités. *Revue Philosophique de la France et de l'Étrangere, 18,* 609–674.
De Rochas, A. (1887). *Les forces non définies: Recherches historiques et expérimentales*. G. Masson.
De Rochas, A. (1899). *L'extériorisation de la sensibilité: Étude expérimentale & historique* (5th ed.). Chamuel.
De Rochas, A. (1902). *Les frontières de la science*. Librairie des Sciences Psychologiques.
Sidgwick, E. M. (1908). [Review of the book La psychologie inconnue]. J*ournal of the Society for Psychical Research, 13,* 285–288.
Tardy de Montravel, A. A. (1785). *Essai sur la théorie du somnambulisme magnétique*. n. p.
Wolffram, H. M. (2005). *On the borders of science: Psychical research and parapsychology in Germany, c. 1870–1939.* Doctoral dissertation, University of Queensland, Australia.

Note on an Early Physiological Index of ESP: John E. Purdon's Observations of Synchronous Pulse Rates*

Carlos S. Alvarado†

The purpose of this Note is to rescue from oblivion the nineteenth-century researches of physician John E. Purdon with measures of pulse rate synchrony between two persons. This was done using a sphygmograph, an instrument that measured pulse and provided graphic tracings on paper. According to Purdon, he found some persons reproduced the tracings of others in conditions that he considered to imply a telepathic transfer. Purdon speculated that one person produced emissions of nervous force that were propagated to others via the ether. While this research may be criticized from the point of view of modern research standards, it is presented here as an interesting and generally unknown early instrumental study of the concept of the detection of ESP via a physiological response.

The use of instrumental monitoring of different physiological processes as an index of ESP functioning is well-known in experimental parapsychology.[1] Some of the earlier work on the topic—such as that conducted by Hettinger (1952, Chapter 9) and by a research committee of the American Society for Psychical Research (Anonymous, 1959)—is not well-known. But even less known is the nineteenth-century work discussed here.[2]

In this Note, I describe research and observations of instrumental pulse measurements conducted by John E. Purdon in the early 1880s that he believed showed evidence of a psychic connection between two persons. Myers referred to this work as an attempt, which he did not find convincing, "to show by sphygmographic tracing the influence of an agent's thought in bringing a percipient's pulse to the same rhythm" (Myers, 1893, p. 32), while American philosopher William Romaine Newbold described the work as cases "in which the pulse-wave of one patient seemed to be telepathically transferred to another, the patients giving identical tracings" (Newbold, 1902, p. 103). I am presenting a short discussion of Purdon's work for its historical value, and not to defend the investigations as evidence for ESP functioning. That is, I write to inform current students about a nearly forgotten example of the use of physiological measures as ESP responses.[3]

John E. Purdon and the Sphygmograph

Purdon

According to Stone (1898, p. 414), John Edward Blakeney Purdon was a physician who was born in Dublin in 1839. He was educated and trained in medicine at Trinity College, Dublin. There he obtained a degree in arts in 1862, having been granted the year before a senior moderatorship (honors

*Republished with permission from *Journal of Scientific Exploration*, *29*, 109–123, 2015.
†I am grateful to the Society for Psychical Research for a grant that funded the writing of this paper, and to Leslie Price, who provided me with a copy of an article by Purdon.

degree) and a gold medal in Experimental and Natural Sciences. In 1863 he obtained two degrees, Bachelor in Medicine and a Masters in Surgery. Finally, he qualified for the M.D. in 1885.

Purdon lived in India serving as a surgeon in the British Army starting in 1865. During the next years he studied, and presumably treated, diseases such as cholera and dysentery. His work in India gained him "the special recognition of the British government ... [and he] was recommended for his zeal and ability" (Stone, 1898, p. 414).

In 1881, when he made his first observations of synchronous pulse rates, he was in charge of a military hospital in Guernsey, the Channel Islands. After retiring from the Army in 1883, Purdon lived in the United States. He was described by Alfred Russel Wallace as "an army surgeon, who has been much in India, and seems a very intelligent man" (Marchant, 1916, p. 195). According to his grave record, he died in 1925 and was buried in California.[4]

By his own admission, Purdon (1892, p. 385) started psychic studies in 1871. This included sittings with medium Florence Cook (Purdon, 1902; see also Marchant, 1916, p. 195). Purdon's name appears in early member lists published by the Society for Psychical Research (Anonymous, 1883, p. 324). In addition to his work with synchronous pulse, Purdon published several papers related to spiritualism and psychic phenomena. These included topics such as materialization phenomena (Purdon, 1881c, 1884, 1902), mesmerism (Purdon, 1881b), physiological observations and ideas about mediumship (Purdon, 1881a, 1885, 1892), and various theoretical ideas (Purdon, 1883, 1893a, 1893b).

The Sphygmograph

Purdon's work on pulse synchrony was done using a sphygmograph. This was a device that became fashionable during the nineteenth century to measure the pulse and to provide a graphic representation on paper of such activity. Interest in such measures was part of the concern many had during the period to develop accurate instruments to measure physiological processes (Reiser, 1978). Aspects of the history of the sphygmograph, and its variations, have been discussed by Frank (1988), Moss (2006), and Reiser (1978), and there are many publications about it by physicians (e.g., Bramwell, 1883; Dudgeon, 1882). Initially a bulky instrument, it was considerably reduced in size into a portable machine by Marey (1860), and eventually others developed several even smaller variations (Lawrence, 1978, 1979).

Many had great hopes for the instrument. For example, in his textbook *The Science and Practice of Medicine*, William Aitken (1872) wrote:

> In the conventional routine of 'feeling the pulse,' the unaided sense of touch is quite unable to distinguish many of the finer features which the sphygmograph enables us now to appreciate ... In place of its being able to take the place of 'feeling the pulse,' it will not only extend our practical knowledge ..., but it will define and greatly extend our knowledge of the more delicate characteristics of the pulse which the sense of touch fails to discover. (Aitken 1872, p. 313)

Others used the instrument in areas such as the study of the effects of drugs (Owens 1885).

But, as with other physiological measurement instruments, there were also measurement and technical problems as well. Frank (1988, p. 239) has shown an incline in medical articles mentioning the sphygmograph from 1855 to 1879, and a decline between 1880 and 1889. As he observed, "sphygmography in the last decades of the Nineteenth Century did not fulfill the great expectations so enthusiastically announced in the 1860s ..." (Frank 1988, p. 224).

While Purdon started writing about his use of the sphygmograph in 1881, when the decline in its use had started, the instrument was still used by many. Interestingly, Purdon rarely mentioned which sphygmograph he used, a point made by a commentator (Gillespie, 1898). In a later paper Purdon (1901, p. 723) stated he had used Dudgeon's sphygmograph.[5]

Purdon's Observations of Synchronous Pulse Phenomena

Purdon published his observations in several places (e.g., Purdon, 1882a, 1882b, 1896, 1898), and presented his work at conventions (Anonymous, 1889, Purdon, 1901). His work attracted some attention and comments in various magazines and journals. Examples include *Current Opinion* (Anonymous, 1893a), *Edinburgh Medical Journal* (Gillespie, 1898), *Medical Age* (Anonymous, 1893b), and the *Journal of the American Medical Association* (Anonymous, 1889).[6]

Purdon said that while he was working in a hospital in Guernsey two soldier patients, Private W. (an epileptic) and Private L. (who suffered from bleeding from a nostril), both who he believed showed an arthritic diathesis,[7] reported unusual knocking sounds around them and "the presence, visible and tangible, of a hand, and the figure of a man …" (Purdon, 1882a, p. 25).[8] He later found out that the apparitions coincided with a "fit" experienced by the wife of a hospital orderly located on the opposite side of the wall of the soldiers's room. She was said to suffer from hystero-epilepsy and had occasional "spasms." The woman, and the soldier, were considered by Purdon to have abnormal nervous systems. Here Purdon shows that he was drawing on the ideas of Charcot (1872-1873) and others (e.g., Richer 1881), which were very influential for a while. Furthermore, and as seen later, Purdon was one of those who combined the idea of abnormal nervous functioning and *real* psychic phenomena, both mental and physical. By *real* I mean here that the phenomena observed were believed by Purdon to be veridical, and not accounted for by conventional processes.

Purdon wrote as follows:

> During the ten days that my observations continued, I took many scores of traces with the sphygmograph finding the likenesses between the curve of Private W … and the young woman next door to be often remarkable. On one occasion I found that Private W … Private L … and myself were showing the same pattern almost exactly. That night our neighbour was eliminated as a disturbing cause, for she was laid up with a very bad sick headache … (Purdon, 1882a, p. 26-27).

In another paper Purdon discussed a "discovery" he made in June of 1881. He wrote:

> I was taking the tracing of a young lady who was lying down with a menstrual headache, her hand being held by an older lady, her first cousin, when I suddenly saw the pulse curve change to that of the other, which I had more than once taken that morning. There could be no mistake about the resemblance, for the tracing of the other person was very characteristic and so familiar to me that such would have been a moral impossibility under the circumstances.
>
> I repeated the observation, taking the tracings of each woman repeatedly, and found more or less resemblance between the tracings of the elder and one side of the younger … This relation had to do in my mind with the state of susceptibility to change, disturbance, or irritation of the nervous system of the younger, as depending upon the presence of the catamenia. I did not consider that the factor of blood relationship played any prominent part in the forced

> resemblance, for in general the tracings were quite dissimilar; nor could any tendon jerk or muscular pressure from the holding of hands account for it, for they were quite quiescent before I started the clock-work of the instrument.
>
> I determined to make an exhaustive study of both pulses, and, during the ensuing month, I made observations every day, or nearly so, and frequently several times a day, night and morning. After the passing away of the menstrual period I was not able to trace any likeness between the pulse tracings of these ladies; and as the time for the return of the same came round I prepared for a careful set of observations. I had everything made ready in the elder lady's room, and succeeded in getting some very sharp tracings, but, strange to say, I did not get the resemblance I had been so earnestly expecting, but a most exact and most perfect reduplication of my own pulse tracing, which was in general quite different from those of either of the two.
>
> Nothing was left to me but to go on observing, and I found that as the days of the periodic disturbance wore away, the tendency to repeat my tracing disappeared also. I continued my observations on these ladies daily for two months more, with complete confirmation of results before obtained; the likenesses being always at the time of the menstrual nisus, and gradually fading away with it.
>
> The younger lady always showed a marked difference in the two wrists at that time, the left being the one which took on the forced likeness, while the right pulse always gave evidence of what I considered to be a hemorrhagic pulse, judging from those I had seen in persons subject to nose bleeding. Be that as it may, the right tracings at the menstrual period were always alike, and always different from the left. I may remark, however, that the tension was much the same, the difference depending on the rhythm of the vaso-motor impulse.
>
> Other observations were done with hospital patients, young and middle-age British soldiers. I was cautious not to be misled by superficial or accidental likenesses, for I made it a rule to regard nothing as a typical likeness where the complete pulsation cycle of the second individual did not fall within the forms of the extremes of the first; that is to say the second man was pronounced *like* the first, when some of his cycles were more like those of the first than the extremes of the first were like one another—and that within a very limited period of time; for the closer the coincidence in time, the more likely was the resemblance to be forced … (Purdon, 1898, p. 333)

Three men were said to show good results. One suffered from urethritis and the other two from rheumatism. According to Purdon:

> Likenesses were observed between the first two named men and also between the second and third; but the most pronounced and truly remarkable resemblances were found to exist when the first-named man influenced the third. (Purdon 1898, p. 335)

Finally, I will present the following observations made by Purdon:

> A gunner of the Royal Artillery, very much broken down in health from Gibraltar fever, was in hospital during the latter part of the year, when I had become pretty expert in the practical application of my method of research. This man on occasions showed very remarkable, I do not exaggerate when I say wonderful, resemblances to my right and left radial traces, always, be it observed, taken at the same time. Peculiar tracings of mine that I could have sworn to in a Court of Justice … were so closely imitated that, if they were mixed up together, I could not say for certain, which were his and which were mine, and that when his ordinary and undisturbed traces

> were absolutely different in every respect from mine. I may add that the patient was always better, in fact at his best, when these similarities were most pronounced.
>
> Another man who suffered from what I regarded as a spurious form of angina pectoris … at times and when I had been brought into close contact with him for some time, as when I had been sitting on his bed for an hour, showed likenesses to my curves which no impartial witness could ascribe to accident. With varying tensions and with frequent adjustments of the instrument, so as to eliminate chance resemblances as much as possible, all the above men were subjected to observation not once or half a dozen, but many scores of times, out of which many true and reliable likenesses showed themselves in each instance of comparison between the selected couples. I felt, therefore, justified in regarding the discovery as proved. (Purdon 1898, p. 336)

Explaining the Pulse Tracings

Purdon's proposal of a physical transmission to explain his pulse tracings took place in the context of many nineteenth-century speculations about brain waves and other physical emanations to account for thought-transference (e.g., Knowles 1869; see also Alvarado 2008) and physical mediumship (e.g., Cox 1872; see also Alvarado 2006).[9] Furthermore, his use of the concept of ether was consistent with ideas in physics at the end of the nineteenth century (Cantor & Hodge, 1981, Schaffner, 1972), and with its application to the concept of telepathy by some writers, an example being the well-known William Crookes (1899; see also Houston, 1892).

For some the ether transcended physics, having metaphysical implications, as seen in Stewart and Tait's *The Unseen Universe* (Tait, 1875; see also Noakes, 2005). It was a concept that attracted speculation from spiritualists. For example, in a lecture it was said that "spiritual beings … may work upon that intermediate ether, and through it … influence material objects" (Anonymous 1884, p. 791). The concept was further extended by others when they imagined the existence of a more spiritual ether (e.g., Blavatsky, 1877), what Hudson Tuttle called a psychic ether, "the medium through which all spiritual phenomena are produced" (Tuttle 1889, p. 20).

Inspired by the idea of ether of James Clerk Maxwell (1878) and others, Purdon argued that the ether could be seen as the way mental events were propagated. He wrote that the

> … medium of communication can be nothing else than the ether in special relation with the two nervous systems, which thus function identically through the presence and agency of sympathetic vibrations. (Purdon 1896, p. 110)

Purdon further affirmed that "when one vaso-motor or cerebral center *acts* upon another, it surely does so physically …" (Purdon, 1898, p. 339).[10]

Purdon was led to speculate about an extrasomatic interaction of nerve centers to account for the above-mentioned phenomena, something that was similar in some ways to the ideas of previous theorists regarding nervous and psychic forces, not to mention the mesmeric literature (Alvarado, 2006, 2008). He advanced the hypothesis of

> … a physical disturbance of a rotational character … propagated through space from the body of the individual in a state of strain, and that there may thereby be a reasonable analogy to the acknowledged principles of magneto-electric action at a distance, but vastly more complex … (Purdon 1882a, p. 28-29)

Regarding the transfer of pulses Purdon wrote:

> The medium of communication can be nothing else than the ether in special relation with the two nervous systems, which thus function identically through the presence and agency of sympathetic vibrations. (Purdon, 1898, p. 110)

Years later Purdon referred to the psychic rapport he had with his wife. The similarity in their pulses led him to think that they both had a

> … similar distribution of the blood [that took place] either through the determination of the unconscious self, or through a nervous attraction preliminary to vital interaction, physical and psychical … It would appear as if the common pulse tracing … is our lower projection view of a transcendental state of affairs … falling outside the limits of our conscious forms of intuition. (Purdon, 1902, p. 224)

Here Purdon may have been influenced by the ideas of Frederic W. H. Myers who argued in many of his publications about the importance of the subliminal mind in the manifestation of telepathy (e.g., Myers, 1884, 1885).[11]

Concluding Remarks

Perhaps it is unfair to comment on Purdon's methodology from the modern point of view. Nonetheless I will make some points that are obvious today but were not so in Purdon's times. By modern standards Purdon's tests are very crude, lacking several methodological precautions considered important today (such as those commented on by Acunzo, Evrard, and Rabeyron [2014]). The evaluation of the results depended on visual inspection of the tracings, something that does not seem to have been done blindly. Furthermore, the reports lack information about checks on the proper functioning of the sphygmograph, potential artifacts related to how the instrument was attached to the arm, the position of the arm and its movements, and environmental stimuli that could have affected the tracings of both subjects. One aspect that was already obvious to some researchers at the time Purdon was working was the need for proper separation between the experimental participants, a problem in some of the tests.

In these current days of "entanglement" and "nonlocality" in which physical transmission models are rejected by many, Purdon's views in which the projection of nervous forces accounted for the mental and physical phenomena of spiritualism and psychical research will appear odd and antiquated to some readers. But both before and during his time there were many such ideas around (Alvarado, 2006, 2008),[12] as there are still today in some quarters.

Current ideas of psi as a normal function are different from Purdon's belief that nervous pathology was related to some genuine psychic manifestations. In earlier writings, such as those of physician B.W. Richmond, abnormal nervous constitutions were associated with "real" psychic phenomena (Brittan & Richmond, 1853; see also Fairfield, 1875; Lombroso, 1909; Morselli, 1908).

Regardless of how we see Purdon's methodology and theoretical ideas, his work deserves to be remembered if only to credit him for an early empirical attempt to detect ESP functioning via physiological measurements.

Notes

1 Some examples of pioneering work in this area are the studies of Figar (1959), Dean (1962), Tart (1963), and Duane & Berendt (1965). Modern examples include the work of Grinberg-Zylberbaum, Delaflor, Attie, & Goswami (1994), Radin (2004), Standish, Kozak, Johnson, & Richards (2004), and Tressoldi, Martinelli, Semenzato, & Cappato (2011). Reviews of this line of research have been published by Beloff (1974), Modestino (2013), Mossbridge, Tressoldi, & Utts (2012), and Palmer (1978).

2 Also of historical interest are various observations that have supported the idea that ESP may manifest via bodily sensations and processes. Charles Lafontaine (1847, p. 87) referred to mesmerized individuals who could feel prickings and other stimuli presented to other people, as well as the pains of the diseased who consulted them. Other examples include early thought-transference experiments to induce pain sensations (Guthrie, 1885), the few cases reported in *Phantasms of the Living* about veridical impressions seemingly related to pain and feelings of illness (Gurney, Myers, & Podmore, 1886), psychics' feeling physical discomfort and pain related to people they were "reading" at a distance (Richet, 1888), and physiological effects that supposedly indicated the effect of drugs and medicines at a distance (Bourru & Burot, 1887). While none of this is proof that actual physiological processes were active expressing ESP—acquired information, they contributed to the idea of the possibility of expressing such information in physiological ways. On the theoretical side, Myers speculated on the possibility "that the telepathic impact may affect some sensitive internal organs ..." (Myers, 1893, p. 32), including vasomotor processes, and stated that motor messages coming from the subliminal mind started "from modifications of the percipient's general organic condition or coenesthesia ..." (Myers, 1893, p. 40).

3 Nicol (1973) made reference to Purdon's work.

4 This date was obtained from *Find a Grave http://www.findagrave.com/*. I believe this refers to our John E. Purdon because of information consistent with Stone (1898, p. 414). This includes his birthdate, birthplace, medical degree, and that he graduated from the University of Dublin.

5 Years later someone wrote that Purdon had sent him sphygmographic tracings done with Dudgeon's instrument (Anonymous, 1917, p. 18). The device, which was smaller and more portable than previous instruments, was described by Dudgeon (1882; see also Lawrence, 1979). According to Dudgeon he introduced the device in 1880 and it was a small model two and a half by two inches in size and its weight was four ounces. He wrote:

> When packed in its leather case it can be easily carried in the pocket. It is adjusted to the wrist, the stud on the free end of the spring being carefully placed upon the radial artery immediately above the styloid process of the radius. The instrument is kept in position by an inelastic strap, which may be secured by a tourniquet or simply held by the fore-finger and thumb of the right hand ... The pressure of the spring is regulated by the excentric wheel, to any amount from one up to five ounces. When the needle is seen to play freely over the centre of the tracing-paper, the machinery of the clockwork which drives the paper through the machine is set in motion by pushing toward the right the small metal handle on the top of the clockwork box ... The instrument is used with equal facility on either arm, and the patient may either stand, sit, or lie. The levers are so adjusted that the movements of the artery are magnified exactly fifty times. The pressure of the spring may be altered without disturbing the instrument. The smoked portion of the paper passes through the instrument in ten seconds; hence six times the number of beats traced on the paper give the number of beats per minute ... (Dudgeon, 1882, p. 29–31).

6 See also mentions of the work in forums open to psychic phenomena such as *The Theosophist* (Anonymous, 1882a), *Psychische Studien* (Anonymous, 1882b), and *Borderland* (Anonymous, 1896).

7 In addition to many earlier discussions of the concept that we cannot cover here, the topic was discussed in British medical journals around the time Purdon started writing. A physician stated that "there is a basic arthritic habit of body, or diathesis, and that from this issue at least two branches, the gouty and the rheumatic stocks" (Duckworth, 1883, p. 194). Another physician referred to arthritic diathesis as a constitutional predisposition to arthritic symptoms that could include such varied things as dyspepsia, renal disease, pneumonia, and skin problems (Hutchinson, 1881). Lemoine (1891) reviewed the topic and stated

that arthritism generates the nervous diathesis but that "the arthritic is not a neuropath yet, but it is on the brink of becoming one and his children frequently are" (Lemoine, 1891, p. 124, my translation).

8 As interesting as the apparitional and physical phenomena were, my focus here is on Purdon's writings about his use of the sphygmograph. But it should be pointed out that Purdon (1882a, p. 27) believed the raps were related to muscular rheumatism and to chorea.

9 Purdon stated: "My sphygmograph studies were first undertaken in the hope of finding some physiological explanation of the Beattie photographs of thirty years ago" (Purdon, 1902, p. 225). This was a reference to photographer John Beattie, who reported obtaining a variety of amorphous luminous forms on photographic plates in the early 1870s (one of Beattie's early reports was transcribed by Houghton, 1882, p. 43–48). It is not clear how the sphygmograph would have helped in elucidation of these phenomena, but perhaps Purdon saw the instrument as the means to detect unknown forces presumably seen in Beattie's photographs (on this see the ideas of force held by Beattie, 1873). Perhaps he made a connection between pulses and invisible forces when he stated that his first exploration was finding a disturbance in the pulse of a sister of medium Florence Cook "on the approach of an apparition visible to herself alone" (Purdon, 1902, p. 225).

10 Referring to physical effects at a distance Purdon wrote later that such effects "can be accounted for in psychics as well as in physics by the assumption of a plenum whose elemental constituents obey laws identical with those which enable the ether to transmit energy" (Purdon, 1902, p. 225).

11 Myers (1892, p. 328) wrote:

> We have … dwelt on the knowledge which reaches us otherwise than through the recognised organs of sense. And it is, I hold, in the subliminal region that such phenomena are initiated, and that such knowledge is primarily gained.

12 Many of the British researchers associated with the Society for Psychical Research, however, did not follow physicalistic approaches (e.g., Gurney, Myers, & Podmore, 1886).

References

Acunzo, D. J., Evrard, R., & Rabeyron, T. (2014). Anomalous experiences, psi, and functional neuroimaging. *Frontiers in Human Neuroscience, 7*, 893.

Aitken, W. (1872). *The science and practice of medicine,* Volume 2 (3rd American ed., from 6th London ed.). Lindsay & Blakiston.

Alvarado, C. S. (2006). Human radiations: Concepts of force in mesmerism, spiritualism and psychical research. *Journal of the Society for Psychical Research, 70,* 138–162.

Alvarado, C. S. (2008). Further notes on historical ideas of human radiations: IV. Mental phenomena. *Psypioneer, 4,* 119–126.

Anonymous (1882a). Psyche. *The Theosophist, 3*, 211.

Anonymous (1882b). Tagesneuigkeiten, Notizen u. dergl.: Die neue 'Psyche' in London und die Himalaya-Brüder. *Psychische Studien, 9*, 182–183.

Anonymous (1883). Members, Associates, Honorary and Corresponding members (*December*, 1883). *Proceedings of the Society for Psychical Research, 1*, 321–330.

Anonymous (1884). The platform: Spiritualism from a scientific point of view. *Medium and Daybreak,* 790–791, December 12.

Anonymous (1889). Society proceedings. *Journal of the American Medical Association, 13*, 714–716.

Anonymous (1893a). Superstitious, unusual and weird. *Current Opinion, 14*, 407–411.

Anonymous (1893b). Psychism of the sphygmograph. *Medical Age, 11*, 596.

Anonymous (1896). Miracles: Catholic and Protestant: III. The miracles of suggestion. *Borderland, 3*, 334–335.

Anonymous (1917). Electronological comments. *Physico-Clinical Medicine, 2*, 9–21.

Anonymous (1959). Report of the research committees for 1958. *Journal of the American Society for Psychical Research, 53*, 69–71.

Beattie, J. (1873). The philosophy of spirit photography. *Spiritual Magazine, 8*, 23–27.

Beloff, J. (1974). ESP: The search for a physiological index. *Journal of the Society for Psychical Research, 47*, 403–420.

Blavatsky, H. P. (1877). *Isis unveiled: A master-key to the mysteries of ancient and modern science and theology: Volume 1: Science*. J. W. Bouton.

Bourru, H., & Burot, P. (1887). *La suggestion mentale et l'action à distance des substances toxiques et médicamenteuses*. J. B. Baillière.

Bramwell, B. (1883). *Student's guide to the examination of the pulse, and use of the sphygmograph* (2nd ed.). Maclachland and Stewart.

Brittan, S. B., & Richmond, B. W. (1853). *A discussion of the facts and philosophy of ancient and modern spiritualism.* Partridge & Brittan.

Cantor, G. N., & Hodge, M. J. S. (Eds.). (1981). *Conceptions of ether: Studies in the history of ether theories, 1740–1900.* Cambridge University Press.

Charcot, J. M. (1872–1873). *Leçons sur les maladies du système nerveux faites à la Salpêtrière* edited by D. M. Bourneville. Adrien Delahaye.

Cox, E. W. (1872). *Spiritualism answered by science* (New Rev. ed.). Longman.

Crookes, W. (1899). Address by Sir William Crookes, F. R. S., V. P. C. S. President. In *Report of the Sixty-Eighth Meeting of the British Association for the Advancement of Science* (pp. 3–38), Bristol, England, September 1898. John Murray.

Dean, E. D. (1966). Plethysmograph recordings as ESP responses. *International Journal of Neuropsychiatry, 2*, 439–446.

Duane, T. D., & Behrendt, T. (1965). Extrasensory electroencephalographic induction between identical twins. *Science, 150*, 367.

Duckworth, D. (1883). The characters of the teeth in persons of the arthritic diathesis. *Medical Press and Circular, 36*, 93–196.

Dudgeon, R. E. (1882). *The sphygmograph: Its history and use as an aid to diagnosis in ordinary practice.* Baillière, Tyndall, and Cox.

Fairfield, F. G. (1875). *Ten years with spiritual mediums: An inquiry concerning the etiology of certain phenomena called spiritual.* D. Appleton.

Figar, S. (1959). The application of plethysmography to the objective study of so-called extrasensory perception. *Journal of the Society for Psychical Research, 40*, 162–172.

Frank, R. G., Jr. (1988). The telltale heart: Physiological instruments, graphic methods, and clinical hopes, 1854–1914. In W. L. Coleman & F. L. Holms (Eds.), *The investigative enterprise: Experimental physiology in nineteenth-century* (pp. 211–290). University of California Press.

Gillespie, A. L. (1898). Recent advances in medical science. *Edinburgh Medical Journal, 4*, 363–366.

Grinberg-Zylberbaum, J., Delaflor, M., Attie, L., & Goswami, A. (1994). The Einstein-Podolsky- Rosen paradox in the brain: The transferred potential. *Physics Essays, 7*, 422–428.

Gurney, E., Myers, F. W. H., & Podmore, F. (1886). *Phantasms of the living* (2 vols.). Trübner.

Guthrie, M. (1885). Further report on experiments in thought-transference at Liverpool. *Proceedings of the Society for Psychical Research, 3*, 424–452.

Hettinger, J. (1952). *Telepathy and spiritualism: Personal experiments, experiences and views.* Rider.

Houghton, Miss [G.] (1882). *Chronicles of the photography of spiritual beings and phenomena invisible to the material eye*. E. W. Allen.

Houston, J. (1892). Cerebral radiations. *Psychical Review, 1,* 150–157.

Hutchinson, J. (1881). Lecture introductory to the study of the arthritic diathesis. *Medical News, 39*, 76–82.

Knowles, J. T. (1869). Brain-waves—A theory. *The Spectator, 42*, 135–137.

Lafontaine, C. (1847). *L'art de magnétiser ou le magnétisme animal considéré sous le point de vue théorique, pratique et thérapeutique.* Germer Baillière.

Lawrence, C. (1978). Physiological apparatus in the Wellcome Museum: 1: The Marey sphygmograph. *Medical History, 22*, 196–200.

Lawrence, C. (1979). Physiological apparatus in the Wellcome Museum: 2: The Dudgeon sphygmograph and its descendants. *Medical History, 23*, 96–101.

Lemoine, G. (1891). Considérations sur l'arthritisme dans ses rapports avec le nervosité. *Gazette Médicale de Paris, 62*, 85–88, 112–114, 122–125, 149–150, 164–166.

Lombroso, C. (1909). *After death—what?* Small, Maynard.

Marchant, J. (1916). *Alfred Russel Wallace: Letters and reminiscences* (Vol. 2). Cassell.

Marey, J. (1860). *Recherches sur le pouls au moyen d'un nouvel appareil enregistreur : Le sphygmographe*. E. Thunot.

Maxwell, J. C. (1878). Ether. *Encyclopaedia Britannica* (9th ed., Vol. 8, pp. 568–572). Adam & Charles Black.

Modestino, E. J. (2013). Physiological responses as unconscious measures of psi. In edited by S. Krippner, A. J. Rock, J. Beischel, H. L. Friedman, & C. L. Fracaso, *Advances in Parapsychological Research 9* (pp. 126–155). McFarland.

Morselli, E. (1908). *Psicologia e "Spiritismo:" Note e Impressioni Critiche sui Fenomeni Medianici di Eusapia Paladino* (2 vols.). Fratelli Bocca.

Moss, S. W. (2006). The sphygmograph in America: Writing the pulse. *American Journal of Cardiology, 97*, 580–587.

Mossbridge, J., Tressoldi, P. E., & Utts, J. (2012). Predictive physiological anticipation preceding seemingly unpredictable stimuli: A meta-analysis. *Frontiers in Psychology, 3*, 390.

Myers, F. W. H. (1884). On a telepathic explanation of some so-called spiritualistic phenomena. *Proceedings of the Society for Psychical Research, 2*, 217–237.

Myers, F. W. H. (1885). Automatic writing. II. *Proceedings of the Society for Psychical Research, 3*, 1–63.

Myers, F. W. H. (1892). The subliminal consciousness: Chapter I. General characteristics of subliminal messages. *Proceedings of the Society for Psychical Research, 7*, 298–327.

Myers, F. W. H. (1893). The subliminal consciousness: Chapter VII: Motor automatism. *Proceedings of the Society for Psychical Research, 9*, 26–128.

Newbold, W. R. (1902). Psychological literature: Hypnotism. *Psychological Review, 9*,102–103.

Nicol, F. (1973). The usefulness of history. In W. G. Roll, R. L. Morris, & J. D. Morris (Eds.), *Research in Parapsychology 1972* (pp. 173–176). Scarecrow Press.

Noakes, R. (2005). Ethers, religion and politics in late-Victorian physics: Beyond the Wynne thesis. *History of Science, 43*, 415–455.

Owens, W. (1885). Jaborandi. In *Proceedings of the Twenty-First Annual Session of of the Homeopathic Medical Society of the State of Ohio*, Cincinnati May 13–14, 1885 (pp. 138 –141). Daily News Books and Job Rooms.

Palmer, J. (1978). Extrasensory perception: Research findings. In S. Krippner, *Advances in Parapsychological Research: Volume 1: Extrasensory Perception* (pp. 59–243). Plenum Press.

Purdon, J. E. (1881a, November 11). Explanatory criticism of the nature of a medical case, with paradoxical temperature. *Spiritualist Newspaper, pp.* 230–232.

Purdon, J. E. (1881b, December 2). An experimental research. *Spiritualist Newspaper,* pp. 271–275.

Purdon, J. E. (1881c, December 16, 23, & 30). A philosophy of materialisation. *Spiritualist Newspaper*, pp. 295–299, 306–310, 317–318.

Purdon, J. E. (1882a, January 20). An experimental research. *Spiritualist Newspaper*, pp. 25–29.

Purdon, J. E. (1882b, January 27). An experimental research, with explanatory criticism. *Spiritualist Newspaper*, pp. 38-41.

Purdon, J. E. (1883). Personality and the universal mind. *Light, 3*, 93, 112–113, 127, 165, 171–172.

Purdon, J. E. (1884, July 5). On the extraordinary space-content with reference to materializations. *Religio Philosophical Journal, 1*, 5.

Purdon, J. E. (1885, December 12). Original psychical research. *Religio Philosophical Journal, 1*, 8.

Purdon, J. E. (1892). The psychical import of variable achromatopsia; an original research. In *Transactions of the Medical Association of the State of Alabama* (pp. 383–394). Brown Printing.

Purdon, J. E. (1893a). The higher spiritualism—Space and matter. *Open Court, 7*, 3770–3772.

Purdon, J. E. (1893b). Psychical dislocation and the theory of mediumism. *Medical and Surgical Reporter, 69*, 467–473.

Purdon, J. E. (1896). Sympathetic vibration in nervous attraction. *Metaphysical Magazine, 3*, 106–110, 202–209.

Purdon, J. E. (1898). Sympathetic and telepathic pulse tracings. *Pacific Medical Journal, 41*, 331–339.

Purdon, J. E. (1901). Transfer of sensori-motor impulses proved by the sphygmograph. In P. Janet (Ed.), *IVᵉ Congrès International de Psychologie* (pp. 713–723). Félix Alcan.

Purdon, J. E. (1902). The problem of 'Katie King.' *Light, 22*, 223-226.

Reiser, S. J. (1978). *Medicine and the reign of technology.* Cambridge University Press.

Radin, D. (2004). Electrodermal presentiments of future emotions. *Journal of Scientific Exploration, 18*, 253–273.

Richer, P. (1881). Études *cliniques sur l'hystéro-épilepsie, ou grande hystérie*. Adrian Delahaye and Émile Lecrosnier.

Richet, C. (1888). Relation de diverses expériences sur la transmission mentale, la lucidité, et autres phénomènes non explicables par les données scientifiques actuelles. *Proceedings of the Society for Psychical Research, 5,* 18–168.

Schaffner, K. (1972). *Nineteenth-century aether theories*. Pergamon Press.

Standish, L. J., Kozak, L., Johnson, L. C., & Richards, T. (2004). Electroencephalographic evidence of correlated event-related signals between the brains of spatially and sensory isolated human subjects. *Journal of Alternative and Complementary Medicine, 10*, 307–314.

Stewart, B., & Tait, P. G. (1875). *The unseen universe of physical speculations on a future state* (2nd ed.). Macmillan.

Stone, R. F. (1898). *Biography of eminent American physicians and surgeons* (2nd Rev. ed). C. E. Hollenbeck.

Tart, C. T. (1963). Physiological correlates of psi cognition. *International Journal of Parapsychology, 5*, 375–386.

Tressoldi, P. E., Martinelli, M., Semenzato, L., & Cappato, S. (2011). Let your eyes predict: Prediction accuracy of pupillary responses to random alerting and neutral sounds. *Sage Open.* doi:10.1177/2158244011420451

Tuttle, H. (1889). *Studies in the out-lying fields of psychic science*. M. L. Holbrook.

Mediumship, Psychical Research, Dissociation, and the Powers of the Subconscious Mind*

Carlos S. Alvarado†

Since the 19th century many psychiatrists and psychologists have considered mediumship to be related to the subconscious mind and to dissociative processes produced mainly by internal conventional processes of the medium's mind. However, some psychologists and psychical researchers active between the last decades of the 19th century and the 1920s expressed a different view. Individuals such as Théodore Flournoy, Cesare Lombroso, Enrico Morselli, Frederic W.H. Myers, Julian Ochorowicz, Charles Richet, Eleanor Sidgwick, and Eduard von Hartmann, argued that some mediums combined dissociation with supernormal phenomena such as knowledge acquired without the use of the senses, and the production of physical effects seemingly beyond the normal bodily capabilities. Depending on the theorist, other issues such as pathology and discarnate agency were also part of the discussions. The supernormal was never accepted by science at large and today is rarely mentioned in the dissociation literature. But ideas related to the supernormal were part of this literature. A complete history of dissociation, and of the subconscious mind, should include consideration of this body of work.

In his book *The Discovery of the Unconscious* Ellenberger (1970, pp. 317–318) argued that by 1900 four main functions of the unconscious mind had been established. These functions were conservative (the repository of memories and perceptions), dissolutive (automatic and dissociative aspects that may interfere with normal functions), creative, and mythopoetic (or fictional fabrications of all sorts). In this paper I will focus on one function not included by Ellenberger, what we would refer to today as "parapsychological." These phenomena were also referred to as psychic, metapsychic, and supernormal. My discussion will focus on theoretical ideas about mediumship and the subconscious mind that include the supernormal, ideas prevalent from the late 19th century to late in the 20th century. The purpose of the paper is to reacquaint contemporary students of dissociation and of mediumship with this nearly forgotten past, a past that at the time interacted with and affected contemporary psychological and psychiatric work toward constructing the concept of dissociation and the idea of hidden powers of the subconscious mind.

To this day the term dissociation has different meanings and conceptualizations (Nijenhuis & Van der Hart, 2011; Spitzer, Barnow, Freyberger, & Joergen, 2006), but it is frequently used to refer to a misunderstood process underlying disruption or separation of memory, identity and sensations from consciousness. The term was not used by the authors discussed in this paper but they evidently believed in such hypothetical process to refer not only to the equally ill-defined mediumistic trance, but to the various manifestations of hypnosis, and hysteria, the latter which some postulated included fugues, amnesia, and so-called "secondary" (or more than two) personalities.

*Republished with permission from *Journal of Parapsychology*, *78*, 98–114, 2014.
†I wish to thank the Society for Psychical Research for a grant that allowed me to prepare this paper. Thanks are also due to Debra H. Weiner for useful editorial suggestions.

Although I (Alvarado, 2002, 2010a) and several others (e.g., Crabtree, 1993; Ellenberger, 1970; Plas, 2000; Shamdasani, 1994) have argued for contributions to the study of psychic phenomena or the supernormal, to psychology and psychiatry, and particularly to ideas about dissociation and concepts about nonconscious levels of the mind, here I focus on ideas that have not received much attention.

Mediumship in Context: Spiritualism, Psychical Research, and Psychiatry

The psychical researchers of the 19th century inherited from previous movements the idea that human beings had powers that could transcend physical limitations (for overviews see Alvarado, 2012; Crabtree, 1993; Inglis, 1992; Méheust, 1999a; Podmore, 1902a, 1902b). The work of the mesmerists—as seen in books such as *Natural and Mesmeric Clairvoyance* (Esdaile, 1852)—promoted the view that some people could influence others at a distance to produce phenomena such as cures and thought transference. In addition to publicizing psychic phenomena, thus creating an intellectual and experiential context for the unorthodox, mesmerism was important for the development of Spiritualism and mediumship in various ways. Among them were the various discussions in the mesmeric literature on nonphysical ideas (Alvarado, 2012, pp. 39–40) and the "mediumistic-like" phenomena reported by some mesmerized individuals (Crabtree, 1993, pp. 196–212).

As social reformer Robert Dale Owen (1860), who lived from 1801–1877, discussed in *Footfalls on the Boundary of Another World*, Spiritualists assumed that some individuals had the ability to perceive and to channel phenomena caused by spirits of the dead. Psychical research emerged as an attempt to continue and systematize the work of the mesmerists and the Spiritualists by exploring hidden dimensions of human functioning and the possibility of spirit agency (Gauld, 1968; Lachapelle, 2011; Moore, 1977; Wolffram, 2009).

While most contemporary scientists seemed to accept a closed model of the mind in which the workings of the subconscious and the phenomena of dissociation were explained by intrapsychic psychological, physiological, and medical factors (including outside influences such as suggestion and trauma), some of the psychical researchers (like the Spiritualists) argued for a model in which the mind was an open system not bound by the limitations of the nervous system and the senses (Gauld, 1968). Although the work in London of the Society for Psychical Research (SPR), founded in 1882, focused on different supernormal phenomena, such as spontaneous and experimental telepathy (e.g., Gurney, Myers, & Podmore, 1886; Guthrie, 1884; see also Gauld, 1968; Le Maléfan, 2008; Luckhurst, 2002), one of the major lines of work that the SPR and researchers outside England conducted was the study of mediumship.

Several historians have chronicled the prominence of mediumship in the 19th century. Some examples are historical studies about spiritualism and mediumship in England (Owen, 1990), Italy (Biondi, 1988), and the United States (Braude, 2001) (see also Alvarado 2010a; Alvarado & Zingrone, 2012; Edelman, 1985; and Galvan, 2010). Some mediums, such as Emma Hardinge Britten (1823-1899) and Cora L.V. Tappan (later Richmond; 1840–1923), were trance or inspirational speakers on social, scientific and philosophical topics (Hardinge, n. d.; Tappan, 1875). Many communications recorded through mediums suggested to some, as one historian wrote, that mediums were in "an elevated state, providing access to spirits and therefore to knowledge of the world beyond inaccessible to conscious human beings" (Braude, 2001, p. 87). The early American spiritualist literature contained many spirit communications about the nature of the afterlife and moral and philosophical topics (e.g., Hammond, 1866; Hare, 1855). Many recorded communications from famous individuals, among them Francis Bacon (1561–1626) and Emanuel Swedenborg (1688–1772) (Edmonds & Dexter, 1853), Thomas Paine (1737–1809; Hammond, 1866), and American presidents George Washington (1732–1799) and Thomas Jefferson (1743–1826; Spicer, 1853). Some, like Allan Kardec (pseudonym of Hippolyte Leon Rivail Denizard, 1804–1869) in France, questioned the spirits through mental mediums (Kardec, 1857). The "spirits" dictated teachings about such issues as God, the spiritual world, reincarnation, the intervention of spirits in life, moral laws dealing with various issues (e.g., society, progress, freedom), evocation of spirits, and mediumship, among many other topics (see also Edelman, 1995; Sharp, 2006). But there were also more specific communications in which mediums presented verifiable information about deceased individuals (e.g., Moses, 1879).

Among the influential phenomena of mediumship were verbal communications, automatic writing (including the production of literary works), as well as visions (e.g., Edmonds & Dexter, 1853; Moses, 1879). Many were impressed by what one author called personification, or "the appropriation or adoption of the name and many times of the character of a personality foreign to that of the medium" (Aksakof, 1890/n. d., p. 30; this and other translations are mine). Such phenomena, reported through the history of Spiritualism and psychical research with many mediums, received much discussion (see Alvarado, 2011b).

In addition to the mental mediums, there were physical mediums thought to manifest spirits through physical manifestations. These phenomena included acoustic ones such as raps (sounds produced on objects) or voices, the movement of objects, luminous effects, the appearance of writing on slates or paper, and materializations of figures, both solid and misty, that supposedly represented the spirits of the dead. Two famous examples were mediums Florence Cook (1856–1904), well-known for her materializations of a "spirit" called Katie King (Corner, Corner, Luxmoore, Tapp, & Harrison, 1873), and D. D. Home (1833–1886), in whose presence sitters reported levitations of tables and of the medium, remarkable beautiful materializations of hands, and immunity to fire, among many other manifestations (Adare, 1869).

From the beginning of mediumship there were many attempts to explain the phenomena in conventional terms, that is, in terms of the closed model of the mind described above. Other than fraud, there were a variety of medical and psychophysiological explanations of mediumship (Alvarado & Zingrone, 2012; Crabtree, 1993; Le Maléfan, 1999; Owen, 1990). These included the view that some mediumistic phenomena represented examples of automatic activities of the nervous system (e.g., Faraday, 1853). Others argued that trances frequently were a disease of the nervous system "in which the cerebral activity is concentrated in some limited region of the brain, the activity of the rest of the brain being for the time suspended" (Beard, 1879, p. 67).

Many physicians wrote about mediumship, particularly mental mediumship, as manifestations of psychopathology. (On mediumship and pathology, see Alvarado & Zingrone, 2012; Le Maléfan, 1999; Moreira-Almeida, Almeida, & Lotufo Neto, 2005; and Owen, 1990.) These works included ideas of uterine pathology (Marvin, 1874). Pierre Janet (1859–1947) wrote that mediumship was related to "a particular morbid state analogous to those that may later become hysteria or insanity: mediumship is a symptom and not a cause" (Janet, 1889, p. 406).

The medical interpretation of mediumship was reinforced by evidence of personality changes that resembled spirit communications in contexts other than mediumship. These included spontaneous changes of personality (e.g., Elliotson, 1846), among them the famous Félida X case (Azam, 1887), as well as seeming secondary personalities that appeared during the hypnotic trance (e.g., Janet, 1889; Lang, 1843), or as the result of suggestion. This is what one researcher referred to as "objectification of types" (Richet, 1883).

The production of these dramas under hypnotic suggestion opened the door to later psychological speculations about mediumship, such as those assuming that some spirit communications were the "product of the medium's subconscious imagination, working from recollections and latent worries" (Flournoy, 1899, p. 144). This and later analyses of the mediumistic romances of a previous life in India and France and of life on Mars produced by the medium Hélène Smith (pseudonym of Catherine Elise Muller, 1861–1929; Flournoy, 1900) supported one of the main assumptions of the medical and psychological model: Mediumistic phenomena were produced by the internal mental resources of the medium, perhaps influenced by suggestion. This is what one writer referred to as the "enormous suggestibility and autosuggestibility of mediums" (Flournoy, 1900, p. 443).

However, there were others who argued that the subconscious mind had more than psychological and pathological functions in mediumship. These individuals proposed the concept of supernormal powers of the subconscious mind to explain mediumistic phenomena. Although ideas along these lines were present earlier during the 19th century (Alvarado, Nahm, & Sommers, 2012; Crabtree, 1993), my focus will be examples published between the late 19th century and the 1920s. I will start with the work of two important and influential pioneers, and will follow with the work of others to account for specific cases of mediumship. My summary of relevant ideas will be confined to a small number of students of the subject, and the reader should be aware that my discussion is not exhaustive.

The Influential Writings of Frederic W. H. Myers and Eduard Von Hartmann

An important early theoretician who influenced thinkers such as Pierre Janet and William James (1842–1910) was Frederic W. H. Myers (1843–1901). Myers—a classical scholar, psychologist and psychical researcher—conducted theoretical work about the subliminal (subconscious) mind and the supernormal in the context of the early SPR. In his view, "the stream of consciousness in which we habitually live is not the only consciousness which exists in connection with our organism. Our habitual or empirical consciousness may consist of a mere selection from a multitude of thoughts and sensations, of which some at least are equally conscious with those that we empirically know" (Myers, 1892a, p. 301). Myers assumed that a subliminal self-manifested in disintegrations of personality as well as in more positive phenomena such as creativity and mediumship. In addition, he believed that the mind was in charge of the body and independent of it, a view different from many of his contemporaries who followed physiological and pathological assumptions (Crabtree, 2003).

Myers argued that mediumship and other phenomena such as creativity and telepathy were expressions of the subliminal mind. This took place largely through sensory and motor automatisms (Myers, 1892b, 1893). Sensory automatisms included visions, voices, dreams, and intuitions, whereas motor automatisms included phenomena such as automatic writing and table turning as well as trance speaking. Both types of automatisms were, according to Myers, conveyors of messages. In his view, "the message which they bring comes from a stratum or phase of our own personality which is chaotic and fragmentary … a message conveyed by automatic action from the subconscious to the conscious or waking self …" (Myers, 1889, p. 535).

In an early paper Myers (1884) argued that many mediumistic communications could be explained without assuming any supernormal ability. For example, automatically produced scripts seemingly done without the conscious knowledge of the automatist could take place, Myers suggested, at will or through low- or high-level unconscious guidance from the automatist's mind. However, Myers also mentioned two other possible causes of these communications that do involve supernormal function: telepathy from the sitters and the influence of discarnate beings. Although he did not discuss the spirit hypothesis in any detail, Myers stated that a few cases suggested thought transference from the sitters attending the séance. This idea was further discussed in a later paper, where he suggested that during motor automatisms a secondary self had a "purposive activity of its own" (Myers, 1885, p. 27). Myers further wrote: "It is the *secondary* self ... which receives or recognises the telepathic impact ... and in some way or other furnishes an intelligent reply" (Myers, 1885, p. 28).

Later Myers discussed the action of spirits of the dead. He argued for "contact between the discarnate mind and the *brain* of the automatist ..." (Myers, 1903, p. 196). The spirit communicator, he believed, used the "capacities" of the medium's brain to communicate, an idea not new with Myers (cf. Kardec, 1863, p. 281). However, in Myers's view the communication process "must be limited by the idiosyncracies of the medium" (Myers, 1903, p. 249). Communications, he argued, generally presented a mix between influences from the medium's subliminal mind and a discarnate agency.

Another influential theoretician in Europe was German philosopher Eduard von Hartmann (1842–1906; see Treitel, 2004, pp. 13–15, 21–22; Wolffram 2009, pp. 41–43). In his view, a medium was a person capable of entering a somnambulistic state either spontaneously or through some induction procedure. Mediums showed "a certain disorganization of the nervous system; that is, the lower and the middle nerve centres are too independent of the highest, reflex-prohibiting centre of consciousness self control; they are, in other words, ... hysterical ..." (Von Hartmann, 1885, p. 406).

According to von Hartmann, mediums showed two types of somnambulism: manifest and masked. In manifest somnambulism mediums had no recollection of the phenomena they produced. The masked type implied that the waking consciousness during mediumistic phenomena had no awareness of the action of a secondary consciousness. Like others before him (for a review see Crabtree, 1993), von Hartmann believed that some of the automatic manifestations of mediumship, such as automatic writing, could take place without any guiding intelligence, being the action of nervous mechanisms without consciousness. But many other manifestations showed a "somnambulistic consciousness accompanying these mechanical material brain processes and enlightening them with real intelligence" (p. 420).

Von Hartmann explained the mediumistic tendency towards symbolization and personifications as the simultaneous action of waking consciousness and enhanced memory access, as well as thought transference and clairvoyance. All of this worked together with the "symbolizing and personifying tendency of the somnambulistic consciousness ... to put these communications in the mouth of an absent person, its dramatic metamorphosing talent must at the same time, succeed in dressing out the communication with all sorts of small external traits appropriate to the person represented" (p. 453).

Von Hartmann also argued that the somnambulistic consciousness could manage nervous forces that, when exteriorized from the body, could cause mediumistic physical phenomena. As he wrote:

> This liberation of directive radiation of nerve force is under all circumstances ... not a function of those parts of the brain which serve as support to the conscious will, but of deeper-lying layers of the brain which either coincide with those supporting the somnambulic consciousness, or are more approximate to them than to the first. It is therefore, no wonder that the development of a magnetic-mediumistic nerve force is stronger in the somnambulistic than in the waking state ... (p. 442).

These ideas are part of an old tradition of ideas of "magnetic," "nervous," or "psychic" forces related to the workings of the human body and considered to be the agent behind the physical phenomena of mediumship (Alvarado, 2006, 2008; Alvarado, Nahm, & Sommer, 2012; Crabtree, 1993).

Speculations on the Mediumship of Leonora E. Piper

In the mid–1880s psychologist and philosopher William James (1842–1910) had an experience with the American medium Leonora E. Piper (1857–1950) that led him to write that "taking everything that I know of Mrs. P. into account, the result is to make me feel as absolutely certain as I am of any personal fact in the world that she knows things in her trances which she cannot possibly have heard in her waking state, and that the definitive philosophy of her trances is yet to be found" (James, 1890b, pp. 658–659). Mrs. Piper was the first mental medium studied under controlled conditions for a prolonged period of time. Many researchers conducted studies with her during the late 19th century.

Mrs. Piper's trance phenomena passed through different stages over time, changing or adding spirit controls including the well-known "Dr. Phinuit" and the George Pelham (really called George Pellew) controls. She communicated through automatic writing and trance speaking. In trance speaking, Piper's spirit control relayed information from a supposed spirit, sometimes answering questions posed by séance participants. In addition, sometimes she seemed to be possessed by the communicating spirit. These performances convinced others besides James that she acquired information beyond the reach of the senses.

Following James, psychical researcher Richard Hodgson (1855–1905) conducted the first systematic investigations of Piper's trance phenomena (see Berger, 1988, pp. 11–33). The following was written by a sitter, Reverend and psychic investigator Minot J. Savage (1841–1918), as reported in Hodgson's (1892) first report showing personation and apparent veridical information. The doctor mentioned was "Dr. Phinuit," the medium's spirit control at that time:

> Immediately on becoming entranced, her control, Dr. Phinuit, said there were many spirit friends present. Among them he said was an old man, whom he described, but only in a general way. Then he said, "He is your father, and he calls you Judson." Attention was called to the fact that he had a peculiar bare spot on his head, and Mrs. Piper put her hand on the corresponding place on her own head ... My father had died during the preceding summer ... He wasn't at all bald, but when quite young had been burned; so that there was a bare spot on the right side of the top of his head, perhaps an inch wide and three inches long, running from the forehead back towards the crown ... This was the spot that Mrs. Piper indicated. Now as to the name by which he addressed me: I was given the middle name, Judson ... father always used, when I was a boy, to call me Judson, though all the rest of the family called me by my first name, Minot. (Hodgson, 1892, p. 100)

In his first report Hodgson (1892) stated his belief that Piper's trance was of the "type where the change to the trance personality involves a partial obliteration of the facts known to the normal waking self" (pp. 55–56). He did not believe that there was enough evidence to support the discarnate agency hypothesis, although he said at the end of the paper that further developments in the Piper mediumship were suggestive of this. Nonetheless, Hodgson concluded that the trances showed "a large residuum to be attributed to some supernormal faculty" (p. 9). Regarding his first six sittings with Piper, Hodgson thought that the medium "had access to portions of my 'subconscious' mind" (p. 10). Still, Hodgson did not think telepathy could explain all the veridical communications. As mentioned below, he later stated his belief in spirit communications.

Another early Piper researcher, classical scholar and banker Walter Leaf (1852–1927; see Anonymous, 1927), argued that in the medium's "abnormal state there is a quite exceptional power of reading the contents of the minds of sitters; but that this power is far from complete" (Leaf, 1890, p. 567). The thought transference process suggested by Leaf was one related to sitters's subconscious minds, that is, content not consciously recollected at the time of the séance. This gave the impression that a spirit was communicating. Others, such as American philosopher William R. Newbold (1865–1926; see Sidgwick, 1926), doubted that Piper's telepathy and clairvoyance could be organized by the medium's mind into a "mosaic of thought, which ... often irrestibly suggests the habits, tastes, and memories of some friend deceased ..." (Newbold, 1898, p. 9).

Frank Podmore (1855-1910; see Dingwall, 1963), an SPR member well–known for his skepticism regarding physical phenomena, was impressed by Piper. In an early statement Podmore (1897) said that the medium presented evidence of "something beyond telepathy" (p. 454). He did not clearly state his belief in the supernormal in a later article (Podmore, 1898), but in his book *Modern Spiritualism* expressed his conviction that Piper's trance utterances provided evidence of supernormal perception (Podmore, 1902b, p. 342). Trance personalities, he concluded, were "illustrations of the plastic powers of the medium's own spirit, rather than as representing alien intelligences" (p. 343). Podmore (1908) argued that it was clear that Piper's changes of personality were shaped in part by suggestion but those suggestions could be psychically conveyed, "telepathically filched" (p. 329) from the sitters (see also Podmore, 1910).

Educator and once principal of Newnham College Eleanor Sidgwick (1845–1936; see E. Sidgwick, 1938) authored an impressive psychological study of Mrs. Piper that also addressed telepathy. As she concluded regarding Mrs. Piper's trance:

> I think it is probably a state of self-induced hypnosis in which her hypnotic self personates different characters either consciously and deliberately, or unconsciously and believing herself to be the person she represents, and sometimes probably in a state of consciousness intermediate between the two. In the trance state her normal powers transcend in some directions those of her ordinary waking self ... And further—what makes her case of great importance—she can obtain, imperfectly and for the most part fragmentarily, telepathic impressions. (Sidgwick, 1915, p. 330)

More than this, Sidgwick argued that telepathy could provide the "material necessary to successful personation" (p. 319). This assumed that a dissociative process (the trance and the personation accompanying it) could incorporate telepathic information.

In Germany, philosopher Traugott Konstantin Oesterreich (1880–1949; see Melton, 2001, p. 1139) was skeptical of the spirit explanation of mediumship. He believed that the subconscious creative imagination of Mrs. Piper was active during her trance, a process "of daily occurrence in modern occultism by reason of traditions and beliefs which are passed on from one medium to another" (Oesterreich, 1923, p. 49). But in his view Piper's subconscious imaginative potential consisted of more.

Oesterreich suggested that Mrs. Piper's veridical communications involved "an elaboration by the creative imagination of Mrs. Piper's telepathically-acquired knowledge and by her telepathic faculty working in conjunction with the minds of others ..." (pp. 44–45). Echoing Leaf, he argued further that the medium's telepathy could tap into the latent thoughts of living people.

Others defended supernormal explanations that related to the spirits of the dead. In his second report on Piper, Hodgson (1898) became convinced that the supernormal content of Mrs. Piper's trances required spirit intervention. Some spirit communicators were more clear than others; Hodgson believed that this should not be the case if thought transference was in operation. In addition, confused communications suggested to Hodgson that they reflected the communicator's illness or other relevant conditions at the time of death. In Italy and in the United States, respectively, others defended the idea of spirit agency to explain Mrs. Piper's veridical trance phenomena (Bozzano, 1926; Hyslop, 1901).

William James, on the other hand, did not seem so sure of the final explanation of the phenomena produced by Mrs. Piper. Studying the Piper communications that allegedly came from the deceased Richard Hodgson, James (1909) was willing to consider their content supernormal. He wrote: "The active cause of the communications is on any hypothesis a will of some kind, be it the will of R. H.'s spirit, of lower supernatural intelligences, or of Mrs. Piper's subliminal ... yet the major part of it is suggestive of something quite different—as if a will were there, but a will to say something which the machinery fails to bring through" (p. 116). This "will," he suggested, could

> ... "tap," possibly the sitter's memories, possibly those of distant human beings, possibly some cosmic reservoir in which the memories of earth are stored, whether in the shape of "spirits" or not. If this were the only will concerned in the performance, the phenomenon would be humbug pure and simple, and the minds tapped telepathically in it would play an entirely passive role—that is, the telepathic data would be fished out by the personating will, not forced upon it by desires to communicate, acting externally to itself. (pp. 116–117)

James expressed the belief that there were traces of a will to communicate coming from Hodgson and that Mrs. Piper's telepathy was not enough to explain the results. But he was willing to speculate on the interactions of many factors. For example, James argued that there could be combinations of two different wills. One was a "will to personate," and another the will to communicate, the latter coming from a discarnate source (p. 117). Furthermore, he also speculated on the interaction of the sitter, the medium and the communicating spirit: "The sitter, with his desire to receive, forms, so to speak, a drainage-opening or sink; the medium, with her desire to personate, yields the nearest lying material to be drained off; while the spirit desiring to communicate is shown the way by the current set up, and swells the latter by its own contributions" (p. 120).

Speculations on the Mediumship of Eusapia Palladino

Eusapia Palladino (1854–1918), a well-known Italian physical medium, has been generally considered to have played an important role in the development of psychical research. Not only did her performances contribute to the development of ideas about mediumship, but she also was instrumental in convincing many researchers that phenomena such as telekinesis and materializations were real (Alvarado, 1993, 2011a; Carrington, 1909).

During a séance Palladino usually sat on one side of a table around which several sitters were posted. Behind her was a "cabinet" formed of a corner or area behind a curtain where objects were sometimes placed to be affected by telekinesis. The following is a typical example:

> The séance began in full light, and whilst the medium was still quite conscious, movements at first slight, then stronger, began in the séance table, which raised three of its feet. In full light the slight outward movements of the curtain on the left were observed. The medium asked by means of the table (five raps) that the light might be lessened; this was done rather slowly, and the strong red light ... fell directly on to the medium's eyes, which occasioned in her a fit of hysteria; she wept and cried out as if demented, hitting her face repeatedly with her fists. This was a genuine fit of hysteria ...

> When the attack was over, Eusapia was no longer in her normal state of consciousness, and no longer spoke in the first person; she spoke as if she were John King ... In the meanwhile, the table on which the toys had been placed, and which we call No. 1, made a noise in the interior of the cabinet, from which it at last came out completely. Then there began to arrive on the séance table many objects from table No. 1: a sheet of paper, a little wooden sheep and a mandoline; the latter was accompanied by the curtain which covered the handle; the curtain ... came back and covered the handle of the mandoline, and a hand, which was not that of the medium or of the sitters, pulled the hair of the person who had pushed back the curtain. At the same time we heard a scratching on the strings of the mandoline. (Aggazzotti, Foà, Foà, & Herlitzka, 1907, pp. 366–368)

Phenomena of this sort were frequently observed by Palladino's investigators, many of whom were convinced of the genuineness of the phenomena while recognizing the medium committed fraud frequently. Three of these researchers were Italian psychiatrist and criminologist Cesare Lombroso (1836–1909), Polish psychologist Julian Ochorowicz (1850–1917), and Italian psychiatrist Enrico Morselli (1852–1929; see Domanski, 2003, Guarnieri, 1988, Knepper & Ystehede, 2013).

In Lombroso's (1892) view, Palladino could produce telekinesis and other phenomena while entranced but she was also a hysteric that showed signs of epilepsy. In his view hysterics and hypnotized individuals had some nervous centers activated at the expense of others that were paralyzed or arrested. This allowed for a transposition and transmission of psychic forces, which in entranced mediums could be exteriorized from the body as a motor force to cause telekinesis and other physical phenomena.

In a later book, translated into English as *After Death—What?,* Lombroso (1909) classified Palladino's phenomena in relation to the medium's mental state. In his experience "the rarer and more important of the phenomena (for instance, apparitions of phantasms), so much the heavier is the trance of the medium" (p. 120). Eventually, Lombroso (1908, 1909) argued that some phenomena were produced by spirits who used the medium's vital force to accomplish such feats as the medium's levitation. In addition to Lombroso, other researchers argued that some of Palladino's phenomena, particularly full body materializations, could not be explained solely by the medium's vital force directed by her subconscious mind (e.g., Carrington, 1909; Venzano, 1907).

Ochorowicz (1896; see also Alvarado, 2010b) did not accept spirit intervention to account for Palladino's phenomena but did accept the force model. He divided the manifestations of mediums into inferior and superior ones using Palladino as an illustrative case. Inferior manifestations were those consisting solely of fraud and automatism; superior manifestations were those produced beyond the confines of the body. Most mediums used fraud frequently due to lax controls and the expectations of the circle. Fraud, according to Ochorowicz, "dominates their repertoire and the habits of their nervous systems" (p. 111).

In Ochorowicz's view, at the beginning of a séance it was important to give the medium time to go through phases of physiological "doubling" or dissociation that would eventually culminate in phenomena beyond conventional dissociation. This doubling referred to unspecified brain centers of automatic action, as well as to consciousness in relation to somnambulistic ideas and autosuggestion. But Ochorowicz was clear that it was possible for Palladino to exteriorize a force from her body to produce telekinesis and materializations and that the process could involve the forces of other sitters as well. This view was discussed in a later publication unrelated to Palladino. Ochorowicz discussed a new and revolutionary form of dissociation shown by mediums. This was a process that took place "between organs and the dynamic principle that animates them; which can go as far as extra-organic manifestations, that is ... out of the body" (Ochorowicz, 1909, p. 757).

Enrico Morselli, whose book *Psicologia e "Spiritismo*" (Morselli, 1908a, 1908) was almost completely dedicated to Palladino's mediumship, also contributed important ideas. Like so many before him, Morselli argued that mediumship was "an abnormal fact of human physio-psychic personality ..." (Morselli, 1908a, p. 95). But he became fully convinced that Palladino produced physical effects such as telekinesis and materializations. According to Morselli (1908a) the low intellectual content of these effects was indicative of psychological disaggregation (or separation of mental processes) because the medium's "inferior personality" (p. 219) manifested at a low intellectual level.

The séances he had with Palladino convinced Morselli that she could project a biopsychic force from her body, a force that could join with other forces coming from the other persons in the mediumistic circle (1908a, p. 350). This force could be imprinted with the "oniric or subconscious thought of the medium" (1908a, p. 243), which constituted the principle guiding telekinesis and shaping materializations. Morselli (1908b) believed that the subconscious thought and will of the medium directed the phenomena (p. 552). However, their uniformity and repetitive nature suggested to him that Palladino had "fixed ideas," or delusional dominant ideas affecting both actions and thought. These ideas probably helped the production of the phenomena by her subconscious mind and also suggested hysteria (1908a, p. 251).

Morselli (1908a) admitted that all these psychological considerations did not really explain the so-called biopsychic effects, that is, that an "unknown modality of energy ... is exteriorized and projected into space" (p. 266). In his view the "constitutional morbidity" of mediums and their trances was not enough to explain physical phenomena nor veridical perceptions (1908b, p. 543). While Morselli believed that the subconscious mind was the domain of abnormal states such as ecstasy, hallucinations and the hypnotic trance, he was unsure if it was involved with the actual exteriorization of force. Physical phenomena, he noticed, could occur in different states of consciousness, such as the waking state or superficial or profound hypnotic states (1908a, p. 268). During superficial hypnotic states "Eusapia ... says incoherent phrases, has muscular shudders, changes the tone of voice, has the fixed and glassy look of an hypnotized person ..." (1908a, p. 272). During profound hypnotic states—a somewhat less developed version of Charcot's lethargic stage of hysteria, visible materializations take place. The exteriorization of the force seemed to Morselli to be stronger the less the medium's consciousness participated in the process. This led him to hypothesize that the trance inhibited the superior centers, leaving the inferior ones to act automatically with the force. This automatic action, Morselli (1908a) considered, was an inferior form of mental activity related to the "narrowing" of consciousness from the conscious mind (p. 322).

Further Speculations on Mediumship

Former Attorney General of Bordeaux, France, and physician Joseph Maxwell (1858–1938; see Evrard, 2009a) was influential in European psychical research (Maxwell, 1903/1905). Like many other "metapsychists" of his times, Maxwell had séances with Palladino and became convinced of the validity of the whole range of mental and physical mediumistic effects.

One of Maxwell's contributions was his discussion of personifications, or the adoption of secondary personalities in mediumistic manifestations (Alvarado, 2011b). This included spirit controls, spirit communicators, and any manifestation that claimed to have a personality of its own. The phenomena,

Maxwell said, "may personify God, the devil, angels, legendary personages, fairies, etc." (Maxwell, 1903/1905, p. 64). These personifications could change with the composition of the mediumistic circle. On occasion, "sort of a collective consciousness is formed" (p. 65). Presumably coming from the sitters themselves, such a phenomenon "forms part of an … undeciphered chapter on the psychology of the crowds" (p. 65). According to Maxwell, this personification could appear with mediumistic communications as well as with physical phenomena such as raps indicating intelligence.

Maxwell saw in the mediums he studied an impressionability or nervous instability favorable for the phenomena. But Maxwell did not mean pathology such as that found in hysteria, neurasthenia, and other nervous affections.

Another important researcher and theoretician was Swiss psychologist Théodore Flournoy (1854–1920). Flournoy wrote about the combination of subliminal and telepathic resources:

> A medium personifies a dead person whom he has never known in a manner so admirable that it carries conviction to the sitters. They do not dream that perhaps one of them carries with him a group of memories which at the very moment that they are organized and flashed upward in the form of a composite portrait of the departed is telepathically reflected in the subconsciousness of the medium, as a living mirror, which immediately translates this image or imprint into words and gestures, portraying without a doubt a certain resemblance, but one in which the defunct has no share.
>
> *Combine*, now, the facts of mental transmission with the products to which memory and subconscious imagination of the sitters can give birth, and you will understand what unforeseen complications may always be expected in spiritistic séances. So extraordinary do the revelations appear that it is very difficult to exclude the possibility that they are due to a play of action and reaction between the medium and the other persons present … (Flournoy, 1911, pp. 212–213).

Flournoy argued that the phenomena of psychical research could be explained by the subconscious powers of the living human mind. These powers, he said, manifested in certain individuals and "under certain psychophysiological conditions (secondary states of consciousness, somnambulism, etc.)" (Flournoy, 1911, p. 323). Flournoy, always open minded, said that this did not mean discarnate agency was not possible, but he emphasized that "before daring to give a verdict in favor of the discarnate, much more must be known as to the foundation and groundwork of our own constitution, with all its resources and endless possibilities …" (Flournoy, 1911, p. 323).

The most scientifically eminent of the writers and researchers to be discussed in this section was the French physiologist Charles Richet (1850–1935). Richet (1883) experimented widely with hypnosis, and he witnessed and induced many changes in personality using suggestion.

Like other individuals discussed in this paper, Richet accepted both mental and physical mediumship as genuine beyond dissociative explanations. Nonetheless, he was not a believer in spiritualism. To the contrary, he was a well-known skeptic on the issue of survival of bodily death in general, and of the question of spirit agency in mediumship in particular, although it is sometimes argued that he changed his view later in life (e.g., Alvarado, 2009).

Richet argued that in mediumship "a new personality is created by auto-suggestion" (Richet, 1923, p. 41). To him, mediums' personifications, including spirit controls, could be explained by the workings of the unconscious mind. Referring to Piper, Richet wrote: "No doubt the personalities that present themselves … showed impressive traits of psychological individuality, and kept them distinctively in writing, voice, style, and thought" (p. 144; see also Richet, cited by Leaf, 1890, pp. 618–620). Many of these cases were seen by Richet to be an example of the "talents of the unconscious," considered to be more creative than the conscious mind (p. 44).

Going beyond typical dissociative phenomena, Richet argued that in some mental mediums "metapsychic cognitions group themselves around the personality created by auto-suggestion" (p. 77). This assumed first the existence of telepathy and clairvoyance (or cryptesthesia, as Richet called it) in normal individuals, shown to occur both in real life as well as under experimental conditions, and secondly, an organization of these cognitions into a personality structure.

Another European psychical researcher, the Italian biologist William Mackenzie (1877–1970; see Melton, 2001, p. 952), published an interesting treatment of this topic in *Metapsichica Moderna*. Like previous writers, Mackenzie (1923) was clear in stating that in mediumship, the dissociative process presented in some cases phenomena beyond current scientific explanations (p. 162). Dissociation sometimes included a supernormal quality whose nature had not been elucidated but that allowed some phenomena to manifest "outside of the somatic system of the subject" (p. 167). This quality or element may be active in normal individuals while awake, in dreams and through intuitions. It may "assume great importance in some hypnotic states and in somnambulism; finally, it may be of maximum importance during the deep *trance* of the completely developed medium" (p. 168).

Regarding table tipping, Mackenzie referred to the "formation of a polypsychic collectivity" (p. 183) formed by the sitters around the table. This psychic *quid* formed during a séance was not the simple addition of the subconscious of the medium and the sitters. Both were necessary to produce phenomena. "But the agent ... is a *product* (and not an addition ...) the polypsychic person'... (p. 286). This was not simply the addition of separate elements but a new collective, a new entity from the dissociated aspects of the medium and the sitters.

Like Ochorowicz before him, Mackenzie theorized that the medium showed two types of dissociation. One was mental dissociation while the other was a new form of dissociation, a dissociation of matter taking place as a "function of a concomitant dissociation of the psyche" (p. 200). This physical dissociation consisted of a molecular and atomic decomposition of the medium's body to create telekinetic and materialization phenomena.

Another psychical researcher who wrote about these ideas was the Frenchman René Sudre (1880–1968; see Evrard, 2009b), who was also known as a science writer. In his textbook *Introduction à la Métapsychique Humaine*, Sudre (1926a) wrote about "prosopopesis," or "brusk, spontaneous or provoked changes of psychological personality" (p. 85). This referred to the appearance of new personalities in mediumship, hypnotic states, possession cases, and in cases of double and multiple personality (see also Sudre, 1926b, 1946). The metapsychic type of prosopopesis was different from other types of dissociative personation phenomena in that sometimes it could be accompanied by phenomena such as "metagnomy" (clairvoyance) or materializations.

According to Sudre the association between metagnomy and prosopopesis made sense because both occurred during dissociation. Metagnomy, he thought, was common during trance and hypnosis, whereas prosopopesis was favored by the reduction and retraction of the waking consciousness. Although the combination of metagnomy and the dramatization of an external personality had convinced many that spirits of deceased individuals communicated through a medium, Sudre believed that metagnomy and prosopopesis, although perhaps sharing a common psychophysiological process, were different, independent functions.

As Sudre wrote, there are phenomena of prosopopesis "free of all supernormal element ... where the subject adopts the speech and manner of a person whom he knows or fancies and by whom he claims to be invaded" (Sudre, 1926b, p. 129), and metapsychic phenomena without personality changes. In his words:

> Between these two extremes come the spiritistic phenomena which proceed from an apparent synthesis of the two functions. But we can always separate them, as does the chemist when he decomposes water into oxygen and hydrogen. We thus show that the medium creates in himself a new personality which is like the character personated in proportion as his faculty of clairvoyance allowed him to get information. If experience did not demonstrate that the two functions exist independently, if there were only spiritistic phenomena, we should not be entitled to make this distinction. (Sudre, 1926b, p. 130)

Physical phenomena were also related to personation and to dissociation. Sudre argued that a force exteriorized from the body was guided by the medium's mind. In his words, "the subject's intelligence, both conscious and unconscious is related to one of the dissociated layers of his personality" (Sudre, 1926a, p. 290).

In addition to some of the above-mentioned individuals, many others accepted that some mediumistic phenomena could be explained by the supernormal powers of the living, while at the same time defending strongly the influence of discarnate spirits on mediumship (e.g., Bozzano, 1926; Delanne, 1902; Hyslop, 1901; Thomas, 1922).

Concluding Remarks

As argued before (Alvarado, 2002; Le Maléfan, 1999; Méheust, 1999b) ideas of the supernormal as regards dissociation and the subconscious were not integrated into the psychology and psychiatry of the times discussed in this paper. Although most medical men held a closed model of the mind (and of dissociation) in which the phenomena were explained mostly by internal resources and a few external influences such as suggestion, few accepted a more open model of mind, such as the one some psychical researchers upheld based on powers that extend sensory and motor capacities beyond the confines of the body. Nonetheless, and as seen in the writings of some such as James (1890a), these psychic or supernormal concepts were part of the same general interest in understanding the mind and its myriad of layers as the more accepted ideas of individuals such as Janet (1889). This situation has been documented by Ellenberger (1970) and by later historians (Crabtree, 1993; Gauld, 1992; Le Maléfan, 1999; Méheust, 1999b; Plas, 2000).

Interestingly, these ideas about the powers or capabilities of the subconscious mind were also connected in some cases to pathology. This was not only the case with those, like Janet (1889), who reduced everything to intrapsychic concepts, but also with those like Lombroso (1909) and Morselli (1908), who admitted the existence of the supernormal as a process related to pathologies such as hysteria. But most of the persons discussed here did not write about pathology.

The topic discussed here is also a reminder that the functions of the subconscious listed by Ellenberger and mentioned at the beginning of the article are incomplete without consideration of the psychical research perspective. In the period discussed here, psychical researchers considered that the functions of the subconscious went beyond memory, pathology, creativity, and imagination. In the case of mediumship, psychical researchers extended current ideas about dissociation (in this case trance and personation) by adding the supernormal to the equation.

We should keep in mind that for the period discussed here "supernormal" meant both the extended abilities of the living, such as telekinesis and telepathy, as well as discarnate agency. In other words, the trances of mediums such as Piper and Palladino were believed to facilitate both extraordinary human faculties and the workings of spirits. These ideas, I must add, were involved in controversy that I have not discussed in this paper. This included the anti-spiritualistic writings of some psychical researchers (Richet, 1923; Sudre, 1926a), the criticisms that believers in spirit action presented about ideas of secondary consciousness, dissociation, and telepathy (e.g., Delanne, 1902; Noel, 1885), and the writings of those skeptical of the supernormal in its totality (e.g., Janet, 1889; Jastrow, 1906).

It is my hope that the material discussed in this paper will remind current students of mediumship of aspects of a past forgotten by many. Furthermore, I hope that my writings and those of others will influence the general historiography of psychiatry and psychology, a trend clear in the work of a few writers (e.g., Crabtree, 1993; Plas, 2000). Currently most of this work refers to the "closed" model of the mind and of dissociation represented by Janet and others. But to limit historical analysis in this way produces an incomplete picture of the past, the details of which are ignored or dismissed by many historians as well as by psychiatrists and psychologists. Regardless of the many subjective aspects of the study of history, attempts to study ideas about the mind should seek to represent the past in its own terms, a history which most certainly includes ideas such as those discussed in this paper.

References

Adare, Viscount (1869). *Experiences in spiritualism with Mr. D. D. Home*. Thomas Scott.

Aggazzotti, A., Foà, C., Foà, P., & Herlitzka, A. (1907). The experiments of Prof. P. Foà, of the University of Turin, and three doctors, assistants of Professor Mosso, with Eusapia Paladino. *Annals of Psychical Science, 5*, 361–392.

Aksakof, A. (n. d., ca. 1906). *Animismo y espiritismo: Ensayo de un exámen crítico de los fenómenos medianímicos* (Vol. 1). Carbonell y Esteva. (Original work published 1890)

Alvarado, C. S. (1993). Gifted subjects' contributions to psychical research: The case of Eusapia Palladino. *Journal of the Society for Psychical Research, 59*, 269–292.

Alvarado, C. S. (2002). Dissociation in Britain during the late nineteenth century: The Society for Psychical Research, 1882–1900. *Journal of Trauma and Dissociation, 3*, 9–33.

Alvarado, C. S. (2006). Human radiations: Concepts of force in mesmerism, spiritualism and psychical research. *Journal of the Society for Psychical Research, 70*, 138–162.

Alvarado, C. S. (2008). Further notes on historical ideas of human radiations: III. The perispirit and mediumistic forces. *Psypioneer, 4*, 85–92.

Alvarado, C. S. (2009). [Review of the book *Charles Richet: O apóstolo da ciência e o espiritismo*, by S. Nunes Magalhães]. *Journal of the Society for Psychical Research, 73*, 120–124.

Alvarado, C. S. (2010a). Classic text No. 84: "Divisions of personality and spiritism" by Alfred Binet (1896). *History of Psychiatry, 21*, 487–500.

Alvarado, C. S. (2010b). Correspondence: Julian Ochorowicz on Eusapia Palladino, dissociation and mediumistic fraud. *Journal of the Society for Psychical Research, 74*, 57–60.

Alvarado, C. S. (2011a). Eusapia Palladino: An autobiographical essay. *Journal of Scientific Exploration, 25*, 77–101.

Alvarado, C. S. (2011b). On mediumistic personation phenomena [Letter to the editor]. *Journal of the Society for Psychical Research, 75*, 59–61.

Alvarado, C. S. (2012). Psychic phenomena and the mind-body problem: Historical notes on a neglected conceptual tradition. In A. Moreira-Almeida & F. S. Santos (Eds.), *Exploring frontiers of the mind-brain relationship* (pp. 35–51). Springer.

Alvarado, C. S., Nahm, M., & Sommer, A. (2012). Notes on early interpretations of mediumship. *Journal of Scientific Exploration, 26*, 855–865.

Alvarado, C. S., & Zingrone, N. L. (2012). Classic text No. 90: "The pathology and treatment of mediomania," by Frederic Rowland Marvin (1874). *History of Psychiatry, 23*, 229–244.

Anonymous. (1927). Obituary: Walter Leaf. *Journal of the Society for Psychical Research, 24*, 52–53.

Azam, [E. E.]. (1887). *Hypnotisme, double conscience et alteration de la personnalité.* Baillière.
Beard, G. M. (1879). The psychology of spiritism. *North American Review, 129*, 65–80.
Berger, A. S. (1988). *Lives and letters in American parapsychology: A biographical history, 1850–1987.* McFarland.
Biondi, M. (1988). *Tavoli e medium: Storia dello spiritismo in Italia.* Gremese.
Bozzano, E. (1926). *A propos de l'introduction à la métapsychique humaine: Réfutation du livre de René Sudre.* Jean Meyer.
Braude, A. (2001). *Radical spirits: Spiritualism and women's rights in nineteenth-century America* (2nd ed.). Indiana University Press.
Carrington, H. (1909). *Eusapia Palladino and her phenomena.* Dodge.
Corner, A., Corner, C., Luxmoore, J. C., Tapp, G. R., & Harrison, W. H. (1873, May 15). Photographing a spirit by the magnesium light. *The Spiritualist*, pp. 200–201.
Crabtree, A. (1993). *From Mesmer to Freud: Magnetic sleep and the roots of psychological healing.* Yale University Press.
Crabtree, A. (2003). "Automatism" and the emergence of dynamic psychiatry. *Journal of the History of the Behavioral Sciences, 39*, 51–70.
Delanne, G. (1902). *Recherches sur la médiumnité.* Librairie des Science Psychiques.
Dingwall, E. J. (1963). Introduction. In F. Podmore, *Mediums of the 19th century* (Vol. 1, pp. v–xxiv). University Books.
Domanski, C. W. (2003). Julian Ochorowicz (1850–1917) et son apport dans le développement de la psychologie du XIXe siècle. *Psychologie et Histoire, 4*, 101–114.
Edelman N. (1995). *Voyantes, guérisseuses et visionnaires en France 1785–1914.* Michel.
Edmonds, J. W., & Dexter, E. T. (1853). *Spiritualism* (Vol. 1). Partridge & Brittan.
Ellenberger, H. F. (1970). *The discovery of the unconscious: The history and evolution of dynamic psychiatry.* Basic Books.
Elliotson, J. (1846). Instances of double states of consciousness independent of mesmerism. *Zoist, 4*, 158–187.
Esdaile, J. (1852). *Natural and mesmeric clairvoyance, with the practical application of mesmerism in surgery and medicine.* Hippolyte Baillière.
Evrard, R. (2009a). Joseph Maxwell: Jurist, physician, psychist (1858–1938). *Psypioneer, 5*(1), 21–27.
Evrard, R. (2009b). René Sudre (1880–1968): The metapsychist's quill. *Journal of the Society for Psychical Research, 73*, 207–222.
Faraday, M. (1853). Experimental investigations of table-moving. *The Athenaeum, 1340*, 801–803.
Flournoy, T. (1899). Genèse de quelques prétendus messages spirites. *Revue Philosophique de la France et de l'Étranger, 47*, 144–158.
Flournoy, T. (1900). *From India to the planet Mars: A study of a case of somnambulism.* Harper.
Flournoy, T. (1911). *Spiritism and psychology.* Harper.
Galvan, J. (2010). *The sympathetic medium: Feminine channeling, the occult, and communication technology, 1859–1919.* Cornell University Press.
Gauld, A. (1968). *The founders of psychical research.* Routledge and Kegan Paul.
Gauld, A. (1992). *A history of hypnotism.* Cambridge University Press.
Guarnieri, P. (1988). Between soma and psyche: Morselli and psychiatry in late–nineteenth-century Italy. In W. F. Bynum, R. Porter, & M. Sheperd (Eds.), *The anatomy of madness: Essays in the history of psychiatry* (Vol. 3, pp. 102–124). Tavistock.
Gurney, E., Myers, F. W. H., & Podmore, F. (1886). *Phantasms of the living* (2 vols.) Trübner.
Guthrie, M. (1884). An account of some experiments in thought-transference. *Proceedings of the Society for Psychical Research, 2*, 24–42.
Hammond, C. (1866). *Thomas Paine's pilgrimage in the spirit world.* Partridge.
Hardinge, E. (n.d., ca. 1861). *"America and her destiny:" Inspirational discourse* (2nd ed.). De Witt.
Hare, R. (1855). *Experimental investigation of the spirit manifestations demonstrating the existence of spirits and their communion with mortals.* Partridge & Brittan.
Hodgson, R. (1892). A record of observations of certain phenomena of trance. *Proceedings of the Society for Psychical Research, 8*, 1–167.
Hodgson, R. (1898). A further record of observations of certain phenomena of trance. *Proceedings of the Society for Psychical Research, 13*, 284–582.

Hyslop, J. H. (1901). A further record of observations of certain trance phenomena. *Proceedings of the Society for Psychical Research, 16,* 1–649.
Inglis, B. (1992). *Natural and supernatural: A history of the paranormal from earliest times to 1914* (Rev. ed.). Prism.
James, W. (1890a). The hidden self. *Scribner's Magazine, 7,* 361–373.
James, W. (1890b). A record of observations of certain phenomena of trance (5). Part III. *Proceedings of the Society for Psychical Research, 6,* 651–659.
James, W. (1909). Report on Mrs. Piper's Hodgson-control. *Proceedings of the Society for Psychical Research, 23,* 2–121.
Janet, P. (1889). *L'automatisme psychologique: Essai de psychologie expérimentale sur les formes inférieures de l'activité humaine.* Alcan.
Jastrow, J. (1906). *The subconscious.* Houghton, Mifflin.
Kardec, A. (1857). *Le livre des esprits* [The book of spirits]. Dentu.
Kardec, A. (1863). *Spiritisme expérimental: Le livre des médiums ou guide des médiums et des évocateurs.* (6th ed.). Didier.
Knepper, P., & Ystehede, P. J. (Eds.). (2013). *The Cesare Lombroso handbook.* Routledge.
Lachapelle, S. (2011). *Investigating the supernatural: From spiritism and occultism to psychical research and metapsychics in France, 1853–1931.* Johns Hopkins University Press.
[Lang, W.]. (1843). *Mesmerism; its history, phenomena, and practice.* Fraser.
Leaf, W. (1890). A record of observations of certain phenomena of trance (3). Part II. *Proceedings of the Society for Psychical Research, 6,* 558–646.
Le Maléfan, P. (1999). *Folie et spiritisme: Histoire du discours psychopathologique sur la pratique du spiritisme, ses abords et ses avatars (1850–1950).* L'Hartmattan.
Le Maléfan, P. (2008). L'hallucination télépathique ou véridique dans la psychopathologie de la fin du XIXème siècle et du début du XXème siècle. *L'Evolution Psychiatrique, 73,* 15–40.
Lombroso, C. (1892). Le spiritisme et la psychiatrie: Explication psychiatrique de certains faits spirites. *Annales des Sciences Psychiques, 2,* 143–151.
Lombroso, C. (1908). Eusapia Paladino and spiritism. *Annals of Psychical Science, 7,* 167–180.
Lombroso, C. (1909). *After death—What? Spiritistic phenomena and their interpretation* (W. S. Kennedy, Trans.). Small, Maynard.
Luckhorst, R. (2002). *The invention of telepathy: 1870–1901.* Oxford University Press.
Mackenzie, W. (1923). *Metapsichica moderna: Fenomeni medianici e problemi del subcosciente.* Librerie di Scienze e Lettere.
Marvin, F. R. (1874). *The philosophy of spiritualism and the pathology and treatment of mediomania.* Butts.
Maxwell, J. (1905). *Metapsychical phenomena: Methods and observations* (L. I. Finch, Trans.). Duckworth. (Original work published 1903)
Méheust, B. (1999a). *Somnambulisme et médiumnité (1784–1930): Vol. 1: Le défi du magnétisme animal.* Institut Synthélabo pour de Progrès de la Connaissance.
Méheust, B. (1999b). *Somnambulisme et médiumnité (1784–1930): Vol. 2: Le choc des sciences psychiques.* Institut Synthélabo pour de Progrès de la Connaissance.
Melton, J. G. (Ed.). (2001). *Encyclopedia of occultism and parapsychology* (5th ed., Vol. 2). Gale.
Moore, R. L. (1977). *In search of white crows: Spiritualism, parapsychology, and American culture.* Oxford University Press.
Moreira-Almeida, A., Almeida, A. A. S., & Lotufo Neto, F. (2005). History of "spiritist madness" in Brazil. *History of Psychiatry, 16,* 5–25.
Morselli, E. (1908a). *Psicologia e "spiritismo:" Impressioni e note critiche sui fenomeni medianici di Eusapia Paladino* (Vol. 1.). Fratelli Bocca.
Morselli, E. (1908b). *Psicologia e "spiritismo:" Impressioni e note critiche sui fenomeni medianici di Eusapia Paladino* (Vol. 2). Fratelli Bocca.
Moses, W. S. [under pseudonym M.A. Oxon]. (1879). *Spirit-identity.* Harrison.
Myers, F. W. H. (1884). On a telepathic explanation of some so-called spiritualistic phenomena: Part I. *Proceedings of the Society for Psychical Research, 2,* 217–237.
Myers, F. W. H. (1885). Automatic writing—II. *Proceedings of the Society for Psychical Research, 3,* 1–63.

Myers, F. W. H. (1889). Automatic writing—IV—The daemon of Socrates. *Proceedings of the Society for Psychical Research, 5*, 522–547.
Myers, F. W. H. (1892a). The subliminal consciousness: Chapter I. General characteristics of subliminal messages. *Proceedings of the Society for Psychical Research, 7*, 298–327.
Myers, F. W. H. (1892b). The subliminal consciousness: Chapter V: Sensory automatism and induced hallucinations. *Proceedings of the Society for Psychical Research, 8*, 436–535.
Myers, F. W. H. (1893). The subliminal consciousness: Chapter VII: Motor automatism. *Proceedings of the Society for Psychical Research, 9*, 26–128.
Myers, F. W. H. (1903). *Human personality and its survival of bodily death* (Vol. 2). Longmans, Green.
Newbold, W. R. (1898). A further record of observations of certain phenomena of trance. Part II. A. *Proceedings of the Society for Psychical Research, 14*, 6–49.
Nijenhuis, E. R., & van der Hart, O. (2011). Dissociation in trauma: A new definition and comparison with previous formulations. *Journal of Trauma and Dissociation, 12*, 416–445.
Noel, R. (1885). Spiritism versus other theories (being an answer to Messrs. Von Hartmann, Myers, and Gurney). *Light, 5*, 514–516, 530–531, 543, 555–556, 568, 587–588, 599–600.
Ochorowicz, J. (1896). La question de la fraude dans les expériences avec Eusapia Paladino. *Annales des Sciences Psychiques, 6*, 79–123.
Ochorowicz, J. (1909). Hypnotisme et mesmérisme. In C. Richet (Ed.), *Dictionnaire de physiologie* (Vol. 8, pp. 709–778). Félix Alcan.
Oesterreich, T. K. (1923). *Occultism and modern science* (from the 2nd German ed.). McBride.
Owen, A. (1990). *The darkened room: Women, power, and spiritualism in late Victorian England.* University of Pennsylvania Press.
Owen, R. D. (1860). *Footfalls on the boundary of another world.* Trübner.
Plas, R. (2000). *Naissannce d'une science humaine: La psychologie: Les psychologues et le "merveilleux psychique."* Presses Universitaires de Rennes.
Podmore, F. (1897). *Studies in psychical research.* Putnam.
Podmore, F. (1898). Discussion of the trance phenomena of Mrs. Piper. I. *Proceedings of the Society for Psychical Research, 14*, 50-78.
Podmore, F. (1902a). *Modern spiritualism: A history and a criticism* (Vol. 1). Methuen.
Podmore, F. (1902b). *Modern spiritualism: A history and a criticism* (Vol. 2). Methuen.
Podmore, F. (1908). *The naturalisation of the supernatural.* Putnam.
Podmore, F. (1910). *The newer spiritualism.* Unwin.
Richet, C. (1883). La personnalité et la mémoire dans le somnambulisme. *Revue Philosophique de la France et de l'Étranger, 15*, 225–242.
Richet, C. (1923). *Thirty years of psychical research: Being a treatise on metapsychics* (S. De Brath, Trans.) Macmillan.
Shamdasani, S. (1994). Encountering Hélène: Théodore Flournoy and the genesis of subliminal psychology. In T. Flournoy, *From India to the planet Mars: A case of multiple personality with imaginary languages* (pp. xi–li). Princeton University Press.
Sharp, L. L. (2006). *Secular spirituality: Reincarnation and spiritism in nineteenth-century France*. Rowman & Littlefield.
Sidgwick, E. (1938). *Mrs. Henry Sidgwick: A memoir.* Sidgwick & Jackson.
Sidgwick, Mrs. H. [E. M.]. (1915). A contribution to the study of the psychology of Mrs. Piper's trance phenomena. *Proceedings of the Society for Psychical Research, 28*, 1–657.
Sidgwick, E. M. (1926). Obituary notice: Professor W. Romaine Newbold. *Journal of the Society for Psychical Research, 23*, 161–162.
Spicer, H. (1853). *Sights and sounds: The mystery of the day: Comprising an entire history of the American "spirit" manifestations.* Bosworth.
Spitzer, C., Barnow, S., Freyberger, H. J., & Grabe, H. J. (2006). Recent developments in the theory of dissociation. *World Psychiatry, 5*, 82–86.
Sudre, R. (1926a). *Introduction à la métapsychique humaine*. Payot.
Sudre, R. (1926b). The role of prosopopesis in psychical research. *Journal of the American Society for Psychical Research, 20*, 129–136.
Sudre, R. (1946). *Personnages d'au-delà.* Société des Editions de Noël.

Tappan, C. L.V. (1875). *Discourses through the mediumship of Mrs. Cora L. V. Tappan.* Burns.

Thomas, C. D. (1922). *Some new evidence for human survival.* Collins.

Treitel, C. (2004). *A science for the soul: Occultism and the genesis of the German modern.* John Hopkins University Press.

Venzano, J. (1907). A contribution to the study of materialisations. *Annals of Psychical Science*, *6*, 75–119, 157–195.

Von Hartmann, E. (1885). Spiritism. *Light*, *5*, 405–409, 417–421, 429–432, 441–443, 453–456, 466–470, 479–482, 491–494.

Wolffram, H. (2009). *The stepchildren of science: Psychical research and parapsychology in Germany, c. 1870–1939.* Rodopi.

The Concept of Survival of Bodily Death and the Development of Parapsychology*, †

Carlos S. Alvarado‡

Some historians of psychology and medicine have argued that concepts and movements considered today to be metaphysical or pseudoscientific had significant influences on later developments. An example in parapsychology is the concept of survival of bodily death. Ideas of survival have been instrumental in defining important moments of the history of parapsychology. Two such moments were the founding and early work of the Society for Psychical Research (SPR) and the development of the work of J. B. Rhine and his associates at Duke University. The concept of survival, embedded within the movement of Spiritualism, offered the SPR a set of phenomena to be investigated, including mediumship, hauntings, apparitions and other manifestations. Work on survival led J. B. and Louisa E. Rhine to Duke University and affected their later emphasis on the study of psi capacities of the living. It is also argued that survival was influential in the development of such non-spirit explanations of mediumship as psi-from-the-living and interferences from the medium's mind. The Spiritualist literature contains more discussions of these issues than is generally acknowledged. Parapsychology did not develop in spite of survival, but to some extent because of it.

Introduction

The issue of survival of bodily death has been one of the classic problems of psychical research. Such phenomena as hauntings, apparitions, deathbed visions, poltergeists, and mediumistic communications have kept this idea alive throughout the years. Survival-related phenomena, especially mediumship, have generated many positions.

Some examples are the opposing views of Charles Richet (1924) and Oliver J. Lodge (1924), and Italian psychical researcher Ernesto Bozzano's (n. d. a., 1926) criticism of René Sudre (1926). Cesar de Vesme provides us with a good characterization of these debates: "When an author publishes a book to maintain the spiritualistic hypothesis, another writer publishes another book to support the contrary thesis, and vice versa. The two doctrines remain in face of one another like two china dogs." (De Vesme, 1928/1931, Vol. 1, p. 283).

*Republished with permission from *Journal of the Society for Psychical Research, 67*, 65–95, 2003.

†This is a revised version of the Gwen Tate Lecture sponsored by the Society for Psychical Research, and presented in London on October 4, 2001.

‡The research for this work was possible thanks to the rich library resources of the Eileen J. Garrett Library of the Parapsychology Foundation. I wish to thank Lisette Coly for useful editorial suggestions.

While I was finishing writing this paper New York City was attacked by terrorists. I wish to dedicate the article to the memory of all the victims of the attack.

The debate over survival has continued to our era and it is not likely to be resolved soon.[1] However, the history of the interest in survival in psychical research can be more than the study of the controversies the idea has generated, and more than just an evaluation of the research conducted. In this paper I will discuss some aspects of the influence of the idea of survival of death on parapsychology. In discussing its importance, I will argue that the concept of survival (through Spiritualism) was a major force in shaping fundamental moments in the history of the field, and in shaping the research agenda. In addition, the survival question has contributed to the development of alternate psychological or parapsychological processes as explanations for survival-related phenomena.

Overarching Concepts in Science and in Psychical Research

The history of science has shown that scientific research is not guided solely by an abstract quest for truth, nor by the mere following-up of our empirical findings with further studies. One of the extra-scientific factors which affects the development of science is the influence of overarching concepts and ideas. These concepts influence the generation of hypotheses, the topics studied, and especially the way in which observations and experimental results have been interpreted. Materialistic and spiritualistic philosophy, for example, have affected science in different ways. Some examples of these are the "mechanical philosophy" of the seventeenth century and the *naturphilosophie* of the nineteenth. A myriad of such concepts as vitalism and evolution have been influential in the development of the natural and the behavioral sciences. One such overarching concept in parapsychology has been the concept of survival of bodily death, and more widely, the concept of transcendence of physical limitations.

There is no question that much of what we call psychical research and parapsychology has been inspired by the search for the transcendental. Catherine Crowe (1848) wrote about the "night-side of nature," by which she meant a spiritual world revealed to us through premonitions, clairvoyance, apparitions of the living and of the dead, poltergeists, and other phenomena. The publications of later researchers have clearly shown that the search for the transcendent, or a spiritual, or non-physical, aspect of humanity has inspired many to become involved in parapsychology. In fact, many of these authors argue that the findings of psychical research support the concept of the soul or of non-physical dimensions of human existence.

In his book, *The Unknown*, French astronomer Camille Flammarion (1900) presented many examples of apparitions and other phenomena. He wrote: "These phenomena prove, I think, that the soul exists, and that it is endowed with faculties at present unknown" (p. 485). Similar statements about the implications of psychical research may be found in Frederic W. H. Myers's *Human Personality and Its Survival of Bodily Death* (1903), in William McDougall's *Body and Mind* (1911), and in Ernesto Bozzano's *Discarnate Influence in Human Life* (n. d. b). In his book, The Reach of the Mind, J. B. Rhine (1947) argued that: "The psi researches show the natural human mind can escape physical boundaries under certain conditions ... Accordingly a distinct difference between mind and matter, a relative dualism, has been demonstrated by the psi experiments ..." (p. 205).

Some may consider these perspectives to be at best, metaphysical, and at worst, unscientific. But regardless of how they should be viewed, such considerations have had important roles to play in the development of scientific research on psychic phenomena in a variety of ways. While this may seem obvious to some, such approaches to the history of science have generated much controversy. In fact, I get the impression that many current parapsychologists seem to think that modern parapsychology represents successful attempts to overcome Spiritualism, the interest in survival and the like. I view the history of the field as complex and interactive, one in which parapsychology developed as a science not in spite of the survival question and Spiritualism, but to some extent because of these factors.

The Influence of Mystical and Occult Ideas on Science

Traditionally, the history of science has been conceptualized as the triumph of reason and rationality over old mystical and occult ideas. Nonetheless, the historiography of the scientific revolution and the seventeenth century has been changing during the last three decades or so. Some of the new historiography holds that Hermeticism, Neoplatonism, astrology, alchemy and other areas of the occult were influential in the development of modern science.

One of the first voices in the new historiography was Frances Yates (1972/ 1978), who argued in her book, *The Rosicrucian Enlightenment*, that "the Hermetic-Cabalistic tradition … in the background of Renaissance science … did not lose force with the coming of the scientific revolution, … it was still present in the background of the minds of figures formerly taken as fully representative of complete emergence from such influences" (p. 232). Although some have considered Yates's position an extreme one (e.g., Vickers, 1984a), such later historians as Allan Debus (1978) have argued that the old Hermetic ideas as well as Paracelsian concepts affected the development of the mechanical philosophy that evolved in the seventeenth century, which had traditionally been accounted for solely by physical, astronomical and biological observations and research (Westfall, 1977). Scholarly attention to the work of Isaac Newton also shows this mixture of traditions especially in relation to alchemy. Richard Westfall (1980) and Betty Jo Dobbs (1991) have argued that Newton's alchemical studies influenced the physics of his *Principia*. However, other historians have been strongly opposed to this view of the history of science. Brian Vickers (1984a), for example, has argued that there were two separate mentalities, a scientific one and an occult one. Vickers believes that old mystical ideas did not influence the development of science in any significant way. There are still other points of view, such as those that accept the influence of the occult on the development of science but postulate a low-level impact (see the anthology edited by Vickers, 1984b). In short, some argue that modern science developed when rationality and empirical observation won out against mystical and occult views of nature (pseudoscience for some), while others see that the mystical and the occult also contributed significantly to what was later called science.

An example of the positive role of so-called pseudoscience is the influence of phrenology on neurology. At one point, historians of neurology had no use for phrenology in their studies. But the early revisionist work of Ackerknecht (1958), and the later work of Young (1970), did much to contribute to the idea that phrenological concepts were important to the development of neurology in that phrenology continued to change the climate of thought and supported notions of localization of sensory and motor functions in the brain.

More relevant to our particular subject matter is the change seen in the historiography of psychiatry and of ideas of the subconscious mind as expounded by Ellenberger (1970) in his book, *The Discovery of the Unconscious*. Ellenberger postulated that spiritism and psychical research positively influenced the development of dynamic psychology and psychiatry in that such mediumistic phenomena as automatic writing (among other factors) provided the impetus for the development of ideas of the subconscious mind. The work of Alfred Binet (1892/1896), William James (1890b), Pierre Janet (1889), and Frederic W. H. Myers (1903), among many others, are examples of this. The more recent work of historians Adam Crabtree (1993), Alan Gauld (1992), Pascal Le Maléfan (1999), and Eugene Taylor (1996) has shown how Spiritualism and psychical research actively interacted with those other fields which studied the mind and human behavior in aspects such as the development of the notion of the subconscious mind. Both Gauld and Crabtree have shown that the mesmeric and spiritualistic literatures were influential in the construction of notions of the human mind. While Taylor argued that psychical research in the United States impacted on psychotherapy around the time of William James, Le Maléfan argued that during the middle part of the nineteenth century French psychiatric nosology in some instances mirrored the claims and phenomena of mediums. Although much more needs to be done to explore the contributions of psychical research to other areas, this work shows a clear-but still not dominant-trend in the history of psychology and psychiatry in which psychical research and Spiritualism are considered to be more than cultural aberrations.

Following this conceptual tradition I will argue—and I make no claim to be original in this assertion—that Spiritualism in general, and the concept of survival of bodily death in particular, have been a factor affecting the development of parapsychology in different ways.

The Influence of Spiritualism on Important Moments in the History of Parapsychology

This part of the paper is perhaps the most obvious and self-evident, particularly for those acquainted with the history of psychical research. The concept of survival was basic for the beginning and development of such key moments in the history of parapsychology as the early work of the Society for Psychical Research and the work of J. B. Rhine and his associates at Duke University.

The Society for Psychical Research

We should do well to keep in mind that Spiritualism was the end process of previous movements and beliefs. The concept of communication with the spirits of deceased persons as well as records of psychic phenomena of all sorts have considerable historical precedence. To find relevant antecedents one only has to study such historical works as J. E. de Mirville's *Pneumatologie: Des Esprits et de leurs Manifestations Fluidiques* (1854), William Howitt's *The History of the Supernatural* (1863), Frank Podmore's *Modern Spiritualism* (1902), Cesar de Vesme's *A History of Experimental Spiritualism* (1928/1931), and the work of other historians (Dingwall, 1930; Inglis, 1977; Paton, 1921). Clearly the phenomena of modern Spiritualism can be found in previous epochs and were strongly influenced by other movements such as mesmerism, among others. Be that as it may, it was Spiritualism, acting on its own and as a filter and conveyor of older beliefs and observations that dictated the agenda for psychical research.

Alan Gauld (1968) makes it clear that the early SPR researchers—such individuals as Frederic W. H. Myers and Henry Sidgwick—were motivated to study a variety of psychic phenomena by Spiritualism and its non-materialistic tenets. Their work represented an attempt to use systematic observation and experiment to determine if there was more to the universe than materialism dictated. As J. Fraser Nicol (1972) reminded us in his review of Gauld's book, some of the men who formed the council of the first SPR were spiritualists, among them William Stainton Moses, Edmund Dawson Rogers and Hensleigh Wedgwood.

The first volume of the *Proceedings of the Society for Psychical Research* presented the agenda of the Society in its now classic "Objects of the Society" (1882). Out of six committees established, the fourth and fifth—on apparitions and haunted houses, and on physical phenomena—were a direct outgrowth from the concerns of British spiritualists during the late nineteenth century.

By the time the SPR was founded in London in 1882, England had had a few decades of both physical and mental mediumship.[2] Mediumship was an important area of discussion in British circles. Books such as the Reverend Charles Maurice Davies's *Mystic London* (1875), a collection of memoirs of the occult in London, remind us of how confusing and incredible Spiritualistic practices looked to some observers in Britain. Davies (1875, p. 290) refers to D. D. Home's famous body elongations, and to such other phenomena as Mrs. Guppy's flights, the materializations of Katie King, and the trance lectures delivered by such well-known spiritualist orators as Mrs. Emma Hardinge Britten and Mrs. Cora L. V. Tappan. Georgiana Houghton (n. d.) recollected in her book, *Evenings at Home in Spiritual Séance*, how in 1859 she was told by her cousin that "there were some persons living near her by whose means the spirits of those we had lost could communicate with us who were still remaining upon earth" (p. 1). This started a lifelong commitment to Spiritualism and to the development of Miss Houghton's own mediumship. During the next years, England saw the performances of such mediums as Florence Cook, William Eglinton, Francis Ward Monck, William Stainton Moses, and a host of others, some of them quite disreputable.

The SPR did not ignore all this interest in mediumship, popularly said to be directed by discarnate entities. An analysis of the content of the *SPR Proceedings* by type of paper shows that, out of 204 papers published between 1882 and 1900, 23% were séance reports. However, this does not reflect the actual number of papers in which survival themes were included. These topics were discussed as well in the other categories, such as theoretical and literature review papers.

Although both Barrett (1886) and Crookes (1889) reported positive evidence for physical mediumship in the *SPR Proceedings*, overall, the evaluations of some of the SPR researchers were negative. Eleanor Sidgwick's (1886b) paper "Result of a Personal Investigation into the Physical Phenomena of Spiritualism," which discussed mediums Kate Jencken (Kate Fox), Annie Eva Fay, Catherine Elizabeth Wood, Annie Fairlamb, and Henry Slade, is an example of this. The paper focused on sittings which took place during the 1870s, before the founding of the SPR. Other negative evaluations of physical mediumship written by Mrs. Sidgwick were her discussion of medium William Eglinton (Sidgwick, 1886a) and of the phenomenon of spirit photography (Sidgwick, 1891).

Mental mediumship was discussed somewhat later, as can be seen in papers about the mediumship of Mrs. Leonora E. Piper published by Richard Hodgson (1892), Walter Leaf (1890), Oliver Lodge (1890), and Frederic W. H. Myers (1890) in the Society's *Proceedings*. This work was essential for the development of all kinds of theoretical issues (although we will see later that, before the SPR was founded, spiritualists discussed these issues in their writings). The SPR work with Piper started to study the possibility of spirit communications, became the first *systematic* attempt to study mediumistic communications under some conditions of control. It was also the first *detailed* analyses of the trance personalities published in the psychical research literature. William James (1886, 1890a) conducted some preliminary work, but his efforts could not compare with the SPR's in terms of organization or detail.

The SPR workers asked such questions as: What was the source of the veridical information that came through Mrs. Piper? Were Mrs. Piper's controls spirits or secondary personalities of the entranced medium? As SPR member Walter Leaf commented on Phinuit, one of Mrs. Piper's controls

> That Dr. Phinuit is only a name for Mrs. Piper's secondary personality, assuming the name and acting the part with the aptitude and consistency which is shown by secondary personalities in other known cases; that in this abnormal state there is a quite exceptional power of reading the contents of the minds of sitters; but that this power is far from complete. … (Leaf, 1890, p. 567)

Many others commented on the consistency of the communicator, studies which give us pioneering insights into the dynamics of mediumship. Oliver Lodge wrote in 1890 that:

> The messages and communications … are usually given through Phinuit as a reporter. And he reports sometimes in the third person, sometimes in the first. Occasionally, but very seldom, Phinuit seems to give up his place altogether to the other personality, friend or relative, who then communicates with something of his old manner and individuality; becoming often impressive and realistic. (Lodge, 1890, p. 453)

In addition, many instances of automatic writing and talking led Frederic W. H. Myers (1884, 1885, 1887, 1889a) to begin his exploration of the subliminal mind and to argue that such mediumistic phenomena could be explained without recourse to the notion of discarnate agency. The title of his 1884 paper, "On a Telepathic Explanation of some so-called Spiritualistic Phenomena", represents an early statement of his ideas. While Myers was not unique in his appeal to unconscious processes as an explanation of such phenomena as mediumistic automatism (e.g., Carpenter, 1877; Von Hartmann, 1885) his concepts had a depth and effectiveness of argument that those of his predecessors did not have. Myers (1903) eventually developed a model that was certainly different from the more mechanical conceptions put forth by the unconscious cerebration theorists. He, in fact, came to argue for the supremacy and independence of the mind in relation to the body. In addition, he conducted unprecedented, careful and detailed analyses of material provided to him by Spiritualists. His analysis of the Reverend P. H. Newnham's wife's automatic scripts (Myers, 1885) is an example of this.[3]

Regarding apparitions and hauntings, one has only to turn to the pages of Catherine Crowe's The *Night-Side of Nature* (1848), William H. Harrison's *Spirits Before Our Eyes* (1879), and Robert Dale Owen's *Footfalls on the Boundary of Another World* (1860) to find a variety of ghost stories that were known to the early SPR pioneers. One still remembers with appreciation the reports by the SPR committee on haunted houses (Barrett et al., 1882; Bushell et al., 1884). This committee recorded many fascinating cases that were influential in later thinking about the subject (e.g., Bozzano, 1919/1925). For example, in the second report of the committee the vicar of a parish house stated that he and his wife heard a sound "like the crash of iron bars falling suddenly to the ground" (Bushell et al., 1884, p. 145). This was the most dramatic of several auditory manifestations. The sound was heard collectively and by visitors who did not know about the haunting. In addition, the sound showed periodicity. It was heard only on Sunday morning at 2:00 am.

Over the years, interest in hauntings and apparitions of the dead continued. R. C. Morton's (R. Despard) classic "Record of a Haunted House" (Morton, 1892) and Eleanor Sidgwick's (1885) earlier paper "Notes on the Evidence, Collected by the Society, for Phantasms of the Dead," are clear examples of this. Mrs. Sidgwick said that the SPR had collected about 370 narratives "of phenomena, not clearly physical, and which believers in ghosts would be apt to refer to the agency of deceased human beings" (p. 70). She outlined several possible explanations for these cases while pointing out that she could not fully accept nor completely reject any particular one. Among these were ideas of spirit influence, such as a physical presence or a telepathic hallucination caused by deceased individuals. Other ideas included telepathic communication between living individuals, and the idea of physical influences on the house perceived by the experimenters. The latter concept came to be known later as the psychometric theory of hauntings, and was discussed many years later in the pages of the *SPR Proceedings* by H. H. Price (1939; see also Bozzano, 1919/1925).

Later publications about apparitions of the dead included fascinating theoretical papers that charted future discussions of apparitions of the dead. The SPR pioneers essentially took the idea of survival that was apparently expressed by these apparitional phenomena and analyzed the problem from the point of view of a variety of possible explanations. Myers's (1889b) paper "On Recognised Apparitions Occurring More than a Year After Death," is one example. In this paper, Myers conceptualized these manifestations in terms of supposed gradations of post-mortem activity and the activity of living spirits. He wrote:

> In the first place, I believe that telepathy ... exists both as between embodied spirits and as between embodied and disembodied spirits. I hold that there is a continuous series of manifestations of such power, beginning with thought-transference experiments and hypnotism at a distance, proceeding through experimental apparitions and apparitions coincident with crisis or death, and ending with apparitions after death;—the results, in my view, of the continued exercises of the same energy by the spirits of the departed. ... (Myers, 1889b, pp. 63–64)

Frank Podmore (1889) proposed a different model in a paper entitled "Phantasms of the Dead from Another Point of View." Following up on one of Mrs. Sidgwick's initial ideas, Podmore argued that evidential cases of apparitions of the dead were telepathic hallucinations. The actual explanation could be found, he wrote, "in the prolonged latency and subsequent emergence of an impression received from the dead man himself before his death; or in telepathy from the minds of other persons still living ..." (Podmore, 1889, p. 308).

This interest in hauntings and apparitions of the dead within the SPR was paralleled by an interest in hallucinations, especially hallucinations of the living. The work of the Literary Committee was certainly influenced by accounts of spontaneous ESP and apparitions of the living from such spiritualistic sources as the above-mentioned books by Crowe, Harrison, and Owen. The third report of the Literary Committee stated

> *Apparitions* ... are an element in nearly every religion known among men; and the discussion of their reality has been a perpetual feature in religious controversy. But the apparitions who have been most associated with religious ideas have been those of the *dead*, and we shall do our best to avoid controversial ground, and also keep our subject within manageable limits, by altogether excluding this class. Let us take only the alleged apparitions of living persons, the commonest of which are death-wraiths, or apparitions of persons near the moment of death. (Barrett et al., 1884a, p. 111)

The early telepathic model of hallucinations, now classically associated to the early SPR work, was discussed in two papers produced by the Literary Committee in 1884 (Barrett et al., 1884a, 1884b). Eventually, these efforts led to the first SPR survey of hallucinations and to studies of the varieties of features of these apparitions of the living, Gurney, Myers and Podmore's *Phantasms of the Living* (1886). As is well known, this interest culminated in the famous "Census of Hallucinations" (Sidgwick et al., 1894). One of the purposes of the 'Census' was to scientifically establish a relationship between a hallucination and the death of the person represented by the hallucination. The notion of survival was the original impetus behind all this work, even if eventually the SPR researchers developed different explanatory models such as that of telepathic hallucinations.

While it may be argued that what I have just discussed is well known, and that such an effect of ideas of survival and of Spiritualism is obvious, we should remember that the sense of what is obvious is often an afterthought. Psychical research would have been very different if it had been affected by movements other than Spiritualism. If mesmerism had had more influence than it had (and it had considerable influence), perhaps the SPR would have paid more attention to the idea of animal magnetism and to similar concepts of force, which might have resulted in an emphasis on the measurement, detection and use of such forces. There were some studies of mesmeric action conducted by the Committee on Mesmerism (Barrett, Gurney, et al., 1883) and by Gurney (1884), but they were not continued beyond the first three years of the SPR's existence. A more mesmerism-based approach might have included more interest in and research on Reichenbach's (1849/1851) Od, which Reichenbach believed was a universal force. Od was perceived by sensitive individuals primarily as lights emanating from crystals, minerals, magnets, and the human body. The SPR abandoned this research topic soon after the founding of the Society (Barrett, Close, et al., 1883). In addition, an animal-magnetism based psychical research might have had more interest in healing, which was generally assumed to involve some form of subtle energy transfer.

If Christianity had been more influential on nineteenth-century SPR work, psychical research might then have had more emphasis on such miracles as healings in shrines (e.g., Myers and Myers, 1893) and Marian apparitions (e.g., Marillier, 1891). Similarly, the work of the SPR would have been different if Theosophy had been more influential than Spiritualism. Instead of mediums and the study of the purported agency of discarnate human beings, the field might have paid more attention to the so-called powers of adepts or spiritual masters and to the study of effects produced by 'non-human spiritual beings' (e.g., Hodgson, 1885).

J. B. Rhine and Associates

Another moment in its history, generally recognized to be crucial for parapsychology, comprised the studies Joseph Banks Rhine and his colleagues conducted at Duke University. Rhine—and his colleague and wife Louisa E. Rhine—was deeply influenced by the idea of survival and the movement of Spiritualism, even if he later came to suggest that parapsychology could not deal with the concept scientifically in any meaningful way (e.g., J. B. Rhine, 1974).[4]

In his book, *New Frontiers of the Mind*, Rhine (1937) recounted how he heard a lecture by Arthur Conan Doyle about Spiritualism in the early 1920s. Although he was not convinced of the tenets of Spiritualism, Rhine was impressed by Doyle's zeal and positive attitude. Rhine wrote, "if there was a measure of truth in what he believed … it would be of transcendental importance" (p. 54).

In 1926, the Rhines had important experiences with mediums. One was a séance with physical medium Margery, who claimed that her dead brother Walter could produce materializations and other phenomena through her. This single séance convinced the Rhines that the performances were fraudulent (Rhine & Rhine, 1927).[5] The same year psychical researcher Walter Franklin Prince offered to pay the Rhines if they would sit with mental medium Minnie Soule (L. E. Rhine, 1982, pp. 104–105), known in the previous literature as Mrs. Chenoweth.[6] Dennis Brian (1982, p.53), in his biography of Rhine, *The Enchanted Voyager*, noted that in these sittings, J. B. Rhine and Louisa had different tasks. While Louisa took verbatim notes in a separate room, J. B. Rhine was in the room with Mrs. Soule, questioning the medium. The results, Louisa recorded in her diary, were disappointing (L. E. Rhine, 1982, p. 105).

In 1927, John F. Thomas, an officer at Detroit's public school system, approached Rhine to see if he would work with him on mediumistic communication records (L. E. Rhine, 1982, pp. 111–113). Thomas was having séances with Soule and other mediums attempting to communicate with his deceased wife.[7] Rhine accepted and Thomas asked him later the same year if he and his wife would go to Duke University to work with William McDougall on his mediumistic records. McDougall was then the head of Duke's psychology department. Eventually the Rhines arrived at Duke, where they were welcomed by McDougall. Their first work at Duke was centered on the Thomas material and only later did they branch out into ESP research.

The Rhines went with Thomas to continue to assist in the evaluation of mediumistic sittings with Mrs. Soule, as well as with such other mental mediums as Eileen J. Garrett and Gladys Osborne Leonard. Thomas eventually obtained a doctoral degree in psychology from Duke University for his study of mediumistic communications. In his books *Case Studies Bearing Upon Survival* (Thomas, 1929) and *Beyond Normal Cognition* (Thomas, 1937), Thomas mentioned that both J. B. and Louisa Rhine helped him in various ways.

The effect of this early mediumship work was to give the Rhines first-hand appreciation of what so many other psychical researchers before them had realized, the difficulties involved in determining the source of the information produced. In a letter he wrote to Prince on November 23, 1927, J. B. Rhine said: "We are just now organizing our thoughts on the question of what we require for proof of the supernormal, how many reasonable hypotheses there seem to be for supernormal production of information, and how we may discover then which of these is the correct one ..." (cited in Brian, 1982, p. 68).

However, later on Rhine was more positive about survival. On March 21, 1929, in a letter to Prince about Thomas's mediumistic records, Rhine said: "We have a very real appreciation for Mr. T. himself, and have been convinced that his material is in part at least, genuinely evidential, that of the hypotheses available to our knowledge certainly the spirit interpretation is the most acceptable" (cited in Mauskopf & McVaugh, 1980, p. 328).

This positive attitude towards survival and its study was also reflected in an idea Rhine developed around 1928 to 1929. This was the establishment of an 'Institute for Experimental Religion' (Mauskopf & McVaugh, 1980, p. 87). Part of the work to be conducted at this Institute was the study of evidence for the existence of the soul, including reports of such phenomena as apparitions suggestive of survival. A few years later, in a 1933 paper published in the *Journal of the Society for Psychical Research* in which he commented on an article about survival written by H. F. Saltmarsh (1932), Rhine (1933a) argued that survival studies should focus on evidence of purpose or motivation. In his words:

> The types of evidence to which I refer as offering superior proof-value to the survival theory are those which clearly show purposes that are appropriate only to one individual, the supposed spirit identified. The point in mind is that peculiar motivation is more identificative of the 'agency' involved than are data from the past life of the individual concerned, facts describing his personality, or physical manifestations claimed to be due to his efforts. ... (p. 36)

Of course this was nothing new. The point of purpose and intention had been argued before by such researchers as Hyslop (1919) and Myers (1903), to name only two prominent examples. While Rhine was not offering anything new, nor any solution to differentiate spirit and psi from the living sources, the paper shows his willingness to consider survival as late as 1933. In fact, it is interesting to notice that in a further communication published later in the same year in the *SPR Journal*, Rhine referred to survival as a question "among the most important we have to discuss in this field" (Rhine, 1933b, p. 125).

While Rhine continued to be interested in survival throughout his life (e.g., Rhine, 1943, 1956, 1960, 1974), when he published his now classic monograph, *Extra-Sensory Perception*, in 1934 he clearly had decided that the survival issue needed to be shelved. Rhine discussed survival in the first chapter of his book. He started classifying the types of parapsychological phenomena. Parapsychical phenomena included ESP in general, including dowsing, psychometry and veridical spirit communications. Such physical phenomena as telekinesis, lights, temperature changes and apports, he designated as parapsycho-physical. The parapsycho-physiological category included materializations, elongation, and stigmatization. Negative possession and healing were considered to be part of parapsycho-pathological phenomena. Finally, parapsycho–literary phenomena included the production of writing or art apparently beyond the means of the individual.

This classification interacted with agency. Corporeal agency was meant to refer to effects from the living and incorporeal agency referred to effects from discarnate spirits. Rhine wrote:

> There seem to be four general cases possible on this principle: one corporeal agent may influence another, as in telepathy, or the one corporeal may be the only personality concerned, as in clairvoyance. The incorporeal agent … may influence a corporeal one, as in the so-called 'mediumistic' experiences. Or, fourth, the incorporeal personality may seem to produce phenomena without the aid of a corporeal one with parapsychological capacities, and in the seeming 'invasions' called 'hauntings.' (J. B. Rhine, 1934a, pp. 8–9)

Rhine stated that his book dealt only with ESP effects by the living produced by two individuals (telepathy tests with a sender) and one individual (clairvoyance tests with no sender). He was unsure about how to classify effects in this system, especially in regard to incorporeal agency. Later in the book Rhine argued that the task at hand was twofold. First, to learn about telepathy and clairvoyance through attempts to relate each phenomenon to the other and to other parapsychological phenomena such as dowsing. Second, to find out more about other variables related to their functioning. Once these tasks were completed the incorporeal phenomena could be explored in more detail following a similar procedure (J. B. Rhine, 1934a, p. 147; see also Rhine, 1934b). But this later step in Rhine's research program, the shifting to a focus on incorporeal agency, never took place—perhaps because the corporeal area proved to be more difficult to explore and map than expected. As Rhine wrote later, the question of survival had to wait for a better understanding of the psi abilities of the living: "For one thing, it is necessary to know the limits and conditions of the operation of the psi process before we can design adequate experiments dealing with the survival hypothesis. It is only when we have evidence of something beyond the range of explanation by ESP and PK that a case for survival begins" (J. B. Rhine, 1947, p. 214).

Unfortunately for proponents of survival, Rhine (1974) ended up arguing that survival was untestable. Nonetheless survival was an important motivator of his early work and a reminder of how certain ideas or movements have had important, but unexpected, effects on the historical development of parapsychology.

Finally, there is another way in which Rhine was affected by Spiritualism. This was his belief that psychic phenomena in general could show us evidence for a non-physical aspect in human beings, that is, for the independence of mind from the body. Rhine discussed these views in his books, *The Reach of the Mind* (1947) and *New World of the Mind* (1953), among other publications.

These ideas did not come only from the results of his experiments, as Rhine (1947) himself argued. Rhine was interested in religion early in his life and planned to be a minister, and thus was led, early on, to beliefs in the nonphysical. Rhine's ideas on this topic can be found in Louisa Rhine's (1982) autobiographical account of her life with J.B., *Something Hidden*. But Rhine was also influenced by the implications of Spiritualism and its phenomena. Being aware of the writings and ideas of such spiritualists as Arthur Conan Doyle, both he and Louisa knew that spiritualists believed that human beings were more than their bodies, that there was a component of human beings that did not depend on physical limitations. As far back as 1865 British spiritualist Benjamin Coleman stated: "Let it be at once recognized that spirit is a living entity when separated from the fleshly body, having a dynamic power over matter, and the great difficulty which enshrouds the materialistic mind vanishes" (Coleman, 1865, p. 128). Similarly, T. P. Barkas (1876) argued from the pages of the *Spiritualist Newspaper*: "If these phenomena be true they suggest very important reflections. Mind is not a mere property of ordinarily organised molecular matter, secreted by the brain … but is independent of any ordinary physical brain …" (p. 261). As mentioned in the introduction, later writers such as Bozzano (n. d.b), Flammarion (1900), and Myers (1903) all argued along similar lines.

Rhine was familiar with some of this literature. In a letter he wrote to the President of the American Society for Psychical Research in 1923 he stated: "Having read Myers' *Human Personality* and some other books of the kind, I have been deeply impressed with the importance of the subject to the human race" (L.E. Rhine, 1982, p. 92). The Rhines were aware of a clear conceptual tradition that certainly gave them hope to find answers about the nature of human beings, and non-physicality. The latter idea was in fact the main tenet of Rhine's ideas about the nature of psi (Beloff, 1982; Iannuzzo, 1983).

Spiritualism and the Complexity of Psychic Phenomena

Survival has influenced psychical research in other, more subtle, ways. One of these is the contribution of spiritualists to our understanding of mediumistic and other phenomena. We sometimes think that spiritualists had simplistic, unitary views about the nature of psychic phenomena. Bruno Fantoni (1974), in *Magia y Parapsicología*, his history of magic and parapsychology, wrote:

> At the beginning spiritists argued that all paranormal phenomena were produced by discarnate beings … With time, they started to admit the possibility of a collaboration between the spirit from the beyond and the medium … Finally, they were forced to admit the existence of paranormal phenomena without the intervention of the dead and that even in those phenomena that supposedly originated in the beyond there may be elements coming from the unconscious of the living. (pp. 319–320, my translation)

While Fantoni's view may represent many individuals, I believe that a study of the primary literature supports a modified view of this process. That is, the writings of some spiritualists show an awareness of theoretical explanations of survival phenomena other than discarnate agency. Indeed, the spiritualist literature contains a rich intellectual discussion of the different possibilities. The history of psychical research sometimes has been written as the history of the triumph of science over the trappings of Spiritualism, but there is room to argue that, from the beginning, Spiritualism was providing us with a variety of alternative explanations for the phenomena in question. More importantly, Spiritualism provided the context for the development of many ideas that actively shaped psychical research conceptually. One of them was psi-from-the-living ideas as an explanation of mediumship.

Psi-from-the-Living Ideas to Explain Mediumship

In her *Journal of Parapsychology* paper "Parapsychology, Then and Now," Louisa E. Rhine (1967) suggested that explanations through ESP from the living were only available or were only realistic after experimental work that started in the 1920s. Rhine gave particular attention to later ESP work at Duke University. In her view: "It was not lack of method that brought to an end the era of mediumistic research on the survival question. It was the establishment of ESP that did it" (p. 238). L. E. Rhine goes as far as to say that those interested and positive about survival in the 1920s "could not then realize that an alternative explanation existed" (p. 248). In this view ESP was not established well enough in the old days to be an effective counter-explanation for the content of veridical mediumistic communications. There is some truth in this in that later experimental ESP work provided more evidence for the existence of this phenomenon and additional information about its workings. But Louisa Rhine exaggerated, especially when she said that no alternative explanations were thought to exist. Rhine did not take into account the fact that from the beginning of Spiritualism and of psychical research there was a long tradition of using ESP explanations to account for mediumistic communications. The fact that the evidence for ESP became better later is not the issue here. What is important in historical terms is that observers of mediums were convinced of the validity of these ESP explanations, a process that was a reality for them. I am arguing here that the early spiritualist literature provides examples of psi-from-the-living explanations, clearly showing that these ideas originated from spiritualists themselves, and in some cases from non-spiritualists who believed in survival.

In his book, *An Exposition of Views Respecting the Modern Spirit Manifestations*, Adin Ballou (1853) wrote: "I believe that departed spirits cause many of these phenomena, but not all of them. I believe that spirits in the flesh,—i.e., the mind of the medium, or the mind of the persons surrounding the medium—sometimes thwart, warp, peculiarize, or modify the manifestations and communications made" (p. 3). For Ballou it was clear that the minds of individuals around the medium could influence the content of the communications, a process he referred to as "mesmeric and psychological influences, from controlling minds near (the medium)" (p. 29).

These ideas were not unique to Ballou. They can also be seen in Andrew Jackson Davis (1853). In his book, *The Present Age and Inner Life,* Davis wrote that "owing to the extraordinary attributes of man's mind, many experiences are by some individuals regarded as spiritually originated; which in truth, are only caused by the natural laws of our being ..." (pp. 160–161). Davis presented a table in his book which listed the possible causes of mediumistic phenomena. In his view 40% were due to "departed spirits." The rest included fraud, neurological, or hysterical explanations, "nervo-psychology" or imaginationists, and "cerebro-sympathy" or epidemic diseases. Eighteen percent referred to what we would call the psychic abilities of the living. This included "vital electricity" coming from the body of mediums, and clairvoyance. While these figures, as most of Davis' writings, were obtained through clairvoyant inspiration, the important point here is that a leader of the early American spiritualist movement offered alternative explanations of mediumship other than spiritual-based ones.

Davis argued that one of the main causes of apparent contradictions in mediumistic communications—meaning confusions and apparent errors—was the simultaneous reception of impressions from two different sources: spirits and the minds of living persons. He wrote: "A medium may obtain thoughts from a person sitting in the circle, or from a mind even in some distant portion of this globe ... , and still be wholly *deceived* as to the source of them" (p. 202).

In later years, Henry J. Atkinson (1871, p. 535), in a paper entitled "Science and Spiritualism", argued that it was important to be clear about the agency behind the phenomenon. That is, was it the action of spirits of the dead or spirits of the living? A later author discussed the problems involved in establishing spirit identity. He said: "The difficulties in respect to spirit identity are very various; as for instance, in the double, or Spirit-issues from the living person; from clairvoyance and thought-transference, or knowledge or memory transference ..." (Atkinson, 1882, p. 249).

English spiritualist William Harrison argued that the thoughts of sitters could affect the content of mediumistic communications. He referred to "thought-reading, or ... the influence of one mind to another" (Harrison, 1873, p. 434) to account for the phenomena.

Helen Dallas (1916), another writer who may be described as a spiritualist, in her book, *Objections to Spiritualism Answered*, commented on the "fact that thoughts telepathically received from those still in the flesh may blend with, or be mistaken for, messages from the discarnate" (p. 70). Similarly, well-known French researcher and theoretician Gustave Geley (n.d.) stated that mediumistic communications sometimes seemed to depend on elements "evidently taken from the *medium* and the sitters of the session, all of them in variable proportions" (p. 102, my translation).

Another interesting example was that of Ernesto Bozzano, probably the best-known European spiritist of his times. Bozzano stated more than once that ESP could account for some cases. In his book, *Animism and Spiritism*, when referring to phenomena suggestive of spirit identity, Bozzano said that "many episodes are explicable by manifestations usually animistic" (Bozzano, n. d.a, p. 47). In his study of hauntings, Bozzano (1919/1925) favored explanations related to discarnate agency for the majority of the cases. However, he accepted telepathic explanations from the living for a small number of cases. In his view, because "not all manifestations between the living are of telepathic origin ... also not all hauntings manifestations seem to have a spirit origin" (p. 305, my translation).

Regarding poltergeists, Bozzano also accepted some agency from the living. He wrote that:

> There are a small number of cases that may be explained through the 'animistic' hypothesis ... the sporadic emission of telekinetic or mediumistic energy controlled by a rudimentary will of subconscious origin. Some cases of little complexity may be classified in this category, ... but it may be said that, in general, 'poltergeist' manifestations are almost never completely 'animistic' nor completely 'spiritistic' ... (Bozzano, 1919/1925, p. 311, my translation)

Others believed that the thoughts of sitters could affect materialization phenomena. So, for example, in the *Spiritualist Newspaper* G. W. Stock wrote that the forms that appeared in séances were "very pliable and capable of being moulded by the thoughts and affections of the sitters" (Stock, 1877, p. 188). A similar view was stated in an unsigned paper, "The Influence of Sitters Upon Spiritual Manifestations," which was presumably written by William H. Harrison (The Influence, 1877).

In fact, the spiritualist publications presented a variety of ideas about the nature of materializations which highlight the complexity of the discussion, one that was not limited to ideas of discarnate agency. Several writers speculated on the exteriorization of the medium's double to account for materializations (e.g., Coleman, 1876; Kislingbury, 1876a, 1876b; Reimers, 1876). One author writing about Katie King's materialization said that Katie "is not an independent spirit, but the spirit, or 'double' of the medium ..." (Spirit Forms, 1873, p. 452). Illustrating the variety of ideas about materializations at the time, spiritualist Emily Kislingbury (1876a, 1876b) suggested that transfiguration of the medium could explain some supposed cases of materializations.

Another way of seeing Spiritualism's theoretical contributions is as a context in which skeptics about survival also developed an important theoretical model. There were many writers who suggested that fluidic substances emanating from the medium's body—animal magnetism, Od, nervous forces—could explain many of the mental, and especially the physical, phenomena of Spiritualism, without recourse to spirit agency. Using the spread of Spiritualism as a justification, and especially the performances of physical mediums that suggested spirit influences, such as movement of objects and materializations, a variety of skeptics of the spirit agency hypothesis postulated a different explanatory model. They believed the phenomena could be explained by a force coming from the medium's nervous system. This literature included John Bovee Dods' *Spirit Manifestations Examined and Explained* (1854), Edward C. Rogers's *Philosophy of Mysterious Agents* (1853), Asa Mahan's *Modern Mysteries Explained and Exposed* (1855), and George Samson's *Spiritualism Tested* (1860). Somewhat later in the nineteenth century such other authors as Edward W. Cox (1872),

Gerry G. Fairfield (1875), and Eduard von Hartmann (1885), continued this line of thinking in which they sought to explain phenomena without recourse to discarnate agency. This line of thought was continued by early twentiethcentury researchers such as Joseph Maxwell (1903/1905), Enrico Morselli (1908), Schrenck-Notzing (1920/1925), and René Sudre (1926). All these writings I have mentioned represent the beginnings of what some modern authors call the super-psi explanation of survival phenomena.

Many of the controversies arising from these ideas were instrumental in outlining the assumptions of spiritualists and their opponents. In his book, *Outlines of Ten Years' Investigations into the Phenomena of Modern Spiritualism*, Thomas P. Barkas (1862) argued that in these concepts of nervous forces "man is converted into a kind of electro-odylic-cerebro-spinal machine" (p. 65). In Barkas' view these ideas of psychic forces were not enough to explain the phenomena. Many critics of the psychic force model expressed this viewpoint. They questioned the ability of these forces to produce intelligent effects, such as those seen in some movements of objects and in materialization phenomena (e.g., Aksakof, 1890/n. d; Dr. Dods and Spiritualism, 1855; Force v. Spiritualism, 1867; Mary Jane, 1863; Review of *What Am I?,* 1874).

However, it is important to recognize that spiritualists themselves also supported the existence of fluidic forces, but emphasized that they were manipulated by the spirits of the dead. An influential concept was that of the perispirit popularized in France by Allan Kardec, the founder of spiritism. In his well-known *"Spirits' Book"*, first published in 1857, Kardec (1875) presented mediumistic communications referring to a "universal fluid which plays the part of intermediary between spirit and matter ..." (p. 9). This substance was called the perispirit. It made the spirit's interaction with the body possible and was the vehicle the spirit used to create apparitions and such phenomena as movements of objects. In a later book, Kardec (1876) gave more details about the production of psychic phenomena via the perispirit. He wrote:

> When an object is set in motion, carried away, or raised into the air, the spirit does not seize it, push it, or lift it, as we do with our hands; the spirit, so to say, *saturates* it with *his own* fluid combined with that of the medium, and the object, being thus vivified for the moment, acts as a living being would act ... (and) it follows the impulsion communicated to it by the will of the spirit. (Kardec, 1876, pp. 76–77)

In an 'inspirational address' about the topic of Spiritualism as a science which was published in the *Spiritualist Newspaper*, British trance medium and trance speaker J. J. Morse (1876) discussed ideas similar to Kardec's notion of the perispirit. In France, this line of thought was further articulated by Gabriel Delanne (1923) and Leon Denis (1922). Similarly, well-known British spiritualist and publisher J. Burns argued in 1872 that there was a force in constant operation in living beings that could come out of the body under certain conditions and with certain individuals so to produce phenomena such as movement of objects. This energy was the same as nerve energy and it conveyed the will to the human organism. In Burns' view: "The peculiarity of the medium is, that he gives off a magnetism with which the spiritual atmosphere surrounding the spirit may become intersphered ..., of the one becoming involved with that of the other ..." (Reed & Woodward, n. d., p. 33).

In some of the pamphlets he published, Burns included leaflets giving instructions about how to conduct séances. One of them was called "How to Investigate Spiritual Phenomena," This leaflet said: "The phenomena are produced by a vital force emanating from the sitters, which the spirits use as a connecting link between themselves and objects" (Appendix, n. d., p. 51).

The spiritualist literature includes many other mentions of these forces. In his book, *The Debatable Land*, American spiritualist Robert Dale Owen (1871) referred to "invisible exudations from the human organisations" (p. 404) to account for materialization phenomena. In reference to vapor observed in materialization séances, William Stainton Moses stated in a meeting of the British National Association of Spiritualists held in November of 1877: "It is the universal pabulum, the raw material used in all operations of its nature ... It is the medium's vital force" (Moses, 1877, p. 254).

Spiritualism-oriented writers also discussed these ideas in the twentieth century. In England, in his book, *Spirit Intercourse*, James Hewat McKenzie (1916) wrote that there was a "psycho-plastic matter" that came out of mediums' bodies to form materializations. In France, Geley argued that ectoplasm consisted of the "anatomo-biologic decentralisation in the medium's body and an externalisation of the decentralised factors in an amorphous state, solid, liquid, or vaporous" (Geley, 1924/1927, p. 358).

As we can see, these ideas of forces and fluids were not unique to the anti-spiritualist writers. Spiritualists were actively involved in the discussion and development of these ideas from the beginning of Spiritualism to our day. This is an important point because this notion—that a force comes from the medium's body to produce the phenomena—was one of the main theoretical models of psychical research between the nineteenth century and the 1920s (Alvarado, 2001). Because the concept has been identified with anti-discarnate-agency explanations, we need to remember that it was not only skeptics who contributed to the literature outlining these influential ideas.

Psychological Influences on Spirit Communications

Spiritualists always have recognized that the medium may influence the communications in different ways. In an article called "Cerebral Influence on Revelation" published in the American journal, *The Shekinah*, S. B. Brittan (1853) argued that mediumistic communications could be influenced by the mediums' thoughts. Brittan asserted: "In all ages, revelations from the Spiritual World have been essentially modified by the physical and mental characteristics of the persons through whom they have been given to mankind. In the process of influx, the elements of two minds are blended, and the revelation is the result of their mingled action" (pp. 39–40).

In Andrew Jackson Davis's (1853) book mentioned above the author argued for the influence of the medium's mind on the communications, especially reflecting the medium's education and customs. The medium's mind, Davis wrote, "is almost certain to unconsciously *alter, modify,* and *arrange* all impressions, from whatever source received, invariably in accordance with the state and style of its own growth and individual culture" (p. 203). This influence could be completely undetected by the medium.

In his *Experimental Spiritism: The Medium's Book, or Guide for Mediums and for Evocations*, Kardec (1876) wrote about the limitations placed on spirits' ability to communicate by the resources of the medium, including such aspects as knowledge of languages. Others also talked about these issues (e.g., Ballou, 1853; Dallas, 1916). Dallas, for example, argued that, even during trance, the "medium's mind ... is not an inanimate mirror upon which other personalities can easily cast the impression of their thoughts; it may rather be compared to a sea moved often by internal currents and ruffled by external winds" (p. 65).

There were also discussions by such authors as Aksakof (1890/n. d.) and Delanne (1902), who, while defending spirit agency, admitted that dissociative mechanisms could account for some phenomena. In Delanne's *Recherches sur la Médiumnité* (1902), a study focusing on automatic writing, he pointed out that there could be different explanations for mediumistic communications. While he believed the source of communications could be distinguished by focusing on their content, even in the best mediums pure psychological automatism could get mixed with mediumship (p. 500). Similarly, Geley argued that, while in trance, the medium's capacity for free will was diminished to the point that mediumistic communications could be affected by "more or less voluntary suggestions of the sitters and will often reflect their own thoughts" (Geley, n.d., p. 108, my translation).

In the United States, James H. Hyslop was well known for his systematic and detailed studies of mental mediumship. In his book, *Contact with the Other World*, Hyslop (1919) argued that even in communications with spiritual entities there could be contamination from the living. He wrote:

> There is nothing clearer to the investigators than the fact that all messages are affected by the mind of the medium, normal or subliminal, according to the conditions under which communication takes place. If the messages come through normal consciousness, the form of the message will be deeply affected. Memories, interpretation, and language determine the form of the message. To some extent the subconscious will affect it in the same way in a trance, when normal consciousness is suspended. (Hyslop, 1919, p. 107)

Hyslop (1906a) devoted his book, *Borderland of Psychical Research*, to those phenomena that were not parapsychological but had the appearance of being so. Among these he included memory problems, hallucinations, and a variety of such dissociative phenomena as secondary personalities. The book, Hyslop said, was intended to prepare future students of the supernormal to discriminate between the "normal and the abnormal, on the one hand, and between both of these and the supernormal on the other" (Hyslop, 1906a, p. viii). He clearly stated that knowledge of psychological mechanisms was essential to the proper evaluation of phenomena that may be indicative of the supernormal in general, and of survival in particular. On many occasions, he insisted, it was not necessary to go beyond conventional psychological explanations. As he wrote

> It is not enough that a phenomenon should be involuntary or unconsciously produced. It must be much more to obtain the credentials of the supernormal. It must bear the stamp of knowledge acquired by some other process than sensory experience. It must also show evidence of more than the imagination may produce in its subliminal creations, and we have at present no criterion for determining the limits of this function. It matters not what characteristics of independent personality are exhibited by secondary states or by the subject of the phenomena claimed to have an external source, if they do not show evidences of personal identity of deceased persons they are referable to subliminal action. Hence secondary personality explains many phenomena that formerly received another explanation, and the criterion for the belief in spirits is made far more stringent. (Hyslop, 1906a, p. 284)

In another book, *Enigmas of Psychical Research*, Hyslop (1906b) stated that secondary personality was a more common phenomenon than 'spirit agency' (p. 343). What is interesting about Hyslop is that he contributed actively as well to the study of these subliminal capacities, processes that he believed interacted with the supernormal. One example is Hyslop's (1913) study about the functions of the subconscious in which he summarized and criticized Myers's ideas about the subliminal mind. Other studies along these lines include Hyslop's analyses of the purported 'Martian' communications of Mrs. Smead (Hyslop, 1918), and his study of unconscious fraud in the production of physical phenomena in the mediumship of Mrs. Burton (Hamilton, Smyth, and Hyslop, 1911).

Another interesting example of how spiritualists contributed psychological explanations of mediumistic communications is in the reaction of some spiritualists to Kardec's ideas about reincarnation. The tenet of reincarnation was a prominent part of Kardec's system. Kardec based his teachings about spiritism and reincarnation on mediumistic communications (Kardec, 1875,

1876). But the idea of reincarnation was not well received by many readers, particularly in England. In 1875 a number of discussions of reincarnation were published in the well-known English *Spiritualist Newspaper* (e.g., Home, 1875; J., 1875; Kislingbury, 1875; Rouse, 1875). In the pages of this publication, medium D. D. Home (1875) ridiculed the concept based on the presence of too many people claiming to have been Napoleon and the absence of people who claimed common previous lives. More importantly, mediumistic communications with a reincarnationist content were attacked by two well-known spiritualists: Alexander Aksakof and William Harrison.

Aksakof (1875) criticized Kardec's reliance on writing mediums because they were well known to "pass so easily under the psychological influence or preconceived ideas ..." (p. 75). He suggested that the reincarnationist content of such automatic scripts were not truly spiritual, but depended instead on the impact of suggestion on the medium.

A much stronger attack was published in an unsigned leading article in the *Spiritualist Newspaper* on October 8, 1875. Presumably William Harrison, the editor of the publication, wrote the article. As the author stated

> Practically speaking the doctrine has not, up to the present time, been taught through any medium of any kind residing in England, and those doctrines which have been taught here have usually (with a few striking exceptions) been strongly coloured by the opinions of the medium, or those of the sitters; in short, it may be laid down as a general principle that about ninety per cent, of spirit messages contain more of the thoughts of the medium than of the thoughts of the communicating spirit. This takes place unconsciously to the medium of course ... We know full well that if the reincarnation doctrine should be agitated in England plenty of spirits will begin to teach it, the reason being that the minds of the various mediums will be set buzzing by the arguments on the subject mooted by persons around them, after which there will be plenty of spirit messages about reincarnation. (Allan Kardec, 1875, p. 170)

Another anonymous speculation, probably written by Harrison as well, asked: "How much of the revelations in Allan Kardec's book were due to his presence at the circles?" (The Inductive Method, 1875, p. 314). The important question here is not that of reincarnation, but the belief some spiritualists had that the ideas expressed by spirit communicators (in this case reincarnation) could be produced artifactually as a function of suggestion on the medium or through the medium's own beliefs.

Mediumistic Communications from the Living

Another contribution of the survival context to the understanding of the complexity of psi phenomena were discussions of mediumistic communications from the living. Far from being unknown or ignored by spiritualists, these communications have been discussed in the spiritualist literature from the beginning. An early mention of this phenomenon appears in Ballou's previously mentioned book. He wrote: "Responses have been made, purporting to come from the spirits of persons deceased,—giving their names, relationship to the living, and various communications,—but afterwards it turned out that the persons represented as dead were alive in the flesh!" (Ballou, 1853, p.29).

In his *Letters and Tracts on Spiritualism*, Judge John Worth Edmonds (1874) discussed the existence of these cases. In a letter written in October of 1857, Edmonds mentioned a case of a communication from a man he had not seen for over fifteen years. He summarized the case as follows: "I had not seen him in several years; he was not at all in my mind at the time, and he was unknown to the medium. Yet he identified himself unmistakably, not only by his peculiar characteristics, but by referring to matters known only to him and me" (Edmonds, 1874, p. 116).

Later on, Allan Kardec (1876) mentioned the evocation of spirits of the living. Both Kardec and his translator Anna Blackwell presented cases of evocations of living spirits (Kardec, 1876, pp. 350–353). In Kardec's views, obtained through mediumistic communications: "The moment most favourable for the evocation of a person in the flesh is during his natural sleep; because his spirit, being then comparatively free, can come to the caller as easily as it can go elsewhere" (Kardec, 1876, p. 345).[8] Later articles published in the 1870s by other authors discussed the existence of communications from the living. These included Nehrer's (1874) "Apparitions of Incarnated Spirits", and Damiani's (1875) "The Double", both of which appeared in the journal, *Human Nature*.

In 1881, in the journal, *Light*, George Wyld wrote: "Spirits of living bodies can, under certain conditions, enter the spirit world and act in all respects as if they were external spirits finally emancipated from the flesh."

From the 1890s on British spiritualist William T. Stead practiced automatic writing (Stead, 1893a, 1893b, 1894). He received messages from supposed deceased persons and from living ones. An example of this telepathic automatism was presented in his little book, *How I Know that the Dead Return*, published in 1909. A lady friend of Stead had spent the weekend at Haslemere, about thirty miles from London. On Monday, Stead sat down to use his automatic writing to see if he could find out if she had left for London. He received the following message:

> I am very sorry to tell you I have had a very painful experience, of which I am almost ashamed to speak. I left Haslemere at 2.27 p.m. in a second-class carriage, in which there were two ladies and one gentleman. When the train stopped at Godaiming the ladies got out, and I was left alone with the man. After the train started he left his seat and came close to me. I was alarmed and repelled him. He refused to go away, and tried to kiss me. I was furious. We had a struggle. I seized his umbrella and struck him, but it broke, and I was beginning to fear that he would master me, when the train began to slow up before arriving at Guildford Station. He got frightened, let go of me, and before the train reached the platform he jumped out and ran away. I was very much upset. But I have the umbrella. (Stead, 1909, pp. 18–19)

The lady later confirmed the story with the exception of one detail. The umbrella was hers, and not her attacker's.

Another fascinating contribution came from astral projector Vincent Turvey. In his book, *The Beginnings of Seership* (n.d., ca 1909), Turvey says he projected out of his body and was able to communicate through mediums. It was reported that the sitters recognized Turvey by the content of the communication.

The assumption made by all of these authors was that just as it was believed possible that spirits of the dead could communicate through a medium, the spirit of a living person could do the same under the proper conditions. These ideas should be seen in the context of other beliefs. In those times many writers had discussed the concept of soul excursions, or of the human double. During the nineteenth century such authors as Crowe (1848), Kardec (1876), Moses (M.A. Oxon., 1876), Nehrer (1874), and Owen (1860) discussed the idea and presented cases of such phenomena as apparitions of the living. It was clearly believed that the spirit of the living could do similar things that the spirit of the dead could do.

The discussion of these incidents illustrates how interest in survival in general, and in Spiritualism in particular, has contributed to the understanding of the complexity of mediumistic communications.

Concluding Remarks

I have argued in this paper that the concept of survival, refracted through the lenses of Spiritualism and mediumship practice, has contributed a context conducive to the development of different aspects of parapsychology. While some of this is well known, I have attempted to present material that is not generally discussed in our literature.

Both the founding of the SPR and the early involvement of J. B. Rhine in parapsychology can, to a great extent, be traced to concerns about survival and about the wider issue of the nature of human beings. Within the SPR, the idea of survival had a positive influence on research and theory. That is, the early SPR researchers appropriated phenomena such as apparitions, haunted houses and mediumship from the survival context that Spiritualism presented in England and this shaped the research agenda of the Society.

In the case of the Rhines, there is no question that, to a large extent, interest in survival led them to the field and to Duke University. But eventually survival had a 'contrary' effect. That is, survival led to later ESP experimental work unrelated to the idea of life after death and, in fact, J. B. Rhine eventually came to the conclusion that survival was an untestable problem.[9] This is an example of how a particular idea or context can be influential in the course of history by contributing to an effect that is different from what is expected. Thus, just as mediumship influenced both the development of the concept of the subconscious mind (Ellenberger, 1970) and of some psychiatric diagnoses (Le Maléfan, 1999), the survival question influenced the development of modern experimental parapsychology. I would not claim that the context of survival was the only factor which led towards the 'new' parapsychology that Rhine and his associates developed through their experimental work (e.g., Mauskopf & McVaugh, 1980; L. E. Rhine, 1971). But it was certainly one of the main initial forces and should be recognized as such.

The contributions of spiritualists to the enterprise were more direct. Among these were their discussions of psi-from-the-living and of psychological explanations for phenomena, as well as recording the existence of mediumistic communications from the living. Spiritualists actively influenced the construction of these concepts, and more broadly put, contributed to the awareness of the complexity of psi phenomena.

Another example of a 'contrary' effect was the initial work of Myers within the SPR. Early in his career Myers published papers that suggested that automatism and telepathy could account for some of the supposed evidence for survival in mediumistic communications (e.g., Myers, 1884). At this stage in his career the idea of survival led Myers to develop a psychology of the subliminal that, while prompted by survival, was not adopting such an explanation for the phenomena. While Rhine abandoned the study of mediums, Myers continued it. But like Rhine, Myers initially did not believe in survival. This was to change later in his career (e.g., Myers, 1903).

There were other direct and indirect and unexpected effects of survival that I have not discussed. Some may be the development of free-response methodology and instrumental studies. The early free-response analysis methods could be seen as a consequence of attempts to evaluate survival by establishing the presence of veridical information. The use of instruments may not have developed directly from the idea of survival, but it was certainly motivated by the study of mediumship. Such ideas await further study.

Some may say that parapsychology started to move forward when the field was able to conquer such superstitious ideas as survival, and such primitive and inefficient methodologies as séance studies. But there is a different way to see these developments. Instead of thinking that parapsychology has progressed because it has discarded the metaphysical and the spiritual, we may assert the opposite. Change has taken place thanks in part to the contributions of such ideas as that of survival of bodily death, and not simply in spite of it. This is similar to the suggestions of some historians of science and medicine as regards the contribution of the role of the Hermetic tradition, mesmerism, and phrenology to science and medicine. The way the influence was transmitted and the way in which it was received is secondary to this argument. The point is that we should be careful in accepting ideas that present science as the simple conquest over what some regard now as unscientific concepts. Without denying the *essential* role of research, especially if it is systematic and programmatic, the growth of science cannot be accounted for solely by research findings, and certainly neither can the growth of parapsychology. A variety of such extra-scientific or social factors as the training and personality of scientists, and the views of what is acceptable or not arc known to bc influential on the course of science. Similarly, such ideas as survival of bodily death have had an effect as well.

Of course we need to be critical of the influence of survival. I am not claiming this was the only factor nor am I claiming that there is no merit in having changed from a predominantly survival-oriented parapsychology to a more secular-based one which relates psychic functioning to psychological and physical variables. I am only concerned with recognizing important aspects of our history that are sometimes forgotten by modern practitioners.[10]

Scientifically trained parapsychologists suffer from this lack of historical memory for a variety of reasons. Some focus on issues such as fraud, which was common among many physical mediums. Others focus on methodological problems, such as the ambiguities in the evaluation of the source of veridical information and the role of chance in mediumistic communications. For such researchers, it is difficult to see beyond the reputation of fraud and the ambiguities of survival evidence. Our past is perceived to be too difficult, too dirty—to use the dirty test tube argument—to be useful for research. Consequently, not only is the area of survival ignored, but there is no interest in learning about the beginnings of our field. While I believe we need to be careful not to fall into extremes, there is certainly some truth in these perspectives.

In addition, some modern critics and parapsychologists see the connection between parapsychology and the ideas of spirituality and survival of bodily death as problematic for our field. James Alcock (1981, 1987) has argued that parapsychologists are merely interested in finding the soul and are not real scientists. In this view, interest in the concept of survival and actual research on the topic are seen as a validation of this metaphysical driving force said to motivate parapsychologists. More recently, Robert L. Morris (2000) has stated that parapsychology is connected to 'problematic' metaphysical origins. This, Morris argues, is a kind of public relations problem for parapsychology. Whether or not we personally find parapsychology's connections to occultism, Spiritualism, and the like embarrassing is a matter each of us needs to resolve. Workers in the field react to this problem according to their training, goals and views of the purpose of the field. But a squeamishness about survival and its place in our history keeps us from recognizing how rich is the historical impact of survival on parapsychology, and how much beyond giving us a starting point and an initial agenda this impact, in fact, goes.

I hope that I have not been misunderstood in my goals. My purpose has not been to glorify Spiritualism nor the concept of survival. I am not arguing that these were the only factors at work. Instead, I hope that their influence will become more visible to contemporary parapsychologists. My goal is difficult to achieve because some of the points discussed in this paper are not clear unless you have access to difficult-to-obtain literature. But it is important to balance views of the history of psychical research in which survival and Spiritualism are only stages along the road to scientific parapsychology. While this is not a completely incorrect view, it is not enough. Concepts of survival in particular and Spiritualism in general are not mere antecedents nor mere stages that have been superseded. Instead, they are rich and complex initiators and contributors to a variety of developments.

It may certainly be argued that a similar paper could have been written about how survival has retarded the growth of parapsychology. I am sure some arguments and examples can be found to defend this position as well. Much more work needs to be done to explore the influence of survival on the development of parapsychology in detail, not to mention the influence of other conceptual traditions such as dualism and vitalism. One approach might use biography by focusing on the lives of survival and anti-survival psychical researchers. Other work might investigate such issues as the development of the concept of mediumship and of ideas about the process behind mediumistic communications.

To conclude, it is my hope that I have been successful in reminding my readers about the importance of survival to parapsychology. While survival is not as important today as it used to be in parapsychology, its past influence is an example of the many factors that have contributed to the development of this field.

Notes

1 See, for example, the discussions between Braude (1992a, 1992b) and Stevenson (1992), and between Cook (1996, 1997) and Almeder et al. (1997).
2 On Spiritualism in England see Oppenheim (1985) and Podmore (1902).
3 It is interesting to notice that contemporary spiritualists were critical of what they believed were Myers's attempts to reduce spiritualistic phenomena to subliminal processes (e.g., Haughton, 1886; Noel, 1886; Wedgewood, 1886).
4 On the early work of the Rhines see Brian (1982), Mauskopf and McVaugh (1980), Rhine and Associates (1965), and L.vE. Rhine (1982). On Rhine and the survival issue see Chari (1982).
5 On Margery's mediumship see Tietze (1973). Regarding Margery and the Rhines see Brian (1982, Ch. 4), Matlock (1987), and Tietze (1973, pp. 107–114).
6 Minnie Soule was an American medium studied before by Lydia Allison (1929) and James H. Hyslop (1910, pp. 722–776). She used the pseudonym of Mrs. Chenoweth (see also Tubby, 1941).
7 On Thomas see Dale (1941).
8 The cases of Blackwell and Kardec—and other examples of evocations of spirits of the living in Kardec's journal *Revue Spirite* (Études, 1860/2001)—were not evidential in any way. Others, however, were (reviews of these cases appear in Bozzano, n. d. b; Curnow, 1927; Dallas, 1924).
9 For discussions about Rhine's ideas about survival and his ESP research see Chari (1982) and Palmer (1982).
10 In addition, we need to remember that many members of the general public are interested in and believe in survival of death. The point is that important issues like this one are not limited to the opinion of the scientifically trained, however capable we think scientists are to evaluate the evidence.

References

Ackerknecht, E. H. (1958). Contributions of Gall and the phrenologists to knowledge of brain function. In F. N. L. Poynter (Ed.). *The history and philosophy of knowledge of the brain and its functions* (pp. 149–153). Charles C Thomas.

Aksakof, A. (1875, August 13). Researches on the historical origin of the reincarnation speculations of French spiritualists. *Spiritual Newspaper,* (pp. 74–75).

Aksakof, A. (n.d., ca 1906). *Animismo y Espiritismo: Ensayo de un Examen Critico de los Fenómenos Medianimicos* (2 vols.). Carbonell y Esteva. (Original work published in German, 1890).
Alcock, J. E. (1981). *Parapsychology: Science or magic?* Pergamon Press.
Alcock, J. E. (1987). Parapsychology: science of the anomalous or a search for the soul? *Behavioral and Brain Sciences, 10,* 553–565.
Allan Kardec's "Spirits' Book". (1875, October 8). *Spiritualist Newspaper,* pp. 169–170.
Allison, L. W. (1929). *Leonard and Soule experiments in psychical research.* Boston Society for Psychic Research.
Almeder, R., Braude, S., Grosso, M., Owens, J. E., Palmer, J. and Taylor, E. (1997). Replies to Dr. Cook's review of *Parapsychology and thanatology. Journal of Parapsychology, 61,* 45–59.
Alvarado, C. S. (2001). *Concepts of force in early psychical research.* Paper presented at the 44th Annual Convention of the Parapsychological Association, August, New York.
Appendix: How to investigate spiritual phenomena (n.d., ca 1872). In Reed and Woodward (Eds.) *Human immortality proved by fact: report of a two nights debate on modern spiritualism,* (pp. 50–52). J. Burns.
Atkinson, H. J. (1871). Science and Spiritualism. *Human Nature, 5,* 534–536.
Atkinson, H. G. (1882). Uncertainties of spirit identity. *Light, 2,* 249.
Ballou, A. (1853). *An exposition of views respecting the modern spiritual manifestations* (from the 2nd American ed.). Edward Howell.
Barkas, T. P. (1862). *Outlines of ten years' investigations into the phenomena of modern spiritualism embracing letters, lectures,* &c. F. Pitman.
Barkas, T. P. (1876, December 29). Additional original researches in psychology. *Spiritualist Newspaper,* pp. 259–262.
Barrett, W. F. (1886). On some physical phenomena, commonly called spiritualistic, witnessed by the author. *Proceedings of the Society for Psychical Research, 4,* 25–42.
Barrett, W. F., Keep, A. P. P., Massey, C. C., Wedgwood, H., Podmore, F. & Pease, E. R. (1882). First report of the Committee on Haunted Houses. *Proceedings of the Society for Psychical Research, 1,* 101–115.
Barrett, W. F., Close, M. H., Lane-Fox, G., Gurney, E., Myers, F. W. H., Myers, A. T., Pease, E. R., Ridley, H. N., Stone, W. H. & Coffin, W. H. (1883). First report of the "Reichenbach" committee. *Proceedings of the Society for Psychical Research, 1,* 230–237.
Barrett, W. F., Gurney, E., Myers, F. W. H., Ridley, H. N., Stone, W. H., Wyld, G. & Podmore, F. (1883). First report of the Committee on Mesmerism. *Proceedings of the Society for Psychical Research, 1,* 217–229.
Barrett, W. F., Massey, C. C., Moses, W. S., Podmore, F., Gurney, E. & Myers, F. W. H. (1884a). Third report of the Literary Committee: a theory about apparitions: Part I. *Proceedings of the Society for Psychical Research, 2,* 109–136.
Barrett, W. F., Massey, C. C., Moses, W. S., Podmore, F., Gurney, E. & Myers, F. W. H. (1884b). Fourth report of the Literary Committee: a theory about apparitions: Part II. *Proceedings of the Society for Psychical Research, 2,* 157–186.
Beloff, J. (1982). J. B. Rhine on the nature of psi. In K. R. Rao (Ed.), *J. B. Rhine: On the frontiers of science* (pp. 97–110). McFarland.
Binet, A. (1896). *Alterations of personality.* D. Appleton. (Original work published 1892).
Bozzano, E. (1925). *Los Fenómenos de encantamiento.* Bauza. (Original work published in Italian, 1919).
Bozzano, E. (n.d. a). *Animism and spiritism: A reply to M. Sudre's Introduction* a *la Métapsychique Humaine.* Arthur H. Stockwell. (Original work published in French, 1926).
Bozzano, E. (n.d. b, ca 1938). *Discarnate influence in human life.* John Watkins.
Braude, S. E. (1992a). Survival or super-psi? *Journal of Scientific Exploration 6,* 127–1 44.
Braude, S. E. (1992b). Reply to Stevenson. *Journal of Scientific Exploration 6,* 151–155.
Brian, D. (1982). *The enchanted voyager: The life of J. B. Rhine.* Prentice-Hall.
Brittan, S. B. (1853). Cerebral influence on revelation. *The Shekinah 2,* 39–43.
Bushell, W. D., Hughes, F. S., Keep, A. P. P., Podmore, F., Wedgwood, H. & Pease, E. R. (1884). Second report of the Committee on Haunted Houses. *Proceedings of the Society for Psychical Research, 2,* 137–151.
Carpenter, W. B. (1877). *Mesmerism and spiritualism,* &c. *historically and scientifically considered.* Longman & Green.
Chari, C. T. K. (1982). J. B. Rhine and post-mortem survival: A reappraisal and vindication. In K. R. Rao (Ed.), *J. B. Rhine: On the frontiers of science* (pp. 83–96). McFarland.

Coleman, B. (1865). Passing events. The spread of spiritualism. *Spiritual Magazine 6,* 110–128.
[Coleman, B.] (1876, July 14). The elimination of further doubtful conditions from materialization manifestation. *Spiritualist Newspaper,* 325.
Cook, E. W. (1996). Survival research today: an essay review of *Parapsychology and Thanatology. Journal of Parapsychology, 60,* 343–355.
Cook, E. W. (1997). Dr. Cook's reply to comments on her review *of Parapsychology and thanatology. Journal of Parapsychology, 61,* 159–167.
Cox, E. W. (1872). *Spiritualism answered by science: With the proofs of a psychic Fforce* (new rev. ed.). Longman.
Crabtree, A. (1993). *From Mesmer to Freud: Magnetic sleep and the roots of psychological healing.* Yale University Press.
Crookes, W. (1889). Notes of séances with D. D. Home. *Proceedings of the Society for Psychical Research, 6,* 98–127.
Crowe, C. (1848). *The night-side of nature: Or, Ghosts and ghost seers* (2 vols). T. Newby.
Curnow, L. (1927). Spirits in the flesh. *Psychic Science 5,* 268–284.
Dale, L. A. (1941). Dr. John F. Thomas (in memoriam). *Journal of the American Society for Psychical Research, 35,* 1–8.
Dallas, H. A. (1916). *Objections to spiritualism answered.* G. Bell.
Dallas, H. A. (1924). Communication from the still incarnate at a distance from the body. *Occult Review 40,* 26–32.
Damiani, G. (1875). The double. *Human Nature 9,* 555–564.
Davies, C. M. (1875). *Mystic London: Or, phases of occult life in the metropolis.* Tinsley Brothers.
Davis, A. J. (1853). *The present age and inner life: A sequel to spiritual intercourse: Modern mysteries classified and explained.* Partridge & Brittan.
Debus, A. G. (1978). *Man and nature in the renaissance.* Cambridge University Press.
Delanne, G. (1902). *Recherches sur la médiumnité.* Librairie des Science Psychiques.
Delanne, G. (1923). *Le spiritisme devant la science.* B.P.S.
Denis, L. (1922). *Dans l'invisible: spiritisme et médiumnité.* Librairie des Sciences Psychiques.
Dingwall, E. J. (1930). *Ghosts and spirits in the ancient world.* Kegan Paul, Trench, Trübner.
Dobbs, B. J. (1991). *The Janus Faces of genius: The role of alchemy in Newton's thought.* Cambridge University Press.
Dods, J. B. (1854). *Spirit manifestations examined and explained: Judge Edmonds refuted; Or, An exposition of the involuntary powers and instincts of the human mind.* De Witt & Davenport.
Dr. Dods and spiritualism. (1855). *Spiritual Telegraph, 7*(n. s.), 319–323.
Edmonds, J. W. (1874). *Letters and tracts on spiritualism.* J. Burns.
Ellenberger, H. F. (1970). *The discovery of the unconscious: The history and evolution of dynamic psychiatry.* Basic Books.
Fairfield, G. G. (1875). *Ten years with spiritual mediums: An inquiry concerning the etiology of certain phenomena called spiritual.* D. Appleton.
Fantoni, B. (1974). *Magia y parapsicología: Historia de las tentativas de explicacion de lo aparentemente inexplicable.* Troquel.
Flammarion, C. (1900). *The unknown.* Harper & Brothers.
Force v. spiritualism. (1867). *Spiritual Magazine 2,* 223–237.
Gauld, A. (1968). *The founders of psychical research.* Routledge & Kegan Paul.
Gauld, A. (1992). *A history of hypnotism.* Cambridge University Press.
Geley, G (1927). *Clairvoyance and materialisation: A record of experiments.* T. Fisher Unwin. (Original work published in French, 1924).
Geley, G. (n.d.). *Ensayo de Revista General y de Interpretacion Sintetica del Espiritismo* (from the 3rd French ed.). Maucci.
Gurney, E. (1884). An account of some experiments in mesmerism. *Proceedings of the Society for Psychical Research, 2,* 201–206.
Gurney, E., Myers, F. W. H. & Podmore, F. (1886). *Phantasms of the living* (2 vols.). Trübner.
Hamilton, W. H., Smyth, J. S. & Hyslop, J. H. (1911). A case of hysteria. *Proceedings of the American Society for Psychical Research, 5,* 1–672.

Harrison, W. H. (1873, December 5). Certain problems connected with mediumship. *The Spiritualist,* p. 436–440.
Harrison, W. H. (1879). *Spirits before our eyes* (2 vols.). W. H. Harrison.
Haughton, G. D. (1886). Correspondence. On the method of research pursued by the Society. *Journal of the Society for Psychical Research, 2,* 25–29.
Hodgson, R. (1885). Report of the Committee appointed to investigate phenomena connected with the Theosophical Society: 2. Account of personal investigations in India, and discussion of the authorship of the "Koot Hoomi" letters. *Proceedings of the Society for Psychical Research, 3,* 207–380.
Hodgson, R. (1892). A record of observations of certain phenomena of trance. *Proceedings of the Society for Psychical Research, 8,* 1–167.
Home, D. D. (1875, October 1). Correspondence. Mr. D. D. Home on reincarnation. *Spiritualist Newspaper,* p. 165.
Houghton, Miss [G.]. (n. d., ca 1881). *Evenings at home in spiritual séance.* London: Trübner.
Howitt, W. (1863). *The history of the supernatural in all ages and nations and in all churches Christian and pagan demonstrating* (2 vols). Robert & Green.
Hyslop, J. H. (1906a). *Borderland of psychical research.* G. P. Putnam's.
Hyslop, J. H. (1906b). *Enigmas of psychical research.* G. P. Putnam's.
Hyslop, J. H. (1910). A record and discussion of mediumistic experiments. *Proceedings of the American Society for Psychical Research, 4,* 1–812.
Hyslop, J. H. (1913). The subconscious and its functions. *Proceedings of the American Society for Psychical Research, 7,* 5–192.
Hyslop, J. H. (1918). The Smead case. *Proceedings of the American Society for Psychical Research, 12,* 5–735.
Hyslop, J. H. (1919). *Contact with the other world.* New York: Century.
Iannuzzo, G. (1983). La rivoluzione "spiritualista" di Joseph Banks Rhine. *Luce e Ombra 83,* 1–11.
The inductive method applied to the doctrines of Allan Kardec (1875, December 31), *Spiritualist Newspaper,* p. 313–315.
The influence of sitters upon spiritual manifestations. (1877, March 9). *Spiritualist Newspaper,* p. 109–110.
Inglis, B. (1977). *Natural and supernatural: A history of the paranormal from earliest times to 1914.* Hodder & Stoughton.
J., B. P. (1875, September 3). Correspondence. The reincarnation controversy. *Spiritualist Newspaper,* p. 117.
James, W. (1886). Report of the Committee on Mediumistic Phenomena. *Proceedings of the American Society for Psychical Research, 1,* 102–106.
James, W. (1890a). A record of observations of certain phenomena of trance (5). Part III. *Proceedings of the Society for Psychical Research, 6,* 651–659.
James, W. (1890b). *The principles of psychology* (2 vols.). Henry Holt.
Janet, P. (1889). *L'automatisme psychologique: Essai de psychologie expérimentale sur les formes inférieures de l 'activité humaine.* Félix Alcan.
Kardec, A. (1875). *Spiritualist philosophy: The spirits' book.* Trübner.
Kardec, A. (1876). *Experimental spiritism: The medium's book, Or, guide for mediums and for evocations.* Trübner.
Kislingbury, E. (1875, September 24). Correspondence. Allan Kardec's "Spirits' Book". *Spiritualist Newspaper,* p. 153.
Kislingbury, E. (1876a, July 28). Correspondence. Form manifestations *versus* materialisations. *Spiritualist Newspaper,* p. 357–358.
Kislingbury, E. (1876b, December 22). Form manifestations. *Spiritualist Newspaper,* p. 242–244.
Leaf, W. (1890). A record of observations of certain phenomena of trance (3). Part II. *Proceedings of the Society for Psychical Research, 6,* 558–646.
Le Maléfan, P. (1999). *Folie et spiritisme: Histoire du discourse psychopathologique sur la pratique du spiritisme, ses abords et ses avatars (1850–1950).* L' Hartmattan.
Lodge, O. (1890). A record of observations of certain phenomena of trance (2). Part I. *Proceedings of the Society for Psychical Research, 6,* 443–557.
Lodge, O. (1924). For and against survival: the possibility of survival from the scientific point of view. *Proceedings of the Society for Psychical Research, 34,* 113–129.

M. A. Oxon [Moses, W. S.] (1876). On the trans-corporeal action of spirit. *Human Nature, 10,* 99–125, 144–157.

M cDougall, W. (1911). *Body and mind: A history and a defense of animism.* Methuen.

McKenzie, J. H. (1916). *Spirit intercourse: Its theory and practice.* Simpkin, Marshall, Hamilton, Kent.

Mahan, A. (1855). *Modern mysteries explained and exposed in four parts.* J. P. Jewett.

Marillier, L. (1891). Apparitions of the Virgin in Dordogne. *Proceedings of the Society for Psychical Research, 7,* 100–110.

Mary Jane (1863). *Spiritual Magazine 4,* 336–352, 385–407.

Matlock, J. G. (1987). Cat's paw: Margery and the Rhines, 1926. *Journal of Parapsychology, 51,* 229–247.

Mauskopf, S. H. & McVaugh, M. R. (1980). *The elusive science: Origins of experimental psychical research.* Johns Hopkins University Press.

Maxwell, J. (1905). *Metapsychical phenomena: Methods and observations.* Duckworth. (Original work published in French, 1903).

De Mirville, J. E. (1854). *Pneumatologie: Des esprits et de leurs manifestations fluidiques.* H. Vrayet de Surcy.

Morris, R. L. (2000). Parapsychology in the 21st century. *Journal of Parapsychology, 64,* 123–137.

Morse, J. J. (1876, May 19). An inspirational address on Spiritualism as a science. *Spiritualist Newspaper,* p. 231–233.

Morselli, E. (1908). *Psicologia e "spiritismo: "Note e impressioni critiche sui fenomeni medianici di Eusapia Paladino* (2 vols.). Fratelli Bocca.

Morton, R. *[pseud.* R. Despard] (1892). Record of a haunted house. *Proceedings of the Society for Psychical Research, 8,* 311–332.

Moses, W. S. (1877, November 30). The British National Association of Spiritualists: Form manifestations. *Spiritualist Newspaper,* p. 254–255.

Myers, F. W. H. (1884). On a telepathic explanation of some so-called spiritualistic phenomena: Part I. *Proceedings of the Society for Psychical Research, 2,* 217–237.

Myers, F. W. H. (1885). Automatic writing. II. *Proceedings of the Society for Psychical Research, 3,* 1–63.

Myers, F. W. H. (1887). Automatic writing. III. *Proceedings of the Society for Psychical Research, 4,* 209–261.

Myers, F. W. H. (1889a). Automatic writing. IV. The daemon of Socrates. *Proceedings of the Society for Psychical Research, 5,* 522–547.

Myers, F. W. H. (1889b). On recognised apparitions occurring more than a year after death. *Proceedings of the Society for Psychical Research, 6,* 13–65.

Myers, F. W. H. (1890). A record of observations of certain phenomena of trance (1). Introduction. *Proceedings of the Society for Psychical Research, 6,* 436–442.

Myers, F. W. H. (1903). *Human personality and its survival of bodily death* (2 vols.). Longman, Green.

Myers, A. T. & Myers, F. W. H. (1893). Mind-cure, faith cure and the miracles of Lourdes. *Proceedings of the Society for Psychical Research, 9,* 160–209.

Nehrer, Dr. (1874). Apparitions of incarnated spirits. *Human Nature, 8,* 145–157.

Nicol, F. (1972). The founders of the S. P. R. *Proceedings of the Society for Psychical Research, 55,* 341–367.

Noel, R. (1886). Hallucination, memory, and the unconscious self. *Journal of the Society for Psychical Research, 2,* 158–171.

Objects of the Society (1882). *Proceedings of the Society for Psychical Research, 1,* 3–6.

Oppenheim, J. (1985). *The other world: Spiritualism and psychical research in England, 1850–1914.* Cambridge University Press.

Owen, R. D. (1860). *Footfalls on the boundary of another world.* Trübner.

Owen, R. D. (1871). *The debatable land between this world and the next.* Trübner.

Palmer, J. (1982). Review of J. B. Rhine's ESP research. In K. R. Rao (Ed.), *J. B. Rhine: On the frontiers of science* (pp. 37–52). McFarland.

Paton, L. B. (1921). *Spiritism and the cult of the dead in antiquity.* Macmillan.

Podmore, F. (1889). Phantasms of the dead from another point of view. *Proceedings of the Society for Psychical Research, 6,* 229–313.

Podmore, F. (1902). *Modern spiritualism: A history and a criticism* (2 vols). Methuen.

Price, H. H. (1939). Haunting and the "psychic ether" hypothesis; with some preliminary reflections on the present condition and possible future of psychical research. *Proceedings of the Society for Psychical Research, 45,* 307–343.

Reed and Woodward (n.d., ca 1872). *Human immortality proved by fact: Report of a two nights' debate on modern spiritualism.* J. Burns.
Reichenbach, C. van. (1851). *Physico-physiological researches on the dynamics of magnetism, electricity, heat, light, crystallization, and chemism, in their relation to vital force* (from German 2ed.). J. S. Redfield. (Original work published in German, 1849).
Reimers, C. (1876, May 19). Correspondence. Mr. Eglinton in Manchester. *Spiritualist Newspaper,* p. 239.
Review of *What Am I? Volume II.* (1874, March 27). *Spiritualist Newspaper,* pp. 152–153.
Rhine, J. B. (1933a). The question of the possibility of proving survival. *Journal of the Society for Psychical Research, 28,* 35–45.
Rhine, J. B. (1933b). Correspondence. On the possibility of proving survival. *Journal of the Society for Psychical Research, 28,* 125–128.
Rhine, J. B. (1934a). *Extra-sensory perception.* Boston Society for Psychic Research.
Rhine, J. B. (1934b). Telepathy and clairvoyance in the normal and trance states of a "medium." *Character and Personality 3,* 91–111.
Rhine, J. B. (1937). *New frontiers of the mind: The story of the Duke experiments.* Farrar & Rinehart.
Rhine, J.B. (1943). Editorial. ESP, PK, and the survival hypothesis. *Journal of Parapsychology,* 7, 223–227.
Rhine, J. B. (1947). *The reach of the mind.* William Sloane.
Rhine, J. B. (1953). *New world of the mind.* William Sloane.
Rhine, J. B. (1956). Research on spirit survival re-examined. *Journal of Parapsychology, 20,* 121–131.
Rhine, J. B. (1960). Incorporeal personal agency: the prospect of a scientific solution. *Journal of Parapsychology, 24,* 279–309.
Rhine, J. B. (1974). Telepathy and other untestable hypotheses. *Journal of Parapsychology, 38,* 137–153.
Rhine, J. B. & Associates (1965). *Parapsychology: From Duke to FRNM.* Parapsychology Press.
Rhine, J. B. & Rhine, L. E. (1927). One evening's observation on the Margery mediumship. *Journal of Abnormal and Social Psychology 4,* 401–42 1.
Rhine, L. E. (1967). Parapsychology, then and now. *Journal of Parapsychology, 31,* 231–248.
Rhine, L. E. (1971). The establishment of basic concepts and terminology in parapsychology. *Journal of Parapsychology, 35,* 34–56.
Rhine, L. E. (1982). *Something hidden.* McFarland.
Richet, C. (1924). For and against survival: the difficulty of survival from the scientific point of view. *Proceedings of the Society for Psychical Research, 34,* 107–113.
Rogers, E. C. (1853). *Philosophy of mysterious agents, human and mundane; Or, the dynamic laws and relations of man.* J. P. Jewett.
Rouse, J. (1875, September 17). Correspondence. The reincarnation controversy. *Spiritualist Newspaper,* p. 143.
Saltmarsh, H. F. (1932). Is proof of survival possible? *Proceedings of the Society for Psychical Research, 40,* 105–122.
Samson, G. W. (1860). *Spiritualism tested; Or, the facts of its history classified and their cause in nature verified from ancient and modern testimonies.* Gould & Lincoln.
Schrenck-Notzing, A. [F.] de (1925). *Les phénomènes physiques de la médiumnité.* Payot. (Original work published in German, 1920).
Sidgwick, H., Johnson, A., Myers, F. W. H., Podmore, F. and Sidgwick, E. M. (1894). Report on the Census of Hallucinations. *Proceedings of the Society for Psychical Research, 10,* 25–422.
Sidgwick, Mrs. H. (1885). Notes on the evidence, collected by the Society, for phantasms of the dead. *Proceedings of the Society for Psychical Research, 3,* 69–150.
Sidgwick, Mrs. H. (1886a). Mr. Eglinton. *Journal of the Society for Psychical Research, 2,* 282–334.
Sidgwick, Mrs. H. (1886b). Results of a personal investigation into the physical phenomena of Spiritualism: with some critical remarks on the evidence for the genuineness of such phenomena. *Proceedings of the Society for Psychical Research, 4,* 45–74.
Sidgwick, Mrs. H. (1891). On spirit photographs: a reply to Mr. A. R. Wallace. *Proceedings of the Society for Psychical Research,* 7, 268–289.
Spirit Forms (1873, December 12th). *The Spiritualist,* pp. 451–454.
Stead, W. T. (1893a). Automatic handwriting: telepathic and otherwise. *Borderland 1,* 340–341.
Stead, W. T. (1893b). Telepathy: A passing note reporting progress in telepathic automatism. *Borderland 1,* 506–508.

Stead, W. T. (1894). My experience in automatic writing: the story of "Julia" and others. *Borderland 1,* 39–49.
Stead, W. T. (1909). *How I know that the dead return.* Ball.
Stevenson, I. (1992). Survival or super-psi: a reply. *Journal of Scientific Exploration 6,* 145–150.
Stock, G. W. (1877, April 20th). A *séance* with Mr. Williams. *Spiritualist Newspaper,* pp. 188–189.
Sudre, R. (1926). *Introduction a la métapsychique humaine.* Payot.
Taylor, E. (1996). *William James on consciousness beyond the margin.* Princeton University Press.
Thomas, J. F. (1929). *Case studies bearing upon survival.* Boston Society for Psychic Research.
Thomas, J. F. (1937). *Beyond normal cognition: An evaluative and methodological study of the mental content of certain trance phenomena.* Bruce Humphries.
Tietze, T. R. (1973). *Margery.* Harper.
Tubby, G. O. (1941). Mrs. Chenoweth (in memoriam). (Mrs. Minnie Meserve Soule, November 12, 1867–April 28, 1936). *Journal of the American Society for Psychical Research, 35,* 31–39.
Turvey, V. N. (n. d., ca 1909). *The beginnings of seership: Or, supernormal mental activity.* Stead.
De Vesme, C. (1931). *A history of experimental spiritualism* (2 vols.). Rider. (Original work published in French, 1928).
Vickers, B. (1984a). Introduction. In Vickers, B. (ed.) *Occult and scientific mentalities in the renaissance.* Cambridge University Press.
Vickers, B. (ed.) (1984b). *Occult and scientific mentalities in the renaissance.* Cambridge University Press.
Von Hartmann, E. (1885). Spiritism. *Light 5,* 405–409, 417–421, 429–432, 441–443, 453–456, 466–470, 479–482, 491–494.
Wedgwood, H. (1886). Planchette writing. *Journal of the Society for Psychical Research, 2,* 189–192.
Westfall, R. S. (1977). *The construction of modern science: Mechanisms and mechanics.* Wiley.
Westfall, R. S. (1980). *Never at rest: A biography of Isaac Newton.* Cambridge University Press.
Wyld, G. (1881). The formative power of spirit imagination and will. *Light 1,* 409.
Yates, F. A. (1978). *The Rosicrucian enlightenment.* Shambhala. (Original work published 1972).
Young, R. M. (1970). *Mind, brain and adaptation in the nineteenth century: Cerebral localization and its biological context from Gall to Ferrier.* Clarendon Press.

Note on Charles Richet's "La Suggestion Mentale et le Calcul des Probabilités" (1884)*

Carlos S. Alvarado

In 1884 French physiologist Charles Richet published an article on "mental suggestion" in the *Revue philosophique de la France et de l'étrangere* that is an early classic of experimental parapsychology. This work is generally remembered for the use of statistical evaluation of ESP experiments. Nonetheless, Richet discussed other issues as well that are generally neglected. This included reanalyses of previously published thought-transference studies, and discussions of topics such as the place of mental suggestion in science, study participants, and the relationship of mediumship to the unconscious mind. Furthermore, in this paper Richet wrote about a variety of issues related to ESP such as its various features, targets, motor automatisms, its unconscious nature, and theoretical issues.

A historian of psychology referred to an 1884 attempt "to make mental suggestion a scientific subject by the use of probability calculations ..." Carroy, 2004, p. 226). This was a reference to one of the most important nineteenth century reports of experimental ESP tests. Published by French physiologist, physician, and psychical researcher Charles Richet (1884), the paper was entitled, "La Suggestion Mentale et le Calcul des Probabilités." It appeared in the December 1884 issue of the *Revue philosophique de la France et de l'étrangere*, a journal that published later several examples of "sleep" induced at a distance, such as the famous work of Pierre Janet (1886a, b) and the observations of others (e.g., Beaunis, 1886; Dufay, 1888).

Richet defined mental suggestion in the paper as the "influence that an individual's thought exerts over a specific sense, without an appreciable exterior phenomenon on our senses, over the thought of a nearby individual" (Richet, 1884, p. 615, this, and other translations, are mine). The term mental suggestion was widely used in France to mean the active sending of thoughts, images, and other effects including commands to induce trance at a distance (for overviews see Ochorowicz, 1887/1891; Plas, 2000, p. 87–109).

Richet's paper received both sympathetic (Gurney, 1884) and unsympathetic (Franklin, 1885) contemporary commentaries. Later discussions on the statistical aspects of the paper include those of historians (Hacking, 1988, p. 438–439) and parapsychologists. Among the latter, J.B. Rhine said that Richet deserved "credit for the first use of the mathematics of chance in evaluating results of telepathy tests ..." (Rhine, 1947, p. 16). Jahn and Dunne (1987) affirmed that Richet's statistical approach "strongly influenced the subsequent analytical strategies" (Jahn & Dunne 1987, p. 41) of

*Republished with permission from *Journal of Scientific Exploration*, *22*, 543–548, 2008.

parapsychology and other disciplines. In this note I briefly discuss additional and generally neglected contributions of Richet in his 1884 paper.

Reanalyses of Previous Thought-Transference Experiments

In addition to the statistical analyses of his own data, Richet's work presents an early example of the statistical reanalyses of previously published experimental studies (pp. 633–634). For example, in some trials of thought-transference studies published by the Society for Psychical Research (Barrett et al., 1882) it was found that there were five consecutive hits. Richet argued that there was one chance in 52 to select the proper card from a deck of playing cards. The successful guessing of a second card was associated with a "probability … of 1/52 × 1/52 … and, in consequence, to state exactly five times the suit of a card, the probability is … 1/16.680.235 …" (p. 633). This, Richet believed, showed that chance did not account for the results.

Regarding other tests in the same report in which eight hits were reported to occur, Richet stated that the probability was "1/528 = 1/7 164 938 643 456" (p. 634). In Richet's view this was equivalent to selecting the single black ball from the remaining 7,164,938,643,455 white balls in an urn.

Targets

Richet not only used playing cards to test for mental suggestion. He also utilized "photographs of paintings, of statues, of antique objects, of scenes, of diverse topics" (p. 635). Richet commented that the photographs "certainly strike the imagination in a way that is more powerful than a simple playing card" (p. 635). There were also tests in which hidden objects and letters served as targets.

Mental Suggestion and the Unconscious

Richet believed that mental suggestion acted on the "unconscious faculties of intelligence" (p. 639). The person receiving the message was not aware of the fact. But such information could manifest through weak unconscious movements. This is what led him to use the dowsing rod and table tilting, as discussed below.

Motor Automatisms

In addition to guessing tasks, Richet used motor automatisms to obtain responses from his participants. He reported tests in which the response was produced through movements produced by table turning. To accomplish this Richet had the persons on the table (designated as C, D, and E) sitting with their backs to two individuals, who sat on a separate table with a board displaying the alphabet. An electric battery was connected to a bell and to the legs of a table so that when any leg was raised the bell would ring. Two other participants were designated as A and B. The person designated as A moved his finger along the alphabet and, when the bell rang (meaning that one of the table's legs rose), B wrote down the letter where the finger was resting. This took place without the table tilters knowing the identity of the letter. Some "quick and repeated movements indicated that the word or the phrase were finished" (p. 653).

To the surprise of C, D, and E, "the word had a meaning, the phrase had a significance" (p. 653). In some tests someone asked for a specific name or reply. Many responses had letters that were either before or after the correct letter in terms of their position in the alphabet and that had the same number of letters, responses that Richet tried to quantify.

Tests were also done using dowsing rods. In one group of tests several pictures representing objects, animals, and persons were placed on a table. Someone concentrated on a picture, while another tried to select the picture using the rod and its movements as responses. The rod was also used in other places and for other tasks, such as trying to find objects placed on a shelf in Richet's library.

Features of Mental Suggestion

Richet noticed the faculty was "very capricious, wandering, uncertain" (p. 616). It manifested "in different degrees with different individuals" (p. 616). Richet referred both to target displacement and declines in the subject's performance. The displacements seemed to be related to consistent confusions of one target for another.

Participants

Good results were obtained with adults "in good health, not hypnotized, nor hypnotizable ..." (p. 632). Most of his tests were done with "non sensitive persons, such as my friends and myself ..." (p. 632). Richet tested himself repeatedly. He posited that two participants in his studies, Mlle. B. and Mme H., were "very sensitive to magnetism" (p. 635), meaning that they were hypnotizable. These individuals were said to have obtained in some tests 22 hits out of 54 trials, where mean chance expectation was 10.

Tests performed with table tilting were done with five of Richet's childhood friends. They were described as educated and intelligent, and lacking in mystical tendencies. Two of them, Gaston Fourier and Henri Ferrari, were said to be mediums. While Richet and the others could not cause the table to move, his two friends could. It should be pointed out that both Fournier and Ferrari participated in many of the above-mentioned tests which Richet said were conducted with non-sensitive persons.

Explanation of Mental Suggestion

Richet said that, regarding the explanation of mental suggestion: "Theory, explanation, is currently quite impossible" (p. 618). Nonetheless, while acknowledging that the process behind such phenomena was an unknown one, he speculated. Richet mentioned the possible existence of a force emitted by an agent, "such that the vibration of the thought of an individual influences the vibration of the thought of a nearby individual" (p. 617).

He further wrote that if a candle could "produce a very clear light at night at 200 meters from us, it seems absurd that at three or four meters of distance cerebral activity shows no action on close-by objects" (p. 668).

Mental Suggestion and Science

From the beginning of the paper Richet let his readers know of the controversial and improbable nature of mental suggestion. He said that the topic at hand was different from the "facts commonly admitted by science" (p. 609). The results of mental suggestion tests are "improbable facts; but their improbability is entirely relative; in the sense that none of them contradict the known facts, acquired by science" (p. 615).

In addition to warning his readers about the incredible nature of the phenomena, he cautioned them to keep in mind the "insufficience and impotence of current science" (p. 609) both to explain many facts of nature as well as mental suggestion.

Mediums

On a different topic, Richet also discussed mediums in terms of the unconscious mind. "In reality," he wrote, "all the intelligent manifestations attributed to the spirits are due to an individual that is unconscious and active at the same time" (p. 650). But such individual (the medium) was not aware of this.

Richet speculated that these persons were in a state of hemisomnambulism in which part of the brain accomplishes some operations, produces thoughts, receives perceptions without the awareness of the self. The consciousness of this individual persists in its apparent integrity: all the very complicated operations are accomplished outside of consciousness, without the voluntary conscious self apparently feeling any modification (p. 650).

In this view a medium was a person showing "partial unconsciousness, a faculty by which part of its intelligence, of her memory, of her will, operates out of consciousness …" (pp. 650–651).

Concluding Remarks

Although Richet published several influential discussions throughout his career about mental suggestion, and what he later called lucidity and the sixth sense (e.g., Richet, 1888, 1889, n. d.), his 1884 paper is still considered a classic of early experimental parapsychology. Clearly, Richet had more to offer in this paper than card guessing tests and statistical analyses, the latter being of considerable importance. He presented information about reanalyses, targets, motor responses to targets, features of mental suggestion, and participants' characteristics, and speculated that mental suggestion acted unconsciously, and that it may be related to the emission of unspecified vibrations.

Richet's views of vibrations were consistent with ideas of human radiations to explain ESP, ideas that preceded and that were discussed around the time he was writing (Alvarado, 2006). Richet continued discussing these ideas in later years. As he wrote in the late 1920s: "The sixth sense is that one which gives us knowledge of a vibration of reality, a vibration which our normal senses are unable to perceive" (Richet, n. d., p. 224).

The involvement of non-conscious levels of the mind in telepathy and mediumship was an idea that started being discussed during the nineteenth century by writers with different conceptions about these hidden levels of the mind. Some had postulated that table-tilters produced the movement with their own hands but without their own awareness (e.g., Chevreul, 1854/1992), and that genuine (and veridical) mediumistic phenomena could take place thanks to unconscious reflex actions of the brain (Rogers, 1853/1856). Earlier in 1884 before Richet's paper was published, there were discussions in publications of the Society for Psychical Research on both the subconscious aspects of motor automatisms and telepathy (Barrett et al., 1884; Myers, 1884). Richet (1886) himself discussed the topic two years later, but his discussions were never as detailed or attentive to the concept of a self-reflective subconscious mind as those of Myers (1884, 1885).

Richet's paper is not only a testament to his creative talents, but also provides us with a fascinating view of concepts and methodology that were developed further in later years.

References

Alvarado, C. S. (2006). Human radiations: Concepts of force in mesmerism, spiritualism and psychical research. *Journal of the Society for Psychical Research, 70,* 138–162.

Barrett, W. F., Gurney, E., & Myers, F. W. H. (1882). First report on thought-reading. *Proceedings of the Society for Psychical Research, 1,* 13–34.

Barrett, W. F., Massey, C. C., Moses, W. S., Podmore, F., Gurney, E., & Myers, F. W. H. (1884). Third report of the Literary Committee: A theory of apparitions: Part I. *Proceedings of the Society for Psychical Research, 2,* 109–136.

Beaunis, H. (1886). Un fait de suggestion mentale. *Revue Philosophique de la France et de L'étrangere, 21,* 204.

Carroy, J. (2004). Playing with signatures: The young Charles Richet. In Micale, M. S. (Ed.), *The Mind of Modernism: Medicine, Psychology, and the Cultural Arts in Europe and America, 1880–1940* (pp. 217–249). Stanford University Press.

Chevreul, M. E. (1992). De la *varilla adivinatoria del pendulo llamado explorador y de las mesas giratorias desde el punto de vista de la historia de la crltica y del metodo experimental* (J. Guerrera Escofet, trans.). Editorial Humanitas. (Original work published 1854)

Dufay, Dr. (1888). Contribution à l'etude du somnambulisme provoque à distance et à l'insu du sujet. *Revue philosophique de la France et de L'étrangere, 26,* 301–312.

Franklin, C. L. (1885). Richet on mental suggestion. *Science, 5,* 132–134.

Gurney, E. (1884). M. Richet's recent researches in thought-transference. *Proceedings of the Society for Psychical Research, 2,* 239–264.

Hacking, I. (1988). Telepathy: Origins of randomization in experimental design. *Isis, 79,* 427–451.

Jahn, R. G., & Dunne, B. J. (1987). *Margins of reality: The role of consciousness in the physical world.* Harcourt Brace Jovanovich.

Janet, P. (1886a). Note sur quelques phénomènes de sonambulisme. *Revue Philosophique de la France et de l'Étranger, 21,* 190–198.

Janet, P. (1886b). Deuxieme note sur le somneil provoque à distance et la suggestion mentale pendant l'etat somnambulique. *Revue Philosophique de la France et de l'Étranger, 22,* 212–223.

Myers, F. W. H. (1884). On a telepathic explanation of some so-called spiritualistic phenomena: Part I. *Proceedings of the Society for Psychical Research, 2,* 217–237.

Myers, F. W. H. (1885). Automatic writing—II. *Proceedings of the Society for Psychical Research, 3,* 1–63.

Ochorowicz, J. (1891). *Mental suggestion* (J. Fitzgerald, trans.). Humbolt. (Original work published 1887)

Plas, R. (2000). *Naissance d'une science humaine: La psychologie: Les psychologues et le "merveilleux psychique."* Presses Universitaires de Rennes.

Rhine, J. B. (1947). *The reach of the mind.* William Sloane.

Richet, C. (1884). La suggestion mentale et le calcul des probabilites. *Revue Philosophique de la France et de l'Étranger, 18,* 609–674.

Richet, C. (1886). Les mouvements inconscients. In Berthelot, M. (Ed.), *Hommage à Monsieur Chevreul a l'occasion de son centenaire 31 aout 1886* (pp. 79–84). Félix Alcan.

Richet, C. (1888). Relation de diverses experiences sur la transmissions mentales, la lucidité, et autres phénomènes non explicables par les données scientifiques actuelles. *Proceedings of the Society for Psychical Research, 5,* 18–168.
Richet, C. (1889). Further experiments in hypnotic lucidity or clairvoyance. *Proceedings of the Society for Psychical Research, 6,* 66–83.
Richet, C. (n.d.). *Our sixth sense.* Rider.
Rogers, E. C. (1856). *Philosophy of mysterious agents, human and mundane; or, the Dynamic laws and relations of man.* J. P. Jewett. (Original work published 1853)

Review of Andrea Graus' *Historical Views of Spiritism and Mediumship in Spain, 1880–1930**

Carlos S. Alvarado

Little is known by non-Spanish speakers about the history of Spiritism and psychical research in Spain. Standard English-language sources such as Frank Podmore's *Modern Spiritualism* (1902) and Arthur Conan Doyle's *The History of Spiritualism* (1926) do not cover developments in that country.[1] There is a useful historical outline of the topic in philosopher and educator Mario Méndez Bejarano's *Historia de la Filoscfía en España Hasta el Siglo XX* (n. d., Chapter 17, Part 14). Much of relevance can be found in the new historiography about the subject in Spain which, like that in some other countries, has grown in recent decades.[2] Other recent studies have included psychical research as well. Particularly useful are the essays compiled by Annette Mülberger (2016) in *Los Límites de la Ciencia: Espiritismo, Hipnotismo y el Estudio de los Fenómenos Paranormales* (1850–1930), and articles about such topics as the attitudes and approaches of specific investigators (Vilaplana Traviera & Mülberger, 2003), turning tables (González de Pablo, 2006), and prominent clairvoyance studies (Mülberger & Balltondre, 2013). Andrea Graus, the author of the book reviewed here, has also made various significant contributions.

Graus, a historian at the Centre Alexandre Koyré, has published various articles about mediumistic investigations, and the ideas of Spanish physicians (e.g., Graus, 2015, 2016). This work has been expanded in the book reviewed here, *Ciencia y Espiritismo en España, 1880–1930.*

Spiritism developed in the second half of the nineteenth century in Spain, following the line of Allan Kardec, who was particularly influential in France (Sharp, 2006). From the 1850s on, several Spanish mediums and students of the subject appeared. The Catholic Church must have felt the movement was growing too much, when on October 9, 1861, they burnt more than 300 spiritist books in Barcelona that came into the country illegally for a French librarian who resided in the city.[3]

By 1888, when the first of various later international spiritist congresses was held in Barcelona, spiritists included important leaders such as writer Amalia Domingo y Soler notary José María Fernández Colavida, philosopher Manuel Sanz Benito, and politician and journalist Viscount Antonio de Torres Solanot y Casas, all of whom took part in the congress (Primer Congreso, 1888).

As stated by one of these leaders, the movement came to answer the questions raised in an age of criticism and skepticism, questions that neither science, nor philosophy, nor religion could answer. Spiritism was a "new element of progress" that arrived at "the twilight of a passing age, and it is the dawn of a coming age" which "*puts us in connection with the invisible world, showing us the future life*" (Torres Solanot, 1875, p. 69, italics in the original; this, and other translations, are mine). This author stated he did not want to impose a belief but instead to invite people to study and experiment. His writings, however, do not show a scientific approach, but rather a missionary perspective that was common among other nineteenth-century writers, both in Spain (Navarro Murillo, 1873–1874) and in other countries (e.g., Brittan, 1851).[4] The individuals covered in the book reviewed here attempted to redefine Spiritism in Spain along more scientific lines.

*Republished with permission from *Journal of Scientific Exploration, 35*(2), 389–404, 2021.

Graus' Book

The author states that "by the end of the XIX century there was a slow appropriation of mediumship from the scientific area, especially within psychiatric and psychological domains" (p. 7). A new conception of mediumship emerged that saw the phenomena as the result of the powers of the living medium, as opposed to discarnate agency. The phenomena "were caused by man, be they through unknown faculties or by natural forces that mediums were able to channel" (p. 7). The book is to some extent about representatives of these ideas in Spain.

Later in the book Graus briefly reviews the psychological, and particularly clinical, approach to mediumship, arguing that the "development of theories about automatism, multiple personalities, or altered states of consciousness was strongly influenced by the study of spiritist mediums, who were transformed into subjects of psychological investigation" (pp. 35–36). This idea has generated a specialized literature that has appeared in forums other than those devoted to history (e.g., Alvarado et al., 2007).

The discussion includes mention of several pioneering non-Spanish writings about the pathology of mediums, such as the ideas about dissociation of French psychopathologist Pierre Janet (p. 41). Janet stated in his classic work *L'Automatisme Psychologique* (1889) that the majority of mediums "are neuropaths, when they are not frankly hysterics" (p. 404). Interestingly, and illustrating Graus' general outlook, an examination of Janet's book shows that he was influenced by psychical researchers. Janet cited the work of well-known English classical scholar and psychical researcher Frederic W. H. Myers to provide examples of dissociation and the phenomena of mediumship (Janet, 1889, pp. 78, 121–122, 135–136, 371, 392–394, 403, 405, 415–419).

He used this material, and writings from spiritists, to provide examples of mediumistic communications in order to construct his model of dissociation, an example of influence from a marginal discipline to a more established one. But the use of Myers's ideas was selective, that is, Janet stripped them from their supernormal component and kept those aspects of it that did not conflict with his views. Incidentally, although Janet did not agree with Myers in several ways, he recognized that Myers had presented a model of dissociation that was more developed than what had been published before (Janet, 1889, p. 403).

Graus starts the first chapter with physician Manuel Otero Acevedo (1865–1920) who was born in Argentina but was educated and worked mainly in Spain. Initially a self-confessed materialist and a skeptic, this physician eventually accepted the reality of psychic phenomena via his own observations and study of the work of others. For example, he conducted observations about mental suggestion and had séances with Eusapia Palladino that convinced him that her phenomena were real. The latter were mentioned in the second volume of his book *Los Espíritus* (Otero Acevedo, 1893–1895). Otero had séances with the medium in Naples in 1888 and 1889. In a section of the book (Vol. 2, pp. 217–255) he classified the phenomena he observed as complete and partial levitations with the medium touching the table; complete and partial levitations of a table when the medium was not touching the table; action on distant objects; changes of weight in tables; levitation of the medium; direct writing; luminous phenomena (small lights and materialized forms); and impressions of fingers, hands, and faces on plaster. Anyone familiar with the literature about this medium will realize that similar effects were reported by many others in later years (e.g., Carrington, 1909).

Otero several times saw violent movements of the séance table. On one occasion he made the medium kneel on a chair and put both hands inside two cups full of water, hoping to control for hand movements, but the table still moved around. He wrote:

[The table] responds to questions I ask with movements and blows, and in turn asks if I am satisfied with the event ... A notable peculiarity: The cups remain firm despite the swings of the table, as if they were attached to the wood ..." (Otero Acevedo, 1893–1895, Vol. 2, p. 221)

The reports of materialized forms were even more impressive. In one of them, Otero reported that the medium started saying her spine was hurting, and she got nervous, yelled and writhed, and the curtains of the mediumistic cabinet moved. He wrote:

> The curtain is shaken again and at the door appeared the outline of an arm that lengthened and quickly withdrew; waves its hand as if saying hello, and disappears. Immediately it leans out by the edge of the curtain, and at a height that corresponds to the screen in the room [a lamp screen], the silhouette of a head, visible up to the neck ... The arm comes out again, the head makes some movements and a shadow crosses the door. The head reappears on the opposite side to the one that it previously occupied, and taking a bow disappeared. (Otero Acevedo, 1893–1895, Vol. 2, pp. 246–247)

Interestingly, Graus makes a comparison between Otero and Lombroso, who shared some correspondence. They both started their study of mediums through Palladino and with an ingrained materialist conviction. This led them to deny, a priori, the spiritist hypothesis. Lombroso was influenced by German materialism and tried to give a physiological explanation for mediumistic phenomena. Both of them attempted to place the phenomena observed with Palladino within "official science," but when they could not find a satisfactory explanation that could account for all the facts, they reached the conclusion that there existed phenomena that seemed to explain the existence of spirit (p. 32).

Also interesting, but beyond the scope of this study, is a topic I have discussed before. I am referring to the influence of individuals such as mediums who generate phenomena, in this case the impact that Palladino had on the development of psychical research (Alvarado, 1993). This included converting many individuals to the belief in real physical phenomena, and, in the case of some, of spiritualistic interpretations. Furthermore, this medium exerted much influence on theoretical ideas of psychic forces via her phenomena and behaviors (in interaction with the ideas and agendas of researchers), and in generating for many people negative images of séance phenomena.

The second chapter is about the physician Víctor Melcior i Farré (1860–1929), from the province of Lleida, in Catalonia. He represented what Graus refers to as an interest that instead of emphasizing spirit action, concentrated on "the interior aspects of the medium, in her subconscious, to try to find the natural cause, psychophysiological, of the spiritist marvels unexplained by science" (p. 36). However, Melcior's approach, as Graus says, differed from the point of view of psychopathologists like Pierre Janet. While Janet only believed in pathology, and not in veridical mental and physical manifestations, Melcior believed in the coexistence of pathology and real phenomena in mediums. This is a conceptual tradition upheld by a few theoreticians, as I have argued in the case of Jules Bernard Luys' ideas of "magnetic" pathology and Cesare Lombroso's explanations of Palladino's physical phenomena (Alvarado, 2019; Alvarado & Biondi, 2017). Interestingly, Graus states that Melcior defended reincarnation following Kardec's ideas (p. 37).

The author writes that Melcior believed that mediumistic communications, and the personality changes in mediums, were explained by dissociation, and the physical phenomena by the projection of vital force from the body of the medium. Neither process involved spirits of the dead. Graus writes:

> According to Melcior, the irradiation of such force did not always manifest with the same intensity, which allowed [him] to classify the subjects into three "psychic types": the weak, the medium,

> and the strong … Melcior defended this stance saying the instability of character and weakness of will facilitated this process … [and he argued that] the passing of psychological doubling to the physical depended on the degree of irradiation of the psychic force. In lower levels it induced creaks, movement of objects, levitation, or apparitions of lights. And last: "in the superior degree of doubling there comes out the phantasmal body of a living person, moving to more or less remote places, and coming to be recognized by the person or persons to whom it appears." (pp. 51–52)

Graus is right to relate these ideas to those of Albert de Rochas, who argued that the exteriorization of forces from the body was associated with a fluidic body or double. This had four phases of the exteriorization of a double, the last one being a physical materialization of a human body. This, according to de Rochas, consisted of "a galvanoplastic transport of the matter of the physical body of the medium, matter that comes from the physical body to occupy a similar position on the fluidic body" (de Rochas, 1897, p. 27).

We are introduced to astronomer Josep Comas i Solà (1868–1937) in the third chapter, and to his séances with medium Carmen Dommguez, who produced, among other phenomena, materializations. While the astronomer may have wanted to bring mediumistic phenomena into science, Graus argues that the spiritists had their own agenda. In her words: "The spiritists did not get in contact with him so that we would confirm the reality of the phenomena, but that, through his authority, he would legitimize them within the scientific sphere" (p. 85). Unfortunately, the whole enterprise did not go well, for Comas accused the medium of fraud, and he entered into controversies about her and the proper way to study mediums, a topic he discussed in his book *El Espiritismo ante la Ciencia* (n. d.).

In this book, Comas argued that the scientific study of natural phenomena would always be legitimate. But a science "based on the study of phenomena that flow from the consciousness of man is condemned, due to its origin, to the infamy of lies" (Comas i Solà, n. d., p. 21), by which he referred to fraud. Interestingly, he went on to discuss physical ideas of matter and energy, from which he speculated on the mechanisms of mediumistic materialization, a phenomenon he did not seem to believe in. In his book, Comas started out assuming that the body of the medium showed a "lack of cohesion or a lack of unity in its organism" (p. 87) that involved the projection of an "individual" from the medium's body. This "new imponderable and invisible individual, completely or partially away from the medium, would have the same forces and the same mentality of the medium, but necessarily diminished" (p. 88) and be similar in shape to the medium's body.

In the fourth chapter we are introduced to physician Humbert Torres i Barberà (1879–1955) who was in contact with French psychical researchers and studied the medium Marcelle Morell. Graus points out that Torres was educated in French metapsychics, and she provides a brief overview of such developments (pp. 92–101).

Torres presented a series of public lectures in 1926 that show he was well-acquainted with the international psychical research literature (De Todas Partes, 1926). The first part, consisting of three presentations, was about phenomena produced by the living, among them telepathy, exteriorization of sensitivity, telekinesis, and materializations. The second part was about phenomena suggestive of discarnate agency. This had two lectures about various mediumistic phenomena and recollection of previous lives.[5] The first included mechanical (table movements and raps), graphic (photographs, automatic writing), spoken (possession, direct writing), plastic (apparitions, materializations) and various other kinds of phenomena (book tests, hauntings).

Graus comments that one of the strategies the French used to separate themselves from Spiritism was a change of terminology, which presented "a view of mediumship that can be defined as 'properly' metapsychic, in that it is destined to show the limits of this field and to be demarcated from Spiritism"

(p. 97). This view, I believe, is consistent with Charles Richet's definition of metapsychics without reference to spirits or nonphysical processes. He proposed calling metapsychics "a science which has as its object mechanical or psychological phenomena due to forces which seem intelligent, or to unknown powers latent in human intelligence" (Richet, 1922, p. 5, italics in original removed). However, Torres was open to discarnate agency as an explanation.

In this chapter Graus presents two organizations that represented attempts to organize metapsychics in Spain. These were the Instituto de Metapsiquismo de Barcelona (founded in 1923) and the Sociedad Espanola de Estudios Metapsíquicos de Madrid (founded in 1924). Both were short-lived and consequently not able to provide much institutional support for psychic investigations. The first one was seen by some of its founders as an attempt to use the scientific investigation of psychic phenomena to assist Spiritism, but it does not seem to have produced research. The second group was founded by Joaquín María Argamasilla de la Cerda y Bayona (1870–1940), known as the marquis of Santa Cara, who believed his son was a clairvoyant.[6] Graus states that, unfortunately, very little of the work of this organization was published. In fact, she suggests that the purpose of the group may have been for Santa Cara to establish his position as the main representative of metapsychics in Spain.

The Sociedad published a journal, *Revista de Estudios Metapsíquicos*, that defined the agenda of the organization as that of atheoretical experimental investigations of psychic phenomena. Announcements appeared in the journal asking the public for information about and access to individuals with psychic faculties. This reminds me of the situation at the beginning of the Society for Psychical Research in London. A letter appeared in *The Times* (of London) on Christmas day of 1883, asking for cases of various types of psychic phenomena to be sent to Edmund Gurney or to Frederic W. H. Myers (Advertisement, 1883). Similarly, the Proceedings of the Society also asked members to conduct thought-transference experiments, and to send information about mediums and haunted houses, as well as published accounts of psychic phenomena found in biographies and in other published sources (To Members, 1883).

Graus reminds us that, in Spain, the relationship between academic psychology and metapsychics was affected by the nascent state of the first discipline. This led some psychologists to engage in boundary work to demarcate between metapsychics and psychology. Here the author introduces the work of psychologist and Jesuit priest Father Fernando María Palmés (1879–1963), who was a strong enemy of metapsychics. "Together with psychologists such as Jastrow in the United States, he argued that only those who were experts in experimental psychology could judge the reality of spiritist phenomena and he assumed the role of guardian of scientific knowledge" regarding metapsychics and Spiritism (p. 113). His attitude, continues Graus, shows that "psychology in Spain still was on fragile ground and struggled for its own scientific legitimacy" (p. 113).[7]

Summary

Graus' book is a valuable contribution to the historiography of both Spanish psychical research and mediumship. Her discussions of the above-mentioned individuals not only enlarge our knowledge of specific investigations and ideas, but also show that the researches she focuses on were connected with what was happening in other countries.

In addition to the individuals she focuses on, Graus also rescues from oblivion other figures such as the above-mentioned Palmés. This is important because in giving space to Palmés she reminds us that the history of psychical research is not only the study of the work of proponents for the reality of the phenomena, but also includes critics, something that is not always recognized by contemporary parapsychologists.

Furthermore, she notices that there is no evidence of connections between the various research projects, or of important institutional developments, even though she mentions some organizations. The fact that their work took place outside academia did not lead the researchers to consider that their work was not scientific. They instead hoped for the development of a new field of study based mainly on the study of mediums. "In this sense, they believed that the investigation of mediums could mean an advance in scientific knowledge, and trusted that their work would one day be recognized as pioneering" (p. 116).

The author also, rightly in my view, questions the use of the term pseudoscience.

> From the historiographic point of view, to be interested in Spiritism and in psychical research is not to ask oneself what turns these fields pseudoscientific, or if they are the mere product of a fraud. The history of the so-called pseudosciences is … a way of getting closer to science, of understanding how knowledge functions in this context and to investigate how scientists mark their terrain and assume positions in society. (p. 117)

Furthermore, Graus sees that the persons she discussed contributed to scientific knowledge during difficult times. That is, when their topics were being highly criticized and when the "professionalization of science defined what and who formed part of a scientific domain" (p. 117).

Graus presents a valuable contribution to the history of psychical research in her discussion of the work and ideas of the above-mentioned men, individuals who have not been well-represented in the international historiography of the subject. She argues at the end of the book that she is not saying that the persons discussed in the book were eccentrics who were simply deceived by mediums. Regardless of the neglect of their work by science at large, these researchers "contributed to the production of a different kind of scientific knowledge, particularly psychological and psychiatric" (p. 117). In conclusion, Graus writes that the role of history is not to determine if a field is pseudoscientific, or if fraud is a likely explanation. In her view the history of the so-called pseudosciences is a way to approach science (p. 117).

Graus' focus on mediumship, and other phenomena, does not emphasize Otero's interest in showing the universality of psychic phenomena in the history of humankind. This is the topic of the first volume of his work *Los Espíritus* (Otero Acevedo, 1893–1895), where he discussed belief and interest in psychic phenomena in past civilizations, such as those of the Assyrians, Chaldeans, Egyptians, Etruscans, Greeks, Hebrews, Indians, Phoenicians, and Romans. Such a massive undertaking is part of a rhetorical tradition present in mesmeric and spiritualist writings to support the reality and importance of psychic phenomena by showing the universality of cases and beliefs across time and cultures (Alvarado, 2014). Otero argued that the then current trends to neglect and deny psychic phenomena show how little humanity has learned about its own history. In his view: "Known from the most remote antiquity, in the first civilizations of which news is preserved today, they have subsisted in all ages, in all times and in all peoples, because they are a manifestation of human organization" (Vol. 1, p. 29).

It should also be mentioned that the second volume of *Los Espíritus* helped to publicize in Spain investigations of various individuals from other countries. There are chapters about the work and ideas of William Crookes, Johann C. F. Zöllner, Aleksandr Aksakov, Ercole Chiaia, and Paul Gibier (Ch. 1–5, respectively). This allows us to see a further dimension of Otero's work, that of popularizer and reviewer of the history of psychical research. A further example is a series of 12 articles that were published in the Spanish newspaper *El Heraldo de Madrid*, in which the author discussed topics such as apparitions of the living, materializations, mental suggestion, and the physical phenomena of Eusapia Palladino (Otero Acevedo, 1891).

Concluding Remarks

There are several minor inconsistencies regarding what certain authors said, and I have some disagreements with some statements, but these shortcomings don't detract from the overall value of the book, the importance of her historical study, or her conclusions. Her work is a pioneering one that I hope will inspire other research efforts in Spain. To restate, *Ciencia y Espiritismo en España, 1880–1930* not only informs us about investigative and theoretical developments in Spain that are generally unknown even to those interested in the histories of Spiritism and psychical research, but it also illuminates social aspects of that history, such as the main figures, their relation to local spiritists, and contacts with foreign figures. The study also shows the existence of Spanish theoretical ideas of pathology, the unconscious mind, and unorthodox concepts of force. All of this shows the influence of foreign concepts (mainly French), and the commonality of conceptual and methodological issues in the international study of mediumship.

Notes

1 For example, Spain is not represented in more recent overviews of spiritualistic and psychical research topics such as Beloff's (1993) general history of parapsychology and Moreman's (2013) anthology of articles about spiritualism and psychical research.

2 Some examples include Abend (2004) and Balltondre and Graus (2016).

3 The burned materials included issues of *Revue Spirite, Revue Spiritualiste*, and books by Allan Kardec, as well as by authors such as Ermance Dufaux, A. Grand, and Ludwig von Guldenstubbe (La Queue, 1861). In the anonymous article its author (probably Kardec), said that it seemed a dream that the fires of the Inquisition were still burning in 1861 (p. 321). In addition, this author also wrote: "Thanks to this reckless zeal, everyone in Spain will hear about Spiritism and will want to know what it is ..." (p. 323). Writing in a Spanish newspaper, an anonymous author considered the book-burning an indication of hypocrisy, fanatism, and barbarism (Untitled Article, 1861).

4 In other publications Torres-Solanot (1872) recognized the value of empirical studies of psychic phenomena.

5 Torres (1923) had previously published an article about reincarnation in which he classified cases in terms of recollections in the waking state, those that were announced via visions, dreams, and spirit communications, and those in which details were given through hypnosis and mediumship.

6 Santa Cara's son, Joaquín María Argamasilla de La Cerda y Elio (1905–1985), received much publicity in Spain and was tested at the Institut Métapsychique International (Mülberger & Balltondre, 2013). For a prominent accusation of fraud outside of the Spanish context, see Houdini (1924). Santa Cara (n. d.) was known in Spain for his studies with clairvoyants.

7 For a discussion of Father Palmés, see Mülberger et al. (2001). I would argue that Palmés' work represents the agendas of at least two groups. He represented psychologists and others who built boundaries between established and unorthodox knowledge regarding psychic phenomena (Brown, 1983; Coon, 1992). In addition, he was part of a tradition of Catholic (and generally Christian) opposition to psychic phenomena, sometimes labelling them as satanic. This opposition is discussed in the context of other countries by Biondi (2013, Chapter 3) and Sharp (2006, pp. 140–145). It must be clarified that not all this opposition came from the clergy, and that many members of the clergy have been positive about the existence of psychic phenomena (Nicol, 1966).

References

Abend, L. (2004). Specters of the secular: Spiritism in nineteenth-century Spain. *European History Quarterly, 34*(4), 507–534.

[Advertisement]. (1883, December 25). *The Times*, p. 1.

Alvarado, C. S. (1993). Gifted subjects' contributions to parapsychology: The case of Eusapia Palladino. *Journal of the Society for Psychical Research, 59*(833), 269–292.

Alvarado, C. S. (2014). On constancy, stability and the antiquity of psychic phenomena. *Paranormal Review, 69*, 3–7.

Alvarado, C. S. (2019). Jules Bernard Luys on magnetic pathology (Classic text no. 119). *History of Psychiatry, 30*(3), 359–374.

Alvarado, C. S., & Biondi, M. (2017). Cesare Lombroso on mediumship and pathology (Classic text no. 110). *History of Psychiatry, 28*(2), 225–241.

Alvarado, C. S., Machado, F. R., Zangari, W., & Zingrone, N. L. (2007). Perspectivas históricas da influência da mediunidade na construção de ideias psicológicas e psiquiátricas. R*evista de Psiquiatria Clínica, 34* (supp. 1), 42–53.

Balltondre, M. & Graus, A. (2016). The city of spirits: Spiritism, feminism and the secularization of urban spaces. In O. Hochadel & A. Nieto–Galan (Eds.), *Barcelona: An urban history of science and modernity, 1888–1929* (pp. 136–157). Routledge.

Beloff, J. (1993). *Parapsychology: A concise history*. Athlone Press.

Biondi, M. (2013). Spiritualism in Italy: The opposition of the Catholic church. In C. Moreman (Ed.), *The spiritualist movement: Speaking with the dead in America and around the world* (Vol. 1, pp. 37–53). Praeger.

Brittan, S. B. (1851). Spiritualism: Its nature and mission. *The Shekinah, 1*(1), 1–12.

Brown, E. M. (1983). Neurology and spiritualism in the 1870s. *Bulletin of the History of Medicine, 57*(4), 563–577.

Carrington, H. (1909). *Eusapia Palladino and her phenomena.* B. W. Dodge.

Comas i Solà, J. (n.d., ca. 1908). *El espiritismo ante la ciencia: Estudio crítico sobre la mediumnidad.* F. Granada.

Coon, D. J. (1992). Testing the limits of sense and science: American experimental psychologists combat spiritualism, 1880–1920. *American Psychologist, 47*(2), 143–151.

de Rochas, A. (1897). Les expériences de Choisy-Yvrec (près Bordeaux du 2 au 14 octobre 1896. *Annales des Sciences Psychiques, 7,* 6–28.

De Todas Partes. (1926). *Lumen, 31*(April), IX–X.

Doyle, A. C. (1926). *The history of spiritualism* (2 vols.). Methuen.

González de Pablo, A. (2006). Sobre los inicios del espiritismo en España: La epidemia psi'quica de las mesas giratorias de 1853 en la prensa médica. *Asclepio, 58*(2), 63–96. https://doi.org/10.3989/asclepio.2006.v58.i2.22

Graus, A. (2015). Los prodigios del hombre encarnado: Víctor Melcior y la redefinición de la mediumnidad (1901). *Dynamis, 35*(1), 83–105. http://doi. org/10.4321/S0211–95362015000100004

Graus, A. (2016). Discovering Palladino's mediumship: Otero Acevedo, Lombroso and the quest for authority. *Journal of the History of the Behavioral Sciences, 52*(3), 211–230. https://doi.org/io.ioo2/jhbs.2i789

Houdini, H. (1924). *Houdini exposes the tricks used by the Boston medium "Margery" to win the $2500 prize offered by the Scientific American: Also a complete exposure of Argamasilla, the famous Spaniard who baffled noted scientists of Europe and America, with his claim to X-ray vision.* Adams Press.

Janet, P. (1889). *L'automatisme psychologique: Essai de psychologie expérimentale sur les formes inférieures de l'activité humaine*. Félix Alcan.

Méndez Bejarano, M. (n. d., ca. 1925). *Historia de la filosofía en España hasta el siglo XX.* Renacimiento.

Moreman, C. M. (Ed.). (2013). *The spiritualist movement: Speaking with the dead in America and around the world.* (3 vols.). Praeger.

Mülberger, A. (Ed.). (2016). *Los límites de la ciencia: Espiritismo, hipnotismo y el estudio de los fenómenos paranormales (1850–1930)*. Consejo Superior de Investigaciones Científicas.

Mülberger, A., & Balltondre, M. (2013). En el umbral de lo desconocido: Un caso de visión extraordinaria en la España de Primo de Rivera. *Dynamis, 33*(1), 195–216. Retrieved from https://doi.org/10.4321/s0211-95362013000100009

Mülberger, A., Astudillo, S., Lorente, S., & Martos, M. (2001). El Padre Palmés contra la metapsíquica: Un análisis histórico de su retórica defensiva. *Revista de Historia de la Psicología, 22*(3–4), 431–438.

Navarro Murillo, M. (1873–1874). El advenimiento de la nueva era de armonía. *Revista Espiritista, 5*(11, 12), 242–246, 257–260; *6*(1, 2, 3), 1–7, 25–32, 49–52.

Nicol, F. (1966). Clerical contributions to parapsychology. *International Journal of Parapsychology, 8*, 227–247.

Otero Acevedo, M. (1891, June 17, 22, 28, July 12, 19, 26, August 2, 9, 16, 22, 29, September 5). Los fantasmas. *El Heraldo de Madrid*, all on p. 1.

Otero Acevedo, M. (1893–1895). Los espíritus (2 vols.). Revista Psicológica "La Irradiación."

Podmore, F. (1902). *Modern spiritualism: A history and a criticism* (2 vols.). Methuen.

Primer Congreso Internacional Espiritista: Representaciones, adhesiones, sesiones públicas, sesiones privadas, conclusiones, documentos, etc.: Reseña completa (1888). Daniel Cortezo.

La queue du moyen âge: Auto-da-fe des ouvrages spirites à Barcelone. (1861). *Revue Spirite, 4*(11), 321–325.

Richet, C. (1922). *Traité de métapsychique*. Félix Alcan.

Santa Cara, Marqués de. (n. d., ca. 1924). *Un tanteo en el misterio (Ensayo experimental sobre la lucidez sonambúlica)*. M. Aguilar.

Sharp, L. L. (2006). *Secular spirituality: Reincarnation and spiritism in nineteenth-century France*. Lexington Books.

To members and associates of the Society for Psychical Research: Circular No. 1. (2nd ed.). On the general work of the Society. (1883). *Proceedings of the Society for Psychical Research, 1*, 295–302.

Torres, H. (1923). La reencarnación. *Lumen, 28*(December), 309–318.

Torres-Solanot, [A.]. (1872). *Preliminares al estudio del espiritismo: Consideraciones generales respecto a lafiloscffa, doctrinay ciencia espiritista*. A. de San Martin.

Torres-Solanot, [A.]. (1872). *Preliminares al estudio del espiritismo: Consideraciones generales respecto a la filosofía, doctrina y ciencia espiritista.* A. de San Martín.

Torres Solanot, [A.]. (1875). El movimiento espiritista. In *Almanaque del espiritismo para el año de 1875* (pp. 68–70). Alcántara.

[Untitled article]. (1861, October 16). *La Discusión*, 1.

Vilaplana Traviera, E., & Mülberger, A. (2003). Espiritismo, metapsíquica y ciencia: Análisis de tres aportaciones catalanas de principios del siglo XX. *Revista de Historia de la Psicología, 24*(3–4), 477–488.

Introducing and Situating Psychical Research: Eleanor M. Sidgwick's Perspective*

Carlos S. Alvarado†

"There exists in England," wrote French philosopher Émile Boirac (1898), "a very large, very successful society, the Society for Psychical Research [SPR], to which the greatest English scientists, physicians, chemists, physiologists, psychologists belong ... and which mission is to collect and control all cases of telepathy, presentiments, second sight, etc." (p. 17). Years later Italian psychiatrist Enrico Morselli (1908) stated that the SPR had finally brought systematization to the study of psychic phenomena, and that the SPR was a "large and luminous affirmation of that civil sentiment of mutual tolerance that today must unite all the true students of the search for Truth" (Vol. 1, p. 72).

While not everyone had the SPR in such high regard, such statements illustrate some of the positive publicity that the work of the SPR received during the nineteenth century, and more importantly, the high regard some had for the Society's achievements. Another example of a discussion of the work of the SPR, and the one reprinted in this paper, appeared in an article that Eleanor M. Sidgwick (1902a) wrote for a reference work.

Discussions of SPR work

In addition to the impact of the work published in the *Proceedings of the Society for Psychical Research* throughout the years, the SPR received much publicity through comments and discussions of its work appearing in various reviews and books. There were many discussions (not always positive) published in scientific and scholarly journals, such as the *American Journal of Psychology* (Hall, 1887), *Science* (Proceedings, 1886), *Journal of Science* (Review, 1882), *Revue Philosophique de la France et de l'Étranger* (Review, 1883), and *Nature* (Wells, 1894). Furthermore, the work of the SPR was presented by psychical researchers themselves and by other students of the subject, as seen in books such as *Les Phénomènes Psychiques Occultes* (Coste, 1895), *Telepathy and the Subliminal Self* (Mason, 1897), and *Studies in Psychical Research* (Podmore, 1897).

Psychical researchers also brought publicity to their work through discussions published in newspapers such as *The Times* (Alvarado, 2007) and in high-level intellectual reviews such as *Nineteenth Century* (e.g., Gurney & Myers, 1884). In addition to the original research reports and other discussions published in the *Proceedings of the Society for Psychical Research*, many publications devoted to psychic phenomena, such as Borderland and Sphinx, published regular articles and reviews about SPR work (e.g., Goodrich-Freer, 1896; Übersinnliche, 1886).

Particularly influential were the writings of well-known figures. One of these, William James, stated in his essay, "What Psychical Research has Accomplished", that the SPR was "destined to be not unimportant in the organization of human knowledge" (James, 1896, p. 303).[1]

*Republished with permission from *Paranormal Review*, *63*, 3–12, 2012.
†Nancy L. Zingrone offered useful suggestions for the improvement of this article.

Part of this dissemination and publicity, both favourable and antagonistic, took place through articles published in reference works, such as encyclopaedias, that were consulted by students and others for basic information. Examples from the old days include discussions about the SPR in entries about psychical research in the *Encyclopaedia Britannica* (Lang, 1911; Schiller, 1922), and in other works, such as the *New International Encyclopedia* (Jastrow, 1907) and the *Encyclopaedia of Religion and Ethics* (Leuba, 1919). These presentations of psychical research were panoramic research summaries, but they also allowed the writers to present their views about the value and importance of the field, as well as the strengths and weaknesses of the movement, among other considerations. In this paper I reprint one such presentation published in an American publication devoted to philosophy and psychology.

Eleanor M. Sidgwick on Psychical Research

The article in question, "Psychical Research," by Eleanor M. Sidgwick (1902a) appeared in the second volume of the *Dictionary of Philosophy and Psychology*, an important reference work compiled by American psychologist James M. Baldwin. Published in three volumes from 1901–1905 (the third volume had two parts devoted to bibliography that were published separately) the book was and still is a standard historical reference source for philosophy and psychology. It has articles by such notables as James Angell, John Dewey, Joseph Jastrow, James McKeen Cattell, C. S. Minot, Josiah Royce, Adolf Meyer, C. Loyd Morgan, Charles S. Peirce, and Edward B. Titchener. Some consulting editors included Yves Delage, Théodore Flournoy, William James, Pierre Janet, Enrico Morselli, Hugo Münsterberg, Edward B. Poulton, Henry Sidgwick, G. F. Stout and Theodor Ziehen. In addition to the general article about psychical research the *Dictionary* had other articles about psychic topics, among them one by Sidgwick about telepathy (Sidgwick, 1902b), and short entries by Joseph Jastrow about automatic writing (Jastrow, 1901a), clairvoyance (Jastrow, 1901b), mediums (Jastrow, 1902a) and premonitions (Jastrow, 1902b).

Considering the well-known antagonism that many American psychologists had for the topic of psychic phenomena (Coon, 1992) it is interesting that Baldwin was willing to have a psychical researcher write the entries about psychical research and telepathy for the dictionary (Sidgwick, 1902a, 1902b), entries that were much longer than those authored by well-known sceptic Jastrow. However, it is easy to speculate on why Sidgwick was selected for the task. By the time her paper on psychical research appeared in the *Dictionary* in 1902 she had become known for her analytical abilities and her skill to summarize and organize large quantities of material related to psychical research.[2] Her work included discussions and case analyses of apparitions and hauntings (Sidgwick, 1885), as well as of cases of physical mediumship (Sidgwick, 1886a, 1886b, 1891b), premonitions (Sidgwick, 1888), clairvoyance (Sidgwick, 1891a), and trance mediumship (Sidgwick, 1900). According to a biographer referring to SPR work, Mrs. Sidgwick "was the perfect practitioner in the collection and sifting of evidence. Her coolness and detachment infused all the activities of the Society and cast both a light of authenticity and a concomitant feeling of mild dullness and respectability over all its proceedings" (Fowler, 1996, pp. 15–16).[3]

As is to be expected from Sidgwick's background, her presentation of psychical research in the *Dictionary* was a carefully guarded but positive one. In her account she saw some progress and expressed hope from recent developments, namely studies conducted by SPR researchers with Mrs. Leonora E. Piper. This does not mean she neglected problems in the field. Sidgwick stated that researchers were not able to produce telepathy at will and she mentioned problems of fraud in connection to physical mediumship. Interestingly, Sidgwick showed in her narrative what I have referred to before as an SPR-centred perspective to discuss the development of psychical research, or a tendency to narrate the history of the field from the point of view of the SPR, its researchers and achievements, to the neglect of other contributions (Alvarado, 2012). The same may be said about reliance on English-language sources. In her bibliography at the end of the entry she mentioned eleven works, out of which eight were in English (e.g., Gurney, Myers, and Podmore, 1886; Podmore, 1894). Three were in other languages (Ermacora, 1898; Flournoy, 1900; Lehmann, 1898), and Richet was mentioned in the text. But such material was not summarized in the article. Neither did Sidgwick think it relevant or necessary to go beyond the SPR *Proceedings* and mention work published in French, German and Italian psychical reviews. It is possible that the selection of her materials was as a result of her belief that SPR standards were higher than those used by researchers in other countries. But regardless of the explanation her discussion situated psychical research as an SPR development, something common in many other English-language overviews and general comments about the field (e.g., James, 1896, pp. 299–327; Leuba, 1919).

It is also clear that she was more interested in mental than in physical phenomena. The Od force of Reichenbach's committee was not even mentioned, even though it was an early interest of the SPR and the subject-matter of one of its early committees (e.g., Barrett et al., 1883). The same may be said of Edmund Gurney's attempts to test for a magnetic emanation in his mesmeric studies (e.g., Gurney, 1884, 1888). Nor is there any mention of specific cases of physical mediumship, perhaps because of their association with fraud in the author's mind, since in earlier publications she reported many suspicious incidents in respect of physical manifestations in the séance room (Sidgwick, 1886a, 1886b, 1891b).

Sidgwick did not discuss in detail the assumptions behind the telepathic explanation of apparitional and other events, but this may have been because she had discussed the topic in her entry about telepathy (Sidgwick, 1902b). The worst omission was of the theoretical ideas developed by Myers. While Myers's important book appeared later (1903), he had presented his ideas in many articles in which automatisms and the subliminal mind were minutely discussed (e.g., Myers, 1892b).

As stated above, the paper ends with a note of hope regarding mental mediumship. This refers to the studies conducted with medium Leonora E. Piper and to what Sidgwick cryptically referred to as "other" inquiries. This may have been a reference to work with Mrs. Thompson (e.g., Myers, 1902) and to the beginnings of the production of the automatic scripts that later became known as cross correspondences (Johnson, 1908).

Regardless of this, Sidgwick was cautious about being enthusiastic, which presumably reflected her personality but perhaps also her awareness that she was writing for a reference work and one she knew was going to be consulted by skeptical psychologists. More positive remarks were published by her in a later lecture about the history of the SPR (Sidgwick, 1932). She wrote: "I may say at once without hesitation that I feel now as I felt when I first engaged in it, before the foundation of the Society, that ours is some of the most important work in which we can engage for the extension of knowledge and the benefit of mankind" (p. 25). She said she believed there was evidence of "occasional communication of an evidential kind between the living and the dead-and some good evidence supporting this has been published in our *Proceedings*" (p. 26). But she did not say more. However, at the end of the lecture, Lord Balfour, who had read it for her, said to the audience: "I have Mrs. Sidgwick's assurance—an assurance which I am permitted to convey to the meeting—that, upon the evidence before her, she herself is a firm believer both in survival and in the reality of communication between the living and the dead" (p. 26).

Sidgwick's Article on Psychical Research

As a technical expression, psychical research owes its origin to the foundation of the English Society for Psychical Research in 1882.[4] The object of the society was, and is, to make an organized and systematic attempt to investigate various sorts of debatable phenomena which are prima facie inexplicable on any generally recognized hypothesis, and which may be regarded as having some bearing on the question of the independent existence and activity of mind apart from body. (Hereafter in this article the society is called the 'SPR').[5]

Some of the principal departments of investigation undertaken by the society are:

1. An examination of the nature and extent of any influence which may be exerted by one mind upon another, otherwise than through the recognized sensory channels. ...
2. The study of hypnosis ... and hypnotism; and an inquiry into the alleged phenomena of clairvoyance. Under this head we may include various forms of automatism, which have engaged the attention of the society, especially crystal vision, automatic writing, and the finding of water by the divining rod.
3. A careful investigation of any reports, resting on testimony sufficiently strong and not too remote, of apparitions coinciding with some external event—as, for instance, a death—or giving information previously unknown to the percipient (veridical hallucinations), or being seen by two or more persons simultaneously (collective hallucinations), or at different times independently.
4. An inquiry into various alleged phenomena apparently inexplicable by known laws of nature, and commonly referred by spiritualists ... to the agency of extra-human intelligences.
5. An inquiry into the evidence for premonitions and previsions.[6]

The aim of the society is to approach these various problems without prejudice or prepossession of any kind, and in the same spirit of exact and unimpassioned inquiry which has enabled science to solve so many problems, once not less obscure nor less hotly debated. The founders of the society have always fully recognized the exceptional difficulties which surround this branch of research; but they nevertheless believe that by patient and systematic effort some results of permanent value may be attained. A similar society was founded in the United States of America in 1884, and incorporated in 1890 with the British society.[7] Societies with somewhat similar aims have been established in Germany and elsewhere, and much assistance has been received from individual workers in various countries. Psychical research has taken an important place among questions discussed at International Psychological Congresses.[8]

The different branches of inquiry described under the four heads above are not of course independent of one another; and, in particular, facts elicited by investigations under heads (2), (3), and (4) form an important part of the evidence bearing upon the subject dealt with under the first head—the influence of mind on mind otherwise than through the recognized sensory channels, or telepathy. But closely connected though many of the subjects considered are, they cover a very wide range of phenomena; and the effort to treat the evidence offered for them in a scientific manner has necessarily led to the adoption of very various methods in different cases.

As regards the first head, the experimental method assumes the most important place; and in applying it, the important thing in the first instance was to establish the fact of telepathy.[9] But the establishment of the fact, that is, the negation of the ordinary channels of communication between mind and mind, is clearly a matter of extreme difficulty, if not impossibility, in any one case—not only on account of the danger of unobserved sensory indications, but on account of the very imperfectly known limits of the human faculties acting through the ordinary channels. The difficulty is increased by the fact that no means have yet been discovered for producing the phenomena of telepathy at will. If, in addition, the honesty of all concerned cannot be assumed—and of course, strictly speaking, it never can be—the problem becomes still harder. As regards probity, indeed, the only course seems to be to encourage as many varied experiments by various persons as possible, so that the widespread attribution of intentional deception which would be necessary to explain them all may ultimately become absurd.

The necessity of guarding against unconscious indications in experiments in thought transference or telepathy has led to a good deal of attention being paid to the possibilities of such means of communication as 'muscle reading' and unconscious whispering.[10] Muscle reading, or the interpretation of slight movements and gestures, is the explanation of those public performances in so-called thought reading in which there is contact between the person 'willing' and the performer; and similar interpretations, often doubtless unconscious, are the most probable explanation of the 'willing game' in private. The proved possibilities of muscle reading render worthless as evidence of telepathy almost all thought-transference experiments in which there is contact between the 'agent' or person trying to transfer his thought, and the 'percipient,' or person trying to read it. Any whispering—even unconscious—by the agent of the idea to be transferred is more easily guarded against.

Notwithstanding the difficulties, a considerable mass of evidence for telepathy has been accumulated by different observers, and it is in this subject that the largest amount of important work has been done by the society.[11]

Under the second head—hypnotism or mesmerism, &c.—interesting work was done by the late Edmund Gurney on certain psychological aspects of hypnotism, and particularly on the relation between more or less disconnected states of consciousness in the same individual.[12] Much attention has, of course, been given of late years, in France and elsewhere, to the psychological aspect of hypnotism without reference to the problems of psychical research.[13] The light thrown by hypnotism on the working of the mind is, however, of great importance in relation to psychical research, because of the opportunities hypnotism affords for the experimental investigation of sensory hallucinations, automatic writing, and other forms of subconscious activities.[14] The hypnotic state also seems favorable to the telepathic process, and some of the most successful experiments in telepathy have been conducted with hypnotized percipients.[15]

Clairvoyance, which we have included under this head, is a term which has been used in several meanings. The two most important are: (1) the perception of things passing at a distance, and known to some living person, but not to any one in direct relation with the percipient; this may be regarded as a form of telepathy. (2) The perception of things unknown to any living person, e.g. a number taken at random from a bag and unseen by anyone. For clairvoyance in this second sense there is not at present much evidence (see experiments by Richet[16]); nor have the SPR obtained much experimental evidence, for the first kind of clairvoyance (see, however, some experiments by A. Backman[17]). For a collection of spontaneous cases see papers by Mrs. H. Sidgwick.[18]

Crystal gazing, which is a method of inducing visual hallucinations more or less at will—in most cases with but a slight disturbance, if any, of the normal consciousness—is a subject to which the SPR has given a good deal of attention.[19] Curious cases occur of the recrudescence through crystal visions of forgotten impressions, and it seems in some cases to be a way of bringing telepathically received impressions to the surface. Some persons who can see visions in crystals can similarly induce hallucination of voices by holding a shell to the ear.

The use of the divining rod for finding water is apparently an instance of automatic and unconscious muscular action resulting from an impression subconsciously received. Whence the impression comes, whether directly through the senses, or by subconscious inference, or by means of some unrecognized sense, is obscure. But there is strong evidence that underground water actually is found by 'dowsers,' where experts have failed to discover it by other means. The evidence has been exhaustively dealt with by W. F. Barrett.[20]

Under the third head enumerated above, a large amount of investigation has been carried out by the SPR into the subject of what are popularly called ghosts.[21] Spontaneous visual and auditory hallucinations—the apparent seeing and hearing of things not forming part of the physical world—are not infrequently experienced by healthy persons; but in most cases there is, of course, no reason to attribute to these apparitions or voices any more importance than to the ordinary deliberately sought crystal visions. In a certain proportion of cases, however, the hallucination is 'veridical' or truth-telling. It coincides, that is, with some external event unknown to the percipient in a way that suggests a causal connection between the two.[22] The most familiar instance is the apparition of a person at the time of his death at a distance. In such cases, after sufficiently establishing the fact of the coincidence, the question we have to ask is whether the coincidences occur more frequently than they would do by the operation of chance alone. The method of investigation becomes therefore statistical. A first attempt to deal with the evidence statistically was made by Gurney in *Phantasms of the Living*—a work in which the evidence up to that time collected for coincidental hallucinations was very fully treated—and for this purpose he made a considerable collection of apparitions coincidental and casual, in order to compare the two classes with each other. It was felt, however, even at the time, that a larger collection was required, and a committee, under the presidency of Henry Sidgwick, appointed at the Paris International Congress of Experimental Psychology in 1889, collected, with the help of friends, answers from 17,000 persons to the inquiry whether they had ever had a sensory hallucination. About 10 per cent of these answered in the affirmative, and their experiences were carefully inquired into and analysed. The results,[23] besides bringing out much interesting matter of other kinds about the spontaneous hallucinations of healthy persons, showed among these 17,000 persons the alleged occurrence of 381 apparitions of persons believed by the percipients at the time to be alive, of which 80 were reported to have occurred within 12 hours of the death of the person seen. Even after making very large allowance for errors of various sorts, described fully in the report, the proportion is far beyond the 1 in 19,000 which, as shown in the report, could be accounted for as due to chance.

Apparitions coinciding with a death lend themselves especially to statistical methods of investigation, because the probability of their occurrence by chance can be exactly calculated. It will be observed, however, that statistical considerations play a large part in most departments of psychical research, even where the investigation is experimental. In experiments in thought transference, for instance, the results are as yet so little under control that the percipient as a rule has more often a wrong than a right impression of the idea the agent endeavours to transform, so that our judgment as to the value of the results depends partly on an estimate of the number of successes that would probably be attained by chance.

Under the head of 'ghosts' the experimental method has been applied in two departments. First, a few persons have succeeded in telepathically causing a percipient at a distance to see an apparition of themselves or others. There is much need of further experiment of this very important kind.[24]

The experimental method has also been applied in the case of houses alleged to be haunted. It is obvious that apparitions seen in a house by one person, or even by different persons at different times, but presenting no marked characteristics unknown to the percipients, do not prima facie differ from ordinary subjective hallucinations. If, however, *B* saw in a house an apparition markedly resembling one seen by *A*, but of which *B* had not previously heard the particulars, there might be some ground for assuming a local cause for that apparition. Various attempts have been made under the auspices of the SPR to discover similar apparitions seen independently in so-called haunted houses—the previous stories being kept secret from the would—be percipients-but so far these experiments have been almost without result.[25]

Under head 4—'spiritualistic phenomena'—widely differing phenomena are included. We have first the physical phenomena of spiritualistic séances—the alleged movement of objects and other mechanical effects, produced in the presence of certain persons called 'mediums' or sensitives, without ordinary physical agency. The SPR has published investigations, conducted before its own foundation by persons of repute, supporting the reality of such phenomena.[26] It has also done useful work in exposing fraud and in demonstrating possibilities of mal-observation. A paper on this latter point by Hodgson and the late S. J. Davey[27] will be found interesting. But there has of late been little opportunity of investigating these phenomena, from a positive point of view, with 'sensitives' against whom there is no well-founded suspicion of fraud.

With these physical phenomena may be classed the alleged marvels which occurred in connection with Madame Blavatsky and the Theosophical Society, for although post-mortem agency was not claimed for them, they were largely similar in character to the phenomena of the séance room. They were carefully inquired into by the SPR, on whose behalf Hodgson visited India in 1884–1885. His investigations ... aided by the confession of some of Madame Blavatsky's accomplices, clearly showed that the marvels were due to trickery.[28]

But what have proved the most fruitful subjects of investigation under this head are the communications received from 'sensitives' in the trance state, and usually claiming to come from deceased persons. Like automatic writing, such trance utterances, even when there is no conscious fraud connected with them, do not as a rule exhibit knowledge or intelligence beyond the sensitives' own. But there are exceptional cases in which the knowledge shown by a person speaking or writing in trance can hardly be supposed to have been acquired by normal means, and where we seem to require at least the hypothesis of telepathy, and sometimes telepathy between the sensitive and persons at a distance in no direct connection with him or her. Some of the communications are found by some writers difficult to explain without assuming post-mortem agency, and some investigators have convinced themselves of the reality of this. The most important publications by the SPR of late years have been detailed accounts of prolonged investigations by Hodgson, W. James, Oliver Lodge, Newbold, Leaf, Myers, and others, with such a trance-speaking sensitive—a Mrs. Piper.[29] Other inquiries, both with this lady and another, are in progress, and it is in this direction that most advance seems at present likely to be made in psychical research.

Notes

1 William James did much to publicize and defend the work of the SPR in his articles for the American public (e.g., James, 1909) and in his publications in the *Psychological Review* (Alvarado, 2009).

2 On Sidgwick's life and work, including psychical research, see Fowler (1996), Johnson (1936) and E. Sidgwick (1938).

3 Further evidence of Sidgwick's analytical mind may be found in publications that appeared after the *Dictionary* was published (e.g., Sidgwick, 1915, 1922, 1932).

4 While it is true that the Society made the term psychical research well known, activities following the same empirical approach existed before in the mesmeric and spiritualist literatures. Two examples from England related to spiritualism are the work of the London Dialectical Society (1871) and of William Crookes (1874).

5 The best discussion of early SPR developments is still Gauld (1968). For other perspectives see Alvarado (2002) and Cerullo (1982).
6 Sidgwick cites papers in volumes 5 and 11 of the *Proceedings of the Society for Psychical Research* (Myers, 1895; Sidgwick, 1888).
7 Regarding the American Society for Psychical Research, an initial organizing committee met in September, October and November 1884 to form the Society. The first meeting was said to have taken place in December, and the organization was finalized in January 1885 (Formation of the Society, 1885).
8 For discussions of psychical research in psychology congresses see Alvarado (2006) and Nuttin (1992)
9 Sidgwick (1902b) discussed the SPR telepathy work, as did Podmore (1894). See also Luckhurst (2002).
10 Much information about these issues appears in Luckhurst (2002). See also Gatchell (1891), and the reflections of one of the most popular of the professional "mind readers" (Cumberland, 1888).
11 The reader was referred to the article about telepathy in the *Dictionary* (Sidgwick, 1902b). The issue of unconscious whispering was a common criticism of thought-transference experiments (Hansen & Lehmann, 1895; but see H. Sidgwick's (1897) reply).
12 See, for example, Gurney (1887a, 1887b, 1887c).
13 Regarding France the relevant literature includes works by Beaunis (1887), Janet (1889), and many others (for overviews see Gauld, 1992; and Nicolas, 2004).
14 As stated by a French student of hypnosis: "Hypnotism constitutes … a genuine method of experimental psychology; it will be for the philosopher what vivisection is for the physiologist" (Beaunis, 1885, p. 1).
15 See Podmore (1894, Chapter 3).
16 Sidgwick refers readers to volumes 5 and 6 of the *Proceedings of the Society for Psychical Research* (Richet, 1888, 1889).
17 See Backman (1891).
18 Sidgwick (1891a).
19 The author refers to papers in *Proceedings of the Society for Psychical Research,* volumes 5, 8, and 10 (Hyslop, 1897; Myers, 1892c; Recent, 1889).
20 Barrett (1900).
21 On apparitions of the dead see Sidgwick (1885) and Myers (1892a).
22 See Gurney, Myers & Podmore (1886).
23 See H. Sidgwick et al. (1894). All of this work with apparitions has been discussed and summarized by Gauld (1968) and McCorristine (2010).
24 For particulars Sidgwick refers us to Gurney et al. (1886), Podmore (1894), and Sidgwick et al. (1894). She also refers readers to a note in *Proceedings of the Society for Psychical Research* in which a case from *Phantasms of the Living* involved a hoax by one of the witnesses (Note, 1898).
25 Sidgwick (1885) contributed an important early paper that touched on hauntings.
26 An example was Crookes' (1889) report of séances with D. D. Home.
27 See Davey (1887) and Hodgson (1887).
28 Sidgwick refers to Report (1885), which has been criticized over the years (e.g., Harrison, 1986; Waterman, 1963).
29 For overviews of the mediumship of Mrs. Piper see her daughter's biography (Piper, 1929) and Gauld's (1982, Ch. 3) convenient concise review. The reports to which Sidgwick refers were published in the *Proceedings of the Society for Psychical Research* (Hodgson, 1892, 1898; James, 1890; Leaf, 1890; Lodge, 1890; Newbold, 1898). Sidgwick's (1915) later study analyzing and summarizing various features of Piper's phenomena is one of the most important studies of the features of mental mediumship on record.

References

Alvarado, C. S. (2002). Dissociation in Britain during the late nineteenth century: The Society for Psychical Research, 1882–1900. *Journal of Trauma and Dissociation, 3,* 9–33.

Alvarado, C. S. (2006). Aspects of the history of parapsychology: I. Psychical research at the 1889 International Congress of Physiological Psychology. Retrieved from http://www.pflyceum.org/162.html

Alvarado, C. S. (2007). Psychical research and telepathy in nineteenth-century issues of *The Times. Paranormal Review, 43,* 3–7.
Alvarado, C. S. (2009). Psychical research in the *Psychological Review,* 1894–1900: A bibliographical note. *Journal of Scientific Exploration, 23,* 211–220.
Alvarado, C. S. (2012). Distortions of the past. *Journal of Scientific Exploration, 26,* 147–168.
Backman, A. (1891). Experiments in clairvoyance. *Proceedings of the Society for Psychical Research,* 7, 199–220.
Baldwin, J. M. (Ed.). (1901–1905). *Dictionary of philosophy and psychology* (3 vols.). Macmillan.
Barrett, W. F. (1900). On the so-called divining rod: A psycho-physical research on a peculiar faculty alleged to exist in certain persons locally known as dowsers. *Proceedings of the Society for Psychical Research, 15,* 130–383.
Barrett, W. F., Close, M., Lane-Fox, St G., Gurney, E., Myers, F. W. H., Myers, A. T., Pease, E. R., Ridley, H. N., Stone, W. H., & Coffin, W. H. (1883). First report of the "Reichenbach" Committee. *Proceedings of the Society for Psychical Research, 1,* 230–237.
Beaunis, H. (1885). L'expérimentation en psychologie par le somnambulisme provoqué. *Revue philosophique de la France et de l'Étranger, 20,* 1–36.
Beaunis, H. (1887). *Le somnambulisme provoqué* (2nd ed.). J. B. Baillière.
Boirac, E. (1898). Leçon d'overture du cours de M. Boirac chargé de cours de philosophie a la Faculté de Lettres de l'Université de Dijon. *Revue Bourguignonne de L'Enseignemment Supérieur, 8,* 1–20.
Cerullo, J. J. (1982). *The secularization of the soul: Psychical research in modern Britain.* Institute for the Study of Human Issues.
Coon, D. J. (1992). Testing the limits of sense and science: American experimental psychologists combat spiritualism, 1880–1920. *American Psychologist, 47,* 143–151.
Coste, A. (1895). *Les phénomènes psychiques occultes: État actuel de la question* (2nd ed.). Camille Coulet.
Crookes, W. (1874). *Researches in the phenomena of spiritualism.* J. Burns.
Crookes, W. (1889). Notes of séances with D. D. Home. *Proceedings of the Society for Psychical Research, 6,* 98–127.
Cumberland, S. (1888). *A thought-reader's thoughts.* Sampson Low, Marston, Searle, & Rivington.
Davey, S. J. (1887). The possibilities of malobservation and lapse of memory from a practical point of view: Experimental investigation. *Proceedings of the Society for Psychical Research, 4,* 405–495.
Ermacora, G. B. (1898). *La telepatia.* Crescini.
Flournoy, T. (1900). *Des indes à la planète Mars.* Félix Alcan.
Formation of the Society (1885). *Proceedings of the American Society for Psychical Research, 1,* 1–2.
Fowler, H. (1996). Eleanor Mildred Sidgwick 1845–1936. In E. Shils & C. Blacker (Eds.), *Cambridge women: Twelve portraits* (pp. 7–28). Cambridge University Press.
Gatchell, C. (1891). The methods of mind-readers. *Forum, 11,* 192–204.
Gauld, A. (1968). *The founders of psychical research.* Routledge and Kegan Paul.
Gauld, A. (1982). *Mediumship and survival.* Heinemann.
Gauld, A. (1992). *A history of hypnotism.* Cambridge University Press.
Goodrich Freer, A. [signed as X.]. (1896). Hypnotism and the Society for Psychical Research: Why hypnotic experiments are made. *Borderland, 3,* 93–95.
Gurney, E. (1884). An account of some experiments in mesmerism. *Proceedings of the Society for Psychical Research, 2,* 189–206.
Gurney, E. (1887a). Recent experiments m hypnotism. *Proceedings of the Society for Psychical Research, 5,* 3–17.
Gurney, E. (1887b). Peculiarities of certain posthypnotic states. *Proceedings of the Society for Psychical Research, 4,* 268–323.
Gurney, E. (1887c). Stages of hypnotic memory. *Proceedings of the Society for Psychical Research, 4,* 515–531.
Gurney, E. (1888). Hypnotism and telepathy. *Proceedings of the Society for Psychical Research, 5,* 216–259.
Gurney, E., & Myers, F. W. H. (1884). Visible apparitions. *Nineteenth Century, 16,* 68–95.
Gurney, E., Myers, F. W. H., & Podmore, F. (1886). *Phantasms of the living* (2 vols.). Trübner.
Hall, G. S. (1887). Review of *Proceedings of the Society for Psychical Research,* and *Phantasms of the living,* by E. Gurney, F. W. H. Myers, and F. Podmore. *American Journal of Psychology, 1,* 128–146.

Hansen, F. C. C., & Lehmann, A. (1895). Ueber unwillkürliches Flüstern, eine kritische und experimentelle Untersuchung der sogenannten Gedakenübertragung. *Philosophische Studien, 11,* 471–530.
Harrison, V. (1986). J'Accuse: An examination of the Hodgson report of 1885. *Journal of the Society for Psychical Research, 53,* 286–310.
Hodgson, R. (1887). The possibilities of malobservation and lapse of memory from a practical point of view: Introduction. *Proceedings of the Society for Psychical Research, 4,* 381–404.
Hodgson, R. (1892). A record of observations of certain phenomena of trance. *Proceedings of the Society for Psychical Research, 8,* 1–167.
Hodgson, R. (1898). A further record of observations of certain phenomena of trance. *Proceedings of the Society for Psychical Research, 13,* 284–582.
Hyslop, J. H. (1897). Some experiments in crystal vision. *Proceedings of the Society for Psychical Research, 12,* 259–276.
James, W. (1890). A record of observations of certain phenomena of trance: Part III. *Proceedings of the Society for Psychical Research, 6,* 651–659.
James, W. (1896). *The will to believe and other essays in popular philosophy.* Longmans, Green.
James, W. (1909). The confidences of a "psychical researcher". *American Magazine, 68,* 580–589.
Janet, P. (1889). *L'automatisme psychologique: Essai de psychologie expérimentale sur les formes inferieures de l'activite humaine.* Félix Akan.
Jastrow, J. (1901a). Automatic writing. In J. M. Baldwin (Ed.), *Dictionary of philosophy and psychology* (vol. 1, pp. 94–95). Macmillan.
Jastrow, J. (1901b). Clairvoyance. In J. M. Baldwin (Ed.), *Dictionary of philosophy and psychology* (Vol. 1, p. 184). Macmillan.
Jastrow, J. (1902a). Medium. In J. M. Baldwin (Ed.), *Dictionary of philosophy and psychology* (Vol. 2, p. 60). Macmillan.
Jastrow, J. (1902b). Premonition. In J. M. Baldwin (Ed.), *Dictionary of philosophy and psychology* (Vol. 2, p. 331). Macmillan.
Jastrow, J. (1907). Psychical research. In D. C. Gilman, H. T. Peck, & F. M. Colby (Eds.), *The new international cncyclopedia* (Vol. 16, pp. 505–506). Dodd, Mead.
Johnson, A. (1908). On the automatic writing of Mrs. Holland. *Proceedings of the Society for Psychical Research, 21,* 166–391.
Johnson, A. (1936). Mrs. Henry Sidgwick's work in psychical research. *Proceedings of the Society for Psychical Research, 44,* 53–93.
Lang, A. (1911). Psychical research. *Encyclopaedia Britannica: A Dictionary of Arts, Science, Literature, and General Information* (11th ed., Vol. 22, pp. 544–547). University Press.
Leaf, W. (1890). A record of observations of certain phenomena of trance (3). Part II. *Proceedings of the Society for Psychical Research, 6,* 558–646.
Lehmann, A. (1898). *Aberglaube und Zauberei van den altesten Zeiten an bis in die Gegenwart.* F. Enke.
Leuba, J. H. (1919). Psychical research. In J. Hastings, with the assistance of J. A. Selbie & L. H. Gray (Eds.), *Encyclopaedia of Religion and Ethics* (Vol. 10, pp. 420–423). Charles Scribner's Sons.
Lodge, 0. (1890). A record of observations of certain phenomena of trance (2). Part I. *Proceedings of the Society for Psychical Research, 6,* 443–557.
London Dialectical Society. (1871). *Report on Spiritualism, of the Committee of the London Dialectical Society.* Longmans, Green, Reader and Dyer.
Luckhurst, R. (2002). *The invention of telepathy 1870–1901.* Oxford University Press.
Mason, R.O. (1897). *Telepathy and the subliminal self.* Henry Holt.
McCorristine, S. (2010). *Spectres of the self: Thinking about ghosts and ghost-seeing in England, 1750–1920.* Cambridge University Press.
Morselli, E. (1908). *Psicologia e "Spiritismo": Note e impressioni critiche sui fenomeni medianici di Eusapia Paladino* (2 vols.). Fratelli Bocca.
Myers, F. W. H. (1892a). On indications of continued terrene knowledge on the part of phantasms of the dead. *Proceedings of the Society for Psychical Research, 8,* 170–252.
Myers, F. W. H. (1892b). The subliminal consciousness: Chapter 1. General characteristics of subliminal messages. *Proceedings of the Society for Psychical Research, 7,* 298–327.

Myers, F. W. H. (1892c). The subliminal consciousness: Chapter 5: Sensory automatisms and induced hallucinations. *Proceedings of the Society for Psychical Research, 8,* 436–535.

Myers, F. W. H. (1895). The subliminal self: IX. The relation of supernormal phenomena to time; — Precognition. *Proceedings of the Society for Psychical Research, 11,* 408–493.

Myers, F. W. H. (1902). On the trance phenomena of Mrs. Thompson. *Proceedings of the Society for Psychical Research, 17,* 67–74.

Myers. F. W. H. (1903). *Human personality and its survival of bodily death* (2 vols). Longmans, Green.

Newbold, W. R. (1898). A further record of observations of certain phenomena of trance. *Proceedings of the Society for Psychical Research, 2,* 6–49.

Nicolas, S. (2004). *L'hypnose: Charcot face a Bernheim: L'ecole de la Salpêtrière face* à *l'école de Nancy.* L'Harmattan.

Note on a case in "Phantasms of the Living". (1898). *Proceedings of the Society for Psychical Research, 14,* 114.

Nuttin, J. R. (1992). Les premiers congres intemationaux de psychologie: Text inedit. In M. Richelle & H. Carpintero (Eds.), *Contributions to the history of the International Congresses of Psychology: A posthumous homage to J. R. Nuttin* (pp. 7–74). Valencia, Spain: 'Revista Historia de la Psicologia' Monographs; Leuven University Press.

Piper, A. L. (1929). *The life and work of Mrs. Piper.* K. Paul, Trench, Trübner.

Podmore, F. (1894). *Apparitions and thoughttransference.* Walter Scott.

Podmore, F. (1897). *Studies in psychical research.* G. P. Putnam's Sons.

Proceedings of the English Society for Psychical Research. (1886). *Science, 8,* 462–463.

Recent experiments in crystal vision. (1889). *Proceedings of the Society for Psychical Research, 5,* 486–521.

Report of the committee appointed to investigate phenomena connected with the Theosophical Society. (1885). *Proceedings of the Society for Psychical Research, 3,* 201–400.

Review of *Proceedings of the Society for Psychical Research.* (1882). *Journal of Science, 4*(s.3), 676–678.

Review of *Proceedings of the Society for Psychical Research.* (1883). *Revue Philosophique de la France et de l'Étranger, 16,* 445–448.

Richet, C. (1888). Relation de diverses expériences sur la transmission mentales, la lucidité, et autres phénomènes non explicables par les données scientifiques actuelles. *Proceedings of the Society for Psychical Research, 5,* 18–168.

Richet, C. (1889). Further experiments in hypnotic lucidity or clairvoyance. *Proceedings of the Society for Psychical Research, 6,* 66–83.

Schiller, F. C. S. (1922). Psychical research. *Encyclopaedia Britannica* (12th ed., Vol. 32, pp. 198–204). Encyclopaedia Britannica.

Sidgwick, E. (1938). *Mrs. Henry Sidgwick: A memoir.* Sidgwick & Jackson.

Sidgwick, H. (1897). Involuntary whispering considered in relation to experiments in thought transference. *Proceedings of the Society for Psychical Research, 12,* 298–314.

Sidgwick, H., Johnson, A., Myers, F. W. H., Podmore, F., & Sidgwick, E. M. (1894). Report on the Census of Hallucinations. *Proceedings of the Society for Psychical Research, 10,* 25–422.

Sidgwick, Mrs. H. [E. M.]. (1885). Notes on the evidence collected by the Society, for phantasms of the dead. *Proceedings of the Society for Psychical Research, 3,* 69–150.

Sidgwick, E. M. (1886a). Mr. Eglinton. *Journal of the Society for Psychical Research, 2,* 282–334.

Sidgwick, H. [E. M.] (1886b). Results of a personal investigation into the physical phenomena of Spiritualism: With some critical remarks on the evidence for the genuineness of such phenomena. *Proceedings of the Society for Psychical Research, 4,* 45–74.

Sidgwick, H. [E. M.] (1888). On the evidence for premonitions. *Proceedings of the Society for Psychical Research, 5,* 288–354.

Sidgwick H. [E. M.]. (1891a). On the evidence for clairvoyance. *Proceedings of the Society for Psychical Research, 7,* 30–99.

Sidgwick, H. [E. M.] (1891b). On spirit photographs: A reply to Mr. A.R. Wallace. *Proceedings of the Society for Psychical Research,* 7, 268–289.

Sidgwick, H. [E. M.] (1900). Discussion of the trance phenomena of Mrs. Piper—II. *Proceedings of the Society for Psychical Research, 15,* 16–38.

Sidgwick, E. M. (1902a). Psychical research. In J. M. Baldwin (Ed.), *Dictionary of philosophy and psychology* (Vol. 2, pp. 378–382). Macmillan.

Sidgwick, E. M. (1902b). Telepathy. In J. M. Baldwin (Ed.), *Dictionary of Philosophy and Psychology* (Vol. 2, pp. 668–672). Macmillan.

Sidgwick, H. [E. M.] (1915). A contribution to the study of the psychology of Mrs. Piper's trance phenomena. *Proceedings of the Society for Psychical Research, 28,* 1–657.

Sidgwick, H. [E. M.] (1922). Phantasms of the living: An examination and analysis of cases of telepathy between living persons printed in the "Journal" of the Society for Psychical Research since the publication of the book "Phantasms of the Living," by Gurney, Myers, and Podmore, in 1886. *Proceedings of the Society for Psychical Research, 33,* 23–429.

Sidgwick, H. [E. H.]. (1932). The Society for Psychical research: A short account of its history and work on the occasion of the Society's jubilee, 1932. *Proceedings of the Society for Psychical Research, 41,* 1–26.

Übersinnliche Gedanken-übertragung nach den Untersuchungen der Society for Psychical Research. (1886). *Sphinx, 1,* 105–129.

Waterman, A. E. [pseudonym of Walter A. Carrithers, Jr.] (1963). *Obituary: The "Hodgson report" on Madame Blavatsky.* Theosophical Publishing House.

Wells, H. G. (1894). Peculiarities of psychical research. *Nature, 51,* 121–122.

Classic Text No. 105: 'Report of the Committee on Mediumistic *Phenomena*,' by William James (1886)*

With an Introduction by

Carlos S. Alvarado

Mediumship was a topic of great interest to some nineteenth-century students of mental phenomena. Together with the phenomena of hypnosis and other manifestations, mediumship was seen by many as a dissociative phenomenon. The purpose of this Classic Text is to present an excerpt of an article about the topic that William James (1842–1910) published in 1886 in the *Proceedings of the American Society for Psychical Research* about American medium Leonora E. Piper (1857–1950). The article, an indication of late nineteenth-century interactions between dissociation studies and psychical research, was the first report of research with Mrs. Piper, a widely investigated medium of great importance for the development of mediumship studies. In addition to studying the case as a dissociative experience, James explored the possibility that Piper's mentation contained verifiable information suggestive of "supernormal" knowledge. Consequently, James provides an example of a topic neglected in historical studies, the ideas of those who combined conventional dissociation studies with psychical research.

The study of dissociation developed rapidly during the nineteenth-century via investigations of phenomena observed in hysteria, hypnosis and various other conditions suggesting the existence of secondary consciousness, including somnambulism, and cases of double and multiple personality (Crabtree, 1993; Ellenberger, 1970; Gauld, 1992; Hacking, 1995). Mesmerist Joseph Philippe François Deleuze (1753–1835) noticed that mesmerized individuals had access to the "recollection of things that were forgotten during wakefulness" (Deleuze, 1813, p. 176), and that things taking place during the somnambulistic state appeared to disappear from the usual consciousness of the individual (see also Bertrand, 1826, p. 409–410). Others reported secondary personalities in magnetized individuals (e.g., Lang, 1843). In later years Pierre Janet (1859–1947) became known for his studies of the apparent secondary streams of thought (or actions) of individuals he regularly hypnotized (Janet, 1886a, 1887, 1888), which were also discussed in his classic *L'Automatisme psychologique* (Janet, 1889).[1] In hypnotic experiments with a woman named Lucie, Janet noticed that when she was entranced during a waking moment:

> … the idea that appeared in her consciousness after a sudden awakening is not the recollection of somnambulism, it is the next part of the act started and interrupted during wakefulness. It is as if somnambulism never existed and the two waking moments seem to join. In the middle of a conversation L. was asleep before she could finish her phrase. After a quarter of an hour of sleep she woke up and calmly finished the conversation started without doubting that she had slept. (Janet, 1886a, p. 579).

*Republished with permission from *History of Psychiatry*, *27*, 85–100, 2016.

But there were also instances of secondary consciousness unrelated to hypnosis, cases which were popularized by various authors, for example Dewar (1823), Elliotson (1846) and also Scottish physician Robert Macnish (1802–1837) in his book *The Philosophy of Sleep* (Macnish, 1834, Ch. 8). Many cases received much publicity, an earlier one being that of Mary Reynolds (1785–1854) (Mitchill, 1817; Plumer, 1860). Particularly well known were the later cases of Félida X. (b. 1843), Louis Vivét (b. 1863) and Ansel Bourne (b. 1826) (see, respectively, Azam, 1887; Bourru & Burot, 1888; Hodgson, 1891).

In a review of phenomena believed to show the existence of the unconscious mind, French physician Jules Héricourt (1850–1938) reminded us about "a state which is neither a hysterical attack, nor an access of somnambulism, … [in which] the conscious and the unconscious appear to have an independent existence, not successive, but simultaneous. It is the state of crisis or the *trance* of mediums" (Héricourt, 1889, p. 265, original italics). The Classic Text below is an article by American philosopher and psychologist William James (1842–1910), which represents an early attempt to study a medium systematically, an attempt that reflected both the then-current interests in the subconscious regions of the mind and the field of psychical research.

Mediumship

While mediumship is an ancient phenomenon, its resurgence in the nineteenth century led to the movement of modern Spiritualism.[2] Mediums presented various manifestations that were both physical (raps, movement of objects, materializations) and mental (communications via verbal means, writing, visions, and other ways).[3] To a great extent mediums, who received much publicity in the press, and some of whom travelled around, provided the means by which Spiritualism spread through the USA and Europe, as well as other countries. Mediums were the ambassadors of the new creed, one that boasted the ability to present empirical evidence for survival of death and of communication with the deceased, as seen in early American developments (Capron, 1855; Hardinge, 1870). One medium stated that she had "travelled and lectured through thirty-two of the United States" (Hardinge, 1870, p. 19). The famous medium Daniel Dunglas Home (1833–1886) travelled to many countries, spreading the idea of a spirit world via his phenomena, many of which consisted of physical manifestations (Home, 1888).

The literature is full of mediumistic communications imparting moral and philosophical messages (e.g., Kardec, 1857; Tappan, 1875), as can be seen in messages from "Thomas Jefferson" and "Calvin" (Spicer, 1853, p. 146–148). Referring to this type of material, American journalist and publisher Horace Greeley (1811–1872) stated that many spirit communications from mediums were "more inane and trashy than it could be if the sages, and heroes, the saints and poets, of by-gone days were really speaking to us through these pretended revelations" (Greeley, 1868, p. 240). However, there were also claims that some spirit communications presented verifiable details (e.g., Anon., 1857; Carlson, 1878; Cooper, 1867, p. 75)—a topic discussed by, among others, English cleric and medium William Stainton Moses (1839–1892) in his book *Spirit-Identity* (1879), and which were seen by some to provide evidence of survival of bodily death.

Many saw mediums as instruments of exploration and study. For example, French spiritist leader and teacher Hippolyte Leon Denizard Rivail (1804–1869), known as Allan Kardec, compared mediums to microscopes. Just as microscopes revealed to us small worlds, mediums "have revealed to us the world of Spirits. With the help of seeing mediums, we have been able to study the invisible world …" (Kardec, 1862, p. 130–131). The belief that mediums granted access to this invisible world obviously affected many popular metaphysical beliefs. Furthermore, as a later historian argued, mediumship "democratized spirit communication and access to the religious authority of higher spiritual beings" (Carroll, 1997, p. 24).

But in addition to helping to build the movement and foster beliefs, mediums, like hysterics and mesmeric subjects, assisted the development of the idea that there were hidden levels of the mind.

Historian of psychiatry Henri F. Ellenberger (1905–1993) was a pioneer in defending the view that phenomena such as mediumship contributed to expand our views of the mind and its hidden dimensions. Ellenberger (1970, p. 85) wrote: "Automatic writing ... was taken over by scientists as a method of exploring the unconscious ... A new subject, the medium, became available for experimental psychological investigations, out of which evolved a new model of the human mind". These ideas, which have been echoed and further developed by others (Alvarado, 2002; Crabtree, 1993; Plas, 2000; Shamdasani, 1993),[4] were based on the writings of many nineteenth-century authors.

Particularly influential was the work of classical scholar Frederic W. H. Myers (1843–1901), who developed a model of the subliminal mind that included mediumship and various other aspects such as dreams, hysteria, hypnosis, creativity and telepathy.[5] In his view, automatic writing and trance speaking were some of the means by which the subliminal conveyed information to the supraliminal (conscious) mind (e.g., Myers, 1884, 1885, 1889, 1903). In many cases, Myers believed, such information came from the medium's mind, but it could also contain "supernormal" information, such as details he conceived could be acquired via telepathy. In later writings Myers accepted the action of spirits of the dead (Myers, 1903, Vol. 2, p. 249).

Also very important was Pierre Janet, mentioned above. In his view, Spiritism "has shown us numerous examples ... of ... mental disaggregation that we have studied experimentally. Mediums ... are the most complete type of division in which the two personalities are completely unaware and develop independently of each other" (Janet, 1889, p. 419). However, Janet, unlike Myers (with some exceptions), did not emphasize pathology. Furthermore, Janet did not include the "supernormal" in his system. Consequently, both men had very different conceptions of the nature of the subconscious mind, and the process of dissociation.

But the idea of subconscious levels of the mind involved in mediumship preceded Janet and Myers (e.g., Baillarger, 1861; Tascher, 1855). French critic and historian Hippolyte Taine (1828–1893) wrote that mediumship showed "the coexistence at the same time, in the same individual, of two thoughts, two wills, two different actions, one of which is conscious, the other of which he is unaware and which he attributes to invisible beings" (Taine, 1878, p. 16). These ideas, in turn, were attempts to explain mediumship in natural ways, part of a nineteenth–century trend to reduce the unusual, the "supernatural", or the spiritual to conventional processes (Gonçalves & Ortega, 2013), something that was clear in attempts to pathologize mediumship and Spiritualism in general (e.g., Burlet, 1863; Hammond, 1876; see also Alvarado & Zingrone, 2012; Le Maléfan, 1999).

In addition to the aforementioned authors, others saw mediumship as an example of dissociation, and as an opportunity to study the levels of the mind (e.g., Binet, 1892; Héricourt, 1889; Richet, 1884, 1886). One early empirical attempt to do so was reported in the excerpt presented below, authored by William James (1886), work which took place both in the context of psychological and psychiatric work, and of psychical research. While some of this work assumed the phenomenon was produced solely by psychological aspects of the medium's mind (Alvarado, 2010; Le Maléfan, 1999), the psychical research work went beyond intrapsychic considerations, admitting, or at least exploring empirically, the possibility that mediumistic mentation could contain information beyond the apparent reach of the senses.

Psychical Research

Psychical research—the study of psychic phenomena such as apparitions, clairvoyance, healing, mediumship, poltergeists and thought-transference—developed in the nineteenth century. To a great extent, the movement inherited from mesmerism and Spiritualism an interest in various unexplained phenomena and, particularly from the latter, an interest in the idea that consciousness may survive death.[6]

An important part of these developments was the work of the Society for Psychical Research (SPR), founded in London in 1882, which included among its members various scholars and scientists, both spiritualists and non-spiritualists (Cerullo, 1982; Gauld, 1968). The SPR soon produced much work about various psychic phenomena (e.g., Gurney et al., 1886; Guthrie & Birchall, 1883; Lodge, 1890; Myers, 1892a), and studies of the subconscious mind, including hypnosis and dissociation in general (e.g., Gurney, 1887; Myers, 1892b; summarized by Alvarado, 2002). One of their main lines of research was telepathy, or the assumption that a mind could communicate with another mind without conventional sensory or inferential means, a topic they followed up via case and experimental studies (for a summary, see Podmore, 1894).

The SPR investigators, and other psychical researchers, were also interested in mediumship. The most important of the early investigations into mental mediumship was the work conducted with the American medium Leonora E. Piper (1857–1950), whose performances assisted psychical researchers to study veridical or verifiable communications. Her case provided the first systematic opportunity to make repeated observations under controlled conditions.[7]

While mental mediumship in the hands of writers such as Janet (1889) and others such as Jules Baillarger (1809–90), Alfred Binet (1857–1911) and, Theodore Flournoy[8] (1854–1920) (Baillarger, 1861; Binet, 1892; Flournoy, 1899, 1900) was presented as the product of the medium's subconscious imaginal processes (see Le Maléfan, 1999), the psychical researchers, as exemplified by Piper, were not only interested in the psychology of mediumship, but also in its "supernormal" content, a topic related to the issue of survival of death. Unlike conventional studies of the subconscious and of dissociation, many of the psychical researchers combined a conventional interest in the psychology of mediums, involving the workings of the subconscious mind, with the possibilities of obtaining veridical information, thus transcending the idea that everything in mental mediumship was produced solely by imaginal processes, as seen, for example, in the early work of Myers (1884, 1885).[9] This particular emphasis was shared by James in the excerpt reprinted here.

William James

James was born in 1842 in New York City, and died in 1910 in New Hampshire. He obtained an MD degree in 1869 from Harvard Medical School, but he did not practice medicine. Instead he is generally known for his work as a philosopher and as a psychologist, as seen in *The Principles of Psychology* (1890b), *Psychology: Briefer Course* (1892a), *The Will to Believe, and Other Essays in Popular Philosophy* (1897), *Human Immortality* (1898a), *Talks to Teachers on Psychology* (1899), The Varieties of Religious Experience (1902), *Pragmatism: A New Name for Some Old Ways of Thinking* (1907b) and *A Pluralistic Universe* (1909c), not to mention many articles (e.g., James, 1879, 1884, 1895a, 1904).[10]

From early on James showed an interest in psychic phenomena.[11] In a book review published in 1869 he stated: "The present attitude of society on this whole question is as extraordinary and anomalous as it is discreditable to the pretensions of an age which prides itself on enlightenment and the diffusion of knowledge" (James, 1869/1960, p. 21). Years later we find him as one of the organizers of the American Society for Psychical Research (ASPR), being present in a meeting in Boston to form the Society in 1884 (Anon., 1885a, p. 1), listed as a member of the Council (Anon.,

1885b, p. 4), and participating in the work conducted by ASPR's committees (James, 1886, 1887b; James and Carnochan, 1886).[12] In 1886 he wrote to German psychologist and philosopher Carl Stumpf (1848–1936) about the work of the London-based SPR, saying: "It is a field in which the sources of deception are extremely numerous. But I believe there is no source of deception in the investigation of nature which can compare with a fixed belief that certain kinds of phenomenon are *impossible*" (H. James, 1920, Vol. 1, p. 248; original emphasis).

In one of his articles James (1890a) referred to the importance of the "unclassified residuum", phenomena such as apparitions, possession and trances, for science. They could, in his view, renovate science, bringing new ideas. In later years we see James reporting on various phenomena (e.g., James, 1889, 1907a, 1909b, 1909d), as well as defending the field (e.g., James, 1896b, 1898b) and popularizing it (e.g., James, 1892b, 1895b). In fact, it may be argued that, more than actual investigations, James' main contributions were to defend psychical research publicly, something he was well suited to do due to his intellectual abilities and his high academic position.

Eventually James became the President of the London-based SPR. He wrote in his Presidential Address about supernormal knowledge, an opinion affected by his experience with Mrs. Piper: "For me the thunderbolt has fallen, and the orthodox belief has not merely had its presumption weakened, but the truth itself of the belief is decisively overthrown" (James, 1896a, p. 884). The SPR, James thought, had made an important contribution: "We have shown some reasonable basis for the most superstitious aberrations of the foretime. We have bridged the chasm, healed the hideous rift that Science, taken in a certain narrow way, has shot into the human world" (p. 887).

Interestingly, and providing further evidence of the effect of SPR work on James, he had high regard for Myers's views about the subliminal self, although he believed there were weak evidential aspects in his system (James, 1901, 1903). According to Taylor (1996, p. 21): "Myers's formulations were, in fact, central to the development of James's psychology and philosophy in the 1890s, and they form the epistemological core of James's scientific activities in abnormal psychology and psychical research."

On a wider view, James followed psychical research in a way consistent with his radical empiricism, and attempting to emphasize facts as opposed to traditional presuppositions. As discussed in a recent article (Junior et al., 2013, p. 73; see also Algaier, 2014):

> Countering classical empiricism, he advanced a set of metaphysical postulates with epistemological consequences, which place experience in its broadest sense as the cornerstone of reality. Consequently, through philosophical reasoning, he was able to encompass any kind of experience, objective or subjective, ordinary or extraordinary, as targets of scientific examinations.

This approach showed that it was natural for James to be interested in psychical research, and in Mrs. Piper, as Ruetenik (2012) has argued in terms of James's pragmatism.

James expressed some disappointment about his understanding of psychic phenomena at the end of his life (James, 1909a). He did not have any explanations for psychic phenomena, although he was open to a panpsychic view about the connections of minds. However, he wrote (p. 580):

> It is hard to believe, however, that the Creator has really put any big array of phenomena into the world merely to defy and mock our scientific tendencies; so my deeper belief is that we psychical researchers have been too precipitate with our hopes, and that we must expect to mark progress not by quarter-centuries, but by half-centuries or whole centuries.

Regarding the topic of the excerpt below, Mrs. Piper was "discovered" for psychical research by William James, who went to see the medium after his mother and his sister-in-law had received what they considered to be evidential communications (James, 1890c). At first James went to see the medium with his wife in 1885 and obtained encouraging results that led him to believe that "Mrs. P. was either possessed of supernormal powers, or knew the members of my wife's family by sight and had by some lucky coincidence become acquainted with such a multitude of their domestic circumstances as to produce the startling impression which she did" (p. 652). This conviction became stronger, as seen in the statement that "taking everything that I know of Mrs. P. into account, the result is to make me feel as absolutely certain as I am of any personal fact in the world that she knows things in her trances which she cannot possibly have heard in her waking state, and that the definitive philosophy of her trances is yet to be found" (pp. 658–659).

The Classic Text is from the first formal report ever published about Mrs. Piper (James, 1886),[13] an important event both in psychical research and in dissociation studies, the latter being an interest of James (e.g., 1889, 1890a; see Alvarado & Krippner, 2010). The year in which it was published, 1886, was an important one for studies of the subconscious mind and dissociation (Crabtree, 1993; Gauld, 1992; Hacking, 1995). Particularly important were developments related to hypnosis. The same year also saw the initial publication of the *Revue de l'Hypnotisme Expérimental & Thérapeutique*, as well as of the important hypnosis studies of Janet (1886a), and the work of many other individuals (e.g., Beaunis, 1886; Bernheim, 1886; Lombroso, 1886), including James (James & Carnochan, 1886), not to mention some of the ideas of Myers (1886) about the value of hypnosis in the exploration of the capabilities of the mind. There were also developments in the study of psychical research, as seen in various works about telepathy and the like, such as Gurney et al.'s (1886) now classic study (see also Dessoir, 1886; Janet, 1886b).

James's (1886) report was a pioneering work for many reasons. First, it started the modern era of scientific mental mediumship studies focusing on both conventional trance phenomena and supernormal aspects, as well as a long line of studies and observations of Piper, as seen in later séance work (see note 6). Second, it pioneered the use of a stenographer to record the statements of the medium, something done more frequently later.[14] Third, James used hypnosis to study possible continuities in consciousness between hypnotic and mediumistic trance, something consistent with the explorations of others regarding trends of thought and memory in and out of hypnosis (Gurney, 1887; Janet, 1889). Fourth, James observed and recorded some features of Piper's trance, which probably inspired later observations (e.g., Hodgson, 1892; see also Sidgwick, 1915). Fifth, James emphasized the importance of work conducted with special participants, which was common in the era in such areas as hypnosis and hysteria (Carroy, 1991; Hustvedt, 2011).

James also had other séances with Piper, including some held between 1893 and 1895 at his home (Hodgson, 1898, p. 482, 494, 525, 525, 526, 528, 534). His experiences with this medium led him to state:

> If you wish to upset the law that all crows are black, you mustn't seek to show that no crows are; it is enough if you prove one single crow to be white. My own white crow is Mrs. Piper. In the trances of this medium, I cannot resist the conviction that knowledge appears which she has never gained by the ordinary waking use of her eyes and ears and wits. (James, 1896a, p. 884)

His final study with Piper was an analysis of communications from Richard Hodgson (1855–1905), one of Piper's main investigators (James, 1909e). James believed there was some "will" coming through the medium's mentation but he did not accept, as Hodgson (1898) and Hyslop (1901) had done in relation to other séances, that there was clear evidence for discarnate action.

The report below, an excerpt from James's (1886) initial study, is an important document heralding later systematic work improving the methodology of earlier spiritualistic observations, as well as an important point in James's intellectual work, when he attempted to bring together both psychology and psychical research.

Classic Text No. 105: 'Report of the Committee on Mediumistic *Phenomena*,' by William James (1886)

To turn to the much simpler and more satisfactory case of Mrs. P.[15] This lady can at will pass into a trance condition, in which she is "controlled" by a power purporting to be the spirit of a French doctor, who serves as intermediary between the sitter and deceased friends.[16] This is the ordinary type of trance-mediumship at the present day. I have myself witnessed a dozen of her trances, and have testimony at first hand from twenty-five sitters, all but one of whom were virtually introduced to Mrs. P. by myself.

Of five of the sittings we have *verbatim* stenographic reports. Twelve of the sitters, who in most cases sat singly, got nothing from the medium but unknown names or trivial talk. Four of these were members of the society, and of their sittings *verbatim* reports were taken.

Fifteen of the sitters were surprised at the communications they received, names and facts being mentioned at the first interview which it seemed improbable should have been known to the medium in a normal way. The probability that she possessed no clew [clue] as to the sitter's identity, was, I believe, in each and all of these fifteen cases, sufficient. But of only one of them is there a stenographic report; so that, unfortunately for the medium, the evidence in her favor is, although more abundant, less exact in quality than some of that which will be counted against her.

Of these fifteen sitters, five, all ladies, were blood relatives, and two (I myself being one) were men connected by marriage with the family to which they belonged. Two other connections of this family are included in the twelve who got nothing. The medium showed a most startling intimacy with this family's affairs, talking of many matters known to no one outside, and which *gossip* could not possibly have conveyed to her ears. The details would prove nothing to the reader, unless printed *in extenso*, with full notes by the sitters. It reverts, after all, to personal conviction. My own conviction is not evidence, but it seems fitting to record it. I am persuaded of the medium's honesty, and of the genuineness of her trance; and although at first disposed to think that the 'hits' she made were either lucky coincidences, or the result of knowledge on her part of who the sitter was and of his or her family affairs, I now believe her to be in possession of a power as yet unexplained.

The most promising way of investigating phenomena like this seems to be that of learning a great deal about one "Subject," who, of course, ought to be a good specimen of the class.[17] Hitherto we have heard a little about a great many Subjects. Stenographic reports are expensive, but they seem indispensable for a conclusive discussion of the facts. They do away with doubts about the veracity of the sitter's memory; and they enable us to make a comparison of different sittings, which without them is hardly possible at all. Questions arise as to the irrelevant names and facts which almost every sitting to some extent contains. Are they improvisations of the moment? Are they in themselves right and coherent, but addressed to the wrong sitter? Or are they vestiges of former sittings, now emerging as part of the automatism of the medium's brain? A reading of the stenographic reports already taken makes it probable that, for some of them at least, this last explanation is correct. "Spirits" originally appearing to me have appeared in the sittings of others who knew nothing either of their persons or their names.

What science wants is a *context* to make the trance-phenomena continuous with other physiological and psychological facts.[18] Curious to ascertain whether there were continuity between the medium-trance and the ordinary hypnotic trance, I made some observations *ad hoc* upon Mrs. P. My first two attempts to hypnotize her were unsuccessful. Between the second time and the third, I suggested to her "Control" in the medium-trance that he should make her a mesmeric subject for me. He agreed. (A suggestion of this sort made by the operator in one hypnotic trance would probably have some effect on the next.) She became partially hypnotized on the third trial; but the effect was so slight that I ascribe it rather to the effect of repetition than to the suggestion made. By the fifth trial she had become a pretty good hypnotic subject, as far as muscular phenomena and automatic imitations of speech and gesture go; but I could not affect her consciousness, or otherwise get her beyond this point. Her condition in this semi-hypnosis is very different from her medium-trance. The latter is characterized by great muscular unrest, even her ears moving vigorously in a way impossible to her in her waking state. But in hypnosis her muscular relaxation and weakness are extreme. She often makes several efforts to speak ere her voice becomes audible; and to get a strong contraction of the hand, for example, express manipulation and suggestion must be practised. The automatic imitations I spoke of are in the first instance very weak, and only become strong after repetition. Her pupils contract in the medium-trance. Suggestions to the "Control" that he should make her recollect after the trance what she had been saying were accepted, but had no result. In the hypnotic-trance such a suggestion will often make the patient remember all that has happened.[19]

No sign of thought-transference—as tested by card and diagram-guessing—has been found in her, either in the hypnotic condition just described, or immediately after it; although her "Control" in the medium-trance has said that he would bring them about.[20] So far as tried (only twice), no right guessing of cards in the medium-trance. She was twice tried with epistolary letters in the medium-trance,—once indicating the contents in a way rather surprising to the sitter; once failing. In her normal-waking state she made one hundred and twenty-seven guesses at playing-cards looked at by me,—I sometimes touching her, sometimes not. Suit right (first guess) thirty-eight times,—an excess of only six over the "probable" number of thirty-two,—obviously affording no distinct evidence of thought-transference. Trials of the "willing game,"[21] and attempts at automatic writing, gave similarly negative results. So far as the evidence goes, then, her medium-trance seems an isolated feature in her psychology. This would of itself be an important result if it could be established and generalized, but the record is obviously too imperfect for confident conclusions to be drawn from it in any direction. Being compelled by other work to abandon the subject for the present, these notes are published merely as a suggestion of lines of inquiry which others may be better fitted than myself to carry out.

If a good trance-subject could be obtained for the society at the outset of her or his career, and kept from doing miscellaneous work until patiently and thoroughly observed and experimented on, with stenographic reports of trances, and as much attention paid to failures and errors as to successes, I am disposed to think that the results would in any event be of scientific value, and would be worth the somewhat high expense which they necessarily would entail. If the friends of spiritualism would contribute money for the thorough carrying out of any such scheme, they would probably do as much as by any one thing could be done, to bring about the "recognition" of trance-mediumship by scientific men.

As for the other kinds of mediumistic phenomena, I have during the past year been very much struck by the volume of evidence which can be collected in their favor. But the mere *volume* of evidence is of no account unless it can be proved that the evidence is likely to be of the ordinary human sort, bad and good mixed together in the usual proportion. If it is possible that it is unusually bad in *quality*, the quantity of it is of little account. Now, that there *are* reasons for believing its quality to be in these matters below the average, no one familiar with the facts can doubt. Only the establishment of one or two absolutely and coercively proven cases—of materialization,[22] for example—will show that the hearsay evidence for *that* phenomenon may be mixed. And only *then* can the volume of evidence already extant on the subject be taken into account by one who has no direct personal experience on which to rely. The ordinary disbeliever rules out all hearsay evidence in advance. The believer accepts far too much of it, because he knows that some of it is good. The committee of the society should first devote itself to the very exact and complete study of a few particular cases. These may consume much labor and time. But if, after studying them, it should reach favorable conclusions, it would do vastly more to make the vaguer testimony already extant influential with the society as a whole, than it could do by discussing such testimony now.

Notes

1 On Janet, see: Crabtree, 1993: Ch. 15; Van der Hart & Horst, 1989.

2 Biondi (1988), Braude (2001), Edelman (1995) and Oppenheim (1985) present overviews of the histories of Spiritualism and Spiritism, as well as aspects of the development of mediumship during the nineteenth century.

3 Examples of early discussions of mediums and their phenomena appear in the works of Ballou (1852), Capron (1855), Clark (1863) and Kardec (1862).

4 See also some of my previous papers (Alvarado, 2010, 2013).

5 On Myers, see: Gauld, 1968, Chs. 12, 13; Kelly, 2007.

6 For overviews, and perspectives from antiquity, see Figuier (1860), Inglis (1992), Podmore (1902). On psychical research in various countries, see Biondi (1988), Lachapelle (2011), Moore (1977), Oppenheim (1985), Wolffram (2009). For a contemporary overview of nineteenth-century psychical research, see Podmore (1897).

7 For overviews of the Piper case, see Tymn (2013), as well as Piper (1929), Sage (1904), and a shorter account by Gauld (1982: Ch. 3). Important work with this medium includes that of Hodgson (1892, 1898), Hyslop (1901), James (1909e), Leaf (1890) and Lodge (1890). But many others had séances as well (e.g., Newbold, 1898; Robbins, 1922; Tanner, 1910; Verrall, 1910). Sidgwick (1915) presented an important analysis of published records with emphasis on the trance and psychological aspects of Piper séances. In addition to Tymn (2013), the case is frequently discussed nowadays (e.g., Alvarado, 2015; Braude, 2003: Ch. 3.2, 3.3; Gauld, 2014; Ruetenik, 2012). The latter author has argued that James's interest in Piper, and psychical research in general, was a natural consequence of his pragmatism.

8 Flournoy actually believed in veridical phenomena, both in mediumistic mentation and in cases of telepathy, but he did not accept survival. Flournoy's (1900) study of Hélène Smith (a pseudonym for Catherine Elise Muller, 1861–1929) has been influential in the development of the concept of creative dissociation. For an overview of Flournoy's work and ideas, see Alvarado et al. (2014).

9 For an overview of the few attempts combining ideas about the subconscious and veridical manifestations during the nineteenth and twentieth centuries, including physical mediumship, see Alvarado, 2014.

10 For a bibliography of James's publications, see Perry (1920). The secondary literature about James in immense; a few examples include: Barnard (1997), Bordogna (2008), Brown (1999), Lamberth (1999), Richardson (2006), Taylor (1996).

11 James's psychical research works have been included in his collected works (Burkhardt, 1986; see also Murphy & Ballou, 1960). Various aspects of this topic have been discussed by Alvarado & Krippner (2010), Bordogna (2008), Ford (1998), Junior et al. (2013), Knapp (2003), Taylor (1996), among others. Blum (2006) covers James in the context of an overview of historical aspects of psychical research.

12 On the early ASPR, see Moore (1977). Taylor (1996) has discussed the organization as an example of an institution supporting early psychological research, and James's involvement with it.

13 The report has been reprinted in Murphy & Ballou (1960) and in Burkhardt (1986), but without the context discussed here.

14 See, for example, Hodgson (1892). Note-taking was used by Hyslop (1901) and by Lodge (1890) in their studies of Piper. Later, verbatim recording was used by Tanner (1910) and by Thomas (1937). For an example of verbatim séance recordings from the mid-nineteenth century, see Simon (1923).

15 Because my emphasis is on mental mediumship, I have omitted here a short section of the beginning of the report in which James refers to materialization sittings with Mrs. Helen Berry. For information about this medium, see Morris (2014).

16 This control was called Dr. Phinuit and many were skeptical about its claim to be a spirit (see Hodgson, 1892, p. 46–58). On Phinuit, and other spirit controls of Piper, see Sidgwick (1915). Myers wrote about the control: "'Phinuit" ... is by no means above "fishing" ... There were some interviews throughout which Phinuit hardly asked any question, and hardly stated anything which was not true. There were others throughout which his utterances showed not one glimmer of real knowledge, but consisted wholly of fishing questions and random assertions" (Myers, 1890, p. 440). Mrs. Piper had other spirit controls, among them George Pellew (whose real name was George Pelhalm).

17 James's emphasis on the investigation of good "subjects" is consistent with nineteenth-century dissociation studies of specific individuals, as seen in the works of Azam (1887), Bourru and Burot (1888), Janet (1889) and others (see also Alvarado, 2009; Carroy, 1991; Kenny, 1986). James was aware of this literature (e.g., James, 1890a). He wrote about many of these cases in his discussion of dissociation in *The Principles of Psychology* (James, 1890b, Vol. 1, p. 379–393), and referred to "curious observations made on hysterical and hypnotic subjects, which prove the existence of a highly developed consciousness in places where it has hitherto not been suspected at all" (p. 201). The use of cases was also evident in James's lectures on exceptional mental states (Taylor, 1984; see also James, 1889). James wrote to Flournoy on 1 January 1900 about the latter's book (Flournoy, 1900) saying that he believed in the importance of "monographic studies of psychic personages" (Le Clair, 1966, p. 90). Much could be said about the importance of "psychic personages" beyond their roles as producers of phenomena (e.g., Alvarado, 1993).

18 The work of Myers (1903) is consistent with this view. See also the discussion of mediumship by James (1890b, Vol. 1, p. 393–400).

19 Hodgson (1892, p. 56) wrote: "I have frequently given Phinuit post-hypnotic suggestions concerning acts to be performed by Mrs. Piper in the waking state, but entirely without result". See also Hyslop (1901, p. Appendix 6).

20 By the time James started his study of Piper in 1885 there had been a tradition of observations supporting the idea of thought-transference (Luckhurst, 2002). The topic actually attracted much attention during the nineteenth century, as seen in the overviews of Ermacora (1898) and Podmore (1894). The SPR had sponsored various thought-transference experiments such as those of Guthrie and Birchall (1883) and Lodge (1884), among many others; see also Richet (1884) in France. It is understandable that James wanted to test Piper for telepathy because, from the beginning of the SPR, there were attempts to demarcate discarnate from living agency psychic phenomena, as seen in the cases of apparitions and mediumship (e.g., Gurney et al., 1886; see also Cerullo, 1982). In fact, explanation of mediumistic phenomena in terms of the psychic powers of the living medium preceded the SPR (Alvarado et al., 2012), and it is a topic that is still discussed in recent times (e.g., Braude, 2003).

21 "The willing game was a dinner party entertainment with a mind-reading twist ... The rules were simple: after guests had gathered, one person would be chosen to leave the parlor. Once he or she had left, a task would be decided on ... Ideally, the chosen person would be 'willed' into the action chosen, following directions sent mentally by others. Often, he or she would be blindfolded before reentering the room, guided by another player. Sometimes the guide would place a hand lightly against the seeker's shoulder or forehead, using touch as an additional aid in "willing" a job to be done" (Blum, 2006, p. 66).

22 Observations of materialization were published frequently during the late nineteenth century, as seen in publications appearing before James's (1886) report such as those of Crookes (1874) and Owen (1871) (see also Sargent, 1876). James (1887a) reported his negative impressions of a séance to produce this phenomenon.

References

Algaier, IV, E. L. (2014). Epistemic sensitivity and the alogical: William James, psychical research, and the radical empiricist attitude. *The Pluralist, 9*, 95–109.
Alvarado, C. S. (1993). The case of Eusapia Palladino, gifted subjects' contributions to parapsychology. *Journal of the Society for Psychical Research, 59*, 269–292.
Alvarado, C. S. (2002). Dissociation in Britain during the late nineteenth century: The Society for Psychical Research, 1882–1900. *Journal of Trauma and Dissociation, 3*, 9–33.
Alvarado, C. S. (2009). Nineteenth-century hysteria and hypnosis: A historical note on Blanche Wittmann. *Australian Journal of Clinical and Experimental Hypnosis, 37*, 21–36.
Alvarado, C. S. (2010). Classic Text No. 84: 'Divisions of personality and spiritism', by Alfred Binet (1896). *History of Psychiatry, 21*, 487–500.
Alvarado, C. S. (2013). Mediumship and psychical research. In: Moreman C (ed.) *The spiritualist movement: Speaking with the dead in America and around the world* (Vol. 2, pp. 127–144). Praeger.
Alvarado, C. S. (2014). Mediumship, psychical research, dissociation, and the powers of the subconscious mind. *Journal of Parapsychology, 78*, 98–114.
Alvarado, C. S. (2015). Charles Richet on Leonora Piper [Letter to the Editor]. *Journal of the Society for Psychical Research, 79*, 56–59.
Alvarado, C. S., & Krippner S (2010). Nineteenth century pioneers in the study of dissociation: William James and psychical research. *Journal of Consciousness Studies, 17*, 19–43.
Alvarado, C. S., Maraldi E de O, Machado, F. R., & Zangari, W. (2014). Theodore Flournoy's contributions to psychical research. *Journal of the Society for Psychical Research, 78*, 149–168.
Alvarado, C. S., Nahm, M. & Sommer, A. (2012). Notes on early interpretations of mediumship. *Journal of Scientific Exploration, 26*, 855–865.
Alvarado, C. S. & Zingrone, N. L. (2012). Classic Text No. 90: 'The Pathology and Treatment of Mediomania', by Frederic Rowland Marvin (1874). *History of Psychiatry, 23*, 229–244.
Anonymous. (1857, July 2nd). Startling evidence of spirit identity. *Banner of Light,* p. 6.
Anonymous. (1885a). Formation of the Society. *Proceedings of the American Society for Psychical Research, 1*, 1–2.
Anonymous. (1885b). Circular No. 1: Issued by the Council. *Proceedings of the American Society for Psychical Research, 1*, 2–4.
Azam, [E. E.]. (1887). *Hypnotisme, double conscience et altération de la personnalité*. J- B. Baillière.
Baillargé, J. (1861). [Communication to the Société Médico-Psychologique]. *Annales Médico-Psychologiques, 7*, 92–93.
Ballou, A. (1852). *An exposition of views respecting the principal facts, causes and peculiarities involved in spirit manifestations*. Bela Marsh.
Barnard, G. W. (1997). *Exploring unseen worlds: William James and the philosophy of mysticism*. State University of New York Press.
Beaunis, H. (1886). *Le Somnambulisme provoque: Études physiologiques et psychologiques*. J.–B. Baillière.
Bernheim, H. (1886). *De la suggestion et de ses applications à la thérapeutique*. Octave Doin.
Bertrand, A. (1826). *Du magnétisme animal en France*. J.- B. Baillière.
Binet, A. (1892). *Les altérations de la personnalité*. Félix Alcan.
Biondi, M. (1988). *Tavoli e medium: storia dello Spiritismo in Italia*. Gremese.
Blum, D. (2006). *Ghost hunters: William James and the search for scientific proof of life after death*. Penguin Press.
Bordogna, F. (2008). *William James at the boundaries: Philosophy, science, and the geography of knowledge*. University of Chicago Press.
Bourro, H., & Burot P (1888). *Variations de la personnalité*. J.- B. Baillière.
Braude, A. (2001). *Radical spirits: Spiritualism and women's rights in nineteenth-century America*. Indiana University Press.
Braude, S. E. (2003). *Immortal remains: The evidence for life after death*. Rowman and Littlefield.
Brown, H. (1999). *William James on radical empiricism and religion*. University of Toronto Press.
Burkhardt, F. H. (ed.). (1986). *Essays in psychical research* (The Works of William James, Vol. 16). Harvard University Press.

Burlet, P. (1863). *Du Spiritisme considère comme cause d'aliénation mentale*. Imprimerie de Richard.
Capron, E. W. (1855). *Modern spiritualism: Its facts and fanatisms, its consistencies and contradictions*. Bela Marsh.
Carlson, J. (1878, January 4th). Correspondence: Spirit identity. *Spiritualist Newspaper*, p. 10.
Carroll, B. E. (1997). *Spiritualism in antebellum America*. Indiana University Press.
Carroy, J. (1991). *Hypnose, suggestion et psychologie: L'invention de sujets*. Presses Universitaires de France.
Cerullo, J. J. (1982). *The secularization of the soul: Psychical research in modern Britain*. Institute for the Study of Human Issues.
Clark, U. (1863). *Plain guide to spiritualism*. William White.
Cooper, R. (1867). *Spiritual experiences, including seven months with the Brothers Davenport*. L. Heywood.
Crabtree, A. (1993). *From Mesmer to Freud: Magnetic sleep and the roots of psychological healing*. Yale University Press.
Crookes, W. (1874). *Researches in the phenomena of spiritualism*. J. Burns.
Deleuze, J. P. F. (1813). *Histoire critique du magnétisme animal* (Vol. 1). Mame.
Dessoir, M. (1886). Experiments in muscle-reading and thought-transference. *Proceedings of the Society for Psychical Research, 4*, 111–126.
Dewar, H. (1823). Report on a communication from Dr. Dyce of Aberdeen, to the Royal Society of Edinburgh, 'On Uterine Irritation and its Effects on the Female Constitution.' *Transactions of the Royal Society of Edinburgh, 9*, 365–379.
Edelman, N. (1995). *Voyantes, guerisseuses et visionnaires en France 1785–1914*. Albin Michel.
Ellenberger, H. F. (1970). *The discovery of the unconscious: The history and evolution of dynamic psychiatry*. Basic Books.
Elliotson, J. (1846). Instances of double states of consciousness independent of mesmerism. *Zoist, 4*, 158–187.
Ermacora, G. B. (1898). *La telepatia*. L. Crescini.
Figuier, L. (1860). *Histoire du merveilleux dans des temps moderns* (4 vols). L. Hachette.
Flournoy, T. (1899). Genèse de quelques prétendus messages spirites. *Revue Philosophique de la France et de l'Etranger, 47*, 144–158.
Flournoy, T. (1900). *From India to the planet Mars: A study of a case of somnabulism*. Harper & Brothers.
Ford, M. (1998). William James' psychical research and its philosophical implications. *Transactions of the Charles S. Peirce Society, 34*, 605–626.
Gauld, A. (1968). *The founders of psychical research*. Routledge & Kegan Paul.
Gauld, A. (1982). *Mediumship and survival: A century of investigations*. Heinemann.
Gauld, A. (1992). *A history of hypnotism*. Cambridge University Press.
Gauld, A. (2014). Two cases from the lost years of Mrs. Piper. *Journal of the Society for Psychical Research, 78*, 65–84.
Gonçalves, V. P., & Ortega, F. (2013). Uma nosologia para os fenomenos sobrenaturais e a construção do cerebro 'possmdo' no seculo XIX. *Historia, Ciencias, Saude-Manguinhos 20*, 373–390.
Greeley, H. (1868). *Recollections of a busy life: Including reminiscences of American politics and politicians*. J. B. Ford.
Gurney, E. (1887). Stages of hypnotic memory. *Proceedings of the Society for Psychical Research, 4*, 515–531.
Gurney, E., Myers, F. W. H., & Podmore, F. (1886). *Phantasms of the living* (2 vols). Trübner.
Guthrie, M., & Birchall, J. (1883). Record of experiments in thought-transference. *Proceedings of the Society for Psychical Research, 1*, 263–283.
Hacking, I. (1995). *Rewriting the soul: Multiple personality and the sciences of memory*. Princeton University Press.
Hammond, W. A. (1876). *Spiritualism and allied causes and conditions of nervous derangement*. G. P. Putnam's.
Hardinge, E. (1870). *Modern American Spiritualism: A twenty year's record of the communion between earth and the world of spirits* (3rd ed). Author.
Héricourt, J. (1889). L'activité inconsciente de l'esprit. *Revue Scientifique, 44*, 257–268.
Hodgson, R. (1891). A case of double consciousness. *Proceedings of the Society for Psychical Research, 7*, 221–255.
Hodgson, R. (1892). A record of observations of certain phenomena of trance. *Proceedings of the Society for Psychical Research, 8*, 1–167.

Hodgson, R. (1898). A further record of observations of certain phenomena of trance. *Proceedings of the Society for Psychical Research, 13*, 284–582.
Home, Mme. D. (1888). *D. D. Home: His life and mission*. Trübner.
Hustvedt, A. (2011). *Medical muses: Hysteria in nineteenth-century Paris*. W.W. Norton.
Hyslop, J. H. (1901). A further record of observations of certain phenomena of trance. *Proceedings of the Society for Psychical Research, 16*, 1–649.
Inglis, B. (1992). *Natural and supernatural: A history of the paranormal from earliest times to 1914* (Rev. ed). Prism.
James, H. (Ed.) (1920). *The letters of William James* (2 vols). Atlantic Monthly Press.
James, W. (1879). Are we automata? *Mind, 4*, 1–22.
James, W. (1884). What is an emotion? *Mind, 9*, 188–205.
James, W. (1886). Report of the Committee on Mediumistic Phenomena. *Proceedings of the American Society for Psychical Research, 1*, 102–106.
James, W. (1887a, February 19th). Letter from Professor James. *Banner of Light*, p. 4.
James, W. (1887b). Reaction-time in the hypnotic trance. *Proceedings of the American Society for Psychical Research, 1*, 246–248.
James, W. (1889). Notes on automatic writing. *Proceedings of the American Society for Psychical Research, 1*, 548–564.
James, W. (1890a). The hidden self. *Scribner's Magazine, 7*, 361–373.
James, W. (1890b). *The principles of psychology* (2 vols). Henry Holt.
James, W. (1890c). A record of observations of certain phenomena of trance (5). Part III. *Proceedings of the Society for Psychical Research, 6*, 651–659.
James, W. (1892a). *Psychology: Briefer course*. Henry Holt.
James, W. (1892b). What psychical research has accomplished. *Forum, 13*, 727–742.
James, W. (1895a). The knowing of things together. *Psychological Review, 2*, 105–124.
James, W. (1895b). Telepathy. In C. K. Adams (Ed.). *Johnson's universal cyclopaedia* (Vol. 8, pp. 45–47). D. Appleton.
James, W. (1896a). Address of the President before the Society for Psychical Research. *Science*, 3, 881–888.
James, W. (1896b). Psychical research. *Psychological Review, 3*, 649–651.
James, W. (1897). *The will to believe and other essays in popular philosophy*. Longmans, Green.
James, W. (1898a). *Human immortality*. Houghton Mifflin.
James, W. (1898b). Mrs. Piper, 'the medium'. *Science, 7*(n. s.), 640–641.
James, W. (1899). *Talks to teachers on psychology*. Henry Holt.
James, W. (1901). Frederic Myers's service to psychology. *Proceedings of the Society for Psychical Research, 17*, 13–23.
James, W. (1902). *The varieties of religious experience*. Longmans, Green.
James, W. (1903). Review of *Human personality and its survival of bodily death. Proceedings of the Society for Psychical Research, 18*, 22–33.
James, W. (1904). Does 'consciousness' exist? *Journal of Philosophy, Psychology, and Scientific Methods, 1*, 477–491.
James, W. (1907a). A case of clairvoyance. *Proceedings of the American Society for Psychical Research, 1*, 221–236.
James, W. (1907b). *Pragmatism: A new name for some old ways of thinking*. Longmans, Green.
James, W. (1909a). The confidences of a 'psychical researcher.' *American Magazine, 68*, 580–589.
James, W. (1909b). Physical phenomena at a private circle. *Journal of the American Society for Psychical Research, 3*, 109–113.
James, W. (1909c). *A pluralistic universe*. Longmans, Green.
James, W. (1909d). A possible case of projections of the double. *Journal of the American Society for Psychical Research*, 3, 253–254.
James, W. (1909e). Report on Mrs. Piper's Hodgson-control. *Proceedings of the Society for Psychical Research, 23*, 2–121.
James, W. (1960). Review of 'Planchette' [1869]. In G. Murphy, & R. O. Ballou (Eds.). *William James on psychical research* (pp. 19-23). Viking Press.
James, W., & Carnochan, G. M. (1886). Report of the Committee on Hypnotism. *Proceedings of the American Society for Psychical Research, 1*, 95–102.

Janet, P. (1886a). Les actes inconscientes et la dédoublement de la personnalité pendant le somnambulisme provoque. *Revue Philosophique de la France et de l'Etranger, 22*, 577–592.
Janet, P. (1886b). Note sur quelques phénomènes de somnambulisme. *Revue Philosophique de la France et de l'Etranger, 21*, 190–198.
Janet, P. (1887). L'anesthésie systématisée et la dissociation des phénomènes psychiques. *Revue Philosophique de la France et de l'Etranger, 23*, 449–472.
Janet, P. (1888). Les actes inconscients et la mémoire pendant le somnambulisme. *Revue Philosophique de la France et de l'Etranger, 25*, 238–279.
Janet, P. (1889). *L'Automatisme psychologique*. Félix Alcan.
Junior, A. S., Araujo, S. de., & Moreira-Almeida, A. (2013). William James and psychical research: Towards a radical science of mind. *History of Psychiatry, 24*, 62–78.
Kardec, A. (1857). *Le livre des esprits*. E. Dentu.
Kardec, A. (1862). *Le livre des mediums* (2nd ed). Didier.
Kelly, E. W. (2007). F. W. H. Myers and the empirical study of the mind-body problem. In E. Kelly, E. W. Kelly, A. Crabtree, A. Gauld, M. Grosso, and B. Greyson. *Irreducible mind: Toward a psychology for the 21st Century* (pp. 47–115), Rowman & Littlefield.
Kenny, M. G. (1986). *The passion of Ansel Bourne: Multiple personality in American culture*. Smithsonian Institution Press.
Knapp, K. D. (2003). *To the summerland: William James, psychical research and modernity*. Doctoral dissertation, Boston College.
Lachapelle, S. (2011). *Investigating the supernatural: From spiritism and occultism to psychical research and metapsychics in France, 1853–1931*. Johns Hopkins University Press.
Lamberth, D. C. (1999). *William James and the metaphysics of experience*. Cambridge University Press.
Lang, W. (1843). *Mesmerism; its history, phenomena, and practice*. Fraser.
Leaf, W. (1890). A record of observations of certain phenomena of trance (3). Part II. *Proceedings of the Society for Psychical Research, 6*, 558–646.
Le Clair, R. C. (Ed.) (1966). *The letters of William James and Theodore Flournoy*. University of Wisconsin Press.
Le Maléfan, P. (1999). *Folie et spiritisme: histoire du discourse psychopathologique sur la pratique du spiritisme, ses abords et ses avatars (1850–1950)*. L'Hartmattan.
Lodge, O. J. (1884). An account of some experiments in thought-transference. *Proceedings of the Society for Psychical Research, 1*, 189–200.
Lodge, O. (1890). A record of observations of certain phenomena of trance (2). Part I. *Proceedings of the Society for Psychical Research, 6*, 443–557.
Lombroso, C. (1886). Studi sull' ipnotismo. *Archivio di Psichiatria, Scienze Penali ed Antropologia Criminale, 7*, 257–283.
Luckhurst, R. (2002). *The Invention of Telepathy 1870–1901*. Oxford University Press.
Macnish, R. (1834). *The philosophy of sleep* (1st US ed). D. Appleton.
Mitchill, Dr. [S L]. (1817). Double consciousness, or a duality of person in the same individual. *Medical Repository* 3: 185–186.
Moore, R. L. (1977). *In search of white crows: Spiritualism, parapsychology, and American culture*. Oxford University Press.
Morris, D. (2014). *Boston in the golden age of spiritualism: Séances, mediums & immortality*. History Press.
Moses, W. S. [under pseudonym, M. A. Oxon] (1879). *Spirit-identity*. W. H. Harrison.
Murphy, G., & Ballou, R. O. (Eds) (1960). *William James and psychical research*. Viking Press.
Myers, F. W. H. (1884). On a telepathic explanation of some so-called spiritualistic phenomena. Part I. *Proceedings of the Society for Psychical Research, 2*, 217–237.
Myers, F. W. H. (1885). Automatic writing. II. *Proceedings of the Society for Psychical Research, 3*, 1–63.
Myers, F. W. H. (1886). Human personality in the light of hypnotic suggestion. *Proceedings of the Society for Psychical Research, 4*, 1–24.
Myers, F. W. H. (1889). Automatic writing. IV. The daemon of Socrates. *Proceedings of the Society for Psychical Research, 5*, 522–547.
Myers, F. W. H. (1890). A record of observations of certain phenomena of trance (1). Introduction. *Proceedings of the Society for Psychical Research, 6*, 436–442.

Myers, F. W. H. (1892a). On indications of continued terrene knowledge on the part of phantasms of the dead. *Proceedings of the Society for Psychical Research, 8*, 170–252.
Myers, F. W. H. (1892b). The subliminal consciousness: Chapter I. General characteristics of subliminal messages. *Proceedings of the Society for Psychical Research, 7*, 298–327.
Myers, F. W. H. (1903). *Human Personality and Its Survival of Bodily Death* (2 vols). Longmans, Green.
Newbold, W. R. (1898). A further record of observations of certain phenomena of trance. Part II. A. *Proceedings of the Society for Psychical Research, 14*, 6–49.
Oppenheim, J. (1985). *The other world: Spiritualism and psychical research in England, 1850–1914.* Cambridge University Press.
Owen, R. D. (1871). *The debatable land between this world and the next.* Trübner.
Perry, R. B. (1920). *Annotated bibliography of the writings of William James.* Longmans, Green.
Piper, A. L. (1929). *The life and work of Mrs. Piper.* Kegan Paul, Trench, Trübner.
Plas, R. (2000). *Naissance d'une science humaine: la psychologie: Les psychologues et le "Merveilleux Psychique."* Presses Universitaires de Rennes.
Plumer, W. S. (1860). Mary Reynolds: A case of double consciousness. *New Monthly Magazine*, I 807–812.
Podmore, F. (1894). *Apparitions and thought-transference.* Walter Scott.
Podmore, F. (1897). *Studies in psychical research.* Kegan Paul, Trench, Trübner.
Podmore, F. (1902). *Modern spiritualism: A history and a criticism* (2 vols). Methuen.
Richardson, R. D. (2006). *William James: In the maelstrom of American modernism.* Houghton Mifflin.
Richet, C. (1884). La suggestion mentale et le calcul des probabilités. *Revue Philosophique de la France et de l'Étranger, 18*, 609–674.
Richet, C. (1886). Les mouvements inconscients. In M. Berthelot (Ed.) *Hommages Monsieur Chevreul a l'Occasion de Son Centenaire 31 Aout 1886* (pp. 79–84). *Félix* Alcan.
Robbins, A. M. (1922). *Past and present with Mrs. Piper.* Henry Holt.
Ruetenik, T. (2012). Last call for William James: on pragmatism, Piper, and the value of psychical research. *The Pluralist, 7*, 72–93.
Sage, M. (1904). *Mrs. Piper and the Society for Psychical Research.* Scott-Thaw (Original work published 1902).
Sargent, E. (1876). *The proof palpable of immortality: Being an account of the materialisation phenomena of modern spiritualism* (2nd ed.) Colby and Rich.
Shamdasani, S. (1993). Automatic writing and the discovery of the unconscious. *Spring, 54*, 100–131.
Sidgwick, Mrs. H (1915). A contribution to the study of the psychology of Mrs. Piper's trance phenomena. *Proceedings of the Society for Psychical Research, 28*, 1–657.
Simon, G. (1923). *Chez Victor Hugo: Les tables tournantes de Jersey: Proces-verbaux des séances.* Louis Conard.
Spicer, H. (1853). *Sights and sounds: The mystery of the day: comprising an entire history of the American 'spirit' manifestations.* Thomas Bosworth.
Taine, H. (1878). *De l'intelligence*, Vol. 1 (3rd rev. ed.) Hachette.
Tanner, A. (1910). *Studies in spiritism.* D. Appleton.
Tappan, C.L.V. (1875). *Discourses through the mediumship of Mrs. Cora L. V. Tappan.* Burns.
Tascher, P. (1855). *Seconde lettre de Grosjean a son évêques au sujet de tables parlantes, des possessions, des sibylles, du magnétisme et autres diableries.* Ledoyen.
Taylor, E. (1984). *William James on exceptional mental states: The 1896 Lowell Lectures.* University of Massachusetts Press.
Taylor, E. (1996). *William James on consciousness beyond the margin.* Princeton University Press.
Thomas, J. F. (1937). *Beyond normal cognition: An evaluative and methodological study of the mental content of certain trance phenomena.* Bruce Humphries.
Tymn, M. (2013). *Resurrecting Leonora Piper: How science discovered the afterlife.* White Crow Books.
van der Hart, O., & Horst, R. (1989). The dissociation theory of Pierre Janet. *Journal of Traumatic Stress, 2*, 397–412.
Verrall, H. de G (1910). Report on the Junot sittings with Mrs. Piper. *Proceedings of the Society for Psychical Research, 24*, 351–664.
Wolffram, H. (2009). *The stepchildren of science: Psychical research and parapsychology in Germany, c. 1870–1939.* Rodopi.

42

Unorthodox Concepts of Force and Psychic Phenomena*

Carlos S. Alvarado

[This paper is based on a review of the works of Raoul Montandon (1927), Hereward Carrington (1939), Alexandre Barety (1887), Albert de Rochas (1899), Hippolyte Baraduc (1896), and Gabriel Delanne (1897).]

There is a long history of unorthodox concepts of force related to the human body, an idea coming from antiquity (Amadou, 1953). The books reviewed here are relatively late examples of such a conceptual tradition used to explain psychic phenomena. I am referring to the idea that there were "vital," "magnetic," or psychic forces, emanating from and surrounding human beings that could serve as carriers of information and as the means to produce healing and other physical actions when projected from the human body.

As I have discussed in recent years (Alvarado, 2006, 2009), such concepts were used in the mesmeric, spiritualistic, and psychical research literatures to explain a variety of phenomena. Following Franz Anton Mesmer (1734–1815), the so-called mesmerists postulated that "animal magnetism" was the means by which trances and healings could be induced, and the media for transmissions of thoughts and feelings at a distance. One of them, Baron Jean du Potet de Sennevoy (1796–1881), argued that:

> The nervous, active atmosphere of the magnetizer, no doubt augmented by the impulse of his will ... enters into rapport with the passive nervous atmosphere of the magnetized person, and augments the latter to the point that, in some cases, it seems that there is a real saturation of the nervous system. (Du Potet, 1868, p. 316; [this and other translations are mine]).

The idea was extended later to account for the phenomena of spiritualism. For example, many individuals writing since the nineteenth century discussed the phenomena of physical mediums as being caused by the exteriorization of some sort of biophysical force coming out from the body of the medium.

In his book *Les Radiations Humaines*, Swiss scholar Raoul Montandon (1877–1950) presented an overview of phenomena believed to be caused by these emanations. The topic of "human radiations" was related to that of subtle bodies in the Introduction. Montandon had chapters about Reichenbach's Od, auras, luminous phenomena, and a variety of other phenomena he believed were manifestations of this force. Some of these phenomena included photographic effects, acceleration in the growth of plants, and movement of objects. The latter included effects on a variety of instruments, many of which had moving needles believed to react to these forces. Such effects, the author wrote, could be caused by "an intra-organic radiation, a human fluid" (Montandon, pp. 373–374).

Montandon concluded that the information presented in the book showed the reality of human radiations, something that supported a vitalistic outlook of existence. He saw human beings as "a detector, an energy transformer and generator ..." (Montandon, 403).

*Republished with permission from *Journal of Scientific Exploration, 25*(1), 121–130, 2011.

Regardless of the validity of this belief in a radiation with physical properties, there is no question that Montandon's work is still a valuable resource to modern readers for its review of a literature that has been forgotten by many. Contemporary readers will find many bibliographical references and summaries of the work of well-known figures (e.g., de Rochas, Joire, Kilner, Ochorowicz, Reichenbach) as well as those who are less-known today (e.g., Barety, Bertholet, Bourg de Bozas, Leger, Tromelin).

British-born Hereward Carrington (1880–1958) who lived most of his life in the United States, was well-known as a researcher and a popularizer of psychic phenomena. He covered some of Montandon's topic in his *Laboratory Investigations into Psychic Phenomena*, but in a briefer way. The value of Carrington's book lies mainly in his report of empirical tests of various devices believed by some to detect unorthodox forces. This work was conducted at the American Psychical Institute directed by himself.

Carrington reported the results of tests with a variety of devices used to detect forces related to the human body via the movement of needles and other parts of the instrument. These instruments have been referred to as "magnetometers," even though they were non-magnetic devices. The results did not support the existence of an unknown force. Carrington stated:

> We have experimented with … more than fifty different varieties of magnetometers. In every case we have been enabled to determine the cause or causes responsible for the movement of the magnetometer needle. (Carrington, [1939], p. 113)

However, Carrington discussed more than unorthodox forces in his book. His book included much information about the use of instruments in psychical research. The first chapter was an overview of this work. In addition, there was a useful list of researchers (pp. 9–14), of instruments used to study "vital radiations" (pp. 49–54), and a chronology of relevant research work (pp. 36–41).

While Montandon's and Carrington's works covered a wide ground, the rest of the books reviewed here were more specific. One such work was Alexandre Baréty's (1844–1918). He was a physician convinced that there was a "neuric" force similar to animal magnetism. In *Le Magnétisme Animal* (1887) probably the most systematic and detailed research monograph of the late neo-mesmeric movement, he defined this force as a dynamic agent

> … probably from the nervous system, which circulates along the nerves or *radiates* out of them … and is susceptible to producing certain sensitive, motor, and psychic modifications on other human bodies. (Baréty, xii)

Baréty divided the book in two sections. In the first one he reported tests conducted with a lady he referred to as Mlle C., while in the second he reported work with other individuals. In Baréty's view the neuric force was projected from the body through passes, as well as through rays coming from the fingers, from eyesight, and from breath. Inside the body the force had properties such as heat and electricity, and once projected from the body and directed toward another person the force produced effects such as trance, anesthesia, hyperesthesia, and the induction or dissipation of contractions. Baréty believed the neuric force propagated through space through the ether and that the force could be transmitted through other objects and could be stored in water and in other things.

Baréty gave many examples of the physiological effects of the force. For example, he treated Mlle. C.'s stomach pains by pointing her fingers at her, which he said caused her pain to disappear in seconds. Baréty also claimed to be successful with Mlle C. in other ways. He was able to "anesthetise and hyperesthesise the integuments of different regions … abolish or exalt one or another sense" (Baréty, p. 326). While Mlle C. was in another room separated from him by a brick wall, Baréty said he was able to induce muscular contractions in one of his subject's wrists and hands by pointing his fingers to the wall.

In Barèty's view the existence and therapeutic value of the neuric force was beyond doubt. Furthermore, he believed that hysteria was related to the force. In his view it was due to a "modification in the direction, the force, and the distribution of nervous or *neuric* currents" (Barèty, p. 627).

Another representative of French neo-mesmerism was Lieutenant Colonel Albert de Rochas (1837–1914), well-known in his day for his numerous publications about hypnosis and psychic phenomena. One of his best-known works was *L Exteriorisation de la Sensibilite*, first published in 1895 but reviewed here in its fifth revised edition.

The opening chapter of de Rochas followed in the tradition of some of the old mesmerists, among them A.A. Tardy de Montravel (1785), who reported that mesmerized subjects saw luminous phenomena, and more particularly the magnetic force emanating from the mesmerizer. De Rochas wrote that his previous studies of the stages of hypnosis led him to conclude that in some hypnotic conditions "some subjects acquire a momentary hyperexcitability of sight that allows them to see effluvia in full light" (de Rochas, p. 6). This included observations of luminous emanations from magnets that, according to de Rochas, were not very consistent. In his words, "the same subject even varies sometimes in the affirmations from one moment to another" (de Rochas, p. 8).

The author conducted much research with sensitive individuals hoping to determine that such perceptions were objective and not the effect of suggestion. Observations made with a subject named Albert L. suggested to de Rochas that the perceptions were objective. For example, in some tests the subject reported lights from the poles of an electromagnet. When the poles were reversed without his knowledge

> … not only the descriptions of the effluvia corresponded perfectly with the operations during the twenty-two tests conducted but the subject even noticed the passage of the current at a time when the operator believed he had removed it. (de Rochas, p. 22)

The second chapter was devoted to the phenomenon of exteriorization of sensibility in which the tactile sensations of the hypnotized or mesmerized subject were projected at a distance from their physical body. In one test, de Rochas used two participants, a sensitive observer (A) and a person who was hypnotized (B). The observer reported seeing what looked like layers positioned a few centimeters from B's skin. The author wrote:

> If I, as magnetizer, act on this layer in any way, B feels the same [sensation] as if I acted on his skin, and he does not sense anything or almost anything if I act in any other place than on the layer; he does not feel much if he is acted upon by a person who is not in rapport with the magnetizer.
>
> If I continue magnetization, A sees forming around B a series of equidistant layers separated by a space from 6 to 7 centimeters [of width] … and B does not feel touches, [or] prickings, … the sensibility diminishes proportionally to its distance from the body. (de Rochas, p. 56).

In the rest of the book, de Rochas discussed spells and other ancient practices and beliefs that may be related to the above-mentioned phenomena of sensibility, including aspects of sympathetic magic. In some of his tests he had projected the sensibility of a person to a photograph and found she felt pain when the photo was pricked. The topic of forces was further discussed in several appendices, one of which was a reprint of an excerpt written by German philosopher Carl du Prel (1839–1899) on the topic of Reichenbach's Od.

Another French student of the subject, and one who received much publicity during his lifetime, was French physician Hippolyte Baraduc (1850-1902). In *L'Ame Humaine* he reported work to detect instrumentally what he believed were manifestations of the soul. While the material, he wrote, manifests "thanks to a solar or artificial exterior solar light, the fluidic invisible manifests by its *own intimate and intrinsic luminous force*" (Baraduc, p. 4). Baraduc described in the book what he believed were ways to show the reality of the "fluidic invisible."

The author started with what he called "biometry," a topic he explored in a previous book (Baraduc, 1893). This referred to the movements of a needle suspended from a thread believed to define certain patterns reflecting the action of the soul on the physical world. He claimed to have found that the "movements of life" showed seventeen different "formulas." The latter refers to numerical readings of the instrument corresponding to the right and left hands, which showed attraction and repulsion of the force, respectively. Baraduc claimed he had more than one thousand observations showing that while the right side of the body attracted "cosmic life," the left one did the opposite, pushed it back. Normal states reflected balance between right attraction and left repulsion. But some "formulas" could indicate particular health problems, including mental conditions.

Baraduc believed that his measures were not due to artifacts coming from environmental or body influences. Instead, he wrote, they were due to "our own animic movements, those of the *Soul* in its physical and psychical manifestations" (Baraduc p. 26).

Other parts of the book were about the photography of invisible forces. With the exception of some electrophotography, this was mainly achieved using conventional photographic equipment taking photos in darkness, hoping that the plaque was affected "by the effluvia, the emanations, the intimate vibrations" (Baraduc, p. 34) of the target object. The soul, usually invisible to the human eye, was believed by Baraduc to be able to impress a photographic plate. He postulated the existence of seven different emanations.

The first photo presented was that of a boy feeling sorry for a dead pheasant. Baraduc claimed that some patterns seen in the photo, similar to marks made by a brush, were a photographic record of the vital force of the child reflecting his animic state. These and many other anomalous photos were seen by the author as proof of the existence of these forces. In addition to Od, which he described as the threads of the cosmic life, he referred to other forces or subtle bodies, among them the ones he called Somod, Psych-icon, and Ob.

In the conclusion, Baraduc hoped that his readers believed that there was a soul. Unfortunately, his language and assumptions were unclear at best. No empirical evidence was presented for countless affirmations about the nature of these forces and their interactions and functions. An example was the assertion that: "The physical soul is the product of the vital instinct of the inferior cosmos" (Baraduc, p. 288). It is actually very difficult to follow the author's way of thinking, and his theoretical assumptions seem to take on a life of their own. Perhaps this is why a reviewer of the book stated: "Currently, the role of the researcher is not to explain, but to accumulate facts" (Battandier, 1896, p. 556). To complicate matters, in the last pages of the book Baraduc related some of his ideas to religious teachings and to concepts of universal life and its essence.

A similar problem appears in the ideas presented by Gabriel Delanne (1857–1926) in *L'Évolution Animique* [1897]. Delanne was an influential French leader in the movement of spiritism. He came into prominence in the movement after the death of the influential French educator Allan Kardec (pseudonym of Hippolyte-Leon Denizard Rivail, 1804–1869). In the book, Delanne discussed aspects of the action of the spirit during its life on Earth. These involved ideas obtained through mediumistic communications that he believed offered a solution to the explanation of many mental and physiological phenomena.

In addition to the physical body and to the spirit, Delanne discussed the "perispirit," which was (and still is) a key explanatory concept in spiritism. He wrote: "All Spirits … are covered with an invisible envelope, intangible and imponderable. This fluidic body is called perispirit" (Delanne, p. 12). Such subtle body or force allowed the spirit to interact with the body and was the instrument through which physical phenomena were produced (e.g., table turning).

Delanne argued that the perispirit was the principle behind memory, and behind what others considered to be the subconscious mind. Instead of postulating brain mechanisms or a psychological subconscious, he believed that recollection and dissociation was a function of this vital principle, one that could act abnormally on occasion. During such abnormal states as epilepsy, or through the use of drugs or hypnosis, the rhythm of the perispirit varied, causing anomalies in the recollection process. The new memories produced in the secondary state were in a different "vibratory plane" (Delanne, p. 226) than the older memories. When the "vital aura" returned to its usual activity, Delanne stated, older recollections came back. In this view it was possible to have more than two memory records, which he believed explained the phenomenon of multiple personalities. These ideas were applied by the author to explain observations about dissociative phenomena, such as the already classic case of Félida X. (b. 1843), and some of the observations reported by Pierre Janet (1859–1947), which were very influential at the time.

But Delanne also believed that the perispirit had morphological functions. He postulated that it served as a blueprint by which the formation of the body was guided in its development from the embryo. The nervous system, Delanne affirmed, was the "material reproduction of the perispirit" (Delanne, p. 175). The perispirit "possesses the organigenic laws that keep the fixity of the organism in the milieu of the unceasing mutations of material molecules" (Delanne, p. 47). Borrowing from the influential French philosopher of physiology and medicine Claude Bernard (1813–1878), Delanne referred to the directing or guiding influence of the perispirit. In his discussion of life, Bernard had mentioned the existence of currently unknown processes different from physico-chemical ones that contained a guiding or directing idea. "In every vital germ," wrote Bernard (1865, p. 162), "there is a creative idea that is developed and that manifests by means of organization." Associating spiritism with Bernard probably served many functions, among which was an attempt to normalize the ideas presented in the book.

The author also affirmed that the fluids described by the spirits would help us to understand matter. Evolution, he also wrote, involved the progress of the spirit over centuries of reincarnations. In its early development

> … the envelope of the soul is crude …; its vibratory movement is of the most inferior form. The work of the soul consists of purifying this envelope, getting rid of its fluidic scoria. (Delanne, p. 358)

The ideas of force and subtle bodies expressed in the above-mentioned books were to a great extent the result of concepts borrowed from a variety of occult-related traditions (Amadou, 1953), as well as from scientific fields of previous times. The latter includes past ideas from neurophysiology and its concepts of nervous fluids (Brazier, 1984) and the explorations of electricity and magnetism of physics (Harman, 1982). In eras where electricity was wondrous and the telegraph extended our reach of communications, it made sense to many to conceptualize psychic phenomena in physicalistic ways involving forces. A late example, among many, was the statement that "psychic waves, like hertzian waves in wireless telegraphy, propagate at a distance" (Denis, 1900, p. 291). Interestingly, many of these ideas of force were not purely physicalistic. Both Baraduc and Delanne referred to the soul in their writings as a higher guiding principle.

These works presented a mix of empirical observations and speculation. The assurances about the existence of certain principles we see in the works of Baréty, Delanne, and de Rochas were not always supported by the observations. In fact, what we see are speculations based on some observations, but growing much beyond the available evidence.

The ideas discussed in this review survive to this day in the New Age, occult, and spiritistic literature and in other movements. But they are not favored in most academic circles, including some of those open to the reality of parapsychological phenomena. A portion of the latter today emphasizes a view of consciousness that is nonphysical and nonlocal, a perspective that considers ideas such as the ones discussed in the books reviewed here as superseded concepts that are not supported by the facts. As I have pointed out before (Alvarado, 2006), with the rise of the influence of the new experimental parapsychology of J. B. Rhine and others, phenomena such as extrasensory perception and psychokinesis were seen by some as nonphysical processes supporting the existence of the mind. Such an emphasis came from the apparent independence these phenomena showed from distance, obstacles, and time.

Regardless of the validity of the ideas discussed in these books, it is important to recognize the existence of this conceptual tradition of unorthodox concepts of force. These were and still are powerful ideas that have been influential over time and that can teach us much about past theoretical thinking to account for psychic phenomena.

References

Alvarado, C. S. (2006). Human radiations: Concepts of force in mesmerism, spiritualism, and psychical research. *Journal of the Society for Psychical Research, 70*, 138–162.

Alvarado, C. S. (2009). Modern animal magnetism: The work of Alexandre Baréty, Emile Boirac, and Julian Ochorowicz. *Australian Journal of Clinical and Experimental Hypnosis*, 37, 1–15.

Amadou, R. (1953). Esquisse d'une histoire philosophique du fluide. *Revue Métapsychique, 21*, 5–33.

Baraduc, H. (1893). *La force vitale: Notre corps vital fluidique, sa formule biométrique*. Georges Carré.

Baraduc, H. (1896). *L'ame humaine: Ses mouvements, ses lumieres, et l'iconographie de l'invisible fluidique*. Georges Carré.

Barety, A. (1887). *Le magnétisme animal: Étudié sous le nom de force neurique rayonnante et circulante dans ses propriétés physiques, physiologiques, et thérapeutiques*. Octave Doin.

Battandier, A. (1896). Photographie de l'invisible. *Cosmos: Revue des Sciences et Leur Applications, 35*, 552–556.

Bernard, C. (1865). *Introduction à l'étude de la medicine expérimentale*. J-. B. Bailliere.

Brazier, M. A. B. (1984). *A history of neurophysiology in the 17th & 18th Centuries*. Raven Press.

Carrington, H. (1939/2006). Laboratory investigations into psychic phenomena. McKay. Reprinted by Kessinger.

de Rochas, A. (1899). *L'extériorisation de la sensibilité: Étude expérimentale & historique* (5th Rev. ed.). Chamuel.

Delanne, G. (1897). *L'evolution animique: Essais de psychologie suivant le Spiritisme*. Chamuel,

Denis, L. (1900). Psychologie expérimentale: Phénomènes d'extériorisation et de dédoublement. *Annales des Sciences Psychiques, 10*, 291–294.

Du Potet, Baron (1868). *Manuel de l'étudiant magnétiseurs* (4th ed.). Germer Baillière.

Harman, P. M. (1982). *Energy, force, and matter: The conceptual development of nineteenth century physics*. Cambridge University Press.

Montandon, R. (1927). *Les radiations humaines: introduction à la démonstration expérimentale de l'existence des corps subtils de l'homme*. Félix Alcan.

Tardy de Montravel, A. A. (1785). *Essai sur le Théorie du Somnambulisme Magnétique*. London.

43

Ambroise Auguste Liébeault and Psychic Phenomena*

Carlos S. Alvarado†

Some nineteenth-century hypnosis researchers did not limit their interest to the study of the conventional psychological and behavioral aspects of hypnosis, but also studied and wrote about psychic phenomena such as mental suggestion and clairvoyance. One example, and the topic of this paper, was French physician Ambroise Auguste Liébeault (1823–1904), who influenced the Nancy school of hypnosis, Liébeault wrote about mental suggestion, clairvoyance, mediumship, and even so-called poltergeists. Some of his writings provide conventional explanations of the phenomena. Still of interest today, Liébeault's writings about psychic phenomena illustrate the overlap that existed during the nineteenth-century between hypnosis and psychic phenomena—an overlap related to the potentials of the mind and its subconscious activity.

In this paper, I will discuss aspects of Liébeault's interests, which more broadly conceived, are consistent with a portion of modem historical writings on hypnosis (Gauld, 1992; Crabtree, 1993; Méheust, 1999a; Plas, 2000). Not only was seemingly "psychic phenomena" a part of the history of psychology and hypnosis, but the investigation of such phenomena, among other factors, contributed to the development of concepts such as dissociation and the subconscious mind (Alvarado, 2002; Ellenberger, 1970; Le Maléfan, 1999; Shamdasani, 1993).

Hypnosis was one of the developments of the nineteenth-century that led a variety of individuals to explore the potentials of the mind, including the existence of the subconscious, the capabilities of memory and its alteration, and the influence of the mind over the body (Crabtree, 1993; Gauld, 1992). In fact, hypnosis was considered a particularly useful exploratory tool for these concerns. In the words of physiologist Henry Beaunis (1830–1921), "hypnotism constitutes ... a true method of experimental psychology; it is for the philosopher what vivisection is for the physiologist" (Beaunis, 1887, p. 115). Such interest consisted mainly in the therapeutic use of hypnosis and in the study of a variety of cognitive, sensory-motor, and physiological functions and processes. Nonetheless, a small part of that hypnosis movement included phenomena that were referred to at the time as supernormal, psychic, or what some French called the "marvelous" (Durand (de Gros), 1894). This paper will focus on Liébeault's observations about these phenomena as they have received little attention. This is due, in part, to the fact that they represented a small part of his overall contributions to hypnosis.

Most contemporary psychologists and students of hypnosis are generally not interested in such phenomena today. Others may take a stronger stance and maintain that the only proper attitude toward psychic phenomena is onc of dismissive skepticism. I believe that the history of hypnosis—and the history of psychology—should be more than an evaluation of the validity and "reality" of past research findings and theory. To have a complete history of our subject we need to pay attention to the so-called marginal and unorthodox. That was the direction of

*Reprinted with permission from *American Journal of Clinical Hypnosis*, *52*, 111–121, 2009.
†Research for this paper was funded by a grant from the Society for Psychical Research (London). I am grateful to Nancy L. Zingrone for editorial suggestions to improve this paper.

Ellenberger (1970) in his study of the influence of mesmerism on the concept of the unconscious mind. Attention to all topics and movements important to the individuals we study has led to a more complex and complete history of psychology and hypnosis (e.g., Alvarado, 2002; Crabtree, 1993; Gauld, 1992; Plas, 2000). Liébeault believed psychic phenomena to be a proper part of the intellectual environment of the individuals he studied. A summary of his writings on psychic phenomena ought to contribute to a broadening of our understanding of what was then considered, by some, to be an acceptable topic of discussion. Willingness to seriously examine Liébeault's concepts and thinking about the so-called psychic phenomena may also reveal a process by which scientific thought evolves.

Hypnosis and Psychic Phenomena

The mesmeric literature contains many descriptions of these phenomena including such manifestations as healing, clairvoyance, and mental suggestion (Crabtree, 1993; Dingwall, 1967–1968; Gauld, 1992; Méheust, 1999a). The hypnosis movement also showed an overlap with psychic phenomena. The Society for Psychical Research (SPR), founded in London in 1882 to study phenomena such as thought-transference, mediumship and apparitions, published in their *Proceedings* much about hypnosis (Gurney, 1884; Gurney & Myers, 1885).[1] The writings of Frederic W. H. Myers (1843–1901) were particularly important regarding the theoretical interface of the supernormal and the hypnotic (e.g., Gurney & Myers, 1885; Myers, 1886).

Journals such as the *Revue de l'hypnotisme et de la psychologic physiologique* published papers about such topics as lucidity (De Rochas, 1889), mental suggestion (Joire, 1898), and mediumship (Lombroso, 1892). Indications of this interest include a section in Max Dessoir's (1867–1947) *Bibliographic des modernen Hypnotismus* (1888, Ch. 7) that presented references which mention the remote action of medicines and drugs, mental suggestion, and telepathy or thought-transference. Many books about hypnosis—such as the writings of Azam (1893, pp. 347–355), Binet and Féré (1887, pp. 40–44), Crocq (1900, Chs, 11, 12, 18, 19), and Moll (1890, pp. 362–366)—referred to some of these phenomena, even if many authors were skeptical of such manifestations.

There are examples of researchers and clinicians generally interested in the conventional phenomena of hypnosis and its clinical application that investigated psychic phenomena. Both Hippolyte Bernheim (1840–1919) and Georges Gilles de la Tourette (1857–1904) mentioned their failed attempts to obtain evidence for mental suggestion (Bernheim, 1888, p. vi; Gilles de la Tourette, 1887, p. 167). Others, such as Beaunis and Charles Richet (1850–1935), were more positive in their assessment (Beaunis, 1887, pp. 267–271; Richet, 1889). Méheust (1999b, pp. 163–174) has discussed many nineteenth-century attempts to explain claims for clairvoyance during the hypnotic trance using hyperesthesia as an explanation.

The above-mentioned publications are evidence of a common history between hypnosis and psychic phenomena in which conventional hypnosis researchers crossed over into psychical research and psychical researchers were concerned with hypnosis. This common history, which included much criticism, came from the fact that some psychic phenomena were thought, and reported, to have taken place under hypnosis. But both psychical and hypnosis research shared the goals of understanding the subconscious mind and human capabilities (Alvarado, 2002; Plas, 2000). A case illustrating these issues is that of Liébeault.

Liébeault and Hypnosis

Ambroise Auguste Liébeault (1823–1904) was a French physician who became known for his use of suggestion for psychotherapeutic purposes (on Liébeault see Barrucand, 1987; Bernheim, 1907; Carter, 2002; Gauld, 1992, pp. 319–324). Liébeault was born in Farrieres, Meurte-et-Moselle, in the Lorraine region of France. He came from a peasant family, and while he attended seminary school and was expected to become a priest, he started medical studies at Strasbourg, obtaining his medical degree in 1850 with a thesis about femorotibial dislocations (Liébeault, 1850). Liébeault became interested in magnetism while he was a medical student but did not pursue this interest for several years. After graduation, he established himself as a country physician at Pont-Saint-Vincent. In 1860 he moved to Nancy and opened a clinic there. He charged for conventional medical treatment but treated patients using hypnosis for free.

His first publication, *Le somneil provoqué et les états analogues considérés surtout au point de vue de faction du moral sur le physique* (1866) focused on similarities between natural sleep and induced sleep (or trance) and on aspects such as the features of hypnotic states, the induction of sleep and its relationship to the nervous system, and such phenomena as hallucinations.[2] A later writer said that Liébeault discussed "all the issues related to the various states of sleep with perfect competence and profound sagacity" (Liégeois, 1889, pp. 71–72). However, the book and the work was largely ignored by the medical profession. Liébeault only achieved prominence later when he was brought to the attention of Nancy physicians in 1882. The most important of these physicians was Bernheim who was instrumental in bringing Liébeault's work to the attention of the medical world (Bemhein, 1907). Influenced by Liébeault, Bernheim eventually became the leading proponent of suggestion to account for hypnotic phenomena. Bernheim (1884, p. 3) argued that while suggestion was proposed by Faria, and was applied by Braid, it was perfected by Liébeault.[3]

This work was further developed and articulated by the Nancy School of Hypnosis headed by Bernheim, a group that included Liébeault as well as others such as the above-mentioned physiologist Henry Beaunis and law professor Jules Liégeois (1833–1908). The Nancy School actively opposed the more somatic and psychopathologically-oriented Salpêtrière School headed by Jean Martin Charcot (1825–1893).[4] Ellenberger (1970, p. 87) argued that while Bernheim was the leader of the Nancy School, Liébeault was the school's spiritual father. There is no question that Liébeault was held in high esteem by many when he died in 1904.[5]

The reader is reminded that what follows represents but a small part of Liébeault's writings, and is not representative of his overall hypnosis work. It illustrates the overlap of interest in hypnosis and psychic phenomena that can be argued to have existed during the nineteenth-century.

Liébeault and Psychic Phenomena

Liébeault was in contact with members of the SPR and sent accounts of what he perceived to be psychic phenomena to the Society. In addition to the above-mentioned Frederic W.H. Myers, other members of the SPR, Edmund Gurney (1847–1888), and Arthur Myers (1851–1894) visited Liébeault and saw some of his patients (Gurney & Myers, 1885, p. 423; Myers, 1886, p. 6). On the recommendation of Myers, Liébeault was elected as a Corresponding Member of the SPR (Meeting of Council, 1885).[6]

What follows will summarize Liébeault's writings about psychic phenomena. This is not to argue for the existence of the phenomena nor to evaluate the methodological conditions under which such work was done, but rather to give specific examples of Liébeault's writings as an illustration of the types of approaches to psychic phenomena taken by some scientists and clinicians interested in hypnosis in Liébeault's day.

The Magnetic Force

Liébeault was part of the late nineteenth-century "magnetic" movement (Alvarado, 2009). In his book. Étude sur le *zoomagnétisme* (1883), he expressed his belief in a physical emanation between magnetizer and patient to account for healing effects on children. He used the term zoomagnetism to refer to this physical influence described as a "neurility exerted by a living being on another living being" (p. 5). After observing healing with small children treated magnetically while asleep, Liébeault stated he had to "admit a direct action of the neurility transmitted from man to man" and that this principle could "restore the physiological functioning of organs" (p. 24). However, in a later publication he accepted that *suggestion*, both direct and indirect, could explain the observed effects (Liébeault, 1891, p. 268). Nonetheless, Carter (2002, p. 18) has argued that Liébeault never completely abandoned his ideas about a magnetic force.

Mental Suggestion and Clairvoyance

The clairvoyance of hypnotized subjects was seen by Liébeault as enhanced sensory functions. He wrote: "I have looked for those phenomena … and when they have presented themselves, I have always found them to be linked to the normal operations of faculties and organs" (Liébeault, 1889/2002a, p. 119).

Some phenomena, Liébeault wrote, were taken by magnetizers to be evidence for a sixth sense. In his view, those magnetizers were not aware "that sleepers in isolation perceive with all their senses what takes place around them and that by asking them questions, on the location of an object for instance, we suggest to them … to direct their focused attention on anything that concerns said object … A whisper, a movement, the agitation of air around them, etc.; nothing they feel escapes their focused attention …" (Liébeault, 1889/2002a, p. 80).

Liébeault believed hypnosis could enhance the senses. Some of his observations included measuring the required distance between the eyes and the pages of a book to assess the effects of hypnosis on vision. He found that in the hypnotic trance several individuals were able to increase the distances when compared in the waking and hypnotic state (Liébeault, 1889/2002a, p. 87). Liébeault also discussed the enhancement of other sensory modalities such as hearing and tactile sensations.

At the end of his book, Liébeault (1889) presented a note (sort of an appendix) recounting two "feats" of mental suggestion he observed at his home in Nancy with a hypnotized woman on January 9, 1886. Present at the tests were several guests, including poet Stanislas de Guaita (1861–1897). It is not clear if Liébeault interpreted the success reported in the note as an example of enhanced sensory perception due to hypnosis. But he stated at the end of the note that there were "facts" recorded in SPR publications "that cannot be explained by a betrayal of thought" (Liébeault, 1889/2002a, p. 263).

Finally, the following is an account of lucidity that Liébeault reported in his book *Thérapeutique Suggestive* (1891; which has been translated, Liébeault, 1891/2002b) that he seemed to believe could not be explained by the principles of enhanced perception previously discussed. The first observation of a young somnambulist called Camille S. was done with Beaunis.' Liébeault wrote:

> First Mr. Beaunis, who had often put her to sleep, acted on her via passess [sic] performed from an adjacent room without her suspecting it, or at least without her conscious self being aware of it. He thus managed to place her in a state of somnambulism quickly, and several times. He repeated this identical experiment on the same person without her knowledge, this time positioning himself on a mound in my garden surrounded by a thick fence of Virginia creeper, some 29 meters from where the subject and I were located. The mound could not be seen, and besides a small wood also separated Mr. Beaunis from his subject. In spite of the obstacles hiding the operator, Camille S. fell into somnambulism 18 minutes after Dr. Beaunis had sent his passes from the mound where he was hiding … (Liébeault, 1891/2002b, p. 292).

In another test, Liébeault reported that his colleague Liégeois had presumably induced a trance using mental suggestion from a distance. Liébeault's consideration of conventional explanations for the phenomena is illustrated by the following: "It can be objected that, the previous experiments having always been conducted between eight and half past nine in the morning, the expecting subject must have fallen into somnambulism out of habit during this short period of time. This objection is not without foundation, but how can one explain why she fell into somnambulistic sleep only on the days we conducted the experiments, which were always kept apart" (Liébeault, 1891/2002b, p. 293)? Liébeault speculated about vibrations transmitted at a distance that could be perceived by special people.

Mediumship and Motor Automatisms

In his 1889 book, Liébeault discussed mediumship and table turning as forms of dissociation and motor automatism that did not require paranormal explanations. Motor automatisms were explained as the function of the doubling of attention and the creation of independent pathways of action and of memory. In terms of the movement of the pendulum, the dowsing rod, and turning tables, Liébeault postulated that the doubling of attention led the mind to produce motor acts unconsciously that were originally present in the conscious mind, although he did not use this terminology.

He felt that the trances of mediums were similar to those of hypnotized individuals. Both showed "concentration of the mind in order to enter their dreams in action, isolation, automatism, insensibility and loss of recall upon waking" (Liébeault, 1889/2002a, p. 224). The ideas mediums recalled during trance allowed them to create fictitious spirit communications. Furthermore, Liébeault believed mediums were not insane, however, he thought they could become so. This was due to their continuous entrance into a passive state—a practice potentially leading to a more permanent passive state that could lead into insanity (Liébeault, 1889/2002a, p. 235).

In a communication sent by Liébeault to the SPR on September 4, 1885, he discussed a case of veridical mediumistic communication. This case appeared in French in the SPR's *Journal* (Liébeault, 1885) and was later published in English (Gurney, Myers & Podmore, 1886, Vol. 1, p. 293; Myers, 1903, Vol. 2, pp. 169–170). Liébeault related a case of a young woman from a French family living in New Orleans. He had successfully treated hypnotically a young Mlle. B, a member of the family, for anemia and a nervous cough. The induction of hypnotic trance suggested to the family and to Mlle. B that she could become a medium (the "lady of the house" was thought to be a medium). The young woman became a writing medium, which she first manifested during breakfast when the impulse to write came over her. Liébeault, who believed the date of the incident was February 7, 1868, wrote:

> She wrote the same words again and again ..., and at last ... it was possible to read that a person called Marguerite was thus announcing her death. The family at once assumed that a young lady of that name, a friend of Mlle B.'s and her companion ... in ... high school, must have just expired. They all came immediately to me ... and we decided to verify the announcement of death that very day. Mlle B. wrote to a young English lady who was also a teacher in that same school. She gave some other reason for writing—taking care not to reveal the true motive of the letter. By return of post we received an answer in English of which they copied for me the essential part ... It expressed the surprise of the English lady at the receipt of Mlle B.'s unexpected and apparently motiveless letter. But at the same time the English correspondent made haste to announce to Mlle B. that their common friend, Marguerite, had died on February 7th at about 8 am ... (Myers, 1903, Vol. 2, pp. 169–170).

A Poltergeist Girl

In another letter Liébeault sent to Myers dated February 1, 1888, he wrote a short account of a case of noises and objects thrown in a closed room. There was also "one young girl, raised from the ground and undressed in the dark, though in the charge of several persons who were holding her" (Liébeault, 1888, p. 227). The girl was taken to Liébeault's so as to deal with her nerves. After hypnosis she left having being calmed. But the manifestations started again and the police became involved, producing a report consistent with the previous account.

Precognitive Information about Death

Myers (1895, pp. 528–529) presented the following case he received from Liébeault. The case, which happened to a patient, also appeared in Liébeault's later book (1891). Liébeault wrote that on December 27, 1879, his patient, then 19 years of age, consulted a "necromancer" and was told that he would lose his father in a year's time to the day. He was also told that he would become a soldier soon, that he would marry, have two children, and will die at 26 years of age. When all the events, except, of course, his own death, had taken place, including the death of his father on December 27, he came to Liébeault hoping to avoid his death. "On this and the following days I tried to send ... [the patient] into profound sleep in order to dissipate the impression that he would die on the February 4, his birthday. (Myers, 1895, p. 529).

Trying to avoid self-suggestion, Liébeault sent the patient to consult one of his somnambulists and was told by him that he would die in 41 years. The patient seemed to cease being worried and he did not die on the 4th of February.

As Liébeault further wrote: "I had forgotten all this, when at the beginning of October I received an invitation to the funeral of my unfortunate patient, who had died on September 30th, 1886, in his 27th year, as ... foretold ... I have since learnt that the unfortunate man had been under treatment for biliary calcuti and died of peritonitis caused by an internal rupture" (Myers, 1895, p. 529).[7]

Liébeault in Context

As mentioned before, Liébeault's writings on psychic phenomena should be seen in the context of his times. While he represents an interest that some of his colleagues involved with hypnosis shared, it was an interest that was by no means universal and, indeed, was controversial at the time. When defending the reality of magnetism, he was part of the late magnetic movement represented by such men as Émile Boirac (1851–1917), Julian Ochorowicz (1850–1917), and Albert de Rochas (1837–1914) (Boirac, 1893; De Rochas, 1887; Ochorowicz, 1887/1891). So, even considering the decline of the magnetic movement in the late part of the nineteenth century, Liébeault was not alone in his initial belief of the influence of a magnetic force on the human body (see Alvarado, 2009).[8]

A similar point can be made about clairvoyance and mental suggestion in late nineteenth-century France (Plas, 2000). Liébeault's explanation of these phenomena in terms of heightened sensory perception in the hypnotized subject also paralleled interesting literature discussing hyperesthesia in the hypnotized and using the concept of hyperesthesia to explain apparent psychic phenomena. Some assumed that enhanced vision could take place to the point that a hypnotized subject could read very small type normally unreadable (Bergson, 1886). A French doctor suggested that enhanced hearing could explain his efforts to induce sleep of subjects placed in an adjoining room (Ruault, 1886). In his view possible changes in the pulse rate of the hypnotizer at the moment of sending a silent command could perhaps produce the effects. Some of this literature was criticized by Myers (1887) for its exaggerated conception of hyperesthesia.

Liébeault also speculated about the transference of information at a distance through vibrations. He only mentioned this in passing but seemed to refer to something different than hyperesthesia. In fact, his ideas seem to belong to that group of nineteenth-century theorists who explained telepathy by physical signals (vibrations, waves) emanating between one person and another (Alvarado, 2008).

In addition to his discussion of observations about enhanced perception to explain clairvoyance, Liébeault's ideas about dissociation and automatisms show that he was part of a French intellectual tradition in which accounts of mediumship and other phenomena could be explained through conventional principles assuming the normal functioning of the human mind. Such tradition has been discussed by Le Maléfan (1999) and includes many other individuals such as the well-known Pierre Janet (1889).

However, Liébeault's observations with Camille, show that he was willing to consider the existence of mental suggestion-at-a-distance which was otherwise unexplained by conventional mechanisms. He may not have been in the same camp as Richet and Myers, but neither was he fully with those who believed solely in conventional explanations.

Concluding Remarks

While Liébeault's cases were interesting and his observations were consistent with those of other authors, there is no evidence to suggest that he conducted systematic studies of these phenomena. In fact, his writings about psychic phenomena represented only a fraction of his intellectual work. Nonetheless, they are an example of the overlap that existed between hypnosis and the supernormal during the nineteenth-century. The work of Beaunis, Janet, and Richet provide other important examples. Such an overlap reflected common interests in the potentials of the human mind, and in the workings of the subconscious.

Interestingly, not all of Liébeault's discussions about psychic phenomena referred to manifestations he believed could not be explained by known principles. He also wrote about the enhancement of sensory perceptions during hypnosis and about unconscious automatisms. These ideas were consistent with the established science of the era.

In reporting observations of the phenomena that were shunned by the establishment Liébeault was consistent with the attitude that led him to champion hypnosis during his early years before he was discovered by Bernheim and others and brought into prominence. That is, his discussions of psychic phenomena illustrated the same pioneering spirit and independence of mind he showed in his writings and therapeutic uses of hypnosis. Although Liébeault's writings about psychic phenomena were not as influential as those of some of his contemporaries, and regardless of the skepticism modem students of hypnosis have for seemingly psychic phenomena, he should be remembered as one of those figures who, on occasion, "walked" the borderline of hypnosis and psychical research.

Notes

1 The standard study of the SPR in the nineteenth-century is Gauld (1968). On SPR work and theory on hypnosis and dissociation see Alvarado (2002) and Gauld (1992, pp. 389–400).

2 Later publications included a revised edition of the 1866 book (Liébeault, 1889). A discussion of the use of suggestion for therapy (Liébeault, 1891) and for other purposes (Liébeault, 1895). Carter (2002) has translated some of Liébeault's writings to English.

3 This was a reference to José Custodio de Faria (1756–1819) and James Braid (1795–1860). On the work of these men see Gauld (1992, pp. 273–277, 279–287).

4 On these schools and the controversies generated see Crabtree (1993, pp. 164–168), Gauld (1992, pp. 324–336, 353–356) and Nicolas (2004).

5 Liébeault received a medal (Leroy. 1899), and his memory was honored in a meeting of the Société de Hypnologie et de Psychologic (Bulletin, 1904. p. 1). After he died there was a ceremony to present a bust of him that involved the attendance of many personalities involved with hypnosis and psychotherapy and the delivery of speeches, the reading of a poem, and a banquet (Inauguration, 1906).

6 Other hypnosis researchers and therapists such as Beaunis, Bernheim, Féré, Janet, Liégeois, and Schrenck-Notzing were also corresponding members of the SPR (List of Members and Associates, 1889).

7 See also Beaunis's (1914) report of observations in which Liébeault was present. On Camille S. see Carroy (1991, pp. 82–84) and Liégeois (1889. pp. 325, 702–709). The latter wrote: "Camille S. ..., 18 years [of age], is a very good somnambulist; M. Liébeault and I have known her for close to four years" (pp. 702–703). An abstract of a conference presentation on the topic appears in Liébeault (1897).

8 For another case see Liébeault (1891, pp. 284–285).

References

Alvarado, C. S. (2002). Dissociation in Britain during the late nineteenth century: The Society for Psychical Research, 1882–1900. *Journal of Trauma and Dissociation, 3,* 9–33.

Alvarado, C. S. (2008). Further notes on historical ideas of human radiations: IV. Mental phenomena. *Psypioneer, 4,* 119–126.

Alvarado, C. S. (2009). Late nineteenth and early twentieth century discussions of animal magnetism. *International Journal of Clinical and Experimental Hypnosis, 57,* 1–16.

Azam, Dr. [E.E.]. (1893). *Hypnotisme et double conscience* [Hypnotism and double consciousness]. Félix Alcan.

Barrucand, D. (1987). Naissance de 1'Ecole de Nancy: Liébeault et Bernheim. *Psychologic Médicale, 19,* 233–235.

Beaunis, H. (1887). *Le somnambulisme provoqué* (2nd ed.). J. B. Baillière.

Beaunis, H. (1914). Deux cas de lucidité télépathique pendant le sommeil hypnotique. *Annates des sciences psychiques, 24,* 33–37.

Bergson, H. (1886). De la simulation inconscient dans 1'hypnotisme. *Revue philosophique de la France de de l'étranger, 22,* 525–531.
Bernheim, Dr. H. (1884). *De la suggestion dans l'état hypnotique et dans l'état de veille*. Octave Doin.
Bernheim, Dr. H. (1888). *De la suggestion el de ses applications a la thérapeutique* (2nd ed.). Octave Doin.
Bernheim, Dr. [H.]. (1907). Le Dr. Liébeault et la doctrine de la suggestion. *Revue médicale de l'Est, 39,* 36–51,70–82.
Binet, A., & Féré, C. (1887). *Le magnétisme animal*. Félix Alcan.
Boirac, E. (1893). *Un essai de classification des phénomènes parapsychiques*. *Annales des sciences psychiques, 3,* 342–354.
Bulletin. (1904). *Revue de l'hypnotisme et de la psychologic physiologique, 19,* 1–3.
Carter, L. (Comp. &Trans.) (2002). *Ambroise-Auguste Liébeault: The hypnological legacy of a secular saint.* College Station, TX: Virtualbookworm.com.
Carroy, J. (1991). *Hypnose, suggestion et psychologie: L'invention de sujets*. Presses Universitaires de France.
Crabtree, A. (1993). *From Mesmer to Freud: Magnetic sleep and the roots of psychological healing*. Yale University Press.
Croq, J. (1900). *L'hypnotisme scientifique*. (2nd ed.). Société d'Éditions Scientifiques.
De Rochas, A. (1887). *Les forces non définies: Recherchés historiques et expérimentales*. G Masson.
De Rochas, A. (1889). Les états profonds de l'hypnose. *Revue de l'hypnotisme et de la psychologic physiologique, 3,* 41–49.
Dessoir, M. (1888). *Bibliographic des modernen Hypnotismus*. Carl Duncker.
Dingwall, E. J. (Ed.) (1967–1968). *Abnormal hypnotic phenomena: A survey of 19th century cases.* Barnes and Noble.
Durand (de Gros), J. P. (1894). *Le merveilleux scientifique*. Félix Alcan.
Ellenberger, H. F. (1970). *The discovery of the unconscious: The history and evolution of dynamic psychiatry*. Basic Books.
Gauld, A. (1968). *The founders of psychical research.* Routledge & Kegan Paul.
Gauld, A. (1992). *A history of hypnotism.* Cambridge University Press.
Gilles de la Tourette, G. (1887). *L'hypnotisme et les états analogues au point de vue médico-légal*. E. Plom Noumt
Gurney, E. (1884). The stages of hypnotism. *Proceedings of the Society for Psychical Research, 2,* 61–72.
Gurney, E., & Myers, F.W.H. (1885). Some higher aspects of mesmerism. *Proceedings of the Society for Psychical Research, 3,* 401–423.
Gurney, E., Myers, F. W. H., & Podmore, F. (1886). *Phantasms of the living* (2 vols.). Trübner.
Inauguration du buste du Dr. Liébeault. (1906). *Revue de I 'hypnotisme et de la psychologic physiologique, 20,* 257–286.
Janet, P. (1889). *L'automatisme psychologique: Essai de psychologic expérimentale sur les formes inferieures de I 'activité humaine*. Félix Alcan.
Joire, P. (1898). De la suggestion mentale: Expériences nouvelles. *Revue de I 'hypnotisme et de la psychologic physiologique, 72,* 104–111.
Le Maléfan, P. (1999). Folie et spiritisme: *Histoire du discourse psychopathologique sur la pratique du spiritisme, ses abords et ses avatars (1850–1950)*. L'Harmattan.
Leroy, M. (1899). L'anniverssaire du Dr. Liébeault, *Revue de l'hypnotisme et de la psychologic physiologique, 14,* 99–101.
Liébeault, A. A. (1850). *Étude sur la désarticulation fémoro-tibiale*. Imprimerie de L. F. le Roux.
Liébeault, A. A. (1866). *Le somneil provoqué et les états analogues considérés surtout au point de vue de faction du moral sur le physique*. V. Masson ct Fils.
Liébeault, A. A. (1883). *Étude sur le zoomagnétisme*. Georges Masson.
Liébeault, A. A. (1885), Cases received by the Literary Committee. *Journal of the Society for Psychical Research, 2,* 67–68.
Liébeault, A. A. (1888), Correspondence. *Journal of the Society for Psychical Research, 3,* 227.
Liébeault, A. A. (1889). *Le sommeil provoqué et les états analogues*. Octave Doin.
Liébeault, A. A. (1891). *Thérapeutique suggestive: Son mécanisme: Propriétés diverses du sommeil provoque et des états analogues*. Octave Doin.

Liébeault, A. A, (1895). Suggestions criminelles hypnotiques: Arguments et faits a l'appui. *Revue de l'hypnotisme et de la psychologic physiologique, 9,* 289–299, 330–336.
Liébeault, A. A. (1897). Communication de pensées par suggestion mentale, *Dritter Intemationaler Congress für Psychologic* (p. 427). J. F. Lehmann.
Liébeault, A. A. (2002a), Induced sleep and states analogous to it. In L. Carter (Comp. & Trans.), *Ambroise-Auguste Liébeault: The hypnological legacy of a secular saint* (pp. 24–275). Virtualbookworm.com,
Liébeault, A. A. (2002b). Lucidity. In L. Carter (Comp. & Trans.), *Ambroise-Auguste Liébeault: The hypnological legacy of a secular saint* (pp. 288–302). Virtualbookworm.com.
Liégeois, J. (1889). *De la suggestion et du somnambulisme dans leurs rapports avec la Jurisprudence et la médecine leígale.* Octave Doin.
List of members and associates (May, 1889). *Proceedings of the Society for Psychical Research, 5,* 590–606.
Lombroso, C. (1892). Les faits spiritiques et leur explication psychiatrique. *Revue de I 'hypnotisme et de la psychologic physiologique, 6,* 289–296.
Meeting of Council. (1885). *Journal of the Society for Psychical Research, 2,* 58.
Méheust, B. (1999a), *Somnambulisme et médiumnité (1784–1930): Vol. 1: Le défi du magnétisme animal.* Le Plessis-Robinson: Institut Synthelabo pour de Progres de la Connaissance.
Méheust, B. (1999b). *Somnambulisme et mediumnite (1784–1930): Vol. 2: Le choc des sciences psychiques.* Le Plessis-Robinson: Institut Synthélabo pour de Progrès de la Connaissance.
Moll, A. (1890). *Hypnotism.* Walter Scott.
Myers, F. W. H. (1886). Human personality in the light of hypnotic suggestion. *Proceedings of the Society for Psychical Research, 4,* 1–24.
Myers, F. W. H. (1887). Note on certain reported cases of hypnotic hyperaesthesia. *Proceedings of the Society for Psychical Research, 4,* 532–539.
Myers, F. W. H. (1895). The subliminal self: Chapter IX: The relation of supernormal phenomena to time. Precognition. *Proceedings of the Society for Psychical Research, 11,* 408–593.
Myers, F. W. H. (1903). *Human personality and its survival of bodily death* (2 vols.). Longmans, Green.
Nicolas, S. (2004). *L'hypnose: Charcot face à Bernhein: L'école de la Salpêtrière face à l'école de Nancy.* L'Harmattan.
Ochorowicz, J. (1891). *Mental suggestion.* Humbolt.
Plas, R. (2000). *Naissance d'une science humaine: La psychologic: Les psychologues et le "merveilleux psychique".* Presses Universitaires de Rennes.
Richet, C. (1889). Further experiments in hypnotic lucidity or clairvoyance. *Proceedings of the Society for Psychical Research, 6,* 66–83.
Ruault, A. (1886). Le mécanisme de la suggestion mentale hypnotique. *Revue philosophique de la France et de L'étranger, 22,* 679–697.
Shamdasani, S. (1993). Automatic writing and the discovery of the unconscious. *Spring, 54,* 100–131.

Nineteenth-Century Suggestion and Magnetism: Hypnosis at the International Congress of Physiological Psychology (1889)*

Carlos S. Alvarado†

Many important conceptual issues related to hypnosis arose during the nineteenth century. Some examples were included in the discussions about hypnosis at the 1889 International Congress of Physiological Psychology. This was the first of a series of international congresses that assisted in the development and professionalization of early psychology. Discussions about hypnosis in the congress included its role in psychological research, as well as terminology, the importance of suggestion, hypnotic sensibility, methodological problems in the study of hypnosis, comparison with sleep, induction techniques, animal hypnosis, mental suggestion, and the existence of magnetic action. Hypnosis papers and discussions from the congress provide us with a reminder of prevalent thought about the subject in 1889, as well as the consensus and controversies of the times.

In August of 1889, a congress of psychology met in Paris. It brought together many of the main psychologists of the world (Congrès International de Psychologie Physiologique, 1890; Nicolas and Meunier, 2002). One of the topics discussed at the congress, and the purview of one of its committees, was hypnosis. Men such as Joseph F. F. Babinski (1857–1932), Hippolyte Bernheim (1840–1919), Joseph R. L. Delboeuf (1831–1896), August Forel (1848–1931), Pierre Janet (1859–1947), Jules Liégeois (1833–1908), Cesare Lombroso (1835–1909), Frederic W. H. Myers (1843–1901), Julian Ochorowicz (1850–1917), Charles Richet (1850–1935), and Albert von Schrenck-Notzing (1862–1929) presented papers or participated as discussants. In this paper I will summarize the main hypnosis discussions that took place at the congress.

Nineteenth-Century Hypnosis and Magnetism

Histories of hypnosis have documented the important developments on the subject that took place during the nineteenth century (e.g. Crabtree, 1993; Gauld, 1992; Nicolas, 2004; Winter, 2000). Such developments in the research and theory of hypnosis were part of the rise of a new empirical psychology which, to a great extent, was attempting to separate itself from philosophy (e.g. Nicolas, 2002; O'Donnell, 1985). Hypnosis provided a tool for the collection of information and theoretical development using special individuals who submitted themselves to all kinds of experiments (Carroy, 1991). In fact, one author wrote: "Hypnotism constitutes ... a genuine method of experimental psychology; it will be for the philosopher what vivisection is for the physiologist"(Beaunis, 1885, p. 1; this, and other translations, are mine).

Some influential examples of these developments included the pioneering work of two men who brought their scientific reputation to the support of the subject, physiologist Charles Richet (1875,

*Republished with permission from *Contemporary Hypnosis*, *27*, 48–60, 2010.
†I wish to thank the Society for Psychical Research for a grant that allowed me to write this paper. I am also grateful to Nancy L. Zingrone for editorial suggestions that improved this paper.

1880, 1883) and the famous neurologist Jean-Martin Charcot (1825–1893; whose writings on hypnosis were collected in Charcot, 1890). In his initial paper, "Du Somnambulisme Provoqué," Richet (1875) argued that in somnambulism "reason is perverted, but their intelligence is visibly overexcited" (p. 358), a state in which the person was open to the "predominant influence of a foreign will" (p. 360). Charcot's interest was related in part to his involvement in pathology and therapy, as seen in his comparison of cases of paralysis that are produced by mental means to the use of suggestion to put ideas "in the mind like a parasite" (Charcot, 1887, p. 336). One of his best-known publications on the subject was a paper presented at the Académie des Sciences entitled "Sur les Divers États Nerveux Déterminés par l'Hypnotisation chez les Hystériques" (1882).

Many other works published during the late nineteenth century attest to the interest in the subject (Dessoir, 1888). Examples representing a variety of theories and methodologies include Azam's *Hypnotisme, double conscience et altération de la personnalité* (1887), Bernheim's *de la suggestion et de ses applications à la thérapeutique* (1888), Gilles de la Tourette's *l'hypnotisme et les états analogues au point de vue médico-legal* (1887), Liébeault's *le sommeil provoqué et les états analogues* (1889), Moll's *der Hypnotismus* (1889), Myers's 'Human Personality in the Light of Hypnotic Suggestion' (1886), Sidis' *the psychology of Suggestion* (1898), Tamburini and Seppilli's 'Contribuzioni allo Studio Sperimentale dell'Ipnotismo' (1881–1882), and Tuckey's *psycho-therapeutics; or treatment by Sleep and Suggestion* (1890). In 1886 the *revue de l'hypnotisme expérimental et thérapeutique* began publication in Paris, edited by Edgar Bérillon (1859–1948). In Berlin, the *Zeitschrift für Hypnotismus* appeared in 1892 under the editorship of J. Grossmann.

The period also saw conflicts between the Salpêtrière and Nancy schools of hypnosis, led by Charcot and Bernheim, respectively. These opposing schools defined most of the French debates and developments regarding hypnosis (Nicolas, 2004). According to a commentator writing in 1887, the work conducted in France and elsewhere laid "the foundation of a true experimental psychology" (Dessoir, 1887, p. 545).

These explorations included different emphases. Some of them used hypnosis in the study of the subconscious mind. This was the case in the investigations of Pierre Janet (1889) on secondary personalities, and Edmund Gurney's (1847–1888) studies of hypnotic memory and creativity (Gurney, 1887b, 1887c). Others focused on the physiological effects of suggestion (Tamburini & Seppilli, 1881–1882) and on its therapeutic uses (Schrenck-Notzing, 1895).

In addition, during the nineteenth century, hypnosis was associated with studies of phenomena more controversial than those previously mentioned. Among these were feats of mental suggestion in which it was believed that telepathy could be used to convey ideas during the hypnotic state or to induce trance (Ochorowicz, 1887; Richet, 1889). Closely related to these ideas of action at a distance were concepts of animal magnetism defended by some students of the subject (Barety, 1887; De Rochas, 1887). Such ideas had by no means disappeared during the late nineteenth century (Alvarado, 2009b), as will be seen in the discussion of the content of the congress.

With the exception of therapeutic concerns, all of these phenomena found their way, if only briefly, into the discussions of hypnosis held in the congress. For this reason, an overview of hypnosis in the congress presents us with a glimpse of the research, ideas, and questions raised about hypnosis in 1889.

The 1889 Congress

In addition to the psychology congress, 1889 also heralded the publication of a number of influential works (Janet, 1889; Liébeault, 1889; Liégeois, 1889; Moll, 1889) and another meeting at Paris on hypnosis (Bérillon, 1889). Many of the papers presented in the 1889 congress of hypnotism were about the therapeutic use of hypnosis in psychological or medical conditions (e.g. Gascard, 1889).

The 1889 International Congress of Physiological Psychology was the first of many congresses representing different aspects of psychology (Nuttin, 1992). It was organized by members of the Société de Psychologie Physiologique, which was founded in 1885. The President of the 1889 congress was Charcot, but he was not present so Théodule Ribot (1839–1916) took his place. Richet was the General Secretary, and members of the congress committee included Henry Beaunis (1830–1921), Francis Galton (1822–1911), William James (1842–1910), Enrico Morselli (1852–1929), Wilhelm Wundt (1832–1920), and Pierre Janet. In addition to hypnotism, which was one of the most widely discussed topics at the congress, the programme of the meeting listed the following subjects: muscular sense, the role of movements in the formation of images, attention and affective states, a statistical study of hallucinations, the appetite of idiots and imbeciles, motor impulses independent of images and ideas in the insane, "psychic poisons" (drugs affecting mental functions), and heredity (Programme du Congrès, 1890).[1]

To a great extent the congress was the result of the development of empirical psychology during the late nineteenth century, as well as attempts to professionalize the field. Similar causes moved psychology in France (Nicolas, 2002) where the congress met during the 1889 Paris Universal Exposition for which the Eiffel Tower was built. These developments were not only concerned with laboratory work, but also with the systematic recording and study of clinical cases, particularly important in the French tradition (Foschi, 2003).

Discussions of Hypnosis in the Congress

Richet on Hypnosis

In a paper about the topics of the congress Richet (1890b) referred to hypnosis as a subject that "empassions all psychologists today" (p. 35). The congress, he said, represented all schools of hypnosis. He wrote about the conflicts between the Salpêtrière and Nancy schools: "We will have achieved great progress if we could reach a reconciliation between the two rival schools ... The moment is close when this rivalry will be regarded as no more than a historical fact rightly relegated among the misunderstandings and errors of the past" (p. 36; but see Babinski's [1890] critiques of Bernheim in the congress).

Richet stated in the same paper that the congress would not cover medical aspects, but would focus instead on the "scientific character" (p. 36) of hypnosis. He wrote: "Hypnotism is an admirable instrument of psychological vivisection. Thanks to the work of physicians and physiologists who have studied hypnotism, we are acquainted with the unconscious, we know that this unconscious accomplishes silently marvelous intellectual operations" (pp. 37–38; such views are consistent with those presented in the congress by Dessoir, 1890).

In Richet's view some questions had been solved: "No one dares to talk anymore of simulation.[2] The influence of suggestion is pretty much universally admitted" (p. 37). But he also reminded his audience that many questions remained unanswered.

Terminology

One of the topics discussed was that of the terminology of hypnosis. Richet (1890b, p. 36) had already stated in the above-mentioned address that it was due to the "defectiveness of language" that errors continued in science. Brissaud and Richet (1890) presented definitions of many relevant terms, among them amnesia, automatism, catalepsy, ecstasy, hypnotism, unconsciousness, lethargy, animal magnetism, memory, simulation, sleep, and somnambulism. Hypnotism was defined as a "somnambulism induced through *physical* actions"[3] and it was added that magnetism was "an induced somnambulism, due to the intervention of an influence or of an *individual* will" (p. 24).

In Brissaud and Richet's view animal magnetism was a vague term used in a variety of ways to refer to the induction of somnambulism. They wrote: "The word magnetism means ... action at a distance; it may be applied to all the actions that bring on somnambulism; for example: the passes, called *magnetic*, producing magnetic sleep. The magnetic sleep is the state of induced somnambulism; the hypnotic state is the same state induced by a cause a little different, that is to say by physical actions, instead of an individual influence" (p. 25).

They wrote about suggestion: "By its etymology, it is the act of suggesting ... an act or an idea" (p. 27). Suggestion may come from a word, a gesture, or from any other indication. It is autosuggestion when it comes from the subject herself. Mental suggestion was defined as a suggestion in which "the person who suggests does not provide the subject with any appreciable indication to the senses or to the normal faculties of knowledge" (p. 27).[4]

Brissaud and Richet's definitions were presented to and discussed by members of the congress in a special meeting (Section de l'Hypnotisme, 1890a). On the term "amnesia," Delboeuf, the Chair of the session, suggested that the following be added to the definition: that "the amnesia is *momentary or complete*" (p. 39). Forel suggested that it was important to determine in what way amnesia could be "partial," and some amnesias could have physiological or dynamic causes.

Richet said that hypnotism was an "induced somnambulism due to physical causes, magnetism is an induced somnambulism due to an individual difference" (p. 41). But Richet also argued, "magnetism and hypnotism indicate the same phenomena" (p. 41). To this Liégeois said: "The two words hypnotism and magnetism have a historical meaning; both words imply a theory" (p. 41).

Bernheim focused on aspects of the meaning of the word "suggestion." In his view a person fell under the influence of a suggestion when they accepted an idea and implanted it in themselves through the abolition of resistance. He further stated: "The word hypnotism is not synonymous with somnambulism or induced sleep" (p. 42). Bernheim said he could produce phenomena—analgesia, hallucinations, catalepsy—without trance: "Hypnosis is nothing but suggestion; all the suggestions can be obtained without sleep" (p. 42).

In Bernheim's view defining hypnosis as "induced sleep" excluded many instances of the phenomenon because such a term only referred to one manifestation. He defined hypnotism as a "*particular psychic state susceptible of being induced and that exalts suggestibility*" (p. 42). He believed the term "induced somnambulism" was ill-defined and "animal magnetism" was also problematic. Hypnotism, he argued, had separated from magnetism and become "an independent scientific branch" (p. 43).

The majority of those attending this discussion session replied negatively when the Chair asked if the terms "hypnotism" and "magnetism" should be used in the same sense. When the Chair asked for agreement with the statement that hypnotism was part of magnetism in the same way that geometry was part of mathematics, six attendees agreed and fifteen did not.

At the end of the session on terminology, Brissaud and Richet's terms were accepted with the following exceptions. It was resolved that the term "animal magnetism" should be reserved for the science dealing with "*nervous phenomena generally included by that term and explaining them in ways other than suggestion*" (p. 43). It was also recommended that hypnotism be defined as the science dealing with phenomena explained by suggestion and autosuggestion, as well as by "analogous reactions" (p. 43).

Errors in the Study of Hypnosis

Léon Marillier (1862–1901) presented a paper about observation errors in the study of hypnosis (Marillier, 1890a). The simulation of the phenomena was a problem, and one, he said, that could be "voluntary or involuntary and half unconscious" (p. 17). Marillier cautioned experimenters about using the same subjects in many experiments,[5] and recommended the changing of experimental conditions on occasion.

Marillier also considered mental suggestion. In his study of this phenomena, he suggested that sources of error came from the observer. Experimenters were cautioned not to give any cues to the subject or "any sign which the subject could interpret, consciously or unconsciously" (p. 17).

Hypnotic Sensibility

Polish psychologist and philosopher Julian Ochorowicz presented several papers on hypnosis. In one of them he discussed hypnotic sensibility, defined as the "aptitude to be influenced by various hypnotization procedures" (Ochorowicz, 1890a, p. 18). Such a propensity could be shown by the facility to induce hypnosis, the depth of the state, the suggestibility of the subject, and the subtlety of the phenomena obtained. In his paper Ochorowicz asked if this sensibility depended on age, sex, race, or social position, or if it was pathological or related to nervousness or sleepwalking. Other questions included: Are there some exterior signs of this sensibility? Are persons showing natural somnambulism more susceptible to hypnosis? Can this sensibility be augmented by chemical means? He concluded: "In summary in the current state of our knowledge, can we say of what *hypnotic sensibility* consists?" (p. 19).

Ochorowicz's topic was discussed by the attendees (*De la Sensibilité Hypnotique*, 1890). Richet argued that non-hysterical subjects could be hypnotized. Bernheim commented that neuropaths were the most difficult to hypnotize. He believed there was an inverse relation between nervousness and suggestibility and that everyone "is hypnotizable, but some people cannot be put into the necessary psychic conditions to sleep" (p. 59). Ochorowicz agreed that neuropathy and hypnotism were different types of sensibilities, and Forel argued that suggestibility depended to a great extent "on the momentary disposition of the subject" (p. 60), a disposition that could change from day to day, or from moment to moment. Other discussants focused on the personal influence of the hypnotizer. This was the case of Bernheim, Delboeuf, Myers, and Richet.

Philosopher Henry Sidgwick (1838–1900), then President of the Society for Psychical Research, stated that he could not hypnotize people and that different hypnotizers may have different influences. To this Richet replied that he had noticed in himself a diminution of his ability to hypnotize, which was stronger when he was younger.

Hypnotic and Normal Sleep

In another paper Ochorowicz (1890b) discussed the comparisons between normal and hypnotic sleep. He wondered if the same phenomena of hypnosis could be produced in someone who was sleeping by establishing rapport with the sleeper. In relation to sleepwalking he said he knew of a person who could be in the state for hours, but who was not hypnotizable. Furthermore, Ochorowicz asked if it was "possible to transform to hypnosis the dream of a person *who is not hypnotizable* in the waking state" (p. 19).

He stated that, unlike normal sleep, hypnosis is an "accidental, abnormal state … which is easily distinguished through the variety of its stages and its symptoms, by the morbidity of its inhibitions and dynamogenies, and finally by its suggestibility, which never acquires such a distinct and marked form during normal sleep" (p. 21).

Ochorowicz pointed out that there were many unanswered questions. These included the similarities and differences in physiological measures between both states, and the possible existence of spontaneous dreams in hypnosis.

Is Suggestion the Only Explanation?

Ochorowicz (1890c) delivered a third paper in which he asked if all of hypnotism could be accounted for by suggestion. He accepted the existence of suggestion but noted that some hypnotists used physical means of induction. There was much discussion of this paper, with some participants commenting that suggestion did not explain everything (Section de l'hypnotisme, 1890c). Ochorowicz asked if some of his observations could be explained by suggestion—an example included obtaining unintended healing effects using suggestion. This was the case in his attempts to cure a nervous tic and accidentally controlling insomnia, or trying to get a hemiplegic to move a paralyzed arm and instead inducing a warming feeling in the feet, which had been cold, and improving circulation. Observations of this sort led Ochorowicz to ask if it was accurate to say that "hypnotic therapy is but a suggestive therapy" (p. 75).

Richet argued that phenomena could be produced by suggestion that could produce "deep modifications in our psychic state" (pp. 75–76). Forel said that "the phenomena of suggestion are physical cerebral phenomena" which, in turn, produce "indisputable physical effects … such as the arrest or production of menstruation" (p. 76). In his view, the fact that Ochorowicz found effects other than those intended did not disprove suggestion, but pointed towards autosuggestion by the subject. He further wrote: "The verbal suggestion … is always completed by the autosuggestion of the hypnotized, that is to say by the way in which it is understood and felt by the subject … Autosuggestion includes phenomena analogous or identical to those produced by suggestion, which the subject produces spontaneously" (p. 76).

According to Bernheim: "There are two opinions represented in this congress: some attribute everything to suggestion, others give a great part to physical influence. But suggestion of a physical action on the brain is not always verbal, it can arise as a result of a touch, when, for example, a hand is placed on the forehead" (p. 79). However, in a paper entitled "La Suggestion Dans l'Hypnotisme," Babinski (1890) disagreed with Bernheim, arguing that "the somatic properties of hypnotism and grand hypnotism may develop independently of all suggestion" (pp. 131–132). He further argued that many of the observations of Charcot and others were confirmed by independent observers. Furthermore, he asked what evidence some researchers thought they had to affirm that suggestion was the only cause of hypnotic phenomena. On Bernheim he said: "The only reason invoked by M. Bernheim consists in saying and repeating, in several different ways, that he has never reproduced in his subjects, without the help of suggestion, the somatic effects observed by M. Charcot and his pupils" (p. 134). Babinski countered by saying that Bernheim was using a different type of hypnotic subject. The "hypnotism of the Salpêtrière is the hypnotism of hysterics" (p. 135); consequently, he argued, it was possible to induce certain phenomena with patients there that could not be obtained with other subjects elsewhere. This difference of opinion between Babinski and Bernheim illustrated the conflict between the Salpêtrière and Nancy schools of hypnosis.

Babinski's presentation was followed by a discussion touching on issues of pathology and suggestion (Discussion of Babinski's paper, 1890). Forel argued that suggestion could produce the appearance of hysterogenic zones.[6] Janet argued that distracted people were the most hypnotizable. In his view "hypnotism is the symptom of a disease, not a physical disease, but a moral disease" (p. 137). But Ochorowicz disagreed. In his view the issue was one of a special sensibility that was not pathological.

Animal Hypnosis

The issue of animal hypnosis also received attention (Danilewski, 1890). Danilewski argued that studies of human beings were not sufficient. Comparative studies with animals, as performed in other areas of science, were important and necessary to understand hypnosis. He argued that, "from the theoretical point of view, the organization of physical and psychic man does not present in general but the highest degree of development of animal organization" (p. 80).

The paper included a long section about frogs in which Danilewski mentioned the inhibition of movements presented as a response to outside stimuli and the suppression of voluntary movements. Other animals discussed included birds, crayfish, crocodiles, fish, octopus, the electrical torpedo (a ray), and serpents. It was said that sea turtles were harder to hypnotize than other animals, but Danilewski wrote: "It is not difficult to induce an access of dyspnea in a hypnotized turtle" (p. 86). In his view, the "exterior hypnotizing influences that, in animals, act on the exterior senses, are replaced in man by psychic influences" (p. 90).

Other Topics

German philosopher Max Dessoir (1867–1947) presented a paper about the double self, a topic that received much discussion during the later nineteenth century (Dessoir, 1890).[7] He saw hypnosis as producing evidence for double consciousness. In his view there were two hypnotic states: one in which the hypnotized person perceived surrounding events but reacted only to the hypnotizer, and another in which only the hypnotizer was perceived. Like Richet (1890b), Dessoir believed that hypnosis could be a valuable instrument of psychological exploration. In his opinion what the field needed was systematic research on specific questions, as opposed to more therapeutic reports or sporadic observations. Research would be of help in the development of theories.

The proceedings also included a summary of a presentation by Albert von Schrenck-Notzing about photographs of hypnotized individuals (Photographies d'Hypnotiques, 1890). In another paper Lombroso (1890) discussed observations of hypnotic phenomena such as hallucinations.

In his address summarizing the topics of the congress, Richet (1890b) stated that there were many questions left unanswered, such as the influence of metals and magnets on the hypnotized,[8] and the issue of lucidity (clairvoyance), consisting of "isolated observations, without being able to determine the conditions [of occurrence], and without even being able to produce a demonstration beyond reproach" (p. 37). There was a general discussion of many of these topics (Discussion of Babinski's paper, 1890, p. 138), in which Myers mentioned the thought-transference experiments conducted by the Society for Psychical Research using hypnotized subjects, and made a call for further work on the subject. Ochorowicz argued that there were several hypnotic states to consider in mental suggestion.

He suggested that a state of monodeism, in which a dominant idea ruled the mind, was a favorable state for the phenomenon (Statistique des Hallucinations, 1890, p. 155). Bernheim indicated his skepticism by referring to "obscure or doubtful phenomena (lucidity, vision at a distance, presentiments, etc.)" (Section de l'Hypnotisme, 1890a, p. 43).

Another issue discussed was that of the existence of a magnetic action in hypnotism. In a session on terminology (Section de Hypnotisme, 1890a), Professor Liégois stated: "Those who believe in the fluid are the magnetizers, those that do not believe [in the fluid] are the hypnotizers" (p. 41). In the same section discussing terminology Forel stated that the word magnetism should be used by those who believed in "fluidism," and the term hypnotism should be reserved for scientists. But Delboeuf argued that some scientists believed in fluidism and that "non-fluidism is not completely demonstrated" (p. 41).

Myers (Section de l'Hypnotisme, 1890b, pp. 61–62) brought to the attention of the group the studies by Gurney (e.g., 1887a), designed to show that the hand of a magnetizer could produce an influence (such as contractions) separate from suggestion. Both Delboeuf and Gilbert Ballet (1853–1918) were skeptical of such an influence. Bernheim also expressed doubts about the existence of a "personal influence" and stated he had never induced contractions if the subjects were not aware of his intentions. Ballet, the Chair of the session, argued that while Bernheim had not observed such facts, he had done so several times. In Ballet's view, "suggestion cannot explain all the facts," and touch could produce contractions "impossible to obtain through suggestion" (p. 63).

Concluding Remarks

Pickren and Fowler (2003) have argued that the content of the early psychology congresses "reflected the heterogeneity of psychology during the period" (p. 535). The same may be said about the discussions of hypnosis at the 1889 congress, which illustrate the variety of ideas and the controversies of the times. Perhaps the most important aspect of the discussions was that no consensus had been reached on either the role or the nature of suggestion. For some attendees suggestion explained all of hypnosis, while others found suggestion to be an incomplete explanation.

The proceedings of the congress also showed how little knowledge or consensus had been reached at the time on specifics such as the relationship of hypnosis to psychopathology and the factors related to hypnotic sensibility, as seen in Ochorowicz's (1890a) paper.

Regardless of Richet's hope for the disappearance of rival schools, the fact is that they were present at the congress. The Salpêtrière position may have been weakened by attacks from the Nancy school, but the war was not over. Babinski's (1890) paper criticizing Bernheim was the main example of this conflict during the congress. But the tension between these two schools did not characterize the whole of the congress' discussions. In fact, one must remember that not everyone interested in hypnosis at the time could be classified either as a follower of the Salpêtrière or of Nancy. Delboeuf, Ochorowicz, and Richet were among those who had not committed to one position or the other.

The congress also illustrates the state of hypnosis culture at the end of the century and its concerns with what some refer to today as the paranormal, such as the occurrence of telepathy during the hypnotic state and other phenomena. There were many individuals—among them Beaunis, Gurney, Janet, Liébeault, Myers, Richet, and Ochorowicz—who explored both hypnosis and psychic phenomena (Alvarado, 2002; Crabtree, 1993). In fact, there were other discussions in the congress related to psychical research, such as those about veridical hallucinations (Marillier, 1890b). However, such an emphasis was barely present at the 1889 hypnosis congress (Berillon, 1889), perhaps because attendees were more concerned with the therapeutic applications of hypnosis. After the 1905 psychology congress, however, psychical research topics were rarely discussed at the meetings. They also disappeared slowly from the agendas of hypnosis researchers and clinicians. Hypnosis itself was also discussed less often in congresses after the turn of the twentieth century.

Conceptually related to the concerns of psychical research are the discussions of magnetic influence in hypnosis, which by the time of the 1889 congress did not have much scientific credence in the eyes of most representatives of established science. Nonetheless, and in opposition to those who believed these ideas had long disappeared from serious circles, the concept of a magnetic action capable of inducing trance and a variety of healing, physiological, and mental effects, was still around in 1889 as can be seen in the discussions in the congress, and in the work of others publishing at the time (Alvarado, 2009a).

The 1889 congress is a window that presents a slice of the history of hypnosis, serving as a reminder of theoretical diversity at the time of the meeting. The efforts of the members of the congress were important to later developments in the empirical study of hypnosis, not to mention in the organization and professionalization of psychology. But such aspects can only be studied in detail by expanding the focus beyond the congress, and considering in more depth aspects such as the psychotherapeutic uses of hypnosis.

Notes

1 For overviews of the congress see James (1889), Marillier (1889), and A. T. Myers (1889).
2 Interestingly, Richet discussed the topic in his first publication on hypnosis (Richet, 1875, pp. 363–370), as well as in later years (Richet, 1880, pp. 337–350).
3 Physical actions included the fixation of the person's gaze on an object (sometimes luminous or shiny), the use of light and sound, pressure on the eyes and on other parts of the body, friction, and the application of magnets (Binet & Féré, 1887, Ch. 4). For earlier discussions see Braid (1843, Ch. 2).
4 Richet (1884, 1888, 1889) was well-known at the time for the study of these phenomena. In fact, he was responsible for bringing leading members of the London based Society for Psychical Research to the congress (Sidgwick & Sidgwick, 1906, p. 515).
5 Repeated use of the same hypnotic subject was common (Carroy, 1991). An example of such "professional" subjects was the career of Blanche Wittmann (Alvarado, 2009a).
6 These are zones which, when pressed, would induce hysterical symptoms, as discussed by Richer (1881, pp. 32–40).
7 Examples include the discussions of Janet (1889), Myers (1892), and Sidis (1898).
8 The issue of metals and magnets has its own interesting place in the history of hypnosis (Harrington, 1988). This also involved the phenomena of transfer studied by Binet and Féré (1885). Richet (1890a) presented a communique about this in the congress in which he asked for new studies on the subject.

References

Alvarado, C. S. (2002). Dissociation in Britain during the late nineteenth century: The Society for Psychical Research, 1882–1900. *Journal of Trauma and Dissociation, 3*, 9–33. DOI: 10.1300/ J229v03n02_02

Alvarado, C. S. (2009a). Nineteenth-century hysteria and hypnosis: A historical note on Blanche Wittmann. *Australian Journal of Clinical and Experimental Hypnosis, 37*, 21–36.

Alvarado, C. S. (2009b). Late nineteenth and early twentieth century discussions of animal magnetism. *International Journal of Clinical and Experimental Hypnosis, 57*, 366–381. DOI: 10.1080/0020–7124

Azam, E. E. (1887). *Hypnotisme, double conscience et altération de la personnalité*. J. B. Baillière.

Babinski, J. F. F. (1890). La suggestion dans l'hypnotisme. *Congrès International de Psychologie Physiologique* (pp. 131–136). Bureau de Revues.

Barély, A. (1887). *Le magnétisme animal: Étudié sous le nom de force neurique rayonnante et circulante dans ses propriétes physiques, physiologiques et thérapeutique*. Octave Doin.

Beaunis, H. (1885). L'expérimentation en psychologie par le somnambulisme provoque. *Revue philosophique de la France et de l'étranger, 20*, 1–36.

Bérillon, E. (ed.), (1889). *Premier Congrès International de l'hypnotisme Expérimentale et Thérapeutique*. Octave Doin.

Bernheim, H. (1888). *De la suggestion et de ses applications a la thérapeutique* (2nd ed.). Octave Doin.

Binet, A., & Féré, C. (1885). L'hypnotisme chez les hystériques: Le transfert. *Revue philosophique de la France et de l'étranger, 19*, 1–25.

Binet, A., & Féré, C. (1887). *Le magnétisme animal*. Félix Alcan.

Braid, J. (1843). *Neurypnology or the Rationale of nervous sleep considered in relation with animal magnetism*. John Murray.

Brissaud, P., & Richet, C. (1890). Essai d'une terminologie dans les questions d'hypnotisme. *Congres International de Psychologie Physiologique* (pp. 24–27). Bureau de Revues.

Carroy, J. (1991). *Hypnose, suggestion et psychologie: L'invention de sujets*. Presses Universitaires de France.

Charcot, J. M. (1882). Sur les divers états nerveux déterminés par l'hypnotisation chez les hystériques. *Comptes-rendus hebdomadaires des seances de l'Academie des Sciences, 94*, 403–405.

Charcot, J. M. (1887). *Leçons sur les maladies du système nerveux faites a la Salpêtrière* (vol. 3). Bureau du Progrès Médical.

Charcot, J. M. (1890). *Oeuvres complètes de J.M. Charcot* (vol. 9, ed.) Bourneville EB. Bureau du Progrès Medical.

Congrès International de Psychologie Physiologique (1890). Bureau de Revues.

Crabtree, A. (1993). *From Mesmer to Freud: Magnetic sleep and the roots of psychological healing*. Yale University Press.

Danilewski, B. (1890). Recherches physiologiques sur l'hypnotisme des animaux. *Congrès International de Psychologie Physiologique* (pp. 79–92). Bureau de Revues.

De Rochas, A. (1887). *Les forces non définies: Recherches historiques et expérimentales*. G. Masson.

De la sensibilité hypnotique (1890). *Congrès International de Psychologie Physiologique* (pp. 59–63). Bureau de Revues.

Dessoir, M. (1887). Hypnotism in France. *Science, 9*, 541–545.

Dessoir, M. (1888). *Bibliographie des modernen Hypnotismus*. Carl Duncker.

Dessoir, M. (1890). Le double moi. *Congrès International de Psychologie Physiologique* (pp. 146–151). Bureau de Revues.

Discussion of Babinski's paper. (1890). *Congrès International de Psychologie Physiologique* (pp. 136–139). Bureau de Revues.

Foschi, R. (2003). L'indagine sulla personnalità alle origini della psicologia scientifica francese (1870–1885). *Physis, 40*, 63–105.

Gascard, A. (1889). Influence de la suggestion sur certains troubles de la menstruation. *Premier Congrès International de l'Hypnotisme Expérimentale et Thérapeutique* (pp. 129–137). Octave Doin.

Gauld, A. (1992). *A history of hypnotism*. Cambridge University Press.

Gilles de la Tourette [G.] (1887). *L'hypnotisme et les états analogues au point de vue médico-legal*. E. Plon, Nourrit.

Gurney, E. (1887a). Recent experiments in hypnotism. *Proceedings of the Society for Psychical Research, 5*, 3–17.

Gurney, E. (1887b). Peculiarities of certain post-hypnotic states. *Proceedings of the Society for Psychical Research, 4*, 268–323.

Gurney, E. (1887c). Stages of hypnotic memory. *Proceedings of the Society for Psychical Research, 4*, 515–531.

Harrington A (1988). Metals and magnets in medicine: Hysteria, hypnosis, and medical culture in finde-siècle Paris. *Psychological Medicine, 18,* 21–38. DOI: 10.1017/S0033291700001859
James, W. (1889). The Congress of Physiological Psychology at Paris. *Mind, 14,* 614–615.
Janet, P. (1889). *L'automatisme psychologique: Essai de psychologie expérimentale sur les formes inferieures de l'activité humaine.* Félix Alcan.
Liébeault, A. A. (1889). *Le somneil provoqué et les états analogues.* Octave Doin.
Liegeois, J. (1889). *De la suggestion et du somnambulisme dans leurs rapports avec la jurisprudence et la médicine légale.* Octave Doin.
Lombroso, C. (1890). Notes sur quelque faits d'hypnotisme. *Congrès International de Psychologie Physiologique* (pp. 139–141). Bureau de Revues.
Marillier, L. (1889). Le congrès de psychologie physiologique de 1889. *Revue philosophique de la France et de l'étranger, 28,* 539–546.
Marillier, L. (1890a). Des causes d'erreur dans l'observation des phénomènes de suggestion hypnotique. *Congrès International de Psychologie Physiologique* (p. 17). Bureau de Revues.
Marillier, L. (1890b). Statistique des hallucinations. *Congrès International de Psychologie Physiologique* (pp. 44–47). Bureau de Revues.
Moll, A. (1889). *Der Hypnotismus.* H. Kornfeld.
Myers, A. T. (1889). International Congress of Experimental Psychology. *Proceedings of the Society for Psychical Research, 6,* 171–182.
Myers, F. W. H. (1886). Human personality in the light of hypnotic suggestion. *Proceedings of the Society for Psychical Research, 4,* 1–24.
Myers, F. W. H. (1892). The subliminal consciousness: Chapter 1. General characteristics of subliminal messages. *Proceedings of the Society for Psychical Research, 7,* 298–327.
Nicolas, S. (2002). *Histoire de la psychologie Française: Naissance d'une nouvelle science.* Edition.
Nicolas, S. (2004). *L'hypnose: Charcot face à Bernheim: L'école de la Salpêtrière face a l'école de Nancy.* L'Harmattan.
Nicolas. S, Meunier F (2002). The causes, course and consequences of the first international psychology congress stand in Paris in 1889. *Teorie & Modelli,* 7, 19–40.
Nuttin, J. R. (1992). Les premiers congrès internationaux de psychologie: Text inedit. In M. Richelle, & H. Carpintero H. (Eds). *Contributions to the history of the International Congresses of Psychology: A posthumous homage to J. R. Nuttin.* Valencia, Spain: 'Revista Historia de la Psicología' Monographs (pp. 7–74). Leuven University Press.
Ochorowicz, J. (1887). *De la suggestion mentale.* Octave Doin.
Ochorowicz, J. (1890a). La sensibilité hypnotique. *Congrès International de Psychologie Physiologique* (pp. 18–19). Bureau de Revues.
Ochorowicz, J. (1890b). Des différences qui existent entre le sommeil hypnotique et le sommeil normal. *Congrès International de Psychologie Physiologique* (pp. 19–21). Bureau de Revues.
Ochorowicz, J. (1890c). Touts les phénomènes de l'hypnotisme peuventils êtres attribués à la suggestion? *Congrès International de Psychologie Physiologique* (pp. 74–75). Bureau de Revues.
O'Donnell, J. M. (1985). *The origins of behaviorism: American psychology, 1870–1920.* New York University Press.
Photographie d'hypnotiques (1890). *Congrès International de Psychologie Physiologique* (pp. 93–94). Bureau de Revues.
Pickren, W. E., & Fowler, R. D. (2003). Professional organizations. In D. K. Freedhein, & I. B. Weiner (Eds) *Handbook of psychology.* Vol. 1: *History of psychology* (pp. 535–554). Wiley.
Programme du Congrès. (1890). *Congrès International de Psychologie Physiologique* (p. 3). Bureau de Revues.
Richer, P. (1881). *Études cliniques sur l'hystéro-épilepsie ou grande hystérie.* Adrien Delahaye et Emile Lecrosnier.
Richet, C. (1875). Du somnambulisme provoqué. *Journal de l'anatomie et de la physiologie normales et pathologiques de l'homme et des animaux, 11,* 348–378.
Richet, C. (1880). Du somnambulisme provoqué. *Revue philosophique de la France et de l'étranger, 10,* 337–374, 462–484.

Richet, C. (1883). La personnalité et la memoire dans le somnambulisme. *Revue philosophique de la France et de l'étranger, 15*, 225–242.
Richet, C. (1884). La suggestion mentale et le calcul des probabilités. *Revue philosophique de la France et de l'étranger, 18*, 609–674.
Richet, C. (1888). Relation de diverses experiences sur la transmission mentales, la lucidite, et autres phénomènes non explicables par les donnees scientifiques actuelles. *Proceedings of the Society for Psychical Research, 5*, 18–168.
Richet, C. (1889). Further experiments in hypnotic lucidity or clairvoyance. *Proceedings of the Society for Psychical Research, 6*, 66–83.
Richet, C. (1890a). Les phénomènes de transfert et de l'action des aimants. *Congrès International de Psychologie Physiologique I* (p. 23). Bureau de Revues.
Richet, C. (1890b). Les travaux du Congrès de Psychologie Physiologique. *Congrès International de Psychologie Physiologique* (pp. 32–38). Bureau de Revues.
Schrenck-Notzing, A. von. (1895). *Therapeutic suggestion in psychopathia sexualis*. F. A. Davis.
Section de L'hypnotisme. (1890a). *Congrès International de Psychologie Physiologique* (pp. 39–43). Bureau de Revues.
Section de l'hypnotisme. (1890b). *Congrès International de Psychologie Physiologique* (pp. 59–63). Bureau de Revues.
Section de l'hypnotisme. (1890c). *Congrès International de Psychologie Physiologique* (pp. 74–79). Bureau de Revues,
Sidgwick, A., & Sidgwick, E. M. (1906). *Henry Sidgwick: A memoir*. Macmillan.
Sidis, B. (1898). *The psychology of suggestion*. D. Appleton.
Statistique des Hallucinations (1890). *Congrès International de Psychologie Physiologique* (pp. 151–157). Bureau de Revues.
Tamburini, A., & Seppilli, G. (1881–1882). Contribuzioni allo studio sperimentale dell'ipnotismo. *Rivista Sperimentale di Freniatria e di Medicina Legale, 7*, 261–300; 8, 268–307, 392–414.
Tuckey, C. L. (1890). *Psychotherapeutics; or, treatment by hypnotism and suggestion* (2nd rev. edn). Baillière, Tindall and Cox.
Winter, A. (2000). *Mesmerized: Powers of mind in Victorian Britain*. University of Chicago Press.

45

Panoramic Memory, Affect, and Sensations of Detachment in the Dying: Discussions Published in France, 1889–1903*

Carlos S. Alvarado†

Between 1889 and 1903, several authors published papers in the French journal *Revue Philosophique de la France et de l'Étranger* and in a few other publications in which they discussed panoramic memory, changes of affect, and a sense of detachment from the body in dying persons. With a few exceptions these publications have been ignored in modern discussion of the phenomena of the dying. Whereas philosopher Victor Egger postulated the psychological explanation that panoramic memory results from the dying person's thoughts of imminent death, physicians Paul Sollier and Charles Féré and psychologist Henri Piéron proposed that it, as well as changes in affect, result from physiological changes in the body sensibility and in the brain. Like many authors today who speculate about near-death experiences, the authors in question did not have much evidence for their explanations. These ideas, and their physiological aspects, were part of a general interest in unusual phenomena and states of consciousness during the 19th century.

In 1896 well-known student of psychopathology, Pierre Janet (1859–1947), commented in the pages of the *Revue Neurologique* about an article the author of which discussed "the often reported fact that the drowned facing imminent death review their whole life in an instant" (Janet, 1896, p. 245; this and other translations in this article are mine). The author in question, French philosopher Victor Egger (1848–1909), started a discussion about sensations of detachment in the dying and what current scholars refer to as panoramic memory that other authors continued and that current scholars of near-death experiences (NDEs) and related phenomena are likely to find interesting. Although the work of Egger has been referenced by some French writers (e.g., Le Maléfan, 1995; Poulet, 1963, pp. 165–205), his writings, and those of the other persons discussed in the present article, have not been cited in general overviews of NDEs (e.g., Agrillo, 2011; Blackmore, 1993; Bonilla, 2011; Greyson, 2000) nor in discussions of theoretical models (Greyson, Kelly & Kelly, 2009) and of the history of the subject (Holden, Greyson, & James, 2009, pp. 2–3). Furthermore, with a few exceptions (Biondi, 2010; Bozzano, 1931, pp. 50–97), writers about panoramic memories have also neglected such publications (e.g., Stevenson and Cook, 1995). This situation may be explained by the fact that the papers in question appeared only in French and that they were published in difficult-to-obtain journals, something that is starting to change with the development of virtual libraries (e.g., Alvarado, 2010).

The purpose of this current article is to discuss Egger and other largely forgotten French writers who, between 1889 and 1903, published about cases of panoramic memory, changes of affect, and floating sensations in the dying. I focus specifically on this period because it was during this particular 15-year

*Republished with permission from *Journal of Near-Death Studies*, *30*, 65–82, 2011.

†The author thanks the Society for Psychical Research for financial support and is grateful to Nancy L. Zingrone, Bruce Greyson, and Janice Holden for useful editorial suggestions for the improvement of this article.

span that certain authors published certain ideas of possible relevance to contemporary scholars in the field of near-death studies but of which they may not be aware. Rather than present detailed evaluation of the validity of these writings and comparisons to more recent ideas, my purpose is to summarize the ideas of these writers so as to bring them to the attention of contemporary students of NDEs.

Interest in Unusual Experiences and in Reports of Phenomena of the Dying

The discussions about panoramic memory presented here were embedded in a variety of intellectual concerns prevalent during the 19th century. One of them was interest in unusual mental states and phenomena such as mesmeric somnambulism, mediumship, ambulatory automatisms, double and multiple personality, and sensory and motor hysterical disturbances. Such topics informed a variety of scholars, scientists, and others about the existence of alterations of consciousness and dissociative phenomena (Cardeña & Alvarado, 2011; Castel, 1998; Crabtree, 1993).

Another topic of relevance was concern with misunderstood memory phenomena, a topic discussed in such well-known books as *Inquiries Concerning the Intellectual Power and the Investigation of Truth* (Abercrombie, 1832), *On Obscure Diseases of the Brain, and Disorders of the Mind* (Winslow, 1860), and *Les Maladies de la Mémoire* (Ribot, 1881). In the last mentioned book philosopher and psychologist Théodule Ribot (1839–1916) wrote on hypermnesia, or exaltation of memories, pointing out that they sometimes took place during acute fevers, ecstasy, hypnosis, and drowning (Ribot, 1881). These and other issues, and particularly the theoretical ideas and empirical observations concerning hysteria and hypnosis, were important catalyzers in the development of French psychology and psychiatry (Foschi, 2003; Nicolas, 2002).

Another intellectual context for the topic of this paper, and a more direct one, was discussions about death. During the 19th century, like in other periods of human history, many authors published books about death and the experiences of the dying. One example is English physician William Munk's (1816–1898) *Euthanasia: Or Medical Treatment in Aid of an Easy Death* (1887); others include Clarke (1878), Cobbe (1877), *Is Death Painful?* (1870), and Lauvergne (1842). In addition, authors discussed what scholars now call NDEs (e.g., Heim, 1892; Myers, 1892; Wiltse, 1889; Winslow, 1860). English classical scholar and psychical researcher Frederic W. H. Myers (1843–1901) stated: "It is possible that we might learn much were we to question dying persons, on their awakening from some comatose condition, as to their memory of any dream or vision during that state" (1892, p. 180).

One writer commented that in some experiences coming close to death, the person "has a complete recollection of its early existence from beginning to end ..." (Jung-Stilling, 1808/1834, p. 62). Nineteenth-century examples of these experiences, later called panoramic memory and life review, were those taking place during falls (Francis, 1896, p. 216; Head, 1860, p. 47; Heim, 1892), war injuries (Derepas, 1883, p. 203), and hanging (Winslow, 1860, pp. 440–441). More relevant to Egger's publications were examples of this phenomenon reported by individuals that survived drowning (e.g., Barrow, 1847, pp. 398–403; Binns, 1842, pp. 271–272; De Quincy, 1864, pp. 234–235; de V., 1893; O., 1855; S., 1868). One of the most remarkable descriptions of this experience was written by the Irish Admiral Francis Beaufort (1774–1857), who survived drowning:

> Though the senses were thus deadened, not so the mind; its activity seemed to be invigorated, in a ratio which defies all description—for thought rose after thought with a rapidity of succession that is not only indescribable, but probably inconceivable, by anyone who has not himself been in a similar situation. The course of those thoughts I can even now in a great measure

> retrace—the event which had just taken place—the awkwardness that had produced it—the bustle it must have occasioned (for I had observed two persons jump from the chains)—the effect it would have on a most affectionate father—the manner in which he would disclose it to the rest of the family—and a thousand other circumstances minutely associated with home, were the first series of reflections that occurred. They took then a wider range—our last cruise—a former voyage, and shipwreck—my school—the progress I had made there, and the time I had misspent—and even all my boyish pursuits and adventures. Thus travelling backwards, every past incident of my life seemed to glance across my recollection in retrograde succession; not, however, in mere outline, as here stated, but the picture filled up with every minute and collateral feature; in short, the whole period of my existence seemed to be placed before me in a kind of panoramic review, and each act of it seemed to be accompanied by a consciousness of right or wrong, or by some reflection on its cause or its consequences; indeed, many trifling events which had been long forgotten then crowded into my imagination, and with the character of recent familiarity (Barrow, 1847, pp. 399–400).

In fact, these experiences during drowning seemed to have been common knowledge, being mentioned in medical reference works (e.g., Herold, 1898, p. 382; Rosse, 1894, p. 800). An anonymous author commented:

> One of the most singular features in Psychology is the fact which is perfectly notorious, that the faculty of memory acquires an activity and tenacity in the cases of persons about being drowned, which it never exhibits under ordinary circumstances (Memory, 1853, p. 250).

The experience was also mentioned in literary works, such as in the following passage written by George Eliot (1819–1880): "The drowning man, urged by the supreme agony, lives in an instant through all his happy and unhappy past: when the dark flood has fallen like a curtain, memory, in a single moment, sees the drama acted over again" (1858, p.151). These memory images of the dying were interesting enough to be featured in 19th century magazines and journals such as the *American and Continental Journal* (Buffet, 1870), the *National Magazine* (Sensations of Drowning, 1853), and the *British Medical Journal* (What Drowning Feels Like, 1894).

The topic was also mentioned by those interested in psychic phenomena. In his book *Man and His Relations*, Universalist minister and spiritualist Samuel B. Brittan (1815–1883) noticed the existence of cases in drowning in which "under the apprehension of immediate death, the mind acts with such incredible rapidity that the whole history of the drowning man passes before him in a single moment" (1854, p. 84, footnote). Similarly, physician George Wyld (1821–1906) wrote in the spiritualist journal *Light* that the "all but drowned man has often flashed before his mental vision the past, and present, and future of his life ..." (1881, p. 68).

French Discussions of Panoramic Memory, Affect, and Sensations of Detachment in the Dying

Most of the papers to be discussed in this section appeared in the French journal *Revue Philosophique de la France et de l'Étranger*. Founded in 1876 by Théodule Ribot, the journal was devoted to psychology, philosophy, sociology, and other social sciences and, like other works by the author, was very influential. A significant part of the new empirical psychology, represented by Ribot (1870) himself, was articulated and publicized in this journal (Meletti Bertolini, 1991). The publication served as a forum that did much to encourage the study of unusual states of consciousness, as seen in important papers discussing hypnosis and dissociative phenomena in general (e.g., Janet, 1886; Richet, 1883). In addition, the journal published some papers about parapsychological phenomena, among them Charles Richet's (1850–1935) well-known and widely-cited article about mental suggestion, "La Suggestion Mentale et le Calcul des Probabilités" (Richet, 1884; see Alvarado, 2008). Considering the openness of this publication to unusual phenomena and its emphasis on the empirical study and analysis of psychological phenomena, it is not surprising that it carried the papers discussed below.

Victor Egger

Before he published his work about the dying, Victor Egger had written about physiological approaches to psychology, mistakes of vision, and dreams (see, respectively, Egger, 1877, 1878, 1895). He was particularly known for his interest in introspection, as seen in his book entitled *La Parole Intérieure* (1881) in which he argued that human beings always carried an internal dialogue. This dialogue, part of human actions and other mental phenomena, represented a "considerable part of the consciousness of every one of us" (p. 1). His analysis included imagery and phenomena such as the hallucinations of Socrates and Jeanne d'Arc. This internal life was explored further in some of his later publications and was part of the French interest in introspection that started to decline in the late 19th century (Brooks, 1998).

In 1895 Egger published an article about dreams in which he referred in passing to "panoramic memory" in a case of drowning. As he wrote, "I imagine that the idea of imminent death may induce a very vivid sense of the self that will cease to exist …" (p. 55).

In a later paper, Egger (1896a) mentioned several published cases of panoramic memory occurring to persons close to death and included a brief mention of the work and experiences of Swiss geologist and alpinist Albert Heim (1849–1937), as reported in a French newspaper (Egger, 1896a, p. 27; see Heim, 1892, and Noyes and Kletti, 1972). In his view, if being close to death produced a strong fear of death, the state was equivalent to a "definitive or temporary death" (Egger, 1896a, p. 27). However, he was skeptical of people who claimed that they had seen all the events of their earlier lives, a claim he considered to be an exaggeration. If death came suddenly, people could develop "concepts and propositions" (p. 30) related to their mortality. The recollections, Egger postulated, represented the "self that is going to end" (p. 30). Their appearance into consciousness meant that that they were produced by the sudden idea of an "imminent death" (p. 30). According to Egger, in some people the self may resist the approach of death. But if they felt death could not be prevented, they were more open to memory images.

In children, Egger (1896a) continued, the sense of self was less developed than in adults. Consequently, children did not experience this phenomenon. Adults, and particularly older people, were more susceptible to panoramic memories because their sense of self was more developed than that of younger people. Egger believed that closeness to death produced what he referred to as a "live self," consisting of "significant and rapid images" (p. 37).

Paul August Sollier

After Egger's (1896a) paper was published, the *Revue* received three letters by authors commenting on the article. Two of them presented further cases of panoramic memory (Keller, 1896; Mouilin, 1896). The French physician Paul August Sollier (1861–1933; see Bogousslavsky and Walusinski, 2011), who had published on a variety of medical topics such as amnesia (Sollier, 1892) and mental illness (Sollier, 1893), insisted that Egger's cases did not involve real death but instead the belief one was going to die (Sollier, 1896). He wrote, "the psychological phenomena that M. Egger tries to explain are connected to the idea that death is coming, but not to the start of death" (Sollier, 1896, p. 304). In his view it was important to know whether there was an organic condition that could cause death or whether or not the case was one in which some exterior circumstance could cause death, such as an accident.

Sollier (1896) presented some cases of drug addicts whom he had observed while they were dying. He noticed that they felt a sensation of detachment from everything as the end approached. For example, he observed a young woman who was close to death on three separate occasions. Although no phenomena were reported in the first instance, the patient had a general sense of wellbeing—which Sollier sometimes called a state of beatitude—and experienced detachment in the second brush with death. On the third occasion, while suffering from peritonitis, she experienced images about her life in chronological order from her youth to her current state, "sort of an inventory of her self" (Sollier, 1896, p. 306).

Panoramic memory was explained by Sollier (1896) as follows. He argued that when an accident took place, all attention was focused on what may cause death. Such distraction induced anesthesia and analgesia, which in turn explained the sense of wellbeing experienced by some persons close to death. "But at the same time we make a violent effort to escape death" (p. 306). In this state, Sollier believed, one's senses gather information using all one's energy. As a by-product one's consciousness may be heightened, including the expression of "previously acquired elements" (p. 306) or memories.

Sollier (1896) postulated that a similar process takes place in physiological death. Weakness could cause sensory isolation, and the sense of self was "reduced to old impressions, the current organic impressions are … annihilated" (p. 307).

Later, Sollier stated in his book *Le Probleme de la Mémoire* [The Memory Problem] that strong emotions such as those evoked by accidents could trigger memories of facts that were not directly related to the event. An example was "panoramic recollections" when people were near death (Sollier, 1900, p. 208). He also mentioned the recollections of hysterics. In his view, in these cases "they are suddenly reviewing … in a real panorama, all their prior existence absolutely as … people who drown" (1900, p. 209).

In a different article Sollier (1903) presented a case of a nervous young woman who was also a morphine addict. While in treatment for addiction, she experienced such symptoms as diarrhea and vomiting. At one point she experienced a sharp burning pain from the head to the back of the neck. Soon after this she had a sensation of wellbeing and:

> … she saw all her existence unfold; this state, she told me later, was as if all the incidents of her life had been printed on a cloth that unfolded the ups and downs [of her life] in front of her. The incidents succeeded in retrograde order, from today to the age of five or six years or less. "Everything I had on the head, I saw … in unparalleled details, accompanied with vague regrets and … a sense of grief, never of joy …, everything was greyish … things were flat; but some facts of my life, the emotions for example, were kind of in relief to me; it was as if you looked at three photographs of people that you knew well; two seemed to be flat and one that you love seems very clear and in great relief" (Sollier, 1903, p. 29).

When the patient recovered, she was anxious, had a very vague feeling of herself, and was completely anesthetic. In addition, she showed contractions and loss of consciousness that she did not have before her crisis. In another occasion she had autoscopic hallucinations in which she saw an image of herself.

As he had argued in his previous paper, Sollier (1903) believed that the loss of sensibility explained both the appearance of the sense of wellbeing and the memory images. In his view: "Each personality state corresponds to a cerebral state, a particular potential. When the potential is reduced from what it is currently to zero, we pass forcefully through all the degrees of potential successively achieved, but in an inverse way" (Sollier, 1903, pp. 30–31). The images a person has are linked to different potential states of the brain, and they appear when this potential is lowered to states that correspond to the images. The images appear in retrograde order following a rapid change in potential.

In Sollier's view the process of recollection in syncopes (fainting episodes that may end in death) is similar to the regression of personality that takes place in hysteria. As he wrote: "The only difference is that, in the case of cerebral exhaustion, the potential is normal and falls from normal to zero, while in hysteria it is below normal and returns to its maximum" (Sollier, 1903, p. 31). But the end result is the same. That is, in both cases the brain presents successive states, a process that includes images of the self.

Sollier (1903) described phenomena taking place during therapy with this patient that he implied validated the above-mentioned explanation. During the treatment she showed "all her old personality states" (p. 31) consisting of recollections of images, actions, impressions, and emotions. Such phenomena referred to the patient's life after nine years of age, after which she started having her first nervous problems such as heart palpitations.

Egger (1896b) wrote a second paper in which he answered Sollier's (1896) first publication and presented new cases, some of them communicated to him directly by persons who had been close to death (e.g., drowning). He questioned Sollier's explanation assuming an "almost complete suppression of general sensibility" (p. 340). Egger argued that Sollier could not explain those cases of people in mortal danger who did not experience anesthesia. Furthermore, Egger said that all of Sollier's cases could be reinterpreted following the idea of imminent death taking hold of the mind of his patients. Such idea was the "necessary condition for the phenomena" to occur (p. 343).

Egger argued further that "imagination and thought are employed in a special direction" (p. 342) related to the idea of imminent death. Such an idea provoked "semi-logical reactions" (p. 342) in the experiencers. In his view, recollections of persons in the shock of being near death, including drowning, were "phenomena analogous to the dreams of sleep" (p. 368).

Charles Féré

Another French contributor to the debates was Charles Féré (1852–1907), well known for his work in hypnosis (Binet and Féré, 1885) and in the interrelations of sensory and motor phenomena (Féré, 1887; on Féré, see Larner, 2011). Before the articles of Egger and Sollier had been published in the *Revue*, Féré had discussed the subject in two publications. In the first article he referred to the phenomenon of "reminiscence" in the dying as a neglected topic but a phenomenon that manifested in natural deaths and in epileptics (Féré, 1889). Sometimes this phenomenon of "panoramic representation" (p. 108) seemed to include all the existence of the individual, whereas on other occasions it included only a few seemingly unimportant events. In Féré's view the recollections represented a "brusque modification of cerebral circulation" (p. 109). Féré (1892) restated this explanation in his book, *La Pathologie des Émotions* [The Pathology of Emotions]. In his view: "The intellectual perversions that arise at the hour of death seem to be connected to certain circulation problems ..." (p. 170). Sudden modifications of cerebral circulation, he argued, could explain the reminiscences seen in drowning cases in which the person sees "unfolding in front of him the picture of his entire life" (p. 171).

In a later article in the *Revue Philosophique de la France et de l'Étranger* Féré (1898) revisited recollections of earlier life events and discussed euphoria close to the moment of death as well. In his view, separate from reacting to the idea of death, the "dying present psychic phenomena in direct relation to physical phenomena" (p. 298), which was also seen in the insane and in "idiots" when going through illnesses involving fever. At death, Féré stated, "the animal tissues and in particular the muscles and the nerves present a period of hyperexcitability in which, due to an equivalent excitation, its reactions are stronger than in the normal state" (p. 301). The brain, Féré believed, should pass through a similar process. As he wrote: "The glimmers of intelligence and euphoria of the dying can be explained by a physiological condition: a momentary hyperexcitability of the nervous elements ..." (p. 302) that makes those elements lose their usual properties. Féré stated that such process took place both in the "nervous central elements as in peripheral nerves" (p. 302). Furthermore, it was stated that the phenomena also depended on individual susceptibilities and aptitudes of the persons in question.

Henri Piéron

French experimental and physiological psychologist Henri Piéron (1881–1964; on Piéron see Reuchlin, 1964) classified the panoramic images in two types, those that were simultaneous and those that were successive and very fast (Piéron, 1901). In his view, images of the first type were probably illusory, and speed of images of the second type were exaggerated. He also speculated that these images came from the subconscious mind. In a note in the *Revue Philosophique de la France et de l'Étranger*, Piéron (1902) summarized a few cases of patients who had sensations of elevation or flying when close to death. He suggested that these sensations could be accounted for by postulating an "anesthesia of the part of the body lying on the bed" (p. 616) due to the slowing of circulation caused by prolonged lying down. Finally, Piéron (1903) noted that the evocation of images was not only associated with dying but with the belief one was going to die. In his view this evocation was due to a "sudden imposition of a focus of attraction of consciousness" that produced an "unforgettable illusion in all those observing the phenomenon" (p. 95).

Discussion

As argued previously, interest in panoramic memory was part of the general interest in France and elsewhere about abnormal psychology and unusual phenomena. This interest also included unusual memory manifestations and the experiences of the dying.

The authors I have discussed defended different explanatory models for the phenomena in question. Egger's approach was psychological, emphasizing the effect of the fear of death on panoramic memory. Sollier, Féré, and Piéron, on the other hand, followed physiological models. It must be recognized that such speculations, even when seen in the context of their times, were not based on good evidence. This situation has been typical of many attempts to explain near-death experiences during the last decades; for overviews see Greyson (2000) and Greyson, Kelly, and Kelly (2009). This has also been the case with other phenomena. The history of psychological and physiological theory illustrates the tendency of some authors to defend interpretations that have very little empirical evidence in their support. Out-of-body experiences (Alvarado, 2009), hallucinations (Asaad, 1990), and depersonalization (Sierra & Berrios, 1997) have been examples of this phenomenon.

In fact, psychologist Alfred Binet (1857–1911) reminded readers that both Egger's and Sollier's views were basically theoretical; he thereby implied a lack of empirical support (Binet, 1897, p. 635). Binet felt that Egger did not explain the fast flow of thoughts in persons who came close to death through accidents. He also criticized Sollier's contention that positive emotions were enhanced at death. In Binet's view, anesthesia and analgesia should produce negative emotions rather than positive ones.

The physiologically-based explanations of Sollier, Féré, and Piéron were typical of 19th century attempts to explain thought and behavior through the functioning of the nervous system (Young, 1970). Similar explanations were proposed for hallucinations (Brierre de Boismont, 1845) and trance (Beard, 1877). In a discussion of the famous double personality case of Félida X. (b. 1843), it was speculated that the changes of memory and behavior were related to problems of cerebral circulation (Azam, 1893, pp. 63–64). Other authors presented similar speculations about mental illness in general (Lewis, 1889, pp. 129–130).

The topic of changes in sensibility was ever-present in the mind of the 19th century physician partly because of its association with hysteria (e.g., Janet, 1892; Richer, 1885, pp. 23–24). Writing about sleepwalking, a physician referred to the "suspension more or less complete of external feeling" (Prichard, 1850, p. 194). Binet hinted that the physical insensibility typical in "doubling" (dissociation) cases, in which two selves appeared to coexist, was assisted by a lack of sensation. That is, such insensibility could help one consciousness function without the interference of the other (Binet, 1892, p. 83). Similarly, Leuba (1902) stated that one of the main characteristics of the temperament of Christian mystics was the unstable nature of their "organic sensibility"—that is, that they alternated "between anesthesia and hyperesthesia" (p. 2).

Closer to the feeling of detachment and elevation that Sollier and Piéron mentioned was the notion of flying sensations attributed to witches as a drug-induced hallucination of the general sensibility of the body (Simon, 1888, p. 132). In an article cited by Piéron, Janet (1900–1901) explained illusions of levitation as occurring because of a hysterical loss of sensibility in the feet of a patient. With this speculation as a background, it is not surprising that some of the authors discussed in this article used physiological arguments related to changes in sensibility in their attempts to explain the phenomena dying persons had reported.

More recent researchers have followed up on the topic of panoramic memory (e.g., Noyes & Kletti, 1977b; Stevenson & Cook, 1995). Some of this work has focused on the experiences of people involved in accidents (e.g., Noyes & Kletti, 1977a; Noyes & Slymen, 1978–1979). To some extent Egger's ideas were similar to the later ideas of Pfister (1930), Ehrenwald (1974), and Noyes (1972; Noyes & Kletti, 1976), who speculated that out-of-body and near-death experiences were a defense mechanism designed to deal with the threat of death. There are also similarities in Egger's and Sollier's ideas to more recent discussions about the distinction between physiologically- and psychologically-induced NDEs (e.g., Gabbard & Twemlow, 1991; Owen, Cook, & Stevenson, 1990; Stevenson, Cook, & McClean-Rice, 1989–1990).

Although the work of Egger, Féré, Sollier, and Piéron has been neglected by more recent students of the subject of panoramic memory and related phenomena near death, it is my hope that this short article will remind current students of the existence of this literature.

References

Abercrombie, J. (1832). *Inquiries concerning the intellectual powers and the investigation of truth* (3rd ed.). Waugh and Innes.

Agrillo, C. (2011). Near-death experiences: Out-of-body and out-of-brain. *Review of General Psychology, 15*, 1–10.

Alvarado, C. S. (2008). Note on Charles Richet's "La Suggestion Mentale et le Calcul des Probabilités" (1884). *Journal of Scientific Exploration, 22*, 543–548.

Alvarado, C. S. (2009). Early and modern developments in the psychological approach to out-of-body experiences. In C. D. Murray (Ed.), *Psychological scientific perspectives on out-of-body and near-death experiences* (pp. 1–22). Nova Science.

Alvarado, C. S. (2010). Online resources for the history of out-of-body experiences and death-related phenomena. *Journal of Near-Death Studies, 28*(3), 143–162.

Asaad, G. (1990). *Hallucinations in clinical psychiatry: A guide for mental health professionals*. Brunner/ Mazel.

Azam, Dr. [E. E.]. (1893). *Hypnotisme et double conscience: Origine de leur étude et divers travaux sur des sujets analogues*. Félix Alcan.

Barrow, J. (1847). *An autobiographical memoir of Sir John Barrow, Bart., late of the Admiralty*. John Murray.

Beard, G. B. (1877). A new theory of trance, and its bearings on human testimony. *Journal of Nervous and Mental Disease, 4*, 1–47.

Binet, A. (1892). *Les altérations de la personnalité*. Félix Alcan.

Binet, A. (1897). État mental des mourants. *L'Année Psychologique, 3*, 629–637.

Binet, A., & Féré, C. (1885). L'hypnotisme chez les hystériques: Le transfert. *Revue Philosophique de la France et de l'Étranger, 19*, 1–25.

Binns, E. (1842). *The anatomy of sleep; or, The art of procuring sound and refreshing slumber at will*. John Churchill.

Biondi, M. (2010). La *life review* nelle NDE second Ernesto Bozzano. *The Missing Link*, No. 4, 90–97. Retrieved from http://www.gruppogrima.it/library/ML04lug2010.pdf

Blackmore, S. J. (1993). *Dying to live: Science and the near-death experience*. Grafton.

Bogousslavsky, J., & Walusinski, O. (2011). Paul Sollier: The first clinical neuropsychologist. In J. Bogousslavsky (Ed.), *Following Charcot: A forgotten history of neurology and psychiatry* (Frontiers of Neurology and Neuroscience, *29*, pp. 105–114). Karger.

Bonilla, E. (2011). Experiencias cercanas a la muerte: Revisión. *Investigación Clínica, 52*, 69–99.

Bozzano, E. (1931). *Indagini sulle manifestazioni supernormali*. (Vol. 1). Dante.

Brierre de Boismont, A. (1845). Des hallucinations ou histoire raisonée des apparitions, des visions, des songes, de l'extase, du magnétisme et du somnambulisme. Germer Baillière.

Brittan, S. B. (1854). *Man and his relations: Illustrating the influence of the mind on the body*. W. A. Townsend.

Brooks, J. I. (1998). *The eclectic legacy: Academic philosophy and the human sciences in nineteenth-century France*. Associated University Presses.

Buffet, E. P. (1870). Is death painful? *American and Continental Monthly, 1*, 359–368.

Cardeña, E., & Alvarado, C. S. (2011). Altered consciousness from the Age of Enlightenment through mid-20th century. In E. Cardeña & M. Winkelman (Eds.), *Altering consciousness: Multidisciplinary perspectives: History, culture and the humanities* (Vol. 1, pp. 89–112). ABC-CLIO.

Castel, P. H. (1998). *La querelle de l'hystérie: La formation du discours psychopathologique en France (1881–1913)*. Presses Universitaires de France.

Clarke, E. H. (1878). *Visions: A study of false sight (pseudopia)*. Houghton, Osgood.

Cobbe, F. P. (1877). The peak in Darien: The riddle of death. *Littell's Living Age, 19*(s.5), 374–379.

Crabtree, A. (1993). *From Mesmer to Freud: Magnetic sleep and the roots of psychological healing*. Yale University Press.

De Quincey, T. (1864). *Confessions of an English opium-eater, and suspiria de profundis*. Tickner and Fields.

Derepas, G. (1883). *Les theories de l'inconnaissable et les degrés de la connaissance*. Ernest Thorin.

de V., H. (1893). Correspondance et chronique: Les impressions d'un ensevel. *Revue Scientifique, 51*, 379–380.

Egger, V. (1877). La physiologie cérébrale et la psychologie physiologique. *Revue des Deux Mondes, 24*, 193–244.
Egger, V. (1878). Sur les lapsus de la vision. *Revue Philosophique de la France et de l'Étranger*, *13*, 286–289.
Egger, V. (1881). *La parole intérieure: Essai de psychologie descriptive*. Germer Baillière.
Egger, V. (1895). La durée apparente des rêves. *Revue Philosophique de la France et de l'Étranger*, *20*, 41–59.
Egger, V. (1896a). Le moi des mourants. *Revue Philosophique de la France et de l'Étranger*, *21*, 26–38.
Egger, V. (1896b). Le moi des mourants: Nouveaux faits. *Revue Philosophique de la France et de l'Étranger*, *21*, 337–368.
Ehrenwald, J. (1974). Out-of-the-body experiences and the denial of death. *Journal of Nervous and Mental Disease*, *159*, 227–233.
Eliot, G. (1858). *Scenes of clerical life*. Harper & Brothers.
Féré, C. (1887). *Sensation et mouvement: Études expérimentales de psycho-mécanique*. Félix Alcan.
Féré, C. (1889). Note pour servir a l'histoire de l'état mental des mourants. *Compte Rendu des Séances de la Société de Biologie*, *9*, 108–110.
Féré, C. (1892). *La pathologie des émotions: Études physiologiques et cliniques*. Félix Alcan.
Féré, C. (1898). L'état mental des mourants. *Revue Philosophique de la France et de l'Étranger*, *45*, 296–302.
Foschi, R. (2003). L'indagine sulla personalità alle origini della psicologia scientifica francese (1870–1885). *Physis*, *40*, 63–105.
Francis, J. R. (1896). *The encyclopedia of death and life in the spirit-world* (Vol. 1). Progressive Thinker.
Gabbard, G. O., & Twemlow, S. W. (1991). Do "near death experiences" occur only near-death? Revisited. *Journal of Near-Death Studies*, *10*(1), 41–47.
Greyson, B. (2000). Near-death experiences. In E. Cardeña, S. J. Lynn, & S. Krippner (Eds.), *Varieties of anomalous experiences: Examining the scientific evidence* (pp. 315–352). American Psychological Association.
Greyson, B., Kelly, E. W., & Kelly, E. F. (2009). Explanatory models for near-death experiences. In J. M. Holden, B. Greyson, & D. James (Eds.), *The handbook of near-death experiences: Thirty years of investigation* (pp. 213–234). Praeger/ABC-CLIO.
Head, F. B. (1860). *The horse and his rider*. London, England: John Murray.
Heim, A. v. S. G. (1892). Notizen über den Tod durch Absturz. *Jahrbuch des Schweitzerischen Alpclub, 27*, 327–337.
Herold, J. (1898). *A manual of legal medicine for the use of practitioners and students of medicine and law.* J. B. Lippincott.
Holden, J. M., Greyson, B., & James, D. (2009). The field of near-death studies: Past, present and future. In J. M. Holden, B. Greyson, & D. James (Eds.), *The handbook of near-death experiences: Thirty years of investigation* (pp. 1–16). Praeger/ABC-CLIO.
Is death painful? (1870). *Putnam's Magazine, 5*(n.s.), 311–318.
Janet, P. (1886). Les actes inconscientes et la dédoublement de la personnalité pendant le somnambulisme provoqué. *Revue Philosophique de la France et de l'Étranger, 22*, 577–592.
Janet, P. (1892). L'anesthésie hystérique. *Archives de Neurologie, 23*, 323–352.
Janet, P. (1896). [Review of the article "Le Moi des Mourants". *Revue Neurologique, 4*, 245–246.
Janet, P. (1900–1901). Une extatique. *Bulletin de l'Institute Générale Psychologique*, *1*, 209–240.
Jung-Stilling, J. H. (1834). *Theory of pneumatology*. Longman, Rees, Orme, Brown, Green, and Longmans. (Original work published 1808)
Keller, A. (1896). L'etat mental des mourants. *Revue Philosophique de la France et de l'Étranger, 21,* 311–313.
Larner, A. J. (2011). Charles Féré (1852–1907). *Journal of Neurology, 258*, 524–525.
Lauvergue, H. (1842). *De l'agonie et de la mort dans toutes les classes de la Société sous le rapport humanitaire, physiologique et religieux* (2 vols.). J.-B. Baillière.
Le Maléfan, P. (1995). Vécu de mort imminente et onirisme: Un chapitre inattendu de l'histoire de la psychologie dynamique. *Information Psychiatrique, 71*, 773–780.
Leuba, J. H. (1902). Les tendances fondamentales des mystiques chrétiens. *Revue Philosophique de la France et de l'Étranger*, *27*, 1–36.
Lewis, W. B. (1889). *A text-book of mental diseases: With special reference to the pathological aspects of insanity*. Charles Griffin.

Meletti Bertolini, M. M. (1991). *Il pensiero e la memoria: Filosofia e psicologia nella "Revue philosophique" di Théodule Ribot (1876–1916)*. Franco Angeli. Memory. (1853). *American Magazine of Homeopathy, 2*, 249–251.
Mouilin, A. (1896). L'état mental des mourants. *Revue Philosophique de la France et de l'Étranger, 21*, 307–310.
Munk, W. (1887). *Euthanasia: Or medical treatment in aid of an easy death.* Longmans, Green.
Myers, F. W. H. (1892). On indications of continued terrene knowledge on the part of phantasms of the dead. *Proceedings of the Society for Psychical Research, 8*, 170–252.
Nicolas, S. (2002). *Histoire de la psychologie française: Naissance dune nouvelle science.* In Press.
Noyes, R. (1972). The experience of dying. *Psychiatry, 35*, 174–184.
Noyes, R., & Kletti, R. (1972). The experience of dying from falls. *Omega: Journal of Death and Dying, 3*, 45–52.
Noyes, R., & Kletti, R. (1976). Depersonalization in the face of life-threatening danger: An interpretation. *Omega: Journal of Death and Dying, 7*, 103–114.
Noyes, R., & Kletti, R. (1977a). Depersonalization in response to life-threatening danger. *Comprehensive Psychiatry, 18*, 375–384.
Noyes, R., & Kletti, R. (1977b). Panoramic memory: A response to the threat of death. *Omega: Journal of Death and Dying, 8*, 181–194.
Noyes, R., & Slymen, D.J. (1978–1979). The subjective response to life-threatening danger. *Omega: Journal of Death and Dying, 9*, 313–321.
O., J. (1855). Replies to minor queries: Sensations in drowning. *Notes and Queries, 12*, 500.
Owen, J. E., Cook, E. W., & Stevenson, I. (1990). Features of "near-death experience" in relation to whether or not patients were near death. *Lancet, 336*, 1175–1177.
Pfister, O. (1930). Shockgedanken und Shockphantasien bei höchster Todesgefahr. *Zeitschrift für Psychoanalyse, 16*, 430–455.
Piéron, H. (1901). Sur l'interpretation des faits de rapidité anormale dans le processus d'évocation des images. In P. Janet (Ed.), *IVe Congres International de Psychologie* (pp. 439–448). Félix Alcan.
Piéron, H. (1902). Contribution a la psychologie des mourants. *Revue Philosophique de la France et de l'Étranger, 27*, 615–616.
Piéron, H. (1903). La rapidité des processus psychiques. *Revue Philosophique de la France et de l'Étranger, 28*, 69–95.
Poulet, G. (1963). *L'espace Proustien.* Gallimard.
Prichard, J. C. (1850). Somnambulism and animal magnetism. In J. Forbes, A. Tweedie, & J. Conolly, revised by R. Dunglison (Eds.), *The cyclopaedia of practical medicine* (Vol. 4, pp. 194–211). Lea and Blanchard.
Reuchlin, M. (1964). Henri Piéron 18 juillet 1881–6 novembre 1964. *Revue de Psychologie Appliquee, 14*, 213–218.
Ribot, T. (1870). *La psychologie anglaise contemporaine (École expérimentale).* Librairie Philosophique de l'Étranger.
Ribot, T. (1881). *Les maladies de la mémoire*. Germer Baillière.
Richer, P. (1885). *Études cliniques sur la grande hystérie ou hystéro-épilepsie*. A. Delahaye and E. Lecrosnier.
Richet, C. (1883). La personnalité et la mémoire dans le somnambulisme. *Revue Philosophique de la France et de l'Étranger, 15*, 225–242.
Richet, C. (1884). La suggestion mentale et le calcul des probabilités. *Revue Philosophique de la France et de l'Étranger, 18*, 609–674.
Rosse, I. C. (1894). Death from submersion in its medico-legal relations. In R. A. Witthaus & T. C. Becker (Eds.), *Medical jurisprudence, forensic medicine and toxicology* (Vol. 1; pp. 793–812). William Wood.
Sensations in drowning. (1853). *National Magazine, 2*, 335–336.
Sierra, M., & Berrios, G. E. (1997). Depersonalization: A conceptual history. *History of Psychiatry, 8*, 213–229.
Simon, P. M. (1888). *Le monde des rêves* (2nd ed.). J. B. Baillière.
Sollier, P. (1892). *Les troubles de la mémoire*. J. Rueff.
Sollier, P. (1893). *Guide pratique des maladies mentales*. G. Masson.
Sollier, P. (1896). L'état mental des mourants. *Revue Philosophique de la France et de l'Étranger, 21,* 303–307.
Sollier, P. (1900). *Les problème de la mémoire*. Félix Alcan.

Sollier, P. (1903). Sur le moi des mourants. *Bulletin de l'Institut Général Psychologique, 3*, 29–32.
S., S. (1868). Experience of the drowned: A personal narrative. *Bible Christian Magazine, 4*(s. 4), 179–181.
Stevenson, I., & Cook, E. W. (1995). Involuntary memories during severe physical illness or injury. *Journal of Nervous and Mental Disease, 183*, 452–458.
Stevenson, I., Cook, E. W., & McClean-Rice, N. (1989–1990). Are persons reporting "near-death experiences" really near death? A study of medical records. *Omega: Journal of Death and Dying, 20*, 45–54.
What drowning feels like. (1894). *British Medical Journal, 2*, 823–824.
Wiltse, A. S. (1889). A case of typhoid fever with subnormal temperature and pulse. *St. Louis Medical and Surgical Journal, 57*, 355–364.
Winslow, F. (1860). *On obscure diseases of the brain, and disorders of the mind.* John Churchill.
Wyld, G. (1881). Clairvoyance in relation to medicinal substances. *Light, 1*, 68.
Young, R. M. (1970). *Mind, brain and adaptation in the nineteenth century: Cerebral localization and its biological context from Gall to Ferrier.* Clarendon Press.

Nineteenth Century Pioneers in the Study of Dissociation: William James and Psychical Research*

Carlos S. Alvarado & Stanley Krippner†

Following recent trends in the historiography of psychology and psychiatry we argue that psychical research was an important influence in the development of concepts about dissociation. To illustrate this point, we discuss American psychologist and philosopher William James's (1842–1910) writings about mediumship, secondary personalities, and hypnosis. Some of James's work on the topic took place in the context of research conducted by the American Society for Psychical Research, such as his early work with the medium Leonora E. Piper (1857–1950). James's work is an example of the influence of psychical research on several aspects of psychology such as early models of the unconscious and of dissociation.

There has been a rise of interest in the concept of dissociation in the last few decades, as well as in the history of this construct and the intellectual factors that permeated these discussions (e.g. Crabtree, 1993; 2007; Gauld, 1992; Hacking, 1995). In this paper we focus on the writings of the well-known American philosopher and psychologist William James (1842–1910), as well as the field of psychical research, of which James was a pioneer.

Our discussion of psychical research follows fairly recent historiographical trends in which a variety of authors have argued that movements such as spiritualism and psychical research that have been considered marginal in the historical development of psychology and psychiatry were in fact influential in the construction of certain aspects of these disciplines (e.g. Alvarado, 2002; Crabtree, 1993; Plas, 2000; Shamdasani, 1993; Taylor, 1996). In fact, an investigation of the work of influential nineteenth century figures in psychology shows that some of them were involved in one way or another with psychical research.[1] One of them was William James, who according to Eugene Taylor (1996), "was informed by early studies in experimental neuropathology, physiological psychology, and psychical research, which, in turn, significantly contributed to the development of the new field of experimental psychopathology" (p. 10).

Historians such as Regina Plas (2000) have argued that the study of psychic (or parapsychological) phenomena was an influential part in the beginnings of empirical psychology. A pioneer in this line of thinking was Henri F. Ellenberger (1905–1993) who, in his monumental book *The Discovery of the Unconscious* (1970), defended the importance of the investigation of mesmerism and spiritualism for the development of ideas about the unconscious, a trend followed by many others (e.g. Alvarado, Machado, Zangari & Zingrone, 2007; Crabtree, 1993; Plas, 2000; Shamdasani, 1993). But there is no doubt that many psychologists of this era were skeptical of the phenomena, suspecting that it represented nothing but conventional psychological functioning or even fraud (e.g. Carpenter, 1877; Janet, 1889; Jastrow, 1889).[2]

In this paper we will summarize James's writings on dissociation, with particular attention to those related to psychical research, and specifically, mediumship and hypnosis. While most of his writings on the subject were published during the nineteenth century, a few appeared in the early years of the twentieth century.

*Republished with permission from the *Journal of Consciousness Studies*, *17*, 19–43.
†The authors gratefully acknowledge the support of Saybrook University's Chair for the Study of Consciousness in the preparation of this paper.

James's Outlook

The study of William James has become an industry. This is obvious when one inspects the number of studies available today about his life and work (e.g. Johnson & Henley, 1990; Proudfoot, 2004; Richardson, 2006; Taylor 1996). Born in 1842 William James studied painting and other topics in Europe. He graduated with an M.D. degree in 1869 from the Harvard School of Medicine. Between 1872 and 1907 he taught, at Harvard, comparative anatomy and physiology, philosophy, and psychology (Courses, n. d.). Over the years James became known for such writings as *The Principles of Psychology* (1890b), *Psychology: Briefer Course* (1892a), *The Will to Believe, and Other Essays in Popular Philosophy* (1897), *Human Immortality* (1898a), *Talks to Teachers on Psychology* (1899), *The Varieties of Religious Experience* (1902), *Pragmatism* (1907), and *A Pluralistic Universe* (1909b) (for writings by and about James see Medd, 2010; Perry, 1920).

James had a clear empirical approach to psychological problems, something related to his well-known interests in pragmatism, radical empiricism, and pluralism. The American psychologist Gardner Murphy (1895–1979) saw James as a pioneer trying to be empirical in his quests in the context of the "new scientific world of the evolutionary period" (Murphy, 1960, p. 4). This empirical outlook, and one attempting to present psychology to a great extent as a metaphysically-free enterprise, was evident in *The Principles of Psychology* (1890b). As James wrote: "This book … assuming that thoughts and feelings exist and are vehicles of knowledge, thereupon contends that psychology when she has ascertained the empirical correlation of the various sorts of thought or feeling with definite conditions of the brain can go no farther—can go no farther, that is, as a natural science. If she goes farther she becomes metaphysical" (Vol. 1. p. vi). But some years later James changed his mind. For example, he stated in his Presidential Address to the American Psychological Association that metaphysical and epistemological considerations should not be kept out of books about psychology (James, 1895, p. 124).

Replying to the belief that James abandoned psychology for philosophy after 1890. Taylor (1996) has argued that what James rejected was a positivist epistemology and that his work in areas such as psychopathology and psychical research, as well as the concept of the unconscious, shows he still operated as a psychologist. Taylor also stated that James defined psychology as a 'person-centered' field, one connected to different fields such as philosophy and the natural sciences, a perspective that could be seen in parts of *The Principles of Psychology*. This stance gave metaphysics a place in the new psychology. As Taylor wrote: "His new position acknowledged the reality of consciousness as an ultimate plurality of states; it shed significant light on then current scientific studies of personality disintegration; it admitted the iconography of the transcendent as a crucial determinant of personality transformation; and it provided James with an analytical tool powerful enough to critique the unexamined assumptions of radical materialism in experimental science" (Taylor, 1996, p. 5; see also Lamberth, 1999).

Even in his early writings, James (1879, 1884) discussed aspects of consciousness. In *The Principles of Psychology*, he wrote that consciousness "does not appear to itself chopped up in bits. Such words as ''chain' or 'train' do not describe it fitly as it presents itself in the first instance. It is nothing jointed; it flows. A 'river' or a 'stream' are the metaphors by which it is most naturally described" (1890b, Vol. 1, p. 239). In a later book, *Talks to Teachers on Psychology*, he referred to "a succession of states, or waves, or fields … of knowledge, of feeling, of desire, of deliberation, etc., that constantly pass and repass, and that constitute our inner life" (James, 1899, p. 15). However, James also noted that there were some disruptions in the flow of consciousness and one of these was dissociation.

Dissociation for James was part of a larger issue, that of consciousness and personality. This is clear in the following statements written as part of an introduction to Boris Sidis's (1867–1923) book *The Psychology of Suggestion*:

> What are the limits of the consciousness of a human being? Is 'self' consciousness only a part of the whole consciousness? Are there many 'selves' dissociated from one another? What is the medium of synthesis in a group of associated ideas? How can certain systems of ideas be cut off and forgotten? Is personality a product, and not a principle? Such are the questions now being forced to the front—questions now asked for the first time with some sense of their concrete import, and questions which it will require a great amount of further work, both of observation and of analysis, to answer adequately. (James, 1898b, pp. v–vi)

Dissociation and Psychical Research

By the time that James had become a well-known scholar, studies of dissociation were well underway. Representing this interest, the French physician Jules Héricourt wrote an overview article in the *Revue Scientifique* entitled 'La Activité Inconsciente de l'Esprit' (1889). He argued that separate from conscious processes there were also unconscious ones that could produce an "apparent doubling of the normal conscious personality" (p. 258; this, and other translations, are ours). Early studies of hypnotic procedures had demonstrated the existence of state specific memories, as argued by authors who identified themselves with Mesmerism (e.g., Deleuze, 1813). Years later the French physiologist Charles Richet induced personality changes in hypnotized participants (Richet, 1883), and other investigators reported cases of hypnotically-induced changes of personality (Azam, 1887), as well as ambulatory dissociations (Hodgson, 1891; Ladame, 1888), indicating that the human psyche had a number of levels of consciousness, many with apparently different memory records.

Many relevant hypnotic observations—state-specific memory, changes of personality—were reported by Pierre Janet in several influential publications (Janet, 1886; 1887; 1888; 1889). In his first paper Janet (1886) referred to hypnotic experiments with his patient Lucie, who, when re-hypnotized, continued talking about the same topic she was conversing about in her previous hypnotic condition (p. 579). In his view hypnotic suggestion was accompanied by "some degree of unconsciousness or rather ... of some doubling of consciousness" (p. 592). Many fascinating observations were reported by Janet in his classic book *L'automatisme psychologique* (1889), such as one with Lucie in which her writing appeared to be childish after Janet "suggested that she was not herself, but that she was a little seven year old child" (p. 412).

The celebrated clinician Jean-Martin Charcot (1825–1893) reported a case in which a woman, designated as Hab, showed a "particular state that we call a *secondary state*, or her B state, broken only by rare returns, both spontaneous and induced, and in any case of short duration, to the previous state, the *primary state* A" (Guinon, Blocq, Souques and Charcot, 1893, p. 172). When recollecting details about her life in her primary state Hab appeared to know about her life prior to 1885, but had no recollections about events that took place between 1885 and 1890. The '*secondary B state*' only could recall memories of some incidents from recent times. The A state could be induced by asking for its appearance, and had less 'hysterical stigmata' (such as anesthesia and visual problems) associated with it than symptoms manifested during the B state.

During this period there were several general discussions of these phenomena that prompted some authors to argue for the existence of an unconscious mind (sometimes referred to as a 'subconscious mind') and for the reality of various dissociative manifestations such as secondary personalities (e.g. Héricourt, 1889; James, 1890a; Newbold, 1896; Prince, 1890). Writing in *Scribner's Magazine* in an article entitled "The Hidden Self" James (1890a) stated: "It seems to me a very great step to have ascertained that the secondary self, or selves, coexist with the primary one, the trance-personalities with the normal one, during the waking state. But just what these secondary selves may be, and what are their remoter relations and conditions of existence, are questions to which the answer is anything but clear" (p. 373).

In addition to the study of dissociation, and other problems of the emerging fields of psychology and psychiatry, the nineteenth century saw the development of what was later called psychical research. The germs of systematic research were present in the movements of mesmerism and spiritualism, which included investigations of phenomena such as apparitions, clairvoyance, healing, and mediumship (Inglis, 1992; Podmore, 1902). But not all of the early works on these topics included serious research efforts; in an attempt to correct this practice, James wrote a book review (1869/1960) in which he made a call for the systematic investigation of these phenomena. In his view, "The present attitude of society on this whole question is as extraordinary and anomalous as it is discreditable to the pretensions of an age which prides itself on enlightenment and the diffusion of knowledge" (p. 21).

The Society for Psychical Research (SPR) was established in London in 1882, an organization having an ambitious program of research (Gauld, 1968). The purpose of the SPR was to pursue "an organized and systematic attempt to investigate that large group of debatable phenomena designated by such terms as mesmeric, psychical, and Spiritualistic" (Objects of the Society, 1882, p. 3). The agenda of the SPR included studies of telepathy, consisting of both experiments (e.g. Guthrie and Birchall, 1883) and analyses of cases taking place in daily life, as seen in one of the central classics of the period, *Phantasms of the Living* (Gurney, Myers & Podmore, 1886). In this study Gurney argued that visual, auditory, and tactile experiences, as well as impressions corresponding to events such as illness and accidents taking place at a distance, were the result of telepathic messages. Such telepathic 'phantasms,' or hallucinations soon became a well-known explanation for such experiences.

Some of the SPR's other work relevant to dissociation were Edmund Gurney's (1847–1888) studies of the stages of hypnosis as well as state-specific hypnotic memory (Gurney, 1884; 1887a, 1887b; 1888). Regarding the latter, Gurney reported the following observation with a person he had hypnotized: "In this condition he was able to read ... After reading a paragraph ... he was then [awakened] completely as usual. But only one word of what he had read could be recalled, and he was very uncertain about that; he recollected distinctly, however, a paragraph that he had recently read in the normal state, and felt satisfied that that was the last one read. Again hypnotized, he had full recollection of the paragraph read in the hypnotic state with open eyes" (Gurney, 1888, p. 10).

Others reported observations about mediumistic trance, including the psychical researcher Richard Hodgson (1855–1905; Hodgson, 1892; 1898) who worked with the Boston medium Leonora E. Piper (1857–1950). Initially the medium showed what seemed to be an initial stage in which she was "dreamily conscious of the sitter, and dreamily conscious of 'spirits'" (Hodgson, 1898, p. 397). This state was followed by the manifestation of what Hodgson referred to as the subliminal consciousness of the medium "which is in direct relation, not so much with our ordinary physical world as with 'another world'" (p. 397). The latter was followed by a state conceptualized as one in which the "subliminal consciousness withdraws completely from the control of her body and takes her supraliminal consciousness with it" (p. 398). Hodgson also noticed that Mrs. Piper came out of trance, reversing the order of appearance of the above-mentioned states.

The work of the classical scholar Frederic W. H. Myers was also very important for the SPR as well as for psychical research and for psychology in general. In his early writings Myers (1884; 1885;

1889) called attention to both sensory and motor automatisms (e.g. hallucinations and automatic writing) as a way in which the subliminal (unconscious) mind communicated. Myers later stated: "I suggest, that the stream of consciousness in which we habitually live is not the only consciousness which exists in connection with our organism. Our habitual or empirical consciousness may consist of a mere selection from a multitude of thoughts and sensations, of which some at least are equally conscious with those that we empirically know" (Myers, 1892, p. 301). He connected the subliminal mind with a variety of dissociative phenomena. Some were what he referred to as phenomena generally accepted by psychology—such as automatisms, hypnosis, and alterations of personality. But he also included manifestations such as telepathy and mediumship that still had not gained general scientific acceptance (Myers, 1903).

As discussed in various historical studies, psychical research was also cultivated in countries other than England. They included France (Plas, 2000), Germany (Treitel, 2003), Italy (Biondi, 1988), and the United States (Moore, 1977). In France the physiologist Charles Richet (1884) explored what the French and others referred to as 'mental suggestion.' In the United States, an organization similar to the SPR, the American Society for Psychical Research (ASPR), was organized in Boston (Formation of the Society, 1885; see also Moore, 1977). The society was part of the SPR until 1906, when it became independent. During its early period its members conducted research on topics such as thought-transference and mediumship (e.g. Bowditch et al., 1886; James, 1886).

James became involved with the SPR, and was its president in 1896. His Presidential Address was published in the opening page of the June 19, 1896 issue of Science (James, 1896a).[3] He pointed out that the field had few active workers and that its phenomena were "fortuitous and occasional" (p. 882). Regardless of this, James believed that the SPR had a record of significant achievements. Among them were the results of its work with hallucinations and mediumship, and the general tendency of the SPR to discuss subject matter using first-hand evidence, something that he believed had not always been the case in previous work. James also praised Myers's writings about automatisms and the subliminal self. He wrote that "thanks to his genius, we begin to see for the first time what a vast interlocked and graded system these phenomena, from the rudest motor automatisms to the most startling sensory apparition, form. Mr. Myers' methodical treatment of them by classes and series is the first great step towards overcoming the distaste of orthodox science to look at them at all" (p. 885).[4]

But regardless of these developments James believed in caution and wrote in the same Presidential Address: "We must … be satisfied for many a year to go without definitive conclusions, confident that if we only keep alive and heap up data, the natural types of them (if there are any) will surely crystallize out; whilst old material that is baffling will get settled as we proceed, through its analogy with new material that will come with the baffling character removed" (p. 886).

James was also involved with the founding of the ASPR in the United States, where we find him on the initial organizing committee (Formation of the Society, 1885, p. 1) and as part of the organization's council (Council of the Society, 1885; Hodgson, 1889, p. 286). In addition, he wrote on a variety of topics in the ASPR's *Proceedings* (James, 1886; 1889a,1889b; James & Bowditch, 1885), including mediumship and hypnosis.

In his book *Human Immortality*, James (1898a) briefly referred to psychic phenomena in relation to his discussion of the production and transmission models of consciousness. That is, he contrasted the idea that the brain produced or created consciousness with the possibility that it was merely an instrument that channeled consciousness, which was basically an independent principle. As he stated:

> A medium … will show knowledge of his sitter's private affairs which it seems impossible he should have acquired through sight or hearing, or inference therefrom. Or you will have

> an apparition of some one who is now dying hundreds of miles away. On the production-theory one does not see from what sensations such odd bits of knowledge are produced. On the transmission-theory, they don't have to be 'produced'—they exist ready-made in the transcendental world, and all that is needed is an abnormal lowering of the brain-threshold to let them through. (James, 1898a, p. 26)

It is also important to acknowledge James's contributions to the popularization and defense of psychical research. This is clear in discussions of the field published in popular reviews such as *Forum* and *American Magazine* (James, 1892b; 1909a), in specialized publications such as *Science* and the *Psychological Review* (e.g. James, 1896a, 1896b), and in his reviews of many published works on the topic.[5]

It is clear that James accepted the existence of some extraordinary phenomena. However, he stated at the end of his life: "I am theoretically no 'further' than I was at the beginning." (James, 1909a, p. 580). James believed psychical researchers had expected too much and that instead they should "mark progress not by quarter-centuries but by half-centuries or whole centuries" (p. 580).

James, Mediumship, and Hypnosis

Mediumship

In one of his articles James (1890a) disagreed with Janet's (1889) view that hypnotically induced secondary selves were pathological. Trances, he believed, were too complex to be able to reduce all of them to a simple explanation, such as Janet's. Furthermore, James wrote: "I know a non-hysterical woman who, in her trances, knows facts which altogether transcend her *possible* normal consciousness, facts about the lives of people whom she never saw or heard of before. I am well aware of all the liabilities to which this statement exposes me, and I make it deliberately, having practically no doubt whatever of its truth" (James, 1890a, p. 373).

This was a reference to the above-mentioned Boston medium Leonora E. Piper, who James (1886; 1890c) studied.[6] James first saw Mrs. Piper in 1885, after his mother and sister-in-law had reported having veridical communications from her. Interested, he went to see the medium with his wife, experiencing firsthand the medium's French 'spirit control', an entity who described himself as a 'Dr. Phinuit.' He wrote about his experience:

> The medium ... when entranced, repeated most of the names of 'spirits' whom she had announced on the two former occasions and added others. The names came with difficulty, and were only gradually made perfect. My wife's father's name of Gibbens was announced first as Niblin, then as Giblin. A child Herman (whom we had lost the previous year) had his name spelt out as Herrin. I think that in no case were both Christian and surnames given on this visit. But *the facts predicated* of the persons named made it in many instances impossible not to recognize the particular individuals who were talked about. We took particular pains on this occasion to give the Phinuit control no help over his difficulties and to ask no leading questions. My impression after this first visit was, that Mrs. P. was either possessed of supernormal powers, or knew the members of my wife's family by sight and had by some lucky coincidence become acquainted with such a multitude of their domestic circumstances as to produce the startling impression which she did. My later knowledge of her sittings and personal acquaintance with her has led

> me absolutely to reject the latter explanation, and to believe that she has supernormal powers. (James, 1890c, p. 652)

James (1886) authored a report of his investigation of Piper as a member of the ASPR's Committee on Mediumistic Phenomena. He mentioned having testimony from 25 sitters, five of whom had verbatim stenographic reports. In addition, James wrote:

> Fifteen of the sitters were surprised at the communications they received, names and facts being mentioned at the first interview which it seemed improbable should have been known to the medium in a normal way. The probability that she possessed no clue as to the sitter's identity was, I believe, in each and all of these fifteen cases, sufficient. But of only one of them is there a stenographic report; so that, unfortunately for the medium, the evidence in her favor is, although more abundant, less exact in quality than some of that which will be counted against her. (James, 1886, p. 103)

James was convinced of Piper's honesty and that she presented genuine trance phenomena. Furthermore, he believed her "to be in possession of a power as yet unexplained" (p. 104). Such an emphasis in the veridical content of mediumship was consistent with the interest of psychical researchers in 'supernormal' knowledge as well as the topic of survival of death, concerns that guided psychical investigations during the nineteenth century.[7] This led James to conduct tests of thought-transference with the medium in hypnosis and out of it, but with no success.

But James was interested in other aspects of Piper's mediumship as well, aspects consistent with the writings of Myers (1884; 1885) on the topic. "What science wants", James (1886, p. 104) wrote, "is a *context* to make the trance-phenomena continuous with other physiological and psychological facts." To explore this James hypnotized Mrs. Piper. After two failed attempts he suggested that her "spirit control" assist in making Mrs. Piper a more "mesmeric" research participant. James wrote in his 1886 report:

> She became partially hypnotized on the third trial; but the effect was so slight that I ascribe it rather to the effect of repetition than to the suggestion made. By the fifth trial she had become a pretty good hypnotic subject, as far as muscular phenomena and automatic imitations of speech and gesture go: but I could not affect her consciousness, or otherwise get her beyond this point. Her condition in this semi-hypnosis is very different from her medium-trance. The latter is characterized by great muscular unrest, even her ears moving vigorously in a way impossible to her in her waking state. But in hypnosis her muscular relaxation and weakness are extreme. She often makes several efforts to speak ere her voice becomes audible; and to get a strong contraction of the hand, for example, express manipulation and suggestion must be practised. The automatic imitations I spoke of are in the first instance very weak, and only become strong after repetition. Her pupils contract in the medium-trance. Suggestions to the 'Control' that he should make her recollect after the trance what she had been saying were accepted, but had no result. (pp. 104–105).

James wrote about Dr. Phinuit's communications both to him and his wife about their own personal shortcomings during which time he was "very different in style from his more usual talk, and probably superior to anything that the medium could produce in the same line in her natural state" (James, 1890c, p. 655). He also noticed that Dr. Phinuit could not understand French but that nonetheless he served as the master of ceremonies in Mrs. Piper's communications with other 'spirits.' Furthermore, James mentioned some instances of direct control of the medium by alleged spirits other than Dr. Phinuit.

In a review of Hodgson's (1898) report James (1898c) commented on Mrs. Piper's trance memory being capable of conversing about topics related to earlier communications even if they had taken place a while back. James wrote: "Mrs. Piper's trance-memory ... is no ordinary human memory; and we have to explain its singular perfection either as the natural endowment of her solitary subliminal self, or as a collection of distinct memory-systems, each with a communicating 'spirit,' as its vehicle" (James, 1898c, p. 423).

In addition to his initial sittings in the 1880s, James held many séances with Piper in later years. For example, in an important report about her mediumship Richard Hodgson mentioned several sittings arranged by James held in his home at Cambridge between 1893 and 1895 (Hodgson, 1898, pp. 482, 494, 525, 526, 528, 534). Years later James (1909c) reported on communications Piper produced purporting to be from Hodgson, who had died in 1905. He considered the content of the communications was 'supernormal' but was not sure of the source of the information obtained. In his view: "The active cause of the communications is on any hypothesis a will of some kind, be it the will of R. H.'s spirit, of lower supernatural intelligences, or of Mrs. Piper's subliminal., yet the major part of it is suggestive of some thing quite different—as if a will were there, but a will to say something which the machinery fails to bring through' (James, 1909c, p. 116).

James seemed to incline towards an outside will, but speculated on the interaction of many factors in the communications. He wrote: "The sitter, with his desire to receive, forms, so to speak, a drainage-opening or sink; the medium, with her desire to personate, yields the nearest lying material to be drained off; while the spirit desiring to communicate is shown the way by the current set up, and swells the latter by its own contributions" (p. 120).

James's openness to different influences affecting mental mediumship was clear in speculations about psychological factors influencing the communications he presented in *The Principles of Psychology* (1890b). He wrote:

> One curious thing about trance-utterances is their generic similarity in different individuals. The 'control' here in America is either a grotesque, slangy, and flippant personage ('Indian' controls, calling the ladies 'squaws,' the men 'braves,' the house a 'wigwam,' etc., etc., are excessively common); or, if he ventures on higher intellectual flights, he abounds in a curiously vague optimistic philosophy-and-water, in which phrases about spirit, harmony, beauty, law, progression, development, etc., keep recurring. It seems exactly as if one author composed more than half of the trance-messages, no matter by whom they are uttered. Whether all sub-conscious selves are peculiarly susceptible to a certain stratum of the Zeitgeist, and get their inspiration from it, I know not; but this is obviously the case with the secondary selves which become 'developed' in spiritualist circles. There the beginnings of the medium trance are indistinguishable from effects of hypnotic suggestion. The subject assumes the role of a medium simply because opinion expects it of him under the conditions which are present; and carries it out with feebleness or vivacity proportionate to his histrionic gifts. (James, 1890b, Vol. 1, p. 394)

Interestingly, James (1889b) reported on other cases of apparent mediumship in his paper "Notes on Automatic Writing," published in the ASPR *Proceedings*. He started his essay by saying that Janet (1886; 1887) had reported anesthesia of the arm used by a participant to produce automatic writing and that he had made similar observations himself. In James's words: "I have actually tested three automatic writers for anaesthesia. In one of them, examined between the acts of writing, no anaesthesia was observed, but the examination was superficial. In the two others, both of them men, the anaesthesia to pricking and pinching, and possibly to touch, seemed complete" (James, 1889b, p. 549).

One of these cases was that of a 21-year-old student who produced writing via a planchette and his hand. While the participant claimed he did not experience the pinchings done by James, his written messages did. James wrote:

> Here, we have the consciousness of a subject split into two parts, one of which expresses itself through the mouth, and the other through the hand, whilst both are in communication with the ear. The mouth-consciousness is ignorant of all that the hand suffers or does; the hand-consciousness is ignorant of pin-pricks indicted upon other parts of the body—and of what more remains to be ascertained. If we call this hand-consciousness the automatic consciousness, then we also perceive that the automatic consciousness may transfer itself from the right hand to the left, and carry its own peculiar store of memories with it. (1889b, p. 551)

James felt these observations had some similarity with Gurney's (1887a) experiments in post-hypnotic suggestion, in which he believed consciousness was split-off and automatically communicated through the participant's hand. This led James to comment: "This dissociation of the consciousness into mutually exclusive parts is evidently a phenomenon destined, when understood, to cast a light into the abysses of Psychology" (James, 1889b, p. 551).

Hysteria and Secondary Consciousness

Like several other American psychologists (e.g. Newbold, 1896; Sidis, 1898), James (1890a, 1890b) was interested in those influential cases of double personality that did much to popularize the concept of unconscious personalities or trains of thought. We are referring to cases such as those of Mary Reynolds (1785-1854), Louis Vivet (b. 1863), Felida X. (b. 1843), and Janet's hypnotized patients.[8] Regarding Leonie (b. 1837), one of Janet's patients, James (1890b, Vol. 1, p. 388) wrote: "Leonie 1 knows only of herself; Leonie 2, of herself and of Leonie 1; Leonie 3 knows of herself and of both the others." Consistent with this, James was of the opinion that "in certain persons at least, the total possible consciousness may be split into parts which coexist, but mutually ignore each other and share the objects of knowledge between them, and—more remarkable still—are complementary" (James, 1890a, p. 369).

Another interesting but less well-known case showing divided consciousness was that of Anna Windsor, who suffered from hystero-epilepsy.[9] James (1889b) reported the case using notes written by Dr. Ira Barrows (1804–1882). Barrows' notes suggested the existence of a second consciousness in Windsor involving different actions and creative endeavors. The record cited by James started on September 17, 1860 with the observation that, in delirium, the patient tore her hair with the left hand while her right hand prevented those actions. On September 29, according to Barrows' notes: "Complains of great pain in right arm, more and more intense, when suddenly it falls down by her side. She looks at it in amazement. Thinks it belongs to some one else; positive it is not hers. Sees her right arm drawn around upon her spine. Cut it, prick it, do what you please to it, she takes no notice of it" (p. 552). Barrow added a note about events five years later stating: "She believes her spine is her right arm, and that her right arm is a foreign object and a nuisance. She believes it to be an arm and a hand, but treats it as if it had intelligence and might keep away from her. She bites it, pounds it, pricks it, and in many ways seeks to drive it from her. She calls it 'Stump; Old Stump' ..." (p. 552).

Other phenomena included apparent writing in her sleep, with no recollection on awakening of having done so. The notes continue:

> February 1 to 11—Under the influence of magnetism writes poetry; personates different persons, mostly those who have long since passed away. When in the magnetic state, whatever she does and says is not remembered when she comes out of it. Commences a series of drawings with her right paralyzed hand, 'Old Stump.' Also writes poetry with it. Whatever 'Stump' writes, or draws, or does, she appears to take no interest in; says it is none of hers, and that she wants nothing to do with 'Stump' or 'Stump's.' I have sat by her bed and engaged her in conversation, and drawn her attention in various ways, while the writing and drawing has been uninterrupted. (p. 552)

Barrow recorded on January 19, 1862 that the right hand was rational and responded to questions in writings, and continued to prevent the patient from tearing clothes and her hair by holding the left hand. The right hand continued to be active during sleep, carrying on conversations, writing poetry, and rapping on the bed's headboard to signal the patient's mother if spasms or other phenomena ensued. The rest of the notes read as follows:

> January, 1863—At night, and during her sleep, 'Stump' writes letters, some of them very amusing; writes poetry, some pieces original. Writes 'Hasty Pudding,' by Barlow, in several cantos, which she had never read; all correctly written, but queerly arranged, as, e.g., one line belonging in one canto would be transposed with another line in another canto. She has no knowledge of Latin or French, yet 'Stump' produces, rhyme of Latin and English.
>
> 'Stump' writes both asleep and awake, and the writing goes on while she is occupied with her left hand in other matters. Ask her what she is writing, she replies, 'I am not writing; that is 'Stump" writing. I don't know what he is writing. I don't trouble myself with "Stump's" doings.' Reads with her book upside down, and sometimes when covered with the sheet. 'Stump' produces two bills of fare in French … (pp. 553–554).

James pointed out that he did not have the records of Windsor's manifestations for the later period of her life. In the rest of the paper, he discussed other cases of automatism in which there were some indications of veridical information being presented.

In 1896 James gave his celebrated Lowell lectures on exceptional mental states (Taylor, 1984). In these presentations he included such topics as hysteria, hypnotism, automatisms, and multiple personality. At the beginning of the lecture on the latter topic James stated: "From the ordinary focus and margin, from the ordinary abstraction, we shade off into phenomena that look like consciousness *beyond the margin*" (Taylor, 1984, p. 73).

Hypnosis

James reminded us that "in the earlier stages of hypnotism the patient remembers what has happened, but with successive sittings he sinks into a deeper condition, which is commonly followed by complete loss of memory" (1890b, Vol. 2, p. 602). Referring to the hypnotic participant when he or she had been suggested to commit crimes he wrote: "His spontaneity is lost only for those systems of ideas which *conflict* with the suggested delusion. The latter is thus "systematized"; the rest of consciousness is shut off, excluded, dissociated from it. In extreme cases the rest of the mind would seem to be actually abolished and the hypnotic subject to be literally a changed personality." (p. 605).

James also mentioned in *The Principles of Psychology* the abolition of pain, and other sensations, as well as perceptions that were not consciously registered. He wrote: "Messrs. Gurney, Janet, and

Binet have shown that the ignored elements are preserved in a split-off portion of the subjects' consciousness which can be tapped in certain ways, and made to give an account of itself" (p. 609). Similarly, some of these authors were said to have demonstrated that suggestions to perform acts were "stored up in consciousness; not simply organically registered, but that *the consciousness which thus retains it is split off, dissociated from the rest of the subject's mind*" (p. 614).

Earlier on James had experimented with hypnosis in his work for the ASPR's Committee of Hypnosis. In their first report (James & Carnochan, 1886) there were some demonstrations using Harvard students. The arm of two subjects (Mrs. Piper being one of them) was made anesthetic. This led the authors of the report to ask: "Is the anesthesia ... produced by suggestion, due to an abolition of sensation or an abolition of "apperception"? Does the subject not *feel?* or [has] he become incapable of *noticing* what he feels? or is his state something more peculiar still?" (p. 96). Several perceptual and hallucinatory tests were conducted. A puzzling effect was that "the hallucination of a colored patch on a real white ground will sometimes be followed by a negative after-image when the gaze is transferred to another place" (p. 98).

In another short paper James (1887b) reported on the effect of hypnosis on reaction time. However, he concluded, "it is clear that there is no simple hypnotic state which can be quoted as having a determinate effect on the reaction-time. There are hypnotic and post-hypnotic *states* which vary very much, and some of which retard, whilst others quicken, the reactions" (p. 248).

James used hypnosis with the Reverend Ansel Bourne (1826–ca 1910) to recover forgotten memories.[10] Bourne, from Greene, Rhode Island, disappeared after withdrawing money from a bank on January 17, 1887. On March 14 a man called A. J. Brown woke up at Norriston, Pennsylvania, where he had been tending a shop for six weeks. Brown did not know where he was and said he was Bourne and the last he remembered was being in a bank withdrawing money. In 1890 James hypnotized him:

> I induced Mr. Bourne to submit to hypnotism, so as to see whether, in the hypnotic trance, his 'Brown' memory would not come back. It did so with surprising readiness; so much so indeed that it proved quite impossible to make him whilst in the hypnosis remember any of the facts of his normal life. He had heard of Ansel Bourne, but 'didn't know as he had ever met the man.' When confronted with Mrs. Bourne he said that he had 'never seen the woman before,' etc. On the other hand, he told of his peregrinations during the lost fortnight, and gave all sorts of details about the Norristown episode. The whole thing was prosaic enough; and the Brown-personality seems to be nothing but a rather shrunken, dejected, and amnesic extract of Mr. Bourne himself. He gives no motive for the wandering except that there was 'trouble back there' and he 'wanted rest.' I had hoped by suggestion, etc., to run the two personalities into one, and make the memories continuous, but no artifice would avail to accomplish this, and Mr. Bourne's skull today still covers two distinct personal selves. (James, 1890b, Vol. 1, pp. 392; for more details see Hodgson, 1891)

Hypnosis was also mentioned by James in the Lowell 1896 lectures on exceptional mental states. In his view suggestibility "is due to the narrowness of the field of consciousness" (Taylor, 1984, p. 27).

Beyond Dissociation

McDermott (1986) has argued that James learned about the margins of consciousness and the artificial separation of experience through psychical research and psychopathology. This is seen in James's (1890b) exploration of consciousness in terms of flow and expansion.

James later emphasized higher dimensions of consciousness, or at least speculated about them. He stated his belief that 'our lives are like islands in the sea, or like trees in the forest' (1909a, p. 589). Using the images of islands and trees James argued that their separation from the rest was illusory due to 'subterranean connections.' In this paper, he went to speculate on the possible collective nature of consciousness and the illusory separation of minds for adaptation purposes (see also James, 1898c; 1909b).

In *The Varieties of Religious Experience* (1902) he speculated on the involvement of 'the higher faculties of our hidden mind' (p. 513) with religious experience. He went on to write: "The whole drift of my education goes to persuade me that the world of our present consciousness is only one out of many worlds of consciousness that exist, and that those other worlds must contain experiences which have a meaning for our life also; and that although in the main their experiences and those of this world keep discrete, yet the two become continuous at certain points, and higher energies filter in" (p. 519). This statement suggests that James's initial interest and more mundane concept of dissociation expanded in a transpersonal way.

Conclusion

James's ideas were congruent with his philosophy of radical empiricism and his concept of pluralism. But our emphasis here has not been on his intellectual evolution in relation to other aspects of his thought (as seen in Lamberth, 1999; Taylor, 1996). Instead, we have focused on his case as an exemplar illustrating the influence of unorthodox phenomena on the study of dissociation.

We are referring to the influence and interaction of psychical research with James's studies of dissociation, a state of affairs that he shared with other figures such as Flournoy, Gurney, Myers, and Richet. The work of these men was nurtured by the conceptual agenda of psychical research. Furthermore, like the influence of hysteria and the performances of specific hysterics (Alvarado, 2009b; Ellenberger, 1970), the phenomenon of mediumship and the performances of particular mediums provided a 'laboratory' and a catalyst for the development of ideas and the recording of observations, a topic discussed elsewhere (Alvarado et al., 2007).

Unlike Janet and others, James did not use dissociation to explain mediumship and related phenomena in the sense of reducing everything to suggestion and the workings of a secondary consciousness. Instead, he adapted ideas, such as Myers's, that assumed the existence of a secondary consciousness and that were not only relevant to pathology, but to the 'supernormal' and the transcendental. James's acceptance of the 'supernormal' in the case of Mrs. Piper represents a break with Janet and other conventional explorers of dissociation. It was in fact a plea to study and accept the possibility that dissociation and consciousness in general could transcend bodily limitations, as argued by other psychical researchers. Such an approach was never widely accepted and remains to this day confined to the field of parapsychology and similar movements.

While we have mentioned the writings of several authors who have 'rescued' the contributions of psychical research to psychology and psychiatry from oblivion, there are unfortunately many modern histories in these fields today that still do not acknowledge such influences. Many of these histories have been concerned only with distinguishing psychology from pseudoscience, and with labelling psychical research as a discredited discipline (e.g. O'Boyle, 2006), while others do not even mention psychical research, as seen in discussions of James (e.g., Mandler, 2007).

Regardless of the above cited body of work much remains unexplored about the history of the interface between dissociation—and psychology and psychiatry in general—and psychical research.

It is our hope that future studies will explore this literature in more detail so as to expand the scope of the historiographies of psychology and psychiatry to include wider currents of influence, as well as the work of neglected individuals such as those uniquely gifted research participants cited in this essay.[11]

Notes

1 This was the case of Ambroise August Liébeault (1823–1904; Alvarado, 2009a), Frederic W.H. Myers (1843–1901; Hamilton, 2009), Sigmund Freud (1856–1939; Fodor, 1971), Carl G. Jung (1875–1961; Fodor, 1971), Pierre Janet (1859–1947; Le Maléfan, 1993), Charles Richet (1850–1935; Wolf, 1993), and Theodore Flournoy (1854–1920; Shamdasani, 1994).

2 Such rejection of psychic phenomena has been documented by several historians (e.g. Brown, 1983; Coon, 1992; Le Maléfan, 1999; Oppenheim, 1985).

3 Science had already a track record of publishing news and reviews of the work of the SPR (e.g., American Society for Psychical Research, 1887; Mrs. Sidgwick and the Mediums, 1886). James's psychical research has been discussed in books (e.g. Blum, 2006; Richardson, 2006; Taylor, 1996), as well as in introductions to James' collected papers (McDermott, 1986; Murphy, 1960), in articles (Gitre, 2006; Gondra Rezola, 2000; Knapp, 2001), and in a dissertation on the topic (Knapp, 2003). For a compilation of the relevant psychical research writings see James (1986).

4 James (1901; 1903) wrote much about Myers and was influenced by him (Taylor, 1996). See also James (1902, pp. 511–512), and some of his correspondence (H. James, 1920, Vol. 2, pp. 57, 141). His attitude, sometimes critical, is reflected in the fact that he said he had a high opinion of "of Myers's constructive gifts, but on the whole a lower opinion of the objective solidity of the system. So many of the facts which form its pillars are still dubious" (H. James, 1920, Vol. 2, p. 186).

5 An example was a review of *Phantasms of the Living* published in Science (James, 1887a). James also published several book and article reviews about psychic phenomena in the Psychological Review (Alvarado, 2009c).

6 Mrs. Piper was the first mental medium the SPR investigated systematically and at length. Reports about her performances during the nineteenth century were published by the SPR (e.g., Hodgson, 1892; 1898; Leaf, 1890; Lodge, 1890). For more information about Mrs. Piper see her daughter's biography (Piper, 1929) and Sage (1902/1904).

7 For examples of interest in what James called 'supernormal phenomena' see studies that have discussed telepathy and clairvoyance (Luckhurst, 2002; Plas, 2000). The interest in survival of death shown by psychical researchers was a direct inheritance from the movement of spiritualism (Podmore, 1902), and reflected the crises of faith typical during the nineteenth century, as seen in Great Britain (Gauld, 1968; Turner, 1974). On the influence of the concept of survival of death on psychical research see Alvarado (2003).

8 For more information on these cases see Carroy (1991), Crabtree (1993), Hacking (1995), and Kenny (1986).

9 This case also deserves study in terms of how it has been cited. Some citations of the case include Myers (1903, Vol. 1, pp. 355–360), Newbold (1896), Prince (1890), and Sidis (1898, pp. 285-288).

10 For an overview of the Bourne case see Kenny (1986). See also Bourne (1858), Hodgson (1891), and James (1890b, Vol. 1, pp. 391–393).

11 Additional figures deserving study include those who wrote later studies of Mrs. Piper (Sidgwick, 1915; Tanner, 1910), and the writings of many others (e.g. Morselli, 1908; Sudre, 1926).

References

Alvarado, C. S. (2002). Dissociation in Britain during the late nineteenth century: The Society for Psychical Research, 1882-1900, *Journal of Trauma and Dissociation, 3*, 9–33.

Alvarado, C. S. (2003). The concept of survival of bodily death and the development of parapsychology, *Journal of the Society for Psychical Research, 67*, 65–95.
Alvarado, C. S. (2009a). Ambroise August Liébeault and psychic phenomena, *American Journal of Clinical Hypnosis, 52*, 111–121.
Alvarado, C. S. (2009b). Nineteenth–century hysteria and hypnosis: A historical note on Blanche Wittmann, *Australian Journal of Clinical and Experimental Hypnosis, 37*, 21–36.
Alvarado, C. S. (2009c). Psychical research in the *Psychological Review*, 1894–1900: A bibliographical note, *Journal of Scientific Exploration, 23*, 211–220.
Alvarado, C. S., Machado, F. R., Zangari, W. & Zingrone, N. L. (2007). Perspectivas historicas da influência da mediunidade na construção de idéias psicológicas e psiquiátricas, *Revista de Psiquiátricas Clínica, 34* (supp. 1), 42–53.
American Society for Psychical Research (1887). *Science, 9*, 50–51.
Azam, E. E. (1887). *Hypnotisme, double conscience et altérations de la personnalité.* J.B. Baillière et Fils.
Biondi, M. (1988). *Tavoli e Medium: Storia dello spiritismo in Italia.* Gremese.
Blum, D. (2006). *Ghost hunters: William James and the search for scientific proof of life after death.* Penguin Press.
Bourne, A. (1858). *Wonderful works of God: A narrative of the wonderful facts in the case of Ansel Bourne.* Moses Cummings.
Bowditch, H. P., Pickering, E. C., Watson, W. M., Hall, E. H., Minot, C. M., Jackson, C. C. & Peirce, J. M. (1886). Report on the Committee of Thought-Transference, *Proceedings of the American Society for Psychical Research, 1*, 106–116.
Brown, E. M. (1983). Neurology and spiritualism in the 1870s, *Bulletin of the History of Medicine, 37*, 563–577.
Carpenter, W. B. (1877). *Mesmerism and spiritualism, & historically and scientifically considered.* Longmans and Green.
Carroy, J. (1991). *Hypnose, suggestion et psychologie: L'invention de sujets.* Presses Universitaires de France.
Coon, D. J. (1992). Testing the limits of sense and science: American experimental psychologists combat spiritualism, 1880–1920, *American Psychologist, 47*, 143–151.
Council of the Society (1885). *Proceedings of the American Society for Psychical Research, 1,* p. 4.
Courses (n.d.). *Courses William James taught at Harvard,* http://www.des.emory.edu/mfp/JamesTeachingSchedule.html.
Crabtree, A. (1993). *From Mesmer to Freud.* Yale University Press.
Crabtree, A. (2007). Automatism and secondary centers of consciousness (pp. 301–306). In E. F. Kelly, E. W. Kelly, A. Crabtree, A. Gauld, M. Grosso, & B. Greyson. (Eds.) *Irreducible Mind.* Rowman & Littlefield.
Deleuze, J. P. F. (1813). *Histoire critique du magnétisme animal.* (Vol. 1). Mame.
Ellenberger, H. F. (1970). *The discovery of the unconscious: The history and evolution of dynamic psychiatry.* Basic Books.
Fodor, N. (1971). *Freud, Jung and Occultism.* University Books.
Formation of the Society (1885). *Proceedings of the American Society for Psychical Research, 1,* 1–2.
Gauld, A. (1968). *The founders of psychical research.* Routledge & Kegan Paul.
Gauld, A. (1992). *A history of hypnotism.* Cambridge University Press.
Gitre, E. J. K. (2006). William James on divine intimacy: Psychical research, cosmological realism and a circumscribed re-reading of *The Varieties of Religious Experience. History of the Human Sciences, 19*, 1–21.
Gondra Rezola, J. M. (2000). William James y la investigation psíquica. *Revista de Historia de la Psicología, 21*, 567–573.
Guinon, G., with Bloc, [no initial], Souques, [no initial] & Charcot, J.B. (eds.) (1893). *Clinique des Maladies du Système Nerveux: M. le Professeur Charcot: Leçons du Professeur, Mémoires, Notes et Observations.* (Vol. 2). Bureaux du Progrès Médical.
Gurney, E. (1884). The stages of hypnotism, *Proceedings of the Society for Psychical Research, 2*, 61–72.
Gurney, E. (1887a). Peculiarities of certain post-hypnotic states, *Proceedings of the Society for Psychical Research, 4*, 268–323.
Gurney, E. (1887b). Stages of hypnotic memory, *Proceedings of the Society for Psychical Research, 4*, 515–531.

Gurney, E. (1888). Recent experiments in hypnotism, *Proceedings of the Society for Psychical Research, 5*, 3–17.
Gurney, E., Myers, F.W.H. & Podmore, F. (1886). *Phantasms of the living*, (2 vols.). Trübner.
Guthrie, M. & Birchall, J. (1883). Record of experiments in thought-transference, *Proceedings of the Society for Psychical Research, 1*, 263–283.
Hacking, I. (1995). *Rewriting the soul: Multiple personality and the sciences of memory*. Princeton University Press.
Hamilton, T. (2009). *Immortal remains: F.W.H. Myers and the Victorian search for life after death.* Imprint Academic.
Héricourt, J. (1889). L'activité inconsciente de l'esprit, *Revue Scientifique, 44*, 257–268.
Hodgson, R. (1891). A case of double consciousness, *Proceedings of the Society for Psychical Research, 7*, 221–255.
Hodgson, R. (1892). A record of observations of certain phenomena of trance, *Proceedings of the Society for Psychical Research, 8*, 1–167.
Hodgson, R. (1898). A further record of observations of certain phenomena of trance, *Proceedings of the Society for Psychical Research, 13*, 284–582.
Hodgson, R. (1889). Meetings of the society. *Proceedings of the American Society for Psychical Research, 1*, 285–286.
Inglis, B. (1992). *Natural and supernatural: A history of the paranormal from earliest times to 1914.* (Rev.). Prism.
James, H. (ed.). (1920). *The letters of William James.* (2 vols.). Atlantic Monthly Press.
James, W. (1869/1960). Review of Planchette. In G. Murphy, & R. O. Ballou. (Eds.) *William James on Psychical Research* (pp. 19–23). Viking Press.
James, W. (1879). Are we automata? *Mind*, 4, 1–22.
James, W. (1884). What is an emotion? *Mind*, 9, 188–205.
James, W. (1886). Report of the Committee on Mediumistic Phenomena, *Proceedings of the American Society for Psychical Research, 1*, 102–106.
James, W. (1887a). Phantasms of the living, *Science, 9*, 18–20.
James, W. (1887b). Reaction-time in the hypnotic trance, *Proceedings of the American Society for Psychical Research, 1*, 246–248.
James, W. (1889a). Note on the foregoing report, *Proceedings of the American Society for Psychical Research, 1*, 285–286.
James, W. (1889b). Notes on automatic writing, *Proceedings of the American Society for Psychical Research, 1*, 548–564.
James, W. (1890a). The hidden self, *Scribner's Magazine*, 7, 161–173.
James, W. (1890b). *The principles of psychology*. Henry Holt.
James, W. (1890c). A record of observations of certain phenomena of trance Part III, *Proceedings of the Society for Psychical Research, 6*, 651–659.
James, W. (1892a). *Psychology: Briefer course*. Henry Holt.
James, W. (1892b). What psychical research has accomplished, *Forum, 13*, 727–742.
James, W. (1895). The knowing of things together, *Psychological Review, 2*, 105–124.
James, W. (1896a). Address of the President before the Society for Psychical Research, *Science, 3*, 881–888.
James, W. (1896b). Psychical research, *Psychological Review, 3*, 649–651.
James, W. (1897). The will to believe and other essays in popular philosophy. Longmans, Green.
James, W. (1898a). *Human Immortality*. Houghton Mifflin.
James, W. (1898b). Introduction (pp. v–vii). In B. Sidis. (Ed.) *The Psychology of suggestion*. D. Appleton.
James, W. (1898c). Review of a "Further record of observations of certain phenomena of trance," by R. Hodgson, *Psychological Review, 5*, 420–424.
James, W. (1899). *Talks to teachers on psychology*. Henry Holt.
James, W. (1901). Frederic Myers' service to psychology, *Proceedings of the Society for Psychical Research, 17*, 13–23.
James, W. (1902). *The varieties of religious experience*. Longmans, Green.
James, W. (1903). Review of "Human personality and its survival of bodily death." *Proceedings of the Society for Psychical Research, 18*, 22–33.

James, W. (1907). *Pragmatism: A new name for some old ways of thinking*. Longmans, Green.
James, W. (1909a). The confidences of a 'psychical researcher.' *American Magazine*, *68*, 580–589.
James, W. (1909b). *A pluralistic universe*. Longmans, Green.
James, W. (1909c). Report on Mrs. Pipers Hodgson-control, *Proceedings of the Society for Psychical Research*, *23*, 2–121.
James, W. (1986). Essays in psychical research. In F. H. Burkhardt (Ed.). *The Works of William James, vol. 16*. Harvard University Press.
James, W. & Bowditch, H. P. (1885). Circular No. 2 issued by the Committee on Work, *Proceedings of the American Society for Psychical Research*, *1*, 5–6.
James, W. & Carnochan, G.M. (1886). Report of the Committee on Hypnotism, *Proceedings of the American Society for Psychical Research*, *1*, 95–102.
Janet, P. (1886). Les actes inconscientes et la dédoublement de la personnalité pendant le somnambulisme provoque, *Revue Philosophique de la France et de L'étranger*, *22*, 577–592.
Janet, P. (1887). L'anesthésie systématisée et la dissociation des phénomènes psychiques, *Revue Philosophique de la France et de L'étranger*, *23*, 449–472.
Janet, P. (1888). Les actes inconscients et la mémoire pendant le somnambulisme, *Revue Philosophique de la France et de L'étranger*, *25*, 238–279.
Janet, P. (1889). *L'automatisme psychologique*. Félix Alcan.
Jastrow, J. (1889). The problem of 'psychic research,' *Harpers New Monthly Magazine*, *79*, 76–82.
Johnson, M. & Henley, T. B. (Eds.) (1990). *Reflections on the principles of psychology*. Earlbaum.
Kenney, M. G. (1986). *The passion of Ansel Bourne: Multiple personality in American culture*. Smithsonian Institution Press.
Knapp, K. D. (2001). WJ, spiritualism, and unconsciousness beyond the margin, *Streams of William James*, *3*(2), 1–5.
Knapp, K. D. (2003). *To the Summerland: William James, psychical research and modernity*. (Ph.D. dissertation, Boston College).
Ladame, D. (1888). Observation de somnambulisme hystérique avec dédoublement de la personnalité, guéri par la suggestion hypnotique, *Revue de L'hypnotisme Expérimental et Thérapeutique*, *2*, 257–262.
Lamberth, D. C. (1999). *William James and the metaphysics of experience*. Cambridge University Press.
Leaf, W. (1890). A record of observations of certain phenomena of trance, part II, *Proceedings of the Society for Psychical Research*, *6*, 558–646.
Le Maléfan, P. (1993). Pierre Janet, le spiritisme et les délires spirites, *L'évolution Psychiatrique*, *58*, 445-452.
Le Maléfan, P. (1999). *Folie et spiritisme: Histoire du Discourse Psychopathologique sur la pratique du spiritisme, ses abords et ses avatars (1850–1950)*. L. Hartmattan.
Lodge, O. (1890). A record of observations of certain phenomena of trance. Part I, *Proceedings of the Society for Psychical Research*, *6*, 443–557.
Luckhurst, R. (2002). *The invention of telepathy 1870–1901*. Oxford University Press.
Mandler, G. (2007). *A history of modern experimental psychology: From James and Wundt to cognitive science*. MIT Press.
McDermott, R. A. (1986). Introduction (pp. xii–xxxvi). In F. H. Burkhardt (Ed.). *Essays in Psychical Research* (*The Works of William James*, Vol. 16). Harvard University Press.
Medd, J. (2010). *William James Cybrary*. http://wjcybrary.net/index.htm.
Moore, R. L. (1977). *In search of white crows: Spiritualism, parapsychology, and American culture*. Oxford University Press.
Morselli, E. (1908). *Psicologia e 'Spiritismo'* (2 vols.). Fratelli Bocca.
Mrs. Sidgwick and the mediums (1886). *Science*, *7*, 554–555.
Murphy, G. (1960). Introduction (pp. 3–18). In G. Murphy, & R. O. Ballou. (Eds.) *William James on Psychical Research*. Viking Press.
Myers, F.W.H. (1884). On a telepathic explanation of some so–called spiritualistic phenomena: Part I. *Proceedings of the Society for Psychical Research*, *2*, 217–237.
Myers, F. W. H. (1885). Automatic writing: Part II. *Proceedings of the Society for Psychical Research*, *3*, 1–63.
Myers, F. W. H. (1889). Automatic writing: The daemon of Socrates. *Proceedings of the Society for Psychical Research*, *5*, 522–547.

Myers, F. W. H. (1892). The subliminal consciousness: Chapter I. General characteristics of subliminal messages. *Proceedings of the Society for Psychical Research, 7*, 298–327.
Myers, F. W. H. (1903). *Human personality and its survival of bodily death.* (2 vols.). Longmans, Green.
Newbold, W.R. (1896). Double personalit. *Appleton's Popular Science Monthly, 50*, 67–79.
Objects of the Society (1882). *Proceedings of the Society for Psychical Research, 1*, 3–6.
O'Boyle, C.G. (2006). *History of psychology: A cultural perspective*. Lawrence Erlbaum.
Oppenheim, J. (1985). *The other world: Spiritualism and psychical research in England, 1850–1914.* Cambridge University Press.
Perry, R. B. (1920). *Annotated bibliography of the writings of William James.* Longmans, Green.
Piper, A. L. (1929). *The life and work of Mrs. Piper*. K. Paul, Trench, Trübner.
Plast, R. (2000). *Naissance d'une Science Humaine: La Psychologie: Les Psychologues et le 'Merveilleux Psychique.'* Presses Universitaires de Rennes.
Podmore, F. (1902). *Modern spiritualism: A history and a criticism*. Methuen.
Prince, M. (1890). Some of the revelations of hypnotism: Post-hypnotic suggestion, automatic writing and double personality. *Boston Medical and Surgical Journal, 122*, 493–495.
Proudfoot, W. (Ed.) (2004). *William James and a science of religions: Re-experiencing the varieties of religious experience.* Columbia University Press.
Richardson, R. D. (2006). *William James: In the maelstrom of American modernism.* Houghton Mifflin.
Richet, C. (1883). La personnalité et la mémoire dans le somnambulisme. *Revue Philosophique de la France et de L'étranger, 15*, 225–242.
Richet, C. (1884). La suggestion mentale elle calcul des probabilités. *Revue Philosophique de la France et de L'étranger, 18*, 609–674.
Sage, M. (1902/1904). *Mrs. Piper and the Society for Psychical Research.* Scott-Thaw.
Shamdasani, S. (1993). Automatic writing and the discovery of the unconscious. *Spring, 54*, 100–131.
Shamdasani, S. (1994). Encountering Helene: Theodore Flournoy and the genesis of subliminal psychology (pp. xi–li). *From India to the planet Mars: A case of multiple personality with imaginary languages.* Princeton University Press.
Sidgwick, E. (1915). A contribution to the study of the psychology of Mrs. Piper's trance phenomena, *Proceedings of the Society for Psychical Research, 28*, 1–657.
Sidis, B. (1898). *The psychology of suggestion.* D. Appleton.
Sudre, R. (1926). *Introduction a la métapsychique humaine*. Payot.
Tanner, A. E. (1910). *Studies in spiritism*. D. Appleton.
Taylor, E. (1984). *William James on exceptional mental states: The 1896 Lowell Lectures.* University of Massachusetts Press.
Taylor, E. (1996). *William James on consciousness beyond the margin.* Princeton University Press.
Treitel, C. (2003). *A science for the soul: Occultism and the genesis of the German modern.* Johns Hopkins University Press.
Turner, F. M. (1974). *Between science and religion: The reaction to scientific naturalism in late Victorian England.* Yale University Press.
Wolf, S. (1993). *Brain, mind and medicine: Charles Richet and the origins of physiological psychology.* Transaction Publishers.

The Psychic Sciences in France: Historial Notes on the *Annales des Sciences Psychiques*[*]

Carlos S. Alvarado & Renaud Evrard[†]

This paper is an overview of aspects of the French journal *Annales des Sciences Psychiques* (*ASP*, 1891–1919). The *ASP* was founded by Charles Richet and Xavier Dariex. The development of the journal was assisted both by the prestige and influence of Richet as a scientist and of Félix Alcan as a publisher. For the nineteenth-century period the journal emphasized cases and experiments over theories. Much of this was about spontaneous telepathy and physical mediumship. Some of the authors included in the pages of the *ASP* were Emile Boirac, Ernesto Bozzano, Albert de Rochas, Giovanni Battista Ermacora, Paul Joire, and Julian Ochorowicz. The journal provided a forum in France to argue about standards in psychical research, discuss controversies, and to bring in information on the topic from foreign countries. This included translations of the work of members of the Society for Psychical Research, such as Frederic W.H. Myers. In 1908 the *ASP* was affiliated with the Sociétè Universelle d'Études Psychiques, becoming its official publication. The *ASP* was important in establishing standards and in providing a forum for the development of psychical research in France.

The March 1891 issue of the *Journal of the Society for Psychical Research* announced the forthcoming appearance of a French periodical—the *Annales des Sciences Psychiques (ASP)*—to discuss psychical research "under the strictest conditions obtainable by accuracy and care" (*Annales des Sciences Psychiques* 1891, p. 46). The *ASP*, discussed in recent writings (e.g., Alvarado, Biondi & Kramer 2006:67, Lachapelle 2011, pp. 88–91, Monroe 2008, p. 207–209), represented an important effort in France to record and disseminate observations and research related to psychic phenomena. In the current paper we will present additional information about the journal focusing on its content, orientation, publisher, and reception. While the journal was published between 1891 and 1919, in some parts of the paper we will focus on its nineteenth-century period. It is our hope that our discussion of the *ASP*, which is meant to present a panoramic view of the topic, will inform readers of aspects of the history of French psychical research that may be difficult to study due to language barriers.

French Interest in Psychic Phenomena

By the time the *ASP* appeared, there was already a long history of French interest in mesmerism and spiritism.[1] These developments were instrumental in defending the existence of, and in popularizing, ideas such as the action of animal magnetism and spirits of the dead.

[*]Republished with permission from *Journal of Scientific Exploration, 26,* 117–140, 2012.
[†]The authors wish to thank Nancy L. Zingrone for useful editorial suggestions and Massimo Biondi for a variety of comments we used to improve this paper.

Physician and popular science writer Louis Figuier (1819–1894) summarized developments from antiquity to the mid-nineteenth century for the French public in his four-volume work *Histoire du Merveilleux dans les Temps Modernes* (1860). Figuier represented the skeptical position, arguing both for humankind's innate love and need for the "marvelous," and for explanations of magnetic and spiritistic manifestations assuming that the "lights of physiology and of medicine suffice" to explain the supposed mysteries (Figuier, 1860, Vol. 1, p. XI). Others such as philologist Émile Littré (1801–1881) similarly reduced phenomena such as table turning and possession to a variety of manifestations showing the "weakening of the nervous system" (Littré, 1856, p. 871). In later years philosopher (later physician) Pierre Janet (1859–1947) discussed mediumship as an example of dissociation, as seen in his influential monograph *L'Automatisme Psychologique* (1889).[2]

But others took a different approach, explaining phenomena through forces said to be directed by discarnate (Kardec, 1863) or human agency (De Gasparin, 1854). Later in the century there was much positive interest and research on mental suggestion at a distance, as seen in physiologist Charles Richet's (1850–1935) classic paper in which, in addition to his celebrated use of statistical evaluation, he reported experiments with various methodologies, and discussed conceptual issues (Richet, 1884, see also Alvarado 2008b). Richet, one of the founders of the *ASP*, became known during the nineteenth century for his important experimental studies of clairvoyance and related phenomena (Richet, 1888, 1889).[3] Other observers documented examples of distant mental influences such as the induction of trance (Janet, 1886), and the effects of drugs at a distance (Bourru & Burot, 1887).

The impact of the mesmeric movement continued during the late part of the century, as seen in the writings of several individuals defending the reality of animal magnetism (Alvarado, 2009). A good example of this line of work was Alexandre Baréty's (1844–1918) *Le Magnétisme Animal: Étudié Sous le Nom de Force neurique Rayonnante et Circulante dans ses Propriétés Physiques, Physiologiques et Thérapeutiques* (1887).

From the early nineteenth century on there was a need to have periodicals for the discussion of unexplained phenomena (Alvarado, Biondi, and Kramer, 2006). Examples of French responses to this need were the *Journal du Magnétisme* (started in 1845), and the *Revue Spirite* (started in 1858). In later years French physicians and others recorded their observations in scholarly and scientific journals such as the *Revue Philosophique de la France et de l'Étranger* (starting in 1876), and in the *Revue de l'Hypnotisme Expérimental & Thérapeutique* (starting in 1887, later the journal changed its title). The creation of the ASP provided French researchers with a specialized forum of discussion, and one modeled to some extent on the influential *Proceedings of the Society for Psychical Research*, published in London since 1882 (Alvarado, Biondi, and Kramer, 2006, p. 65–66).

The Annales des Sciences Psychiques

Beginnings and Founding Principles

An important force behind the *ASP* was the above-mentioned Charles Richet. Although Richet was well-known for his scientific research in physiology, among other areas, he also was interested in scientific journalism and in the popularization of science. According to one biographer:

> Richet immersed himself in this journalistic undertaking with great enthusiasm. He immensely enjoyed his work as a editor and, according to his grandson, Gabriel, he was as enthusiastic about journalism as about science. (Wolf, 1993, p. 56)

Richet had considerable experience as an editor since he edited the *Revue Scientifique* between 1880 and 1902. This was a semipopular science journal addressed to both educated laymen and scientists.

The *ASP* appeared in 1891, and was the joint project of Richet and Xavier Dariex, an opthalmologist at the Hôpital des Quinze-Vingt in Paris. In some ways the *ASP* was a continuation of Richet's interest in disseminating scientific work in the pages of the *Revue Scientifique*, but this time the emphasis was psychical research. However, the initiative did not come from Richet himself but from Dariex. Initially, Richet was reluctant to get involved in the journal. He did not seem to have much regard for Dariex, whom he described as "a small man, thin, timid, hesitant, and lacking in charm" (Richet, unpublished Mémoires, quoted by Wolf 1993, p. 59). But collaboration ensued and the first issue of the journal appeared in 1891.

Before the journal was published, Richet had been the general secretary of the Sociétè de Psychologie Physiologique. This society had the famous neurologist Jean-Martin Charcot (1825–1893) as President, and its purpose was the examination of psychological phenomena, among them those of hypnosis and psychical research, following the model of the London-based Society for Psychical Research (SPR). But the Sociétè de Psychologie Physiologique did not fully achieve its agenda and disappeared soon after having organized the International Congress of Physiological Psychology in 1889, the first international meeting of psychology.[4]

The *ASP* was another attempt by Richet to develop French psychical research. He hoped that the journal, similar to the publications of the SPR, would serve as a repository of observations of "so-called occult facts" that had supportive evidence (Richet, 1891, p. 4). In 1890 Richet founded the Sociétè des Annales Psychiques with Dariex to publish the *ASP*.

While the term "psychic sciences" was used in the journal, "psychical research" also appeared in the text frequently. This was probably an attempt to separate the field, and the *ASP*, from French spiritism. In fact, writing many years later, Richet (1922) argued that, like the SPR *Proceedings*, the *ASP* established a proper "balance between the credulity of the spiritist journals and the blind ignorance of the compendiums of official psychology" (p. 37).

The *ASP* addressed a more popular audience than the one targeted by more academic journals such as the influential *Revue Philosophique de la France et de l'Étranger*. While the journal included articles written by known figures from psychology and from other fields, the contributions were shorter in length and less scholarly than those presented in the *Revue*.[5] The ASP was open to everyone, a situation reflecting the status of psychical research. As stated by Lachapelle (2011):

> Psychical research would be a science in its presentation, and its rigor, but it would be a different kind of science. It would be accessible and inclusive: an open enterprise. Anyone could subscribe to the *Annales*, which was aimed at a broad audience rather than a restricted group with specific disciplinary credentials. Psychical phenomena could be observed or experienced by everyone, and readers were encouraged to participate by reporting their own psychical experiences to the *Annales*.[6] (Lachapelle 2011, pp. 86–87)

Dariex (1891) discussed how to produce a reliable report about psychic phenomena and asked readers to prepare written reports of psychic phenomena. However, Dariex warned them to be aware of problems such as the unreliability of memory.

The first issue of the journal opened with a letter Richet (1891) addressed to Dariex. Such an introduction was important for at least two reasons. First, Richet's association with the journal probably gave respectability to the enterprise and attracted both subscribers and writers. This was the case because Richet was very prominent during his lifetime. Not only did he belong to French high society, but he was a recognized figure in areas such as physiology and literature, not to mention psychical research (Carroy, 2004, Wolf 1993).

Second, Richet set the tone for the new journal. He acknowledged the many methodological issues involved in the study of psychic phenomena, thus presenting the *ASP* from the beginning as an attempt to contribute to solving this problem. Most previous work, he argued, consisted of "incomplete facts, defective observations, ridiculous experiences, rough and weak attempts" (Richet, 1891, p. 2). While he believed that conventional explanations could not account for all claims of psychic phenomena, he cautioned readers that the journal would contain only raw facts. Theory, he stated, was simply premature. Richet believed that, while it was easy to propose theories, it was hard to establish a fact well. Theoretical explanations would come later, as more facts were established.[7] Consequently, experiments and observations of cases would be emphasized.

Following the example of the SPR, and their *Proceedings*, Richet stated that the *ASP* would report "all the serious observations" addressed to them about "so-called occult facts" (Richet, 1891, p. 4). He listed the following topics to be discussed in the journal: telepathy, lucidity, presentiments, movement of objects, and objective apparitions, or those apparitions that were unaccountable by hallucination. This included "photographs of phantoms" and collectively perceived apparitions (p. 6). However, Richet recognized that the classification was incomplete.

Dariex (1891) commented on the topic along similar lines:

> Our ambition ... is to contribute to throw a bit of light on the profound darkness that still surrounds psychic phenomena, and to encourage their study (Dariex, 1891, p. 10)

Like Richet, he emphasized research over theory:

> We will not be spiritists, swedenborgeans, nor theosophists, nor occultists. We will be modest researchers of facts and very humble worshipers of the truth ... (Dariex, 1891, pp. 29–30)

In a later communication Dariex (1894) argued that the purpose of the journal was the search for truth through science. He expressed the hope that others would follow the ASP in the "cult of truth" (p. 2).

Reports of Cases, Experiments, and Séances

An editorial note stated that the *ASP* started with mental phenomena but would include physical manifestations later as new evidence for the phenomena accumulated (Dariex, 1892a, p. 64). Indeed, and as mentioned below, later volumes included other topics, such as more séance reports.

The first year of publication showed much activity. An analysis of the first volume of the journal, published in 1891, revealed that out of 48 articles 40% were reports of cases of such phenomena as telepathy and apparitions. The rest consisted of performances or tests of telepathy and clairvoyance (19%), book reviews and notices of publications (19%), editorial comments (10%), discussions of methodology (6%), theory and concepts (4%), and séance reports (2%).

Many of the papers were reports of cases. One of the most remarkable cases published was lawyer M.G. Morice's (1892–1893) account of an auditory haunting. Other contributions—some of which appeared in later years—included presentations and discussions of cases of "bilocation" (Bozzano, 1911), premonitions (Desbeaux, 1899), telepathic hallucinations (Hallucinations Télépathiques, 1891), presentiment (Héricourt, 1895), and faces seen on a wall (Maxwell, 1905b).

There were also papers about telepathy and clairvoyance experiments. German physician and psychical researcher A. von Schrenck-Notzing (1862–1929) reviewed recent studies on the topic (Schrenck-Notzing, 1891). Others presented observations of psychic dreams (Ermacora, 1895), and mental suggestion at a distance (Joire, 1897), among other topics. Richet's pupil Jean Charles Roux (1872–1942) (1893) conducted card studies, and Richet (1893b) analyzed them statistically in a note on chance and probability.

Table 47.1. Examples of Papers about Eusapia Palladino Published in the *Annales des Sciences Psychiques*

Reference	Topic
Ciolfi (1891)	Séances
Lombroso (1892)	Theoretical ideas
Aksakof et al. (1893)	Séances
Richet (1893a)	Séances
Dariex (1896)	Séances
Ochorowicz (1896)	Fraud and dissociation
Sabatier et al. (1896)	Séances
De Rochas (1897)	Séances
Bottazzi (1907)	Séances using instrumental recording
Morselli (1907)	Variety and reality of phenomena
Imoda (1908)	Action on an electroscope
Lombroso (1908)	Séances and clinical observations
De Fontenay (1908)	Photo of materialized hands
De Rochas (1908)	Materialized hands

Writing from the United States some years after the period considered here, Hereward Carrington (1880–1958) pointed out that most reports about Italian medium Eusapia Palladino (1854–1918) were to be found in the *ASP* (Carrington, 1907, p. 11). The journal, indeed, was required reading at the time to be able to evaluate Palladino's mediumship. The report of the famous Milan Commission, formed by Alexander Aksakof (1832–1893) and others such as Carl du Prel (1839–1899) and Giovanni Battista Ermacora (1869–1898), Richet, and Cesare Lombroso (1835–1909) appeared in the journal (Aksakof et al., 1893). The studies were held in 1892 and involved the use of instruments such as balances to weigh the medium. The report included phenomena observed under light and in darkness. These consisted of movements of the table while the medium was touching it, and movements of objects at a distance. Table 47.1 lists many papers about Palladino that were published in the *ASP*.

Physical phenomena were also discussed by Dariex (1892b, 1893, 1900). In the later paper he noted that the supposed agent behind the phenomena was a servant suspected to be a medium. This servant had a delicate health and suffered from gastro-intestinal problems of possible nervous origin.

Theoretical Papers

While theory was not emphasized, it was discussed more frequently than the journal founders recognized. For example, Albert de Rochas (1837–1914) mentioned his interest in concepts of force, a topic he had discussed before the ASP was founded (e.g., De Rochas, 1887). He argued for the existence of a fluidic body capable of leaving the physical body to produce physical phenomena:

1. There is in man a spiritual and fluidic body destined to serve as intermediary between the soul and the material body …
2. This fluidic body, which during life is the mold of the material body, can under some circumstances momentarily abandon the material body, and be perceived, even at a distance, by some of the human senses.

3. Some persons enjoy the property of secreting the substance that forms the fluidic body in fairly great quantity and with enough density for this substance to be perceived in the form of a luminous cloud … (De Rochas, 1895b, p. 125)

Some ideas of emanations believed to come from the body of mediums were briefly discussed in papers about Palladino (e.g., De Rochas, 1897; Lombroso, 1892). Polish philosopher Julian Ochorowicz (1850–1917) speculated on nervous forces, dissociation, and the ideas of the circle to explain Palladino's phenomena (Ochorowicz, 1896).[8]

Others discussed similar ideas to explain telepathic manifestations (e.g., Baudoin, 1900, A. Denis, 1895; Goupil, 1897; Héricourt, 1891). Léon Denis (1846–1927) wrote that:

> Thought vibrations may propagate through space like light and sounds and may affect other organisms that are in affinity with the one manifesting. The psychic waves, like hertzian waves in wireless telegraphy, propagate at a distance … (L. Denis 1900, p. 291)

There were other theoretical discussions, such as a review of theories of premonitions (Ermacora, 1899). Finally, psychologist Théodore Flournoy (1854–1920) presented speculations about mediumistic communications. He referred to the "subconscious imagination of the medium, working through recollections or latent worries" (Flournoy, 1899, p. 19).[9]

Philosopher Emile Boirac (1891–1917) presented a classification of psychic phenomena, which he called "parapsychic" (Boirac, 1893). He divided them into those that could be explained by known principles, and those that required other explanations. The first group included "psychopathy" (mental and physiological effects of suggestion and the manifestations of hysteria) and "cryptopsychism" (or intelligent subconscious action expressed through automatism). The second order were phenomena consisting of action on matter or on biological organisms under the name of "psychodynamism." Boirac believed these effects were caused by a force different from the known forces of nature. When the action took place at a great distance the phenomena were called "telepsychic," such as cases of telepathy. Finally, "hyloscopy" included phenomena where matter seemed to exert an influence on humans. This included agents such as "atmospheric currents," and magnetism from the ground and from magnets, metals, and other substances.

Overviews and Controversies

As seen in Table 47.2, there were papers on many other topics. Such variety shows that the *ASP* was open to practically all topics of psychical research.

The *ASP* also presented notices and reviews of the work of the SPR and other foreign societies.[10] Regarding the SPR this included a long review of Richard Hodgson's (1855–1905) writings about medium Leonora E. Piper (1857–1950) (Mangin, 1898), reprints of cases of telepathic hallucinations (Hallucinations Télépathiques, 1891), and papers about various phenomena such as physical mediumship (Myers, 1896), poltergeists (Podmore, 1897 1898), and clairvoyance (Sidgwick, 1891–1892). Furthermore, one of Frederic W.H. Myers' (1843–1901) multi-part papers about the subliminal mind was also translated and published in the *ASP* (Myers, 1897–1903).

In fact, Myers received much attention in the journal, something that helped to spread his ideas in France (e.g., Mangin, 1903, 1904; Review, 1903). When Myers died, two obituary notices of him appeared in the *ASP* (Erny, 1901; Richet, 1901). Richet made it clear that he admired Myers, and pointed out that the man combined the "faith of the mystics" with "scientific sagacity and precision" (Richet, 1901, p. 173).

Table 47.2. Various Topics Discussed in the *Annales des Sciences Psychiques*

Reference	Topic
De Rochas (1894)	Perceptions of "effluvia" during the hypnotic state
Boirac (1895)	Exteriorization of sensibility
Boirac (1896)	Induction of trance at a distance
Boucher (1895)	Healing case at Lourdes
De Rochas (1895a)	Exteriorization of the double
Erny (1900)	Case of premonition
De Rochas (1901)	Levitation of human body
Regnault (1901)	Role of vasomotor system in religious healing
Petrovo-Solovovo (1902)	Séances with Sambor
De Rochas (1902)	Long fasts
Joire (1903)	Case of crystal vision
Lombroso (1904)	Thought-transference
Waller (1905)	Crystal visions
Wijk (1905)	Rapping poltergeist
Durville (1908)	Projection of double
Duchatel (1914)	Psychic photography
Osty (1914)	Psychometry
Geley (1916)	Self-premonition of death
Lodge (1917)	Personal conviction of survival of death
Flammarion (1918)	Seeing the future and free will

In addition, the *ASP* provided a forum for the discussion of controversies and differences of opinions. A good example was Ochorowicz's (1896) strong critique of Richard Hodgson and other SPR researchers' investigation of Palladino at Cambridge. Another was the polemics about Richet's (1905b) observations of materializations (e.g., Maxwell 1906).[11]

Also interesting, and showing differences of opinion about conceptual and methodological issues that are part of every serious discipline, were Bozzano's (1905a) defense of critiques of the mediumship of William Stainton Moses (1839–1892), and critiques about such topics as the views of Frederic W.H. Myers (Mangin, 1903), Camille Flammarion (1842–1925) (Erny, 1900), and Enrico Morselli (1852–1929) (de Vesme, 1908).

Frequent Authors

Some individuals were frequent authors in the journal. Richet was prolific, as seen in Table 47.3. French physician and jurist Joseph Maxwell (1858–1938) also contributed several articles on various topics, among them the work on the automatisms of Michel Eugène Chevreul (1786–1889), a haunting, and intuition (Maxwell, 1904, 1905b, 1913). Another frequent contributor, Italian scholar Cesar de Vesme (1862–1938), wrote many papers about such topics as specific mediums, publications, and the phenomena of phantom armies and battles (see, respectively, de Vesme, 1905, 1908, 1915-1916).

A remarkable series of multi-part papers was published by the above mentioned Julian Ochorowicz. The papers were about the physical phenomena of Polish medium Stanislawa Tomczyk. Ochorowicz

Table 47.3. Examples of Papers published by Charles Richet in the *Annales des Sciences Psychiques*

Year of Publication	Topic
Richet (1891)	Introduction to the journal
Richet (1892a)	Reply to a critic
Richet (1892b)	The future of psychology
Richet (1893b)	Statistical analysis of an ESP test
Richet (1900)	Case of a musical prodigy
Richet (1901)	Obituary of F. W. H. Myers
Richet (1902)	Case of near-death experience from antiquity
Richet (1903)	Case of premonition
Richet (1905b)	Materialization phenomena
Richet (1905c)	Automatic writing in Greek
Richet (1908a)	Call for premonition cases
Richet (1908b)	Incredulity
Richet (1914)	On reason and science
Richet (1919)	Lucidity

included in the papers many observations about telekinesis, the photographic detection of "fluidic" hands and forces, and speculations about a variety of forces believed to exteriorize from the medium to produce phenomena (Ochorowicz, 1909a, 1909b, 1910, 1911, 1911–1912, 1912). Another example was Italian student of psychic phenomena Ernesto Bozzano (1862–1943). He published several papers about topics such as animals and psychic phenomena (Bozzano, 1905b), deathbed visions (Bozzano, 1906), symbolism and psychic phenomena (Bozzano, 1907), "bilocation" (Bozzano, 1911), and premonitions (Bozzano, 1912–1913).

The Annales and the Félix Alcan Publishing House

Up until 1904 the *ASP* was published by Félix Alcan, a well-known French publishing house that produced and disseminated countless works in philosophy and in the natural and social sciences (Tesniere, 1990, 2001). In addition to the *ASP* the press published several journals such as the *Annales de l'École Libre des Sciences Politiques,* the *Bulletin de la Sociétè de Psychologie Physiologique*, the *Revue Historique*, the *Revue de Medicine*, and the *Revue Philosophique de la France et de l'Étranger*.

Alcan published several series of books. Some of them were the *Bibliothèque de Philosophie Contemporaine* (Library of Contemporary Philosophy), which in addition to philosophy included psychiatry, criminology, and sociology, as well as the *Collection Historique des Grands Philosophes* (Historical Collection of the Great Philosophers), the *Bibliothèque d'Histoire Contemporaine* (Library of Contemporary History), and the *Bibliothèque Scientifique International* (International Scientific Library). Many eminent authors were represented in these collections. Among the Frenchmen, and in addition to Charles Richet and Pierre Janet, were Gilbert Ballet (1853–1916), Henri Bergson (1859–1941), Alfred Binet (1857–1911), Charles Féré (1852–1907), Paul Janet (1823–1899), Etienne J. Marey (1830–1904), and Hippolyte Taine (1828–1893). Foreign translated authors included Alexander

Bain (1818–1903), John Stuart Mill (1806–1873), Arthur Schopenhauer (1788–1860), Herbert Spencer (1820–1903), James Sully (1842–1923), John Tyndall (1820–1893), and Wilhem Wundt (1832–1920).

In addition, the press published psychical research books. This included abridged translations of Gurney, Myers, and Podmore's *Phantasms of the Living* (1886, 1891), and of Myers' *Human Personality and Its Survival of Bodily Death* (1903, 1905). There were, of course, other works on the topic published by Alcan that were originally written in French (e.g., Flournoy, 1900, Gyel, 1899).[12]

The prominence of the publisher helped bring attention to the *ASP*. Alcan advertised the journal widely in the catalog of its works included at the end of many books.[13] In addition, there were advertisements of the journal in English-language publications such as *Mind* (Advertisement, 1896), and the *Philosophical Review* (Advertisement, 1898).

Citations of the *Annales*

In France, the journal was criticized for having the word "science" in its title, because the *ASP* was seen as a publication "which contains but tales" (Verdier, 1892, p. 707). However, the critic recognized that the editors would perform a good service for science if they could uncover the laws behind telepathy and other phenomena.

Most books on psychic phenomena published in France after the founding of the *ASP* cited or mentioned the journal. Examples include the publications of figures associated with spiritism and psychical research (e.g., Bois, 1907, p. 22, 175, 369; Delanne, 1897, p. 60; Flammarion, 1900, p. 159, 160; Maxwell, 1905a, p. 16, 93, 170). Even critics paid attention to the journal (e.g., Grasset, 1908, p. 21, 22, 52, 57). Attention to the *ASP* continued even after the journal had ceased publication (e.g., Richet, 1922, p. 19,735; Warcollier, 1921, p. 40, 55, 128, 184).

While the *ASP* was very important in France, it also received some attention in other countries. In England it was mentioned in the *Journal of the Society for Psychical Research* (*Annales des Sciences Psychiques*, 1891). In the United States a writer in the Monist showed some reservations about the cases reported in the journal (Arreat, 1891). Some years later another writer in the same publication considered that, like the *Proceedings of the Society for Psychical Research*, the *ASP* presented a "record of the highest distinction for observations of this kind" (Vaschide, 1902, p. 282).

"The French," wrote someone in charge of news on the journal *Medical Record*, published in New York, "have joined in the investigation of ghosts, telepathy, haunted houses, etc., and have begun the publication of a journal called *Annales des Sciences Psychiques* in which to record their work. ... We trust that their work will be fruitful" (News of the Week, 1891, p. 46).

Several writers paid attention to the nineteenth-century issues of the *ASP*, as did Frederic W.H. Myers in his *Human Personality and Its Survival of Bodily Death* (1903, p. Vol. 1, p. 533, Vol. 2, p. 136, 212). Some, like Andrew Lang (1894, p. 159), Edmund Parish (1897, p. 85), and Frank Podmore (1894, p. 80–81, 119–120, 140–142) cited cases from the *ASP* in their writings. William James (1894) reviewed an 1893 issue of the *ASP* in the *Psychological Review*, bringing the publication to the attention of American psychologists.

Issues of the journal were listed in some library catalogs (e.g., *A List of Periodicals*, 1897, p. 9). It was also included in several bibliographies (e.g., Bibliographie der Psycho-Physiologischen, 1898, p. 353–354; Fletcher, 1891, p. 283). Articles from the journal were listed in the *Revue Scientifique*.

The *ASP* was featured in the journal among the publications of disciplines such as biology, geography, physiology, and zoology in a section about the main periodicals presenting original essays (Bibliographie: Sommaires, 1891, p. 223). All of this shows that the *ASP* was known beyond psychical research circles.

One can only speculate on the impact the journal had on specific individuals, particularly those involved in psychical research. One individual about whom we have information is Italian student of psychic phenomena Ernesto Bozzano. He wrote in an autobiographical essay:

> In the year 1891 … I had my initiation into metapsychical research, Professor Ribot, director of the *Philosophical Review* [*Revue Philosophique*], having sent me the first number of "The Annals of Psychical Science," to read and send him my judgment upon. I read: Therein was talk of telepathy, of clairvoyance, and of telekinesis. I was scientifically scandalized! I wrote in this tone to Professor Ribot. He answered, exhorting me to re-read and reflect more quietly, for he saw that the existence of the facts could not be denied. In deference to the Director of the *Revue Philosophique*, I re-read, thought it over, and decided to acquire works of this nature. Result: the complete defeat and demolition of my *misoneism*. (Bozzano, 1924, p. 153–154).

A Look into the 1901–1919 Period

During the twentieth century the role of the *ASP* in French psychical research grew and changed in quality. Dariex wrote in 1901 that the journal, initially created to examine psychical phenomena with impartiality, and to present them to the scientific world with credibility, had succeeded in its mission by careful consideration of phenomena with little theoretical discussion. The *ASP* was now ready to enter a new phase of existence:

> We will not abandon this line of conduct and the *Annales des Sciences Psychiques* will continue to be what they have been; but now that the goal has been accomplished, now that we have done all that we could to bring attention to these phenomena and their study, we will abandon our strictness—what some impatient minds would say is our exclusiveness—and we will widen our program. (Dariex 1901, p. 2)

In 1904, the *ASP* incorporated the *Revue des Études Psychiques* and began to appear every month (as opposed to every two months). Dariex was the only person listed as director but it was stated that Cesar Baudi De Vesme (1862–1938), formerly director of the *Revue*, became editor-in-chief of the *ASP* (Dariex 1904).[14] A new editorial committee was formed. It consisted of Camille Flammarion, Marcel Mangin (1852–1915), Joseph Maxwell, and Albert de Rochas for France. In addition, the following men represented other countries: William Crookes (1832–1919), Cesare Lombroso, Enrico Morselli (1852–1929), Julian Ochorowicz, Francesco Porro (1861–1937), and Albert von Schrenck-Notzing. However, Richet's name continued to appear on the cover of later issues as one of the directors of the journal.

An English edition of the *ASP* appeared between 1905 and 1910 (Crabtree, 1988, p. 302). The cover of the first bound volume (January-June 1905) lists De Vesme as editor, but in subsequent years the editor is listed as Laura I. Finch.[15] Dariex and Richet are listed as Directors and there is an editorial committee of eleven individuals, among them the above-mentioned De Rochas, Lombroso, Maxwell, Ochorowicz, and Schrenck-Notzing. While there was overlap between the French and the

English editions, they were not identical. The order of the articles varied and the sections of news and comments were also somewhat different.

In 1908, the *ASP* became the official publication of the Sociétè Universelle d'Études Psychiques (SUEP), a society founded in Lille in 1901 by physician Paul Joire (1856–1930) to study psychical phenomena scientifically (La fusion, 1914). The journal included many accounts of conferences, meetings, and research related to the SUEP (e.g., Actes de la Sociétè, 1908a, 1908b).

With this new format, the *ASP* became more popular and accessible for the French general public. Its pages now had evocative pictures and illustrations, news, and a more varied content. Lachapelle (2011) has argued that such changes led to a loss of the original purpose of the journal. She wrote:

> Gone were the days when the journal limited most of its activities to the sober discussions of telepathic occurrences; it had become a truly popular enterprise. The more accessible it became, however, the less likely it was to incorporate the scientific world. Ultimately, the creators of the *Annales* failed in the mission they had set out for themselves. (Lachapelle, 2011, p. 91)

While it is true that the topics were more varied and that there were many illustrations, Lachapelle's perspective is somewhat exaggerated. Even reports of sensational phenomena, such as papers about materializations and their photographs in the cases of mediums Marthe Beraud (Richet, 1905b) and Eusapia Palladino (de Fontenay, 1908), were attempts to learn about these phenomena. In other words, the phenomena, and some of the illustrations, may have been sensational in appearance, but the intention of the authors was a serious and critical one, even if many were not convinced. While it is possible to criticize methodology, it is problematic to equate seriousness and scientific outlook on the basis of "sober discussions of telepathic phenomena" when the subject matter of the field also included physical phenomena that appeared incredible to many. Was the journal supposed to ignore some topics just because they seemed sensational to some, or because they were difficult to investigate scientifically?

Regardless of methodological and interpretation aspects, and of the illustrations, several twentieth-century authors presented various attempts to learn from the phenomena. In addition to the above-mentioned work by Bozzano and Ochorowicz, we may mention publications about premonitions (Geley, 1916) and lucidity (Osty, 1914). The investigations of Ochorowicz (1910, 1911, 1911–1912, 1912), in which he tried to determine empirically the characteristics of a force he believed was exteriorized by medium Stanislawa Tomczyk, represent one of the most systematic observations published in the *ASP*.

The *ASP* lost Dariex, its founding editor, after his having been involved with the *ASP* for twenty years. He was replaced by De Vesme. In later years, during World War I, the journal's activities were considerably slowed down and only a few issues appeared between 1914 and 1918. The last issue was published in 1919. At that time, the Institut Métapsychique International (IMI), which had just been created, took over the affairs of the *ASP* and the SUEP (De Vesme, 1924).

The transition from the *ASP* to the *Revue Métapsychique* (RM), the journal published by IMI, was difficult because IMI wanted to have a high intellectual content with articles and experimental reports written by the elite researchers.[16] The place left to popular science, more prominent in the *ASP*, was reduced. It was suggested that readers of the *ASP* would subscribe to the *RM*, with no competition between them. But De Vesme (1921–1922) tried to negotiate with the board of IMI a merging of the *ASP* and the *RM* in which he would obtain some financial compensation. Although by this time the *ASP* was no longer published, De Vesme affirmed that he would start its publication again because it was his "moral duty."

Concluding Remarks

Like so many other journals dedicated to psychical research, the *ASP* belongs to a previous generation and thus has been forgotten by many current students of the subject. The same may be said about the work of authors represented in the journal such as Bozzano, Boirac, Dariex, de Rochas, Ermacora, Ochorowicz, and Richet, among many others.

Our comments by no means represent all that can be said about the journal. Certainly, more can be written about its content. This not only includes a discussion of the topics emphasized, but also of the methodologies and approaches represented, and the affairs of the SUEP. In addition, there is more to say about the contributors. Even the papers of such a frequently discussed figure as Richet have not been studied in detail (see Table 47.3).

The journal, or its editors, did much to inform French readers about foreign developments. For example, there were many news reports about the SPR, and translations of articles written by SPR members. In fact, it may be argued that the *ASP* was one of the vehicles by which British psychical research was spread in France.

It is a matter of speculation how much influence the *ASP* had on the development of French psychical research. One author has stated that the journal assisted in the process of bringing together "scattered and non-centralized researches" about psychic phenomena (Marmin, 2001, p. 157). Another was more emphatic and perhaps overstated her case when she said: "Psychical research officially began in France with the founding of the *Annales des Sciences Psychiques* in 1891" (Lachapelle, 2011, p. 86). There is no question that the journal stimulated and supported the field in France by providing a forum of discussion separate from spiritist and occult periodicals. In addition, the *Annales des Sciences Psychiques* was one of the factors that assisted the development of later French studies of psychic phenomena, when the former "science psychique" was called "la métapsychique," showing the continuous influence of Richet.[17]

Notes

1 For reviews see Brower (2010), Edelman (1995), Lachapelle (2011), Meheust (1999a, 1999b), Monroe (2008), and Plas (2000).

2 On conventional explanations of mediumship in France, see Le Maléfan (1999), and, to some extent, Alvarado, Machado, Zangari, and Zingrone (2007). On Janet, see Ellenberger (1970) and Carroy and Plas (2000).

3 For general studies of Richet see Estingoy (2003), Lewer (2006), Schneider (2001), and Wolf (1993). His involvement with psychical research has been discussed by several authors (e.g., Brower, 2010, p. Chapter 4; Le Malefan, 1999, pp. 85–88, 273–278; Lachapelle, 2011; Monroe, 2008, p. 208, 211, 253; Plas, 2000, pp. 54–55, 89–93, 99–109, 125–126, 150–154; Tabori, 1972, p. 98–132).

4 On the Société, see Plas (2000). Regarding the Congress, see Alvarado (2006a, 2010b) and Nicolas and Meunier (2002).

5 The *Revue* was founded by philosopher and psychologist Théodule Ribot (1839–1916). In addition to papers about topics such as philosophy, sociology, and education, the journal represented the new empirical psychology in France (Bertolini, 1991; Nicolas, 2002, p. 113–118). The *Revue* carried important papers about psychic phenomena during the nineteenth century, such as those of Janet (1886) and Richet (1884).

6 In England SPR leaders asked the general public to send them cases, as seen in the pages of *The Times* (Advertisement, 1883; Gurney, 1883). They also issued instructions to conduct experimental work (To Members, 1883).

7 To some extent, such an attitude toward theory was followed by Richet in later publications (e.g., Richet, 1922). But this does not mean that Richet was completely theory-free, as one of us has discussed before (Alvarado, 2008a, 2008b).
8 This paper has been summarized elsewhere (Alvarado, 2010a). On the topic of magnetic, psychic, or vital forces used in the past to explain psychic phenomena, see Alvarado (2006b).
9 Flournoy (1900, 1911) is well-known for having developed these ideas further in later publications.
10 SPR work was also disseminated in France through the translation of works (Gurney, Myers, and Podmore, 1891, Myers 1905), and through discussions of investigations in other publications (Delanne, 1897, p. 91–93, 143, 145–149; Gibier, 1891, p. 36–39; Richet, 1884, p. 633–635).
11 This was probably the most controversial episode in Richet's career in psychical research. For an overview, see Le Maléfan (2002).
12 E. Gyel was the pseudonym of French physician and psychical researcher Gustave Geley (1868–1924).
13 Some examples include Berthelot (1891), Binet (1892), Lefèvre (1893), and Proal (1892).
14 The *Revue* was the French version of the Italian *Rivista di Studi Psichici*, which was founded in 1895 by Giovanni Battista Ermacora and by Giorgio Finzi (Alvarado, Biondi, & Kramer, 2006, pp. 67–68). During 1902–1903, the *Revue* was the French version of the *Rivista*, and it ceased publication in 1903 (we owe these last two points to Massimo Biondi). On De Vesme, see Warcollier (1938).
15 Finch was said to be the Mme. X who produced automatic scripts for Richet (1905c). See Bozzano (1932, p. 46) on her psychic abilities. See Fodor (n.d./1966, p. 61).
16 The first volume of the Revue Métapsychique appeared under the title Bulletin de l'InstitutMétapsychique International.
17 Richet (1905a) presented the term *métapsychique* in his Presidential Address to the Society for Psychical Research. While he admitted there was a precedent for the use of the term (Richet, 1905a, p. 13, footnote), it was popularized by his influence. His later and extremely influential *Traité de Métapsychique* (1922), published by Félix Alcan, also helped to popularize the term in later years. The term was adopted by the Institut Métapsychique International (founded in 1919), and used in its journal. Many French authors used the term in articles and books (e.g., Maxwell 1907, Sudre 1926).

References

Actes de la Sociétè Universelle d'Études Psychiques (1908a). *Annales des Sciences Psychiques, 18,* 198–204.

Actes de la Sociétè Universelle d'Études Psychiques (1908b). *Annales des Sciences Psychiques, 18,* 237–244.

Advertisement (1883, December 25). *The Times*, p. 1.

Advertisement (1896). *Mind, 5,* (unnumbered frontmatter).

Advertisement (1898). *Philosophical Review, 7,* (unnumbered frontmatter).

Aksakof, A., Schiaparelli, G., Du Prel, C., Brofferio, A., Gerosa, G., Ermacora, G. B., Finzi, G., Richet, C., & Lombroso, C. (1893). Rapport de la commission reunie a Milan pour l'etude des phénomènes psychiques. *Annales des Sciences Psychiques, 3,* 39–64.

Alvarado, C. S. (2006a). Aspects of the history of parapsychology: I. Psychical research at the 1889 International Congress of Physiological Psychology.

Alvarado, C. S. (2006b). Human radiations: Concepts of force in mesmerism, spiritualism, and psychical research. *Journal of the Society for Psychical Research, 70,* 138–162.

Alvarado, C. S. (2008a). Charles Richet on "The Limits of Psychic and Metapsychic Science." *Psypioneer, 4,* 198–207.

Alvarado, C. S. (2008b). Note on Charles Richet's "La Suggestion Mentale et le Calcul des Probabilites" (1884). *Journal of Scientific Exploration, 22,* 543–548.

Alvarado, C. S. (2009). Modern animal magnetism: The work of Alexandre Barèty, Emile Boirac, and Julian Ochorowicz. *Australian Journal of Clinical and Experimental Hypnosis, 37,* 1–15.

Alvarado, C. S. (2010a). Correspondence: Julian Ochorowicz on Eusapia Palladino, dissociation, and mediumistic fraud. *Journal of the Society for Psychical Research, 74,* 57–60.

Alvarado, C. S. (2010b). Nineteenth-century suggestion and magnetism: Hypnosis at the International Congress of Physiological Psychology (1889). *Contemporary Hypnosis, 27*, 48–60.

Alvarado, C. S., Biondi, M., & Kramer, W. (2006). Historical notes on psychic phenomena in specialised journals. *European Journal of Parapsychology, 21*, 58–87.

Alvarado, C. S., Machado, F. R., Zangari, W., & Zingrone, N. L. (2007). Perspectivas históricas da influência da mediunidade na construção de idéias psicológicas e psiquiátricas. *Revista de Psiquiatria Clínica, 34* (Supplement 1), 42–53.

Annales des Sciences Psychiques (1891). *Journal of the Society for Psychical Research, 5*, 45–46.

Arréat, L. (1891). Literary correspondence. *Monist, 1*, 590–596.

Barety, A. (1887). *Le Magnétisme Animal: Étudié Sous le Nom de Force neurique Rayonnante et Circulante dans ses Propriétés Physiques, Physiologiques et Thérapeutiques.* Octave Doin.

Baudoin, M. (1900). Un cas de télépathie: Manifestations d'une mourante sur sa soeur a l'état de veille constatée par un médicin en visite et charactérisée par un phénomène physique. *Annales des Sciences Psychiques, 10*, 129–142.

Berthelot, M. (1891). *La synthèse chimique* (7th ed.). Félix Alcan.

Bertolini, M. M. (1991). Il Pensiero e la Memoria: Filosofi a e Psicologia nella "Revue Philosophique" di Théodule Ribot (1876–1916). Franco Angeli.

Bibliographie der Psycho-Physiologischen Literatur des Jahres 1897 (1898). *Zeitschrift für Psychologie und Physiologie der Sinnesorgane, 18*, 337–468.

Bibliographie: Sommaires des Principaux Recueils de Mémoires Originaux (1891). *Revue Scientifique, 48*, 223–224.

Binet, A. (1892). *Les altérations de la personnalité.* Félix Alcan.

Boirac, E. (1893). *Essai de classification des phénomènes parapsychiques. Annales des Sciences Psychiques, 3*, 341–354.

Boirac, E. (1895). Expériences sur l'extériorisation de la sensibilité. *Annales des Sciences Psychiques, 5*, 169–173.

Boirac, E. (1896). Un cas de somneil provoqué a distance. *Annales des Sciences Psychiques, 6*, 56–58.

Bois, J. (1907). *Le miracle moderne.* Société d'Éditions Littéraires et Artistiques.

Bottazzi, F. (1907). Dans les régions inexplorées de la biologie humaine: Observations et expériences sur Eusapia Paladino. *Annales des Sciences Psychiques, 17*, 553–571, 645–663, 681–704, 749–770.

Boucher, Dr. (1895). Quèlques cas de guérisons dites miraculeuses: I. Lourdes et un cas de tuberculose aiguë généralisée. *Annales des Sciences Psychiques, 5*, 156–158.

Bourru, H., & Burot, P. (1887). La Suggestion Mentale et l'Action a Distance des Substances Toxiques et Médicamenteuses. J. -B. Baillière.

Bozzano, E. (1905a). Pour la défense de la mémoire de William Stainton Moses. *Annales des Sciences Psychiques, 15*, 76–129.

Bozzano, E. (1905b). Perceptions psychiques et animaux. *Annales des Sciences Psychiques, 15*, 422–473.

Bozzano, E. (1906). Des apparitions des défunts au lit de mort. *Annales des Sciences Psychiques, 16*, 144–182.

Bozzano, E. (1907). Symbolisme et phénomènes métapsychiques. *Annales des Sciences Psychiques, 17*, 617–644, 705–739.

Bozzano, E. (1911). Considerations et hypothéses sur les phénomènes de "bilocation." *Annales des Sciences Psychiques, 21*, 65–72, 109–116, 143–152, 166–172.

Bozzano, E. (1912–1913). Des phénomènes prémonitoires. *Annales des Sciences Psychiques, 22*, 257–265, 295–309, 324–339, 363–373, *23*, 15–24, 47–57, 77–85, 109–117, 140–148, 172–176, 202–210, 232–243, 261–271.

Bozzano, E. (1924). Autobiographical sketch. *Journal of the American Society for Psychical Research, 18*, 153–155.

Bozzano, E. (1932). *Polyglot mediumship (Xenoglossy).* Rider.

Brower, M. B. (2010). *Unruly spirits: The science of psychic phenomena in modern France.* University of Illinois Press.

Carrington, H. (1907). *The physical phenomena of Spiritualism: Fraudulent and genuine.* Herbert B. Turner.

Carroy, J. (2004). Playing with signatures: The young Charles Richet. In M. S. Micale (Ed.), *The mind of modernism: Medicine, psychology, and the cultural arts in Europe and America, 1880–1940* (pp. 217–249). Stanford University Press.

Carroy, J., & Plas, R. (2000). La genèse de la notion de dissociation chez Pierre Janet et ses enjeux. *Évolution Psychiatrique*, *65*, 9–18.
Ciolfi, E. (1891). Les expériences de Naples. *Annales des Sciences Psychiques*, *1*, 326–332.
Crabtree, A. (Ed.) (1988). *Animal magnetism, early hypnotism, and psychical research, 1766–1925: An annotated bibliography*. Kraus International.
Dariex, X. (1891). De la méthode dans les observations de télépathie. *Annales des Sciences Psychiques*, *1*, 9–30.
Dariex, X. (1892a). [Reply to letter]. *Annales des Sciences Psychiques*, *2*, 63–64.
Dariex, X. (1892b). Expériences sur les mouvements d'objets sans contact. *Annales des Sciences Psychiques*, *2*, 189–208.
Dariex, X. (1893). Quelques expériences sur certains phénomènes d'ordre physique. *Annales des Sciences Psychiques*, *3*, 32–38.
Dariex, X. (1894). Avant-propos. *Annales des Sciences Psychiques*, *4*, 1–2.
Dariex, X. (1896). Expériences sur Eusapia Paladino faite a Paris en Septembre 1896. *Annales des Sciences Psychiques*, *6*, 321–374.
Dariex, X. (1900). De diverse expériences sur les mouvements d'objets matériels provoqués sans contact par une force psychique agissant a distance. *Annales des Sciences Psychiques*, *10*, 257–266.
Dariex, X. (1901). Avant-propos. *Annales des Sciences Psychiques*, *11*, 1–2.
Dariex, X. (1904). Importantes modifications introduites dans les Annales des Sciences Psychiques. *Annales des Sciences Psychiques*, *14*, 321.
De Fontenay, G. (1908). Le fraude et l'hypothèse de l'hallucination dans l'étude des phénomènes produits by Eusapia Paladino. *Annales des Sciences Psychiques*, *18*, 49–57.
De Gasparin, Cte A. (1854). *Des tables tournantes: Du surnaturel en général et des esprits* (2 volumes). E. Dentu.
Delanne, G. (1897). *Le phénomène spirite: Témoignages des savants* (5th ed.). Chamuel.
Denis, A. (1895). Essai d'une théorie de la télépathie. *Annales des Sciences Psychiques*, *5*, 14–32.
Denis, L. (1900). Psychologie expérimentale: Phénomènes d'extériorisation et de dédoublement. *Annales des Sciences Psychiques*, *10*, 291–294.
De Rochas, A. (1887). *Les forces non défi nies: Recherches historiques et expérimentales*. G. Masson.
De Rochas, A. (1894). Objectivité des effluves percus sous forme de lumière dans l'état hypnotique. *Annales des Sciences Psychiques*, *4*, 129–162.
De Rochas, A. (1895a). Les fantômes des vivants. *Annales des Sciences Psychiques*, *5*, 257–275.
De Rochas, A. (1895b). Review of Essai de Spiritisme Scientifique, by D. Metzger, and Le Psychisme Expérimental, by A. Erny. *Annales des Sciences Psychiques*, 5, 119–126.
De Rochas, A. (1897). Les expériences de Choisy–Yvrec (prés Bordeaux) du 2 au 14 octobre 1896. *Annales des Sciences Psychiques*, *7*, 6–28.
De Rochas, A. (1901). La lévitation du corps humain. *Annales des Sciences Psychiques*, *11*, 17–47.
De Rochas, A. (1902). Les longs jeunes. *Annales des Sciences Psychiques*, *12*, 65–96.
De Rochas, A. (1908). Les mains fluidiques d'Eusapia. *Annales des Sciences Psychiques*, *18*, 277–283.
Desbeaux, E. (1899). Trois cas de prémonition. *Annales des Sciences Psychiques*, *9*, 65–70.
De Vesme, C. (1905). Étude critique des séances du médium Ch. Bailey à Milan e à Rome. *Annales des Sciences Psychiques*, *15*, 218–242.
De Vesme, C. (1908). Le nouvel ouvrage du Professeur H. Morselli "Psychologie et Spiritisme." *Annales des Sciences Psychiques*, *18*, 341–349.
De Vesme, C. (1915–1916). Armées, flottes et combats fantômatiques. *Annales des Sciences Psychiques*, *25*, 247–261, *26*, 1–12.
De Vesme, C. (1921–1922). Letters to Gustave Geley about the Institut Métapsychique International's absorption of the *Annales des Sciences Psychiques*. Archives of the Institut Métapsychique International. Box 3, dossier 8.
De Vesme, C. (1924). Aux anciens abonnés des *Annales des Sciences Psychiques*. *Revue Métapsychique*, *4*, 172–173.
Duchatel, E. (1914). Quelques nouvelles expériences de photographie de la pensée. *Annales des Sciences Psychiques*, *24*, 109–122.
Durville, H. (1908). Nouvelles expériences sur les fantômes des vivants à la Société Magnétique de France. *Annales des Sciences Psychiques*, *18*, 224–230.

Edelman, N. (1995). *Voyantes, Guérisseuses et Visionnaires en France 1785–1914.* Albin Michel.
Ellenberger, H. F. (1970). *The discovery of the unconscious: The history and evolution of dynamic psychiatry.* Basic Books.
Ermacora, G. B. (1895). Rêves télépathiques. *Annales des Sciences Psychiques, 5*, 321–349.
Ermacora, G. B. (1899). Sur la possibilité des théories rationnnelles de la prémonition. *Annales des Sciences Psychiques, 9*, 38–57.
Erny, A. (1900). Cas curieux de premonitions. *Annales des Sciences Psychiques, 10*, 22–35.
Erny, A. (1901). In memoriam F. W. Myers. *Annales des Sciences Psychiques, 11*, 179–183.
Estingoy, P. (2003). De la creativite chez le chercher: Un regard transversal sur l'oeuvre de Charles Richet. *Histoire des Sciences Medicales, 37*, 489–499.
Figuier, L. (1860). Histoire du Merveilleux dans les Temps Modernes (4 vols). L. Hachette.
Flammarion, C. (1900). *L'Inconnu: The Unknown.* Harper and Brothers.
Flammarion, C. (1918). La prévision de l'avenir et le libre arbitre. *Annales des Sciences Psychiques, 27*, 42–43.
Fletcher, R. (1891). A quarterly bibliography of anthropological literature. *American Anthropologist, 4*, 283–289.
Flournoy, T. (1899). Genèse de quelques prétendus messages spirites. *Annales des Sciences Psychiques, 9*, 199–216.
Flournoy, T. (1900). *Des Indes à la Planète Mars.* Félix Alcan.
Flournoy, T. (1911). *Spiritism and psychology*. Harper & Brothers.
Fodor, N. (1966). *Encyclopedia of psychic science*. University Books. (Original work published, circa 1933)
La fusion de la S.U.E.P. avec la Société des annales des sciences psychiques (1914). *Annales des Sciences Psychiques, 24*, 213–217.
Geley, G. (1916) Un cas remarquable d'auto-premonition de mort. *Annales des Sciences Psychiques, 26*, 125–130.
Gibier, P. (1891). *Le Spiritisme (Fakirisme Occidental)* (third revised edition). Octave Doin.
Goupil, A. (1897). Expériences de transmissions mentales avec M. Lauriel (Lauri-Ali). *Annales des Sciences Psychiques, 7*, 129–138.
Grasset, J. (1908). *L'occultisme hier et aujourd'hui* (second revised edition). Coulet et Fils.
Gurney, E. (1883, December 17). The Society for Psychical Research. *The Times*, p. 10.
Gurney, E., Myers, F. W. H., & Podmore, F. (1886). *Phantasms of the living* (2 vols.). Trübner.
Gurney, E., Myers, F. W. H., & Podmore, F. (1891). *Les hallucinations télépathique.* Félix Alcan.
Gyel, E. (1899). *L'Être Subconscient*. Paris: Félix Alcan.
Hallucinations Télépathiques (1891). *Annales des Sciences Psychiques, 1*, 41–60, 163–177, 362–370.
Héricourt, J. (1891). Review of *Les Hallucinations Télépatiques*, by E. Gurney, F. W. H. Myers, and F. Podmore. *Annales des Sciences Psychiques, 1*, 313–319.
Héricourt, J. (1895). Observation de pressentiment. *Annales des Sciences Psychiques, 5*, 155.
Imoda, Docteur [E.] (1908). Action d'Eusapia Paladino sur l'electroscope. *Annales des Sciences Psychiques, 18*, 196–197.
James, W. (1894). Review of *Annales des Sciences Psychiques*, September-October 1893. *Psychological Review, 1*, 317–318.
Janet, P. (1886). Note sur quelques phénomènes de somnambulisme. *Revue Philosophique de la France et de l'Étranger, 21*, 190–198.
Janet, P. (1889). *L'automatisme psychologique: Essai de psychologie expérimentale sur les formes inférieures de l'activité humaine*. Félix Alcan.
Joire, P. (1897). De la suggestion mentale: Expériences nouvelles. *Annales des Sciences Psychiques, 7*, 193–212.
Joire, P. (1903). Expérience de vision dans le cristal. *Annales des Sciences Psychiques, 13, 129*–130.
Kardec, A. (1863). *Spiritisme experimental: Le livre des mediums ou guide des mediums et des évocateurs* (sixth edition). Didier.
Lachapelle, S. (2011). Investigating the supernatural: From Spiritism and occultism to psychical research and metapsychics in France, 1853–1931. Johns Hopkins University Press.
Lang, A. (1894). *Cock lane and common-sense*. Longmans, Green.
Lefèvre, A. (1893). *Les races et les langues.* Félix Alcan.

Le Maléfan, P. (1999). Folie et Spiritisme: Histoire du Discourse Psychopathologique sur la Pratique du Spiritisme, ses Abords et ses Avatars (1850–1950). L'Hartmattan.
Le Malefan, P. (2002). Richet Chasseur de Fantômes: L'Épisode de la Villa Carmen. In B. Bensaude-Vincent & C. Blondel (Eds.), *Des Savants Face à l'Occulte 1870–1940*. La Découverte.
Lewer, N. (2006). Charles Richet: Medical scientist, innovator, peace thinker, and savant. *Medicine, Conflict, & Survival, 22*, 145–158.
A List of Periodicals, Newspapers, Transactions, and Other Serial Publications Currently Received in the Principal Libraries of Boston and Vicinity (1897). Trustees of the Public Library.
Littré, E. (1856). Des tables parlantes et des esprits frappeurs. *Revue des Deux Mondes, 26,* 847–872.
Lodge, O. (1917). Comment j'ai acquis la conviction de la survivance humaine. *Annales des Sciences Psychiques, 27*, 17–22.
Lombroso, C. (1892). Le spiritisme et la psychiatrie: Explication psychiatrique des certain faits spirites. *Annales des Sciences Psychiques, 2*, 143–151.
Lombroso, C. (1904). Transmission de la pensée. *Annales des Sciences Psychiques, 14*, 257–275.
Lombroso, C. (1908). Eusapia Paladino et le spiritisme. *Annales des Sciences Psychiques, 18*, 29–37.
Mangin, M. (1898). Compte rendu analytique des expériences de M. Hodgson avec Mme Piper. *Annales des Sciences Psychiques, 8*, 228–254, 268–294.
Mangin, M. (1903). Objections aux théories de Myers. *Annales des Sciences Psychiques, 13*, 240–244.
Mangin, M. (1904). La personnalité humaine et sa survivance après la most du corps. *Annales des Sciences Psychiques, 14*, 35–55.
Marmin, N. (2001). Métapsychique et psychologie en France (1880–1940). *Revue d'Histoire des Sciences Humaines, 4*, 145–171.
Maxwell, J. (1904). L'étude de Chevreul sur la baguette divinatoire et les tables tournantes. *Annales des Sciences Psychiques, 14*, 276–290, 337–358.
Maxwell, J. (1905a). *Metapsychical phenomena: Methods and observations*. Duckworth. Original work published in French, 1903.
Maxwell, J. (1905b). Note sur quelques faits anormaux survenus dans une maison de environs de Bordeaux. *Annales des Sciences Psychiques, 15*, 42–45.
Maxwell, J. (1906). Les séances de la Villa Carmen et leurs critiques. *Annales des Sciences Psychiques, 16*.
Maxwell, J. (1907). Psychologie et métapsychique. *L'Année Psychologique, 13*, 100–113.
Maxwell, J. (1913). Le problème de l'intuition. *Annales des Sciences Psychiques, 23*, 310–315, 342–346.
Méheust, B. (1999a). *Somnambulisme et médiumnité (1784–1930). vol. 1.: le défi du magnétisme animal.* Institut Synthélabo pour de Progrès de la Connaissance.
Méheust, B. (1999b). *Somnambulisme et médiumnité (1784–1930): Vol. 2: Le Choc des Sciences Psychiques.* Institut Synthélabo pour de Progrès de la Connaissance.
To Members and Associates of the Society for Psychical Research: Circular No. 1. (1883). *Proceedings of the Society for Psychical Research, 1*, 295–302.
Monroe, J. W. (2008). *Laboratories of faith: Mesmerism, spiritism, and occultism in modern France*. Cornell University Press.
Morice, M. G. (1892–1893). Exposé des phénomènes étranges du Chateau de T. *Annales des Sciences Psychiques, 2*, 211–223, *3*, 65–90.
Morselli, H. (1907). Eusapia Paladino et la réalité des phénomenènes médiumniques. *Annales des Sciences Psychiques, 17*, 225–264.
Myers, F. W. H. (1896). Expériences de W. Stainton Moses. *Annales des Sciences Psychiques, 6,* 204–229, 289–304, 350–369.
Myers, F. W. H. (1897–1903). De la conscience subliminale. *Annales des Sciences Psychiques, 7*, 276–301, *8*, 170–185, 196–227, *9*, 152–172, 225–236, 290–319, *10*, 36–52, 96–118, 332–348, *11*, 184–192, 223–239, 278–301, *12*, 337–353, *13*, 209–240.
Myers, F. W. H. (1903). *Human personality and its survival of bodily death* (2 vols.). Longmans, Green.
Myers, F. W. H. (1905). *La Personnalité humaine, sa survivance, ses manifestations supranormales.* Félix Alcan.
News of the Week (1891). *Medical Record, 40*, 46–48.
Nicolas, S. (2002). *Histoire de la psychologie Française: Naissance d'une nouvelle science*. In Press Editions.

Nicolas, S., & Meunier, F. (2002). The causes, course, and consequences of the first international psychology congress in Paris in 1889 [in Italian]. *Teorie & Modelli*, *7*, 19–40.
Ochorowicz, J. (1896). La question de la fraude dans les expériences avec Eusapia Paladino. *Annales des Sciences Psychiques*, *6*, 79–123.
Ochorowicz, J. (1909a). Un nouveau phénomène médiumique. *Annales des Sciences Psychiques*, *19*, 1–10, 45–51, 65–77, 97–106, 129–133.
Ochorowicz, J. (1909b). Les phénomènes lumineux et la photographie de l'invisible. *Annales des Sciences Psychiques*, *19*, 193–201, 235–241, 275–282, 298–300, 334–339.
Ochorowicz, J. (1910). Les rayons rigides et les rayons Xx: Études expérimentales. *Annales des Sciences Psychiques*, *20*, 97–105, 129–136, 172–178, 204–209, 225–231, 257–263, 295–302, 336–344, 357–370.
Ochorowicz, J. (1911). Nouvelle étude expérimentale sur la nature des rayons rigides et du courant médiumnique. *Annales des Sciences Psychiques*, *21*, 161–166, 199–203, 230–236, 276–280.
Ochorowicz, J. (1911–1912). Radiographies des mains (monographie expérimentale). *Annales des Sciences Psychiques*, *21*, 296–303, 334–341, *22*, 1–8.
Ochorowicz, J. (1912). Les mains fluidiques et la photographie de la pensée. *Annales des Sciences Psychiques*, *22*, 97–104, 147–153, 164–170, 204–210, 232–240.
Osty, E. (1914). Un fait de lucidité en la condition dite "psychometrique." *Annales des Sciences Psychiques*, *24*, 97–107.
Parish, E. (1897). *Hallucinations and illusions*. Walter Scott.
Petrovo-Solovovo, M. (1902). Le médium Sambor: Nouvelles et dernières expériences. *Annales des Sciences Psychiques*, *12*, 257–302.
Plas, R. (2000). *Naissance d'une science humaine: La psychologie: Les psychologues et le "merveilleux psychique."* Presses Universitaires de Rennes.
Podmore, F. (1894). *Apparitions and thought-transference*. Walter Scott.
Podmore, F. (1897–1898). Esprits tapageurs. *Annales des Sciences Psychiques*, *7*, 161–175, 216–254, 353–367, *8*, 25–44.
Proal, L. (1892). *Le Crime et la Peine*. Félix Alcan.
Regnault, F. (1901). Guérison miraculeuse de maladies d'apparance organique: Rôle du système vaso-moteur. *Annales des Sciences Psychiques*, *11*, 120–128.
Review of Human Personality and Its Survival of Bodily Death, by F. W. H. Myers (1903). *Annales des Sciences Psychiques*, *13*, 125.
Richet, C. (1884). La suggestion mentale et le calcul des probabilités. *Revue Philosophique de la France et de l'Étranger*, *18*, 609–674.
Richet, C. (1888). Relation de diverses expériences sur la transmission mentales, la lucidité, et autres phénomènes non explicables par les données scientifiques actuelles. *Proceedings of the Society for Psychical Research*, *5*, 18–168.
Richet, C. (1889). Further experiments in hypnotic lucidity or clairvoyance. *Proceedings of the Society for Psychical Research*, *6*, 66–83.
Richet, C. (1891). Des phénomènes psychiques: Lettre a M. Dariex. *Annales des Sciences Psychiques*, *1*, 1–8.
Richet, C. (1892a). A propos du mysticisme moderne: Réplique a M. Rosenbach. *Annales des Sciences Psychiques*, *2*, 293–301.
Richet, C. (1892b). L'avenir de la psychologie. *Annales des Sciences Psychiques*, *2*, 341–350.
Richet, C. (1893a). Expériences de Milan. *Annales des Sciences Psychiques*, *3*, 1–31.
Richet, C. (1893b). Le hasard et la probabilite: Note relative aux expériences de M. Roux. *Annales des Sciences Psychiques*, *3*, 209–211.
Richet, C. (1900). Un cas remarquable de précocité musicale. *Annales des Sciences Psychiques*, *10*, 324–331.
Richet, C. (1901). In memoriam Frederic W. H. Myers. *Annales des Sciences Psychiques*, *11*, 173–178.
Richet, C. (1902). Occultisme dans l'antiquité. *Annales des Sciences Psychiques*, *12*, 310–312.
Richet, C. (1903). Étude sur un cas de prémonition. *Annales des Sciences Psychiques*, *13*, 65–71.
Richet, C. (1905a). La métapsychique. Proceedings of the Society for Psychical Research, 19, 2–49.
Richet, C. (1905b). De quelques phénomènes dits de matérialisations. *Annales des Sciences Psychiques*, *15*, 649–671.
Richet, C. (1905c). Xenoglossie: L'écriture automatique en langues étrangères. *Annales des Sciences Psychiques*, *15*, 317–353.

Richet, C. (1908a). Enquète sur les premonitions. *Annales des Sciences Psychiques, 18*, 42.

Richet, C. (1908b). Des limites de l'incrédulite. *Annales des Sciences Psychiques, 18*, 97–101.

Richet, C. (1914). L'éloge de la raison. *Annales des Sciences Psychiques, 24*, 79–81.

Richet, C. (1919). Lucidité. *Annales des Sciences Psychiques, 29*, 49–53.

Richet, C. (1922). *Traité de métapsychique.* Félix Alcan.

Roux, J. C. (1893). Quelques expériences de lucidité. *Annales des Sciences Psychiques, 3*, 198–209.

Sabatier, A., De Rochas, A., de Gramont, A., Maxwell, J., Dariex, X., & de Watteville, C. (1896). Expériences de l'Agnelas sur Eusapia Paladino. *Annales des Sciences Psychiques, 6*, 1–55.

Schneider, W. H. (2001). Charles Richet and the social role of medical men. *Journal of Medical Biography, 9*, 213–219.

Schrenck–Notzing, [A.] (1891). Le récent travaux sur la télépathie et la clairvoyance. *Annales des Sciences Psychiques, 1*, 65–97.

Sidgwick, Mme H. (1891–1892). Essais sur la preuve de la clairvoyance. *Annales des Sciences Psychiques, 1*, 204–230, 268–294; *2*, 11–47. (Original work published in English, 1891)

Sudre, R. (1926). Introduction à la métapsychique humaine. Payot.

Tabori, P. (1972). *Pioneers of the unseen.* Souvenir Press.

Tesnière, V. (1990). L'histoire aux éditions Alcan (1874–1939). *Vingtième Siècle: Revue d'Histoire, 28*, 15–28.

Tesnière, V. (2001). *Le quadrige: Un Siècle d'Édition Universitaire, 1860–1968.* Presses Universitaires de France.

Vaschide, N. (1902). Experimental investigations of telepathic hallucinations. *Monist, 12*, 273–307.

Verdier, C. (1892). La philosophie au temps présent. *Revue des Facultés Catholiques de l'Ouest, 2*, 689–717.

Waller, E. (1905). Une aventure romanesque de vision dans crystal. *Annales des Sciences Psychiques, 15*, 133–142.

Warcollier, R. (1921). *La Télépathie: Recherches Expérimentales.* Félix Alcan.

Warcollier, R. (1938). César de Vesme (1862–1938). *Revue Métapsychique*, Nos. 4/5, 241–245.

Wijk, H. (1905). Karin: Étude expérimentale sur les phénomènes de frappement spontané. *Annales des Sciences Psychiques, 15*, 517–550.

Wolf, S. (1993). *Brain, mind, and medicine: Charles Richet and the origins of physiological psychology.* Transaction Publishers.

Gifted Subjects' Contributions to Psychical Research: The Case of Eusapia Palladino*

Carlos S. Alvarado†

A historical view of psychical research should consider the contributions of gifted subjects (psychics, mediums) beyond their roles as generators of the phenomena that researchers in the field study. The Italian medium Eusapia Palladino (1854–1918) provides a case in point. Her performances are seen here as an active agent in the production of images of psychical research, and of unorthodox concepts of force in explanations of physical phenomena. Palladino's influence was felt not only in the production of phenomena, but through their characteristics and through behaviors such as acts of fraud, and verbal statements about the nature of the phenomena. Her influence shows how we may extend our conceptions of who has been important to psychical research history by going beyond studies of researchers' contributions. In addition, some of Palladino's actions show the importance of social and behavioral aspects of gifted subjects' performances in the development and construction of ideas held in psychical research.

Traditionally, history has been written from the perspective of a small group of people: the élites in power. Well-known politicians, statesmen, kings, generals, writers or scientists have constituted the main voices of the past. The tendency of history to focus on élites began to change during the last two decades with the shift of social history's emphasis to a variety of marginal groups, an approach sometimes referred to as 'history from below' (Sharpe, 1991). The new historiography includes much work on women, as well as on other individuals and groups who have received scant attention as makers of history. Among these are 'radical' political and religious groups, the working classes, slaves, strikers, delinquents and the homeless, and residents of rural areas.[1] The implications of this new approach are clear: it is assumed that the experiences and actions of the collective are also important in shaping the development of the world as we know it. Doing 'history from below' opens our past to a different set of protagonists, to different voices, each with something important to say.

In such human sciences as psychiatry, psychology and psychical research these neglected voices may be found, for example, among patients and research subjects.[2] Ellenberger (1970) has argued that the history of dynamic psychiatry is "inseparable from the contributions of a gallery of eminent patients ..." (p. 893). This point is amply evident in the role patients such as Blanche Wittman, Anna O. and Léonie have played in the work of Jean-Martin Charcot, Joseph Breuer, and Pierre Janet, respectively (Drinka, 1984; Ellenberger, 1970). The history of psychical research has also been profoundly influenced by subjects who claimed to have psychic abilities. Examples include D. D. Home (Jenkins, 1982), Eusapia Palladino (Inglis, 1977, Chaps. 35, 38), Charles Bailey (Irwin, 1987), Eileen Garrett (Angoff, 1974), Rudi Schneider (Gregory, 1985), and Margery (Tietze, 1973). However, most of the studies about these individuals have not clearly articulated the importance

*Republished with permission from *Journal of the Society for Psychical Research*, *59*, 269–292, 1993.

†This is a revised version of a paper presented at the 1992 Parapsychological Association Convention held in Las Vegas. I wish to thank Nancy L. Zingrone for useful suggestions for the improvement of this paper.

of casting psychics and mediums as agents of change, persons contributing to the field in the same active way psychical researchers do, though perhaps through different means. In the current history of psychical research, the unwritten assumption is that the field changes mainly because of the actions of the intellectual élite (i. e., psychical researchers). Gifted subjects, on the other hand, are only passive generators of phenomena, the production of which becomes knowledge by the order imposed by the researcher.

In this paper I argue that mediums' and psychics' performances actively contributed to the development of public images of the field, and of concepts and methods of research, performances that forced psychical research through continuous change. Of course, gifted subjects have not worked in isolation. They acted within particular social and cultural systems governed by such factors as belief in and skepticism about psychic phenomena, the influence of religious and intellectual movements such as spiritualism, and the needs and agendas of psychical researchers. I am not arguing that gifted subjects can be separated from these systems or other factors, but rather that they are important and, too often, ignored elements, whose contributions go beyond the simple production of phenomena. Mediums, because of their personality and performances, are catalyzers, focusers of the attention of intellectual communities, while at the same time they are active influencers of public opinion and theoretical speculation. By seeing psychics and mediums as more than producers of phenomena we can begin to conceptualize them as important agents of change in both the discourse and the practice of psychical research.[3]

Gifted subjects are an active social source of influence or persuasion, a "focus of authority" (Nelson, 1969, p. 242) capable of engaging, promoting, or maintaining particular images of psychic phenomena and of psychical research. This, as Jordanova (1989) has argued in a different context, is an example of how scientific disciplines "tell stories and produce images that convince both 'experts' and others, that act as sources for other social and cultural relationships, that satisfy people in the accounts they are able to give …" (p. 158). Such influence implies interactions with researchers and the wider social context in which the subject exists (e.g., Kenny, 1986). But we should not forget that the idiosyncrasies of gifted subjects, such as desire for fame, practice of fraud, personality traits, or particular behaviors and statements associated with the phenomena they produce, act as important shapers of images of the field regardless of the explanation of the phenomena in question.

To illustrate this point, I will focus on the Italian medium Eusapia Palladino (1854–1918). Born in Minervino-Murge, Bari, Italy, Palladino was studied for nearly half her life by psychical researchers, as well as by other scientists and intellectuals.[4] Her phenomena, mainly of the physical type, were so varied that they were classified by Enrico Morselli (1907), an Italian psychiatrist, as: mechanical phenomena with and without contact with the object affected, alteration of the weight of bodies (e.g., levitation of the medium), thermal effects, acoustic phenomena, lasting effects on inert matter (e.g., direct writing), visible and invisible materializations, and luminous phenomena. She certainly had enough of a repertoire to keep the interest of a generation of researchers. In fact, her mediumship has been considered by some of these researchers as vital for the reality of physical phenomena. It has been argued that her mediumship "may now be said to culminate and focus the whole evidential case for the physical phenomena of spiritualism" (Carrington, 1909a, p. 4). Another author wrote that even if Palladino was the only physical medium in existence "her manifestations would suffice to establish scientifically the reality of telekinesis and ectoplasmic forms" (Richet, 1923, p. 34). In recent years discussions about Palladino's mediumship have also centered on evidential issues. Some have defended the phenomena (e.g., Cassirer, 1983), while others have discussed it as an example of fraud and delusion (e.g. Hansel, 1989, pp. 237–243). The recent discussions in the *Journal of the Society for Psychical Research* revolving around Wiseman's (1992) critique of the methodology and reporting standards of the well-known study of Palladino by Feilding, Baggally and Carrington

(1909) have also focused on evidential issues (Barrington, 1992; Fontana, 1992; Martinéz-Taboas & Francia, 1993). In this paper, however, I will argue that Palladino's mediumship was influential in ways other than the establishment of evidential claims for physical phenomena.

Palladino as a Publicist for Psychical Research

Public Discussions of Palladino's Mediumship

Palladino's mediumship was important because it provided an immense amount of publicity (not always positive) for psychical research. Many researchers were convinced of the reality of physical phenomena by her mediumship, among them Hereward Carrington, Camille Flammarion, Cesare Lombroso, Oliver Lodge, and Enrico Morselli. Their interest ignited a chain reaction among believers and disbelievers as these men actively researched, wrote about, and defended physical mediumship. The cases of Lombroso and Carrington are particularly telling.[5]

The well-known Italian psychiatrist and criminologist Cesare Lombroso was converted to Palladino's phenomena after sitting with her in 1891 (Ciolfi, 1891; Lombroso, 1892). In these séances Lombroso "saw extremely heavy objects transferred through the air without contact, from that time on I consented to make the phenomena the subject of investigation" (Lombroso, 1909, p. 39). Others have argued that Lombroso's involvement with Palladino brought her to the attention of the international intellectual community. The historian of Italian psychical research, Massimo Biondi, wrote: "Lombroso's name was of no little consequence in bringing Eusapia Palladino to the consideration and curiosity of many illustrious exponents of ... positivistic science ..." As a consequence, "a semi-literate [person] had around her the highest names in science and in European culture" (Biondi, 1988, p. 140, my translation).

Partly because of Lombroso's endorsement Palladino took center stage in the famous Milan Commission sittings of 1892 (Rapport, 1893; Richet, 1893). Among the researchers present were Lombroso, the German philosopher Carl du Prel, the Italian astronomer Giovanni Schiaparelli, the French physiologist Charles Richet, and Alexandre Aksakov, Councilor of State to the Emperor of Russia. Lombroso's influence is evident in the opening words of the Commission's report:

> Taking into consideration the evidence of Professor Lombroso on the subject of mediumistic phenomena produced through Mme. Eusapia Paladino, the undersigned met at Milan for the purpose of holding a series of séances with her with the object of verifying the phenomena, by submitting her to experiments and to observations as rigorous as possible.[6]

The Milan sittings convinced most of the gathered savants that Palladino's mediumship presented something valuable to be investigated. In their opinion: "What we have seen and ascertained is sufficient to prove to us that these phenomena are well worth the attention of scientists" (Joire, n. d., ca. 1916, p. 413). The repercussions of these séances may be discerned in the attention they received in the contemporary literature. Soon after the publication of the commission's report Frank Podmore discussed it at a meeting of the Society for Psychical Research in London (General Meeting, 1893). Podmore also published a review of the report in the Society's *Proceedings* (Podmore, 1894). The report was reprinted in the German periodical *Psychische Studien* (Bericht, 1893), where it generated further discussion (du Prel, 1893; Wittig, 1893). Reprints also appeared in the United States (Comey, 1894; Science and the Spirits, 1893). The Milan Commission's report marked the beginnings of formal research on Palladino. These sittings were followed by much activity during the rest of the nineteenth century and into the twentieth. Among these later studies were the investigations by SPR members (e.g., Feilding, Baggally and Carrington, 1909; Lodge, 1894), by the Institut Général Psychologique in Paris (Courtier, 1908), by the Italian psychiatrist Enrico Morselli (1908), by the Polish psychologist Julian Ochorowicz (1910, pp. 204–207), and the so-called American sittings held in New York (Carrington, 1954), among many others (e.g., Barzini, 1984; Bottazi, 1907; Bozzano, 1903; Flammarion, 1909; de Fontenay, 1898; de Krauz, 1894; de Rochas, 1896; Schrenck-Notzing, 1928).

Lombroso's own writings (e.g. 1892; 1908a; 1908b; 1909) were also influential in spreading his belief and underscoring his authority regarding the genuineness of Palladino's phenomena specifically and the legitimacy of psychical research in general. In his book, *Ricerche sui Fenomeni Ipnotici e Spiritici*, translated into English as *After Death—What?* (1909), Lombroso endorsed Palladino's phenomena vigorously. He discussed her mainly in Chapters 2–4, including not only his own experiences but also those of others such as Morselli. Lombroso described the scientific nature of his investigations and those of others by focusing on instrumental studies of Palladino's phenomena. "The great mediumistic problem cannot be solved without the assistance of those accurate instruments by the use of which we are saved from every possible error of judgment" (p. 72), he reminded his readers. Lombroso also mentions dynamometers, cardiographs, electroscopes and balances in an attempt to show how the instrumentation of science could conquer the "spirits". Similarly, Lombroso devoted considerable space to the studies of Palladino's physiology and mental health. He eventually accepted the spirit hypothesis as an explanation for some of her phenomena, as seen in his statement that in some cases "a third will may intervene, which is not that of the medium nor of the sitters, but is opposed to the will of all these" (p. 164). *After Death—What?* received considerable publicity (e.g., Jastrow, 1909). To this day it remains one of Lombroso's most frequently cited psychical research publications.

The conversion of Hereward Carrington also had important consequences for the popularization of Palladino's mediumship, and, ultimately, for psychical research. Carrington, a British-born psychical researcher who operated most of his life from the United States, was skeptical of Palladino until he sat with her in Naples in 1908 (Feilding et al., 1909). In a note he appended to the report of these séances Carrington said that the Naples sittings led him to "absolute conviction of the reality of at least some of the phenomena; and the conviction … that the results witnessed by us were not due to fraud or trickery on the part of Eusapia" (p. 555).

After his conversion Carrington started what was, in a sense, an unintentional publicity campaign for Palladino. He wrote two books about her, *Eusapia Palladino and her Phenomena* (1909a) and *The American Séances with Eusapia Palladino* (1954). The former resembled Lombroso's in that Carrington took great pains to argue for the importance of Palladino to psychical research and to maintain that research with her was conducted along critical and scientific lines. In his "Historical Résume of the Palladino Case" Carrington listed a myriad of séances held with the medium, and devoted several chapters to explanatory theories and to "Biological and Psychological Considerations."

But Carrington did not limit his writing to these books. He also published a variety of articles and notes, such as one which labelled Palladino "the despair of science" (Carrington, 1909b; see also 1910a; 1910b; 1910c; 1910d; 1911a; 1939b). In addition, he described the medium's phenomena and her investigations in many book chapters and sections (Carrington, 1913; 1919; 1920; 1931; 1939a; 1946). Because of all this work the medium, specifically, and physical phenomena in general, were kept in the public's mind.

Both Lombroso and Carrington interacted with Palladino's performances to bring respectability to the subject matter by reporting serious and systematic research on the occurrence of telekinetic and materialization phenomena. Palladino's actions, recasted by the above-mentioned researchers, were made to look scientific, to wear an image of respectability. However, the opposite was the case in some of the newspaper coverage of the medium's activities.

Palladino was also in the limelight when her séances were covered by a variety of newspaper stories in many countries. Biondi (1988) has discussed aspects of the involvement of the Italian press in the early Palladino séances. Among these was the spiritualist Ercole Chiaia's 1888 public invitation to Lombroso to study Palladino published in the Milan newspaper *Fanfulla della Domenica* (pp. 127–131) and journalist Eugenio Torelli Viollier's 1892 attack on the medium in a series of articles in the *Corriere della Sera* (pp. 149–151). These publications stimulated both polemics and further research by bringing Palladino to the attention of scientists and other individuals.

After the 1895 Cambridge sittings sponsored by the SPR many English papers carried reports about her mediumship, through which the public got a glimpse of the séance room usually reserved for spiritualists and psychical researchers. Gauld (1968, chapter 10) discussed the impact these sittings had on the SPR, an impact that reinforced the negative impression of physical mediumship many leaders of the Society had formed.[7]

But no other period of Palladino's mediumship created so much publicity as her sittings in New York from November 1909 to June of 1910 arranged by Carrington. In an analysis of articles, notes and reports on psychic phenomena published in *The New York Times* during Palladino's visit, the majority were found to be centered on the Italian medium. During her stay the public's conception of psychic phenomena and its investigation was shaped by Palladino's performances, or, more accurately, by the continuous and frequently sensational reports of her séances. A brief overview of *The New York Times* shows that, if anything, Palladino gave psychical research a bad name.[8] Following are some examples of the news headlines about Palladino published in the *New York Times* (1909–1910) that cast a negative light on her mediumship.

- Paladino Tells About Her Stunts (11/13/1909, p. 3)
- Paladino Meets a Firm Skeptic (11/17/1909, pp. 1–2)
- The Palladino Tricks (11/18/1909, p. 10)
- Paladino Used Phosphorous (11/19/1909, p. 6)
- Sidelights on the Paladino Delusion (11/21/1909, pt. 5, pp. 1–2)
- Calls Paladino a Fraud (1/20/1910, p. l)
- Palladino Tricks All Laid Bare (5/12,1910, pp. 1–2)
- Easily Wrought Palladino Wonders (5/20/1910, p. 3)

Palladino's first séance in New York took place on November 14, 1909 (Irwin, 1909). Before her arrival the *Times* had prepared the American public for the medium by announcing that Palladino was "about to visit these shores with her stock of trickery and supernatural pretensions" (Eusapia Palladino, 1909b). In addition, Palladino's previous history was discussed in the newspaper's pages (Davis, 1909; Eusapia Paladino, 1909a), with the focus on her controversial personality and practice of trickery. "Nobody," an editorial stated, "... denies that she has been caught again and again in fraud, deliberate and intentional" (Topics of the Times, 1909a).

Criticism was quick to come after the first séance. An editorial (Topics of the Times, 1909b) depicted Palladio's performance as:

> ... more variants of those to be seen any Sunday afternoon for 50 cents or a dollar in scores of shabby back parlors haunted by the dupes or less notorious 'mediums' ... The wonder was that such a woman, by doing such things, should ever have received the attention of men in one branch or another of science really eminent.

Negative images of Palladino—and of psychical research—were clearly visible in the *Times*' emphasis on accusations of fraud, such as those made by an anonymous sitter (Paladino Meets, 1909), by psychologist Hugo Münsterberg (Calls Paladino, 1910), and by the professors who participated in the Columbia University sittings (Miller, 1910). As a result of the latter investigation Palladino was called a "symbol of sophistry" (Miller, 1910, p. 1) because it was believed that "this greatest of spiritualistic impostors in history was unmasked" (A Famous Medium, 1910).

Psychical research's image further suffered when the events were carnivalized by offers of money from magicians who entered the scene. Skeptic Joseph F. Rinn offered $1,000 if Palladino could produce results under his conditions, among which was his request that the medium perform from within a sack (Palladino Ready, 1910). On the opposing side, Howard Thurston (1910), convinced that the medium could produce genuine manifestations, offered the same amount of money to a charity if it could be shown that Palladino "cannot levitate a table without resort to trickery or fraud".

The public image of psychical research also suffered when researchers such as Carrington and James H. Hyslop, the latter well known to the public for his activities on behalf of the American Society for Psychical Research, had disagreements in the *Times*' pages.[9] After Hyslop criticized Carrington by saying that he did not expect much of scientific value to be obtained (Close Watch, 1909), Carrington accused Hyslop of being a "dog in a manger" (Paladino Used, 1909). In a later communication, Hyslop argued that Carrington's approach was not scientific because Carrington did not treat the medium as the hysteric Hyslop considered her to be, and because Carrington courted publicity in his management of Palladino. In Hyslop's view "no scientific man will resort to vaudeville methods for proving his position to the public" (Hyslop, 1909). Hyslop was hinting that he considered Carrington's approach sensational, that is, involving journalists and using newspapers to express his views. In the end the whole affair had little scientific success. The public did not know whom to trust, and the controversy spawned a circus of opposing opinions, described in the *Times* as the "battle between the anti-Palladinoists and the pro-Palladinoists ..." (Palladino Test, 1910, p. 1).

As a result of these exposures in the press many scientists, especially psychologists, became more distrustful of psychical research than ever before. According to Deborah J. Coon (1992), during this period many psychologists tried to offer natural explanations for psychic phenomena, focusing on issues such as credulity, belief, and the psychology of deception. The psychologist Joseph Jastrow's reprint of a previously-published essay on Palladino (Jastrow, 1910) in his *The Psychology of Conviction* (1918) illustrates how Palladino's mediumship was used in this way. In Jastrow's view Palladino highlighted the importance of the attitudes and beliefs of the persons around the medium. In his words (1918, p. 121):

> It becomes clear, when one thinks below the surface of the Paladino situation, that perhaps the largest single factor contributing to her reputation and to the excitement which her very simple and vulgar performances aroused, has been the strong inherent tendency to believe the hypothesis which she encouraged in regard to her 'manifestations.'

Others such as Leuba (1909) and Münsterberg (1910) also showed skepticism to paranormal explanations of Palladino's phenomena.

For psychical researchers the New York affair was a cause of embarrassment and ambiguity. William James described the situation in a letter written to the Swiss psychologist Théodore Flournoy in April of 1910 as one unsuccessful "from the point of view of investigation ... Eusapia's trip to the U.S. will simply have spoiled her, and discredited everyone else" (Le Clair, 1966, p. 230).

In England the Society for Psychical Research devoted space in their *Journal* to negative coverage of Palladino's American visit. They reprinted accusations of fraud (Eusapia Palladino, 1910; Sittings, 1910), published one paper that discussed the tricks of the medium (Krebs, 1910), and another that argued that Palladino's trick performances were not done unconsciously (Kellogg, 1910). In addition, Feilding and Baggally (1910), believers in Palladino's phenomena since the 1908 Naples sittings, commented that, in general, fraud was let go unchecked in some séances with the purpose of detecting her. They argued—and in this there was an implicit criticism—that they themselves had taken a better course in their research because they had controlled for trickery as soon as it appeared. Also, in the pages of the *SPR Journal*, Hereward Carrington (1910c) had to admit that, even though he believed in the medium's genuineness, "at the lowest estimate—the evidence stands just where it was before" the American séances (p. 372).

In the United States the *Journal of the American Society for Psychical Research* (JASPR) also presented a negative view of the Palladino séances. Davis (1910) devoted a whole article to a discussion of observations of trickery and of suspicious circumstantial details in some of the New York séances in which he participated. In Hyslop's (1910, pp. 182–183) view:

> The Palladino case, as it has been managed, is not calculated to influence intelligent people who have no time to spend years and fortunes on it. It only excites dispute and many of the facts asserted of it are so closely related to fraud that even the apology of hysteria has little effect.

The bad publicity was bound to affect the American Society for Psychical Research (ASPR). According to Hyslop (1914) three hundred ASPR members left the Society because of the "Palladino affair" (p. 18). A review of information about membership available in the *Journal* of the Society does not confirm Hyslop's figures, but shows a loss of membership after 1909 consistent with his evaluation.

Further Examples of Palladino's Disorderly Conduct

As is apparent in the preceding paragraphs, the issue of fraud was paramount in the public's mind during Palladino's New York visit. But such discussions were not unique to the New York episode of her career. The Palladino literature is replete with instances of trickery, mentioned on many occasions even by her staunchest defenders. For example, Lombroso (1909) stated: "Many are the crafty tricks she plays, both in the state of trance (unconsciously) and out of it ..." (p. 102). These tricks involved mainly the substitution of hands and feet, as was the case when Morselli saw the medium reach for a trumpet when he mistakenly thought he had her controlled (Barzini, 1984, p. 89).

Carrington (1909a), among others, saw the medium "release the right hand and arm, place it behind her into the cabinet, catch hold of the curtains on that side and throw it out over the table" (p. 182). Others reported that they saw Palladino using hairs to move balances (Courtier, 1908, p. 521; Flammarion, 1909, pp. 200–201) and using a nail to produce tracings on paper (Courtier, 1908, p. 523). Such reports made it difficult for many to evaluate Palladino's performances even when there appeared to be good conditions of control.

However, Palladino's conduct was not limited to trickery. Her behavior in and out of trance also generated images of disorder that affected the evaluation of her séances. For example, Schiaparelli pointed out to Flammarion (1909, p. 64) that the 1892 séances in Milan were not true scientific experiments because of the "unfavorable circumstances imposed by the medium." Some years later, Myers (1895) noted that "Eusapia persistently threw obstacles in the way of proper holding of the hands. ... Moreover, she repeatedly *refused* any satisfactory test other than holding". In addition, she was said to hate the novelty of the testing situation (Barzini, 1984, pp. 33, 64).

On one occasion Palladino objected when Carrington checked her feet during one of the séances conducted in Naples by the SPR committee in 1908. As a result: "She worked herself up into a passion and covered us with rich Neapolitan reproaches for our suspicion and inexperience of her phenomena. The storm raged for about an hour ..." (Feilding et al., 1909, p. 522). Similarly, another writer stated that: "She does not allow for doubt regarding her extraordinary powers and interrupts any discussions about this, uttering the most picturesque and energetic insults of the flowery Neapolitan dialect" (Barzini, 1984, p, 33, my translation; see also Bottazzi, 1907, pp. 395–396).

In addition, Palladino was reported to be so "violent and impulsive as actually to fly at her adversaries and beat them" (Lombroso, 1909, p. 112).

Palladino's trance behavior was also considered to be extravagant, and certainly pathological (hysterical). Flammarion (1909, p. 90) mentioned her "inflamed looks" and "satanic smile", while de Rochas (1896, p.19) remarked that she showed "movements characteristic of erotic ecstasy". Other observers at the séances described Palladino's inflamed face and hysterical laugh as she gradually acquired the "expression of an intense ecstasy, generally of a voluptuous and erotic nature ..." (de Krauz, 1894, p. 172, my translation). After the séance, the medium falls "on the arms of the men sympathetic to her ... The embrace generally manifests in a desire for caresses ..." (de Krauz, 1894, p.172, my translation). Palladino, as stated by de Krauz, has admitted to having voluptuous sensations during these experiences.

It was also stated (Schrenck-Notzing, 1928, p. 79, my translation) that:

> Frequently success in producing something on request induces pleasurable sensations (voluptuosity?) in the medium, who is in a hysterosomnambulistic state. There is a slight erotic aspect in her attitude regarding those around her. She says at the end of the experience: "I feel so happy ..."[10]

All this behavior could do no less than relate Palladino's performances to uncontrolled, pathological and carnalistic experiences. In plain terms, these images of disorderly conduct alienated many from this area of research. As Schiaparelli commented regarding difficulties of control: "All that kind of thing excites distrust" (Flammarion, 1909, p. 65).

Palladino and the Nature of Physical Mediumship

Concepts of Force Derived from Palladino's Mediumship

Palladino also served as a beacon or catalyst for developments in theoretical speculation about the hypothetical force that some psychical researchers believed were behind telekinesis, materializations and other physical phenomena. As Frank Podmore (1902) pointed out in his account of the development of spiritualism and psychical research, there is a long history of concepts of force used to explain psychic phenomena predating the arrival of Palladino on the psychic scene. The history of this 'fluid', as traced by Robert Amadou (1953), goes back to ancient times. During the eighteenth century it appeared in Franz Anton Mesmer's concept of animal magnetism. Mesmer's force was defined in 1784 as a "fluid which surrounds all that exists and which serves to maintain the equilibrium of all the vital functions" (Mesmer, 1980, p. 81). Changing concepts of this force—albeit assuming its connection to the human body—were used to explain all types of psychic phenomena and trances. The work of such people as Gregory (1851), Lafontaine (1847) and Petetin (1808) provides evidence of this, as does the research conducted by Baron Karl von Reichenbach (1851) on what he called the "od" force.

Early students of the phenomena of the séance room, such as Dods (1854), Mahan (1855), and Rogers (1853), accepted the existence of a magnetic or electric-like force as the agent behind such phenomena as the movement of objects without contact. Some, like Allan Kardec (1874), described this force as a fluidic body connected to the human body of mediums, which he called "perispirit". Kardec argued that discarnate spirits could use the perispirit of living persons to cause physical manifestations in or out of the séance room (e.g., poltergeists).

Such writers as Dods and Rogers associated the concept of a force with the nervous system, a line of thought developed by Edward William Cox (1872), whose speculations on the 'psychic force' conceptually influenced William Crookes (1874) in his experiments with the medium D.D. Home. These ideas developed to such an extent that they formed a widely influential conceptual tradition that survives to this day.[11] Examples include the French hypnotist and psychical researcher Albert de Rochas (1887), who argued that phenomena such as the polarity of human magnetism, levitation of the human body, movement of objects without contact, and the induction of particular hypnotic states were evidence for the "existence in the human body of a force similar to electricity and capable of projecting itself out of it. ..." (p. 387, my translation). In the opinion of researchers like Hyppolite Baraduc (1896) this force could be classified in different types of emanations, could be photographed, and was related to mental and physiological states of the persons producing it.

Years later Carrington (1939a, p. 21) wrote:

> Modern psychic investigators are now inclined to think that supernormal physical phenomena ... depend upon the externalization, from the medium's body, of a subtle energy, which is capable of affecting matter in its immediate environment, and is also seemingly capable, at times, of moulding matter into the semblance of living organisms ...[12]

Palladino's mediumship clearly did not originate the psychic force model of PK, but she was of great importance in stimulating researchers to develop ideas of this sort. Her availability for research at a time period that bridged the nineteenth and twentieth centuries made her a virtual theoretical concept generator. More precisely, she both inspired and actively participated in the development of concepts of force that nurtured the 'fluidic' model for many years.

One of Palladino's early supporters and publicists, Ercole Chiaia, argued in a paper he read at the 1889 International Congress of Spiritism and Spiritualism in Paris that "an invisible fluidic force ... emanates from this woman; it comes out from all the pores of her fingers ..." (Chiaia, 1890, p. 328, my translation). Later, other researchers developed this idea in greater detail, basing their speculations about psychic forces completely or partly on Palladino's phenomena.

Lombroso (1892) speculated that the externalization of a nervous force from Palladino might be due to abnormal functioning of the medium's nervous system, an aberration that let loose the energy of the motor centers of the brain. Years later Lombroso (1909) was still writing about the "projection and transformation" of the medium's energy (p. 156), but he argued that this force was not enough to explain all the phenomena. Discarnate agency was required to explain many of the phenomena of the séance room, Lombroso claimed, particularly those manifestations that seemed to require a will different from the medium's.

The English physicist Oliver Lodge (1894) was also led to speculate on unorthodox concepts of force as he tried to explain the phenomena, he witnessed with Palladino in 1894. According to Lodge there were "temporary prolongations" from the medium's body that were an example of vital power channeled in an unusual way. In his words (pp. 334–335):

> … instead of action at a distance in the physical sense, what I have observed may be said to be more like vitality at a distance—the action of a living organism exerted in unusual directions and over a range greater than the ordinary.
>
> The reason why I speak of temporary prolongations from the medium's body is because I myself have been frequently touched by something which might most readily be described as such a prolongation or formation, and have sometimes seen such a thing while it was touching another person. But the effect on an observer is usually more as if the connecting link, if any, were invisible and intangible, or as if a portion of vital or directing energy had been detached, and were producing distant movements without any apparent connexion with the medium.

Another, similar, concept was proposed by Albert de Rochas. As may be seen from the titles of two of de Rochas's main books—*L'Extériorisation de la Sensibilité* (1895) and *L'Exteriorisation de la Motricité* (1896)—the French researcher believed that the human body contained a fluid intimately related to nervous impulses that could be projected out of the body during hypnosis or during mediumistic trance. In the latter book—in which Palladino's séances play a prominent part—de Rochas suggested that this force could be directed to do specific things by the will of the subject. In a later article about Palladino he expanded his ideas (1909, p. 227):

> … with certain persons … the adhesiveness of the nervous fluid to the carnal organism is feeble, so that they may even, under various influences, project this nervous fluid outside of their bodies. Experiment has shown that, ordinarily, this tenuous substance tends to regain, when it has been projected, the form which it had in the physical body, of which it bathed all parts, and that it then re-crystallizes itself according to the same system … This fluidic body is able to model itself under the influence of the will. … and thus to present the form of this or that personage called up by the thought of the medium or that of the magnetizer.

The last point, in de Rochas's opinion, explained the variety of the forms that Palladino imprinted on clay placed at a distance from her body.

Another eminent European researcher, the French astronomer Camille Flammarion, also used concepts of psychic force to explain the phenomena he witnessed with Palladino. In his opinion this invisible force emanated not only from the medium but from the sitters attending the séance as well. As Flammarion (1897, p. 746) wrote:

> This force is not immaterial. It may be a substance, an agent, emitting radiations having wave lengths which do not affect our retina … In the absence of light rays this force can concentrate itself, materialize, even assume a certain resemblance to a human body, act like our organs, knock violently on a table, touch us.

Flammarion (1909) later referred to this phenomenon as a "prolongation of the muscular and nervous force of the subject" (p. 424), and as a "fluidic and condensable double [having] the power of gliding momentarily out from the body of the medium …" (pp. 424–425).

There were, of course, many other researchers who used this model to explain Palladino's phenomena. Ochorowicz (1910, pp. 204–207) discussed them in terms of mediumistic currents and threads projecting out from the medium's hands. Some merely referred to radioactive emanations (Aggazzotti, Foà, Foà &, Herlitzka, 1907), while others wrote about 'vital' and 'nerve' forces

(Barzini, 1984; Maxwell, 1905; Morselli, 1908; Schrenck-Notzing, 1928). Like Lombroso (1909), there were those who thought that some intelligent manifestations (e.g. materializations) required more than Palladino's 'fluids' to be explained. Bozzano (1903), Carrington (1909a) and Venzano (1907) believed that these forces could emanate from the medium and from the sitters, but that, in some cases, its intellectual agency was that of discarnate entities.

Phenomena and Behavior Supporting Unorthodox Force Concepts

As an individual, Palladino was singularly important in the development and maintenance of beliefs in such concepts of force because of the character of her phenomena and because a variety of her behaviors continuously reinforced such ideas.

The characteristics of some of the phenomena suggested to many researchers that something was coming out of the medium's body. There were reports of luminous emanations from Palladino's fingers (Flammarion, 1909, p. 198) and mention of a breeze coming from the scar of an old head wound (Carrington, 1910a, p. 312; Maxwell, 1905, p. 115). Others saw hands and arms receding into the medium's body (Bottazzi, 1907, p. 413; Carrington, 1910a, p. 314). Venzano (1907) reported a séance that took place in 1905 in which a "hand and an arm covered by a dark sleeve [was seen to] issue from the front and upper part of the right shoulder of the medium" (p. 100). After moving a glass, the arm was seen to "disappear as if it returned into the shoulder from which we had seen it issue" (p. 101).

Similarly, another researcher reported seeing some "*sort of excrescence* coming out from the top part of [Palladino's] body ... the excrescence seemed to be alive; it moved toward the instrument [a music box], and offered resistance to touch" (Schrenck-Notzing, 1928, p. 87, my translation).

In addition to such reports, Palladino exhibited other behaviors that helped to support the psychic force model. One was her well-known tendency for 'synchronisms,' or muscular movements that corresponded to telekinetic or materialization manifestations. As reported by Oliver Lodge (1894), on one occasion Palladino "made several spasmodic movements, each of which was accompanied or followed by violent movements of the neighbouring round table" (p. 350), an observation that was frequently reported in the literature.[13] Bozzano (1903, pp. 98–99) thought that this coincidence of motor activity and telekinetic phenomena was due to a 'fluidic' connection between the medium's body and the phenomena produced at a distance.

Another behavior that supported these ideas, and one closely related to synchronisms, was Palladino's use of hand movements over objects to be moved, such as small tables (e.g., Feilding et al., 1909, p. 390) and balances (e.g., Bottazzi, 1907, p. 398; Maxwell, 1905, p. 100). After all, if PK phenomena followed hand movements it was logical to think that some emanation or connection between the hands and the targets existed.

Support for these unorthodox concepts of force came also from Palladino's exhaustion and other unpleasant after-effects she claimed to experience after the séances, clearly supporting the idea that the phenomena depended on the medium's physiology (e.g., Barzini, 1984, pp. 73–74; Flammarion, 1909, pp. 7, 210; Lombroso, 1909, p. 115). As Carrington (1909a, p. 315) noted:

> During a sitting ... a large amount of Eusapia's energy is sapped ... After a séance, Eusapia is indeed a pitiable object. She appears shrunken together, weak, nauseated, with loss of memory of much that has transpired, her face deeply lined and sallow—giddiness, and general uncertainty as to her surroundings ...[14]

Palladino also kept the idea of forces alive by referring frequently to it or to related issues, references that served in part to give validity to the concepts of force in question by keeping them constantly in the minds of researchers and others interested in physical mediumship.[15] Some of these related to her inner sensations. According to de Rochas (1896, p. 22—I am using the translation in Flammarion, 1909, p. 143):

> She suddenly experiences an ardent desire to produce the phenomena; then she has a feeling of numbness and the goose flesh sensation in her fingers; these sensations keep increasing; at the same time she feels in the inferior portion of the vertebral column the flowing of a current which rapidly extends into her arm as far as her elbow, where it is gently arrested. It is at this point that the phenomenon takes place.

She also mentioned mediumistic 'currents' frequently. According to Courtier (1908, p. 487) Palladino referred to two types of current: one coming from the sitters (which had different feelings to it according to which sitters produced it) and another coming from the cabinet, which was usually formed in a comer of the room. Palladino also commented on problems of interference (de Krauz, 1894, p. 13), of weak currents (Carrington, 1910d, p. 135), of 'countercurrents' (Mille, 1908), of having "little force" (Ochorowicz, 1896, p. 81), or of having great power in a particular séance (Flammarion, 1909, p. 88).

The concepts of force that Palladino helped to support and to construct through her phenomena and behaviors were present in a great number of twentieth-century treatises and articles.[16] These ideas were clearly articulated in Ochorowicz's (1910) research with Stanislawa Tomczyk, in Crawford's (1916) studies with Kathleen Goligher (and her circle), in Geley's (1927) work with Eva C., Jan Guzyk and Franek Kluski, and in Osty and Osty's (1931–32) investigations of Rudi Schneider. In addition, an immense amount of work was carried out by many individuals, who tried to detect some hypothetical force by using a variety of meters (e.g., Joire, 1905), photography (e.g., Kudriavtzeff, 1909), and hypnotic-like interventions (e.g., Alrutz, 1922). The wide range of such work clearly shows the extent of the influence of the concept of psychic force, a tradition which Palladino nurtured and sustained, both directly and indirectly, during the long period when she was the main physical medium active in Europe. Her mediumship was so prominent and presented so many anomalies that psychical researchers were forced to 'explain' her case using the already old tradition of psychic forces. Her contribution, however, may also be traced to the social side of her performances, through which she helped to keep the notion of psychic forces alive.

Concluding Remarks

In this paper I have provided an example of how we can extend our net in our studies of parapsychology's past to capture more fully the range of the individuals who contributed to the field's development. It is also a defense of the idea that gifted subjects can have profound influence on the field beyond the evidence for the reality of the phenomena under study. In this case I have argued that Palladino's performances helped to publicize physical phenomena and psychical research (sometimes in negative ways) because of the controversies she created. I have also argued that she provided a context for the extension and nurturing of concepts of force put forth to account for physical phenomena. None of this was unique to Palladino, except perhaps in the magnitude of interest her mediumship generated.

But these actions were not limited to stimulating researchers. Palladino's personality and idiosyncrasies were clearly influential in shaping the development of images of the field and of the concepts of psychic force. Her actions or performances (e.g., practice of fraud, verbal statements about forces) remind one of those that Clifford Geertz (1983) has discussed in relation to the social construction of power in political situations. In these situations, the governing élite (p. 124)

> … justify their existence and order their actions in terms of a collection of stories, ceremonies, insignia, formalities, and appurtenances that they have inherited or … invented. It is these—crowns and coronations, limosines and conferences—that mark the center as center and give what goes on there its aura of being not merely important but in some odd fashion connected with the way the world is built.

In Palladino's case we may see her behaviors as actively contributing to the formation and maintenance of images and concepts, shaping and outlining them through actions that were consistent with a wider social context (e.g. skepticism about mediumship, belief in forces). I am not arguing against the existence of the telekinesis and materializations that figured so prominently in Palladino's life, but rather calling for a consideration of additional forces involved in the construction of ideas in psychical research and elsewhere. Palladino's phenomena may be conceptualized as part of a general field of actions, actions that, although different from each other, are intimately related to the context of the séance room. Consequently, the lines in the diagram are permeable, since it is precisely their interactions which were instrumental in the creation of the above-mentioned images and theoretical concepts of the field.

Like an actress, Palladino offered a performance that shaped and constructed views of psychical research. Some of these views (or images) attempted to be scientific, based on the controlled exploration of the medium's phenomena (as seen in the work of Lombroso and Carrington). But they were also controversial, erratic and disordered, as seen in the sensationalist newspaper coverage of Palladino's séances, and in her fraudulent, 'hysterical' and erotic behaviors. These behaviors provide us with a text by which we may get a glimpse of the factors that contributed to form the negative evaluations of psychical research emphasized by such writers as Jastrow (1910), Leuba (1909) and Münsterberg (1910). Similarly, the character of Palladino's phenomena, together with her verbal statements about forces and other behaviors consistent with such ideas, contributed to concepts of force prevalent at the time. All these resources, which are not necessarily in contradiction with the factual (parapsychological) claims for the phenomena, illustrate what Klaniczay (1990) means when he writes about the formation of charisma from a conglomerate of factors, "where various resources of supernatural power … are put together, exploited and manipulated by the charismatic person himself and by the group around him, who impute extraordinary qualities to him" (p. 9).

Eventually, perspectives such as this may expand the historiography of this field, by enriching our appreciation of the range of individuals who have made psychical research history, and of the variety of ways by which they have had an impact on the field.

Notes

1 See, respectively, Cott and Pieck (1979), Hill (1985), Kessler-Harris (1982), Kulikoff (1986), Pico (1983), and Poos (1991).

2 They may also be found among researchers, as I have argued in the case of women in parapsychology (Alvarado, 1989).

3 Another way of including mediums and psychics in history is to study their careers from their own point of view. That is, considering their experiences, motivations, needs, expectations, and opinions regarding psychic phenomena and their performance as mediums or psychics (for a discussion in the context of medical patients see Porter, 1985). For example, recent historical studies have discussed the social and political function of mediumship for women during the nineteenth century (Braude, 1989; Owen, 1990).

4 Much has been written about Palladino. For reviews of her career see Alippi (1962), Amadou (1957, pp. 57–101), Carrington (1909a), Dingwall (1950, Chap. 5), Hansel (1989, pp. 237–243) and Inglis (1977, Chaps. 35, 38). Morselli (1908, Vol. 1, pp. 134–170; Vol. 2, pp. xvii–xviii) presents an extensive bibliography up to 1907. See also the bibliographies of Alvarado (1987, pp.67–72) and Dingwall (1950, pp. 215–217).

5 Tabori (1972, pp. 24–60, 173–210) has discussed the psychical research career of these men. Rogo (1975) has discussed some of the controversies created by Palladino.

6 I am quoting from Joire (n. d., ca. 1916, p. 389), who presents an English translation of the report.

7 Psychical research periodicals discussed séances held with Palladino reported in newspapers (e.g. Further Experiments, 1907; Lang, 1893). Italian journalist Luigi Barzini collected several of his newspaper articles about Palladino into his book *Nel Mondo dei Misteri con Eusapia Paladino* (1984).

8 Other analyses using a wider selection of newspapers should be done before any conclusion is reached. But the fact remains that the *Times* was one of the main papers of the period, boasting a daily circulation on weekdays for 1909–1910 of over 170,000 (Berger, 1951, p. 569). In addition, the same negative tone prevalent in the *Times* may be found in the intellectual reviews of the time (e.g. Jastrow, 1910; Leuba, 1909; Münsterberg, 1910).

9 These disagreements were carried into the pages of the *Journal of the American Society for Psychical Research* (e.g. Carrington, 1911b; Hyslop, 1911). See also Carrington (1910b) opposing opinions, described in the *Times* as the "battle between the anti-Palladinoists and the pro-Palladinoists …" (Palladino Test, 1910, p. 1).

10 These séances also say much about power and gender roles when it is noticed that a low-class woman was surrounded (mostly) by men from the higher classes.

11 For reviews see Carrington (1939a, pp. 45–58), González Quevedo (1971, Vol. 1, Chap. 1), Montandon (1927), and Sudre (1960, Chap. 6). Some recent examples of these ideas include publications from China (for a review see Zha & McConnell, 1991) and the work of Andrade (1983) and Motoyama (1991).

12 The latter is a reference to the problem of ectoplasm, and, more generally, to materialization phenomena (see the reviews of Dingwall, 1921; González Quevedo, 1971, Vol. 1, Chaps. 9–10; Vol. 2, Chaps. 1–6; and Sudre, 1960, Chap. 8.

13 Other reports include Barzini (1984, p. 68), Bottazzi (1907, pp. 275, 285), Carrington (1910a, p. 313), and Flammarion (1909, pp.72, 208).

14 Feelings of exhaustion were also reported by some sitters (e.g., Feilding et al., 1909, p. 554; Carrington, 1909a, pp. 315–316). Albert de Rochas (1896, p. 20) affirmed that the medium sometimes touched sitters as if to extract "magnetic force." Lodge (1894, pp. 326–327) and Morselli (1908, Vol. 1, pp. 316–319, 351–352) reported dynamometric measures of hand grip as a way of measuring possible expenditure of energy by the medium and the sitters.

15 On the importance of verbal statements in relation to increasing the impact of and belief in psychic or spiritual readings see Heeren and Mason (1984).

16 Some clear discussions of this model may be found in Carrington (1922), de Coudenhove (1909), Gruber (1926), Joire (n. d., ca. 1916), Mackenzie (1923), and Sudre (1960).

References

Aggazzotti, A., Foà, C., Foà, P. & Herlitzka, A. (1907) The experiments of Prof. P. Foà, of the University of Turin, and three doctors, assistants of Professor Mosso, with Eusapia Paladino. *Annals of Psychical Science 5,* 361–392.

Alippi, T. (1962). Eusapia Palladino. *Luce e Ombra 62,* 126–155, 210–240, 283–310.

Alrutz, S. (1922). Problems of hypnotism: an experimental investigation. *Proceedings of the Society for Psychical Research, 32,* 151–178.
Alvarado, C. S. (1987). Historical notes on a séance with Eusapia Palladino in 1912. *Zetetic Scholar Nos. 12/13,* 61–72.
Alvarado, C. S. (1989). The history of women in parapsychology: a critique of past work and suggestions for further research. *Journal of Parapsychology, 53,* 233–249.
Amadou, R. (1953). Esquisse d'une histoire philosophique du fluide. *Revue Métapsychique 21,* 5–33.
Amadou, R. (1957). *Les grandes mediums.* Denoel.
Andrade, H. G. (1983). *Morte, renascimiento, evoluqao: Uma biologia transcendental.* Pensamento.
Angoff, A. (1974). *Eileen Garrett and the world beyond the senses.* William Morrow.
Baraduc, H. (1896). *L'ame humaine: Ses mouvements, ses lumieres et l'iconographie de l'invisible fluidique.* Georges Carrel.
Barrington, M. R. (1992). Palladino and the invisible man who never was. *Journal of the Society for Psychical Research, 58,* 324–340.
Barzini, L. (1984). *Nel mondo dei misteri con Eusapia Paladino.* Longanesi. (Original work published 1907).
Berger, M. (1951). *The story of The New York Times: 1851–1951.* Simon & Schuster.
Bericht über die zu Mailand mit Eusapia Paladino von fünf italienischen Gelehrten und Dr. du Prel auf Einladung des Herausgebers im September und October 1892 angestellten Experimente. (1893). *Psychische Studien, 20,* 1–28.
Biondi, M. (1988). *Tavoli e medium: Storia dello spiritismo in Italia.* Gremese.
Bottazzi, P. (1907). The unexplored regions of human biology: observations and experiments with Eusapia Paladino. *Annals of Psychical Science, 6,* 149–156, 260–290, 377–422.
Bozzano, E. (1903). *Ipotesi spiritica e teorie scientifiche.* A. Donath.
Braude, A. (1989). *Radical spirits: Spiritualism and women's rights in nineteenth century America.* Beacon Press.
Calls Paladino a fraud: Prof. Münsterberg says he has detected tricks of the medium. (1910, January 20). *New York Times,* p. 1.
Carrington, H. (1909a). *Eusapia Palladino and her phenomena.* B. W. Dodge.
Carrington, H. (1909b). Eusapia Palladino: the despair of science. *McClure's Magazine 33,* 660–675.
Carrington, H. (1910a). American notes. *Annals of Psychical Science, 9,* 304–316.
Carrington, H. (1910b). Correspondence: Prof. Hyslop and Eusapia Palladino. *Annals of Psychical Science, 9,* 304–316.
Carrington, H. (1910c). Eusapia Palladino and fraud. *Journal of the Society for Psychical Research, 14,* 370–372.
Carrington, H. (1910d). A reply to Mr. Podmore's criticism of the Paladino report. *Light, 30,* 135–136.
Carrington, H. (1911a). An account of Eusapia Palladino's American séances. In I. K. Funk (Ed.), *The widow's mite and other psychic phenomena* (3rd ed., pp. 523–544). Funk & Wagnalls.
Carrington, H. (1911b). Correspondence: Eusapia Palladino and the Burton case. *Journal of the American Society for Psychical Research, 5,* 487–488.
Carrington, H. (1913). *Personal experiences in spiritualism* (Including the Official Account and Record of the American Palladino Séances). T. Werner Laurie.
Carrington, H. (1919). *Modern psychical phenomena: Recent researches and speculations.* Dodd, Mead.
Carrington, H. (1920). *The coming science.* Small, Maynard.
Carrington, H. (1922). Physical and psycho-physiological researches in mediumship. In C. Vett (Ed.). *Le Compte Rendu Officiel du Premier Congrès International des Recherches Psychiques à Copenhague* (pp. 123–141). No publisher.
Carrington, H. (1931). *The story of psychic science (Psychical Research).* Ives Washburn. (Original work published 1930).
Carrington, H. (1939a). *Laboratory investigations into psychic phenomena.* David McKay.
Carrington, H. (1939b). Some personal experiences with Eusapia Palladino. *Journal of the American Society for Psychical Research, 33,* 238–249.
Carrington, H. (1946). *The invisible world.* Beechhurst Press.
Carrington, H. (1954). *The American Séances with Eusapia Palladino.* Garrett Publications.

Cassirer, M. (1983). The fluid hands of Eusapia Palladino. *Journal of the Society for Psychical Research, 52,* 105–112.
Chiaia, E. (1890). Expériences medianimiques. *Compte Rendu du Congres Spirite et Spiritualiste International,* 326–334. Librairie Spirite.
Ciolfi, E. (1891). Les expériences de Naples. *Annales des Sciences Psychiques, 1,* 326–332.
Close watch on Paladino séances. (1909, November 12). *New York Times,* p. 12.
Comey, A. M. (1894). The psychical experiments at Milan. *Psychical Review, 2,* 45–64.
Coon, D. J. (1992). Testing the limits of sense and science: American experimental psychologists combat Spiritualism, 1880–1920. *American Psychologist, 47,* 143–151.
Cott, N. F., & Pieck, E. H. (Eds.). (1979). *A heritage of her own: Toward a new social history of American women.* Simon & Schuster.
de Coudenhove, Count A. (1909). Concerning physical phenomena in mediumship. *Annals of Psychical Science, 8,* 467–483.
Courtier, J. (1908). Rapport sur les séances d'Eusapia Palladino a l'institut General Psychologique. *Bulletin de l'Institut General Psychologique, 8,* 415–546.
Cox, E. W. (1872). *Spiritualism answered by science* (New Rev. ed.). Longman.
Crawford, W. J. (1916). *The reality of psychic phenomena: Raps, levitations, etc.* John M. Watkins.
Crookes, W. (1874). *Researches in the phenomena of Spiritualism.* J. Burns.
Davis, W. S. (1909, October 17). An analysis of the exploits of Madame Palladino. *New York Times,* Pt. 5, p. 2.
Davis W. S. (1910). *The New York* exposure of Eusapia Palladino. *Journal of the American Society for Psychical Research, 4,* 401–424.
Dingwall, E. J. (1921). The plasma theory. *Journal of the American Society for Psychical Research, 15,* 207–219.
Dingwall, E. J. (1950). *Very peculiar people.* Rider.
Dods, J. B. (1854). *Spirit manifestations examined and explained: Judge Edmons refuted; or, an exposition of the involuntary powers and instincts of the human mind.* New York: De Witt & Davenport.
Drinka, G. F. (1984). *The birth of neurosis: Myth, malady, and the Victorians.* Simon & Schuster.
Ellenberger, H. F. (1970). *The discovery of the unconscious: The history and evolution of dynamic psychiatry.* Basic Books.
Eusapia Paladino: the woman who has mystified the scientists of Europe soon to submit herself to a series of tests in America. (1909a, September 26). *New York Times,* Pt. 6, p. 9.
Eusapia Palladino. (1909b, October 6). *New York Times,* p. 8.
Eusapia Palladino in America. (1910). *Journal of the Society for Psychical Research, 14,* 265–275.
A famous medium exposed. (1910, May 12). *New York Times,* p. 10.
Feilding, E., & Baggally, W. W. (1910). Note on the above. *Journal of the Society for Psychical Research, 14,* 343–345.
Feilding, E., Baggally, W. W., & Carrington, H. (1909). Report on a series of sittings with Eusapia Palladino. *Proceedings of the Society for Psychical Research, 23,* 309–569.
Flammarion, C. (1897). A séance with Eusapia Paladino: Psychic forces. *Arena, 18,* 730–747.
Flammarion, C. (1909). *Mysterious psychic forces: an account of the author's investigations in psychical research, together with those of other European savants.* Small, Maynard. (Original work published in French, 1907).
Fontana, D. (1992). The Feilding Report and the determined critic. *Journal of the Society for Psychical Research, 58,* 341–350.
de Fontenay, G. (1898). *A propos d'Eusapia Paladino.* Societe d'Editions Scientifiques.
Further experiments with Eusapia Paladino. (1907). *Annals of Psychical Science 5,* 208–213.
Gauld, A. (1968). *The founders of psychical research.* Routledge and Kegan Paul.
Geertz, C. (1983). *Local knowledge: Further essays in interpretive anthropology.* Basic Books.
Geley, G. (1927). *Clairvoyance and materialisation: A record of experiments.* T. Fisher Unwin. (Original work published in French,1924).
General Meeting. (1893). *Journal of the Society for Psychical Research, 6,* 78–79.
González Quevedo, O. (1971). *Las fuerzas fisicas de la mente* (2 vols.). Sal Terrae. (Original work published in Portuguese,1969).
Gregory, A. (1985). *The strange case of Rudi Schneider.* Scarecrow Press.

Gregory, W. (1851). *Letters to a candid enquirer, on animal magnetism.* Taylor, Walton and Maberly.
Gruber, K. (1926). The problem of materialization, and its significance. *Journal of the American Society for Psychical Research, 20,* 279–289, 342–351.
Hansel, C. E. M. (1989). *The search for psychic power: ESP and parapsychology revisited.* Prometheus.
Heeren, J. W., & Mason, M. (1984). Seeing and believing: a study of contemporary spiritual readers. *Semiotica, 50,* 191–211.
Hill, C. (1985). *The world turned upside-down: radical ideas during the English revolution.* Penguin Books. (Original work published, 1972).
Hyslop, J. H. (1909, November 21). Paladino and science: Prof. Hyslop replies to Mr. Carrington's allegations. *New York Times,* Pt. 2, p. 12.
Hyslop, J. H. (1910). Eusapia Palladino. *Journal of the American Society for Psychical Research, 4,* 169–185.
Hyslop, J. H. (1911). Editor's reply. *Journal of the American Society for Psychical Research, 7,* 488–494.
Hyslop, J. H. (1914). Editorial: the financial conditions of the Society. *Journal of the American Society for Psychical Research, 8,* 18–25.
Inglis, B. (1977). *Natural and supernatural: A history of the paranormal from earliest times to 1914.* Hodder and Stoughton.
Irwin, H. J. (1987). Charles Bailey: A biographical study of the Australian apport medium. *Journal of the Society for Psychical Research, 54,* 97–118.
Irwin, W. (1909, November 15). Paladino does her marvels. *New York Times,* pp. 1–2.
Jastrow, J. (1909). The case of Lombroso. *Dial, 47,* 284–286.
Jastrow, J. (1910). The case of Paladino. *American Review of Reviews, 42,* 74–84.
Jastrow, J. (1918). *The psychology of conviction: A study of beliefs and attitudes.* Houghton Mifflin.
Jenkins, E. (1982). *The shadow and the light: A defence of Daniel Dunglas Home, the medium.* Hamish Hamilton.
Joire, P. (1905). Modifications in the nervous force externalised, according to the state of health of the subjects. *Annals of Psychical Science, 2,* 219–234.
Joire, P. (n. d., ca. 1916). *Psychical and supernormal phenomena.* Frederick A. Stokes. (Original work published in French, 1909).
Jordanova, L. (1989). *Sexual visions: Images of gender in science and medicine between the eighteenth and twentieth centuries.* University of Wisconsin Press.
Kardec, A. (1874). *Experimental Spiritism: Book on mediums; or, guide for mediums and invocations.* Colby and Rich. (Original work published in French, 1861).
Kellogg, J. L. (1910). Does Eusapia trick unconsciously? *Journal of the Society for Psychical Research, 14,* 386–388.
Kenny, M. G. (1986). *The passion of Ansel Bourne: Multiple personality in American culture.* Smithsonian Institution Press.
Kessler-Harris, A. (1982). *Out to work: A history of wage-earning women in the United States.* Oxford University Press.
Klaniczay, G. (1990). *The uses of supernatural power: The transformation of popular religion in medieval and early-modern Europe.* Princeton University Press.
de Krauz, C. (1894). Expériences medianiques de Varsovie. *Revue de l'Hypnotisme Expérimental et Thérapeutique, 9,* 1–20, 42–45, 70–79, 106–111, 143–150, 169–179.
Krebs, S. L. (1910). Trick-methods of Eusapia Paladino; major and minor. *Journal of the Society for Psychical Research, 14,* 297–317.
Kudriavtzeff, K. (1909). Human radiations and their application to healing. *Light 29,* 175–178.
Kulikoff, A. (1986). *Tobacco and slaves: The development of southern cultures in the Chesapeake, 1680–1800.* University of North Carolina Press.
Lafontaine, C. (1847). *L'Art de magnetiser: Ou, le magnetisme animal considere sou le point de vue theorique, pratique at therapeutique.* Germer Baillière.
Lang, V. R. (1893). Neue expérimente mit Eusapia Paladino: Nach dem Berichte des Dr. Julian Ochorowicz im "Kurjer Warszawski". *Psychische Studien, 20,* 417–425.
Le Clair, R. C. (Ed.). (1966). *The letters of William James and Theodore Flournoy.* University of Wisconsin Press.

Leuba, J. H. (1909). Eusapia Paladino: A critical consideration of the medium's most striking performances. *Putnam's Magazine, 7*, 407–415.
Lodge, O. J. (1894). Experience of unusual physical phenomena occurring in the presence of an entranced person (Eusapia Paladino). *Journal of the Society for Psychical Research, 6*, 306–336, 346–360.
Lombroso, C. (1892). Les faits spiritiques et leur explication psychiatrique. *Revue de I'Hypnotisme Experimental et Therapeutique, 6*, 289–296.
Lombroso, C. (1908a). Eusapia Paladino and spiritism. *Annals of Psychical Science, 7*, 167–180.
Lombroso,C. (1908b). Psychology and spiritism. *Annals of Psychical Science, 7*, 376–380.
Lombroso, C. (1909). After death—what? Spiritistic phenomena and their interpretation. Small, Maynard.
Mackenzie, W. (1923). *Metapsichica moderna: Fenomeni Medianici e promlemi del subconsciente.* Libreria di Scienze e Lettere.
Mahan, A. (1855). *Modern mysteries explained and exposed.* J. P. Jewett.
Martinéz-Taboas, A., & Francia, M. (1993). The Feilding Report, Wiseman's critique and scientific reporting. *Journal of the Society for Psychical Research, 59*, 120–129.
Maxwell, J. (1905). *Metapsychical phenomena: Methods and observations.* Duckworth. [Original work published in French, 1903].
Mesmer, F. A. (1980). Catechism on animal magnetism. In Bloch, G. J. (Ed. & Trans.). *Mesmerism: A translation of the original scientific and medical writings of F. A. Mesmer* (pp. 81–86). William Kaufmann. (Original work published in French, 1784).
Mille, P. (1908). Esquisses d'aprés nature: Eusapia Palladino. *Les Temps (le 6 fevrier)*, 2.
Miller, D. (1910, May 12). Paladino tricks all laid bare. *New York Times*, pp. 1–3.
Montandon, R. (1927). *Les radiations humaines: Introduction à la démonstration expérimentale de l'existence des corps subtils de l'homme.* Félix Alcan.
Morselli, E. (1907). Eusapia Paladino and the genuineness of her phenomena. *Annals of Psychical Science 5*, 319–360.
Morselli, E. (1908). *Psicologia e "Spiritismo: Impressioni e note critiche sui fenomeni medianici di Eusapia Palladino"* (2 vols.). Fratelli Bocca.
Motoyama, H. (1991). *The correlation between psi energy and ki: Unification of religion and science.* Human Science Press.
Münsterberg, H. (1910). My friends the spiritualists: some theories and conclusions concerning Eusapia Palladino. *Metropolitan Magazine, 31*, 559–572.
Myers, F. W. H. (1895). Reply to Mr. Page Hopps, concerning Eusapia Paladino. *Journal of the Society for Psychical Research, 7*, 164.
Nelson, G. K. (1969). *Spiritualism and society.* Routledge and Kegan Paul.
New York Times (1975). *The New York Times Index for the Published News of 1909* (Vol. 12, prior series). New York Times.
New York Times (1976). *The New York Times Index for the Published News of 1910* (Vol. 13, prior series). New York Times.
Ochorowicz, J. (1896). La question de la fraude dans les expériences avec Eusapia Paladino. *Annales des Sciences Psychiques, 6*, 79–123.
Ochorowicz, J. (1910). Les rayons rigides et les rayons Xx: études expérimentales. *Annales des Sciences Psychiques, 20*, 97–105, 129–136, 172–178, 204–209, 225–231, 257–263, 295–302, 336–344, 357–370.
Osty, E. & Osty, M. (1931–32). Les pouvoirs inconnus de l'esprit sur la matière. *Revue Métapsychique No. 6*, 393–427; *1*, 1–59; *2*, 81–122.
Owen, A. (1990). *The darkened room: Women, power and spiritualism in late Victorian England.* University of Pennsylvania Press.
Paladino meets a firm skeptic. (1909, November 17). *New York Times*, p. 1.
Paladino used phosphorous. (1909, November 19). *New York Times*, p. 6.
Palladino ready for a strict test. (1910, May 14). *New York Times*, pp. 1–2.
Palladino test won't take place. (1910, May 27). *New York Times*, pp. 1–2.
Petetin, J. H. D. (1808). *Electricité animâtes, prouvée par la découverte des phénomènes physiques et moraux de la catalepsie hystérique, et des variétés* (2nd ed.). Brunot-Labbe.
Picó, F. (1983). *Los gallos peleados.* Huracán.

Podmore, F. (1894). Review of "Expériences de Milan," by C. Richet, and of "Rapport de la commission réunie à Milan pour l'etude des phénomènes psychiques." *Proceedings of the Society for Psychical Research, 9,* 218–225.
Podmore, F. (1902). *Modern spiritualism: A history and a criticism* (2 vols.). Methuen.
Poos, L. R. (1991). *A rural society after the black death: Essex 1350–1525.* Cambridge University Press.
Porter, R. (1985). The patient's view: doing medical history from below. *Theory and Society, 14,* 175–198.
du Prel, C. (1893). In Sachen der Mailänder spiritistischen Sitzungen: Berichtigung und Abwehr. *Psychische Studien, 20,* 42–47.
Rapport de la commission réunie à Milan pour l'etude des phénomènes psychiques. (1893). *Annales des Sciences Psychiques, 3,* 39–64.
Reichenbach, C. von (1851). *Physico-physiological researches on the dynamics of magnetism, electricity, heat, light, crystallization, and chemism, in their relation to vital force.* J. S. Redfield. (Original work published in German, 1845).
Richet, C. (1893). Expériences de Milan. *Annales des Sciences Psychiques, 3,* 1–31.
Richet, C. (1923). *Thirty years of psychical research: Being a treatise on metapsychics.* Macmillan. (Original work published in French, 1922).
de Rochas, A. (1887). *Les forces non definies: Recherches historiques et expérimentales.* G. Masson.
de Rochas, A. (1895). *L'extériorisation de la sensibilité: Etude expérimentale et historique.* Chamuel.
de Rochas, A. (1896). *L'exteriorisation de la motricite: Recueil d'experiences et d'observations.* Chamuel.
de Rochas, A. (1909). The fluidic hands of Eusapia. *Annals of Psychical Science, 8,* 219–228.
Rogers, E. C. (1853). *Philosophy of mysterious agents, human and mundane; Or, The dynamic laws and relations of man.* J. P. Jewett.
Rogo, D. S. (1975). Eusapia Palladino and the structure of scientific controversy. *Parapsychology Review, 6(2),* 23–27.
Schrenck-Notzing, A. de (1928). *Los fenomenos de la mediumnidad.* No publisher given. (Original work published in German, 1920).
Science and the spirits. (1893). *Scientific American Supplement 35,* 14327–14330.
Sharpe, J. (1991). History from below. In P. Burke (Ed.). *New perspectives on historical writing* (pp. 24–41). Pennsylvania State University Press.
Sittings with Eusapia Palladino in America. (1910). *Journal of the Society for Psychical Research, 14,* 329–343.
Sudre, R. (1960). *Parapsychology.* Citadel Press. (Original work published in French, 1956).
Tabori, P. (1972). *Pioneers of the unseen.* Taplinger.
Thurston, H. (1910, May 14). Believers in Palladino: magician Thurston offers $1,000 if it be shown she depends on fraud. *New York Times,* p. 2.
Tietze, T. R. (1973). *Margery.* Harper and Row.
Topics of the times: Mme. Paladino and her investigators. (1909a, November 12). *New York Times,* p. 8.
Topics of the times: So this is the famous Paladino! (1909b, November 16). *New York Times,* p. 8.
Venzano, J. (1907). A contribution to the study of materialisations. *Annals of Psychical Science, 6,* 75–119, 157–195.
Wiseman, R. (1992). The Feilding Report: A reconsideration. *Journal of the Society for Psychical Research, 58,* 129–152.
Wittig, G. C. (ed.). (1893). Zur vorgeschichte des münchener zeitungs—Angriffes auf den Mailänder Collectiv—Bericht und der darauf folgenden Berichtigung und Abwehr. *Psychische Studien 20,* 29–42.
Zha, L., & McConnell, T. (1991). Parapsychology in the People's Republic of China: 1979–1989. *Journal of the American Society for Psychical Research, 85,* 119–143.

Théodore Flournoy on Veridical Hallucinations: A Reprint and Historical Note*

Carlos S. Alvarado†

While Swiss psychologist Théodore Flournoy's (1854–1920) interest in psychical research has received some attention[1] there is little information about the beginnings of his interest on the subject. In this brief paper I will present a translation of an early example of Flournoy's interest in psychic phenomena that has not been discussed in the above-mentioned literature.

According to Édouard Claparède (1873–1940), Flournoy's colleague and cousin, Flournoy had some early brushes with the topic in the early 1890s. One of them was a visit in 1893 to Flournoy's laboratory of a man whose daughter supposedly had thought-transference abilities, but whose performance showed the whole thing depended on verbal cues (Claparède, 1921, p. 68). Another was a lecture Flournoy presented in 1894 about "occult psychology" (p. 36).

Flournoy is generally remembered in psychical research history for his study of medium Hélène Smith (whose real name was Catherine Élise Müller, 1861–1929; see Shamdasani, 1994). This work was reported in his important book *Des Indes à la Planète Mars: Étude sur un Cas de Somnambulisme avec Glossolalie,* also published in English (Flournoy, 1900a, 1900b).[2] In addition to this work Flournoy is known to have published earlier discussions of mediumship (Flournoy, 1897, 1899a),[3] and later papers (e.g., Flournoy, 1901b, 1903, 1909) and a book related to psychical research which, in addition to some new material, had reprints of previously published articles (Flournoy, 1911).

The material translated and reprinted here has escaped mention in most writings about Flournoy's interest in psychical research. This is the case regardless of it been listed in Flournoy's bibliography compiled by Claparède (1921, p. 121). But this commission may be due to the fact that the title of Flournoy's work did not refer to psychic phenomena.

The paper, or more properly, the abstract of a presentation given by Flournoy, was entitled "Sur les Hallucinations a l'état Normal" [On Hallucinations in the Normal State] (1891b). Flournoy presented it to the Société de Physique et d'Histoire Naturelle de Genève, an important scientific and scholarly Swiss institution founded at the end of the eighteenth-century (Société, n.d.). It was read at a session held on December 18, 1890, and the abstract appeared in 1891 in the *Archives des Sciences Physiques et Naturelles*, the journal of the Society.

The abstract is presented here as an example of an early psychical research contribution by Flournoy, and one that reflected the interest the topic of veridical hallucinations generated during the nineteenth-century.

*Republished with permission from *Psypioneer Journal, 9*, 163–170, 2013.

†I wish to thank the Society for Psychical Research for a grant that supported the writing of this paper and Nancy L. Zingrone for useful editorial assistance.

Nineteenth-Century Psychical Research and Veridical Hallucinations

Although veridical hallucinations have been of interest before the founding of the Society for Psychical Research (SPR), the topic acquired more prominence and was more widely discussed during the late nineteenth-century thanks to the work of the SPR (Le Maléfan, 2008; on apparitions in general in the British context see McCorristine, 2010). SPR workers discussed veridical hallucinations as "truth-telling" hallucinations. These were observed to "coincide with some crisis in the life of the person whose image is seen, and which, therefore, as we contend, though they are in one sense hallucinations, yet have some reality behind them—some origin exterior to the eyes and brain of the person who sees them" (Barrett, Massey, Moses, Podmore, Gurney & Myers, 1884a, pp. 49–50).[4]

In an early volume of the Society's *Proceedings* it was stated in reports by their Literary Committee that some veridical apparitions and other experiences were probably explained by telepathy (Barrett et al., 1884b, 1884c). The idea, as well as the collection and analyses of cases, eventually culminated in the publication of the first major SPR project and a nineteenth-century classic of psychical research, the book *Phantasms of the Living* (1886) authored by Edmund Gurney (1847–1888), Frederic W.H. Myers (1843–1901), and Frank Podmore (1856–1910), which was followed by what became known as the Census of Hallucinations (Sidgwick, Johnson, Myers, Podmore, & Sidgwick, 1894).[5]

Discussions of the topic transcended the British context when the Census and veridical hallucinations were discussed in international psychology congresses (e.g., Mariller, 1890; Sidgwick, 1892), and when others wrote and commented about these manifestations. An example were French discussions (e.g., Binet, 1894; Paulhan, 1892), including some by Myers (1886a, 1886b). 1891 was an important year in the French context. An abridged translation of *Phantasms of the Living* was published in 1891 in French under the title *Les Hallucinations Télépathiques* (Gurney, Myers, & Podmore, 1891), and included a preface by Charles Richet (1850–1935), who by that time was well known in psychical research circles.[6] The same year saw the publication of cases from *Les Hallucinations Télépathiques* in the *Annales des Sciences Psychiques* (Hallucinations Télépathiques, 1891; Hallucinations Télépathiques Expérimentales, 1891), and the publication of the abstract of Flournoy's presentation in Switzerland.

Théodore Flournoy

By the time Flournoy presented his paper on veridical hallucinations he had started his career in psychology (Claparède, 1921). He obtained his initial baccalaureate degrees in literature, mathematics and physical and natural sciences between 1872 and 1875, and then studied theology briefly and eventually qualified as a physician. Later he studied philosophy at Leipzig, where he took courses with Wilhelm Wundt (1832–1920).

The 1890s were the beginnings of Flournoy career in psychology. In his first major work Flournoy (1890a) called for empirical approaches to psychology and for the abandonment of metaphysical concerns such as speculations about the spirit and its relation to the body. In 1891 he obtained a chair in experimental psychology which, different from other European psychology chairs, was not located within a philosophy faculty, but was instead part of the faculty of sciences. Further developments included a laboratory of psychology founded in 1892 which, according to Flournoy (1896) was not limited to German-type measurement oriented psychology but included other research approaches.

His paper on veridical hallucinations (Flournoy, 1891b) was presented in a period in which he was very active studying various psychological phenomena. In fact, this paper, essentially a psychical research paper, was part of his early development and work as a psychologist. Other examples of his early work about specific psychological phenomena include his publications about synesthesia (Flournoy, 1890b, 1893), reaction time (Flournoy, 1892a, 1892b), and mental activity and physiology (Flournoy, 1891a). As stated before, the paper about veridical hallucinations was published as an abstract in 1891.

Flournoy's "Sur les Hallucinations a l'État Normal" (1891)

We have given the name of *veridical* hallucinations to those which correspond to a real event out of the range of the senses of the subject.[7] For example, an individual has all of a sudden the apparition of an absent person, and it is learned later that this person died precisely at this time. In their *Phantasms of the Living* (London 1887)[8] Mrs. Gurney, Myers and Podmore published several hundreds of cases of this kind. The strangeness of these facts, and on the other hand the impossibility of treating them as simple coincidences, considering the number and guarantees of authenticity of many of them, have driven the Society for psychical [*sic*] Research, and following its lead the International Congress of Experimental Psychology, to organize, both in Europe as in America, a little understood survey of hallucinations with normal persons awake and healthy.[9] Mr. Flournoy gave an account of some of the observations which he made for this occasion.

With the first hundred persons questioned seventeen were found which had hallucinations (two tactile, four visual, eleven auditory). Only one of them was in the category of hallucinations said to be *veridical*: it was about a nurse who, being awake and occupied with the care of her profession, believed she was called in the middle of the night by the voice of her brother, who she knew was sick at eight miles from there. The following day a dispatch informed her that he had died during the night at the same time that she had heard his voice. It would be pointless to draw any conclusion from this isolated fact. The detailed analysis of six other cases seems to indicate that other people in good health and of sound mind can have hallucinations. Under the influence of various causes (concern, tiredness, perhaps light unperceived drowsiness by the subject), the working of the nervous centers which should not produce images but exceptionally reaches a degree of intensity which corresponds to a real sensation; there is thus a hallucination, immediately rectified by reason or by the control of the other senses. The Christian name of the subject and the voice of loved ones, who died after some time, seems particularly apt to leave from the sphere of a simple memory to sometime acquire the force and the vivacity of external perceptions.

Concluding Remarks

While Flournoy's paper does not add much to the historical study of veridical hallucinations, it provides us with generally neglected information about his early interest in psychical research. Similarly, his paper provides us with another example of discussions on the subject in a scholarly context, in this case the Société de Physique et d'Histoire Naturelle de Genève. This parallels other discussions in forums such as the international congresses of psychology (Alvarado, 2010b), and in mainstream publications (e.g., Alvarado, 2009), something that does not imply general acceptance of the topic.

Finally, the material presented here is yet another example of how some of the pioneers of European psychology were involved with the phenomena and ideas of psychical research, a topic that has received some discussion in recent decades (e.g., Alvarado, 2010a; Plas, 2000; Crabtree, 1993). Like other figures—among them Pierre Janet (1859–1947) and Charles Richet (Plas, 2000)—Flournoy showed interest in psychic phenomena early in his career. This indicates the importance of the topic in nineteenth-century Europe.

These, and other developments, keep reminding us that the study of psychical research and other "rejected" disciplines and ideas have become part of our modern attempts to understand the past.

Notes

1 See Caratelli (1996), Cifali (2001), Claparède (1921), Goldsmith (1979), and Shamdasani (1994). For studies of other aspects of Flournoy see Alexandre (2011) and Nicolas and Charvillat (1998).
2 Flournoy (1901a) also published another study of this medium reporting later developments that is less known than his book.
3 This includes parts of *Des Indes* presumably appearing before the book was released (Flournoy, 1899b, 1899c).
4 Not all veridical hallucinations referred to crises or to death, as seen in cases of arrival and experimental apparitions (Gurney, Myers, & Podmore, 1886).
5 On these SPR studies see Cerullo (1982), Gauld (1968), and McCorristine (2010).
6 On Richet and psychic phenomena see Alvarado (2008) and Lachapelle (2011).
7 The expression "veridical hallucinations" appears in early issues of the *SPR Proceedings* and *Journal* (Barrett et al., 1884a, p. 48, 1884c, p. 168; General Meeting, 1884, pp. 4, 37).
8 *Phantasms* was first published in 1886.
9 Marillier (1892) reported on surveys in French speaking counties. The full SPR report appeared in their *Proceedings* (Sidgwick et al., 1894).

References

Alexandre, K. (2011). La correspondance d'Alfred Binet a Théodore Flournoy: Témoignage inédit d'une collégiale amitié. *Bulletin de Psychologie, 64*, 239–250.

Alvarado, C. S. (2008). Note on Charles Richet's "La Suggestion mentale et le calcul des probabilités" (1884). *Journal of Scientific Exploration, 22,* 543–548.

Alvarado, C. S. (2009). Psychical research in the *Psychological Review*, 1894–1900: A bibliographical note. *Journal of Scientific Exploration, 23,* 211–220.

Alvarado, C. S. (2010a). Classic text No. 84: 'Divisions of personality and spiritism' by Alfred Binet (1896). *History of Psychiatry, 21*, 487–500.

Alvarado, C. S. (2010b). Nineteenth-century suggestion and magnetism: Hypnosis at the International Congress of Physiological Psychology (1889). *Contemporary Hypnosis, 27*, 48–60.

Barrett, W. F., Massey, C. C., Moses, W. S., Podmore, F., Gurney, E., & Myers, F. W. H. (1884a). Second report of the Literary Committee. *Proceedings of the Society for Psychical Research, 2*, 43–55.

Barrett, W. F., Massey, C. C., Moses, W. S., Podmore, F., Gurney, E., & Myers, F. W. H. (1884b). Third report of the Literary Committee: A theory of apparitions: Part I. *Proceedings of the Society for Psychical Research, 2*, 109–136.

Barrett, W. F., Massey, C. C., Moses, W. S., Podmore, F., Gurney, E., & Myers, F.W.H. (1884c). Fourth report of the Literary Committee: A theory of apparitions: Part II. *Proceedings of the Society for Psychical Research, 2*, 157–186.
Binet, A. (1894). Recensement des hallucinations. *L'Année Psychologique, 1*, 494–500.
Caratelli, G. (1996). *Psicología psicoanalisi parapsicología*. Sovera.
Cerullo, J. J. (1982). *The secularization of the soul: Psychical research in modern Britain*. Institute for the Study of Human Issues.
Cifali, M. (2001). Théodore Flournoy, le savant et l'occulte. *Campus, 52*, 6–7.
Claparède, E. (1921). Théodore Flournoy: Sa vie et son oeuvre. *Archives de Psychologie, 18*, 1–125.
Crabtree, A. (1993). *From Mesmer to Freud: Magnetic sleep and the roots of psychological healing*. Yale University Press.
Flournoy, T. (1890a). *Métaphysique et psychologie*. H. Georg.
Flournoy, T. (1890b). Note sur l'audition coloree. *Archives des Sciences Physiques et Naturelles, 23*, 352–354.
Flournoy, T. (1891a). Activité psychique et physiologie générale. *Revue Philosophique de la France et de l'Etranger, 31*, 506–509.
Flournoy, T. (1891b). Sur les hallucinations a l'état normal. *Archives des Sciences Physiques et naturelles, 25*, 135–136. (Summary)
Flournoy, T. (1892a). Temps de réaction aux impressions auditives. *Archives des Sciences Physiques et Naturelles, 27*, 575–577. (Summary)
Flournoy, T. (1892b). Temps de reaction simple chez un sujet de type visuel. *Archives des Sciences Physiques et Naturelles, 28*, 319-331.
Flournoy, T. (1893). *Des phénomènes de synopsie (audition coloree): Photismes-schemes visuels-personnifications*. Félix Alcan.
Flournoy, T. (1896). *Notice sur le Laboratoire de Psychologie de l'Universite de Geneve*. Ch. Eggimann.
Flournoy, T. (1897). Quelques faits d'imagination subliminale chez les mediums. *Dritter Internationaler Congress fur Psychologie* (pp. 419–420). Munich: J.F. Lehmann.
Flournoy, T. (1899a). Genèse de quelques prétendus messages spirites. *Revue Philosophique de la France et de l'Étranger, 47*, 144–158.
Flournoy, T. (1899b). Somnambulisme et spiritisme. *La Semaine Litteraire*, November 18, 555–558.
Flournoy, T. (1899c). Sur un cas de glossolalie somnambulique. *Archives des Sciences Physiques et Naturelles, 8*, 90–92.
Flournoy, T. (1900a). *Des indes a la planète Mars: Etude sur un cas de somnambulisme avec glossolalie*. Félix Alcan.
Flournoy, T. (1900b). *From India to the planet Mars: A study of a case of somnabulism*. Harper & Brothers.
Flournoy, T. (1901a). Nouvelles observations sur un cas de somnambulisme avec glossolalie. *Archives de Psychologie, 1*, 101–255.
Flournoy, T. (1901b). Observations psychologiques sur le spiritisme. In P. Janet (Ed.), *IV Congres International de Psychologie* (pp. 102–112). Félix Alcan.
Flournoy, T. (1903). Myers et son ouvre posthume. *Archives de Psychologie, 2*, 269–296.
Flournoy, T. (1909). Esprits et mediums. *Bulletin de l'Institut Général Psychologique, 9*, 357–390.
Flournoy, T. (1911). *Esprits et mediums: Mélanges de métapsychique et de psychologie*. Kundig.
Gauld, A. (1968). *The founders of psychical research*. Routledge & Kegan Paul.
General meeting. (1884). *Journal of the Society for Psychical Research, 1*, 3–6, 35–38.
Goldsmith, R. E. (1979). *The life and work of Théodore Flournoy, 1854–1920*. PhD dissertation, Michigan State University.
Gurney, E., Myers, F. W. H., & Podmore, F. (1886). *Phantasms of the living* (2 vols.). Trübner.
Gurney, E., Myers, F. W. H., & Podmore, F. (1891). *Les hallucinations télépathiques*. Félix Alcan.
Hallucinations télépathiques (1891). *Annales des Sciences Psychiques, 1*, 41–62, 163–177, 362–370.
Hallucinations telepathiques experimentales. (1891). *Annales des Sciences Psychiques, 1*, 101–110.
Lachapelle, S. (2011). *Investigating the supernatural: From spiritism and occultism to psychical research and metapsychics in France*, 1853–1931. Johns Hopkins University Press.
Le Maléfan, P. (2008). L'hallucination télépathique ou véridique dans la psychopathologie de la fin du XIXeme siecle et du debut du XXeme siecle. *L 'Evolution Psychiatrique, 73*, 15–40.

Marillier, L. (1890). Statistique des hallucinations. *Congrès International de Psychologie Physiologique* (pp. 44–47). Bureau de Revues.
Marillier, L. (1892). Rapport sur l'enquête statistique sur les hallucinations (France et pays de language française). *International Congress of Experimental Psychology* (pp. 62–67). Williams & Norgate.
McCorristine, S. (2010). *Spectres of the self: Thinking about ghosts and ghosts-seeing in England, 1750–1920.* Cambridge University Press.
Myers, F.W.H. (1886a). Des certaines formes d'hallucination. *Revue Philosophique de la France et de l'Etranger, 21*, 214–215.
Myers, F.W.H. (1886b). Des hallucinations véridiques. *Revue Philosophique de la France et de l'Etranger, 21*, 434.
Nicolas, S., & Charvillat, A. (1998). Théodore Flournoy (1854–1920) and experimental psychology: Historical note. *American Journal of Psychology, 111*, 279–294.
Paulhan, F. (1892). Les hallucinations véridiques et la suggestion mentale. *Revue des Deux Mondes, 62*(s. 3), 65–100.
Plas, R. (2000). *Naissance d'une science humaine: La psychologie: les psychologues et le "merveilleux psychique."* Presses Universitaires de Rennes.
Shamdasani, S. (1994). Encountering Hélène: Théodore Flournoy and the genesis of subliminal psychology. In T. Flournoy, *From India to the planet Mars: A case of multiple Personality with Imaginary Languages* (pp. xi–li). Princeton University Press.
Sidgwick, H. (1892). Statistical inquiry into hallucinations. *International Congress of Experimental Psychology* (pp. 56–61). Williams & Norgate.
Sidgwick, H., Johnson, A., Myers, F. W. H., Podmore, F., & Sidgwick, E. M. (1894). Report on the Census of Hallucinations. *Proceedings of the Society for Psychical Research, 10*, 25–422.
Société de Physique et d'Histoire Naturelle de Geneve. (n.d.). Online: http://www.unige.ch/sphn/

Telepathic Emissions: Edwin J. Houston on "Cerebral Radiation"*

Carlos S. Alvarado†

Interest in telepathy during the Nineteenth Century developed in the context of ideas of magnetic, nervous, and psychic forces said to project from the physical body to cause various phenomena, as seen in the literatures of mesmerism, Spiritualism, and psychical research. An article about cerebral radiations authored by American electrical engineer Edwin J. Houston in 1892 is reprinted here and commented upon. Houston speculated that cerebral waves were projected to other brains via the ether, a process involving resonance with a similarly disposed brain. These ideas were affected by concepts from physics dealing with such forces as magnetism and constructs like the ether. In fact, the phenomena of thought-transference stimulated many speculations involving ideas of brain waves and radiations that were part of a tendency to reduce unexplained phenomena to physical and physiological principles, or in this case biophysical ones. Houston's paper is one of the most detailed presentation of ideas of this sort published in the Nineteenth Century. Nonetheless, Houston showed no familiarity with the literature of his time about telepathy. While his article did not originate ideas of this sort, it is representative of speculations of the period about what today we refer to as physical transmission models of ESP.

> *Let it be granted that whensoever any action takes place in the brain ... an atomic movement occurs ... Let it also be granted that there is ... [an] "Ether" ... But if these two assumptions be granted ... should it not follow that no brain action can take place without creating a wave or undulation ... in the ether ... Each acting, thinking brain then would become a centre of undulations transmitted from it in all directions through space ... with the varying nature and force of brain actions* ... James T. Knowles (1869:136)

In his book *The Kingdom of Man*, English zoologist and biologist E. Ray Lankester (1847–1929) wrote that wireless telegraphy did not offer support to the idea of thought-transference because:

> ... the important factors in such human intercourse—namely, a signaling-instrument and a code of signals—have not been discovered, as yet in the structure of the human body ... (Lankester 1907, p. 88)

The idea of such signals was inspired by the fast popularization during the Nineteenth Century of communication technology and the establishment of various physical processes, such as the various forms of radiation (L'Annunziata, 2007). This affected conceptions of psychic phenomena, producing a corpus and conceptual tradition of physical and biophysical ideas that, in turn, were part of attempts to naturalize the unusual during the Nineteenth Century (e.g., Gonçalves & Ortega 2013, Meheust 1999). Such concepts ranged from accepted principles and forces—such as electricity and magnetism—to a

*Republished with permission from *Journal of Scientific Exploration, 29*, 467–490, 2015.

†I wish to thank the Society for Psychical Research for financial support. Massimo Biondi and Michael Nahm were helpful with references.

variety of unorthodox ideas of human magnetism, nervous and psychic forces, kind of a psychical physics offering explanations for the mental and physical phenomena of psychical research.[1] These ideas were part of modernism, in the sense that various physical and psychical forces were important for technology, for beliefs, as well as for social and cultural developments, including the arts (Enns & Trower, 2013).

Such physical transmission ideas are still around, as seen in modern speculations about ESP (e.g., Marciak-Kozlowska & Kozlowski, 2013; Vasilescu & Vasilescu, 1996). However, speculations involving hypothetical physical, or biophysical processes, were prevalent during the late Nineteenth Century (and even later), which is the topic of this paper, in which I focus on physical explanations of telepathy.

My purpose is to present a reprint of an article relevant to the history of these ideas. It is a paper published in 1892 by American engineer and electrician Edwin J. Houston about speculations of cerebral radiations to explain telepathy. The excerpt presented here is a good example of early examples of physical transmission models of ESP. The article is, in fact, one of the most detailed discussions of such ideas of the time.

In addition to being a good representative of old transmission models, the paper is of interest as well for other reasons. First, it was written by a prominent individual who was not identified with psychic phenomena, but with other disciplines. Second, the paper, while not widely cited in psychical research circles, was published in several non-psychic American publications, thus helping to popularize psychic phenomena. Third, Houston's article reminds us that, in addition to ideas of nonphysicality and mind-body independence emphasized by some parapsychologists,[2] and certainly prominent both in the past as in the present, the Nineteenth Century also had its share of physicalistic assumptions.

The Context: Forces and Psychic Phenomena

Psychic Forces

Nineteenth-Century physics brought us much information about forces of nature, among them electricity, light, electromagnetism, and concepts such as the ether and the conservation of energy.[3] In his work *When Physics Became King*, Morus (2005) documents how such work transcended scientific circles and influenced society in many ways. I argue, as others have done before (Luckhurst, 2002), that this was the case as well with physical concepts and psychic phenomena, in this case telepathy.

The so-called imponderables, principles such as magnetism and electricity that had a subtle physical nature (Heilbron, 1993), inspired many speculations about psychic phenomena. An important early one involved the concept of animal magnetism, a universal force interacting with physical and biological matter, discussed by Franz Anton Mesmer (1734–1815; 1779) and by his followers, which formed the movement of mesmerism.[4]

The construct of animal magnetism suggested new ways in which human beings were related to nature, a more intimate connection with the surrounding forces, the forces of existence. This magnetism, Segala (2001) has suggested, connected humans more with the cosmos and was a symbol of universal harmony, while pointing to the idea of the unity of forces. Animal magnetism (Mesmer, 1779), which some believed was part of human physiology, and the principle of life itself, was described sometimes as a fluid:

> The magnetic fluid continuously escapes us: It forms an atmosphere around our body … which … does not act noticeably on individuals around us; but when our will pushes and directs it moves with all the strength that we impart: It moves like light rays sent out by bodies ablaze. (Deleuze, 1813, p. 89; this, and other translations, are mine).

Another mesmerist stated: "Man is a congeries of forces all under the regulation of magneto-electric laws. He is, in fact, a magnet ..." (Ashburner, 1867, p. 193). It was this force, or radiation, or fluid, that was believed to act from the mesmerist to the mesmerized person (or somnambule) and cause healings and other phenomena such as the transmission of the thoughts of the mesmerizer (for a pictorial representation of animal magnetism).

Many mesmerists believed that magnetized individuals could perceive the thoughts of others. In Italy it was stated that after the magnetizer imparted his vital fluid to his subject, both shared a common vitality that allowed the latter to feel "different sensations experienced by the magnetizer" (Guidi, 1854, p. 228). Such transmissions were believed by a mesmerist in the United States to be due to the fact that "the magnetic fluid passes from the brain and eye ... of the *magnetizer* to the eye ... and brain of the magnetic somnambulist ..." (Durant 1837, p. 79). In addition to this literature, and to later neo-mesmeric developments that included the work of Alexandre Barėty (1844–1918) and Julian Ochorowicz (1850–1917) (e.g., Barėty 1887, Ochorowicz 1891), over the years there were many discussions about human radiations to explain various phenomena.

These ideas of nervous and vital forces flourished in the context of Spiritualism and, later, in psychical research. The medium, instead of the somnambule, was the dynamo generating forces to produce all sorts of phenomena, including physical ones such as movement of objects and malerializalions.[5] As stated in an early classic of table turning:

> If my brain, active as a Leyden jar, emits and directs a fluidic current through my nerves, if the other members of the [mediumistic] chain follow similarly, it is evident that it would not be long for us to form sort of an electric battery, by which the influence will be felt according to our thoughts; we will produce a rotation, we will produce, also at a distance, vigorous liftings. (De Gasparin, 1854, Vol. 1, p. 514)

Various physical forces were adopted by Spiritualists to explain mediumistic phenomena. One was electricity, which soon was being discussed in terms of the transmission similarities between telegraphy and mediumship. In one case, mediums were seen as electrical conductors in the production of physical phenomena, acting "on principles strictly analogous to the magnetic telegraph" (Davis 1855, p. 66; see also the discussions of Carroll, 1997 and Thurschwell, 2001). In turn, these speculations were conceptually related to older concepts (Amadou, 1953), and to ideas of electrophysiology (Clarke & Jacyna, 1987), and animal magnetism.

Later in the century other forms of radiation were highly influential. In fact, the 1890s brought important developments, such as the discovery of X-rays. From the beginning X-rays captured the popular imagination (Knight, 1986; Pamboukian, 2001), and they were soon connected by many to psychic phenomena such as telepathy (Crookes, 1897; Sibley, 1898; see also Henderson, 1988; Nalale, 2011). "The discovery of the famous X-rays that pass through opaque materials," wrote a commentator, "could well also put us on the path to a rational explanation of clairvoyance" (Bois, 1896, p. 355). In the same year, another author who was discussing X-rays saw these new radiations as analogous to phenomena such as telepathy and clairvoyance and asked if the latter should also be generally accepted (Bixby, 1896, p. 880).

But the 1890s, the decade in which Houston was writing, also brought other ideas of body radiations from psychical researchers. These included: Cesare Lombroso's (1836–1909) belief that cerebral forces could be exteriorized from the body to cause physical phenomena due to the inhibition of centers where that agent was normally used; Hippolyte Baraduc's (1850–1902) studies of instrumental detection of a vital force emanating from the body; and Albert de Rochas' (1837–1914) studies of exteriorization of sensibility (or the projection of a neural principle which had sensation properties) (Baraduc, 1893; De Rochas, 1895; Lombroso, 1892b). The period also presented the use of photography to show the existence of invisible psychic vibrations and fluids, as seen in the work of Baraduc (1896) and others (e.g., Luys & David, 1897).[6]

Thought Transference in the Nineteenth Century

Houston's ideas in the excerpt reprinted below appeared in the context of Nineteenth Century interest in thought-transference (Luckhurst, 2002; Wiley, 2012). An important development was the experimental study of the subject, initially called thought-reading, mind-reading, thought-transference, and eventually telepathy. Following on the observations of mesmerists and others (e.g., Brittan, 1854, Chapter 24), and in the considerable interest brought in by the public performances of mind-readers such as Washington Irving Bishop (1856–1889; Romanes, 1881), many tests were conducted by members of the Society for Psychical Research (SPR) in England. Among them were those reported with the Creery Sisters by Barrett, Gurney, and Myers (1882), and several others published through the end of the Nineteenth Century (e.g., Gurney, Myers, & Barrett, 1884; Guthrie & Birchall, 1883; Lodge, 1884). But there was also work conducted in other countries, among them, Italy (Lombroso, 1891), France (Richet, 1884), and Germany (Schrenck-Notzing, 1891).[7]

The results of this research, it is important to say, were criticized by many who argued that the claims for the reality of the transference of thoughts could have alternate explanations, among them fraud, muscle reading, and other sensory perceptions (e.g., Hall, 1887; Jastrow, 1895). Expressing skepticism, psychologist Edward B. Titchener (1867–1927) stated in *Science*: "No scientifically-minded psychologist believes in telepathy" (Titchener, 1898, p. 897).

As seen in the epigraph at the beginning of this paper, an author writing in 1869 in *The Spectator*, published in London, mentioned transmissions of thought at a distance caused by brain waves moving through the ether (Knowles, 1869; see also Andrew, 1876; and Despine, 1880). Others mentioned the possibility of induction (W. F. Barrett, 1876; McGraw, 1875). Physicist William F. Barrett (1844–1925) speculated that "just as a vibrating tuning fork or string spends its energy most swiftly when it is exciting another similar fork or string in unison with itself, so the activity of the brain may be more speedily exhausted by the presence of other brains capable of sympathetic vibration with itself" (W.F. Barrett, 1882, p. 62).

Many had similar ideas which were published before the paper by Houston discussed here (e.g., C., 1887; Coues, 1885; Haig, 1874; Mancini, 1891). "A candle burning in the night 200 meters away," wrote French physiologist Charles Richet (1850–1935), "produces a very clear light, it seems absurd that at three or four meters of distance cerebral activity shows no action on close-by objects ... If we consider this emissive power absurd, it is only because we do not see it" (Richet, 1884, p. 668).

In a prominent example about what he referred to as "mental telegraphy," Mark Twain (1835–1910) stated in *Harper's New Monthly Magazine:* "Doubtless the something which conveys our thoughts through the air from brain to brain is a finer and subtler form of electricity ..." (Twain 1891, p. 101). But such analogies about thought-transference and the telegraph were not new with Twain, having been used or implied before by others (e.g., Brittan, 1864; Mitchell, 1872). An earlier example was the ideas of a Spanish author who stated that

> [the soul] has in the surrounding electricity a telegraph that is always in immediate contact with our organism which uses it to send the expression of its thoughts to the person it wishes to regardless of distance. (Vergés, 1857, p. 14)

Similarly, many others continued discussing such concepts during the 1890s (e.g., Astere, 1895; Wagstaff, 1892). Lombroso (1892a) wrote about the projection of cortical activity carrying thoughts through the ether. English chemist and physicist William Crookes (1832–1919) speculated on the possibility that the brain may transmit and receive "electrical rays of wavelengths hitherto undetected by instrumental means" (Crookes, 1892, p. 95), which may account for thought-transference.

But it should also be stated that not everyone followed physical transmission models. In later writings about telepathy, some of the early SPR researchers were skeptical of explanations such as physical waves or radiations and saw the process as a psychical one, even though this idea did not involve a clear explanation (e.g., Gurney, Myers, & Podmore, 1886). "If there really is a physical counterpart to the fact of transmission," wrote the authors of the SPR's Third Report of the Literary Committee, "that counterpart remains wholly unknown to us. The physical analogies hitherto suggested for telepathic impulses are aids to imagination and nothing more" (Barrett, Massey, Moses, Podmore, Gurney, & Myers, 1884, p. 135). Others, such as Italian physicist Giovanni Battista Ermacora (1869–1898), offered more specific critiques of physical transmission ideas of telepathy (Ermacora, 1892). In his view such process was not proven, and the waves, if present, should weaken considerably with distance. He also pointed out that such ideas did not explain the intellectual content and selective nature of telepathy, asking why other people did not receive the transmission as well.

Edwin J. Houston

Edwin James Houston (1847–1914) was an educator, an electrical engineer, and an inventor.[8] He was born in Alexandria, Virginia, and taught most of his professional life at the Central High School of Philadelphia, where he had earlier obtained a master's degree. He later taught civil engineering there and was given a chair of natural philosophy, which he held until 1914, when he died. It has been said that Houston brought "to his lectures an extensive knowledge of electricity and regularly illustrated them with elaborate apparatus" (Carlson, 1991, p. 33).

Houston held many honors. He was a member of the electrical commission appointed by the U.S. government in 1884, President of the American Institute of Electrical Engineers (1893–1895), President of the electrical section of the Franklin Institute, and President of Section C of the Electrical Congress held in Chicago in 1893. In addition he taught physics at the Franklin Institute and the Medico-Chirurgical College, both in Philadelphia. He obtained an honorary Ph.D. from Princeton University in 1894.

Working with English engineer and inventor Elihu Thomson (1853–1937), Houston developed various projects such as the Thomson-Houston system of arc lightning, and was co-founder of the Thomson-Houston Electric Company in 1883. After many developments, this eventually led to the creation of General Electric in 1892 (Carlson, 1991).

Houston authored many books. Some examples are *A Dictionary of Electrical Words, Terms and Phrases* (Houston, 1889), *Electricity and Magnetism* (Houston, 1893b), and *The Electric Transmission of Intelligence* (Houston, 1893a). With electrical engineer Arthur E. Kennelly (1861–1939) as co-author, Houston published various treatises such as *Magnetism* (Houston & Kennelly, 1896), *Electric Telegraphy* (Houston & Kennelly, 1897), *Electricity in Electro-Therapeutics* (Houston & Kennelly, 1898), & *Electric Arc Lighting* (Houston & Kennelly, 1906). In addition, Houston was known for his many lectures. In an announcement of a presentation about electricity, he was described as a "most interesting and instructive lecturer" (Anonymous, 1892b, p. 540). Another example was a lecture Houston presented at a meeting of the New York Electrical Society in December of 1892, where he covered topics such as early knowledge about magnetism, magnetic effluvia, Faraday's ideas, magnetic induction, methods of magnetization, and causes of the earth's magnetism (Anonymous, 1892e).

Like others involved with technology and science in the late Nineteenth Century, Houston had a progressive view. In his Inaugural Address before the Congress of the American Institute of Electrical Engineers, held in New York in 1893, Houston commented on how common electrical technology had become among the public (Houston, 1893c). But even though this was taken for granted by many, there was still the possibility of important advancements. This was the case, Houston, wrote, about developments that took place between the Philadelphia International Exhibition (1884) and the World's Fair of Chicago (1893).[9] Houston lived in an era of, and was an active participant in, the rapid technological development of the Nineteenth Century in the United States and elsewhere, as seen particularly in electrical developments, including the internationally known work of Thomas Alva Edison (1847–1931) and Nikolas Tesla (1856–1943) (Carlson, 2013; Freeberg, 2013).[10]

But Houston's interests went beyond electricity, magnetism, and their associated technologies. This was evident in books he wrote about chemistry (Houston, 1883), natural philosophy (Houston, 1884), forestry (Houston, 1893d), and geography (Houston, 1901), as well as in the paper discussed here. In fact, his paper about telepathy may be seen as a connection between his general interests and his work with electricity and magnetism, particularly that which related to communication (Houston, 1893a; Houston & Kennelly, 1897).

Houston does not seem to have published anything about thought-transference before or after he published this paper. The article reprinted here was first presented at a meeting of the Electrical Section of the Franklin Institute in March of 1892 (Anonymous, 1892d). Entitled "Cerebral Radiations," it was published in various journals. These include the *Journal of the Franklin Institute* (Houston, 1892b), from which I copied the article, as well as the *American Gas Light Journal* (Houston, 1892a), *Psychical Review* (Houston, 1892c), *La Science Française* (Houston, 1892g), *Scientific American Supplement* (Houston, 1892d), and *Western Electrician* (Houston, 1892e). The author explained thought-transference: "Cerebral energy … is dissipated by imparting wave motions to the surrounding ether, and such waves are sent out in all directions from the brain" (Houston, 1892b, p. 490).

The Houston Excerpt

Here is most of Houston's (1892b) article.

> I have thought it possible that it might interest you to consider some rather wild speculations in which I have indulged for a number of years past, but which I have heretofore refrained from publishing … Although the suggestions I have to offer as a basis for a hypothesis of the mechanism of cerebration, are confessedly incomplete, and, perhaps improbable, yet I have concluded to place them on record as of possible interest to the scientific world …
>
> Postulating the existence of the universal or luminiferous ether, which is now generally accepted in scientific circles, and bearing in mind the fact that this ether passes through even the densest matter, as easily as water through a sieve, it follows that the brain atoms or molecules that are here assumed as the cause of cerebration, are completely surrounded by the ether.[11] Now, since the ether is a highly elastic, easily movable medium, it would follow that thought or cerebration, if attended by vibrations, must necessarily develop in the ether wave-motions, which have the brain atoms or molecules for their centres …

The exact nature of the motions that are assumed to attend an active condition of the brain must necessarily remain unknown as long as we are ignorant of the exact nature of the mechanism that is moved …

Cerebral energy … is dissipated by imparting wave motions to the surrounding ether, and such waves are sent out in all directions from the brain, possibly in greater amount, or of greater amplitude from some of the brain openings, as, for example, those of the eyes.

Let us assume, then, that cerebral radiations or waves are given off from every sentient or active brain, and that these waves pass into the space around the brain something like the waves that are imparted to the air around a sounding tuning-fork …

If such waves, which I would call thought-waves or cerebral-waves, be present in ether that fills all space, it will be interesting to inquire what phenomena they might be expected to produce …

An active brain may … be regarded as moulding the ether around it into thought-waves, that are spreading outwards from it in all directions. In this respect, it is not unlike a conductor through which an oscillatory discharge is passing, producing those waves which Hertz has so beautifully demonstrated as resembling the vibrations that produce light.

Assume, then, that the cerebral radiations partake of the nature of thermal, luminous, electric, or magnetic radiations, and the following explanation of telepathy, or thought transference, is, to say the least, not improbable.

I would explain the possibility of the transference of specific cerebral vibrations from an active brain, to a passive or receptive brain, by the simple action of what is known in science as sympathetic vibrations.

Take the case of a vibrating tuning-fork sending off its waves across the space which separates it from a second tuning-fork, not as yet in motion, but tuned so as to be able to vibrate in exact unison with it. As is well known, the exact correspondence between the period of the active or transmitting-fork, and the passive or receptive-fork, is such that the vibrations of one fork are gradually taken up by the other fork, so that the energy of the motion of the one is transferred or carried across the space existing between them, by means of pulses or waves, set up in the air which surrounds them …

Or, similarly, take the case of the sympathetic vibrations excited by waves of light. Solar energy is radiated or transferred across the space existing between the sun and the earth by waves or oscillations in the luminiferous ether …

Or, take the still more interesting case of what Hertz calls electric resonance. As already mentioned, it is now generally recognized by electricians that a conductor, which is the seat of an oscillatory electric discharge, is sending into the space around it electric waves or oscillations which travel with the velocity of light, and which are, in fact, of exactly the same nature as light itself. If these electric waves meet a circuit so tuned as regards the period of oscillation of the circuit in which they originally occurred, as to be in consonance with them, electric oscillations will be set up in this circuit, of exactly the same nature as those exciting it.

In view of these facts, it does not seem improbable to me, that a brain engaged in intense thought should act as a centre of cerebral radiations, nor that these radiations proceeding outwards in all directions from such brain should affect other brains on which they fall, provided, of course, that such brains are tuned to vibrate in unison with them. In such cases the absorption of energy by the recipient brain may be either a species of selective absorption, in which its train of thought is only modified, or it may be absolute, in which case the recipient brain has excited in it an exact reproduction of the thoughts of the exciting brain …

If such a hypothesis be true, then these cerebreal [sic] vibrations or radiations must travel through space with exactly the velocity of light. This is of course on the assumption that the vibrating or oscillating brain molecules or atoms set up vibrations similar to those of light. Of course, this equality between the velocity of cerebral wave propagation and that of light is true only for free ether. In the ether which fills the interatomic or intermolecular spaces of gross matter, or, as it is technically called, combined ether, the velocity of wave propagation varies according to the particular character of the matter with which it is associated. A retardation or decrease in the velocity of the assumed cerebral waves would doubtless be experienced while passing through the materials of the skull and head.

If thought travels along waves in the ether similar to waves of light, it would be able to travel along any path by which rays of lights can pass. It can therefore travel along rays of light, i.e. along paths in the ether through which rays of light are moving.

There is a well-known experiment in hypnotism, in which the patient, placed in a state of semi- or complete unconsciousness, has his brain called into a more or less active condition by the suggestions of the hypnotizer, which might seem to somewhat favor the hypothesis of cerebral radiation.

It might be interesting, in view of the above suggestions, to see whether a hypnotizer placed in such a position as regards the hypnotized that flashes of light falling on his eyes shall afterwards fall on the eyes of the patient, to observe whether or not acts of suggestion are more readily perceived by the brain of the hypnotized along such rays of light than without the aid of such rays.

If the preceding speculations be regarded as wild, and that this is true I have already granted, what may not be said as to the following?

If thought radiations partake of the nature of ether-waves, then there should presumably exist in the thought radiations or waves, phenomena corresponding to the various phenomena of thermal, luminous, electric, or magnetic radiation; even the phenomena of reflection, refraction, and possibly even of dispersion of such waves, would appear to be a possibility. In this connection, it is of interest to imagine the analysis or separation of a complex wave of thought into its component or elementary waves, corresponding to the separation of a beam of light, by means of a prism ...[12]

If thought radiations or waves partake of the nature of light, then it would seem among the remote possibilities of science—to obtain, say by means of a lens—a photographic impression of such thought-waves on a suitably sensitized plate, somewhat after the manner of the ordinary photo graphic picture.[13] Such a thought-record, suitably employed, might be able to awaken at any subsequent time in the brain of a person submitting himself to its influences, thoughts identical to those recorded.

Of course, I am aware of the improbability of such a record being obtained in the near future, and of the exceeding difficulties that would seem to stand in the way of ever obtaining it.

Until we know something more definite concerning the nature of these assumed cerebral vibrations and of their lengths, we must necessarily be seriously handicapped as how to best permanently fix them on a suitable record-surface, and how afterwards to cause such record-surface to interpret its peculiarities to the brain. I merely throw it out as a possibility of what science may have in store for those who come after us. I would suggest, in this connection, that 100 years ago it would probably have been regarded as quite impossible that the telephone or the phonograph could have been produced.

Such a thought-record, however, if obtained would not be an image of the thought itself, or of the particular groupings of the particles, whose to-and-fro movements attend or produce thought, any more than the tracings of the phonograph record form an image of the spoken words. They would merely represent the to-and-fro motions of the ether set in motion by the thought or cerebrations.

An eye looking at such an image would not be influenced thereby. If, however, ether waves similar to those recorded could be reproduced by causing light to pass through such photographic images of the to-and-fro motions of thought-waves, such waves might be caused to influence the brain and thereby awaken thoughts similar or identical to those recorded …

Probably one of the most serious objections to the hypothesis is to be found in the fact that the phenomena of telepathy and thought transference are not of more frequent occurrence. This I must frankly acknowledge to be a most serious objection. I would suggest, however, that the comparative infrequency of the phenomena may possibly be explained by the presence in the human body of a shield which protects the brain or the nerve centres from the effects of cerebral radiations. It is not impossible the sheathes of the nerves act as screens to prevent the reception by the brain of these thought radiations …

If there be any truth in the hypothesis I have briefly outlined, there should be what I would term a kind of vital radiation going on and passing outwards from the body of a healthy person, which may not improbably excite by sympathetic vibrations in the bodies of weaker persons around them, vibrations of a normal or more healthy type than those present in the sick person.

If this be true, the old belief of the efficacy of the laying on of hands, or of magnetic healing, may find some foundation, in fact, apart from what is most probably the general explanation of such causes, viz., hysteria.

I have thrown out the above hypothesis of cerebral radiations with considerable doubt and hesitation as a suggestion only to those working in the field of telepathy or thought transference, in the hope that I may thereby call the attention of such investigators to some phenomena in this very obscure field of research.

Comments About Houston's Paper

Houston's discussion was considered of interest to students of psychic phenomena to the point of being reprinted in the *Psychical Review* (Houston, 1892c)[14] and in one of the books of Albert de Rochas (1895, p. 206–216) in which he referred to the vibrations of the "fluid" of a person affecting another. It was also briefly mentioned by Angelo Brofferio (1893, p. 140–141). However, I have not found mention of it in issues of the *Annales des Sciences Psychiques*, the *Journal* and *Proceedings of the Society for Psychical Research*, nor the Psychische Studien published between 1892 and 1899. However, some later writers on psychic topics mentioned him briefly (Carrington no date, pp. 60–61; Stocker, 1906, p. 18, 26).

A commentator in the *English Mechanic and World of Science* agreed with Houston that his ideas were wildly speculative, but stated that "they are based upon proper scientific analogies, and hence must be taken seriously" (Anonymous, 1892c, p. 371). Commenting about this in the theosophical journal *Lucifer*, an anonymous author wrote:

> Theosophical students will find them [Houston's ideas] familiar and even elementary, but, as they have often been derided for saying the same thing, they may be amused to see their own teachings welcomed with respect when they fall from lips scientific. (Anonymous, 1892f, p. 353)

Being unaware of the serious study of the topic, the commentator in *Electrical Engineer* praised Houston because he believed that the study of psychic phenomena had been left to visionaries. In his view, Houston's ideas "opened an enormous field for labor upon lines already familiar to men skeptical as to spooks, but intensely alive to the importance of all that bears upon the questions of everyday life." He also hoped that Houston "will not be content to stop at suggestions" (Anonymous, 1892a, p. 604, for both quotes).

Houston's article was summarized in French newspapers (Bataillard, 1892; Lucet, 1892), in the *Revue Scientifique* (Anonymous, 1892g), and in the Spiritualist publication *Light*, where the writer merely endorsed Houston's hope that his idea would be considered by researchers in the area (Anonymous, 1893). A few years later Reverend T.E. Allen (1895) agreed with Houston's basic idea. Furthermore, the article was listed in bibliographies published during the second decade of the Twentieth Century under the headings of "Theories of the Ether" (Anonymous, 1912) and "Thought-Transference" (Anonymous, 1913).

Concluding Remarks

Simple transmission models based on radiations and waves such as Houston's have been criticized in the past as failing to explain the evidence for ESP (e.g., Braude, 2002, Chapter 4, Section D). Nonetheless, historically it is important to pay attention to ideas such as Houston's because the study of past developments in parapsychology, and of any other scientific field, should not be limited to what is believed today to be correct. To understand the factors that shaped the development of the discipline, and its state in particular periods, it is essential to consider what we label today as superseded or rejected knowledge, and to avoid focusing only on aspects of the past that resemble our current interests and beliefs.[15]

While I do not claim that Houston's article had an important impact on the study of ESP (the reverse seems to be the case), a discussion of its content contributes to our understanding of the assumptions surrounding past ideas on the subject. In this case it is clear that Houston was influenced by the then current concepts of physics (or by extensions of these concepts), which included constructs such as brain-generated radiations and the ether. The influence of physics on parapsychology, it is interesting to see, continues to recent times (e.g., Radin, 2006).

Regardless of the few above-mentioned citations of Houston's work in writings about psychic phenomena, including the reprint of the article in *Psychical Review* (Houston, 1892c), there is no evidence to say that Houston's ideas were influential in the concepts of others, or that they generated research. While his ideas seem to me more detailed than previous ones, his main postulate, that of brain radiations transferred via the ether, was hardly original. Perhaps Houston would have been more influential if he had addressed his ideas directly to the psychical research community and if he had conducted research himself.

Regarding psychical research, the paper has no reference at all to previous studies on the topic. Houston's work is, in fact, the work of someone who showed no evidence that he was familiar with the phenomenon he was trying to explain. Nowhere in his paper did he mention the ideas and studies of telepathy published before his article. Knowledge of this literature would have allowed him to discuss the actual things that were believed to be transmitted from mind to mind, including images, thoughts, emotions, and physical sensations. Interestingly, some of this literature, and particularly the work of the SPR, was discussed in many American publications that Houston must have had access to (e.g., Courtenay, 1891; Hovey, 1885; Prince, 1887), not to mention the publications of the SPR.

Many ideas of physical transmission continued to be discussed after the appearance of Houston's 1892 paper in the Nineteenth Century (e.g., Astere, 1895; Crookes, 1899). Examples of Twentieth-Century discussions include magnetist Hector Durville's (1849–1923) graphic representation of the aura showing the constant reception and projection of "thoughts in the form of rays or waves". In addition, there was the research and theories of Naum Kotik (1908) on psychophysical radiant energy and of Italian neuropathologist Ferdinando Cazzamalli (1887–1958) on cerebral waves (Cazzamalli, 1925/1926). The radio analogy was discussed by many, perhaps more famously by American author and social activist Upton Sinclair (1878–1968) in his *Mental Radio* (1930).

The well–known French psychical researcher René Warcollier (1881–1962) speculated on resonance and vibrations from the nervous system, and on wireless telegraphy (Warcollier, 1938).[16] Ideas of physical transmission exist in more recent times (e.g., Marciak-Kozlowska and Kozlowski, 2012; Vasilescu & Vasilescu, 1996), but these are outside the range of this paper.[17] As pointed out before, there were some who were not convinced of the applicability of physical models to explain telepathy (e.g., Gurney, Myers, & Podmore, 1886). In fact, such thinking characterized most of the early SPR researchers. Initially open to consider physical models, Barrett changed his mind. After writing about the brain wave idea to explain telepathy, he stated that "supernormal phenomena … do not belong to the material plane, and therefore the laws of the physical universe are inapplicable to them" (W.F. Barrett 1911, p. 109). Over the years many others opposed wave and radiation models (e.g., Rhine, 1934; Tischner, 1920/1925). As I have pointed out before (Alvarado, 2006), physical transmission models declined in parapsychological circles with the rise of the Rhinean paradigm and ideas from modern physics.[18]

To conclude, Houston's article allows us to see in detail a type of theory that has been prevalent throughout the history of interest in telepathy. In fact, his paper is probably the most detailed discussion of the topic in the later Nineteenth Century. Houston's ideas were part of a long conceptual tradition that has been influential both in parapsychological concepts, as well as in popular conceptions of telepathy.

Notes

1 I have discussed this conceptual tradition in various articles (e.g., Alvarado, 2006; Alvarado & Nahm, 2011). On physics and psychic phenomena in the British context, see Noakes (2004, 2008). In addition to ideas coming from physics, the concept of telepathy was also part of the late Nineteenth-Century interest in the subconscious mind, as discussed by Luckhurst (2002) and Plas (2000).

2 Regarding the nonphysicality tradition of previous times, see Alvarado (2009, 2012b). The position is represented today by individuals such as Dossey (2013), Kelly, Kelly, Crabtree, Gauld, Grosso, & Greyson (2007), and Tart (2009).

3 For overviews, see Buchwald & Fox (2013), Harman (1982), and Purrington (1997). More specific studies include those of Buchwald (1985, 1989) and Smith (1998). Much has also been written about relevant topics such as the ether (Cantor & Hodge, 1981), and about cultural aspects of the impact of physics and its associated ideas, practices, and technology (Marvin, 1988; Morus, 2005; Simon, 2005).

4 On the concept of animal magnetism, and mesmerism in general, see Crabtree (1993), Gauld (1992), and Méheust (1999). A similar concept was Karl von Reichenbach's (1788–1869) Od (Reichenbach, 1851), which was considered by some to be the vehicle of telepathic phenomena. A late example of this was German philosopher Carl du Prel (1839–1899) in his *Die Magie als Naturwissenschaft* (du Prel, 1899). Relevant to this paper is his discussion of wireless telegraphy and telepathy (Vol. 1, p. 20–34).

5 There are many examples of the use of the concept of nervous and vital forces to explain physical mediumship (Alvarado, 2006). This includes authors writing in France (Chevillard, 1869), England (Cox, 1872), Germany (von Hartmann, 1885), and the United States (Rogers, 1853), among others. Years later German physician Albert von Schrenck-Notzing (1862–1929) discussed mediums and referred to "an emanation or projection [of] vital energies beyond the limits of the human organism" (Schrenck-Notzing, 1920, p. 180).

6 This, in turn, was part of the wide use of photography in Nineteenth-Century science to make visible the invisible (Canguilhem, 2004; Keller, 2008). In fact, the topic of "photography of the invisible"—both in conventional science and in psychic studies—has an interesting scientific and cultural history (Nowotny & Weiss, 2000). These developments also follow on early attempts to photograph spirits, thoughts, and "fluids" (Cheroux, Fischer, Apraxine, Canguilhem, & Schmit, 2005).

7 Ermacora (1898) and Podmore (1894) present overviews of this work. They cover observations in the normal and in the hypnotic state, as well as the transference of images, feelings, sounds, and tastes, and the induction of trance at a distance. Some of the early SPR work with the Creery Sisters was qualified later when evidence for fraud was obtained (Gurney 1888, p. 269).

8 For biographical information, see Anonymous (1906, 1911, 2013).

9 The World's Columbian Exposition—also known as the Chicago's World Fair—had remarkable exhibits of electrical instruments, showing the progress in that area (J.P. Barrett, 1894). Some of the exhibits, and the then current technology, included incandescent and arc lighting, dynamos, motors, switchboards, telegraphy, telephony, electro-therapeutics, batteries, and clocks. Connected to the Exposition was the International Electrical Congress. Houston was a member of the Electrical Congress' Advisory Council, and Chairman of its Section C (Pure Practice) (Anonymous, 1894, p. v, 338).

10 On late Nineteenth-Century electrical developments, and particularly in the United States, see Carlson (1991), Freeberg (2013), Klein (2008), and Marvin (1988).

11 As mentioned before, the ether was considered before by others in relation to thought-transference (Andrew, 1876; Despine, 1880; Knowles, 1869; Lombroso, 1891). The idea of the ether was not only important for the transmission of physical signals, but was also involved with political and religious issues (Noakes, 2005).

12 According to Mesmer (1779), animal magnetism was "augmented and reflected by mirrors" (p. 78). See also Baréty's (1887) studies of animal magnetism, or neural force, in relation to a prism (pp. 14, 16–17) and to refraction on things such as mirrors (pp. 12, 110, 302–303).

13 Referring to the brain waves mentioned in the epigraph, Knowles (1869) speculated on their photographic detection and on the possibility of obtaining a "dim portrait of thought" (p. 136). On the use of photography in Nineteenth-Century science to detect invisible processes and various forms of psychic photography, see Note 6. See also Reichenbach's (1862) early attempts to photograph Od. Houston (1892f, 1892h) showed interest in the use of photography, as seen in his discussions of the configuration of magnetic fields using photography of iron fillings. Consistent with his interest in technology (e.g., Houston, 1888, 1893b; Houston & Kennelly, 1897), Houston continued to speculate about technological ways to record thoughts. Discussing future developments related to electricity, he mentioned that he saw "dimly outlined through the clouds, an apparatus for the automatic registration of unwritten, unspoken thought" (Houston, 1894, p.199). Interestingly, there were other Nineteenth-Century discussions of the instrumental recording of thoughts (Anonymous, 1896, 1897). Somewhat related were Alexander Graham Bell's (1847–1922) speculations about the transference of thoughts via electricity in two persons wearing helmets connected with wires (Moffett, 1893, p. 41–42).

14 The *Psychical Review* was published by the American Psychical Society (not to be confused with the American Society for Psychical Research). Its officers for 1892 were writer Hamlin Garland (1860–1940) (President), journalist Benjamin O. Flower (1858–1918) (Vice-President), and Reverend Thomas E. Allen (1858–1930) (Secretary and Treasurer).

15 On this topic, see Alvarado (2012a, p. 619–621).

16 The historically minded reader may remember many other early Twentieth-Century speculations (Alvarado, 2008). One was French physiologist Charles Richet's (1850–1935) vague idea of vibrations to explain the sixth sense:

> The sixth sense is that one which gives us knowledge of a vibration of reality, a vibration which our normal senses are unable to perceive. (Richet, no date/1928, p. 224).

For the ideas of Hans Berger (1873–1941), see Millett (2001). More interesting, but less well-known, was French physician's Charles Binet-Sanglé's (1868–1941) belief in brain waves:

> Each thought corresponds to a particular system of ethereal waves ... In this way, by means of brain waves, every thought of the radiant brain awakens the same thought in some people ... In my view, the direct transmission of visual images is but a particular case of telephotography, the direct transmission of auditory images, a special case of wireless telephony. (Binet-Sanglé, no date, p. 25)

17 It has not been possible to discuss in detail the vast early Twentieth-Century popular literature discussing telepathic vibrations, waves, and the like. This includes little-known works such as *Practical Mind Reading* (Atkinson, 1908), *Telepathy, Mental Telegraphic Communication* (Stocker, 1906), and *The Call of the Soul* (Freyer, 1926). There were also several articles in magazines, among them one in the Catholic review *America*, where one author stated:

> Since the brain, however, is the seat of thought and consists of cells, there is no obvious reason why the activity of those cells could not cause a subtle wave and eject it into the outside world. (Murphy, 1915, p. 88)

18 On ideas of nonphysicality of the Rhinean paradigm, see Rhine and Pratt (1957) and Zingrone (1985). It is not possible to discuss here the influence of physics on modern parapsychology, but see Oteri (1975).

References

Allen, T. E. (1895). A theory of telepathy and the light it throws upon the problem of immortality. *Arena, 12*, 116–122.

Alvarado, C. S. (2006). Human radiations: Concepts of force in mesmerism, spiritualism and psychical research. *Journal of the Society for Psychical Research, 70,* 138–162.

Alvarado, C. S. (2008). Further notes on historical ideas of human radiations: IV. Mental phenomena. *Psypioneer*, *4*, 119–126.

Alvarado, C. S. (2009). Discussions of telepathy and nonphysicality by early members of the Society for Psychical Research. *Psypioneer*, *5*, 373–379.

Alvarado, C. S. (2012a). Distortions of the past. *Journal of Scientific Exploration, 26,* 611–633.

Alvarado, C. S. (2012b). Psychic phenomena and the mind-body problem: Historical notes on a neglected conceptual tradition. In *Exploring Frontiers of the Mind-Brain Relationship edited by A. Moreira-Almeida and F. S. Santos.* Springer Science+Business Media, pp. 35–51.

Alvarado, C. S., & Nahm, M. (2011). Psychic phenomena and the vital force: Hereward Carrington on "Vital Energy and Psychical Phenomena." *Journal of the Society for Psychical Research, 75*, 91–103.

Amadou, R. (1953). Esquisse d'une histoire philosophique du fluide. *Revue Métapsychique, 21,* 5–33.

Andrew, H. M. (1876). Brain waves. *Melbourne Review, 1*, 105–110.

Anonymous (1892a). Prof. Houston on cerebral radiation. *Electrical Engineer, 13*, 604.

Anonymous (1892b). Prof. Houston to lecture in Brooklyn. *Electrical Engineer, 13*, 540.

Anonymous (1892c). Shall we ever have a "thought-machine?" *English Mechanic and World of Science, 55,* 371.

Anonymous (1892d). Society and club notes. *Electrical Engineer, 13*, 438.

Anonymous (1892e). Society and club notes. *Electrical Engineer, 14*, 533.

Anonymous (1892f). On the watch-tower. *Lucifer, 10*, 353–360.

Anonymous (1892g). Les radiations cerebrales. *Revue Scientifique*, *50*, 59–60.

Anonymous (1893). Cerebral radiation. *Light, 13*, 100–101.

Anonymous (1894). *Proceedings of the International Electrical Congress Held in the City of Chicago.* American Institute of Electrical Engineers.

Anonymous (1896). The thought machine. *Journal of the American Medical Association, 26*, 834835.

Anonymous (1897). Thought machine records mental emotion. *The Phonoscope, 1*(10), 5–6.

Anonymous (1906). *The National Cyclopaedia of American Biography* (Volume 13). James T. White.

Anonymous (1911). Edwin James Houston. *Electrical Review and Western Electrician, 63*, 125.

Anonymous (1912). *Royal Society of London Catalogue of Scientific Papers 1800–1900: Subjects Index: Volume III: Part I.: Generalities, Heat, Light. Sound.* University Press.

Anonymous (1913). *Index-Catalogue of the Library of the Surgeon's General's Office, United States Army: Authors and Subjects: Second Series* (Vol, 18). U.S. Office of the Surgeon-General.

Anonymous (2013). Edwin Houston. In *IEEE Global History Network.* Retrieved from http://www.ieeeghn.org/wiki/index.php/Edwin_Houston

Ashburner, J. (1867). *Notes and studies in the philosophy of animal magnetism and spiritualism: with observations upon catarrh, bronchitis, rheumatism, gout, scrofula, and cognate diseases.* H. Baillière.

Astere, D. (1895). Essai d'une theorie de la télépathie. *Annales des Sciences Psychique, 5*, 14–32.

Atkinson, W. (1908). *Practical mind reading: A course of lessons on thought-transference, telepathy, mental-currents, mental rapport, etc.* Advanced Thought.

Baraduc, H. (1893). *La force vitale: notre corps vital fluidique, sa formule biométrique.* G. Carré.

Baraduc, H. (1896). *L'ame humaine: Ses mouvements, ses lumières et l'iconographie de l'invisible fluidique.* Georges Carré.

Baréty, A. (1887). *Le magnétisme animal: Etudie sous le nom de force neurique rayonnante et circulante dans ces propriétes physiques, physiologiques et thérapeutique.* Octave Doin.

Barrett, J. P. (1894). *Electricity at the Columbian exposition: Including an account of the exhibits in the electricity building, the power plant in machinery hall, the arc and incandescent lighting of the grounds and buildings, the transmission of power for the operation of machinery, the subway and conduits, electric fountains, search lights, intramural road, electric launches, electric elevators, lighting of the ferris wheel, corona lighting of the manufactures building, etc.* R. R. Donnelley & Sons.

Barrett, W. F. (1876). On some phenomena associated with abnormal conditions of mind. *Spiritualist Newspaper,* September 22, 85–88.

Barrett, W. F. (1882). Appendix to the report on thought-reading. *Proceedings of the Society for Psychical Research, 1*, 47–64.

Barrett, W. F. (1911). *Psychical research.* Henry Holt.

Barrett, W. F., Gurney, E., & Myers, F. W. H. (1882). First report on thought-reading. *Proceedings of the Society for Psychical Research, 1*, 13–34.

Barrett, W. F., Massey, C. C., Moses, W. S., Podmore, F., Gurney, E., & Myers, F. W. H. (1884). Third report of the Literary Committee: A theory of apparitions: Part I. *Proceedings of the Society for Psychical Research, 2*, 109–136.

Bataillard, L. (1892). La activité cérébrale. *La Science Française*, October 13, 102–103.

Binet-Sanglé, C. (no date, circa 1922). *La Fin du Secret: Applications de la Perception Directe de la Pensée.* Albin Michel.

Bixby, J. T. (1896). Professor Roentgen discovery and the invisible world around us. *Arena, 15*, 871–885.

Bois, J. (1896). L'âme scientifique. *Revue Spirite: Journal d'Études Psychologiques, 39*, 352–355.

Braude, S. E. (2002). *ESP and psychokinesis: A philosophical examination* (Rev. ed.). Brown Walker Press.

Brittan, S. B. (1864). *Man and his relations: Illustrating the influence of the mind on the body.* W. A. Townsend.

Brofferio, A. (1893). *Per to Spiritismo* (2nd ed.). Domenico Briola.

Buchwald, J. (1985). *From Maxwell to Microphysics: Aspects of electromagnetic theory in the last quarter of the nineteenth century.* University of Chicago Press.

Buchwald, J. (1989). *The rise of the wave theory of light: Optical theory and experiment in the early nineteenth century.* University of Chicago Press.

Buchwald, J. Z., & Fox, R. (Eds.) (2013). *The Oxford handbook of the history of physics.* Oxford University Press.

C., N. (1887). *Psychometry and thought-transference: With practical hints for experiments.* Esoteric Publishing Company.

Canguilhem, D. (2004). *Le Merveilleux Scientifique: Photographies du Monde Savant en France, 1844–1918.* Gallimard.

Cantor, G. N., & Hodge, M. J. S. (Editors) (1981). *Conceptions of ether: Studies in the history of ether theories, 1740–1900.* Cambridge University Press.

Carlson, W. B. (1991). *Innovation as a social process: Elihu Thomson and the rise of general electric, 1870–1900.* Cambridge University Press.
Carlson, W. B. (2013). *Tesla: Inventor of the electrical age*. Princeton University Press.
Carrington, H. (no date, circa 1939). *Laboratory investigations into psychic phenomena.* Rider.
Carroll, B. E. (1997). *Spiritualism in Antebellum America.* Indiana University Press.
Cazzamalli, F. (1926). Telepsychic phenomena and cerebral radiations. *Journal of the American Society for Psychical Research, 20*, 1–17. (Original work published in French, 1925)
Chéroux, C., Fischer, A., Apraxine, P., Canguilhem, D., & Schmit, S. (2005). *The perfect medium: Photography and the occult.* Yale University Press.
Chevillard, A. (1869). *Études expérimentales sur le fluide nerveux et solution définitive du probleme spirite.* Victor Masson.
Clarke, E., & Jacyna, L. S. (1987). *Nineteenth-century origins of neuroscientific concepts*. University of California Press.
Coues, E. (1885). An explanation of telepathy. *The Nation, 40*, 54.
Courtenay, R. (1891). Telepathy. *Eclectic Magazine of Foreign Literature, Science, and Art, 54*(n. s.), 324–334.
Cox, E. W. (1872). *Spiritualism answered by science* (New rev. ed.). Longman.
Crabtree, A. (1993). *From Mesmer to Freud: Magnetic sleep and the roots of psychological healing*. Yale University Press.
Crookes, W. (1892). Some possibilities of electricity. *Little's Living Age, 78*(s. 5), 93–97.
Crookes, W. (1897). Address by the President. *Proceedings of the Society for Psychical Research, 12*, 338–355.
Crookes, W. (1899). Address by Sir William Crookes, F.R.S., V.P.C.S., President. In *Report of the sixty-eighth meeting of the British Association for the Advancement of Science held at Bristol in September 1898* (pp. 3–38). John Murray.
Davis, A. J. (1855). *The present age and inner life: A sequel to spiritual intercourse: Modern mysteries classified and explained.* Partridge & Brittan.
De Gasparin, Comte A. (1854). *Des tables tournantes: Du surnaturel en général et des esprits* (2 vols.). E. Dentu.
Deleuze, J. P. F. (1813). *Histoire critique du magnétisme animal* (Vol. 1). Mame.
De Rochas, A. (1895). *L'extériorisation de la sensibilité: Etude expérimentale et historique* (2nd ed.). Chamuel.
Despine, P. (1880). *Etude scientifique sur le somnambulisme: sur les phénomènes qu'il présente et sur son action thérapeutique dans certaines maladies nerveuses.* F. Savy.
Dossey, L. (2013). *One mind: How our individual mind is part of a greater consciousness and why it matters.* Hay House.
Du Prel, C. (1899). *Die magie als naturwissenschaft* (2 vols.). Costenoble.
Durant, C. F. (1837). *Exposition, or a new theory of animal magnetism with a key to the mysteries: Demonstrated by experiments with the most celebrated somnambulists in America.* Wiley & Putnam.
Durville, H. (1921). *Magnétisme personnel ou psychique: Éducation de la pensée, développement de la volonté* (6th ed.). Henri Durville.
Enns, A., & Trower, S. (Editors) (2013). *Vibratory modernism*. Palgrave Macmillan.
Ermacora, G. B. (1892). *I Fatti Spiritici e le Ipotesi Affrettate: Osservazioni Sopra un Articolo del Prof. Lombroso*. Fratelli Drucker.
Ermacora, G. B. (1898). *La Telepatia.* L. Crescini.
Freeberg, E. (2013). *The age of Edison: Electric light and the invention of modern America*. Penguin Press.
Freyer, E. C. (1926). *The call of the soul: A scientific explanation of telepathy and psychic phenomena, with specific instructions for developing thought-transference, psychometry, mind-reading, automatic writing, mental broadcasting and other psychic phenomena*. Auto-Science Institute.
Gauld, A. (1992). *A history of hypnotism.* Cambridge University Press.
Gonçalves, V. P., & Ortega, F. (2013). Uma nosologia para os Fenômenos sobrenaturais e a construção do cérebro 'possuiclo' no século XIX. *História, Ciências, Saúde-Manguinhos, 20*, 373–389.
Guidi, F. (1854). *Trattato Teorico-Practico diMagnetismo Animale Considerate sotto il Punto di Vista Fisiologico e Psicologico.* Carlo Turati.
Gurney, E. (1888). Note relating to some of the published experiments in thought-transference. *Proceedings of the Society for Psychical Research, 5*, 269–270.

Gurney, E., Myers, F. W. H., & Barrett, W. F. (1884). Fourth report of the Committee on ThoughtTransference. *Proceedings of the Society for Psychical Research, 2,* 1–11.
Gurney, E., Myers, F. W. H., & Podmore, F. (1886). *Phantasms of the living* (2 vols.). Trübner.
Guthrie, M., & Birchall, J. (1883). Record of experiments in thought-transference. *Proceedings of the Society for Psychical Research, 1,* 263–283.
Gutierrez, C. (2009). *Plato's ghost: Spiritualism in the American renaissance*. Oxford University Press.
Haig, J. R. (1874). Spiritual apparitions. *Notes and Queries, 1*(s. 5), 381–382.
Hall, G. S. (1887). Review of *Proceedings of the Society for Psychical Research*, and *Phantasms of the Living*, by E. Gurney, F. W. H. Myers, and F. Podmore. *American Journal of Psychology, 1*, 128–146.
Harman, P. M. (1982). *Energy, force and matter: The conceptual development of nineteenthcentury*. Cambridge University Press.
Heilbron, J. L. (1993). Weighing imponderables and other quantitative science around 1800. *Historical Studies in the Physical and Biological Sciences, 24*(No. 1 Supplement), 1–33, 35–277, 279–337.
Henderson, L. D. (1988). X Rays and the quest for invisible reality in the art of Kupka, Duchamp, and the Cubists. *Art Journal, 47*, 323–340.
Houston, E. J. (1883). *The elements of chemistry for the use of schools, academies and colleges.* Eldredge & Brother.
Houston, E. J. (1884). *Intermediate lessons in natural philosophy*. Eldredge & Brother.
Houston, E. J. (1888). The gramophone. *Journal of the Franklin Institute, 95*(s. *3*), 44–55.
Houston, E. J. (1889). *A dictionary of electrical words, terms and phrases.* W. J. Johnston.
Houston, J. (1892a). Cerebral radiations. *American Gas Light Journal, 57*, 186.
Houston, J. (1892b). Cerebral radiations. *Journal of the Franklin Institute, 133*, 488–497.
Houston, J. (1892c). Cerebral radiations. *Psychical Review*, *1*, 150–157.
Houston, J. (1892d). Cerebral radiations. *Scientific American Supplement, 34*, 13801–13802.
Houston, J. (1892e). Cerebral radiations. *Western Electrician, 10*, 333–334.
Houston, E. J. (1892f). A graphic representation of the magnetic field. *Electrical Engineer, 14*, 60–63.
Houston, E. J. (1892g). La radiation cérébrale. *La Science Française,* September 29, 66–68.
Houston, E. J. (1892h). Some additional notes on the graphic representation of magnetic fields. *Electrical Engineer, 14*, 229.
Houston, E. J. (1893a). *The electric transmission of intelligence and other advanced primers of electricity.* W. J. Johnston.
Houston, E. J. (1893b). *Electricity and magnetism: Being a series of advanced primers of electricity.* W. J. Johnston.
Houston, E. J. (1893c). The International Electrical Congress and World's Fair of 1893. In *Transactions of the American Institute of Electrical Engineers* (Vol.10, pp. 464–468). American Institute of Electrical Engineers.
Houston, E. J. (1893d). *Outlines of forestry; or, the elementary principles underlying the science of forestry.* J. B. Lippincott.
Houston, E. J. (1894). The edge of the future in science: Professor Edwin J. Houston, of the Thomson-Houston Company, on the future of electricity. *McClure's Magazine, 2*, 199.
Houston, E. J. (1901). *The elements of physical geography, for the use of schools, academies, and colleges* (Rev. ed.). Eldredge & Brother.
Houston, E. J., & Kennelly, A. E. (1896). *Magnetism*. W. J. Johnston.
Houston, E. J., & Kennelly, A. E. (1897). *Electric telegraphy*. W. J. Johnston.
Houston, E. J., & Kennelly, A. E. (1898). *Electricity in electro-therapeutics* (2nd ed.). McGraw.
Houston, E. J., & Kennelly, A. E. (1906). *Electric arc lighting*. McGraw.
Hovey, W. A. (1885). *Mind reading and beyond.* Lee and Shepard.
Jastrow, J. (1895). The logic of mental telegraphy. *Scribner's Magazine, 18*, 571–576.
Keller, C. (Editor) (2008). *Brought to light: Photography and the invisible, 1840–1900*. Yale University Press.
Kelly, E. F., Kelly, E. W., Crabtree, A., Gauld, A., Grosso, M., & Greyson, B. (2007). *Irreducible mind: Toward a psychology for the 21st century*. Rowman and Littlefield.
Klein, M. (2008). *The power makers: steam, electricity, and the men who invented modern America.* Bloomsbury Press.

Knight, N. (1986). The new light: X rays and medical futurism. In J. J. Corn (Ed.), *Imagining tomorrow: History, technology, and the American future* (pp. 10–34), MIT Press.
Knowles, J. T. (1869). Brain-waves—A theory. *The Spectator, 42*, 135–137.
Kotik, N. (1908). *Die Emanation der psychophysischen Energie*. Bergman.
Lafontaine, C. (1852). *L'Art de magnétiser: Ou le magnétisme animal considères sous le point de vue théorique, pratique et thérapeutique* (2nd ed.). Germer Bailliere.
Lankester, E. R. (1907). *The kingdom of man*. Archibald Constable.
L'Annunziata, M. F. (2007). *Radioactivity: Introduction and history*. Elsevier.
Lodge, O. J. (1884). An account of some experiments in thought-transference. Proceedings of the *Society for Psychical Research, 1*, 189–200.
Lombroso C. (1891). Inchiesta sulla transmissione del pensiero. *Archivio di Psichiatria, Scienza Penali ed Antropologia Criminale, 12*, 58–108.
Lombroso, C. (1892a). I fatti spiritici e la loro spiegazione psichiatrica. *Vita Moderna,* February *7*, 1–2.
Lombroso, C. (1892b). Le spiritisme et la psychiatrie: Explication psychiatrique de certains faits spirites. *Revue de l'Hypnotisme et de la Psychologie Physiologique, 6*, 289–296.
Lucet, R. (1892). Tablettes du progrès: L'irradiation cérébrale. *Le XIXe Siècle*, July 16, 2.
Luckhurst, R. (2002). *The invention of telepathy 1870–1901*. Oxford University Press.
Luys, [J. B.], & David, [E.] (1897). Note sur l'enregistrement photographique des effluves qui se dégagent des extrémités des doigts et du fond de l'oeil de l'être vivant, a l'état physiologique et a l'etat pathologique. *Comptes Rendus Hebdomadaires des Séances et Mémoires de la Société de Biologie, 4*(s. 10), 515–519.
Mancini, V. (1891). *La trasmissione del pensiero secondo le teorie fisiche.* Cagnacci.
Marciak-Kozlowska, J., & Kozlowski, M. (2013). Heaviside's quantons as the carriers of the extrasensory perception phenomena. *NeuroQuantology, 11, 209–222.*
Marvin, C. (1988). *When old technologies were new: Thinking about electric communication in the late nineteenth century.* Oxford University Press.
McGraw, T. A. (1875). On mind-reading and allied morbid phenomena. *Detroit Review of Medicine and Pharmacy, 10*, 451–470.
Meheust, B. (1999). *Somnambulisme et médiumnité (1784–1930): Volume 1: Le défi du magnetisme animal.* Institut Synthélabo pour de Progrès de la Connaissance.
Mesmer, F. A. (1779). *Mémoire sur la découverte du magnétisme animal.* Didot.
Millett, D. (2001). Hans Berger: From psychic energy to the EEG. *Perspectives in biology and medicine, 44*, 522–542.
Mitchell, T. (1872). *Non spiritus: The philosophy of spiritualism*. Weed, Parsons.
Moffett, C. (1893). An interview with Professor Alexander Graham Bell. *McClure's Magazine, 1*, 39–43.
Morus, I. R. (2005). *When physics became king*. University of Chicago Press.
Murphy, E. F. (1915). Lodge, Hyslop and telepathy. *America, 13*, 87–89.
Natale, S. (2011). The invisible made visible: X-rays as attraction and visual medium at the end of the nineteenth century. *Media History, 17*, 345–358.
Noakes, R. (2004). The "bridge which is between physical and psychical research": William Fletcher Barrett, sensitive flames, and Spiritualism. *History of Science, 42*, 419–464.
Noakes, R. (2005). Ethers, religion and politics in late-Victorian physics: Beyond the Wynne thesis. *History of Science, 43*, 415–455.
Noakes, R. (2008). The 'world of the infinitely little': Connecting physical and psychical realities circa 1900. *Studies of the History and Philosophy of Science, 39*, 323–334.
Nowotny, H., & Weiss, M. (Editors) (2000). *Shifting boundaries of the real: Making the invisible visible*. Zurich: Vdf Hochschulverlag AG an der ETH.
Ochorowicz, J. (1891). *Mental suggestion*. Humbolt. (Original work published in French1887)
Oteri, L. (Ed.) (1975). *Quantum physics and parapsychology*. Parapsychology Foundation.
Pamboukian, S. (2001). "Looking radiant": Science, photography and the X-ray craze of 1896. *Victorian Review, 27*, 56–74.
Plas, R. (2000). *Naissance d'une science humaine: la psychologie: Les psychologues et le "merveilleux psychique."* Presses Universitaires de Rennes.
Podmore, F. (1894). *Apparitions and thought-transference: An examination of the evidence for telepathy.* Walter Scott.

Prince, M. (1887). Thought-transference. *Boston Medical and Surgical Journal, 116*, 107–112.
Purrington, R. D. (1997). *Physics in the nineteenth-century*. Rutgers University Press.
Radin, D. (2006). *Entangled minds: Extrasensory experiences in a quantum reality*. Paraview Pocket Books.
Reichenbach, C. von (1851). *Physico-physiological researches on the dynamics of magnetism, electricity, heat, light, crystallization, and chemism, in their relation to vital force* (from German 2nd ed.). J. S. Redfield (Original work published in German1849)
Reichenbach, K. von (1862). *Odische Begebenheiten zu Berlin in den Jahren 1861 und 1862*. Schroeder.
Rhine, J. B. (1934). *Extra-sensory perception*. Boston Society for Psychic Research.
Rhine, J. B., & Pratt, J. G. (1957). *Parapsychology: Frontier science of the mind*. Charles C Thomas.
Richet, C. (1884). La suggestion mentale et le calcul des probabilités. *Revue Philosophique de la France et de l'Etranger, 18*, 609–674.
Richet, C. (no date). *Our sixth sense*. Rider. (Original work published in French 1928)
Rogers, E. C. (1853). *Philosophy of mysterious agents, human and mundane*. John P. Jewett.
Romanes, G. J. (1881). "Thought-reading." *Nature, 24, 171–172.*
Schrenck-Notzing, A. von (1891). Experimental studies in thought-transference. *Proceedings of the Society for Psychical Research, 7*, 3–22.
Schrenck-Notzing, A. F. (1920). *Physikalische phaenomene des mediumismus: Studien zur erforschung der telekinetischen vorgänge*. Ernst Reinhardt.
Segala, M. (2001). Électricité animale, magnétisme animal, galvanisme universel: À la recherche de l'identité entre l'homme et la nature. *Revue d'Histoire des Sciences, 54*, 71–84.
Sibley, N. W. (1898). Psychical research and the roentgen and other X rays. *Westminster Review, 49*, 211–213.
Simon, L. (2005). *Dark light: Electricity and anxiety from the telegraph to the x-ray*. Harcourt.
Sinclair, U. (1930). *Mental radio*. Author.
Smith, C. (1998). *The science of energy: The construction of energy physics in the nineteenthcentury*. Athlone Press.
Stocker, R. D. (1906). *Telepathy, mental telegraphic communication: What it is and how it is done* (3rd ed). L. N. Fowler
Tart, C. T. (2009). *The end of materialism: How evidence of the paranormal is bringing science and spirit together*. New Harbinger Publications.
Thurschwell, P. (2001). *Literature, technology and magical thinking, 1880–1920*. Cambridge University Press.
Tischner, R. E. (1925). *Telepathy and clairvoyance*. Harcourt, Brace. (Original work published in German 1920)
Titchener, E. B. (1898). The 'feeling of being stared at.' *Science, 8*(n. s.), 895–897.
Twain, M. (1891). Mental telegraphy: A manuscript with a history. *Harper's New Monthly Magazine, 84*, 95–104.
Vasilescu, E., & Vasilescu, E. (1996). The mechanism of telepathy. *Journal of the Society for Psychical Research, 61*, 289–310.
Vergés, A. (1857). *Tratado de la electricidad, correo del pensamiento, de las simpatasy antipatfas, y en ocasiones del acierto ó desacierto.* Imprenta de de Mariano y Puyol.
Von Hartmann, E. (1885). *Spiritism*. Psychological Press.
Wagstaff, E. W. (1892). A theory of brain waves. *National Review, 20*, 140–144.
Warcollier, R. (1938). *Experimental telepathy*. Boston Society for Psychic Research.
Wiley, B. H. (2012). *The thought reader craze: Victorian science at the enchanted boundary*. McFarland.
Zingrone, N. L. (1985). Non-physicality and meaning in parapsychology: To teach an old science new tricks. In M. C. Rose (Editor), *Mysticism, creativity and psi: A search for a new science* (pp. 47–57). Academy of Religion and Psychical Research.

Classic Text No. 119: Jules Bernard Luys on Magnetic Pathology*

Carlos S. Alvarado

In the mesmeric movement, one of the phenomena cited to defend the existence of magnetic and nervous forces was the visual perception of them in the form of luminous emanations from people, or effluvia. This Classic Text is an 1892 article by French neurologist, Jules Bernard Luys (1828–1897), about the observation of such effluvia by hypnotized individuals. Interestingly, the luminous phenomena perceived from mentally diseased individuals and from healthy ones had particular properties. Luys' interest in this and other unorthodox phenomena were consistent with ideas of animal magnetism in the late neo-mesmeric movement, as well as with some physicalistic conceptions of hypnosis and the nervous system held at the time.

The theory and practice of mesmerism, and its concept of animal magnetism, produced at least three main ideas, which had varied and profound implications. One of them was a psychological current of thought that contributed to the exploration of various states of consciousness as well as to the construction of the idea of an unconscious mind. The other two were movements emphasizing medical applications of mesmerism, and phenomena later referred to as parapsychological (Crabtree, 1993; Gauld, 1992). Of particular relevance to this article are the last two aspects, and the idea that magnetism was involved in pathology. This Classic Text is about the ideas of French physician Jules Bernard Luys, who, among other things, explored the perception of magnetic effluvia by hypnotized individuals.

Human Magnetism

Although there are old ideas of concepts similar to animal magnetism, I will focus here on the mesmeric movement, as it developed from the eighteenth century to later into the nineteenth and twentieth centuries.[1] This concept was discussed by Franz Anton Mesmer (1734–1815) in his 1779 *Mémoire sur la Découverte du Magnétisme Animal*, in which he presented 27 propositions about animal magnetism. This force was conceived as a "fluid universally spread & continued … the subtlety of which allows no comparison, & which, by its nature, is liable of receiving, propagating, & communicating all the impressions of movement …" (Mesmer, 1779, p. 74). This universal fluid, Mesmer continued, affected the human body via the nerves, showed polarity on the body, could be communicated to inanimate objects, could act at a distance without intermediaries, was enhanced and propagated by mirrors and sounds, could be stored and moved, and could be used for healing. The latter was particularly important for Mesmer, who commented that these ideas would allow

*Republished with permission from *History of Psychiatry, 30*, 359–374, 2019.

physicians "to judge properly the degree of health of each individual, & to preserve him from the diseases to which he might be exposed. The art of healing will thus reach its final perfection" (p. 83).[2]

> Over the years after Mesmer, a great number of writers—individuals such as Louis Joseph Jules Charpignon (1815–86), Joseph-Philippe-François Deleuze (1753–1835) and William Gregory (1803–58)—continued this magnetic tradition, believing that animal magnetism, or vital and nervous forces, were able to produce various manifestations (Charpignon, 1848; Deleuze, 1813; Gregory, 1851). This included the induction of trance, and various psychological and physiological manifestations, not to mention cases of distant diagnoses, healings, travelling clairvoyance, and transpositions of the senses.

One writer believed that "Man is a congeries of forces all under the regulation of magneto-electric laws. He is, in fact, a magnet ..." (Ashburner, 1867, p. 193), while another argued that:

> The nervous, active atmosphere of the magnetizer, no doubt augmented by the impulse of his will ..., enters in rapport with the passive nervous atmosphere of the magnetized person, and augments the latter to the point that, in some cases, it seems that there is a real saturation of the nervous system ... (du Potet, 1868, p. 316)

These ideas continued in the neo-mesmeric movement which flourished during the late nineteenth century and part of the twentieth.[3] This was evident in the work of Luys, featured in this Classic Text, and in the works of individuals such as French magnetists Alexandre Barety (1844–1918), Emile Boirac (1851–1917), Albert de Rochas (1837–1914) and Hector Durville (1849–1923), among others (Barety, 1887; Boirac, 1908; de Rochas, 1899; Durville, 1895–1896). For example, Barety defended the existence of a neuritic (*neurique*) force that originated "probably from the nervous system, which *circulates* along the nerves or *radiates* out of them ... and is susceptible of producing certain sensitive, motor and psychic modifications on other human bodies" (Barety, 1887, p. xii, original italics). Similar beliefs were held by magnetist and psychical researcher de Rochas (1887, 1899), who magnetized persons who saw emanations from magnets and human beings, and who believed that the tactile sensibility of his subjects could be projected beyond the body's periphery so as to perceive touch and pain at a distance from it. This force, the magnetist Durville (1895–1896) postulated, emanated from the body "like the undulations produced by a stone falling on the surface of still water" (Vol. 1, p. 169).

Interestingly, these unorthodox concepts of force were also part of psychical research, an example being theorization about the phenomena of physical mediums – ideas that extended from the nineteenth century into the twentieth (e.g., Crookes, 1874; de Rochas, 1897; Morselli, 1908; von Hartmann, 1885).[4] Many believed that various instruments, as well as photographic plates, were able to detect this force. Luys belonged to this tradition, and even attempted to use photography for this purpose (Luys & David, 1897a, 1897b).[5]

One of the phenomena that assisted in the maintenance of the belief in animal magnetism, and the topic of the article by Luys reprinted here, was the visual perception of the magnetic fluid by magnetized individuals. Perceptions of luminous forces seen by magnetic somnambules were recorded several times in the mesmeric literature, to the point that Deleuze (1813, p. 82) stated: "Most somnambulists see a luminous and brilliant fluid surround their magnetizer, [which] leaves with more strength from his head and his hands." An early example read as follows: "I put the thumb of my right hand in opposition to the thumb of the left hand of my patient, and separated our two hands horizontally; she saw the fluid out of her thumb & mine; she distinguished very well the two fluids ..." (Tardy de Montravel, 1785, p. 27–28).

Several other examples were recorded in the literature (e.g., Buckland, 1850, p. 43–44; Elliotson, 1848, p. 225; Olivier, 1849, p. 36). Such perceptions were consistent with Charpignon's experiments where magnetized individuals saw luminous forms corresponding to fluid projected inside bottles. He wrote about one test:

> Having magnetized an empty bottle and having presented it to another somnambulist, she declared that she saw a luminous vapour which evaporated as soon as contact had taken place. When other people in turn magnetized this bottle, the somnambulist saw a different fluid each time, more or less bright, according to their nervous force and according to their sex, and naming the person from whom it had come when a magnetic rapport had been established. (Charpignon, 1848, p. 56)

In later years, Karl von Reichenbach (1788–1869), who discussed the Od force, popularized even more the idea that some sensitive individuals could see (or feel) emanations from magnets, minerals and people (von Reichenbach, 1849/1851). One of these sensitives was a 29-year-old woman named Barbara Reichel, who suffered from nervous attacks and episodes of somnambulism. In one instance, "When a magnet was laid before her in darkness, she saw *it emit light, not merely when open, but when it was closed, like a horseshoe, by the armature*" (p. 28, original italics). Von Reichenbach wrote about this woman:

> As I saw Miss Reichel ... with closed eyes, playing in a sort of half sleep with the magnet flame, which always gave her great pleasure, I interposed my outstretched hand, in the darkness, between the magnet and the patient. She immediately began to play in the same manner with the tips of my fingers, and to talk to the bystanders of five little flames, which leaped up and down in the air. She did not perceive my hand itself, and took the movement of my fingers, on the points of which she saw the flames, for an independent movement of the latter. (p. 114).

This work inspired de Rochas (1887, 1899) to conduct more tests with magnets and people. In a series of tests with a young man called Albert Lévy, de Rochas used an electromagnet with which he could turn off and on, or change the position of, the magnetic poles, without Lévy's knowledge. According to the summary of the results, "not only are the descriptions of the effluvia perfectly consistent with these operations in the twenty-two experiments carried out, but the subject even noticed the passage of the current at a moment when the operator thought he had suppressed it" (de Rochas, 1899, p. 22). Interestingly, de Rochas (p. 7) met Lévy at the Charité, where he was a subject in some of Luys' tests.[6]

Magnetic Pathology

In his book *Traité Clinique et Thérapeutique de l'Hystérie*, physician Paul Briquet (1796–1881) affirmed that "most of the so-called magnetic somnambules, are hysterical women" (Briquet, 1859, p. 413); this is consistent with the beliefs expressed by many other later writers during the nineteenth century who believed that susceptibility to hypnosis was related to nervous problems, and to hysteria in particular (e.g., Charcot, 1882; Richer, 1885, p. 535). Similarly, many mesmerists assumed that pathological conditions were related to magnetism. Some emphasized that disease of bodily weakness made the person sensitive to magnetism, while others, like Luys, argued that bodily problems were reflected in the person's magnetic force.

The first idea was discussed in a work in which it was assumed that sensitiveness to magnetism was higher in "weak individuals, with a lymphatic and nervous temperament" and in those with chronic and organic problems" (Pigeaire, 1839, p. 282). Ethereal vibrations, speculated Prosper Despine (1812–1892), could explain thought transference if the receiving person was in a state of "extreme sensibility, abnormal, pathological", which was a rare state (Despine, 1880, p. 226). In Despine's view, the parts of the body most affected by disturbances, and those with the most nerves (such as the head, the upper abdomen, the arms and the neck), are the most affected by magnetic passes.

Physicians H. Bourru and P. Burot (1887) assumed the existence of a magnetic field around the human body to account for the influence of drugs at a distance. They wrote: "There is no doubt this zone exists in all individuals, with considerable differences in power, and would reach its maximum impressionability in certain morbid states, hysteria and induced somnambulism" (p. 252). They also wrote that those who were open to the influence of drugs and metals were individuals whose nervous systems were unbalanced.[7]

But there were also some who believed that magnetic processes could cause some afflictions. In his *Electricité Animal*, J.H.D. Petetin (1744–1808) presented observations of a woman suffering from cataleptic somnambulism who showed the phenomena of transposition of the senses. According to Petetin (1808, p. 58), such phenomena were caused in part by "the excessive mobility of the electric fluid contained in the nerves of the cataleptics". The disordered action of magnetism was said by another writer to cause parts of the human system "to become unhealthy in their action, and thus cause disease" (Baistow, 1846, p. 146), while another stated: "Derangement of the magnetic forces, in the mental organs, produces monomania, insanity, and madness" (Sunderland, 1842, p. 57).

The idea of pathology was also found in the literature about the Od force. Von Reichenbach (1852/1860) stated that, while there were healthy Od sensitives, others had health issues. Many had sleep disturbances such as somnambulism. Others "often have sick headaches, frequently have short fits of colic, [and] complain of nervous irritability" (p. 24). A later student of Od believed that "disturbances in odic circulation, or its abnormal accumulation in vital organs, give rise to symptoms and pathological states adverse to those of health in its most lively forms" (Eadon, 1885, p. 279).

Physician Alexandre Barèty (1844–1918) was a well-known student of the neuric force, a force circulating via the nerves which he believed could be exteriorized to cause various phenomena. He connected this idea with hysteria and wrote that hysteria was related to "a change in the direction, strength and distribution of nervous or neural currents" (Barèty, 1887, p. 627).

A somewhat later physician, Hippolyte Baraduc (1850–1902), reported tests with his biometer, an instrument consisting of a needle hanging from a thread covered by a cylinder (Baraduc, 1893). The movements of the needle presented the action of a vital force that could be measured as "formulas" or patterns of the functioning of the vital force, which represented the physical action of the soul. These formulas were based on numerical measures of movements representing attraction and repulsion caused by the right and left hands. A pattern of double attraction from both hands was considered to be a hypotension of the vital body, corresponding to weakness in the physical, something which was frequent in neurasthenia and exhausted individuals. Furthermore, hysteria, Baraduc wrote, "is an animic affection, a weakness of the fluidic body" (p. 141, original italics), which shows "oscillation, ... lack of fixity and the variability of the formula" (p. 152).

In the literature on Spiritism, related ideas appeared about the concept of the perispirit, or a semi-fluidic envelope surrounding the spirit and connecting it to the physical body.[8] One of the French spiritist leaders, engineer Gabriel Delanne (1857–1926), discussed the topic, apparently using as his source spirit the communications received via mediums. In his view, the perispirit was the place where memories were stored. Dissociation could be produced when the perispirit was out of balance. This could take place during hypnosis, under the effects of drugs, or during epileptic attacks. Under these influences, the perispirit could show abnormal vibratory manifestations that affected recollections

(Delanne, 1897, p. 226). Delanne believed there could be more than one memory record, which was important in order to account for secondary personalities. In this regard, he mentioned the well-known case of Félida X. (b. 1843), and some of the work of Pierre Janet (1859–1947) (Janet, 1889).[9]

Another writer who theorized on the basis of perispiritual pathology was Spanish physician Víctor Melcior y Farré (1860–1929). Considering the perispirit as a principle capable of storing memories, Melcior argued that it could store many different memories. Mental obsessions were seen by him as "vices" of the perispirit produced by habits of action and thinking (Melcior y Farré, 1900, p. 209).

Jules Bernard Luys

Jules Bernard Luys (1828–1897) was a French physician who specialized in the study of the nervous system and its pathology.[10] He was the son of wealthy parents living in Paris; he obtained a medical degree in 1857 with a thesis about tuberculosis. By 1862 he had become a hospital physician and worked at the Salpêtrière, and soon he was in charge of a well-known mental health facility, the Maison de Santé d'Ivry. In 1886 he moved to another important hospital, La Charité.

Luys, who was widely recognized as a major contributor to the study of the nervous system, made various original contributions. An important early publication was *Recherches sur le Système Cérébro-Spinal, sa Structure, ses Fonctions et ses Maladies* (Luys, 1865). Here Luys divided his discussions in three sections. These were anatomy (convergent inferior and superior nervous fibres, commisurant fibres), physiology (unconscious and conscious sensory impressions, cerebral functions in intellectual operations, the nervous system and movement, and sleep and the nervous centres), and clinical issues (pathological anatomy, effects of lesions in spinal-cerebral axis, dynamic problems in the nervous system, and semiological value and summary of morbid nervous manifestations).

Another major work was the fifth edition of the textbook *Le Cerveau et ses Fonctions*, in which Luys (1876) presented 33 chapters discussing the brain. The book had three general sections about brain anatomy, properties of the nervous components of the brain, and the evolution of processes of brain activity. Other works about the nervous system and medical topics included his books *Iconographie Photographique des Centres Nerveux* (2 vols., 1873), *Études de Physiologie et de Pathologie Cérébrale* (1874), *Leçons sur la Structure et les Maladies du Système Nerveux* (1875), *Traite Clinique et Pratique des Maladies Mentales* (1881) and *Le Traitement de la Folie* (1893a). He also published many articles on topics such as ossification of the dura-mater, nervous over-excitation, the structure of the cerebral cortex, and the brain hemispheres (see, respectively, Luys, 1855, 1882, 1883, 1888a).

In addition to his research and clinical work, Luys was also a journal editor. Two of the journals he edited were *L'Encéphale: Journal des Maladies Mentales et Nerveuses*, and the *Annales de Psychiatrie et d'Hypnologie dans leurs Rapports avec la Psychologie et la Médicine Légale*.

Luys' work on the nervous system was recognized at the time. His 1865 book *Recherches sur le Système Cérébro-Spinal: Sa Structure, ses Fonctions et ses Maladies* was praised by a committee of the Academie des Sciences which awarded him a Montyon Prize (Anon., 1866, p. 523–525). He was also granted the titles of Knight and Officer in the Légion d'Honneur, and was elected to the Académie de Médicine.

Luys' interest in unusual phenomena may have started with his participation in studies to test the claims of metalloscopy (Charcot, Luys & Dumontpallier, 1877, 1878).[11] In his later reports of phenomena with hypnotized individuals, Luys wrote about the transmission of the effects of drugs, medicines and other substances at a distance, as evaluated by changes of emotions and attitudes (Luys, 1886, 1887a, 1887b, 1887c, 1887d, 1890b); this subject was also explored by others (Bourru and Burot, 1887), but some were critical.[12] According to Luys (1887b, p. 61), "The subject in a state of hypnotism becomes a veritable apparatus of exquisite sensibility; it is a veritable reagent of extreme refinement, which is set in motion by way of infinitesimal vibrations of the surrounding environment".[13]

Luys (1887c) published a summary of this research in the *Bulletin de l'Academie Nationale de Médicine*. As is evident in the ensuing comments about the paper (Academie Nationale de Médicine, 1887), Luys wanted the Academie to investigate the subject. This actually took place, but the Académie's official report did not confirm Luys' positive results (Dujardin-Beaumetz, 1888); Luys (1888b) strongly disagreed with the report.

Luys' interest in hypnotism extended his neurological ideas to a new area. In his view:

> Hypnotism is an extra-physiological experimental state of the nervous system. It is an artificial neurosis that is developed in a predisposed subject, a pseudo sleep that is imposed, and during which the subject having the experience loses the notion of its own existence and of the external world. (1890c, p. 5–6, italics removed)

According to Luys, during hypnosis automatic nervous processes were active when the subject entered the lethargic state, and then the person proceeded into two more hypnotic stages, catalepsy and somnambulism—stages similar to Charcot's (1882). The hypnotized individual, he wrote, is "torpid and silent *only in appearance*, and obeys silent influences in a given direction.—*Hypnotism is therefore a veritable physiological process in evolution*" (Luys, 1890c, p. 7, original italics). Furthermore, the hypnotized, Luys thought, had changes in the body's nervous currents that refocused in new regions of the body. These changes involved "truly extra-physiological energies; – new phenomena, develop in a purely experimental way, which form in the hypnotized subject completely new conditions of life and of perception of the exterior world ..." (p. 14).

Luys' interests in new forms of perception can also be appreciated from the papers by other authors published in one of the journals he edited, the *Annales de Psychiatrie et d'Hypnologie* ... There were papers about mental suggestion (Bourget, 1895), the action of drugs at a distance (Peter, 1894), and other topics (Boirac, 1895; Goudard, 1895).

In addition, Luys explored other unorthodox phenomena which suggested to him the existence of little-explored sensibilities in the hypnotized.[14] This included the study of the effects of magnets and electrical currents on emotions (Luys, 1890a); of phenomena in which an iron crown that was moved from one patient to another was said to cause a transfer[15] of mental conditions (Luys, 1894; Luys & Encausse, 1890); and the perception by hypnotized individuals of luminous effluvia emanating from a person (Luys, 1892a, 1892b).[16] In another paper, Luys referred more directly to unorthodox forces, where his purpose was the photographic detection of "the effluvia which are released ... from the ends of the fingers, as well as those which emerge from the back of the eye" (Luys & David, 1897a, p. 515). This was seen by Luys as the objective demonstration of forces that had been discussed for a long time. In the words of the authors, "The fluids of the magnetizers,—the fluid mentioned by Reichenbach under the name of Od,—Barety's neuric force,—etc., etc., will thus find their certificate of scientific reality" (p. 517).[17]

Although writers with beliefs in unorthodox forces similar to those of Luys held his work in high regard (e.g., Leymarie, 1897), many others were skeptical. These studies were not received as well as Luys' previous physiological research had been. In fact, it was even said that because of this work Luys lost some of his scientific reputation (Vermey, 1897).

A contemporary of Luys, writer Léon Daudet (1867–1942), wrote years later that Luys' hypnotic demonstrations were deceptions by his subjects, who even practiced their performances in advance (Daudet, 1915, p. 86–89). Another negative evaluation came from English physician Ernest Hart (1835–1898), who was the editor of the *British Medical Journal*. In several issues of the journal, Hart (1893) summarized his evaluation of Luys' work, some of which he had seen himself. In his view, much could be explained by suggestion and simulation, and he complained about Luys' "incredible looseness in his method of experiment" (p. 261).

Another critical physician wrote:

> Does it not strike one at once that the subjects of Dr. Luys' laboratory, who as it were, breathe an atmosphere of suggestion, who hear daily, conversations about, and explanations of, the phenomena of transfer; who read the literature of the subject, and are permitted to witness the experiments, may … be more affected by the suggestions (unconsciously given by the operator) than by the magnet? (Kingsbury, 1891, p. 148)

Furthermore, an obituarist commented that Luys had not been able to distinguish the true from the false, and that confirmation of the existence of "odic effluvia" had to wait for the results of future studies (Toulouse, 1897). Luys did not help his case by presenting sensational public demonstrations of hypnosis (Lepelletier, 1887). Some of his work was also perceived by the press as astounding, as was the case of his transfer tests using crowns, which evoked the thought that "one really seems to find oneself in the world of sorcery" (Anon., 1894).

Commentaries about Luys' work have continued to modern times. Gauld (1992, p. 34–36) presents it as highly extravagant examples of the neo-mesmeric movement, while Plas (2000, p. 57) says that the bizarre character of Luys' work brought him accusations of charlatanism and credulity. More recently, Luys' writings were pictured as an entrance "into the world of the irrational" (Parent & Parent, 2011, p. 134). But regardless of present-day evaluations of correctness, such work should be seen in context.

In the opinion of Plas (2000, p. 77), Luys always had a physiological orientation in his hypnosis related work, similar to his earlier clinical-pathological studies.[18] Perhaps it may be argued that Luys extended his conventional neurology based on internal processes to an unorthodox one, beyond the limits of the body, where the "nervous system is placed in extraphysiological conditions", thus showing "reactions of an exceptional finesse which constitute a new field of study for observers" (Luys, 1895, p. 353).

Luys' work was inspired in part by the assumptions of the Salpêtrière School of hypnosis with its emphasis on the nervous system (as seen in Richer, 1885). Some members of this school used magnets and performed transfer experiments, for example Alfred Binet (1857–1911) and Charles Féré (1852–1907). These men believed that a magnet could induce "a faint electric current on the nervous system, and produces a continuous peripheral excitement" (Binet and Féré, 1887, p. 262). In their view, magnets were "the great modifier of the nervous system" (Binet and Féré, 1885, p. 16). All this was consistent with Luys' ideas. In fact, his work and ideas may be seen as a combination and further developments of Salpêtrière ideas, influenced as well by mesmeric ideas and by his longstanding interest in the nervous system.

Luys and Magnetic Effluvia in Pathology

Like others before him, Luys considered nervous forces were related to pathology, and that they acted differently from the forces of normal individuals. This was evident in his writings about visual perception of effluvia by hypnotized persons (Luys, 1892a, 1892b), the second of which is translated and reprinted below.

Writing in a different publication, Luys (1895) stated that the effluvia seen around normal healthy persons was strong, but that it was weak with people suffering from various disturbances such as paralysis and hemiplegia. Those with brain lesions not only showed weak effluvia, but also "clusters of *dark* spots in the peripheral sub-orbital and frontal regions of the face" (p. 362, original italics). He wrote further:

> A large number of neuropathic states (hysterics, neurasthenics) are characterized by a weakening of red effluvia on the right side.—These effluvia, especially in hysterics (women and men), are violet, and the blue side of the left side, instead of being dark blue, is pale blue.—As a consequence, the encroachment of the violet on the right is a sign of general weakening of the nervous force.—As the subjects heal, the red coloration which returns in the right eye is a sign of recovery of nervous forces. (pp. 360–361)

The paper reprinted here is entitled "De la visibilité par les sujets en état hypnotique des effluves dégagés par les êtres vivants" (On the visibility to subjects in the hypnotic state of effluvia emitted by human beings). It was published in *Annales de Psychiatrie et d'Hypnologie* ... (Luys, 1892b).[19] The paper appeared after a similar article had been published in the same journal (Luys, 1892a; see also Luys, 1893b).

The phenomena described by Luys were in the mesmeric tradition. It may be argued that they also belonged to ideas about the aura, or the perception of various luminous shapes around the human body reported by non-hypnotized individuals such as mediums, psychics and others, a topic discussed frequently over the years. The aura, according to some writers, reflected the mental and physiological state of the person around whom it was seen, an idea also espoused by Luys.[20]

Classic Text No. 119
Jules Bernard Luys on Magnetic Pathology

Not only do hypnotized subjects have the attribute of seeing the magneto-electric effluvia which emerge from physical devices (as I have explained in a previous lecture),[21] but they can also ... recognize the effluvia that are released from the eyes, ears, nostrils and the lips of living beings – [and can] distinguish them, those on the right side and those on the left side, putting the blue colour on the left and red on the right. Thus they distinguish in the human body and in animals a half which corresponds to the north pole, and another half which corresponds to the south pole of a magnetic bar or of a magneto-electric apparatus. The previous investigations of Decle[22] on the different human polarities on the left and right sides are thus directly confirmed.

The hypnotized subject, whose eyes have been prepared and verified by the assistance of the ophthalmoscopic examination of which we have spoken,[23] can thus be employed as a real living reagent to recognize the differences in the coloration of the effluvia on the left side and those on the right side. In healthy, well men, the irradiated effluvia of the eye and the organs of the senses of the left side appear with a very intense blue coloration – those on the right side with a red carmine coloration. The intensity of the emitted effluvia seems to indicate the maximum energy of the nervous forces – indeed:

In hemiplegics, the effluvia irradiated from the eye of the paralysed side are very weak.

In chronic tabetics, very markedly weakened, the intensity of the effluvium is greatly diminished on both sides.

In neuropaths and in hysterics of both sexes, the red coloration of the effluvia of the right eye becomes violet; this is a diagnostic sign which in certain cases has allowed me to detect states of latent hysteria, and the eyes of these subjects appear incapable of moving upwards until they can form a red color. The effluvia of the ears, nostrils and lips maintain their red coloration.

In this matter I have been able to make a fortunate application of magnetized crowns, and thus restore the red effluvia in subjects with purple effluvia. I put, in fact, a magnetic crown on the head of the subject; under these conditions, the blue north pole is applied on the right side (violet) of the diseased subject, as if they were magnetic bars, the poles of opposite name are attracted, and poles of similar name are repelled. I was able to verify with a human being the physical law of the actions of the magnets, and to observe that, after fifteen or twenty minutes, by the action of this magnetized crown, arranged as opposite magnets, the blue rays of the violet eye were repulsed, and the red rays, attracted; so that in some cases I have been able to restore the magnetic effluvia to their physiological conditions.[24] (I am continuing this research from the point of view of an application to the treatment of hysteria.)

In subjects affected with multiple sclerosis, and with various tremors, the eyes on the right side of these subjects almost always emit yellow-coloured effluvia analogous to those of which we have spoken, which appear on the induction coils.

And this is still a very interesting point, which brings the study of the magnetic effluvia of living beings to that of the magneto-electric apparatus, since it shows us a special modality of the electromagnetic force which appears on both sides by a yellowish colour.[25]

These new studies, applied to the field of mental pathology, have enabled me to record interesting facts, which I shall communicate later.

I will add that I have continued my research on different types of the animal kingdom and, in horses, guinea pigs, dogs, cats, birds, fish, I have found, in the same way, that they emitted blue effluvia from their left sides, and that they have red effluvia on the right side. These details were clearly indicated by the hypnotized subject, without the least hesitation.

I will also add that, in a new series of experiments, the magnetic effluvia disappear at death, and are gradually extinguished.

Thus, out of four cadavers examined from this special point of view in the autopsy room, I have observed that in two of them, pronounced dead for twenty-four hours, the effluvia were completely wanting, and that in two others they were still apparent in the form of small blue or red glimmers.

Later, I will publish new details about this interesting subject.[26]

Notes to the Introduction

1 Much has been written about mesmerism and the concept of animal magnetism, as seen in bibliographies: Alvarado, 2008b; Crabtree, 1988; Dessoir, 1888. Also, in the studies of: Crabtree, 1993; Gauld, 1992; Meheust, 1999. On similar force concepts before Mesmer, see Podmore, 1909, p. Chap. 2.

2 The early mesmerists were particularly concerned with the use of magnetism for healing. Many of the *journals of magnetism*, such as the Journal du Magnétisme, devoted a good number of pages to magnetic

healing cases. For examples of medical applications of magnetism, see Mialle's (1826) long list of cases, and the works of: Ashburner, 1867: Ch. 11; Elliotson, 1843; Esdaile, 1846.

3 Aspects of the neo-mesmeric movement have been discussed by: Alvarado, 2009a, 2009b; Crabtree, 1993; Dingwall, 1967–1968; Harrington, 1988a; Plas, 2000.

4 For overviews, see my previous articles: Alvarado, 2006, 2016a, 2016b; Alvarado & Nahm, 2011.

5 On the various attempts to physically detect unorthodox forces emanating from the body, see Carrington, n. d.; Chéroux, 2005; Montandon, 1927; Ungaro, 1992.

6 For other relevant positive and negative observations using magnets, see Nahm, 2012, pp 393–401.

7 During the late nineteenth century, there were several reports of ostensible psychic phenomena of different sorts reported with individuals described as hysterical or having nervous disturbances, e.g., Dailey, 1894; F., 1894; Fontan, 1887; G., 1892; Giacchi, 1893; Mason, 1894; Tolosa-Latour, 1893. There were also some who saw the phenomena of physical mediums as caused by instability and pathology of the nervous system, as Lombroso (1892, 1909) argued about the physical medium Eusapia Palladino (1854–1918). I have discussed Lombroso's ideas elsewhere. (Alvarado, 2017; Alvarado & Biondi, 2017).

8 For early discussions of the perispirit based on spirit communications, see Kardec, 1857, p. 44, 67–68; 1862, p. 5–6, 55–57, 62–66. The same author stated: "The incarnate Spirit has two envelopes, the material one which is the [physical] body, the other semi-material and indestructible which is the perisprit. On leaving the first one, it preserves the second, which constitutes for him a kind of body, but its properties are essentially different. In its normal state it is invisible to us, but it can become momentarily visible and even tangible: this is the cause of the phenomenon of apparitions"; Kardec 1859, p. 2. See also Alvarado, 2008a, p. 85–86.

9 Both the Félida X. case, reported by Azam (1887), and Janet's work were extremely influential in France, and elsewhere; Ellenberger, 1970; Foschi, 2003.

10 On Luys' life and work, see: de Gassicourt, 1897; Escalard, 1984; F., 1897; Gautier, 1898; Parent and Parent, 2011; Vapereau, 1893, p. 1027; Vermey, 1897.

11 This referred to the effects of metals on hysterics and hypnotized patients, a phenomenon of particular interest to members of the Salpêtrière psychiatric community; Harrington, 1988b; Plas, 2000, p. 46–48. On the pioneering work on this topic by Victor Burq (1822–84), see Walusinski, 2018.

12 Luys interpreted his results as evidence of direct influence of the substances on the experimental participants. But a critic speculated on the possible role of suggestion and mental suggestion in the interpretation of these results; Dumontpallier, 1886, p. 429. Commenting on similar research (Bourru & Burot, 1886), physiologist Charles Richet (1850–1935) also speculated on the effects of suggestion and mental suggestion, but in addition he suggested that the experimenter should be blind as to the substance used in specific tests, and that attention should be paid to physiological reactions specific to the substances used, and not to general reactions (such as stupor). Furthermore, he suggested that these tests should employ a small number of substances, for a better assessment of the probability of chance results; Richet, 1886, p. 323.

13 Luys also wrote: "By virtue of this exquisite receptivity of the hypnotized subject, by virtue of these incessant vibrations of the molecules of moving matter, each group of these molecules will produce similar reactions by a mechanism analogous to that of magnetic vibrations"; Luys, 1890c, p. 261. Highly hypnotizable persons had an unstable nervous system that allowed such sensitiveness. For this reason, Luys worked with special patients. He wrote: "The main subject, Esther, who has been used in all these researches, is of exquisite sensibility, and of a very special impressionability"; Luys, 1887b, p. 70. She was described as being 20 years old and as a patient presenting hystero-epileptic attacks treated by Luys at the Salpêtrière and at the Charité. Conventional treatments were not effective, but she seemed to improve when hypnotized; pp. 71–72. Luys (1887b) presented at the end of his book various photographs of Esther, one in her normal state and various others under the influence of substances and drugs. On nineteenth century interest in vibrations and forces to convey information, sometimes at a distance, see: Alvarado, 2015; Enns and Trower, 2013. The latter anthology of articles also relates the topic to art and science.

14 For overviews see: Gauld, 1992, p. 334–336; Méheust, 1999, p. 126–128; Parent and Parent, 2011, p. 132–134; Plas, 2000, Chap 3. Luys was also discussed by some of his contemporaries, e.g., Croq, 1900, pp. 162–163, 167–168, 177–178, 196–197; Foveau de Courmelles, 1890, Chap. 4; Hart, 1893; Sicard de Plauzoles, 1893.

15 The word "transfer" was used to refer to the moving of physical or mental phenomena (such as paralysis and hallucinations) from one side of the body to the other. This was soon extended to transfers from one person to another. For a discussion, see Gauld 1992, pp. 333–334; Harrington, 1988b.
16 This paper also appeared in the prestigious *Compte Rendu Hebdomadaires des Séances et Mémoires de la Société de Biologie:* Luys, 1892c.
17 This research is part of a history of attempts to photograph fluids or psychic forces using photography; Chéroux, 2005; Girod, 1912. Perhaps the best-known early work in this area was conducted by Baraduc, 1896. The methodology of Luys and David was criticized in terms of artefacts such as heat; Martin, 1897; Yvon, 1898. However, the authors defended their results; Luys and David, 1897b.
18 In his book *Leçons Cliniques sur les Principaux Phénomènes de l'Hypnotisme dans Leurs Rapports avec la Pathologie Mentale*, Luys (1890c) stated that he tried to demonstrate that the phenomena of hypnotism were "for the most part, reducible to simple laws derived from the principles of normal physiology …" (p. vi).
19 It was also published as Luys, 1892c.
20 Some nineteenth-century examples are: Baraduc, 1896; Leadbeater, 1895; Marques, 1896. Later discussions include the work of Kilner (1920) and Leadbeater (1902), among others.
21 See Luys, 1892a.
22 Charles Dècle wrote, with Louis T. Chazarain, about magnetic phenomena, emphasizing polarity in the human body (Chazarain & Dècle, 1887). Several other neo-mesmerists wrote about polarity as well, e.g., Barέty, 1887; Durville, 1895–1896, as did Mesmer, 1779, p. 76.
23 Luys (1895) stated that the eyes of the hypnotized persons who participated in his studies acquired an uncommon sensitivity. He wrote: "If we examine their retina at this moment with the opthalmoscope, we find an extraordinary hyperaemia of the vessels, a dilation of the veins, a state of special erethism of the circulation, which in turn put the sensory properties of the cells of the retina into a state of extreme exaltation …" (p. 354). This, Luys said, was found by him and by other physicians in 18 participants tested.
24 On the use of crowns in transfer tests, see Luys and Encausse, 1890.
25 Luys added this note here: "The hypnotized subjects are still able to reveal the disorders in the circles of the eye which they examine. Thus, in certain cases of amaurosis, glaucoma, cataracts, the subjects reveal special modifications in the state of the eyes under their examination."
26 Luys (1893b, p. 640) briefly described further observations in another paper. He said a sensitive saw lights in the exposed brain of a dog but ceased seeing them when the dog died. Then he asked the same hypnotic subject to observe cadavers in a hospital. The glimmers of light perceived diminished 24 hours after the body's death, but on occasion some were seen.

References

Académie Nationale de Médicine (1887). [Discussion of Luys's paper presented at the Académie Nationale de Médicine]. *Bulletin de l'Académie Nationale de Médicine, 18*(s. 2), 303–306.

Alvarado, C. S. (2006). Human radiations: Concepts of force in mesmerism, spiritualism and psychical research. *Journal of the Society for Psychical Research, 70*, 138–162.

Alvarado, C. S. (2008a). Further notes on historical ideas of human radiations: III. The perispirit and mediumistic forces. *Psypioneer,* 4, 85–92.

Alvarado, C. S. (2008b). Mesmerism online: A bibliographic review. *Australian Journal of Clinical and Experimental Hypnosis, 36*, 115–120.

Alvarado, C. S. (2009a). Late 19th- and early 20th-century discussions of animal magnetism. *International Journal of Clinical and Experimental Hypnosis, 57*, 1–16.

Alvarado, C. S. (2009b). Modern animal magnetism: the work of Alexandre Barέty, Émile Boirac, and Julian Ochorowicz. *Australian Journal of Clinical and Experimental Hypnosis, 37*, 1–15.

Alvarado, C. S. (2015). Telepathic emissions: Edwin J. Houston on "Cerebral Radiation." *Journal of Scientific Exploration, 29*, 467–490.

Alvarado, C. S. (2016a). Human radiations. In R. McLuhan (Ed.) *Psi Encyclopedia*. London: Society for Psychical Research. Retrieved from http://psi-encyclopedia.spr.ac.uk/articles/human-radiations

Alvarado, C. S. (2016b). On psychic forces and doubles: the case of Albert de Rochas. *Journal of Scientific Exploration,* 30, 63–84.
Alvarado, C. S. (2017). Correspondence: Cesare Lombroso's "psychiatric explanation" of Eusapia Palladino. *Journal of the Society for Psychical Research, 81*, 142–144.
Alvarado, C. S., & Biondi M (2017). Cesare Lombroso on mediumship and pathology (Classic Text No. 110). *History of Psychiatry, 28*, 225–241.
Alvarado, C. S., & Nahm M (2011). Psychic phenomena and the vital force: Hereward Carrington on "Vital Energy and Psychical Phenomena." *Journal of the Society for Psychical Research,* 75, 91–103.
Anonymous. (1866). Prix de médicine et de chirugie fondé par M. de Montyon: rapport sur le concours de l'année 1865. *Comptes Rendus Hebdomadaires des Séances de l'Académie des Sciences, 62,* 519–529.
Anonymous. (1894). "Couronne magique": l'emmagasinement des activités cérébrales. *Le Matin,* (30 Aug.), 1.
Ashburner, J. (1867). *Notes and studies in the philosophy of animal magnetism and spiritualism*. H. Baillière.
Azam, E. E. (1887). *Hypnotisme, double conscience et altérations de la personnalité*. J.- B. Baillière.
Baistow, C. (1846). A suggestion. *The Saint Louis Magnet, 2,* 146–149.
Baraduc, H. (1893). *La force vitale: Notre corps vital fluidique, sa formule biométrique*. G. Carré.
Baraduc, H. (1896). *L'ame humaine: Ses Mouvements, ses Lumières, et l'Iconographie de l'Invisible Fluidique*. Georges Carré.
Barety, A. (1887). *Le magnétisme animal: Étudié sous le nom de force neurique rayonnante et circulante dans ces propriétes physiques, physiologiques et thérapeutique*. Octave Doin.
Binet, A., & Féré, C. (1885). L'hypnotisme chez les hystériques: Le transfert. *Revue Philosophique de la France et de l'Étranger* 19, 1–25.
Binet, A., & Féré C. (1887). *Animal magnetism*. Kegan Paul, Trench.
Boirac, E. (1895). Une nouvelle méthode d'expérimentation pour vérifier l'action nerveuse à distance. *Annales de Psychiatrie et d'Hypnologie dans leurs Rapports avec la Psychologie et la Médicine Légale, 5*, 325–330.
Boirac, E. (1908). *La psychologie inconnue: Introduction et contribution à l'étude expérimentale des sciences psychiques*. Félix Alcan.
Bourget, P. (1895). Un cas de suggestion mentale. *Annales de Psychiatrie et d'Hypnologie dans leurs Rapports avec la Psychologie et la Médicine Légale, 5*, 95–96.
Bourru, H., & Burot P. (1886). Les premières experiences sur l'action des médicaments à distance. *Revue Philosophique de la France et de l'Étranger, 21*, 311–321.
Bourru H., & Burot P. (1887). *La suggestion mentale et l'action à distance des substances toxiques et médicamenteuses*. J.– B. Baillière.
Briquet, P. (1859). *Traité clinique et thérapeutique de l'hystérie*. J.- B. Baillière.
Buckland, T. (1850). *The handbook of mesmerism* (2nd ed.). H. Baillière.
Carrington, H. (n.d., *c*.1939). *Laboratory investigations into psychic phenomena*. Rider.
Charcot, J. M. (1882). Sur les divers états nerveux déterminés par l'hypnotisation chez les hystériques. *Comptes Rendus Hebdomadaires des Séances de l'Academie des Sciences, 94*, 403–405.
Charcot, J-M, Luys, J., & Dumontpallier, A. (1877). Rapport fait à la Société de Biologie sur la métalloscopie du Docteur Burq. *Comptes Rendus des Séances et Mémoires de la Société de Biologie,4*(s. 6), 1–24.
Charcot, J-M, Luys, J., & Dumontpallier, A. (1878). Second rapport fait à la Société de Biologie sur la métalloscopie et la métallothérapie du Docteur Burq. *Comptes Rendus des Séances et Mémoires de la Société de Biologie* 30, i–xxxii.
Charpignon, J. (1848). *Physiologie, médecine et métaphysique du magnétisme*. Germer Baillière.
Chazarain, L. T., & Dècle, C. (1887). *Les courants de la polarité dans l'aimant et dans le corps humain.*
Chéroux, C. (2005). Photographs of fluids: an alphabet of invisible rays. In C. Chéroux, *The perfect medium: Photography and the occult* (pp. 114–138). Yale University Press. (Original work published in French, 2004.)
Crabtree, A. (ed.). (1988). *Animal magnetism, early hypnotism, and psychical research, 1766–1925: An annotated bibliography*. Kraus International.
Crabtree, A. (1993). *From Mesmer to Freud: Magnetic sleep and the roots of psychological healing*. Yale University Press.
Crookes, W. (1874). *Researches in the phenomena of spiritualism*. J. Burns.
Croq, J. (1900). *L'hypnotisme scientifique* (2nd ed.). Société d'Éditions Scientifiques.
Dailey, A. H. (1894). *Mollie Fancher, The Brooklyn enigma*. Press of Eagle Book Printing Department.

Daudet, L. (1915). *Devant la douleur: Souvenirs des milieux littéraires, politiques, artistiques et médicaux de 1880 a 1905* (Vol. 2). Nouvelle Librairie National.

de Gassicourt, C. (1897). Obsèques de M. Luys. *Bulletin de l'Académie de Médicine 38*(s. 3), 98–200.

de Rochas, A. (1887). *Les forces non définies: Recherches historiques et expérimentales*. G. Masson.

de Rochas, A. (1897). Les expériences de Choisy-Yvrec (près Bordeaux) du 2 au 14 octobre 1896. *Annales des Sciences Psychiques, 7*, 6–28.

de Rochas, A. (1899). *L'Extériorisation de la sensibilité: Etude expérimentale & historique* (5th ed.). Chamuel.

Delanne, G. (1897). *L'Evolution animique: Essais de psychologie suivant le spiritisme*. Chamuel.

Deleuze, J. P. F. (1813). *Histoire critique du magnétisme animal* (Vol. 1). Mame.

Despine, P. (1880). *Étude scientifique sur le somnambulisme, sur les phénomènes qu'il présente et sur son action thérapeutique dans certaines maladies nerveuses*. F. Savy.

Dessoir, M. (1888). *Bibliographie des modernen hypnotismus*. Carl Duncker.

Dingwall, E. J. (Ed.). (1967–1968). *Abnormal hypnotic phenomena: A survey of nineteenth-century cases* (4 vols.). J. &. J. Churchill.

du Potet [de Sennevoy J]. (1868). *Manuel de l'étudiant magnétiseur* (4th ed.). Germer Baillière.

Dujardin-Beaumetz, G. (1888). Sur les recherches et experiences communiquées par M Luys, membre de l'Académie, à la séance du 30 août 1887, concernant la solicitation expérimentale des phénomènes émotifs chez les sujets en état d'hypnotisme, au nom d'une commission composée de MM Hérard. Bergeron. Brouardel, Gariel et Dujardin-Beaumetz. *Bulletin de l'Académie Nationale de Médicine, 19*, 330–350.

Dumontpallier, A. (1886). Remarques sur le communication de M. Luys. *Compte Rendu Hebdomadaires des Séances et Mémoires de la Société de Biologie, 3*(s. 8), 428–429.

Durville, H. (1895–1896). *Traité expérimental de magnétisme* (2 vols.). Librairie du Magnétisme.

Eadon, S. (1885). Natural sensitives and our lunatic asylums. *Light, 5*, 279–281.

Ellenberger, H. F. (1970). *The discovery of the unconscious: The history and evolution of dynamic psychiatry*. Basic Books.

Elliotson, J. (1843). *Numerous cases of surgical operations without pain in the mesmeric state*. H. Baillière.

Elliotson, J. (1848). Cure of a true cancer of the female breast with mesmerism. *Zoist, 6*, 213–237.

Enns, A., & Trower, S. (Eds). (2013). *Vibratory modernism*. Palgrave Macmillan.

Escalard, B. (1984). Un méconnu de l'hystérie: Jules Bernard Luys. Unpublished MD thesis, Université de Caen.

Esdaile, J. (1846). *Mesmerism in India, and its practical application in surgery and medicine*. Longman, Brown, Green, and Longmans.

F. J. H. P. (1894). Expériences sur la transmission mentale. *Annales des Sciences Psychiques, 4*, 67–74.

F. M. (1897). Le Docteur Luys. *Le Figaro*, (25 Aug.), 3.

Fontan, J. (1887). Hystéro-épilepsie masculine, suggestion-inhibition-transposition de sens. *Revue Philosophique de la France et de l'Étranger, 24*, 213–221.

Foschi, R. (2003). L'indagine sulla personalità alle origini della psicologia scientifica francese. (1870–1885). *Physis, Rivista Internazionale si Storia della Scienza*, (1–2), 63–105.

Foveau, de Courmelles, F. V. (1890). *L'hypnotisme*. Hachette.

G. A. (1892). Notes sur une série d'expériences relatives à la télépathie poursuivies en 1888. *Annales des Sciences Psychiques, 2*, 317–337.

Gauld, A. (1992). *A history of hypnotism*. Cambridge University Press.

Gautier, E. (1898). Necrologie, le Docteur Luys. In *L'Année Scientifique et Industrielle* (Vol. 41, p. 407). Hachette.

Giacchi, O. (1893). Communication sur les faits de télépathie. *Annales des Sciences Psychiques, 3*, 302–306.

Girod, F. (1912). *Pour photographier les Rayons Humain*. Bibliothèque Gènèrale d'Éditions.

Goudard, H. (1895). Sur la réalité objective des effluves lumineux magnétiques perçus par certains sujets. *Annales de Psychiatrie et d'Hypnologie dans leurs Rapports avec la Psychologie et la Médicine Légale, 5*, 14–15.

Gregory, W. (1851). *Letters to a candid inquirer, on animal magnetism*. Blanchard and Lea.

Harrington, A. (1988a). Hysteria, hypnosis and the lure of the invisible, the rise of neo-mesmerism in fin-desiècle French psychiatry. In W. F. Bynum, R. Porter, R. & M. Shepherd (Eds,) *The anatomy of madness, essays in the history of psychiatry, Vol. 3: The asylum and its psychiatry* (pp. 226–246). Tavistock Press.

Harrington, A. (1988b). Metals and magnets in medicine, hysteria, hypnosis and medical culture in fin-de-siècle. *Psychological Medicine, 18*, 21–38.

Hart, E. (1893). Notes on the new mesmerism. *British Medical Journal, 1*, 77–78, 127–130, 198–200, 261–263, 301–303, 369–364.

Janet P. (1889). *L'Automatisme psychologique, essai de psychologie expérimentale sur les formes inférieures de l'activité humaine*. Félix Alcan.

Kardec, A. (1857). *Le livre des esprits*. E. Dentu.

Kardec, A. (1859). A S.A. le prince G. *Revue Spirite, Journal d'Études Psychologiques 2*, 1–7.

Kardec, A. (1862). *Spiritisme expérimental, le livre des médiums* (2nd ed.) Didier.

Kilner, W. J. (1920). *The human atmosphere (the Aura)* (2nd rev. ed). Kegan Paul, Trench, Trübner.

Kingsbury, G. C. (1891). *The practice of hypnotic suggestion*. John Wright.

Leadbeater, C. W. (1895). The aura. *The Theosophist, 17*, 134–141.

Leadbeater, C. W. (1902). *Man, visible and invisible, examples of different types of men as seen by means of trained clairvoyance*. John Lane.

Lepelletier, E. (1887). Les nouveaux dieux. *Gil Blas* (11 Nov.), 1–2.

Leymarie, P. G. (1897). Photographies par immersion, effluves perispritales rendues visibles. *Revue Spirite, 40*, 524–528.

Lombroso, C. (1892). Le spiritisme et la psychiatrie, explication psychiatrique de certains faits spirites. *Annales des Sciences Psychiques, 2*, 143–151.

Lombroso, C. (1909). *After death – what? Spiritistic Phenomena and their Interpretation*. (W. S. Kenney, trans., from *Ricerche sui Fenomeni Ipnotici e Spiritici*). Small, Maynard.

Luys, J. (1855). Ossifications de la dure-mère, recueillies chez une femme de 68 ans, à la Salpêtrière. *Comptes Rendus des Séances et Mémoires de la Société de Biologie 2*(s. 2), 105–106.

Luys, J. (1865). *Recherches sur le système cérébro-spinal, sa structure, ses fonctions et ses maladies*. J.- B. Baillière.

Luys, J. (1873). *Iconographie photographique des centres nerveux*. (2 vols.). J.- B. Baillière.

Luys, J. (1874). *Études de physiologie et de pathologie cérébrale*. J.- B. Baillière.

Luys, J. (1875). *Leçons sur la structure et les maladies du système nerveux*. J.- B. Ballière.

Luys, J. (1876). *Le cerveau et ses fonctions*. J.- B. Baillière.

Luys, J. (1881). *Traité clinique et pratique des maladies mentales*. Delahaye et Lecrosnier.

Luys, J. (1882). Des conditions somatiques de la surexcitation nerveuse. *L'Encéphale, Journal des Maladies Mentales et Nerveuses, 2*, 569–577.

Luys, J. (1883). Recherches sur la structure de l'écorce cérébrale d'après la méthode microphotographique. *L'Encéphale, Journal des Maladies Mentales et Nerveuses, 3*, 140–155.

Luys, J. (1886). Sur l'action de médicaments à distance chez les sujets hypnotisés. *Compte Rendu Hebdomadaires des Séances et Mémoires de la Société de Biologie, 3*(s. 8), 426–428.

Luys, J. (1887a). Les émotions chez les sujets en état d'hypnotisme, études de psychologie expérimentale faites à l'aide de substances médicamenteuses ou toxiques impressionant à distance les réseaux nerveux périphériques. *L'Encéphale, Journal des Maladies Mentales et Nerveuses, 7*, 513–544.

Luys, J. (1887b). *Les émotions dans l'état d'hypnotisme et l'action à distance de substances médicamenteuses ou toxiques*. J.- B. Baillière.

Luys, J. (1887c). De la sollicitation expérimentale des phénomènes émotifs chez les sujets en état d'hypnotisme. *Bulletin de l'Académie Nationale de Médicine, 18*(s. 2), 291–303.

Luys, J. (1887d). Phénomènes produits par l'action des médicaments à distance. De l'exorbitis expérimental. *L'Encéphale, Journal des Maladies Mentales et Nerveuses, 7*, 74–80.

Luys, J. (1888a). Étude sur le dédoublement des operations cérébrales et sur le rôle isolé de chaque hemisphere dans les phénomènes de la pathologie mentale. *L'Encéphale, Journal des Maladies Mentales et Nerveuses, 8*, 404–424, 516–537.

Luys, J. (1888b). Sur la sollicitation expérimentale des phénomènes émotifs chez les sujets en état d'hypnotisme. *Bulletin de l'Académie Nationale de Médicine, 20*(s. 3), 246–261.

Luys, J. (1890a). Action psychique des aimants, des courants électro-magnétiques, et des courants électriques continus. *Compte Rendu Hebdomadaires des Séances et Mémoires de la Société de Biologie, 2*(n. s.), 143–146.

Luys, J. (1890b). *Hypnotisme expérimental, les émotions dans l'état d'hypnotisme et l'action à distance de substances médicamenteuses ou toxiques*. J.- B. Baillière.

Luys, J. (1890c). *Leçons cliniques sur les principaux phénomènes de l'hypnotisme dans leurs rapports avec la pathologie mentale*. Georges Carré.

Luys, J. (1892a). De la visibilité des effluves magnétiques & électriques chez les sujets en état hypnotique. *Annales de Psychiatrie et d'Hypnologie dans leurs Rapports avec la Psychologie et la Médicine Légale, 2*, 193–195.

Luys, J. (1892b). De la visibilité par les sujets en état hypnotique des effluves dégagés par les êtres vivants. *Annales de Psychiatrie et d'Hypnologie dans leurs Rapports avec la Psychologie et la Médicine Légale, 2*, 321–323.

Luys, J. (1892c). De la visibilité, par les sujets en état hypnotique, des effluves dégagés par les êtres vivants. *Compte Rendu Hebdomadaires des Séances et Mémoires de la Société de Biologie, 4*(s. 9), 657–659.

Luys, J. (1893a). *Le traitement de la folie*. Rueff.

Luys, J. (1893b). De la visibilité directe des effluves cérébraux. *Compte Rendu Hebdomadaires des Séances et Mémoires de la Société de Biologie, 5*(n.s.), 638–641.

Luys, J. (1894). De l'emmagasiment de certaines activités cérébrales dans une couronne aimantée. *Annales de Psychiatrie et d'Hypnologie dans leurs Rapports avec la Psychologie et la Médicine Légale, 4*, 65–67.

Luys, J. (1895). Nouvelles recherches sur les facultés réactionnelles des sujets mis en état d'hypnotisme. *Annales de Psychiatrie et d'Hypnologie dans leurs Rapports avec la Psychologie et la Médicine Légale, 5*, 353–364.

Luys, J., & David E (1897a). Note sur l'enregistrement photographique des effluves qui se dégagent des extrémités des doigts et du fond de l'oeil de l'être vivant, à l'état physiologique et à l'état pathologique. *Comptes Rendus Hebdomadaires des Séances et Mémoires de la Société de Biologie, 4*(s. 2), 515–519.

Luys, J., & David, E. (1897b). Fixation par la photographie des effluves que se dêgagent de l'appareil auditif. Réponse à certaines objections concernant l'émission des effluves digitaux. *Comptes Rendus Hebdomadaires des Séances et Mémoires de la Société de Biologie, 4*(s. 2), 676–678.

Luys, J., & Encausse, G. (1890). Du transfert à distance à l'aide d'une couronne de fer aimanté, d'états névropathiques variés, d'un sujet à l'état de veille sur un sujet à l'état hypnotique. *Comptes Rendus Hebdomadaires des Séances et Mémoires de la Société de Biologie, 3*(n.s), 599–602.

Marques, A. (1896). *The human aura, a study*. Office of Mercury.

Martin, C. (1897). De l'importance des actions physico-chimiques dans l'obtention d'épreuves photographiques par le procédé de MM. Luys et David. *Comptes Rendus Hebdomadaires des Séances et Mémoires de la Société de Biologie, 4*(s. 2), 722–723.

Mason, R. O. (1894). Case of hysteria, catalepsy and unstable consciousness accompanied by supernormal perception. *Journal of the Society for Psychical Research, 6*, 361–365.

Méheust, B. (1999). *Somnambulisme et mediumnité (1784–1930). Vol. 1, Le défi du magnétisme animal.* Le Plessis-Robinson, Institut Synthélabo pour de Progrès de la Connaissance.

Melcior, y Farré, V. (1900). *La enfermedad de los místicos (patología-psíquica)*. Juan Torrens y Coral.

Mesmer, F. A. (1779). *Mémoire sur la découverte du magnétisme animal*. Didot.

Mialle, S. (1826). *Exposé par ordre alphabétique des cures opérées en France par le magnétisme animal, depuis Mesmer jusqu'à nos jours (1774–1826)* (2 vols.). J. G. Dentu.

Montandon, R. (1927). *Les radiation humaines, introduction à la demonstration expérimentale de l'existence des corps subtils de l'homme*. Félix Alcan.

Morselli, E. (1908). *Psicologia e "spiritismo," impressioni e note critiche sui fenomeni medianici di Eusapia Paladino* (2 vols.). Fratelli Bocca.

Nahm, M. (2012). The sorcerer of Cobenzl and his legacy, the life of Baron Karl Ludwig von Reichenbach, his work and its aftermath. *Journal of Scientific Exploration, 26*, 381–407.

Olivier, J. (1849) *Traité de magnétisme suivi des paroles d'un somnambule et d'un recueil de traitements magnétiques*. L. Jougla.

Parent, M., & Parent A. (2011) Jules Bernard Luys in Charcot's penumbra. In J. Bogousslavsky (Ed.) *Following Charcot, A forgotten history of neurology and psychiatry* (Frontiers of Neurology and Neuroscience, Vol. 29, pp. 125–136). Karger.

Peter, [M]. (1894). Action de médicaments à distance. *Annales de Psychiatrie et d'Hypnologie dans leurs Rapports avec la Psychologie et la Médicine Légale, 4*, 150–153.

Petetin, J. H. D. (1808). *Électricité animale* (2nd ed.). Brunot-Labbé.
Pigeaire, J. (1839). *Puissance de l'électricité animale, ou, du magnétisme vital et de ses rapports avec la physique, la physiologie et la médecine*. Dentu.
Plas, R. (2000). *Naissance d'une science humaine, la psychologie, les psychologues et le "merveilleux psychique."* Presses Universitaires de Rennes.
Podmore, F. (1909). *Mesmerism and Christian science, a short history of mental healing*. George W. Jacobs.
Richer, P. (1885). *Études cliniques sur la grande hystérie ou hystéro-épilepsie* (2nd ed.). Adrien Delahaye et Émile Lecrosnier.
Richet, C. (1886). L'action des substances toxiques et médicamenteuses à distance. *Revue Philosophique de la France et de l'Étranger, 21,* 321–323.
Sicard de Plauzoles, J. (1893). Les expériences du Dr Luys et de M. de Rochas sur l'extériorisation de la sensibilité. *Annales de Psychiatrie et d'Hypnologie dans leurs Rapports avec la Psychologie et la Médicine Légale, 3,* 52–57.
Sunderland, L. R. (1842). Life, health, disease, and death. *The Magnet, 1,* 55–57.
[Tardy de Montravel, A. A]. (1785). *Essai sur la théorie du somnambulisme magnétique*. n. p.
Tolosa-Latour, M. (1893). Expériences de suggestion mentale à distance. *Annales des Sciences Psychiques, 3,* 268–273.
Toulouse, E. (1897). Mélanges et nouvelles, nécrologie. *Travaux de Psychiatrie (Médicine Mentale, Neurologie, Psychiatrie), 1,* 254.
Ungaro, J. (1992). *Las radiaciones humanas, historia de la radiónica*. Club de Estudio.
Vapereau, G. (ed.). (1893). *Dictionnaire universel des contemporains* (6th ed.). Hachette.
Vermey, A. (1897). Necrologie, le docteur Luys. *La Science Illustrée* (No. 497), 291.
von Hartmann, E. (1885). *Spiritism*. Psychological Press.
von Reichenbach, C. (1851). *Physico-physiological researches on the dynamics of magnetism, electricity, heat, light, crystallization, and chemism, in their relation to vital force* (2nd ed.). J. S. Redfield. (Original work published in German1849).
von Reichenbach, Baron, C. (1860). *Odic-magnetic letters*. Calvin Blanchard. (Original work published in German,1852).
Walusinski, O. (2018). The scientific illusion of Victor Burq (1822–1884). *European Neurology, 79,* 135–149.
Yvon, P. (1898). Des causes d'erreur inhérentes à la production du voile en photographie. *Comptes Rendus Hebdomadaires des Séances et Mémoires de la Société de Biologie, 5*(s. 2), 120–123.

Classic Text No. 84: '*Divisions of Personality and Spiritism*' by Alfred Binet (1896)*

Carlos S. Alvarado†

During the nineteenth century such individuals as Alfred Binet (1857–1911), who is the author of this Classic Text, conducted clinical and research work that led to the development and refinement of ideas about the subconscious mind and dissociation. The work concentrated on hysterical blindness, hypnosis, spontaneous somnambulism, and double and multiple personality. Another phenomenon that focused thinking on the topic was mediumship. The Classic Text is an excerpt from Binet's writings that illustrates how a representative of French abnormal psychology used mediumship to defend his particular ideas about the mind. The excerpt is taken from the English language translation, published in 1896, of Binet's *Altérations de la personnalité* (1892).

In his book *Recherche sur la médiumnité* (1902), the French spiritist leader Gabriel Delanne (1857–1926) criticized the nineteenth-century French tendency to reduce the phenomena of mental mediumship to psychopathology, the workings of the subconscious mind, and dissociation. In his view, those he criticized were too hasty to explain away what Delanne considered to be the manifestation of spirit agency. His book is an indirect reminder of a medical and psychological tradition that attempted to explain mediumship by postulating the action of conventional psychological processes. The purpose of this Classic Text is to bring this nineteenth-century conceptual tradition to the attention of current students of dissociation through the presentation of an excerpt from the writings of Alfred Binet.

Mediumship, the Subconscious Mind and Pathology

The explanations to which Delanne referred were part of the rise of the concept of the subconscious mind and its various manifestations. The notion of non-conscious mental activity was particularly developed during the nineteenth century through observations of a variety of such phenomena as hysterical anesthesia, hypnotic state-specific memory, somnambulism, amnesia, and spontaneous and hypnotically induced secondary personalities (Crabtree, 1993; Ellenberger, 1970; Foschi, 2003; Hacking, 1995). These phenomena were of special interest to French physicians and others who specialized in the study of subjects such as somnambulists, hysterics and gifted hypnotic individuals (e.g., Azam, 1887; Bourru & Burot, 1888; Charcot, 1891; Janet, 1889). This tradition was mainly of pathological orientation. In the words of Alfred Binet, a French researcher:

*Republished with permission from *History of Psychiatry*, *21*, 487–500, 2010.
†Research for this study was funded by a grant from the Society for Psychical Research (London). I am grateful to Nancy L. Zingrone for editorial suggestions to improve this Introduction.

> With relatively few exceptions, the psychologists of my country have left the investigations of psychophysics to the Germans, and the study of comparative psychology to the English. They have devoted themselves almost exclusively to the study of pathological psychology, that is to say psychology affected by disease ... they have sought in the pathology of the mind or in the pathology of nervous action, the data to render intelligible the mechanism of the normal state. (Binet, 1890a, p. 12–13)

Such a trend, another French author wrote, represented the functioning of the 'unconscious activity of the mind' (Héricourt, 1889).[1]

The emergence of spiritualism in the USA and spiritism in France brought the phenomena of mediumship to this equation, generally dividing the practice into the production of physical effects and communications from spirits.[2] Although there were many examples of physical mediums—those said to produce phenomena such as raps and table levitations—mental manifestations were of more relevance for psychology and psychiatry. One writer described these phenomena in this way:

> There are mediums for writing, some by impression, and some are mechanically influenced; mediums who are wholly entranced, and some who are partly or in whole conscious; mediums who see spirits, and describe them to be identified by their friends; mediums who are influenced to personify departed friends, and go through scenes of past experience ... mediums who describe disease ...; mediums who are impelled to execute music, paint, sing, speak, and manifest other gifts not apparent in the normal state; mediums who prophesy, speak and write in tongues, give warnings, presentiments, describe past life, incidents, accidents, events, traits of character, offer counsels and cautions, etc. (Clark, 1863, p. 52–53).

In France the development of spiritism, led by Allan Kardec (the pseudonym of Hippolyte Leon Denizard Rivail, 1804–1859), popularized the figure of the medium.[3] In a widely read book, Kardec (1862, p. 195) asserted: "Every person who feels in any degree the influence of spirits is ... a medium." Such a quality, Kardec believed, presented different levels of sensitiveness. Very many people were exposed to Kardec's book *Le Livre des esprits* (1857), in which mediums conveyed information from "spirits" about such topics as God, the world of spirits, reincarnation and a variety of "moral laws" concerning society and behavior. The teachings presented in the book consisted of the answers that mediums gave to questions addressed to the supposed discarnate agents. It seems that mediums, as stated by an anonymous author, were the prophets of spiritism (Anon., 1863, p. 418).

The movement and its phenomena received much criticism in the French literature (e.g., Lemoine, 1861; Littre, 1856). A physician argued that mediums were "weak beings, impressionable and excitable" who exploited credulous people in salons and among high-class people (Bouchut, 1864, p. 44). Soon there were attempts to characterize mediumship as manifestations of the subconcious.[4] According to Ellenberger (1970, p. 85):

> The advent of spiritism was an event of major importance in the history of dynamic psychiatry, because it indirectly provided psychologists and psychopathologists with new approaches to the mind. Automatic writing, one of the procedures introduced by the spiritists, was taken over by scientists as a method of exploring the unconscious ... A new subject, the medium, became available for experimental psychological investigations, out of which evolved a new model of the human mind.

Influenced by the writings of Kardec and others, as well as of critics, several French students of the mind wrote about mediumship (Le Maléfan, 1999). Mediums were seen as an exemplar of subconscious functioning, implicating dissociation. In a communication presented at a meeting of the Société Médico-Psychologique in 1860, mediumship was described as a "doubling of personality similar to that produced during a dream" (Baillarger, 1861, p. 93). The French critic, philosopher and historian Hippolyte Taine (1828–1893) referred to mediumship when he wrote that some spiritistic manifestations showed "coexistence at the same time, in the same individual, of two thoughts, two wills, two distinct actions, one which is conscious, another which is not conscious" and which claims to come from the spirit world (Taine, 1878, p. 16). The concept found resonance in the writings of other students of the mind (e.g., Janet, 1889; Liébeault, 1889).

One of them wrote that the medium had a "series of ideas completely different from the series of ideas of the conscious person, who ignores all that takes place in his unconscious" (Richet, 1886, p. 93). In later years Edgar Bérillon (1859–1948) continued these speculations. In his view, a medium he was writing about showed "variations of personality analogous to those that we can induce experimentally with the hypnotized" which resulted in a "particular mental state that manifests by unconscious and automatic phenomena ..." (Bérillon, 1900, p. 251).

Some relevant studies of and writings about mediums came from the field of psychical research which, during the late nineteenth century, developed to study mediumship, as well as phenomena such as apparitions, hauntings and telepathy.[5] The early psychical researchers—such as those grouped around the London-based Society for Psychical Research (Gauld, 1968)—were interested in mediumship as a dissociative phenomenon (Alvarado, 2002). This was also evident in various discussions published in psychical research journals in France (Ochorowicz, 1896) and in the USA (James, 1889). But, in the case of mental mediums, they also conducted studies to determine if the manifestations supported the belief that the medium could obtain information about deceased and living persons transcending conventional explanations such as fraud, coincidence and cold reading. Examples of this were studies conducted with the US medium Leonora E. Piper (1857–1950; e.g., Hodgson, 1892; Lodge, 1890). Writing about his sittings with this woman, William James (1842–1910) stated that: "knowledge of her sittings and personal acquaintance with her has led me ... to believe that she has supernormal powers" (James, 1890b, p. 652).

An important and influential member of the Society for Psychical Research, classical scholar Frederic W. H. Myers (1843–1901), believed that "*some* of the effects which Spiritualists ascribe to spirits are referable to the unconscious action of the writer's own mind" (Myers, 1884, p. 237; original emphasis), ideas he developed in later publications (e.g., Myers, 1885, 1889). Myers did not share the pathological orientation of the French researchers. Furthermore, he believed that some mediums could obtain veridical information, and eventually was convinced that mediums could contact the dead (e.g., Myers, 1903).[6]

In addition to ideas about the subconscious in relation to mediumship, there were early discussions of the pathology of the phenomenon (e.g., Burlet, 1863; Marvin, 1874).[7] US physician William Hammond (1828–1900) stated that many tactile phenomena attributed by mediums to spirits:

> ... are merely symptoms of nervous derangement of some kind, often slight in character, but not infrequently of serious moment. In the former case they may generally be dissipated by a few doses of the bromide of potassium or half a dozen applications of galvanism; in the latter, they are often precursors of organic disturbance of the brain or spinal cord, leading to paralysis, epilepsy or mental derangement. (Hammond, 1876, p. 118)

Another US physician, George M. Beard (1839–83), believed that trance "is a morbid state, consisting in a concentration of the cerebral force in some limited region of the brain, the activity of other portions being meanwhile suspended" (Beard, 1877, p. 6). He also believed that mediums became more susceptible to trance the more they experienced it. According to Beard (1877, p. 8) "there is … in this disease, the same periodicity oftentimes that has long been observed in neuralgia".

Famous student of dissociation Pierre Janet (1859–1947) noticed that many mediums showed nervous crises.[8] He believed they were "neuropaths, if not frankly hysterical" (Janet, 1889, p. 404). Mediumship, he wrote, "depends on a particular morbid state" (p. 406) similar to those that may turn into hysteria or madness. But "mediumship is a symptom and not a cause" (p. 406). Ideas of mediumistic pathology continued into the twentieth century (e.g., Lévy-Valensi, 1910).

Alfred Binet

French psychologist Alfred Binet (1857–1911) was one of several students of the mind who discussed mediumship in their writings.[9] Binet, who came from a well-to-do family, finished law studies in 1878 and obtained a doctorate in natural sciences in 1894. That year was an important one for Binet, who became the Director of the Laboratory of Physiological Psychology of the École Pratique des Hautes Études in Paris, and founder of the journal *L'Année psychologique* (Nicolas, Segui & Ferrand, 2000). Nevertheless, for various political reasons, Binet never held a formal teaching position (Nicolas & Ferrand, 2002).

While Binet is now remembered mainly for his work on the measuring of intelligence (e.g., Binet, 1903; Binet & Simon, 1905), during the nineteenth century he explored a wide variety of topics. His early work included the study of hypnosis at the Salpêtrière (e.g., Binet & Féré, 1885, 1886) which he summarized in his well-known book—written with colleague and friend Charles Féré (1852–1907)—*Le Magnétisme Animal* (Binet & Féré, 1887). The book, a classic textbook on the subject, representing the views of the Salpêtrière school of hypnosis, had sections on the history of the topic, and on induction procedures, symptoms, suggestion, paralysis and other subjects.

Throughout his career Binet studied many topics. His book *Études de psychologie expérimentale* (1888a) includes chapters on the fetishism of love, the life of micro-organisms, the intensity of mental images, and the writing of hysterics. He also published on hallucinations (Binet, 1884), reasoning (Binet, 1886), mathematical prodigies (Binet, 1894), hysterical anesthesia (Binet, 1888b), the movements of infants (Binet, 1890b), synesthesia (Binet and Philippe, 1892), memory for words (Binet and Henri, 1894), and the influence of mental processes on blood pressure (Binet & Vaschide, 1897).

Binet was a good representative of the French interest in dissociation and the subconscious mind (Foschi and Cicciola, 2006a). He had the opportunity to observe many of the hysterics at the Salpêtrière, as seen in his studies of hypnosis (Binet & Féré, 1885, 1887) and the alteration of consciousness (Binet, 1889a) and sensibility (Binet, 1888b, 1889b). In his book *On Double Consciousness* (1890a), Binet reprinted various previously published papers about subconscious actions and trains of thought, some of which included observations and discussions of hysterical blindness and automatic writing. On the latter, he wrote: "Automatic writing does not only serve to express sensations perceived by the second consciousness; it is likewise able to express the thoughts that this second consciousness spontaneously combines" (Binet, 1890a, p. 29).

In a later book, *Les Altérations de la personnalité* (1892; translated as *Alterations of Personality*, 1896), Binet focused on dissociative phenomena such as multiple personality, motor automatisms and mediumship, articulating the general nineteenth-century trend to relate the phenomena to pathology and to the workings of the subconscious mind. He argued that "a genuine breaking up of consciousness occurs both in cases of disease and also of subjects under experiment; and now and then, often with the assistance of a slight suggestion, one of these consciousnesses has succeeded in attaining the dignity of a veritable personality" (Binet, 1896, p. 347). The existence and behaviors of these personalities had been documented by many French clinicians (e.g., Azam, 1887; Janet, 1889), as Binet discussed in the book.

The book is devoted to observations suggesting that, in some circumstances, "the normal unity of consciousness is broken up and several distinct consciousnesses are formed, each of which may have its own system of perceptions, its own memory, and even its own moral character" (Binet, 1896, p. x). Divided into three parts, the first part, "Successive Personalities," includes spontaneous cases of somnambulism and of double and multiple personalities, as well as of induced somnambulism. The second part, "Coexistent Personalities", has chapters about the insensibility of hysterics, their automatic writing, and such topics as distraction, ideas of subconscious origin, and the plurality of consciousness in normal individuals. The last includes studies with one common feature: "they throw a person into such a condition that without intending it, and often without knowing it, they tell their most secret thoughts. In other words, the person is induced to perform unconscious movements" (p. 220). The third, and final section, is about "Alterations of Personality in Experiments on Suggestion." Binet concludes by saying: "we have seen that a genuine breaking up of consciousness occurs both in cases of disease and also of subjects under experiment; and now and then, often with the assistance of a slight suggestion, one of these consciousnesses has succeeded in attaining the dignity of a veritable personality" (p. 347).

All of this indicated to Binet that: (a) aspects that normally constitute the self may disaggregate; (b) these elements always have a consciousness associated with them even if the self is not aware; (c) in some special conditions such elements can constitute secondary personalities. Our apparent unity, Binet (1896, p. 349) believed, "is to be sought in the co-ordination of the elements which compose it." Such a view, as Binet himself pointed out, was shared by Théodule Ribot (1839–1916), as seen in the conclusion of his influential *Les Maladies de la personnalité* (1888). Interestingly Foschi and Cicciola (2006a, p. 369) have pointed out that, unlike Janet (1889), Binet's views were not based on deficiency. They argued that his concept of double consciousness is the beginning of a change in the French emphasis on the study of pathology to understand the normal mind, a topic deserving detailed study.

One of the phenomena included in the third and last section of Binet's book is mediumship. Like others before him (e.g., Baillarger, 1861; Janet, 1889), in this book Binet sees mediums as an example of double consciousness, a dissociation that could be pathological. Unlike Myers and others (e.g., Hodgson, 1892; James, 1890b; Lodge, 1890; Lombroso, 1892) who were willing to accept the supernormal in some mediums, Binet was skeptical about this, which was consistent with his opinion that mental suggestion was a question of perceiving all kinds of sensory cues (Binet & Féré, 1887). In a later article about a case of telepathy, he stated that his attitude was one of "benevolent scepticism" (Binet, 1895, p. 199). This was consistent with other skeptical views about psychic phenomena prevalent in French circles, as has been documented in previous studies (Le Maléfan, 1999, 2008; Monroe, 2008; Plas, 2000).

Binet's views on mediumship are presented in the following excerpt. This is taken from the third part of the English translation of his book on dissociative phenomena, from the seventh chapter, entitled "Divisions of Personality and Spiritism" (Binet, 1896, p. 325–343; for a previous discussion see Binet, 1891, p. 851–854). This excerpt illustrates that, in addition to the phenomena of hypnosis, and of cases of somnambulism, amnesia, double and multiple personality, mediumship was important to some nineteenth-century researchers as a tool by which to study and conceptualize dissociation.

Classic Text No. 84: 'Divisions of Personality and Spiritism' by Alfred Binet (1896)

Recent researches have thrown new light upon [the] phenomena of spiritism, or so-called "spiritualism," by showing that these phenomena are due largely to mental disaggregation or division. There is no essential difference between the experiments—[conducted with] hysterical patients and the more spontaneous experiments that the spiritists practise upon themselves. The principal differences lie in the minor or, one might almost say, anecdotal conditions—i.e., in the medium, the terms employed, the imagined explanations, etc. ...

As a matter of fact, careful study of the phenomena shows that automatic handwriting proceeds from a thought other than the conscious thought of the medium. There are within him at a given time two thoughts that are unaware of each other, the only communication between them being by the automatic movements of handwriting. To be more exact, there are two coexisting personalities, for the thought that guides the automatic handwriting is by no means an isolated and detached thought; it has a character of its own, and it even bears the name of the spirit whose presence has been invoked.

We find here, therefore, a new and curious example of mental disaggregation and division of personality. One of the authors who understands the true nature of spirit phenomena best, Mr. Meyers.[10] summed up the theory of multiple personality very exactly—at a time when M. Janet's studies on somnambulism and my own on hysterical insensibility—which tend to the same result - were not yet begun.[11] This new coincidence, added to so many others, confirms the results, and proves that notwithstanding the imperfections and errors of detail that must exist in these researches, as in all others, the conclusion is fundamentally correct.

As with experiments in suggestion, those in spiritism succeed best on a certain class of subjects, among whom hysterical patients hold an important place. Hysterical patients, and somnambulists generally, furnish the greater part of the good mediums.[12] One may see that by glancing over the works on spiritism. Every now and then the most discreet author finds himself obliged to say that such and such an excellent medium had a nervous crisis or was soon fatigued, in consequence of delicate health. It is, moreover, generally admitted that spiritist performances predispose to nervous complications. Charcot reported a striking example of this very thing ...[13]

It follows from these results that the division of consciousness only breaks up the thinking processes. It remains within the province of ideation. No phenomena yet discovered show the sensibility of the peripheral organs in any way modified, as is the case with hysterical patients. Spiritist writers rarely mention this point. They are generally enthusiasts and mystics, ill prepared for methodical investigation. Moreover, it is probable that the question whether the medium's arm becomes insensible in writing would seem to them an utterly insignificant question and quite devoid of interest. When endeavouring to converse with the souls of the dead, one should not disgrace himself by looking out for insensibility to pin pricks. It is nevertheless worth notice that in many cases the medium, relating his own feelings, declares that he has not felt the movements of his hand in writing. Others perceive clearly that the hand moves, but do not know what it has written until they see the paper. These observations are not invariable, for in other cases the medium seems to have been conscious of the whole experiment. Nevertheless it is probable that with some subjects the medium's writing induces a certain degree of anaesthesia ...[14]

The division of consciousness is clearly established, therefore, at least with many mediums. It is no longer possible to entertain doubt on this point. A peculiar feature of these experiments is the illusion that seems to dominate the subconscious person. To understand this illusion clearly we must remember how the facts present themselves in the quiet experiments in the laboratory, which lack almost all dramatic character. When we come to detect the unconscious person that the anaesthesia of an hysterical patient reveals, we are in the presence of a little group of elementary phenomena which scarcely form a subconsciousness and not a personality at all. In a state of induced distraction this secondary consciousness, as we have also seen, is much more developed. It is distinct from the principal consciousness, and often curiously calls it the other. It is very easy to get it to accept a different name. This name, it should be noticed, does not by any means apply to a fictitious personality. It groups together very real phenomena – elements of a psychological life which has really been experienced. Under the name of Adrienne, for example, M. Janet's subject described part of his present and past life taken out of his whole existence.[15] It is just here that the difference is clearly shown between our experiments and those of the spiritists. The subconscious person of the spiritist bears a fictitious names—Socrates, or Napoleon, or some other spirit, called up. In any case this person does not consider himself as a part of the medium, and does not apply his special memories to the medium. This difference is characteristic and contributes largely to a special and very original appearance which the spiritist manifestations present.

Why, then, these conditions of mental *melieu [sic]* which are so important in experiments of this kind? Because the medium who takes the pen does not by any means remain, as our hysterical patients do, indifferent and ignorant of the end to be attained; he has his plan and his expectations. He believes in spirits and in the possibility of calling them up. He is dominated by a powerful preconception. Moreover, it is he or the audience who generally chooses the spirit with whom he is to come into communication. Even when such a choice is not made ... the medium still expects to converse with an intelligence distinct from his own. In a word, he is in the most favourable conditions for autosuggestion.

Only there is one curious thing: the ego who consents to the performance of the suggestion is not the normal ego, but the secondary ego. It is this latter who receives the suggestion that he is such or such a person, and who, sustaining this illusion or obligingly complying with it—for we do not know exactly how it occurs—goes on to write messages in the style of the person conjured up, whose name he signs. In M. Richet's curious experiments, which have now become classic, a person is transformed thus by suggestion and forced to represent a fictitious personality.[16] Everything takes place as if one had been able during a moment of distraction to communicate with the subconscious and impose a new personality upon it.

The subconscious person can express this suggested personality in different ways. In the first place by writing, and this is usually what is done. It is to this means of communication that we owe the tiresome messages with which the spiritist journals are filled. The mediums have often pointed out the fact that this handwriting does not resemble their own. That is natural enough, for as Richet's, Ferrari's, and Héricourt's experiments show, the suggestions that transform the personality also modify the handwriting in the same way.[17] If the subconscious personality becomes much developed he will not be content with merely guiding the movements of the hand. There will be a tendency to possess himself of other means of expression; he will shake the subject's head, make him make grimaces, and even set him to talking. In this case, which has sometimes been observed, the medium pronounces words of which his normal ego is not conscious. Further, sometimes in the midst of an experiment the medium has been known to rise, gesticulate, assume a dramatic position, and represent the personality that has been called up. The medium, meanwhile, is not conscious of the part that he is playing, and when it is all done his normal consciousness retains no memory of it, for, properly speaking, it is not he that has acted; it is the subconscious personality. We have already seen so many similar situations that further remark on it is unnecessary. It is sufficient to remember that with many subjects the somnambulistic ego comes upon the scene at the time when the post-hypnotic suggestion is performed, and advances toward the footlights, while the normal ego goes into the background or disappears behind the scenes.

So by uniting together two experiments—first, suggestion of transformation of personality in the somnambulistic state; and, second, suggestion whose performance is deferred until after waking – we arrive at the same result as those reached by the spiritist experiments.

But though the result is alike, the causes are somewhat different. In our former studies we saw the division of consciousness result from two principal causes, hysterical anaesthesia and distraction. In the spontaneous phenomenon of the conjuring up of the spirit by a medium, we do not find either of these two causes in action. Undoubtedly mental modifications occur which are less simple and less easy to describe. The medium's concentration of thought, his conviction that a second intelligence is going to take possession of his hand, autosuggestion, in short, is what produces the division of his consciousness, and it would be possible by communicating the same condition of mind to an hysterical patient to reproduce all the results. ...

Now, the normal consciousness does not directly know the secondary consciousness. In order that the medium know[s] the spirit's reply he has to read his writing. So, in this way the dialogue may continue. The subconscious personality, on the contrary, needs no external signs in order to grasp the thought of the normal consciousness. This thought that cannot be uttered aloud, and which is often only mentally formulated, is seized, understood, and responded to by the subconscious personality. It is he who really takes the principal role in spiritist experiments. We grow accustomed also to find him playing an important part in the collaboration. In complicated suggestions it will be remembered it is he who assumes the responsibility for the more delicate operations. He knows everything, while the normal ego knows nothing. In the same way, in successive personalities, the ego of the second condition often knows the ego of the first, while the latter believes that he alone exists.

All these analogies should serve as our guide and inspiration in such difficult questions. And it is by this method of comparison, I think, that future researches should be conducted ...

Notes

1 On French studies of dissociation and related matters, see: Alvarado, 2009b; Carroy, 1991; Foschi. 2003; Hacking, 1995; Leblanc, 2001. Literature about French studies of hypnosis include general surveys of hypnosis (Crabtree, 1993; Gauld, 1992) and more specific studies (Alvarado, 2010; Barrucand, 1967; Carroy, 1991; Nicolas, 2004). The French and German approaches to psychology are discussed by Carroy and Schmidgen, 2006.

2 On the history of these movements and of mediumship, see: Biondi, 1988; Braude, 2001; Edelman, 1995; Owen, 1990.

3 On French spiritism, and on Kardec, see: Castellan, 1954; Edelman, 1995; Monroe, 2008; Sharp, 2006.

4 Shamdasani (1993) discusses the subconscious, while several other authors focus on pathology: Le Maléfan, 1999; Moreira-Almeida, Silva de Almeida and Lotufo Neto, 2005; Owen, 1990; Zingrone, 1994. An overview of both topics appears in Alvarado, Machado, Zangari, and Zingrone, 2007.

5 There are several studies of the early history of psychical research in various countries: Biondi, 1988; Moore, 1977; Oppenheim, 1985; Plas, 2000; Treitel, 2004.

6 While Myers's writings in the veridical aspects of mental mediumship were generally ignored outside psychical research, his ideas about a subliminal mind and writings about automatisms were widely cited in his day. Hamilton (2009) presents an overview of his life and work. See also: Crabtree, 1993, Chap. 16; Gauld, 1968, pp. 38–44, 89–114, 116–36, Chaps. 12–13; Kelly, 2007. Alvarado (2009a) presents a short overview of writings about Myers.

7 Le Maléfan (1999) discusses French ideas about the pathology of mediumship.

8 Janet's influence on psychology and psychiatry has been documented by Ellenberger (1970, Chap. 6), and by later historians, e.g. Carroy and Plas, 2000; Fiedler, 2006. On Janet and mediumship, see Le Maléfan, 1993, 1999, pp. 66–84.

9 Binet has been discussed in various studies, among them: Cicciola, 2008, 2009; Fancher, 1998; Foschi and Cicciola, 2006a, 2006b; Nicolas and Ferrand, 2002; Wolf, 1973. On Binet's place in French psychology, see Nicolas, 2002. Carroy (2001) discusses aspects of the book that I have emphasized. [Notes to Binet's Text by C. S. Alvarado]

10 This is a reference to Frederic W. H. Myers (1885). Janet (1889, 403) stated that he believed Myers was the author who had done the most to "develop the scientific study of spiritistic phenomena." Myers (1892) complained that while both Binet and Janet mentioned him, they "have omitted to state that I have published … a number of automatic messages, oral and written, which do in my view probably contain information not acquired by the automatist in any normal manner; but acquired at any rate by telepathic transmission from other living minds, if not by penetration into or commerce with some source still more unexpected or remote." (p. 420).

11 See: Binet, 1890a; Janet, 1889.

12 Binet did not accept there were phenomena beyond those produced by motor automatisms or subconscious personalities. However, others have postulated pathology while accepting the existence of supernormal manifestations such as veridical communications and physical phenomena; e.g., Fairfield, 1875; Lombroso, 1892.

13 See Charcot, 1888, pp. 1–12.

14 Janet (1887, 1892, pp. 423–424) and Raymond and Janet (1898, p. 175) also referred to anesthesia in automatic writers. According to James (1890a, vol. 1, pp. 398–399): "I have found the hands of two automatic writers anaesthetic during the act. In two others I have found this not to be the case. Automatic writing is usually preceded by shooting pains along the arm-nerves and irregular contractions of the arm-muscles. I have found one medium's tongue and lips apparently insensible to pin-pricks during her (speaking) trance." See also James, 1889.

15 Adrienne was a secondary personality of Lucie, who Janet (1889, p. 491) described as a twenty-year-old woman in an appendix of his book. See also Janet, 1886.

16 See Richet, 1883. This was the famous French physiologist Charles Richet (1850–1935; see Wolf, 1993), who was well known for his interest and work in many topics, including psychical research (Alvarado, 2008a, 2008b).

17 See Ferrari, Héricourt and Richet, 1886.

References

Alvarado, C. S. (2002). Dissociation in Britain during the late nineteenth century: The Society for Psychical Research, 1882–1900. *Journal of Trauma and Dissociation* 3, 9–33.

Alvarado, C. S. (2008a). Aspects of the history of parapsychology. II. Charles Richet's (1850–1935) work in psychical research. https://www.PFLyceum.org

Alvarado, C. S. (2008b). Note on Charles Richet's "La Suggestion Mentale et le Calcul des Probabilités" (1884). *Journal of Scientific Exploration,* 22, 543–548.

Alvarado, C. S. (2009a). Frederic W.H. Myers, psychical research and psychology, an essay review of Trevor Hamilton's *Immortal longings, F. W. H. Myers and the Victorian search for life after death. Journal of the Society for Psychical Research, 73,* 150–170.

Alvarado, C. S. (2009b). Nineteenth-century hysteria and hypnosis, a historical note on Blanche Wittmann. *Australian Journal of Clinical and Experimental Hypnosis, 37,* 21–36.

Alvarado, C. S. (2010). Nineteenth-century suggestion and magnetism: hypnosis at the International Congress of Physiological Psychology (1889). *Contemporary Hypnosis, 27*, 48–60.

Alvarado, C. S., Machado F. R., Zangari W., & Zingrone N. L. (2007). Perspectivas históricas da influência da mediunidade na construção de idéias psicológicas e psiquiátricas. *Revista de Psiquiatria Clínica* 34 (suppl.1), 42–53.

Anonymous. (1863). Sciences morales et politiques. *L'anne littéraire et dramatique, 5*, 374–426.

Azam, [E. E.]. (1887). *Hypnotisme, double conscience et altérations de la personnalité*. J.B. Baillière.

Baillarger J. (1861). [Communication to the Société Médico-Psychologique]. *Annales medico-psychologiques, 7*, 92–93.

Barrucand, D. (1967). *Histoire de l'hypnose en France*. Presses Universitaires de France.

Beard, G. M. (1877). A new theory of trance, and its bearings on human testimony. *Journal of Nervous and Mental Disease, 4*, 1–47.

Bérillon, Dr. [E.]. (1900). Dédoublement de la personnalité et phénomènes subconscients provoques par des manœuvrés de spiritisme. *Revue de l'hypnotisme et de la psychologie physiologique* 14, 251–252.

Binet, A. (1884). L'hallucination. *Revue philosophique de la France et de l'étranger, 17*, 377–412, 473–502.

Binet, A. (1886). *La Psychologie du raisonnement*. Félix Alcan.

Binet, A. (1888a). *Etudes depsychologie expérimentale*. Octave Doin.

Binet, A. (1888b). Recherches sur l'anesthésie hystérique. *Compte rendus hebdomadaires des séances de l'Académie des Sciences* 107, 1008–1010.

Binet, A. (1889a). Recherches sur les altérations de la conscience chez les hystériques. *Revue philosophique de la France et de l'étranger,* 27, 135–170.

Binet, A. (1889b). Recherches sur les mouvements volontaires dans l'anesthésie hystérique. *Revue philosophique de la France et de l'étranger,* 28, 470–500.

Binet, A. (1890a). *On double consciousness: Experimental psychological studies.* Open Court. (Original articles published 1889–1890)

Binet, A. (1890b). Recherches sur les mouvements chez quelques jeunes enfants. *Revue philosophique de la France et de l'étranger, 29*, 297–309.

Binet, A. (1891). Les altérations de la personnalité d'après les travaux récens. *Revue des deux mondes,* 103, 839–855.

Binet, A. (1892). *Les Altérations de la personnalité*. Félix Alcan.

Binet, A. (1894). *Psychologie des grands calculateurs et joueurs d'échecs.* Hachette.

Binet, A. (1896). *Alterations of personality* (H. G. Baldwin, Trans.; J. M. Baldwin, Notes & Preface). D. Appleton. (Original work published 1892)

Binet, A. (1903). *L'Étude expérimentale de l'intelligence.* Schleicher.

Binet, A., & Féré, C. (1885). L'hypnotisme chez les hystériques: le transfert. *Revue philosophique de la France et de l'étranger, 19*, 1–25.

Binet, A., & Féré, C. (1886). Expériences d'hypnotisme sur les images associées. *Revue philosophique de la France et de l'étranger, 21*, 159–163.

Binet, A., & Féré, C. (1887). *Le magnétisme animal*. Félix Alcan.

Binet, A., & Henri, V. (1894). La mémoire des mots. *L'Année psychologique,* 1, 1–23.

Binet, A., & Philippe, J. (1892). Etude sur un noveau cas d'audition colorée. *Revue philosophique de la France et de l'étranger, 33*, 461–464.

Binet, A., & Simon, T. (1905). Méthodes nouvelles pour le diagnostic du niveau intellectuel des anormaux. *L'Anne psychologique, 11*, 245–366.

Binet, A., & Vaschide, N. (1897). Influence des différents processus psychiques sur la pression du sang chez l'homme. *Compte rendus hebdomadaires des séances de l'Académie des Sciences, 124*, 44–46.

Biondi, M. (1988). *Tavoli e medium: Storia dello spiritismo in Italia.* Gremese.

Bouchut, E. (1864). *Histoire de la médicine et des doctrines médicales*. Germer Baillière.

Bourru, H., & Burot, P. (1888). *Variations de la personnalité.* J. B. Bailliére.

Braude, A. (2001). *Radical spirits: Spiritualism and women's rights in nineteenth-century America.* Indiana University Press.

Burlet, P. (1863). *Du Spiritisme considère comme cause d'aliénation mentale.* Imprimerie de Richard.

Carroy, J. (1991). *Hypnose, suggestion et psychologie: L'invention de sujets.* Presses Universitaires de France.

Carroy, J. (2001). “Le rappel des personnalites anciennes par suggestion;” presentation. *Champ Psychosomatique,* (21), 9–24.

Carroy, J., & Plas, R. (2000). La genèse de la notion de dissociation chez Pierre Janet et ses enjeux. *Evolution psychiatrique, 65*, 9–18.

Carroy, J., & Schmidgen, H. (2006). Psychologies expérimentales: Leipzig-Paris-Wurzburg (1890–1910). *Mil neuf cent, 24*, 171–204.

Castellan, Y. (1954). *Le Spiritisme*. Presses Universitaires de France.

Charcot, J. M. (1888). *Clinical lectures on certain diseases of the nervous system*. Geoge S. Davis.

Charcot, [J- M]. (1891). Du somnambulisme spontané avec double personnalité. *Revue de l'hypnotisme et de la psychologie physiologique,* 5, 343–347.

Cicciola, E. (2008). Alfred Binet e le prime “misure” dell'intelligenza (1905–1908). *Physis: Rivista Internazionale di Storia della Scienza, 45*, 165–203.

Cicciola, E. (2009). Alfred Binet e il laboratorio di psicologia fisiologica della Sorbonne. In H. Gundlach, E. Lafuent, M. Sinatra, M. Sokal & G. Tanucci (Eds.). *Psicotecnica: Ieri! Oggi? Domani?? Atti del I Congresso Internazionale* (pp. 67–80). (Vol. I). Aracne.

Clark, U. (1863). *Plain guide to spiritualism*. William White.

Crabtree, A. (1993). *From Mesmer to Freud: Magnetic sleep and the roots of psychological healing*. Yale University Press.

Delanne, G. (1902). *Recherches sur la médiumnité*. Librairie des Sciences Psychiques.

Edelman, N. (1995). *Voyantes, guérisseuses et visionnaires en France 1785–1914*. Albin Michel.

Ellenberger, H. F. (1970). *The discovery of the unconscious: The history and evolution of dynamic psychiatry*. Basic Books.

Fairfield, F. G. (1875). *Ten years with spiritual mediums*. D. Appleton.

Fancher, R. E. (1998). Alfred Binet, general psychologist. In Kinble GA & Wertheimer M (Eds.) *Portraits of pioneers in psychology* (pp. 67–83). (Vol. 3). American Psychological Association.

Ferrari, H., Héricourt, J., & Richet, C. (1886). La personnalité et l'écriture. *Revue philosophique de la France et de l'étranger, 21*, 414–424.

Fiedler, P. (ed.). (2006). *Trauma, dissoziation, personlichkeit: Pierre Janets Beitrage zur modernen psychiatrie, psychologie und psychotherapie*. Past Science Publications.

Foschi, R. (2003). L'indagine sulla personality alle origini della psicologia scientifica francese (1870–1885). *Physis: Rivista Internazionale si Storia della Scienza,* (1–2), 63–105.

Foschi, R., & Cicciola E. (2006a). The notion of ‘double consciousness’ in Alfred Binet's psychological experimentalism. *Physis: Rivista Internazionale si Storia della Scienza,* 43, 363–372.

Foschi, R., & Cicciola, E. (2006b). Politics and naturalism in the 20th century psychology of Alfred Binet. *History of Psychology, 9*, 267–289.

Gauld, A. (1968). *The founders of psychical research*. Routledge and Kegan Paul.

Gauld, A. (1992). *A history of hypnotism*. Cambridge University Press.

Hacking, I. (1995). *Rewriting the soul: Multiple personality and the sciences of memory.* Princeton University Press.

Hamilton, T. (2009). *Immortal longings: Frederic W. H. Myers and the Victorian search for life after death.* Imprint Academic.

Hammond, W. A. (1876). *Spiritualism and allied causes and conditions of nervous derangement*. G.P. Putnam's.

Héricourt, J. (1889). L'activité inconsciente de l'esprit. *Revue Scientifique, 44*, 257–268.

Hodgson, R. (1892). A record of observations of certain phenomena of trance. *Proceedings of the Society for Psychical Research, 8*, 1–167.

James, W. (1889). Notes on automatic writing. *Proceedings of the American Society for Psychical Research,* 1, 548–564.

James, W. (1890a). *The principles of psychology.* (Vol. 1.) Henry Holt.

James, W. (1890b). A record of observations of certain phenomena of trance (5). Part III. *Proceedings of the Society for Psychical Research* 6, 651–659.

Janet, P. (1886). Les actes inconscientes et le dédoublement de la personnalité pendant le somnambulisme provoqué. *Revue philosophique de la France et de l'étranger, 22*, 577–592.

Janet, P. (1887). L'anesthésie systématisée et la dissociation des phénomènes psychiques. *Revue philosophique de la France et de l'étranger,* 23, 449–472.
Janet, P. (1889). *L'Automatisme psychologique: Essai de psychologie expérimentale sur les forms inferieures de l'activité humaine*. Félix Alcan.
Janet, P. (1892). Le spiritisme contemporain. *Revue philosophique de la France et de l'étranger, 33*, 413–442.
Kardec, A. (1857). *Le Livre des esprits*. E. Dentu.
Kardec, A. (1862). *Spiritisme expérimental: Le livre des mediums* (2nd ed.) Didier.
Kelly, E. W. (2007). F. W. H. Myers and the empirical study of the mind-body problem. In Kelly, E., Kelly, E.W., Crabtree, A., Gauld, A., Grosso, M., & Greyson, B., *Irreducible mind: Toward a psychology for the 21st century* (pp. 47–115). Rowman & Littlefield.
Leblanc, A. (2001). The origins of the concept of dissociation: Paul Janet, his nephew Pierre, and the problem of post-hypnotic suggestion. *History of Science, 39*, 57–69.
Le Maléfan, P. (1993). Pierre Janet, le spiritisme et les délires spirites. *L'Evolution Psychiatrique, 58*, 445–452.
Le Maléfan P. (1999). *Folie et spiritisme: Histoire du discours psychopathologique surla pratique du spiritisme, ses abords et ses avatars (1850–1950)*. L'Hartmattan.
Le Maléfan, P. (2008). Les hallucinations télépathiques dans la psychologie et la psychopathologie françaises. *L'Evolution Psychiatrique,* 73, 15–39.
Lemoine, A. (1861). Le spiritualisme et le spiritisme. *Revue européenne,* 17, 512–549.
Levy-Valensi, J. (1910). Spiritisme et folie. *L'Encéphale, 5*, 696–716.
Liébeault, A. A. (1889) *Le Sommeil provoque et les états analogues*. Octave Doin.
Littré, E. (1856). Des tables parlantes et des esprits frappeurs. *Revue des deux mondes, 26*, 847–872.
Lodge, O. (1890). A record of observations of certain phenomena of trance (2). Part I. *Proceedings of the Society for Psychical Research, 6*, 443–557.
Lombroso, C. (1892). Le spiritisme et la psychiatrie, explication psychiatrique des certain faits spirites. *Annales des sciences psychiques,* 2, 143–151.
Marvin, F. R. (1874). *The philosophy of spiritualism and the pathology and treatment of mediomania*. A. K. Butts.
Monroe, J. W. (2008). *Laboratories of faith: mesmerism, spiritism and occultism in modern France*. Cornell University Press.
Moore, R. L. (1977). *In search of white crows: Spiritualism, parapsychology, and American culture*. Oxford University Press.
Moreira-Almeida, A., Silva de Almeida, A. A., & Lotufo Neto, F. (2005). History of 'spiritist madness' in Brazil. *History of Psychiatry, 16*, 5–25.
Myers, F. W. H. (1884). On a telepathic explanation of some so-called spiritualistic phenomena. Part I. *Proceedings of the Society for Psychical Research, 2*, 217–237.
Myers, F.W.H. (1885). Automatic writing. II. *Proceedings of the Society for Psychical Research, 3*, 1–63.
Myers, F. W. H. (1889). Automatic writing. IV. The daemon of Socrates. *Proceedings of the Society for Psychical Research, 5*, 522–547.
Myers, F. W. H. (1892). Review of *Les alterations de la personnalité*, by A Binet. *Mind, 1*, 417–421.
Myers, F.W.H. (1903). *Human personality and its survival of bodily death*, 2 vols. Longmans, Green.
Nicolas, S. (2002). *Histoire de la psychologie française, Naissance d'une nouvelle science*. In Press.
Nicolas, S. (2004). *L'Hypnose, Charcot face a Bernheim*. L'Harmattan.
Nicolas, S., & Ferrand, F. (2002). Alfred Binet and higher education. *History of Psychology,* 5, 264–283.
Nicolas, S., Segui, J., & Ferrand, L. (2000). *L'Année Psychologique*, history of the founding of a 100-year-old French journal. *History of Psychology, 3*, 44–61.
Ochorowicz J. (1896). La question de la fraude dans les expériences avec Eusapia Paladino. *Annales des sciences psychiques, 6*, 79–123.
Oppenheim, J. (1985). *The other world, spiritualism and psychical research in England, 1850–1914*. Cambridge University Press.
Owen, A. (1990). *The darkened room, women, power and spiritualism in late Victorian England.* University of Pennsylvania Press.
Plas, R. (2000). *Naissance d'une science humaine, la psychologie, les psychologues et le "merveilleux psychique."* Presses Universitaires de Rennes.
Raymond, F., & Janet, P. (1898). *Nevroses et idees fixes* (Vol. 2.) Félix Alcan.

Ribot, T. (1888). *Les maladies de la personnalité*, 2nd edn. Félix Alcan.
Richet, C. (1883). La personnalité et la mémoire dans le somnambulisme. *Revue philosophique de la France et de l'étranger, 15*, 225–242.
Richet, C. (1886). Les mouvements inconscients. In *Hommages Monsieur Chevreul à l'occasion de son centenaire, 31 aout 1886.* Félix Alcan, 79–94.
Shamdasani, S. (1993). Automatic writing and the discovery of the unconscious. *Spring,* 54, 100–131.
Sharp, L. L. (2006). *Secular spirituality, reincarnation and spiritism in nineteenth-century France*. Lexington Books.
Taine, H. (1878). *De l'Intelligence.* (Vol. 1., 3rd rev. enlarged ed.) Hachette.
Treitel, C. (2004). *A science for the soul, occultism and the genesis of the German modern.* Johns Hopkins University Press.
Wolf, S. (1993). *Brain, mind and medicine, Charles Richet and the origins of physiological psychology.* Transaction Publishers.
Wolf, T. H. (1973). *Alfred Binet*. University of Chicago Press.
Zingrone, N. L. (1994). Images of women as mediums, power, pathology and passivity in the writings of Frederic Marvin and Cesare Lombroso. In Coly L. & White R. A. (Eds.) *Women and Parapsychology* (pp. 90–121). Parapsychology Foundation.

53

Eusapia Palladino Anthologized*

Carlos S. Alvarado

In the last decade we have seen the publication of various books about physical mediums. The authors of these studies have done much to rescue from oblivion the careers of individuals such as Indridi Indridasson from Iceland (Haraldsson & Gisurarsson, 2015), William Mumler from the United States (Kaplan, 2008), and Franek Kluski from Poland (Weaver, 2015). One medium who needs discussion, so as to be reintroduced to new generations, is the Italian Eusapia Palladino.

Unlike the above-mentioned studies and overviews of the careers of mediums, the present work, compiled by Scott Dickerson, is more limited in scope. It is an anthology of various English-language articles and sections of books about Palladino. *Eusapia Paladino: Materialisations and Intellergetic Phenomena in Physical Mediumship* is part of a series entitled "Lost Foundations of Parapsychology and Psychical Research." Unfortunately, the book has no information about this series, but its Amazon page states that the series "endeavors to provide the interested public with authoritative investigative accounts from the period of research prior to the rise of the statistical approach to parapsychology championed by J. B. Rhine, coming to prominence in the later 1930s."

Why Palladino?

The mediumship of Eusapia Palladino has continued to be relevant among those who take physical mediumship seriously. Unfortunately, Dickerson does not introduce the book (nor any of the articles reprinted) in any way, limiting himself to presenting the articles with no additional information. Such a course of action does not help those readers who are not familiar with the medium to understand her importance in psychical research, nor to realize from the beginning of the book the variety of phenomena shown by her (Alvarado, 2016).

Palladino is important for various reasons. First, her case has long been considered evidential by many. For example, Charles Richet (1922, pp. 38–39) stated in his celebrated *Traité de Métapsychique*, that even assuming that Palladino was the only medium in the world, her séances would suffice to scientifically establish both telekinesis and materializations. A more recent example is Stephen E. Braude, who has written:

> The crucial issue is not whether there are instances in which the medium cheated, but whether there are instances in which the evidence is strong that no cheating occurred. And in that respect, Eusapia's case is exceptionally good. (Braude, 2007, p. 47)

The medium's cheating, which was repeatedly reported (e.g., Carrington, 1909, p. 182, Courtier, 1908, p. 521–540), has created much skepticism among modern parapsychologists, some of whom

*Book review of *Eusapia Paladino: Materialisations and Intellergetic Phenomena in Physical Mediumship* compiled by Scott Dickerson, republished with permission from *Journal of Scientific Exploration, 31*(3), 467–476, 2017.

tend to ignore the case (Irwin & Watt, 2007), or present highly imaginative fraudulent explanations for particular séances (Wiseman, 1992). Such skepticism is not unique about Palladino, since other past physical mediums also are neglected. Many people appear to have a general distrust about accepting old séance reports as documentation for the reality of physical phenomena.

Second, and as I have argued before (Alvarado, 1993), Palladino's case was historically important for reasons other than evidential concerns. In addition to projecting influential negative images of mediumship with some of her fraudulent, flamboyant, and apparently hysterical behaviors, her performances contributed to the development of theoretical concepts, and of research standards involving controls and the use of instruments to record physical phenomena.[1]

Palladino's importance is evident in the coverage of her mediumship in overviews of the history of parapsychology, such as Gutierez and Maillard's *Les Adventuriers de L'Esprit* (2004, pp. 82–100, 117–138) and Inglis' *Natural and Supernatural* (1992, chaps. 35–38). There is much information about her in Biondi's history of spiritism and psychical research in Italy (1988, pp. 96–100, 121–129, 134–159). Furthermore, there are other examples of scholarship about her such as the work of Gauld (1968, chap. 10), Giuditta (2010), and Sommer (2012). Palladino has been a particular interest of mine, as seen in various articles I have written about topics such as her influence on psychical research (Alvarado, 1993), Julian Ochorowicz's ideas about her fraud and dissociation (Alvarado, 2010), her biography (Alvarado, 2011), and Lombroso's writings about her (Alvarado & Biondi, 2017).

But to learn about this medium in detail, it is necessary to go to the original séance reports. Many examples could be presented. In addition to very early mentions of the medium (Damiani, 1872), there are various nineteenth-century reports. These include those about the famous sittings Cesare Lombroso had with the medium (Ciolfi, 1891), as well as those conducted at Milan (Aksakof, et al. 1893), and elsewhere (e.g., Lodge, 1894). The subsequent literature is vast, including the reports of Bottazzi (1909/2011), Carrington (1954), Courtier (1908), Feilding, Baggally, & Carrington (1909), and Morselli (1908).

The Anthology

The anthology opens with Cesare de Vesme's article "The Spiritistic and Spiritualistic Explanation of Mediumistic Phenomena" (de Vesme, 1907, p. 1–39, these and other page ranges refer to the anthology reviewed here). I wonder why this article was chosen to open the volume since it barely mentions Palladino. It consists mainly of ideas about the study of psychic phenomena in general. Some examples are sections about "a priorism in scientific language," the use of explaining phenomena with one hypothesis, and cases that "appear to be spiritistic." While in principle such issues are related to many phenomena and specific cases in psychical research, including Palladino's, the medium is little discussed in the article.

This is followed by a much-neglected article by physician and student of mediumship Giuseppe (called Joseph in the report) Venzano, "A Contribution to the Study of Materialisations" (pp. 41–138), taken from the *Annals of Psychical Science* (Venzano, 1907).[2] This is a good selection because it includes more dramatic materializations than those usually reported with this medium. The following is an example reported in a séance that took place on December 29, 1900, which included various individuals, among them Venzano and astronomer Francesco Porro:

> Suddenly Dr. Venzano, who held the medium with his left hand, she resting her head, visibly to all, on the shoulder of Professor Porro, saw forming to his left, at about a hand's breadth from his face, as it were a globular, vaporous, whitish mass, which condensed into a more decided form,

> that of an oval, which gradually assumed the aspect of a human head, of which the nose, the eyes, the moustache, and the pointed beard could be distinctly recognised. This form came and touched his face, and he felt a warm and living forehead press against his own and remain there for a second or two. Then he felt the contact of the whole profile of the face against his own, with a pressure as of a caress, then the imprint of a kiss, after which the mass seemed to vanish into vapour near the curtains. The other sitters, meanwhile, were only aware of a vague luminosity in the direction of Dr. Venzano; but they distinctly perceived the sound of the kiss. (p. 91)

Other observations were even more dramatic, involving the appearance of apparently whole-body figures. All of these observations were made in Italy, at the Circolo Scientifico Minerva in Genoa. Several reports of phenomena seen in this group appear in books published in Italian by Ernesto Bozzano (1903), Enrico Morselli (1908), and Luigi Arnaldo Vassallo (1902).

The third chapter, "Eusapia Paladino" (pp. 139–144), is taken from William F. Barrett's *On the Threshold of the Unseen* (1917). He mentions at the beginning the negative conclusions of the investigation of the medium at Cambridge University by members of the Society for Psychical Research (see Sidgwick, 1895). Unfortunately, the account does not even begin to acknowledge the magnitude of the controversies created, as seen in Gauld's (1968, Chap. 10) discussion of the subject.

But Barrett discussed other issues as well. He stated:

> Like other psychics ..., she is most sensitive to "suggestion," even when unexpressed; and in the trance, when her consciousness and self-control are largely inhibited, she is the easy prey of external influences. In the absence of the steadying, though subconscious, influence of a high moral nature, she unblushingly cheats whenever the conditions are unfavourable for the production of supernormal phenomena. We have no right to assume that she is wholly conscious of so doing ... If they are due, as some have thought, to an externalization of the nerve force of the psychic, it is not improbable that the degree of this externalization will vary with the favorable or unfavorable mental state of those present. We may even conceive that when this psychic force is restricted or not externalized, it may create movements of the limbs of the psychic which will cause her to perform by normal actions (in perhaps a semi-conscious state) what under good psychical conditions would be done supernormally. This would produce the impression of intentional fraud. (pp. 143–144)

However, these interesting ideas were not original with Barrett. Julian Ochorowicz (1896) discussed these years before, but the lack of contextual information in this anthology does not help the reader realize this.

Some of the work of Enrico Morselli is covered in "Experiments Made with Eusapia Paladino at Genoa by Professor Morselli" (pp. 145–169), taken from a chapter from *Psychical and Supernormal Phenomena* by Paul Joire (1909/circa 1916, Chap. 37), who mainly cites Morselli. From the so-called Feilding report (Feilding, Baggally, & Carrington, 1909), the compiler presents the conclusions of each of the authors (pp. 170–191): Hereward Carrington, W.W. Baggally, and Everard Feilding. Carrington wrote:

> As a result of the ten sittings held by us at Naples, November 21st–December 15th, 1908—being the ten séances attended by me—I beg to record my absolute conviction of the reality of at least some of the phenomena; and the conviction, amounting in my own mind to complete certainty, that the results witnessed by [us] were not due to fraud or trickery on the part of Eusapia. (p. 170)

Carrington's statement is interesting because it shows his conversion to the reality of the medium's manifestations. It is important to remember, and this is something that the compiler does not mention, that Carrington was not only skeptical of Palladino, but of most physical mediums. This is clear in his book *The Physical Phenomena of Spiritualism* (Carrington, 1907). But the 1908 Naples sittings made him change his mind about the Italian medium. He stated in the book's second edition: "Since this book was first issued, I have seen Eusapia Palladino, and witnessed what I believe to be many genuine and remarkable physical manifestations" (Carrington, 1920, p. vi).

There were important consequences. As I have documented before (Alvarado, 1993, 273–274), Carrington became a defender of Palladino, providing much publicity for the medium. Furthermore, Carrington brought the medium to the United States in 1909, something that generated many controversies (Carrington 1954).

The book being reviewed here also has excerpts presenting negative and positive views from Frank Podmore and Cesare Lombroso. The excerpt by Podmore (pp. 193–201) comes from his well-known book *Modern Spiritualism* (Podmore, 1902, Vol. 2, 198–203), a study showing much skepticism to physical phenomena. In addition to some general background, Podmore stated:

> Finally, if we decide to reject the evidence in favour of Eusapia's supernormal powers, that decision is in the last analysis justified. The justification is that the results attained are not sufficiently free from ambiguity to weigh against the presumption derived from an examination of all previous evidence upon the subject. (p. 200)

Cesare Lombroso's discussion (pp. 203–239), including personal experiences with the medium, was taken from his book *After Death—What?* (1909). There is no discussion in the anthology of the importance of Lombroso's acceptance of her phenomena, which included publicizing her with his fame in psychiatry and criminology, and bringing her to the attention of others who then conducted many séances with her. For example, the first major investigation of her mediumship, conducted in Milan, stated:

> Taking into consideration the testimony of Professor Cesare Lombroso about the topic of mediumistic phenomena that occur through Mme. Eusapia Paladino, the undersigned gathered here in Milan to do with her a series of studies in order to verify these phenomena by submitting them to experiments and observations as rigorous as possible. (Aksakof et al., 1893, p. 39)

But Lombroso was also important in another way. His writings about Palladino spread a "mixed" perspective of mediumship, also held by a few others (e.g., Morselli, 1908). This view consisted of the idea that Palladino suffered from hysteria but also showed genuine physical phenomena such as movement of objects and materializations (Lombroso, 1892, 1909), a topic I discuss with a colleague elsewhere (Alvarado and Biondi, 2017).

In the excerpt presented in the anthology, Lombroso describes many examples of phenomena. Here is one of them:

> At Naples, in 1895 …, I again tried these experiments in a room in our inn chosen expressly for the purpose. And here, in full light, we saw a great curtain which separated our room from an alcove adjoining (and which was more than three feet distant from the medium) suddenly move out toward me, envelop me, and wrap me close. Nor was I able to free myself from it except with great difficulty. A dish of flour had been put in the little alcove room, at a distance of more than four and a half feet from the medium, who, in her trance, had thought, or at any rate spoken, of sprinkling some of the flour in our faces. When light was made, it was found that the dish was bottom side up with the flour under it. This was dry, to be sure, but coagulated like gelatin … When the lights had been turned on, and we were all ready to go, a great wardrobe

> that stood in the alcove room, about six and a half feet away from us, was seen advancing slowly toward us. It seemed like a huge pachyderm that was proceeding in leisurely fashion to attack us, and looked as if pushed forward by someone. (pp. 217–218)

Perhaps the most dramatic one was the séance in which Lombroso's deceased mother was said to appear. He wrote, after being told she would come:

> I saw detach itself from the curtain a rather short figure like that of my mother, veiled, which made the complete circuit of the table until it came to me, and whispered to me words heard by many, but not by me, who am somewhat hard of hearing … I was almost beside myself with emotion and begged her to repeat her words. She did so, saying, "*Cesar, fio mio*!" (I admit at once that this was not her habitual expression, which was, when she met me, "*mio fiol*"; but the mistakes in expression made by the apparitions of the deceased are well-known, and how they borrow from the language of the psychic and of the experimenters), and, removing the veil from her face for a moment, she gave me a kiss.
>
> After that day the shade of my mother (alas! only too truly a shadow) reappeared at least twenty times during Eusapia's séances while the medium was in trance; but her form was enveloped in the curtain of the psychic's cabinet, her head barely appearing while she would say, "My son, my treasure," kissing my head and my lips with her lips, which seemed to me dry and ligneous like her tongue. (pp. 224–225).

Furthermore, the book also includes a summary (pp. 241–253) of a biographical article written by Paola Lombroso (1907b) originally published in Italian (P. Lombroso, 1907a). This is a good selection for the anthology because it includes much personal and anecdotal information about the medium's personality.

Finally, the anthology includes some articles published about Palladino's performances during her visit to New York, published in issues of the newspapers *The New York World, The New York Times,* and *The New York Herald* (pp. 255–284). All this illustrates the complexity of this case, particularly in the New York séances. In fact, I would argue that this is an episode of the medium's career that deserves further study, particularly using the New York newspapers. I once copied from microfilm (before the advent of modern PDF databases) everything I could find about Palladino's New York séances from 1909–1910 issues of *The New York Times* and can attest to the complexity of the discussions. But one must remember, as seen in the current anthology, that there were several other newspapers at the time in New York covering the séances as well.

Evaluation

I have argued throughout this Essay Review that the anthology is problematic in many ways. To start, the book clearly needs more contextual information to introduce the reader to Palladino, since not all potential readers can be expected to know much about her. This information could have been provided with an initial essay presenting an overview of the medium's career, including biography, phenomena typical of the séances, controversies (evidence for fraud), and other aspects of this important mediumship case.

It would have also helped to have short introductions to each chapter with information about its authors. After all, not everyone today knows who Barrett, Carrington, de Vesme, Feilding, Lombroso,

Podmore, and Venzano were, to name a few. Similarly, the book would have been improved if a bibliography of published primary and secondary literature about Palladino had been included.

It would also have been helpful to readers if essays appearing later in the volume, such as those of Barrett and Podmore, would have been placed at the beginning, since they present more general perspectives. The same may be said about the summary of the Paola Lombroso essay, consisting of biographical notes about the medium.

While the anthology could have been better crafted, particularly for those with little background on the topic, it still has much to offer. Several of its chapters present useful information about Palladino that will inform readers about her phenomena and other aspects of her career. This includes the work of Lombroso, Venzano, and Morselli, among others. Similarly, readers will learn about the opinions of Carrington, Baggally, and Feilding, aspects of the New York séances, and about doubts and controversies such as those discussed by Podmore. All in all, within the above-mentioned limitations, this anthology can assist readers to obtain information about the legendary Eusapia Palladino.

Notes

1 The main theoretical concept I am referring to is the idea of biophysical forces coming out of the body of mediums to produce physical phenomena (Alvarado, 2006). Both Morselli (1908) and Carrington (1909) are examples of theoreticians of this sort of material. There is much about instruments and controls in Courtier (1908) and Feilding, Baggally, and Carrington (1909).

2 The article (Venzano, 1907) is not only in the August issue of the journal, as indicated in the anthology (p. 41), but also in the September issue. It is a two-part article.

References

Aksakof, A., Schiaparelli, G., du Prel, C., Brofferio, A., Gerosa, G., Ermacora, G. B., & Finzi, G. (1893). Rapport de la commission réunie à Milan pour l'étude des phénomènes psychiques. *Annales des Sciences Psychiques*, *3*, 39–64.

Alvarado, C. S. (1993). Gifted subjects' contributions to psychical research: The case of Eusapia Palladino. *Journal of the Society for Psychical Research*, *59*, 269–292.

Alvarado, C. S. (2006). Human radiations: Concepts of force in mesmerism, spiritualism, and psychical research. *Journal of the Society for Psychical Research*, *70*, 138–162.

Alvarado, C. S. (2010). Julian Ochorowicz on Eusapia Palladino, dissociation and mediumistic fraud [Letter to the Editor]. *Journal of the Society for Psychical Research*, *74*, 57–60.

Alvarado, C. S. (2011). Eusapia Palladino: An autobiographical essay. *Journal of Scientific Exploration*, *25*, 77–101.

Alvarado, C. S. (2016). Eusapia Palladino: III. Variety of phenomena. *Parapsychology: News History, Research*, December 17. https://carlossalvarado. wordpress.com/2016/12/17/eusapia-palladino-iii-variety-of-phenomena/

Alvarado, C. S., & Biondi, M. (2017). Classic Text No. 110: Cesare Lombroso on mediumship and pathology. *History of Psychiatry*, *8*(2), 225–241.

Barrett, W. F. (1917). *On the threshold of the unseen* (second revised edition). Kegan Paul, Trench, Trübner.

Biondi, M. (1988). *Tavoli e medium: Storia dello spiritismo in Italia*. Gremese.

Bottazzi, F. (2011). Mediumistic phenomena: Observed in a series of sessions with Eusapia Palladino. ICRL Press. [Original work published in 1909]

Bozzano, E. (1903). *Ipotesi spiritica e teorie scientifiche*. A. Donath.

Braude, S. E. (2007). *The gold leaf lady and other parapsychological investigations*. University of Chicago Press.
Carrington, H. (1907). *The physical phenomena of spiritualism: Fraudulent and genuine*. Herbert B. Turner.
Carrington, H. (1909). *Eusapia Palladino and her phenomena*. B. W. Dodge.
Carrington, H. (1920). *The physical phenomena of spiritualism: Fraudulent and genuine* (2nd rev. ed.). Dodd, Mead.
Carrington, H. (1954). *The American séances with Eusapia Palladino*. Garrett Publications.
Ciolfi, E. (1891). Les expériences de Naples. *Annales des Sciences Psychiques, 1*, 326–332.
Courtier, J. (1908). Rapport sur les séances d'Eusapia Palladino à l'Institut Général Psychologique. *Bulletin de l'Institut Général Psychologique, 8*, 415–546.
Damiani, G. (1872). Spiritualism in Italy—Mazzini a Spiritualist. *Human Nature, 6*, 220–224.
de Vesme, C. (1907). The spiritistic and spiritualistic explanation of mediumistic phenomena. *Annals of Psychical Science, 6*, 493–518.
Feilding, E., Baggally, W. W., & Carrington, H. (1909). Report on a series of sittings with Eusapia Palladino. *Proceedings of the Society for Psychical Research, 23*, 309–569.
Gauld, A. (1968). *The founders of psychical research*. Routledge & Kegan Paul.
Giuditta, A. (2010). The 1907 psychokinetic experiments of Professor Filippo Bottazzi. *Journal of Scientific Exploration, 24*, 495–512.
Gutierez, G., & Maillard, N. (2004). *Les aventuriers de l'esprit: Une histoire de la parapsychologie*. Presses du Châtelet.
Haraldsson, E., & Gissurarson, L. R. (2015). *Indridi Indidason: The Icelandic physical medium*. White Crow Books.
Inglis, B. (1992). *Natural and supernatural: A history of the paranormal from earliest times to 1914* (Rev. ed.). Prism Press.
Irwin, H. J., & Watt, C. (2007). An introduction to parapsychology (5th ed.). McFarland.
Joire, P. (circa 1916). *Psychical and supernormal phenomena: Their observation and experimentation*. Frederick Stokes. [Original work published in French1909]
Kaplan, L. (2008). *The strange case of William Mumler, spirit photographer*. University of Minnesota Press.
Lodge, O. J. (1894). Experience of unusual physical phenomena occurring in the presence of an entranced person (Eusapia Paladino). *Journal of the Society for Psychical Research, 6*, 306–336.
Lombroso, C. (1892). Le spiritisme et la psychiatrie: Explication psychiatrique de certains faits spirites. *Annales des Sciences Psychiques, 2*, 143–151.
Lombroso, C. (1909). *After death—What?* Small, Maynard.
Lombroso, P. (1907a). Eusapia Paladino: Cenni biografici. *La Lettura, 7*, 389–394.
Lombroso, P. (1907b). Eusapiana. *Annals of Psychical Science, 6*, 215–224.
Morselli, E. (1908). *Psicologia e "spiritismo": Impressioni e note critiche sui fenomeni medianici di Eusapia Paladino* (2 vols.). Fratelli Bocca.
Ochorowicz, J. (1896). La question de la fraude dans les expériences avec Eusapia Paladino. *Annales des Sciences Psychiques, 6*, 79–123.
Podmore, F. (1902). *Modern spiritualism: A history and a criticism* (Vol. 2). Methuen.
Richet, C. (1922). *Traité de métapsychique*. Félix Alcan.
Sidgwick, H. (1895). Eusapia Paladino. *Journal of the Society for Psychical Research, 7*, 148–159.
Sommer, A. (2012). Psychical research and the origins of American psychology: Hugo Münsterberg, William James, and Eusapia Palladino. *History of the Human Sciences, 25*, 23–44.
Vassallo, L. A. (1902). *Nel mondo degli invisibli*. Enrico Voghera.
Venzano, J. (1907). A contribution to the study of materialisations. *Annals of Psychical Science, 6*, 75–119, 157–195.
Weaver, Z. (2015). *Other realities: The enigma of Franek Kluski's mediumship*.
Wiseman, R. (1992). The Feilding Report: A reconsideration. *Journal of the Society for Psychical Research, 58*, 129–152.

Psychical Research in the *Psychological Review,* 1894–1900: A Bibliographical Note*

Carlos S. Alvarado†

While there was much conflict during the 19th century between psychology and psychical research, the latter was occasionally discussed in psychology journals. The purpose of this paper is to provide a guide to existing discussions of psychical research and related topics in the American journal *Psychological Review*. Many of the discussions were authored by individuals favorably disposed to psychical research, such as William James and James H. Hyslop, but also by such skeptics as James McKeen Cattell and Joseph Jastrow. With a few exceptions, the majority of the authors were critical of psychical research. This reflected the hostility on the topic shown by many psychologists at the time.

Many works discuss the interactions between 19th-century psychology and psychical research (e.g., Alvarado, 2002; Coon, 1992; Oppenheim, 1985; Plas, 2000). Some of the primary literature on the subject appeared in a variety of intellectual reviews and psychology journals, such as the *Psychological Review*. While some general information about the historical context of the material is presented, the purpose of this note is to provide bibliographical guidance for those interested on the topic by identifying papers and book reviews about psychical research published in the *Review*.

Psychical research during the 19th century was on the rise, as can be seen in the work of members of the Society for Psychical Research (SPR) in England (Gauld, 1968), and the work of individuals in other countries.[1] Several prominent figures in psychology, such as William James (1896d), Julian Ochorowicz (1887), and Charles Richet (1884), defended the validity of some of the claims of psychical research. In addition, psychical researchers contributed to the study of the subconscious mind, of dissociation, and of hallucinations. The work of members of the SPR (e.g., Myers, 1884; Sidgwick et al., 1894) provides examples of this.

While aspects of the work of the SPR were controversial and rejected by many psychologists, several of these individuals were acquainted with it (e.g., Janet, 1889; Jastrow, 1889). One indication that the SPR work was well-known was the fact that educator, psychical researcher, and SPR member Eleanor Mildred Sidgwick (1902) contributed a summary of the work of the SPR for the well-known reference work *Dictionary of Philosophy and Psychology*. Furthermore, members of the SPR, and psychical research itself, appeared often at 19th-century congresses of psychology (Alvarado, 2006; Nutting, 1992). Psychical research was also discussed frequently in the journal *Science* and in prominent newspapers (e.g., Mason, 1893; "Psychical Research," 1884; "The Society for Psychical Research," 1884).

In the United States William James was the most prestigious defender and popularizer of psychical research during the 19th century.[2] James wrote in the *Psychological Review* that psychical research "has ... many enemies, fair and foul, to elude before she gets her scientific

*Republished with permission from *Journal of Scientific Exploration, 23*(2), 211–220, 2009

†I wish to thank Nancy L. Zingrone for useful editorial suggestions for the improvement of this paper.

position recognized ..." (James, 1896d, p. 649). Many of those enemies were psychologists who reduced telepathy and mediumship to known natural processes. Mediumship was reinterpreted by Pierre Janet (1889) as a dissociative phenomenon, while others argued that telepathy could be accounted for by unconsciously perceived sensory cues (e.g., Hansen & Lehmann, 1895; Rualt, 1886). There was also a literature in which psychical researchers were considered to lack the necessary scientific training to conduct their studies, a situation that was believed to lead to the use of improper methodology (e.g., Jastrow, 1889; Scripture, 1897; see also Coon, 1992).

In addition to complaints about methodology and theoretical interpretation of unexplained phenomena, professional psychologists rejected the anti-materialistic ideas some psychical researchers used to explain their phenomena (on the latter see Gurney et al., 1886). The new empirical psychology, in an attempt to separate itself from metaphysical ideas about the soul, embraced a materialistic view in which the mind was the product of the nervous system.[3] Working under this assumption, action at a distance (such as telepathy), and the idea that the mind could be independent of the body, was unlikely to be accepted as part of psychology.

Several of these topics, as well as the phenomena of psychical research, were occasionally discussed in leading psychology journals, among them the American journal *Psychological Review*.

The *Psychological Review*

The *Psychological Review* was founded in 1894 by James Mark Baldwin and James McKeen Cattell, who were both the owners and the editors (in alternate years) of the journal between 1894 and 1903 (Calatayud et al., 1987; Kintsch and Cacioppo, 1994; Sokal, 1997). From the beginning, the *Review* became a prominent journal that represented the new empirical psychology then prevalent in American universities (O'Donnell, 1985). The first volume, published in 1894, included contributions by such authors as James R. Angell, Mary Whitton Calkins, John Dewey, Christine Ladd Franklin, William James, Joseph Jastrow, George H. Mead, Hugo Münsterberg, Edward W. Scripture, and Lightner Witmer, among others. In addition to articles, the book review section of the journal informed the American public of the wide range of available literature from psychology, as well as from areas such as philosophy and sociology. The journal, still in print today, currently publishes theoretical papers.

Psychical Research in the *Psychological Review*

Articles

One of William James' (1896d) papers was a reply to James McKeen Cattell's (1896) critique of James' (1896a) presidential address to the SPR.[4] To counter James' view that groups of apparitions cases were more impressive than single cases, Cattell argued:

> When we have an enormous number of cases, and cannot find among them all a single one that is conclusive, the very number of cases may be interpreted as an index of the weakness of the evidence. The discovery of a great many gray crows would not prove that any crows are white, rather the more crows we examine and find to be black or gray, the less expectation have we of finding one that is white.[5] (p. 582)

Cattell was not impressed by James' assessment of Mrs. Piper as his "white crow." In a critical tone, Cattell (1896: 582–583) stated: "The ablest of men have followed alchemy and astrology, have worshiped strange gods, have consulted witches and burned them. Geese have before now been mistaken for swans, and often to the honor of those who made the mistake. One white crow is enough, but its skin should be deposited in a museum."

James (1896d) disagreed with Cattell's argument of the weakness of accumulated cases, arguing that he did not have any evidence of "erroneousness," but instead was working on the assumption common to some scientists that the evidence against psychic phenomena was too strong to be questioned. In other words, he implied that Cattell was talking from prejudice and not from actual evidence or conventional explanations. James further wrote:

> The presumption has remained presumption merely, the scientist saying, "I can't believe you're right," whilst at the same time he has been unable to show how or where we were wrong, or even except in one or two cases to point out what the error most probably may have been. … Professor Cattell says: Can the exhibition of any number of gray crows prove that any crows are white? But our reports are not of gray crows; at the very worst they are of white crows without the skins brought home …; and where there are such obvious reasons why it must be easier to see a wild beast than to capture him, who can seriously maintain that continued reports of merely seeing him tend positively to decrease the probability that he exists? … Continued reports, far from strengthening the presumption that such things cannot exist, can only detract from its force. (p. 650)

In a long paper, philosopher and psychical researcher James H. Hyslop (1898) discussed "psychical research and coincidence." He argued that the coincidental phenomena studied by the SPR "has done much to strengthen the interest and belief in the possible meaning of such phenomena, especially when they take a certain form" (Hyslop, 1898, p. 362). Hyslop, aware of veridical cases and cases with supporting testimony, was not convinced that chance coincidence and illusions explained all the cases reviewed. However, he believed he found in some cases "evidence of an extraordinary combination of emotional interests and a predisposition to automatisms to simulate supernormal phenomena" (Hyslop, 1898, p. 386).

Hyslop (1899) also criticized Hugo Münsterberg's critiques of the evidence for psychic phenomena, which generated a counter reply (Münsterberg, 1899a).[6] In a short note complaining that the newspapers had distorted his statements about the immortality of the soul, Hyslop (1900b, p. 65) stated that the time was past for ridiculing the study of psychic phenomena: "Scientific method must control the study of these phenomena or lose its prestige and authority where it has the supreme right …"

In a fascinating paper, University of Iowa's psychologist G.T.W. Patrick (1898) discussed secondary personalities. He criticized the assumption of discarnate agency presented by Hodgson (1898, p. 556) as an illegitimate hypothesis that failed to "connect the phenomena in question with any other known facts or laws." Similarly, he criticized the lack of attention experimental psychologists had dedicated to the topic, and to automatism in general, perhaps designed to "maintain the dignity of experimental psychology" (1898, p. 556).

Patrick believed these phenomena could throw much light on the workings of the mind, and called for the investigation of simple cases to further understand the more complicated ones. Expressing the typical skepticism of psychologists to survival of bodily death and the ideas of Frederic W. H. Myers, Patrick wrote that the former were similar to Descartes' concept of "animal spirits," while the latter's concepts about the mind, and its telepathic dimensions, were essentially a "metaphysical, not a psychological hypothesis" (1898, p. 562). However, Patrick touched on many topics previously discussed by Myers without any acknowledgement. Some examples were the "remarkable activity of the constructive imagination" (1898, p. 573), the suggestibility of secondary personalities, and the low intellectuality of some of them.

Patrick referred to the veridical statements of mediumistic personalities as a "happy intuition." This did not imply the action of either spirits or telepathy because he believed other explanations could be forthcoming when the "characteristics of the secondary personality become subject to accurate scientific description" (1898, p. 576).

Following on the topic of conventional explanations, E.E. Slosson (1899), from the University of Wyoming, discussed the power of suggestion to produce hallucinations. He reported that during a lecture to students he was able to induce an olfactory hallucination in three-fourths of the audience. Hallucinations of sensations of temperature and pain, he said, "are easily induced by suggestion in susceptible individuals by the use of magnets. ... It is of course, necessary that the subject should have hazy ideas about magnetism. ... Sensations of heat may be produced by the north pole of the magnet, and cold by the south, or one pole may be made to give a tingling or smarting pain in the right hand and side of the body, and the south pole on the left ..." (1899, pp. 407–408).[7]

Book and Article Reviews

The rest of the discussions consist of book and article reviews, such as those of William James. In some of these writings James criticized criticisms of work with veridical hallucinations (James, 1895a, 1897c), and commented on SPR work on the subject (James, 1895c, 1895d). In addition, James (1896b) summarized the paper in which Hansen and Lehmann (1895) attempted to redefine experimental thought-transference as an exercise in involuntary whispering.[8]

Other reviews were about discussions of telepathy (James, 1895b, 1896c, 1897b), possession (James, 1895e), the subliminal self (James, 1896e), involuntary whispering and thought-transference (James, 1897a), and Mrs. Piper (James, 1898b). James also brought attention to publications in languages such as French (James, 1894), German (James, 1895a), and Italian (James, 1897b). All of these writings contributed to the popularization of psychical research topics among American psychologists.

John Grier Hibben (1897), from Princeton University, commented on William Crookes' SPR Presidential Address. Referring to Crookes's (1897) hypothesis that ether waves affecting the brain could account for telepathy, Hibben commented that the concept was not even a hypothesis: "At best he establishes merely the possibility of his speculation, for he presents no facts to indicate its probability or to save it from being relegated to the sphere of bare conjecture" (1897, p. 536).

In his discussion of two books about stage magic and illusions, Cattell (1899) continued his critical attitude, arguing that suggestibility and the psychology of the crowd are topics for psychological study. The books in question "should certainly be read by those interested in 'psychical research'" (Cattell, 1899, p. 554).

The psychology and physiology of the dying, including reports of panoramic memory, were reviewed as well. H. N. Gardiner (1896a, 1896b, 1897, 1898), from Smith College, commented on several articles on the topic published in France. The reviewer was skeptical of ideas in which a psychological self was held to react to the experience of being near-death by producing past memories.

Finally, Joseph Jastrow (1900), from the University of Wisconsin, a well-known critic of psychical research (e.g., Jastrow, 1889), reviewed the French edition of Théodore Flournoy's psychological study of medium Hélène Smith, which was translated into English (Flournoy, 1900). The medium produced communications about past lives in India, descriptions of planet Mars, and a Martian language.[9] The main value of the book, Jastrow stated, was the "success with which the various phases of these 'mediumistic' phenomena have been described and traced to natural and tangible points" (1900, p. 406). Flournoy's tracing of the medium's Martian language, Jastrow commented, was a "truly classical instance of the psychological comprehensiveness of the automatic self in exceptional cases" (1900, p. 411). He wrote further:

> The dangers of a false interpretation of this "psychic" tale are many, and are certain to mislead many who's interest in and powers of comprehension of cases of this kind are not equally developed ... It seems probable that when a sufficient number of these cases have been collected, that their general nature and law-abiding character will be understood, that a rational group of associations may be clustered about the term 'mediumistic,' (sic) and that the temptation to magnify the doings of some of this class into a bundle of miracles will gradually pass away—all of which would be welcome consummations for the progress of Psychology. (p. 411)

Concluding Remarks

The contents of the *Psychological Review* reflect the hostile position many psychologists took towards psychical research during the 19th century. As argued elsewhere (e.g., Alvarado, 2006; Coon, 1992), psychical research was generally rejected by psychologists of the time for a variety of reasons, one of which involved psychology's own struggle to be recognized as a science. Coon (1992, p. 150) has stated: "Psychologists were stationed at the periphery of science, and therefore they were the most threatened by challenges to the boundary and the most susceptible to cultural anxieties about what it meant to be 'scientific.'" Psychic phenomena represented one of these threats, both in terms of expertise and the non-materialistic explanations of telepathy and other manifestations.

Some of those openly critical of psychical research in the Review were Cattell, Jastrow, Münsterberg, and Patrick. These authors redefined psychic phenomena as the operation of sensory cues, hallucinations, and a variety of subconscious phenomena that included secondary personalities and automatic writing, among others.

Nonetheless, there were a few exceptions. The most notable was the work of James. But Hyslop also defended the field.[10]

It is my hope that the above comments will guide interested readers to the psychical research content of the *Psychological Review*. However, the study of this literature needs to be extended to contributions appearing in several other journals. Interested readers should also consider publications such as the *American Journal of Psychology, Mind*, and the *Revue Philosophique de la France et de l'Étranger*.

Notes

1 For reviews of developments in different countries see Biondi (1988), Moore (1977), Oppenheim (1985), Plas (2000), and Wolffram (2005).

2 This is clear in the material referenced below, as well as in critiques (James, 1886) and reviews of specific works (James, 1887). Recent discussions of James and psychical research include the work of Blum (2006) and Knapp (2003). For a collection of his psychical research writings see James (1986).

3 This process, intimately related to the study of localization of functions in the nervous system (Clarke & Jacyna, 1987), has been discussed in general overviews of the history of psychology (e.g., Boring, 1950), as well as in histories devoted to specific countries (e.g., Nicolas, 2002; O'Donnell, 1985).

4 There were other controversies between James and Cattell. In response to criticisms about research with medium Leonora E. Piper (Cattell, 1898a) in the pages of *Science*, James (1898a) wrote a letter to the journal, which was answered by Cattell (1898b).

5 This was a reference to James' famous comment about Mrs. Piper: "If you wish to upset the law that all crows are black, you mustn't seek to show that no crows are; it is enough if you prove one single crow to be white. My own white crow is Mrs. Piper" (James, 1896a, p. 884).

6 Münsterberg (1899b) was a well-known critic of psychical research. He was criticized by Hyslop (1908) and Schiller (1908).

7 This should be seen in the context of 19th-century interest in the influence of magnets to induce a variety of phenomena on human beings (e.g., Binet & Féré, 1885; Durville, 1895).

8 Hansen and Lehmann's (1895) paper was very influential. It was cited by many psychologists either implying that the study took care of the evidence for telepathy (e.g., Titchener, 1898, p. 897), or directly saying so (Scripture, 1897, p. 63–68, 259–260). As another psychologist wrote a few years later, this study showed "that much of the alleged transfer of thoughts might be accounted for by hints and suggestions given …" (Stratton, 1903, p. 206). See also the important critical comments of Sidgwick (1897), and the controversy between William James and Edward B. Titchener in the pages of Science (James, 1899a, 1899b; Titchener, 1899a, 1899b).

9 The medium's real name was Catherine Élise Müeller. Her performances, and Flournoy's work, have been discussed by Shamdasani (1994).

10 In later years Hyslop became even better known than James in the United States as a defender of psychic phenomena from its numerous critics (e.g., Hyslop, 1909). His work as a popularizer of psychical research is evident in his books (e.g., Hyslop, 1905), and in ideas discussed in newspapers ("Mrs. Piper, Trance Medium," 1900), and magazines (Hyslop, 1900a).

References

Alvarado, C. S. (2002). Dissociation in Britain during the late nineteenth century: The Society for Psychical Research, 1882–1900. *Journal of Trauma and Dissociation, 3,* 9–33.

Alvarado, C. S. (2006). *Historical perspective in parapsychology: I. Psychical research at the 1889 International Congress of Experimental Psychology.* http://www.pflyceum.org/162. html.

Binet, A., & Féré, C. (1885). L'hypnotisme chez les hystériques: Le transfert. *Revue Philosophique de la France et de l'Étranger, 19,* 1–25.

Biondi, M. (1988). *Tavoli e medium: Storia dello spiritismo in Italia.* Gremese.

Blum, D. (2006). *Ghost hunters: William James and the search for scientific proof of life after death.* Penguin Press.

Boring, E. G. (1950). *A history of experimental psychology* (2nd ed.). Appleton-Century-Crofts.

Calatayud, C., Carpintero, H., Peiro Silla, J. M., & Tortosa, F. M. (1987). La psicología americana a través del *Psychological Review* (1894–1945). *Revista de Historia de la Psicología, 8,* 39–65.

Cattell, J. M. (1896). Review of Presidential Address to the SPR, by W. James. *Psychological Review, 3,* 582–583.

Cattell, J. M. (1898a). Mrs. Piper, the medium. *Science, 7*(n.s .), 534–535.

Cattell, J. M. (1898b). Mrs. Piper, "the medium." *Science, 7*(n. s.), 641–642.

Cattell, J. M. (1899). Review of *Magic, stage illusions and scientific diversions*, by A. F. Hopkins, and *Spirit slate writing and kindred phenomena*, by W. B. Robinson. *Psychological Review, 6,* 554.

Clarke, E., & Jacyna, L. S. (1987). *Nineteenth-century origins of neuroscientific concepts*. University of California Press.

Coon, D. J. (1992). Testing the limits of sense and science: American experimental psychologists combat spiritualism, 1880–1920. *American Psychologist, 47,* 143–151.

Crookes, W. (1897). Address by the president. *Proceedings of the Society for Psychical Research, 12,* 338–355.

Durville, H. (1895). *Application de l'aimant au traitement des maladies* (5th ed.). Librairie du Magnétisme.

Flournoy, T. (1900). *From India to the planet Mars: A study of a case of somnambulism*. Harper & Brothers.

Gardiner, H. N. (1896a). Review of "L'état mental des mourants," by P. Sollier, A. Moulin, and A. Keller. *Psychological Review, 3,* 454–455.

Gardiner, H. N. (1896b). Review of "Le moi des mourants," by V. Egger. *Psychological Review, 3,* 236–237.

Gardiner, H. N. (1897). Review of "Le moi des mourants," by V. Egger. *Psychological Review, 4,* 101–102.

Gardiner, H. N. (1898). Review of "L'état mental des mourants," by C. Féré. *Psychological Review, 5,* 530–532.

Gauld, A. (1968). *The founders of psychical research*. Routledge and Kegan Paul.

Gurney, E., Myers, F. W. H., & Podmore, F. (1886). *Phantasms of the living* (2 vols.). Trübner.

Hansen, F. C. C., & Lehmann, A. (1895). Ueber unwillkürliches flüstern, eine kritische und experimentelle untersuchung der sogenannten gedakenübertragung. *Philosophische Studien, 11,* 471–530.

Hibben, J. G. (1897). Review of Presidential Address to the Society for Psychical Research, by W. Crookes. *Psychological Review, 4,* 535–536.

Hodgson, R. (1898). A further record of observations of certain phenomena of trance. *Proceedings of the Society for Psychical Research, 13,* 284–582.

Hyslop. J. H. (1898). Psychical research and coincidence. *Psychological Review, 5,* 362–387.

Hyslop, J. H. (1899). Professor Münsterberg on mysticism. *Psychological Review, 6,* 192–298.

Hyslop, J. H. (1900a). From India to the planet Mars. *North American Review, 171,* 734–747.

Hyslop, J. H. (1900b). Newspaper science. *Psychological Review, 7,* 64–65.

Hyslop, J. H. (1905). *Science and a future life*. H. B. Turner.

Hyslop, J. H. (1908). Professor Muensterberg and Dr. Hodgson. *Journal of the American Society for Psychical Research, 2,* 23–42.

Hyslop, J. H. (1909). Professor Newcomb and occultism. *Journal of the American Society for Psychical Research, 3,* 255–289.

James, W. (1886). Professor Newcomb's address before the American Society for Psychical Research. *Science, 7,* 123.

James, W. (1887). Phantasms of the living. *Science, 9,* 18–20.

James, W. (1894). Review of *Annales des Sciences Psychiques*, September–October 1893. *Psychological Review, 1,* 317–318.

James, W. (1895a). Review of *Ueber die Trugwahrnehmung*, by E. Parish. *Psychological Review, 2,* 65–67.

James, W. (1895b). Review of *Apparitions and thought transference*, by F. Podmore. *Psychological Review, 2,* 67–69.

James, W. (1895c). Review of "Report of the Census of Hallucinations." *Psychological Review, 2,* 69–75.

James, W. (1895d). A correction. *Psychological Review, 2,* 174.

James, W. (1895e). Review of *Demon possession and allied themes*, by J. L. Nevius. *Psychological Review, 2,* 529–531.

James, W. (1896a). Address of the president before the Society for Psychical Research. *Science, 3*(n.s.), 881–888.

James, W. (1896b). Review of "Ueber unwillkürliches Flüstern," by F. C. C. Hansen and A. Lehman. *Psychological Review, 3,* 98–99.

James, W. (1896c). Review of "Telepathic dreams experimentally induced," by G. B. Ermacora. *Psychological Review, 3,* 99–100.

James, W. (1896d). Psychical research. *Psychological Review, 3,* 649–652.

James, W. (1896e). Review of "Subliminal Self, or Unconscious Cerebration?" by A. H. Pierce; Reply to this paper, by F. Podmore; *Ueber spaltung der persönlichkeit*, by Dr. Schrenck–Notzing; and *Die mehrheit geistoger persönlichkeiten in einem individuum*, by S. Lanmann. *Psychological Review, 3,* 682–684.
James, W. (1897a). Review of "Involuntary whispering considered in relation to thought-transference," by H. Sidgwick. *Psychological Review, 4,* 654–655.
James, W. (1897b). Review of *I fenomeni telepatice e le allucinazione veridiche,* by E. Morselli. *Psychological Review, 4,* 655–657.
James, W. (1897c). Review of *Zur kritik telepatischen Beweimaterials*, and *hallucinations and illusions,* by E. Parish. *Psychological Review, 4,* 657–658.
James, W. (1898a). Mrs. Piper, "the medium." *Science, 7*(n. s.), 640–641.
James, W. (1898b). Review of "A further record of observations of certain phenomena of trance," by R. Hodgson. *Psychological Review, 5,* 420–424.
James, W. (1899a). Discussion and correspondence: Messrs. Lehmann and Hansen on telepathy. *Science, 9*(n. s.), 654–655.
James, W. (1899b). Discussion and correspondence: Telepathy once more. *Science, 9*(n. s.), 752–753.
James, W. (1986). Essays in psychical research. In Burkhardt, F. H. (Ed.), *The Works of William James* (Vol. 16). Harvard University Press.
Janet, P. (1889). *L'automatisme psychologique: Essai de psychologie expérimentale sur les formes inférieures de l'activité humaine.* Félix Alcan.
Jastrow, J. (1889). The problem of "psychic research." *Harper's New Monthly Magazine, 79,* 76–82.
Jastrow, J. (1900). Review of *Des Indes à la planète Mars*, by T. Flournoy. *Psychological Review, 7,* 406–411.
Kintsch, W., & Cacioppo, J. T. (1994). Introduction to the 100th anniversary issue of the *Psychological Review. Psychological Review, 101,* 195–199.
Knapp, K. D. (2003). *To the Summerland: William James, psychical research and modernity*. Ph.D. dissertation, Boston College.
Mason, R. O. (1893). In the field of psychology: Reports of the scouts who have been exploring. *New York Times,* 22 October, p. 20.
Moore, R. L. (1977). *In search of white crows: Spiritualism, parapsychology, and American culture*. Oxford University Press.
Mrs. Piper, trance medium: Prof. Hyslop, at Columbia, talks of her manifestations. (1900). *New York Times,* 14 February, p. 3.
Münsterberg, H. (1899a). Professor Hyslop on mysticism. *Psychological Review, 6,* 408–410.
Münsterberg, H. (1899b). Psychology and mysticism. *Atlantic Monthly, 83,* 67–85.
Myers, F. W. H. (1884). On a telepathic explanation of some so-called spiritualistic phenomena: Part I. *Proceedings of the Society for Psychical Research, 2,* 217–237.
Nicolas, S. (2002). *Histoire de la psychologie Français: Naissance d'une nouvelle science*. In Press.
Nutting, J. (1992). Les premiers congrés internationaux de psychologie: Test inedit. In Richelle, M. & Carpintero, H. (Eds.), *Contributions to the history of the International Congresses of Psychology: A posthumous homage to J. R. Nutting* (pp. 7–74). Valencia: *Revista Historia de la Psicología* Monographs. Leuven University Press.
Ochorowicz, J. (1887). *De la suggestion mentale*. Octave Doin.
O'Donnell, J. M. (1985). *The origins of behaviorism: American psychology, 1870–1920*. New York University Press.
Oppenheim, J. (1985). *The other world: Spiritualism and psychical research in England, 1850–1914.* Cambridge University Press.
Patrick, G. T. W. (1898). Some peculiarities of the secondary personality. *Psychological Review, 5,* 555–578.
Plas, R. (2000). *Naissance d'une science humaine: La psychologie: Les psychologues et le "merveilleux psychique."* Presses Universitaires de Rennes.
Psychical research. (1884). *The Times,* 29 January, p. 6.
Richet, C. (1884). La suggestion mentale et le calcul des probabilités. *Revue Philosophique de la France et de l'Étranger, 18,* 609–674.
Rualt, A. (1886). Le mécanisme de la suggestion mentale hypnotique. *Revue Philosophique de la France et de l'Étranger, 22,* 679–697.

Schiller, F. C. S. (1908). Comments by F. C. S. Schiller on a criticism of Prof. Hyslop. *Journal of the Society for Psychical Research, 13,* 163–167.

Scripture, E. W. (1897). *The new psychology*. Walter Scott.

Shamdasani, H. (1994). Encountering Hélène: Théodore Flournoy and the genesis of subliminal psychology. In Flournoy, T., *From India to the Planet Mars: A Case of Multiple Personality with Imaginary Languages* (pp. xi-li). Princeton University Press.

Sidgwick, E. M. (1902). Psychical research. In Baldwin, J. M. (Ed.), *Dictionary of Philosophy and Psychology* (Vol. 2, pp. 378–382). Macmillan.

Sidgwick, H. (1897). Involuntary whispering considered in relation to experiments in thought-transference. *Proceedings of the Society for Psychical Research, 12,* 298–314.

Sidgwick, H., Johnson, A., Myers, F. W. H., Podmore, F., & Sidgwick, E. M. (1894). Report on the Census of Hallucinations. *Proceedings of the Society for Psychical Research, 10,* 25–422.

Slosson, E. E. (1899). A lecture experiment in hallucinations. *Psychological Review, 6,* 407–408.

The Society for Psychical Research. (1884). *Science, 4,* 40–43.

Sokal, M. (1997). Baldwin, Cattell and the *Psychological Review*: A collaboration and its discontents. *History of the Human Sciences, 10,* 57–89.

Stratton, G. M. (1903). *Experimental psychology and its bearing upon culture*. Macmillan.

Titchener, E. B. (1898). The 'feeling of being stared at.' *Science, 8*(n. s.), 895–897.

Titchener, E. B. (1899a). Discussion and correspondence: Professor James on telepathy. *Science, 9*(n. s.), 686–687.

Titchener, E. B. (1899b). Discussion and correspondence: The telepathic question. *Science, 9*(n. s.), 787.

Wolffram, H. M. (2005). *On the borders of science: Psychical research and parapsychology in Germany, c. 1870–1939*. Ph.D. dissertation, University of Queensland.

On Psychic Forces and Doubles: The Case of Albert de Rochas[*]

Carlos S. Alvarado[†]

In nineteenth and early twentieth centuries' psychical research literature, there were many speculations to explain physical mediumship consisting of the projection of nervous and vital forces from the body. The purpose of this paper is to present an example of these ideas and a translation of part of an article published by Albert de Rochas in 1897 in the *Annales des Sciences Psychiques*. The article was devoted to séances with Eusapia Palladino, and de Rochas suggested the projection of forces to explain telekinesis and materializations, a concept also involving the idea of a fluidic double. The ideas are presented in the context of previous speculations, and of the life and work of its author. The point of this article is not to defend or criticize the validity of the concept, but to contribute to the history of these ideas by rescuing de Rochas from oblivion, which in turn also shows French contributions to nineteenth-century psychical research.

In a book German physician Albert von Schrenck-Notzing published in 1920 about physical mediumship, he referred to "an emanation or projection of vital energies beyond the limits of the human organism" (Schrenck-Notzing, 1920, p. 180). This idea was related to concepts of vital forces coming from antiquity (Amadou, 1953) and to the movement of mesmerism. Starting in the late Eighteenth century, many individuals representing such movement popularized the concept of animal magnetism. Franz Anton Mesmer (1779) referred to it as a universal fluid capable of acting at a distance and of affecting inorganic and organic matter. Regarding the latter, Baron Jean du Potet de Sennevoy wrote:

> The nervous, active atmosphere of the magnetizer ... enters in rapport with the passive nervous atmosphere of the magnetized person, and augments the latter to the point that, in some cases, it seems that there is a real saturation of the nervous system. (Du Potet. 1868, p. 316; this and other translations are mine).[1]

Such magnetic phenomena, which included a variety of physiological and psychological effects, informed an interesting model developed during the nineteenth century and later to explain psychic manifestations, which is the topic of this paper. The basic concept was that what was variously referred to as "magnetic," "vital," "fluidic," and "nervous" bodily forces, could cause phenomena such as thought-transference, movement of objects, raps, luminous effects, and materializations when projected from the human body.[2] Interestingly, such ideas of human radiations were a particular interest of various French researchers, a tradition that began with mesmerism and continued in later years. This was exemplified by many publications, among them overviews such as *La Force Psychique* (Bonnaymé, 1908), *Magnétisme Vital* (Gasc-Desfossés, 1897), *Pour Photographier les Rayons Humaines* (Girod, 1912), and *Les Radiations Humaines* (Montandon, 1927). The purpose of

[*]Reprinted with permission from *Journal of Scientific Exploration, 30*, 63–84, 2016.
[†]I wish to thank Massimo Biondi for taking the time to trace an article in Italian about de Rochas.

this paper is to present a translation of an account of one of these ideas, postulated by Albert de Rochas in the late nineteenth century, which was actually a late formulation of concepts of emanations from the body to account for physical phenomena, and part of the neo-mesmeric movement that continued the old mesmeric tradition.[3] De Rochas was one of several French neo-mesmerists who continued writing about magnetism during the late Nineteenth century and later, among them Émile Boirac (1908), Hippolyte Baraduc (1896), Alexandre Barèty (1887), and Hector Durville (1895–1896).

The translation and presentation of an excerpt from one of de Rochas' articles is of interest today for various reasons. First, it is a reminder of a conceptual tradition of vital, psychic, and nervous forces (Alvarado, 2006, 2008) that, while still present today, are not considered by many current workers in parapsychology who emphasize ideas of nonphysicality (e.g., Kelly, 2015; Tart, 2009). Second, it is an opportunity to present to modern readers, many of whom presumably are unacquainted with the topic, a fragment of French psychical research theorization from the nineteenth century. Third, I briefly present an overview of the work of de Rochas, a figure who is not frequently discussed today.

Magnetic, Nervous, and Fluidic Forces, and Doubles

As seen in the literature of mesmerism and the work of Reichenbach (1849/1851), the conceptual ground for de Rochas' theorization had actually been prepared by others before him. Later ideas of emanations from the human body included those of many writers who proposed various concepts to explain the phenomena of Spiritualism, particularly the physical ones. A few early examples from the United States were B. W. Richmond (Brittan & Richmond, 1853), Asa Mahan (1855), and E. C. Rogers (1853).

Several other examples appeared as explanations of the phenomenon of table turning (De Gasparin, 1854; Thury, 1855), which created much publicity. As the well-known French investigator of table-turning Agénor de Gasparin wrote in his classic *Des Tables Tournantes*:

> If my brain, active as a Leyden jar, emits and directs a fluidic current through my nerves, if the other members of the [mediumistic] chain follow similarly, it is evident that it would not be long for us to form sort of an electric battery, by which the influence will be felt according to our thoughts; we will produce a rotation, we will produce, also at a distance, vigorous liftings. (De Gasparin, 1854, Volume 1, p. 514).

A variety of similar ideas continued to be postulated and further developed later. This included various sorts of speculations such as those appearing in *Spiritualism Answered by Science* (Cox, 1872) and in *Spiritism* (Von Hartmann, 1885), and in the twentieth century (e.g., Morselli, 1908; Sudre, 1926) to account for physical mediumship. According to German philosopher Eduard Von Hartmann, the projection of nerve force by mediums was

> … not a function of those parts of the brain which serve as support to the conscious will, but of deeper-lying layers of the brain which either coincide with those supporting the somnambulic consciousness, or are more approximate to them than to the first. (Von Hartmann, 1885, p. 51)

Consequently,

> … the development of magnetic-mediumistic nerve force is stronger in the somnambulic than in the waking state … (Von Hartmann, 1885, p. 51)

Somewhat earlier, English physicist William Crookes helped popularize ideas of force through his writings about the physical phenomena of medium D. D. Home. He wrote:

> Being firmly convinced that there could be no manifestation of one form of force without the corresponding expenditure of some other form of force, I for a long time searched in vain for evidence of any force or power being used up in the production of these results.
>
> Now, however, having seen more of Mr. Home, I think I perceive what it is that this psychic force uses up for its development ... after witnessing the painful state of nervous and bodily prostration in which some of these experiments have left Mr. Home—after seeing him lying in an almost fainting condition on the floor, pale and speechless—I could scarcely doubt that the evolution of psychic force is accompanied by a corresponding drain on vital force. (Crookes, 1874, p. 40–41).

Many also speculated about the process underlying materialization. A twentieth-century example was French researcher Gustave Geley, who argued that the phenomenon consisted of an

> ... anatomo-biologic decentralisation in the medium's body and an externalisation of the decentralised factors in an amorphous state, solid, liquid, or vaporous. (Geley, 1924/1927, p. 358).

There were also speculations to account for mental phenomena. Various other forms of bodily radiations or biophysical emanations were postulated in different time periods to account for telepathy (for an overview and bibliography, see Alvarado, 2008, 2015).

Interestingly, such ideas were also related to the concept of subtle bodies, or fluidic doubles, believed by many to be able to exteriorize from the body. This was an ancient concept (Mead, 1919; Poortman, 1954/1978), and one discussed by de Rochas in the Excerpt presented below (for the purpose of this paper, I will not get into discussion of different types of subtle bodies).

The idea of doubles, and more generally, subtle bodies of different sorts, has a long literature, and one that has been connected to psychic phenomena (Alvarado, 2009a; Vesme, 1898). Various authors such as Adolphe d'Assier (1883/1887) and Carl du Prel (1899/1908) helped to keep alive the concept, not to mention the writings of well-known occultists such as Gerard Encausse (1890) and Annie Besant (1896). Alexander Aksakof (1890/1895) defended the existence of spontaneously produced doubles, seen as apparitions, with some degree of materiality.

In ideas that preceded the concept of a fluidic double discussed by de Rochas as applied to physical mediumship, several nineteenth-century writers speculated that the medium's double produced materializations (e.g., Coleman, 1865, p. 127–128). Referring to the double, a later writer stated that "the substance composing this counterpart is, to a certain extent, the nucleus around which all spirits materializing are developed or clothed" (Brackett, 1886, p. 126).[4]

Various writers from different branches of occultism also discussed astral bodies and materializations, as seen in *La Magie et l'Hypnose* (Encausse, 1897, p. 143) and in *The Ocean of Theosophy* (Judge, 1893, p. 150). Considering the cause of magical action on human beings, German philosopher Carl du Prel referred to the astral body. This agent, "when it manifests as an apparition; (double, phantom, materialization) reproduces the outline of the exterior man" (Du Prel, 1899/1908, p. 394).

In the de Rochas' excerpt reprinted below, he defended the idea of a semi-physical principle between the spirit and the physical body. This idea was by no means new with him. Limiting references to the nineteenth century, some examples are the "life" principle of Chardel (1818), the "psychode" of Thury (1855), and the "perispirit" of Kardec (1863).[5] Several other French writers who were contemporaries of de Rochas discussed the existence of semi-physical fluidic doubles, showing the topic received much attention in some circles. This included, among others, Gabriel Delanne (1909), Hector Durville (1909), and Louis-Sophrone Fugairon (1907).

Interestingly, all these ideas of forces and subtle bodies were interrelated. In a book about "human radiations," Raoul Montandon (1927, pp. 4–5) stated that the existence of the double was vital to "the understanding of nearly all the manifestations which occupy Occultists, Metapsychists, Spiritists, etc."

Albert de Rochas

In 1914 it was announced that a group of students of psychic phenomena and scientists formed a committee to express their "admiration and sympathy towards the veteran of metapsychic studies" Albert de Rochas (Anonymous, 1914), whose scientific jubilee was due. That the man was held in high esteem was evident by the names of these individuals, which included, among others known for their interest in psychic phenomena, physicians Gustave Geley, Eugene Osty, and Albert von Schrenck-Notzing, physiologist Charles Richet, philosophers Henri Bergson and Emile Boirac, and astronomer Camille Flammarion.

Colonel Eugène-Auguste-Albert de Rochas d'Aiglun (1837–1914), who had the title of Count, is one of those psychical researchers in need of study, and a figure forgotten by many contemporary parapsychologists.[6] According to biographical sources, de Rochas was from an old family from Provence, France. His initial education took place at the Lyceum of Grenoble, and he obtained in 1856 an honorary mention in mathematics. He entered the École Polytechnique in 1857, and in the following years he was in the military service, rising steadily in rank and holding different posts. By 1888 he became the administrator of the École Polytechnique, after having become Lieutenant Coronel. He hoped this position would provide time for scientific studies, and this was the case until a military superior proclaimed that occult practices were not proper in a military school (de Rochas, 1895a, p. 183; see also Gaillard, 1902). In a later edition of the of de Rochas' book (1895a), he replied that "as the name indicates, the École Polytechnique was not only a military school and that all sciences were occult before being discovered," and unfortunately "from that moment, I had to abandon the experiments I had initiated in one of the physics laboratories of the institution ..." (de Rochas, 1899, p. 190). Forced to retire, de Rochas found himself with the freedom to do what he wanted (see also Anonymous, 1915; Curinier, no date).

Many of his studies were on topics of military and science history, fortifications, and other issues, among them *La Science des Philosophes et l'Art des Thaumaturges dans l'Antiquité, a study of the pneumatics of Heron and Philo* in which he translated these authors from Greek (de Rochasm 1882b), and *La Science Dans l'Antiquité: Les Origines de la Science et Ses Premières Applications* (de Rochas, no date circa 1883), about science and technology in ancient times.[7] Some of this work led him to receive several distinctions and awards. Among others, gold medals from the Society for Greek Studies in 1872 and from the National Congress of Geography Societies in 1882 were conferred on him. In addition, he was elected an Officer of the Legion of Honor (Curinier, no date, p. 10).

De Rochas believed that phenomena considered through history to be unexplained would eventually be accounted for as our knowledge of the workings of nature increased. Some phenomena, he stated, were due to unknown principles related to "the nervous organization of exceptionally constituted individuals" (de Rochas, 1897a, p. 379). But he was also aware of the tendency of many to dispute the existence of some phenomena "because they rarely occur and we consider the accounts about them as simple legends due to the natural tendency of the human mind towards the marvellous" (de Rochas, no date circa, 1883, p. 5).

He participated in séances with many mediums and published various books. Several of them were about psychic forces, a topic to which he became an important contributor, and included: *Les Forces non Définies* (1887a), *Le Fluide des Magnetiseurs* (1891), *L'Extériorisation de la Sensibilité* (1895a), and *Les Frontieres de la Science* (1902).

His first studies included a follow-up to Reichenbah's work regarding perceptions of lights in magnets and in human beings (De Rochas, 1895a, Chap. 1). De Rochas, like other neo-mesmerists, held the belief that humans had a "fluid that circulates along the nerves like electricity circulates along the metallic wires of a telegraphic network" (de Rochas, 1895a, p. 58). He stated that such fluid exteriorized through the breath, and through the eyes, fingers, ears, and other parts of the body.

Such beliefs were related to de Rochas' work regarding the "exteriorization of sensibility," in which a magnetized person projected their tactile sensibility to objects or to the surrounding environment (de Rochas, 1892a, Chap. 3, 1892b; 1895a, p. Chap. 2). While such exteriorization was invisible, it was perceived by some experimental subjects.

Although many accepted the literal exteriorization explanation (e.g., Gasc-Desfossés, 1897, pp. 97–105), others mentioned the possible effects of suggestion (e.g., Boirac, 1896, p. 215; Croq, 1900, Chap. 11, Part 3), something considered by de Rochas but apparently not controlled for in many tests.[8] In any case, de Rochas' exteriorization work was widely discussed in both popular (de Rochas, 1892b) and scientific (Boirac, 1896) forums, including public lectures (Anonymous, 1899), giving him much publicity in France and abroad (for an example in the United States, see Gaullieur, 1895).

De Rochas also published books about physical phenomena, such as *L'Extériorisation de la Motricité* (1896), and *La Lévitation* (1897c), and about various other topics (e.g., de Rochas, 1904b). He wrote about hypnosis, exploring its stages and effects, and the properties of magnetic procedures and suggestion to induce various manifestations, some of a psychic nature (de Rochas, 1892a, 1893, 1895b, 1900). Hypnotism, he wrote (de Rochas, 1892a, p. 75), "is but the entrance hall to a vast and marvelous building ..."

Other topics covered by this researcher in his writings were medium Eusapia Palladino (de Rochas, 1897b), stigmatization (de Rochas, 1903), magnetic/hypnotic regression (de Rochas, 1905a), spirit photography (de Rochas, 1905b), apparitions and materializations (de Rochas, 1906b), auras and luminous phenomena (de Rochas, 1911b), recollections of previous lives (de Rochas, 1911c), and what he referred to as the "suspension of life," or cases of lack of food intake and prolonged sleep for long periods, and apparent death (de Rochas, no date circa 1914).

De Rochas' Excerpt

Article About Eusapia Palladino

The article from which the excerpt below is taken (de Rochas, 1897b) is about the Italian medium Eusapia Palladino, who was at the height of her career during the 1890s.[9] It is a report of séances de Rochas had with the medium in France held between October 2 and 14 of 1896. The French researcher had many séances with Palladino (e.g., de Rochas, 1897b; Sabatier, de Rochas, de Gramont, Maxwell, Dariex, and de Watteville, 1896), and devoted more than half of his book *L'Extériorisation de la Motricité* (1896, pp. 1–315) to her, a discussion that is probably the most complete overview of the medium and her phenomena published during the Nineteenth century.

The 1897 article from which the following excerpt is taken was mainly a report of séances, which included discussions of the effects of magnetic passes on the medium, which are summarized by the observation that the medium showed behaviors similar to those of other magnetized individuals. It was also said that there seemed to be an invisible sensitive link or connection between her and the objects moved. According to de Rochas, the medium had her arms extended with her fists closed toward a table that was moving. He pinched the surrounding air between the table and Palladino's fists and she uttered a cry and remonstrated him (de Rochas, 1897b, p. 10).

It was also reported that the medium's sensitivity was exteriorized, because under magnetization she said she saw on her right side "sort of a phantom and that it was at the location of this phantom that her sensibility was localized" (de Rochas, 1897b, p. 7). Such phantoms were also seen by various individuals magnetized by de Rochas, such as the young man Laurent (de Rochas, 1895b), and the young woman Maria Mayo (de Rochas, 1905a).

Observations of this sort and of the exteriorization of sensibility recorded before 1897 prepared the ground for the ideas appearing in the excerpt reprinted here, and can be found at the end of that article under the heading "Hypotheses" (pp. 22–28).

Excerpt from de Rochas (1897b)

The moment seems to come for me to attempt a synthesis of all these facts, and I will go from the *postulatum* that in the living man there is a SPIRIT and a BODY.

The spirit we cannot apprehend; all we know is that from it come the phenomena of will, thought, and feeling.

As for the body, it is pointless to define it, but we will distinguish two things: the raw material (bones, flesh, blood, etc.) and an invisible agent which, single or double, transmits to the mind the sensations of the flesh and to the muscles the orders of the mind.

Intimately linked to the body that secretes it during life, it is halted, in most, on the surface of the skin and escapes only through more or less intense effluvia, depending on the individual, through the sense organs and the most prominent parts of the body, such as the fingertips. This at least are the frequent assertions of subjects who have acquired by certain processes a momentary visual hyperesthesia, which was admitted by the old magnetisers ....[10]

In some people called *subjects* the adherence of nervous fluid to the fleshly organism is weak, so that it can be moved with extreme ease and produce the known phenomena of hyperesthesia and complete insensitivity due either to self-suggestion, that is to say, to the action of the spirit of the subject itself on its fluidic body, or at the suggestion of another person whose mind has contacted the fluidic body of the subject.

Some subjects, even more sensitive, can project their nervous fluid, under certain conditions, out of the skin, and so produce the phenomenon that I studied under the name of *exteriorization of sensibility*.[11] It is understood easily that a mechanical action exerted by these effluvia, *out of the body*, can propagate thanks to them and thus go up to the brain.

The exteriorization of motricity[12] is more difficult to understand and I cannot, trying to explain, but resort to a comparison.

Suppose that, in some way, we prevent the nerve agent to reach our hand; it will become a corpse, an inert material as a piece of wood, and nonetheless it will come back under the control of our will when we have given to this inert material the exact proportion of fluid it takes to animate. Let's concede that a person can project the same fluid on a piece of wood in sufficient quantities to soak it in the same proportion; it will not be absurd to believe that, by an unknown mechanism of attractions and electrical repulsions, this piece of wood will act as an extension of the body of this person.[13]

This also explains the movements of tables under the fingers of those called *mediums*, and in general all the movements *with contact* produced on light objects by many sensitives, without significant muscular effort. These movements have been thoroughly studied by Baron de Reichenbach and described by him in five lectures given in 1856 ....[14]

It even includes the production of movements requiring a force greater than that of the medium through the chain which puts at his disposal part of the force of the assistants.

But such a simplistic hypothesis does not account for the formation of hands,[15] and one is led to complete it as follows.

The nerve agent spreads along the sensory and motor nerves in all parts of the body. So we can say that it presents on the whole the same shape as the body, since it occupies the same portion of space, and is called the *fluidic double* of man, without leaving the domain of positive science.

Many experiments, which unfortunately had as guarantor only the evidence of subjects (at least those I have made),[16] appear to establish that this double may reconstitute outside the body, after a sufficient externalization of nerve impulses, such as a crystal is reformed into a solution when it is sufficiently concentrated.

Thus exteriorized the double continues to depend on the spirit and it obeys it with even more ease since it is now less hindered by its adherence to the flesh, so that the subject can move it and build up the material on one or another of its parts in order to make this part perceptible to the ordinary senses.

In this way Eusapia forms the hands that are seen and felt by the spectators.

Other experiments, which are less numerous and, consequently, we should not accept but with great reservations, tend to prove that the exteriorized fluidic matter can be modeled due to the influence of a fairly powerful will, as clay is shaped under the hand of a sculptor.

Presumably Eusapia, after passing through various spiritist environments, conceived in her imagination a John King,[17] ... and managed to give forms to her own fluidic body, when she made us feel big hands which she produced at a distance, on clay, [and the] impressions of a man's head ....[18]

Thus, everything that my colleagues and I have seen with Eusapia can be explained (even the lights, which would be but very intense condensations of the nervous substance) without the intervention of a spirit other than hers.[19]

But if nothing has shown us that John exists, nothing has proved to us either that he does not exist ...

We obtain in effect a first stage of the release of the fluidic body in the exteriorization of sensibility in the form of concentric layers around the body of the subject. The materiality of the effluvia is demonstrated by the fact that they dissolve in some substances such as water and fat; but, like odor, the reduction of body weight given off is immeasurable by our instruments.

The second stage is given by the coagulation of these effluvia in a sensitive double, but not visible yet to ordinary eyes.

The third stage is visible and tangible materialization, but only of a part of the body. The psychic matter emitted by the medium seems to be able to produce these effects on the condition that it appears in a place sheltered from light vibrations and of the sitter's gaze. The medium may remain in the light, but the materialization forms in a dark recess and very close.

> Finally, the fourth stage is the materialization of an entire human form. Here it is almost always that the medium herself is away from light and from the gaze of the sitters; as in the previous case the form only shows up when it acquires a sufficient degree of materiality, but this materiality can be intense enough to withstand several hours of disorganizing influences …
>
> In the third and the fourth stages, it is as a galvanoplastic transport of the matter of the physical body of the medium, matter that comes from the physical body to occupy a similar position on the fluidic body. It has been found with a balance, *a very large number of times*, that the medium lost some of its weight and that this weight went into the materialized body …[20]
>
> The most curious case, which so far is unique, is that of Mistress d'Espérance with whom this transport was done with such intensity that some of her own body had become invisible. There was only in its place but a fluidic body of which the double is only an emanation; the spectators could pass their hand across, but she felt it.[21] This phenomenon, taken to its extreme limit, would lead to the complete disappearance of the body of the medium and its appearance in another place, as is reported in the lives of saints.
>
> In full body materialization, the body is almost always animated by an intelligence different from that of the medium. What is the nature of these intelligences? To what degree of materialization can they intervene to direct the exteriorized psychic matter? These are issues of great interest, but which are not yet resolved.

Concluding Remarks

De Rochas' ideas, which he also presented in other publications (e.g., de Rochas, 1895c, 1909), have been forgotten by many, but they received some attention in his day. They were an extension of earlier concepts derived from the writings of the mesmerists, Reichenbach, and many others interested in various forms of psychic phenomena, such as mediumship. This was the case for both ideas of an exteriorized force and a fluidic double, which for de Rochas, and others, were not different concepts.

The theoretical part of the 1897 paper does not seem to have been cited directly, but the ideas were referred to occasionally (e.g., Anonymous, 1897; Carrington, 1909, p. 269; Flammarion, 1907, p. 409), providing support for later similar speculations. In later years, de Rochas (1902, Chap. 1; 1909) discussed the same ideas that appear in the excerpt, in part using the same words. In a letter he wrote in 1901 to a French writer, de Rochas defended the view that many psychic phenomena supported the idea of the exteriorization of thought, as well as of the sensory and motor powers of the body. This, he believed,

> … proved the existence of several emanations of various nature which the magnetizers confused under the name of *magnetic Fluid*, and which agree with the theories of the Orientals, of the ancient Greek philosophers, and the first Fathers of the Church about the *fluidic body or soul*, which serve as an intermediary between the Spirit and the Body. (de Rochas, 1904b, p. 26)

While de Rochas (1896, p. 477) said he was preparing a book about phantoms of the living discussing the concept of fluidic bodies, he later stated he was not going to publish such a work (de Rochas, 1902, p. 1). In later publications he continued to discuss the astral body and attempts to project it from the physical body (de Rochas, 1905a, 1906a, 1910, 1911a), but this did not involve out-of-body experiences in the sense that the magnetized person was conscious of being located out of their physical body (as stated by Bozzano, 1911, pp. 157–168). De Rochas (1900, Chap. 4, 1908) was also interested in the photographic detection of this subtle body, as were other contemporaries, such as Hector Durville (1909).[22] Interestingly, the close relationship between the projected sensibility and the concept of a double was supported by sensations perceived by the subject. Similar to those instances in which someone felt pain when an object in which his or her sensibility was embedded was pricked, pain (and other) sensations were also felt when the double, only seen by the experimental participant, was touched at the position where it was reported to be (de Rochas, 1905a, p. 5, 7; 1910, p. 291, 293, 294).

These ideas influenced later writers about subtle bodies, among them Delanne (1909), Durville (1909), and Lefranc (1911a). Bozzano (1904) argued that de Rochas' work on exteriorization of sensibility contributed to the recognition of the existence of a fluidic double and, in turn, to the recognition that this double could leave the body, showing the spiritual nature of man.[23]

Ideas of forces (without emphasis on a double) to explain physical mediumship also continued after de Rochas' 1897 paper. In Germany, Schrenck-Notzing (1920) wrote under the assumption of such concepts, as did Sudre (1926) in France, and Carrington (1921) in the United States. Several others continued this tradition, and some of them, like de Rochas, presented their ideas as explanations of Palladino's mediumship (e.g., Carrington, 1909; de Fontenay, 1898; Morselli, 1908).

The preceding Excerpt is part of the history of ideas about doubles, but also of attempts to explain materializations, and psychokinesis in general. But such ideas, while part of current popular culture, do not appear to interest many modern parapsychologists, particularly those representative of the experimental approach. As pointed out before (Alvarado, 2006), some academic parapsychologists have moved away from this biophysical or psychoenergetic tradition, preferring instead ideas based on as yet unspecified non-materialistic concepts (e.g., Kelly, 2015; Tart, 2009). Others have suggested physical approaches that do not assume force-like mechanisms like the ones postulated by de Rochas and others (e.g., Walker, 1975; Jahn & Dunne, 2001). The same may be said about semi-physical subtle bodies. For example, recent academic discussions of out-of-body experiences have emphasized psychological and neurological-informed speculations, as I have reviewed elsewhere (Cardeña & Alvarado, 2014, pp. 189–191).

Seen from this perspective, de Rochas' ideas probably appear to some of our contemporaries as antiquated and of little relevance to explain the riddle of psychic phenomena (and physical phenomena in particular), although there is still interest and belief in such ideas, an example being modern spiritist discussions (Loureiro, 1998), which do not seem to interact with current parapsychology.

My interest, however, has not been in the validity of de Rochas' ideas, be they magnetic effluvia or fluidic doubles. My purpose has been that of rescuing from oblivion ideas that are sometimes forgotten by parapsychologists today because they have fallen out of fashion (even if still believed in by some groups), or because they are considered today to be wrong. A history of attempts to understand physical phenomena, however, should not consist only of the things believed to be "correct" today. Such a perspective reflects current conceptions but do not do justice to the actual developments of the past. De Rochas' theoretical model, bringing together ideas of biophysical emanations and fields, and of subtle bodies, are a reminder of a different era and of different conceptions that provide us with a more complete view of past attempts to understand physical mediumship.

Notes

1 The mesmeric movement, and its concept of animal magnetism, is discussed by Crabtree (1993), Gauld (1992), and Méheust (1999). Also important was the work of Karl von Reichenbach (1849/1851), whose ideas about a force he called Od perceived by some individuals around crystals, magnets, and human beings were widely influential (see Nahm, 2012).

2 I have reviewed in various papers aspects of the development of ideas of body emanations or radiations to explain psychic phenomena (e.g., Alvarado, 2006, 2009b, 2011b; Alvarado & Nahm, 2011). See also the overviews of Amadou (1953) and Ungaro (1992), and the earlier publications of individuals such as Aksakof (1890/1895, pp. 1–21), Montandon (1927), Servadio (1932), and Sudre (1926, Chap. 6).

3 On the neo-mesmeric movement, see Alvarado (2009b, 2009c) and Harrington (1988).

4 Several observations were reported about instances where a materialized figure looked like the medium (e.g., Anonymous, 1879, p. 133), what some interpreted to be the medium's double. In later years Polish philosopher and psychologist Julian Ochorowicz (1911–1912) used the idea to explain the invisible hands he photographed with medium Stanislawa Tomczyk, arguing that her astral body could "manifest exteriorly and materialize in a manner sufficient to influence a photographic plate" (Ochorowicz, 1911–1912, p. 335).

5 In an article in a mesmeric journal, it was affirmed that magnetism connected matter and spirit:

> The soul touches the fluid and the fluid touches the body, it is through this channel that these two essentially different substances communicate. (Berruyer, 1852, p. 170)

The concept of the perispirit was further developed in later years in the spiritist literature (e.g., Delanne, 1899), and is still discussed in some circles (Loureiro, 1998).

6 For general information about de Rochas, see Anonymous (1914), Curimier (n. d. pp. 9–10), Fodor (no date, p. 332), and Marzorati (1914). See also Alvarado (2009b, pp. 373–374), Castellan (1955/1960, pp. 60–62), Lachapelle (2011, pp. 56–58), and Peter (1915).

7 See also works about an engineer (de Rochas, 1867), fortifications (de Rochas, 1881), artillery (de Rochas, 1882a), synesthesia (de Rochas, 1885), geography and the ancient Greeks (de Rochas, 1887b), and messenger pigeons (de Rochas, 1890). De Rochas used two versions of his name in his publications, but for convenience I have listed them chronologically in the references, not alphabetically.

8 Another critic also mentioned that most of the persons participating in the experiments were familiar with mesmeric ideas, or were experienced subjects, or individuals who had participated in many tests (Dariex, 1895). The implication was that subjects could be trained to produce specific phenomena, which may reflect the demands of the environment they were working in. Much of the work of de Rochas was done with such subjects, something that was also common as well with many "star" hysterics and hypnotic subjects during the nineteenth century (Alvarado, 2009d; Carroy, 1991).

Interestingly, de Rochas (1895c, Chap. 3, 1904a) speculated that such exteriorization accounted for the long tradition of spells. This was the case with attempts to influence someone using some object representing them, an object imprinted with their "sensibility."

9 The prominence of Palladino as a research medium during the nineteenth century can be appreciated from the overviews of Carrington (1909, pp. 28–72) and de Rochas (1896, pp. 1–315). Many were the reports about her phenomena during this period, among them those of Aksakof, Schiaparelli, du Prel, Brofferio, Gerosa, Ermacora and Finzi (1893), de Fontenay (1898), Lodge (1894), and Sidgwick (1895). Interestingly, Palladino inspired many others in addition to de Rochas to develop ideas to explain physical phenomena, as I have discussed elsewhere (Alvarado, 1993).

10 Regarding observations of luminous effluvia by mesmerized individuals, an early mesmerist stated: "Most somnambulists see a bright luminous fluid surround their magnetizer, coming out stronger from his head and hands" (Deleuze, 1813, p. 82). For particular examples, see Buckland (1850, p. 43), Elliotson (1848, p. 225), and Tardy de Montravel (1785, pp. 27–28). Luys (1892) reported similar observations in later years. In this part of the text the author refers to the first chapter of one of his books entitled "On the Objectivity of Effluvia Perceived in the Form of Light during the Hypnotic State" (de Rochas, 1895a; see also de Rochas, 1894). He also cited a French edition of lectures delivered in 1866 by Reichenbach (no date) in Vienna (see also De Rochas, 1891).

11 For example, in his studies with Mrs. Lux (pseudonym for Mrs. L. Lambert), de Rochas stated:

> I charged a photographic plate with her effluvia and placed it first between her hands … [after the plate was developed] Mrs. Lux felt when I touched the plate, but she felt nothing when MB [the person who developed the plate] touched it, unless I touched MB myself … I pricked on the image of one of her hands: Mrs. Lux fainted. (de Rochas, 1895a, pp. 104–105).

Lefranc (1911b) reported an instance of "repercussion" in which Mrs. Lambert felt her double was grabbed by an invisible hand. Next day she showed swollenness and redness of the forearm. Photographs of the bruise were presented.

12 In his book *L'Extériorisation de la Motricité*, de Rochas (1896, p. ii) defines the term as the induction of movements on stationary objects via a force coming from the body.

13 Similarly, Chevillard (1869) wrote in relation to turning tables that:

> The table is truly magnetized by the medium's will … The table becomes an organ of the medium-magnetizer, as his arm, his ear, and it will obey for the same reason … that my arms obey, when my will commands. (Chevillard, 1869, p. 14–15).

14 De Rochas cites the French edition of these lectures, entitled *Les Effluves Odiques* (Reichenbach, no date). The first part of the book has a long introduction by de Rochas entitled "Notice Historique sur les Recherches Relatives aux Effets Mécaniques de l'Od." Regarding table turning, see de Rochas' (1896, Part 2, Chap. 1) discussion of the work of Agenor de Gasparin (1854) and Marc Thury (1855).

15 This is a reference to materializations of hands. De Rochas (1897b, p. 20) reported this phenomenon with Palladino, saying that "fluidic hands," as well as movement of objects, "must be considered a fact definitively acquired by positive science." He wrote about materialized hands later (de Rochas, 1909). Appearances of hands in séances were well-known before the time when our author was writing (e.g., Adare, 1869, p. 135).

16 Here he cites his article about phantoms of the living (de Rochas, 1895b; on de Rochas and doubles see Alvarado, 2011a). This work, and that of visual perceptions of lights from magnets and layers of sensibility (de Rochas, 1895a), depended on the reports of the magnetized experimental participants.

17 This was the medium's spirit control. As de Rochas (1896) wrote:

> This John King says he is the brother of Crookes' Katie King and that he was Eusapia's father in another existence. It is John who speaks when Eusapia is in a trance; he speaks of her calling her 'my daughter' and gives advice on how she should be treated. (de Rochas, 1896, p. 16)

Katie King was a full body materialization observed by William Crookes with medium Florence Cook (Crookes, 1874, p. 102–112).

18 De Rochas (1896, pp. 132–133) had referred to imprints on clay with Palladino in a previous publication. Describing what happened in an instance in which a clay mould of clenching fingers was obtained, he wrote:

> Eusapia groaned, writhed and all her limbs trembled; however, her hands did not leave ours for a moment. Then she said: It is done. (de Rochas, 1896, p. 132)

Bozzano (1911, p. 167) interpreted imprints of Palladino's facial features on clay as the influence of "her 'etheric body,' doubled and materialized." Interestingly, de Rochas recounted in a different publication an instance in which he believed that the medium was in a deep hypnotic state and she saw, "to her great surprise, on her right, a blue phantom. I asked her if it was John; she replied no, but that it was that which John used" (de Rochas, 1896, p. 17).

19 Explanations of physical mediumship based on concepts of nervous forces without recourse to discarnate agency were frequent in the literature before de Rochas published his ideas (e.g., Rogers, 1853; Von Hartmann, 1885).

20 Most of the weighing tests with mediums conducted before de Rochas' article was published do not support this (but see Aksakof, 1890/1895, p. 243, and Harrison, 1878). Regarding stages of materialization, Alexander Aksakof (1894–1896/1898, p. 13) postulated that there were three of them. This consisted of formations not visible to the naked eye, visible incomplete formations, and materializations of complete bodies.

21 On d'Espérance, see Fodor (no date, pp. 83–85). Aksakof (1894–1896/1898) has discussed the apparent instance of dematerialization mentioned by de Rochas (see also D'Esperance, no date). There have been other reports of dematerialization of the whole body of mediums (e.g., Roberts, 1876).

22 de Rochas added in a footnote:

> Some people, especially sensitives, perceive it by sight or touch. I photographed it again with [photographer Paul] Nadar, but I could not repeat the experiment. The spirit photographs appear to be due to the action, on the plate, of the double of the subject modeled by a foreign intelligence, but still invisible in this state. (de Rochas, 1897a, p. 27)

See, on photographs of the astral body and its emanations, de Rochas (1900, Chap. 4, 1908). The idea of capturing the spirit of living individuals in photos was present in the early spiritualist literature (e.g., Carter, 1875; Moses, 1876). Furthermore, there was much interest in the photographic detection of invisible vital or nervous forces (e.g., Baraduc, 1896; Luys and David, 1897; see also the overviews of Cheroux, 2005 and Krauss, 1995).

23 Bozzano developed these ideas in later publications (e.g., Bozzano, 1911, 1934/1937), connecting different forms of nonconscious projections (such as autoscopy and many apparitions of the living) to the conscious experience of feeling out of the body, and to the idea of transcending the body and surviving its physical death (see also Alvarado, 2005). De Rochas's work was one strand of evidence cited to argue for the existence of a double independent of physical constraints.

References

Adare, V. [1869]. *Experiences in spiritualism with D. D. Home*. Thomas Scott.

Aksakof, A. (1895). *Animisme et spiritisme: Essai d'un examen critique des phénomènes médiumniques.* P. G. Leymarie. (Original work published 1890)

Aksakof, A. (1898). *A case of partial dematerialization of the body of the medium: Investigation and discussion.* Banner of Light. (Original work published 1894–1895)

Aksakof, A., Schiaparelli, G., du Prel, C., Brofferio, A., Gerosa, G., Ermacora, G. B., & Finzi, G. (1893). Rapport de la commission réunie à Milan pour l'étude des phénomènes psychiques. *Annales des Sciences Psychiques, 3,* 39–64.

Alvarado, C. S. (1993). Gifted subjects' contributions to psychical research: The case of Eusapia Palladino. *Journal of the Society for Psychical Research, 59,* 269–292.

Alvarado, C. S. (2005). Ernesto Bozzano on the phenomena of bilocation. *Journal of Near-Death Studies, 23,*207–238.

Alvarado, C. S. (2006). Human radiations, Concepts of force in mesmerism, spiritualism and psychical research. *Journal of the Society for Psychical Research, 70,*138–162.

Alvarado, C. S. (2008). Further notes on historical ideas of human radiations: IV. Mental phenomena. *Psypioneer, 4,* 119–126.

Alvarado, C. S. (2009a). Historical notes on doubles and travelling spirits: I—Introduction. *Paranormal Review, 50,* 6–15.

Alvarado, C. S. (2009b). Late nineteenth and early twentieth century discussions of animal magnetism. *International Journal of Clinical and Experimental Hypnosis, 57,* 366–381.

Alvarado, C. S. (2009c). Modern animal magnetism: The work of Alexandre Baréty, Émile Boirac, and Julian Ochorowicz. *Australian Journal of Clinical and Experimental Hypnosis, 37,* 1–15.

Alvarado, C. S. (2009d). Nineteenth-century hysteria and hypnosis: A historical note on Blanche Wittmann. *Australian Journal of Clinical and Experimental Hypnosis, 37,* 21–36.

Alvarado, C. S. (2011a). Historical notes on doubles and travelling spirits: X. Albert de Rochas. *Paranormal Review, 60,* 3–6.

Alvarado, C. S. (2011b). Unorthodox concepts of force and psychic phenomena. *Journal of Scientific Exploration, 25,* 121–130.

Alvarado, C. S. (2015). Telepathic emissions: Edwin J. Houston on "Cerebral Radiation." *Journal of Scientific Exploration, 29,* 467–490.

Alvarado, C. S., & Nahm, M. (2011). Psychic phenomena and the vital force: Hereward Carrington on "Vital Energy and Psychical Phenomena." *Journal of the Society for Psychical Research, 75*, 91–103.
Amadou, R. (1953). Esquisse d'une histoire philosophique du fluide. *Revue Métapsychique, 21,* 5–33.
Anonymous (1879). Materialisation manifestations. *Spiritualist Newspaper*, March 2, 133–134.
Anonymous (1897). X.—Some stories of mediums and their exploits: II. Eusapia Paladino and her "astral" hands. *Borderland, 4*, 49–50.
Anonymous (1899). Spectacles & concerts. *Le Figaro*, January 5, 4.
Anonymous (1914). Echos et nouvelles: Pour le jubilé scientifique de M. de Rochas. *Annales des Sciences Psychiques, 24*, 217.
Anonymous (1915). Nécrologie: Albert de Rochas. *Annales des Sciences Psychiques, 25*, 243–245.
Anonymous (n. d.). Albert de Rochas papers: Background note. http://amphilsoc.org/mole/view?docId=ead/Mss.Ms.Coll.106-ead.xml#bioghist
Baraduc, H. (1896). *L'ame humaine: Ses mouvements, ses lumières et l'iconographie de l'invisible fluidique*. Georges Carré.
Baréty, A. (1887). *Le magnétisme animal: Étudié sous le nom de force neurique rayonnante et circulante dans ses propriétés physiques, physiologiques et thérapeutiques*. Octave Doin.
Berruyer, A. (1852). De l'union de l'ame et du corps. *Journal du Magnétisme, 11*, 169–191.
Besant, A. (1896). *Man and his bodies*. Theosophical Publishing Society.
Boirac, E. (1896). Review of *L'Extériorisation de la Sensibilité*, by A. de Rochas. *Revue Philosophique de la France et de l'Étranger, 41*, 212–216.
Boirac, E. (1908). *La psychologie inconnue: Introduction et contribution à l'étude expérimentale des sciences psychiques*. Félix Alcan.
Bonnaymé, Docteur [E.] (1908). *La force psychique: L'agent magnétique et les instruments servant à les mesurer* (2nd ed.). Librairie du Magnétisme.
Bozzano, E. (1904). Contribution a l'étude des phénomènes d'extériorisation de la sensibilité. *Revue d'Études Psychiques, 4*(2), 149–158.
Bozzano, E. (1911). Considerations et *hypothèses sur les phénomènes de "bilocation." Annales des Sciences Psychiques, 21*, 65–72, 109–116, 143–152, 166–172.
Bozzano, E. (1937). *Les phénomènes de bilocation*. Jean Meyer. (Original work published 1934)
Brackett, E. A. (1886). *Materialized apparitions: If not beings from another life, what are they?* Colby and Rich.
Brittan, S. B., & Richmond, B. W. (1853). *A discussion of the facts and philosophy of ancient and modern spiritualism*. Partridge & Brittan.
Buckland, T. (1850). *The handbook of mesmerism*. Hippolyte Baillière.
Cardeña, E., & Alvarado, C. S. (2014). Anomalous self and identity experiences. In E. Cardeña, S. J. Lynn, & S. Krippner (Eds.), *Varieties of Anomalous Experiences* (2nd Ed., pp. 175–212). American Psychological Association.
Carrington, H. (1909). *Eusapia Palladino and her phenomena*. B. W. Dodge.
Carrington, H. (1921). Vital energy and psychical phenomena. *Psychic Research Quarterly, 1*, 271–277.
Carroy, J. (1991). *Hypnose, suggestion et psychologie: L'Invention de sujets*. Presses Universitaires de France.
Carter, A. G. W. (1875). Experiences in spirit-photography. *Banner of Light*, July 31, 3.
Castellan, Y. (1960). *La metapsíquica*. Paidós. (Original work published 1955)
Chardel, C. (1818). *Mémoire sur le magnétisme animal, presenté a l'académie de Berlin, en 1818*. Badouin.
Chéroux, C. (2005). Photographs of fluids: An alphabet of invisible rays. In C. Chéroux et al., *The perfect medium: Photography and the occult (*pp. 114–138). Yale University Press. (Original work published 2004)
Chevillard, A. (1869). Études expérimentales sur *le fluide nerveux et solution définitive problème spirite*. Victor Masson.
Coleman, B. (1865). Passing events: The spread of Spiritualism. *Spiritualist Magazine, 6*, 110–128.
Cox, E. W. (1872). *Spiritualism answered by science* (Rev. ed.). Longman.
Crabtree, A. (1993). *From Mesmer to Freud: Magnetic sleep and the roots of psychological healing*. Yale University Press.
Crookes, W. (1874). *Researches in the phenomena of spiritualism*. J. Burns.
Croq, J. (1900). *L'hypnotisme scientifique* (2nd ed.). Société d'Éditions Scientifiques.
Curinier, C. E. (Ed.) (n. d). *Dictionnaire National des contemporaines* (Vol. 4). Office General d'Édition.

Dariex, X. (1895). Review of *L'Extériorisation de la Sensibilité*, by A. de Rochas. *Annales de Sciences Psychiques, 5*, 184–192.
D'Assier, A. (1887). *Posthumous humanity: A study of phantoms.* George Redway. (Original work published1883)
Deleuze, J. P. F. (1813). *Histoire critique du magnétisme animal* (Vol. 1). Mame.
D'Espérance, E. (n.d., circa 1897). *Shadow land: Or, light from the other side.* George Redway.
De Fontenay, G. (1898). *A propos d'Eusapia Paladino: Les* séances *de Montfort-l'Amaury (25–28 Juillet 1897).* Société d'Éditions Scientifiques.
De Gasparin, Cte A. (1854). *Des tables tournantes: Du surnaturel en général et des esprits* (2 vols.). E. Dentu.
Delanne, G. (1899). *L'ame est immortelle: Démostration expérimentale.* Chamuel.
Delanne, G. (1909). *Les apparitions matérialisées des vivants & des morts: Volume 1: Les fantômes de vivants.* Librairie Spirite.
Deleuze, J. P. F. (1813). *Histoire critique du magnétisme animal* (Vol. 1). Mame.
de Rochas, A. (1867). *D'Arcon: Ingénieur militaire: Sa vie et ses écrits.* J. Dumaine.
de Rochas, A. (1881). *Principes de la fortification antique.* Ducher.
de Rochas, A. (1882a). L'artillerie chez les anciens. *Bulletin Monumental ou Recueil de Documents et de Mémoires Relatifs aux Différentes Branches de l'Archéologie, 10*(5), 154–177.
de Rochas, A. (1882b). *La science des philosophes et l'art des thaumaturges dans l'antiquité.* G. Masson.
de Rochas, A. (n. d., circa 1883). *La science dans l'antiquité: Les origines de la science et ses premières applications.* G. Masson.
de Rochas, A. (1885). L'audition colorée. *La Nature, 13*, 306–307, 406–408.
de Rochas, A. (1887a). *Les forces non définies: Recherches historiques et expérimentales.* G. Masson.
de Rochas, A. (1887b). Découverte de la géographie chez les Grecs et origine de cette science. *Cosmos: Revue des Sciences et de Leurs Applications, 7*(n. s.), 79–80.
de Rochas, A. (1890). Les pigeons messagers en orient. *Revue Scientifique, 45*, 754–759.
de Rochas, [A.] (1891). *Le fluide des magnétiseurs: Précis des expériences du Baron de Reichenbach sur ses propriétés physiques et physiologiques.* Georges Carré.
de Rochas, A. (1892a). *Les états profonds de l'hypnose.* Chamuel.
de Rochas, A. (1892b). L'extériorisation de la sensibilité. *Le Temps*, May 27, 3.
de Rochas, A. (1893). *Les états superficiels de l'hypnose.* Chamuel.
de Rochas, A. (1894). Objectivité des effluves perçus sous forme de lumière dans l'état hypnotique. *Annales des Sciences Psychiques, 4*, 129–162.
de Rochas, A. (1895a). *L'extériorisation de la sensibilité: étude expérimentale et historique* (2nd ed.) Chamuel.
de Rochas, A. (1895b). Les fantômes des vivants. *Annales des Sciences Psychiques, 5*, 257–275.
de Rochas, A. (1895c). Review of *Essai de spiritisme scientifique*, by D. Metzger, and *Le psychisme expérimental*, by A. Erny. *Annales des Sciences Psychiques, 5*, 119–126.
de Rochas, A. (1896). *L'extériorisation de la motricité: Recueil d'expériences et d'observations.* Chamuel.
de Rochas, A. (1897a). M. de Rochas, son opinion. *Revue Spirite: Journal d'Études Psychologiques, 40*, 379–380.
de Rochas, A. (1897b). Les expériences de Choisy-Yvrec (près Bordeaux) du 2 au 14 octobre 1896. *Annales des Sciences Psychiques, 7*, 6–28.
de Rochas, A. (1897c). *La lévitation.* P. G. Leymarie.
de Rochas, A. (1899). *L'extériorisation de la sensibilité: Étude expérimentale & historique* (fifth edition) Chamuel.
de Rochas, A. (1900). *Les sentiments, la musique et le geste.* Librairie Dauphinoise H. Falque et F. Perrier.
de Rochas, A. (1902). *Les frontières de la science* (Vol. 1). Librairie des Sciences Psychologiques.
de Rochas, A. (1903). Un cas de stigmatization. *Annales des Sciences Psychiques, 13*, 1–15.
de Rochas, A. (1904a). *Le envoutement: Documents historiques et expérimentaux* (2nd Rev. ed.). Chacornac.
de Rochas, A. (1904b). *Les frontières de la science* (Vol. 2). Librairie des Sciences Psychologiques.
de Rochas, A. (1905a). The regression of memory: Case of Mayo. *Annals of Psychical Science, 2*, 1–52.
de Rochas, A. (1905b). Concerning spirit photography. *Annals of Psychical Science, 2*, 216–218.
de Rochas, A. (1906a). New experiments relative to the astral body and the magnetic "rapport." *Annals of Psychical Science, 4*, 120–125.
de Rochas, A. (1906b). Revenants & fantomes. *Je Sais Tout, 2*, 337–345.

de Rochas, A. (1908). My experiments with M. de Jodko in 1896. *Annals of Psychical Science, 7*, 80–88.
de Rochas, A. (1909). The fluidic hands of Eusapia. *Annals of Psychical Science, 8*, 219–228.
de Rochas, A. (1910). Répercussion sur le corps physique des actions exercées sur le corps astral. *Annales des Sciences Psychiques, 20*, 289–295.
de Rochas, A. (1911a). Expériences relatives au "corps du désir." *Le Monde Psychique, 1*, 257–266.
de Rochas, A. (1911b). Les radiations lumineuses du corps humain. *Annales des Sciences Psychiques, 21*, 264–268.
de Rochas, A. (1911c). *Les vies successives: Documents pour l'étude de cette question*. Chacornac.
de Rochas, A. (no date circa 1914). *La suspension de la vie*. Dorbon-Ainé.
du Potet, Baron (1868). *Manuel de l'étudiant magnétiseur* (4th ed.). Germer Baillière.
du Prel, C. (1908). *La magie: Science naturelle* (Vol. 2). H. Vaillant. (Original work published 1899)
Durville, H. (1895–1896). *Traité expérimental de magnétisme* (2 vols.). Librairie du Magnétisme.
Durville, H. (1909). *Le fantôme des vivants: Anatomie et physiologie de l'âme: recherches expérimentales sur des dédoublement du corps de l'homme*. Librairie du Magnétisme.
Elliotson, J. (1848). Cure of a true cancer of the female breast with mesmerism. *Zoist, 6*, 213–237.
Encausse, G. [under the pseudonym of Papus] (1890). Le corps astral. *L'Initiation, 7*, 502–516.
Encausse, G. [under the pseudonym of Papus] (1897). *La Magie et l'hypnose: Recueil de faits et d'expériences justifiant et prouvant les enseignements de l'occultisme*. Chamuel.
Flammarion, C. (1907). *Mysterious psychic forces: An account of the author's investigations in psychical research, together with those of other European savants*. Small, Maynard.
Fodor, N. (no date). *Encyclopaedia of psychic science*. Arthurs Press.
Fugairon, L. S. (1907). *La Survivance de l'ame ou la mort et la renaissance chez les êtres vivantes: Études de physiologie et d'embryologie philosophiques*. Librairie du Magnétisme.
Gaillard, J. (1902). Monsieur de Rochas. *Revue Spirite: Journal d'Études Psychologiques, 45*, 418–419.
Gasc-Desfossés, E. (1897). *Magnétisme vital: Expériences récentes d'enregistrement, suivies d'inductions scientifiques et philosophiques*. Société d'Éditions Scientifiques.
Gauld, A. (1992). *A history of hypnotism*. Cambridge University Press.
Gaullieur, H. (1895). The wonder of hypnotism and the transfer of sensitiveness from man to inert substances. *Arena, 15*, 33–41.
Geley, G. (1927). *Clairvoyance and materialisation*. London: T. Fisher Unwin (Original work published 1924)
Girod, F. (1912). *Pour photographier les rayons humains: exposé historique et pratique de toutes les méthodes concourant à la mise en valeur du rayonnement fluidique humain*. Bliothèque Générale d'Éditions.
Harrington, A. (1988). Hysteria, hypnosis and the lure of the invisible: The rise of neo-mesmerism in fin-de-siècle French psychiatry. In W. F. Bynum, R. Porter, & M. Shepherd (Eds.), *The anatomy of madness: Essays in the history of psychiatry: The asylum and its psychiatry* (Vol. 3, pp. 226–246), Tavistock Press.
Harrison, W. H. (1878). Weighing a medium during the production of spiritual manifestations. *Spiritualist Newspaper*, May 3, 211–216.
Jahn, R. G., & Dunne, B. J. (2001). A modular model of mind/matter manifestations (M5). *Journal of Scientific Exploration, 15*, 299–329.
Judge, W. Q. (1893). *The ocean of theosophy* (2nd ed.). The Path.
Kardec, A. (1863). *Spiritisme expérimental: Le livre des médiums* (sixth edition). Didier.
Kelly, E. (2015). Parapsychology in context: The big picture. In E. Cardeña, J. Palmer, & D. Marcusson-Clavertz (Eds.), *Parapsychology: A handbook for the 21st century* (pp. 30–41). McFarland.
Krauss R. H. (1995). *Beyond light and shadow: The role of photography in certain paranormal phenomena: An historical survey*. Nazraeil Press.
Lachapelle, S. (2011). *Investigating the supernatural: From spiritism and occultism to psychical research and metapsychics in France, 1853–1931*. Johns Hopkins University Press.
Lefranc, L. (1911a). Les états du sommeil magnétique du fantôme du vivant ou corps ethérique. *Le Monde Psychique, 1*(2), 3–7.
Lefranc, L. (1911b). Cas fortuit de répercussion sur le corps physique d'une lésion produite sur le fantôme d'un sujet. *Le Monde Psychique, 1*(3), 84–88.
Lodge, O. J. (1894). Experience of unusual physical phenomena occurring in the presence of an entranced person (Eusapia Paladino). *Journal of the Society for Psychical Research, 6*, 306–336, 346–360.
Loureiro, C. B. (1998). *Perispírito: Natureza, funções e propriedades*. Mnêmio Tulio.

Luys, J. (1892). De la visibilité par les sujets en état hypnotique des effl uves dégagés par les êtres vivants. *Annales de Psychiatrie et d'Hypnologie dans Leurs Rapports avec la Psychologie et la Médicine Légale, 2*, 321–323.

Luys, [J.], & David, [E]. (1897). Note sur l'enregistrement photographique des effl uves qui se dégagent des extrémités des doigts et du fond de l'oeil de l'être vivant, a l'état physiologique et a l'état pathologique. *Comptes Rendus Hebdomadaires des Séances et Mémoires de la Société de Biologie, 4*(10), 515–519.

Mahan, A. (1855). *Modern mysteries explained and exposed in four parts*. Boston: J. P. Jewett.

Marzorati, A. (1914). Alberto de Rochas. *Luce e Ombra, 14,* 565–570.

Mead, G. R. S. (1919). *The doctrine of the subtle body in western tradition*. J. M. Watkins.

Méheust, B. (1999). *Somnambulisme et mediumnité (1784–1930): Volume 1: Le défi du magnétisme animal.* Institut Synthélabo pour de Progrès de la Connaissance.

Mesmer, F. A. (1779). *Mémoire sur la découverte du magnétisme animal.* Didot.

Montandon, R. (1927). *Les radiation humaines: Introduction à la démonstration expérimentale de l'existence des corps subtils de l'homme*. Félix Alcan.

Morselli, E. (1908). *Psicologia e "spiritismo:" Impressioni e note critiche sui fenomeni medianici di Eusapia Paladino* (2 vols.). Fratelli Bocca.

Moses, W. S. [under pseudonym M. A. Oxon] (1876). Photographing the spirit of a medium in Paris, while his body was asleep in London. *Spiritualist Newspaper*, March 5, 119.

Nahm, M. (2012). The sorcerer of Cobenzl and his legacy: The life of Baron Karl Ludwig von Reichenbach, his work and its aftermath. *Journal of Scientific Exploration, 26*, 381–407.

Ochorowicz, J. (1911–1912). Radiographies des mains (monographie expérimentale). *Annales des Sciences Psychiques*, *21*, 296–303, 334–341; *22*, 1–8.

Peter, J. (1915). Albert de Rochas. *Psychiche Studien, 42*, 97–99.

Poortman, J. J. (1978). *Vehicles of consciousness: The concept of hylic pluralism (Ochema)* (4 vols.). Theosophical Society in the Netherlands. (Original work published 1954)

Reichenbach, C. von (1851). *Physico-physiological researches on the dynamics of magnetism, electricity, heat, light, crystallization, and chemism, in their relation to vital force* (from German 2nd ed.). J. S. Redfield. (Original work published1849)

Reichenbach, Baron de (no date circa 1897). *Les effluves odiques*. Ernest Flammarion.

Roberts, J. M. (1876). Spirit–materializations in the light of common sense. *Banner of Light*, September 30, 1–2.

Rogers, E. C. (1853). *Philosophy of mysterious agents, human and mundane*. John P. Jewett.

Sabatier, A., de Rochas, A., de Gramont, A., Maxwell, J., Dariex, X., & de Watteville, C. (1896). Expériences de l'Agnelas sur Eusapia Paladino. *Annales des Sciences Psychiques, 6*, 1–55.

Schrenck-Notzing, A. F. (1920). *Physikalische phaenomene des mediumismus: Studien zur erforschung der telekinetischen vorgänge*. Ernst Reinhardt.

Servadio, E. (1932). Proofs and counter-proofs concerning human "fluid." *Journal of the American Society for Psychical Research, 26*, 168–173, 199–206.

Sidgwick, H. (1895). Eusapia Paladino. *Journal of the Society for Psychical Research, 7*, 148–159.

Sudre, R. (1926). *Introduction à la métapsychique humaine.* Payot.

Tardy de Montravel, A. A. (1785). *Essai sur le théorie du somnambulisme magnétique*. No publisher named.

Tart, C. T. (2009). *The end of materialism: How evidence of the paranormal is bringing science and spirit together*. New Harbinger Publications.

Thury, M. (1855). *Les tables tournantes: Considerées au point de vue de la question de physique générale qui s'y rattache.* J. Kessmann.

Ungaro, J. (1992). *Las radiaciones humanas: Historia de la radiónica.* Club de Estudio.

Vesme, C. (1898). La dimostrazione sperimentale dell'esistenza del corpo fluidico. *Rivista di Studi Psichici, 4*, 147–155, 175–182.

Von Hartmann, E. (1885). *Spiritism*. Psychological Press.

Walker, E. H. (1975). Foundations of paraphysical and parapsychological phenomena. In L. Oteri (Ed.), *Quantum Physics and Parapsychology* (pp. 1-44). Parapsychology Foundation.

Nineteenth Century Psychical Research in Mainstream Journals: *The Revue Philosophique de la France et de L'Étranger*[*]

Carlos S. Alvarado & Renaud Evrard[†]

While there were several psychical research journals operating during the nineteenth century, many interesting discussions about psychic phenomena also took place in a variety of intellectual reviews and scholarly and scientific journals of various disciplines. One such example was the French journal *Revue Philosophique de la France et de L'Étranger*, founded in 1876 by Théodule Ribot. Reflecting the various interests of psychologists during the nineteenth century, many topics were discussed in the Revue, among them hypnotic phenomena as well as mental suggestion and mediumship. The journal provided an important forum for French discussions in psychology and in the social sciences in general that helped the development of those disciplines. The same may be said about psychic phenomena, which were discussed in the pages of the *Revue* by authors such as Émile Boirac, Victor Egger, Théodore Flournoy, Jules Héricourt, Pierre Janet, Léon Marillier, Julian Ochorowicz, Charles Richet, and Albert Ruault. We present summaries of some of these writings which we hope will bring some of this material to the attention of non-French readers.

Much of the spread of psychical research and the dissemination of its results during the nineteenth century was due to such specialized journals as the *Annales des Sciences Psychiques*, the *Proceedings of the American Society for Psychical Research*, the *Proceedings of the Society for Psychical Research, Psychischen Studien*, and the *Rivista di Studi Psichici* (Alvarado, Biondi, & Kramer, 2006; Alvarado & Evrard, 2012). In fact—and as has been the case in other disciplines (Cantor & Shuttleworth, 2004)—such spread during the nineteenth century was assisted by the proliferation of numerous magazines, intellectual reviews, and scholarly and scientific journals which carried articles, book reviews, and news about the investigation of psychic phenomena.[1]

In this paper we present an overview of discussions of this topic in the well-known French journal *Revue Philosophique de la France et de l'Étranger*. Our purpose is to bring to the attention of English-language readers important bibliographical material relevant to the history of psychical research that is frequently neglected, most likely because of the language barrier.[2] It is our hope that this brief overview, which covers the nineteenth century period when the journal was most influential and contained many papers related to psychic phenomena, will help improve the situation. In addition, the paper is an outline of past developments in psychical research, mainly in France. We emphasize this journal not only because the material published in its pages about psychic phenomena is important and widely cited, but because the *Revue* was a significant influence on France's development in psychology and the social sciences in general.

[*]Republished with permission from *Journal of Scientific Exploration, 27*, 655–689, 2013.

[†]The first author is grateful for financial support provided by the Society for Psychical Research. Both authors would like to thank Massimo Biondi for suggestions for the improvement of this paper, and Lori Derr for helping us find a paper cited in our article.

The Conceptual Background

Magazines, Journals, and Psychic Phenomena

Psychical research received much publicity during the nineteenth century through articles in magazines and reviews. Some of these consisted of positive accounts, among them an influential group of articles authored by French astronomer and psychical researcher Camille Flammarion (1842–1925) in the *Annales Politiques et Littéraires*, discussing apparitions, telepathy, and mediumship (Flammarion, 1899). Such papers remind us that there were positive articles in intellectual reviews written by psychical researchers themselves. Some of the best-known in English were those written by prominent members of the Society for Psychical Research (SPR) in publications such as *Nineteenth Century* (Gurney & Myers, 1884), *Forum* (James, 1892), and elsewhere (Podmore, 1895). But many other papers, such as those appearing in the *Harper's New Monthly Magazine* (Jastrow, 1899), the *North American Review* (Minot, 1895), and the *Revue des Deux Mondes* (Paulhan, 1892) were negative discussions of the topic.

More relevant to the theme of the current paper were publications about psychical research in scholarly and scientific journals, a type of publication that carried many discussions about psychic phenomena, usually negative, during the nineteenth century. This included skeptical comments in journals such as the *Psychological Review* (Alvarado, 2009e), as well as Science (Cattell, 1898), the *American Journal of Psychology* (Hall, 1887), and *Nature* (Wells, 1894).

There were always exceptions to these negative views in important academic journals, as seen in William James's (1842–1910) open-minded and positive discussions of psychical research in two of the above-mentioned publications (e.g., James, 1896a, 1896b). Other exceptions were the articles of Cesare Lombroso (1835–1909) and others in the *Archivio di Psichiatria, Scienze Penali ed Antropologia Criminale* (Lombroso, 1891, 1896), a journal he edited and the pages of which he opened to psychic phenomena.[3] However, overall, most discussions in prominent academic journals tended to be negative. The *Revue* had its share of critical and skeptical material, but also contained many positive discussions and presentations of cases.

Psychic Phenomena in France

By the time the *Revue* was founded in 1876, much work had taken place in France in relation to psychic phenomena. As in other countries, there were many developments connected to movements such as mesmerism and spiritism. This was evident in French works discussing both movements from various perspectives, such as Bersot's *Mesmer et le Magnétisme Animal* (1864), and Blanc's *Le Merveilleux dans le Jansénisme, le Magnétisme, le Méthodisme et le Baptisme Américains, l'Epidémie de Morzine, le Spiritisme* (1865). The developments were narrated by physician, chemist, and popularizer of science Louis Figuier (1819–1894) in his *Histoire du Merveilleux dans les Temps Modernes* (1860), not to mention in many modern scholarly works.[4] Mesmerism in France, as documented in Dingwall's (1968) detailed discussion, was full of claims of psychic phenomena in mesmerized individuals. As stated by student of mesmerism J.P.F. Deleuze (1753–1835) in his *Histoire Critique du Magnétisme Animal*:

> Somnambules are more or less clairvoyant … they present various phenomena: but the faculty of seeing with the eyes closed, the intimate rapport with their magnetizer, the development of

> intellectual faculties, the sight of their interior, the prevision of their coming woes, almost always accompany their condition. Moreover, and this is extremely remarkable, most somnambules see and describe the fluid in the same way. (Deleuze 1813, p. 165–166; this, and other translations, are ours)

This fluid, conceptualized as animal magnetism, was at the center of the late French mesmeric movement which continued into the twentieth century (e.g., Chazarain & Declé, 1886, De Rochas, 1887; see also Alvarado, 2009b). There were also other phenomena, such as the claims of cures and of vision at a distance, making the mesmeric literature a veritable catalog of unexplained phenomena.

Many figures of later hypnosis literature were also interested in psychic phenomena (e.g., Carroy, 1991; Gauld, 1992). One example was physician Ambroise Auguste Liébeault (1823–1904), who influenced the Nancy school of hypnosis (Liébeault, 1889, part 2, Chapters 2–6, note C; see also Alvarado, 2009a). Another important figure, who we will discuss in more detail below, was physiologist Charles Richet (1850–1935), who conducted work in areas such as mental suggestion and clairvoyance (e.g., Richet, 1884, 1888b, 1889).

A similar catalog of unexplained phenomena, including a variety of physical manifestations and claims of communication with the dead, were part of spiritism, as seen in works such as Allan Kardec's (1860, 1863) famous books of spirits and of mediums.[5] In the latter work, Kardec considered many phenomena related to mediums, or individuals believed to be capable of being in contact with the deceased. This included verbal, visionary, and written mediumistic communications, but also the movement of objects, raps, apports, materializations, and direct writing. Spiritism became a popular topic of discussion during the nineteenth century (e.g., Bonnamy, 1868; Delanne, 1897). Probably the most popular manifestation associated with spiritism in France was the phenomenon of table turning, described by Figuier in the *Dictionnaire Universel des Connaissances Humaines* as: "Strange phenomena that occupy much of the public, as well as the savants" (Figuier, 1859, p. 289).[6]

A topic that attracted the attention of many was mental suggestion, which was discussed by Polish psychologist and philosopher Julian Ochorowicz (1850–1917) in his widely cited book *De la Suggestion Mentale* (1887). According to one author, mental suggestion was "the transmission of thought or sensations of an individual to another without perceptible exterior signs to our senses" (De Rochas, 1887, p. 372). The concept included the effects of drugs and medicine at a distance, a topic popularized by Bourru and Burot in their book *La Suggestion Mentale et l'Action à Distance des Substances Toxiques et Médicamenteuses* (1887b). Furthermore, mental suggestion was believed to involve the transmission of ideas, images, and thoughts, and the induction of trance and behaviors at a distance. Much work along similar lines was conducted outside France, by, among others, members of the SPR, who used the terms thought-transference and telepathy.[7]

Mental suggestion, like other psychic phenomena, was controversial. As stated by one commentator:

> Unfortunately, these facts are not conclusive. The vast majority of them leave room for multiple interpretations. Can they, however, all be explained by random or strange coincidences? The dominant view of contemporary psychologists and physiologists is certainly contrary to the existence of mental suggestion. (Yung, 1890, p. 94)

Both mesmerism and animal magnetism, not to mention occultism in general, were the subjects of many magazines and journals. Three of them published in France were the *Journal du Magnétisme* (started in 1845), the *Revue Spirite* (started in 1858), and *L'Initiation* (started in 1888). The Revue Spirite, edited in its beginnings by Kardec, presented much information in its pages about psychic phenomena, particularly summaries of cases discussed in the press and opinions about phenomena and other topics authored by supposed discarnate spirits communicating through mediums.

In 1874 the *Revue de Psychologie Expérimentale* began publication. The journal covered such varied topics as spiritualism, somnambulism, and hypnosis. It was edited by physician and botanist Timothée Puel (1812–1890), a pioneer of hypnotism who had published work on catalepsy (Puel, 1856). The journal was short-lived, stopping publication in 1876 (Lachapelle, 2011, p. 29–30).

In later years the *Annales des Sciences Psychiques* (which started in 1891) became the main publication of French psychical researchers (Alvarado & Evrard, 2012). Because psychic phenomena were considered controversial (e.g., Richet, 1892a), there were few mainstream journals that opened their pages to the topic in a positive way.[8]

The *Revue Philosophique de la France et de l'Étranger*

The Revue[9] was founded in 1876 by philosopher and psychologist Théodule Ribot (1839–1916), an important figure in late nineteenth century French psychology who insisted the field should be empirical, based on systematic observation and connected to physiological concepts (Ribot, 1879).[10] It is not well-known that Ribot also had a life-long scientific interest in psychic phenomena (Gumpper, 2013). Indeed, he was a corresponding member of the Society for Psychical Research from November 1886 to his death. Ribot was a close friend of Richet, and stood at his side during some attempts to institutionalize psychical research, and even participated in some in some experiments (Richet, 1888b, p. 70). He helped to bring discussion of this research to an academic level in France.[11]

Although the journal had the word *philosophy* in its title, its contents covered many disciplines. Thirard's (1976) analysis of 508 original articles published in the journal for the 1876–1890 period showed discussions of psychology (37%), history of philosophy (26%), philosophy, history of science, and logic (9%), sociology and human sciences (7%), metaphysics (7%), morality and philosophy of education (6%), esthetics (5%), and physiology (3%). While she argued that psychology was the most frequent topic when we consider esthetics, metaphysics, and other aspects of philosophy combined with other topics (morality, philosophy of science), philosophy needs to be considered at least on a par with psychology. Nonetheless, there is no question that psychology was a prominent topic in the journal.

Before the founding of *L'Année Psychologique* in 1894 (Nicolas, Segui, & Ferrand, 2000), the *Revue* was probably the main French forum for the publication papers of psychological topics. Other existing journals were either short-lived and of limited circulation (e.g., *Bulletin de la Société de Psychologie Physiologique*) or were too specialized (e.g., *Annales Medico-Psychologiques* and *Revue de l'Hypnotisme Expérimental & Thérapeutique*). In fact, it has been argued that the Revue "was the instrument of diffusion of French 'experimental' psychology; therefore it represents the main historiographical source to understand the characteristics of the rising psychological research in that country" (Foschi, 2003b, p. 46).

The first volume of the *Revue* included articles by such noted figures as Paul Janet (1823–1899), George H. Lewes (1817–1878), John Stuart Mill (1806–1873), Herbert Spencer (1820–1903), Hippolyte Taine (1828–1893), Eduard Von Hartmann (1842–1906), and Wilhelm Wundt (1832–1920). There were also many reviews of books published in a variety of languages.

French historian of psychology Serge Nicolas has argued that while the new generation of French psychologists followed an empirical approach that dominated the *Revue*, the dialogue between scientific and philosophical psychologists was kept open in the journal. Nicolas further argued that the journal was a contributing factor in the development of nineteenth century empirical psychology (Nicolas, 2002, p. 118). An important aspect was that the *Revue* was a forum for work on abnormal psychology and hypnotic phenomena that contributed to the development of the concepts of the subconscious mind and of dissociation.[12] While Ribot argued for methodological improvements to deal specifically with mental phenomena, others conducted the necessary research (for an overview, see Brower, 2010, p. 39–44).

An important figure in this task was Pierre Janet (1859–1947), who became well-known for his studies of hypnosis and dissociation in general.[13] Three of Janet's papers about phenomena such as automatic writing and state-specific memory in a small number of hypnotized mental patients published in the *Revue* were particularly important and influential (Janet, 1886a, 1887, 1888b). In the first work, which dealt with unconscious acts and the doubling of personality during hypnosis, Janet (1886a) wrote about a hysterical woman named Lucie, referred to as "L." in the article. Put into a somnambulistic (hypnotic) state during the middle of a conversation, L. stopped talking, but resumed the conversation when she awakened.

> The same phenomenon has taken place elsewhere in somnambulism. Once she goes back to sleep, L. continues sometimes the act began during the previous somnambulism. We could have as well two conversations very strangely interrupted and resumed, one during the waking states, the other during somnambulisms. (Janet, 1886a, p. 579)

Different personalities communicated through L.'s automatic writing, one which adopted the name Adrienne at Janet's suggestion. On other tests Janet found that L. could keep track of numbers in her somnambulistic state. These and other observations led Janet to believe that: "Evidently there exists in the head of L. important psychological operations outside of her normal consciousness" (Janet, 1886a, p. 586).

Also important was the work of Richet, who explored memory states and personality changes during hypnosis and published his findings and ideas in the *Revue* (Richet, 1880, 1883).[14] Richet stated that the hypnotized showed "a dissociation of their psychic elements" in which the "*self* is retained, while amnesia of personality is complete" (Richet, 1883, p. 233).

In addition to Janet and Richet, many other writers discussed the phenomena of hypnosis in the pages of the *Revue* (Beaunis, 1885; Bergson, 1886; Bernheim, 1885; Bourru & Burot, 1885; Delboeuf, 1886; Sauvaire, 1887). Hypnosis was seen by many in France as a tool to explore non-conscious levels of the mind, as well as the mind in general (e.g., Héricourt, 1889). As stated in the *Revue*: "Hypnotism constitutes … a genuine method of experimental psychology; it will be for the philosopher what vivisection is for the physiologist" (Beaunis, 1885, p. 1).

All of this work took place not only with hypnosis, but with the study of other phenomena. Outside the *Revue* there were many French explorations of various hysterical disturbances (Richer, 1885) and spontaneous dissociative episodes of different sorts such as the famous case of Félida X. (b. 1843) (Azam, 1887), among others (e.g., Bourru & Burot, 1888; Dufay, 1876; Guinon in collaboration with Bloq, Souques, & Charcot, 1893, p. Chapter 29). As others have noted, phenomena such as amnesia, somnambulism, and double and multiple personality cases, implying the idea of secondary states, were important in shaping parts of French psychology (Carroy & Plas, 1993; Foschi, 2003a).[15] It was part of a general belief that the pathological and the unusual could illuminate the formation of normal personality (e.g., Ribot, 1888).

As argued by Plas (2000), all this interest in non-conscious levels of the mind was not limited to amnesia, natural and induced (hypnotic) somnambulism, and secondary personalities. It also included what some referred to as psychic phenomena or what many in France referred to as the marvelous (e.g., Durand (de Gros), 1894; Figuier, 1860). All of this was discussed in the *Revue*.

Commenting about the *Revue*, Wilhelm Wundt stated that topics such as hypnosis, telepathy, and animal magnetism were discussed "not as if they were mere curiosities" (Wundt, 1905, p. 43). In fact, and as discussed below, the *Revue* was unusually open to the topic, which may have reflected Ribot's interests in unusual phenomena. He went on record at the Fourth International Congress of Psychology that "supernormal" phenomena were the "advanced, adventurous parts of experimental psychology, but not the less attractive" (Ribot, 1901, p. 46).

Psychic Phenomena in the *Revue*

Mental Suggestion

The most frequently discussed phenomenon in the *Revue* was mental suggestion. Richet (1884) authored an influential paper on this topic in the *Revue* in which he introduced statistical evaluation to the subject. His studies included guessing tasks of cards, photographs of statues, objects, and scenes, and tests in which motor responses were elicited using the dowsing rod and table turning. Richet concluded:

> The method that I have adopted is that of probabilities; it poses the problem thus: *Given an arbitrary designation whose probability is known; does the probability of this designation change by the fact of mental suggestion?* To this question our experiments allow us to reply affirmatively: For playing cards, the answer by chance should be 458, and it was 510 with suggestion on 1833 tests. For photographs and pictures, the probable number was 42, and the acquired number was 67 on 218 tests. For experiments with the dowsing rod, the probable number was 18, and the real number was 44 on 98 tests. For experiments called spiritistic, the probable number was 3, but the real number was 17 on 124 tests. The results acquired by the calculation of serial probability are more conclusive still. (Richet, 1884, p. 668–669).

Regarding the latter, Richet stated: "It is completely implausible that chance, on about 300 experiments, can give me so many times these remarkable series" (Richet, 1884, p. 669). Overall, he concluded that his results were not explained by chance. Paraphrasing Pascal, Richet wrote:

> *If it was necessary to opt for the reality or not reality of mental suggestion, I would let luck decide; but I would give two chances to the hypothesis that suggestion exists, and one chance only to the opposite hypothesis.* (Richet, 1884, p. 670, Richet's italics).

Assuming the reality of mental suggestion, Richet queried, would this mean that the phenomena would bring a "new era" to science? Not in his opinion. He believed the phenomenon "changes nothing in our actual knowledge about living or inert matter" (Richet, 1884, p. 671).

As discussed elsewhere (Alvarado, 2008), the article included other interesting topics such as the reanalysis of previously published telepathy studies and the relationship of mental suggestion to the unconscious mind. According to Richet, mental suggestion acted on the "unconscious faculties of intelligence" (Richet, 1884, p. 639). There was no awareness that a message had been received, but the information could find expression through means such as unconscious movements associated with dowsing and table tilting. But the tests and statistical analyses of mental suggestions were the aspects most widely cited in this paper, and the reason why this article is still remembered and cited today.[16]

But what may have been more influential to open parts of the academic French scene to mental suggestion were the famous attempts to induce trance and behavioral effects at a distance reported by Pierre Janet (1886b, 1886c), a phenomenon one author referred to as telepathic hypnotism (Myers, 1886d) and what the French called sleep or somnambulism induced at a distance. In two papers Janet reported tests conducted with Le Havre physician Joseph Gibert (1829–1899) in which he attempted to induce trance at a distance on Mme B., an alias for the famous subject/patient Léonie Leboulanger (b. 1837).[17]

This work was presented in meetings held at the Société de Psychologie Physiologique, which was founded in 1885, an event mentioned in the *Revue* (Société de Psychologie Physiologique de Paris 1885). The Société, which was presided over by neurologist Jean-Martin Charcot (1825–1893), and had the above-mentioned Ribot and philosopher Paul Janet as Vice-President and Richet as General Secretary, was devoted to various problems of psychology, among them those of psychical research (see Plas, 2000, p. 54–55).

Janet's first paper had a simple title merely referring to "some phenomena of somnambulism," while the second one referred to sleep induced at a distance and mental suggestion. We will use the published English translation of the two papers (Janet, 1886/1968a, 1886/1968b) and present several quotes from them.

In the first paper Janet (1886/1968a) reported observations made in 1885. He started by admitting that the phenomena were unusual and "far from being admitted [to] by all those who concern themselves with these questions" (1886/1968a, p. 124). Then he proceeded to describe his subject, Mme. B. (Léonie Leboulanger), whom he characterized as essentially a healthy countrywoman during her usual state, but who presented moments of somnambulism starting in childhood during which "she was able to speak of and describe the unique hallucinations that she experienced" (1886/1968a, p. 124). Janet described one of the tests conducted as follows:

> Without warning Mrs. B. of his intention, Dr. Gibert went into an adjoining room and placed himself six or seven meters from his subject. From this other room, he tried mentally to give her the order to sleep. I remained with the subject and noticed that after a few minutes her eyes closed and sleep began. But what seemed particularly strange to me was that in her lethargy she was not at all under my influence. I could not provoke in her either contracture or attraction, although I was in her presence when she went to sleep. On the other hand, she completely obeyed Dr. Gibert who was not present, and finally it was Dr. Gibert who had to awaken her. This proved that it was he who had to put her to sleep. (Janet, 1886/1968a, p. 127)

In another test Janet stated that he had visited Gibert in his office and asked him to suggest sleep to B., who was in another house 500 meters away. B. had never been affected in this way at this time of the day, something Janet mentioned to show he was aware of the influence of expectation. Janet went to see B. and said there had been no apparent effect. But he wrote that she said:

> I know that Dr. Gibert wanted to put me to sleep … but when I felt it coming I found some cold water and put my hands in it … I did not want him to put me to sleep this way … I could have been talking to someone and that would disturb me and make me appear stupid … (Janet, 1886/1968a, p. 127).

On another occasion Janet repeated the same test, going to Gibert's place once again, and this time B. was asleep. "The sleep was not a natural one because she was completely insensible, and one could not awaken her" (Janet, 1886/1968a, p. 128).

Gibert also suggested some complicated acts to be performed:

> These acts were evidently too complicated to be executed, but at the exact moment when Dr. Gibert ordered her to do them from Graville, I saw with my own eyes the effect that these commands produced at a distance of 2 kms and a real beginning of their execution. It really seemed that Mrs. B. could somehow sense these orders, that she had resisted them, and that she was only able to disobey when Dr. Gibert was in some way distracted. (Janet, 1886/1968a, p. 129).

In another test, silent suggestions were given from close by. Gibert mentally suggested to B. by bringing his forehead close to B.'s. He silently willed her to lock the doors of the house at 12 o'clock the next day. According to Janet:

> The next day, when I arrived at a quarter to twelve, I found the house gates closed and the door locked. I found out that it was Mrs. B. who had closed them. When I asked her why she had done this strange thing, she answered in the following way: "I felt very tired and I didn't want you to enter the house, and put me to sleep." (Janet, 1886/1968a, p. 130)

Janet seemed to be open-minded about the phenomena he observed. But he stated he had no explanations for his results.

The report of the tests continued in the second paper (Janet, 1886/1968b). Once again, Janet attempted a distant test from his office separated from B. by four or five hundred meters. Janet was dubious of the result of the test. He wrote:

> To my great astonishment, the people in the house warned me that Mrs. B. had been extremely indisposed for about an hour. She had been overtaken by fatigue and forced to interrupt her housework. In order to pull herself together, she had had to drink a glass of water and wash her hands and face. Mrs. B. herself told me of her indisposition, which she was unable to explain. (Janet, 1886/1968a, p. 259).

In another distant test when Janet went to B.'s place he found her "stretched out on a sofa in a very deep sleep" (Janet, 1886/1968a, p. 260). Several tests seem to have been failures and some partial successes. Janet further wrote:

> On the 14th of April I put her to sleep without touching her, but at the time I was in the same room with her. On the 18th, which was a Sunday, I was alone and ... I tried to put her to sleep from my place. I was completely successful. She was asleep 10 minutes after I began to think of putting her to sleep. On Monday, the 19th, my uncle, Dr. Paul Janet,[18] had just arrived at Le Havre. I wanted first of all to show him the somnambule before trying any experiments. He preferred, with no one being warned, to ask Dr. Gibert to immediately put her to sleep from his place. Caught unaware, Dr. Gibert tried to do this at 4 o'clock. We found Mrs. B. completely asleep at 4, p. 15. On the 20th, a Tuesday, Dr. Gibert put her to sleep from a distance, this time at 8 o'clock in the evening in front of Dr. Paul Janet and made her come to his place using mental suggestion. (Janet, 1886/1968a, p. 262).

Another test took place involving Janet's brother, Dr. Jules Janet (1861–1945).[19] This time Gibert willed B. to sleep and to come to his place.

> A few minutes after nine, Mrs. B. abruptly left her house. She was not wearing any hat, and her walk was rather precipitated. I went up to her and saw that her eyes were completely closed and that she showed all the signs which I knew to be typical of her somnambulistic state. She avoided all obstacles

> with a dexterity that reassured me but it took her quite a long time to recognize me. At the beginning she avoided me and stated that she did not want to be accompanied. After about 200 meters, she knew who I was, and seemed pleased with my presence. However, several times, I was rather frightened by the hesitation of her walk. She would stop and balance back and forth as if she was going to fall. I was afraid she might quickly enter into a period of lethargy or catalepsy which would have made the trip very difficult. This did not occur. She pulled herself together and arrived without any further difficulty. She had barely arrived when she fell into an armchair in a very profound state of lethargy. This lethargy was only interrupted for a moment by a period of somnambulism in which she murmured: "I came … I saw Dr. Janet … I thought it would be better if I didn't take the rue d'Étretat, there were too many people … (She had taken another street on her own volition.) A man threw himself in front of me … He said that I was blind, how stupid of him …," and she remained asleep for a long time. Later she again fell into a somnambulistic state and said that she had felt a great deal of fatigue and hesitation during the trip. She believed that this was due to the fact that Dr. Gibert had not thought continually enough of making her come. She had fallen asleep, as I was told afterwards, several minutes before 9 o'clock, that is to say the hour Dr. Gibert had thought of, but she began her walk only 5 or 6 minutes later. (Janet, 1886/1968a, p. 265–266).

Several tests took place in the presence of other observers, such as physician Arthur T. Myers (1851–1894), classical scholar and psychical researcher Frederic W.H. Myers (1843–1901), student of religion Léon Marillier (1862–1901), and the above-mentioned Julian Ochorowicz. These have been described elsewhere in more detail (Myers, 1886d; Ochorowicz, 1887, p. 121ff).

Summarizing his work with Gibert, Janet stated that out of 22 experiments, 16 were successful and six were failures. In the second paper, as in the first, Janet did not offer any theoretical explanations for the reported effects. He merely finished the article by saying: "One must continue to gather facts which are more precise and more numerous on this delicate subject which is as interesting to psychology as it is to physiology" (Janet, 1886/1968a, p. 267).[20]

Janet's papers were very influential in late nineteenth century psychical research, cited by many inside and outside of France (e.g., Gurney, Myers, & Podmore, 1886, Vol. 2, p. 679–682; Ochorowicz, 1887, p. 118; Paulhan, 1892, pp. 71–72; Senillosa, 1891, pp. 256–260). This work, particularly that reported in the first paper, opened the door to the publication of similar cases in the *Revue* by other authors, accounts that were also presented in the meetings of the Société de Psychologie Physiologique. Both Richet and physician Jules Héricourt (1850–1938) reported on old observations they made in the 1870s (Héricourt, 1886; Richet, 1886a). Richet (1886a) commented: "If, therefore, the phenomenon exists—and I think it is difficult to deny it absolutely—it is extremely rare, and occurs only in special circumstances which so far elude scientific determination" (p. 200).

Héricourt (1886) described his case as consisting of observations of a 24-year-old woman of Spanish origin who was a widow and mother of a five-year-old, of dark complexion, and with no discernible hysterical problem. As he wrote about his attempts to induce trance using mental suggestion, the first test was successful after a period of ten minutes in which he looked at her and held her thumbs.[21] "Subsequently, the same result was obtained, either only by looking at or touching the head or the hand for barely a few seconds, and then finally, by even less …" (Héricourt, 1886, p. 201; for more information about this case, see Héricourt, 1931).

Others reported various observations as well to the Société (Beaunis, 1886; Dufay, 1888; Gley, 1886; Richet, 1888a). However, these reports were not as systematic as those authored by Janet.

Furthermore, many commented about these phenomena. In an essay review about publications on "mental suggestion and mental action at a distance" Marillier concluded:

> Apparent mental suggestion is a dialogue between the subject's unconscious and the unconscious of the experimenter and the greatest service that these new studies can make is to attract the attention of psychologists on a class of phenomena where we can find the solution of a good number of problems which confuse very much the science of the mind. (Marillier, 1887, p. 422).

Ochorowicz (1886) listed several variables that needed to be controlled in order to obtain acceptable evidence for mental suggestion. Among them were chance, involuntary verbal and other forms of suggestion, and hyperesthesia of the senses. But he affirmed the existence of the phenomena and listed disease, pain, objective sensations, feelings, ideas, and well as things that could be transmitted from one person to another.

On the skeptical side, physician Albert Ruault (1850–1928) assumed that sensory unconscious communication explained the phenomena (Ruault 1886). He believed that, "In general, the experiences of mental suggestion are much more successful when the hypnotist is in the presence of the subject than when he is away at some distance" (Ruault, 1886, p. 396). But he did not satisfactorily address the issue of distance in tests such as those of Janet and Gibert. In his view, "The thought of the hypnotizer doing the mental suggestion is manifested thanks to his interior word [thoughts], which is always accompanied by movements ..." (p. 687). Given this, Ruault argued, "The movements are perceived unconsciously by the subject, whose sensory hyper acuity is then extreme" (p. 687). He suggested that this hyperacuity could include the hypnotist's pulse rate, which accelerates when an effort of mental will is done. "Is it not therefore reasonable to assume that vasomotor phenomena, or other of our unknown signs may be unconsciously perceived by the subject, and produce in him these vague sensations which he attributes in effect to a personal influence of the hypnotist?" (p. 693).[22]

Effects of Drugs and Medicines

Another line of research was the work of physicians Henri Bourru (1840–1914) and Prosper Burot (1849–1888), who were well-known for their claim that patients were able to show the effect of medicines and drugs when they were presented to the patients without mention of their physiological properties (Bourru & Burot, 1887a, 1887b). Both these authors & Richet discussed the topic in the *Revue* (Bourru & Burot, 1886; Richet, 1886b). Bourru & Burot (1886) asked if it was possible to induce "by a simple external application, the physiological action" (p. 313) of drugs and medicine on research subjects.

In one case, a hysterical patient had a piece of opium wrapped in paper put on his head, after which he closed his eyes, relaxed his muscles, and fell asleep. "On repeating the experience by changing the place of application: on the front, the neck, the left or right side of the head, the h&, and [up] to the soles of the feet, the effect is always the same" (Bourru & Burot, 1886, p. 313).

It was also observed that when "A vial of atropine is put in contact with the sole of the foot; after three seconds, the subject remains motionless, the eyes open; soon the eyelids will close, the eyes convulse, and after a few moments the pupils dilate. There is photophobia while awake" (Bourru & Burot, 1886, p. 314).

In another test they used two packets prepared by a colleague without knowing their content. They wrote: "The first produced sleep, with yawning and nausea while awake: It contained opium. The second produced an intolerable burn: It was a mercury salt. We consider this experience is of very great importance" (Bourru & Burot, 1886, p. 315).

The authors were aware of critiques such as that the subjects could perceive smells of the substances or that they could learn from the experimenters what effects to produce, objections they rejected. In a comment following the paper, Richet (1886b) was worried about smells perceived by the subjects and commented on expectation and the possibility of mental suggestion, as opposed to the direct action of drugs (such as the idea of vibrations emanating from the drugs and medicine, favored by Bourru and Burot (1887b, p. 254). He ended by suggesting that future researchers should conduct tests while the experimenter did not know the nature of the substance used and that the results should be evaluated directly from the symptoms presented. In addition, he suggested the use of a limited number of substances, listing four possible candidates. He pointed out that in that case the probability of making an accurate diagnosis was one out of four, so after a few tests it could be evaluated "if one has a better diagnosis than could [be] given by chance" (Richet, 1886b, p. 323).

Other Hypnotic Phenomena

In addition to Ruault, others discussed the hyperacuity of the senses in the hypnotized (Bergson, 1886; Sauvaire, 1887). But one of the most interesting hypnotic phenomena was that of transfer, which took place mainly within the Salpêtrière school of hypnosis and generated many controversies (Nicolas, 2004).[23] As seen in a *Revue* paper by Alfred Binet (1857–1911) and Charles Féré (1852–1907), this consisted of the "transfer" of sensory and motor phenomena (e.g., hallucinations, paralysis) from one side of the body to another through the application of magnets (Binet & Féré, 1885). Their subjects were generally hysterical patients who were hypnotized.

The authors presented several examples of this transfer, such as the following with the famous hysteric/hypnosis subject Blanche Wittman (b. 1859):[24]

> Wit … is in a state of somnambulism, sitting on a chair. We suggested to her to scratch the arm of the chair with the left index [finger]; the magnet was applied at some distance from the right hand, and then we woke the patient. The movement still existed on the left, but if slightly, so that the patient did not see it. At the end of 30 seconds, the two indexes were beginning to fiddle slightly; the movement was growing to the right, while it decreased to the left. The transfer was complete at the end of a minute. (Binet & Féré, 1885, p. 8).

In another test, the same patient was hypnotized and was suggested to write numbers with her right hand. "We woke her; a magnet was hidden in the vicinity of her left hand. She wrote up to the number twelve with the right hand, and then she hesitated, changed the hand with the pen, and began to write with the left hand" (p. 10). The numbers were correctly written in reverse from left to right and the left hand made similar movements to those of the right hand. This was considered to be evidence that the magnet induced a transfer. "It should be pointed out that while she writes with her left hand, it is impossible to write with the right hand, she became left-handed with her right hand" (p. 10).

Binet and Féré believed that the magnet produced the transfer, being "the great modifier of the nervous system" (p. 16). In their view, they had accounted for suggestion and expectations in different ways.

In later work reported in the *Revue*, physician J.J.F.F. Babinski (1857–1932) extended transfer phenomena beyond the patient's body (Babinski, 1886). Instead of transfers from one side of the body to another, the phenomena was reported to take place from one person to another. This work was continued by others in work published elsewhere (Luys and Encausse, 1890).

Of course, transfer demonstrations brought criticism from those such as Hippolyte Bernheim (1840–1919), who believed that suggestion, rather than the physical action of the magnet, explained the experiments of Binet and Féré (Bernheim 1885). "Among no hypnotized … have I seen any transfer produced *by the single application of the magnet, before the idea of the phenomenon had entered their brain*" (p. 312).[25]

As was to be expected, members of the Salpêtrière School did not pay much attention to these objections. An example was physician Paul Richer's (1849–1933) review of a book by Binet and Féré (1887) published in the *Revue* (Richer 1887).

Mediumship

Swiss psychologist Théodre Flournoy (1854–1920) authored an important paper on mediumship in which he presented two cases of mediumistic communications that were interpreted to be the "product of the subconscious imagination of the medium, working with recollections and latent worries" (Flournoy, 1899, p. 144). This was the beginning of Flournoy's (1900b, 1911) well-known psychological analyses of mental mediumship.[26]

Flournoy argued that his cases represented subliminally-produced romances by means of the mediums' memories and of a "curious faculty of dramatization and personification" (p. 157).[27] Furthermore, Flournoy concluded that in some normal persons, the practice of mediumship may disturb their mental balance and "engender an automatic activity [whose] results simulate in the most complete way communications coming from the beyond, although in reality they are but the result of the subliminal workings of ordinary faculties of the subject" (pp. 157–158).[28]

In an early paper Pierre Janet stated: "All suggestions must be accompanied by some degree of unconsciousness or instead … by some doubling of consciousness. All the phenomena of spiritism that are frequent are but the development of analogous facts" (Janet, 1886a, p. 592). Janet developed these ideas further in other publications and returned to the topic in a later paper in the *Revue* in which he presented remarks about mediumship and spiritist publications.[29]

In this paper Janet (1892) argued that spiritists had neglected the psychological study of mediums. On the other hand, he credited them for bringing a useful technique to the attention of students of the mind.[30] "We persist in believing," wrote Janet (1892, p. 413), "that spiritists were the first to bring attention to subconscious movements and to the manifestations … of mental disaggregation."[31] He had written in the *Revue* years before that automatic writing was a "method of psychological analysis," the means to "penetrate further into the thought of somnambules" (Janet, 1887, p. 452).

In his view, both mediums and hysterics displayed a "serious problem in the mental operation of perceptions" indicative of "psychological disaggregation" (Janet, 1892, p. 419). Some of them, Janet pointed out, showed lack of sensibility in their right side while doing automatic writing. Nonetheless, Janet did not think that mediums were always hysterics. He observed a case of somnambulism and automatic writing that did not show hysteria, but presented fixed ideas, doubts, and insanity. In such cases he considered "mental disaggregation as a disease larger than hysteria that may manifest through hysterical symptoms but that may also manifest in other forms" (p. 424).

Mediumship was also discussed in a review of a book by Flournoy authored by magnetizer and psychical researcher Colonel Albert de Rochas (1837–1914; De Rochas, 1900; see also Flournoy, 1900a). There were also reviews of books that featured the mediumship of Eusapia Palladino (1854–1918; Boirac, 1897) and Henry Slade (1835–1905; Review of *La Physique Transcendentale* 1880).

Near-Death Experiences and Panoramic Memory

Two papers by French philosopher Victor Egger (1848–1909) on "the self of the dying" focused on panoramic memory[32] (Egger, 1896a, 1896b). Egger postulated that being close to death produced in the experiencer a "live self," consisting of "significant and rapid images" (1896a, p. 37). A sudden threat of death, he believed, could trigger "concepts and propositions" (p. 30) related to the person's mortality.

His discussion was followed by other articles and notes in which other cases and theoretical discussions were presented. Two readers of the *Revue* presented further cases of panoramic memory (Keller, 1896; Moulin, 1896). Other ideas were discussed by French physicians Paul August Sollier

(1861–1933) and Charles Féré. Sollier (1896) speculated instead that the panoramic images were caused by an effort to escape death and a loss of bodily sensibility. Egger (1896b) was critical of Sollier's physiological ideas and argued that the idea of imminent death was actually the "necessary condition for the phenomena" to take place (p. 343). Féré (1898) also argued for a physiological explanation of memories. In his view they were caused by "a momentary hyper-excitability of the nervous elements …" (p. 302).

Critical Views

As mentioned before, some papers were critical of the phenomena or attempted to present conventional explanations for them such as sensory cues (Bergson, 1886; Ruault, 1886) and suggestion (Bernheim, 1885).

The reviewer of a book by British physician William B. Carpenter (1813–1885) considered the phenomena of mesmerism and spiritualism to be absurd, and expressed his belief that scientific education would decrease belief in the "marvelous" (Levoix, 1877, p. 443). On the other hand, historian of physiological psychology Jules Soury (1842–1915) reviewed Wundt's critical ideas about spiritism and Hermann Ulrici's (1806–1884) views, as well as the latter's reply, publications presenting negative and positive views about spiritualistic phenomena, respectively (Soury, 1879).

Frederic Paulhan (1856–1931), a librarian at Nimes, did not review serious psychical research work, but was critical of superstitions and the claims of spiritism. In his view, some spiritistic manifestations could be explained by recourse to the "beautiful experiences of M. Pierre Janet [showing] that the doubling of the mind of the medium is the only real cause" (Paulhan, 1890, p. 495).

A stronger critic, P. Rosenbach (1892), referred to psychical research as an example of "modern mysticism." In his view, the Society for Psychical Research tried to "demonstrate the possibility of a supernatural and spiritual rapport between men …" (p. 156). Such an approach contrasted to what Rosenbach considered to be the far more scientific approach of psychophysics and "scientific experimental psychology." He believed that when psychic phenomena were examined scientifically they lost their mysterious, "mystical" character.

Richet (1892b) replied to Rosenbach, pointing out that he was wrong in thinking that psychical researchers embraced the concept of the supernatural. Furthermore, Richet stated that Rosenbach misrepresented the goal of psychical research and that he had a narrow view of science.

Other Topics

French philosopher Émile Boirac (1851–1917), once chancellor of the Académie de Grenoble and of the Université de Dijon, discussed what he referred to as "cryptoid" phenomena, or phenomena at the margins of science. In his view, science should be able to find truth and grow conceptually, and eventually "recognize the reality of certain phenomena that it has considered before to be imaginary and chimeric …" (Boirac, 1899, p. 51).

The above-mentioned English classical scholar and psychical researcher Frederic W.H. Myers authored two notes on veridical hallucinations (Myers, 1886a, 1886b), a topic studied by researchers connected to the London-based SPR (Gurney, Myers, & Podmore, 1886). The phenomenon was defined as hallucinations that "without having a material reality, correspond nevertheless to real fact, that has determined, by a process as yet unknown, the moment and the nature of such hallucination" (Myers, 1886a, p. 214). Myers wrote:

> A large number of observations ... were collected, in which the hallucination of A coincided exactly with the disease or the death of B. In most cases collected by us:
>
> 1. There has never been any other hallucination;
> 2. Neither death nor the disease of B were likely;
> 3. The death and disease of B could not be known to A. (Myers, 1886a, p. 214–215)

Furthermore, aspects of the work of the Society were reviewed in a discussion of Gurney, Myers, and Podmore's *Phantasms of the Living* (1886) (Marillier, 1887) and in a note about the Society's further work on hallucinations (Society for Psychical Research, 1889). There were also short summaries of the content of the *Proceedings* of the Society (Review of Proceedings, 1883, 1884a, 1884b).

A few other topics deserve mention. Among these are a discussion of Marian apparitions reported in Dordogne in 1889 (Marillier, 1891) and, following the old French tradition of animal magnetism, ideas of "odic" and "neuric" forces, and what de Rochas called the exteriorization of sensibility and motricity (Boirac, 1896, 1897; Janet, 1888a; Lechelas, 1887; Société de Psychologie Physiologique, 1890).[33]

Concluding Remarks

We have summarized the nineteenth century content of the *Revue* relevant to the study of psychic phenomena. While the journal still carried relevant publications in later years (e.g., Boirac, 1911; Janet, 1923), there were many more discussions of psychic phenomena during the nineteenth century. This is consistent with the view (seen from many studies) that the nineteenth century was a particularly important period for the topic in terms of research and methodological developments as well as the formation of the first institutions and journals (e.g., Alvarado, Biondi & Kramer, 2006; Gauld, 1968; Lachapelle, 2011).

The Revue included much material in support of specific phenomena such as mental suggestion. But like other publications it also had its share of critical outlooks and outright rejection of specific claims and ideas. In this way the *Revue* was not much different from more specialized publications such as the *Proceedings of the Societ0y for Psychical Research.*

The Revue was also different from most academic journals—from France or from other countries—in that it regularly opened its pages to psychic phenomena. Perhaps this reflected both the interest of the times in the subconscious mind and unusual mental phenomena in France. This, as argued by others (e.g., Carroy, 1991; Plas, 2000) included psychic phenomena, but the majority of the efforts focused on dissociation in general, and more specifically on the variety of sensory-motor manifestations of hysteria and hypnosis.[34]

This interest in mental phenomena may explain the lack of papers about physical phenomena in the *Revue*. There were, however, brief mentions of the topic in comments about published works (e.g., Boirac, 1897; Janet, 1892).

The critical views of Paulhan and Rosenbach may suggest a change in the openness of the *Revue* to psychical research. Whereas since Richet's 1884 article, many issues of the Revue contained studies on controversial phenomena of hypnotism and psychical research, in 1890 we find only Paulhan's article about the new mysticism and Binet's review of *L'Automatisme Psychologique* of Janet (Binet, 1890), a book without his most "disturbing" experiments in Le Havre, yet positively received by many at the time. In 1892, Janet published his critical article on "contemporary spiritism," showing a skeptical view that was not evident in his previous reports of experimental studies on mental suggestion.

It seems that, with some exceptions, the wave of interest and openness about this topic inside the *Revue* extends primarily from Richet's 1884 article to Marillier's 1889 review of the First International Congress of Physiological Psychology. We have few clues to understand this change, which is exemplified by Janet. It may be speculated that the 1889 Congress marked the beginning of the failure of the integrative and eclectic strategy of the founders of the Société de Psychologie Physiologique. At this event, presided over by Ribot, questions of psychology, hypnotism, and psychical research were intertwined, as they were in the *Revue*. But the discussion of hypnosis and related topics at the 1889 congress received some criticisms, particularly in Germany (Sidgwick, 1892, p. 284).[35] Ribot, who derived part of his legitimacy from his promotion of the German positivist model of psychology (Ribot, 1879), may have found himself stuck. The *Revue*, like Janet, seems to have eventually made the choice to side with the psychological orthodoxy.

The Société de Psychologie Physiologique severely declined after the 1889 Congress. Both Wolf (1993) and Plas (2000) indicate that it was Richet's emphasis on the "marvelous" that alienated Charcot and caused his lack of support of this society. Indeed, it was this society which brought initial openness to psychical research in France. Its meetings and *Bulletin* provided a forum for discussions of mental suggestion which were also published in the *Revue* (e.g., Gley, 1886; Héricourt, 1886). It was not until 1900 that a similar dynamic developed at the Institut Général Psychologique (Brower, 2010, Chapter 3). Meanwhile, the *Annales des Sciences Psychiques* was founded in 1891 as a new forum of discussion (Alvarado & Evrard, 2012). But while the *Annales* was an important specialized journal representing organized French psychical research, it was not a mainstream resource.

One of the topics that could have been discussed further here is the reception of the work mentioned. While a detailed study of this is beyond the scope of the present paper, it is an important topic that deserves further consideration in order to understand the impact of the material published in the *Revue*. While this paper has not studied this in detail, it is apparent that the importance of the *Revue* gave much visibility to the articles in question. We have already presented references to citations of Janet's (1886b, 1886c) research about the induction of trance at a distance. Similarly, the paper published by Richet (1884) about mental suggestion became a new representative of the scientific interest in psychic phenomena at the time, as seen in studies about developments in France (e.g., Plas, 2000). But there were also citations of this work in many other publications beyond the French context (e.g., Gurney, 1884).

A case could also be made about the impact and frequent citation of other papers mentioned. This includes articles about hypnotic transfer phenomena (Binet & Féré, 1885), mediumistic communications (Flournoy, 1899), and spiritism and the psychological study of mediums (Janet, 1892).

Depending on the reader's interest, the material reviewed here will serve different purposes. Those interested in the reality of psychic phenomena will use these materials to assess the evidential value of the old work. In contrast, those interested in the historical aspects of psychical research will see these papers and book reviews as examples of important primary sources for the study of nineteenth century psychical research. From either perspective—and perhaps from the perspective of those interested in both views—there is no question that the Revue is an important source of information for the study of nineteenth century psychical research, particularly in France.

Notes

1 There were also many books published during the nineteenth century in which authors presented observations of phenomena as well as theoretical concepts (e.g., Aksakof, 1895; Gyel, 1899; Gurney, Myers & Podmore, 1886; Ochorowicz, 1887). Some overviews of psychical research included those by Coste (1895) and Podmore (1897). We will not consider here discussions of psychical research in newspapers (e.g., Alvarado, 2007).

2 A possible example of this is that references to Richet's (1884) important paper about ESP and its statistical evaluation published in the Revue, and discussed below, generally rely on secondary English-language sources (e.g., Irwin & Watt, *2007*, p. 49; Radin, 2006, p. 64).

3 Between 1896 and 1898 this journal had a section entitled "Hypnotic and Mediumistic Research," which was devoted mainly to psychic phenomena. In later years the section was called "Mediumship."

4 Crabtree (1993) presents an overview of some of these developments. On French work see Brower (2010), Carroy (1991), Dingwall (1967/1968), Edelman (1995), Lachapelle (2011), Meheust (1999a, 1999b), Monroe (2008), Plas (2000), and Sharp (2006). See also various general books about psychic phenomena and spiritism published in France during the late nineteenth century (e.g., Coste, 1895; Delanne, 1897; Erny, 1895; Gibier, 1887).

5 Spirits of the dead were also claimed to be seen in the visions of magnetic somnambules (Alvarado, 2009c; for an overview see Crabtree, 1993, p. 196–212). Allan Kardec was the pseudonym of educator Hippolyte Léon Denizard Rivail (1804–1869). For information about him see the detailed study by Wantuil and Thiesen (1984) and the more recent writings of Edelman (1995), Monroe (2008), and Sharp (2006).

6 Wantuil (n.d.) has presented a detailed study of table turning that is not well-known outside Brazil (see also Figuier 1860, Vol. 4, and Monroe, 2008, Chapter 1). Some examples of French writings on the topic by scientists include Arago (1854, p. 456–458), Babinet (1854), and Chevreul (1854). Perhaps the best-known work on table turning is by De Gasparin (1854).

7 Plas (2000, p. 87–109) presents an overview of French work on mental suggestion (see also Caratelli, 1996, Chapter 7). Additional examples of discussions on the topic published in France include Alliot (1886), Féré (1887, Chapter 18), Liébeault (1889, note c), and Paulhan (1892). The nineteenth century work of the SPR on the topic is summarized by Podmore (1894; see also Luckhurst 2002).

8 For some exceptions, see Bourru and Burot (1887a), Lombroso (1891), and Luys (1886).

9 Nineteenth century issues of the *Revue* are freely available online in Gallica (http://gallica.bnf.fr/), Google Books (http://books.google.com/), and in the Hathi Trust Digital Library (http://www.hathitrust.org/). On the journal see Meletti Bertolini (1991), Mucchielli (1998), Nicolas (2002, p. 113–118), and Thirard (1976).

10 On Ribot see Brooks III (1998, Chapter 2), Guillin (2004), Nicolas (2002, p. 104–118), and Nicolas and Murray (1999).

11 Ernesto Bozzano (1862–1943) credited Ribot with getting him interested in psychical research, having sent him an issue of the *Annales des Sciences Psychiques* (Bozzano, 1924). Historian of Italian psychical research Massimo Biondi believes that Bozzano's memory may be faulty about this (Personal communication to CSA, 2/29/2012). This is consistent with other early problematic autobiographical recollections of Bozzano (Iannuzzo, 1983).

12 On this general interest in France see Alvarado (2010), Carroy (1991), Crabtree (1993), Foschi (2003a, 2003b), Gauld (1992), Hacking (1995), and Nicolas (2002).

13 Janet has been discussed by many authors (e.g., Carroy & Plas, 2000; Crabtree, 1993, Chapter 15; Ellenberger, 1970, Chapter 6; Foschi, 2003b). On Janet and psychic phenomena see Kopell (1968) and Le Maléfan (1999, p. 66–84). Carbonel (2008) discusses Janet in the context of the psychical research movement.

14 Gauld (1992, p. 298–302) has summarized Richet's hypnosis work. Wolf (1993) discusses his life and his scientific and scholarly work. For his psychical research see Alvarado (2008), Brower (2010, Chapter 4), Le Maléfan (1999, p. 85–88, 273–278), and Tabori (1972, p. 98–132).

15 Many 19th century authors reviewed the topic in publications appearing in France, among them Héricourt (1889), Laurent (1892), and Liégeois (1889, Chapter 9). Probably the best-known French work on secondary states was Janet's widely cited L'Automatisme Psychologique (1889).

16 For discussions of this paper in the *Revue* see Lechelas, Tannery, and Richet (1885). Richet's paper was discussed in many publications appearing in France (e.g., Gilles de la Tourette, 1889, p. 166–167; Ochorowicz, 1887, p. 65–69), and in other countries (e.g., Franklin, 1885; Gurney, 1884). Recent citations of the paper include Irwin and Watt (2007, p. 49) and Radin (2006, p. 64).

17 For earlier examples of this phenomenon in the mesmeric literature, see Burdin and Dubois (1841, p. 415–416) and Esdaile (1852, p. 227). Janet's papers have been translated into English (Janet, 1886/1968a, 1886/1968b). Gibert's work as a physician is discussed by Carbonel (2006). On Leboulanger see Richet's studies (1888a, 1888b, p. 32–42, 1889, p. 67–83) and Gauld's overview (1996). Plas (2000, p. 107–109) has discussed the dual role Leboulanger played in France as a subject of psychological and psychic experimentation.

18 Paul Janet was a well-known and influential philosopher. He presented Pierre's first mental suggestion paper at the Société de Psychologie Physiologique (Ochorowicz, 1887, p. 118).

19 Pierre's brother was a physician who was also interested in dissociation and hysteria (e.g., Janet, 1888). He was a urologist and published works on the subject (e.g., Janet, 1890).

20 Years later, Janet (1930) wrote in his autobiography that the tests had never seemed conclusive to him. He referred to the multiple citations of his work as an "abuse of my former observations" (p. 126). Janet was amazed that these authors did not ask his opinion of the matter.

> I should have answered that already at that time, and even more so now, I doubted the interpretation of the facts and was disposed to criticize them myself, regarding them as a simple departure from more profound studies." (Janet, 1930, p. 126).

Janet may have later seen this work as a "simple departure from more profound studies," but if put in the context of the times it may be argued, as Plas (2000) has done, that mental suggestion had clear conceptual connections to the study of the subconscious mind emphasized by Janet in his early work (Janet, 1886a, 1887, 1888b, 1889); see also Myers (1886d) and Richet (1884) for connections between mental suggestion and the subconscious. Mental suggestion was a manifestation of the subconscious mind in the eyes of many at the time. Consequently, we should be skeptical of Janet's later attempt to play down the conceptual significance of mental suggestion work.

21 This practice probably comes from the old mesmeric belief in the importance of thumbs in the projection of animal magnetism. Deleuze (1825) wrote: "It is through the end of the fingers, and especially by the thumbs, that the fluid escapes with the most activity" (p. 31).

22 Referring to Janet and Gibert's tests, Myers (1887) said he found it "hard to believe that a peasant woman is sent to sleep by 'the sound of a going' in the arteries of an elderly physician, at a distance of half a mile" (p. 156). Presumably the reference to an elderly physician applied to Gibert, who was actually in his late 50s.

23 On transfer phenomena see Gauld (1992, p. 333–334), Harrington (1988), and Nicolas (2004, p. 18–21). See also Myers's (1886c, p. 449) suggestions of things to consider in conducting tests on the subject.

24 For recent discussions of Wittmann see Alvarado (2009d) and Hustvedt (2011, Chapter 3).

25 Bernheim's critiques were part of the paradigmatic conflicts between the Nancy and the Salpêtrière schools of hypnosis (Nicolas, 2004). These conflicts centered over specific hypnotic phenomena, among them the phases of hypnosis and transfer. More dramatic for the attention they got in the press were the supposed cases of hypnotically induced crimes (Bogousslavsky, Walusinski, & Veyrunes, 2009). Referring to transfer, Bernheim (1888, p. 128) accused his opponents of suffering from "experimental illusions."

26 On Flournoy and mediumship see Shamdasani (1994). The cases presented in the *Revue* paper appear in English elsewhere (Flournoy, 1911, p. 72–86).

27 On such ideas before and after Flournoy see Alvarado (2011a).

28 For discussions of the issue of pathology and mediumship, also relevant to Janet's ideas presented below, see Alvarado, Machado, Zangari, and Zingrone (2007), Alvarado and Zingrone (2012), Le Maléfan (1999), and Moreira-Almeida, Almeida, and Lotufo Neto (2005).

29 On Janet and mediumship see Le Maléfan (1999, p. 66–84). Janet discussed the topic in *L'Automatisme Psychologique* (1889, Chapter 3), where he argued that mediumship was similar to hysteria and hypnotic somnambulism in that all of them showed the "disaggregation of personal perception and … the formation of several personalities that are both successive and simultaneously developed" (p. 413). He believed that mediums were predisposed to have nervous problems and that their condition depended on a morbid state similar to one shown by those who develop hysteria and insanity. But mediumship was "a symptom and not

a cause" (p. 406). Janet (1894, p. 59) further wrote that automatic writing was a procedure that accessed the subconscious mind and that a medium was a person who had lost awareness of his or her internal mental activity (Janet, 1898, p. 395).

30 Janet was influenced here both by Hippolyte Taine (1828–1893) and by Myers (Janet 1886a, p. 587, 588).

31 Janet frequently credited non-scientific movements with influencing psychology. In his discussion of the use of crystal gazing to access the subconscious he stated his belief that "ancient superstition" may help psychology "today to guide our investigations" (Janet, 1898, p. 408). Such a view of the importance of past practices was expressed in his later discussions of hypnosis (Janet, 1919).

32 For a more detailed discussion of the writings of Egger and others see Alvarado (2011b) and Le Maléfan (1995).

33 On the late nineteenth century neo-mesmeric movement see Alvarado (2009b).

34 For overviews see Carroy (1991), Foschi (2003a), Hacking (1995), Hustvedt (2011), and Nicolas (2002).

35 On psychic phenomena in the 1889 congress see Alvarado (2006). The reactions to the first congress were but the beginning stages of rejection of psychic phenomena in the congresses. This continued and reached a critical point in the 1900 congress when many openly questioned the inclusion of spiritism and psychic phenomena (Janet, 1901).

References

Aksakof, A. (1895). *Animisme et Spiritisme: Essai d'un Examen Critique des Phénomènes Médiumniques, Spécialement en Rapport avec les Hypothèses de la "Force Nerveuse," de l'"Hallucination" et de l' "Inconscient."* P. G. Leymarie. (Original work published 1890).

Alliot, E. (1886). *La Suggestion Mentale et l'Action des Médicaments à Distance.* J. B. Baillière.

Alvarado, C. S. (2007). Psychical research and telepathy in nineteenth century issues of *The Times. Paranormal Review, 43*, 3–7.

Alvarado, C. S. (2006). *Aspects of the history of parapsychology: I. Psychical research, proceedings from the 1889 International Congress of Physiological Psychology*. Parapsychology Foundation

Alvarado, C. S. (2008). Note on Charles Richet's "La Suggestion Mentale et le Calcul des Probabilités" (1884). *Journal of Scientific Exploration, 22*, 543–548.

Alvarado, C. S. (2009a). Ambroise August Liébeault and psychic phenomena. *American Journal of Clinical Hypnosis, 52*, 111–121.

Alvarado, C. S. (2009b). Late 19th- and early 20th-century discussions of animal magnetism. *International Journal of Clinical and Experimental Hypnosis, 57*, 366–381.

Alvarado, C. S. (2009c). Mesmeric mediumship: The case of Emma. *Psypioneer, 5*, 44–51.

Alvarado, C. S. (2009d). Nineteenth-century hysteria and hypnosis: A historical note on Blanche Wittmann. *Australian Journal of Clinical and Experimental Hypnosis, 37*, 21–36.

Alvarado, C. S. (2009e). Psychical research in the *Psychological Review*, 1894–1900: A bibliographical note. *Journal of Scientific Exploration, 23*, 211–220.

Alvarado, C. S. (2010). Classic text No. 84: Divisions of personality and spiritism by Alfred Binet (1896). *History of Psychiatry, 21*, 487–500.

Alvarado, C. S. (2011a). On mediumistic personation phenomena. *Journal of the Society for Psychical Research, 75*, 59–61.

Alvarado, C. S. (2011b). Panoramic memory, affect, and sensations of detachment in the dying: Discussions published in France, 1889–1903. *Journal of Near-Death Studies, 30*, 65–82.

Alvarado, C. S., Biondi, M., & Kramer, W. (2006). Historical notes on psychic phenomena in specialised journals. *European Journal of Parapsychology, 21*, 58–87.

Alvarado, C. S., & Evrard, R. (2012). The psychic sciences in France: Historical notes on the *Annales des Sciences Psychiques*. *Journal of Scientific Exploration, 26*, 117–140.

Alvarado, C. S., Machado, F. R., Zangari, W., & Zingrone, N. L. (2007). Perspectivas históricas da infl uencia da mediumidade na construção de idéias psicológicas e psiquiátricas. *Revista de Psiquiatria Clínica, 34*(Supplement 1), 42–53.

Alvarado, C. S., & Zingrone, N. L. (2012). Classic Text No. 90: "The Pathology and Treatment of Mediomania" by Frederic Rowland Marvin (1874). *History of Psychiatry, 23*, 229–244.

Arago, F. (1854). *Oeuvres Complètes de François Arago* (J. A. Barral, ed.). (Vol. 4). Gide and J. Baudry.

Azam, E. E. (1887). *Hypnotisme, double conscience et altération de la personnalité*. J. B. Baillière.

Babinet, J. (1854). Des tables tournantes au point de vue de la mécanique et de la physiologie. *Revue des Deux Mondes, 24*, 408–419.

Babinski, J. (1886). Recherches servant a établir que certaines manifestations hystériques peuvent être transférées d'un sujet à un autre sujet sous l'influence de l'aimant. *Revue Philosophique de la France et de l'Étranger, 22*, 697–700.

Beaunis, H. (1885). L'expérimentation en psychologie par le somnambulisme provoqué. *Revue Philosophique de la France et de l'Étranger, 20*, 1–36.

Beaunis, H. (1886). Un fait de suggestion mentale. *Revue Philosophique de la France et de l'Étranger, 21*, 204.

Bergson, H. (1886). De la simulation inconsciente dans l'hypnotisme. *Revue Philosophique de la France et de l'Étranger, 22*, 525–531.

Bernheim, H. (1885). L'hypnotisme chez les hystériques. *Revue Philosophique de la France et de l'Étranger, 19*, 311–316.

Bernheim, H. (1888). *De la Suggestion et de ses Applications à la Thérapeutique* (2nd ed.). Octave Doin.

Bersot, E. (1864). *Mesmer et le Magnétisme Animal: Les Tables Tournantes et les Esprits* (3rd ed.). L. Hachette.

Binet, A. (1890). Review of *L'Automatisme Psychologique* by P. Janet. *Revue Philosophique de la France et de l'Étranger, 29, 186*–200.

Binet, A., & Féré, C. (1885). L'hypnotisme chez les hystériques: Le transfert. *Revue Philosophique de la France et de l'Étranger, 19,* 1–25.

Binet, A., & Féré, C. (1887). *Le magnétisme animal.* Félix Alcan.

Blanc, H. (1865). *Le Merveilleux dans le Jansénisme, le Magnétisme, le Méthodisme et le Baptisme Américains, l'Epidémie de Morzine, le Spiritisme: Recherches Nouvelles.* Henri Plon.

Bogousslavsky, J., Walusinski, O., & Veyrunes, D. (2009). Crime, hysteria and *Belle Époque* hypnotism: The path traced by Jean-Martin Charcot and Georges Gilles de la Tourette. *European Neurology, 62*, 193–199.

Boirac, E. (1896). Review of *L'extériorisation de la Sensibilité* by A. de Rochas. *Revue Philosophique de la France et de l'Étranger, 41*, 212–216.

Boirac, E. (1897). Review of *L'extériorisation de la Motricité* by A. de Rochas. *Revue Philosophique de la France et de l'Étranger, 43*, 321–326.

Boirac, E. (1899). Les phénomènes cryptoïdes. *Revue Philosophique de la France et de l'Étranger, 47*, 42–62.

Boirac, E. (1911). L'étude scientifique du spiritisme. *Revue Philosophique de la France et de l'Étranger, 71*, 367–383.

Bonnamy, M. (1868). *La raison du spiritisme* (3rd ed.). Librairie Internationale.

Bourru, H., & Burot, P. (1885). De la multiplicité des états de conscience chez un hystéro épileptique. *Revue Philosophique de la France et de l'Étranger, 20*, 411–416.

Bourru, H., & Burot, P. (1886). Les premières expériences sur l'action des médicaments à distance. *Revue Philosophique de la France et de l'Étranger, 21*, 311–321.

Bourru, H., & Burot, P. (1887a). L'action à distance des substances toxiques et médicamenteuses: Résultats pratiques et interprétation. *Revue de l'Hypnotisme Expérimentale & Thérapeutique, 2*, 109–115.

Bourru, H., & Burot, P. (1887b). *La suggestion mentale et l'action à distance des substances toxiques et médicamenteuses*. J. B. Baillière.

Bourru, H., & Burot, P. (1888). *Variations de la personnalité.* J. B. Baillière.

Bozzano, E. (1924). Autobiographical sketch. *Journal of the American Society for Psychical Research, 18*, 153–155.

Brooks III, J. I. (1998). *The eclectic legacy: Academic philosophy and the human sciences in nineteenth-century France*. Associated University Press.

Brower, M. B. (2010). *Unruly spirits: The science of psychic phenomena in modern France*. University of Illinois Press.

Burdin, C., & Dubois, F. (1841). *Histoire académique du magnétisme animal accompagnée de notes et de remarques critiques*. J. B. Baillière.

Cantor, G., & Shuttleworth, S. (Eds.). (2004). *Science serialized: Representation of the sciences in nineteenth-century periodicals.* MIT Press.

Caratelli, G. (1996). *Psicologia psicoanalisis parapsicologia.* Sovera.
Carbonel, F. (2006). Un jalon pour l'émergence de la psychologie scientifi que: Pierre Janet et les médecins aliénistes du Havre (22 février 1883-août 1889). *Janetian Studies, 3.* http://pierre-janet.com/JanetianStudiesBody.htm
Carbonel, F. (2008). Au-delà de Paris et Nancy, l' "École de Charles Richet" selon Pierre Janet: Son impact et ses réseaux, ses membres et son hétérodoxie de l'appel à un Congrès International de Psychologie (1881) à la fondation d'un Institut Psychique (1900). *Janetian Studies, 5.*
Carroy, J. (1991). *Hypnose, suggestion et psychologie: L'Invention de sujets.* Presses Universitaires de France.
Carroy, J., & Plas, R. (1993). La méthode pathologique et les origines de la psychologie française au XIXe siècle. *Revue Internationale de Psychopathologie, 12*, 603–612.
Carroy, J., & Plas, R. (2000). How Pierre Janet used pathological psychology to save the philosophical self. *Journal of the History of the Behavioral Sciences, 36*, 231–240.
Cattell, J. M. (1898). Mrs. Piper, the medium. *Science, 7*(n. s), 534–535.
Chazarain, L. T., & Declé, C. (1886). *Découverte de la polarité humaine ou demonstration expérimentale des lois suivant lesquelles l'application des aimants, de l'electricité et les actions manuelles ou analogues du corps humain.* Octave Doin.
Chevreul, M. E. (1854). *De la baguette divinatoire, du pendule dit explorateur et des tables tournantes.* Mallet-Bachelier.
Coste, A. (1895). *Les phénomènes psychiques occultes: État actuel de la question* (second edition). Camille Coulet.
Crabtree, A. (1993). *From Mesmer to Freud: Magnetic sleep and the roots of psychological healing.* Yale University Press.
De Gasparin, Cte A. (1854). *Des tables tournantes: Du surnaturel en général et des esprits* (2 vols.). E. Dentu.
Delanne, G. (1897). *Le phénomène spirite: Témoignages des savants* (5th ed.). Chamuel.
Delboeuf, J. (1886). La mémoire chez les hypnotisés. *Revue Philosophique de la France et de l'Étranger, 21*, 441–472.
Deleuze, J. P. F. (1813). *Histoire critique du magnétisme animal* (Vol. 1). Mame.
Deleuze, J. P. F. (1825). *Instruction Pratique sur le Magnétisme Animal.* J. G. Dentu.
De Rochas, A. (1887). *Les forces non définies: Recherches historiques et expérimentales.* G. Masson.
De Rochas, A. (1900). Review of *Des Indes à la Planéte Mars* by T. Flournoy. *Revue Philosophique de la France et de l'Étranger, 49*, 650–654.
Dingwall, E. J. (1968). Hypnotism in France. In E. J. Dingwall's (Ed., *Abnormal hypnotic phenomena: A survey of nineteenth-century cases* (Vol. 1, pp. 1–328). Barnes & Noble. (Original work published 1967).
Dufay, Dr. (1876). La notion de la personnalité. *Revue Scientifique de la France et de l'Étranger, 11*(s. 2), 69–71.
Dufay, Dr. (1888). Contribution à l'étude du somnambulisme provoqué à distance et à l'insu du sujet. *Revue Philosophique de la France et de l'Étranger, 26*, 301–312.
Durand (de Gros), J. P. (1894). *Le merveilleux scientifique.* Félix Alcan.
Edelman, N. (1995). *Voyantes, guérisseuses et visionnaires en France 1785–1914.* Albin Michel.
Egger, V. (1896a). Le moi des mourants. *Revue Philosophique de la France et de l'Étranger, 41*, 26–38.
Egger, V. (1896b). Le moi des mourants: Nouveaux faits. *Revue Philosophique de la France et de l'Étranger, 41*, 337–368.
Ellenberger, H. F. (1970). *The discovery of the unconscious: The history and evolution of dynamic psychiatry.* Basic Books.
Erny, A. (1895). *Le psychisme expérimental: Étude des phénomènes psychiques.* E. Flammarion.
Esdaile, J. (1852). *Natural and mesmeric clairvoyance.* Hippolyte Baillière.
Féré, C. (1887). *Sensation et mouvement: Études expérimentales de psycho-méchanique.* Félix Alcan.
Féré, C. (1898). L'état mental des mourants. *Revue Philosophique de la France et de l'Étranger, 45*, 296–302.
Figuier, L. (1859). Tables tournantes. In B. Luna (Ed.), *Dictionnaire universel des connaissances humaines* (Vol. 7, pp. 289–298). Magiaty.
Figuier, L. (1860). *Histoire du merveilleux dans des temps modernes* (4 volumes). L. Hachette.
Flammarion, C. (1899). Les problèmes psychiques et l'inconnu. *Annales Politiques et Litteraires, 32*, 3–5, 35–36, 67–69, 99–101, 131–133, 164–165, 195–196, 227–230, 259–261, 291–293, 338–341.

Flournoy, T. (1899). Genèse de quelques prétendus messages spirites. *Revue Philosophique de la France et de l'Étranger, 47*, 144–158.
Flournoy, T. (1900a). Correspondence. *Revue Philosophique de la France et de l'Étranger, 50*, 111.
Flournoy, T. (1900b). *From India to the planet Mars: A study of a case of somnabulism.* Harper & Brothers.
Flournoy, T. (1911). *Spiritism and psychology.* Harper & Brothers.
Foschi, R. (2003a). L'indagine sulla personalità alle origini della psicologia scientifica francese (1870–1885). *Physis, 40*, 63–105.
Foschi, R. (2003b). La psicologia sperimentale e patologica di Pierre Janet e la nozione di personalità (1885–1900). *Medicina & Storia, 3*, 45–68.
Franklin, C. L. (1885). Richet on mental suggestion. *Science, 5*, 132–134.
Gauld, A. (1968). *The founders of psychical research.* Routledge & Kegan Paul.
Gauld, A. (1992). *A history of hypnotism.* Cambridge University Press.
Gauld, A. (1996). Notes on the career of the somnambule Léonie. *Journal of the Society for Psychical Research, 61*, 141–151.
Gibier, P. (1887). *Le spiritisme (fakirisme occidental): Étude historique, critique et expérimentale.* Octave Doin.
Gilles de la Tourette, G. (1889). *L'hypnotisme et les états analogues au point de vue médico-legal* (2nd ed.). E. Plon, Nourrit.
Gley, G. (1886). A propos d'une observation de sommeil provoqué à distance. *Revue Philosophique de la France et de l'Étranger, 21*, 425–428.
Guinon, G., with the collaboration of Bloq, [no initial], Souques, [no initial], & Charcot, J. B. (Eds.) (1893). *Clinique des maladies du système nerveux: M. le Professeur Charcot: Leçons du professeur, mémoires, notes et observations* (Vol, 2). Bureaux du Progrès Médical.
Guillin, V. (2004). Théodule Ribot's ambiguous positivism: Philosophical and epistemological strategies in the founding of French scientific psychology. *Journal of the History of the Behavioral Sciences, 40*, 165–181.
Gumpper, S. (2013). Théodule Ribot. In S. Gumpper & F. Rausky (Eds.), *Dictionnaire de Psychologie et Psychopathologie des Religions.* Bayard.
Gurney, E. (1884). M. Richet's recent researches in thought-transference. *Proceedings of the Society for Psychical Research, 2*, 239–264.
Gurney, E., & Myers, F. W. H. (1884). Visible apparitions. *Nineteenth Century, 16*, 68–95.
Gurney, E., Myers, F. W. H., & Podmore, F. (1886). *Phantasms of the living* (2 volumes). Trübner.
Gyel, E. [Geley, G.] (1899). *L'Être subconscient.* Félix Alcan.
Hacking, I. (1995). *Rewriting the soul: Multiple personality and the sciences of memory.* Princeton University Press.
Hall, G. S. (1887). Review of *Proceedings of the Society for Psychical Research*, and *Phantasms of the Living*, by E. Gurney, F. W. H. Myers, and F. Podmore. *American Journal of Psychology, 1*, 128–146.
Harrington, A. (1988). Metals and magnets in medicine: Hysteria, hypnosis and medical culture in fin-de-siècle Paris. *Psychological Medicine, 18*, 21–38.
Héricourt, J. (1886). Un cas de somnambulisme à distance. *Revue Philosophique de la France et de l'Étranger, 21*, 200–203.
Héricourt, J. (1889). L'activité inconsciente de l'esprit. *Revue Scientifique, 44*, 257–268.
Héricourt, J. (1931). Une observation de sommeil hypnotique provoqué à distance. *Revue Métapsychique*, No. 3, 177–182.
Hustvedt, A. (2011). *Medical muses: Hysteria in nineteenth-century Paris.* W. W. Norton.
Iannuzzo, G. (1983). *Ernesto Bozzano: La vita e l'opera* (Le monografi e di *Luce e Ombra*, No. 2). Luce e Ombra.
Irwin H. J., & Watt, C. A. (2007). *An introduction to parapsychology* (fifth edition). McFarland.
James, W. (1892). What psychical research has accomplished. *Forum, 13*, 727–742.
James, W. (1896a). Address of the president before the Society for Psychical Research. *Science, 3*, 881–888.
James, W. (1896b). Psychical research. *Psychological Review, 3*, 649–651.
Janet, J. (1888). L'hystérie et l'hypnotisme, d'après la theorie de la double personnalité. *Revue Scientifique, 25*, 616–623.
Janet, J. (1890). *Les troubles psychopathiques de la miction: Essai de psycho-physiologie normale et pathologique.* Librairie Lefrançois.

Janet, P. (1886a). Les actes inconscients et la dédoublement de la personnalité pendant le somnambulisme provoqué. *Revue Philosophique de la France et de l'Étranger, 22*, 577–592.
Janet, P. (1886b). Note sur quelques phénomènes de somnambulisme. *Revue Philosophique de la France et de l'Étranger, 21*, 190–198.
Janet, P. (1886c). Deuxième note sur le sommeil provoqué à distance et la suggestion mentale pendant l'état somnambulique. *Revue Philosophique de la France et de l'Étranger, 22*, 212–223.
Janet, P. (1887). L'anesthésie systématisée et la dissociation des phénomènes psychiques. *Revue Philosophique de la France et de l'Étranger, 23*, 449–472.
Janet, P. (1888a). Review of *Le magnétisme animal étudié sous le nom de force neurique* by A. Barėty. *Revue Philosophique de la France et de l'Étranger, 25*, 91–95.
Janet, P. (1888b). Les actes inconscients et la mémoire pendant le somnambulisme. *Revue Philosophique de la France et de l'Étranger, 25*, 238–279.
Janet, P. (1889). *L'automatisme psychologique: Essai de psychologie expérimentale sur les formes inférieures de l'activité humaine*. Félix Alcan.
Janet, P. (1892). Le spiritisme contemporain. *Revue Philosophique de la France et de l'Étranger, 33*, 413–442.
Janet, P. (1894). *État mental des hystériques: Les accidents mentaux*. Rueff.
Janet, P. (1898). *Névroses et idées fixes: I.: Études expérimentales sur les troubles de la volonté, de l'Attention, de la Mémoire, sur les Émotions, les Idées Obsédantes et lei Traitement.* Félix Alcan.
Janet, P. (Editor) (1901). *IVe Congrès International de Psychologie proceedings*. Félix Alcan.
Janet, P. (1919). *Les médications psychologiques: Études historiques, psychologiques et cliniques sur les méthodes de la psychothérapie* (Vol. 1). Félix Alcan.
Janet, P. (1923). A propos de la métapsychique. *Revue Philosophique de la France et de l'Étranger, 96*, 5–32.
Janet, P. (1930). Autobiography of Pierre Janet. In C. Murchison (Ed.), *A history of psychology in autobiography* (pp. 123–133). Clark University Press.
Janet, P. (1968a). Report on some phenomena of somnambulism. *Journal of the History of the Behavioral Sciences, 4*, 124–131. (Original work published 1886)
Janet, P. (1968b). Second observation of sleep provoked from a distance and the mental suggestion during the somnambulistic state. *Journal of the History of the Behavioral Sciences, 4*, 258–267. (Original work published 1886)
Jastrow, J. (1889). The problem of "psychic research." *Harper's New Monthly Magazine, 79*, 76–82.
Kardec, A. (1860). *Philosophie spiritualiste: Le livre des esprits* (2nd ed.). Didier.
Kardec, A. (1863). *Spiritisme expérimental: Le livre des médiums* (6th ed.). Didier.
Keller, A. (1896). L'état mental des mourants. *Revue Philosophique de la France et de l'Étranger, 41*, 311–313.
Kopell, B. S. (1968). Pierre Janet's description of hypnotic sleep provoked from a distance. *Journal of the History of the Behavioral Sciences, 4*, 119–123.
Lachapelle, S. (2011). *Investigating the supernatural: From spiritism and occultism to psychical research and metapsychics in France, 1853–1931.* Johns Hopkins University Press.
Laurent, L. (1892). *Des états seconds: Variations pathologiques du champ de la conscience*. Ve Cadoret.
Lechelas, G. (1887). Review of *Les forces non définies*, by A. de Rochas. *Revue Philosophique de la France et de l'Étranger, 24*, 91–93.
Lechelas, G., Tannery, P., & Richet, C. (1885). La suggestion mentale et le calcul des probabilités. *Revue Philosophique de la France et de l'Étranger, 19*, 112–118.
Le Maléfan, P. (1995). Vécu de mort imminente et onirisme: un chapitre inattendu de l'histoire de la psychologie dynamique. *L'information psychiatrique, 71*, 773–780.
Le Maléfan, P. (1999). *Folie et spiritisme: Histoire du discours psychopathologique sur la pratique du spiritisme, ses abords et ses avatars (1850–1950)*. L'Harmattan.
Levoix, E. (1877). Review of *Mesmerism, Spiritualism, &c.*, by W. Carpenter. *Revue Philosophique de la France et de l'Étranger, 4*, 440–443.
Liébeault, A. A. (1889). *Le sommneil provoqué et les états analogues*. Octave Doin.
Liégeois, J. (1889). *De la suggestion et de somnambulisme dans leurs Rapports avec la jurisprudence et la médicine légale*. Octave Doin.
Lombroso, C. (1891). Inchiesta sulla transmissione del pensiero. *Archivio di Psichiatria, Scienza Penali ed Antropologia Criminale, 12*, 58–108.

Lombroso, C. (1896). Caso singolare di premonizioni. *Archivio di Psichiatria, Scienza Penali ed Antropologia Criminale, 17*, 128–130.
Luckhurst, R. (2002). *The invention of telepathy 1870–1901*. Oxford University Press.
Luys, J. (1886). Sur l'action des médicaments a distance chez les sujets hypnotisés. *Comptes Rendus Hebdomadaires des Séances et Mémoires de la Société de Biologie, 3*(s. 8), 426–428.
Luys, J., & Encausse, P. (1890). Du transfert a distance, à l'aide d'une couronne de fer aimanté, d'états névropathiques variés, d'un sujet à l'état de veille sur un sujet à l'état hypnotique. *Comptes Rendus Hebdomadaires des Séances et Mémoires de la Société de Biologie, 2*(8), 599–602.
Marillier, L. (1887). La suggestion mentale et les actions mentales à distance. *Revue Philosophique de la France et de l'Étranger, 23*, 400–422.
Marillier, L. (1889). Le Congrès de Psychologie Physiologique. *Revue Philosophique de la France et de l'Étranger, 28*, 539–546.
Marillier, L. (1891). Les apparitions de la Vierge dans la Dordogne en 1889. *Revue Philosophique de la France et de l'Étranger, 32*, 422–432.
Méheust, B. (1999a). *Somnambulisme et médiumnité (1784–1930): Vol. 1.: Le défi du magnétisme animal.* Le Plessis-Robinson: Institut Synthélabo pour le Progrès de la Connaissance.
Méheust, B. (1999b). *Somnambulisme et médiumnité (1784–1930): Vol. 2: Le choc des sciences psychiques.* Le Plessis-Robinson: Institut Synthélabo pour le Progrès de la Connaissance.
Meletti Bertolini, M. (1991). *Il pensiero e la memoria: Filosofi a e psicologia nella "Revue Philosophique" di Théodule Ribot (1876–1916).* Franco Angeli.
Minot, C. S. (1895). The psychical comedy. *North American Review, 160*, 217–231.
Monroe, J. W. (2008). *Laboratories of faith: Mesmerism, spiritism, and occultism in modern France*. Cornell University Press.
Moreira-Almeida, A., Almeida, A. A. S., & Lotufo Neto, F. (2005). History of spiritist madness in Brazil. *History of Psychiatry, 16*, 5–25.
Moulin, A. (1896). L'état mental des mourants. *Revue Philosophique de la France et de l'Étranger, 41*, 307–310.
Mucchielli, L. (1998). Aux origines de la psychologie universitaire en France (1870–1900): Enjeux intellectuels, contexte politique, réseaux et stratégies d'alliance autour de la *revue philosophique* de Théodule Ribot. *Annals of Science, 55*, 263–289.
Myers, F. W. H. (1886a). De certaines formes d'hallucination. *Revue Philosophique de la France et de l'Étranger, 21*, 214–215.
Myers, F. W. H. (1886b). Des hallucinations véridiques. *Revue Philosophique de la France et de l'Étranger, 21*, 434.
Myers, F. W. H. (1886c). Report on the General Meeting. *Journal of the Society for Psychical Research, 2*, 443–453.
Myers, F. W. H. (1886d). On telepathic hypnotism, and its relation to other forms of hypnotic suggestion. *Proceedings of the Society for Psychical Research, 4*, 127–188.
Myers, F. W. H. (1887). On a case of alleged hypnotic hyperacuity of vision. *Mind, 12*, 154–156.
Nicolas, S. (2002). *Histoire de la psychologie Française: Naissance d'une nouvelle science*. Editions In Press.
Nicolas, S. (2004). *L'Hypnose: Charcot face à Bernheim.* L'Harmattan.
Nicolas, S., & Murray, D. J. (1999). Théodule Ribot (1839–1916), founder of French psychology: A biographical introduction. *History of Psychology, 2*, 277–301.
Nicolas, S., Segui, J., & Ferrand, L. (2000). *L'année psychologique*: History of the founding of a hundred-year-old French journal. *History of Psychology, 3*, 20–43.
Ochorowicz, J. (1886). Sur le problème de la suggestion mentale. *Revue Philosophique de la France et de l'Étranger, 22*, 208–212.
Ochorowicz, J. (1887). *De la suggestion mentale*. Octave Doin.
Paulhan, F. (1890). Le nouveau mysticisme. *Revue Philosophique de la France et de l'Étranger, 30*, 480–522.
Paulhan, F. (1892). Les hallucinations véridiques et la suggestion mentale. *Revue des Deux Mondes, 114*, 65–100.
Plas, R. (2000). *Naissance d'une science humaine: La psychologie: Les psychologues et le "merveilleux psychique."* Presses Universitaires de Rennes.
Podmore, F. (1894). *Apparitions and thought-transference*. Walter Scott.

Podmore, F. (1895). What psychical research has accomplished. *North American Review, 160*, 331–344.

Podmore, F. (1897). *Studies in psychical research.* G. P. Putmam's Sons.

Puel, J. T. (1856). *De la catalepsie.* J. B. Baillière.

Radin, D. (2006). *Entangled minds: Extrasensory experiences in a quantum reality.* Paraview Pocket Books.

Review of *La Physique Transcendentale* by F. Zollner (1880). *Revue Philosophique de la France et de l'Étranger, 10*, 566–567.

Review of *Proceedings of the Society for Psychical Research* (1883). *Revue Philosophique de la France et de l'Étranger, 16*, 445–448.

Review of *Proceedings of the Society for Psychical Research* (1884a). *Revue Philosophique de la France et de l'Étranger, 17*, 239–240.

Review of *Proceedings of the Society for Psychical Research* (1884b). *Revue Philosophique de laFrance et de l'Étranger, 18*, 604–605.

Ribot, T. (1879). *La psychologie Allemande contemporaine (École Expérimentale).* Germer Baillière.

Ribot, T. (1888). *Les maladies de la personnalité* (2nd ed.). Félix Alcan.

Ribot, T. (1901). La psychologie de 1896 a 1900. In P. Janet (Editor), *IVe Congrès International de Psychologie* (pp. 40–47). Félix Alcan.

Richer, P. (1885). *Études cliniques sur la grande hystérie ou hystéro-épilepsie* (2nd ed.). Adrien Delahaye and Émile Lecrosnier.

Richer, P. (1887) Review of *Le Magnétisme Animal* by A. Binet and C. Féré. *Revue Philosophique de la France et de l'Étranger, 23*, 633–635.

Richet, C. (1880). Du somnambulisme provoqué. *Revue Philosophique de la France et de l'Étranger, 10*, 337–374, 462–484.

Richet, C. (1883). La personnalité et la memoire dans le somnambulisme. *Revue Philosophique de la France et de l'Étranger, 15*, 225–242.

Richet, C. (1884). La suggestion mentale et le calcul des probabilités. *Revue Philosophique de la France et de l'Étranger, 18*, 609–674.

Richet, C. (1886a). Un fait de somnambulisme à distance. *Revue Philosophique de la France et de l'Étranger, 21*, 199–200.

Richet, C. (1886b). L'action des substances toxiques et médicamenteuses à distance. *Revue Philosophique de la France et de l'Étranger, 21*, 321–323.

Richet, C. (1888a). Expériences sur le sommeil à distance. *Revue Philosophique de la France et de l'Étranger, 25*, 435–452.

Richet, C. (1888b). Relation de diverses expériences sur la transmission mentale, la lucidité, et autres phénomènes non explicables par les données scientifiques actuelles. *Proceedings of the Society for Psychical Research, 5*, 18–168.

Richet, C. (1889). Further experiments in hypnotic lucidity or clairvoyance. *Proceedings of the Society for Psychical Research, 6*, 66–83.

Richet, C. (1892a). L'avenir de la psychologie. *Annales des Sciences Psychiques, 2*, 341–350.

Richet, C. (1892b). A propos du mysticisme moderne. *Revue Philosophique de la France et de l'Étranger, 34*, 417–422.

Rosenbach, P. (1892). Étude critique sur le mysticisme moderne. *Revue Philosophique de la France et de l'Étranger, 34*, 113–158.

Ruault, A. (1886). Le mécanisme de la suggestion mentale hypnotique. *Revue Philosophique de la France et de l'Étranger, 22*, 679–697.

Sauvaire, C. (1887). Hyperesthésie dans l'état hypnotique. *Revue Philosophique de la France et de l'Étranger, 23*, 333–335.

Senillosa, F. (1891). *Concordancia del espiritismo con la ciencia* (Vol. 1). Martin Biedma.

Shamdasani, S. (1994). Encountering Hélène: Théodore Flournoy and the genesis of subliminal psychology. In T. Flournoy, *From India to the planet Mars: A case of multiple personality with imaginary languages* (pp. xi–li). Princeton University Press.

Sharp, L. L. (2006). *Secular spirituality: Reincarnation and spiritism in nineteenth-century France.* Lexington Books.

Sidgwick, H. (1892). The International Congress of Experimental Psychology. *Journal of the Society for Psychical Research, 5*, 283–293.

Société de Psychologie Physiologique de Paris (1885). *Revue Philosophique de la France et de l'Étranger, 19,* 591–592.
Société de Psychologie Physiologique de Paris (1890). *Revue Philosophique de la France et de l'Étranger, 30,* 223.
Society for Psychical Research (1889). *Revue Philosophique de la France et de l'Étranger, 28,* 111.
Sollier, P. (1896). L'état mental des mourants. *Revue Philosophique de la France et de l'Étranger, 41,* 303–307.
Soury, J. (1879). Review of *Der Spiritismus* by W. Wundt, and *Der Sogenannte Spiritimus eine Wissenschaftliche Frage* by H. Ulrici. *Revue Philosophique de la France et de l'Étranger, 8,* 660–668.
Tabori, P. (1972). *Pioneers of the unseen.* Souvenir Press.
Thirard, J. (1976). La fondation de la "Revue philosophique." *Revue Philosophique de la France et de l'Étranger, 166,* 401–413.
Wantuil, Z. (n.d.). *As mesas girantes e o espiritismo.* Federação Espirita Brasileira.
Wantuil, Z., & Thiesen, F. (1984). *Allan Kardec* (3 vols., 2nd ed.). Federação Espirita Brasileira.
Wells, H. G. (1894). Peculiarities of psychical research. *Nature, 51,* 121–122.
Wolf, S. (1993). *Brain, mind and medicine: Charles Richet and the origins of physiological psychology.* Transaction Publishers.
Wundt, W. (1905). *Hypnotisme et suggestion: Étude critique* (3rd ed.). Félix Alcan.
Yung, E. (1890). *Hypnotisme et spiritisme (Les faits positifs et les faits présumés).* R. Burkhardt.

Mesmerism Online: A Bibliographic Review*

Carlos S. Alvarado†

With the development of digital libraries, the availability of historical books and articles has considerably increased. One example is the online library Google Book Search (http://books.google.com), which has been discussed in the past in terms of dissociation (Alvarado, 2008) and other phenomena (Alvarado, 2007). In this bibliographical note, I would like to focus on some of the holdings of the collection about mesmerism published during the nineteenth century. My purpose is not to discuss the material in detail, but to offer brief comments so as to bring a variety of books and articles to the attention of readers interested in the history of the subject.

Histories and Overviews

A good general overview of the early history of mesmerism was provided by science populariser Louis Figuier (1819–1894) in the third volume of his *Histoire du merveilleux dans temps modernes* (Figuier, 1860). The volume's 17 chapters were dedicated to the topic, with the last two focusing on hypnosis. The general focus of Figuier was France, and the first 10 chapters were about Franz Anton Mesmer (1734–1815) and the reception of his work.

The collection also includes several books that combine historical information with discussions of the practice and theory of mesmerism. One of them is the first volume of *Histoire crititique du magnétisme animal* (Deleuze, 1813). In the book Joseph Philippe François Deleuze (1753–1835) started with Mesmer, and went on to discuss aspects such as the magnetic fluid, healing, problems and dangers of mesmerism, and personally observed phenomena. Other useful overviews in the collection are *Animal Magnetism: Its History to the Present Time* (1841), *Du magnétisme animal en France* (Bertrand, 1826), *An History of Magic, Witchcraft, and Animal Magnetism* (Colquhoun, 1851), *Isis Revelata: An Inquiry into the Origin, Progress and Present State of Animal Magnetism* (Colquhoun, 1836), *Mesmer et le magnétisme animal* (Bersot, 1864), *Versuch einer Darstellung des animalischen Magnetismus als Heilmittel* (Kluge, 1815), and several other works (e.g., Binet & Féré, 1887/1894; Leger, 1846; Teste, 1840/1843).

German physician and poet Justinus Kerner (1786–1862) discussed Mesmer in his *Franz Anton Mesmer aus Schwaben, Entdecker des thierischen Magnetismus* (Kerner, 1856). The collection also has one of Mesmer's (1814) books, *Mesmerismus oder System der Wechselwirkungen,Theorie und Anwendung des thierischen Magnetismus*.

There is much information about early magnetism in the United States in the account that Charles Poyen (1837) presented in his Progress of Animal Magnetism in New England. He wrote:

> "At the time when the writer commenced lecturing in New England, he found the subject almost universally unknown ... Nineteen months have elapsed since that period; and already Animal

*Republished with permission from *Australian Journal of Clinical and Experimental Hypnosis, 36*(2), 115–129, 2008.
†I wish to thank Andreas Sommer for his assistance in translating German book titles.

Magnetism has sprung, from a complete state of obscurity and neglect, into general notice, and become the object of a lively interest throughout the country" (p. 35).

Many authors presented overviews of different aspects of the mesmeric movement (e.g., Buckland, 1850; Deleuze, 1825/1850; Dupotet de Sennevoy, 1838; Esdaile, 1852; Gregory, 1884; Lee, 1866; Lowe, 1822; Teste, 1840/1843). One of them was Italian Francesco Guidi, who wrote in his *Trattato Teorico-Pratico di Magnetismo Animale*: "Magnetism … cannot be well defined: it is an unexplained protean; now visible, now invisible" (Guidi, 1854, p. 2; this, and other translations, are mine).

The collection also has many article reviews on the topic (e.g.,"*Animalischer Magnetismus*," 1823; "*Animal Magnetism*," 1838; Eve, 1845; Herfner, 1844; Knight, 1867, pp. 584–588; "*Magnetismo Animal ó Mesmerismo*," 1842; "Mesmerism," 1843; Ripley & Dana, 1858, pp. 593–598). The author of a paper entitled "*Quelques Reflexions sur le Magnétisme Animal*" called for research and speculated on the role of imagination to explain mesmeric phenomena (Le Boyer, 1823).

Phenomena

The travelling magnetiser Charles Lafontaine (1803–1892) referred to physiological and psychological effects of magnetism in his book *L'art de magnétiser ou le magnétisme animal* (Lafontaine, 1847/1852). The first were such effects as the closing of the eyes, perspiration, spasms, convulsive tremors, partial or complete insensibility or paralysis, catalepsy, somnolence, attraction, trance, and induction of trance at a distance. The second were thought-transmission, sight with closed eyes and through matter, and ecstasy.

Commenting about magnetic sleep Poyen (1837) stated: "Those who have been put into the magnetic sleep in this country, belong to both sexes, and they are persons of almost every age. The writer of these pages had himself alone the opportunity of observing twenty-eight" (p. 59). Others discussed the memory of the magnetised somnambules. Alphonse Teste (1840/1843) wrote in his book *A Practical Manual of Animal Magnetism*: "From the beginning, most somnambulists recollect with astonishing precision all the events which have occurred to them; sometimes, too, from so long a date back, that they had absolutely lost the recollection of them during the state of being awake" (pp. 58–59). British physician William Gregory (1803–1858) wrote about the same topic:

> "As a general rule … the sleeper does not remember, after waking, what he may have seen, felt, tasted, smelled, heard, spoken, or done during his sleep; but when next put to sleep, he recollects perfectly all that has occurred, not only in the last sleep, but in all former sleeps, and, as in the ordinary state, with greater or less accuracy, although usually very accurately indeed" (Gregory, 1884, p. 5).

There is an interesting report of observations of insensibility to induced pain observed at the Asylum for the Deaf and Dumb of Philadelphia. One of the descriptions about phenomena obtained with a 16-year-old boy reads as follows:

> When the boy was asleep, several of the party were asked to pinch his flesh as hard as they thought proper, to see whether he would awake; but, though some pressed their nails so as to imbed them in his flesh, he never moved a muscle. A pin was then thrust through his flesh, making a complete hole in it; but to this he was as insensible as to all the rest. (Buckingham, 1841, pp. 387–391)

French physician Alexandre Bertrand (1795–1831) wrote that some of his somnambules said they could see "the fluid coming out of my fingers" (Bertrand, 1826, p. ix), a phenomenon he attributed to the imagination. Some mesmerised subjects said they "could see an aura, or fluid, passing into, along, and out of the magnet" (Haddock, 1851, p. 168). The collection also has the classic work of Carl Ludwig Reichenbach (1788–1869) on sensitives claiming to see lights around magnets, crystals and minerals, Physico-Physiological Researches on the Dynamics of Magnetism, Electricity, Heat, Light, Crystallization, and Chemism, in their Relation to Vital Force (Reichenbach, 1849/1851). While Reichenbach did not mesmerise his subjects, his writings were quoted by many mesmerists (e.g., Ashburner, 1867, pp. 36, 83). Later publications in the collection were about luminous emanations from magnets conducted using magnetic procedures, an example being the paper "Mémoire relatif a certaines radiations perçues par les sensitifs" (De Rochas, 1891).

There were also accounts of clairvoyance (Barth, 1849; Elliotson, 1849). Other authors discussed phenomena such as the production of a variety of effects on mesmerized individuals through silent suggestions (Adams, 1849; Ashburner, 1847).

British physician Joseph Haddock (1800–1861) reported observations of the spiritualistic type with his subject Emma. As he wrote in *Somnolism & Psycheism*: "Frequently during the spring and summer of 1848, Emma would, in the mesmeric state, speak of the scenery and nature of the spirit-world" (Haddock, 1851, p. 181). Similar mediumistic phenomena were discussed in detail by Louis Alphonse Cahagnet (1809–1885) in *The Celestial Telegraph* (Cahagnet, 1848–1854/1851).

The digital library has discussions of phenomena representing the late nineteenth-century neo-mesmeric movement. A well-known representative of this trend was French Colonel Albert de Rochas (1837–1914). In his book *L'extériorisation de la sensibilité* he stated that "the human body … emitts effluvia likely to act on the senses of certain persons" (De Rochas, 1895, p. 47). In this book, he also discussed the "exteriorisation of sensibility," a phenomenon in which, in magnetised subjects, "the sense of touch, instead of being excerted, as ordinarily, on the surface of the skin, is extended outside of the body" (p. 50). Other publications in the collection that were part of French neo-mesmerism include *Les courants de la polarité dans l'aimant et dans le corps humain* (Chazarain & Dècle, 1887) and *Traité expérimental de magnétisme* (Durville, 1895–1896).

Medical Appplications

Many authors focused on the medical applications of mesmerism. This included discussions about the control of pain during procedures such as amputations and the removal of tumors (Elliotson, 1843, 1846), and dental operations (Purland, 1859). The author of *The Mighty Curative Powers of Mesmerism* presented cases cured by mesmeric procedures in chapters about rheumatism, neuralgia, toothache, sprains, paralysis, headaches, noises in the head, epilepsy, St Vitus's Dance, inflammations, affections of the eyes, loss of voice, throat and chest complaints, affections of the heart, affections of the stomach, emaciation and debility in children (Capern, 1851).

Physician James Esdaile (1808–1859), reported on his medical use of mesmerism in several publications (Esdaile, 1846a, 1846b, 1852). He concluded in his *Mesmerism in India*:

> That in the mesmeric trance the most severe and protracted surgical operations can be performed, without the patients being sensible of pain.
>
> That spasms and nervous pains often disappear before the mesmeric trance.

> That it gives us a complete command of the muscular system, and is therefore of great service in restoring contracted limbs.
>
> That the chronic administration of Mesmerism often acts as a useful stimulant in functional debility of the nerves. (Esdaile, 1846b, p. 271)

Several cases of claimed cures were published in the Zoist, an English journal devoted to mesmerism some of which volumes are in the collection. Some of the articles were: "Cure of a Large Polypus of the Uterus" (Ashburner, 1851), "Cure of Long-Standing Intense Pains and Other Sufferings and Extreme Debility, with Mesmerism, after the Failure of Endless and Distressing Measures" (Elliotson, 1847), "Cure of Deafness" (Evans, 1849), and "Cures of Severe Female Chronic Ailments, with Mesmerism" (Hands, 1846).

Critiques

La Verdad Católica, a Catholic magazine published in Cuba, had an anonymous article about animal magnetism as seen by the Church. According to the writer, "the Church, a watching sentinel in matters of faith and customs, has expressly prohibited the consultations made to somnambulism" (O., 1861, p. 111).

The author of an overview of mesmerism published in 1844 in the *Dublin University Magazine* stated that: "Mesmerism … cannot with any propriety be said to have as yet attained to the rank of a science. Its procedure is not sure: there is something in it still of a shooting-at-random, predictive of an appearance of caprice or inconstancy in the results" (Herfner, 1844, p. 49). Another author was even more negative. In his view, belief in mesmerism was a "stupid delusion" and "the science is a humbug; its practitioners knaves, and its believers dupes" (Reese, 1838, p. 62).

In an editorial in the British medical journal Lancet, possibly written by the well-known critic of mesmerism Thomas Wakley (1795–1862), it was stated that mesmerism's "arrogant pretensions and gross falsehoods have often been detected and exposed" (Mesmeric humbug and quackery, 1851, p. 155).

Defenders of the animal magnetic movement, such as Elliotson (1843) and Sandby (1848), discussed the opposition of many to the claims of mesmerism, much of which came from physicians. English writer, abolitionist and women's rights defender Harriet Martineau (1802–1876) wrote in her *Letters on Mesmerism* about the skepticism of physicians:

> The systematic disingenuousness of some Medical Journals on this subject, and the far-fetched calumnies and offensive assumptions with which it is the regular practice of a large number of the Faculty to assail every case of cure or relief by Mesmerism, looked very much as if they were in conflict with powerful truth, and as if they knew it. (Martineau, 1845, pp. vi–vii)

Similarly, a writer in *Mechanic's Magazine, Museum, Register, Journal, and Gazette* stated:

> "In a subject confessedly so little understood as the physiology of the nerves, the very men who at one moment confess their almost total ignorance of its laws, are found the next obstinately refusing to examine with their own eyes and ears the new phenomena" (H., 1849, p. 150).

There were, or course, many defenses of mesmerism. Two examples from France were *Défense du magnétisme animal contre les attaques don't il est l'objet dans le Dictionnaire des Sciences Médicales*

(Deleuze, 1819) and *Le magnétisme animal devant les savants, devant le raisonnement, devant les faits* (Rabache, 1854).

Many of the critiques were expressed in the form of defenses of theoretical explanations other than the magnetic fluid. Examples of these discussions in the collection appear in the next section.

Explanatory Concepts

Most mesmerists emphasized the physical nature of the magnetic fluid. James Esdaile (1852) discussed the concept in his *Natural and Mesmeric Clairvoyance*: "Man … in an abnormal state … like the electric fish … can … project his nervous fluid … by his will, beyond the surface of his body, and in the direction desired" (p. 234). Deleuze stated: "The magnetiser can communicate his fluid to many objects, and these objects become either the conductors of his action, or proper instruments of its transmission, and produce magnetic effects upon persons with whom he is in communication" (Deleuze, 1825/1850, p. 212). Lafontaine (1847/1852) commented on the "vital or nervous fluid that is essentially necessary to life, which can be communicated to another body to produce the phenomena known by the name of animal magnetism" (p. 17). This principle, Lafontaine believed, was affected by the will of the magnetist. It was projected from the magnetizer's nervous system to the system of the persons being influenced, where it produced different effects.

The concept of a fluid, wrote an anonymous author, seemed too convenient to account for phenomena whose nature are unknown. The idea was considered to be "repugnant to common sense" (Magnetismo animal ó mesmerismo, 1842, p. 130). Others presented alternative explanations to the concept of a magnetic force. Etienne Félix Henin de Cuvillers (1755–1841) believed that this force was not real, but the product of the imagination. The magnetisers, he asserted in *Le magnétisme animal retrouvé dans l'antiquité*, proposed the concept of animal magnetism "gratuitously, and on their own authority" (Henin de Cuvillers, 1821, p. 134). In another publication, Henin de Cuvillers (1820) argued that animal magnetism as a force did not produce magnetic sleep, "it is the fixed gaze of the magnetiser that fatigues and puts to sleep the person … ; this is added to gestures and passes, which often frighten, or at least cause a vivid emotion … Up to now it is not necessary to suppose an emission of a material fluid" (p. 76).

English physicians Thomas Laycock (1812–1876) and William B. Carpenter (1813–1885) also discussed the subject. The first felt that mesmerism was an example of ideas becoming a reality in the mind of the mesmerised (Laycock, 1857, p. 136), while the second referred to the influence of susceptibility and belief (Carpenter, 1877, p. 26).

Perhaps the most influential of the nineteenth-century conventional theorists was Scottish physician James Braid (1795–1860). He wrote in his classic book *Neurypnology*:

> The phenomena of mesmerism were to be accounted for on the principle of a derangement of the state of the cerebro-spinal centres, and of the circulatory, and respiratory, and muscular systems, induced … by a fixed stare, absolute repose of body, fixed attention, and suppressed respiration, concomitant with that fixity of attention … arising from the causes referred to, and not at all on the volition, or passes of the operator, throwing out a magnetic fluid, or exciting into activity some mystical universal fluid or medium. (Braid, 1843, pp. 19–20)

In a later work, Braid (1852) referred to the possibility that, in some individuals involved in experiments of electro-biology, the ideas and suggestions from others could "even in the waking condition … change physical action, and produce the expected results" (p. 2). Furthermore, such observations showed that, "through the influence of suggestion, existing predominant ideas may be removed" (p. 42).

There are several other examples in this digital library of authors skeptical about animal magnetism as a physical agent (e.g., Estlin, 1843; Eve, 1845; Madden, 1857). A late critique came from English physician Ernest Hart (1836–1898), who wrote in his book *Hypnotism, Mesmerism, and the New Witchcraft:*

> I may say … that the conditions induced … may be shown to be due to a nervous condition or mental state arising in the individual subject either from physical or mental excitation; and further that such conditions … are not and never were due to any healing power or to any fluid or magnetic influence or mesmeric or hypnotic power resident in the operator. (Hart 1896, p. 34)

Of course, not all magnetizers agreed with the "imagination" explanation. As stated by one of them:

> The influence of the imagination and of the imitative principle seem, at first sight, much more capable of affording an adequate explanation of the facts; but the activity of these principles in the magnetic process is rejected as absurd by every practical magnetiser, as well as by every intelligent opponent of the system; and, besides, many of the phenomena are of such a nature, that they cannot be rationally accounted for upon any such theory. (Colquhoun, 1833, p. 91)

Anti-Materialistic Views

In *An History of Magic, Wichcraft, and Animal Magnetism*, Colquhoun (1851) argued for the religious implication of animal magnetism. In his view:

> Animal Magnetism … is eminently calculated to confirm our Christian faith, and to increase our rational devotion towards the great Creator and Preserver of all things; for there is no subject of philosophical inquiry which has a more direct tendency to elevate our thoughts to the contemplation of our present endowments and ultimate destiny—to increase our admiration of the power, and wisdom, and beneficence of the Supreme Being, in the creation and government of the universe, and to prepare us for the enjoyment of another, a better, and a more spiritual state of existence. (Vol. 2, pp. 299–300)

Colquhoun (1836) argued further in another work that animal magnetism refuted materialistic ideas. This was the case because its phenomena presented evidence for the soul's existence. These phenomena were "capable of exercising its various functions … without the assistance or co-operation of any of those material organs, by means of which it usually maintains a correspondence with the external world" (Vol. 2, p. 166).

Writers, such as Haddock (1851) and Ashburner (1867), also related animal magnetism to ideas of the soul. The same may be said about the German physician Johann Heinrich Jung-Stilling (1740–1817), as discussed in his *Theory of Pneumatology* (Jung-Stilling, 1808/1851). French magnetiser Jules Dupotet de Sennevoy (1796–1881) presented animal magnetism as a doctrine capable of elevating man closer to God, as seen in his *Essai sur l'ensegnement philosophique du magnétisme* (Dupotet de Sennevoy, 1845). In addition to the above-mentioned authors, others in the collection have argued against materialism based on mesmeric phenomena (Chardel, 1826; Wienholt, 1805/1845).

Miscellaneous Material

Some publications in the collection present studies or observations of particular individuals. This was the case of *The Seeress of Prevorst* (Kerner, 1829/1845), in which were recorded many observations of Friedericke Hauffe (1801–1829). Suffering from a variety of problems, the "physician prescribed magnetic passes and medicines; but she fell into the magnetic sleep, and prescribed for herself" (p. 45). There are also writings about other magnetic somnambules, such as Ellen Dawson (Barth, 1849), Bruno Binet (Cahagnet, 1848–1854/1850), Alexis Didier (Elliotson, 1849), Emma (Haddock, 1851), Cynthia Ann Gleason (Poyen, 1837), and Loraina Brackett (Stone, 1837).

The interaction of mesmerism and phrenology was commented on by several writers—a topic called phreno-magnetism. As described by a commentator, phrenology postulated that "the brain contains or consists of a great number of distinct organs, each destined to be the seat of particular moral feelings and separate mental operations," while in phreno-magnetism "it is conceived that it is possible to magnetise particular cerebral organs, to call forth the evidence of the operation of particular moral qualities, or to excite the action of certain intellectual faculties" (Review of the books *Human Magnetism and Letters on Mesmerism*, 1845, p. 223). One observer mesmerised a subject and wrote: "On my touching the region of Tune, she broke forth in a strain of melody as sweet as it was loud and clear; and gave a few equally striking indications of the functions of other faculties" (Hall, 1845, p. 8). Other relevant observations in the collection appear in *The Phreno-Magnet and Mirror of Nature*, edited by Spencer T. Hall (1812–1885) ("Private Experiments in Phreno-Magnetism," 1843; Sunderland, 1843).

Several reviews of books can be found in the collection (e.g., Review of the book *Animal Magnetism and Homeopathy*, 1838; Review of the book *Facts in Mesmerism*, 1841; Review of the book *Illustrations of Modern Mesmerism*, 1846; Review of the book *Mesmerism and Its Opponents*, 1844; Review of the book *Mesmerism in India*, 1847). These are particularly useful when assessing the reception of ideas about mesmerism.

The collection also has a few bibliographies useful for research. German surgeon C. A. F. Kluge (1782–1844) discussed mesmeric literature in a long essay (Kluge, 1815, pp. 16–210). Other works listed many useful titles (*The Bibliography of Progressive Literature*, 1899, pp. 32–35; De Ploucquet, 1809, pp. 2–4; Grässe, 1843, pp. 43–46; Pauly, 1872, pp. 787–799; Rand, 1905, pp. 1059–1067).

Finally, the digital library has issues of relevant specialized journals such as *Archives du Magnétisme Animal, Magikon, Le Magnétiseur, The Phreno-Magnet and Mirror of Nature*, and Zoist.

Conclusion

These are but a few examples of the contents of Google Book Search about mesmerism. I have attempted to present in this essay both well-known works, and less-known and generally neglected writings. The latter include articles from magazines and medical journals. While I have not covered all possible references or topics in the collection, the resources of this digital library are of great value for the historical study of mesmerism. Readers are encouraged to use the library's search engine to find additional materials, many of which are to be found in non-mesmeric literature such as medical and general-interest periodicals.

In addition, the collection contains many papers and books on other topics. There are numerous materials about hypnosis, and much that is relevant to the histories of psychology, psychiatry, general medicine, and many other disciplines.

References

Adams, N. (1849). Remarkable mesmeric phenomena. *Zoist, 7*, 79–80.

Alvarado, C. S. (2007). Online historical materials about psychic phenomena. *Journal of Scientific Exploration, 21*, 607–615.

Alvarado, C. S. (2008). Note on online books and articles about the history of dissociation. *Journal of Trauma and Dissociation, 9*, 107–118.

Animalischer magnetismus [Animal magnetism]. (1823). *Leipziger Literatur Zeitung, 113*, 897–901.

Animal magnetism. (1838). *Family Magazine, 5*, 265–267.

Animal magnetism: Its history to the present time. (1841). G. B. Dyer.

Ashburner, J. (1847). On the silent influence of the will. *Zoist, 5*, 260–273.

Ashburner, J. (1851). Cure of large polypus of the uterus. *Zoist, 9*, 265–273.

Ashburner, J. (1867). *Notes and studies in the philosophy of animal magnetism and spiritualism*. H. Baillière.

Barth, E. H. (1849). Ellen Dawson's clairvoyance. *Zoist, 7*, 95–101.

Bersot, E. (1864). *Mesmer et le magnétisme animal.* (3rd ed.). L. Hachette.

Bertrand, A. (1826). *Du magnétisme animal en France*. J. B. Baillière.

The bibliography of progressive literature. (1899). New Epoch Publishing Company.

Binet, A., & Féré, C. (1894). *Animal magnetism*. D. Appleton. (Original work published 1887).

Braid, J. (1843). *Neurypnology, or, the rationale of nervous sleep*. John Churchill.

Braid, J. (1852). *Magic, witchcraft, animal magnetism, hypnotism, and electro-biology* (3rd ed.). John Churchill.

Buckingham, J. S. (1841). *America historical, statistical and descriptive* (Vol. 1). Harper & Brothers.

Buckland, T. (1850). *The handbook of mesmerism*. H. Baillière.

Cahagnet, L. A. (1851). *The celestial telegraph; or, secrets of the life to come, revealed through magnetism* (1st American ed.). J. S. Redfield. (Original work published 1848–1854).

Capern, T. (1851). *The mighty curative powers of mesmerism*. H. Baillière.

Carpenter, W. B. (1877). *Mesmerism, spiritualism, &c.* D. Appleton.

Chardel, C. (1826). *Esquisse de la natura humaine expliquée par le magnétisme animal*. Bureau de l'Encyclopédie Portative.

Chazarain, L. T., & Dècle, C. (1887). *Les courants de la polarité dans l'aimant et dans le corps humain.* Authors.

Colquhoun, J. C. (1833). *Report of the experiments on animal magnetism, made by a committee of the medical section of the French Royal Academy of Sciences*. Robert Cadell.

Colquhoun, J. C. (1836). *Isis revelata: An inquiry into the origin, progress and present state of animal magnetism* (2 vols). Maclachlan & Stewart.

Colquhoun, J. C. (1851). *An history of magic, witchcraft, and animal magnetism* (2 vols). Longman, Brown, Green, & Longman.

Deleuze, J. P. F. (1813). *Histoire crititique du magnétisme animal* (Vol. 1). Mame.

Deleuze, J. P. F. (1819). *Défense du magnétisme animal contre les attaques don't il est l'objet dans le Dictionnaire des Sciences Médicales*. Belin-Leprieur.

Deleuze, J. P. F. (1850). *Practical instructions in animal magnetism* (4th ed., T. C. Hartshorn, Trans.). Hippolyte Baillière. (Original work published 1825)

De Ploucquet, G. G. (1809). *Literatura medica digesta sive repertorium medicinae practicae chirurgiae actque rei obstetricae* (Vol. 3). Joannem Georgium Cottam.

De Rochas, A. (1891). Mémoire relatif a certaines radiations perçues par les sensitifs *Revue de l'Hypnotisme et de la Psychologie Physiologique, 5*, 204–208, 300–306.

De Rochas, A. (1895). *L'extériorisation de la sensibilité* (2nd ed.). Chamuel.

Dupotet de Sennevoy, Baron [J.]. (1838). *An introduction to the study of animal magnetism*. Saunders & Otley.

Dupotet de Sennevoy, Baron [J.]. (1845). *Essai sur l'ensegnement philosophique du magnétisme*. A. René.

Durville, H. (1895–1896). *Traité expérimental de magnétisme.* (2 vols). Librairie du Magnétisme.

Elliotson, J. (1843). *Numerous cases of surgical operations without pain in the mesmeric state.* H. Baillière.

Elliotson, J. (1846). Accounts of more painless surgical operations. *Zoist, 4*, 1–59.

Elliotson, J. (1847). Cure of long-standing intense pains and other suffering and extreme debility, with mesmerism, after the failure of endless and distressing measures. *Zoist, 5*, 103–123.

Elliotson, J. (1849). Clairvoyance of Alexis Didier. *Zoist, 6*, 417–420.
Esdaile, J. (1846a). Alleged painless operations by mesmerism. *Medical Times, 15*, 32–33, 68–69, 145–147.
Esdaile, J. (1846b). *Mesmerism in India, and its practical application in surgery and medicine.* Longman, Brown, Green, and Longmans.
Esdaile, J. (1852). *Natural and mesmeric clairvoyance*. Hippolyte Baillière.
Estlin, J. B. (1843). An address on mesmerism. *Provincial Medical Journal and Retrospect of the Medical Sciences, 6*, 303–308.
Evans, T. (1849). Cure of deafness. *Zoist, 7*, 89.
Eve, P. F. (1845). Mesmerism. *Southern Medical and Surgical Journal, 1*(n. s.), 167–192.
Figuier, L. (1860). *Histoire du merveilleux dans les temps modernes. Vol. 2. Le magnétisme animal.* (2nd ed). L. Hachette.
Grässe, J. G. T. (1843). *Bibliotheca magica et pneumatica.* Leipzig: W. Englemann.
Gregory, W. (1884). *Animal magnetism; or mesmerism and its phenomena.* Psychological Press Association and E. W. Allen.
Guidi, F. (1854). *Trattato teorico-pratico di magnetismo animale*. Carlo Turati.
H., A. (1849). Possibilities and probabilities in physical science. *Mechanic's Magazine, Museum, Register, Journal, and Gazette, 51*, 150–154.
Haddock, J. W. (1851). *Somnolism & psycheism* (2nd ed.). James S. Hodson.
Hall, S. T. (1845). *Mesmeric experiences*. H. Baillière.
Hands, D. (1846). Cures of severe female chronic ailments, with mesmerism. *Zoist, 4*, 75–82.
Hart, E. (1896). *Hypnotism, mesmerism, and the new witchcraft* (rev. ed.). D. Appleton.
Hénin de Cuvillers, Baron [E. F.]. (1820). Introduction. *Archives du Magnétisme Animal, 1*, 1–252.
Henin de Cuvillers, Baron [E. F.]. (1821). *Le magnétisme animal retrouvé dans l'antiquité.* (2nd ed.). Barrois.
Herfner, I. (1844). Mesmerism. *Dublin University Magazine, 23*, 37–53, 286–301.
Jung-Stilling, J. H. (1851). *Theory of pneumatology* (S. Jackson, Trans.). J. S. Redfield. (Original work published 1808)
Kerner, J. (1845). *The seeress of Prevorst: Being revelations concerning the inner-life of man* (C. Crowe, Trans.). J. C. Moore. (Original work published 1829)
Kerner, J. (1856). *Franz Anton Mesmer aus Schwaben, Entdecker des thierischen Magnetismus.* (3rd ed.). Literarische Anstalt.
Kluge, C. A. F. (1815). *Versuch einer darstellung des animalischen magnetismus als heilmittel*. F. Staar.
Knight, C. (1867). *Arts and sciences or fourth division of "The English Ciclopedia"* (Vol. 5). Bradbury, Evans.
Lafontaine, C. (1852). *L'art de magnétiser ou le magnétisme animal* (2nd ed.). Germer Baillière. (Original work published 1847)
Laycock, T. (1857). *Lectures on the principles and methods of medical observation and research.* Blanchard and Lea.
Le Boyer, J. (1823). Quelques reflexions sur le magnétisme animal. *Le Lycée Armoricain, 2*, 97–107, 205–214.
Lee, E. (1866). *Animal magnetism and magnetic lucid somnambulism.* Longmans, Green.
Leger, T. (1846). *Animal magnetism, or psycodunamy.* D. Appleton.
Lowe, M. (1822). *A treatise on the phenomena of animal magnetism*. G. Schulze.
Madden, R. R. (1857). *Phantasmata or illusion and fanatisms of protean forms productive of great evils* (2 vols). T. C. Newby.
Magnetismo animal ó mesmerismo. (1842). La Colmena, 1, 48–52, 127–132.
Martineau, H. (1845). *Letters on mesmerism* (2nd ed.). Edward Moxon.
Mesmer, F. A. (1814). *Mesmerismus oder System derWechselwirkungen, Theorie und Anwendung des thierischen Magnetismus als die allgemeine Heilkunde zur Erhaltung des Menschen.* Nikolaische Buchhandlung.
Mesmeric humbug and quackery. (1851). *Lancet, 2*, 154–155.
Mesmerism. (1843). *New Age, and Concordium Gazette, 1*, 17–18, 25–26, 33–35.
O., R. A. (1861). El magnetismo animal juzgado por la iglesia. *La Verdad Católica, 7*, 111–114.
Pauly, A. (1872). *Bibliographie des sciences médicales*. Librairie Tross.
Poyen, C. (1837). *Progress of animal magnetism in New England.* Weeks, Jordan.
Private experiments in phreno-magnetism. (1843). *The Phreno-Magnet, and Mirror of Nature, 3*, 147–149.
Purland, Dr. (1859). Dental and other operations in the mesmeric trance. *Dental Review, 1*, 234–242.

Rabache, C. (1854). *Le magnétisme animal devant les savants, devant le raisonnement, devant les faits*. Feret Fils.
Rand, B. (1905). Bibliography of philosophy, psychology, and cognate subjects. In J. M. Baldwin (Ed.), *Dictionary of philosophy and psychology* (Vol. 3, Part 2, pp. 543–1192). Macmillan.
Reese, D. M. (1838). *Humbugs of New York*. John S. Taylor.
Reichenbach, C. von. (1851). *Physico-physiological researches on the dynamics of magnetism, electricity, heat, light, crystallization, and chemism, in their relation to vital force* (from German 2nd ed). J. S. Redfield. (Original work published 1849)
[Review of the book *Animal magnetism and homeopathy*]. (1838). *Monthly Review*, 2, 471–490.
[Review of the book *Facts in mesmerism*]. (1841). *Southern Literary Messenger, 7*, 807–808.
[Review of the books *Human magnetism and Letters on mesmerism*]. (1845). *Edinburgh Medical and Surgical Journal, 64*, 190–227.
[Review of the book *Illustrations of modern mesmerism, from personal investigation*]. (1846). *Metropolitan, 45*, 112–113.
[Review of the book *Mesmerism and its opponents*]. (1844). *Gentleman's Magazine*, 22(n. s.), 58–60.
[Review of the book *Mesmerism in India*]. (1847). *Western Journal of Medicine and Surgery*, 7(n.s.), 66–67.
Ripley, G., & Dana, C. A. (1858). *The new American cyclopedia: A popular dictionary of general knowledge* (Vol. 1). D. Appleton.
Sandby, G. (1848). *Mesmerism and its opponents* (2nd ed.). Longman, Brown, Green, and Longmans.
Stone, W. L. (1837). *A letter to Dr A. Brigham, on animal magnetism*. George Dearborn.
Sunderland, L. R. (1843). Phreno-magnetic discoveries. *Phreno-Magnet, and Mirror of Nature, 3*, 3–8.
Teste, A. (1843). *A practical manual of animal magnetism* (D. Spillan, Trans.). Hyppolyte Baillière. (Original work published 1840)
Wienholt, A. (1845). *Seven lectures on somnambulism* (J. C. Colquhoun, Trans.). Adam and Charles Black. (Original work published 1805)

Index

Note: Page numbers in italics refer to figures and tables. Endnotes are indicated by the page number followed by "n" and the endnote number: e.g.; 151 n.2 refers to endnote 2 on page 151.

About the Editors and Contributors

Carlos S. Alvarado, PhD, (1955–2021) obtained an MS in parapsychology from John F. Kennedy University (USA), an MA in history from Duke University (USA), and a PhD from the University of Edinburgh (UK). Over his life, he received grants and awards from the Fundacão Bial (Portugal), the Perrott-Warrick Fund, and the Society for Psychical Research (UK), among others. He contributed 20 articles to the *Psi Encyclopedia* and 14 articles to the *History of Psychiatry.* He published numerous letters to the editor and book reviews, as well as theoretical, research, and literature review articles in a variety of other publications in English, Spanish, and Portuguese, including the *Australian Journal of Clinical and Experimental Hypnosis, Ciencias de la Conducta, Psi Communicación,* the *European Journal of Parapsychology,* the *Journal of Parapsychology,* the *Journal of Scientific Exploration,* the *Journal of the Society for Psychical Research, Imagination, Cognition and Personality,* the *International Journal of Parapsychology,* and *Psychology of Consciousness.* He served nine years on the Board of Directors of the Parapsychological Association, including two terms as president in 1995 and 2002–2003. He also served as the chairman of domestic and international programs at the Parapsychology Foundations from 2000 through 2008, volunteered from 2008 through 2014, and was named the foundation's first research fellow in 2015. In addition to various other positions, he was appointed assistant professor of research at the Division of Perceptual Studies at the University of Virginia from 2003 to 2011 and the scholar in residence at Atlantic University from 2010 through January 2013.

Etzel Cardeña is the Thorsen Professor of Psychology at Lund University, Sweden, where he is director of the Centre for Research on Consciousness and Anomalous Psychology (CERCAP). He has served as president of the Society of Psychological Hypnosis, and the Society for Clinical and Experimental Hypnosis. He is the current editor of the *Journal of Parapsychology*. The Parapsychological Association honored Cardeña with the 2013 Charles Honorton Integrative Contributions Award. His publications include the books *Altering Consciousness* and *Varieties of Anomalous Experience.*

Renaud Evrard is a clinical psychologist and associate professor of psychology at the University of Lorraine. His main interests are in clinical practice with exceptional experiences and the history of heterodox psychology. He has been president of the Parapsychological Association and president of the association AnHomalies.

Stanley Krippner, PhD, has held faculty appointments at Akamai University, Fordham University, Kent State University, New York University, Saybrook University, Sofia University, the University of Puerto Rico, Wagner College, and the California Institute of Integral Studies. He is the former director of the Child Study Center, Kent State University, in Kent, Ohio, and of the Dream Laboratory, Maimonides Medical Center, in Brooklyn, New York. He has received lifetime achievement awards from the Parapsychological Association, the International Association for the Study of Dreams, and the Society for Humanistic Psychology. He is the past president of all three groups as well as the Society for Psychological Hypnosis, which awarded him its 2002 Award for Distinguished Contributions to Professional Hypnosis. Krippner is a fellow of the Society for the Scientific Study of Religion, the Society for the Scientific Study of Sexuality, and five divisions of the American Psychological Association, which granted him its 2002 Award for

Distinguished Contributions to the International Development of Psychology. He is coauthor of the award-winning book *Personal Mythology* and coeditor of the award-winning book *Varieties of Anomalous Experience* and has published over 1,000 peer-reviewed articles. Since 2010, he has held international certification as an Advanced Alcohol and Other Drugs Counselor.

Pascal Le Maléfan is a French teacher-researcher in clinical psychology, a psychologist, and a psychoanalyst. He is the author of *Spiritisme et folie. Histoire du discours psychopathologique sur la pratique du spiritisme, ses abords, ses avatars (1850–1950)* (1999). This work is a partial rewrite of his thesis, defended in 1989 at EHESS-Paris V Descartes and directed by Professor Georges Lantéri-Laura. He has published several articles on the links between clinical psychology, psychopathology, and paranormality.

Sonali Bhatt Marwaha earned her MA and MPhil in psychology from the S.N.D.T. Women's University (Mumbai) and PhD from Andhra University (Visakhapatnam, India). Her recent publications include *The Star Gate Archives: Reports of the United States Government Sponsored Psi Program, 1972–1995* (four volumes) and the Multiphasic Model of Informational Psi. She is a recipient of the Parapsychological Association's 2022 Outstanding Contribution Award.

Michael Nahm, PhD, is a biologist and research associate at the Institute for Frontier Areas of Psychology and Mental Health (IGPP) in Freiburg, Germany. His research interests focus on under-researched and unconventional phenomena in frontier areas of the sciences of life. These include various near-death phenomena, terminal lucidity, reincarnation cases, physical mediumship, hauntings and poltergeists, unidentified anomalous phenomena (UAP), philosophical implications of such fringe phenomena, as well as theories and the history of parapsychology and biology. Nahm has published five monographs and more than 100 articles on these subjects.

Andreas Sommer is a historian working on the interrelations of the sciences and the occult. His doctoral thesis (University College London, 2013) reconstructed the links between psychical research and experimental psychology in the 19th and early 20th centuries, and it won an award from the International Union of History and Philosophy of Science and Technology. He has held various research posts at the University of Cambridge, England, and published numerous articles in peer-reviewed journals and chapters in edited scholarly volumes. He is also running "Forbidden Histories" (https://www.forbiddenhistories.com) as an effort to communicate work in the academic history of science and the occult to a broader audience.

Nancy L. Zingrone, PhD, earned her MSEd in higher education with a teaching specialty in psychology from Northern Illinois University (USA) and her PhD in psychology from the University of Edinburgh (Scotland). Her recent publications include "Women and Parapsychology 2022: An Online Survey" with coauthors Gerhard Mayer and Cedar S. Leverett in the *Journal of Anomalistics* (2022), "An Overview of Modern Developments in Parapsychology" with coauthors Carlos S. Alvarado and Gerd H. Hövelmann in *Parapsychology: A Handbook for the 21st Century* (2015), and "A Brief History of Psi Research" with coauthor Carlos S. Alvarado in *Extrasensory Perception: Support, Skepticism, and Science: Vol. 1: History, Controversy, and Research* (2015). She served two terms as president of the Parapsychological Association in 2000–2001 and 2003–2004 and was awarded the Parapsychological Association's Outstanding Contribution Award in 2015.